Perception

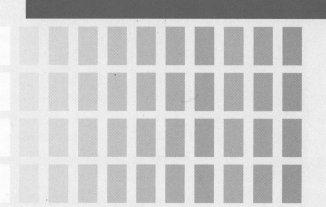

FIFTH EDITION

Perception

FIFTH EDITION

Randolph Blake
Vanderbilt University

Robert Sekuler
Brandeis University

Boston   Burr Ridge, IL   Dubuque, IA   Madison, WI   New York   San Francisco   St. Louis
Bangkok   Bogotá   Caracas   Kuala Lumpur   Lisbon   London   Madrid   Mexico City
Milan   Montreal   New Delhi   Santiago   Seoul   Singapore   Sydney   Taipei   Toronto

Higher Education

PERCEPTION

Published by McGraw-Hill, a business unit of The McGraw-Hill Companies, Inc., 1221 Avenue
of the Americas, New York, NY 10020. Copyright © 2006, 2002, 1994, 1990 by The McGraw-Hill
Companies, Inc. All rights reserved. Copyright © 1985 by Alfred A. Knopf, Inc. All right
reserved. No part of this publication may be reproduced or distributed in any form or by any
means, or stored in a database or retrieval system, without the prior written consent of The
McGraw-Hill Companies, Inc., including, but not limited to, in any network or other electronic
storage or transmission, or broadcast for distance learning.
Some ancillaries, including electronic and print components, may not be available to customers
outside the United States.

This book is printed on acid-free paper.

1 2 3 4 5 6 7 8 9 0 CCW/CCW 0 9 8 7 6 5

ISBN 0–07–111272-3

About the Authors

RANDOLPH BLAKE is Centennial Professor of Psychology at Vanderbilt University, Nashville, Tennessee, where he is also a Fellow of the Kennedy Center for Research in Human Development, a member of the Vision Research Center and the Center for Cognitive and Integrative Neuroscience. He served as chair for the department of Vanderbilt's psychology department from 1988 to 1996. For fourteen years before coming to Vanderbilt he was on the faculty of Northwestern University. Blake received his Ph.D. from Vanderbilt in 1972 and then spent two years as a postdoctoral fellow in the Sensory Sciences Center at the University of Texas Graduate School of Biomedical Sciences.

Blake has published extensively in major psychology and neuroscience journals and has contributed chapters to edited books, including *Models of the Visual Cortex, Frontiers of Visual Science, Early Vision and Beyond, and the Primate Visual System* (with Sekuler), and coedited the recently published book *Binocular Rivalry.* His research, supported by grants from the National Science Foundation and the National Institutes of Health, focuses on visual perception with particular emphasis on binocular vision, motion perception, and perceptual grouping. In recent years, Blake's research has expanded to include functional brain imaging of visual areas involved in perception of human activity.

In recognition of his research contributions, Blake received a Career Development Award from the National Institutes of Health, and the American Psychological Association's Early Career Award for Distinguished Scientific Contribution. In 2002, he received the Sutherland Award for Research Accomplishment from Vanderbilt University. Blake is an elected Fellow of the American Association for the Advancement of Science, the American Psychological Society, and the John F. Kennedy Center for Research on Human Development. He is a past member of the Committee on Vision of the National Academy of Sciences/National Research Council and the Sensory Sciences Advisory Panel of the National Science Foundation. During 1992 and again during 2004, he was a Fellow of the Japan Society for the Promotion of Science, and in 1995, he held the William Evans Professorship in Psychology at Dunedin University, New Zealand. His professional memberships include the Association for Research in Vision and Ophthalmology, Sigma Xi, the Vision Sciences Society, the American Association for the Advancement of Science and the American Psychological Society.

ROBERT SEKULER is the Louis and Frances Salvage Professor of Cognitive Neuroscience at Brandeis University and Consultant in Neurosurgery at Children's Hospital (Boston). At Boston University, he is Adjunct Professor of Cognitive and Neural Sciences, and a member of the NSF-funded Center of Excellence for Learning in Education, Science, and Technology. At Brandeis, where he served as the university's provost, Sekuler is now a member of the Volen National Center for Complex Systems, an interdisciplinary center for the study of the brain, and the Program in Neuroscience, which he has chaired. After earning his Ph.D. at Brown University in 1964, he held an NIH postdoctoral fellowship at the Massachusetts Institute of Technology. For the following 24 years, Sekuler was on the faculty at Northwestern University, where he was John Evans Professor of Neuroscience, and held the rank of professor in the departments of psychology, ophthalmology, and neurobiology and physiology. After chairing Northwestern's department of psychology for six years, he went on to serve five years as Associate Dean in the College of Arts and Sciences.

A leader in the fields of motion perception and age-related changes in perception, Sekuler has published more than 200 scientific papers and has contributed chapters to various books including the *Handbook of Perception,* the *APA Encyclopedia of Psychology,* the *Handbook of Sensory Physiology, Stevens' Handbook of Experimental Psychology,* and the *Oxford Textbook of Geriatric Medicine.* He chaired the National Academy of Sciences' Committee on Vision, and directed the Academy's study entitled "Aging Workers and Visual Impairment" as well as its study of "Vision and Aging."

Those projects led to his coedited book, *Aging and Visual Function*. In recent years, Sekuler's research program, funded by the National Institutes of Health and the National Sciences Foundation, has expanded to include functional brain imaging and electrophysiological studies of visual memory and visual cognition.

In 2000, Sekuler was a visiting scientist at the Rotman Research Institute of Toronto's Baycrest Centre for Geriatric Care, and a visiting professor of psychology at the University of Toronto. He has served on the board of the Hugh Knowles Center on Hearing and its Preservation, and on the Sensory Physiology of Advisory Panel of the National Science Foundation. Sekuler is an elected fellow of the American Psychological Society and the American Association for the Advancement of Science; he is a member of the Psychonomic Society, the Vision Sciences Society, the Society for Neuroscience, and the Association for Research in Vision and Ophthalmology.

In addition to this book, Blake and Sekuler coauthored the award-winning *Star Trek on the Brain: Alien Minds, Human Minds* (1998; paperback and Japanese editions 1999).

Contents

APPENDIX

Behavioral Methods for Studying Perception 553

From the moment you awake in the morning until you nod off at night, your mental and physical activities are guided by the barrage of environmental information supplied by your senses. All your activities—driving, reading, eating, conversing, typing, exercising—are strongly influenced by what you see, hear, feel, touch, smell, and taste. Perception is crucial to everything you do. But unlike the many abilities that you work hard to master, perception comes naturally and effortlessly: everyone is a natural-born perceptual genius. In fact, perception's effortlessness belies its complexity, and that is one reason teaching or writing about perception can be challenging: it is not immediately obvious that there is anything to be explained. If you ask a friend how he or she goes about solving a jigsaw puzzle, your friend will be able to list the steps involved (turn all the pieces face side up, arrange them in piles according to color, and so on). But if you ask the same person to explain how he or she goes about reading the words on this page, the person is likely to shrug, pause a moment, think, and then say something such as, "I just look at the page and read." Perception seems easy and automatic, but this greatly underestimates the complexity, beauty, and remarkable achievements of perception.

Goals of this Textbook

In first writing and then revising our textbook one of our consistent goals was to help readers appreciate the complexity and intelligence of all the processes that make perception possible. Our book introduces readers to the exciting behavioral and biological research that illuminates the remarkable achievement we call perceiving. Our aims have remained constant over five editions: *By conveying science's cumulative progress, we want to give readers a fresh, new perspective on their own seeing, hearing, touching, smelling, and tasting.* Following the pattern set by its predecessors, this latest edition of **Perception** emphasizes the field's exciting new developments. In preparing this edition we listened carefully to feedback from users of previous editions and tried to accommodate their advice and suggestions. The result? A new edition that is substantively and significantly different from previous ones. The following sections highlight the ways in which we've tried to improve this fifth edition of **Perception.**

Organization and Coverage

The first chapter summarizes the motivations that inspire people to study perception, as well as the various approaches that such study takes. It also outlines the framework on which the entire text is constructed. Chapters 2 through 8 discuss seeing—the biological bases of vision and the perception of pattern, color, and depth. The treatment of seeing concludes in Chapter 9 with an essay on the perception of visual events, particularly visual motion. Chapters 10, 11, and 12 provide a sweeping introduction to hearing, with special emphasis on speech and music (Chapter 12). Chapter 13 explores the sense of touch, and the book's last two chapters deal with the chemical senses, Smell and Taste (Chapters 14 and 15).

Two chapters are new to this edition, and other chapters have been revised substantially to capture and communicate the accelerating pace of significant new discoveries. Recent exciting developments in speech and music perception demanded that we devote an entire, new chapter (Chapter 12) to those topics. And dramatic growth in research on the chemical senses required such an expansion of coverage that we had to replace the previous edition's single combined chapter with two larger, separate chapters, one on smell and one on taste (Chapters 14 and 15). Material on cognitive influences on perception has been updated and expanded; in this edition, as in the previous one, we have integrated this material into the text, rather than consigning it to its own, separate chapter as was done in the first three editions. When it comes to important methodological details and techniques, we continue to believe that this material is best introduced within the context of substantive problems. So readers will be exposed to techniques such as direct scaling and multidimensional scaling within the body of the text. We do, however, offer more concentrated coverage of those techniques in the Appendix.

Special Features of the Fifth Edition

This fifth edition of ***Perception*** has several noteworthy features. First, attentive readers may notice that the order of authors has been reversed, from Sekuler and Blake, to Blake and Sekuler. This change should communicate that despite the order used in all preceding editions, we have been equal partners throughout. Second, the format and layout of the book have been greatly improved. The new large format gives the book a more contemporary look, makes the text easier to read, and leaves more space for those important notes that readers will want to make in the book's margins. Third, as explained above, the book's chapter count has grown by two. We recognize that in many courses the expansion of the text makes it less likely that the entire text will be assigned reading. However, chapters have been carefully constructed so that readers would be able to sample portions of chapters without necessarily reading the whole thing. In this way, we hope that readers will be able to get a sense of important developments in topics that they might not otherwise be exposed to. Fourth, the text embeds central topics firmly in their historical context. This allows us to present today's perception research for what it really is: the product of an unfolding, continuing intellectual process. At the same time, our source materials are frankly biased toward recently published material. Because we want readers to appreciate developments at the frontiers of perception, we give thorough coverage to "hot," rapidly developing topics, at the same time ensuring that such coverage is closely integrated with its intellectual origins. For example, one chapter provides a comprehensive treatment of recent discoveries concerning natural scene statistics, and the ways in which properties of the natural world are mirrored in the properties of perception; others highlight the amazing plasticity of sensory systems; and still other chapters detail the latest thinking on genetic determinants of color vision, the chemical senses, and what is popularly known as tone deafness. In almost every chapter, pivotal ideas are illustrated by studies that exploit the technology and insights of functional neuroimaging. Our special emphasis on recent work and the most up-to-date techniques testifies, again, that perception is a dynamic and growing field.

Illustration Program

The extensive program of several hundred illustrations, many brand new and all substantially revised for this edition, is another of this book's most important features.

And the number of all-important color plates has almost doubled from the previous edition. Our own years of teaching experience, more than six decades combined at last count, have taught us that readers don't always see in a diagram or graph exactly what was intended. In fact, the ability to read a graphic is a skill that, like any other skill, requires practice. So instead of merely directing readers to look over the figure, we crafted and coordinated the text, figures, and figure captions to ensure proper interpretation of the illustrative material. In addition, we have given extra care to the graphic presentation of complex ideas. Such ideas are often conveyed in this book by a short series of illustrations, with each illustration in a series introducing additional concepts. This approach enables every reader to get the point—even those who are novices at interpreting graphs and diagrams. Finally, illustrations that depict previously published experimental results have been adapted and redrawn to maximize clarity and consistency of presentation.

Vocabulary and Methods of Perceptual Research

Because the study of perception draws upon a number of distinct disciplines—physics, chemistry, anatomy, psychology, computer science, and some branches of medicine, among others—its technical vocabulary incorporates the terminology of those disciplines. Beginning students of perception can feel bewildered by the flood of new terms they must master. Because we do not want technical vocabulary to obscure the book's important messages, we introduce only those terms that are absolutely necessary to the discussion. Where it is likely to aid memory or understanding, we explain the term's origin. Also, each term is carefully defined when it is first used, and all these terms appear at the end of each chapter and in a glossary at the back of the book.

We have kept detailed, abstract descriptions of research methods to a minimum. Where appropriate, we explain particular methods in enough detail that all of our readers can appreciate the methods and whatever constraints they impose on results and conclusions. Various methods for studying perception are discussed within the context of the specific problems that they were designed to solve. By integrating methods and results, we hope to facilitate the reader's genuine appreciation of both.

An appendix provides much additional information about conventional behavioral methods for studying perception. The appendix also describes contemporary variants of those methods: forced-choice procedures, signal detection theory, and adaptive psychophysical methods.

Like the rest of the book, the appendix grounds its presentation in historical context, enabling the reader to understand not only the methods but also the reasons for their development.

Links to Everyday Life

In "Talks to Teachers" (1892), William James advised teachers how best to adapt the principles of psychology to the classroom. In one chapter, James urged teachers to recognize and exploit the natural interests that students bring to any topic. He suggested that abstract facts and new ideas are most readily assimilated when they have been linked to matters that students find inherently interesting, particularly matters that relate to their own lives. In our own classrooms and while writing this book, we kept James's advice in mind. Perception is not just an abstract, scientific discipline, but an integral and fascinating part of everyday life. Recognizing this fact, our book consistently relates scientific research on perception to the reader's own perceptual experiences. To underscore the relationship between science and everyday experience, we present many interesting demonstrations that readers can perform on their own with little or no equipment.

In order to anchor the discussion in the reader's own experience, the text emphasizes the everyday behavioral needs that seeing, hearing, smelling, tasting, and touching are designed to satisfy—the functions of perception. This functional approach to perception is highlighted by the many discussions, throughout the text, of clinical disorders and their intriguing perceptual consequences. Some students will be interested in learning about these disorders for personal reasons; all students should find that the study of perceptual disorders provides insight into the nature of normal perception.

Integration

William James also advised that teachers take care to connect new ideas and facts with what students have already learned. Associate the new with the old in some natural and telling way, so that the interest, being shed along from point to point, finally suffuses the entire system of objects of thought. In his own textbook, *The Principles of Psychology,* James followed this counsel, to great success. As we wrote and revised this book, we thought of James's advice and have attempted to make our treatment of perception an integrated one, in part by linking ideas across chapters. These linkages reflect the fact that different areas of perception often utilize similar techniques and related theoretical ideas. Our text is integrated in another way, blending anatomy, physiology, and psychophysics. The information and ideas from each of these three approaches have been carefully selected to ensure a coherent, complete presentation. Structure and function become more comprehensible and memorable when they are integrated. We like to think that James would approve.

Although our book is not meant to be a comprehensive reference volume, we know from experience that many readers will want to follow up with additional reading on some point that particularly caught their interest. To help this process, we provide a comprehensive list of references, with more than 1,700 entries. Scrutiny of the list reveals that 20 percent of those references are *new* to this edition; many older references from the previous edition were eliminated because they were outmoded or superceded by new references. Nearly all of the new references represent contributions published in the last three years, including 79 published in 2004 and 7 published in 2005. In addition, we have provided Web links to many exciting sites where readers can experience perception-related demonstrations and can learn more about topics introduced in the text. These Web links, which will be regularly updated, can be found at http://www.mhhe.com/blake5.

Supplements

Instructor's Manual and Test Bank

Prepared by Robert O'Shea (University of Otago), the Instructor's Manual provides many useful teaching tools. For each chapter, a general overview, learning objectives, detailed chapter outline, teaching tips and activities, and a summary are provided. The Test Bank also prepared by Robert O'Shea, includes matching, multiple choice, true-false, and essay questions for each chapter. Both the Instructor's Manual and Test Bank are available on an Instructor's Resource CD-ROM. In addition, The Instructor's Manual can be found on the password-protected instructor's side of the book-specific Online Learning Center www.mhhe.com/blake5.

EZ Test

The Test Bank is also available in computerized format on the Instructor's Resource CD-ROM. McGraw-Hill's EZ Test is a flexible and easy-to-use electronic testing program. The program allows instructors to create tests from book specific items. It accommodates a wide range of question types and instructors may add their own question. Multiple versions of the test can be created and any test can be exported for us with course management systems such as WebCT, BlackBoard, or PageOut. EZ Test Online give you a place to easily administer your EZ Test created exams and quizzes online. The program is available for Windows and Macintosh environments.

Online Learning Center

The Online Learning Center website for *Perception,* Fifth Edition, includes a number of resources for instructors and students to enhance the teaching and learning experience. The Student Center includes learning objectives, chapter outlines, practice quizzes (prepared by Robert O'Shea), web links, flashcards, and other tools. Visit the Online Learning Center at www.mhhe.com/blake5.

Acknowledgments

In preparing various editions of the book, we benefited greatly from many people's comments and suggestions. Special credit, though, should be given to those individuals who either reviewed various chapters and sections or educated us on relevant topics. These individuals include:

Edward Adelson, *Massachusetts Institute of Technology*

Jo-Anne Bachorowski, *Vanderbilt University*

Linda Bartoshuk, *Yale University*

Patrick Bennett, *McMaster University*

Irving Biederman, *University of Southern California*

Anne Blood, *Massachusetts General Hospital,*

Wendy Bourque, *University of New Brunswick*

Geoff Boynton, *University of California, San Diego*

William Cain, *University of California, San Diego*

David Calkins, *University of Rochester*

Marisa Carrasco, *New York University*

Vivien Casagrande, *Vanderbilt University*

Peter Dallos, *Northwestern University*

Barbara Dillenburger, *Max Planck Institute, Tuebingen*

Vincent Ferrara, *Columbia University*

John Flowers, *University of Nebraska*

Perry Fuchs, *University of Texas, Arlington*

Isabel Gauthier, *Vanderbilt University*

Wilson Geisler, *University of Texas, Austin*

Asif Ghazanfar, *Max Planck Institute, Tuebingen*

Pierre Gosselin, *University of Ottawa*

Troy Hackett, *Vanderbilt University*

Michael Hall, *University of Las Vegas*

Michael Hawken, *New York University*

Rachel Herz, *Brown University*

Jon Kaas, *Vanderbilt University*

Donald Katz, *Brandeis University*

Richard Kruk, *University of Manitoba*

Ilona Kovács, *Rutgers University*

Joseph Lappin, *Vanderbilt University*

Susan Lederman, *Queen's University*

Mark McCourt, *North Dakota State University*

Dennis McFadden, *University of Texas, Austin*

Julie Mennella, *Monell Chemical Senses Center*

Claire Murphy, *San Diego State University*

Ken Nakayama, *Harvard University*

Hiroshi Ono, *York University*

Robert O'Shea, *University of Dunedin*

Thomas Papathomas, *Rutgers University*

Francesco Pavani, *University of Trento*

Isabel Peretz, *Université de Montréal*

Todd Preuss, *Emory University*

Dario Ringach, *University of California, Los Angeles*

Anna Roe, *Vanderbilt University*

Mickey Rowe, *University of California, Santa Barbara*

Philippe Schyns, *University of Glasgow*

Allison Sekuler, *McMaster University*

David Sheinberg, *Brown University*

Steve Shevell, *University of Chicago*

Eero Simoncelli, *New York University*

Noam Sobel, *University of California, Berkeley*

James Todd, *Ohio State University*

Benjamin Wallace, *Cleveland State University*

Brian Wandell, *Stanford University*

Fred Wightman, *University of Louisville*

Steve Yantis, *Johns Hopkins University*

Qasim Zaidi, *College of Optometry, State University of New York*

Robert Zatorre, *McGill University*

While we worked on the book's first two editions we were fortunate in having adjoining offices and laboratories. That physical proximity made it easy for us to share materials, ideas, comments, and suggestions, and to strengthen our friendship. It also enabled us to do much of the writing while we both sat at a single computer that was specially outfitted with twin keyboards—in the style of pianists playing music for four hands. Because our academic bases now are separated by 1,640 kilometers, we have resorted to other means to continue our close, highly interactive collaboration. We've made intense, but fun home-to-home visits—Blake to Concord, Massachusetts, and Sekuler to Nashville, Tennessee. For our more usual interaction, though, we depended upon the Internet, most recently taking advantage of Apple's iSight and iChat technologies for video visits.

Our electronic virtual closeness gave each of us complete pride of ownership for the entire text. Of course, files, comments, and drawings shared over an electronic network are not the same thing as sitting side by side, but they proved to be an acceptable substitute. Both of us have vivid memories of weekend marathons during which we carried on prolonged, high-speed electronic dialogues over some matter or other. Even as we wrap up this fifth edition, we are working interactively, though separated by 14 time zones (Blake in Japan, Sekuler in Massachusetts). Researchers are adapting computer technology to create what is known as virtual reality, computer-mediated experiences that substitute for—and sometimes improve upon—the real thing. In this spirit, we have been delighted that the speed and ease of our largely electronic collaboration enables us to continue to be close colleagues, if only mostly of the virtual variety.

Thanks are owed to our students, colleagues, and especially our families for their tolerance and good humor during our preoccupation with this labor of love. We are also grateful to the McGraw-Hill editorial and production team, especially Judith Kromm, Senior Developmental Editor, and Cathy Iammartino, Project Manager, whose serious commitment to this new edition has made our work enjoyable and, we think, highly productive.

Introduction to Perception

The world is filled with objects and events that generate a torrent of potential information. Though much of that information is irrelevant to people's daily needs, some is absolutely essential. To exploit this information effectively, human beings are equipped with specialized machinery that captures the information and translates it into the language of the nervous system. The brain refines this translated information into neural "descriptions" of behaviorally relevant objects and events in the environment. Some of these descriptions reach conscious awareness, allowing us to formulate deliberate plans for subsequent intractions with those objects; other descriptions guide immediate or reflexive reactions to objects and events.

Perception puts us in contact with the world we live in; it shapes our knowledge of that world, and knowledge is power. Our chances of survival improve markedly if we can detect objects and events in our environment and if we can, then, distinguish the safe from the dangerous, sort out the desirable from the undesirable. Knowing about our world allows us to predict the consequences of our actions, a critical skill in a constantly changing world.

Perception doesn't have to provide us with an accurate view of the world, perfectly detailed in every respect. What is crucial is that perception provide us with a *useful*

view of the world, where useful means being able to interact safely and effectively within our environment. As you will learn, perception accentuates the important and diminishes, or even ignores, the irrelevant. Perception may even misrepresent an object's true appearance, if that misrepresentation improves our chances of interacting effectively with that object. Sensory illusions represent an example of misrepresentation, and you'll be seeing many examples of sensory illusions as we move through the chapters. These illusions can be construed as perceptual mistakes that, paradoxically, work in our favor.

The environment generates a powerful stream of sensory information. In fact, there are so many objects and events that our perception cannot possibly process and respond to each one. Nonetheless—and fortunately for us—perception does work. Our perceptual systems overcome this potential sensory overload in several ways. For one, the world in which we live is full of regularities dictated by the physical nature of matter and energy. Those regularities make it easier to detect objects and to discriminate one object from another. For example, our visual system evolved in a world where light nearly always comes from above and, consequently, we unconsciously use that knowledge to interpret shapes of objects based on shadows. (You will see an example of this constraint in Chapter 8.) Perception can exploit this and many other environmental regularities to make educated guesses about what in the world gave rise to a particular pattern of sensory stimulation.

There is a second effective way that perception deals with the environment's overwhelming complexity: it simply ignores much of what is going on in the world. Much of what the environment has to offer is simply of no interest to us. It is not important, for example, to sense the minute electrical fields generated by other biological creatures (including other people). Humans' keen sense of vision makes "electroreception" superfluous for members of our species. Consequently, our perceptual systems are tuned to those sensory events that are biologically relevant (or, more correctly, *were* biologically relevant to our primate ancestors). As you will learn throughout this book, animal species differ in their behavioral goals, and the goals of some species require sensitivity to sensory stimulation that falls outside our reality.

Perception arises from a complex interplay of mutually interdependent events. To understand perception completely—and no one yet does—requires knowing all the components involved in the process and the ways those components interact. To begin, we must specify the nature of the environment in which we live, for this environment determines *what* there is to perceive. Aspects of the environment are specified using terms derived from physics, because stimulation comes in various forms of physical energy: thermal, mechanical, chemical, acoustic, and electromagnetic. The physical energy that initiates the chain of events is called a **stimulus** (plural, "stimuli").

Next, it is necessary to understand how the nervous system converts patterns of physical energy into neural events. Known as **sensory transduction,** this conversion process requires an understanding of the specialized sensory receptors (such as those contained in eyes and ears) that convert physical energy into bioelectrical signals. Once this transduction has been achieved, objects and events are represented solely as patterns of neural impulses within the various sensory nerve fibers. From this point on, all further elaboration and editing of the sensory information must be performed using this neural representation.

Of course, the brain plays a central role in perception. So a full understanding of perception also requires knowing about various brain areas specialized for processing patterns of neural impulses arising from the various senses. A full understanding also requires knowledge of how the activity distributed among those many areas is combined to form our unified sense of the world. How, for example, do the neural signals conveying information about the sounds from an object combine with the signals generating the visual impressions of that object? In addi-

tion, we need to discover how neural activity signaling the presence of objects is used to control our behavioral and emotional reactions to those objects.

A complete account of perception must incorporate a thorough description of the appearances of objects and events: we have to be able to describe systematically the sights, sounds, smells, and tastes that populate our conscious experiences. In addition to describing how things appear to us, we must also specify how our abilities to detect, discriminate, and recognize objects are governed by the information available to our senses. And, in a similar vein, we must understand the behavioral consequences of sensory stimulation, for our actions will modify those very patterns of sensory stimulation.

These tasks represent formidable challenges. Not surprisingly, scientists have developed diverse techniques for systematically cataloging the performance of our perceptual systems and relating that information to patterns of physical stimulation. The enterprise of relating physical stimulation to perceptual events is known as **psychophysics.** By specifying the relation between physical and perceptual events, psychophysics provides important clues to understanding the various steps leading from objects and events to perception.

Perception constitutes a whole sequence of events, beginning with things that happen in the physical world external to the perceiver. From that start, perception proceeds through the translation of external events into patterns of activity within the perceiver's nervous system, culminating in the perceiver's experiential and behavioral reactions to those events. Those reactions, in turn, can affect the very same sensory events that triggered those reactions. All of this forms a closed loop in which perception alters behavior, and behavior, in turn, alters perception. This dynamic, continuous loop is schematized in Figure 1.1. Let's now consider several important implications of this way of thinking about perception.

Perception Is a Biological Process

In this book, we approach perception as a *biological* process. To be perceived, *any* information about events in the world must be registered by the sensory nervous system. The noted neuroscientist Vernon Mountcastle has vividly described this constraint:

> Each of us lives within . . . the prison of his own brain. Projecting from it are millions of fragile sensory nerve fibers, in groups uniquely adapted to sample the energetic states of the world around us: heat, light, force, and chemical composition. That is all we ever know of it directly; all else is logical inference. (1975, p. 131)

FIGURE 1.1 | Perception registers and interprets sensory information from the environment, in this case light, that guides behavior, which, in turn, shapes the nature of input to the senses.

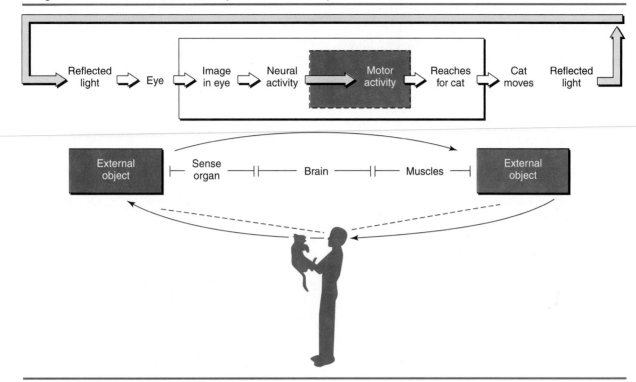

Mountcastle points out that sensory nerve fibers provide our only link to the external world; they alone represent our communication channels to reality. If environmental events fall outside the sensitivity range of our sensory channels, we will not experience those events directly. Now, it may be possible to detect some of these events indirectly, using specialized instruments that work in one of two ways. Some instruments *amplify* physical energy, making otherwise weak, undetectable signals strong enough to stimulate the senses. A microscope, for example, can magnify objects too small to be seen by the naked eye. This is the only way we're able to know what bacteria actually look like. Other instruments *convert* energy that is outside the normal bounds of any of our senses into a form that falls within those bounds. Geiger counters can warn about the presence of radioactivity, a form of energy that cannot be sensed directly by most creatures; the Geiger counter converts imperceptible radiation energy into audible sound or visible deflections of a gauge. Box 1.1 actually shows you what ordinarily invisible optical information may look like. Whether amplifying or converting energy, these specialized instruments all perform the same function—they extend the reach of our sensory systems into realms of physical reality that are normally beyond our perceptual grasp.

It may be difficult to accept that your rich perceptual world encompasses only a tiny, restricted portion of the objects and events in the natural environment. Because one's conception of reality is so intimately determined by subjective experience, it seems unnatural to distinguish between one's perception of the world and the world itself. Roger Sperry (1964) cast this distinction with beautiful clarity: "Before brains there was no color or sound in the universe, nor was there any flavor or aroma and probably little sense and no feeling or emotion." To understand perception fully, then, you have to make this distinction. Perhaps a few examples will enable you to appreciate what we mean by the limited scope of your perceptual world.

Consider, for instance, how different species of animals experience the world. It is well documented that not all animals have the same sensory systems. Consequently, various species have access to different universes of physical events (Hughes, 1999). You probably know that dogs can hear sounds in regions of the frequency spectrum where humans are deaf. You may not know, however, that bees can navigate using a quality of light, polarization, that is outside the realm of human visual experience; sharks hunt their prey by following electrical trails given off by their potential meal; bats use

BOX 1.1 Seeing the Invisible

Have you ever heard the adage, "There's more to the world than meets the eye" ? It's certainly true, for our world is awash with radiant energy that falls completely outside the range of sensitivity of our eyes. Take, for example, electromagnetic radiation in the portion of the spectrum called infrared. This form of radiation is usually associated with heat, including the body heat of living creatures. If infrared is sensed at all, it is experienced as warmth on the skin. Although some animals, notably certain snakes, have specialized sense organs that allow them to detect and respond to objects on the basis of the infrared energy radiated by those objects, humans are fairly insensitive to infrared.

To give you some idea of what it might be like to see infrared radiation, we have prepared the two accompanying photographs. The photograph on the left shows a scene taken with ordinary black-and-white film; this film

is about as *in*sensitive to infrared as the human eye. That is why pictures taken with such film look "normal." The photograph on the right shows the same scene taken with film that is sensitive to infrared; it reveals things in the scene (areas of heat and cold) that humans ordinarily would not see. Thus, for instance, the water in the right-hand photo appears dark because it is cold.

Although the differences between these pictures are interesting, we can't really claim that the photographs provide much insight into the experiences of those infrared-sensitive snakes. In some cases, their infrared-sensitive organs are not even part of their eyes. It's more likely that they *feel* infrared energy rather than *see* it. The photographs do remind us, though, that the human perceptual world is limited to that sample of objects and events with physical energy falling within the range of sensitivity of our sensory systems.

self-produced, ultrasonic echoes to navigate in complete darkness; snakes can detect and orient toward infrared radiation; trout have tiny biomagnets in their heads that let them exploit the earth's magnetic field to orient their navigation; zebra finches rely on ultraviolet light to select mates; moths can sense chemical substances, that are entirely odorless to humans. In general, there is no single "environment" in which all animals live. Members of different species interact with their physical worlds in ways that reflect their own unique requirements and capabilities.

How can we get a glimpse of the perceptual world of other animals? In a now famous essay, philosopher Thomas Nagel (1974) reasoned that one must actually *become* that creature in order to understand what it is like to *be* that creature. (Nagel's essay is available on the Web, and can be accessed from www.mhhe.com/blake5.) In fact, Nagel wasn't the first to endorse this idea. In T. H. White's book *The Sword in the Stone* (1939), Merlyn the magician wanted Arthur, future King of England, to experience a variety of perspectives on the world he would eventually rule. To provide that experience, Merlyn

4

magically turned Arthur into a bird, a fish, an ant, and a badger. Although a magician living in the Middle Ages couldn't possibly have read Nagel's twentieth-century essay, Merlyn nonetheless was anticipating Nagel's philosophy. Although we are not magicians like Merlyn, we want to enable you to imagine what it's like to be another creature, particularly a creature with perceptual abilities very different from yours. So throughout the book's chapters you'll be challenged to imagine the perceptual world of creatures very different from humans.

For that matter, not even all humans experience the same perceptual world. Some people, for example, have eye defects that prevent them from experiencing the full range of colors that most people see; you'll meet some of these people in Chapter 7. Many elderly people are unable to hear some high frequency sounds that are clearly audible to younger individuals; you'll learn about the consequences of this deficit in Chapter 11. Certain people cannot taste one of the bitter substances in coffee or grapefruit juice; Chapter 15 tells you why these people have limited taste perceptions. These and similar examples appearing throughout this book underscore the dependence of perception on the function of the sensory nervous system.

Recognition of perception as a biological process underscores another important point: perception entails symbolic representations. A symbol is something that stands for something other than itself. Hermann Helmholtz, an influential nineteenth-century contributor to physics, physiology, and perception, emphasized this point when he wrote: "Our sensations are for us only symbols of the object of the external world, and correspond to them in such way as written characters or articulate words correspond to the thing they denote" (quoted in Park, 1999, p. 8). A road map, for instance, is a symbol of the highways and terrain over which you may wish to travel. Running your finger along some highway on a map is very different from traveling the actual road, but the map symbolizes the reality. The words on this page are symbols, denoting objects, actions and relations among them. When you read the letters Z-E-B-R-A, they symbolize a kind of animal with which you're familiar. The letters don't magically conjure up an actual zebra, but they surely might conjure up in your mind's eye the image of a horselike animal with black and white stripes. Words are useful for spoken and written communication because they have a sufficiently narrow range of referents that can be recognized by large groups of human beings.

Your perceptual experiences are associated with characteristic patterns of neural activity in your brain (hence we say that perceptual states are produced by brain states). This fact makes perception a symbolic process. Suppose you hear a bird chirping outside your window. Your perceptual experience of that sound is certainly not the same as the actual event that gives rise to the sound, in this case the acoustic energy produced by the bird. However, your perceptual experience does represent important qualities of that acoustic event. In the case of perception, the symbols are not the sort we usually think of—a screech of brakes, the trill of a bird, the crescendo of an orchestra. Instead, the symbols are the various brain states that stand for these sounds. Just like other kinds of symbols, however, the properties of these symbols are not the same as the properties of the things being symbolized: in your brain, the representation of a loud explosion is neither loud nor explosive. What the neural responses *can* retain, however, is important information about the spatial or temporal structure of the objects and events the neural symbols represent. Thus, the beginning and end of neural patterns in your brain evoked by the bird's chirping will generally coincide with the beginning and end of the bird's call; the temporal structure of the neural activity mirrors the temporal structure of the event. Viewing a single, isolated star in the sky will create a more spatially compact pattern of neural activity in your brain than will viewing a whole cluster of stars; the spatial structure of the neural activity thus mirrors the spatial structure of the objects being viewed.

At least while you're awake, your brain expects to receive more or less continuous sensory input stimulated by events in the external world. When that input is reduced or eliminated, the sensory systems lapse into a kind of disorderly conduct that can be quite bizarre. Input to the brain can be shut off by placing a person in an environment that virtually eliminates sensory stimulation (Bexton, Heron, and Scott, 1954; Siegel, 1984). Although this may sound like a relaxing, pleasant situation, it's not: placed in sensory deprivation, people become anxious and begin to hallucinate. A less severe but nonetheless disturbing condition arises when a particular sensory channel has diminished function because of disease. For example, in about 10 to 15 percent of people with serious eye disease, the impaired vision evokes realistic and complex visual hallucinations (Schultz and Melzack, 1991). In this condition, known as **Charles Bonnet syndrome,** the hallucinations come from impaired sensory systems, not from dementia, as was once assumed. Similarly, following amputation of a body part, many people experience "phantom limbs," compelling and very painful hallucinations that the missing body part is still present. The visual hallucinations and the phantom limbs are both generated by activity within the brain, in this case, activity uncoupled from normal sensory input.

But let's return to brain activity that produces normal perception, triggered by sensory events. It is really remarkable how deceptively simple and self-evident our perceptions of the world seem. If you were asked to describe how you solve a jigsaw puzzle, you might give an account of the steps involved: "Turn all the pieces right side up, arrange the pieces into little piles according to color," and so on. Likewise, many of you can probably describe what you do when brewing fresh coffee ("Grind the beans, place a filter in the coffeemaker," etc.). But what answer would you give to the following: How do you read the words on this page? Most people would probably say, "I open my eyes and look at the page." Of course, this simple description belies the truly complex nature of the process, but it does dramatize the point we wish to make: normal perception occurs rapidly and without much effort.

But we shouldn't be fooled. Even the simplest perceptual experiences result from a complex series of neural events involving extensive interactions among numerous brain cells. These interactions, which bear a formal resemblance to interactions in an electronic circuit, can be thought of as computations. The computations that shape the symbolic representations in the brain work on environmental information picked up by the eyes, ears, and other sensory organs. Using this information, the brain computes the properties of objects and events (such as their size or their distance from the point of observation).

The philosophy that guides contemporary work in perception is termed **materialism**—it asserts that perceptual experience depends on the operation of the nervous system, with no requirement for the involvement of some noncorporeal force. The materialistic viewpoint has been well expressed by the late Roger Sperry, a Nobel Prize–winning brain scientist. According to Sperry, perceptual experience is a "functional property of brain processing, constituted of neuronal and physicochemical activity, and embodied in, and inseparable from, the active brain" (1980, p. 204).

Although materialism holds that perception is based on neural events in the brain, it does not imply that one could dissect a brain and thereby locate those experiences. Again, Roger Sperry put it quite well:

> Once generated from neural events, the higher order mental patterns and programs have their own subjective qualities and progress, operate and interact by their own causal laws and principles which are different from and cannot be reduced to those of neurophysiology. (1980, p. 201)

To illustrate further what he had in mind, Sperry offered the example of a wheel rolling downhill. The wheel

> "carries its atoms and molecules through a course in time and space and to a fate determined by the overall system properties of the wheel as a whole and regardless of the inclination of individual atoms and molecules. The atoms and molecules are caught up and overpowered by the higher properties of the whole. One can compare the rolling wheel to an ongoing brain process or a progressing train of thought in which the overall organizational properties of the brain process, as a coherent organizational entity, determine the timing and spacing of the firing patterns within its neuronal infrastructure." (1980, p. 201)

In other words, though one's experiences have a physical basis, they cannot be entirely reduced to a set of physical components; equally important are their spatial organization, what they communicate to one another, and how both spatial organization and communication change with time. If another analogy would help, consider what would happen if you took a television set completely apart and examined all its components in an effort to understand how it worked. The proper function of the television set demands a particular spatial arrangement of parts as well as a certain sequence of signals in time. The "secret" of the set's operation would have completely eluded you and could not be found in the pile of parts left after the set had been dismantled. And certainly from the parts alone, it would be impossible to deduce the function of a television set.

Not everybody agrees with the materialistic perspective. Some prominent scientists, including the late Sir John Eccles (1979), another Nobel Prize winner, subscribe to an alternative view. This alternative, **dualism,** is often associated with the seventeenth-century French philosopher René Descartes. Dualism holds that perceiving (like any "mental" function) is not solely a phenomenon of the physical brain. Instead, it also entails some special, nonphysical substance—the mind or the soul—that interacts with the brain. Many people find dualism persuasive because they are unconvinced that perception, a personal, subjective experience, can be fully explained by brain processes, which are certainly not experiences. They object to materialism's basic claim: a quantity of one sort—neural activity—can cause a quantity of so different a sort—perception.

According to philosopher John Searle (1987), though, no logical barrier prevents cause-and-effect relationships between entities of radically different sorts. In fact, denying that such relationships are possible betrays a misunderstanding of cause and effect itself. To drive his point home, Searle draws on examples from physics. Physicists commonly distinguish between large-scale macro phenomena and smaller-scale micro elements, postulating causal relationships between the two, even though macro and micro entities are quite different from one another. Take some examples offered by Searle. Heat and lightning are macro-level phenomena; molecular movements and electrical discharges are elements on the micro level. Physics teaches us that a macro phenomenon can be *caused* by the behavior of micro elements: we say that heat is caused by molecule movements or that lightning is caused by electrical discharge. Moreover, either of these macro phenomenon can be equated to the behavior of its micro elements. Therefore, we can say that heat is the mean kinetic energy of molecule movements or that lightning is an electrical discharge.

Paul Churchland elaborated the main arguments against dualism (1988). Here we'll mention two of them. Against the claim that perception is independent of what happens in the brain, Churchland cites numerous instances in which changes in the brain's condition dramatically alter the content and quality of perception. Throughout the following chapters, we give many examples of perception disordered by brain damage. Against the claim that perception is far too complicated to be the product of things as simple as nerve cells, research on neural networks shows that one can create extraordinarily complex, sophisticated systems out of very simple components, undercutting the need to postulate other, more intelligent agents. As a result, one can account for complex, intelligent aspects of perception without recourse to elements that are themselves complex or intelligent.

Searle expresses the view most investigators in the field of perception have adopted:

> Mental phenomena, whether conscious or unconscious, whether visual or auditory, pains, tickles, itches, thoughts, and all the rest of our mental life, are caused by processes going on in the brain. Mental phenomena are as much a result of electrochemical processes in the brain as digestion is the result of chemical processes going on in the stomach and the rest of the digestive tract. (1987, p. 220)

Within contemporary psychology and neuroscience, perception is an area of scientific research that has made major advances in explaining the relation between brain and mind. Adoption of the materialist position has greatly facilitated those advances.

Perception Involves Action

Perceiving usually requires some action on the perceiver's part. You look around in order to see, searching the visual environment until the desired object of regard is located. Likewise, to make a faint sound audible, you may turn your ear in the direction of the sound. When touching an object, you're better able to identify it if you actively explore it by moving your fingers over it. All these examples remind us that perception is an *active* process, an idea especially championed by James J. Gibson (1966), who expressed this idea succinctly when he wrote, "We must perceive in order to move, but we must also move in order to perceive" (1979, p. 223).

Active perception accomplishes several goals. First, we sample our environment purposefully, rather than waiting on sensory events to drop into our laps, so to speak. Our sampling behavior—looking, listening, touching, and so on—is usually guided by our needs (Are you hungry, sleepy, afraid, or what?). Perception, in other words, has purpose. Once active sampling uncovers an object of potential interest, we must decide whether to approach it or to avoid it. Here, again, active perception helps us make intelligent decisions. By actively exploring an object we're able to improve the quality of the sensory information we receive. As you investigate an unfamiliar object with your hand, your fingers are directed to the most informative parts of that object, looking for telltale signs of the object's shape, size, texture, and, ultimately, its identity. Having identified the object, you may elect to discard it or to keep it. The same kinds of exploratory activities occur with the other senses, including vision and hearing. Your behavior depends on *what* is perceived, and what is perceived depends on your behavior.

Active perception, useful as it is, introduces a potential confusion that the brain must sort out, namely distinguishing self-produced patterns of stimulation from externally produced ones. An example should make this point clear. Hold the index finger of one hand in front of your face and look straight at it (see Figure 1.2). Now shift your gaze back and forth, looking to the left and the right of your finger. This action causes the image of your finger to sweep back and forth over the light-sensitive surface on the back of your eye. Now modify the exercise by moving your finger back and forth while staring straight ahead without moving your eyes. This also causes the image of your finger to sweep back and forth over the back of your eye. So here are two distinct situations—a stationary object and a moving object—that can produce comparable patterns of eye stimulation. How

FIGURE 1.2 │ While holding your finger in front of your face, shift your gaze from the left to the right of your finger. As you do this, the image of your finger sweeps back and forth over the back of your eye, much the same as it does when you hold your gaze steady and move your finger back and forth.

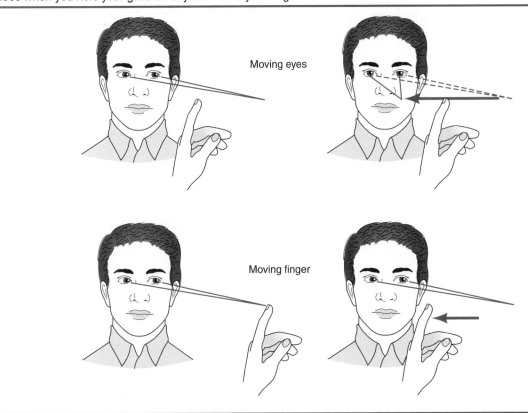

does the visual nervous system distinguish one from the other? We'll postpone details of the answer until Chapter 9, but suffice it to say the brain solves the potential dilemma by keeping track of motor commands sent to the eye muscles. A neural copy of those commands can be sent to visual areas of the brain thereby "vetoing" the implication of signals arriving from the eye. This kind of sensorimotor feedback is probably used whenever we distinguish self-produced stimulation from externally produced stimulation.

Perception's links to action orientation produces an interesting distinction among the various senses that has to do with the proximity of the perceiver to the object of perception. Touch and taste require direct contact between the perceiver and the source of stimulation. Because of this restriction, taste and touch can be considered **near senses.** The sense of smell is also effectively a near sense, at least for humans. Volatile chemicals from an odorous substance are diluted with distance, so smell works more effectively for substances in the general vicinity of the nose.[1] In contrast, for us humans, seeing and hearing can be thought of as **far senses,** or **distance senses.** The eyes and ears can pick up information originating from remote sources. In this respect, they function like a ship's radar. They allow one to make perceptual contact with objects located too far away for immediate grasp. They extend your perceptual grasp out into the world beyond your fingertips and your nose. Vision and hearing serve as able substitutes for actual locomotor exploration of the environment. These two far senses let you explore your surroundings vicariously. They provide ad-

---

[1]Actually, this is not true for all species: some animals possess a highly acute sense of smell that allows them to detect odors over great distances, as you'll learn in Chapter 14.

vance warning of approaching danger, and they guide the search for friends and desired objects. In general, hearing and seeing open up to you the large world that lies outside your reach. Imagine how vulnerable you would feel if you were denied access to all information picked up by your far senses. Your whole world would shrink to the area within arm's reach. You would be able to sense objects only when you touched them or when they touched you. It is not surprising, therefore, that blindness and deafness, losses of the far senses, are considered so devastating.

Incidentally, this distinction between the near and far senses has an important behavioral consequence. Any crucial reaction called for by taste or touch must be executed swiftly. There is no time to decide whether a bitter substance is toxic—you spit it out reflexively. Nor do you first try to judge what is causing a burning sensation before you remove your hand from a hot object. In these cases, you act first and then consciously think about what it was that triggered your reflex action. However, in the case of the far senses—seeing and hearing—you're often dealing with objects located some distance away. This distance permits you the luxury of evaluating the potential consequences of your actions.

One final note about active perception. The ability to explore the world actively requires fine motor control over the body parts used for exploration. You could think of your fingers as finely tuned calipers that adjust their grip force to suit the object you're holding. You're able to do this because the muscles in your fingers contain specialized sensory receptors that gauge the strength of contraction and, hence, the tightness of your grip. Without those internal sensory receptors to monitor grip strength, you'd have trouble squeezing the right amount of toothpaste from a tube, and you could crush a delicate flower before you knew what you were doing. Called **kinesthesia,** this internal sense of muscular contraction is intimately involved in coordinating all sorts of motor activities, including walking, dressing, eating, and typing. We won't dwell on the mechanisms of kinesthesia, but you should keep in mind that the nervous system also includes specialized sensory systems that monitor the internal "perceptual" states of your body's interior parts.[2]

---

[2]One could also construe internal regulatory mechanisms as "sensory" systems, in that they monitor physiological states such as hormone and glucose levels and blood oxygen. When those levels drift out of balance, compensatory reactions are triggered (e.g., a change in heart rate). Thus, these internal mechanisms also form sensory/action loops. We won't include internal monitoring systems in this book, for we're concerned with sensory systems that allow us to interact with our external environment.

Why Study Perception?

Over the years, people have studied perception for a variety of reasons. Some of these reasons, as you will see, stem from practical considerations, such as the need to solve a particular problem. Other reasons do not involve practical concerns, but arise from simple intellectual curiosity about ourselves and the world we live in.

Practical Reasons for Studying Perception

The human senses evolved under environmental conditions in many ways quite different from those we now live in. Many of the challenges confronting the human senses today didn't exist in the more primitive environments for which these senses were designed. It's very important to know just what kind of perceptual demands can reasonably be placed on the human senses without compromising safety and sanity. There is an optimum range of sensory stimulation within which the majority of people work and play most effectively. Intense stimulation—such as excessive noise, glaring light, and harsh smells—can impair immediate performance as well as damage the sensory nervous system. Through the study of perception, one can identify and correct potentially hazardous environmental conditions that threaten the senses and impair the ability to make decisions.

In a related vein, studying perception enables one to design devices that ensure optimal perceptual performance. Just think how often each day you come in contact with devices designed to communicate some message to you. Traffic lights, alarm clocks, telephones, and video displays are just a few of the myriad inventions that people rely on during work, play, study, even sleep. To be effective, these devices should be tailored to human sensory systems. It would be unwise, for example, to use a high-pitched tone as a fire alarm in a hotel because most elderly people have difficulty hearing such tones. Similarly, a traffic sign with blue lettering on a green background would be inefficient, because the contrast between these two colors makes letters more difficult to distinguish than, say, red letters on a green background. In general, we want the signs and signals in the environment to be easy to see and hear, and this requires an understanding of human perceptual capacities and limitations.

Understanding perception also makes it possible to design devices to help individuals with impaired sensory function. Take hearing aids as an example. For decades hearing aids amplified not only the sounds the user wanted to hear—such as a person's voice—but also other, unwanted sounds, such as traffic noises. Recognizing this problem, Richard L. Gregory developed a procedure that selectively amplifies just speech sounds (Gregory and Drysdale, 1976). This invention, which is now in wide use, grew out of earlier work on the ear's ability to respond selectively to particular sounds. And recently we've seen the development of devices that boost hearing by direct stimulation of the auditory nerve, using implants driven by speech processors embedded on microchips (Wilson et al., 1991). This device has been a boon to thousands of hearing-impaired children, but the design of such aids requires a solid understanding of mechanisms of normal perception.

Also in a practical vein, companies in the food and beverage industry carefully test the perceptual appeal—the taste, smell, and appearance—of their products before marketing them. Advertising, too, capitalizes on perception research to package and market products in ways that will bring those products to the attention of consumers. There are even claims that subliminal sensory messages—pictures or words presented too briefly or too faintly to be consciously seen or heard—can improve one's memory or enhance self-esteem, although these claims are questionable (Greenwald et al., 1991).

So far, our practical reasons have focused on human perception. But as the following examples show, there are solid reasons for studying animal perception, too. For one thing, animals can be trained to perform jobs that are beyond the sensory limits of humans. Dogs, because of their keen sense of smell, are adept at detecting odors too faint for the human nose. This is why dogs are frequently employed to sniff out illegal drugs or to trace the footsteps of a fleeing suspect. In other instances, knowledge of an animal's sensory apparatus allows one to control that animal's behavior. For instance, agricultural scientists control cotton bollworms—moth larvae that damage cotton crops—by spraying crop fields with a chemical that fools adult male moths into mating with moths of a different species. This chemical overwhelms the smell cues that normally guide mating behaviors. As a result, the moths engage in promiscuous and ineffective mating behavior. As a final example, scientists study animals whose sensory capacity is impaired by congenital disorders or by some experimental manipulation such as sensory deprivation (Kaas and Florence, 1996). These studies, in turn, lead to valuable ideas concerning the bases and treatment of comparable sensory disorders in humans.

Perception and Pleasure

In more primitive lifestyles (such as those of nonhuman primates) the lion's share of perceptual processing was probably devoted to survival—being on the alert to distinguish friends from foes and trying to locate the next meal. As civilization developed, these pressing demands relaxed. Consequently, civilized people enjoy the freedom to develop pastimes, such as the visual arts, music, and cuisine, that engage their perceptual machinery in pleasurable, amusing, and creative ways. Each of these pastimes involves the stimulation of the senses. Besides their immediate aesthetic and sensual qualities, these kinds of sensory experiences play an important role in the cultural heritage of societies. Through various forms of art, people share the joys and pains experienced by others, and they can savor vicariously the thrill of discovery that originally inspired the artist. In brief, art embodies much of a culture's wisdom and transmits that wisdom from one generation to the next by means of shared sensory experience.

Interestingly, however, artistic creations can also provide insight into the nature and mechanisms of perception. After all, artistic works are the creations of people whose perceptual systems obey the same principles as yours; the artist's eyes, ears, and brain are not fundamentally different from yours, either. So the artistic creations of those talented individuals, inspired as they may seem, must be guided by the same rules of perception that govern the way the rest of us experience the world. If art is going to communicate ideas and feelings to an audience, that artwork must work within the constraints of the perceptual systems of the audience members. At the same time, artists can exploit perceptual tricks to create captivating effects, both in visual art and in music. You'll see examples of these tricks in Chapters 5, 7, 8, 11 and 12. In general, it has become increasingly evident that we can learn a lot about perception by studying art (Livingstone, 2002; Zeki, 1999).

Perception and Intellectual Curiosity

Practical and pleasurable concerns aside, learning about perception satisfies an intellectual curiosity about ourselves and the world in which we live. Perception can be regarded as each individual's personal theory of reality, the knowledge-gathering process that defines our view of the world. Because this perceptual outlook guides our mental and behavioral activities, we naturally find it fascinating to inquire about the bases of perception. At the same time, people hold some odd theories about perception that need to be replaced by knowledge grounded in fact, not in intuition. We were surprised to learn, for example, that a large number of college students believe that our eyes emit the light that illuminates objects in the environment (Winer et al. 2002).

Natural curiosity leads to a variety of conjectures about perception. When looking at a newborn child, for instance, one cannot help speculating about what that infant sees and hears. Likewise, one is curious to know whether blind people really can hear sounds that escape the ears of sighted people. You may have wondered why colors seem to change depending on the time of day. As dusk approaches, greens take on a deeper richness, while yellows and reds lose some of their brilliance. And why does everyone effectively become color-blind in dim light? One would like to know what sensory cues enable a displaced pet to journey hundreds of miles, eventually returning to its old home. And one grudgingly marvels at how adept mosquitoes are at locating a person's bare skin in total darkness.

People are intrigued by their everyday experiences and are curious about the bases of those experiences. This curiosity was long ago formalized in philosophy. For centuries, philosophers argued about how human beings can know the external world. Their arguments reflected a concern about the validity of sense experiences. Though our concept of the world derives from the information of our senses, can we rely on those senses to tell the truth? Might we not be deceived about the world? Perhaps, as Plato suggested in Book VII of *The Republic,* we are like prisoners in a cave, cut off from the world, so that we can see only shadows created by objects and events outside.

In fact, from earliest times on, people have known that their senses were fallible. Realizing that sensory information was not totally dependable, philosophers became increasingly skeptical about anyone's ability to know the world as it really is. This skepticism reached full bloom during the late seventeenth and early eighteenth centuries. During that time, the British philosopher John Locke (1690/1924) made a crucial observation: water in a basin can feel either warm or cool to the touch, depending on where your hand has just been. If your hand has been in cold water, the basin's water would feel warm; if your hand has been in hot water, the water in the basin would feel cool. The apparent warmth or coolness of the water does not reside in the water itself; it is a quality that depends on the perceiver's own state. Because, to him, some perceived qualities of the external world seemed more subjective than others, Locke distinguished between primary qualities (that is, real qualities, actually present in the object) and secondary qualities (that result from an object's power to produce various sensations in us). Primary qualities include the bulk, number, motion, and shape of objects. Locke's secondary qualities include an object's color, sound, taste, and smell. Locke thought we can rely on primary qualities to reflect accurately the nature of objects in the real world, but we must be cautious, or skeptical, about relying on secondary qualities in the same way.

This skepticism about the information of the senses was carried to greater extremes by David Hume in *A Treatise of Human Nature* (1739/1963). Hume rejected the distinction between primary and secondary qualities, banishing all sense experiences to the realm of the subjective and unreliable. Hume's pessimism about the possibility of ever understanding perception is represented quite well by the following comment from his *Treatise:*

> As to those impressions which arise from the senses, their ultimate cause is, in my opinion, perfectly inexplicable by human reason, and it will always be impossible to decide with certainty whether they arise immediately from the object, or are produced by the creative power of the mind, or are derived from the author of our being. (Book I, Part III, Section V, p. 75)

There is good reason, though, to question Hume's skepticism (Schlagel, 1984). As knowledge of our senses has deepened, we have come to understand that lawful processes are responsible for what previously seemed to be mysterious sensory caprice. We know that holding one's hand in a basin of hot water initiates a process called adaptation, an alteration in the skin's temperature receptors. This process produces the thermal paradox that so perplexed Locke. If we understand adaptation—how it grows with time, how long it lasts, and so on—Locke's paradox becomes less of a reason for skepticism. Or suppose you put on a pair of colored sunglasses. If they're strongly tinted, they'll temporarily alter the overall color appearance of the world. But that's no reason to dismiss vision as inherently undependable. If you understand how the sunglasses alter the light that reaches your eyes, and if you understand enough about color vision itself, you'll be able to explain this change in the world's color appearance. In fact, the senses are actually quite dependable—as long as you understand how they operate. For instance, you would be able to take any pair of sunglasses and predict quite accurately how the world will look through those glasses, or you'd be able to take any person's hand and any basin of water and predict exactly how warm that water will feel. The scientific study of perception overcomes some of the skeptic's doubts.

Inasmuch as we are discussing attitudes about the relation between perception and reality, this is a good time to introduce a view we'll mention from time to time in this book. This view, called **naive realism,** is common among laypersons and beginning students of perception. "Naive realism is the view that what we know about the world is both unadulterated and unexpurgated with respect to even

FIGURE 1.3 | The perspectives of these two transparent figures appear to fluctuate. The darkened surface in each figure seems sometimes to be an inner surface and sometimes an outer surface. The fluctuations of the rhomboid (left) were first noticed by L. A. Necker about 150 years ago while he was examining some crystals. Today these figures are known as Necker's rhomboid and The Neckers cube.

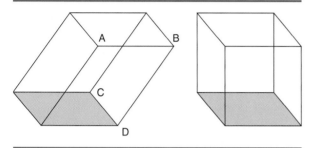

its most subtle details" (Shaw and Bransford, 1977, p. 18). In other words, the world *is* always exactly as it appears.

A simple test can determine whether someone is a naive realist. When asked, "Why does the world look to you the way it does?" the naive realist will answer, "Because it *is* that way." In other words, the properties of experience can always be completely and easily explained by the properties of the world itself. But this simple view of perception is mistaken. For one thing, it cannot explain why different people experience the same environmental event differently. And this does happen, as you'll discover throughout this book. We know, for example, that infants cannot see small objects that adults can see; that young adults can hear some sounds that older adults cannot; and that certain people are completely oblivious to odors that others have no trouble smelling. These individual differences challenge naive realism. We all live in the same *physical* world. If naive realism were a valid viewpoint, wouldn't our *perceptual* worlds be identical?

There's another reason to reject naive realism: a single, unchanging physical stimulus can fluctuate in appearance from one moment to the next. A classic example of this is the **Necker cube,** named after Swiss naturalist Louis Albert Necker (see Figure 1.3). Note how the rhomboid at the left seems to switch between two alternative perceptual interpretations. At one moment line segment AB appears closest to you, while at another moment segment CD appears closest. The appearance of the figure at the right undergoes similar fluctuations. This figure is said to be perceptually bistable. Now if perception were determined solely by the physical properties of the figure, its appearance should be un-

changing. Such examples clearly demonstrate that one's perceptions have qualities not present in the physical attributes of the stimulus. You'll see more examples of bistable figures in the forthcoming chapters.

At the other extreme from naive realism is **subjective idealism,** the view that the physical world is entirely the product of the mind, a compelling mental fiction. This philosophical position is associated with the Irish philosopher George Berkeley, who capsulized the idea in the phrase "to be is to perceive." In other words, the world exists only as a result of perception; no perception, no world. Carried to its extreme, this position leads to **solipsism,** the notion that only your mind exists and all other worldly objects are perceptions of your mind. This position can be entertaining to discuss among friends but is scientifically sterile. If the world in which we exist were not real, there would be no reason to study the relation between perceiving and that (imaginary) world.

Having rejected naive realism and solipsism, what do we propose about the relations between human perceptions and the real world? As stressed earlier, we readily acknowledge the existence of the real world and assert that its existence does not depend on a perceiver. At the same time, we recognize the perceiver's special contribution to the process of perception. The perceiver's view of the world is not perfectly accurate, of course, because the perceiver's sensory system both *limits* the information that is available and *augments* that information.

To show you more exactly what we mean by the perceiver's contribution, consider a familiar question: Does a tree falling in the forest make a sound if there is no one around to hear it? According to a solipsist, no tree, no forest, and no sound would exist in the absence of a perceiver. But according to our view, not only would the falling tree still exist even though no perceiver happened to be around, its fall would create acoustic energy in the form of air pressure waves. But would this constitute sound? If the term *sound* means a perceptual experience, then clearly the falling tree would not produce a sound. For the tree to produce a sound requires the presence of some organism with a sensory system capable of registering the available acoustic energy. But even this does not guarantee that the resulting experience would be what is normally called "sound." It's conceivable that the organism that is present might not be able to hear because it has no ears, but instead could *feel* the energy produced by the falling tree (in the same way that you can literally feel the beat of a bass drum). To qualify as sound, the energy must strike the ears of a human—or some other creature with a nervous system like that of a human. What this boils down to is that the quality of one's sensory experience depends on events within the nervous system, as Box 1.2 underscores.

Seeing and hearing are qualitatively different perceptual experiences. This is shown by the fact that people never confuse sight and sound. The same can be said for touch, taste, and smell. In fact, these qualitative differences form the basis for the classic five-part division of the senses—touch, taste, smell, hearing, and seeing. Our assumption in this book is that these subjectively different experiences are products of neural events within the brain. And yet those events, it is known, all boil down to patterns of nerve impulses within the brain. Since different experiences are represented by the same sort of events, how does the brain manage to distinguish one type of experience from another—sight from sound, and taste from smell? Let's consider this question as it applies to sight and sound.

It is tempting to answer by pointing out that sound waves, the stimulus for hearing, are fundamentally different from light energy, the stimulus for seeing. However, this argument is not adequate because the brain does not directly *receive* either sound waves or light energy. It receives only tiny electrical signals called neural impulses. In other words, from the brain's perspective, all incoming signals are equivalent. But, you might point out, although they resemble one another, those neural impulses *arise* from different sources, namely, the eyes and the ears. And, you might continue, those sources *are* fundamentally different—they are specially designed to respond only to particular kinds of physical stimulation. Because of their specialized receptors, the eyes respond to light but not to sound, while the opposite is true for the ears. So, you might well conclude, the distinctiveness of seeing and hearing depends on the difference between the eyes and the ears.

This explanation, however, is not adequate either because sensations of light and sound can be produced without the participation of eyes and ears. One can bypass them and stimulate the brain directly. During the course of brain surgery on awake, alert humans, neurosurgeons sometimes need to stimulate the brain's surface electrically to determine exactly where they are working. Depending on the area of the brain stimulated, patients report vivid sensations that seem quite real (Penfield and Perrot, 1963). For instance, stimulation at a point in the back of the brain can elicit sensations of light flashes, whereas stimulation at the proper spot on the side of the brain can cause the patient to hear tones.

Here, then, are examples of qualitatively distinct sensations that arise from exactly the same sort of stimulation—a mild electric current. Note, though, that the patients did not *feel* the electric current, they "heard" it or "saw" it, depending on the brain region stimulated.

These observations force a surprising conclusion: the critical difference between hearing and seeing depends not so much on differences between the eyes and the ears but on *where* in the brain the eyes and ears send their messages and how those brain areas are organized. This is actually a very old idea, dating back to Johannes Müller, a nineteenth-century German physiologist. Müller's theory, called the doctrine of **specific nerve energies,** states that the nature of a sensation depends on the particular set of nerve fibers stimulated. According to this doctrine, activity in the nerve from the eye will invariably produce visual sensations, regardless of how that activity is instigated. Nowadays, it is recognized that sensory nerves travel to specific brain areas: the nerve from the eye travels to one place, the nerve from the ear to another. Thus, the emphasis has shifted from the nerves themselves to their projection sites in the brain. It is now widely believed that the distinctiveness of sight and sound is related to the unique properties of the neural connections within different regions of the brain, connections that are established during early brain development (von Melchner, Pallas, and Sur, 2000).

Müller's doctrine suggested a provocative thought experiment to William James (1892, p. 12). To paraphrase his idea, suppose you were able to reroute the nerve from your eye, sending it to the part of your brain that normally receives input from your ear. Suppose that while you were at it, you also rerouted the nerve from your ear, sending it to that part of your brain that normally gets visual information. Now imagine that with this revised nervous system, you are caught in a thunderstorm. A flash of lightning, which stimulates the eyes, should evoke auditory sensations, while the subsequent sound of thunder, which stimulates the ears, should evoke visual sensations. But don't expect the light-evoked auditory sensations to sound like thunder or the sound-evoked visual sensations to resemble lightning—the train of neural impulses carried by the optic nerve and the auditory nerve are unlikely to establish the precise patterns of brain activity associated with thunder and lightning.

To sum up: In order to understand perception as fully as possible, one must study not only the properties of the physical world but also those of the perceiver.

Complementary Approaches to the Study of Perception

At the outset of this chapter we stated that perception entails a sequence of interrelated events that mutually influence one another. Furthermore, we said that to understand perception requires knowing something about each component of the sequence. Understanding these components requires the combined knowledge from several different scientific disciplines, ranging from biophysics to psychology. These disciplines use different levels of analysis, from the microscopic (studying the behavior of molecules) to the macroscopic

(studying the behavior of whole organisms and groups of organisms). For a complete picture, then, one needs to analyze perception at several different levels, each offering a unique and necessary perspective. To illustrate metaphorically what we mean by "levels of analysis," look at Figure 1.4. It shows an aerial photograph taken over the Peruvian desert from a very great height. From this altitude, one can see a mammoth sand carving thought to be a thousand years old. The carving, made by people lost to history, is a figure nearly 1,600 meters long. It is so huge that it can be recognized only from a great height. Standing on the ground, you would be able to see only small portions of the carving, never the entire thing. And at a really close level of scrutiny, you would see only the hills and valleys in the ground's surface. Thus, to appreciate the carving's entire pattern requires a particular level of analysis, namely, far above

FIGURE 1.4 | Aerial photograph of sand carving on Peruvian desert.

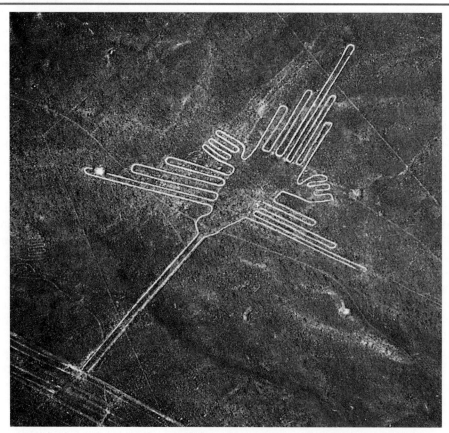

the carving. Suppose, though, that you wanted to understand just how the carving had been done. Then you would need to examine the details of the carving and what it was made of. Such an examination would require a radically different perspective, one focused on the details of the carving.[3]

This beautiful and mysterious desert carving dramatizes a point about perception: one must adopt different levels of analysis in order to answer all the significant questions about the subject. Consequently, we'll be adopting various levels of analysis in our examination of perception. The three main levels of analysis that we'll explore are the *psychological, biological,* and *theoretical.*

Distinguishing among the psychological, biological, and theoretical approaches will help organize the discussion that follows. We repeat, though, that these approaches are not mutually exclusive, but are complementary. One simply cannot learn all one wants to know about perception from just one approach.

Psychological Approaches

Psychological approaches can take many different forms, but all have in common the use of some behavioral measure as a gauge of perception. Those behavioral measures can be verbal responses ("Yes, I hear it"), manual reactions ("Press this button when you hear it"), or reflexive reactions ("Did he flinch when the sound was produced?"). Those behavioral reactions to stimuli are taken as indices of whether those stimuli can be detected or whether they can be discriminated from other stimuli. For instance, one might attempt to train a bird to fly to a red perch but not to a green perch. If the bird succeeds in learning this task, one might infer that the bird can discriminate red from green. To justify this conclusion, however, requires additional tests to ensure that the bird is actually relying on color, not other visual cues such as position or brightness.

Similarly, a human being can be instructed to push one button whenever a red object is presented and to push another button whenever a green object is presented. For birds and humans, behavior is used to infer something about perception. There are actually many specific techniques for studying perception, and we'll

---

[3]It is strange to realize that the creators of this carving were never able to see the entire fruits of their labor, since they could never enjoy a view from a perspective anything like the one shown in Figure 1.4.

describe some of those techniques as the need arises. Now, however, let's not focus on the details of particular behavioral techniques. Instead, let's analyze the methods along more general lines, grouping them according to their degree of *formality.* By "formality" we mean the extent to which stimuli and reactions to them are structured or controlled.

The Phenomenal/Naturalistic Approach The least formal is the phenomenal/naturalistic method. "Phenomenal" (sometimes called "phenomenological") means that the data used to learn about perception consists of one's own conscious experiences which, of course, can be communicated to others only using verbal descriptions. "Naturalistic" means that the evidence pertains to perceptual experiences occurring within our everyday environment; there is no effort to induce, modify, or control the objects or events triggering perceptual experience.

This "informal" approach to perception has some strengths. For one thing, it relies on the most readily available data, the steady stream of perceptual experiences evoked by naturally occurring events. Such experiences might include the deeply saturated colors experienced around sunset, the rising and then falling pitch of an ambulance's siren as the vehicle speeds past you, the funny taste of orange juice after you've brushed your teeth. We all have countless experiences like these throughout our waking hours. To study perception, then, you could collect and organize these experiences. Going one step further, you could discuss your perceptual experiences with other people, for purposes of comparison. But what limitations would you encounter by following this program?

First, by restricting yourself to phenomenal descriptions, you would be unable able to study perception in animals and preverbal infants, a serious limitation. Second, even working with humans who *can* verbalize their experiences, you would need to be wary. Verbal reports can be fallible and misleading. For one thing, not all people use words in the same way. For instance, many colorblind people have learned to label colors much as color-normal people do, even though their experiences are surely very different.

Because verbal descriptions are typically made with great confidence (after all it is *your* experience you're describing), one can be misled into believing verbal descriptions provide an accurate and complete picture of perceptual experience. That assumption, however, is unwarranted: there is reason to doubt whether individuals

FIGURE 1.5 | Look at this drawing for a while. If you cannot discern an animal, look at Figure 1.6 on page 18.

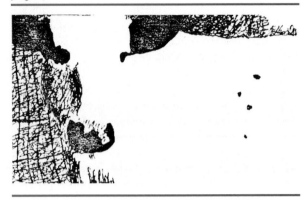

can accurately describe their experiences, motives, and thought processes (Nisbett and Wilson, 1977). Factors of which we're completely unaware can profoundly influence what we perceive. As you will learn as we move through the book's chapters, these unconscious influences include expectations, prior experience, and motivations (see Figure 1.5). Although such factors are integral to the nature of perceptual experience, the phenomenal approach would foreclose identifying them: you cannot possibly describe aspects of perception that transpire outside your awareness.

In a related vein, verbal reports of perceptual experience can unwittingly force someone to categorize a perceptual experience in a way that belies the true nature of that experience. Take, for example, the simple question, Did you hear that faint, rattling sound when you started the car? The question calls for a binary decision—yes or no—but the sensory experience upon which that decision must be based is probably far more subtle. Your binary answer can thus depend on the possible implications of your answer as well as on your prior knowledge about the status of your car. Fortunately, there are procedures allowing us to assess the influence of these "criterion" effects on sensory decisions (see Box 1.3).

There's another reason why verbal reports cannot always be trusted. In some instances, people are motivated to avoid telling what they consider to be the truth about their experiences. Here's one example. A *malingerer* is someone who pretends to have an illness or disability to get some special gain or to avoid some re-

sponsibility. Feigned deafness is one form of malingering. Ask such a malingerer if he can hear, and you'll get no answer unless the question is communicated in writing, lip reading, or sign language. Then, the malingerer will assure you that he can't hear (a misleading verbal report). But there is a very clever, foolproof way to catch the malingerer: delayed auditory feedback. While the person is reading aloud, record his speech and, following a very short delay, play it back into his ears. If he is genuinely deaf, and not a malingerer, delayed auditory feedback will have no influence on his reading. But if he *can* hear, the delayed feedback of his own voice will invariably disrupt his speech.

The word *feigns* denotes that someone is purposely lying or pretending. But there are instances where a person's erroneous verbal reports don't really constitute lying. One such instance is **Anton's syndrome,** which was first described by Gabriel Anton more than a hundred years ago (Foerstl, Owen, and David, 1993). This syndrome, as rare as it is bizarre, involves complete blindness coupled with denial (the blind person denies that he or she is blind). The condition supposedly arises because two different areas of the brain have been damaged: the one needed for seeing and the one needed for knowing that you're seeing. This damage to the brain occurs quite suddenly—usually as the result of a cerebral vascular accident (a stroke)—and the victim of Anton's syndrome may walk around for quite some time bumping into things and having other mishaps until he or she becomes convinced that something is wrong. But immediately following damage to the brain, victims of Anton's syndrome confidently insist that they can see. Asked to describe what they see, the victims may give very detailed answers, which are utter fabrications, as evidenced by their lack of correspondence to objective reality.

Anton's syndrome not only underscores the potential unreliability of verbal reports about perception, but also points up a more general fact: perceptual experiences and knowledge of those experiences are two quite separate things.

Despite its limitations, the phenomenal/naturalistic approach to perception has an important role to play. For more than a hundred years, careful and thoughtful observers have used this informal approach as a basis upon which to build a more formal study of perception. Although this book will emphasize these more formal approaches, many of the ideas for formal study derive from this less formal method.

Just about everyone has had this maddening experience. While taking a shower, you faintly hear what sounds like the telephone ringing. Because of the shower's steady noise, though, you're not sure it *is* the phone. So do you decide to run, dripping wet, to answer it? Or do you conclude that it's only your imagination?

Your behavior in this situation depends on factors other than the loudness of the ringing sound. For instance, if you are expecting an important call, you will in all likelihood scurry out of the shower to see whether the phone is actually ringing. If, in contrast, you're not expecting a call, you're more likely to attribute the ringing sound to the shower's own noises. Your decision about the reality of the sound, then, is influenced by your expectations. This example illustrates a significant principle, namely, that one's interpretation of sensory data depends significantly on nonsensory factors.

This dependence affects the way in which results from perceptual studies are interpreted. Imagine testing a person's hearing by presenting faint sounds and having the person say whether or not she could hear the sound. Performance on such a test can vary from one person to the next, and not just because some people have better hearing than others. Some people are simply more willing to take a gamble, asserting that they heard something even if they're not 100 percent certain (these people might also want to impress the tester with their keen hearing, say, if the hearing test is part of a job application). There are also more conservative people, who are not gamblers. In the hearing test, such people might require a much louder sound before they are willing to say they heard it. Suppose that two people took a hearing test, one a conservative type, the other a gambler. On the basis of their performance on the hearing test, the tester might mistakenly conclude that the conservative had inferior hearing.

People *do* differ in the sensitivity of their sensory systems. Some individuals, for instance, have a keener sense of smell than do others. But people *also* differ in their motivations, expectations, and willingness to gamble. As an aggregate, these latter differences can be labeled "motivational differences." In studies of perceptual abilities, it is important to distinguish between an individual's sensitivity and motivation. Toward this end, psychologists have developed several strategies for separating the two.

To tell whether a person can *really* hear an extremely faint sound, one needs more to go on than the fact that she is constantly saying that she hears a sound. Logically, one must also ensure that she does not make exactly the same claim when no sound whatever has been presented (Goldman, 1976). Many experiments on hearing, then, randomly intermix two types of test trials. On one type of trial, a weak sound is presented; on the other, no sound is presented. After each trial, the person says whether or not she heard a sound. Someone really interested in impressing the tester might say, "Yes, I hear it," after every single trial. Of course, she'd be right on every trial in which a sound actually occurred, but she'd be wrong with respect to every trial in which no sound occurred. From this result, the tester should realize that this person could not discriminate the presence of sound from the absence of sound. Omitting the sound and noting the subject's failure to recognize that omission allows the tester to separate the person's sensitivity to sound from other possible factors, such as the motivation to impress.

This general strategy is not limited to the study of hearing; similar methods are used with the other senses as well. To implement the strategy, psychologists have developed a set of sophisticated statistical techniques collectively known as *signal detection theory*. The appendix provides additional details of signal detection theory. For a more thorough treatment of this topic, we suggest you consult Wickens (2001), MacMillan and Creelman (2004), or Swets, Tanner, and Birdsall (1961). Meanwhile, before showering the next time, take the phone off the hook.

Experimental Approaches   The phenomenal/naturalistic approach works with objects and events as they occur in nature, without trying to control or manipulate them. This approach is simple but not entirely satisfactory. For one thing, to study a particular aspect of perception often requires creation of a class of stimuli that is not available naturally. To give an example, nearly all sounds in the natural world comprise a broad range of acoustic energy spread throughout the audible frequency spectrum. But to understand our ability to hear natural sounds, it is essential to study hearing's sensitivity to different, isolated frequencies, and that requires generating those sound frequencies artificially in the laboratory. Moreover, it is sometimes necessary to use a whole series of

FIGURE 1.6 | Outline drawing of the same animal depicted in Figure 1.5. Note how seeing this figure helps you interpret Figure 1.5. Surprisingly, this effect lasts for months.

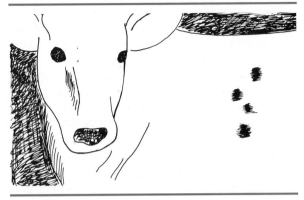

stimuli to compare each to the effects produced by its fellows. And the specific series you want might never occur naturally. For example, suppose you want the members of a series of sound tones to differ in only one attribute (such as pitch) with all others (such as loudness) held constant. This would make it easy to ascribe any resulting change in perception to the varied attribute. If several attributes varied simultaneously (as is usually the case with naturally occurring stimuli), you would have trouble knowing how much each attribute contributed to perception.

In a related vein, naturalistic stimuli do not often repeat themselves precisely. We mentioned previously that the study of perception should be general: It should measure the perceptual responses of more than one person (generalizability), and it should measure those responses multiple times in the same person (replicability). To satisfy these needs requires repeated measures of perception in response to the same stimuli presented multiple times under controlled conditions.

Control and careful manipulation of the stimulus also allow one to identify exactly *what* aspect of the stimulus underlies some perceptual experience. Here's one illustration: Some rare individuals are able to discriminate among thousands of different wines by taste alone. To determine the basis of this remarkable ability, you could create a series of specially constituted wines that varied in their composition, and using this set of controlled stimuli you could isolate the cues enabling such individuals to distinguish what most people cannot.

Control over sensory stimuli represents a key requirement for two kinds of experiments that are the foundation of the scientific study of perception: matching experiments and detection experiments. *Matching experiments* ask people to adjust one stimulus until it appears identical to another. This obviously requires stimuli that can be manipulated precisely. *Detection experiments* measure the weakest stimulus that a person can detect. Again, such experiments require stimuli whose intensities can be controlled. The appendix describes some of the formal, structured methods for performing these kinds of experiments. In addition, throughout the book, you'll encounter descriptions of various methods in the context of the research problems for which they were designed.

So, to control and manipulate stimuli, one usually synthesizes specially designed stimuli not found in the natural environment. Such stimuli are sometimes criticized as being nonecological, because they are not the objects and events for which perceptual systems evolved. Researchers widely agree, however, that simple, artificial (nonecological) stimuli can be valid because they often clarify the effects of more complex, naturally occurring stimuli. This point is well documented throughout this book. There is merit, though, to studying perception using ecologically representative stimuli. In recent years, perception research has increasingly tried to relate simple, laboratory-created stimuli to the objects and events ordinarily encountered in the natural environment. In fact, one relatively new branch of perception focuses explicitly on quantitative descriptions of the visual world and the auditory world in which we live. Called **natural scene statistics** (Nelken, 2004; Kersten, Mamassian, and Yuille, 2004), these descriptions can provide powerful links between psychophysical data and results generated using any of several biological approaches that you'll learn about in the next section.

Another "non-ecological" characteristic of the experimental approach is the tendency to study a given sensory modality in isolation of the others. In fact, entire journals are devoted to research on single modalties (e.g., *Vision Research, Hearing Research, Chemical Senses*). This parceling of perception into sensory systems is also reflected in the organization of this textbook, with separate chapters devoted to vision, hearing, touch, taste, and smell. Yet our perceptual experiences in the natural environment are nearly always multimodal in character, with information from the separate modalities merged to form a coherent perceptual experience. For that reason, throughout this book you will repeatedly encounter examples underscoring the interdependence of perceptual experience on information from multiple sensory systems.

So despite its limitations, the psychological approach is essential in the study of perception. Nonetheless, it leaves unanswered important questions about neural processes underlying perception. In the next section we turn to a complementary approach that addresses those questions.

Biological Approaches

Throughout the history of scientific research on perception, an enduring theme has been the dependence of perceptual events on neural events, within sensory receptors and within the brain. An overriding goal, then, has been to investigate the linkages between perceptual and biological phenomena. Though such investigations can be challenging to carry out, their outcomes often yield information fundamental to understanding perception. Here we'll sketch out some of the strategies used to relate physiology to behavior, without going into the details or the outcomes. In subsequent chapters, you'll learn how these strategies provide answers to specific questions about perception.

Lesion Technique   A wound or an injury to a delimited part of the brain can destroy neurons within that part of the brain. This loss of brain cells produces what is called a **lesion,** and by studying the consequences of that lesion one can draw inferences about the function of the neural tissue in that region of the brain. Lesions can occur naturally, from disease or trauma, or lesions can be created in experimental animals specifically for research purposes. Restricted lesions can be produced by applying electrical current to a targeted area of the brain, by injecting a chemical that kills nerve cells, or by surgically removing brain tissue. Usually, such lesions are permanent, and irreversible.

Regardless of how the lesion occurs, a researcher can measure resulting changes in perceptual function. Interpreted with proper caution, these studies can help identify the anatomical locus of neural structures crucially involved in a given perceptual ability. There are, however, limitations to the conclusions that can be drawn from lesion studies, especially because lesions disrupt more than just the neural operations associated with the lesioned brain region. Consider this analogy: A mammoth snowfall on the Massachusetts Turnpike's eastern end can seriously interfere with the economic activity throughout the Boston area, but we wouldn't conclude that economic activity is localized *on* the Massachusetts Turnpike. Likewise, lesioning a particular brain area may destroy an animal's ability to recognize a certain class of

visual objects such as faces, but it would be misleading to state that this brain region was solely responsible for analyzing that class of objects. By the same token, an animal may recover function following the destruction of brain tissue, but this doesn't mean that the lesioned area does not normally participate in that function. Other brain areas may have taken over for the destroyed area. The perceptual consequences of naturally occurring lesions in humans have been used for centuries to gain insights into the neural basis of human perception (Boring, 1942). Lesion results from human studies, however, can be especially difficult to interpret (Rorden and Karnath, 2004). Disease or trauma usually creates brain damage in multiple areas of the brain, so naturally occurring lesions may offer only limited help in pinpointing the neural basis of perceptual function. So, results from lesion studies can be strongly suggestive but seldom definitive.

Before turning to the next biological approach, we want to mention a relatively new technique, **transcranial magnetic stimulation** (TMS), that can be construed as a safe, reversible form of the lesion technique. As you probably know, brain activity consists of tiny electric signals generated by the brain's billions of neurons. A lesion, of course, destroys that electrical activity by destroying the neurons themselves. TMS, in contrast, disrupts neural activity by briefly but potently altering the biophysical events underlying generation of those electrical signals. Specifically, TMS involves the delivery of a brief, strong pulse of magnetic energy through a probe resting on a person's scalp. These bursts of magnetic radiation easily penetrate the scalp and skull, thereby inducing small electrical currents within the brain tissue directly below the probe. Those electrical currents interfere with normal, ongoing neural activity within cells located at the site of the TMS pulse and, thereby, disrupt whatever function those neurons ordinarily subserve. Laboratories are now beginning to use TMS to study the role of different brain regions in perception (Stewart et al., 2001). It is crucial, of course, to use this technique with great caution, to ensure that the currents induced by TMS remain within safe levels and to be certain that people with any history of epileptic seizure do not participate in a TMS study (Anand and Hotson, 2002).

Evoked Potential Technique   Another widely used procedure relates perceptual judgments made in response to a given stimulus with the electrical brain activity evoked by that same stimulus. Measured through small electrodes placed on the surface of a person's scalp, this brain activity is termed an **evoked potential** (EP) or,

FIGURE 1.7 | Photograph of a human volunteer with a multi-electrode array attached to the scalp. Each electrode is capable of picking up tiny electrical signals generated by the brain.

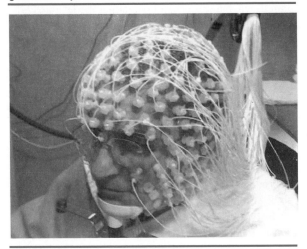

alternatively, an **event-related potential (ERP).** This procedure requires sensitive electronic amplifiers to boost the electrical signals measured from the scalp and skull. These signals are called massed responses because they reflect the varied activity among the thousands of brain cells located near each electrode. In recent years, ERPs have been measured using an array of electrodes distributed over a large region of the scalp (see Figure 1.7). By recording electrical signals from all these electrodes simultaneously, researchers can more accurately localize the source of brain activity associated with a given stimulus. Moreover, using multiple electrodes makes it possible to monitor how brain activity builds and spreads from one location to another.

Over the years, ERPs have been measured in a variety of tasks. In some instances, researchers want to know whether the magnitude of the ERP correlates with a person's subjective impression of the stimulus's intensity. In other cases, researchers measure the ERP in response to unanticipated or novel stimulation. A particularly intriguing application of the ERP technique looks for brain activity in response to visual or auditory events that, in fact, are not perceived. For example, Luck, Vogel, and Shapiro (1996) found that unexpected words still elicited a strong "novelty" response in the ERP, even when the presence of those words could not be reported because the person's attention was temporarily distracted.

The ERP technique is also useful for studying nonverbal perception in infants and in animals, individuals unable to report their perceptions verbally. When ERPs to a given stimulus can be recorded from the brain of an infant or an animal, we can safely conclude that the brain is responsive to that stimulus. We cannot, of course, conclude that the individual actually perceives the stimulus, but we can be certain that a necessary condition for perception has been satisfied. Using ERPs, researchers have harvested important facts about the visual world of infants (e.g., Atkinson and Braddick, 1998) and of animals (e.g., Berkley and Watkins, 1971).

This technique also has its drawbacks. For one, the *failure* to record an ERP doesn't necessarily mean the brain fails to register the evoking stimulus—the neural signals may just be too weak to be picked up or the recording electrodes may be misplaced on the scalp. For another, it is very difficult to pinpoint in exactly what region of the brain ERP activity is arising. So, it is important to realize that the evoked potential provides a rather diffuse measure of brain activity picked up from tiny signals generated by large numbers of brain cells; the evoked potential reflects omnibus brain activity.

Brain Imaging Techniques   In the past decade, perception research has profited substantially from imaging techniques that generate detailed pictures of the human brain in action. When measured under appropriately designed experimental conditions, images produced by these methods can reveal specific regions of the human brain uniquely activated while a person is engaged in a specific perceptual task. Currently in use are three powerful forms of brain imaging: **positron-emission tomography (PET) scan, functional magnetic resonance imaging (fMRI), and magnetoencephalography (MEG).** Each of these techniques has produced remarkably revealing "snapshots" of brain regions engaged in various acts of perception.

MEG exploits the fact that active nerve cells produce tiny electrical currents, which, in turn, generate minute, localized magnetic fields. The skull and scalp are essentially transparent to these magnetic fields, so an array of several hundred ultra-sensitive detectors around the head can pick up the magnetic fields.[4] Sophisticated software then analyzes the spatial and temporal distribu-

---

[4]The brain's magnetic fields are less than one hundred millionth of earth's normal magnetic field. As a result, MEG requires a magnetically shielded room and ultra-sensitive detectors that must be cooled to the temperature of liquid helium, about −270 degrees Celsius.

tion of the magnetic field, and can localize the brain regions that gave rise to the field. Because MEG does not depend upon relatively slow metabolic changes in the brain, as PET and fMRI do, it can resolve very fast changes in brain activity. With a temporal resolution about a thousand times better than that of the other techniques, MEG can tell apart distinct stages of processing that contribute to perception (Finney et al., 2003; Liu, Harris, and Kanwisher, 2002), including stages involved in short-term memory of what has been perceived (Lu, Williamson, and Kaufman, 1992). Compared to fMRI, MEG is less often used as an imaging technique, in part because of the great expense of the necessary facilities and the extreme vulnerability of the measured signals to extraneous noise. Also, compared to fMRI, MEG lacks the spatial precision to pinpoint activity to a small area in the brain. Technological advances will undoubtedly reduce these problems, however, which means we can expect MEG to play a growing role in the study of perception.

PET capitalizes on the fact that activated regions of the brain temporarily require additional amounts of glucose and oxygen. PET tracks this increased metabolic demand by applying a radioactive "tag" to glucose or to oxygen atoms in water, both of which are required for increased metabolism. Sensors can then register the temporary accumulation of this radioactively labeled chemical in particular brain regions. In one version of the procedure, a person first inhales a mixture of air and radioactively labeled carbon dioxide. From the person's lungs, trace amounts of the radioactive material enter the bloodstream and then rapidly dissipate. For a few minutes or so after inhalation, regions of the brain with heightened metabolic activity will attract a strong local flow of blood, bringing with it additional radioactive material. Using radioactive sensors arrayed around the head, one can record an image of the distribution of radioactively "tagged" blood within the brain. Going one step further, the person can now engage in a particular perceptual task (e.g., detect changes in the color of a geometric form) while the PET scan is being performed. It thus becomes possible to relate neural activity in specific brain regions with the execution of particular perceptual tasks (Corbetta et al., 1991; McIntosh et al., 1999). PET has some noteworthy limitations, however. First, the technique has limited spatial resolution: PET cannot distinguish differences in activity between small brain areas that adjoin one another. Second, safety and health regulations limit the amount of radioactive exposure an individual can receive, making it impossible to test the same person repeatedly un-

FIGURE 1.8 | Photograph of an MRI scanner, a device capable of measuring tiny fluctuations in a magnetic field produced by increased blood flow in the brain. Called *functional magnetic resonance imaging,* this technique has developed into the premier method for studying brain activations associated with cognitive function, perception included. The volunteer participant lies on the table (shown here outside of the scanner), and the table is moved into the scanner so that the person's brain is centered inside the donut-shaped "bore" of the scanner.

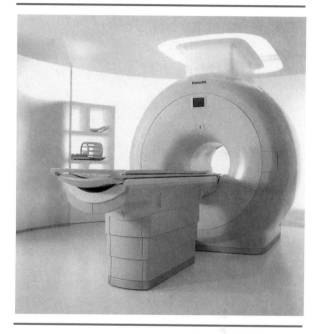

der different conditions. For these reasons, recent brain imaging work has favored another technology that we turn to next, fMRI.

fMRI exploits the same principle as PET: increased neural activity triggers a temporary increase in metabolic demand at the site of activation. But unlike PET, fMRI tracks the consequences of this increased demand without the need for a radioactive labeling agent. fMRI capitalizes on the fact that oxygenated blood has different magnetic properties from deoxygenated blood. Thus, it's possible to detect and localize brief surges in oxygenated blood within the brain, thereby inferring sites of increased neural activity. An fMRI scanner, then, allows researchers to measure fluctuations in the magnetic fields of well-defined areas of the brain (see Figure 1.8). These measurements can be made at the same

FIGURE 1.9 | This is an image of the left hemisphere of the brain of an adult human (that human happens to be Randolph Blake, a coauthor of this textbook). The checkered overlay at the back of the brain (the right-hand portion of image) denotes regions activated when this individual viewed a rotating checkerboard figure. Other areas within interior regions (not visible in this picture) were also activated by this visual pattern. Regions of activation were identified by the brain imaging technique called *functional magnetic resonance imaging,* or fMRI.

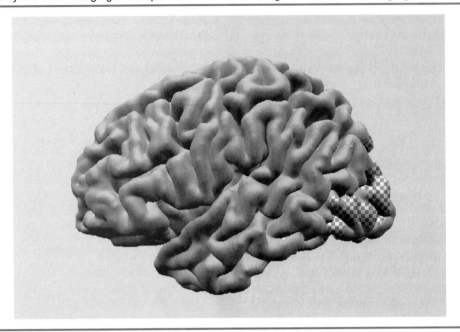

time that an individual engages in a perceptual task, making it possible to correlate fluctuations in an fMRI signal with performance of the task (see Figure 1.9). A nice primer on fMRI can be found on the Web (accessible at www.mhhe.com/blake5).

Depending on the scanner's sensitivity, fMRI can pinpoint regions of neural activation with very high spatial accuracy (Wandell, 1999). As fMRI requires no radioactive material, it can be repeated on the same individual, which makes it possible to examine aspects of perception, such as learning, that may take days to develop. As powerful as it is, fMRI does have its limitations, however. First and foremost is the relatively poor temporal resolution of the technique. The hemodynamic changes in response to increased neural activity are themselves relatively slow, meaning that it can take several seconds for blood flow to increase in those parts of the brain where neural activity has gone up. This makes it difficult to pinpoint with high accuracy exactly when activity increased and whether activation in one area

started before activation in another area. Besides its relatively poor temporal resolution, fMRI also suffers from our incomplete understanding of the nature of the signal being measured by the technique. There's no doubt that fMRI is indexing neural activity, but at present there is no way to know what proportion of that activity corresponds to output signals from a brain region compared to input signals to that brain region. For that matter, we aren't sure about the exact nature of the physiological events triggering increased blood flow. Those events could involve any number of component processes that go into the generation of neural activity, and the interpretation of fMRI results can depend on what those components are (Logothetis, 2002). Fortunately, these questions are going to be answered in the near future, thereby sharpening the conclusions we can draw from fMRI experiments. Despite these limitations, the technique remains quite popular and is highly useful in the study of perception; throughout the coming chapters, you'll read about many results obtained using fMRI.

Single Cell Techniques   The techniques discussed so far all operate on a fairly coarse scale, in which the grain comprises thousands of neurons. Techniques that provide finer grain analysis are excellent supplements to what we have characterized as coarser techniques. In one fine-grain approach, the physiological responses of individual neurons are recorded while an alert behaving animal, usually a monkey, engages in some perceptual task. For example, while varying the complexity of the task, the researcher tries to identify single neurons whose responses are strongly correlated with the animal's performance. Correlated activity suggests that those neurons form part of the neural machinery involved in the perceptual task. To be successful, this approach must draw upon prior evidence about the locus of neurons thought to register information utilized in the task. Otherwise, the research would degenerate into an unguided search for a needle in a haystack.

Once an investigator has identified a set of neurons that is believed to mediate a particular perceptual judgment, that hypothesis can be tested more directly. One can artificially stimulate the neurons by passing weak electrical current into them. If activity in those neurons is crucial, this boost in activity should alter an animal's performance on an associated perceptual task (Newsome, Britten, and Movshon, 1989; Cohen and Newsome, 2004). You will see examples of revealing results using this technique in several chapters to come. Note, however, that electrical stimulation activates not only those neurons in contact with the electrode but also other neurons nearby. So it would be a mistake to assume that activity in those neurons *alone* is affecting the animal's behavior.

Incidentally, just because these recording techniques gather information from individual neurons it doesn't mean that researchers are limited to gathering that information from just one neuron at a time. In recent years, it has become possible to perform multielectrode recordings, capturing the activity of dozens or more neurons simultaneously (Nicolelis and Ribeiro, 2002; Katz, Nicolelis, and Simon, 2002). This great advance allows us to examine entire neural circuits in action, and to understand the flow of neural information from one part of the circuit to another.

Theoretical Approaches

The previous two sections outlined strategies by which perception and its underlying neural events can be studied and ultimately related to one another. Borrowing terminology from computer science, we might say that these sections dealt with the *input* for perception, the *hardware* of the perceptual process, and its *output*. This metaphor, however, ignores a crucial element: the *program*. Here, "program" refers to the set of instructions or rules that transform input into output.

Sometimes people confuse the program with the hardware on which it runs. This confusion obscures an important distinction between the two. To reinforce the distinction between hardware and program, consider philosopher Daniel Dennett's discussion of an abacus.

> "Its computational task is to do arithmetic: to yield a correct output for any arithmetic problem given to it as input. At this level, then, an abacus and an electronic calculator are alike; they are designed to perform the same "information-processing task." The algorithmic description of the abacus is what you learn when you learn how to manipulate it—the recipe for moving the beads in the course of adding, subtracting, multiplying, and dividing. Its physical description depends on what it is made of: It might be wooden beads strung on wires in a frame; or it might be poker chips lined up along the cracks in the floor; or something accomplished with a pencil and good eraser on a sheet of lined paper." (1991, p. 276).

In his influential book *Vision*, David Marr (1982) argued the value of studying perception on three complementary levels of abstraction. From most to least abstract, the levels are as follows: one can analyze perception as an information-processing problem; one can examine the set of rules (the program) used to solve the information-processing problem; finally, one can study the neural machinery of perception and how that machinery executes the program. Marr insisted that some effort on the most abstract level ought to precede work on the other two levels.

If, like Marr, one describes perception as a solution to a problem, one needs to appreciate exactly what the problem is. An analogy may help. Suppose a friend tells you that she is thinking of a number between 1 and 20. Your job is to identify that number. You get one clue: the number is odd. Obviously, the clue does not give enough information to identify the number with certainty; it *under specifies* the solution (as opposed to being told, for instance, that the number is the largest prime number in the set). Generally speaking, the information provided to our sense organs under specifies the true nature of objects in the world. Somehow, though, despite significant under specification, the perceptual process manages to yield high-quality, useful representations of those objects.

A researcher may sometimes want to identify not only the processes that make it possible to perform a particular perceptual task, but also how efficiently humans perform that task. The theoretical goal is to identify any aspect of the perceptual process that fails to exploit fully whatever information might be available. One strategy is to compare human performance of a perceptual task against what could be expected from an "ideal perceiver" who was able to utilize all the available information. Often the "ideal perceiver" is a computer-generated model that processes information optimally, with none of the quirks, biases, blindspots, or inefficiencies of human perception (Geisler, 1989). Comparisons of human performance against theoretically ideal benchmarks make it possible to identify aspects of perceptual processing that limit actual performance.

Any computation, whether carried out by an ideal observer, by an electronic device, or by a biological device, is only as good as its data and its processing rules. The brain's perceptual computations may be accurate or they may be in error, depending on the quality of information supplied by the senses and on the brain's predisposition to process that information in certain ways. But if certain processing rules can lead to errors, why would the brain be predisposed to use those rules?

The information picked up by the senses is not merely a series of unrelated, incoherent data. Instead, sensory information closely conforms to predictable, structured patterns (Snyder and Barlow, 1988). These patterns arise from the very nature of the physical world itself, the world in which our senses have evolved. For instance, in our world, objects tend to be compact. The various parts of any object tend to be near one another, not scattered at random all over the landscape (Geisler et al., 2001). In our world, the surface color or texture of most natural objects tends to change gradually rather than abruptly (Kersten, 1987). In our world, light tends to come from above rather than from below (Gregory, 1978). In our world, the hardness of a surface determines how sound energy is reflected from that surface (Handel, 1989).

If the brain's processing rules embodied these regularities, or constraints, that characterize the natural world, the brain's perceptual operation could be more efficient and rapid (Kersten, Mamassian, and Yuille, 2004). Just as processing rules can be embodied within the microchips of an electronic device, rules that assume these regulari-

FIGURE 1.10 │ Subjective, or illusory, square.

ties of the natural world could be embodied in the hardware of our brains (Ramachandran, 1988). We'll illustrate this with an example.

Look at Figure 1.10, one of many interesting figures devised by Gaetano Kanizsa (1976). This **Kanizsa figure** conveys a strong impression of a white square resting atop four black circles. However, in creating the figure, we had only to make the four sectored disks. Your perceptual system did the rest by creating the white square. It is widely believed that subjective figures, like the one seen in Figure 1.10, occur because the visual system makes the quite reasonable assumption that nearer objects tend to occlude objects located farther away.

Now, in principle, there's no reason why perception has to include a square in its interpretation of Figure 1.10—a perfectly reasonable alternative would be for you to see four sectored disks, period. In fact, that's exactly what you *do* see when you look at Figure 1.10, a set of four objects seen against a white background. So why does perception fabricate a square in Figure 1.10? Because perception takes into account the likelihood of the layout of objects within a scene when interpreting that scene. For you to see just the four sectored disks and no square in the figure, those disks would have to be precisely arranged *in the world* with their missing sectors forming perfect right angles relative to one another. Because such an experience is unlikely, our perceptual apparatus prefers the alternative interpretation of four complete disks partially occluded by a square. Perception, in other words, behaves as if it knew the likelihood of various environmental configurations. In the words of Horace Barlow (1998, page 886), "Learning the ways of the world consists of learning what does NOT happen as much or more than learning what does."

**FIGURE 1.11 | Photographs of natural objects occluding one another.

Because vision is designed to deal with partial occlusions within naturally occurring scenes (see Figure 1.11), visual perception automatically treats Kanizsa's figure as though it were one object (a white square) occluding other, more distant objects (four black disks).

In the preceding paragraphs, we focused on perception from an information-processing approach, one aimed at specifying the computational problems facing perception. This represents one form of theorizing within the field of perception. In general, the development of theories of perception, whether computational or not, sharpens our thinking, often translating qualitative observations into quantitative statements. These kinds of quantitatively explicit theories then serve to guide the design and implementation of experiments in perception. Good theories tell us what to look for and, often, where to look.

Recurring Themes

Running throughout the following chapters are some recurring themes that transcend a given perceptual modality. To provide a framework for integrating the material you encounter in the following chapters, we'll finish our introductory comments with a summary of five of those major themes.

Sensory Transduction   Each of the various sensory modalities we will examine—vision, hearing, touch, taste, and smell—is designed to pick up information in the environment about a particular class of stimulus objects and events. The physical nature of the information depends on the modality under consideration. Vision, for example, is triggered by photons of electromagnetic energy ("light" as we call it) that stimulate the eye's light-sensitive photoreceptors. Smell is triggered by an entirely different class of stimulation, volatile molecules that interlock with proteins within the nasal cavity. These are just two examples of the process known as sensory transduction: the conversion of some form of physical energy (photons and volatile molecules, in the examples just given) into electrical signals within biological tissues called sensory receptors. Your understanding of perception is not complete without an appreciation of the nature of the physical stimulus associated with a given modality and the nature of the biological processes that register the presence and nature of that stimulus.

Variations in Perception among People and Animals   The study of perception tends to focus on normal adult human beings. Given that students of perception nearly all fall in this category, that focus is understandable and sensible. But some of the most revealing lessons about perception can be achieved by studying individuals who fall outside of the "normal adult" category. For example, we can examine perception *developmentally* by studying newborn infants, young children, and, at life span's other end, elderly people. Systematic changes in perception accompany developmental changes in the sense organs and central nervous system. Thus, studying developmental changes in perception offers one way to understand the relation between sensory systems and perceptual experience (Teller, 1997).

Normal perception can be compromised by inherited disorders, by disease, or by injury. And just as studying pathology illuminates the processes of health, studying the abnormal perception can illuminate the normal processes of perception. Some of our most remarkable discoveries about perception have come from clinical case studies in which a perceptual disorder has been traced to a physiological abnormality. A classic example of this strategy comes from color vision, where the genetics of color vision were revealed by studying people with deficient color vision. Even when the cause of a perceptual disorder is not fully understood, one can still acquire useful clues about possible causes by determining what other aspects of perception are unaffected. For example, a person with misaligned (crossed) eyes can have diminished depth perception but still be able to see objects and to judge whether those objects are moving or stationary. These kinds of selective perceptual losses indicate that the affected perceptual ability depends on structures within the nervous system different from those mediating the unaffected perceptual abilities (Hebb, 1949; Brindley, 1970).

The study of human perception can also profit from learning about perception in nonhuman animals. Although special, sophisticated techniques are required to study animal perception (Blake, 1998), such work expands our appreciation of the mechanisms of perception. In this book, some of what you will learn about human perception comes from animal studies. A good deal is known about the anatomy and physiology of the sensory systems of several nonhuman species.

FIGURE 1.12 | Zöllner's illusion of orientation.

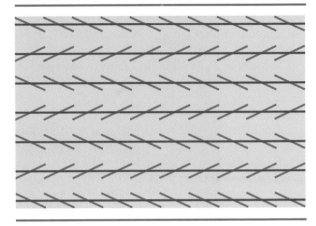

This knowledge takes on added significance when it can be related to studies of perception in the same species.

Illusions and Errors of Perception   It is natural to assume that perception works best when it provides an accurate, veridical view of the world. Yet there are numerous, fascinating examples where perception makes mistakes, sometimes glaring ones. In the case of vision, we may grossly misjudge the size of an object; in hearing, we may swear that a person is uttering one word when, in fact, he's saying something different; and in touch, we may judge a stimulus as cold when touching it with one hand but hot when touching it with the other hand. In all the chapters in this book you'll run into these so-called **illusions** of perception, where the appearance of a stimulus departs notably from the actual nature of the evoking stimulus. Figure 1.10 illustrates one such illusion, and Figure 1.12 illustrates another. Here the long horizontal lines appear tilted relative to one another, but in fact they are perfectly parallel. This illusion of orientation, invented by Franz Zöllner in 1860, disappears when the radially oriented lines are removed leaving just the horizontal ones, and this reveals an important clue to illusions: when they occur, illusions are usually attributable to the context in which the illusory figures appear. In fact, illusions and the conditions producing them provide genuine insights into the operations of normal perception. Illusions, in other words, highlight the ordinary processes underlying normal perception. Throughout the book, you'll have opportunities to experience these fascinating curiosities. You also should visit some of the websites on illusions available at http://www.mhhe.com/blake5.

Perception Is Modifiable Many of our perceptual skills improve with experience, and these improvements occur without special effort on our part: the mere act of using perception sharpens our vision, hearing, touch, taste, and smell. For example, you're able to distinguish subtle differences in speech sounds (e.g., the utterances "bill" and "bell") that can baffle the ears of a nonnative English speaker. Moreover, we can purposefully set about educating our perceptual systems, achieving levels of discriminability that far exceed those of the average individual. Among wine aficionados and aficionadas exist individuals whose broad repertoire of tasting experiences allow them to identify accurately the grape from which a wine is made, the region within a given country where that grape was grown, and the year in which the grapes were harvested. These individuals have spent years learning all the nuisances—color, odor, taste—that distinguish wines from one another. Perception psychologists have long recognized that the senses can be educated to a remarkable degree, and you will see evidence of this theme in many of the coming chapters. You will also learn what kinds of changes occur within the nervous system to promote those perceptual changes.

Perception Is Supplemented by Cognitive and Affective Influences The purpose of perception is to inform us about the objects and events in our immediate environment that can intelligently guide our behavior in a busy, potentially dangerous world. Should the information guiding our perceptual decisions be limited solely to the sensory data gathered by the peripheral receptors? Or should sensory data be tempered or amplified by expectations? Reflexive actions based on sensory signals work adequately for some species, including frogs, whose very limited behavioral repertoire requires little in the way of interpretation of that sensory data. If a frog is hungry and a small black moving object is within its field of view, the frog will mindlessly flick its long tongue at the black object on the assumption that it's an insect. But humans constantly make more refined behavioral decisions based on the perceptual data bombarding us. Those behavioral decisions are guided by knowledge that places the perceptual information in context and by emotional factors that help us anticipate the impact of different perceptually guided decisions. Perception, in other words, can be shaped by knowledge and expectations and can be tinged by affective reaction. Thus, your perceptual reaction to the appearance of a person at your door depends on whether the person's visit was expected and whether the person is a friend or a stranger. Perception is susceptible to all sorts of nonsensory influences, and we will highlight those influences throughout the upcoming chapters.

With these introductory comments in place, we're now ready to tackle a question that has fascinated and puzzled philosophers, scientists, and curious laypeople for centuries: how is it that we establish perceptual contact with the world in which we live?

SUMMARY AND PREVIEW

This chapter lays the framework for our analysis of perception, including the philosophical assumptions we'll be making. We have mentioned some of the practical and theoretical reasons for wanting to know more about perception. And we have outlined three distinct, though complementary, ways of understanding perception: the psychological, biological, and theoretical approaches. Now that this general framework is in place, the next chapter will begin to fill in the pieces, starting with some fundamentals about the organ we use for seeing—the eye. Although this book also covers hearing, taste, smell, and touch, it devotes more space to seeing. We know more about vision than the other senses, and we believe vision represents the richest source of environmental information. This preeminence of vision is mirrored in the large portion of the human brain devoted to vision.

K E Y   T E R M S

Anton's syndrome
Charles Bonnet syndrome
dualism
event-related potential (ERP)
evoked potential (EP)
far or distance senses
fMRI (functional magnetic
    resonance imaging)
illusions
Kanizsa figure
kinesthesia

lesion
materialism
MEG (magnetoencephalography)
naive realism
natural scene statistics
near senses
Necker cube
perception
PET (positron-emission
    tomography) scan

psychophysics
sensory transduction
solipsism
specific nerve energies
stimulus
subjective idealism
transcranial magnetic stimulation
    (TMS)

The Human Eye

You are relaxing on a sunny beach, soaking up the sun's rays (while wearing lots of sunscreen, of course), and gazing out at the boats on the water. Later that night you find yourself in a dimly lit movie theater, and manage to navigate the aisle to find a seat. In both environments you're able to use your eyes to see what's around you and, when needed, to get up and move about. But these two environments could not be any more different in terms of the available light—your visual system is working effectively at light levels that differ by a factor of about 100 million! To build an optical/video device to operate over such a huge range of intensities—dynamic range, as it's called—represents an almost insurmountable engineering challenge. And yet, our eyes perform this miracle every day and night. In this chapter you will learn about some of the biological tricks that nature has used to allow the human eye to work so efficiently.

The visual system of all vertebrates, humans included, consists of three major components: *eyes,* which capture light and convert it into neural messages; *visual pathways,* which modify and transmit those messages from the eye to the brain; and *visual centers of the brain,* which interpret the messages in ways useful for guiding behavior. All three components are crucially involved in

seeing, so each component's structure and function must be understood in order to comprehend how an organism sees. This chapter and the next one concentrate on the first of these components, the human eye; they discuss its anatomy (structure) and physiology (how it works). These chapters emphasize how the eye is built, how it captures light, and how it turns that light into neural messages the brain can interpret. Chapter 4 will discuss the remaining two major sections of the vertebrate visual system, the visual pathways to the brain and the brain's visual centers.

Each of these three chapters has features that require special comment here. First, we don't spend time talking about anatomy simply because we are fascinated with structure per se. Structure is important because it influences how and what we can see. Second, although mainly interested in the *human* eye, we also consider the eyes of other animals, particularly animals whose environments and lifestyles differ from those of humans. Understanding the diversity of vision—and the uniqueness of human vision—will heighten your appreciation of the processes involved in seeing. Finally, we also consider how various defects impair vision. Besides being fascinating in their own right, visual defects illuminate the intimate connection between structure and function.

In writing these chapters we were very much influenced by Gordon Walls's book *The Vertebrate Eye and Its Adaptive Radiations* (1942). Walls wrote eloquently about the eye, as the following statement demonstrates:

> Everything in the vertebrate eye means something. Except for the brain, there is no other organ in the body of which that can be said. It does not matter in the least whether a liver has three lobes or four, or whether a hand has five fingers or six, or whether a kidney is long and narrow or short and wide. But if we should make comparable changes in the makeup of a vertebrate eye, we should quite destroy its usefulness. Man can make optical instruments only from such materials as brass and glass. Nature has succeeded with only such things as leather and water and jelly; but the resulting instrument is so delicately balanced that it will tolerate no tampering. (Walls, 1942, pp. iii–iv)

Walls's credo underscores that we cannot understand vision without first understanding the eye's structure. We'll begin our actual discussion of the eye with general questions about the nature of vision—*why* vision took the form that it did.

Designing the Organ of Vision

The Diversity of Eyes in Nature

Chapter 1 distinguished between near senses and distance senses, putting vision in the latter category. By definition, a distance sense allows you to detect and recognize objects without having to come close to those objects. Both hearing and seeing give us this capacity. But vision enjoys a major advantage over hearing: it allows us to detect and recognize objects that make no sounds. (Hearing offers its own special advantages, including the ability to register the presence of things that cannot be seen—but we'll get to that in Chapters 10 and 11.) Vision also provides important information about objects, information that is simply beyond the reach of hearing. It's sight, not hearing, that can tell us about the color of a piece of fruit, the shape of a cup we're about to grasp, the likelihood of threat posed by an approaching stranger and countless other useful pieces of information about objects and events in our environment.

To appreciate vision's power, all we have to do is look at the diversity of creatures that possess eyes and the diversity of design of those eyes (see Figure 2.1). Many species, including all varieties of birds and fish, have eyes that follow the same basic design as ours, and

are every bit as complicated. Other species, however, possess eyes that are very different from ours. Some insects, such as butterflies, have eyes consisting of hundreds of tiny cameralike lenses each focusing light on its own cluster of light-sensitive cells. This array of miniature optical systems is packaged in a single large eye, sometimes mounted on the end of a long stack protruding from the creature's head. These so-called compound eyes work very differently from our eyes, which possess a single optical system (see Figure 2.2). But given the long-standing history of the compound eye and its ubiquity among living creatures, we can safely assume that compound eyes allow their owners to see what is important to them. In still other species, including some worms, "eyes" consist of nothing more than a patch of photosensitive pigment somewhere on the surface of the skin. By reacting to the presence of light, these light-sensitive spots tell the creature whether it's day or night. It's arguable whether we should refer to this as "vision," but there's no doubt that these creatures are sensing light. In fact, patches of photosensitive pigment in these kinds of primitive creatures almost certainly represent the precursors for the variety of eyes found in other, more advanced animals.

Take a look at the unusual caterpillar pictured in Figure 2.3. If you didn't know better, you'd swear it was staring at you. That's exactly what natural selection—the designer of this caterpillar—wants you to think. This menacing "eye," however, is nothing more than pigmentation on the caterpillar's back. Its real eyes are those tiny pinholes located on the side of its body. This adaptive ornamentation deters potential predators, warning them to be wary about trying to sneak up on the caterpillar. These examples from nature remind us that eyes are not only the organ of sight; they also communicate clear messages to others, who may be looking at us: "I can see you, so be careful what you do."

Evolution seems to have invented and reinvented the sense of vision dozens of different times throughout the animal kingdom (Mayr, 1982). Each time vision arose, the process has been lengthy and complicated. Indeed, the complex structure of the human eye has led some to conclude that it simply couldn't have arisen by natural selection. Instead, they argue, the grand design of the eye reveals the hand of God in creation. Others, however, have traced out plausible scenarios for the evolution of eyes through the force of natural selection acting in concert with chance mutations (Dawkins, 1996). Our purpose here isn't to quarrel about the "designer" of eyes but, rather, to instill in you an appreciation for the

FIGURE 2.1 | Examples of the variety of eyes in nature.

FIGURE 2.2 | Two fundamentally different designs for eyes in nature. The left-hand panel (A) shows a compound eye, made of many individual light sensors each with its own, independent optical system that focuses light onto a small number of receptors. Compound eyes are typical among insects and crustaceans. The right-hand panel (B) shows a chambered eye, which contains a single optical system (cornea and lens, in most cases) that forms a single image on the back of the eye where there are millions of receptors. Chambered eyes are common among mammals, birds, and fish.

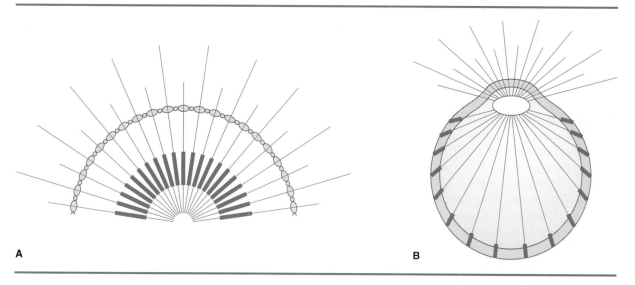

A

B

FIGURE 2.3 | Pigmented spots on the back of a caterpillar resemble eyes.

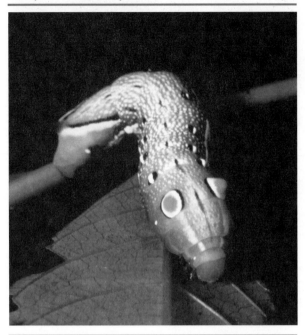

quality and service provided by that design. Toward that end, we must start with some basics about light, the messenger that bridges the distance between you and the objects you see.

Why Have Eyes That Use Light?

Light is defined as **electromagnetic radiation** falling within a small region of electromagnetic (EM) spectrum (see Figure 2.4). Other familiar forms of electromagnetic radiation include radio waves, infrared and ultraviolet radiation, microwaves, and X-rays. All of these are forms of radiating energy produced by the oscillations of electrically charged material. Since virtually all matter consists of oscillating (that is, wavelike) electrical charges, electromagnetic energy exists in abundance. An animal that can sense electromagnetic radiation benefits in two important ways.

First, electromagnetic radiation travels very rapidly (in empty space, at 186,000 miles, or approximately 300,000 kilometers, per second). Any creature able to detect such radiation can pick up information from distant sources with minimal delay. Thus, we receive opti-

cal information about objects and events almost instantaneously (except, of course, for extraterrestrial events transpiring millions of miles away). Second, electromagnetic radiation tends to travel in straight lines. This means that images created by this radiation retain important geometrical characteristics of the objects that reflect that radiation toward the eyes. We'll return to this point in a moment.

The frequency of electromagnetic radiation depends on the oscillation frequency of the material that emitted the radiation. In fact, electromagnetic radiation can be scaled (or arranged) along a spectrum according to the frequency of oscillation. This frequency, or oscillation rate, of light energy can be converted into units termed *wavelengths*. **Wavelength** is defined by how far the radiation travels between oscillations. High rates of oscillation mean that radiation travels a very short distance between oscillations, hence a short wavelength. Figure 2.4 underscores an important point: Light, the form of radiation on which we depend for sight, occupies only a very small portion of the electromagnetic spectrum. Actually, radiation from other portions of this spectrum *could* have been used to bridge the distance between the perceiver and objects of visual perception. So why do the eyes rely solely on this one, very narrow portion of the entire electromagnetic spectrum, the part we call light?

One reason that eyes use light as their medium is that, thanks to our solar system's sun, the world has a lot of it. That abundance ensures that terrestrial creatures will have ample opportunity to exploit their light-sensing apparatus. It wouldn't have made much sense for early vertebrate "eyes" to depend on wavelengths in the ultraviolet range, for example, because most (but not all) of sunlight's energy in this short wavelength region of the spectrum is absorbed by molecules in the earth's atmosphere (mainly nitrogen and oxygen). Consequently, most of the sun's ultraviolet rays never reach objects in terrestrial or aquatic environments. Second, light is useful as a medium of information about the world because light interacts with the surface molecules of many objects we're interested in seeing. These interactions, in the form of reflection and absorption, allow light to convey information not only about the presence and absence of objects, but also about the structure of those objects and their surfaces (Gibson, 1966). Energy from outside the "light" portion of the electromagnetic spectrum—because of the length of the constituent waves—interacts very differently with the solid objects that are relevant to behaving organisms. For example, longer wavelengths, including microwave energy, penetrate opaque objects

FIGURE 2.4 | The spectrum of electromagnetic energy. The region containing visible light is shown enlarged.

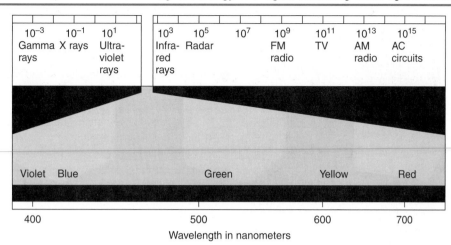

rather than being reflected by them. (By penetrating them, microwaves can more evenly heat objects and therefore are useful in cooking.)

To sum up, eyes are a good idea, and eyes that make use of light are an even better one.

The Message and the Messenger: Inverse Optics

As we progress through this discussion of vision, keep in mind that light is the *carrier* of visual information. It delivers messages from environmental objects to your eyes. But light itself is seldom the message of interest. It's the objects we want to see.

In a nutshell, the eye receives patterns of light energy reflected from the surfaces of objects in the environment. Those patterns of energy depend on a host of factors, including the surface properties of objects, the distance from the eye to those objects, and the source of light illuminating the objects. Whenever you change the angle of vision between yourself and any object, for example, you alter the pattern of light energy falling on your eyes (see Figure 2.5). Whenever you view an object in natural sunlight and then move indoors to look at the same object under artificial lighting, you change the wavelength composition of light energy arriving at your eyes (artificial light isn't identical to sunlight). In short, the same object can convey countless different optical messages to your eyes; the optical messages are ambiguous. But it's the object you're interested in, not the varying optical patterns arising from that object.

So how do the eyes and brain work from the ambiguous optical patterns they receive to specify which object or objects produced a given pattern of light energy? That's really what these next three chapters are all about. You will learn how the eye and brain are able to work backward, or inversely, starting with patterns of light and culminating in descriptions of objects in the world. This backward approach, which vision accomplishes automatically and effortlessly, is called **inverse optics.**

As you will learn, solving the inverse optics problem requires that the eye and brain make some assumptions about the objects and events we're likely to encounter in our environments. Fortunately, those assumptions are fairly safe ones because the physical nature of matter imposes constraints on the properties of objects, and vision can exploit those constraints. For example, light cannot pass through opaque objects, which means that when one object partially blocks the view of another, we automatically see the partially occluded one at a greater distance than the occluding object (this constraint is discussed in more detail in Chapter 8). In addition, those constraints don't change over time. Nature has exploited this stability to develop shortcuts for solving the problem of inverse optics. We'll be describing some of these shortcuts throughout this book.

Where Should the Eyes Be Placed?

Recognizing that animals would do very well to have eyes that exploit light, we must now decide *where* those eyes should go in the body. Because embryologically the

FIGURE 2.5 | Imagine walking in a clockwise direction around a box resting on the ground. As you change your viewpoint, the image of the box on the back of your eye will change. These six drawings simulate the images associated with six different viewing positions.

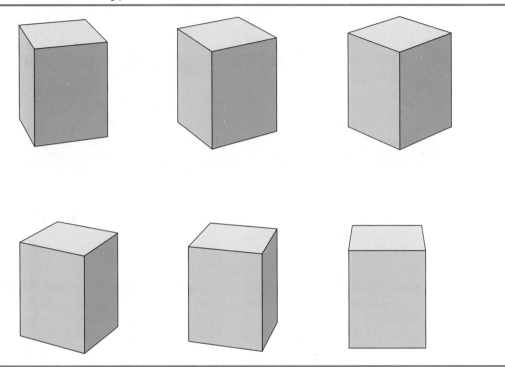

eyes are an outgrowth of the brain, their most natural location is in the head, near the brain. But where exactly in the head should the eyes go?[1] Surveying the animal kingdom, we find a variety of different eye placement schemes. In some ocean-dwelling creatures, for example, the eyes are situated in the back of the head; these are the bottom-dwelling fish who need to monitor what (or who) is above them. Among most vertebrates, there are two popular designs for outfitting the head with a pair of eyes: they can be located in a *frontal* position, as are those of a leopard or a human being; or they can be located in a more *lateral* position, as are those of a deer or a rabbit (see Figure 2.6). Each strategy carries its own advantage: frontal eyes improve depth perception (as you will learn in Chapter 8), whereas lateral eyes make it possible to take in more of the visual world at one time. As a rule, predatory animals—those that hunt and eat other animals—have frontally placed eyes. Those that are

prey—animals frequently taken as food—have laterally placed eyes. In other words, those needing excellent depth perception to stalk and capture have considerable binocular overlap of the two visual fields. Those needing a more panoramic view of the environment in order to watch for predators have little binocular overlap. Incidentally, the caterpillar in Figure 2.3 is "prey" for other creatures (e.g., birds), but this insect is trying to masquerade as a predator with its pair of simulated eyes with implied frontal overlap.

Why Should the Eyes Be Able to Move?

Because we humans lack panoramic vision, what we see at any given moment is rather limited. (Compare the fields of view of the human and the rabbit, as shown in Figure 2.7.) And there is no guarantee that our eyes will always be directed toward things in the environment that we need to see. Fortunately, we can compensate for our relatively narrow field of vision by turning the head and eyes. This is what you do when you look both ways before crossing a street. You also move your eyes because they are not uniformly sensitive. Some parts of the eye

---

[1]This discussion of eye placement is restricted to creatures with a pair of eyes but, in fact, there are insects—such as the jumping spider—and invertebrates—such as the horseshoe crab—that have more than two eyes.

FIGURE 2.6 | Note the placement of the eyes in the head of the leopard (frontal eye placement) and in the head of the deer (lateral eye placement).

FIGURE 2.7 | The extent of visual field of view for a rabbit and for a human. Note that the rabbit has almost completely panoramic vision, whereas the human's field of view encompasses only about 180 degrees.

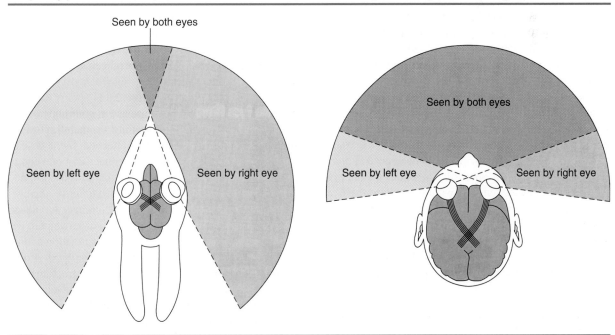

provide much better detail vision than other parts. Think for a moment what you do when something suddenly appears out of the corner of your eye. To see exactly what has grabbed your attention, your eyes reflexively move so that you're looking directly at whatever caught your attention.

Animals use various strategies for changing their field of view: they can move their bodies, turn their heads, or merely move their eyes. Some animals, owls for one, have very limited ability to move their eyes (Steinbach and Money, 1973). This comes about because their eyes are large and fit tightly into their sockets. Rather than depending on eye movements, the owl moves its entire head and they can literally rotate their heads 90 degrees or more in a fraction of a second. Still, from a human standpoint the owl's method may seem effortful and conspicuous.

Not all birds are our inferiors when it comes to eye movements, however. For example, the European starling, now so numerous as to be a nuisance in most North American and European cities, owes some of its success to its eye movements. Most birds, as they forage on the ground, need to look sideways in order to see what they're about to peck at. But starlings, whose skulls are quite narrow and whose eyes are extremely mobile, can turn their eyes far enough forward so that they can actually see between their opened beaks. Equally important (and amazing) is the starling's ability to instantly swing its eyes up and back to scan the skies behind its head for possible predators (Martin, 1987). Because it can watch for predators without having to turn its head, the starling remains relatively unobtrusive, another element of protection. With eye movements so well designed both for fruitful foraging and self-protection, it's no wonder that in a mere 100 years the starling population of North America has gone from approximately 100 European imports to more than 200 million birds.

Although we humans can't match the starling's ability to shift its eyes without moving its head, we can shift the position of our eyes with enormous speed. For instance, it takes less than one-fifth of a second for our eyes to turn from their extreme leftward position to their extreme rightward position. When we execute this movement, our eyes are briefly traveling 700 degrees per second! (To make this figure more concrete, think of the moon's rotation. If the moon rotated at this speed, it would complete two revolutions in one second.) Not only do the eyes move rapidly, they move with great accuracy as well. For example, as you read these lines, your eyes skip along from one place of interest to another, alighting

FIGURE 2.8 | A view of the eye muscles attached to the left eye. For ease of visualization, a portion of the lateral rectus muscle has been removed so you can see structures that would otherwise be obscured from view. Note, too, that the medial rectus, the muscle closest to the nose, is partially obscured by the globe. Also shown in this figure is the optic nerve, which comprises axons of the eye's ganglion cells.

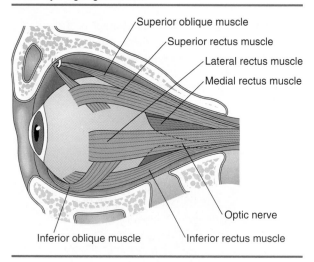

Superior oblique muscle
Superior rectus muscle
Lateral rectus muscle
Medial rectus muscle
Optic nerve
Inferior oblique muscle
Inferior rectus muscle

with great precision on the desired letter or space. The cooperative interaction among the **extraocular muscles** (six for each eye) makes this rapid and accurate eye movement possible; the diagram in Figure 2.8 shows the approximate positions of these six muscles for the left eye. Through their combined actions, the extraocular muscles enable movement of the eyes in all directions. Let's consider the mechanical arrangement that makes this possible.

How the Eyes Move   Every muscle in your body works by contracting and thereby pulling on the structure or structures to which the muscle is attached. In the case of the extraoculars, each muscle is connected at one end to an immovable structure, the eye socket of the skull, and at the other end to an object that is free to move, the eyeball. So when an extraocular muscle contracts, it pulls on the eyeball and moves it. The *amount* of movement depends on the strength of the muscle's contraction and on the action of the other muscles. The *direction* of movement depends on the place at which the contracting muscle is attached to the eyeball and skull, and on which other extraocular muscles are also contracting. Because each extraocular muscle is attached to the eyeball at a different position, contraction of any particular muscle turns the eyeball in a characteristic direction. The following is a brief and simplified description of what the extraoculars do. As we move through this material, keep in mind that the extraocular muscles are among the busiest in the entire body: it is estimated that we make more than 100,000 eye movements a day!

Each eye's muscles can be divided into two groups, one with four muscles and one with two. The larger group, the **rectus muscles,** run straight back from the eyeball. Muscles in the other, smaller group run obliquely back from the eyeball. We can understand the general principles of the eye's movements by looking just at the muscles in the larger group.

Each rectus muscle is attached to the eyeball at a different location, toward the front of the eyeball (see Figure 2.8). The other end of each rectus muscle is attached to the rear of the bony cavity holding the eyeball; this is the immovable end of the muscle. Whenever a rectus muscle contracts, it pulls the eyeball toward the place at which that muscle connects to the eyeball. When a rectus muscle relaxes, the eye turns back toward its original position.

One muscle, the *medial* rectus, attaches to the side of the eyeball closest to the nose. When it contracts, the medial rectus rotates the eye toward the nose. Another muscle, the *lateral* rectus, has exactly the opposite effect. It is connected to the side of the eyeball farthest from the nose, so its contraction turns the eyeball laterally, away from the nose. The *superior* rectus muscle connects to the top of the eyeball, and its contraction elevates the eyeball, causing you to look upward. The superior's opposing muscle, the *inferior* rectus, is attached to the lower portion of the eyeball and its contraction lowers the eye, causing you to look down.

Now let's consider how these muscles cooperate to move the eyes. Imagine that while looking straight ahead, you decide to glance leftward. Both eyes must move to the same degree and in the same direction. In order for you to look to the left, the medial rectus of the right eye and the lateral rectus of the left eye must both contract, while both the lateral rectus of the right eye and the medial rectus of the left eye relax. You should be able to figure out for yourself what will happen if you now decide to glance rightward.

For the eye movements just described, both eyes have moved in the same direction—upward, leftward, and so on. Eye movements of this type are called **conjugate** eye movements, and they preserve the angle between the two eyes. But the eyes are capable of other types of movements as well. The eyes can move in opposite directions: Both may turn inward or both may turn outward. These are called **vergence** eye movements, and they produce variation in the angle between the eyes. For example, the left eye can turn rightward while the right eye turns leftward. As a result, both eyes turn inward, toward the nose. This movement aims the two eyes at a very close object straight ahead of you. This particular type of vergence movement is called a *convergent eye movement.* To accomplish it, the medial rectus muscles of both eyes contract, while the lateral rectus muscles of both eyes relax. If you look at an object at arm's length and then bring it closer to you, your eyes converge, tracking the object. When the object moves away from you, your eye muscles will engage in the opposite behavior, resulting in a divergent eye movement.

Even when you do not intend to move them, your eyes constantly jitter back and forth by tiny amounts. These small, imperceptible eye movements are not attributable to sloppy eye muscle control but, instead, are programmed muscular actions that literally keep you from going blind. To observe these tiny eye movements and learn what role they play in vision, see Box 2.1.

Much more can be said about eye movements and their role in vision, particularly in reading, and we'll return to these roles in later chapters. But for now, we want to stress that eye movements alone are insufficient to compensate for our limited field of view. To experience this for yourself, try a simple exercise. Hold your head very steady, close one eye, and then look around in all directions by moving your open eye. Notice how limited this monocular field of vision really is. Repeat the exercise using your other eye. When the Austrian scientist and philosopher Ernst Mach (1838–1916) performed this exercise, he made a sketch of what he saw. Figure 2.9 shows you what Mach drew. Mach firmly believed that scientists should confine themselves to descriptions of phenomena that can be perceived by the senses. In this particular case, Mach's senses revealed a seldom realized truth: Because we're accustomed to moving our eyes and heads, we seldom realize how limited our actual view of the world is at any given moment. Our grasp on the whole of visual reality comes in bits and pieces assembled over time.

How Should the Eyes Be Protected?

Vertebrate eyes are fragile, complicated devices occupying a very exposed position in the head. Fortunately, various mechanisms have evolved to protect the eyes, and an outline of these protective mechanisms provides a good introduction to the overall structure of the eye.

BOX 2.1 **Eyes That Never Stand Still**

Contractions of the extraocular muscles pull and tug on the eyeballs, guiding their direction so objects of interest can be fixated. But even when you try to keep your eyes absolutely still, small random contractions of the extraocular muscles keep the eyes moving. These involuntary eye movements are usually too minor for you to be aware of, but they are important for seeing. Before learning why they're important, though, try this simple trick that will let you see your own involuntary eye movements.

The trick requires a pattern like the grid in the accompanying figure (Verheijen, 1963). First carefully fixate on the black dot in the center of the pattern for about 30 seconds, keeping your eyes as still as possible. Then quickly move your eyes to the white dot. Again, keep your eyes as still as possible. You'll see an illusory pattern, called an **afterimage,** that jiggles slightly. The jiggling of the afterimage is caused by the movements of your eyes. You can prove this to yourself by making large, intentional eye movements; the afterimage follows your eyes. The afterimage itself arises from the differential adaptation of neurons in your retina responding to the light and dark parts of the figure. Of course, the adapted neurons are fixed in place in the eye's retina; it is as if a negative image of the grid is temporarily imprinted on the back of the eye. Thus, whenever you see the afterimage move, you're in fact witnessing your eyes moving—whether you intended them to or not. The slight jiggling of the afterimage even when you try to fixate is the consequence of your own involuntary eye movements.

These small random eye movements are actually very important for vision; when they are eliminated, vision changes dramatically. For example, special optical systems have been developed that move whatever you're looking at in step with the movements of your eyes. This scheme produces a motionless, stabilized image on your retina. Here is one way to produce a stabilized retinal image. A small photographic transparency of some object is mounted on a special high-power contact lens that focuses the image on the retina. Since the contact lens moves along with the eye, the image of the transparency

attached to this lens is stabilized on the retina. And the perceptual result is remarkable—within a few seconds, the object begins to fade from view, as if the brightness on a television screen were being reduced. Eventually the object disappears entirely, leaving nothing but a homogeneous gray field. So when the effects of normal involuntary eye movements are eliminated, vision is eliminated, too (Pritchard, Heron, and Hebb, 1960; Riggs et al., 1953).

The disappearance of stabilized retinal images is actually quite fortunate. If this didn't happen, you'd constantly be annoyed by the images produced in your eyes by blood vessels. Because they are in the path of light, these blood vessels cast shadows on your retina. Since the vessels move along with your eye, their shadows are stabilized retinal images and, consequently, are invisible to you. However, you can temporarily "destabilize" them by moving a beam of light back and forth across the vessels. This causes their shadow to move back and forth slightly, enough to make them visible. The simplest way to produce this effect is with a small flashlight (a penlight). Looking straight ahead with eyes closed, place the penlight against the corner of your eye—the corner away from your nose, as is shown in the illustration. Gently rock the penlight back and forth. After a second or two you should begin to see what look like the branches of a tree. These are the shadows of blood vessels in your eye. Once you get them into view, stop moving the flashlight and the branches will disappear within a few seconds, as the image returns to its normal, stabilized condition.

FIGURE 2.9 | Ernst Mach's view of his study, after drawing in Mach (1959).

The eye is partially protected by virtue of its location within the **orbit,** a bony depression in the skull. Within the orbit, each eyeball is surrounded by a substantial cushion of fat. Without this orbital fat, blows to the head would be transmitted directly to the eye. But by absorbing such shocks, orbital fat protects the eye against all but the most severe jolts. The eye is also protected by eyelids, movable folds of tissue. The position of the upper lid relative to the lower one determines the opening through which the front of the eye is visible. The lids move in concert with one another in various modes. For instance,

in a fraction of a second, they can open and close (blink). Such blinks usually occur spontaneously, without thought. Blinks clean and moisten the front of the eye to keep it from drying out. The lids can also execute reflexive blinks that protect the eye when it is touched by a foreign object, or when an object is on a collision course with the head. In addition to involuntary and reflexive blinks, we can also voluntarily blink our eyes or, for that matter, close them entirely when we want to go to sleep.

Under normal circumstances, a blink occurs about once every four seconds. This figure varies from person to person, depending on emotional state and the environmental conditions. When the air is very dry, we tend to blink our eyes more often, ensuring that the delicate front surface of the eye doesn't dry out.

A blink, measured from the instant the lids begin to close until they reopen, takes roughly one-third of a second. For about half this time, the lids are completely closed, reducing the light by over 90 percent (Crawford and Marc, 1976). If the room lights were momentarily dimmed by this amount, the resulting blackout would be very noticeable. Why is it, then, that we never notice the same blackout when it's caused by a blink?

Volkmann, Riggs, and Moore (1980) offered an intriguing answer to this question. They hypothesized that when the brain signals the lids to close, it also produces an ancillary neural signal that suppresses, or temporarily shuts off, vision for the duration of the blink. And it is this brief suppression of vision, so they surmise, that keeps you from noticing that a blink had occurred. This hypothesis, although intriguing, is difficult to test. The appropriate test would be to measure the eye's sensitivity to light during a blink without the lid closure actually affecting the intensity of the eye's exposure to that light. Volkmann and colleagues developed the following ingenious way to stimulate the eye so that the light reaching the retina would not be affected by lid closure.

The eyes lie directly above the roof of the mouth. Thus, a strong light focused on the roof of the mouth under one eye can penetrate this tissue and stimulate the retina—you're actually able to see light delivered through the roof of your mouth whether or not your lids are closed. This procedure makes it possible to measure the ability to see a dimming of the light at various times relative to a blink.

Volkmann and colleagues used a bundle of optical fibers to carry light to the roof of a person's mouth. By abruptly dimming the light, they determined the smallest reduction in light intensity visible to that person. Remember: All the light that could be seen came through the person's mouth, bypassing the lids. At the same time, Volkmann and colleagues attached electrodes to the skin near the eyelids to monitor the occurence of blinks. Since a blink is produced by muscle contractions, it's easy to detect the electrical activity of the lid muscles and know from that activity when a blink begins and ends. These researchers found that dimming was much harder to see *during* a blink than *between* blinks. To be detected during a blink, the light had to be dimmed by an amount five times greater than it did between blinks.

These results suggest that the brain suppresses vision just before and during each blink, keeping us from noticing the visual blackouts. Without this suppression, which occurs in tandem with the typical blink rate of 10 to 15 times per minute, we would be bothered by profound blackouts. To our relief, the visual system uses a temporary, well-timed suppression to protect us from the annoying but necessary behavior of our eyelids.

Our social environment also affects the behavior of our eyelids. We tend to blink more often during casual conversation than when we're alone. And during a heated discussion, our blink rate skyrockets. In addition to our blink rate, the size of the opening between the lids provides a reliable clue as to how interested your listener is. Watch a friend's eyes closely; the opening between the lids will average 8 millimeters (about 1/3 inch). You'll probably notice a change in that opening as your friend's attention varies. When interest is high, the opening between the lids increases to about 10 millimeters. Similarly, drowsiness or boredom reduces the size of the opening. And, of course, we immediately recognize the social message conveyed when someone looks directly at us and gives an exaggerated blink with one eye. A wink speaks volumes.

Tears also convey social messages, such as sadness, pain, great joy, and more. But tears protect the eyes as well. Although usually associated either with emotional states or with slicing raw onions, tears irrigate the eyes' exposed surfaces. Tears are secreted from a gland situated in the upper, front portion of each orbit (under the upper lid). From there, they pass down over the eye's front surface, moistening it, and then drain through small openings in the lower nasal portion of each orbit. Finally, the tears drain onto the mucous membrane lining the nose's inner surface. This nasal membrane acts as an evaporator for the tears, which explains why you have to blow your nose when you've been crying. Tears contain an antimicrobial agent that helps protect the eye from bacteria present in the environment. In addition, the regular flow of tears flushes away debris, such as dust. Tears also lubricate the surface of the eyes so that blinking won't abrade the lids or scratch the front of the eyeball. The constant, very thin film of tears over the front of the eye minimizes the wear and tear produced by constant lid movement. In many older adults, the secretion of tears slows down, producing a condition called "dry eyes." Fortunately, the regular application of ophthalmic drops to the eyes provides relief.

Having covered its ancillary features, we are now ready to discuss the structure of the eye itself. As we move through this material, you can supplement your understanding of the anatomy and physiology of the retina by visiting the excellent website called "WebVision," created by Helga Kolb, Eduardo Fernandez, and Ralph Nelson. This website, which can be accessed via www.mhhe.com/blake5, confirms the adage that a picture is worth a thousand words.

FIGURE 2.10 | Cross section of human eye, showing major layers and structures.

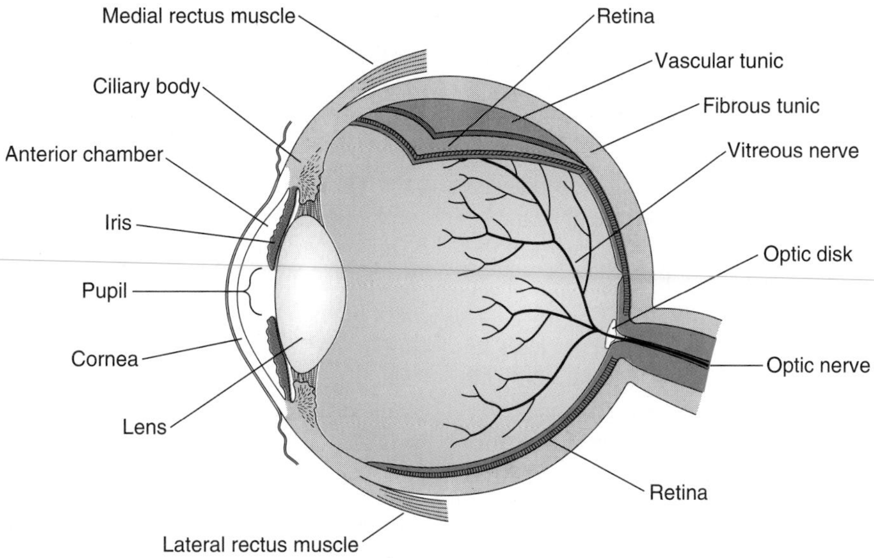

The Structure of the Human Eye

To understand the human eye, let's start with an overview tour of the major features. We'll ignore the details, however, until the second stage of our discussion. By that time you'll have a good idea where those details fit into the eye's grand scheme. In portraying these details, incidentally, people often draw an analogy between the eye and a camera. This analogy is apt, but only to a point. Certainly, both are optical devices designed to record visual images on light-sensitive material (film, in the case of the camera; photoreceptors, in the case of the eye). And the two do have components in common (mechanical, in the case of the camera; biological, in the case of the eye). So where appropriate, we will point out these commonalities. But don't be misled. A camera merely records optical images on film. The eyes do much, much more. Besides recording images, eyes recode those images, extract biologically meaningful information from the recoded signals, and transmit that information to the brain for interpretation and reaction. In this and the next few chapters, we'll point out other instances where the analogy fails. For now, let's start with an overview of the eye's major features.

The human eye is very nearly spherical, with a diameter of approximately 24 millimeters (nearly 1 inch), or slightly smaller than a Ping-Pong ball. It consists of three concentric layers, each with its own characteristic appearance, structure, and functions. From outermost to innermost, the three layers are the **fibrous tunic,** which protects the eyeball; the **vascular tunic,** which nourishes the eyeball; and the **retina,** which detects light and initiates neural messages bound for the brain. Figure 2.10 illustrates this three-layered arrangement. In this figure you can see that the eye is partitioned into two chambers, a small anterior chamber and a larger vitreous chamber. Thus, the basic layout is three concentric layers and two chambers, plus the iris, pupil, and lens.

The Outermost, Fibrous Tunic

When looking directly at someone's eye, you see only about one-sixth of its outer surface. The rest is tucked into the bony orbit, hidden behind the lids and other protective structures. The "white" of the eye is part of the outermost, fibrous coat. Because this white part is made of tough, dense material, it is called the **sclera,** from a Greek root meaning "hard."[2]

---

[2]Most parts of the eye have names related to their character or appearance. Knowing the origin of some of these names can help you appreciate the structure of the eye. Our explanations come from a book entitled *On Naming the Parts of the Human Body,* written in the first century AD by Rufus of Ephesus. Ephesus is an ancient city located in what is now Turkey. We have drawn on an excellent partial translation by Stephen Polyak (1941, p. 96).

The sclera averages about 1 millimeter in thickness, and microscopic inspection reveals that it's made of tightly packed, interwoven fibers running parallel to the sclera's surface. These densely packed fibers give the sclera its toughness. Actually, the sclera needs to be tough because pressure inside the eyeball is double that of the atmosphere. If the sclera were more elastic, that pressure differential could cause the eyeball to become deformed. As a result, the quality of one's sight would be greatly diminished. We'll return to the importance of the shape of the eyeball later, when we discuss the eye as an optical instrument.

At the very front of the eye, this outer coat loses its white coloring and becomes so transparent that it's difficult to see in the mirror. However, if you look at someone else's eye from the side, you will notice a small bulge on the front of the eye. This bulge is called the **cornea,** from a root word meaning "like an animal's horn." (The cornea is composed of tissue comparable to that of an animal's horn.) The cornea's transparency is crucial for vision. It allows light to enter the eyeball unimpeded. The neat and orderly arrangement of the cornea's fibers is the primary reason that the cornea is transparent. In addition, greater transparency is made possible because the cornea has no internal blood supply of its own. Since blood and the requisite vessels could reduce the passage of light, the cornea draws its nourishment from the clear fluid in the anterior chamber.

The transparent cornea plays a crucial role in the formation of images on the back of the eye. Anything that disturbs the cornea's transparency, therefore, will reduce the quality of these images and, hence, the quality of vision. For self-protection, the cornea has extremely high sensitivity to touch. When contacted by foreign bodies, such as dust particles or a misguided finger, the cornea initiates a sequence of protective responses, including lid closure and tear production. There's one reflexive response, however, that should be avoided: As our mothers used to tell us, "Never rub your eye except with your elbow"—these words of wisdom mean leave your eyes alone, for most "remedies" simply do further damage.

The Middle, Vascular Tunic

For most of its course, the vascular tunic hugs the wall of the eyeball, and only toward the front of the eyeball does it pull away from the wall. We'll begin by considering the rear two-thirds of this middle layer, the part that fits snugly against the wall of the eyeball.

Most of the middle layer consists of a heavily pigmented, spongy structure called the **choroid.** The choroid averages about 0.2 millimeters in thickness and contains a network of blood vessels, including capillaries. Blood from these capillaries nourishes one particular class of cells in the retina, the photoreceptors that turn light into neural signals. Without their nourishing blood supply, these vital photoreceptor cells would starve to death from lack of oxygen.

The choroid's heavy pigmentation also reduces light scatter, the tendency for light to be reflected irregularly around inside the eyeball; light scatter would reduce the sharpness of images formed inside the eye. The choroid's dark pigmentation reduces scatter by harmlessly absorbing light that isn't captured by the photoreceptors. Incidentally, this is the same reason the inside of a camera is painted flat black. The paint absorbs scattered light and protects the sharpness of images on the film.

The Anterior Chamber

Toward the front of the eye, this middle, choroidal layer curls away from the wall of the eyeball and runs more or less parallel to the front surface of the eye. Over this part of its course, the middle layer forms a long slender structure called the **ciliary body.** This spongy network of tissue manufactures **aqueous humor,** the watery fluid that fills the smaller, anterior chamber of the eye located behind the cornea and in front of the lens. The aqueous humor serves a number of important maintenance functions. It transports oxygen and nutrients to several of the structures it bathes, and it carries away their waste products. The eye's crucial optical components—the cornea and lens—rely on the aqueous humor as their source of nourishment.

The aqueous fluid also helps maintain the shape of the eyeball. If there is too little fluid in the anterior chamber, the eye will become deformed, like an underinflated soccerball. Constant pressure is maintained, however, because cells in the ciliary body are constantly producing new aqueous to keep the supply of nutrients from becoming exhausted. The creation of new fluid also prevents the buildup of high concentrations of waste products.

For pressure to remain constant, of course, a balance must be achieved between the rate at which aqueous fluid is created and the rate at which it is drained from the eye. Sometimes this dynamic balance cannot be maintained and too much aqueous accumulates in the eye, thus elevating intraocular pressure. Excess aqueous accumulates either because of overproduction or because of improper drainage out of the anterior chamber. Drainage can be blocked or slowed down if the outlets for aqueous (which lie at the junction of ciliary body and cornea) become squeezed shut or clogged. Pressure builds up within the eye, and if the pressure remains high for too long, vision can be impaired permanently. Increased intraocular pressure—the condition called **glaucoma**—is the single most common cause of blinding eye disease in North America. Fortunately, glaucoma can be treated if the condition is detected early enough. For this reason, eye doctors routinely measure the intraocular pressure in eye examinations these days.

The Iris, Pupil and Lens

The Iris   As it curls inward, away from the wall of the eye, the ciliary body gives rise to the **iris,** that circular section of tissue that gives your eye its characteristic color: brown, blue, green, gray, and so forth. This variety of colors makes the name *iris* very appropriate because iris comes from the Greek word for rainbow.

The iris actually consists of two layers, an outer layer containing pigment, and an inner layer containing blood vessels. If the outer layer is heavily pigmented, the iris will appear brown. But if this outer layer is lightly pigmented, the inner layer becomes partially visible through the outer one. In this case, the iris will look more lightly colored. Thus, the color of one's eyes results from a combination of the pigmentation of the outer layer and the color of the blood vessels in the inner layer. If the iris's outer layer has no pigment, the inner layer becomes very noticeable, giving the eye a pinkish hue. This condition occurs in albino humans, who, because of a genetic defect, have greatly reduced pigmentation.

The Pupil   Looking in a mirror at the center of your own iris, you'll see a round black region, the **pupil.** The pupil is actually an opening, or gap, within two sets of muscles. The inner set runs circularly around the pupil. When this circular band of muscles contracts, the pupil gets smaller. Another set of muscles runs radially out from the edge of the circular muscles, away from the pupillary opening. When the radial muscles contract, the pupil widens, or dilates. These changes in pupil size regulate the amount of light reaching the back of the eye.

The size of the pupil at any given moment depends on several factors. First, it depends on the light level to which the eye is exposed: The size of the pupil decreases as the level of light increases. In young adults, the pupil diameter varies from about 8 millimeters down to less than 2 millimeters, a fourfold variation in diameter. The amount of light passing through the pupil is proportional

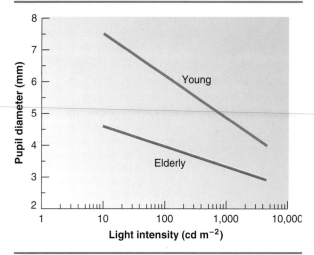

FIGURE 2.11 | Pupil size varies according to both light intensity and age. (cd m^{-2} stands for candelas per square meter, a common unit of light intensity.)

to the pupil's *area,* which is itself proportional to the square of pupil's diameter. Thus, as the pupil diameter varies over a range of 4 to 1, the amount of light passing through the pupil varies over a range of 16 to 1. The pupils of older adults change size in response to light in different proportions than their younger counterparts. In dim light, the pupil of an 80-year-old person is only about half that of a 20-year-old (see Figure 2.11). As a result, less light reaches the retinas of elderly people. This undoubtedly explains why older people frequently complain about the dim lighting in restaurants. Notice, by the way, that light intensity is plotted on a logarithmic (base 10) scale in this figure; the log scale allows us to plot results over a very wide range of values (light intensity, in this case) without having to make the abscissa (horizontal axis) unmanageably large.

Besides light level, the size of the pupil also varies in response to events that stimulate the autonomic nervous system. Anything that induces excitement, fear, or sexual interest can change the size of the pupil. Some people, such as seasoned poker players, are quite adept at sensing an opponent's excitement on the basis of their opponent's pupil size. An opponent's widened pupils are a dead giveaway that he or she has drawn a potentially winning card. Realizing the potential cue involuntarily provided by their eyes, professional poker players wear dark glasses to hide their telltale pupils, and also to obscure raised eyebrows, twitches, and changes in blink rate.

FIGURE 2.12 | The degree of blur in a picture depends on the size of the aperture of the camera. The sharp photo on the right was taken through a smaller aperture than was used in taking the photo on the left, thus increasing the depth of field in the right-hand photograph.

Although large pupils allow more light into the eye, smaller pupils can sometimes offer an advantage. Suppose you are looking at an object located several meters in front of you. While you're looking at that object, other objects—those much closer or much farther away—will tend to appear somewhat blurred. The range of distances over which objects will appear sharply focused varies inversely with the size of the pupil. This range of sharp vision is called the **depth of field.** The easiest way to demonstrate depth of field is to substitute a camera for your eye. In taking the photographs shown in Figure 2.12, the photographer varied the size of the camera's aperture to simulate the effects of changing pupil size. The photograph on the left was taken with a large aperture; the one on the right, with a small aperture. In both instances, the camera was focused on the object centered in the picture. Note that on the left, the picture taken with the larger aperture, very few objects appear sharp. The photograph on the right was taken without changing the focus but with a smaller aperture. Now, more objects appear well focused—the range of distances over which objects appear in sharp focus has increased. This range defines depth of field. Whether we're talking about cameras or about eyes, depth of field is determined by pupil (or aperture) diameter.

The Lens   One very important optical element of the eye, the **crystalline lens,** lies right behind the iris. The lens takes its name from its resemblance to a lentil, or bean. In adults, the lens is shaped like a very large aspirin tablet, about 9 millimeters in diameter and 4 millimeters in thickness. The lens consists of three distinct parts: an elastic covering, or *capsule;* an *epithelial layer* just inside the capsule; and the *lens* itself. As you might expect, each of these parts has its own job to do.

In fact, the thin, elastic capsule around the lens has two jobs. First, it moderates the flow of aqueous humor into the lens, helping the lens retain its transparency to light. Second, the elastic capsule molds the shape of the lens—varying its flatness and, thereby, the lens's optical power. This variation in optical power is called **accommodation.**

The lens never stops growing. Throughout your life span, the outer, epithelial layer of your lens continues to produce protein fibers that are added to the surface of the lens. Consequently, those protein fibers nearest the center of the lens are the oldest (some were present at birth), whereas the fibers on the outside are the youngest. Between birth and age 90 years, the lens quadruples in thickness and attains a weight of 250 milligrams (Paterson, 1979). In the center of the lens, the old fibers become more densely packed, producing **sclerosis,** or hardening, of the lens. We'll describe the significance of sclerosis later in this chapter.

For good vision, the lens must be transparent—light must be able to pass through it easily, without loss or deviation. Like the cornea, this transparency depends on the material out of which the lens is made. Of all the body's parts, the lens has the highest percentage of protein, and its protein fibers are lined up parallel to one another, maximizing the lens's transparency to light. Anything that disturbs this alignment, such as excess fluid inside the lens, reduces transparency.

An opacity (or reduced transparency) of the lens is called a **cataract.** Whereas some cataracts are minor, barely reducing the transmission of light, others undermine vision to the point of blindness. In some cases, cataracts can be traced to cumulative exposure to ultraviolet radiation present in sunlight (Schein et al., 1994), which helps explain why cataracts are more common in elderly people. But not all young people are spared from cataracts. In fact, certain populations (Arabs and Sephardic Jews, for instance) have a very high incidence of congenital cataracts—lens opacities at birth. These opacities severely degrade the stimulation received by the eye, and this can be serious. At birth, the visual nervous system is immature, and its proper development depends on normal stimulation of the eye. Deprived of that proper stimulation, the immature visual nervous system develops abnormally (Hubel, Wiesel, and LeVay, 1977). Realizing this consequence of visual deprivation, physicians now recommend removal of congenital cataracts as early in life as possible.

Surgical removal of a cataractous lens has become more or less routine today. Because the lens contributes to the total optical power of the eye, removal of the lens must be accompanied by some form of optical compensation. Powerful spectacles or contact lenses can be worn, or alternatively, a plastic lens can be surgically inserted into the eye, replacing the missing biological lens (Applegate et al., 1987). None of these alternatives, however, restores the ability to accommodate. People who have had such surgeries must use different glasses for near versus far vision.

Not all of us will develop cataracts, fortunately, but we can all count on our lenses gradually yellowing with age. Called brunescence, this condition arises from the accumulation of yellow pigment in the lens. This yellowing is hastened by exposure to ultraviolet light, such that the extent of yellowing depends on how much sunlight exposure you receive (Lindsey and Brown, 2002). You might come to think that the world should have a yellow cast to it because older individuals are effectively viewing the world through eyes with yellow "filters" in them. But the yellowing process occurs so gradually that one is never aware of any changes in color appearance. That is, until a lens is removed for surgical reasons. Then the world initially appears to have an overall blue cast to it, and if the lens removal is unilateral (meaning one eye only), the comparison between eyes is dramatic. Experts have debated whether these ocular changes influence the way color names are used by people living near the equator, where ultraviolet (UV) exposure is high, compared to people living significant distances away from the equator, where UV exposure is less.

The Vitreous Chamber

The vitreous chamber accounts for nearly two-thirds of the total volume of the eye. This larger of the eye's two chambers is bounded by the lens in front and the retina on the sides and in the rear. This chamber is filled with a transparent fluid called **vitreous,** a gellike substance with the consistency of egg white.

Encased in a thin membrane, the vitreous is anchored to the inner wall of the eyeball. Unlike the aqueous, the vitreous is not continuously renewed, which means that debris can accumulate within it. Sometimes you become aware of this debris, in the form of **floaters,** small opacities that float about in the vitreous. If you look at a bright, uniform surface, floaters cast shadows on the back of the eye, producing little dark spots that dart about immediately in front of you. Thanks to gravity, floaters tend to settle to the bottom of the vitreous chamber, out of the line of sight. Although floaters are usually harmless, dense or persistent floaters may be a symptom of retinal detachment, a vision-threatening condition that requires treatment.

FIGURE 2.13 | Cross section of the retina. The small box in the inset at the base of the eyeball shows the region of the eye represented in the enlarged drawing.

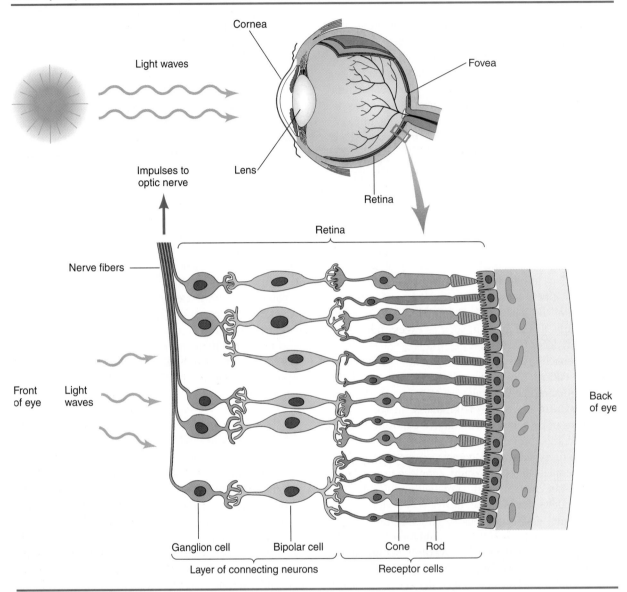

The Retina

The innermost of the eye's three layers, the **retina,** resembles a very thin, fragile meshwork, which explains its name—*rete* is Latin for "fisherman's net." Although it is no thicker than a postage stamp, the retina has a complex, layered organization (Wässle, 2004). Figure 2.13 shows how a section of the retina would look if magnified greatly and viewed from the side. The arrows denote the direction taken by incoming light. From this perspective, you can see that the cells comprising the retina have a peculiar arrangement: Light must pass through a complex network of neural elements before reaching the **photoreceptors,** which are actually responsible for converting light energy into neural signals. Moreover, the light-

FIGURE 2.14 | German scientist Hermann von Helmholtz, who invented the ophthalmoscope, illustrated on the right.

 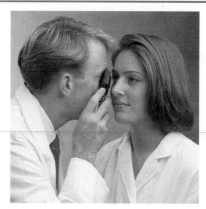

sensitive part of each photoreceptor, called the **outer segment,** actually faces away from the incoming light and toward the back of the eye. This seemingly backward arrangement has one distinct advantage. Photoreceptor outer segments, which have high metabolic demands, end up snuggled into the choroid, which, as we mentioned, contains a rich blood supply.

The neural signals generated by the photoreceptors, in turn, pass through a network of cells—**bipolar, amacrine,** and **horizontal cells**—that collect and recombine the photoreceptor signals. These collected, transformed signals are then passed on to the **retinal ganglion cells,** where biologically important information about the distribution of light over space and time is extracted and recoded. The recoded neural messages are then carried by the axons of the ganglion cells out of the eye and into the brain. As you can already begin to appreciate, crucial events underlying visual perception are inaugurated in this complex neural network, the retina.

To a large degree, the retina's complexity reflects its origins. Embryologically, the retina arises from the same tissue that spawns the billions of cells comprising the brain. So the retina is actually a direct extension of the central nervous system. This affinity with the brain has one unfortunate aspect, though: damaged retinal cells, like damaged brain cells, cannot be repaired. The visual consequences of damage are permanent, which is why it's so important to protect the eyes from excessive light exposure (by wearing sunglasses), from trauma (by wearing goggles when playing sports), and from disease (by having a routine, periodic eye examination).

The eye is not just a window to the outside world, it is also a window through which another person can look directly inside your body and view your nervous system. In fact, the eye is the *only* place where the nervous system and blood supply can be viewed directly, without surgery. If you were to look directly into another person's pupil, however, you wouldn't be able to see anything except a dark hole because your head obstructs the light necessary for seeing the back of the eye. Essentially, you're looking through a peephole into a dark chamber. Thanks to the nineteenth-century physicist, physician, mathematician, and philosopher, Hermann von Helmholtz (1821–94), it's possible to illuminate the eye while at the same time look into it (see Figure 2.14). Helmholtz invented a simple, clever device called an **ophthalmoscope,**[3] which allows us to visualize the interior of the living human eye, including its retina and blood supply. Doctors use this instrument to examine millions of patients every year, usually employing a handheld, battery-powered model that you've probably encountered during a routine vision exam.

---

[3]Actually, Charles Babbage, who developed a mechanical digital computer in the middle of the eighteenth century, made a working model of an ophthalmoscope some years before Helmholtz but didn't pursue the project (Rucker, 1971).

FIGURE 2.15 | Photograph showing the inside of the back of the human eye. The dark spot in the middle is the macula, the region where cone photoreceptors are concentrated. The blood vessels can be traced to a single location at the far right of the photograph, the region called the optic disk. The optic disk is displaced from the macula toward the nasal side of the retina, which tells us that this is a view of the right eye.

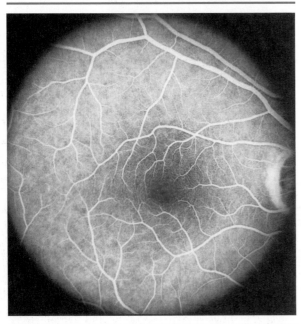

Retinal Landmarks and Blood Supply   Figure 2.15 illustrates what is seen when looking into a normal human eye using an ophthalmoscope. Because the living retina is virtually transparent, the ophthalmoscope primarily reveals structures lying in front of the retina—such as the central retinal artery—and structures lying behind it—such as the choroid. Although it does not provide a complete view of the entire retina, this photograph does highlight several of the retina's most significant features. Look first at the dark, nearly circular area in the center. Measuring roughly 1.5 millimeters in diameter, this region is called the **macula.** When you look directly at objects such as the words on this page, the images of those objects are centered within the macula of each eye. Vision is most acute in the center of the macula, for reasons you'll discover shortly.

Consider another landmark shown in Figure 2.15, the **optic disk.** Located at the far right-hand edge of the photograph, this is the region of the eye where optic nerve fibers (the axons of the ganglion cells) exit the retina, carrying in-

formation to the brain. Also, blood vessels within the retina enter and leave the globe at the optic disk. Normally, the optic disk has a pinkish color because of small blood vessels on its surface; these blood vessels nourish part of the optic nerve. Loss of this pink color can signify the presence of a circulatory problem that could eventually starve the optic nerve and destroy vision. Fortunately, such changes in color can be detected quite easily with the ophthalmoscope, allowing corrective measures to be taken where possible.

The retina has the highest metabolic rate of any part of the body, so its access to blood—for oxygen and nutrition—is vital. To supply the entire retina with blood is a challenge because metabolically active cells need to be in extremely close contact with the capillaries that nourish them. To meet this challenge, the eye contains two blood supplies: one that primarily nourishes the photoreceptors (the choroidal circulation system), and the other that nourishes the remaining cells of the retina (the retinal circulation system).

As we have already indicated, the choroid and its blood supply are located behind the photoreceptors and, therefore, are out of the path of light that stimulates the photoreceptors. This isn't true, however, for the retinal circulatory system. In Figure 2.15, note the network of large blood vessels (arteries and veins) that appear in the photograph as white, branching structures; these vessels comprise the retinal circulatory system. They fan out from the optic disk, dispersing into a fine network of capillaries spread throughout the inner part of the retina. Because they're situated in front of the retina, these blood vessels lie directly in the path of incoming light. This arrangement may strike you as odd, but it's the only way to get the blood vessels in close proximity to the outer portions of the retina that require nourishment.

You may also notice in Figure 2.15, however, the clever rerouting of the arteries and veins around the macula. Within this most important region for seeing, therefore, light is not obstructed on its route to the photoreceptors. But what about the other parts of the retina? Why don't we see the blood vessels and nerve tissue in the other parts through which light must pass? The simple exercise at the end of Box 2.1 (page 38) gives the answer and also allows you to see what you've probably never seen before: the blood vessels in your own eye.

Because its metabolic activity is so high, the retina is crucially dependent on normal blood flow. This makes the retina particularly vulnerable to diseases or disorders that impede the flow of blood. What sorts of things might interrupt the retina's blood supply? For one thing, feeder arteries can become clogged, blocking the flow of blood to and within the inner retina. This happens in arteriosclerosis (hardening of the arteries), and sometimes in sickle cell disease, a condition common among Africans and people of African descent.

Impairment of the blood supply to the outer, choroidal system can also have disastrous consequences. The outermost sheath of the retina consists of a single layer of cells, the **pigment epithelium,** which forms a barrier through which choroidal blood must pass to nourish the outer segments of the photoreceptors. The pigment epithelium transfers oxygen, nourishment, and vitamin A from the choroidal circulation to the photoreceptors. A steady supply of vitamin A is required for the synthesis of the receptors' light-sensitive pigment, a detail we'll return to later.

The pigment epithelium is also responsible for the disposal of metabolic waste products. Molecular garbage shed by the receptors is taken up and recycled within the pigment epithelium. If uncollected debris accumulates, it can eventually impede the transfer of nutrients. So anything that keeps pigment epithelium cells from performing their tasks will cause photoreceptor starvation and, eventually, death.

One natural enemy of the pigment epithelium is aging, and one of the most potentially devastating consequences of aging is macular degeneration. Indeed, age-related macular degeneration is the leading cause of impaired vision in the Western world and accounts for about one-half the cases of blindness among the elderly. Macular degeneration can seriously impair a person's ability to read, to drive an automobile, and even to get around on foot (Hazel et al., 2000). Currently, a minority of cases of age-related macular degeneration can be arrested, but not reversed, if treated early by means of laser surgery. You can see simulations of the devastating effect of macular degeneration on vision by using the web resources at www.mhhe.com/blake5.

Diabetes is another common disease that can affect the retina's blood supply. This disease is marked by disordered insulin metabolism that causes too much sugar to accumulate in the diabetic's blood. For reasons not completely understood, the excess sugar can promote the development of a cataract in the eye's crystalline lens. Cataracts, as you've learned, can blur vision to the point of blindness. In addition to cataracts, diabetes can have another serious consequence for vision. In some diabetics, the retina's blood supply is severely reduced. Sensing that it is being starved for oxygen (carried in the blood), the retina generates a chemical that stimulates the growth of new, larger blood vessels. Although growing new blood vessels may seem like an excellent solution to

the problem, this growth produces devastating consequences: The thick new vessels grow out of control, blocking light and eventually causing blindness. Fortunately, lasers can successfully cauterize these new vessels, to stop their growth.

Having presented an overview of the neural and vascular parts of the retina, we now need to consider how images are formed on the back of the eye. These images provide the raw ingredients for the process of vision. It is to that topic—optics—that we turn next.

The Eye as an Optical Instrument

Obviously, to see objects in the environment around you, your eyes must capture light reflected by those objects. But simply capturing the light itself isn't sufficient. The pattern of light reaching the retina must mirror the distribution of light in the scene being viewed if vision is to be useful. This light distribution, or **retinal image** as it's called, provides the raw material on which the retina operates, and high-quality vision is impossible without high-quality raw material. So, what determines the fidelity of the retinal image? Image quality is governed by the interactions between patterns of light arriving at the eye and various ocular structures that influence the passage of that light to the back of the eye where the photoreceptors are located. Appreciating the workings of the eye's retina, then, requires understanding something about the image it receives. So let's start there, with the formation of images on the back of the eye.

Light conveys to the eyes information about objects in the environment. But how does light acquire that information in the first place? Initially, light originates from a source such as the sun or a light bulb. This is called *emitted light,* and it's certainly a necessary antecedent for vision: We cannot see in the dark. But emitted light per se isn't the stimulus for vision. Rather, we are interested in seeing *objects,* and for that to happen our eyes must pick up and register light reflected off the surfaces of those objects. It is reflected light that conveys biologically important information about the appearance—and hence the identity—of objects. How does this come about?

The surfaces of objects absorb some, but not all, of the light illuminating them; the portion of light not absorbed is reflected by those surfaces.[4] Objects with high

---

[4]Actually, absorption and reflection do not exhaust the possibilities. For some objects, a portion of the incident light can be transmitted (pass through the object). The three options are often summarized by the mnemonic RAT.

FIGURE 2.16 | The top drawing illustrates how abrupt changes in reflectance signal the presence of an edge and, in this example, the boundary between two objects abutting one another. The two bottom images show how highlights on the surface of an object can signify the smoothness of that surface. The shiny appearance of the sphere on the left signifies a glossy surface while the dull appearance of the one on the right denotes a matte surface.

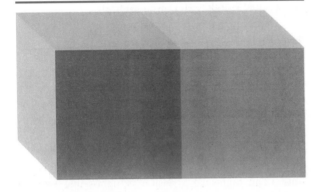

Surfaces can sculpt the patterns of reflected light in other ways, too, depending on the material forming those surfaces. For example, you have no trouble distinguishing wood from plastic, or paper from metal. This is because those surfaces have characteristic ways of reflecting light, with some reflecting light evenly in many different directions and others reflecting light in a narrow range of directions. Surfaces reflecting light diffusely lack highlights, they appear dull or matte. Surfaces reflecting light strongly in one range of directions can appear to have highlights, making them appear glossy or specular (Greenberg, 1989; Fleming, Dror, and Adelson, 2003). The two spheres in the bottom portion of Figure 2.16 show examples of a glossy surface and a dull surface.

So, reflected light is structured by objects in the environment, and this optical structure conveys potential information about those objects and the composition of their surfaces. But before that potential can be realized, three prerequisites must be satisfied. First, the light must be sufficiently intense to penetrate the eye, reaching the photosensitive material in the retina. In fact, about 50 percent of all light striking the cornea is reflected or absorbed before reaching the retina.

Second, the distribution of light imaged on the retina must be properly focused. Consider the sharp contours forming this pair of letters: GO. To produce a sharp image of these letters, light reflected from that region of the page must form small, well-defined replicas of those contours on the retina. Blurred replicas would be created if each small, sharp contour were imaged as a larger, spread-out distribution of light on the retina. As a result, different parts of the retinal images of the contours would overlap, blurring one another's boundaries and making it difficult to see separate, individual letters, in which case reading would be impossible. Take a look at Figure 2.17 to see how blur confounds reading (some of us need only remove our glasses to produce blurring comparable to that simulated in this figure).

Third, the pattern of light falling on the retina must preserve the spatial structure of the object from which it is reflected. If that spatial structure is preserved, light arising from two adjacent regions in space—from neighboring parts of an object, for instance—will fall on adjacent parts of the retina. A distribution of light that preserves the spatial ordering of locations in space is called an **image.** If the light distribution on the retina were scrambled so as to be spatially random, it would be useless as a source of information about the structure and layout of objects.

So how does the eye satisfy these three prerequisites? The material in the next section provides the answer.

reflectance usually appear light, whereas objects with low reflectance tend to appear dark. For example, the white portions of this page have a reflectance of about 80 percent, while the dark print on this page has a reflectance of about 10 percent. Abrupt changes in reflectance usually signal discontinuities in a surface, such as the letters on this page or the edges and corners that demarcate object boundaries (see the top drawing in Figure 2.16). More gradual changes in reflectance usually correspond to curved surfaces (see the objects in the bottom part of Figure 2.16). Light that is reflected from an object, in other words, is sculpted by the surfaces of the objects illuminated by that light, where "sculpted" refers to differential reflection of the light from different portions of the objects and their backgrounds.

FIGURE 2.17 | Effect of blur on the legibility of text. (For a legible version, you can find these paragraphs on page 49.)

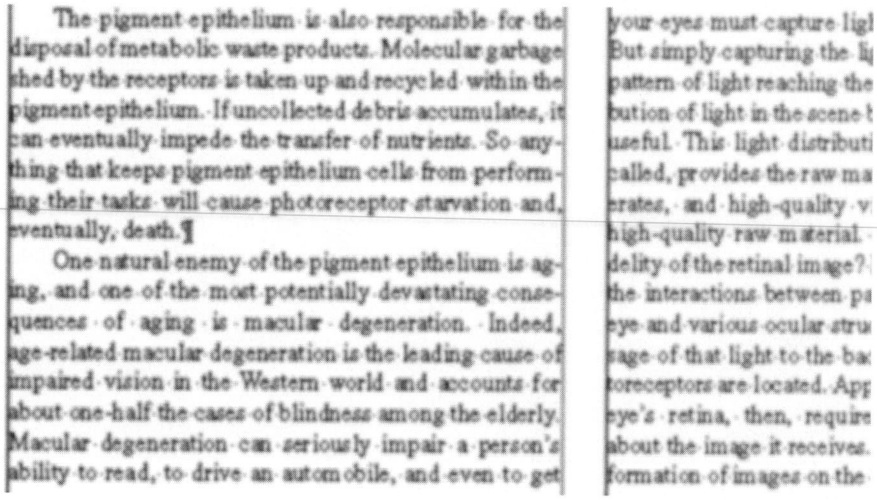

The pigment epithelium is also responsible for the disposal of metabolic waste products. Molecular garbage shed by the receptors is taken up and recycled within the pigment epithelium. If uncollected debris accumulates, it can eventually impede the transfer of nutrients. So anything that keeps pigment epithelium cells from performing their tasks will cause photoreceptor starvation and, eventually, death. ¶

One natural enemy of the pigment epithelium is aging, and one of the most potentially devastating consequences of aging is macular degeneration. Indeed, age-related macular degeneration is the leading cause of impaired vision in the Western world and accounts for about one-half the cases of blindness among the elderly. Macular degeneration can seriously impair a person's ability to read, to drive an automobile, and even to get

your eyes must capture ligh
But simply capturing the li
pattern of light reaching the
bution of light in the scene t
useful. This light distributi
called, provides the raw ma
rates, and high-quality v
high-quality raw material.
delity of the retinal image?
the interactions between pa
eye and various ocular stru
age of that light to the bac
toreceptors are located. App
eye's retina, then, require
about the image it receives.
formation of images on the

Image Formation in the Human Eye

The sharpness of images formed on the retina depends mainly on two factors. The first is the optical power of the cornea and crystalline lens (where "optical power" means ability to bend, or refract, light). The other factor controlling image sharpness is the size of the eyeball, particularly the eyeball's length from front to back. In a camera, a good picture requires that the film be just the right distance from the lens. In the eye, the same thing holds true: the retina must be the right distance from the crystalline lens. Some eyes are too short, others are too long; either condition impairs vision.

The optical power of the eye is not constant, though. By changing its shape somewhat, the crystalline lens changes its optical power and, hence, the overall focus of the eye. This shape change, called **accommodation,** helps one see objects clearly, regardless of their distance from the eye. To appreciate how these components of the eye contribute to vision, we'll have to consider the behavior of light and its interaction with these components. To simplify our analysis of image formation we'll begin with a very small object: a single point in space that emits light. The same analysis works for other, more complex visual objects, since we can think of them as consisting of a large set of points. But dealing with just one point will simplify our explanation of the rudiments of image formation.

In the eighteenth century, Thomas Young showed that light behaved as though it consisted of waves. Consider the oft-used metaphor of a pebble dropped into a pond. When this happens, you see wave fronts spreading out from the place where the stone hit the water. The stone corresponds to our point of light, and radiating out from that point is a set of spherical wave fronts (see Figure 2.18). Light that spreads out in this way is said to be **divergent.** Divergent light cannot form a well-focused image—a point—unless something is done to reverse its divergence. How does the eye accomplish this feat of reversing the path of light? Like a camera, the eye counteracts light's tendency to diverge using a convex lens, which gets its name from its shape. Once a diverging wave front passes through a strong convex lens, the paths of neighboring points on the wave front get progressively closer together and eventually converge to a single point. After passing through this point, light diverges once again. Figure 2.19 illustrates this effect of a convex lens.

Lenses differ in their ability, or power, to converge light. A highly convex lens converges light more strongly than does a mildly convex lens. As Figure 2.20 shows, rays that pass through a convex lens of lower power are focused at some distance farther from the lens, whereas rays that pass through a convex lens of high power are focused close to the lens. The distance at which a lens

FIGURE 2.18 | Light waves radiate out from a source of light in a way that resembles the ripples produced when a pebble is dropped into a pond.

FIGURE 2.19 | A convex lens focuses diverging light.

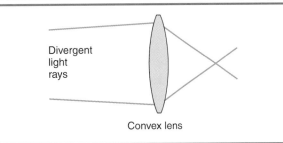

Divergent light rays

Convex lens

FIGURE 2.20 | Convex lenses of different power bring light to focus at different distances. If the light rays striking the lens are parallel, the spot at which the light converges to a point is called the *focal point*.

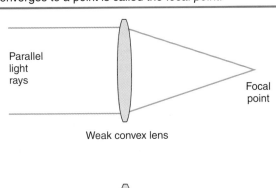

Parallel light rays

Focal point

Weak convex lens

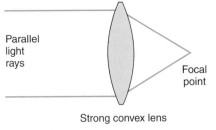

Parallel light rays

Focal point

Strong convex lens

brings light to focus depends on both the power of the lens itself and the degree of light divergence striking the lens. To converge the light, a convex lens must overcome, or null, the light's divergence. This is demonstrated in Figure 2.21: A lens of constant power is shown converging light of three different degrees of divergence. The most strongly divergent light comes from the source positioned closest to the lens, while the most weakly divergent light comes from the source farthest from the lens. In addition, each object is focused at a different distance from the lens: The most divergent light is focused farthest from the lens, and the least divergent light is focused closest to the lens.

With these optical principles in mind, consider a human eye that is looking at an object sufficiently far away that light coming from that object has essentially zero divergence (in this case we say the object is located at optical infinity). To form a useful image, light from the object must be focused on the retina. Since cornea and crystalline lens both contribute to image formation, let's lump them together, calling the combination the optics of the eye. How powerful should those optics be to produce a sharp retinal image of that distant object? For the retinal image to be sharply focused, the power of the optics

FIGURE 2.21 | The spot at which a convex lens brings light to a point depends on the degree of divergence of the light arriving at the lens.

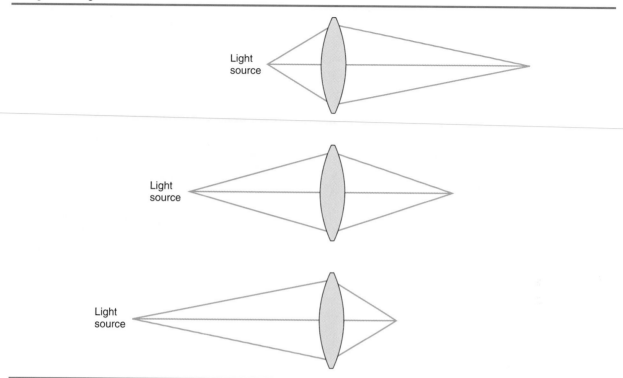

must match the length of the eyeball—specifically, the distance from the lens to the retina.

This idea is illustrated in Figure 2.22. The eyeball in the top of the figure is precisely the right length, given the power of its optics. As a result, the distant object is brought to focus exactly on the retina. Such an eye is said to be **emmetropic** (meaning in the right measure or size).

The middle panel shows an eye that is too long, given the strength of its optics. Although an image *is* formed, that image is formed in front of the retina, rather than on it. In fact, the rays have begun to diverge again by the time they reach the retina, so the image on the retina is blurred. Such an eye is described as **myopic,** or nearsighted, because near objects will be in best focus.

The bottom panel in Figure 2.22 shows an eye that is too short for its optics; an image is formed on the retina, but it, too, is not well focused and hence the image is blurred. Actually, for this eye the best-focused image would lie behind the retina if light were able to pass through the retina. Such an eye is described as **hyperopic,** or farsighted, because far objects will be in best focus.

What are the perceptual consequences of a mismatch between an eye's length and its optics? You've seen that in myopic or hyperopic eyes, light does reach the retina, but it is not sharply focused. When an eye of the wrong size looks at a distant point, the resulting image on the retina will be a circular patch, not a point. Thus, the point in space will appear blurred, or indistinct.

The degree of blur depends on the extent to which the eye is too short, or too long: The greater the mismatch between the eye's optics and its length, the worse the blur. The photographs in Figure 2.23 illustrate how the world might appear to a properly focused eye (panel A), to an eye that is only one-third of a millimeter too long (panel B), and to an eye that is 2 millimeters too long (panel C). Remember that when we describe an eye as too long or too short, we mean this in relative terms. "Too long" and "too short" are defined relative to the power of the eye's optics.

The blur in panels B and C is so striking that it is hard to imagine that many people actually suffer unwittingly for years with that much blur or more. They go through their entire childhood and adolescence never realizing that their

FIGURE 2.22 | Image formation in emmetropic, myopic, and hyperopic eyes.

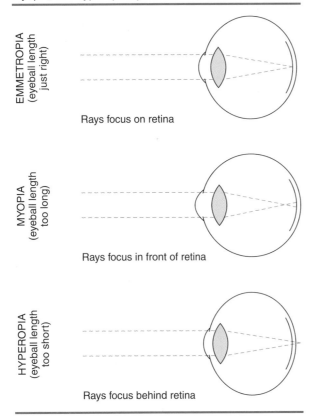

EMMETROPIA (eyeball length just right)

Rays focus on retina

MYOPIA (eyeball length too long)

Rays focus in front of retina

HYPEROPIA (eyeball length too short)

Rays focus behind retina

FIGURE 2.23 | Focus influences the quality of the image. Panel A simulates the image formed by an emmetropic eye; panel B, by a mildly myopic eye; and panel C, by a more severely myopic eye.

A

B

C

vision is defective. For reasons that we will explain, if their vision is blurred from myopia, they may have trouble seeing the blackboard clearly. If the blur comes instead from hyperopia, they may have trouble reading for prolonged periods. Unfortunately, the difficulties they experience in school may be mistakenly attributed to poor learning abilities rather than to poor vision.

Since about half the human race is afflicted with these problems, it's worth our time to consider hyperopia and myopia, and what steps can be taken to correct those problems.

Hyperopia Imagine an eye whose length and optical power are properly matched. For that eye, a distant object would be in proper focus on the retina. Recall that proper focus demands an object just far enough from the eye so that wave fronts from the object, when they strike the eye, will diverge at the right rate. If that same eye were shortened—making it hyperopic—by even a fraction of a millimeter, the distant object would no longer be focused as

FIGURE 2.24 | Mild hyperopia can be overcome either by accommodation or by placing a convex lens in front of the eye.

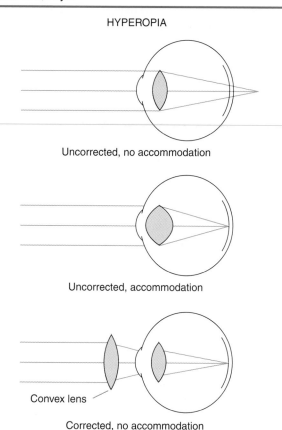

HYPEROPIA

Uncorrected, no accommodation

Uncorrected, accommodation

Convex lens

Corrected, no accommodation

well on the retina. The plane in which the image would be focused best would lie behind the retina, not right on it (see the top panel of Figure 2.24). In its shortened state, this eye's optics would be too weak even for light coming from an object so distant that it is not diverging at all. If it has to deal with light from closer objects (even more strongly diverging), the eye will misfocus the light all the more.

A person with hyperopia—a hyperope—can alleviate this problem by accommodating, increasing the eye's optical power. This enables the hyperope to produce focused images of objects, provided the eye is not too hyperopic and provided the objects are not too close. Accommodation makes the lens more convex, thereby increasing its power and allowing well-focused images to be formed on the retina. The middle panel of Figure 2.24 shows how accommodation helps the hyperope bring an object into better focus on the retina.

But the hyperope pays a price for constant accommodation. First, there are limits to the amount of accommodation that the human eye can produce. As a result, if the eye is much too short and the resulting hyperopia substantial, the hyperope may be unable to accommodate enough for close work, such as reading. Second, even if the hyperope *could* accommodate enough to read, accommodation requires maintained muscular effort. The very strong, prolonged accommodation, as might be required in order to read, can cause eyestrain, headaches, and even nausea (Daum, 1983).

Fortunately, there is an alternative. Because the hyperopic eye cannot make incoming light converge strongly enough, the light is not focused on the plane of the retina. The problem can be corrected by placing a convex lens in front of the cornea. With such a lens, the total optical power of the eye will be approximately the sum of the eye's own inherent optical power plus the power of the supplementary lens. This increased total optical power allows distant objects to be focused on the retina with little or no accommodation. As a result, the hyperope will need less accommodation when doing close work and will suffer less accommodative strain. The bottom panel of Figure 2.24 illustrates how this added convex lens helps the hyperope see near objects without accommodation.

Myopia Next let's consider an eye that is too long relative to its optical power. Such an eye is myopic, meaning that an object at optical infinity would be sharply focused somewhere in front of the retina, not at the plane of the retina (see the top panel of Figure 2.25). This situation could be rectified if we moved the object closer to the myopic person, or conversely, if we moved the myopic person closer to the object. Sometimes, of course, neither of these approaches is practical. Nor is it possible for the blur to be corrected by accommodation. In fact, increasing the power of the crystalline lens increases the overall optical power of the eye, worsening the blur. Fortunately, there is an effective solution to myopia: Alter the effective optical power of the eye by placing the proper spectacle lens in front of, or the proper contact lens on, the eye.

What sort of corrective lens would a myopic eye need? We could correct the myopic eye by adding a concave lens (which causes light to *diverge,* combating the myopic eye's tendency to make light *converge* too much). The bottom panel of Figure 2.25 shows how such a lens helps to focus an otherwise misfocused target on a myope's retina.

FIGURE 2.25 | A concave lens in front of the eye can correct myopia.

MYOPIA

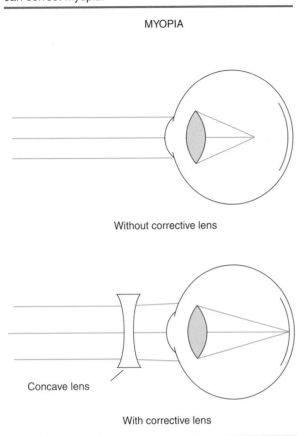

Without corrective lens

Concave lens

With corrective lens

FIGURE 2.26 | The *near point*—the closest distance at which an object can be seen without blur—increases with age. Note that the Y axis is scaled such that closer near point values (implying a wider range of sharp vision) appear more toward the top of the axis.

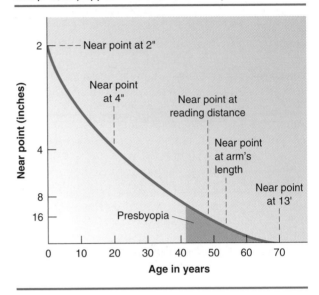

In many countries, myopia is so common that it poses a costly public health problem. Myopia means that you cannot see distant objects in sharp focus without glasses or contact lenses (NRC, 1989). It is important to note, however, that the prevalence of this vision problem is not the same in all populations, which points to considerable genetic influence on development of myopia (Zadnik et al., 1994). Also, comparisons of monozygotic and dizygotic twins show stronger correlation between the degree of myopia in identical twins than in their non-identical counterparts (Hammond et al., 2001; Morgan, 2003). But genetics is not the entire story. The prevalence of myopia also depends upon environmental factors, including the visual demands of a person's occupation or leisure time activities. People who do a great deal of near work, for instance, show an increased incidence of myopia. Sailors who serve for long stretches aboard submarines are an excellent case in point. These submariners are cooped up for months on end in very small quarters, with little or no op-

portunity for distance vision (Kinney et al., 1980); myopia is one consequence of their enforced diet of near vision. Reviewing numerous studies from around the world, Morgan and Rose (2004) documented the rising rate of myopia, which appears to reflect, in part, changes in the amount of time children are indoors, reading, playing computer games, or watching television. The importance of environmental factors in producing myopia is clinched by a study in which monkeys spent their waking time on the equivalent of near work. In order to simulate near work, newborn monkeys were reared so that there was nothing for them to see more than 50 centimeters from their eyes. Over a three-year period, these rearing conditions led to severe, permanent myopia (Young, 1981). As Box 2.2 describes, certain conditions produce a temporary, reversible form of myopia.

Presbyopia Myopia and hyperopia affect many individuals. But the eye's focus can be disturbed in yet another way that *everyone* who lives long enough will experience sooner or later.

As people get older, their ability to accommodate decreases. As Figure 2.26 shows, the trend begins very early in life and continues until about age 70 (Carter, 1982). For the average 20- or 30-year-old, this loss has no

Some conditions have the power to diminish even the best vision, converting emmetropes into myopes, though only temporarily. Because this error in the eye's optical power is temporary, it differs from myopia. But as you'll see, the transitory nature of this condition, called **anomalous myopia,** does not reduce its potential seriousness.

It has been known for 200 years that some people who are blessed with perfectly good eyesight during the day become quite nearsighted at night or at twilight. You may have experienced this yourself: Nearby objects are seen clearly, but distant ones are not. Wide differences exist among individuals in the severity of anomalous myopia—some people show virtually no myopia at low light levels, while others become extremely nearsighted.

Low light is not the only condition that elicits a temporary myopia. Even in daylight, many individuals become myopic in featureless environments, such as a large open field, or when viewing a clear, cloudless sky. The amount of nearsightedness an individual experiences in such a featureless environment is strongly related to the nearsightedness experienced at twilight. One suspects then that both "open field myopia" and twilight myopia arise from a common cause. Both are subsumed under a single general rubric, anomalous myopia.

What causes this condition? Thanks to the efforts of Herschel Leibowitz and Fred Owens (1975), we know the answer. At low light levels or in open fields, there is no powerful stimulus to control the amount of accommodation. Freed from stimulus control, accommodation returns to a preferred neutral, or resting, level. The eye becomes myopic because that resting level is more suited to seeing near objects rather than very distant ones. In other words, the resting state of accommodation in many people does not produce a perfectly relaxed lens with minimal optical power. Instead, the resting state of accommodation leaves the lens focused for relatively nearby distances. Using laser-based instrumentation, Leibowitz and Owens confirmed that in the dark, most people's eyes tended to focus at some intermediate distance, not optical infinity. The actual distance varied widely among individuals, with an average viewing distance of about 0.67 meter.

The existence of anomalous myopia poses a potentially serious safety threat (Owens, 1984). Imagine you are the pilot of an airplane flying through the nighttime sky or the driver of a car speeding over a dark country road. In both conditions, accommodation will revert to its resting level. This will tend to blur and diminish the visibility of any object that appears within the field of view at a distance other than that associated with the resting level. If you are a pilot, the blurred object might be another aircraft; if you are a driver, it could be a pedestrian.

Like other refractive errors, anomalous myopia can be remedied optically. Leibowitz and Owens (1976) measured the resting level of accommodation for various individuals and then fitted them with concave corrective lenses of the appropriate power. These glasses, although inappropriate for daylight or nonmyopic conditions, produced impressive improvements in drivers' nighttime vision. Perhaps, sometime in the future, drivers and pilots will be routinely outfitted with individually prescribed glasses for nighttime use. The benefits, in lives saved, could be substantial.

---

practical consequence; people that age still have sufficient ability to accommodate. But upon reaching the mid-40s, the average person can no longer accommodate sufficiently to bring very close objects into focus. Reduced accommodation arises from various sources, including sclerosis of the lens and reduced elasticity of the lens's capsule. Severely diminished ability to accommodate is called **presbyopia,** meaning "old sight." In addition, an old lens is very sluggish in executing even the small shape changes that are still within its capabilities. This lengthens the time required to change gaze from near to distant objects, and vice versa, causing potential problems in driving and other tasks that entail rapid shifts in focus at different distances.

You have probably seen signs of presbyopia in people who are beyond 40 years of age but have yet to wear glasses or contact lenses. To see clearly, these individuals have to hold their reading material at arm's length, and some eventually complain that their arms need to grow longer. A relatively easy solution is readily available. A convex lens can be placed in front of the eye to substitute for the crystalline lens's own diminished ability to become sufficiently convex.

Benjamin Franklin was about 47 years old when he found that he could no longer read without spectacles. However, his reading glasses made distant objects too blurred. Constantly having to switch from one pair of glasses to another annoyed him, so

BOX 2.3

Seeing Under Water

The next time you go swimming, try this experiment. Hold your hand under water and, with your head out of the water, look at your hand. Keeping your hand where it was, put your face into the water with your eyes open. When you look at your hand, you'll notice it doesn't look as sharp and clear as it did when your eyes were out of the water. The reason is that the cornea has effectively been eliminated as part of the eyes' optical system.

When light moves from air into the cornea, the path it travels is altered. This alteration, or bending, of light is called **refraction.** The amount of refraction depends on the difference between air and the material out of which the cornea is made. Under water, light enters the eye not from air but from the water itself. Because of the strong similarity between water and the material out of which the cornea is constructed (a large percentage of the cornea is water) light from the water is bent very little as it enters the cornea. Thus, when under water, the eye has effectively no cornea. Putting your face under water has reduced the optical power of your eye by about two-thirds, so it's no wonder you can't see so well. Of the eye's usual optical system, only the crystalline lens remains functional. But steps can be taken to restore the effectiveness of your cornea underwater. A transparent diving mask keeps water away from direct contact with your corneas, allowing them to work just as they did with your face out of water.

Other creatures also need to use their eyes underwater but don't have access to face masks. How do they do it? If an animal spends all of its time underwater there's no problem; its eye is designed so that the cornea contributes little optical power anyway. The lens is strong enough to do all the necessary light bending. Most fish eyes have extremely powerful convex crystalline lenses—a perfect adaptation to their aquatic world.

But what about animals who spend some time above water and some below? They face the same problem that humans do. We'll consider two particularly interesting creatures who solve this challenge in different ways. Think about the problem that a diving bird faces. Flying along, it looks for fish swimming near the surface of the water below. When it spots a fish, the bird dives into the water and tries to snatch the fish. But as soon as it enters the water, the bird's cornea will lose its optical power, handicapping the bird visually. Some diving birds avoid this effect by using the equivalent of an adjustable face mask. The cormorant, for instance, has thick but partially transparent eyelids that close when the bird enters the water. Keeping water from coming into contact with the bird's corneas, the lids preserve much of the cornea's optical power.

But some animals face a situation that is even more optically demanding. Instead of going into and out of the water, these creatures are simultaneously both in and out of the water. The most famous of these creatures is *Anableps anableps,* a freshwater fish found in South and Central America. Because some of its food supply consists of insects above the water, anableps swims along the surface of the river, its eyes half under water and half above water. Anableps has a rather interesting adaptation to this peculiar environmental niche. The upper portion of anableps's eye (the part that is exposed to air) is distinct from the lower portion (the part that is exposed to water). Anableps has two pupils in each eye (one below and the other above the water), but relies more on aerial vision than on its aquatic vision (Albensi and Powell, 1998). In addition, the lower half of its lens is more powerful than the upper half (Sivak, 1976). Anableps is commonly referred to as *cuatro ojos* (Spanish for "four eyes"), but having four eyes rather than two suits the anableps's lifestyle very well indeed.

Franklin invented bifocals, which are glasses having two separate lenses in front of each eye, with the more strongly convex lens filling the bottom of the frame. Looking down at reading material, Franklin could take advantage of the extra help given by that lens. Looking slightly upward, he could see the world through a less powerful convex lens, allowing him clear vision of distant objects.

Astigmatism   So far, our discussion of image formation in the eye has emphasized the role of the crystalline lens. The cornea, though, contributes more to the formation of sharp images on the retina than the lens does. To be more precise, the cornea contributes about two-thirds of the eye's total optical power, with the crystalline lens contributing the rest (see Box 2.3). As in the case of the lens, the cornea's shape determines its power—the more spherical the cornea, the more strongly it will converge incoming light. When the cornea is misshapen, the retinal image will be distorted. The most common distortion of shape produces a visual problem called **astigmatism.**

You can test yourself for astigmatism by using the spoke pattern in Figure 2.27. Look at the center of the

FIGURE 2.27 | Chart for testing astigmatism.

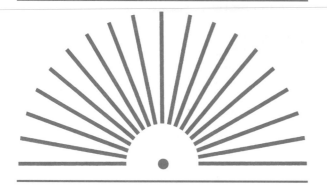

spoke pattern. Without shifting your gaze, note whether some lines look fainter or have fuzzier edges than others. If they do, you may have astigmatism. This condition is not uncommon. It's caused when the cornea is more sharply curved along one axis than it is along another. These differences in curvature mean that the cornea cannot sharply focus two different line orientations simultaneously on the retina. You may be wearing glasses that correct an astigmatism. To find out, remove your glasses, look through just one lens and slowly rotate the glasses through a 90-degree angle. If the lines on the test chart change in appearance, your glasses contain a correction for astigmatism. People with astigmatism who wear contact lenses automatically have their vision corrected. The contact lens itself is perfectly spherical, and it is cushioned snuggly against the eye by a thin film of tears. The contact lens thus compensates for any irregularity in the cornea's shape and, thereby, nullifies any astigmatism.

Almost all eyes have some degree of astigmatism because the cornea is almost never perfectly spherical. But for some people the astigmatism may be severe enough to interfere with perception. Figure 2.28

FIGURE 2.28 | The photograph at the right was taken using a lens that simulates astigmatism.

FIGURE 2.29 | A highly magnified view of a portion of the human retina.

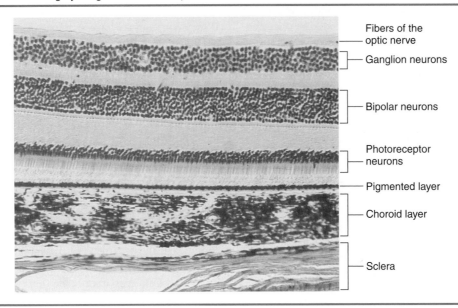

Fibers of the optic nerve

Ganglion neurons

Bipolar neurons

Photoreceptor neurons

Pigmented layer

Choroid layer

Sclera

illustrates how severe astigmatism can distort the appearance of a common, everyday scene. Astigmatism can be corrected by providing a lens that compensates for the cornea's distortion by an equal and opposite distortion of its own.

In addition to correcting optical defects using glasses or contact lenses, optometrists and ophthalmologists now also use a technique called LASIK surgery. LASIK stands for laser-assisted in situ keratomileusis, and the procedure involves resculpting the cornea by removing thin layers from portions of the cornea, thereby altering its shape and hence its refractive power. The laser acts as an extremely sharp knife that literally vaporizes small portions of corneal tissue. The procedure has been used successfully to correct myopia, hyperopia, and astigmatism; it is not, however, a solution to presbyopia. There are risks involved, including the development of glare and annoying halos. And LASIK treatment doesn't always completely correct refractive error, forcing the patient to use mild refractive correction to make up the difference. For additional information you can visit the FDA-sponsored website on LASIK surgery, the link for which is available at www.mhhe.com/blake5.

This finishes our overview of the optical components responsible for forming images on the back of the eye. Now we're ready to resume looking at the back portion of the eye—the retina—which serves as the screen on which the image is cast. As mentioned previously, this screen is actually located *behind* a complex network of nerve cells. The carefully formed image must pass through this network before the image can be registered by the photoreceptors. Let's take a look at this odd but obviously successful arrangement.

A Sideways Look at the Retina

Figure 2.29 shows a thin slice of the retina viewed from its side. To create this slice, the retina was carefully removed from the eye, stretched out on a flat surface, and cut downward, through the thickness of the retina. (Special chemical dyes applied to this tissue make different types of retinal cells visually conspicuous under a microscope.)

The cross section in Figure 2.29 was taken from a region a few millimeters from the center of the retina, just outside of the macula. This cross section is arranged so that if it were actually in an animal's eye, incoming light would first pass through the *top* part of the cross section. Notice that the photoreceptors are situated toward the *bottom* of the drawing. This drawing again reminds us that before light can reach the photoreceptors and initiate the responses that result in vision, light must traverse the entire thickness of the retina.

FIGURE 2.30 | Shown on the left is a highly magnified picture of a few rod and cone photoreceptors. On the right are drawings of a rod and a cone, with their major parts labeled.

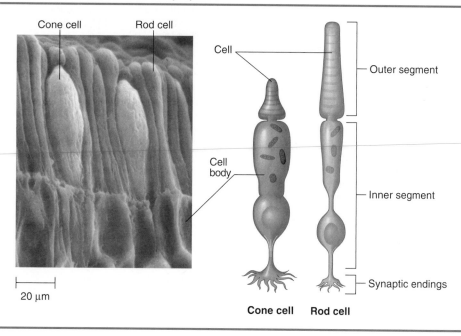

Not all regions of the retina have the same thickness. Within the macula at the very center of the retina, the layers of tissue thin out, forming a pit called the **fovea** (in Latin, *fovea* means "pit"). The retina in the foveal neighborhood is thin because some overlying structures have been pushed to the margins of the foveal pit. There's a good reason for this small clearing around the fovea. As light passes through the retina, some of it is absorbed or scattered before it can reach the photoreceptors. The thinness of the retina's fovea minimizes absorption and scatter, thus eliminating the obstacles to the passage of light to this particularly important region of the retina.

With this overview of image formation and the retina firmly in mind, let's now consider how the photoreceptor cells in the retina sense the presence of light and initiate the process of seeing.

The Photoreceptors

The human eye contains two major classes of photoreceptors: **rods** and **cones.** In humans, each eye contains about 100 million rods and approximately 5 million cones (Wandell, 1995). Figure 2.30 shows an example of rod and cone photoreceptors, and from their shapes you can see where they get their names. The tip of a cone is tapered, resembling a teepee or an upside-down ice cream cone. In contrast, the tip of a rod has straighter sides and a blunt end—it looks like a rod. But their differences go well beyond shape. In fact, functional differences between the two types of photoreceptors determine the lifestyles of their owners. Creatures who have a preponderance of rods in their retinas, such as the owl, tend to be most active at night. (We call such creatures nocturnal animals.) Creatures who have a preponderance of cones, such as the squirrel, tend to be active only during daylight hours. (We call them diurnal.) We humans have duplex retinas, containing both rods and cones; we're called "arhythmic" since our activities are not limited to just one part of the day/night cycle.

Think back to the analogy between the eye and a camera. The eyes' photoreceptors are analogous to the camera's film. Because human eyes contain two types of photoreceptors, they resemble a camera that holds two different kinds of film at once. The type of film in a camera—

FIGURE 2.31 | Distribution of rods and cones over the extent of the retina of the right eye, as seen from above. In the left eye, the nasal and temporal areas of the retina would appear reversed, but the relative distributions of rods and cones would be the same. Note the complete absence of rods within the fovea, where cones abound.

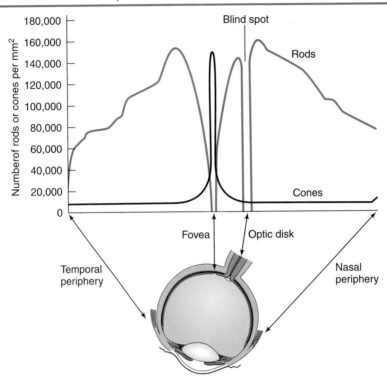

color versus black and white—determines what kind of pictures are produced. Our eyes are simultaneously loaded with two different kinds of "film" (rods and cones). The duplex nature of the human eye produces some interesting idiosyncrasies in the way that we see. These idiosyncrasies will become apparent as we survey the differences between the rods and cones.

The Distribution of Rods and Cones

Rods and cones are not uniformly distributed throughout the retina: Cones predominate in central vision, and rods predominate in peripheral vision. This differential distribution is shown in Figure 2.31, which plots the density of rods and cones in samples taken from different parts of the retina. In the very center of the macula, only cones are found. There, the cone's tips are thinner than elsewhere and they're very tightly packed. About

150,000 cones occupy an area 1 millimeter square. As we move away from the macula, the number of cones decreases while, at the same time, the number of rods increases. In fact, about 7 millimeters away from the fovea—moving along the retina in a direction toward the nose—rods reach a density approximately the same as that found for cones in the center of the macula. This difference in geographical distribution of rods and cones means that central and peripheral parts of the retina are useful for different aspects of vision. We'll get to those differences in a moment, but first let's consider a small, inconspicuous island of complete blindness found within each and every eye.

Notice the interruption in the plots shown in Figure 2.31. This gap denotes the complete absence of photoreceptors at the optic disk, the part of the retina where the nerve fibers exit the eye. Because you cannot see without photoreceptors, you're actually "blind" to any image

The optic disk—that place where the axons of the retinal ganglion cells come together to form the optic nerve—contains no photoreceptors. Consequently, it cannot support vision: It is literally a blind spot. Note that we're distinguishing between a region defined anatomically, the optic disk, and a region defined perceptually, the blind spot. Before we go on about the blind spot, you may want some proof that it actually exists.

Of course you cannot *see* a blind spot (though you can see an optic disk, using an ophthalmoscope). What you can see are the consequences of your blind spot—an object imaged within this blind region of your retina will be invisible. The accompanying figure will help you see the consequences of this blind spot. Making sure that the book is propped up at right angles to the tabletop, view the figure from a distance of about 60 centimeters (about 2 feet). Close your left eye and, using only your right eye, stare at the fixation cross in the figure. At this viewing distance, the black disk to the right of the cross should fall on your optic disk, and therefore disappear. Because the location of the optic disk varies from one person to the next, you may have to stare at a point slightly different from the fixation cross.

The demonstration of the existence of a blind spot represented a milestone in understanding the eye. Edmé Mariotte, the French scientist who discovered the blind spot in 1668, did not simply stumble upon it by accident (Mariotte, 1668/1948). Instead, his dissection of human eyes suggested to him that vision might be impaired in the region of the optic disk. This was the first time that anyone had predicted a previously unknown perceptual phenomenon simply from an anatomical observation. From the geometry of the eyeball, including the location of the optic disk, Mariotte correctly predicted where stimuli would have to be placed relative to a fixation point in order for the image to fall on the optic disk. Mariotte also confirmed that there were individual variations in the precise location of the blind spot, corresponding to individual variations in the optic disk itself.

It's been claimed that England's "merry monarch," Charles II, exploited the retina's blind spot to "behead" symbolically members of his court who were in disfavor (Rushton, 1979). After placing them at the right distance from his throne, Charles would adjust his gaze so that the head of his "victim" was imaged on the optic disk. Although this is an intriguing story, the more so because Charles I, the father of Charles II, had been beheaded, Adam Reeves (1982) describes the story as "a baseless canard" against Charles II. Frankly, we're not sure who's correct.

While you were looking for your own blind spot, you may have noticed something else strange. When the black disk disappeared, you weren't left with a "hole" in your visual field. Instead, the background appeared uniformly white. This phenomenon is called completion or "filling in." Blind spot completion has been cleverly exploited by Ramachandran (1992) to study the filling-in phenomenon in more detail. His article, which contains some delightful demonstrations, concludes that completion of vision across the blind spot is just one instance of a more general process called interpolation, an aspect of perception we will take up in Chapter 7.

X

Fixation cross

falling within this area of the retina devoid of receptors. We referred previously to an analogy between the photoreceptors and photographic film. Following this analogy, the optic disk would correspond to a defective area of the film, on which the factory neglected to put any light-sensitive chemical. If that defective film were used in a camera and developed, the resulting picture would have a noticeable blank region. Surprisingly though, we almost never notice the large gap that the optic disks create in our retinas. Box 2.4 will help you see what you've been missing all these years.

Let's now return our attention to those parts of the retina that contain photoreceptors. The array of approximately 105 million photoreceptors in each eye converts the optical image on the retina into a neural image that will be transmitted to the brain. But as Figure 2.31

shows, the density of photoreceptors varies regionally throughout the retina. This means, therefore, that the optical image is not being uniformly sampled by the photoreceptors. Again using the film analogy, it is as if our camera were loaded with film in which the light-sensitive chemical emulsion were unevenly spread over the film's surface. As a result, parts of our photograph would contain sharp detail (where the emulsion was dense) while other parts would appear grainy and blurred (where the emulsion was sparse). Photographic film isn't made this way, of course, but the retina is: It does unevenly register the spatial detail in the image formed on it. In the fovea where cones alone exist, the image is very finely sampled, while out in the periphery, sampling is coarse. You can easily preview the consequence of these sampling differences by trying to read small text out of the corner of your eye—the image of that text is not registered with sufficient detail to convey the identities of individual letters.

If one knows how densely the photoreceptors are packed, it's possible to calculate the finest pattern that any particular array of receptors could reproduce (Yellott, 1982). In the foveas of most young adults, the photoreceptors are packed very densely, in an orderly arrangement that produces a near-constant distance between neighbors. As one progresses away from the center of the retina, the distances increase between neighboring receptors and the orderliness of the packing diminishes (Hirsch and Miller, 1987). When the photoreceptors are photographed from the end, they suggest a carefully laid mosaic, such as one made out of small, hexagonal tiles. In the center of the retina, this remarkably orderly and tightly packed mosaic allows the photoreceptor array to reproduce the finest details that the eye's optics can transmit to the retina. To see what this mosaic actually looks like, turn to Plate 13 in the middle of the text. This is a highly magnified view of a small portion of the photoreceptor mosaic from one person's eye; the image was acquired from a perspective that has you looking directly into the mosaic. You're seeing, in other words, just the tips of the photoreceptors. We'll explain in a later chapter what the different colors denote, but for now notice how regular the spacing is.

We've commented admiringly on the exquisite packing of photoreceptors in the central retina of the human adult and on the contribution of that packing to the excellence of vision. The situation is quite different, though, for young infants. It takes about four years for an infant's retina to reach its final, adult state. During that time, photoreceptors migrate toward the center of the retina from the periphery, a migration that creates the pit known as the fovea. Even as late as 15 months of age, the distance between neighboring photoreceptors of the central retina is twice the comparable value in the adult eye (Yuodelis and Hendrickson, 1986). Although some of the infants' poor visual acuity arises from the immature state of their brains, most of their poor vision results from immaturity at the retinal level (Banks and Bennett, 1988; Teller and Movshon, 1986).

An analogous, though far less dramatic, change occurs at the other end of the life span. In old age, the packing of receptors in the central retina changes because of cell death (Weale, 1986). Undoubtedly, this contributes to the drop in acuity that accompanies aging (Owsley, Sekuler, and Siemsen, 1983).

Although retinal anatomy and retinal function follow parallel courses, retinal anatomy and retinal function are permanently arrested at the infant stage in some humans. These individuals, whose skin, hair, and eyes lack pigmentation, have a genetic disorder known as albinism. Melanin, the pigment that gives color to skin, hair, and eyes, is particularly abundant in the macular region of the normal retina. The melanin promotes the inward migration of photoreceptors and the formation of the foveal pit. The albino eye, lacking melanin, does not have much receptor migration and never develops a foveal pit. As a result, the number of photoreceptors per unit area in the central retina of the albino eye is far below that of pigmented adults. Hugh Wilson and colleagues have studied the vision of human albinos and liken their central retinal anatomy and function to that of a normal 10-month-old (Wilson et al., 1988). All of these unusual cases—infants, the aged, and albinos—reinforce the idea that the retina's photoreceptor mosaic sets important limits on the information that can be extracted from the retinal image.

The First Step toward Seeing

Light registers its presence on the retina by interacting with special light-sensitive molecules contained within the photoreceptors. These molecules, called **photopigments,** are contained in the membrane portions of an array of discs that are tightly packed within the outer segment of each and every photoreceptor (see Figure 2.32). Light passing through these discs triggers a cascade of biochemical events that culminate in the generation of electrical signals within the photoreceptor.

FIGURE 2.32 | Highly magnified photograph of an outer segment of a rod photoreceptor from a monkey's eye. The array of thin horizontal stripes are stacks of tightly packed disks that house the photosensitive molecules responsible for generating electrical signals when stimulated by light.

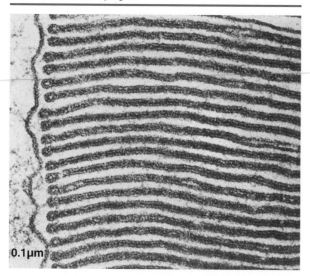

0.1 μm

We'll start by considering the chemical basis of the photopigment molecules.

Each photopigment molecule consists of two components: a very large protein, *opsin;* and another component, *retinal,* derived from vitamin A. Normally, the two components are tightly connected, producing a stable molecule that won't break up spontaneously. But when light strikes one of these molecules, some of the light's energy is imparted to the molecule, causing it to change shape, or *isomerize.* Once this shape change occurs, the photopigment molecule is no longer stable and its two components undergo a series of changes, eventually splitting apart.

This change in shape alters the flow of electric current in and around the photoreceptor. In the absence of light, electrical current flows into the stack of discs within the photoreceptor's outer segment. This inward current flow, then, signifies that the eye is in darkness. Photopigment isomerization, triggered by the presence of light, briefly reduces this flow of current. That change in current flow signifies the presence of light. The greater the amount of light, the larger the number of molecules

isomerized and the greater the resulting change in electrical potential.

This change in current moves down the length of the photoreceptor to its terminal end, where specialized chemical messengers, called **transmitter substances,** are housed. In the photoreceptors, these messengers are glutamate molecules. In the absence of light, glutamate is continuously released by the photoreceptor into the very small gap that separates the photoreceptor from the cells with which they are in chemical communication.[5] The presence of light—through its effect on the photopigments and the electrical current flow—reduces the rate of glutamate released into the synapse. Light, in other words, turns *down* the release of chemical messages by the photoreceptors. Like the photoreceptors pointing backward into the eye, this is another one of those counterintuitive ways that nature constructs biological mechanisms. But obviously it works, and very efficiently. The entire chain of events, from absorption to isomerization to current flow is called **phototransduction.** It occurs in less than a thousandth of a second. In the next chapter, we'll learn how the cells in communication with the photoreceptors make sense of these odd messages.

Not all light wavelengths are equally effective in triggering phototransduction. Whereas retinal is the same for all human photopigments, opsin comes in several different molecular forms, each with its own unique sensitivity to lights of different wavelengths. These different molecular forms are genetically determined, and genetic mutation can and does alter the form of the opsins in some individuals. The various sensitivities of opsins to light wavelengths is fundamentally important for vision, but we'll postpone discussing that until the next chapter. For now, let's survey the different types of photoreceptors as defined by their wavelength sensitivity.

Exposing a photoreceptor to light from various regions of the wavelength spectrum makes it possible to measure how much of that light is actually absorbed and, therefore, how much that wavelength stimulates the photoreceptor. When this is done, one finds that for any given receptor there is one wavelength of light that most strongly stimulates the receptor. There is, in other words, one wavelength to which the receptor is most sensitive. Rods give their biggest response when stimulated with

---

[5]The junctions between nerve cells are called **synapses;** these are the sites cells transfer neurochemical messages.

FIGURE 2.33 | Graph showing how the amount of light absorbed by rod photoreceptors varies with the wavelength of the light. The absorption values plotted on the Y axis are expressed relative to the maximum, which in this graph occurs near 500 nanometers; all other values are expressed as a percentage of this value.

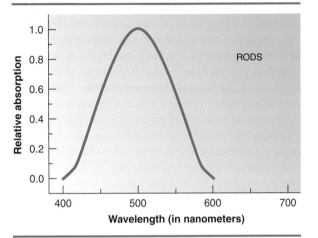

FIGURE 2.34 | Graph showing how the amount of light absorbed by each of three types of cone photoreceptors varies with wavelength. As in the previous graph, the absorption values for each of the three curves are expressed relative to the maximum value for each curve.

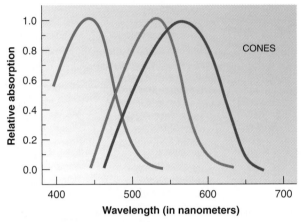

approximately 500 nanometers (the wavelength of light is measured in **nanometers,** billionths of a meter); shorter or longer wavelengths give a diminished response. A summary of the rod's spectral sensitivity is graphically illustrated in Figure 2.33. To appreciate the stimulus to which rods are most sensitive, you should know that under daylight conditions, light of 500 nanometers looks bluish green.

The corresponding story for cones is more complicated because the wavelength at which sensitivity is optimum depends on *which* type of cone is being studied. There are three distinct classes of cones. One is maximally responsive to light of about 440 nanometers, a second class responds best to light of 530 nanometers, and a third class has its peak response at 560 nanometers. The responses of these three classes of cones are shown in Figure 2.34 as functions of the wavelength of stimulating light. Again, to give some reference points, under daylight conditions, light of 440 nanometers looks violet, light of 530 nanometers looks green, and light of 560 nanometers looks yellow. We should emphasize that the graphs in Figures 2.33 and 2.34 plot sensitivity in terms of *relative* absorption, with a value of 1.0 in each graph denoting the wavelength producing the greatest percentage of light ab-

sorption for that photoreceptor type. In fact, rod photoreceptors are, overall, more sensitive than the cones. A given amount of light produces a considerably larger electrical response in rods than it does in cones and, consequently, rods require less light than do cones to produce reliable neural signals. That is why rods work better under dim light conditions, which we'll talk more about in the next chapter. Cones, however, have the advantage of working effectively over a much, much larger range of illumination than do rods. Once cones receive enough light to produce phototransduction, they continue to function even when the level of illumination is raised to extremely high levels. To borrow Rodieck's colorful way of putting it, "In principle, the light level can increase until the cones cook" (Rodieck, 1998, p. 147). Rods, on the other hand, operate within a very narrow range of light levels, and once the upper limit of that range is exceeded (corresponding to twilight levels), the rods cease responding. So now you have a better idea of why our eyes have both rods and cones: Being creatures that move about at night and during the day, we place great demands on our photoreceptors in terms of their required sensitivity and dynamic range. Evidently, nature has not yet discovered how to create a single type of photoreceptor able to operate over the enormous range of illumination characteristic of our visual habits.

So, our vision operates over an enormous range of illumination. At the same time, our vision is confined to a rather narrow range of visible wavelengths. Looking again at Figures 2.4, 2.33, and 2.34, we are reminded that our photopigments are insensitive to infrared radiation (wavelengths longer than 700 nanometers). We're also unable to see into the ultraviolet region of the spectrum (wavelengths shorter than about 380 nanometers). For at least a portion of this region of the spectrum, our inability to see ultraviolet light is owing primarily to the filtering properties of our lens, not to insensitivity of our photopigment. The lens absorbs very short wavelengths and, thus, screens the eye's photoreceptors from these very short wavelengths. In those rare individuals in which the lens is surgically removed, the spectral sensitivity function extends into the ultraviolet range, allowing them to see wavelengths normally invisible to the human eye. The ability of aphakic humans (those without a lens) to see ultraviolet light confirms that at least one category of photoreceptors are responsive into this region of the spectrum. Looking at the curves in Figure 2.34, one suspects that it is primarily the cones whose peak sensitivity occurs around 450 nanometers that provide aphakic humans with these glimpses of ultraviolet light. In nature, there are many species that routinely see in the ultraviolet range even with their lenses intact. Some of these animals, such as gerbils, have a specialized photoreceptor for detecting ultraviolet light (Jacobs, 1992), whereas others, such as some species of bats, have a single photoreceptor whose broad spectral absorption curve stretches into this region (Winter, Lopez, and von Helversen, 2003). Their ability to see into the ultraviolet range probably allows these animals to detect surface markings on flowers and fruits.

We have been focusing on photoreceptors and their signals, but within the visible portion of the wavelength spectrum, "seeing" requires more than just a change in a photoreceptor's electrical state. Messages about the presence of light must be transmitted from the receptors to the intermediate network of bipolar, amacrine, and horizontal cells and then to the retinal ganglion cells, which communicate the outcome of all this neural analysis to the brain. In the next chapter, we'll look in detail at how photoreceptor signals are transformed by this neural network in ways that shape how things look to us. But before turning to that, we need to introduce you to one more concept—**visual angle**—to pave the way for the other chapters on vision.

Computing Visual Angle

Throughout the forthcoming chapters on vision we will refer to the sizes of objects and to the distances between objects. We could express these dimensions in physical units such as centimeters ("This pencil I'm holding is 18 centimeters long"), but it makes more sense to express these values in units that refer to the images of those objects on the back of the eye. Needless to say, a pencil 18 centimeters long doesn't produce an image on the back of the eye that is 18 centimeters long—the image of the pencil on the back of the eye is much, much smaller. Moreover, the size of the image of the pencil (or any other object) depends not only on the actual size of the object but also the distance between you and the object you're viewing. A pencil held at arm's length produces an image on the back of the eye that's half the size of the image produced by the very same pencil held at half-an-arm's length. Image size, in other words, is inversely proportional to viewing distance.

So we need a metric of image dimensions that takes into account both the size of the object and the viewing distance from the eye to that object. To accomplish this, vision scientists express image sizes and distances in units called degrees of visual angle (see Figure 2.35). To understand this unit of measure, think of the image of an object properly focused on the back of the eye. The eye, being a curved surface, has a radius of curvature, and the image of an object occupies, or subtends, a given portion of the eye's interior radius of curvature. The size of the image, in other words, can be expressed in angular units which, for our purposes, are angular degrees. Likewise, two objects spatially separated in the world will form two spatially separated images on the back of the eye, and the distance between these images also can be expressed in degrees of visual angle.

The following is a simple formula based on trigonometry that very closely approximates the angular dimension(s) of the image of any object:

Visual angle (degrees) =
57.3 * object size / viewing distance

When using this formula, it is crucial that the values for size and distance be expressed in the same units of measure (e.g., centimeters). To see the formula in action, let's compute the angular subtense of our pencil held at arm's length (which, in the case of our arms, equals 50 cm).

Visual angle = 57.3 * 18 / 50 = 20.6 degrees

FIGURE 2.35 | The size of the image of an object on the back of the eye is inversely proportional to the distance between the object and the eye. Image size is expressed in units termed *visual angle,* expressed in units called *degrees.*

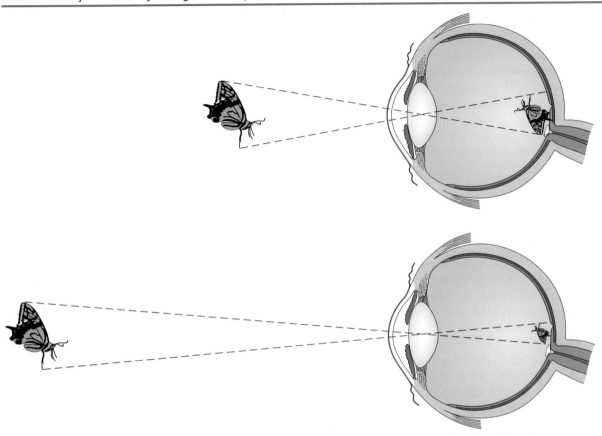

As long as we're at it, let's compute the angular subtense of the width of the pencil (which in metric units is 0.7 cm):

Visual angle = 57.3 * 0.7 / 50 = 0.80 degrees

You should appreciate that the angular subtense of the image of the pencil will grow to 41.2 degrees (length) by 1.6 degrees (width) when you move the pencil closer to your eyes by 25 centimeters, for you have reduced the value of the denominator by half and, thus, you have doubled the angular subtense values.

The same formula can be used to compute the distances between objects in your field of view. Suppose you hold two pencils at arms' length in front of you, one in each hand, and suppose you hold your two hands 10 centimeters apart. The distance between the two images of the pencils on the back of your eye will be 11.46 degrees. Halve the distance between your two hands, and this angular separation shrinks to 5.73 degrees. Now move both hands closer to your eyes, keep-

ing your hands 5 centimeters apart. How close do you have to move them to reproduce the angular separation of 11.46 degrees?

Now you're ready to think about dimensions and distances in terms of their values in angular degrees on the back of the eye. For amusement, try estimating the visual angle of an 18-foot-long trailer viewed from 25,000 feet in the air (on a clear day, you can be in the window seat of an airplane at this altitude and still see vehicles this size driving on freeways). Now compute the visual angle subtended by this punctuation mark — • — viewed from ordinary reading distance.

Before closing our lesson on visual angle, let's consider just how small images really are on the back of the eye. Think about viewing a dime on the ground, with the distance between you and the dime being about 1 meter. The diameter of the image of the dime would subtend roughly 1 degree visual angle, and on the back of your eye, 1 degree corresponds to a diameter of only

0.3 millimeter (also known as 300 microns). If you looked directly at this dime so that its image fell directly on your fovea where cones are maximally concentrated, its image would encompass approximately 25,000 cone photoreceptors. Each one of those individual cones, viewed on end, has a diameter of approximately 0.0083 degrees of visual angle. When numbers get this small, vision scientists break degrees into smaller units termed "minutes" of arc (with 60 minutes = 1 degree); thus, the cone's diameter can also be expressed as 0.5 minutes of arc. This sounds quite small—and it is—but we're able to see objects much tinier than this. If you want to be totally amazed, compute the visual angle of the width of a single strand of human hair viewed from a distance of 1 meter. Then, the next time you notice such a hair on your bathroom floor, you'll have an even greater appreciation for the keenness of human vision.

SUMMARY AND PREVIEW

This chapter laid out the basic design of the human eyeball, emphasizing the good fit between its structure and the job it must do. Because vision depends on an interaction between light and the eye, we also considered how light itself manages to capture information about the environment, information that is conveyed by light. This led us to a discussion of the eyeball's optical characteristics and various common imperfections in those characteristics. The chapter then covered the capture of light by photopigment molecules and the first step toward seeing—photoreceptor responses that are communicated to other neurons in the retina and eventually to the brain. The next chapter follows these messages as they pass from one retinal neuron to the next. You already know that your vision mirrors the properties of your photoreceptors; the next chapter will show you how other elements in the retina also control what you see.

KEY TERMS

accommodation
afterimage
amacrine cells
anomalous myopia
aqueous humor
astigmatism
bipolar cells
cataract
choroid
ciliary body
cones
conjugate
cornea
crystalline lens
depth of field
divergent
electromagnetic radiation
emmetropic
extraocular muscles

fibrous tunic
floaters
fovea
glaucoma
horizontal cells
hyperopic
image
inverse optics
iris
macula
myopic
nanometers
ophthalmoscope
optic disk
orbit
outer segment
photopigments
photoreceptors
phototransduction

pigment epithelium
presbyopia
pupil
rectus muscles
refraction
retina
retinal ganglion cells
retinal image
rods
sclera
sclerosis
synapse
transmitter substances
vascular tunic
vergence
visual angle
vitreous
wavelength

The Eye and Seeing

To appreciate how complex the eye actually is, talk to an engineer who has tried to build a bionic eye using electronic components. The first stage in the visual process—registering the presence of light within an image—is not so difficult for the engineer to implement using an array of special light-sensitive transistors called *photodiodes*. These tiny devices produce voltages that accurately represent the amount of light impinging on them, just like the photoreceptors in your eye do. But then what? How do you make any sense out of an array of voltage values? How does the artificial eye figure out what objects in the world produced particular patterns of voltage values in its array of photodiodes?

To accomplish this feat engineers have turned to nature, which holds all the patents on the most successful eye designs on earth. Using ideas borrowed from biological eyes, engineers working together with physicians have created wafer-thin silicon microchips whose circuitry mimics some of the neural processing accomplished by the retina. Implanted into the eye, these tiny electronic sensors can provide an otherwise blind person with serviceable visual information for walking around and avoiding objects. Still, the performance of an artificial retina pales in comparison to the real thing: The circuitry embedded in these microchips cannot hold a candle to the neural circuitry packaged in the retina of your eyes. In this chapter, we're going to try to think as

design engineers do, examining the circuitry and neural computations performed by the retina.

By way of preview, here's an abbreviated parts list for the retina of one human eye: just over 100 million photoreceptors (rods and cones); 10 million horizontal, amacrine and bipolar cells; and 1.25 million ganglion cells.[1] And these millions of parts have to be packaged just right, segregated into different layers of a retina not much thicker than an ordinary sheet of paper (recall Figure 2.29). Our goal in this chapter is to see how the retina's parts work together to generate biologically useful descriptions of the retinal image for the brain to interpret. To start, let's briefly review what photoreceptors do inasmuch as they kick off the series of neural events that culminate in visual perception.

Millions of Points of Light

Each and every photoreceptor performs one simple job: It gauges how much light is falling on it. Photoreceptors perform these measurements by generating electrical currents proportional to the amount of light absorbed by

---

[1]These are just a couple of the numerical values associated with the structure of the eye. For even more values, navigate to Brian Wandell's Web page, a link to which can be found at www.mhhe.com/blake5.

the photopigment contained in their outer segments. Over the entire retina, this operation results in millions of separate measurements, each one specifying the level of light falling on the tiny region of the eye occupied by a photoreceptor. Viewed this way, we can characterize the photoreceptor matrix as a two-dimensional array comprising millions of cells. At any given moment, each cell is generating its own unique response to the light that is striking that cell; the magnitude of that response reflects the degree to which the electrical current in that photoreceptor cell has been altered. That alteration in current is directly related to the amount of light absorbed by the photoreceptor pigment. The matrix of photoreceptors, then, generates an array of numerical values, with each value being proportional to the amount of light stimulating a given photoreceptor. This enormously large matrix of numbers constitutes the "data" registered by one eye, and together the left and right eye matrices comprise the raw ingredients from which vision is constructed (see Figure 3.1).

But vision doesn't consist of tiny points of light signaled by our photoreceptors. The objects we see in nature aren't like the pictures printed in newspapers, where images are synthesized from clusters of tiny light and dark dots. The array of light measurements registered by the photoreceptors get passed on to a network of neurons that reorganize those millions of raw measurements into more efficient, behaviorally relevant messages about the distribution of light in the retinal image. Individual light measurements are transformed into visually important information about the contrast, color, edges, and textures, as well as the ingredients, or features, that comprise objects. To understand those transformations, we need to define exactly what is meant by "information about objects."

Think back to our discussion of image formation in the preceding chapter. There we noted that objects absorb some of the light hitting their surfaces and reflect the rest. In effect, objects in our environment "sculpt" the light that arrives at our eyes. The optics of the eye maintain that sculpted spatial structure, forming an image of the sculpted light on the retina. Thus, when it reaches the retina, the amount of light reflected from an object usually differs from the amount of light reflected from the object's surroundings. The key word here is *differs*. If there were some way of registering when neighboring retinal regions were being illuminated by different amounts of light, one would be well on the way to identifying an object's edges or borders—places where the amount of reflected light varies. If one is in-terested in objects and edges, one is *not* interested in regions of the retina over which the light level remains constant. Homogeneous, uniformly illuminated regions of the retina probably do not represent the image of an edge. To identify an edge, the retina needs to note where there are differences between the light levels at adjacent locations. As you'll see, many retinal cells are designed to do precisely that: respond to differences between adjacent levels of light.

Our immediate goal, then, is to understand how the retina condenses and reorganizes the array of light measurements generated by the photoreceptors. Then we will consider how these editing operations actually affect the appearance of objects and their surfaces.

Eventually, we need to examine the neurons forming the middle layers of the retina: the bipolar, amacrine, and horizontal cells. They are the circuit elements that radically transform the photoreceptors' signals into something more complex and useful than mere light measurements. But for the moment, let's skip to the **retinal ganglion cells,** the neurons responsible for the last stage of processing within the eye itself. Once you understand what the ganglion cells do, you'll find it easier to see how those middle layer cells make the visual process possible.

During our discussion, keep in mind two important facts about the ganglion cells. First, although they respond to visual stimulation, ganglion cells do not themselves absorb light; they are not photoreceptors. Ganglion cells process neural information that the other retinal cells have received from the photoreceptors. Without input from those other neural components, the ganglion cells would be blind to everything happening in the visual world.

Second, ganglion cells can only signal the outcome of their processing by generating **action potentials,** brief electrical discharges carried by the nerve fibers of the ganglion cells to the central visual stages within the brain. So whatever a ganglion cell has to "say" about a visual stimulus must be expressed using this one-"word" vocabulary. This restriction actually applies to all further stages of visual processing—almost all neurons talk to one another in a language composed entirely of action potentials, or neural impulses, as they are sometimes called. Particular neurons speak with a burst of impulses only when certain types of visual stimuli appear. By virtue of their early position in this chain of visual processing, retinal ganglion cells set this neural dialogue in motion. Let's examine what the ganglion cells have to say.

FIGURE 3.1 | Photoreceptors generate electrical signals proportional to the amount of light impinging on them. The array of spots on the left depicts a portion of the image of a human face as "seen" by an array of photoreceptors; the shade of gray of each spot mirrors the amount of light in the image striking a given photoreceptor. The matrix on the right contains numerical values representing electrical signals. The value of each "signal" is proportional to the intensity of light striking a given photoreceptor. Notice the spatial correspondence between intensity levels and signal values in the matrix.

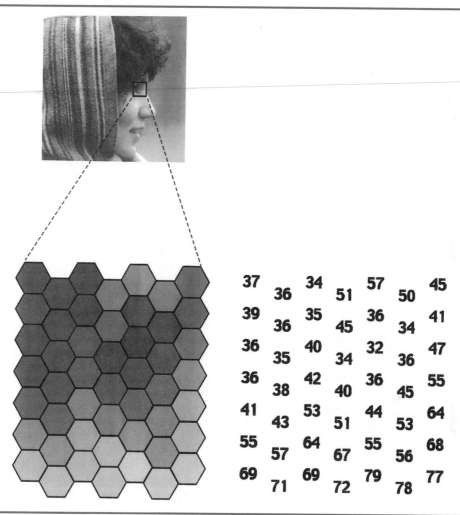

The Retinal Ganglion Cells

The human eye contains an estimated 1.25 million retinal ganglion cells. Comparing this figure to the roughly 100 million receptors in the eye, you know from the outset that ganglion cells, being far less numerous, must be condensing the raw messages from the receptors. Imagine you are handed a 1,000-word essay (about four double-spaced, typed pages) and told to edit it down to 12 or 13 words (one or two sentences) without losing the essentials of its message. To meet this challenge, you must identify the essay's major points and then rephrase them, condensing in a way that preserves the essence of the original. Retinal ganglion cells face the same kind of problem: They must collate messages from the more numerous photoreceptors and—with help from the horizontal, amacrine, and bipolar cells—summarize those messages in a biologically relevant way. How do the ganglion cells accomplish this?

FIGURE 3.2 | Laboratory setup for recording action potentials from single neurons. An experimental animal (a monkey, in this example) faces a video monitor upon which visual images are presented. The monkey's eye position remains steady, so the experimenter always knows where the animal is looking. An extremely thin wire with only its tip exposed—the "electrode"—is inserted into the animal's brain through a tiny hole drilled in the skull. The precise placement of the recording electrode governs which stage of the visual nervous system will be examined. The signals from the electrode are fed to electronic circuitry that amplifies the action potentials, records them to computer data files, and displays them on a second video monitor so that the experimenter may visualize the neural activity produced by the images on the video monitor the animal is viewing. It should be stressed that the surgical procedures required for this kind of experiment are performed under sterile conditions while the animal is anesthetized. And the experiment itself cannot use any procedure that causes the animal unrelieved pain or discomfort. All investigators who perform these experiments must be certified to work with animals, and the experiments themselves must be evaluated and approved by an investigative committee responsible for overseeing the safety and well-being of the animals.

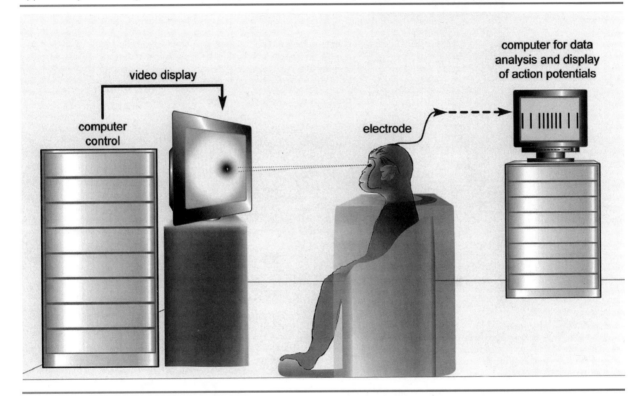

The most direct way to address this question is to determine what kinds of visual stimuli are best able to activate ganglion cells. Figure 3.2 illustrates the experimental procedure for determining a visual cell's preferred stimulus. An experimental animal, a monkey in this case, is shown facing a video monitor. (For these kinds of experiments, incidentally, monkeys are often studied, since their eyes and the visual parts of their brain are quite similar to a human's.) A tiny, fine-tipped wire called a **microelectrode** is surgically and painlessly inserted into the part of the visual system under study; for our purposes here, we'd target the optic nerve, because that bundle of fibers comprises the axons of the ganglion cells in which we're interested. The probe can be positioned close enough to an individual ganglion cell **axon** (the portion of the cell that carries its impulses out of the retina) so that the electrode picks up the action potentials (neural impulses) arising from just that cell. One can then monitor the number of action potentials generated by this single cell and try to influence the cell's activity level by presenting various sorts of visual stimuli on the screen. This technique, called **single cell recording,** has been success-

FIGURE 3.3 | Neural activity (shown as vertical lines) of retinal ganglion cells. See the text for a full discussion.

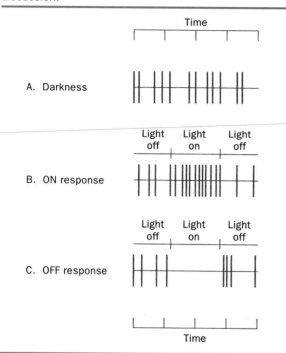

fully employed to determine what kinds of visual stimuli activate cells at different stages within the visual system. Here we are interested in the retina. In effect, we wish to ask the ganglion cells, "What sort of visual stimulus do you reliably respond to?"

Before presenting anything on the video monitor, you discover that the ganglion cell is already active. The electrode is picking up an irregular but persistent chatter of action potentials from the cell. This spontaneous activity continues even when the monkey is in complete darkness. The occurrence of individual action potentials over time is plotted in Figure 3.3. In each of the three panels, the small vertical lines represent single action potentials from one retinal ganglion cell. Time is traced out along the horizontal axis. Looking at panel A, you see the impulses occurring in the absence of visual stimulation: This is the cell's spontaneous activity.

Because it is spontaneously active when no light is present, the cell must signal the presence of light by changing its *level* of activity. Suppose your job is to discover what it takes to produce that change from spontaneous activity. Knowing that photoreceptors (from which the ganglion cells receive input via those middle layer

cells) are small, you start by moving a small spot of light in small steps over the screen in front of the monkey. By doing this, you are moving the light over the monkey's retina, stimulating clusters of photoreceptors wherever you move the spot. So, in effect, your job is to search for an area of the retina where the image of the spot of light will influence the ganglion cell's level of activity.

As we proceed with our example, it is very important to keep the following in mind: Different regions on the screen in front of the monkey correspond to different areas on the monkey's retina. To maintain this correspondence, the monkey's eye must remain perfectly still. If the monkey moved its eye around during the experiment, you could never be certain when your spot of light fell on its retina. Monkeys can be trained to hold their fixation very steady, but sometimes investigators use a drug that temporarily stabilizes the eye during the experiment. Once the monkey's eye position is stable, the location of the visual stimulus presented on the monitor can be placed wherever it is desired relative to the monkey's center of gaze (which, as you've learned, corresponds to the macula). With this in mind, let's start our experiment.

By moving the spot of light around on the screen, you discover a region of the retina where the spot causes an increase in the recording cell's activity. Concentrating on this region, you find that the cell generates a burst of impulses when you turn the light on this area. When you turn the light off, the cell's activity quickly settles back to its background (spontaneous) level. This outcome is shown in panel B of Figure 3.3. Next, you test a neighboring area of the retina in the same way. Now you find just the opposite result—turning the light on causes the activity level to drop *below* the background level. But when you turn the light off, the cell emits a short, vigorous burst of impulses. This second outcome is illustrated in panel C. So, this cell responds in two antagonistic ways, depending on where you place the light on the screen and, hence, on the retina. In one region it responds to an *increase* in light, whereas in the other it responds to a *decrease* in light. To distinguish these two kinds of responses, let's call the first an "ON response" and the second an "OFF response."

While still recording from this same cell, suppose you now test at other, nearby locations on the retina. You find that ON responses can be elicited from anywhere within a relatively small region roughly circular in shape. In fact, enlarging your spot so it just fills this circular region produces a very vigorous response. The regions giving an OFF response, however, form a ring that completely surrounds the circular ON region. So a single spot of light

FIGURE 3.4 | A single ON-center retinal ganglion cell (A) responding to uniform illumination (B), to a dark/light edge (C), to a vertical bar of light (D), and to an oblique bar of light (E).

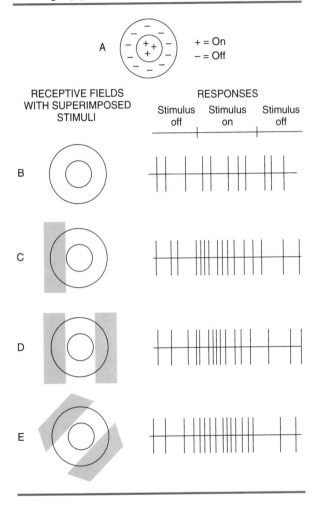

tivity may be influenced. (The term *receptive field* was coined by Keffer Hartline [1938] in his classic work on retinal ganglion cells in frogs.) You should also understand that the small region of the retina of a given cell's receptive field corresponds to a given region of visual space somewhere within the animal's field of view. Relocating the spot of light in visual space relocates the image of that spot of light on the retina and, thus, moves it out of one ganglion cell's receptive field and into the receptive field of another ganglion cell. The important concept to keep in mind here is that the center/surround region of a ganglion cell's receptive field corresponds to a circumscribed region in visual space that maps onto a given region of the retina. Different ganglion cells have receptive fields located at different regions of visual space. Thus, the approximately 1.25 million ganglion cells within the human eye, provide 1.25 million small "windows onto the world" distributed over the region of space visible to that eye.

The concept of a receptive field is extremely important for understanding visual processing. As you will come to appreciate in this chapter and several ones that follow, the receptive field serves as a kind of template with which a cell gauges the pattern of light falling within a restricted area of the retina. That pattern of light must match the location, size, and spatial details of the receptive field in order to activate a cell. Because the cell responds best when the image matches the cell's receptive field template, these receptive fields are sometimes referred to as "filters" (the notion being that the receptive field allows neural messages to be generated and passed on to the brain only when rather specific stimulus conditions are present in the visual image). Vision scientists also use the term *computation* to refer to the operation performed by these receptive fields—the neuron is "computing" the difference in illumination within different parts of its receptive field to generate a "value" (expressed in action potentials) proportional to this difference in illumination.

To illustrate this filtering or computation, consider the receptive field mapped out in panel A of Figure 3.4. These ON and OFF regions were mapped using a tiny spot of light located sequentially at different positions, but now that we know the overall layout of these regions let's think about what larger stimulus would best activate this cell. Can you picture an optimal visual stimulus, one that would produce the most vigorous increase in neural activity in the cell? First, imagine illuminating the entire retina, in effect filling the cell's receptive field with light. As shown in panel B of Figure 3.4, the cell gives only a weak response to uni-

can have two opposite, or antagonistic, effects: one effect produced by light in the spot's center, and the opposite effect by the surrounding area (which we can denote as "the surround"). If you label these two regions using plus signs (for ON) and minus signs (for OFF), the composite looks like a small circle of plus signs surrounded by a ring of minus signs, as shown in panel A of Figure 3.4.

Light placed anywhere outside this donut-shaped composite has no influence whatsoever on this cell's activity. In other words, only light falling in this limited, concentrically shaped area of the retina is registered by this ganglion cell. This area constitutes that cell's **receptive field**—the patch of retina within which a cell's ac-

Because of its spontaneous activity, an ON-center cell sends the brain a stronger message when no light falls in its receptive field than it does when its surround alone is illuminated. This curious state of affairs suggests the possibility that some light may actually appear darker than no light at all. In fact, surrounding a dim area with a sufficiently intense light makes that dim area appear darker than an area that contains no light whatever. Probably the intense surround drives the activity of ON-center ganglion cells *below* their spontaneous levels, signaling the brain that something blacker than black is present (Brown and Mueller, 1965).

The consequences of this spontaneous activity show up in everyday life. Think about what it's like to wake up in the middle of the night in an absolutely dark room. Usually the room doesn't appear totally black. In fact, many people experience dim, illusory, swirling lights, the result of spontaneous activity in the visual system (Hurvich and Jameson, 1966).

Some artists exaggerate discontinuities in intensity in order to highlight the outline of figures in their work. If an artist wants to create the deepest possible black region in some painting, he or she must do more than simply use black paint. Even if that black paint reflected no light at all (which isn't really possible with paint), receptive fields in which the black paint was imaged would still be sending spontaneous messages to the brain. To reduce those messages to a minimum, the artist surrounds the black paint with an area of white or other light-colored paint. The contrast between the two areas intensifies the blackness produced by the dark paint. Ratliff (1972) provides a good introduction to the uses of lightness illusions in art.

The same effect is exploited by your television set and your computer monitor. The screen cannot get any darker than it is when the power is off. Yet the screen doesn't look black when the video monitor is off—it looks dark gray. So how is it that black objects are produced when the monitor is on? Gray regions appear black when surrounded by other, light-colored regions.

Some parents and children also take advantage of light's ability to create darkness, often unwittingly. Many children have a hard time falling asleep unless conditions are just right. Not only must it be past their appointed bedtime, but conditions outside must also confirm that it is bedtime—it must *look* sufficiently dark outside. Some wise parents take advantage of a lightness illusion to hasten bedtime—as some children realize. The Finnish-American poet Anselm Hollo captured this idea in this imaginary request from an imaginary 4-year old:

> *switch on the light*
> *so it gets dark outside*
> *and we can go*
> *to bed.*
> *(1977, p. 30)*

form illumination. This is because such a stimulus produces opposite effects in the center and the surrounding area. The two antagonistic regions compete with one another, resulting in a near standoff. This interaction between antagonistic regions is called **lateral inhibition.**

Now imagine what happens when an edge is positioned in the manner shown in panel C of the figure. The ON-center portion of the receptive field receives an increase in light, its preferred stimulus, while a good portion of the surround receives a reduced level of light, its preferred stimulus. The net result is a vigorous response from the cell. As panels D and E show, the cell would also respond well to bars of light positioned appropriately within the receptive field. Incidentally, because these center/surround areas are nearly always concentrically arranged, ganglion cells will respond well regardless of whether the edge is oriented vertically, horizontally, or diagonally. The orientation of an edge or bar is irrelevant so long as the edge or bar is positioned appropriately within the receptive field.

So, it is this antagonistic arrangement of center and surround within the receptive field that enables the retinal ganglion cell to perform its filtering. Lateral inhibition has enabled the cell to condense the messages from a patch of photoreceptors into a single statement: "I detect a light/dark boundary." By accenting the *difference* in light levels on adjacent areas of the retina, the cell has begun the process of extracting perceptually relevant information.

Nearly all ganglion cells have concentrically arranged receptive fields, composed of a center and a surround that respond in an antagonistic fashion. Some of those cells have ON centers and OFF surrounds, like the receptive field illustrated in Figure 3.4. (Box 3.1 discusses one interesting perceptual phenomenon thought to result

FIGURE 3.5 | A receptive field of an OFF-center retinal ganglion cell.

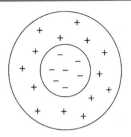

from these cells.) Other cells have just the opposite layout, with an OFF center and an ON surround. An example of this latter type of cell is shown in Figure 3.5.

Over the entire ensemble of 1.25 million ganglion cells, there are about as many ON-center cells as there are OFF-center cells. Moreover, both types respond best to light/dark boundaries, although they differ in terms of the spatial arrangement of those boundaries. As you read the words on this page, different combinations of ON-center and OFF-center ganglion cells are being activated as the numerous contours making up the letters of these words sweep through those cells' receptive fields. Don't imagine, though, that the activity generated within ON cells cancels the activity within OFF cells, and vice versa. At higher stages of the visual system, information from ON-center and OFF-center cells remains segregated, allowing information from both types to be used (Wässle, Peichl, and Boycott, 1981).

The Neural Architecture of ON and OFF Regions

We have lots more to say about ganglion cells and their center/surround properties. But now is a good time to look more closely at the cells in the intermediate layers of the retina, for it is those cells that are responsible for the spatial layout of ON and OFF regions. Look at Figure 3.6, a highly magnified schematic of the arrangement of the retina's parts at one small location. Let's concentrate on the three types of cells that lay between the photoreceptors and the ganglion cells.

First, notice that the photoreceptors (shown pointing upward in the drawing) are interconnected by laterally spreading cells, aptly named **horizontal cells.** Any given horizontal cell can be in contact with dozens of neighboring photoreceptors, and each photoreceptor makes contact with several horizontal cells. Each and every horizontal cell does only one thing: It modifies the strength of the signals generated by its neighboring photoreceptors.

It's an ingenious arrangement. Any one horizontal cell receives input from a cluster of photoreceptors and, in turn, provides input back to those very photoreceptors. Horizontal cells turn down (attenuate) the strength of the signals generated by those individual photoreceptors. This attenuation most strongly affects those photoreceptors whose signals are the weakest to begin with. The more active photoreceptors are less affected and, hence, their signals become relatively larger. Thus, when one small cluster of photoreceptors within the neighborhood is more active than the rest, the horizontal cell accentuates the strength of their signals relative to the signals in the other, less active photoreceptors. This feedback arrangement accentuates differences in photoreceptor signals, differences that can be traced to locations in the retinal image where there are transitions in the spatial distribution of light. Horizontal cells, in other words, amplify photoreceptor signals associated with edges; they are a fundamental part of the lateral inhibition previously described.

But how are these modified photoreceptor signals conveyed to the ganglion cells? Here's where the **bipolar cells** enter the picture. As you can see in Figure 3.6, they, too, make synaptic contact with the photoreceptors. Their receiving ends are tucked into the spaces at the terminal ends of the photoreceptors where the transmitter substance glutamate is released. The bipolar cells generate electrical signals, and the strength of those signals is proportional to the amount of glutamate they receive. Of course, the amount of glutamate they receive is determined by the amount of light energy captured by the photoreceptors. Interestingly, the bipolar cells come in two varieties: One type responds positively to *decreases* in glutamate concentration, and the other responds positively to *increases* in glutamate concentration. Remember that photoreceptors release glutamate in inverse proportion to the amount of light they receive: The more light received, the less glutamate put out. The more light, the less glutamate, and vice versa. So bipolar cells that respond positively to a *drop* in glutamate levels are signaling an *increase* in light level, whereas bipolar cells that respond to an *increase* in glutamate levels are signaling a *decrease* in light level. Now we can begin to understand how photoreceptor signals are transformed into the ON and OFF components within the receptive fields of ganglion cells—the bipolar cells provide the circuitry for the two types of ganglion cells.

FIGURE 3.6 | A magnified view of retinal cells. In this diagram, the back of the eye would be located at the bottom of the drawing, meaning that light entering the eye travels through a network of cells before reaching the photoreceptor cells.

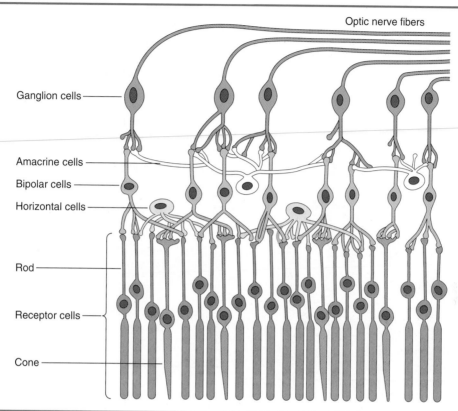

Actually, there are at least a dozen different kinds of bipolar cells in the human retina. They differ in both size and the patterns of connections they make with rod and cone photoreceptors and with ganglion cells. But they all do essentially the same thing: combine photoreceptor signals (which have been modified by horizontal cell connections) and pass those combined signals to the ganglion cells.

What about the **amacrine cells?** We know that amacrine cells receive inputs from bipolar cells and, in turn, modify the responses of those bipolar cells. (In this respect, amacrine cells behave like feedback cells, comparable to the horizontal cells.) It is thought that amacrine cells influence the temporal dynamics of ganglion cells, meaning how vigorously ganglion cells respond over time. Amacrine cells also serve as "switches" that control whether ganglion cells receive bipolar cell signals from the rods or from the cones; this switching

function is necessary because, as we have already mentioned, there are so many more photoreceptors than there are ganglion cells, forcing at least some optic nerve fibers to carry signals arising from either rods or cones.

In summary, the network of cells in the retina's intermediate layer form the circuitry underlying the center/surround layout of ganglion cell receptive fields. Figure 3.7 shows how these elements are thought to be interconnected within the circuitry for one ON-center ganglion cell. The central portion of the cell's receptive field is constructed from signals collected from a relatively small, circular patch of neighboring photoreceptors. For an ON-center cell like the one we're considering, those photoreceptors' signals are registered by inverting-type bipolar cells, which become more electrically positive when their contributing photoreceptors become more electrically negative (as they do when light levels increase). These positive electrical responses are passed

FIGURE 3.7 | Schematic showing how a center/ surrounding area receptive field is "constructed" through interconnecting retinal cells.

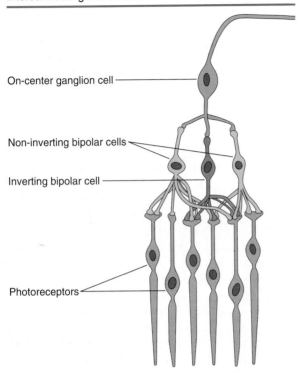

On-center ganglion cell

Non-inverting bipolar cells

Inverting bipolar cell

Photoreceptors

FIGURE 3.8 | Sensitivity profile of a retinal ganglion cell with center/ surround area organization. The excitatory center portion is shown by the sharp peak in the middle of the figure and the inhibitory surround portion is shown by the shallower trough running throughout the entire receptive field. If you were able to look directly down on this profile you would be looking at the donut-shaped center/surround portions as shown in Figures 3.4 and 3.5. The optimum stimulus for activating this cell would be a light region imaged in the center surrounded by darker regions falling within the surround.

ON - center ganglion cell receptive field

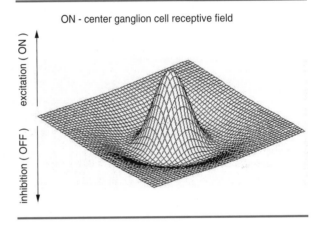

excitation (ON)

inhibition (OFF)

on to the ganglion cell, giving that cell its ON-center response. The surround portion of this ON-cell's receptive field arises from signals collected from a larger, concentrically arranged circular patch of photoreceptors. The signals from this larger collection of photoreceptors are registered by noninverting-type bipolar cells that become electrically more negative when the photoreceptors decrease their responses. These negative electrical responses are passed on to the ganglion cell, giving the cell its OFF-surround response. Note, by the way, that the central interior of this surrounding region includes the same photoreceptors that contribute to the center. The surround, in other words, actually encompasses the entire region of the receptive field, with its influence being weaker than the center region where the two overlap.

To show the net outcome of this center/surround arrangement, we can plot the sensitivity of the ON-center and OFF-surrounding regions in the manner shown in Figure 3.8. It is conventional to use a pair of bell-shaped curves (called Gaussian curves) to depict the responsiveness of the center and surrounding portions. The center

and surrounding Gaussian curves subtract from one another, yielding a resultant called the difference of Gaussians (or **DoG curve,** for short). A DoG curve provides a good approximation of the spatial layout of most retinal ganglion cells. It is simple to apply the same scheme to the construction of an OFF-center receptive field, just by inverting the signs of the two Gaussians contributing to the center and surround.

This completes our overview of the intermediate circuitry within the retina, and we'll refer back to this stage of processing in subsequent discussions. But armed with this expanded view, we're now ready to return to the ganglion cells, to learn more about the neural messages they encode and transmit to the brain. To do this, we'll need to map the individual receptive fields from a large sample of ganglion cells, and this will entail repositioning our microelectrode periodically to access different cells. Our aim now is to learn what visual pattern of light produces the most vigorous responses in each cell. In the course of this exercise, we would discover several important receptive field properties.

FIGURE 3.9 | Graph showing how the sizes of receptive field centers increase with distance from the fovea. The size of the entire receptive field is larger than just the center diameter, since the entire receptive field consists of a center *and* a surround. The large circles plot center diameters for M cells and the small circles plot center diameters for P cells (these two classes of retinal ganglion cells are described in the next section of this chapter). These results are redrawn based on data described by Rodieck (1998).

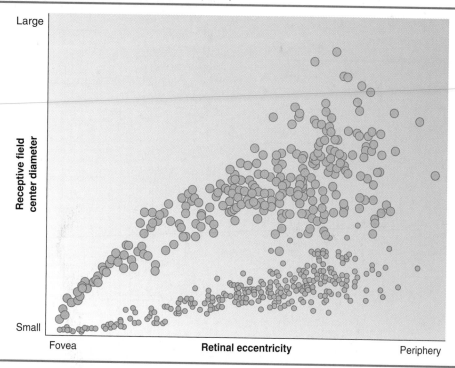

Receptive Field Size

The sizes of receptive fields vary systematically with retinal location (Wiesel and Hubel, 1960; de Monasterio and Gouras, 1975). Receptive fields in the center of the retina, within the macula, are quite small, with some having diameters subtending on the order of 0.01 millimeters on the retina. Cells with these small, centrally placed receptive fields monitor tiny areas of the visual world wherever the observer (a monkey in our hypothetical experiment) is looking. As you move away from the macula into the periphery of the retina, you find that the receptive fields grow increasingly larger. In fact, 10 millimeters away from the fovea, receptive field centers may be as large as 0.5 millimeters (roughly the diameter of the end of a paper clip), 50 times larger than their foveal counterparts. Cells with these peripherally placed receptive fields, in other words, collect information from larger areas of the retina. Figure 3.9 graphs the relation between receptive field size and retinal location. The hor-izontal axis represents the retinal location around which the receptive field was centered; "fovea" stands for the center of the macula. The vertical axis is the diameter of the center portion of the receptive field. Note that with increasing **eccentricity**—deviation from the center of the retina—the size of receptive fields tends to increase. You'll also notice two groups of dots in this graph, distinguished by the sizes of the circles. We'll explain the meaning of these two groups in a moment, but for now notice that cells in both groups show the same trend: Receptive field size increases with eccentricity.

Because receptive fields are quite small in and around the fovea, it naturally takes more ganglion cells to cover a given area of retina in the fovea compared to more peripheral parts of the retina. In fact, the fovea accounts for only about 2 percent of the total retinal area, whereas about 33 percent of all ganglion cells are devoted to the neural analysis of image features within this small, but critically important, retinal territory.

FIGURE 3.10 | A single ON-center receptive field responding to bars of light of varying width.

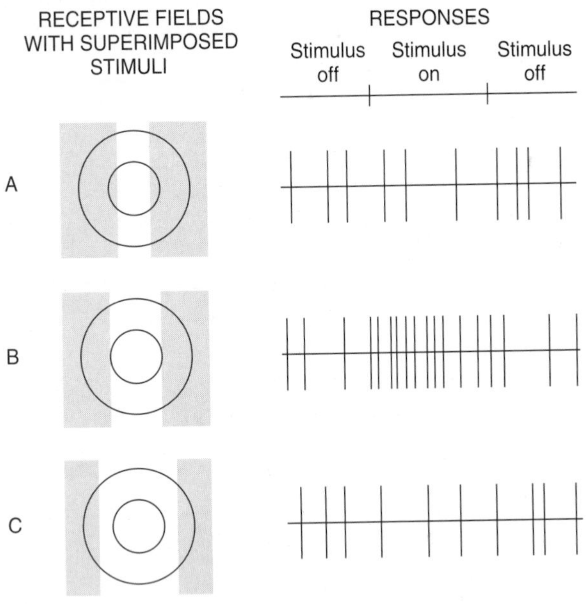

RECEPTIVE FIELDS WITH SUPERIMPOSED STIMULI	RESPONSES
	Stimulus off / Stimulus on / Stimulus off

A

B

C

FIGURE 3.11 | Three ON-center receptive fields with different-sized receptive fields responding to bars of light of matching width.

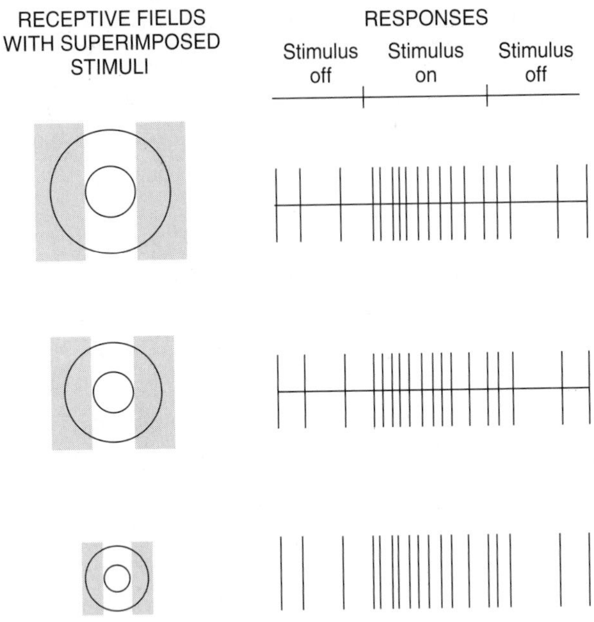

RECEPTIVE FIELDS WITH SUPERIMPOSED STIMULI	RESPONSES
	Stimulus off / Stimulus on / Stimulus off

The graph in Figure 3.9 also reveals another important fact. At each of the various eccentricities, we have data for more than just a single receptive field. Comparing data collected at the same eccentricity, we see that not all receptive fields at that eccentricity have exactly the same size. Because these size differences occur at a single locality on the retina, the phenomenon is known as *local variation*. So the sizes of receptive fields differ in two ways: First, they vary with retinal eccentricity; second, they vary locally.

Think what this variation in receptive field size means for the sort of stimulus that would be best suited to activate a particular cell. As shown in Figure 3.10, there is one bar width size (panel B) that elicits the best response from that cell. Bars smaller (panel A) or larger (panel C) than this produce a less than optimum response. As you can see in Figure 3.11, cells with small receptive fields will respond best to small objects, while those with large receptive fields will prefer larger objects. This principle suggests that analysis of object size may be inaugurated in the retina.

Three Types of Retinal Ganglion Cells

So far we've distinguished retinal ganglion cells on the basis of receptive field size and center type (ON versus OFF). But retinal ganglion cells differ in other ways, some

of which are particularly relevant for understanding vision. These differences form the bases for classifying ganglion cells into one of three groups, the **M cells,** the **P cells,** and the **K cells** (Hendry and Calkins, 1998). *M* stands for magnocellular, *P* for parvocellular[2] and *K* for koniocellular. These three terms refer to the three classes of brain cells to which the M, P, and K cells relay their neural impulses. Table 3.1 summarizes these three classes of cells, and in the following paragraphs we'll describe some major differences among cells in these three classes. We'll start by contrasting the M and P cells, which have been studied in much more detail than the K cells.

Seen under a microscope, M cells are larger than P cells, and the M cell's axon is thicker. Because of this, neural impulses travel more rapidly to the brain over M cell axons, since the conduction velocity of neural impulses increases with axon thickness. A second difference is that these two types of cells differ greatly in number, with approximately 80 percent of all primate ganglion cells belonging to the P class. Third, at any

---

[2]Some researchers refer to the P and M ganglion cells as parasol and midget cells, respectively. These terms are derived from the anatomical shapes of these two classes of ganglion cells.

TABLE 3.1 | Physiological Properties of P, M, and K Cells

Characteristic	P Cells	M Cells	K Cells
Cell size	Small	Large	Very small
Conduction velocity	Slow	Fast	Slow/variable
Cell population (percentage)	80%	10%	~10%
Spatial resolution	High	Low	Moderate
Temporal resolution	Low	High	High
Contrast sensitivity	Low	Good	Modest

given retinal eccentricity, the receptive fields of P cells are several times smaller than the receptive fields of M cells. (This difference is responsible for much of the vertical scatter in receptive field size seen in Figure 3.9.) The difference in field size between P and M cells means that P cells will respond better to small objects than will M cells (recall Figure 3.11). Fourth, M cells respond well to very small differences in light levels in center and surround. P cells require greater contrasting difference in light between center and surround portions of the receptive field before they will respond strongly (Kaplan, Shapley, and Purpura, 1988). This distinction between cell types suggests that M cells may be especially important for the perception of objects of low contrast, such as dark gray letters on a medium gray background. P cells may be more important for seeing high-contrast objects, such as black letters on a white background. Fifth, M cells respond well even when a visual stimulus is turned on and off very quickly, whereas P cells respond poorly if at all to such a temporally modulated stimulus. This difference in temporal sensitivity means that M cells are better able to register transient visual events, such as the presence of a rapidly moving object.

The sixth difference between M and P cells is especially intriguing, since it probably relates to color vision. For P cells, an excitatory response is evoked only when the receptive field is stimulated with light of a particular color (for example, red). P cells are inhibited by the presence of another, quite different color (for example, green). For M cells, in comparison, color makes no difference. They respond to light regardless of color. To illustrate this important difference between P and M cells, imagine looking for a ripe, red apple lying on a lawn of green grass. If the apple and grass reflect the same amount of light (that is, if they are equal in lightness), the M ganglion cells would fail to signal the presence of the apple. Everywhere you look, the responses of the M cells would be the same. The P cells, however, would solve the problem: As your gaze roams over the grass, a P cell sensitive to red would be silent until your gaze brought the image of the apple into the P cell's receptive field, thus evoking a robust response.

Not as much is known about the third class of cells, the ones comprising the koniocellular pathway. Cells in this pathway get their name from the neurons that they innervate in the lateral geniculate nucleus, which we will learn about in Chapter 4. Those geniculate neurons are extremely small (*konis* is Greek for "dust") and, therefore, very difficult to isolate for physiological study. In terms of their response properties, K cells more closely resemble P cells, in that their responses depend on the color of light within their receptive fields. In particular, most K cells are excited by blue light and inhibited by yellow light (Dobkins, 2000). K cells may also play a role in shutting down vision temporarily whenever we rapidly move or blink our eyes. Detailed reviews of the K cells are provided by Casagrande (1994) and by Hendry and Reid (2000).

Although P, M, and K cells constitute the lion's share of neurons in the retina (over 90 percent of the total), there are other, less researched cell types. These other cell types send their axons to phylogenetically older regions of the brain that are probably involved in the control of eye and head movements. These other cell types are also thought to provide the visual information that drives circadian rhythms and influences your sleep–wake cycle (see Box 3.2). In contrast, the P, M, and K cells project to higher, phylogenetically newer brain centers mediating visual perception. As you will learn, nature has gone to great lengths to keep separate the information carried to these higher centers by these three classes of cells. In the next chapter, we will learn more about the separate visual pathways that originate from the retina's P, M, and K cells, and will discuss further their possible roles in visual perception.

This completes, then, our abbreviated survey of retinal ganglion cells. By examining the workings of the retinal ganglion cells, you have learned several important things about the eye's processing of visual information. You now know that this processing begins with the photoreceptors, which act like an array of tiny photocells, each specifying the level of light falling within the purview of the photoreceptor. These 100 million messages about light intensity are then passed on to a complex network of intermediary cells that integrate information from groups of neighboring photoreceptors. The results of this integration are conveyed to the retinal ganglion cells. Because of the center/surround

BOX 3.2   **Your Daily Dose of Light**

We have repeatedly stressed that vision isn't concerned with seeing light but, instead, with seeing objects and events. We have characterized light as the messenger that carries optical information from the environment to our eyes. There is one easily overlooked aspect of vision, however, where light itself *is* the message. Light calibrates the internal, neural clock that our brains use to regulate our sleep/wake cycles, our appetites, and our hormone levels. It's this clock that temporarily gets out of whack when we travel overseas.

Called **circadian rhythms,** these periodic activities and bodily functions are normally coupled to our 24-hour light/dark cycle. In the absence of light, however, the clock that regulates circadian rhythms can drift out of synch. Thus, rats placed in complete darkness for weeks at a time, or humans who voluntarily live in dark caves for several months slip into sleep/wake cycles that deviate significantly from the normal solar cycle. Once these light-deprived individuals return to environments with normal light exposure, their clocks quickly resynchronize. The eyes are critical for this resetting of the clock.

One would naturally expect either rod or cone photoreceptors to be responsible for setting the daily clock, but recent evidence suggests this is not the case. Mice lack both rod and cone photoreceptors, and yet they maintain normal activity cycles and their light-dependent hormone levels remain normal (Freedman et al., 1999). We now know that the eye contains a special type of retinal ganglion cell that behaves like photoreceptors: These special cells respond to light directly, with no need for input from rods or cones. They have their own photopigment (called melanopsin), and this pigment's spectral sensitivity curve covers the same range of wavelengths as those contained in the light that governs circadian rhythms. Moreover, axons of these unique ganglion cells project to the suprachiasmatic nucleus, a structure in the hypothalamus thought to be the internal clock that regulates our sleep/wake cycles (Provencio, Rollag, and Castrucci, 2002). Like the eye's rods and cones, the number and distribution of these special ganglion cells are under genetic control, which means people may differ in the proportion of "circadian" ganglion cells within their eyes. Could the tendency for some people to have trouble regulating their sleep/waking habits be related to a paucity of "circadian" cells in their eyes?

---

organization of their receptive fields, the vast majority of ganglion cells are designed to detect differences in light level, or *contrast,* as it is called. These cells are unconcerned with the overall level of light; instead, they "look" for local regions in the image containing edges and contours (see Figure 3.12).

In some of these cells, this center/surround organization is designed to extract information about color contrast. This kind of local receptive field analysis is performed over the entire retina by the 1.25 million or so ganglion cells in the eye. Hence, everything you see must have registered its presence within this retinal machinery. The particulars of this machinery necessarily influence the *way* you see. There is no other route to visual perception but through the retinal ganglion cells.

The remainder of this chapter relates certain properties of vision to events occurring in the retina. A few of these events transpire in the photoreceptors, while others occur at the level of the retinal ganglion cells. It's important that you understand what we mean when we claim that some property of vision is "caused by" the idiosyncrasies of some retinal cell. We are not saying that conscious visual perception occurs in the retina. Most visual scientists think that the processes underlying what we call "vision" actually take place in the brain and not in the eye.

Instead, we're saying that events in the retina *shape* vision by emphasizing some information (such as differences in light level) and by deemphasizing other information (such as uniformities). For example, retinal ganglion cells respond very strongly to discontinuities in illumination, and this operating principle reveals itself, sometimes vividly, in visual experience. Potentially important information, in other words, gets accentuated. In contrast, retinal cells fail to respond to images composed of wavelengths longer than 700 nanometers, meaning that the brain receives no information about such images. So some information gets ignored. Thus, even though sight occurs in the brain, the retina preordains much of what we can and cannot see. Brindley (1970) and Teller (1989) discuss the logical bases for attributing perceptual events to the behavior of certain physiological processes.

FIGURE 3.12 | Whatever you look at, the distribution of light falling on your retina is analyzed by retinal ganglion cell receptive fields with center/surround organization. When you look at this picture of a woman's face, for example, tens of thousands of ganglion cell receptive fields are engaged in the process of seeing the face. Cells with small receptive fields register the fine details in the image (such as the thin stripes on the hood of the woman's coat) while, at the same time, cells with bigger receptive fields register the larger regions of uniform lightness in the image (such as the woman's cheek). The ON cells (shown schematically by white lines) are sensitive to borders with light regions in their centers and OFF cells (shown schematically by black outlines) are sensitive to borders with dark regions in their centers. This figure simulates just a tiny fraction of the actual number of ganglion cell receptive fields that would be activated when you look at this picture.

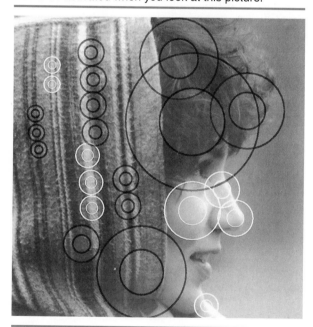

Perceptual Consequences of Center/Surround Antagonism

The preceding section emphasized the antagonism between the center and the surround of a retinal ganglion cell's receptive field. The net response of such a cell is the sum of these two opposing influences. This antagonistic arrangement reorganizes the receptors' raw information into neural signals associated with light/dark boundaries

(such as with edges and contours). In the process, center/surround antagonism accentuates those boundaries and, at the same time, deemphasizes regions where light intensity is uniform. This differential boost given to edge information has led to the popular but controversial idea that the perceived lightness over regions of a surface is related to activity in retinal ganglion cells. In the next few pages, we consider a couple of intriguing perceptual illusions that suggest the operation of center/surround antagonism in human vision.

From the outset of this discussion, we need to clarify the distinction between the terms "brightness" and "lightness." These terms, both of which refer to perceptual qualities, are sometimes used interchangeably, but they should be differentiated. Among vision researchers, the term **brightness** refers to the amount of light that appears to come from some self-luminous, light-emitting object. For instance, a light bulb, the sun and a computer monitor all generate and give off light—we may speak of the brightness of these sources. **Lightness,** though, refers to an aspect of the appearance of the surfaces of objects that themselves do not emit light. Thus, we may speak of the lightness of a piece of paper or the lightness of a person's skin. According to this definition, it is technically correct to refer to the lightness, not the brightness, of the moon, since the moon does not emit light. Note that because lightness depends on the amount of light reflected from the surface of an object, it depends upon both the amount of light illuminating the object and the amount of illumination reflected by that surface. Stated succinctly, brightness is a perceptual response to emitted light from a self-luminous object whereas lightness is a perceptual response to light reflected from a surface. In most instances, it is the lightness of a surface with which we are concerned. Our everyday activities entail recognizing objects, not light, and surface lightness is one property that aids recognition.

With this distinction in mind, let's take a look at some intriguing visual illusions that have been devised to test retinal mechanisms involving local spatial interactions.

The Hermann Grid

In the nineteenth century, Ludimar Hermann, a German neurophysiologist, had a very disturbing experience. While reading a book on crystal structure, Hermann noticed that one of the book's illustrations went through peculiar, dynamic changes whenever he looked at it. With the aid of Figure 3.13 you can experience the very thing that so disturbed Hermann: illusory spots in most of the

FIGURE 3.13 | Three conventional versions of Hermann grids.

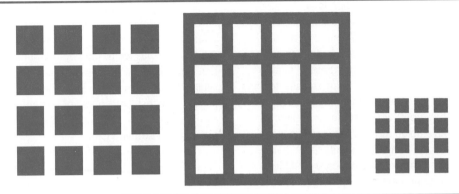

intersections between the horizontal and vertical white stripes. Note, too, that when you move your eyes to look *directly* at one of these phantom spots, the spot disappears—until you look away again. A pattern that induces these hide and seek spots is known as a **Hermann grid.**

The properties of these dynamic, changing spots vary with the characteristics of the grid. Looking at the left-hand grid, you'll notice dark spots located in most of the intersections of white horizontal and vertical stripes. Looking at the middle grid (a photographic negative of the other), you'll notice light spots in most of the intersections of black horizontal and vertical stripes. Looking at the right-hand grid (a smaller version of the one on the left), you'll see dark spots at *all* the intersections. Although they are vivid, these spots—every one of them—

are illusory. Where, then, do they come from? Why do they appear where they do? And why are they sometimes dark and sometimes light? It is generally accepted that these illusory spots arise, at least in part, from center/surround antagonism within receptive fields of retinal ganglion cells (Spillmann, 1994).

We'll use the properties of ON-center receptive fields to explain why spots are seen in the left-hand grid. We ask two questions. First, why are the spots that you see located only at intersections between horizontal and vertical stripes, not elsewhere? Second, why do you *not* see a spot located in an intersection when you look directly at it? To answer the first question, we've drawn receptive fields on Hermann's grid (Figure 3.14). This allows you to compare how the retinal image of the grid would affect

FIGURE 3.14 | A possible neural explanation of Hermann grids.

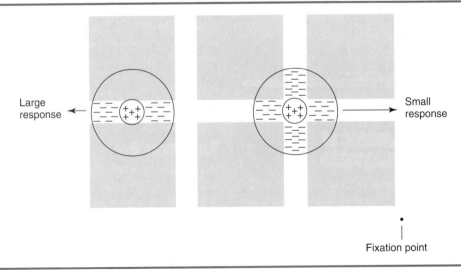

FIGURE 3.15 | A possible neural explanation for the absence of local dimming of Hermann grids at the point of fixation.

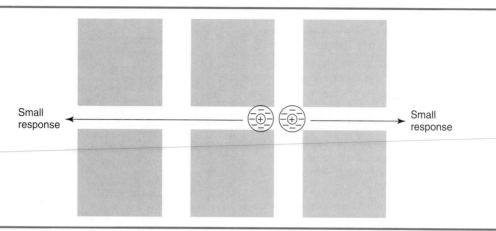

Small response ←   → Small response

the two receptive fields shown, one being stimulated by an intersection and the other stimulated by part of a white stripe that is not at an intersection.

To determine the response of either retinal ganglion cell, we must analyze how each of its components—the center and the surrounding area—would be affected by the grid pattern.[3] Assume that a viewer gazes steadily on the spot labeled "fixation point." Now, note that the centers of both receptive fields receive the same amount of light, but the surrounds receive different amounts. Remember that light falling in an OFF portion of a receptive field reduces that cell's activity. This means that the cell whose receptive field is centered on the intersection will respond less than the cell whose receptive field is centered between intersections. Consequently, between intersections, the white stripes will look comparatively lighter. Since the reduced response is confined to cells with receptive fields centered on the intersections, one experiences dimming at such locales—gray spots.

Why, though, don't you see a spot in the intersection when you look directly at it? Recall that receptive fields vary in size according to their eccentricity (Figure 3.9), with the smallest receptive fields coinciding with the fovea. When you look directly at an intersection, you are using receptive fields whose centers and surrounds are so small that *both* fit completely within the width of a stripe. We've illustrated this in Figure 3.15.

Assume that a person fixates on the right-hand intersection of the grid. As you can see, these small receptive fields all receive the same amount of stimulation within their centers and surround. Consequently, all the cells around the region of fixation will give the same response, whether on the intersection or not. As a result, there will not be any local dimming at that intersection.

To test your understanding of these ideas, see if you can apply this same line of reasoning to the middle grid in Figure 3.13, where the illusory spots appear light against the dark background. Finally, see if you can explain why spots are seen at every intersection, including the one that you are fixating, in the right-hand grid in Figure 3.13.

You might also try looking at Figure 3.13 under very dimly lit conditions. (Be patient; you must let your eyes adapt to the darkness.) You'll be amazed to see that the phantom spots, unlike most apparitions, actually disappear when the lights are low (Wist, 1976). Why should this happen? To give you a clue, remember that the illusory spots arise because of the surround portions of the receptive fields, which are differentially stimulated depending on what part of the grid they are analyzing. If we were to eliminate the surround's contribution to each cell's response, the spots should disappear. Evidently that's exactly what happens: The surround portions of ganglion cell receptive fields become ineffective at low-light levels, leaving only the center region to generate responses (Barlow, Fitzhugh, and Kuffler, 1957).

Some features of the Hermann grid illusion aren't easily explained by the responses of ganglion cells (Wolfe, 1984). For one thing, the number of intersections present in the figure influences the strength of the illu-

---

[3]The following analysis applied to ON-center cells. A corresponding, separate analysis can be made for OFF-center cells whose increased activity signals increasing darkness.

sory spots at those intersections. Specifically, increasing the number of intersections strengthens the illusion. For another thing, the regularity of the intersection's spacing also modulates the strength of the illusion, with the illusory spots appearing dimmer when irregularities are introduced into the spacing. Finally, the illusory spots are weaker when the Hermann grid is rotated 45 degrees, so that the intersections run diagonally (Spillmann, 1994; de Lafuente and Ruiz, 2004). You can verify this latter observation by viewing Figure 3.13 with the book turned obliquely. These various observations imply that far-reaching influences, not just local center/surround interactions, also play a role in creating these phantom spots. Before leaving this topic, we want to mention a website where you can interactively explore this peculiar illusion, the Hermann grid. You can find a link to that website by navigating to www.mhhe.com/blake5.

Let's turn from illusory spots to another peculiarity of human vision that suggests the involvement of center/surround antagonism, Mach bands.

Mach Bands

In Chapter 2 you were introduced to Ernst Mach, the Austrian physicist and philosopher who made important contributions to a number of scientific disciplines during the last part of the nineteenth century and the early part of the twentieth. We're concerned here with one small part of his work. The interested student will find an excellent, highly readable account of Mach's life and work in Ratliff (1965).

Mach became interested in the connection between the intensity of reflected light ("lightness" by our convention) and the sensation it engendered. To explore this interest, Mach created various patterns out of paper that portrayed gradients of light, ranging from white through gray to black. Mach carefully studied whether perception of the gradients conformed to the actual distribution of light reflected from those patches of paper. In some instances, the two did not correspond. Mach had the great insight that these idiosyncrasies of perception were caused by antagonistic influences within the retina. Because we have much more information about retinal physiology and anatomy than was available to Mach, we are able to infer that these idiosyncrasies could be caused by the center/surround antagonism evidenced in the receptive fields of retinal ganglion cells.

The upper portion of Figure 3.16 shows one of the kinds of patterns Mach developed. The graph below the pattern plots the actual intensity distribution of light re-

FIGURE 3.16 | The lightness of each stripe in the pattern (upper portion of the figure) varies even though the intensity of each stripe is constant (lower portion of the figure).

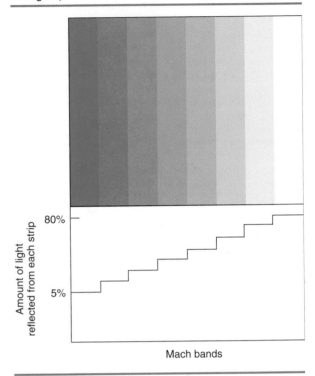

flected from the pattern. The horizontal axis of the graph represents spatial position in the pattern. The vertical axis shows how much light the pattern reflects at that position. From left to right, the graph shows the level of intensity in the pattern increasing in a stepwise fashion. Thus, the pattern really consists of a series of bars, each of uniform intensity and each giving way abruptly to another level.

When you look at the pattern itself, though, you'll notice some things that don't seem to correspond with the graph. In particular, the lightness of each bar does not appear uniform. Take, for example, one of the bars in the middle. One edge—near the bar's left-hand, darker neighbor—seems extra light, whereas the other edge—near the bar's right-hand, lighter neighbor—seems extra dark. In other words, the lightness within the bar's interior varies even though the intensity of light reflected from the page does not. Most people describe the edges of each bar as having bands, extra dark and extra light regions. These bands are called **Mach bands** in honor of the first person to study them systematically.

FIGURE 3.17 | Possible neural explanation of Mach bands.

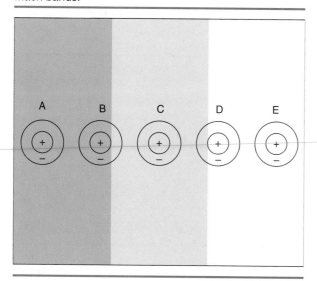

These bands, no matter how vivid they may seem, are illusory. They don't exist on the paper, only in your head. To understand the classic explanation of where they come from, consider how the retinal ganglion cells respond to such a pattern of bars. When one looks at the pattern in the upper portion of Figure 3.16, a distribution of light is produced on the retina similar to the distribution shown by the graph in the lower part of Figure 3.16. This distribution of light is broad enough so that it extends across the receptive fields of many retinal ganglion cells. To simplify the discussion, let's consider only three adjacent bars from the pattern (see Figure 3.17). Suppose that the image of the three bars falls on some small number, say five, of ON-center receptive fields (though this assumption is not crucial to our point). These ganglion cells are each responsible for signaling the brain about the intensity of light falling within their individual receptive fields. What sorts of messages would the brain get if these cells were stimulated by the pattern shown in the upper part of Figure 3.16?

To see what response any cell would give, we must weigh how much light falls in each of its two regions. (Remember the convention: plus indicates an ON region, minus indicates an OFF region.) Let's take the three easiest ones first. Receptive field A (leftmost ganglion cell in Figure 3.17) receives the least light, field E the most, and field C an intermediate amount of light. Each cell's response will be proportional to the amount of light falling

within its receptive field. So the bar A "sees" will seem the dimmest; the one E "sees," the brightest; and the one C "sees," appearing intermediate to the two. That leaves B and D as the interesting cases.

Receptive field B's center is stimulated by the same level of light as A's. Their respective surrounds, however, are *differentially* stimulated. All of A's surround is dimly illuminated, thereby producing little antagonism to combat the response produced by the center. Although the left part of B's surround is similarly illuminated, the right part is stimulated by the higher light level of the middle bar. As a result, the surround of B generates more antagonism than does the surround of A, *diminishing* the overall response of B to a level below that of A. Consequently, the region B "sees" appears darker than A "sees." B creates a dark Mach band.

Now consider D and E. The net response from D will be larger than that from E because D's surround is partially stimulated by the reduced light from the center bar, rather than by the higher level from the right-hand bar. As a result, D's surround generates *less* antagonism to its center's response, yielding a net response that is *greater* than that from E. So the region D "sees" will appear lighter than that E "sees." D creates a light Mach band.

So, center/surround interations provide a plausible account of Mach bands and the conditions under which they do and do not occur. Actually, Mach himself deserves credit for dreaming up this explanation, for he speculated that the illusory bands he described arose from neural processing within a system exhibiting spatially antagonistic interactions. Numerous investigators after Mach have endorsed this idea and, going one step further, have identified that system as the retinal ganglion cells (for example, Cornsweet, 1970; Ratliff, 1984; Hubel, 1988; Dowling, 1998).

Despite the plausibility of this simple, elegant theory, recent work challenges the idea that center/surround antagonism in the retina provides a complete account of lightness illusions such as Mach bands. Even when the pattern of retinal stimulation remains constant, the vividness of illusory Mach bands varies depending on how you interpret the surface upon which the intensity gradient appears (Lotto, Williams, and Purves, 1999). If the gradient is construed to be a shadow on a flat surface, Mach bands are not nearly as salient as when that same gradient is associated with a curved surface (see Figure 3.18). The same light intensity profile, in other words, is perceived differently simply by changing what it is you *think* you're looking at. There is no obvious reason why the responses of retinal ganglion cells in the eye should be susceptible

FIGURE 3.18 | The vividness of Mach bands depends on how you interpret the figure. Looking at panel A, compare the lightness of the curved edge of the box (the upper outlined region in panel B) with the shadow cast on the textured floor (the lower outlined region in panel B). The two parts of the image are physically identical (as denoted by the graph in panel B), but the Mach band seems more pronounced in the region associated with the surface of the object than in the region of the shadow.

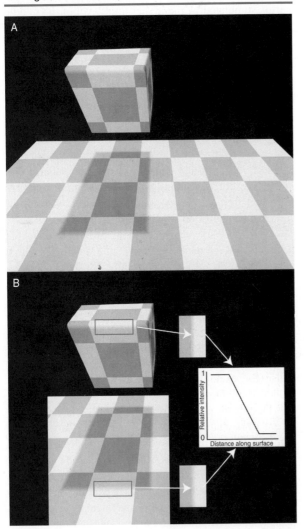

FIGURE 3.19 | Graph showing the response of an ON-center ganglion cell to light of varying intensity falling on the center of the cell's receptive field. The three curves represent the effect of different intensities of surrounding stimulation.

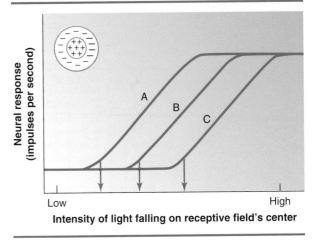

to this kind of "cognitive" influence. Consequently, vision scientists now believe that while center/surround antagonism in retinal ganglion cells contributes to Mach bands, such antagonism cannot be the complete explanation.

Next let's consider another illusion of surface lightness, known as simultaneous lightness contrast. To set the stage for this illusion, let's perform a few more experiments on the retinal ganglion cells we've been talking about.

Two More Center/Surround Experiments

In the first experiment, we'll compare how a retinal ganglion cell responds when its center is stimulated by light of different intensities while its surround is subjected, in turn, to no illumination, some illumination, and finally, intense illumination. Suppose that we are recording from a retinal ganglion cell of the ON-center variety. Finding the cell's receptive field center, we focus a small spot of light within just that area, avoiding the surround altogether. The test spot is turned on for a second, and the resulting number of impulses is recorded. After repeating this procedure with test spots of varying intensities, we plot the results as the curve labeled *A* in Figure 3.19. The graph's vertical axis represents the number of impulses. The horizontal axis represents the light intensity that evoked each response.

The spontaneous activity of the cell (the activity when no light is present at all) is plotted at the extreme

FIGURE 3.20 | Two graphs showing the response of an ON-center ganglion cell to light of varying intensity falling on the center of the cell's receptive field. The left graph shows that a single, constant response (broken horizontal line) can be produced by several different intensities, depending on the amount of light falling on the cell's surround. The right graph shows that a fixed intensity of light (broken vertical line) can produce several different levels of neural response.

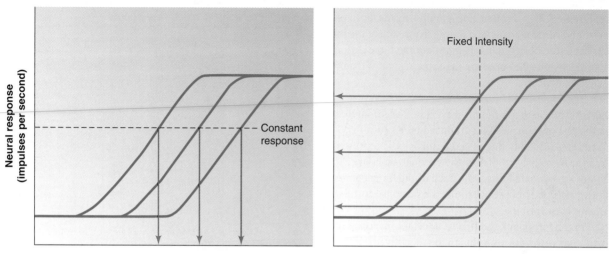

Intensity of light falling on receptive field's center

left of the horizontal axis. The graph reveals that very weak intensities of light fail to change the cell's spontaneous activity. Notice the arrow extending from curve *A* to the horizontal axis of the figure. It indicates the weakest intensity of light that will evoke a response appreciably different from that occurring with no light at all. In a sense, this is the minimum amount of light that this cell can "distinguish" from complete darkness.

As the spot's intensity increases, the cell's response grows larger. Finally, at some high intensity, the response of the cell *saturates,* meaning that further increases in intensity fail to produce corresponding increases in response. As far as this cell is concerned, all spots more intense than the point of saturation are indistinguishable from one another. From the cell's viewpoint, all such spots are equally intense.

Now suppose we repeat this experiment with one notable modification. The small spot again falls in the receptive field center, but now the surround is also illuminated. Again, we vary the intensity of the spot in the receptive field center, holding the surround illumination constant. The cell's response under this condition is shown by curve *B* in Figure 3.19. What are the differences between curves *A* and *B*? For both, arrows extending to the horizontal axis indicate the dimmest intensities that will produce an appreciable change in the cell's spontaneous response rate.

As you can see, when the surround is illuminated, the center must be more strongly stimulated in order to change the cell's response. More generally, adding light in the surround reduces the response produced by any given intensity of light in the center. This is another demonstration of antagonistic forces at work: light has opposite effects on the ganglion cell's activity, depending on where the light strikes within the cell's receptive field.

Before considering how these antagonistic forces might influence vision, let's repeat the same basic experiment one more time. Again, the surround is illuminated constantly, but now with a more intense light than was used before. The results of the cell's response to various intensities of light in the center are shown by curve *C* in Figure 3.19. With this strongest light in its surround, the cell requires an even more intense light in its center before its response can noticeably increase.

Lightness Contrast and Constancy

How would vision be affected by ganglion cells that behave in the manner shown in Figure 3.19? Suppose the magnitude of a ganglion cell's response is signaling the brain about the light intensity within its receptive field, with large responses signaling high light levels. With this assumption in mind, consider Figure 3.20. The two graphs in this figure add several features to what you saw in Figure 3.19. The left-hand graph indicates the three different intensities of light that produce the same response—a *constant response*—from the ganglion cell with various surrounds. This line of constant response is represented by a broken line parallel to the horizontal axis. The vertical arrows extending from each of the three curves to the horizontal axis point out the three different spot intensities that produce the same response from the ganglion cell.

The right-hand graph of Figure 3.20 analyzes the cell's response in a different way. Here we are interested in the response magnitude produced by a central spot of *fixed intensity*. This line of fixed intensity is represented by a broken line parallel to the vertical axis. The horizontal arrows extending from each of the three curves to the vertical axis point out the cell's response to this intensity with various surrounds.

In the left panel, the line of constant response indicates that with various lights in the receptive field's surround, different intensities of center stimulation are required to produce the same response. Alternatively, in the right panel, the line of fixed intensity indicates that with various lights in the surround, the same intensity of center stimulation will produce different responses. Both panels highlight the same idea: The cell's response to a stimulus falling in its receptive field center is affected by the level of stimulation in the receptive field surround. Thus, the messages that the brain will get about exactly the same stimulus will vary depending on how much light is falling in the receptive field of the surround.

From the behavior illustrated in these two panels, one might conclude that ganglion cell responses provide unreliable information about lightness. Does this seeming unreliability disqualify ganglion cells as carriers of lightness information? The answer is no. Although the cell's behavior (as represented in Figure 3.20) would certainly produce errors of perception, the errors would have two sorts of consequences, one good and one not so good. Let's consider the not-so-good one first.

The right-hand panel of Figure 3.20 shows that a retinal ganglion cell could send the brain rather different messages about a spot of fixed intensity, depending on what other light happens to fall in the cell's surround. Translating this into perceptual terms, objects identical in intensity could appear different in lightness. In fact, such an outcome is experienced. Figure 3.21 demonstrates this effect, called **lightness con-**

FIGURE 3.21 | Demonstration of simultaneous lightness contrast. The two circles in this figure are physically identical—both reflect exactly the same amount of light from the page to your eye. They look different in lightness because of the influence of the surrounds against which they appear.

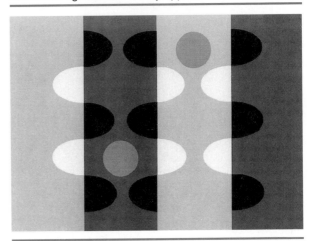

trast. The two circular regions in this drawing are equal in *physical* intensity, but they appear different in lightness. To verify that both circles are identical, you must eliminate the influence of their surrounds. In a piece of paper, cut a hole just slightly smaller than either circle. Position the hole over each circle in turn, occluding the surround in each case. By looking only at the circles, without contamination by their surrounds, you will see that both are identical in lightness. This proves that the different surrounds are responsible for the differences in perceived lightness. This perceptual outcome means that one's judgments about lightness can be in error by a substantial amount—a seemingly disadvantageous consequence.

Lightness contrast represents a case where the same physical intensity can yield differences in perceived lightness. The converse also occurs—different physical intensities can yield the same lightness. This routinely happens when you view an object under different levels of light. Under such conditions, your perception of lightness tends to remain constant despite variations in the amount of light falling on the retina. This phenomenon is called **lightness constancy.** You can demonstrate lightness constancy for yourself. Hold an object, such as an aspirin tablet, under strong light, and notice how light the object looks. Then dim the lights. As the amount of light falling on the aspirin falls, so does the amount of light reflected from the aspirin to your eye. Nonetheless, its lightness remains unchanged over a fairly wide range of light levels. This constancy of perceived lightness is the good perceptual error alluded to above.

Why do we characterize constancy as "good"? You might argue that lightness constancy means the human visual system is flawed—perception of light intensity fails to keep pace with the actual changes in light reflected from the aspirin tablet. But in fact, it's lucky that perception fails in this manner, for it allows an object to be recognized even though the level of illumination changes drastically. Because of this "flaw," the surface appearance of an object remains constant despite changes in the surface's level of illumination. After all, we are more concerned with seeing objects than with judging the level of illumination of those objects.

To understand how lightness constancy works, return once more to retinal ganglion cells. Let's measure the response of the retinal ganglion cell when a light of intensity x is flashed inside a surround several times more intense than the spot. For example, let the surround be three times the intensity of the spot, or $3x$. We now vary *both* the spot and the surround intensities, being careful to keep them in a ratio of 3 to 1. So long as this ratio remains constant, the ganglion cell will give the same neural response when the spot appears within the center. Assuming the retinal ganglion cell's response signals lightness, this invariant response means that lightness of the spot will remain constant even though the actual light from the spot is changing. The same result holds for most other ratios between the spot and its surround. This explanation of lightness constancy in ratio terms was suggested by Hans Wallach (1963), a pioneer in the field of human perception.

Now let's apply this ratio principle to the illumination of real objects, not just circular spots of light. Lay a dark-colored pen down on a piece of white paper. Because the paper reflects more light, it looks lighter than the pen. No surprise here. Using a light meter, we could actually measure the amount of light reflected by these objects. Typically, a clean piece of white paper reflects about 80 percent of the light falling on it; depending on its color, the pen might reflect about 10 percent, giving us a ratio of 8 to 1.

Now take a strong desk lamp and shine its light on both pen and paper. More light is falling on the pen than before you turned the lamp on. Consequently, more light is being reflected from the pen into your eyes. But the pen looks no lighter than before (lightness constancy). The reason is that with the lamp on, more light is also being reflected from the paper. Since the ratio of light from the paper to light from the pen (8:1) is unchanged, with more light coming from *both,* perceived lightness remains unchanged. Recent research shows just how robust the ratio explanation can be. Under the proper conditions, observers exhibit lightness constancy, even though the overall level of illumination varies by more than 1 million to 1 (Jacobsen and Gilchrist, 1988). Of course, if you did something to alter that ratio (such as illuminating just the pen), lightness constancy would fail: The lightness of the pen would change as you varied the amount of light falling on it alone. As Box 3.3 shows, under certain conditions, lightness constancy does indeed fail.

Although the ratio between the amounts of light reflected from two adjacent retinal areas can explain many aspects of lightness constancy (and its failures), these ratios don't tell the whole story. Alan Gilchrist (1977, 1988) has identified several conditions where lightness constancy and lightness contrast are influenced by factors that have nothing to do with retinal mechanisms. In one study, for instance, Gilchrist showed that the perceived lightness of a piece of gray paper varied dramatically, depending on whether it was perceived to lie in front of or behind the background against which it was viewed. When the paper rested directly on a dark background, it appeared light. But when it was positioned some distance in front of the background, the gray paper appeared darker. These changes in perceived lightness occurred even though the amount of light reflected to the eye from the paper and from the background remained unchanged. Here, then, lightness perception varied even though adjacent retinal areas were receiving unchanging amounts of light. This finding is reminiscent of Mach bands, where the illusion's strength depended on what you thought you were seeing.

Edward Adelson (1993) published an equally dramatic demonstration of the effect of knowledge on perceived lightness. A version of his illusion is shown in Figure 3.22. Look first at the array of patches in the left-hand part of the figure, and compare the appearance of the patches labeled a_1 and a_2. Patch a_1 appears much darker than a_2 but, in fact, they're identical. (If you find this hard to believe, punch two small holes in a piece of paper and view the two patches in isolation from their surroundings.) Next, look at the right-hand part of the figure, this time comparing patches b_1 and b_2. This pair

BOX 3.3 **When Lightness Constancy Fails**

Usually lightness constancy works, keeping you from erroneous interpretations of what you are seeing. But when constancy fails, the failure can be dramatic—and sometimes upsetting. Some years ago, one of us (R.S.) woke up, looked at his sleeping wife lying next to him, and was shocked. Overnight, a large patch of her hair had turned silvery white (it had been brown the night before). He could not imagine what terrible nightmare could possibly have made a patch of her hair go white in just a few hours.

Reaching over to touch the strange patch, he discovered the silvery appearance was illusory. In fact, when he touched her hair, his hand also turned silvery. Despite this temporary disfigurement of his hand, he was relieved that he wouldn't have to break the news about her hair to his wife when she awoke.

But why did this illusion occur? The partially open shutters passed a narrow beam of light into the room, illuminating part of his sleeping wife's hair without illuminating anything else in the room. In 1929, the psychologist Adhemar Gelb showed that this sort of arrangement—illumination confined to one object with no illumination of its surrounding area—tends to defeat lightness constancy. Perhaps you've had a more common version of this experience while walking in a forest dappled with sunlight. Suddenly, you come upon a large, shiny coin on the ground. Bending down to pick it up, you discover it is a leaf that had

been illuminated by a narrow beam of light coming through the branches of a tree. Here, again, constancy failed. The lightness of the leaf was so much inflated relative to its background that the leaf appeared to shine like silver.

Some researchers have tried to relate this breakdown of lightness constancy to the viewer's lack of knowledge, a cognitive explanation. Usually, these researchers follow the line of Hermann Helmholtz, who said that lightness constancy depends on an "unconscious inference" about the true conditions of stimulation. According to this theory, constancy breaks down when the viewer is confused about the actual level of illumination (Williams, McCoy, and Purves, 1998). It would seem to follow, then, that lightness judgments should be corrected if the confusion is eliminated. Yet this doesn't necessarily happen. For instance, even after R.S. recognized the illusory nature of his nighttime experience, the silvery appearance of his wife's hair persisted. Knowledge of the correct stimulus conditions did not override the illusory perception of lightness (see also Hurvich and Jameson, 1966).

These failures of lightness constancy, and the inability of mental effort to remedy them, reinforce the idea that lightness constancy depends, at least in part, on lateral interactions within the visual system, interactions that are initiated by the registration of different amounts of light from adjacent areas of the field.

FIGURE 3.22 | The vividness of simultaneous lightness contrast depends on how you interpret the 3D layout of the scene; see text for details.

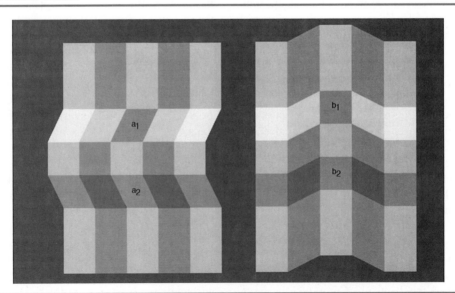

looks much more similar, yet they're physically identical to patches a_1 and a_2. Your perception of these patches is being strongly influenced by the three-dimensional appearance of the image. In the configuration on the left, patch a_1 appears to be a dark gray patch that is brightly illuminated, whereas patch a_2 is a light gray patch that is dimly illuminated. In the configuration on the right, however, both patches appear to receive the same level of illumination and, therefore, appear about equal in lightness. Retinal ganglion cells know nothing about the three-dimensional layout of objects. Thus, these cells should be insensitive to the global context in which the patches appear. Evidently, then, retinal mechanisms cannot fully account for illusions of surface lightness. We must look beyond the eye to the brain for a complete account of these illusions (for clues about brain areas that might be involved in perception of surface lightness, see Rossi, Rittenhouse, and Paradiso, 1996).

Despite what these demonstrations may seem to indicate, the retina does play a role in signaling lightness levels within local regions of the image. Even with his compelling demonstrations, Adelson (1993) acknowledges that retinal processes contribute to illusions of lightness and brightness. No one would deny that retinal signals are crucially involved in registering information about surface perception. To the contrary, retinal ganglion cells are the *only* vehicles for communicating visual information from the eye to the brain. Everything that we see—whether veridical or illusory—must be represented in the neural activity among the 1.25 million ganglion cells of each eye. Without a doubt, their receptive field properties help shape the world that we see.

In this section we have focused on possible perceptual consequences of center/surround antagonism. Now let's turn to another aspect of retinal ganglion cell organization, a feature that governs how well those cells perform on two seemingly incompatible visual tasks.

Sensitivity versus Resolution

Aspects of Convergence

Earlier we noted that over the entire retina, signals from 100 million photoreceptors converge on about 1.25 million retinal ganglion cells. This suggests an average convergence, over the entire retina, of about 80 photoreceptors to 1 ganglion cell. But this summary statistic is misleading.

Suppose we examine the number of receptors and the corresponding number of ganglion cells locally in different small patches throughout the retina, ranging from the macula to the periphery. For each patch of retina, we can calculate the degree of convergence by taking the ratio of receptors to retinal ganglion cells. This calculation reveals two important facts. First, the convergence ratio varies widely and systematically from one part of the retina to another. Second, near the center of the macula, the convergence ratio approaches unity—about one photoreceptor per ganglion cell—whereas in the periphery of the retina, the ratio is several hundred to one. In other words, there is a strong connection between retinal eccentricity and the amount of convergence. The connection is so strong that it suggests the operation of some grand plan. What might that plan be? To answer this question, we need to explain what is gained and what is lost by this neural convergence. As we proceed, keep in mind that the extent of receptor to ganglion cell convergence is directly related to the ganglion cell's receptive field size. The greater the number of receptors contributing to the receptive field of a given ganglion cell, the larger that cell's receptive field. This principle is illustrated schematically in Figure 3.23. Two ganglion cell receptive fields are shown schematically in the top panel, one small (*left*) and one large (*right*). Note that fewer photoreceptors contribute input to the small receptive field compared to the larger receptive field. We'll get to the bottom part of the drawing in a moment.

To picture the consequences of convergence, consider an extreme example. Suppose your eye had only a single retinal ganglion cell—a convergence ratio of 100 million to 1. In effect, your entire retina would be the receptive field for this solitary cell. How would your vision differ from its present form? It's certain that your vision would be changed in two ways, one for the good, one for the bad.

We'll start with the bad. With only one retinal ganglion cell to tell your brain what the eye saw, you would not be able to read or watch television. In fact, you would be virtually blind. Imagine the problem the brain faces with this solitary retinal ganglion cell as its only link to the visual world. The brain would be unable to distinguish different distributions of light falling on the back of the eye; all distributions would have the same effect on the cell. You would confuse letters of the alphabet and be unable to recognize your friends by sight. In brief, your resolution would be awful—not a good situation.

FIGURE 3.23 | A ganglion cell receiving input from just a few receptors (left-hand example) has a smaller receptive field and thus responds well to a smaller stimulus and responds poorly, if at all, to larger stimulus. A ganglion cell receiving input from a larger array of neighboring receptors (right-hand example) has a larger receptive field and responds poorly to a small stimulus but vigorously to large one. The larger receptive field, because it pools signals over a larger area, can also register the presence of weak levels of light.

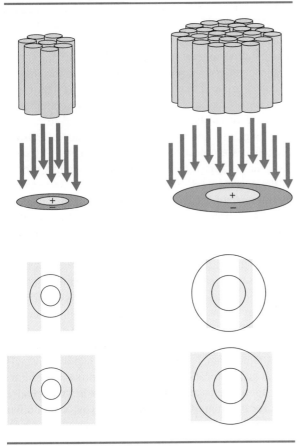

Resolution refers to the ability to distinguish differences in the spatial distribution of light in an image. The best-known measure of resolution is **visual acuity,** which we will discuss in a moment. With only one retinal ganglion cell to "describe" the image on the retina, your resolution would be nil. Regardless of the total light falling on the retina, you wouldn't be able to distinguish one letter of the alphabet from another—even with extremely large, headline type. You don't need to go to the extremes of our single-ganglion-cell example to discover that convergence is incompatible with good resolution. Generally, greater degrees of convergence lead to poorer resolution. That's because when visual information from a large region of space converges onto a single ganglion cell, the visual system inevitably loses track of exactly where within that region of space the information originated. That is why *convergence is the enemy of resolution.*

To see this enemy in action, look at the patterns of light within the ON and OFF regions of the two receptive fields shown in the bottom panel of Figure 3.23; one pattern consists of narrow, small contours and the other consists of broader, larger contours. Although the cell with the larger receptive field receives input from a larger number of receptors, responses to the narrow dark and light contours would cancel one another. As a result, this cell would fail to respond to the smaller contours. In contrast, the cell with the smaller receptive field, receiving input from fewer receptors, would give a vigorous response to the narrow pattern because the light and dark portions of the pattern "fit" within this cell's receptive field profile. The smaller receptive field thereby has superior visual acuity because convergence—the enemy of resolution—is more limited for this cell. To activate the cell with the larger receptive field, the pattern would have to consist of broader contours; those broad contours would not activate the cell with the smaller receptive field.

Now for the good news about convergence. Let's begin with two hypothetical ganglion cells, *A* and *B*. Suppose *A* receives input from a relatively small cluster of neighboring receptors (such as the ganglion cell in the upper left of Figure 3.23) while *B* received input from a larger array of neighboring receptors (such as the ganglion cell in the upper right of Figure 3.23). How well are these two different ganglion cells able to signal the presence of dim light? In other words, how sensitive to light are the two cells? You've learned that for a ganglion cell's activity to change, it must receive a sufficient amount of transmitter substance from the bipolar cells. In effect, a retinal ganglion cell weighs all the neurochemical evidence it receives and decides whether the cumulative evidence exceeds some minimum threshold. If that threshold is exceeded, the ganglion cell's activity level is altered, signaling the brain that a visual event is occurring. In weighing the cumulative evidence, the ganglion cell disregards which particular bipolar cells (and, hence, which photoreceptors) provide the individual pieces of evidence. From the ganglion cell's perspective, only the total is important. With this in mind, let's compare the abilities of ganglion cells *A* and *B* to inform the brain about the presence of dim light imaged on the retina.

For this comparison, we'll use a large but dim spot of light that can be centered on either ganglion cell's receptive field. Let's start with ganglion cell *A,* the one receiving input from a small cluster of photoreceptors. Even though the image of the dim spot fills this cell's receptive field, the receptors would give a weak response to the light. Some of these weak photoreceptor messages get passed along to cells in the intermediate layers of the retina, but those cells, too, will generate weak messages at best. As a result, ganglion cell *A* may well receive too little transmitter substance to disturb its spontaneous activity. So this ganglion cell will fail to inform the brain that a dim spot of light is present.

What about ganglion cell *B,* the one receiving input from a larger array of photoreceptors? These photoreceptors will also give a weak response because the light is dim. But there will be substantially more photoreceptors contributing weak signals to the ganglion cell via the bipolars. The ganglion cell, therefore, will receive more transmitter substance ("evidence"), thereby increasing its chances of being activated. Consequently, the brain is much more likely to receive messages about the dim spot of light.

The principle is simple: Increasing the number of receptors contributing input to a retinal ganglion cell allows weak signals to be summed, yielding a total input strong enough to change the activity of that ganglion cell. A retinal ganglion cell sums weak signals originating from an array of retinal locations, an ability known as **spatial summation.** Spatial summation enables you to see very dim light. In other words, it enhances the sensitivity of your eyes. Because summation depends on convergence, one can say that *convergence is the ally of sensitivity.*

Now you can appreciate the conflict. On the one hand, convergence is a prerequisite for high sensitivity; on the other, convergence interferes with good resolution. To design an eye that detects very dim lights *and* possesses good spatial resolution represents a real challenge.

The Duplex Solution   So how do your eyes manage to resolve these two conflicting demands—resolution and sensitivity? To answer this question, let's return to an

analogy we've already used, the analogy between the eye and a camera.

Photographers face the same kinds of problems we've been discussing. Some types of film, such as those used for nighttime surveillance, have extremely large grains of photosensitive material and, thereby, a high sensitivity to light. This makes such film usable at very low light levels. (As you may know, a film's light sensitivity is indexed by its ISO or ASA rating.) Highly sensitive films usually have relatively poor resolution, and so they don't produce very sharp photographs.

Other types of film, such as the microfilm used by librarians, have exceedingly small grains of photosensitive material and therefore produce very sharp photographs (even in huge enlargements). However, these types of film work properly only at relatively high light levels. With film, then, as with the eye, there is a trade-off between resolution and sensitivity. The photographer can solve this dilemma by simply changing the film in the camera, matching the film to the available light. The eye, however, doesn't allow the capability of loading and unloading different types of film as needed. In fact, this is unnecessary because the "film" in the eye is **duplex,** meaning that the eye contains two types of photosensitive elements (or films). One—associated with the rod photoreceptors—provides high sensitivity to light; the other—associated with the cone photoreceptors—provides high resolution. In the human eye, the two types of film occupy somewhat different locations along the back of the eye.

To see how this duplex arrangement works, think back to the convergence of receptors onto ganglion cells. Recall that the central region of the eye (where cones predominate) has very little convergence. Hence, it has excellent resolution but only average sensitivity to light. Peripheral regions of the retina (where rods predominate) have high degrees of convergence, hence poor resolution but good light sensitivity. (For further discussion of high sensitivity, see Box 3.4.)

The preceding chapter pointed out that the center of the primate retina contains mainly cones and very few rods. As a result, activity of retinal ganglion cells with receptive fields near the center of the retina reflects mainly the responses of cones. Because of the predominance of rods in the retinal periphery, the activity of ganglion cells with receptive fields in that region reflects mainly the influence of rods. As you are about to learn, rods and cones differ in numerous ways important to vision. This means that ganglion cells in the rod-dominated periphery make different contributions to

BOX 3.4 Adding Photons Over Time and Space

Multiple factors govern the eye's sensitivity. Some have already been discussed—the wavelength of light, its intensity and spatial pattern, and where on the retina the stimulus falls. But there are two other, very important variables: its duration and its size.

To understand the importance of duration and size, we must consider exactly what events need to occur before one can detect a very weak stimulus. Suppose that seeing the stimulus requires that the photoreceptors absorb some small number of photons—a **photon** being the smallest unit of light energy. (The actual number of photons doesn't matter so long as it is greater than 1.) Imagine that we split the stimulus into two installments, both intense enough to cause the receptors to absorb exactly one-half the total number of photons needed for seeing. Now let's introduce one condition: allow one hour to elapse between delivery of the first and second installments of photons. Will you see the stimulus? No, because by the time the second installment of photons arrives, the effects of the first installment will have long since disappeared.

Granting that an hour's delay is unreasonable, how much time can elapse between installments of photons before the effects of the first installment completely dissipate? Photoreceptors have a limited memory—called **temporal summation**—with the rods' "memory" being somewhat longer than that of the cones. But whichever system is stimulated, the shorter the interval between the two installments, the greater the chances that the residue of the first installment will be available to add to the effects of the second. Delivering all the photons within a very short time period guarantees that effects

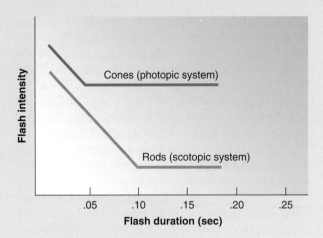

produced by the earliest photons will add to those of the later ones. If the stimulus is stretched out in time, a greater *total* number of photons must be delivered to the eye, since losing the advantage of temporal summation makes each photon less efficient.

This fact has been formalized as **Bloch's law,** which states that a constant product of light intensity and time will be equally detectable. Sometimes Bloch's law is expressed as

$$I \times T = C$$

where *I* stands for intensity, *T* for time, and *C* for constant visual effect. Bloch's law says that time can be traded for intensity. Lengthening the presentation of some relatively weak light makes it just as visible as another, more in-

vision than do ganglion cells in the cone-dominated central region of the retina. Many ganglion cells receive inputs from both rods and cones (Enroth-Cugell, Hertz, and Lennie, 1977), so that both classes of photoreceptors share communication pathways to the brain. However, rod and cone signals to these mixed input ganglion cells get switched from all-cone to all-rod inputs depending on the overall level of light. As pointed out previously, this switching function is thought to be accomplished by the amacrine cells.

Rod-dominated ganglion cells support vision even when light levels are several hundred times less than that required by their cone-dominated counterparts. This re-

sults partly from the rods' own greater sensitivity (Detwiler, Hodgkin, and McNaughton, 1980), as well as greater convergence on rod-dominated retinal ganglion cells. Vision under dimly lit conditions is termed **scotopic** (from the Greek words *skotos,* meaning "darkness," and *opsis,* meaning "sight"). We'll use the term *scotopic vision* to signify vision that depends on rod photoreceptors. You must keep in mind that these rod signals are still passed through the intermediate retinal layers to ganglion cells, which send those rod-mediated messages to the brain.

The cones require somewhat higher light levels in order to function properly. Thus, vision using this class of photoreceptors is described as **photopic** (from the tense light that is presented only briefly. So long as each has the same product (of intensity and time), the two stimuli contain the same total energy and will be equally detectable. These relationships are depicted in the figure at the end of this box. There, the vertical axis represents the stimulus intensity that is just barely detectable (I), and the horizontal axis represents the stimulus's duration (T). Two lines are shown on the graph, one representing the behavior of the scotopic system, the other representing the behavior of the photopic system. Bloch's law predicts that data should fall on an oblique line, a 45-degree slope. Note that in both lines this prediction holds when the durations are relatively short.

For the rods, Bloch's law breaks down at about one-tenth of a second. For cones, it breaks down much earlier, at about one-twentieth of a second or less (Hood and Finkelstein, 1986). These values reflect the temporal memories—temporal summation—of the two systems. Incidentally, Bloch's law also pertains to contrast, not just luminance: It is possible to interchange exposure duration with stimulus contrast to yield constant visual effects, within limits (Harley, Dillon, and Loftus, 2004).

There is a *spatial* analog to the *temporal* law just discussed. We mentioned previously that many photoreceptors will share a single ganglion cell. In other words, the ganglion cell adds together signals from spatially separate sources—two or more photoreceptors—a capacity referred to in the text as spatial summation.

Suppose we take a very small stimulus and by trial and error determine how intense it must be in order to be just detectable. This stimulus causes the absorption of a minimum, or threshold, number of photons. If we distribute that same number of photons widely over the retina, seeing will not result. The spatially dispersed photons stimulate photoreceptors that do not contribute to the same ganglion cells. As a result, the opportunity for co-operative effect is reduced.

Within certain limits, all stimuli having the same product of intensity *and* area will be equally detectable. This is not completely surprising since any two stimuli having the same product of area and intensity contain identical amounts of total light. This trade-off between intensity and area is known as **Ricco's law.** Ricco's law holds only in the fovea, and even there, it holds only for very small stimuli.

We don't want to leave you with the idea that the visual system responds *solely* to the number of photons gathered over time and space. If it did respond that way, you'd confuse long, weak flashes with brief, intense ones. This confusion would be particularly strong when flashes of different durations contained the same total number of photons, since according to Bloch's law, they would be equally detectable. However, even when two flashes contain the same total number of photons (and hence, are equally detectable), people can still discriminate between a long, weak flash and a brief, intense one (Zacks, 1970). In other words, the visual system registers more than just the total number of photons. It also discriminates how those photons are distributed over time. At present, though, it is not known how the visual system manages this discrimination.

Greek word *photos,* meaning "light"). Figure 3.24 indicates the light levels considered photopic and those considered scotopic. This is an important distinction because, as you'll see later, photopic and scotopic vision differ in a number of significant ways. There is a narrow, intermediate range of light levels where both rods and cones operate, and vision in this very limited range is termed **mesopic** (from the Greek word *mesos,* meaning "middle"). In this chapter, we shall concentrate on vision in the much larger photopic and scotopic ranges.

As noted earlier, the eye must satisfy two competing goals: good resolution and good sensitivity. We now discuss each of these goals in turn.

Resolution

Since convergence is the enemy of resolution, the photopic system, having less convergence, should have better resolution. It is estimated that 33 percent of all the retina's ganglion cells receive input from cones occupying the fovea, which itself accounts for only 2 percent of the retina's total area. Thus, we expect resolution to be best in the center of the macula, where the ratio of cones to ganglion cells is about 1 to 1. We do not yet know precisely how the convergence of the cone system changes across the retina (the extensive physiological measurements required to answer that question have yet to be performed). Instead, we must infer the answer using related information: the density of cones at various places on the

FIGURE 3.24 | Scale of light intensity expressed in units called "candelas per square meter," a measure of light energy.

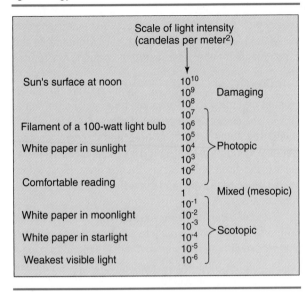

FIGURE 3.25 | Graph showing how visual acuity and the number of cone photoreceptors covary with retinal eccentricity. In this graph, a visual acuity of 1.0 corresponds to an image of about 0.005 millimeters in diameter on the retina. Values less than 1.0 correspond to larger images on the retina and, hence, poorer acuity.

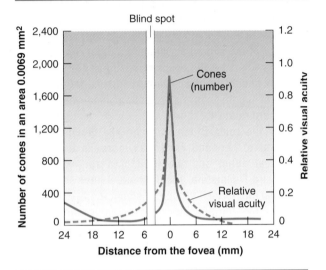

retina. The solid line in Figure 3.25, labeled "Cones (number)," shows how the number of cones per square millimeter decreases with distance from the fovea (eccentricity). The dotted curve in the same graph shows visual resolution measured for various regions of the retina. This second curve, showing "Relative visual acuity," comes from measurements taken from humans who tried to read a well-lit eye chart while directing their gaze at various distances away from the center of the chart. Fixating in this way causes the letters on the chart to be imaged at different, known places on the retina. Note the fairly good correspondence between the perceptual measurements of resolution (visual acuity) and the anatomical measurements (the number, or density, of cones).

You can see one consequence of the variation in acuity with eccentricity by gazing steadily at any letter on this page. You'll have little trouble recognizing that letter. However, if you're careful not to move your eyes, you'll notice that letters in the periphery appear less distinct. Only the bigger letters, such as those used for the section headings, can be read without looking directly at them. Figure 3.26 (created using a technique described by Anstis, 1998) shows a pair of pictures, one in clear focus and the other progressively blurred from the center outward. The blurred picture simulates the falloff in vi-

sual acuity with eccentricity. Stare directly at the center of the focused picture, maintaining your fixation on the word *stare* in bold. Then stare at the center of the blurred picture, at the word *stare* in bold. If you're careful to maintain strict fixation each time, the text in the two pictures should look indistinguishable. That's because your visual system is effectively blurring the details in the top picture everywhere except in the central region where you're looking. The bottom picture, in other words, simulates what you're actually seeing when you stare at the top picture.

Another good example of our blurred peripheral vision can be seen in Figure 3.27 (this one created by Wilson Geisler). The middle photo is the original, which is sharply focused. Take a moment to look at the eagle's eye and talons in this middle photo. The picture on the left simulates what you're actually seeing when you gaze directly at the eagle's eye in that middle picture. The version on the right simulates what you're actually seeing when you shift your gaze to the eagle's talons in the middle picture. Again, the spatial detail is significantly obscured for portions of the scene falling outside your fovea. It's remarkable how unaware we are of our relatively poor spatial resolution in the visual periphery (Perry and Geisler, 2002). To learn how these simulation images were pro-

FIGURE 3.26 | Pair of pictures demonstrating the fall-off in visual resolution in the periphery. Follow the instructions given in the text.

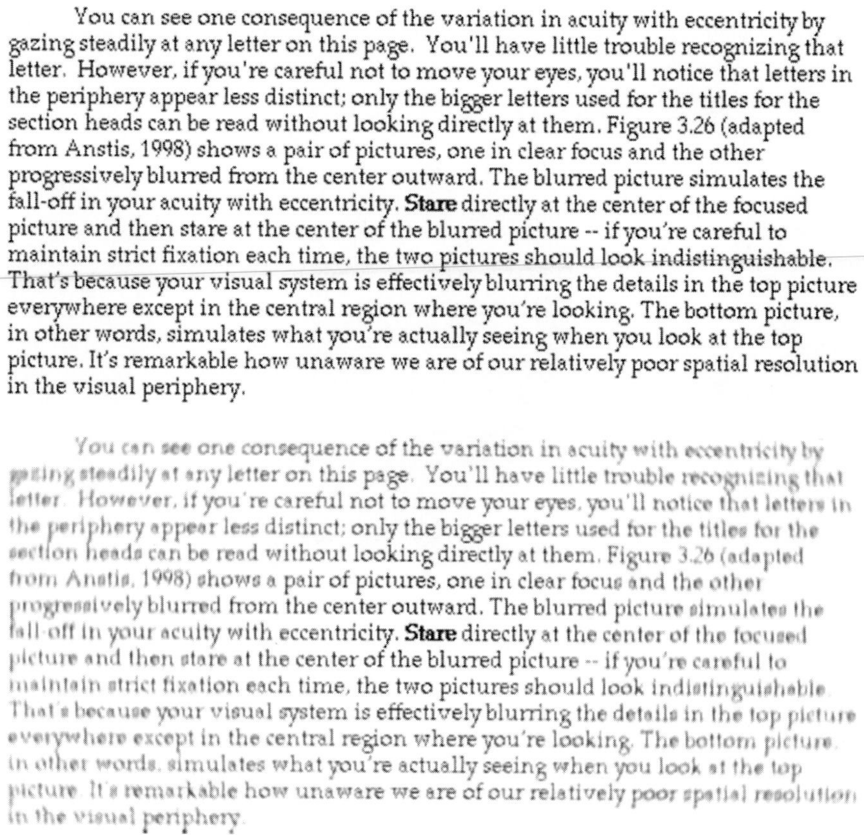

You can see one consequence of the variation in acuity with eccentricity by gazing steadily at any letter on this page. You'll have little trouble recognizing that letter. However, if you're careful not to move your eyes, you'll notice that letters in the periphery appear less distinct; only the bigger letters used for the titles for the section heads can be read without looking directly at them. Figure 3.26 (adapted from Anstis, 1998) shows a pair of pictures, one in clear focus and the other progressively blurred from the center outward. The blurred picture simulates the fall-off in your acuity with eccentricity. **Stare** directly at the center of the focused picture and then stare at the center of the blurred picture -- if you're careful to maintain strict fixation each time, the two pictures should look indistinguishable. That's because your visual system is effectively blurring the details in the top picture everywhere except in the central region where you're looking. The bottom picture, in other words, simulates what you're actually seeing when you look at the top picture. It's remarkable how unaware we are of our relatively poor spatial resolution in the visual periphery.

You can see one consequence of the variation in acuity with eccentricity by gazing steadily at any letter on this page. You'll have little trouble recognizing that letter. However, if you're careful not to move your eyes, you'll notice that letters in the periphery appear less distinct; only the bigger letters used for the titles for the section heads can be read without looking directly at them. Figure 3.26 (adapted from Anstis, 1998) shows a pair of pictures, one in clear focus and the other progressively blurred from the center outward. The blurred picture simulates the fall-off in your acuity with eccentricity. **Stare** directly at the center of the focused picture and then stare at the center of the blurred picture -- if you're careful to maintain strict fixation each time, the two pictures should look indistinguishable. That's because your visual system is effectively blurring the details in the top picture everywhere except in the central region where you're looking. The bottom picture, in other words, simulates what you're actually seeing when you look at the top picture. It's remarkable how unaware we are of our relatively poor spatial resolution in the visual periphery.

duced, navigate to Geisler's Web page on "space variant imaging" where you can read about the techniques and see more examples including animations; the Web page address is available at www.mhhe.com/blake5.

Stuart Anstis was interested in how the ability to recognize letters varies depending on how far from the fovea the letters are imaged. With a person seated 57 centimeters (about 22 inches) from a bright, white screen, Anstis moved a letter inward from the edge of the screen. Starting far enough away from a fixation point so the person could not identify the letter, Anstis brought the letter in, toward the fovea, until the person could recognize the letter. After he did this with letters of various sizes, Anstis found that small letters had to be brought much nearer to the fixation point than did larger letters (Anstis, 1974).

Figure 3.28 demonstrates Anstis's results. Hold the chart a little less than arm's length away from your eyes and stare steadily at the dot in the center. All the letters should be equally legible because the size of the letters increases at the same rate that your visual acuity decreases.

Although the data in Figure 3.25 demonstrate a close connection between visual acuity and the density of cones, cone density is not the entire explanation of visual acuity. Ganglion cell density also falls off with eccentricity, whereas the receptive fields of the 1.25 million ganglion cells of the eye enlarge as we move from the fovea to the periphery. These two factors—decreased cell density and increased receptive field sizes—also guarantee that acuity will be poorer in the periphery. It is estimated that the eye would have to contain 35 million ganglion cells in order to support uniform, high acuity throughout the retina. To accommodate this many ganglion cells, each of your eyes would have to be as large as your whole head!

FIGURE 3.27 | The photographs on the left and the right simulate the degraded spatial detail present when you fixate on the middle picture.

FIGURE 3.28 | All letters in this chart should be equally legible when you fixate on the small dot in the center of the chart.

Acuity also decreases appreciably as the level of illumination drops (you probably already know this from your own difficulty reading a menu in a dimly lit restaurant). Yet it's obviously not the number of cones or the density of ganglion cells that changes with light level. The reduction in acuity with decreasing illumination is probably caused by changes in the spatial layout of receptive fields of the ganglion cells. As the overall level of illumination drops, the surrounding portions of ganglion cell receptive fields become less effective and, consequently, the center regions become larger (Barlow, Fitzhugh, and Kuffler, 1957; Maffei and Fiorentini, 1973). Box 3.5 completes the story by describing additional influences on visual acuity.

Sensitivity

Scotopic Vision   Under ideal conditions, rod photoreceptors operate at the theoretical limit of their sensitivity, generating measurable electrical signals when only a single photon is absorbed by a given rod's photopigment (Lewis and Del Priore, 1988; Hecht, Shlaer, and Pirenne, 1942; Rodieck, 1998). But the capture of a single photon does not constitute seeing. In order for light to generate a visual sensation, more than one rod, though not many more, must

Visual Acuity: The Meaning of 20/20 Vision   BOX 3.5

Visual acuity can be defined in several different ways. One common definition relates acuity to the smallest target, such as a letter, that can be correctly recognized. A person able to recognize smaller letters is said to have better acuity. You may have heard someone comment with pride about having 20/20 visual acuity. What exactly do these numbers mean?

When optometrists and ophthalmologists began quantifying acuity more than a century ago, they created eye charts containing letters of various sizes. Patients tried to read ever smaller letters, until they came to letters so small that reading was impossible. One Dutch doctor, Hermann Snellen, tested hundreds of people who had no eye diseases (so-called "normals") and found that half these people were unable to see details smaller than a certain size. He designated this size—details whose images on the retina were about 0.005 millimeters high—as "normal." For any given detail, the viewing distance is crucial. If you move far enough away, even headlines become impossible to read. So visual acuity is expressed in relation to the distance at which the eye chart is read, usually 20 feet. Someone is said to have normal visual acuity if, while standing 20 feet from the chart, that individual can read the same letters that the average healthy person can read at 20 feet. Hence, the notation "20/20." The metric equivalent of 20/20 is 6/6, since testing is carried out at a viewing distance of 6 meters.

Acuity can be either better or worse than 20/20. If you cannot see small print, your acuity may be only 20/60. This means that you must get as close as 20 feet in order to read what the average person can read from 60 feet. Likewise, if you have really sharp eyes, your vision may be 20/15 or even 20/10. This means that you can read letters at a distance of 20 feet that the average person cannot. He or she has to move closer to the letters in order to read them: within 15 feet in the first case, 10 feet in the second.

But 20/20 is not good enough. A normal, healthy young person should have vision *better* than 20/20. The graph shown in the right-hand column shows that for young people, visual acuity is on average better than 20/20. Acuity declines as we get older. Part of this decline is owing to the reduced size of an older person's pupils, which allows less light to reach the retina (Owsley, Sekuler, and Siemsen, 1983). Older people also have particular difficulty with eye charts whose letters are of low contrast. On such charts the test letters are printed in various shades of gray rather than in black. Tony Adams of the University of California's School of Optometry used a low-contrast eye chart to

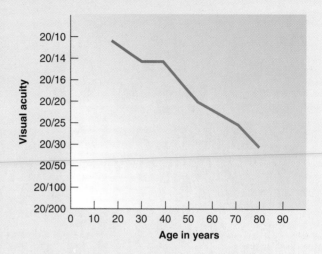

measure the acuities of young and old people, all of whom had 20/20 acuity when tested with the normal, high-contrast eye charts. Adams and his colleagues (1988) found that the older observers showed a far greater decline in acuity at low contrast. This result bears on the design of work and home environments in which older persons have to function.

Visual acuity varies with factors other than age and light level. Some people have particular trouble reading eye charts composed of letters bunched together. They'll be able to read smaller letters on a less crowded line of the eye chart, even though they fail with a line of larger letters that are crowded together. You can see this **crowding effect** in an eye chart prepared by Stuart Anstis. Compare the legibility of this crowded chart to the legibility of the chart shown in Figure 3.28. They are almost the same, except that Anstis has added many extra letters to the chart in this box.

Visual acuity scores may also be affected by cognitive factors, including memorization of the eye chart (by someone who is particularly anxious to "pass" an eye test). Sometimes these cognitive factors play a role even though neither patient nor doctor intend them to. Erica, the youngest daughter of one of the authors (R.S.), was having her eyes examined by a well-meaning though inexperienced ophthalmologist who, to make matters worse, was in a hurry. Wanting to measure acuity separately for each eye, the ophthalmologist asked Erica to close her left eye

(continued)

BOX 3.5 **Visual Acuity: The Meaning of 20/20 Vision** *(continued)*

and read the five small letters at the bottom of the chart, using only her right eye. After she had finished a perfect rendition of the requested letters, she was told to switch eyes, now using her left eye to read the letters. Since the doctor had not bothered to change the chart, she asked him incredulously, "Do you want me to read the *same* letters again?" Of course, most people would have no difficulty remembering the five letters they'd read aloud only a few seconds before. But the doctor urged her on. No surprise: Her second rendition of the letters was every bit as good as her first. When the testing procedure was complete, she almost—her good manners alone stood in the way—offered to read the bottom line with *both* eyes closed. The moral? Although tests of acuity are supposed to assess only one's vision, they can be influenced by other factors as well if the tester is not careful.

FIGURE 3.29 | When fixating on the X, the test spot falls in the periphery of the retina.

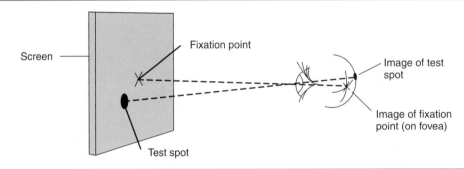

catch at least one photon each. To efficiently activate the small number of rods needed for seeing, conditions must be exactly right. Examining some of these conditions gives a very good introduction to scotopic vision in general, so let's consider the conditions that optimize sensitivity to light.

The first requirement is that the eye have a full supply of photopigment molecules. Exposure to light uses up these molecules, much as exposure to light consumes the light sensitivity of film. Since we're exposed to light just about every waking moment, our eyes rarely maintain a full supply of unused molecules (except when we sleep). To restore the full supply of photopigments (without going to sleep) requires keeping the person you're

going to test in complete darkness for about 35 minutes. This period of adapting to the dark suffices to build the rod photopigments to maximum levels.

Second, the photons need to be imaged on an area of the retina where rods are plentiful. Thus, it makes no sense to present the stimulus to the fovea, where there are no rods. Rods are most plentiful in a region slightly more than 3 millimeters away from the fovea. To stimulate this retinal region requires knowing where the person is actually looking. So the person is asked to fixate on a small, continuously visible spot. As illustrated in Figure 3.29, knowing where someone is fixating makes it possible to situate the test stimulus at the appropriate distance from

FIGURE 3.30 | Visual sensitivity of the rod-based scoptopic system and the cone-based photopic system varies with the wavelength of the test light. The vertical axis plots the reciprocal of the minimum light intensity necessary to detect the test flash of light (with intensity expressed in standard photometric units.

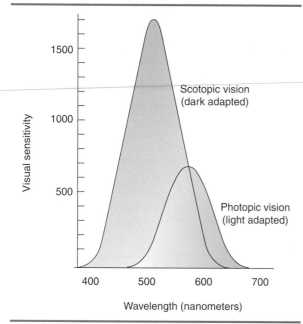

Photopic Vision   Though sensitivity is not the speciality of photopic vision, it's worth considering photopic sensitivity so that we can compare it to scotopic sensitivity. To measure *photopic* sensitivity requires imaging the target on a retinal area containing only cones; rods should play no role. Again, for stimuli of different wavelengths, we want to determine the minimum number of photons required for photopic vision.

The curve labeled "photopic vision" in Figure 3.30 is the photopic sensitivity curve, again with sensitivity plotted as a function of stimulus wavelength. (Box 3.6 discusses one very practical implication of this curve's shape). Comparing the two curves, note that scotopic sensitivity is greater than photopic sensitivity at all except the longest wavelengths, the "red" end of the spectrum. Note also that the peaks of the two curves occur at different wavelengths. Maximum scotopic sensitivity occurs around 510 nanometers, whereas photopic sensitivity peaks at 550 nanometers.

The Purkinje Shift   The difference between the wavelengths at which the photopic and scoptopic curves peak has an interesting perceptual consequence, one that you may have experienced. This effect was first described by Johannes Evangelista von Purkinje, a Bohemian physiologist of the early nineteenth century (Kuthan, 1987). During the day, when vision is photopic, objects close to 550 nanometers in wavelength tend to appear lighter than objects of 500 nanometers. As night falls and vision becomes scotopic, the situation will be reversed; objects reflecting 500 nanometers become lighter than those reflecting 550 nanometers. This variation in relative lightness with time of day is known as the **Purkinje shift.**

Fortunately, the Purkinje shift can be easily seen under rather pleasant conditions. Get a comfortable chair and a good book, and sit in a flower garden on a nice, warm day. Compare the lightness of yellow daisies to the lightness of the green foliage. During the day, the daisies will look lighter because their reflected wavelengths fall closer to the peak of the photopic sensitivity curve. But as twilight falls, the foliage will appear lighter, since it reflects wavelengths closer to the peak of the scotopic sensitivity curve. This is the Purkinje shift.

Dark Adaptation   The retina's duplex nature produces the differences between photopic and scotopic vision. We've already explored some of these differences. The duplex retina also affects vision by controlling the recovery from exposure to light, a process called **dark adaptation.**

that fixation spot. The test stimulus must be fairly small so that it stimulates only the desired retinal region.

Remember that the goal is to determine the dimmest light necessary for detection. The fewer photons needed for vision, the higher one's visual sensitivity is said to be. Not all wavelengths of light are equally effective in stimulating rods. Therefore, to find the wavelength to which the scotopic system is most sensitive, we must stimulate the eye with various wavelengths of light, noting how many photons are needed to detect each wavelength.

The curve in Figure 3.30 labeled "scoptopic vision" shows the results of such testing. The horizontal axis shows the wavelength of light used to stimulate the eye. The vertical axis shows sensitivity (scaled in units of the reciprocal of light intensity at threshold). The curve represents the sensitivity of the rod-based system and is usually called the scotopic sensitivity function. The scotopic sensitivity function peaks at 510 nanometers, with the eye being less sensitive when stimulated by either shorter or longer wavelengths of light. In daylight and at sufficient intensity, light of 510 nanometers appears blue- green. To the person whose scoptopic vision is being tested, however, the faint test target will appear colorless (the explanation for this failure of color vision is given in Chapter 7).

BOX 3.6 **Do You Get Your Money's Worth from the Electric Company?**

The bill from your electric company has just arrived. Shocked by the numbers, you want to know if you're getting your money's worth. A dollar value cannot be placed on the pleasure you may have gotten from your X-Box, TV, and microwave oven, so let's ignore those uses of electricity. Stick to one we can say something about—the use of electricity to produce light for reading.

Because only the photopic system affords reasonable resolution, we use that system when reading. So we can begin the analysis by looking at the photopic sensitivity curve (see Figure 3.30). Since the photopic system is most sensitive to light whose wavelength is 550 nanometers, your electricity dollars would be most efficiently spent if

they were used to produce radiation of only that wavelength. Electricity devoted to producing ultraviolet or infrared radiation is, of course, wasted because you can't see either one. Moreover, any electricity spent to produce visible radiation at wavelengths other than 550 nanometers is not being used as efficiently as it could be.

Suppose you use only ordinary, tungsten light bulbs for reading. How could you determine the effectiveness of each dollar spent to power one of these bulbs? The answer depends on the spectral distribution of the light emitted by these bulbs. If they emitted only at 550 nanometers, they'd be highly efficient—putting out light precisely at the wavelength that has the greatest impact on the human visual sys-

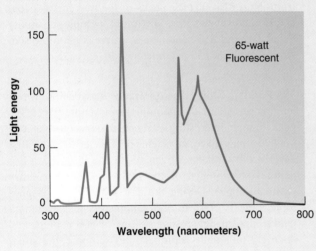

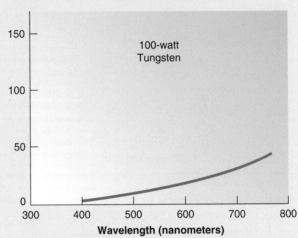

Every time you go to the movies you are experiencing dark adaptation. Upon first entering the darkened theater from the bright lobby, you have difficulty finding a seat or seeing the faces of people around you. After a while, though, you get used to the dark and can see better. A small part of your improved vision can be traced to changes in your pupil. In darkness, the pupil dilates, allowing more light into the eye. But dark adaptation cannot be explained solely by pupillary dilation. For one thing, as you adapt to the dark, your sensitivity to light may improve by a factor of 100,000 or more, whereas the change in pupil area is relatively small, a factor of 16 at most. Moreover, your sensitivity may continue to improve for 30 to 40 minutes, whereas the pupil reaches its maximum size within a matter of seconds.

When dark adaptation is studied in the laboratory, it is possible to measure the recovery time of vision. Such ex-

periments are numerous and have revealed a lot about vision's duplex nature. We'll present some of the highlights here; for a more extensive treatment, see Reeves (2004).

Studies of dark adaptation typically begin by exposing a person to a strong light, called the *adaptation stimulus*. The idea is to determine how quickly a person's visual sensitivity recovers from exposure to that strong light. After the adaptation stimulus has been extinguished, the person sits in complete darkness and tries to detect a very dim, briefly flashing light (the *test stimulus*), which is presented about once per second. The test light's intensity slowly increases until the light becomes visible to the person. At that point, the intensity of the light is immediately dropped so it becomes invisible again. This cycle is repeated over and over, for up to 1 hour. Each time the test stimulus becomes visible, two values are recorded: the *intensity* of that just visible stimulus and the *time* at which tem. The left graph in the accompanying figure shows the spectral distribution of the radiation emitted by a typical tungsten bulb. Note that most of the radiation that you pay for consists of wavelengths that you can't see, let alone use, for reading. For quantification, we must turn to **Abney's law** (named for a British physicist of the early twentieth century).

Abney's law describes the effectiveness of a stimulus that simultaneously contains many different wavelengths, which is certainly the case for light from a tungsten bulb. For each wavelength present in such a stimulus, Abney's law instructs one to take the product of two quantities: the amount of light present at that wavelength and how sensitive the photopic system is to that wavelength. The first of these quantities can be obtained from measuring devices (spectrum analyzers of various sorts); the second can be obtained from a table of the photopic sensitivity function's numerical value at various wavelengths. After these products are obtained for each wavelength in the stimulus, Abney's law requires that one sum up all the products. The resulting sum is a numerical statement of the visual effectiveness of the spectrally complex stimulus. Stated simply, Abney's law says that one can predict the impact of a complex stimulus composed of many wavelengths by evaluating the effectiveness of each of its component wavelengths and then adding together their separate effects.

To make quantitative sense of the outcome, though, we need some reference point, such as a stimulus that represents 100 percent efficiency, the maximum obtainable. Since that's the best you could achieve, let's say that

such a stimulus gave you a full dollar's worth of light for each dollar spent on electricity. Compared to that standard, you get only 3 cents worth of light for each dollar put into electricity for a tungsten bulb. Some tungsten bulbs do a little better—5 cents return per dollar spent—but these lamps tend to burn out quickly.

We can apply the same analysis to another common type of light used for reading—fluorescent lamps. The spectrum of a typical fluorescent lamp is shown in the right-hand graph in the accompanying figure. Compared to the tungsten bulb, the fluorescent lamp emits far more of its radiation within the visually effective band (400 to 700 nanometers) and far less in the infrared (which is experienced as heat, not light). Applying Abney's law to the spectrum of a fluorescent lamp, we find that you get 10 cents' worth of reading light for each dollar's worth of electricity, a much better buy.

Oddly enough, the most efficient light source for reading is one that doesn't require any electricity at all. One vision scientist pointed out that fireflies and glowworms emit light very near the peak wavelength of the photopic sensitivity curve (LeGrand, 1968, p. 82). Because fireflies achieve very high photopic efficiencies, a lamp full of fireflies would certainly give you your money's worth of reading light.

We don't usually tell you things that we don't want you to remember. But for your own peace of mind, the next time you have to pay an electric bill, maybe you should forget how few of your dollars are going for something you actually used.

it was seen (that is, the time elapsed since the person entered into darkness). The general outcome can be described simply: The longer the person stays in the dark, the less intense the test stimulus needs to be in order to be seen. To put it another way, the person's sensitivity steadily increases the longer he or she spends in the dark.

Now suppose that we wanted to measure the recovery of rod sensitivity separately from the recovery of cone sensitivity. How might that be done? You could capitalize on the uneven distribution of these two types of photoreceptors to isolate their separate behaviors. To measure dark adaptation using cones only, the test stimulus could be presented to the fovea. To do the same for rods, the test stimulus could be presented in the periphery, where the rods predominate.

The left-hand panel of Figure 3.31 shows how dark adaptation measurements turn out when the test stimulus

is presented to the fovea. The drop in the curve over time shows an improvement in photopic sensitivity the longer one remains in darkness. The middle panel shows the results of a comparable experiment in which the test stimulus is imaged away from the fovea. Because the stimulus is imaged on a portion of the retina predominated by rods, the curve reflects the changing sensitivity over time of the scotopic system.

Compare the two curves. Note that at 0 time, the scotopic curve (middle panel) is higher than the photopic curve (left-hand panel). Immediately after entering darkness, in other words, the scotopic system is less sensitive (it needs more light to see) than the photopic system. Now compare the curves later in time, say at 20 minutes. Here the scotopic system is more sensitive than the photopic system, the opposite of what we just saw. The greater scotopic sensitivity after prolonged darkness is consistent

FIGURE 3.31 | Graphs showing changes in sensitivity relative to the length of time in darkness.

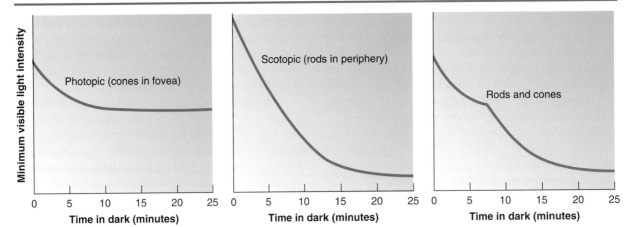

Returning to the dark adaptation curves in Figure 3.31, note that the scotopic system starts out less sensitive than the photopic system but ends up more sensitive. After an interval of about 8 to 10 minutes, their *relative* sensitivities reverse. One other point emerges from these curves. The photopic system completes its recovery from the adaptation stimulus rather quickly (since the curve stops declining after 5 to 6 minutes). The scotopic system takes a lot longer to recover completely (the curve doesn't stop declining until at least 15 minutes have elapsed).

Next, suppose we modify the previous study by imaging the test stimulus on a retinal region that contains both rods and cones. Measuring recovery from the same adaptation stimulus as before, the outcome will resemble the curve shown in the right-hand panel of Figure 3.31.

Compare the curve in this panel to the others, noting the kink in this new curve. For the first 8 minutes or so of dark adaptation, things seem to go along smoothly, with the recovery of sensitivity seeming to have leveled off. Then all of a sudden, around the 8-minute mark, recovery starts up again, eventually subsiding once more at about the 15-minute mark. What is going on here? Notice that the left-hand part of the kinked curve bears a striking resemblance to the early part of the photopic dark adaptation curve (the left panel in Figure 3.31), whereas the rest of the kinked curve resembles the late part of the scotopic curve (the middle panel in Figure 3.31). The explanation of the kinked curve, then, is simple. Because in this third case the test stimulus affects both cones and rods, we have measured both types of adaptation simultaneously. Early in dark adaptation, the photopic system

is more sensitive, so it alone determines the threshold. Later in dark adaptation, the scotopic system is more sensitive, so it alone determines the threshold.

The exact outcome of these studies depends on a number of experimental details, notably the strength of the initial adaptation stimulus, the size of the test stimulus, and the wavelength of light used in the test stimulus. All these variables as well as many others (including an individual's diet, as Box 3.7 indicates) change the curve of dark adaptation in ways that are predictable from understanding the retina's duplex nature.

You don't need special equipment to verify some of these observations. Pick a clear night, and just before going outside, stand for a few moments in a brightly lit room. Then quickly go outside and look at the sky. At this point you probably won't be able to see any stars. Keep looking, though, and after a while some will become visible. The first ones you'll be able to see will probably be right around the location you're fixating on because early in dark adaptation the photopic system is more sensitive than the scotopic. After a short time, your scotopic system will catch up and then exceed the photopic system's sensitivity. At that point you'll be able to see very dim stars using the rod-dominated periphery of your retina.

After you've adapted to the dark for a few minutes, you can verify that the rod-dominated periphery of your retina is more sensitive than the cone-dominated central region. Glance slowly around the sky, stopping when you can just barely see some very dim star that lies away from the spot you're looking directly at. If the star is just barely visible using the most sensitive part of your retina (where rods are most numerous and convergence is greatest), that star will become invisible when you look directly at it (imaging it on a less sensitive part of the retina).

When people compare the human eye to a camera, they liken the retina to the camera's film. But in one sense, the retina is more like videotape than film—both the retina and videotapes are reusable. Even this analogy is inadequate, though, because unlike videotape, the retina can be used and reused millions of times. Wilhelm Kühne, a German physiologist and one of the first to study the retina's recovery, commented that,

> bound together with the pigment epithelium, the retina behaves not merely like a photographic plate, but like an entire photographic workshop in which the workman continually renews the plate by laying on new light-sensitive material, while simultaneously erasing the old image. (Translation by Wald, 1950, p. 33)

How does the retina renew itself, recovering sensitivity after being exposed to light? When a photopigment molecule breaks up, it is said to have become "bleached," an apt term. When Franz Boll first studied this process, he noticed that the retina of the frog was usually intensely red. But when the frog's eye was exposed to light, the color of the retina disappeared; that is, it was bleached. Now we know that this loss of color is associated with the splitting apart of the retina's photopigment molecules.

In the 1880s, Kühne was struck by the analogy between the retina and the photographic plate, then still a novelty. Kühne exploited this resemblance scientifically, using retinas to make "retinal photographs" or, as he called them, "optograms." An optogram treats the retina as though it were a photographic plate or piece of film, actually developing and fixing the image on the retina using special chemicals (Kühne, 1879/1977). Kühne used this approach to examine the image that various objects cast on the retina.

To make one particularly imaginative but gruesome optogram, Kühne got the cooperation of a man sentenced to die on the guillotine. The man's eyes were shielded from light for several hours before the execution, allowing light-sensitive material to accumulate in the retina. Then, just before the beheading, his eyes were uncovered. Immediately after the execution, Kühne removed the eyes and chemically treated the retinas to preserve the image of the last thing the man had seen (Wald, 1950). Unfortu-nately, the optogram was ambiguous, perhaps because instead of staring fixedly at just one object, the condemned man understandably moved his eyes around, taking his "last look" at one thing after another.

How does the retina manage to process millions of images over a lifetime? The secret lies in the retina's ability to restore its own sensitivity to light through a complex biochemical process (Stabell, Stabell, and Fugelli, 1992). Remember Boll's observation on bleaching in the frog's eye? He also noticed that the retina regained its normal, reddish color if the frog stayed in the dark for a short time (Boll, 1877/1977). We know now that the reddish color returns because new photopigment molecules have been created. This restoration is just as important for the visual process as the bleaching. If photopigment could not be restored, an animal would quickly become blind because when all the available photopigment molecules became bleached, they would be unable to signal the presence of light.

To produce new photopigment after light has bleached part of the retina requires that a derivative of vitamin A diffuse through the retinal pigment ephithelium and combine with protein available within the retina. Since all the body's vitamin A comes from the food one eats, a serious deficiency of vitamin A in the diet slows down the restoration of photopigments. In vitamin A deficiency, once a photopigment molecule is bleached, its return to the unbleached state is slowed. A person with a vitamin A deficiency is described as "night blind" because he or she typically experiences difficulty seeing at night or in other dim light (Dowling, 1966). Such people might have extreme difficulty seeing after entering a darkened theater, be unable to recognize friends on the street in a dim light, or be unable to see clearly while driving at night.

Vitamin A deficiency is common in developing countries, where diet is often inadequate and vitamin supplements rare. Even people in developed countries are not immune to poor diet and night vision problems. For example, many years ago, one-third of a test sample of medical students showed diminished night vision that was attributable to their diet (Jeghers, 1937). These medical students were simply too busy to eat proper quantities of carrots and leafy vegetables.

S U M M A R Y   A N D   P R E V I E W

This chapter outlined how various aspects of visual perception are shaped by the properties of the retina, notably the center/surround antagonism of retinal ganglion cells and the differences between the photoreceptors that feed the ganglion cells. Clearly, though, not all vision is determined by the retina. We encountered several visual phenomena that defy explanation at the retinal level, and there are lots more where those came from. To broaden our understanding of vision, we have to push farther into the nervous system, following the messages generated by the retina, back into the brain itself. There you'll see that these messages originating in the retina are further refined and reorganized in ways that account for still other properties of the way you see the world.

K E Y   T E R M S

Abney's law
action potentials
amacrine cell
axon
bipolar cell
Bloch's law
brightness
circadian rhythms
crowding effect
dark adaptation
DoG curve
duplex
eccentricity

Hermann grid
horizontal cell
K cells
lateral inhibition
lightness
lightness constancy
lightness contrast
M cells
Mach bands
mesopic
microelectrode
P cells

photon
photopic
Purkinje shift
receptive field
resolution
retinal ganglion cells
Ricco's law
scotopic
single cell recording
spatial summation
temporal summation
visual acuity

The Brain and Seeing

In this chapter we'll forge ahead into the brain as we continue our examination of vision's neural machinery. By way of preview, you'll see that visual areas of the brain work out the details of the form, color, and locations of objects within your field of view. The eye, which you learned about in Chapters 2 and 3, provides the raw material for vision, but it's the brain that digests that raw material and derives meaning from it. This chapter gives an overview of the neural machinery by which this process of "digestion" occurs. But before moving to that overview, let's take a moment to consider some of the visual products of that neural machinery. Take a look at the series of drawings in Figure 4.1. Each reveals an essential characteristic of visual perception. Because these characteristics operate in the background of our visual awareness, they ordinarily escape our attention. Here's a chance to see what is normally hidden.

As you look at panel A in Figure 4.1, what do you see? Most people readily perceive a white square resting on four black disks. But if you take away the disks you discover that the white square disappears, too. This square is a figment of the visual processing machinery in your brain—the visual portions of your brain have fabricated the square from the bits and pieces of contour information contained in the drawing. This so-called illusory figure underscores the constructive nature of visual perception: The brain goes beyond the optical information provided by the eye and generates plausible interpretations of the visual layout that gave rise to that optical information. That's the first characteristic to keep in mind: perception is constructive.

Next look at panel B of Figure 4.1. The serpentine, segmented curves at the top of each panel have been duplicated and embedded in the tangle of random lines below them (the left-hand snake within the tangle at the left, and the right-hand snake within the tangle at the right). Take a moment to search for each hidden snake. Although both embedded curves are exactly the same length and composed of the same number of segments, the one on the right is quite conspicuous, but the one on the left is hard to see. Why? Adjacent segments making up the conspicuous snake differ in orientation by only 30 degrees from one another, while those comprising the inconspicuous snake differ by 60 degrees. The similarly oriented segments are more strongly unified and, hence, form a more salient figure. Evidently, the brain does not concentrate on individual features in isolation but, instead, exploits relationships among features as contextual clues about how those features ought to be knitted together. That's the second characteristic to remember: perception is context dependent.

FIGURE 4.1 | Vision depends on more than the patterns of light striking the eye, as these four figures illustrate. See text for instructions.

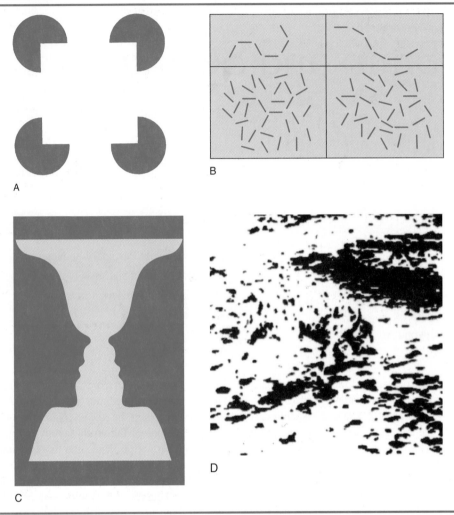

Now look at the drawing in panel C of Figure 4.1. Here you'll probably have trouble deciding what you're looking at because the figure's appearance keeps changing. At one moment the figure appears to be a white vase against a dark background but then, without warning, it turns into a pair of dark faces looking at each other against a white background. This so-called ambiguous figure illustrates that the same optical information can generate multiple perceptual interpretations. So, perception involves interpretation, the third characteristic, and when more than one interpretation is plausible, perception fluctuates over time between the alternatives.

Finally, look at the seemingly random collection of black splotches in panel D of Figure 4.1. While initially indecipherable, the splotches will eventually become or-ganized into a meaningful scene. Take a moment to study the figure before reading on. Can you tell what the scene depicts? Don't be discouraged if the answer escapes you—a more recognizable version of this figure is provided at the end of this chapter. To make sense of this picture, your visual system must synthesize contour and texture information gathered from a large portion of the picture, and it must figure out which pieces of the image go together. This illustrates a fourth characteristic of vision: There is a strong tendency to group bits and pieces of information into meaningful forms, even when those forms are suggested only vaguely by the bits and pieces.

These illustrations all converge on the same general principle: Visual perception depends on more than just the pattern of light striking the retina. Vision, rather than being

FIGURE 4.2 I Drawing of the left hemisphere of the brain, showing the locations of the visual cortex within the occipital lobe and the lateral geniculate nucleus and superior colliculus, both of which are situated within the interior brain and not on its surface (which is why their locations are shown with dotted lines). At the very back of the occipital lobe is the primary visual cortex (also referred to as visual area V1). Additional visual areas are situated in front of (anterior to) V1. Color plate 2 shows another view of the visual cortex, viewed from the interior surface of the right hemisphere.

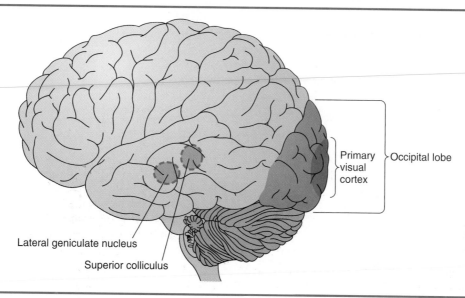

a mindless process of measuring how much light enters the eye, is an intelligent activity of a finely tuned brain. To paraphrase Donald Hoffman (1998), we are all visual virtuosos, but unaware of our talent for constructing what we see. Some of those "talents" are embodied in the neural elements within the eye itself, as you learned in the two previous chapters. But the eyes are just launching stages for our marvelous visual talents. In this chapter we continue tracing the flow of information within the visual nervous system, and we'll concentrate on the areas of the brain collectively known as the visual cortex (see Figure 4.2). You'll learn how visual information about objects and events in the world is carried to the brain and distributed to different sets of neurons in the visual cortex. You'll also see how patterns of activity within these brain cells can be related to various aspects of visual perception.

Let's begin by examining the **optic nerve,** the bundle of fibers carrying information from the eyes to various processing areas in the brain.

The Optic Nerve

Each eye's optic nerve comprises the axons from its whole collection of retinal ganglion cells. Thus, the optic nerve from each eye resembles a cable that contains approximately 1.25 million individual wires. Multiplied by two eyes, this means that the brain receives visual input from 2.5 million separate channels, with each channel carrying information about a small region of the visual world. That may seem like a huge number of communication lines, but it is really quite modest compared to the hundreds of millions of neurons populating the visual areas of the brain. Keep in mind that all neural processing of visual information within the brain depends on the optic nerves for input data. The optic nerves provide the brain with visual perception's raw material. Any neurological condition that interrupts the flow of that information to the brain, such as a tumor impinging on the optic nerve, can destroy vision.

Within the eye itself, the axons of ganglion cells are not covered by **myelin.** As you may know, myelin is a membrane that both insulates the axon from activity in neighboring axons and speeds the conduction of nerve impulses. Presumably, axons within the eye remain unmyelinated in order to reduce the clutter through which light must pass to reach the receptors (a coating of myelin could double the diameter of an axon). Once outside the eye, though, this restriction is removed, and individual axons acquire a coating of myelin.

FIGURE 4.3 | The projections of the optic fibers from the two eyes to the two hemispheres of the brain. The fibers represented by the solid black lines originate from the nasal retina of both eyes; they cross at the optic chiasm to the opposite hemisphere and are called contralateral fibers. The fibers represented by the hatch marks originate from the temporal retina of both eyes; they remain on the same side of the brain and are called ipsilateral fibers.

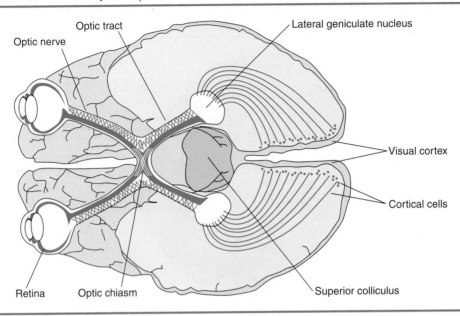

Within each optic nerve, fibers from different regions of the retina congregate in an orderly fashion, with fibers carrying information from neighboring regions of the retina running adjacent to one another within the nerve (Torrealba et al., 1982). From the point it leaves the eye, the optic nerve travels approximately 5 centimeters (2 inches) before rendezvousing with the optic nerve from the other eye.

The optic nerves from the two eyes converge at the **optic chiasm.** The term chiasm comes from the Greek word meaning "cross," and a glance at Figure 4.3 shows why this term is appropriate. At the chiasm, there is a wholesale rearrangement of the constituent fibers. Using Figure 4.3, carefully trace the fibers from different regions of either eye as those fibers enter and leave the optic chiasm. Notice that some fibers always remain on the same side of the brain—these are called uncrossed or **ipsilateral fibers** ("ipsi" means "same"; "lateral" refers to side). Regardless of which eye they come from, these ipsilateral fibers originate from that eye's temporal retina ("temporal" refers to that half of the retina nearest the temples). Other fibers cross to the opposite side of the brain at the optic chiasm. These are the crossed or **contralateral fibers,** and they come from the nasal retina of each eye ("contra" means "opposite"; "nasal" refers to the half of

the retina closest to the nose). Thus, the optic nerve from each eye branches into two segments—one crossed, the other uncrossed. Within the chiasm, crossed fibers from one eye join with uncrossed fibers from the other eye, producing two new combinations of retinal axons. These new combinations, which run from the chiasm to structures deeper in the brain, are known as **optic tracts.** Don't be fooled by the terminology: An optic tract is still composed of axons from ganglion cells; the change in name from "nerve" to "tract" is simply a convention used by anatomists. The important thing to understand is that each optic tract contains fibers from both eyes, from the temporal retina of one eye and from the nasal retina of the other.

The proportion of crossed and uncrossed fibers in the optic tract varies among species, according to the position of the animal's eyes within its head. In animals with laterally placed eyes, such as the deer or the rabbit, nearly all of the axons cross to the opposite side of the brain. In humans, about 50 percent of the axons from each eye cross at the chiasm, while the other 50 percent remain uncrossed. This division between crossed and uncrossed occurs along an imaginary vertical seam bisecting the fovea.

But why should eye position in the head be related to the percentage of crossing fibers? To figure out the answer, think about the relation between the position of an object

FIGURE 4.4 | Objects to the right of the point of fixation cast images on the nasal retina of the right eye and the temporal retina of the left eye. Fibers from these two retinal areas project to the left side of the brain (left drawing). Objects to the left of the point of fixation cast images on the nasal retina of the left eye and the temporal retina of the right eye. Fibers from these two retinal areas project to the right side of the brain (right drawing).

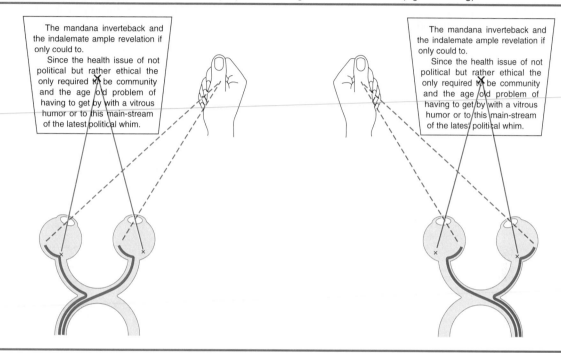

The mandana inverteback and the indalemate ample revelation if only could to.

Since the health issue of not political but rather ethical the only required to be community and the age old problem of having to get by with a vitrous humor or to this main-stream of the latest political whim.

in space and the position of that object's image on the retina. The following exercise will help (see Figure 4.4). While looking at the center of this page, place your thumb on the right-hand edge of the page. The image of your thumb will now fall on the temporal retina of your left eye and nasal retina of your right eye. Looking at Figures 4.3 and 4.4, you will see that fibers from these regions of the two retinas wind up together in the optic tract on the left side of the brain. Keeping your gaze on the center of the page, place your thumb on the page's left-hand edge. Now your thumb is imaged on the nasal retina of your left eye and the temporal retina of your right eye. Figures 4.3 and 4.4 show that both these regions send their fibers to the right side of the brain.

As this exercise demonstrates, there is a general rule to describe how inputs from the two halves of the visual field are distributed to the occipital lobes in the two hemispheres of the brain: The right hemisphere receives information from the left visual field, while the left hemisphere receives information from the right visual field. Those portions of the left and right eyes that look at the *same* area of visual space send their nerve fibers to the *same* region of the brain. The partial crossing of ax-

ons at the chiasm makes this possible. Rerouting the axons sets the stage for combining information from the two eyes, a process we'll learn more about shortly.

In animals with eyes on the side of their heads, the two eyes look at *different* areas of visual space. For these animals, it would be extremely maladaptive to mix information from the two eyes because such information specifies different objects located in different regions of the visual field. Mixing information from the two eyes could lead to serious confusion about the location of those objects. To avoid this potential for confusion, the optic fibers from the two eyes remain strictly segregated, crossing in their entirety at the optic chiasm. This serves to route information from the two laterally placed eyes to different halves of the brain.

With these facts in our grasp, we can resume tracing the destination of the fibers of the optic tract. Remember we're still talking about the axons of the ganglion cells located back in the retina. About 80 percent of the fibers project to a cluster of cell bodies known as the **lateral geniculate nucleus.** The remaining 20 percent of optic tract fibers project to several neighboring structures in the midbrain, the most prominent being the **superior**

colliculus (Figure 4.3 shows the relative locations of these structures within the interior of the brain). Since the superior colliculus and the lateral geniculate nucleus are both regions of the brain to which retinal axons project, these places are referred to as *projection sites.*

To make it easier to follow the flow of visual information from the optic tract, we'll discuss the two major branches of the optic tract separately. We'll first briefly describe the branch to the superior colliculus and then cover in more detail the other branch, to the lateral geniculate nucleus and its projection site, the visual cortex. But don't let our separate treatment of these areas of the brain mislead you. These visual centers are richly interconnected, and their functions can be carried out only when all the components work in harmony. Moreover, there are several other midbrain structures—thought to be involved in control of pupil size, registration of self-motion, and postural adjustments—omitted from our discussion.

The Superior Colliculus

Tucked away at the top of the brain stem, the superior colliculus is a phylogenetically older, more primitive visual area than the visual cortex. In many lower animals, such as frogs and fish, the superior colliculus represents *the* major brain center for visual processing. In humans and other mammals, however, the phylogenetically newer visual cortex has supplanted the superior colliculus as the dominant visual area. Nonetheless, even in these higher animals, the superior colliculus plays a prominent role in orienting an organism toward novel, potentially important stimuli. Several lines of evidence point to this conclusion.

For one thing, cells in the superior colliculus have receptive fields with rather poorly defined ON and OFF regions. These cells will respond to just about any visual stimulus—edges, bars of any orientation, light flashes—suddenly appearing within their receptive fields, regardless of the shape or orientation of that stimulus (Goldberg and Wurtz, 1972). These properties suggest that the colliculus is not concerned with precisely *what* the stimulus is but rather with *where* it is.

For another thing, cells in the superior colliculus clearly are involved in controlling eye movements (Schall 1991; Horwitz and Newsome, 1999). Many cells in the superior colliculus emit a vigorous burst of activity just before the eyes begin to move. This burst of activity occurs, however, only if the eyes move in order to fixate on a light flashed in the visual periphery. Eye movements made in darkness evoke no activity in these cells. So the *intention* to move the eyes toward some ob-

ject seems to be critical for the cells' responsiveness. Besides initiating eye movements, the superior colliculus also plays some role in guiding the direction and extent of those eye movements (Carpenter, 1992). Thus, damage to the superior colliculus impairs the accuracy of visually guided eye movements in monkeys (Gandhi and Sparks, 2004) and in humans (Heywood and Ratcliff, 1975). However, the superior colliculus is just one of several brain areas playing a role in the guidance of eye movements; other prominent areas include the visual cortex (Seagraves et al., 1987) and the frontal eye-field situated in the frontal lobe (see Schall, 1991, for an excellent review of this literature on neural control of eye movements). Eye movements themselves will be discussed in more detail in Chapter 8.

Besides receiving visual input, cells in the superior colliculus also receive auditory input from the ears, as evidenced by their responsiveness to sound stimulation (Gordon, 1972). Because they receive sensory input from the eyes *and* ears, these are called *multisensory cells.* For these multisensory cells to respond, the auditory and visual stimulation must originate from the same region of space. For example, if a particular multisensory cell responds to a spot of light appearing in the upper right portion of the visual field, that cell will respond to a sound only if it, too, comes from the same vicinity. Additionally, when visual and auditory inputs occur simultaneously, a multisensory cell responds more strongly than when either input occurs alone. Because of this property, a weak auditory input can amplify the effects of a weak visual input, producing a strong combined response. As a result, sight and sound can reinforce one another in these multisensory cells, enabling an animal to detect the location of feeble environmental events (Stein, Wallace and Meredith, 1995; Stein, Jiang, and Stanford, 2004).

In summary, the superior colliculus seems designed to detect objects located away from the point of fixation and to guide orienting movements of the eyes and head toward those objects (Sparks, 1988). The colliculus does not, however, contain the machinery necessary for a detailed visual analysis of such objects. That job, instead, belongs to the other branch of the optic tract, the one projecting to the lateral geniculate nucleus and then on to the visual cortex. It is to those sites that we turn next.

The Lateral Geniculate Nucleus

In this section we will first consider the interesting structure of the lateral geniculate nucleus (LGN), and the way in which retinal input is distributed throughout that structure. Then we'll describe the receptive field properties of geniculate neurons and speculate about the role of these neurons in vision. The top part of Figure 4.5 indicates where within the brain the LGN is located.

Structure of the LGN

The LGN is one portion of the thalamus, which is a sub-cortical structure that receives sensory information from the eyes (vision), the ears (hearing), the tongue (taste), and the skin (touch); the visual portions of the thalamus are located laterally within this structure (thus the term *lateral*). This portion of the thalamus has a very distinct, layered appearance, as you can see in the middle panel (b) of Figure 4.5. These layers have a bend to them, like the bent posture of a knee (thus the term *geniculate*, which means "with bent knee," as in "genuflect"). The layers of the LGN consist of cell bodies, and the number of layers in the LGN varies from one species to another. In humans, the LGN on each side of the brain contains six layers stacked on top of one another, with the bend in the middle. For purposes of discussion, let's number the successive layers 1, 2, 3, 4, 5, and 6, going from the bottom to the top of the structure. Cells in layers 1 and 2 are larger than those in layers 3 through 6. These two large-cell layers are termed the **magnocellular layers,** and the four small-cell layers are called the **parvocellular layers** (the prefixes of these two terms come from the Latin words *magnus,* meaning "large," and *parvus,* meaning "small"). You will recall the P and M retinal ganglion cells from the previous chapter. The P ganglion cells provide the input to the parvocellular layers of the LGN while the M cells feed into the magnocellular layers of the LGN. Recall also that the P and M cells differed in the kinds of visual stimuli to which they respond best; those response differences are maintained at the level of the LGN, as we will discuss in a moment. Also shown in this diagram are the K cells mentioned in Chapter 3. In the

LGN, these very small K cells are sandwiched between the successive layers of M and P cells.

Let's take a closer look at the LGN, beginning with the pattern of connections between fibers of the optic tract and cells in the different layers of the lateral geniculate

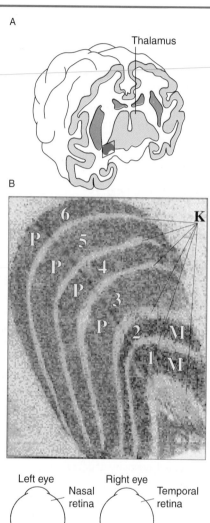

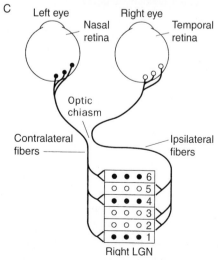

FIGURE 4.5 | Lateral geniculate nucleus (LGN). (A). Drawing of a cross section of the brain showing the location of the thalamus and, within the thalamus, the LGN (indicated by the outline box). (B). Magnified picture of a cross section through the LGN showing its distinct layers; the numbers and letters denote the different layers, described in the text (David Calkins.) (C). Diagram showing projections from both eyes to the right LGN; a corresponding diagram could be drawn for the projections to the left LGN. Numbers correspond to the numbers shown in the photograph, and the filled and open circles correspond to ipsilateral and contralateral layers, respectively.

nucleus. Remember that each optic tract contains a mixture of fibers from both eyes, the temporal retina of the ipsilateral eye and the nasal retina of the contralateral eye. These fibers become very strictly segregated when they arrive at the lateral geniculate nucleus: the contralateral fibers contact only the cells in layers 1, 4, and 6, whereas the ipsilateral fibers contact only the cells in layers 2, 3, and 5. Take a moment to study Figure 4.5 to be sure you understand this pattern of input to the various layers. In sorting out these projections, keep in mind that the brain contains a pair of lateral geniculate nuclei, one located in the left hemisphere and the other in the right hemisphere. This paired arrangement means that a single eye provides contralateral input to one lateral geniculate nucleus and ipsilateral input to the other. Now let's look at how retinal input is registered within these layers.

Retinal Maps in the LGN

Each layer of the LGN contains an orderly representation, or map, of the retina. This point is illustrated in Figure 4.6. As you can see, axons that carry information from neighboring regions of the retina connect with geniculate cells that are themselves neighbors. This way of distributing retinal information within any layer of the LGN creates a map of the retina within that layer. Since such a map preserves the topography of the retina, it is known as a **retinotopic map.** Each of the six layers contains its own complete retinotopic map, and these layers are stacked in such a way that comparable regions of the separate maps are aligned with each other. For instance, the foveal parts of adjacent layers are situated on top of one another.

Receptive Field Properties of P and M LGN Cells

Like their retinal counterparts, LGN cells have approximately circular receptive fields, subdivided into concentric center and surround components. As in the retina, these two components interact antagonistically. Some cells have ON centers paired with OFF surrounds, whereas others have exactly the opposite configuration. There is an important difference, though, between the LGN and retina: The surround of an LGN receptive field exerts a stronger inhibitory effect on its center than does the surround of a retinal ganglion cell (Maffei and Fiorentini, 1973). This means the LGN cells amplify, or accentuate, differences in illumination between neighboring retinal regions even more than do retinal ganglion cells. Incidentally, because their fields are circular in shape, LGN cells, like their retinal counterparts, will respond to borders or contours of any orientation.

This center/surround layout of LGN receptive fields is characteristic of essentially all LGN cells, regardless of whether they are located in a parvocellular layer or a

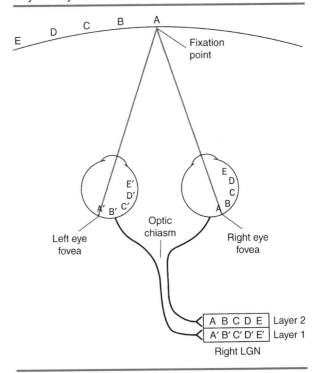

FIGURE 4.6 | Drawing showing how different areas of the visual field are mapped onto the two retinas and then onto various layers of the right LGN. For simplicity, only two layers are shown.

magnocellular layer. There are, however, major differences between cells in the magnocellular layers and cells in the parvocellular layers (Livingstone and Hubel, 1988; Schiller and Logothetis, 1990), differences that relate to the P versus M ganglion cell inputs to these layers. Most importantly, these differences strongly imply that the two subdivisions—magnocellular and parvocellular—make unique contributions to visual perception.

Color Nearly all parvocellular cells (that is, the cells in layers 3 through 6) are differentially sensitive to the *color* of light imaged within their receptive fields (De-Valois et al., 1958; Wiesel and Hubel, 1966; Dreher, Fukada, and Rodieck, 1976). A vigorous response can be evoked from these cells only if the center of the field is illuminated by one particular color (for example, red). When the center is illuminated by a different color (for example, green), the cell's activity is inhibited. When the surround is illuminated by the same color as the center (for example, red), the cell's response is reduced. But when the surround is illuminated with a different color (for example, green), the cell's response is augmented. Because of their unique response to the pairing of "opposite" colors, these cells are called *color opponent cells.* Some opponent cells exhibit red/green organization, while others exhibit blue/yellow organization. We'll consider these opponent cells in greater detail in Chapter 7. Just to reiterate, the color opponent cells in the parvocellular layers are thought to receive their inputs from the P cells in the retina.

Cells in the magnocellular layers (and a small fraction of cells in the parvocellular layers) respond to all colors. Their response depends solely on the relative intensity of light falling in the center and surround portions of their receptive fields. To reiterate, cells in the magnocellular layers are thought to receive their inputs from the M cells in the retina.

Acuity Within each of the six layers of the LGN, receptive fields vary systematically in size. The smallest fields are devoted to representation of the fovea (mirroring the size/eccentricity relationship seen in retinal ganglion cell receptive fields). For a given region of the retina, cells in the magnocellular layers have receptive fields that are two or three times larger than receptive fields for cells in the parvocellular layers (again, mirroring the M and P cell differences seen in the retina). Hence, parvocellular cells analyze spatial information at a finer level of detail than do magnocellular cells.

Temporal Variation Magnocellular cells respond vigorously to rapid, abrupt fluctuations of light intensity within their receptive fields, whereas parvocellular cells respond sluggishly, if at all, to such fluctuations. Abrupt changes in light intensity are produced by rapid motion of objects within the visual field, so it is most likely magnocellular cells, not parvocellular cells, that are able to signal the presence of rapid movement.

But what about the K cells occupying the interlayer regions of the LGN? It's not so easy to speculate about what they contribute to vision, for relatively few studies have measured their receptive field properties. K cells in the LGN do have relatively large receptive fields compared to M and P cells, and some K cells respond to sound as well as to visual stimulation. One clue to their possible role in vision is provided by the regions of the cortex to which they project. (We'll discuss K cell projections shortly.)

These three distinct populations of LGN neurons—M, P, and K cells—all send their axons to the visual cortex. As we will discover shortly, however, those axons terminate in different parts of the visual cortex, thus maintaining the functional segregation of information found within these different layer types. Before moving up to the cortex, though, let's spend a moment speculating about the importance of the LGN for vision.

Possible Functions of the LGN

You now have a thumbnail sketch of the chief characteristics of the LGN, the relay station between the retina and higher visual areas in the brain. What do the various anatomical and physiological properties we've discussed suggest about the LGN's role in vision? As just described, cells in the LGN are primarily concerned with differences in intensity of light between neighboring regions of the retina, and in some instances with the wavelength composition of that light. These cells are unconcerned with the overall level of light. In other words, LGN cells are designed to register the presence of edges in the visual environment. This alone, however, does not represent a unique contribution to vision. Retinal cells have already accomplished the job of signaling the presence of edges. So we are led to ask: Does the LGN seem uniquely suited for some other role? Or does it merely relay messages broadcast from the retina straight to higher brain sites, with no editing or censorship? There are good reasons for thinking the LGN is considerably more than just a relay station.

For one thing, the LGN receives input not only from the retina, but from the **reticular activating system** as well. Buried in the brain stem, the reticular activating system governs an animal's general level of arousal. Hence, the flow of visual information from the LGN to higher visual centers could be modified by the animal's state of arousal. The LGN may operate like the volume control on a radio, modulating the intensity of retinal inputs according to the animal's current state of arousal. In support of this idea, Livingstone and Hubel (1981) found that when an animal was in a drowsy state (as evidenced behaviorally and by brain-wave recordings), the overall level of activity in the LGN was low. The reduced level of LGN activity meant that the higher visual centers of the drowsy animal were receiving signals that were attenuated compared to those they would have received had the animal been more alert. This interplay between arousal level and the strength of signals going to the higher visual centers could promote attentiveness to visual information.

For another thing, a subset of cells in the LGN—the K cells—may also play a modulatory role in visual processing (Hendry and Reid, 2000), serving to boost or to diminish signals carried by P and M cells. K cells receive strong inputs from the superior colliculus which, as pointed out earlier in this chapter, is the subcortical structure thought to be involved in the generation and control of eye movements. Vivien Casagrande (1994), a neuroanatomist who has argued for the importance of this overlooked category of cells, believes that K cells may serve to shut down vision temporarily whenever gaze is shifted rapidly from one part of the visual scene to another. According to her scheme, at the time the superior colliculus begins generating signals to move the eyes it also activates K cells in the LGN. They, in turn, briefly turn down the activity of cortical cells to which they project, thereby muting the neural consequences of the abrupt shift in the retinal image accompanying a rapid eye movement.

In addition to input from the reticular activating system and the superior colliculus, the LGN also receives a large input from the visual cortex. You may find this intriguing, since the visual cortex itself *receives* a substantial amount of its input from the LGN. In effect, the LGN formulates a message and transmits it to the cortex. The cortex, in turn, sends back a reply to the LGN, thereby allowing that message to be altered. This kind of arrangement is known as a *feedback loop,* and it is widely used in electronics to regulate electrical current within a circuit. At present, the biological purpose of the visual feedback between the cortex and the LGN is not known, although intriguing speculations have been advanced (Martin, 1988; Sherman and Guillery, 2002).

The highly organized arrangement of this structure and the distinct physiological differences between magnocellular and parvocellular layers strongly suggest that the LGN plays another crucial role in vision. Recall that information about color is processed exclusively in the parvocellular layers, while information about large, rapidly moving intensity contours falls within the domain of the magnocellular layers. This orderly sorting of visual information sets the stage for the next level of processing occurring in the visual cortex. An analogy may help clarify what we mean.

Think for a moment about the most efficient way to assemble a complex jigsaw puzzle. You usually begin by sorting the jumble of pieces into groups, according to some shared property. You might locate and place all the pieces that make up the border into one pile, the pieces of comparable color into another pile, and so on. In general, before assembling the puzzle pieces into a picture, you will organize them so that the solution emerges with minimal trial-and-error effort. The lateral geniculate nucleus may perform an analogous sorting operation, segregating as it does the P and the M cells as well as the left-eye and the right-eye retinotopic maps. There is even some evidence that the LGN may segregate retinal ON cells and OFF cells into separate P layers (e.g., Schiller and Colby, 1983). The orderly arrangement of information within the LGN could help the next stage of visual processing begin piecing the puzzle together. And this next stage of processing takes place in the primary visual cortex, our next destination.

The Visual Cortex

The visual cortex is located at the back of the cerebral hemispheres (see Figure 4.2), the bulk being within that portion of the brain called the **occipital lobe.** If you place your cupped hand on the back of your head just above the base of your skull, your hand will be resting over the occipital region. Actually, the occipital lobe consists of a cluster of neighboring brain regions each devoted to neural analyses of some aspects of the visual scene. Together, these areas comprise the bulk of the visual cortex. One portion of the visual cortex—the primary visual cortex—receives input from the LGN (and sends signals back to the LGN), and it is anatomically more complex than the LGN. This anatomical complexity is paralleled by an increase in physiological complexity, particularly in the variety of receptive fields exhibited by cortical cells. But before tackling the anatomical and physiological details of this fascinating region of the brain, let's consider some important findings from clinical neurology, for it was these findings that first pointed to the primary visual cortex as a major visual center.

Cortical Blindness

By the middle of the last century, neurologists had developed a keen interest in how the brain was subdivided. To examine its subdivisions, they removed localized regions of tissue from animals' brains and noted the behavioral consequences (this is the lesion technique described in Chapter 1). Using this technique, neurologists observed that an animal seemed to be blind after destruction of the posterior area of its cerebral hemispheres.

At about the same time, case records began appearing in the medical literature describing permanent loss of vision in humans who had suffered brain damage in this area (Glickstein, 1988). This evidence also pointed to the occipital lobe as the visual center in humans. The most thorough set of case studies was published by the Irish neurologist Gordon Holmes. Most of his patients were veterans of World War I with localized brain damage from gunshot wounds. Holmes (1918) measured areas of blindness within the visual field of each patient by moving a small spot of light throughout the field of view while the patient stared at a stationary point. The patient reported when the light was visible and when it was not. Holmes was thus able to locate patches of blindness, or **scotomas,** within the patient's visual field. (Recall from Chapter 2 the simple demonstration of the small scotoma in *your* visual field, associated with the optic disk; also, see Box 4.1.) Holmes compared the size and location of

Damage to different parts of the visual system produces predictable losses of vision within regions of the **visual field.** A visual field is easy to envision: While staring at some point straight ahead of you, your visual field is the entire region of space that is visible to you. Your attention is naturally focused on the center of the visual field, but you are aware of events occurring on the periphery as well.

Physicians and vision researchers use a routine procedure to measure a visual field; it is called **perimetry** (from the roots *peri,* meaning "around," and *metron,* meaning "measure"). While an individual has one eye covered and the open eye staring at a fixed point, a small, dim exploring spot is moved around slowly in front of that person's open eye, and the individual reports when the spot disappears. The positions where the spot disappears are traced out on a map of visual space. The map

shows areas of sight (unshaded regions) and areas of blindness (shaded regions). Keep in mind that a visual field map describes visual space, not the retina. (To draw the map based on retinal geography requires inverting and reversing the map of visual space.)

A normal visual field map for each eye looks like the pair numbered 1 in the accompanying figure (for simplicity, the blind spot has been omitted). Note that the nose obscures the right portion of the left eye's view and the left portions of the right eye's view. Now suppose that because of some accident the left optic nerve was completely severed. This would totally eliminate the left eye's field, leaving the right eye's field intact. This situation is shown by the pair of maps numbered 2.

Let's consider a more complicated visual field loss. In humans, the pituitary gland lies immediately behind the

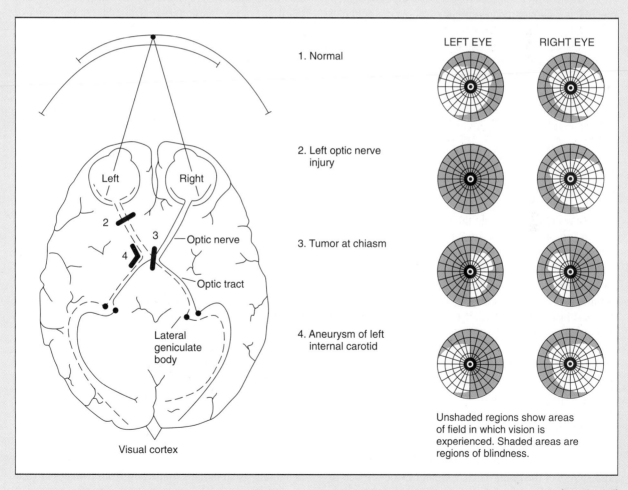

Left

Right

2

3

4

Optic nerve

Optic tract

Lateral geniculate body

Visual cortex

LEFT EYE RIGHT EYE

1. Normal

2. Left optic nerve injury

3. Tumor at chiasm

4. Aneurysm of left internal carotid

Unshaded regions show areas of field in which vision is experienced. Shaded areas are regions of blindness.

(continued)

BOX 4.1   **Look Both Ways Before Crossing** *(continued)*

middle of the optic chiasm. A tumor in the pituitary gland can press this structure against the chiasm, damaging the fibers that cross through the chiasm. These fibers, you will recall from Figures 4.3 and 4.4, originate from the nasal portion of each retina. The resulting visual field loss will resemble that shown in the pair of maps numbered 3. The lost regions of visual space are those that are normally represented within the fibers originating from the nasal retinas.

Consider a case that is virtually the opposite of the one just described. The internal carotid arteries, branches of the prominent arteries in the neck, pass very near to the sides of the chiasm. These arteries can develop an **aneurysm,** a balloonlike bulge of the arterial wall. This bulge can push against the fibers that form the outer margin of the chiasm (recall that these are *un*crossed fibers). Thus, for example, an aneurysm of the left internal carotid artery would affect uncrossed fibers coming from the left eye; that is, fibers carrying information about the right half of the left eye's field. In this case, the visual field map would resemble the fourth pair of maps. See whether you can determine the visual field loss produced when *both* left and right internal carotid arteries have developed aneurysms, a condition that does occur at times.

This close connection between visual field loss and disease makes perimetry a very useful diagnostic tool.

But there's one surprising aspect to visual field loss, even for severe cases such as those noted here: The person exhibiting the loss is often unaware of it! Apparently, by moving the eyes around, a person's residual visual field can provide coverage that is adequate for most situations. But sometimes the coverage proves inadequate, and the outcome may be fatal, as the following study documents.

Freytag and Sachs (1968) examined the records for a specific category of traffic accidents in Baltimore: pedestrians killed under circumstances suggesting that the victims should have seen the vehicle that struck and killed them. Autopsies revealed that the visual systems of some accident victims had been damaged *before* the accident. In these cases, the location and extent of that damage implied a visual field loss that explained the accident. In one case, for instance, a man was struck and killed by a car approaching from his right. Autopsy showed that his right optic nerve was completely atrophied. Consequently, if this man were looking straight ahead, a car approaching from his right would fall within the blind portion of his visual field. Thus, while this man's vision was probably good enough for his activities at home, his unsuspected visual deficit proved lethal when he had to cross the street.

---

the scotoma with the extent and position of the damage within the occipital cortex.

His results showed that the visual field (and, by extension, the retina) is represented within the cortex in a very orderly, topographic fashion. The center of the visual field maps onto the posterior region of the occipital lobe, and the periphery of the field maps onto more anterior portions. The upper portion of the visual field is represented in the lower portion of the occipital lobe, and vice versa, as shown schematically in Figure 4.7. (The drawing in this figure, incidentally, shows the medial bank of the occipital lobe of the left hemisphere, which would only be visible by pulling apart the two hemispheres to expose the interior surface of each. Nature has situated most of the primary visual cortex within a portion of the brain that is ordinarily unexposed.)

Holmes found that visual disturbances always appeared in the visual field contralateral to the damaged hemisphere of the brain. Thus, a wound to the left occipital lobe would be accompanied by blindness somewhere within the right visual field. Holmes also observed that

the cortical map of the visual field appeared greatly distorted. Based on the pattern of distortions, Holmes correctly deduced that the amount of cortical tissue devoted to the central portion of the field far exceeded the amount devoted to the periphery. This distortion, in which representation of the center of the field is highly exaggerated, has come to be known as **cortical magnification.** From a retinal perspective, cortical magnification means that a large portion of the cortex is devoted to a very small area of the retina (Azzopardi and Cowey, 1993). That area of the retina is the *fovea,* on which the central portion of the visual field is imaged (see Figure 4.8). Thus, the lion's share of the cortex is devoted to that region of the retina responsible for highly acute vision.

Holmes's clinical work provided the earliest description of the retinotopic map on the visual cortex. Since these pioneering studies, many other neuroscientists (such as Teuber, Battersby, and Bender, 1960) have cataloged the visual deficits that result from damage to various brain centers. We will describe some of these unusual and informative syndromes later in this and other chap-

FIGURE 4.7 | This drawing shows how upper and lower portions of the visual field are mapped onto the primary visual cortex located in the rear-most portion of the occipital lobe. Central vision, including the fovea, is represented on the most posterior (rearward) portion of the occipital lobe, and more peripheral portions of the visual field, corresponding to locations to one side of the fovea, are represented on more anterior (forward) portions of the occipital lobe. The upper portions of the visual field are located in the lower banks of the lobe, and the lower portions of the visual field are represented in the upper banks of the lobe. These portions of the occipital lobe are actually located on the medial (interior) walls of the left and right hemispheres, so to actually see them the two hemispheres would have to be pulled apart so their normally hidden, interior walls could be visualized. (Modified from Rodieck, 1998).

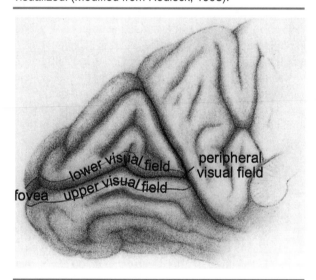

FIGURE 4.8 | Imagine looking at the right-hand edge of a checkerboard pattern (a). The resulting retinal image will look something like the upper portion of panel b. Notice the position of the fovea in this image. By means of the processes described in Chapters 2 and 3, this retinal image is converted into neural signals and is conveyed to the visual cortex via the LGN (represented by arrows in b). The bottom portion of drawing b depicts how this retinal image is transcribed into neural activity within the visual cortex. The size of each square in the cortical representation is proportional to the number of cortical cells activated by any given square on the checkered surface being viewed. Notice that the squares near the point of fixation are expanded in the cortical representation. This expansion reflects the disproportionately large number of cortical cells devoted to neural representation of information falling on and near the fovea. Conversely, squares located far from the point of fixation activate a relatively small number of cortical cells devoted to the peripheral retina. It is important to note that this diagram is not meant to imply that a checkered pattern appears in the cortex, nor does the perceived square look distorted. The figure only shows schematically how the volume of neural tissue in V1 activated by the image of an object is biased toward the region of that object currently imaged on the fovea. Our impression of the figure and the actual shape of the figure are in fact isomorphic.

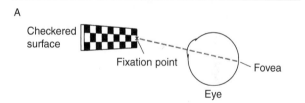

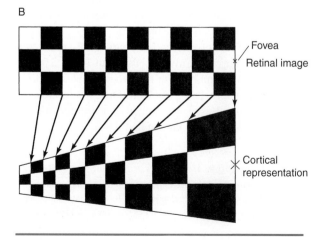

ters. In general, the unfortunate victims of accidents have greatly advanced scientific understanding of the anatomy of vision. As Box 4.2 indicates, even the study of persons who are totally blind can shed light on the neural basis of visual perception. Now let's look in more detail at the structures that are implicated in Holmes's clinical work.

Structure of the Visual Cortex

The primary visual cortex is that portion of the occipital lobe receiving input from the lateral geniculate nucleus. It is sometimes referred to as area V1, in recognition of its being the first in a hierarchy of cortical visual areas. Other names for this area include area 17 (based on a postal-codelike

BOX 4.2

Some Insights on Blindness

Everyone knows what the word *blindness* means—an inability to see. However, two recent developments in neurology (the branch of medicine concerned with the nervous system) and ophthalmology (the branch of medicine concerned with disorders of vision and the eye) are forcing a reconsideration of the conception of blindness. One of these developments comes from an attempt to design an artificial eye that would permit the blind to see. The second development concerns the ability of people, who, despite blindness due to visual cortical damage, can still "see" in one sense. Let's consider each of these intriguing developments in more detail.

First, keep in mind that loss of sight can result from disease or injury affecting the photoreceptors in the retina, the fibers of the optic nerves, or various areas of the brain. If damaged photoreceptors are the cause of blindness, then in principle one could install a tiny electronic microcircuit that stimulated the ganglion cells directly, at least crudely mimicking the inputs from photoreceptors. Efforts to create such a device are underway (Rizzo and Wyatt, 1997). But if it's the ganglion cells themselves that are damaged, visual information cannot be relayed to higher brain centers that, in fact, may still be functional. In such cases, it is the absence of input that prevents sight.

For several decades researchers have been exploring the possibility of directly stimulating the visual cortex in blind patients with nonfunctioning eyes, thus bypassing the defective route to the cortex (Schmidt et al.,

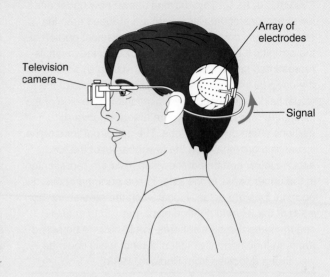

1996). The scheme would work something like this. The blind person would be outfitted with a small video camera that converted optical images of the environment into a pattern of electrical signals. This pattern of signals would then be applied directly to the person's visual cortex, through an array of electrodes placed directly on the surface of the brain (see the accompanying illustration). It has long been known that direct stimulation of the visual cortex generates conscious visual sensations (Dobelle and Mladejovsky, 1974; Brindley and Lewin, 1968). Called *phosphenes,* these sensations are said to

labeling scheme, whereby neighboring, anatomically defined areas of the brain are sequentially numbered) and striate cortex (owing to the region's faintly striped appearance when seen under a low-power microscope). But the terms *V1 area 17, striate cortex,* and *primary visual cortex* all refer to the same portion of the brain.

Like the rest of the cerebral cortex, the visual area consists of a layered array of cells about 1.5 to 2.0 millimeters thick. Combined for the two hemispheres, there are approximately 1×10^9 (1 billion) cells in area V1 (Stevens, 2001). Based on volumetric measurements (not actual cell counts), it is known that the size of V1 varies widely among normal people.[1]

Figure 4.9 is a magnified image of human brain tissue from V1. The tiny black dots denote the cell bodies of neurons located throughout the 2-millimeter thickness of the cortex. Here you can see that the different layers vary in thickness and that the concentration of cells varies from layer to layer. The million or so axons arriving from the six layers of the LGN connect with cortical cells within layer 4 of the visual cortex. The axons of cells from the magnocellular layers of the LGN make their contacts within an upper subdivision of cortical layer 4, while LGN axons from the parvocellular LGN layers contact the lower subdivision of layer 4. From here, connections within the cortex carry information to neurons in other layers above and below layer 4 and, eventually, to other areas within the brain.

Recall that the regions between layers of the LGN are populated with the small K cells. Their axons, too, project to area V1 where they synapse with cortical cells in layers 1, 2, and 3.

---

[1] People in whom area V1 is exceptionally large also tend to have unusually large LGNs and large optic tracts. It is not known whether these people have superior visual abilities (Andrews, Halpern, and Purves, 1997).

resemble small, glowing spots or grains of rice. Increasing the duration of the stimulating pulse makes the phosphenes brighter; occasionally, even colored phosphenes are reported, but most appear white. When several phosphenes are evoked simultaneously, patients describe seeing crude but recognizable shapes. Conceivably, this could provide the patient with useful information about the identity and location of objects in the environment. Before this procedure can be perfected, however, more work must be done to determine the number and placement of electrodes necessary to convey useful pattern information. In the meantime, this research very clearly demonstrates that the visual cortex *can* generate conscious visual sensations in the absence of input from the eyes.

Perhaps even more intriguing are the residual visual abilities of some cortically blind people. In these individuals, the eyes and optic nerves remain intact. Their permanent loss of sight results from damage to the visual cortex caused by an accident or stroke. The extent of the region of blindness (the *scotoma*) depends on the size of the damaged area of cortex. By definition, light flashed anywhere within this scotoma elicits no sensation of vision. Yet when asked to guess where a light is flashed within this blind region by pointing to it, these individuals can do so with reasonable accuracy. At the same time, they deny seeing any hint of the flash and describe the exercise as rather silly. Some patients can even direct their gaze toward an unseen light, can report the color or orientation of a visual stimulus, and can adjust their hands and fingers to grasp an object they cannot see! These puzzling abilities, summarized by Weiskrantz (1995), are all instances of what is termed **blindsight.**

The common denominator in all these studies is the use of **forced-choice testing** (see the appendix). With this procedure, an individual doesn't describe what is seen but rather judges where a stimulus is presented or when it is presented, guessing if necessary.

By what means can a blind person accurately guess the location of a flash he or she never saw? Think back to the superior colliculus, that subcortical area of the brain thought to be involved in visual orienting reflexes. Because it lies below the cerebral hemispheres, the superior colliculus could be unaffected by injury to the visual cortex and hence remain available to provide visual information for the guidance of hand or eye movements (Rafal et al., 1990). Because in blindsight, behavior is divorced from awareness, we might even conclude that subcortical brain regions process visual information at an unconscious level. Some scientists are skeptical about this hypothesis, however, arguing instead that small islands of cortical tissue are still intact, and provide crude but usable visual information for guidance of the eyes or hand (Fendrich, Wessinger, and Gazzaniga, 1992).

What this picture cannot convey is the remarkable transformations of visual information occurring within this cortical area. To appreciate these transformations you must know something about the visual stimuli necessary to activate these cortical cells. This brings us to the research of David Hubel and Torsten Wiesel, neurobiologists whose pioneering studies of the visual cortex earned them a Nobel Prize in 1981. Their discoveries and the subsequent work stimulated by those discoveries have very greatly expanded our understanding of the neural machinery of visual perception. The following paragraphs highlight some of those major findings.

Retinal Maps in the Cortex

The first notable property of cortical cells is that each cell responds to stimulation of a restricted area of the retina; this area constitutes that cell's receptive field. You will recognize this property as a continuation of the processing scheme inaugurated in the retina and carried forward in the LGN: At each of these processing stages, individual cells analyze information from a limited area on the retina.

Considered as a group, the receptive fields of cells in each hemisphere of V1 form a topographic map of the contralateral visual field. This cortical map, like its counterpart in the LGN, is said to be *topographic* because adjacent regions of visual space are mapped onto adjacent groups of cells in the visual cortex (recall Figure 4.6). The map in each hemisphere is said to represent the *contralateral* visual field because the left half of the visual field is represented in the right hemisphere, and vice versa.

Now let's consider *how* this map of the visual field is distributed over the cortex. Recall that Holmes's studies of brain-damaged people implied that a great deal of cortical area is devoted to representation of the fovea. This implication has since been confirmed by actually

FIGURE 4.9 | Magnified picture of a section of brain tissue from the human visual cortex, with the various layers labeled. The top of the brain is situated just above layer 1. Below layer 6 lies the white matter of the brain, tissue consisting of the incoming axons from the LGN. Those LGN axons make connections with cortical neurons in layer 4. There's some disagreement among neuroanatomists about the exact boundary between layers 3 and 4. The labels in this figure show the version (Hässler, 1967) endorsed by Casagrande and Kaas (1994). For our purposes, this controversy is beside the point: Everyone acknowledges that layer 4 is the area that receives input from the P and M portions of the LGN, with K cells projecting to upper layers.

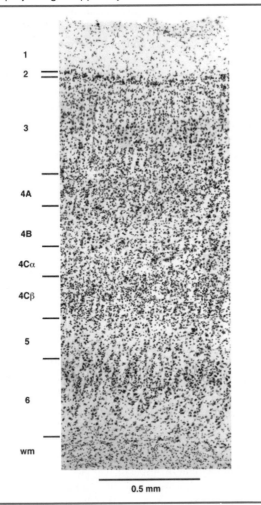

0.5 mm

plotting the locations of receptive fields of cells sampled from throughout the primate visual cortex (Hubel and Wiesel, 1974a). It is estimated that about 80 percent of the cells in the visual cortex are devoted to representing the central 10 degrees or so of the visual field (Drasdo, 1977). Previously we pointed out that this exaggerated cortical mapping of central vision is referred to as cortical magnification.

Some of this bias toward the central portion of the visual field is inherited from the retina and the LGN. Remember from our discussion of the retina, that the number of ganglion cells subserving the fovea is considerably larger than the number devoted to the rest of the retina, even though in terms of area the periphery dwarfs the fovea. This foveal bias appears in the LGN's retinotopic map, too, where it is even further exaggerated (Malpelli and Baker, 1975). Moving on up to the cortex, the foveal representation swells to even greater proportions.

This magnified foveal representation makes sense when we consider the sizes of receptive fields of cortical cells representing different retinal eccentricities. Cells concerned with the fovea may be "looking at" a retinal area covered by no more than a few photoreceptors, whereas cells devoted to the periphery "look at" areas hundreds of times larger. Because foveal receptive fields are so small, it stands to reason that many cells may be required to cover a given patch of retina. In the representation of the periphery, a comparably sized patch of retina may be monitored by relatively few cells (recall Figure 4.8). This principle explains why local damage to visual cortex (from a bullet wound, for example) may produce scotomas of different size. Damage within the foveal representation will destroy cells with small receptive fields, yielding a small scotoma in the center of vision. Damage within the peripheral representation may destroy the same number of cells, but the resulting scotoma will be considerably larger because those cells have bigger receptive fields. This large scotoma will also, of course, be located away from the center of gaze.

So, in effect, the bulk of the machinery in the visual cortex processes information about objects that are viewed directly. This is why head and eye movements play such a prominent role in seeing: Such movements turn the eyes toward objects of current interest. These newly fixated objects then cast their images on the fovea, ensuring that those objects will receive the most detailed visual analysis possible by the visual cortex.

So far we've considered the orderly layout of cortical receptive fields and the resulting topographic map. Our discussion focused on *where* in the visual field different cortical cells are "looking." Now let's ask *what*

FIGURE 4.10 | Response of a single cortical cell to bars presented at various orientations. The graph summarizing response magnitude as a function of orientation is called a tuning curve, with the peak of the curve denoting the preferred orientation for that cell (vertical in this example).

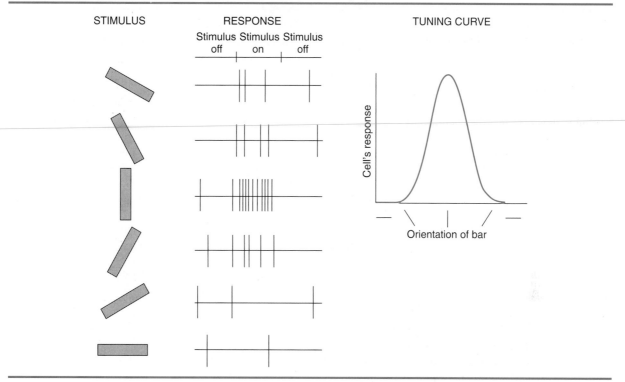

Functional Properties of Cortical Cells

each cell is "looking for." To answer this question, we need to repeat the kind of experiment illustrated in Figure 3.2, whereby we record neural activity from cells responding to visual stimulation presented on a video monitor viewed by our experimental subject. Only now our recording electrode will be placed in visual area V1, toward the very back of the animal's brain. Exactly what kind of visual stimulus must be present within a cell's receptive field in order to evoke activity in that cell?

On the basis of your knowledge of the retina and the geniculate, you can probably anticipate one fact: Cortical cells are unconcerned about overall levels of illumination. Simply increasing or decreasing the ambient illumination has no appreciable impact on a cortical cell's activity. Instead, cortical cells respond best to gradients in light intensity, such as those produced by borders, edges, and lines. In this respect, cortical cells behave like their retinal and geniculate relatives from whom they inherit input. But cortical cells exhibit several notable characteristics not present in their precortical relatives, characteristics described in the following section.

Orientation Selectivity   One of the most striking characteristics of cortical cells is their **orientation selectivity.** Recall that retinal and geniculate cells, because of their circular-shaped receptive fields, respond indiscriminately to all orientations (look back at Figure 3.4). In marked contrast, most cortical cells are very fussy about the orientation of a contour or an edge. As shown in Figure 4.10, any particular cell will respond only if the orientation of an edge or line falls somewhere within a rather narrow range. Each cortical cell has a "preferred" orientation, one to which it is maximally responsive. If a line tilts a little away from this optimum, the cell's response is markedly decreased; if the line tilts even more, the cell no longer responds at all. This behavior can be summarized by graphing a cell's response strength as a function of orientation. The resulting "tuning curve" resembles a teepee with its peak defining the cell's preferred orientation (see the right-hand portion of Figure 4.10).

The preferred orientation of a V1 cell can typically be sharply defined. In many cells, a tilt of no more than 15 degrees away from the optimum orientation is sufficient to abolish that cell's response completely. An angular deviation this small corresponds to about the difference in position of a clock's hand at 12:00 and at 12:03! Just about all V1 cells are selective for orientation, although those in cortical layer 4 are not nearly so finely tuned for orientation as those outside of layer 4 (Leventhal et al., 1995). Likewise, regularly spaced patches of cells near the cortical surface show only coarse orientation selectivity. In all other regions of V1 outside these restricted areas, orientation matters greatly.

Let's take a look at the layout of ON regions and OFF regions comprising the receptive fields of some cortical cells. From these layouts you should be able to see why these cells are selective for orientation. Some representative cortical receptive fields are shown in Figure 4.11. There, you can see that receptive fields are elongated, not circular, as in retinal and geniculate cells. Notice, too, that the discrete zones of ON and OFF activity are arranged differently depending on the particular cell. Simply by inspecting these various arrangements, you should be able to picture what kind of oriented stimulus would evoke the best response from a given cell. For this reason, cortical cells with these well-delineated zones are called **simple cells:** There is a simple relation between their receptive field layout and their preferred stimulus. For cells of this type, a properly oriented bar or edge must be positioned exactly within the receptive field to yield a large neural response. Changing either the orientation or position of the stimulus will reduce the cell's response. This specificity of response means that simple cells are able to signal the orientation of a stimulus falling within a particular region of the visual field.

Other cortical cells do not have such well-defined ON and OFF zones, yet they also exhibit a preference for a particular orientation. These are called **complex cells** because it is more complicated to predict just what stimulus will optimally activate them. Unlike simple cells, the receptive fields of complex cells don't have well-defined "on" and "off" zones, yet, complex cells do respond preferably to a given contour orientation. And unlike simple cells, that oriented contour can fall anywhere within the boundaries of the receptive field. Precise location is not nearly so important for a complex cell, so long as the stimulus falls anywhere within its receptive field and remains properly oriented.

There is a third category of cortical cells, called **hypercomplex cells,** whose responses depend not only on contour orientation but contour length as well. These

FIGURE 4.11 | Layout of ON regions (+) and OFF regions (−) of several representative cortical receptive fields. The ON regions are sometimes called excitatory zones and the OFF regions are called inhibitory zones. Cells in which these regions can be mapped are called simple cells, and the layout of the ON and OFF regions predicts the cells' preferred orientation.

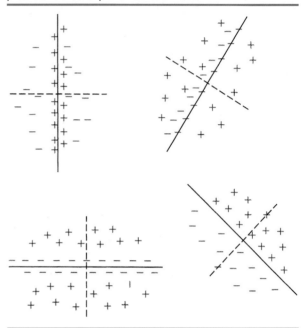

cells give their maximum response to an appropriately oriented bar whose length and width "fits" their receptive field. Extending the bar's length beyond this optimum value dramatically reduces the cell's response.

Within area V1, preferred orientation varies from cell to cell and within an ensemble of cells, all orientations are represented. However, the distribution of preferred orientations is not uniform. Recordings made from many cells in the visual cortex of the monkey reveal a distinct bias in favor of the principal axes, vertical and horizontal. Figure 4.12 (adapted from Mansfield, 1974) illustrates this finding. In this graph, each line represents the preferred orientation of a single cortical cell. As you can see, while all orientations are represented, there is a clustering of cells preferring vertical and another clustering of cells preferring horizontal. This bias in favor of vertical and horizontal is most pronounced among cells with receptive fields close to and within the fovea (see also Li, Peterson, and Freeman, 2003). This raises two intriguing questions: What are the perceptual consequences of this bias and what factors produce this bias in the first place? The following section addresses these two questions.

FIGURE 4.12 | The distribution of orientation selectivity from a sample of neurons in the primary visual cortex (V1) of a monkey. Each line designates a given neuron's preferred orientation. Note the bias in favor of cells tuned to orientations at and near vertical and horizontal. (Redrawn from Mansfield, 1974.)

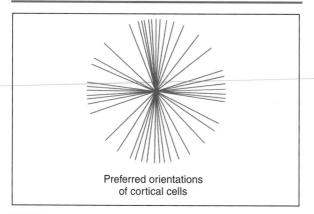

Preferred orientations
of cortical cells

FIGURE 4.13 | Test figures for experiencing the oblique effect. Follow the instructions given in the text.

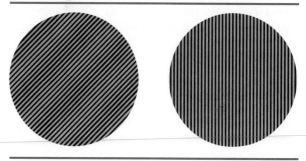

The Oblique Effect Long before the discovery of orientation-selective cortical cells, vision scientists had noted that horizontal and vertical lines can be detected more easily and identified more rapidly than can lines oriented obliquely. For instance, visual acuity is highest for vertical and horizontal lines, and lowest for lines oriented 45 degrees in either direction from vertical. Compared to horizontal or vertical lines, oblique lines are also more difficult to see when the contrast of the lines is faint. (**Contrast** refers to the difference in intensity between the dark lines and their light background.)

You can experience the oblique effect by looking at the two bar patterns in Figure 4.13. Prop the book up so that you can view the pair of patterns from a distance. Backing away from the book, you should discover that at some distance the thin vertical bars remain visible while the diagonal ones blend together and are, thus, unresolvable. By turning the book sideways, you can repeat this exercise, now comparing horizontal to diagonal.

This general superiority in the visibility of horizontal and vertical is called the **oblique effect.** Although most people experience the oblique effect, some do not. In fact, some individuals show the opposite tendency: they see oblique lines of a particular orientation *more* clearly. Usually, those who fail to experience the oblique effect or who show a reverse oblique effect have some degree of astigmatism. Recall from Chapter 2 that astigmatism (an irregularly curved cornea) causes contours of certain orientations to appear blurred while

other orientations appear sharply focused. Depending on the direction of the astigmatism, this condition can nullify the normal oblique effect, and it can also lead to a superiority in vision for oblique lines, a sort of reverse oblique effect. Interestingly, in cases where oblique is favored, the bias endures even when the astigmatism is optically corrected, thereby making all orientations equally sharp on the retina (Mitchell et al., 1973). This condition is called **meridional amblyopia** (amblyopia literally means "dull vision," and refers to a visual loss that cannot be corrected optically). Apparently the astigmatism, prior to optical correction, altered the brain in a direction favoring oblique over horizontal and vertical. In fact, animals made artificially astigmatic exhibit just such alterations—cortical cells in these animals prefer orientations centered around the one most clearly focused, with many fewer cells responding preferentially to the blurred, astigmatic orientation (Freeman and Pettigrew, 1973). The ability of biased visual experience to alter the orientation preferences of cortical cells provides a ready explanation for meridional amblyopia. Presumably, people with this condition have fewer cortical cells tuned to the previously blurred orientation. But why do people who are *not* astigmatic see horizontal and vertical *more* clearly?

At present, there are two general theories. One attributes the bias to the carpentered environment in which most people grow up (Annis and Frost, 1973). According to this idea, people receive more exposure to vertical and to horizontal contours than to oblique contours, because horizontal and vertical exist in abundance within an urban landscape of houses and buildings. Indeed, measurements have confirmed an overabundance of horizontally oriented and vertically oriented contours in both our indoor and outdoor environments (Coppola et al., 1998). This biased visual exposure, the theory continues, influences the development of orientation preferences among the cortical cells. This theory is supported by animal studies demonstrating that the brain *is* susceptible to biased visual experience early in life (Blakemore and Cooper, 1970; Hirsch and Spinelli, 1970). The carpentered environment theory also receives support from studies testing the vision of people who grew up in agrarian environments where no particular orientation predominates. These individuals *fail* to exhibit an oblique effect (Annis and Frost, 1973), presumably because their brains did not receive a heavy dose of vertical and horizontal contours.

As an alternative to this environmental theory of the oblique effect, another view attributes the neural bias for horizontal and vertical to unspecified genetic factors that operate to favor the development of cortical cells tuned to horizontal and vertical (Timney and Muir, 1976). Those who favor this genetic theory point to the fact that infants only a few months old exhibit an oblique effect (Leehey et al., 1975). It is hard to imagine, this theory argues, how visual experience could already have shaped the brains of infants so young.

The debate about origins of the oblique effect is really part of a larger concern with the genesis of orientation selectivity of neurons in the visual cortex. Is experience necessary for the development of oriented cortical cells, or is orientation selectivity an intrinsic property of the visual cortex present from birth? As we so often see in science, the emerging consensus appears to be a compromise of both views: some degree of orientation selectivity is specified by genetically controlled, intrinsic connections, but these connections are modifiable by environmentally determined experience (Sengpiel, Stawinski, and Bonhoeffer, 1999). For another interesting twist on the link between visual-orientation perception and cortical physiology, see Box 4.3.

Selectivity for Direction of Motion   Besides preferring contours of a particular orientation, a substantial fraction of cortical cells also respond best when those contours *move* through their receptive fields. Among these movement-sensitive cells, simple cells tend to prefer relatively slow-moving contours, while complex cells can respond even when contours travel rapidly across the receptive field. Movement-sensitive cells typically respond robustly to one *direction* of motion only. For instance, a cortical cell (like the complex cell illustrated in Figure 4.14) might give a burst of activity when a vertical contour moved from left to right, but would remain unresponsive when that same contour moved in the opposite direction, right to left. A different cell might respond only to a contour moving from

FIGURE 4.14 | Response of a complex cell to a bar moving through the cell's receptive field (shown in outline) either from left to right or from right to left.

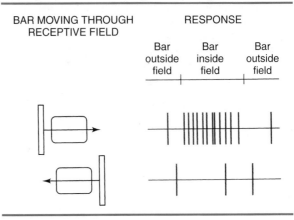

right to left. This property, known as **direction selectivity,** suggests that this class of cells plays an important role in motion perception. We'll return to this idea when we discuss motion perception in Chapter 9.

In area V1, direction-selective cells respond vigorously when an appropriately oriented contour sweeps through their receptive fields. These cells also respond when an eye movement sweeps the receptive field across a stationary contour. In both cases, the image of the contour moves through the cells' receptive fields and the cells respond to this movement. Their responses, in other words, are ambiguous with respect to the source of image motion (Ilg and Thier, 1996). Yet, as you look about the world, you don't usually confuse image motion caused by eye movement with image motion caused by a moving object. Evidently, at a later stage of processing, the motion signals generated in V1 cells are rendered unambiguous.

Size Selectivity   We've already mentioned that receptive fields of cortical cells vary in size, with those in the fovea being smallest, and those in the periphery, the largest. This is true for both simple and complex cells. Moreover, in any given region of the visual field there is also some variation in field size. Thus, some cells have receptive fields favoring, say, a narrow vertical bar, while others prefer a wider bar. This is reminiscent of the situation in the retina (recall Figures 3.9 and 3.11) and the LGN. But in the cortex, size selectivity is combined with orientation selectivity. In Chapter 3 we characterized receptive fields as filters that respond only when particular stimulus features are present in the retinal image. Cortical filters, then,

If you were asked to point your index finger in the upward direction, you'd probably point to the ceiling. You'd do the same thing if you were lying on your side or on your back, or, for that matter, if you were standing on your head. We tend to interpret *up* in terms of gravitational coordinates. The fixed reference frame for *up* is possible because our brain keeps track of gravity's pull, using information from the vestibular system housed in the inner ear. (The vestibular system registers the body's movements and its position in space.)

Now, what about the orientation of the contours on the left- and right-hand sides of this box? You'd immediately label them *vertical* and you'd be correct. But tilt your head sideways (keeping the book stationary), and look at the contours. What is the orientation of the contours now? If you're like most people, you'd stick with "vertical" because you reference their orientation with respect to gravity. This tendency to judge orientation based on gravity is called **orientation constancy** because an object's perceived orientation remains constant even when we turn our heads.

Are the orientation-selective cells in area V1 of your brain smart enough to keep track of which way your head is tilted? Does a cell that prefers vertical when your head is upright continue to prefer "vertical" when your head is tilted? To find out, suppose we perform the following experiment.

We train an alert monkey to remain seated in a chair with its eyes fixated on the center of a video monitor. From an electrode implanted in area V1 of the monkey's brain, we record responses from orientation-selective cells. With the monkey sitting upright, suppose we locate a cell whose preferred orientation is vertical (see Figure 4.10). This cell's response dwindles considerably when the contour within its receptive field deviates from vertical by as little as 25 degrees in either direction. Now suppose we tilt the chair in which the monkey is sitting,

rotating the monkey's body and head 25 degrees clockwise from upright. Unlike the monkey, the video monitor isn't rotated, so now the vertical contour on the monitor is oriented 25 degrees counterclockwise on the monkey's retina. What happens to the V1 cell's response? Does the cell continue to respond vigorously, taking into account the head's tilted position? Or does the cell fall silent because the image of the contour no longer matches the retinal coordinates of its receptive field? For nearly all V1 cells studied, the preferred orientation is tied to retinal coordinates. Turning the head silences the cells. To resurrect their responses, the orientation of the contour must be tilted by an amount sufficient to match the body's tilt. This means, then, that V1 cells don't know whether the orientation of a contour has changed or whether the tilt of the head has changed. Evidently, V1 cells don't have access to the vestibular information necessary to specify orientation in gravitational coordinates.

Fortunately, visually activated cells in other regions of the brain are not so uninformed. Cells in a higher visual area, called V3, do respond to orientations specified in gravitational coordinates (Sauvan and Peterhans, 1999). Tilting the monkey tilts the preferred orientation of those cells. Evidently, these cells do receive information about gravity necessary to compensate for bodily rotation.

Think back to the oblique effect described in the text. Our perceptual bias for horizontal and vertical contours, like the responses of V1 neurons, is tied to retinal coordinates. When you tilt your head sideways 45 degrees, oblique contours are more visible than vertical ones (where oblique and vertical refer to gravitationally defined orientations). This is strong evidence that the oblique effect originates within the V1 area. On other, more complex, tasks that involve vertical, horizontal, and oblique contours, however, human performance *is* governed by gravitationally defined orientation (Marendaz et al., 1993). So, what's *up* depends on what you're up to.

---

are tuned for size and orientation, two fundamental building blocks for specifying the identity of objects.

Binocularity   Recall that information from the two eyes is distributed in separate layers of each LGN, with individual cells receiving input from either one eye or the other. This ocular segregation is retained in layer 4, the cortical layer receiving input from the LGN. Only now the left and right eye cells are segre-

gated into snakelike stripes, which can easily be visualized by injecting specially labeled dye into area V1 (Horton and Hocking, 1996). Figure 4.15 shows a magnified view of ocular dominance stripes in postmortem tissue from human area V1. The interdigitated stripes of cells innervated by the right and left eyes appear as alternating light and dark gray bands. This approximately 1-millimeter-wide banded slice of tissue cuts across layer 4.

FIGURE 4.15 | Magnified photograph showing the ocular dominance stripes of a piece of postmortem tissue from layer 4 of human area V1. The alternating light and dark bands correspond to the array of cells receiving input from the right and left eyes, respectively. Each stripe is approximately 1 millimeter in width.

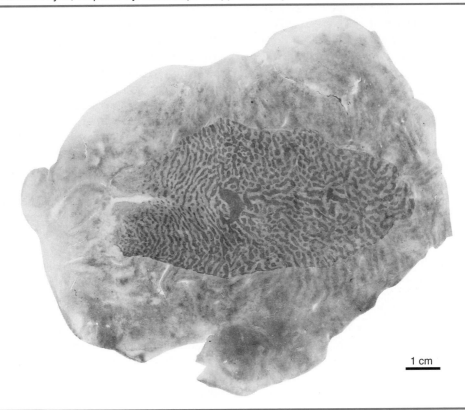

1 cm

Cells in layer 4, in turn, send signals to other cortical layers immediately above them, and at this stage, **monocular** (meaning "one eye") *segregation* gives way to **binocular** (meaning "two eyes") *integration*. Within area V1, and outside layer 4, individual cells, with few exceptions, are innervated from both eyes.

Figure 4.16 shows how a typical cortical cell responds to stimulation of the two eyes. We can see the map of the ON and OFF regions, meaning this is a simple cell, and the light and dark bars denote presentation of an optimally oriented bar to the left eye (upper plot), right eye (middle plot), and both eyes (lower plot). As you can see, this particular cell responds moderately well to a contour presented to either eye alone, but its response is even stronger when both eyes are stimulated simultaneously. Unlike this cell, some respond more vigorously to stimulation of the left eye, whereas others favor right-eye stimulation. This variation in the activation strength produced by the two eyes is called **ocular**

dominance. Any cell that can be excited through both eyes, regardless of its ocular dominance, is called a **binocular cell;** only a small fraction of V1 cells are monocular, meaning that the cell can only be activated by stimulation of one eye or the other but not both. And as previously mentioned, the bulk of these monocular cells reside in layer 4.

Because they can be excited by either eye, all binocular cells actually have two receptive fields: one for the left eye and one for the right eye. The two fields of a binocular cell are nearly always matched in type (simple or complex), preferred orientation, and preferred direction of motion. If, for instance, the cell responds best to a horizontal line moving upward in front of the left eye, then upward movement of a horizontal line will evoke the largest response via the right eye as well.

The two receptive fields for any particular binocular cell also fall on approximately equivalent regions of the two eyes. Thus, if one field is located to the right of

FIGURE 4.16 | Response of a single cortical cell to stimulation of the left eye only, the right eye only, and both eyes simultaneously. The plus and minus signs show the receptive field layout for this cell, and the light and dark bars signify presentation of the stimulus.

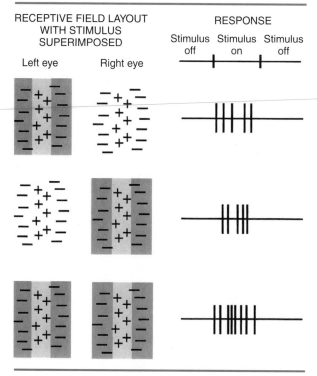

RECEPTIVE FIELD LAYOUT WITH STIMULUS SUPERIMPOSED

Left eye   Right eye

RESPONSE

Stimulus off   Stimulus on   Stimulus off

image of the object no longer falls within the right eye's receptive field. In fact, there is no single position *on* the viewing screen where one object could simultaneously stimulate both the left and right eyes' receptive fields. But there is a position *in front of* the screen that could accomplish this, as shown in panel C. When the object is at a specific location in front of the screen (and hence closer to the eyes), both receptive fields are stimulated.

If we were to repeat these measurements for a large sample of binocular cells, we would find that different cells respond to objects placed at different distances relative to the plane of fixation. Some cells, such as the one shown in Figure 4.17, respond best to objects located closer in depth relative to the fixation plane, and other binocular cells respond best to objects located farther away in depth relative to the plane of fixation. Still other binocular cells respond best to objects at the same depth as the plane of fixation. For each binocular cell, in other words, there will be one position in three-dimensional space where the two receptive fields can be simultaneously stimulated. This position varies from cell to cell, depending on the retinal placement of the pair of receptive fields for a given cell.

Take a minute to be sure you understand why this is so. A little extra effort at this point will pay nice dividends when we talk about binocular depth perception in Chapter 8. As you will learn then, the layout of binocular receptive fields plays an important role in one's ability to judge the distance from one object to another. For now, though, you should appreciate two properties of binocular cells: They respond preferentially to the same type of stimulus in both eyes, and the relative positions of the two receptive fields of a cell specify the location of the stimulus that will optimally excite the cell.

the fovea in one eye, the other field will fall to the right of the fovea in the other eye. In general, binocular cortical cells respond most strongly when the appropriate regions of each eye are stimulated by forms of corresponding size and orientation.

Keeping in mind that a binocular cell has two receptive fields (one associated with each eye), think for a moment about where a single object must be situated in the world in order to maximally activate a binocular cell. To begin, suppose the two eyes fixate a point in the center of a viewing screen, as shown in Figure 4.17. In order for stimulation of the right eye to activate a binocular cell, let's suppose that an object has to be located within the area of the screen labeled "right eye" (see panel A). Note, though, that at this position the image of that object does not fall within the cell's receptive field in the left eye. So at this position, stimulation of the left eye would not activate the binocular cell. To be imaged within the left eye's receptive field and therefore activate this cell, the object must be displaced laterally on the screen, closer to the point of fixation (see panel B). Note, however, that in this location the

Color Besides orientation, direction of motion and binocularity, some cortical cells in area V1 also register information about color. Some of these color-sensitive cells are concentrated in bloblike regions regularly spaced throughout the upper layers of visual cortex (Livingstone and Hubel, 1984), while others are found outside these regions (Lennie, Krauskopf, and Sclar, 1990). Each of these so-called **blobs** contains neurons that receive their inputs from the lower subdivision of layer 4, the one innervated by color-selective cells of the parvocellular pathway. Cells in the blobs constitute one of the unusual cortical groups that show no strong preference for contour orientation. Blob cells do, however, exhibit a complex form of color opponency, wherein the effect of a color (excitatory versus inhibitory) depends on whether that color falls within the center or the surround of the

FIGURE 4.17 | This series of drawings illustrates why a single object must be situated in a particular location in visual space to optimally stimulate both receptive fields (RFs) of a single binocular cell. For details, see the text.

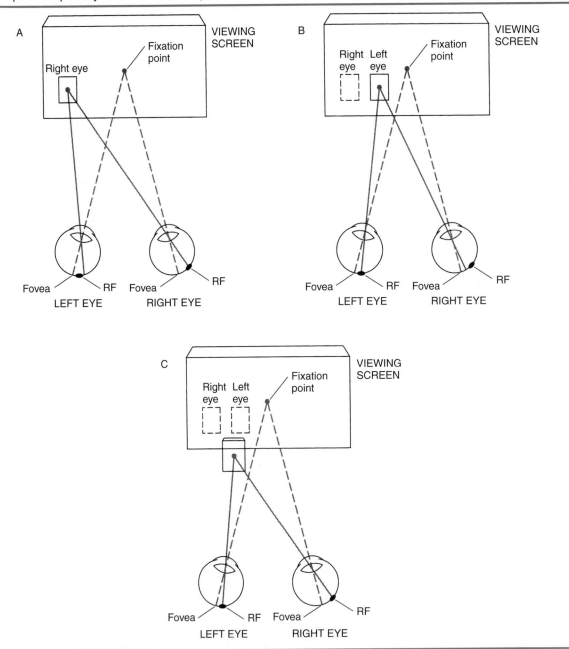

cell's receptive field. The functional significance of these color-selective cells will be discussed in Chapter 7.

Having summarized the major response properties of V1 cells, let's look at how two of these properties—orientation and binocularity—are anatomically arranged within the cortex.

Columns and Hypercolumns

Earlier we mentioned that cortical cells vary in their preferred orientations, some responding best to vertical, others to horizontal, and still others to orientations in between. These orientation-selective cells are not haphazardly arranged; they are grouped in a very orderly fashion within the cortex. To envision this grouping, imagine we are able to unfold the visual cortex so that this thin, layered sheet of tissue is lying flat. Now suppose we randomly select a position somewhere on the surface of this unfolded cortex. Starting here, we gradually move straight downward through the various layers in a direction perpendicular to the surface of the cortex. Throughout our short, 2-millimeter journey we carefully catalog the preferred orientation of each cell encountered. After penetrating all six cortical layers, we will discover that all cells along the path of this penetration have identical preferred orientations (except for cells in layer 4, which respond to *all* orientations). Along the way, there may be variation in the size of these cells' receptive fields, and some are likely to prefer edges while others prefer bars. But *all* cells will exhibit the same orientation preference.

Suppose we now repeat this sampling procedure, this time beginning at a position just a fraction of a millimeter away from our initial penetration. Now we will find that all cells in a perpendicular penetration prefer an orientation approximately 10 degrees different from the one encountered in the first sample. If we continue repeating this sampling procedure over and over, always being careful to make the penetrations perpendicular to the cortical surface, we will uncover a regular sequence of preferred orientations. Each time we make a new penetration, spacing it about 0.05 millimeter from the last one, the preferred orientation will change by about 10 to 15 degrees. By the time we have sampled a strip of cortex less than a millimeter in width, the sequence of preferred orientations will have progressed through one complete rotation. This regular progression through a complete set of orientations is comparable to the range of positions assumed by the second hand of a clock as it advances from vertical (at 12:00) to horizontal (at 3:00) and back to vertical (at 6:00). This tidy packaging of orientation-selective cells recurs throughout the visual cortex (Hubel and Wiesel, 1974b). Figure 4.18 shows schematically how orientation is systematically "mapped" within a slab of cortical tissue.

As we make these repeated samplings, another intriguing regularity emerges: Within a given penetration perpendicular to the cortical surface, all cells have the same ocular dominance. If the first cell encountered responds strongest to stimulation of the right eye, all cells in that sequence will be right-eye dominant (with the exception of the monocular cells in layer 4). Moreover, if we now make another sampling penetration right next to the first one, the cells encountered will exhibit a different pattern of ocular dominance, perhaps responding equally

FIGURE 4.18 | Orientation and ocular dominance columns in the visual cortex. All cells in a column have the same orientation preference and the same ocular dominance. An aggregate of columns representing a complete range of preferences is known as a hypercolumn.

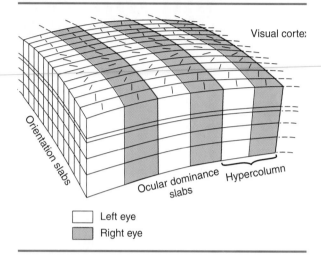

well to stimulation of either eye. So ocular dominance—like preferred orientation—varies systematically as we move laterally over the cortex. This, too, is illustrated in Figure 4.18.

At first, all these facts may seem bewildering. But taken together, they produce an interesting and coherent picture. The visual cortex appears to be composed of columns of cells, with each column consisting of a stack of cells all preferring the same orientation and exhibiting the same ocular dominance.[2] Altogether, it takes roughly 18 to 20 neighboring columns to cover a complete range of stimulus orientations and ocular dominance. This aggregation of adjacent columns is collectively known as a **hypercolumn.** Each hypercolumn contains tens of thousands of cells whose receptive fields all overlap on the same retinal territory. The hypercolumns themselves are all uniform in size throughout the cortex, but the hypercolumns devoted to the central retina deal with a much

---

[2] Besides containing columns for orientation and ocular dominance, area V1 also contains an orderly map of preferred directions of motion (Weliky, Bosking, and Fitzpatrick, 1996). Thus, neighboring cells respond best to similar but not identical directions of motion. The systematic map of direction selectivity is interdigitated with the orientation map in a manner that divides a given orientation column into cells preferring opposite directions of motion.

FIGURE 4.19 | Schematic showing a sequence of oriented bars (called a "grating") presented successively over time. The size and location of the grating remain the same; only the orientation of the contours comprising the grating changes over time. If you were to view this sequence of changing orientations, what would transpire within visual area V1 of your brain? The answer is shown in color plate 1 (located in the middle of the book).

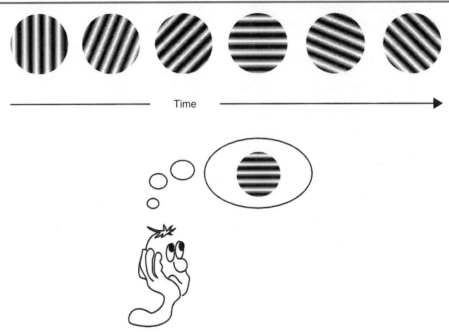

Time

smaller area of retina than do the hypercolumns concerned with the peripheral retina. This emphasis on central vision, you will recognize, is the principle of cortical magnification described previously in this chapter.

Hence each hypercolumn contains neural machinery for analyzing visual information within a local region of the retina. Throughout the entire visual cortex there are many such hypercolumns, each receiving input from different portions of the retina. Working simultaneously, the hypercolumns analyze multiple aspects of the retinal image—orientation, direction of motion, binocularity, size—in a local, piecemeal fashion. Each hypercolumn provides a "description" of that portion of the image falling within its own, restricted field of view. This description is embodied within the activity of cells in the constituent columns of the hypercolumn.

At the end of this chapter we will consider how these cells might participate in various aspects of visual perception. For the moment, though, let's consider what might transpire within the visual cortex when you stare with both eyes open at a figure composed of regularly spaced light and dark contours (a "grating" as the figure is called). Suppose that the contour's orientation changes

over time in regular steps, such that you eventually end up seeing a range of different orientations (see Figure 4.19). For any given orientation, the grating should maximally activate those cells in the cortex responsive to that currently displayed orientation, with cells selective for all other orientations responding much less vigorously or not at all. (In Figure 4.19, you're currently looking at the horizontal contours.) As both eyes are open, ocular dominance preference should not matter. Now suppose we could look directly at area V1 of your cortex and visualize those cells activated by the different orientations as they appear over time. On the basis of what you have just learned about the organization of the cortex, can you imagine what we would see?

Because the orientation and ocular dominance columns are more or less evenly spaced throughout the entire cortex, we should see, at any given time, regular patches of active cells interspersed among patches of inactive ones. And over time, the locations of these active and inactive patches should shift in your cortex, as different orientation-selective cells are brought into action. And, in fact, this is exactly what is seen when this kind of experiment is performed on animal subjects. Investigators can actually identify active neurons within V1 using an optical imaging procedure to measure local blood flow in the animal's visual cortex. (Optical imaging resembles functional magnetic resonance imaging, except that its spatial resolution is much better because the measurements are taken directly from the surface of the brain.) In a typical experiment, the animal views a large display, and the bars of the grating are moved back and forth to ensure that the visual cortex receives a healthy dose of visual stimulation. Over time, various orientations are shown successively.

Color plate 1 (color plates appear on pages in the middle of the book) shows what is typically found using optical imaging. The series of color-coded maps indicate regions of active and inactive patches of cortex associated with viewing different orientations. Each of the eight maps shown in color plate 1 shows precisely the same region of V1, the region whose neurons have receptive fields located where the grating is situated on the video monitor. Within each map, yellow and red denote regions of high activity, while blue indicates regions of low activity. For starters, look at the activation map associated with viewing vertical contours (the left-hand activation map in color plate 1). The array of red and yellow patches corresponds to the columns of cortical cells activated by the vertical bars. Note, too, the regions within the map where activation is very low (the blue regions), denoting areas of cortex containing cells unresponsive during stimulation by vertical. Next look at the activation map for horizontal (the right-hand map in the color plate). Notice in particular that the *active* patches in this map very closely match the *inactive* patches in the "vertical" map; likewise, the *inactive* patches in the "horizontal" map correspond to the *active* patches in the "vertical" map. In general, comparing activation patterns in maps for the different orientations confirms what you would predict: Different orientations activate different regions within the cortical map. Measuring the distance between the centers of the active patches within any given map yields a value close to half a millimeter. This corresponds nicely to the dimension of an individual hypercolumn estimated from physiological recordings of cortical cells. These imaging experiments confirm what single-cell recordings implied, namely that orientation-selective neurons are packed in regularly structured columns within V1 (Kenet et al., 2003).

This completes our overview of the receptive field properties of cells in V1 and the architecture of hypercolumns in this visual receiving area. As mentioned at the outset of this section, our survey hit only the high-

lights of this stage in visual processing. Neurophysiologists have studied cortical cells in considerably greater detail than we've gone into here. They have also begun to unravel the neural circuitry (that is, the connections between cortical cells) underlying such receptive field properties as orientation selectivity. But visual processing doesn't stop at V1. On the contrary, V1 can be construed as the distribution center where information about rudimentary visual features—contour size, orientation, color, direction of motion—gets transmitted to higher stages of processing. It is within these higher stages that these rudimentary features are transformed into neural representations of objects and events, and it is to these higher visual stages that we now direct our attention.

Visual Processing Beyond Area V1

From visual area V1, neural information is distributed over a number of pathways to higher visual areas of the brain. Figure 4.20 represents one attempt to summarize the connections among the multitude of brain areas that can be visually activated (Felleman and Van Essen, 1991). Each labeled box represents a different visual area, starting with the retina (RGC), LGN and V1 at the bottom. These visual areas are distributed widely throughout the cerebral cortex.

Most of the details of this wiring diagram are not essential for our purposes; they simply underscore the large number and hierarchical arrangement of these brain areas associated with vision. However, the pathways denoted by thick lines are important, for they represent significant components of the neural pathways formed by the P and M systems. From our earlier discussion of inputs to V1 from LGN, you will recall that the P and M cells remain segregated within area V1. This segregation remains in effect through the first several stages of processing following V1. Thus, the M pathway projects through V1 via certain parts of V2 and V3 to area MT. The P pathway, in contrast, projects to an anatomically distinct area of V2 and then on to V4. There are also direct M projections from V1 to MT and direct P projections from V1 to V4. Within each of these areas—V1, V2, V3, V4, and MT—exists an orderly retinotopic map, with neighboring regions of the visual field mapped onto neighboring regions of cortical tissue. Moreover, receptive fields in these higher visual areas are significantly larger than those found in V1 and, as a consequence, a stimulus may appear anywhere within a relatively large regions of visual space and still activate a given neuron. Cells in these higher visual areas, in other words, exhibit what is

FIGURE 4.20 | Diagram showing the hierarchical arrangement of visual processing stages, starting with the retina (bottom of diagram) and moving up through the multiple visual areas of the brain. The bold lines show the first parts of the P and M pathways discussed in the text.

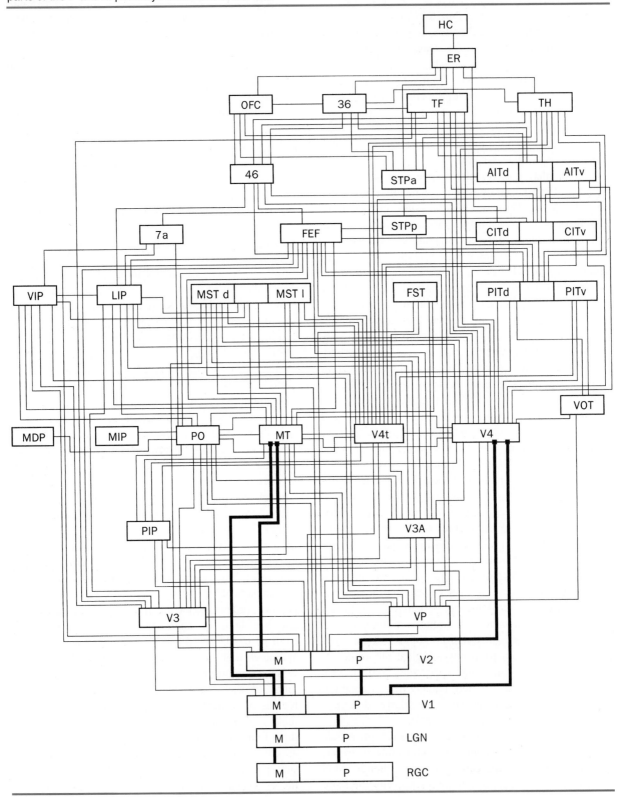

termed **position invariance**, meaning they are less particular about the exact location of a stimulus.

The flow of information within this complex network is not unidirectional. Every cortical region receiving input from another region also sends feedback connections back to that other region. Thus, for example, portions of area V1 provide input to area V4, which, in turn, sends neural messages back to V1. Portions of V2 send signals to area MT, which broadcasts its own signals back to V2. In addition, those visual areas activated by the P and M pathways are richly interlinked, with the neural operations carried out in one set of areas influencing the operations carried out within the others (see the review by Gegenfurtner, Kiper, and Fenstemaker, 1996).

Judging from cells' receptive field properties in various areas (Maunsell and Newsome, 1987; Merigan and Maunsell, 1993), some areas appear specialized for analyzing information about color (for instance, area V4) and about object shape (areas forming the IT complex in the upper right portion of Figure 4.20), whereas other areas are more concerned with motion (areas MT and MST). There is a brain region (the two areas labeled STP in Figure 4.20) containing neurons responsive only to human faces viewed from particular angles (Perrett et al., 1991; Desimone, 1991). Neurons in the region labeled FEF (toward the upper, middle part of the diagram) participate in the identification of objects of interest within the visual field and, then, in the guidance of eye movements that direct the center of gaze toward those objects. There are even brain regions with neurons whose responses seem designed to register the remembered location of visual objects within three-dimensional space, neurons that can temporarily retain instructions about where the animal should eventually turn its eyes and head in order to see an object. An overview of these visual areas, with anatomical pictures, can be found on the "Functional Brain Areas" Web page whose link is available at www.mhhe.com/blake5. We will be returning to some of these brain areas in subsequent chapters, as we cover specific components of visual perception in more detail. For now, you should appreciate that vision is the culmination of neural activity spread over a wide territory of the brain, with different areas tackling the analysis and representation of different aspects of vision. In the next few sections we will weigh some of the evidence pointing to this division of labor among brain areas.

The Duality of Visual Processing

The idea that vision consists of multiple, distinct pathways is deeply ingrained in contemporary thinking. The roots for this idea can be traced back to the 1960s, when vision scientists spoke about an "ambient" system that

registered where objects were located in space and a "focal" system that registered the identities of those objects (Schneider, 1969). The focal system was often identified with cortical structures and the ambient system with subcortical structures. In the 1980s focal and ambient vision gave way to another version of this "dual systems" hypothesis, a version positing the existence of two separate cortical pathways, or streams, as they were sometimes called (Mishkin, Ungerleider and Macko, 1983). One pathway, the so-called **parietal stream,** consisted of visual areas laid out along a trajectory leading from occipital to parietal brain regions (recall Figure 4.2). This stream, it was thought, is concerned with the locations of objects in space. Some researchers termed it the *where pathway.* The second pathway, the **temporal stream,** comprised a network of visual areas spanning the occipital and temporal lobes. This stream was thought to be involved in object identification and, therefore, was often referred to as the *what pathway.* You will sometimes see the parietal pathway referred to as the **dorsal stream** since it projects into more dorsal parts of the cerebral cortex (dorsal refers to the upper parts of the brain). The "temporal" pathway, in this nomenclature, is dubbed the **ventral stream** because it projects into more ventral (lower) parts of the cortex.

You can probably see the similarity between the what/where model and the earlier focal/ambient model—the two differ primarily in terms of the anatomical structures embodying the separate pathways. Looking again at Figure 4.20 you may also deduce that the what and where pathways are more or less synonymous with the P and M pathways. As originally proposed by Livingstone and Hubel (1988), the P and M pathways were thought to carry information about color and form (P pathway) and about depth and motion (M pathway). As we will discuss in a moment, behavioral experiments have provided qualified support for some parts of the P/M model.

More recent, detailed anatomical studies reveal, however, that the P and M systems do not remain strictly segregated throughout the visual cortex (Sawatari and Callaway, 1996); contributions from both P and M cells can be traced into both the parietal and temporal pathways.

The latest incarnation of the dual systems hypothesis provides a somewhat different interpretation of the functions of the parietal and temporal pathways (Goodale and Milner, 1992). According to this version of the hypothesis, our visual awareness of objects and events arises from activity in structures comprising the temporal pathway. This pathway would constitute the machinery responsible for the "seeing" aspect of vision that we ordinarily associate with perception. Activity in the parietal pathways, in contrast, is responsible for directing and guiding our activities within the visual environment, activities such as orienting toward and reaching for objects of interest. This constitutes the "action" part of vision.

In our everyday lives, we don't stop to think that these two aspects of vision—seeing and acting—might be dissociated. Yet brain damage to certain regions within the parietal system can throw the two aspects into sharp relief. Goodale and Milner (1992) describe a tragic case where a young woman suffered localized brain damage caused by anoxia from inadvertent carbon monoxide poisoning. Fortunately, this woman retained her intellectual and social skills, but her vision was permanently impaired in a bizarre and revealing way. When shown objects and asked to describe them, she gave no sign that she could even see them. She utterly failed to distinguish shapes as simple as cylinders and blocks. Yet when asked to pick up an object, she deftly moved her hand toward it, and her fingers began conforming to the shape of the object before she ever made contact with it. Notice what your hand and fingers do when you reach for a cup or a pencil—that's exactly what this patient did. The parts of her brain controlling her motor actions seemed to know what she was reaching for, even though she was visually unaware of what she was doing. This intriguing case, in turn, has led to other studies documenting that our visually guided actions seem to be mediated by neural processes that are distinct from those providing us with visual awareness of the objects of those actions (see Goodale and Humphrey, 1998, for an excellent review of this literature).

So the "seeing versus acting" model continues the legacy that vision consists of multiple pathways specialized for different visual tasks. The different versions of this dual systems hypothesis all seem to acknowledge that the temporal stream is doing something rather different from the parietal stream. There is also agreement that, at least in its early stages, vision can be subdivided into P and M cell systems that are inaugurated in the retina. Let's take a moment to examine evidence showing the specializations of these two systems.

P and M Cell Contributions to Vision

Direct evidence for the role of P and M pathways in vision comes from studies in which one pathway—either the P or the M—is rendered inoperative by lesioning it, leaving only the other to mediate vision. This section summarizes the consequences of those selective lesions

To examine the visual contributions of P and M pathways, Schiller and Logothetis (1990) created localized lesions in either parvocellular or magnocellular layers of

the LGN of monkeys and then measured the perceptual consequences. (A lesion at this level of the LGN interrupts processing within this and subsequent stages of the pathways subserved by that cell type.)

Schiller and Logothetis adapted a behavioral technique that was both sensitive and highly versatile, enabling them to study many different aspects of vision. While comfortably seated in a setup like the one pictured in Figure 3.2, monkeys were trained to stare at a central spot on a television monitor. In discrimination tests, stimuli were presented in a circular array, centered about the fixation spot. The monkeys had to move their eyes from the fixation spot toward the one target in the array that differed from the others. In the detection tests, just one target appeared, in a randomly chosen location. On these trials, the monkeys simply shifted the eyes from the central fixation spot to the location of that target. Some of the stimulus arrangements employed by Schiller and Logothetis are illustrated in Figure 4.21.

Results of LGN lesions suggest that P and M pathways do tend to be associated with particular functions. For example, texture discrimination and color discrimination are severely impaired with parvocellular lesions; these same functions are unaffected by lesions of the magnocellular layers. Conversely, discrimination of high rates of flicker is greatly impaired by lesions in magnocellular layers, but not at all affected by parvocellular lesions. Schiller and Logothetis's principal results are given in Figure 4.22.

Although the figure captures the broad outlines of P and M pathway specialization, it misses some important nuances. Consider the case of color. The parvocellular lesions (and only parvocellular lesions) destroyed the ability to make subtle color discriminations (for example, one color patch versus another color patch when the patches have the same brightness), but those same lesions did not diminish the ability to locate a single, large target whose color differed from that of its background even when the target and background were equal in brightness. Presumably, this detection task is also accomplished by using color information, but apparently the M pathway is able to support such tasks even when the parvocellular layers have been damaged.

Or consider the case of a patch that flickers on and off repetitively. As Figure 4.22 shows, only magnocellular lesions impact the discrimination of flicker. But, if the flicker rate is low, the same lesion has no effect. Evidently, the P pathway does have some capacity to process temporal modulation, so long as the modulation rate is not high.

These exceptions should not obscure the importance of the generalizations that can be made. First, under many

FIGURE 4.21 | Illustration of some of the displays used by Schiller and Logothetis (1990) to test visual capacities of monkeys in which the P or the M pathway was inactivated.

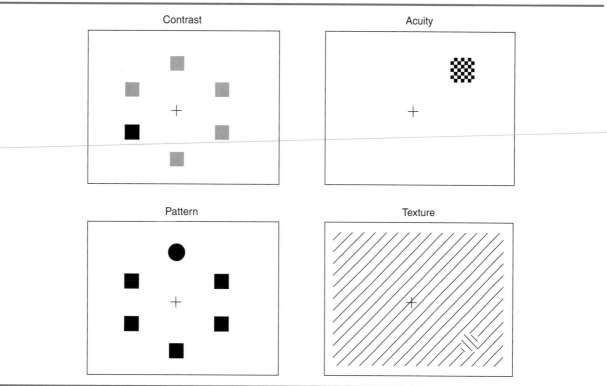

Contrast

Acuity

Pattern

Texture

FIGURE 4.22 | Visual consequences of lesioning the P or the M cells in the LGN.

Function Tested	Result of Lesion in P-pathway	Result of Lesion in M-pathway
Color vision	**Deficit**	Normal
Texture perception	**Deficit**	Normal
Pattern perception	**Deficit**	Normal
Acuity	**Deficit**	Normal
Contrast perception	**Deficit**	Normal
Flicker perception	Normal	**Deficit**

conditions, the P pathway is primarily responsible for perception of color, spatial detail, and texture. Second, under many conditions, the M pathway is primarily responsible for motion and flicker. Third, when the tests are made increasingly more subtle, by employing smaller details or lower contrast between the test object and its background, the division of specialization becomes sharper.

The anatomical diagram in Figure 4.20, the physiological measures of receptive field properties, and the lesion experiments described in the last few paragraphs all involved the study of nonhuman primates, principally the monkey. But several lines of evidence point to the existence of similarly organized, multiple visual areas in the human brain, too.[3] We'll summarize just some of that evidence in the next section.

---

[3] Although they are comparable in general organization, monkey visual cortex and human visual cortex differ in terms of the fine structure of the layers of the cortex (Preuss, Qi, and Kaas, 1999; Preuss and Coleman, 2002). At present, we do not know whether these anatomical differences have perceptual consequences.

Specialized Visual Areas in Human Vision?

One line of evidence is provided by the puzzling visual disorders experienced by people with lesions confined to specific areas of the brain. You've already been introduced to Goodale and Milner's female patient with damage within her temporal pathways. Although unable to recognize objects, she could readily reach and grasp for them. There are other, equally fascinating cases. For example, damage to portions of the brain located on the interior part of the occipital lobe near its junction with the temporal lobe can produce **achromatopsia**—permanent loss of color vision (Cowey and Heywood, 1995). Damage to specific portions of the temporal lobe (which includes the visual areas in the upper right-hand portion of Figure 4.20) can produce **prosopagnosia**—the inability to recognize previously familiar faces even though visual acuity and general intellect remain intact (Damasio, Tranel, and Damasio, 1990). And brain damage confined to the vicinity of area MT can interfere with motion perception, a condition termed **akinetopsia** (Vaina, 1998). The selective nature of these visual disorders suggests that the damaged area was responsible for processing information relevant for the impaired ability. We will return to each of these interesting disorders in subsequent chapters.

The tentative conclusions derived from studies of people with brain damage are buttressed by investigations using the modern neuroimaging techniques (described in Chapter 1). These studies reveal that distinct brain regions are metabolically active during performance of different sorts of visual tasks. Color plate 2 gives one interpretation of the layout of these brain regions (Tootell et al., 1998). Shown in this diagram are two views of the right hemisphere of the human brain, the top view showing the medial surface (visible only by lifting away the left hemisphere) and the bottom view showing the lateral surface of the right hemisphere. The colored regions with labels denote visual areas identifiable by their unique activation to some aspect of the visual scene.[4] Thus, for example, area V8 in the lower part of the occipital lobe is highly active when a person views multicolored displays (Hadjikhani et al., 1998). In the lateral view of the occipital lobe, we see area MT. It's activated when a person watches objects such as dots or lines moving around within the visual field (Tootell et al., 1995). Area V3A, toward the top of the occipital lobe, is also activated by motion, especially if the moving elements

are arranged to form a shape (Tootell et al., 1997). Turning to more complex visual objects, pictures of human faces will activate specific regions within the folds of the temporal lobe (Kanwisher, McDermott, and Chun, 1997), located (but not labeled) just in front of area V8. Viewing scenes depicting rooms, landscapes, and buildings activates a different set of structures within the temporal lobe, situated forward in the brain closer to the hippocampus (Epstein and Kanwisher, 1998). Area V1, in comparison, is activated by all sorts of visual displays—faces, moving dots, colored patches, complex scenes—with the distribution of activation highly dependent on the region of the visual field stimulated (Engel, Glover, and Wandell, 1997). The ubiquitous activation of V1 merely confirms that it serves as the distribution center to these other, more specialized visual areas. In subsequent chapters, we will return to the idea of cortical specialization.

So we have seen converging lines of evidence for the existence of separate visual areas, each specialized for processing a particular aspect of the visual scene. But what is nature's motive for distributing visual processing among multiple areas of the brain? Research in computer science suggests one possible advantage. To quote from one of the most influential writers on this topic:

> Any large computation should be split up and implemented as a collection of small sub-parts that are as nearly independent of one another as the overall task allows. If a process is not designed in this way, a small change in one place will have consequences that become multiplied within many other places. This means that the process as a whole becomes extremely difficult to debug or to improve, whether by a human designer or in the course of natural evolution, because a small change to improve one part has to be accompanied by many simultaneous compensating changes elsewhere. (Marr, 1976, p. 485)

Just how many distinct visual areas exist remains a guess, and much remains to be learned about how activity in these separate areas is orchestrated to guide our actions in the world. An even more perplexing question remains unanswered: How does activity in visually activated neurons produce visual perception? In the next section, we consider this thorny question in more detail.

Relating Visual Perception to Neurophysiology

The previous sections summarized some of the response properties of neurons at various stages along the visual pathways, with particular emphasis on V1. What can be

---

[4] There are fewer labeled areas in color plate 2 than in Figure 4.20 simply because neuroimaging studies have yet to explore many of the cortical territories identified by single cell recordings and anatomical tracing techniques used to construct Figure 4.20. Additional areas in color plate 2 will get filled in as neuroimaging expands its horizons.

said about the role played by these neurons in visual perception? That is the question we take up in this section.

No one doubts that visual cortex is crucially involved in visual perception. This involvement is sadly evidenced by the blindness accompanying damage to visual area V1 and by the unusual visual deficits accompanying damage to visual areas elsewhere in the dorsal and ventral streams. The crucial involvement of visual cortex is further underscored by the fact that visual sensations can be evoked by brief pulses of electric current applied directly to cortical cells (Schmidt et al., 1996). In these cases of direct brain stimulation, people see flashing spots and lines, sometimes colored and sometimes moving, at various locations in their visual fields. The specifics of the visual sensation depend on where brain stimulation is directed (Lee et al., 2000). Because they occur even with the eyes closed or in total darkness, these **phosphenes,** as the sensations are called, must arise entirely from within the person's visual system. Visual hallucinations experienced under the influence of psychoactive drugs (Gregory, 1979) and visual auras experienced during migraine headaches (Richards, 1971) may also reflect the abnormal discharge of cells in the visual cortex.

Another piece of evidence underscoring the tight link between vision and the visual cortex comes from the technique described in Chapter One, called **transcranial magnetic stimulation** (TMS). With this technique, a strong but brief pulse of magnetic energy is directed to a small region on the scalp. If the pulse is strong enough—about 20,000 times greater than the earth's normal magnetic field—and if it is narrowly focused, TMS can selectively disrupt neural activity within a highly restricted region of the brain (Walsh and Cowey, 1998). Using this technique, investigators have created temporary scotomas by applying TMS to the region of the scalp overlying the occipital lobe (Kamitani and Shimojo 1999; Kammer, 1999) and have interfered with visual motion perception by applying TMS to the scalp region over area V5 (Hotson et al., 1994).

Although these observations are intriguing, they merely demonstrate that certain areas of the brain are active during visual perception. They don't prove that these cells actually cause perception. What more can we say about the cellular events that actually mediate vision? How much of what you see can be explained by the activity of brain cells that "prefer" various kinds of visual stimuli? To answer these questions intelligently requires that you be familiar with the various aspects of visual perception—movement, color, form, and so on. Since you will read about these topics in the following chapters, it is premature for us to consider the above questions in specific detail now. However, it *is* worthwhile to consider what sort of activity in visual neurons would most likely explain visual perception.

What Cortical Cells Do

It is tempting to think that the activity of a cortical cell asserts something very specific about the nature of an object located at a particular region of visual space. This idea was well developed by Horace Barlow (1972), who coined the term *feature detector* to characterize visual neurons with very specific stimulus requirements. According to this idea, feature-detecting neurons at higher and higher levels of visual processing become increasingly refined, to the point where they respond only to one very specific object (such as your grandmother's face) or event (such as Barry Bonds swinging a baseball bat).

But this line of reasoning runs headlong into a stumbling block: It requires there to be as many feature detectors as there are unique, recognizable objects and events. These feature detectors would even have to be prepared to construe novel objects or events that had never before been seen by anyone. Even the enormously large number of brain cells available for this task would hardly seem adequate to cover the repertoire of visual experiences that most people will enjoy in their lifetimes.

We run into another problem when talking about cortical cells as feature detectors. Ideally, such a detector would respond only when the requisite feature was present in the visual image, and in the presence of any other feature it would remain completely silent. To behave otherwise would introduce ambiguity into the detector's message, for one could never be sure which feature had activated the cell. Yet real neurons suffer from exactly this **ambiguity problem.** Here is what we mean. As you learned earlier in this chapter, the responses of cortical cells may vary depending on such stimulus features as orientation and direction of motion. A change in any one of those features would be sufficient to reduce the level of activity in such a cell. But purely on the basis of such a reduction in the level of activity of that cell, we could never be sure *which* stimulus feature, or features, had actually changed.

Let's illustrate this problem of ambiguity with an example. Suppose a single vertical line moves slowly from left to right in front of you. Presumably this event will produce a burst of activity in those cortical cells maximally responsive both to slow rates of movement and to vertically oriented contours. Panel A of Figure 4.23 illustrates how one such cell might respond to this stimulus. We can go so far as to presume that activity in cells such as the one illustrated *causes* you to see the moving line. But now suppose the same vertical line moves more rapidly from left to right. This increased speed will reduce the neural activity within your set of cortical cells, for they prefer slower motion. Such a reduction is illustrated in panel B of Figure 4.23. But an equivalent reduction in

FIGURE 4.23 | The response of one cortical cell to different combinations of speed and orientation of a moving bar.

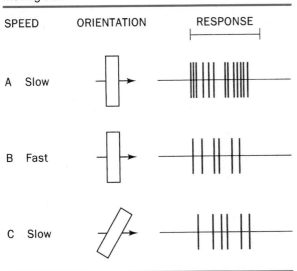

neural activity could be produced another way as well. We could present the line at the preferred, slow rate of movement but change the orientation of the line slightly, so that it was no longer exactly vertical. As panel C of Figure 4.23 shows, this change in orientation also reduces the cell's response. Thus, changing either orientation or speed of movement would diminish the level of activity in cells such as the one illustrated. Just looking at the activity level of a small set of cells, then, we cannot tell which stimulus event actually occurred. The activity level of a cell provides an ambiguous message.

Neurons in the visual cortex cannot really be called feature detectors, then, because individual cells cannot signal the presence of a particular visual feature with certainty. The ambiguity inherent in the response of a single cell can be overcome, however, by *collaboration* among an ensemble of neurons. To illustrate, let's reconsider the example involving a moving line. When the line is tilted slightly away from the vertical, neurons preferring vertical will show a drop in activity, just as we previously pointed out. But at the same time, neurons preferring the new orientation will show an increase in their level of firing. By comparing the levels of neural activity in these two sets of cells, each tuned to slightly different orientations, we could infer that the line had changed in orientation, not in speed. In other words, ambiguity within single neurons can be overcome by considering the pattern of activity within an ensemble of neurons tuned to different

values along a stimulus dimension such as orientation. To amplify this idea of ensemble coding, let's apply it to a visual illusion of orientation that you can experience.

We start with the observation that cells in the visual system, like those in other sensory systems, undergo a process called **adaptation.** When stimulated intensely for a period of time, they become temporarily adapted and are, therefore, less responsive (Movshon and Lennie, 1979). What might be the perceptual consequences of temporarily reducing the responsiveness of the orientation-selective cells of the visual cortex? One consequence may be the **tilt aftereffect,** a temporary change in the perceived orientation of lines. First you should experience this intriguing illusion, and then we can consider how it might be explained in terms of neural fatigue, or adaptation, within an ensemble of cortical neurons.

To begin, look at the three sets of bar patterns shown in Figure 4.24. Note that the circular patch of bars in the middle set (the "test" pattern) are oriented straight up and down. Now stare for a minute or so at the left-hand pattern, the one where the central patch of bars tilt counterclockwise. Let your gaze wander around the circle within the pattern while you are adapting to it. At the end of this period of adaptation, quickly look back at the test pattern in the middle. You will see that the vertical bars within the interior now appear tilted ever so slightly clockwise. (The change in perceived orientation may be most obvious by comparing the orientation of the bars in the central patch to those within the surrounding, annular region; but be sure to keep your gaze directed at the center of the figure at all times.) This illusory distortion in orientation wears off rather quickly, so you can repeat this adaptation procedure as soon as the entire test pattern looks perfectly vertical again. This time, adapt for a minute to the tilted bars in the right-hand pattern, again being careful to move your eyes around the circle. After you have adapted to this clockwise orientation, the bars within the interior of the test pattern will appear rotated in a counterclockwise direction.

So you have learned that the apparent orientation of the test bars deviates *away* from the orientation of the adapting bars. Now let's consider how this tilt aftereffect may be explained. Recall our discussion of the ambiguity inherent in the response of any single cell. We concluded that this problem could be circumvented if stimulus properties such as orientation were represented by the relative activity within an ensemble of orientation-selective cells. In the case of vertical lines, this activity profile might look like that shown in the left-hand portion of Figure 4.25. In the upper part of the diagram, below the test pattern, each

FIGURE 4.24 | Displays for generating the tilt aftereffect. Follow the instructions in the text.

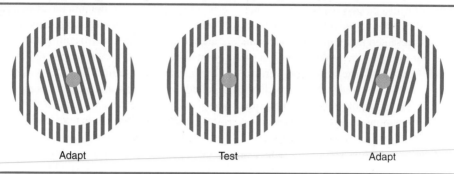

Adapt   Test   Adapt

FIGURE 4.25 | Possible explanation for the tilt aftereffect, based on the concept of ensemble coding of orientation information. The left-hand portion of the drawing shows neural activity evoked by vertical bars prior to adaptation. The right-hand portion shows activity evoked by vertical bars after adaptation to bars tilted slightly clockwise.

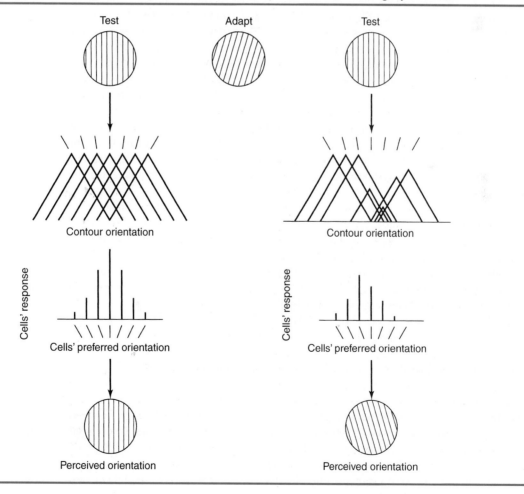

teepee-shaped curve represents the orientation tuning curve for a cortical cell with a particular preferred orientation (recall Figure 4.10). The preferred orientation for each of the cells shown is represented just above the peak of the cells' tuning curve. For example, the middle tuning curve corresponds to a cell maximally responsive to vertical. When this ensemble of cells is stimulated by vertical test bars, the cells within the ensemble respond unequally. Cells with preferred orientations at vertical respond most vigorously, and those with preferred orientations slightly removed from vertical respond less vigorously. This distribution of responses is depicted in the left-hand bar graph, just below the tuning curves. Because this distribution of activity peaks at vertical, this is the perceived orientation of the test pattern.

Suppose we now adapt this array of cells to bars tilted clockwise from vertical (the pattern labeled "Adapt"). With prolonged exposure, the cells activated by this orientation will be fatigued. The cells maximally responsive to the adapting orientation will be maximally fatigued and hence least responsive following adaptation. The upper right-hand portion of the diagram shows what will result when the partially adapted array of cells is again confronted with vertical. Notice that cells maximally stimulated by the tilted adaptation pattern are now fatigued and hence less able to respond to the vertical test. These fatigued cells include ones whose preferred orientation is vertical. Thus, the distribution of responses produced by the vertical test pattern (which is shown in the right-hand bar graph) is no longer centered around vertical. Instead, the peak of this distribution is centered on those cells whose preferred orientation is slightly counterclockwise to vertical. For this reason, the test bars, though physically vertical, seem tilted counterclockwise to vertical. Evidently, the fatigued cells recover quickly, since the tilt aftereffect lasts for a very short time.

See whether you can apply the same reasoning to explain why adapting to an orientation counterclockwise to vertical generates a clockwise tilt aftereffect. Using this theory, predict what will happen if you alternately adapt to both orientations by looking at one for 5 seconds and then the other for 5 seconds and so on, until a minute has elapsed. Presumably, this should fatigue cells on both sides of vertical. After you have derived your prediction, you can test it by actually adapting in that alternating fashion.

The neural coding scheme we've been discussing assumes that information is coded as an activity profile. In this scheme stimulus features are specified by patterns of neural responses within ensembles of cells. But can we say anything about the *number* of ensemble cells needed to register the presence of a given stimulus? There are two reasons for thinking that the number of cells active at any given moment is quite small relative to the hundreds of millions of cells potentially available within visual cortex. First, neurons require metabolic energy to generate action potentials and to convey those action potentials down the neurons' axons. Lennie (2003) has tallied up all the many energy-demanding stages of neural activity and calculated just how much energy is required to produce a given level of activity within a cell. His calculations reveal that for the brain to operate within sustainable levels of energy demand, only a few percent of all cortical neurons can be active at any given time. If this level were exceeded, the brain would quickly burn up its available energy. So metabolic efficiency is one good reason for limiting the ensemble size of active neurons to a minimum. Fortunately, this is not an unreasonable limitation, which brings us to the second reason for believing that ensembles can be relatively small. The receptive field properties of cortical neurons are well matched to regularities associated with images of objects in our natural environment (e.g., Simoncelli and Olshausen, 2001; Simoncelli, 2003). As a result, a relatively sparse set of neurons can efficiently represent the features comprising any given object encountered in the visual world. In subsequent chapters, we'll encounter specific instances where the statistical properties of the world are well matched to the perceptual mechanisms used to register and interpret those properties. For now, however, we can be satisfied that **sparse coding,** as it's sometimes called, makes it possible for the brain to work effectively within the metabolic limitations imposed by the high cost of producing action potentials.

According to an activity profile scheme of information coding, then, stimulus features are specified by patterns of activity within an ensemble of cells. And this coding scheme solves the ambiguity inherent in the responses of individual cells, implying that the visual cortex *does* contain a neural representation of biologically relevant features, such as oriented lines and edges. This brings us back to the intriguing figures introduced in the very beginning of this chapter. Let's reconsider those figures in light of what we now know about cortical processing.

Cortical Neurons and Visual Perception

Vision Is Constructive

Look again at the illusory square resting on top of the four black disks (panel A, Figure 4.1). The contours defining the outlines of this square seem visually distinct, even within the white regions of the figure. Yet those contours are fabrications, not real ones—their existence underscores the

FIGURE 4.26 | Two versions of illusory contours that activate cortical cells in visual areas V1 and V2.

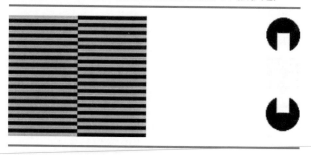

constructive nature of visual perception. It appears, however, that the construction process is undertaken by neurons in V1. Approximately half of the orientation selective cells in this area respond to illusory contours defined by discontinuities in a series of abutting lines like those shown in the left-hand portion of Figure 4.26 (Grosof, Shapley, and Hawken, 1993). The cells are not responding to the horizontal lines themselves but, instead, to the illusory vertical "edge" defined by the offset between the two sets of lines. In visual area V2, which receives input from V1, cells have been found that respond to an illusory contour created by sectored disks such as that shown in the right-hand part of Figure 4.26 (von der Heydt, Peterhans, and Baumgartner, 1984). And, in humans, illusory contours such as these produce enhanced fMRI signals in visual cortical areas immediately adjacent to V1, areas likely to include V2 (Hirsch et al., 1995).

These observations imply that cortical cells in V1 and V2 aren't just replicating features present in the retinal image but, instead, are deducing the locations and orientations of object boundaries. These are crucial first steps in describing the identity and layout of objects within the visual scene.

Vision Is Context Dependent

Next, look back at panel b in Figure 4.1, the one illustrating the impact of context on visual perception. In one context, the snake is conspicuous, but in the other, the snake is hard to locate. Evidently, when linking together the segments making up the snake, the brain is influenced by the contextual relationships among those segments (Field, Hayes, and Hess, 1993). But how does this context effect come about?

As you've learned, a V1 neuron responds best to an appropriately oriented contour located within its receptive field. Thus, for example, a cell preferring vertical

responds vigorously when an upright bar is imaged within its receptive field. By definition, that cell does not respond when that vertical bar (or one of any other orientation) is positioned *outside* the cell's receptive field. However, for many cells in area V1 of the monkey's brain, the cell's response to an oriented bar appearing *within* its receptive field is strongly influenced by the simultaneous presence of other contours just *outside* its receptive field (Das and Gilbert, 1999). Although these interactions can take several different forms, one form of context effect is especially relevant for understanding the visibility of the snakes in Figure 4.1, panel b.

A cell's response to an optimally oriented line within its receptive field is amplified when a neighboring line outside the receptive field has approximately the same orientation and is roughly collinear with the optimally oriented line. Once the line orientation outside the receptive field differs by 60 degrees from the line within the receptive field, this neural facilitation disappears (Kapadia, Westheimer, and Gilbert, 1999). This enhanced response is even stronger if the bar activating the cell is the central figure within an array of oriented contours. If the bar is simply one of the background elements, its response is more muted (Lamme, 1995). Attention to a given figure, in other words, can amplify cortical responses to that figure (Ito and Gilbert, 1999).

These observations demonstrate that V1 cells are performing rather sophisticated neural operations. Instead of merely registering the locations of simple features, these cells can highlight particular features and segregate them from background elements (e.g., Súper et al., 2003). And, in addition to its dependence on context, this highlighting operation is guided by the organism's intentions. Thus, individual neurons respond even more vigorously to features imaged within their receptive fields when those features are the object of the organism's attention (e.g., Luck et al., 1997). As John Maunsell put it, "[T]he cortex creates an edited representation of the visual world that is dynamically modified to suit the immediate goals of the viewer (1995, p. 768)." By the way, the consequences of this dynamic modification can also be seen in neuroimaging experiments with humans. An unchanging visual figure can evoke extra large metabolic activity in visual brain areas when that figure is the focus of a person's attention (Tootell et al., 1998).

Let's continue with the visual objects introduced in Figure 4.1, considering a couple of phenomena that present more formidable challenges for V1 neurons.

Vision and the Ambiguity of Perception

The vase/face figure in panel c in Figure 4.1 documents that a single figure, although physically invariant, can be seen in two strikingly different ways. Figure 4.27 shows another well-known ambiguous figure introduced into the scientific literature by E. G. Boring (1930).[5] If you look at the picture for a few moments, you may appreciate why it's known as the "Wife and Mother-in-Law" figure. Sometimes the figure looks like a shy young woman and at other times it appears to be an unattractive old woman. These fluctuations in the figure's appearance occur even though the stimulus information reaching your eyes remains unchanged. Recall that in the vase/face illusion, the ambiguity concerned which part of the drawing constitutes the figure and which part is the background. With the young/old woman drawing, however, it's not figure and ground that swap places in perception, it's the interpretation of the figure itself that fluctuates.

From what we know about the response properties of V1 cells, their activity should not be changing over time as you stare at these ambiguous pictures—the contour information comprising the figures remains invariant. It is generally assumed that the neural events responsible for the spontaneous changes in the appearance of the figures arise at a higher level of processing, far beyond the primary visual cortex (Logothetis, 1998a; Leopold and Logothetis, 1999). This idea is bolstered by the effect of prior knowledge on the perception of ambiguous figures. Perceptual reversals are far more frequent when people are told ahead of time that a figure can be seen in either of two ways and when they are given some idea of what those alternatives look like (Rock and Mitchener, 1992).

So where in the hierarchy of visual areas (Figure 4.20 and color plate 2) does knowledge exert its influence on visual interpretation? Studies of brain-damaged patients suggest that the kind of knowledge promoting perceptual reversals is embodied neurally in the frontal regions of the brain, well beyond the occipital lobe at the back of the brain where V1 resides. Frontal lobe damage limits an individual's ability to switch between alternative visual interpretations of an ambiguous figure (Ricci and Blundo, 1990; Cohen, 1959; Meenan and Miller, 1994). And in alert, behaving monkeys trained to "report" fluctuations in visual

---

FIGURE 4.27 | An ambiguous figure, which can be seen in either of two ways (an old woman or a young woman).

perception, cells whose activity waxes and wanes in synchrony with perception are readily found in visually activated regions located more toward the front of the brain, but not in area V1 of the occipital cortex (Logothetis, 1998a; Leopold and Logothetis, 1999).

Integration of Local Features

Still stumped by the last drawing in panel d of Figure 4.1? It's an overexposed black-and-white photo of a scene containing, among other things, an animal. Van Tonder and Ejima (2000) showed this very image to a dozen people who had never seen it before, asking them to describe what they saw. Most said that the upper right portion of the figure showed a dark circular ring, with a tree sticking up from its center. Ten of the 12 people described seeing a bulging object in the middle of the image, which they took to be an animal. They described this animal variously, as a lion cub, an iguana, a dog with a tiny head, a human runner doing stretches, and an elephant. Although people disagreed on *what* they saw, curiously, all 10 agreed on the mystery animal's general location: below and to the left of the dark ring.

Incidentally, the animal actually caught by the camera for this image was neither a lion, an iguana, nor a human being; it was a Dalmatian dog with its head pointed downward, nose sniffing the ground. It's easy to understand the image feature that causes people to see the dark ring, but what in the image triggers the perception of an animal? And why do people see so many different animals? Van Tonder and Ejima hypothesized that the answer lay with the dark blobs in the region where the dog is located. In particular, they suspected, that the blobs' orientations gave away the existence of a convex object.

To test their idea, van Tonder and Ejima (2000) randomized the orientation of each individual blob on the animal's body in the image. They showed this randomized image to a new group of people and asked them to describe what they saw. Fewer than half of the people saw a bulging object. The randomly oriented blobs on the animal's body now tended to blend into the randomly oriented blobs in the background, which effectively camouflaged the animal. This brings us to why the individuals in van Tonder and Ejimi's original experiment saw so many different animals, rather than the Dalmatian dog that was the photograph's actual subject. Because the dog's spots are relatively sparse, there are large areas of its body (such as its left hind leg) within which orientation information is weak. The shape and orientation of such areas are therefore ambiguous, and are consistent with varying interpretation. Also, some parts of the dog's body occlude other parts, which further undermines the quality of information available in the image. Finally, the dappled, blotchy background in the image blends smoothly into the dappling on some parts of the dog, such as the dog's dorsal surface and butt. As a result, there is even more uncertainty about the animal's precise outline and species.

Incidentally, if you still can't see the Dalmatian in panel D of Figure 4.1, look at Figure 4.28, which shows the dog in outline. Be forewarned, however, once you find the dog, it'll never go away! If you come back to Figure 4.1 weeks, months, or even years from now you'll spot the Dalmatian immediately.

Looking at only local regions of the picture, as V1 cells do, would never lead one to recognize the scene and the central object within that scene. Rather, we see the scene and the object because of some more widespread, or global, comparison of local contour information. Moreover, knowledge of what to look for dramatically simplifies the job of realizing what you are looking at. It is doubtful whether V1 neurons possess the "knowledge" and "memory" necessary to assemble these pieces into a dog. For that accomplishment, we must look to higher visual areas. But once those higher areas have discovered the overall organization to the pieces, feedback from those areas to V1 may well reinforce activity in some neurons and suppress activity in others (Murray et al., 2002).

FIGURE 4.28 | The figure from panel D in Figure 4.1, now with the mystery animal highlighted for you.

To sum up, it would be a mistake to imagine that the primary visual cortex bears the entire burden of visual perception. This region of cortex is elegantly designed to derive information concerning the shapes and locations of boundaries in the retinal image—an important early step in the process of seeing (Marr, 1982). But seeing involves more than this. Rather than experiencing a conglomeration of unconnected contours scattered throughout the field of view, we see these contours organized into whole objects whose sizes and shapes remain constant. This organization in perception mirrors the organization of real objects as they actually exist. The correspondence between perceptual experience and the objects represented in that experience is not accidental (Campbell, 1974; Shepard, 1981). After all, the visual system did evolve for a purpose, namely to inform us about the objects with which we need to interact. Presumably, natural selection has sponsored this correspondence between perception and the physical world. William James (1892) put this idea succinctly: "Mind and world . . . have evolved together, and in consequence are something of a mutual fit" (p. 4).

SUMMARY AND PREVIEW

These last two chapters have provided an overview of some of the neural machinery of visual perception, including the multiple visual areas scattered throughout the brain. We are now ready to shift the focus to perception itself. In the next several chapters, we are going to examine different aspects, or qualities, of vision. These qualities of vision—shape, color, movement and depth—serve to differentiate objects from one another. In discussing each of these qualities of vision, we will treat them as the final product of the visual system's processing. We will also consider what sort of mechanism would be needed to yield this product. However, the major emphasis will be on *what* you see, rather than on *how* you see.

KEY TERMS

achromatopsia
adaptation
akinetopsia
ambiguity problem
aneurysm
binocular
binocular cell
blindsight
blobs
complex cells
contralateral fibers
contrast
cortical magnification
direction selectivity
dorsal stream
forced-choice testing
hypercolumn

hypercomplex cells
ipsilateral fibers
lateral geniculate nucleus
magnocellular layers
meridional amblyopia
monocular
myelin
oblique effect
occipital lobe
ocular dominance
optic chiasm
optic nerve
optic tracts
orientation constancy
orientation selectivity
parietal stream
parvocellular layers

perimetry
phosphenes
position invariance
prosopagnosia
reticular activating system
retinotopic map
scotomas
simple cells
sparse coding
superior colliculus
temporal stream
tilt aftereffect
transcranial magnetic stimulation
   (TMS)
ventral stream
visual field

Spatial Vision and Form Perception

We rely on vision for just about everything we do: reading a menu, looking out for vehicles when crossing a busy street, kicking a football, using a mirror to put on makeup, selecting ripe apples at a roadside stand, spotting a friend in a crowded airport, and all the countless other activities we engage in every day. As these examples suggest, visually guided activities nearly always revolve around *objects*. Some tasks entail picking out an object from its surroundings, such as spotting the evening's first star in the twilight sky. We can call this process **detection.** Other tasks require the additional step of distinguishing one object from another, such as selecting a quarter from the pile of coins on your desk. We can call this second, more refined process **discrimination.** Or you may need to identify with precision a particular object or a specific person. Finding your picture in the college yearbook requires this level of specificity. This third process we can call **identification.** To deal with the environment successfully, people must be able to accomplish all three tasks rapidly and accurately: detect, discriminate, and identify. Detection reveals the presence of an object or objects; discrimination and identification serve more refined, complicated purposes. For example, visual discrimination allows an organism to sort important objects from unimportant ones. Of course, importance varies with one's current needs.

Overwhelming hunger means you'd better be able to distinguish the edible from the inedible; when preparing a research paper, you must be able to distinguish potentially relevant books from irrelevant ones. For some animals, it is imperative to discriminate potential mates who are in heat from those who are not. Identification demands one more step—not only must one object be distinguished (discriminated) from others, the precise identity of that object must be specified. To find *your* red Miata in a crowded parking lot, you must discriminate the red cars from all the rest *and* then identify yours based on other familiar, more specific cues such as the small dent in the hood.

These examples suggest a hierarchy of processes in which discrimination builds on detection, and identification, in turn, builds on discrimination. Of course, you do not consciously step through this sequence. The perceptual act of identifying some object in a complex scene often occurs effortlessly, in the blink of an eye, and mostly without your being aware. Nonetheless, the stimulus information required for the three processes differs, with each successive process requiring more refined information.

Even the seemingly simple act of detection has prerequisites. To be detected, an object must differ from its surroundings in at least one of several possible ways. The differences can involve color (a ripe, red berry against the green leaves of its bush), movement (an ant crawling on your ice cream), shape (a chocolate-covered cherry in a box of mixed chocolates), or depth (an aspirin that has fallen on a white tile floor). Usually, several of these sources of information are available at the same time, which facilitates detection. For example, a breeze causes some red berries to move relative to the green leaves, making the berries even more conspicuous. But once the berries are detected, ripe ones must be discriminated from the unripe, which can require judging subtle color differences. And, of course, to guard against poisoning, it's a very good idea to identify the type of berry you're about to eat. Identification entails comparing the current environmental stimulus with stored knowledge about categories of berries.

This chapter and the four that follow deal with visual information that makes detection and discrimination possible. These chapters also go into the details of how the nervous system registers and processes that information. The present chapter examines how an object's spatial properties influence detection and discrimination. We use the term *spatial properties* to refer to those attributes of an object that determine the perceived size and shape of the object. Defined in this way, the term *spatial properties* is more or less synonymous with the often-used terms *form* and *visual pattern*. In this chapter, we'll be focusing on what some experts would characterize as "early vision," a term used to denote the initial stages of image analysis that, in turn, are used for more refined description of a visual scene. In the following chapter, we'll move to the rules governing that more refined description. Of course, objects have color and three dimensionality, and some characteristically move about in the environment—these are aspects of vision that are discussed in Chapters 7, 8, and 9, respectively.

We should start by defining what is meant by an "object." To do that, let's start with a real-world problem.

What Defines an Object?

On January 4, 2004, the planet Mars had its second human-made visitor, a sophisticated robotic vehicle named Spirit. (Spirit's robotic forbearer was a compact little gadget named Sojourner, the first human-made vehicle to move across Mars's surface back in 1997.) Spirit was deposited in the middle of the Gusev crater, a region of the Martian landscape of particular interest to NASA scientists because of its diverse geological composition. From high-altitude photographs, scientists suspected that Gusev's rocks and sediment held important clues to the origin and evolution of Mars, including the possible existence of water on Mars eons ago. Spirit's assignment was to navigate

Gusev's treacherous terrain, collecting invaluable images and geological samples. To accomplish this daunting task, Spirit was outfitted with an array of sensitive instruments including a stereo camera that captured detailed color images of the Martian surface in vivid 3D. Electronic signals from this pair of cameras were transmitted back to earth, where Spirit's human colleagues issued commands guiding Spirit's explorations.[1]

Information from Spirit's "eyes" arrived on earth as a torrent of numbers: numerical snapshots of what Spirit encountered from moment to moment. In any snapshot, a single number represented how much light fell on a particular place on the robot's cameras during that snapshot. A large number signified a lot of light, a small number meant very little light; in this respect, Spirit's camera is like the photoreceptor matrix in the human eye (recall Figure 3.1). The numbers held the secrets to locating objects within the Martian environment—the hills, valleys, rocks, and boulders of the red planet. But how could those secrets be unlocked so that scientists, back here on earth, can reconstruct the objects that Spirit encountered?

Figure 5.1 shows the collection of numbers produced when Spirit had its camera-eyes fixed on the distinctive rock formation that NASA scientist fancifully named Sashimi.[2] To transform the numbers into meaningful descriptions of Martian objects, researchers perform operations much like ones the human visual system performs when our eyes gather information from some complex scene here on earth. Of course, operations on data from Mars are carried out numerically, by powerful computers, but our visual system performs analgous operations neurally, using even higher-powered biological brains.

Spirit's numerical snapshots convey to us something about Martian objects. But how can we sift through the numbers to find signs that an object was present? For the answer to this question, we must exploit physical properties of matter. As described in Chapter 2, the patterns of light reflected from objects depend on the surface properties of those objects. Suppose that an object, let's say a rock, is composed of different material from its surroundings, say the dust-covered surface of Mars. Now, different materials (e.g., rocks and dust) usually differ in

---

[1] There are websites devoted to Spirit's activities on Mars, and these sites include some remarkable photos taken by the device's camera. Some of those websites are available through links at www.mhhe .com/blake5.

[2] Sashimi, as you probably know, is a Japanese delicacy consisting of slices of raw fish. Geological structures encountered on Mars are typically named on the basis of their resemblance to familiar objects on earth. Imagination plays a large role in this naming process.

FIGURE 5.1 | At the upper part of the figure is an image of a rock (named Sashimi) encountered at Gusev crater site on the Martian surface; the photograph was taken by one of the onboard cameras of the Martian Rover Spirit. Light levels of the pixels in a small square section of the image (outlined in white) were measured and digitized (converted into numerical values). The results of digitization are shown in the array of numbers at the bottom of the figure. High numerical values represent brighter pixels; low values represent dimmer pixels. You should have no trouble seeing the correspondence between clusters of numbers of regions in the image. This photograph, of course, is black and white, so the numbers just refer to light levels. For color photographs, each cell in the matrix of numbers would have three values specifying the amount of light at different bands of wavelength.

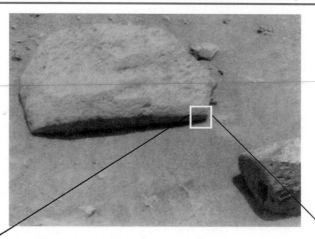

174	168	160	159	168	171	187	193	192	172	161	97	50	108	129	120	130
175	173	171	171	170	158	166	178	189	181	172	127	101	121	130	137	139
154	161	168	169	171	155	149	152	159	161	158	144	131	128	138	148	137
144	153	161	158	154	149	146	143	141	146	149	158	140	129	133	155	153
123	125	139	143	135	120	112	102	120	128	131	156	148	152	148	157	163
155	156	140	121	92	100	123	134	129	109	124	150	142	149	155	163	161
130	119	102	94	94	109	111	104	111	136	169	156	145	154	164	169	162
70	58	49	49	47	50	44	38	47	69	116	136	152	165	167	168	168
20	17	7	6	7	5	11	12	7	6	57	130	151	167	163	165	178
3	8	9	8	16	15	13	3	2	4	62	136	148	166	162	170	191
0	10	6	0	9	4	3	9	11	6	73	140	148	162	161	170	186
2	2	6	6	7	14	5	8	2	17	92	139	148	156	156	161	169
0	6	2	5	3	5	2	3	12	39	97	137	152	146	148	161	173
7	7	8	9	0	13	16	4	10	66	139	159	152	145	147	159	164
2	3	3	9	16	12	21	46	77	120	148	139	153	153	152	158	165
7	22	32	42	69	90	105	125	144	141	145	164	159	169	165	158	167
81	98	111	122	130	146	145	146	164	168	159	164	152	169	168	158	171
139	139	136	137	130	136	148	148	152	164	164	159	152	164	167	167	175
132	133	134	140	158	149	157	158	158	163	161	160	167	167	167	168	169
143	149	152	160	156	157	157	152	160	160	144	148	160	154	152	152	157

the amounts of light they reflect and in the wavelengths contained in that reflected light; those differences in light reflection thus can distinguish an object from its surroundings based on color, texture, lightness, and shape. A properly programmed computer can find regions in Spirit's Martian snapshots where clusters of numbers differ systematically from surrounding numbers. The computer, in other words, can "detect" an object (or parts of an object).

So, one of vision's basic aims is to identify regions where clusters of numbers (if done by computer image processing) or neural signals (if done by biological hardware) differ appreciably from surrounding numbers or neural signals. There are several ways that light reflected from an object can differ from the light reflected by the object's immediate surroundings. For example, the two might differ in intensity (bright versus dim light), spectral content (long wavelengths versus short wavelengths), or in the way that the reflected light is patterned (uniform versus uneven). These three kinds of differences produce perceptual qualities that are called lightness, color, and glossiness (recall Figure 2.16). Success in detecting an object or a part of an object depends on the *difference* between the light reflected by the object and the light reflected from its surroundings.[3] As Chapters 3 and 4 noted, neurons at multiple stages of the visual system are well suited to register such differences. The numerical array in the bottom part of Figure 5.1 summarizes the light levels within the tiny portion of the image of Sashimi outlined by the white square. Within this array of numbers you can easily see regions where the light levels change abruptly, suggesting the presence of different surfaces and, perhaps, different objects. So, identifying distinctive areas within an image is a crucial first step in machine vision and in biological vision, but of course it's not the only step. After all, distinctive areas do not by themselves tell us what we're looking at. Spirit's clusters of numbers are meaningless without further analysis, and the same is true for the cluster of intensity and wavelength values registered by the eye. The next step is to translate information about distinctive regions into information about form.

---

[3] As the intensity of an object's background increases, light reflected from that object must be more intense in order for the object to be seen. This is why you cannot see the stars in the daytime sky even though they are present and give off just as much light as they do at night. This is an example of the general principle known as Weber's law, which is discussed in the appendix.

What Defines "Form"?

You probably have some intuition about what is meant by an object's "form." The term typically refers to the attributes of size and shape. All objects have form. For nebulous ones such as clouds, the form may be changeable. For most biological objects, such as a person or an orange, however, stable form is more long-lasting. And for many nonbiological objects, such as the Martian rock named Sashimi, form is really long-lasting. Are there universal laws governing the perception of form? Is it useful to consider a given visual form as some composite of more elementary features? And if so, what are those features? How does the visual system extract form information from the retinal image? These questions are explored in the next several sections.

From the outset, keep in mind an important caveat about the study of form perception. Like other aspects of visual perception, form is the culmination of many processing steps, most of which transpire without your effort or awareness. Just looking at an object tells you nothing about the steps involved in deriving your impression of that object's form (Snyder and Barlow, 1988). To make this point concrete, consider an analogy. The end product of cooking can be a sophisticated dish, but just tasting the dish does not disclose the steps involved in preparing the dish. Complete understanding of the cooking process requires knowing the ingredients as well as the recipe by which those ingredients were prepared and combined. The same requirement applies to understanding form perception.

As we move through this and the next chapter, it is useful to distinguish between processing carried out within local spatial neighborhoods and processing carried out on a more widespread, global basis. This local/global distinction will become clearer as we move through this and the following chapter, but for now an analogy should help. The text on this page consists of words composed of letters constructed from simple lines and curves. Obviously to read the text requires that vision register the simple features comprising individual letters. We can construe that registration process as local since it deals with simple features in local regions of the retinal image of the page. But reading also involves clustering of letters into larger, coherent groups: words and then sentences. These grouping processes assemble local features into more global patterns that are meaningful to our task.

Our exploration of spatial vision and form perception begins with short-range, local analysis of the retinal image, and then proceeds to longer-range, global analysis. For starters, we'll consider the question of form and its components from an historic perspective.

What Are the Components of Visual Form?

The structuralist tradition, which germinated in Europe during the late nineteenth century and flowered after being transplanted to the United States, had a simple guiding notion, namely, that ideas and perceptions are created by combining fundamental components. According to this view, simple sensations constitute the building blocks of perceived form. Seems reasonable, but how do we identify these simple sensations? Edward Bradford Titchener, a leader of the structuralist movement, championed a very simple method, called **analytic introspection.** He trained people to ignore all aspects of an object except its immediate, primary qualities. By attending only to an object's appearance and nothing else, people tried to enumerate the various sensations evoked by that object. For example, a person looking at an apple might report seeing four different colors and 13 different levels of lightness, with both color and lightness distributed over the apple's surface. According to the structuralists, these ingredients constituted the sensations from which perception of the apple was built. After analytic introspection had been in use for a while, the number of approved "elementary" sensations ballooned out of control, to more than 40,000 (Boring, 1942). Compared to the relatively modest number of chemical elements in the periodic table (currently, a few shy of 120), a set of 40,000 perceptual elements seemed excessive. To make matters worse, one person's reported elementary sensations often differed from those of another person. These disagreements were particularly striking because they involved people working in different laboratories. This suggests that the technique of introspection is susceptible to nonperceptual influences such as motivation and instruction. As you might imagine, what people *say* they see depends partly on what they *expect* to see ("Aren't apples typically red?").

In addition to the drawbacks just mentioned, introspection suffers from a logical flaw as well. Even if someone can learn to recognize a particular sensation when it occurs all by itself, there's no guarantee that the person will be able to recognize it when that sensation occurs in combination with other sensations. Is an apple's particular shade of red really independent of the glossiness of its skin or the color of the surface upon which the apple is resting? These difficulties seriously undermine the usefulness of analytic introspection as a tool for identifying "components" of perception. Nonetheless, one can embrace the structuralists' idea that perceptions are built from elementary sensations without subscribing to introspection as the method for isolating those sensations. But how can we identify the units of sensation with minimal contribution from our prejudices and expectations about what those units *ought* to be (Harris, 1998) and thus be confident we've got the right answer? One approach is to use physiological and psychophysical experiments that force the visual system itself to tell us the answer, even if those experiments produce answers that go against our intuitions.

A Local Analysis: Differences between Neighbors

Figure 5.2a is a photograph of downtown Nashville, Tennessee. Like other environments, natural or human-made, this scene comprises a range of different levels of spatial information, from coarse to very fine (Field, 1987; Tolhurst and Tadmor, 1997). Each level of spatial information defines a **scale.** To illustrate this idea, we have used a computer to break down the scene into three different sets of spatial scales, extracting and then displaying each scale separately.[4] The photograph in panel b captures the content of the scene on the broadest scale, the proverbial "big picture." Panel d contains the smallest scale of structural information from the scene—the scene's details. Panel c shows the scene's information on a scale intermediate to the other two. In panel e, you can see what happens when the three isolated scales, in panels b, c, and d, are put back together. The result is identical to the original. The differences in scale of the three images emphasize different aspects of the scene: the top image (b) emphasizes the broad layout of the scene, with skyline distinct from the river in the foreground; the middle (c) highlights individual buildings; and the bottom (d) image spotlights architectural details.

The objects we encounter every day contain spatial information on multiple spatial scales, and the features represented on those different scales harmonize with one another. But to highlight the concept of spatial scale, hybrid images can be created in which the various scales are in conflict with one another. An example of such an

---

[4] Any scene, this one included, actually contains a continuum of scales, not just three. We are working with three for ease of illustration.

FIGURE 5.2 | Photograph of Nashville, Tennessee, skyline (a) decomposed, or filtered, into component parts (b–d) depicting different spatial scales present in the original. Recombination of those filtered images recreates the original (e).

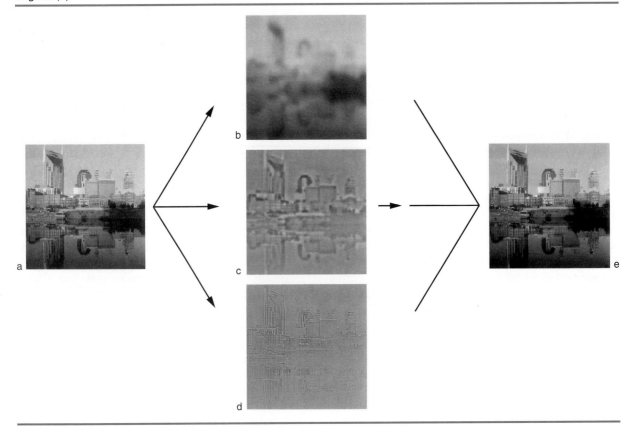

image is shown in Figure 5.3. Upon looking at this photograph, most people see the unsmiling face of a man. But this indicates that they're actually seeing only half of the picture. To create this photograph, Philippe Schyns and Aude Oliva blended two different faces—one an unsmiling male (carried by fine scale information), the other a smiling female (carried by low scale information). Although the image contains both faces, the unsmiling male is what we see because his face has been computer-processed to make it dominate the blend. Want to see the other member of the composite? Try squinting or defocusing your eyes as you look at the figure—you should see the other face, a smiling female. If you wear glasses, simply removing them may do the trick. If none of these tricks works for you, try dimming the lights or moving farther away from the picture until the smiling face appears. All of these maneuvers—squinting, dimming the lights, and so forth—alter the

balance of information in the two composites, reducing the effectiveness of the small scale (detailed) information and allowing the form carried by the lower scale information to emerge. Ordinarily, of course, information registered at low spatial scale is concordant with information registered at high spatial scale, so you'd never see this kind of perceptual competition.

As we noted before, objects and scenes in the natural environment typically contain information at multiple spatial scales, from very fine to very coarse. A viewer's goals determine what components of this blend are paramount. Sometimes it's important to see the forest, (the overall, "global" view), while at other times it's the trees or even the leaves that interest us (the detailed, "local" view). Ideally, then, your brain's neural representation of a scene would contain information from all scales simultaneously.

To probe vision's flexibility in using information on different scales, Schyns and Oliva (1997) employed hy-

FIGURE 5.3 | Two superimposed faces, one portrayed at a coarse spatial scale (smiling woman) and the other at a fine spatial scale (unsmiling man). Under normal viewing conditions, you will probably see that the male's face dominates the percept. The text explains how you can tip the balance in the direction of the other, female face.

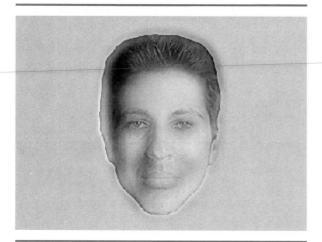

FIGURE 5.4 | The puzzle piece on the right fits somewhere in the complete puzzle on the left. Can you find the piece's location?

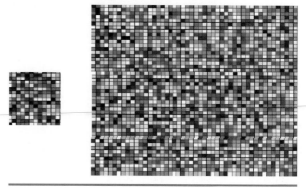

brid images like the one in Figure 5.3. After each hybrid was briefly presented, observers reported what they saw. From these reports Schyns and Oliva inferred which spatial scale observers were relying on. For example, if you look at Figure 5.3 and report seeing a smiling woman, you must be accessing the figure's coarse scale of spatial information.

In the first phase of Schyns and Oliva's experiment, observers were sensitized to one scale of information—for some people this was the coarse scale, for the others, it was the fine scale. During this sensitization phase, observers saw hybrids containing meaningful information on only one scale; the other scale constituted a meaningless pattern. The aim of this sensitization phase was to "tune" or "prime" each observer's visual system to one scale or the other. Then, without warning to the observer, the composition of the hybrids changed. In this phase of the experiment, each hybrid contained meaningful images on both scales, coarse and fine. Nonetheless, observers continued relying on the scale they had been sensitized to ("coarse" for those sensitized to coarse, and "fine" for those sensitized to fine). So the sensitization experience dramatically influenced how observers saw the ambiguous test hybrids. Moreover, after the experiment, virtually all observers were surprised to learn that

the test hybrids actually contained two different meaningful images since they were aware of seeing just one.

Access to representations of scenes and objects at different spatial scales allows the visual system to solve problems that would be intractable using just a single representation (Hildreth, 1986). You will learn about some of those potentially intractable problems in later chapters. For now, a simple analogy may illustrate the utility of creating neural representations of a visual scene on several different scales simultaneously. Think about the optimum strategy for assembling a complex jigsaw puzzle (a thought experiment we introduced in Chapter 4, when speculating about the lateral geniculate nucleus's function). Before attempting to fit together small, individual pieces of a puzzle, most people sort them into larger clusters based on common features. For example, we gather all the light blue pieces in a pile, knowing that they probably all go together to represent the sky; the dark brown pieces are placed in a separate pile because they'll make up the large tree trunk in the foreground. The large dark regions (foreground) and the large light regions (background) define the image's coarse spatial information. In effect, you're exploiting spatial scale information to get a head start on the assembly process. If you started by trying to assemble the pieces based on the picture's fine detail, the task would be overwhelming.

To illustrate spatial scale's utility, we've created a special jigsaw puzzle that's unusually hard to assemble. The assembled puzzle is shown in the right-hand part of Figure 5.4, and as you can see the puzzle portrays an irregular array of black, white, and gray checks. Notice that

FIGURE 5.5 | This is the same puzzle and piece as in Figure 5.4, only now portrayed at a coarse spatial scale.

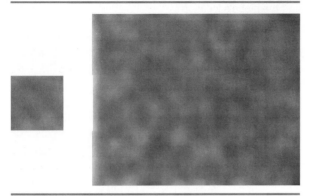

FIGURE 5.6 | A sinusoidal grating pattern.

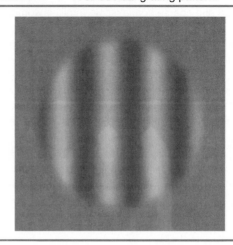

there is no meaningful structure in the layout of these checks. Shown on the left of Figure 5.4 is one small, square piece of this puzzle, and this piece appears somewhere within the completed puzzle on the left. Can you figure out where the piece originated? Taking a hint from the visual system, we've recreated the puzzle and the piece as they might be represented at some coarser spatial scale—these modified images are shown in Figure 5.5. Note that operating on coarse scale information, the task becomes easier—you probably have less trouble locating where this piece came from.

But this analogy is a little misleading. Assembling a puzzle involves figuring out which pieces interlink with one another. You begin by randomly shuffling the pieces to scramble their spatial arrangement. In vision, however, the two-dimensional spatial layout of the image is preserved; no scrambling is involved. But here's a key: There are neural operations in vision where the brain must compare the spatial arrangement of "pieces" from one image and match them to the spatial arrangement of "pieces" in another image. This is true for binocular vision (where the separate images are formed in the two eyes), and it's true for motion perception (where the successive images are formed over time); you'll learn about both in Chapters 8 and 9, respectively. For now, you should have a clearer understanding of the concept of spatial scale and its potential utility when it comes to image analysis.

But how is this multiscale analysis actually implemented in human vision? In 1968, two vision scientists, Fergus Campbell and John Robson, hypothesized that the

visual system uses neurons with different-sized receptive fields to create a series of neural representations on different scales. Their theory was inspired by physiological studies of neurons in the visual system. At different levels of the visual system, responses of various neurons form a neural representation of the light that is falling on the retina. As discussed in Chapters 3 and 4, because receptive fields vary in size among neurons, the responses of different subsets of neurons constitute a neural representation at different spatial scales. Each subset of neurons conveys a characteristic kind of information defined by the spatial scale, so each set comprises an information *channel*. Because Campbell and Robson's theory relates vision of spatial form to activity within many such channels, it is known as the **multichannel model.**

To test their hypothesis, Campbell and Robson (1968) needed visual patterns whose properties could be varied systematically in ways that would have a varying, but predictable, impact on neurons in the visual cortex. Because cortical neurons are tuned to stimulus orientation and to spatial scale (size), the researchers needed patterns whose orientation and scale could be varied systematically. In addition, knowing that neurons' responses vary with image contrast (the difference between adjacent regions' light levels), they needed to specify and vary contrast as well. The visual pattern shown in Figure 5.6 satisfies these requirements. Such patterns, called **gratings,** can be generated on a computer monitor or television display. The one in Figure 5.6 is called a **sinusoidal grating** because the intensity of its light and dark bars varies gradually across the grating's width, in a sinusoidal fashion.

Gratings as Tools for Exploring Form Perception

What Are Gratings?

Gratings have four defining characteristics: **spatial frequency, contrast, orientation,** and **spatial phase.** These characteristics can vary independently of one another, which means that one can be changed without affecting the others. Let's examine these characteristics one by one.

Spatial frequency refers to the number of light and dark regions imaged within a given distance on the retina. One third of a millimeter is a convenient unit of retinal distance because an image that size subtends one degree of visual angle (recall the discussion of visual angle at the end of Chapter 2). To give you an idea of this angular unit of size, your index fingernail forms an image one degree in width when your finger is viewed at arm's length; a typical human thumb, not just the nail, but the entire width at the widest point, forms an image about twice as big, two degrees of visual angle (O'Shea, 1991). Recall from Chapter 2 that the size (or visual angle) of the retinal image cast by an object depends on the distance of that object from the eye. As the distance between the eye and the object decreases, the object's image subtends a greater visual angle.

The unit employed to express spatial frequency is the number of cycles that fall within one degree of visual angle (one cycle consists of one dark and one light bar). A grating of high spatial frequency—many cycles within each degree of visual angle—is made up of narrow bars. A grating of low spatial frequency—fewer cycles within each degree of visual angle—contains wide bars. Because spatial frequency is defined in terms of visual angle, a grating's spatial frequency changes with viewing distance. As this distance decreases, each bar casts a larger image. As a result, the grating's spatial frequency decreases as the distance decreases. To give you an example, when held at arm's length, the grating in Figure 5.6 has a spatial frequency of about 1.0 cycle per degree of visual angle. Doubling the viewing distance doubles the grating's spatial frequency to 2.0 cycles per degree.

Contrast is related to the intensity difference between the light and dark bars of the grating. If this difference is great, the grating's contrast is high; a small difference means the contrast is low. If the contrast is low enough, the bars of the grating may not even be visible. At sufficiently low contrast, the computer monitor or television screen would appear uniform and unpatterned; the grating contrast would be "below the threshold for visibility." At higher contrasts, the pattern would be visible. In Figure 5.3, the image of the unsmiling male face tends to predominate because the contrast of that image exceeds that of its companion female face image.

Quantitatively, contrast runs from 0 percent (when there is no difference at all between the intensity of the light and dark bars) to 100 percent (when the difference between light and dark bars is at its maximum).[5] The contrast of the print you are reading is about 90 percent; the contrast in the grating shown in Figure 5.6 is about 40 percent.

Orientation refers to the axis of the grating's bars. The grating in Figure 5.6 is a vertical grating. If it were rotated through 90 degrees, it would become a horizontal grating.

Spatial phase refers to a grating's position relative to some landmark. A convenient landmark is the left edge of the display. Looking at that edge, we can say that a grating "begins" with a dark bar, a light bar, or something in between. The gratings at the top and bottom of Figure 5.7 are in opposite phase; one begins with a light bar, the other with a dark one. The phase of the middle grating is midway between those at the top and bottom.

Phase specifies how components of an image relate to one another, which is a crucial aspect of form perception. In fact, when we create hybrid gratings composed of two components, the appearance of the hybrid depends on the relative spatial phase of the two. Figure 5.8 shows a pair of hybrid gratings consisting of a 1 cycle/degree grating added to a 3 cycle/degree grating (these spatial frequencies assume viewing at arm's length). In the right-hand hybrid, the two components were added so that their bright bars in the middle of the figure were superimposed. In the left-hand hybrid, the middle bright bar of one coincides with a dark bar of the other. Notice that these two hybrids are noticeably different even though they are composed of identical components; phase affects the appearance of the combination.

Manipulating these four properties of gratings—spatial frequency, contrast, orientation, and phase—we can construct any visual pattern, including a human face. To start, let's see how far we can get using just two orientations. Our plan is to start with a pair of gratings, one with bars oriented diagonally clockwise (CW) and the other with bars oriented diagonally counterclockwise (CCW), and add pairs of higher-frequency grat-

---

[5] There are several formulae for computing contrast. For gratings, though, contrast is equal to the difference between the light intensity of the lightest part of the grating and the light intensity of the dimmest part, divided by the sum of these two quantities.

FIGURE 5.7 | These three gratings differ in phase only.

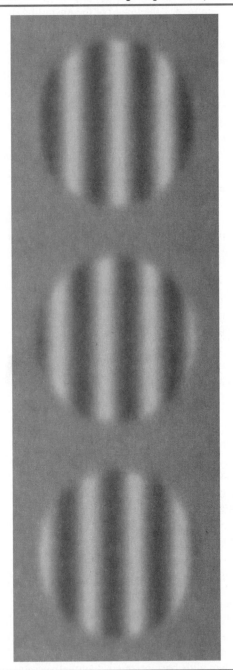

FIGURE 5.8 | The same components added in different phases yield distinctly different compound gratings.

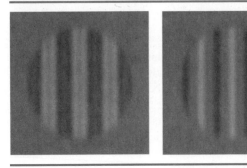

a pair of obliquely oriented gratings of a particular frequency. Note two things about C's evolution. First, from A through C, the combination begins to resemble a plaid. Here, interactions between components are creating visual structures (diamonds) that are not associated with the individual components themselves. Second, from A through C, the diamonds become more sharply defined, even though only sinusoidal components with no sharp edges were used. Repeating a point made previously when discussing introspection, you cannot always tell what elementary components make up a pattern.

Now let's try to synthesize an even more complex figure, a photograph of a natural scene. This synthesis requires that we use more than just two orientations. Because it would take a great many frequency components to synthesize the natural scene, it would be tedious to show each individual step of the process. Instead, at each stage we'll add whole clusters of frequencies. Looking at Figure 5.10, A shows the frequency and orientation cluster that we'll start with. From this point, we follow the same procedure used in Figure 5.9, successively adding the clusters shown in 1 and 2 to create B and C. Note how each cluster makes its own unique contribution to the final product, C. Bear in mind that this complex scene results from adding various simple components that differ in frequency, contrast, orientation and phase. Notice, incidentally, that A, 1, and 2 represent the low, medium, and high spatial frequency information of the final product.

As just shown, spatial frequency components can be used to create a visual scene. Because they provide a vocabulary rich enough to express important aspects of visual form, gratings became a popular tool for studying

ings, each additional pair consisting of a CW and a CCW component. Looking at Figure 5.9, in A you see the first two gratings superimposed. Adding in the next two components (1) results in B. Adding to this the next two components (2) produces the pattern shown in C. In each case, the added components are nothing more than

FIGURE 5.9 | Steps involved in generating a plaid.

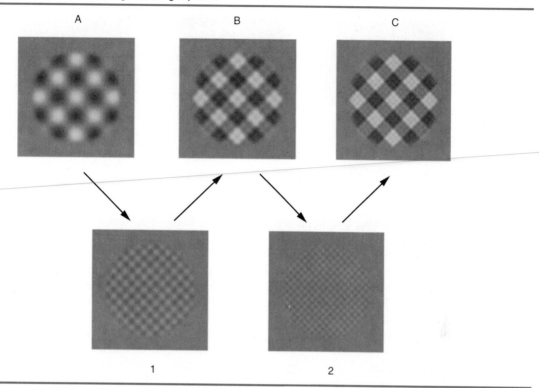

FIGURE 5.10 | Steps involved in generating a natural scene, in this instance, a photograph of flowers.

FIGURE 5.11 | Which of these three gratings appears highest in contrast and which appears lowest in contrast?

form perception. However, just because the photographic image of a scene can be synthesized from spatial frequency components does not mean that the visual system analyzes the scene into those components. Later in this chapter, we will consider evidence for scale-dependent analysis in human vision. Eventually, we'll show you how gratings are used to explore human pattern perception. However, since *human* vision is rather complicated, we begin with a much simpler system.

As you already know from Chapters 2 and 3, there are many parallels between the eye and a camera. As an entrée to human form perception, then, let's see how the performance of a camera's lens might be measured. A lens, as you know, is the optical component responsible for producing a focused image on the plane of the film or, with a digital camera, on the plane of the charge-coupled device (CCD). The quality of that image is only as good as the optical quality of the lens. The following section explains the technique we can use to measure the optical quality of a lens, a technique that can be generalized to measurement of the quality of human vision.

Using Gratings to Measure Performance

Measuring a lens's performance requires two steps. First, we use the lens to create an image of an object, preferably one like a grating whose spatial content can be quantified. Then we compare the image produced by the lens with the actual object. For example, using a lens, we would create an image of a grating of specified spatial frequency and contrast. We could then determine how good an image the lens had created. But "good" is an extremely vague term. How can we quantify it?

One approach is simply to judge the appearance of the image. But subjective impressions can be mislead-

ing. To illustrate, look at the three gratings in Figure 5.11 and rank them in terms of their apparent contrast (these gratings differ in spatial frequency). Most people would rank them in the order shown, with the leftmost grating deemed lowest in contrast. But this is wrong, for all three gratings have precisely the same physical contrast. In a moment, we'll consider why the perceived contrast differs from the actual contrast. But first, let's explore in greater detail this problem of evaluating image quality. A better, more objective way to assess the quality of images such as the one in Figure 5.11 is by means of a photometer, an instrument that measures light levels. The following example shows how this can be accomplished.

Suppose we use an expensive, high-quality lens to cast an image of a "target" grating on a clean, white paper. We can use the photometer to determine the intensity of the light and dark portions in the image and, hence, the contrast of the image of the grating produced by the lens. We'll repeat these measurements for different spatial frequencies, always using target gratings of the same contrast. We can graph the results in the following way. The horizontal axis of the graph will show spatial frequency; the vertical axis will show the image's contrast (as a percentage of the target's contrast). The resulting plot is termed a **transfer function,** because it specifies how contrast is transferred through the lens. Typical graphs of this kind are shown in Figure 5.12.

Look first at the curve labeled "clean lens" in the graph. Note that up to a certain spatial frequency the contrast in the image is identical to that of the target. For these frequencies, the lens faithfully reproduces the target. However, for still higher spatial frequencies, the contrast in the image is reduced even though the contrast in the target is constant. For these spatial frequencies, the lens reproduces the target less faithfully. The frequency

FIGURE 5.12 | Two transfer functions for a lens. The curves specify how contrast in the image formed by the lens is related to contrast in the object.

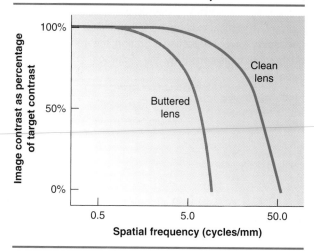

But few people dedicate their cameras exclusively to taking photographs of gratings. To see how transfer functions such as those of Figure 5.12 can be applied to photographs of more natural scenes, the information in the scene must be related to gratings.

One method for doing this comes from the work of Jean Baptiste Fourier, a nineteenth-century French mathematician who happened also to be a friend and an associate of Napoleon. As part of a prestigious mathematics contest, Fourier had to develop equations expressing how heat is transferred from one body to another. He recognized that extremely complex equations would be needed and that those equations would have to be general enough to apply to a wide variety of different bodies. To satisfy these requirements, Fourier developed a powerful simplification. He showed that if some quantity (such as heat) changed in a complex manner over time, that complex function of time could be approximated by a series of simple sinusoidal functions. This simplification was an enormous breakthrough because it allowed Fourier to simplify a mathematically difficult function down into less complex, more tractable components. From here, the problem could be solved by working with the simple components (incidentally, Fourier won the contest). In recognition of his accomplishment, his technique is known as **Fourier analysis** (Bracewell, 1989; see also the websites at www.mhhe.com/blake5).

But how does Fourier's solution enable us to relate simple sinusoidal functions to a photograph of some scene taken through some lens? First, we treat the scene as the sum of a series of simple sinusoidal components. Then, using the lens's transfer function, we evaluate how the lens would image each of those components individually.

Consider the lens whose transfer function is given by the lighter line in Figure 5.12 (the lens smeared with butter). If we used that lens to photograph a scene containing many *very* fine details, the resulting image would be low in contrast and would appear *very* washed out. This is because fine detail is equivalent to high spatial frequency. As the transfer function shows, the buttered lens does a poor job of transferring high spatial frequencies. It reduces the contrast of any high spatial frequencies contained in a scene. Although this lens could faithfully represent the general shape of a large target (such as a tree that is near the camera), it would not be adequate for fine details (such as the wrinkles in the tree's bark). This illustrates that sinusoidal targets can predict the quality of a photograph produced by a lens.

at which the image contrast falls to zero is called the **cutoff frequency.** Once the frequency in an actual target exceeds this value, the image will no longer contain any contrast whatsoever—the target itself might as well have zero contrast.

Now look at the curve labeled "buttered lens" in Figure 5.12. This curve connects the points we would observe if we repeated the experiment after having made one messy modification: smearing the lens by running a buttery finger over its surface. At very low spatial frequencies, the smear makes little difference in the performance of the lens. However, at intermediate and high spatial frequencies, butter on the lens degrades the contrast in the image. This is shown by the difference between the curves for the lens in its buttered and unbuttered states. Note also that the cutoff frequency for the buttered lens is lower than that for the clean lens. This difference between the curves makes intuitive sense: a high-quality lens excels at imaging fine spatial detail *and* coarse spatial detail, whereas a low-quality lens images only the latter. Incidentally, rubbing butter on a lens isn't the only way to degrade the lens's quality—smudges from fingerprints and accumulations of dust will have the same effect. (For those of you who wear glasses, think about how much sharper the world looks when you clean the lenses on your spectacles.)

To reiterate, several steps are involved. First, we determine the transfer function of the lens. Second, we analyze the visual scene into its spatial frequency components. With these pieces of information in hand, we determine which spatial frequency components will be preserved in the image of that scene and which will not. The first step, measuring the transfer function, is straightforward in the camera. But how easy is it to measure a transfer function for a visual system such as your own? If we did know your transfer function, we could predict the visibility of scenes you might look at. As we'll describe later, these predictions confer some practical benefits. Our next goal, then, is to derive a transfer function for human vision comparable to the one we derived for a lens.

The Contrast Sensitivity Function as a Window of Visibility

The Human Contrast Sensitivity Function

There's one major stumbling block to measuring a transfer function for human vision: We cannot duplicate with humans the procedure employed with a lens. While we can produce sinusoidal gratings of known contrast, it's difficult to measure the image such gratings produce because that image is inside the eye. Besides, measuring this image would give only part of the visual system's complete transfer function. While describing the eye's *optical* components, this transfer function would not reflect the *neural* components of the visual system. And since we are interested in visual perception, not just the image formed in the eye, we must be concerned with the *perceptual* transfer function, which depends both on the optical transfer function and on the neural transfer function.

How, then, can we measure the perceptual transfer function? If your visual system (both its optical and its neural components) did a good job of transferring some particular spatial frequency, it stands to reason that you'd need little contrast to see a grating of that frequency. In other words, you'd be relatively sensitive to that frequency. However, if your visual system did a poor job of transferring that spatial frequency, you'd need more contrast to see it. You'd be relatively *in*sensitive to that frequency. In general, the sensitivity of the visual system determines the threshold contrast needed to detect a given spatial frequency. By measuring **contrast thresholds** for different spatial frequencies, we

FIGURE 5.13 | A contrast sensitivity function for an adult human. The horizontal axis is scaled in units specifying the number of pairs of light and dark bars of the grating falling within 1 degree of visual angle on the retina. The vertical axis on the left specifies the contrast necessary for just detecting a grating; the vertical axis on the right plots sensitivity, the reciprocal of contrast threshold.

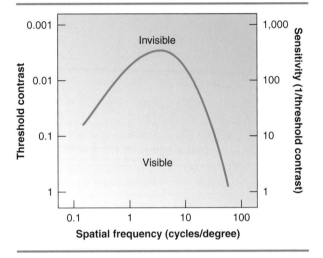

can derive a curve that describes the entire visual system's sensitivity to contrast. We call this curve the **contrast sensitivity function (CSF),** to distinguish it from the transfer function of a lens. The term *sensitivity* is a reminder that we are dealing with a property of the visual system, not just a property of the stimulus. As you'd expect from everyday usage of the term *sensitivity,* someone is said to have high sensitivity if that person requires little contrast to see a pattern. By the same token, someone is said to have low sensitivity if that person requires considerable contrast to see a pattern. Defined in this way, sensitivity is inversely related to threshold contrast.

Figure 5.13 shows a CSF for a human adult. This curve defines the adult's **window of visibility.** Before explaining the importance and usefulness of the CSF, let's describe how it can be measured. A test grating is created electronically on a specially designed and calibrated television screen. The screen displays a grating of fixed spatial frequency. Using a knob (like the contrast control on a television set), the observer adjusts the contrast until the bars of the grating are just barely visible—turning down the contrast any further would reduce the grating to invisibility.[6] This barely visible contrast value is then recorded, and the procedure is repeated several more times to produce multiple estimates of the visibility threshold for that spatial frequency; the average of these settings is defined as the "contrast threshold" for that test grating. Now we repeat the entire procedure for other test spatial frequencies, generating contrast threshold values spanning a range of spatial frequencies. The resulting set of threshold values are plotted in the graphical format shown in Figure 5.13. The horizontal axis specifies the grating's spatial frequency, plotted as the number of cycles within a degree of visual angle. The vertical axes plot the minimum contrast required to see the grating, with the left-hand axis plotting these values in units of contrast and the right-hand axis plotting values as the inverse of this contrast value (defined as sensitivity). To see your own CSF, use the web resources listed for Chapter 5 at www.mhhe.com/blake5.

This curve defines a window of visibility: The region underneath the curve represents combinations of contrast and spatial frequency that can be seen, while the region above the curve represents combinations that cannot be seen. To clarify this idea, pick any point on the CSF curve. Because this point is the threshold contrast for seeing that pattern, decreasing the pattern's contrast (moving upward from the curve) renders the pattern invisible. Conversely, increasing the pattern's contrast (moving downward from the curve) makes the pattern more visible.

Note that in one respect the *shape* of the human CSF resembles the shape of the transfer function of a lens (Figure 5.12): Both curves display a high-frequency cutoff. However, in another respect the two are different. In particular, the CSF drops at low frequencies, whereas the function for the lens does not. The visual system, in other words, is less sensitive to very low spatial frequencies than it is to intermediate ones. As a result, there is a range of spatial frequencies, toward the center of the horizontal axis in Figure 5.13, where humans are maximally sensitive. Gratings are less visible if they lie on either side of this optimum spatial frequency; a person requires higher contrast in order to see them. The same line of reasoning can be applied to a visual scene or photograph of that scene. If the objects in a scene have most of their spatial frequency information

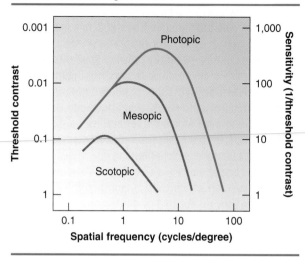

FIGURE 5.14 | Contrast sensitivity functions measured at three light levels.

around the optimum point on the CSF, those objects will be clearly visible even when they are low in contrast. If those objects contain only very low spatial frequencies (very large objects) or only very high spatial frequencies (very small objects or fine details), they will be less visible and their contrast will have to be high in order for those objects to be seen. This also explains why the gratings in Figure 5.11 *appear* different in contrast: their apparent contrast varies with the sensitivity to different spatial frequencies.

You know from experience that you are able to see better under some conditions than others. If the CSF and your ability to see are importantly related, conditions that change one should also change the other. In fact, this is precisely what happens. Let's consider one such condition.

As discussed in Chapter 3, resolution is poor under scotopic conditions. That is why it's hard to read in dim light. Because resolution involves seeing fine detail, we'd expect decreased light to affect particularly that portion of the CSF corresponding to fine detail. Indeed this happens, as the curves in Figure 5.14 illustrate. The upper curve shows the CSF measured under photopic (daytime) light levels; the middle curve shows a CSF measured under mesopic (twilight) conditions; the lowest curve depicts the CSF associated with scotopic (dim light) viewing conditions. As the level of light decreases from daylight to twilight, visual sensitivity drops primarily at high spatial

---

[6] This method of measuring visibility thresholds is called the *adjustment method,* and it is described in the appendix. Also in the appendix are other techniques for estimating visibility thresholds.

BOX 5.1 **Putting the CSF to Work**

The contrast sensitivity function captures aspects of human vision that escapes measures such as visual acuity. Visual acuity, as described in Chapter 3, is a measure of the finest spatial detail that the visual system can resolve. Visual acuity measures only the spatial (size) factors that limit vision, so other factors are optimized. For instance, when an eye chart is printed with very light gray ink on a gray card stock rather than with very black ink on a white card stock, the letters are harder to see (Regan, 1988). In this case, the reduced contrast of the letters limits visual acuity, preventing one from assessing performance on the basis of size alone. When measuring visual acuity, then, one tries to optimize contrast and illumination so they do not limit performance.

When measuring visual acuity, one is interested in how size *alone* limits vision. When measuring the CSF, one is interested in how *both* contrast and size limit vision. In fact, two people can have exactly the same visual acuity but have different contrast sensitivities, as the following demonstrates.

Arthur Ginsburg and his associates used the CSF to predict how well pilots would be able to see objects in the air and on the ground. At least under conditions of reduced visibility (twilight or fog, for example), visual acuity gives a poor account of a pilot's visually guided performance. In fact, very fine details that might normally be seen are invisible at twilight or in fog. Ginsburg found that a pilot's CSF was a good predictor of the pilot's ability to see targets on the ground from the air.

Ginsburg tested pilots in a sophisticated aircraft simulator that provided a panoramic view through the plane's windscreen. Pilots flew simulated missions and then landed. On half of their landings, an obstacle (another plane) blocked the runway, requiring the landing to be aborted. Ginsburg determined how close each pilot came to the obstacle before aborting the landing. Even though all were experienced jet pilots, they varied in the distance at which they could spot the obstacle. The best pilots saw the obstacle three times farther away than did the worst. Significantly, pilots with the highest contrast sensitivities were able to see the obstacle from the greatest distances. Pilots with the lowest contrast sensitivities had to get closer to the obstacle before it became visible. Visual acuity was unrelated to the performance of the pilots on this test (Ginsburg, Evans, Sekuler, and Harp, 1982).

In another application of contrast sensitivity, Mary Jo Nissen measured the CSFs of patients with Alzheimer's disease (Nissen et al., 1985). Although this progressive disease of the brain is best known as a destroyer of memory, in many patients, Alzheimer's disease brings other symptoms, including diminished vision. Nissen's patients showed substantial but varying degrees of contrast sensitivity loss, affecting both coarse (low frequency) and fine (high frequency) patterns. These findings raise the possibility that some portion of the cognitive losses shown by Alzheimer's patients results from diminished vision (Sekuler and Sekuler, 2000).

These are just two examples of CSF's usefulness in predicting visual performance in everyday settings. Other uses include predicting how well various visually impaired people can get around in their environments (Marron and Bailey, 1982), gauging the disabling effects of glare from various types of lighting sources (Carlsson et al., 1984), and enhancing printed materials for use by the visually impaired (Peli and Peli, 1984).

---

frequencies; lower frequencies are little affected. But when light levels drop even further to nighttime values, sensitivity decreases at low frequencies, too.

Think about what these curves imply for your vision as conditions of illumination change. Driving at night, you may be unable to see the fine details (high frequencies) of the shrubs alongside the road. At the same time, you probably will be able to see larger objects (low frequencies), such as another car, just about as well as you do under daylight conditions. If you park your car in an unlit place and turn off your headlights, you will be operating under light conditions like those producing the scotopic curve. Under such conditions, even large objects will be difficult to see. Box 5.1 gives several examples of practical and medical uses of the CSF.

In summary, the CSF characterizes the ease with which people are able to detect objects of various sizes and perceive the structural detail, such as texture, of those objects. Conditions that alter the CSF, such as light level, change the visibility and appearance of objects. In a sense, these conditions thrust one into a different visual world. From this it follows that creatures with different CSFs must actually perceive different visual worlds. The next two sections develop this intriguing possibility.

FIGURE 5.15 | Apparatus for testing the cat's contrast sensitivity.

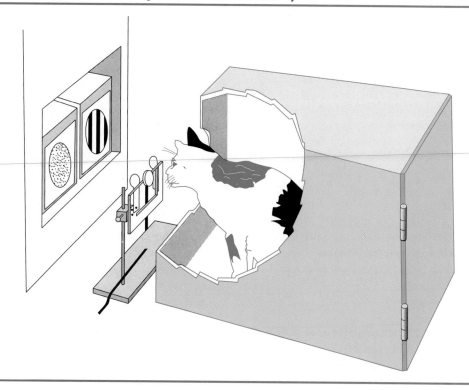

CSFs of Other Species

Cats are notorious for seeming to watch things that their human owners can't see, as if there were ghosts present. Such inexplicable behavior enhances the cat's reputation for spookiness. While we don't deny that cats can be spooky, it may well be that under certain conditions they actually do see things that are real, though invisible to their owners (Blake, 1988a). We'll explain what we mean by this, and in so doing, show how the CSF allows you to compare your vision to that of other animals.

Just as it does for humans, the CSF defines a window of visibility for other species. Provided they have sufficient contrast, objects producing retinal images composed of spatial frequencies falling within the range of a creature's CSF will be visible to that creature. Objects producing images composed of frequencies outside that CSF will be invisible, regardless of their contrast. Thus, if you know some animal's CSF, you can predict what that animal will be able to see and what it won't be able to see. But how do you measure the CSF in a nonverbal animal such as the cat? The basic problem is to determine

how little contrast a cat needs to distinguish a grating from a uniform field of the same brightness. One setup for doing this is illustrated in Figure 5.15.

The cat faces two adjacent television screens, one displaying a grating, the second a uniformly bright field. The cat is rewarded with a morsel of food if it pushes against a small plastic nose-key located just in front of the television displaying the grating. The experimenter randomly presents the grating on the left or right television screen. When the contrast of the grating is above the cat's threshold, a hungry cat will respond correctly on virtually every trial. When the contrast falls below the cat's threshold, the animal will simply guess and will be correct only half the time. The cat's threshold, then, is defined as the contrast that allows it to respond correctly on 75 percent of the trials, a level of performance midway between chance and perfection. This threshold contrast can be measured for different spatial frequencies, and the cat's CSF can then be plotted in the same way as it is for humans. (This procedure, incidentally, constitutes a forced-choice threshold test, and the details of this method are covered in the appendix.)

FIGURE 5.16 ┃ Contrast sensitivity functions for cats and human beings.

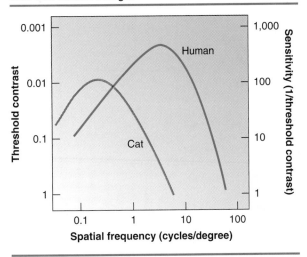

FIGURE 5.17 ┃ Contrast sensitivity functions for five species.

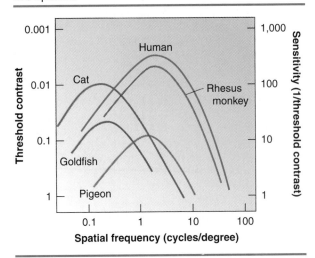

Figure 5.16 shows a typical CSF for a cat (grey line) and for a human (colored line) tested under comparable conditions. Note first the area common to the two CSFs. This overlapping region defines combinations of spatial frequencies and contrasts that both you and a cat can see. Next, note the regions where the two CSFs do not overlap. Within these two regions, one creature—you or the cat, depending on which one has the higher sensitivity—can see patterns that are invisible to the other. At high spatial frequencies, your sensitivity is better than the cat's; at low spatial frequencies, the reverse is true. Now suppose that a cat is sitting on your lap. If you are watching television, you will be able to see fine details in the picture that your cat cannot see. This is because those fine details are composed of high spatial frequencies that fall outside the cat's window of visibility. At the same time, if something large and very low-contrast appears in the room—say, an indistinct shadow on a wall—the cat may see it even though you cannot. In this instance, the shadow falls outside your window of visibility. These large, low-contrast objects could be the invisible "ghosts" that enhance the cat's reputation for spookiness.

CSFs have been measured for more than a dozen different species, and it's instructive to compare them. Figure 5.17 shows several representative curves. Look first at the curve labeled "Human"; this is the human adult CSF that you've seen in several previous figures. Next note the curve labeled "Rhesus monkey." Like several other nonhuman primates that have been studied, the rhe-

sus monkey's CSF is highly similar to that of a human, suggesting that the world would probably appear very similar to you and to a monkey sitting on your lap. It is certainly unlikely that you'd see things that the monkey could not, or vice versa. Next note that the goldfish's CSF is displaced toward lower spatial frequencies, a fact that makes sense considering where the goldfish lives. Its aquatic environment prevents high spatial frequencies from ever reaching the fish's eye (Lythgoe, 1979). Like the cat, the goldfish is equipped for seeing either very large objects or smaller ones that are quite nearby. In general, there seems to be a good fit between what an animal uses its eyes for and where its CSF lies along the spatial frequency scale.

Age and the CSF

On the basis of differences between the CSFs of various species, we've pictured what the world might look like to the owners of these CSFs. In the same way, we can consider how the world might appear to human individuals at various points in their lifetimes. To begin, suppose while you are reading this book, someone puts a human infant on your lap (where previously you've held a cat and a monkey). How does your visual world compare to that of the infant? This question, incidentally, has intrigued philosophers and parents for centuries.

It is hard to know what very young, preverbal infants see. Obviously, you can't use the same methods to study

FIGURE 5.18 | An infant's preference for looking at a pattern can be used to measure the infant's contrast sensitivity.

FIGURE 5.19 | Contrast sensitivity functions for an infant and for an adult.

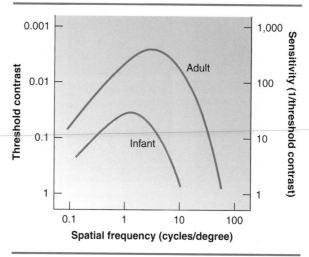

infant vision that you use with cooperative, attentive adults. To get around this limitation, researchers have exploited a naturally occurring tendency exhibited by infants: they prefer to look at complex rather than dull scenes, and this preference can be exploited to measure the infant's ability to see gratings (Atkinson and Braddick, 1998). Here's how it works.

Confronted with a patch of grating and a patch of uniform brightness, an infant prefers to look at the grating, presumably because the presence of the contours makes the grating more interesting than the blank patch (see Figure 5.18). During testing, the bars of the grating can be made sufficiently low in contrast that the infant cannot detect the contours and, therefore, cannot tell the difference between the patch of grating and the blank patch. In this case, the infant will show no preference for the grating over the uniform field. So, we can estimate the infant's contrast threshold for a given spatial frequency by fixing the grating spatial frequency and varying its contrast over a series of trials. By doing this, we can discover the minimum contrast at which the infant exhibits a preference for looking at the grating—this value defines the infant's contrast threshold at that spatial frequency. And by repeating this procedure at different spatial frequencies, we can derive the entire CSF for the infant.

The basic findings are summarized in Figure 5.19, which shows CSFs for an infant somewhere between 3 to 6 months old and for a typical adult. Note that the infant's window of visibility is very different from the adult's. An infant held on your lap will not be able to see fine spatial details visible to you. In this respect, the infant more closely resembles a cat. But unlike a cat, the infant does not have an advantage over you at low frequencies: You should be able to see everything that the infant can see. Also, even for spatial frequencies visible to both of you, the infant will require more contrast than you do.

The CSF in Figure 5.19 delimits the range of visible spatial frequencies visible to the infant, but it doesn't portray what the infant sees when looking about the natural environment. To get some idea of what the world looks like through an infant's eyes, we have simulated infants' quality of vision at several different ages. The simulations, shown in Figure 5.20, are grounded in measurements of contrast sensitivity (Teller, 1997).

In a sense, these simulations confirm what some parents have noticed: Their very young infants seem oblivious to everything except very large, high-contrast objects (Banks, 1982). Incidentally, the lack of sensitivity to high frequencies does not stem from optical causes but from the fact that the infant's immature visual nervous system fails to encode high frequencies. In effect, infants are best suited for seeing objects located close to them (recall that spatial frequency is distance dependent), which makes sense from a behavioral standpoint.

The infant's CSF improves steadily over the first year or so of its life. However, this improvement stalls at an immature level if the infant does not receive normal visual experiences. Several visual disorders can alter the quality

FIGURE 5.20 | This series of photographs shows what the world would look like through the eyes of infants at different stages of development. As acuity improves with age, the infant is able to see finer and finer spatial detail.

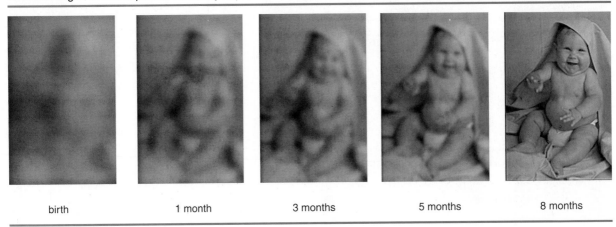

| birth | 1 month | 3 months | 5 months | 8 months |

of visual experiences received by an infant and hence keep spatial vision from its normal course of development. First of all, any condition that chronically blurs the images reaching the infant's retina will limit the information available to the visual system. Optical blur of this sort can result from myopia or hyperopia, or from congenital cataracts or corneal scars (recall our discussion of optics in Chapter 2). Misalignment of an infant's two eyes can also retard the development of good spatial vision. When its eyes are not properly aligned, an infant must suppress or ignore visual input from one eye in order to avoid seeing double (a condition we will discuss in Chapter 8). For reasons still to be learned, continuous suppression of one eye can lead to a loss in spatial vision, a condition called *amblyopia* (a visual disorder introduced in Chapter 4).

Fortunately, infants afflicted with any of these disorders can recover normal spatial vision, providing the disorder is corrected sometime during the first few years of life (von Noorden, 1981; Maurer et al., 1999). But if correction is postponed until the child reaches school age, the prognosis for full recovery is much poorer. Apparently there is a critical period early in life when the visual nervous system requires normal input to mature properly. During this period, neural connections are still being formed. This critical period of neural development ends by the time a child reaches 3 or 4 years of age. If the visual nervous system arrives at this stage incompletely developed because of inadequate visual experience, any neural abnormalities are irrevocably preserved throughout the remainder of life.

Because early visual experience is crucial to the brain's normal development, visual disorders in infants must be detected and then corrected as early as possible. The realization that early detection and intervention are

FIGURE 5.21 | Contrast sensitivity functions for three age groups.

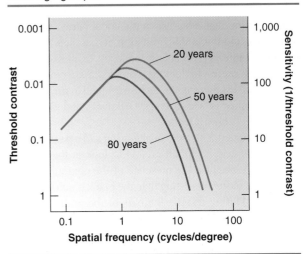

vital has revolutionized the way that pediatric ophthalmology and pediatric optometry treat human infants. For example, if congenital cataracts are left untreated for several years, the development of normal connections in a child's brain is retarded, and even if surgery is done later in life, the quality of vision is unlikely to be optimal.

So far our discussion has focused on spatial vision in infants and young children. Consider now what happens to the CSF during the remainder of the life span. The CSF remains more or less stable through young adulthood, but after age 30, systematic changes in the CSF begin reappearing. Figure 5.21 shows how the CSF changes from age 20 to age 80 (Owsley, Sekuler, and Siemsen, 1983).

By now you should have no trouble interpreting what a CSF implies about a person's ability to see. Suppose an elderly aunt takes the place of that infant on your lap; you should be able to predict from Figure 5.21 how her visual world might differ from yours.

At least some of your aunt's diminished sensitivity to high frequencies results from optical changes in her eyes. For example, as she has grown older, her pupil has become smaller, which means that her retina receives considerably less light than yours (Weale, 1982). This reduced illumination of her retina mimics changes that would be seen in your CSF as you went from photopic to mesopic conditions (see Figure 5.14). Still, there remains some degree of loss in contrast sensitivity that cannot be accounted for by optical factors, implicating age-related neural changes (Bennett, Sekuler, and Ozin, 1999). Whatever its origins, changes in the CSF as well as in other measures of vision (Haegerstrom-Portnoy, Schneck, and Brabyn, 1999) document that people experience very different visual worlds at different stages of their lives. Society needs to be aware of these visual changes, so that older people can be helped to adjust to their changing visual world. To give just a couple of simple suggestions, providing large-print menus in restaurants can be very helpful to an older person whose reduced acuity makes it more difficult to read fine print. And providing extra illumination for reading that menu is a good idea, too, since the older person's smaller pupil is effectively reducing the illumination for that individual.

The Structural Basis of the CSF

As we mentioned previously in this chapter, Campbell and Robson (1968) proposed that the human visual system contains sets of neurons, each capable of responding to targets over only a restricted range of spatial frequencies. This range of "preferred" frequencies varies from one set of neurons to another. According to this hypothesis, the sensitivities of these frequency-tuned neurons, or channels, together determine the overall CSF (see Figure 5.22).

One reason for believing that the CSF depends on several different channels is the fact that certain conditions can alter one portion of the CSF without affecting others. As Box 5.2 explains, diseases attacking the visual system can produce this frequency-selective change in the CSF. (Evidently, subsets of neurons are differentially affected by disease.) But we don't have to wait for disease to change the CSF. We can change it intentionally, using a technique called **selective adaptation.** This procedure, mentioned in Chapter 4 in the context of orientation, produces a temporary loss of sensitivity to particular spatial frequencies.

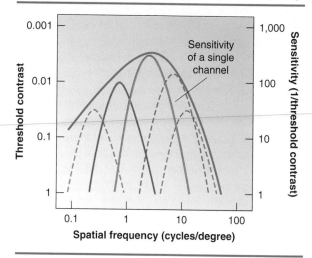

FIGURE 5.22 | The overall contrast sensitivity function is determined by the individual sensitivities of neurons responsive to limited ranges of spatial frequency.

Measurement of selective adaptation entails several steps. First, you assess the person's CSF. Then, the person views a high-contrast grating for a minute or so, thereby adapting to one spatial frequency at a given orientation. Steady viewing of this adaptation grating decreases responses from visual neurons that respond to the grating (Movshon and Lennie, 1979; Albrecht, Farrar, and Hamilton, 1984). After the person has adapted to this grating for a minute or two, you redetermine the CSF (interspersing threshold measurements with additional adaptation to keep the level of adaptation high). The typical outcome of such experiments (for example, Blakemore and Campbell, 1969) is shown in Figure 5.23. In each panel, the arrow on the horizontal axis indicates the frequency to which the person adapted. Note that the notch carved in each CSF is centered about the adaptation frequency. So adapting to one spatial frequency diminishes sensitivity to that frequency and neighboring ones, leaving more remote frequencies unaffected. This process of selective adaptation works even when the adaptation frequency is contained in a complex pattern.

To understand how selective adaptation works, look again at Figure 5.22. If just one of the channels is fatigued by adaptation, that channel will respond more weakly when its preferred spatial frequency is presented. This means that a grating of that preferred spatial frequency would look somewhat washed out compared to its normal appearance (Blakemore, Muncey, and Ridley, 1973). A low-contrast grating that is normally visible will stimulate the adapted channel so weakly that the

BOX 5.2 **When Things Go Wrong with Pattern Vision**

The way in which diseases affect vision can provide clues about the structural basis of the CSF. Some neurological cases can produce a notch in the CSF—a loss of contrast sensitivity limited to a certain range of target sizes. Moreover, the location and severity of sensitivity loss can vary from one patient to the next.

In a study by Ivan Bodis-Wollner (1972), patients' notch losses resulted from stroke damage to the visual cortex. (A stroke, is caused by an interruption of the blood supply to a portion of the brain.) Other diseases can produce similar losses. The most common of these diseases is multiple sclerosis, a disease that attacks the myelin on nerve fibers, including fibers that make up the optic nerve. Even though their visual acuity is good, some multiple sclerosis patients complain that the world appears "washed out." Presumably, this washed-out appearance is related to the nervous system's diminished capacity to code contrast.

In addition, about 30 percent of all people who have multiple sclerosis experience Uhthoff's symptom, a condition first described by Wilhelm Uhthoff, an eminent late nineteenth century ophthalmologist. For individuals with Uhthoff's symptom, exercise or emotional strain heightens their visual problems for several minutes. No one yet understands how emotional or physical strain or exercise causes these effects. But these conditions offer a unique opportunity to study the visual system under conditions of transient impairment. In one study (Sekuler, Owsley, and Berenberg, 1986), a 30-year-old accountant with Uhthoff's symptom reported that when he was emotionally upset his vision grew hazy and objects lost much of their apparent contrast. For example, during a confrontation at work, his boss's face appeared totally washed out and featureless. Surprisingly, during these episodes the patient retained his ability to read columns of small numbers, an important part of his job. Thus, he seemed to suffer a size-selective loss, retaining the ability to see fine details while losing the ability to see larger objects.

This strange set of symptoms was confirmed by comparing the patient's contrast sensitivity before and immediately after he exercised. Contrast sensitivity for high spatial frequencies was unchanged by exercise, but sensitivity for intermediate frequencies dropped. Longer periods of exercise produced an even greater loss of vision: Not only was contrast sensitivity drastically reduced at all frequencies, but visual acuity was seriously impaired as well.

We do not yet understand the specific physiological basis for these restricted losses in the CSF. But such losses do imply that the CSF—and the ability to see patterns of different sizes—depends on the coordinated responses of different sets of visual cells, any one of which may be attacked and damaged by disease.

FIGURE 5.23 | Adapting to a particular spatial frequency produces a temporary depression in the contrast sensitivity function at and near the adapting spatial frequency.

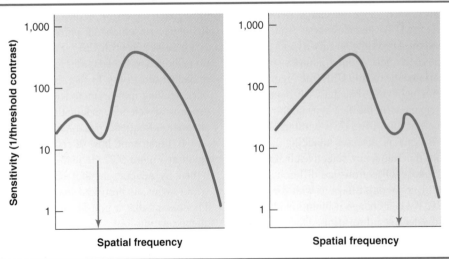

FIGURE 5.24 | By following the instructions in the text, you can experience the consequences of selective adaptation.

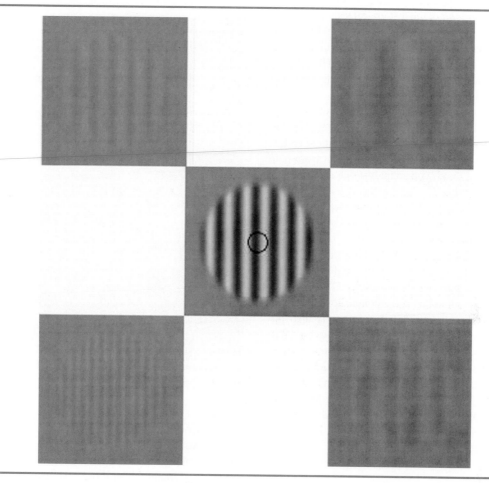

grating will be below threshold. In order to attain visibility, this grating's contrast will have to be boosted, resulting in a dip in the CSF. The width of this dip depends on the selectivity of the fatigued channel. Presumably, unaffected regions of the CSF depend on channels that were not fatigued by the adaptation grating.

You can demonstrate selective adaptation for yourself. Figure 5.24 shows several different low-contrast test gratings and one high-contrast adaptation grating. Before looking at the adaptation grating (in the center of the figure), note the apparent contrast of the test gratings surrounding it. Now inspect the high-contrast grating for about a minute. Don't stare fixedly, but allow your eyes to roam around the circle in the grating's center. Then, without delay, look at one test grating and note its apparent contrast. After looking back at the adaptation grating for another minute, note the apparent contrast of another

test grating. By adapting and then examining each test grating in turn, you'll find that adapting alters the appearance of only some test gratings. Now you've seen for yourself that spatial frequency adaptation is selective.

Selective adaptation probably occurs in visual cortical cells (Albrecht, Farrar, and Hamilton, 1984). Such cells are selective for spatial frequency (size), but as Chapter 4 showed, they are also selective for orientation. As a result, you might expect grating adaptation to be selective for both orientation *and* spatial frequency. The logic behind this assertion resembles that used to explain spatial frequency selective adaptation.

You can demonstrate for yourself that this adaptation effect really is selective for orientation. Rotate this book by 90 degrees (turn it sideways) and then adapt to the high-contrast grating in Figure 5.24. This maneuver will orient the contours in that grating horizontally. After adapting for a minute, quickly return the book to its upright position and look at the vertically oriented test gratings. Unlike before, *all* of the test gratings should remain visible. In other words, adapting to horizontal has no effect on the contrast threshold for detecting vertical, regardless of similarities in spatial frequency. This implies that the cells adapted by the horizontal grating are not at all involved in detecting vertical contours.

This demonstration is a reminder of one of the properties exhibited by visual cortical cells: orientation selectivity. Recall that another characteristic of cortical cells is their binocularity: Most of them receive input from *both* eyes. This implies that if you adapt just one eye to a grating, you will be able to observe the consequences of adaptation while looking through either the adapted eye or the unadapted eye (Blake and Fox, 1972). You can use Figure 5.24 to verify this fact also.

These adaptation effects imply that different neural channels are used to detect different spatial frequencies, since it is possible to affect the sensitivity of one without altering the others. And this same conclusion—different channels for different spatial frequencies—is also implied by results obtained using other techniques (see Wilson and Wilkinson, 2004, for a succinct review of those results). We'll not go into that additional evidence and, instead, we'll turn to evidence showing that these distinct channels strongly interact with one another. We'll start with a demonstration of this interaction and then consider why these interactions are a good idea in terms of visual object perception.

Interaction among Channels and Contrast Normalization

Look at Figure 5.25 and see if you can perceive a familiar object. Need some help? Try squinting your eyes, a maneuver that blurs your vision and thus reduces the high-frequency details in the retinal image of this picture (if you wear glasses, try viewing the photo with glasses off). Once those details are attenuated, the remaining low frequency information becomes relatively stronger and the object becomes conspicuous. In effect, the high frequency details contained in the edges of the blocks were camouflaging the lower frequency pattern that is present in Figure 5.25. (To understand how this block portrait was created, see Figure 5.26.)

This demonstration is just one piece of evidence pointing to the existence of strong interactions among the multiple channels revealed by selective adaptation. Results using the adaptation procedure point to the same con-

FIGURE 5.25 | Can you tell what is pictured here?

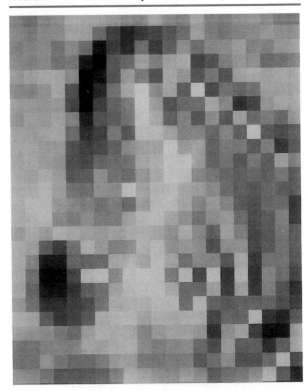

clusion. Consider, for example, the apparent contrast of a grating. Adaptation to, say, a set of horizontal contours *reduces* the apparent contrast of gratings of all orientations, not just horizontal, when those gratings are high in contrast; the same is true when the adaptation and test gratings differ in spatial frequency (Snowden and Hammett, 1996). So the perception of patterns at clearly visible levels of contrast, unlike their appearance at the contrast threshold of visibility, seems to depend on activity across multiple channels tuned to different orientations and to different spatial frequencies. This cross-channel interaction occurs, however, only among spatial frequencies and orientations imaged at the same location within the visual field. We know this because perceived contrast of a pattern at a given location is not altered by adaptation occurring within another portion of the visual field.

But what purpose do these interactions serve? One idea is that the responses of channels tuned to different spatial frequencies and orientations within a given, local region of an image are "normalized" based on the overall contrast among these components (Heeger, 1992). According to this idea of **contrast normalization,** visual re-

FIGURE 5.26 | The picture in the previous figure was constructed by setting the light level of each block so that it was the average intensity of the region covered by the block. Squinting (thus blurring the high frequencies) should make the detail in the two photographs more nearly equivalent.

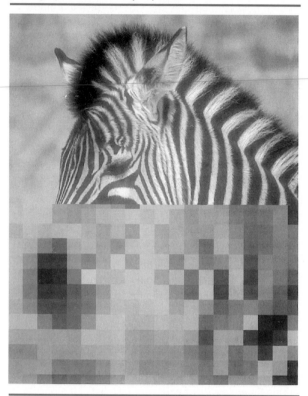

FIGURE 5.27 | Many natural scenes contain some regions where the local contrast among contours is relatively low and other regions where contrast is high. Visual neurons can respond to only a limited range of contrast variations, but through contrast normalization that range can be dynamically shifted to operate efficiently within the prevailing levels of contrast. The two graphs in the lower part of this figure show the contrast-response curves for visual neurons with receptive fields stimulated by relatively low contrast images (left-hand curve) and by relatively high contrast images (right-hand curve).

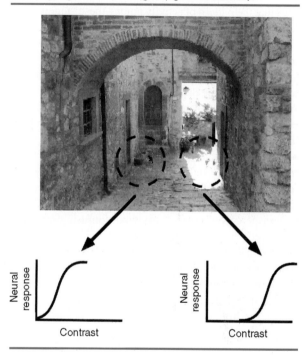

sponses are combined from all active neurons whose receptive fields fall within a local neighborhood, and this combined signal, in turn, modifies the individual responses of those active neurons; this process can occur very quickly. But what is the advantage of normalizing neural responses based on some combined level of responsiveness? There are two reasons for doing this (summarized in Schwartz and Simoncelli, 2001). The first reason has to do with maximizing the ability of neurons to respond over a wide range of contrast values. The response of a visual neuron increases with contrast, but a neuron can respond only so vigorously after which its response levels off at its maximum value. Because of the limited response range of the neuron, the range of contrasts over which the neuron's activity level varies is relatively narrow compared to the complete range of contrast values encountered during ordinary vision. It is as if the neuron has a limited

range of numbers with which to specify any value within a broad range of numbers. Through contrast normalization, however, the neuron can adjust its range of responsiveness to cover the prevailing level of contrast within a local region of the image. This normalization process is illustrated schematically in Figure 5.27. In effect, neurons monitoring a given, restricted region of an image adjust their responsiveness to ensure that they can represent the contrast levels contained within that region of the image. It is important for normalization to be spatially restricted and to not extend over the entire image, because the entire field of view is very likely to contain a range of contrast values much too wide to be effectively accommodated by global normalization applied to all regions of the image (see the image in the top part of Figure 5.27).

That's the first reason for pooling responses across multiple channels. The second reason has to do with maintaining the stimulus selectivity of visual neurons. Recall that a given neuron selectively responds only to a narrow range of orientations and a limited range of sizes (or spatial frequencies). In Chapter 4 you saw examples of orientation selectively summarized in the form of a "tuning curve" (recall Figure 4.10), where the peak of the curve signaled the preferred orientation and the breadth of the curve represented the range of orientations capable of stimulating that neuron. Moreover, we saw in Figure 4.25 that the pattern of activity among these "tuned" neurons could signal the orientations of contours. Now, if the shapes of the neurons' tuning curves were to vary depending on the contrast of the contours activating those neurons, the patterns of activity produced by a given contour would change depending on the contour's contrast. And that would not be visually desirable, for then we could mistake changes in contrast for changes in orientation. Fortunately we don't make that mistake, and that's because tuning curves *retain* their shapes despite variations in contrast. And they retain their shapes because the responses of those neurons are normalized for contrast. In effect, the visual system is willing to tolerate slight errors in perceived contrast to avoid confusing errors in perceived orientation.

Contrast normalization also offers one possible explanation for why the object in Figure 5.25 is difficult to see unless you blur the image. The sharp edges of the blocks in Figure 5.25 contain strong contrast signals within the high spatial frequency range of the picture. These strong signals bias the normalization process toward higher contrasts and, thus, effectively weaken the contrast signals within the low spatial frequency components contained in the image. By blurring the image, the high spatial frequencies are removed, their contribution to contrast normalization is weakened, and the low spatial frequency contrast signal is boosted. (For other possible factors involved in this phenomenon, see Hess, 2004.)

To sum up, recent studies of detection and pattern visibility converge on a common view of the human visual system. In this view, detection of any spatial target depends on responses generated in a set of visual neurons tuned to contours of particular sizes and orientations. Each set of neurons is responsible for signaling the presence of targets on a particular scale and orientation. Moreover, the responses of those neurons are adjusted based on the level of contrast contained within the region of the image being stimulated by those neu-

rons. In the next sections, we'll see how this model of spatial vision may account for other aspects of form perception as well.

Form Discrimination

You've now learned how the CSF defines a window of visibility within which objects can be seen. Our emphasis was on form detection as determined by an observer's sensitivity to contrast and spatial frequency. Now we are ready to extend our analysis of spatial vision to form discrimination, which is the ability to tell one object from another. Before getting into details, though, it will be useful to specify what must go on within the visual system to make discrimination possible.

The perception of pattern, or spatial structure, depends on the responses of cells in the visual system. This dependence sets limits on what stimuli will appear different and what stimuli will look alike. It stands to reason that all stimuli producing *identical* patterns of neural activity within the visual system will be indistinguishable from one another.[7] But if stimuli produce different activity patterns, potentially you have some basis for telling them apart. Whether you actually can tell them apart depends on how different the neural responses are. In Chapter 4 you read that the response of any one cell, say a simple cell in the visual cortex, provides ambiguous messages about the characteristics of visual features of objects in the visual world. In all likelihood, the visual appearance of objects depends on the pattern of activity within an *ensemble* of cells, not just one cell alone.

Metamers

If you look at two exact duplicates of the same object, each produces precisely the same effects on your visual system, and they will look identical. But two objects that are physically different can also have identical neural effects and, therefore, appear identical. In other words, things need not *be* identical to *look* identical. Two objects that are perceptually indistinguishable from one another, despite their physical differences, are called **metamers.**

---

[7] In principle, "identical patterns" of neural activity means that the very same neurons produce the very same sequence of action potentials in response to two or more stimuli. Of course, it is highly unlikely that precisely the same neurons produce precisely the same pattern of activity upon repeated presentation of the *same* stimulus. So practically speaking, "identical" really means equivalent in a statistical sense, that is, with insignificant variability.

FIGURE 5.28 | The two photographs are identical except that frequencies falling above the cat's high-frequency cutoff have been eliminated from the right-hand photograph.

We can learn about neural processing in human vision by determining which visual patterns are metamers and which are not. Metamers exist because two or more stimuli, although different along some dimension (e.g., size) are insufficiently different to produce distinctive responses within the visual nervous sytem—whatever dimension distinguishes those stimuli is too subtle for the neurons responsive to those stimuli. Consequently, we are "blind" to the differences between the stimuli. When your visual system generates identical responses to two objects, the objects will appear identical, even if they are physically different; those two objects are said to be metameric. The following simple exercise will introduce you to one example of metamers, in this case a pair of pictures.

In Figure 5.28, the two photographs are identical except for the presence of high spatial frequency information in the left-hand photograph. You are probably able to see that the two photos are slightly different because, from this reading distance, these high spatial frequencies are visible to you; in other words, the two photographs are *not* metameric. But now prop the book up on a table and view these two photographs from a distance of about 15 feet. Now the high frequencies in the left-hand photograph will fall beyond the limits of your acuity, rendering the two photographs metameric: they appear identical even though the two are physically different. At the greater viewing distance, both photographs produce equivalent patterns of activity in your visual system. Viewing these

two photographs under dim light illumination will also render them metameric even at ordinary reading distance. Looking back at Figure 5.14, you should understand why.

Incidentally, if a cat were to view this same pair of photographs from your normal reading distance under good illumination (conditions where you can tell the photos apart), the high frequencies in the left-hand photograph would be outside of the cat's window of visibility. Thus, the two photographs would be indistinguishable to a cat, meaning the pair would be metamers for the cat at both viewing distances.

But it's not only light level or distance that determines whether two stimuli are metameric. Any condition that alters the response of the nervous system can influence whether stimuli are metameric. You've already seen one example of this principle at work, when you experienced the temporary invisibility of a low-contrast grating following adaptation (Figure 5.24). Adaptation momentarily reduced the responsiveness of neurons tuned to that spatial frequency and orientation, to the point where those neurons were no more active than they are when confronted with an uncontoured, uniform gray field. The low-contrast grating, as a consequence of adaptation, was temporarily metameric with an uncontoured field.

Let's consider another visual phenomenon where we use adaptation to alter the responsiveness of the visual nervous system and, thereby, to change stimuli from metameric to nonmetameric. To do this, we turn to the

FIGURE 5.29 | A neural account of how contour size is encoded in the visual system. (See text for details.)

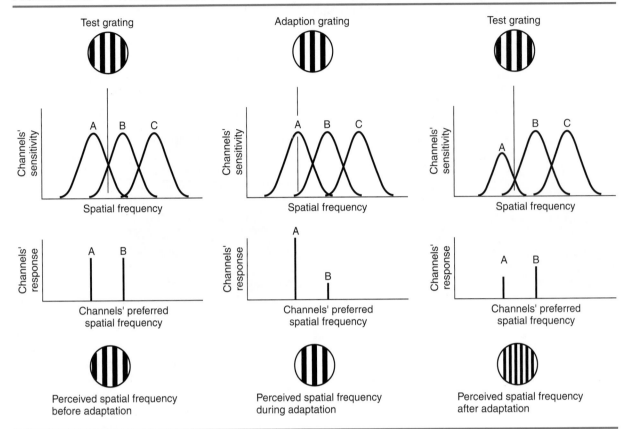

size aftereffect, which is robust and easy to induce. Before experiencing the size aftereffect, let's preview why the effect happens. We start with the widely accepted theory that the visual system represents size by the patterns of neural activity among channels tuned to spatial frequencies (Blakemore, Nachmias, and Sutton, 1970). Figure 5.29 shows how a simplified version of this theory applies to the perceived size (i.e., spatial frequency) of a grating. In the upper two graphs, the horizontal axes represent spatial frequency and the vertical axes represent sensitivity. These curves, you may notice, correspond to several of the multiple channels we talked about previously (recall Figure 5.22). To make the argument easier to follow, only three channels are shown. As the upper left panel indicates, channel A prefers the lowest frequency of the three, B prefers an intermediate frequency, and C prefers the highest frequency.

Suppose we present a test grating whose frequency is halfway between the preferred frequencies of channels A and B. (This condition is not crucial for the argument; it merely simplifies the description.) Note that the test

grating produces equal responses within channels A and B (bottom left panel). According to the theory, this neural code—equal activity in A and B—determines the way the grating looks.

But if we did something to change the distribution of activity produced by that test grating, the grating's appearance would be altered. Producing a change in activity can be accomplished using an adaptation procedure much like the one already described. First, a person looks at a grating and judges its spatial frequency. We'll refer to this as the "test grating." Next, the person adapts to a high-contrast grating whose spatial frequency is lower than that of the test grating. We'll call this the "adaptation grating." Finally, after a minute or so of adaptation, the person looks back at the test grating and again judges its spatial frequency. Does the test grating still look the same? To answer this question, consider how adaptation would have affected the neural code previously described.

As we have pointed out, the test grating produces equal responses in channels A and B prior to adaptation. Suppose also that the adaptation grating is one to which

FIGURE 5.30 | These samples cause the viewer to experience the size-shift aftereffect. (Follow the instructions given in the text.)

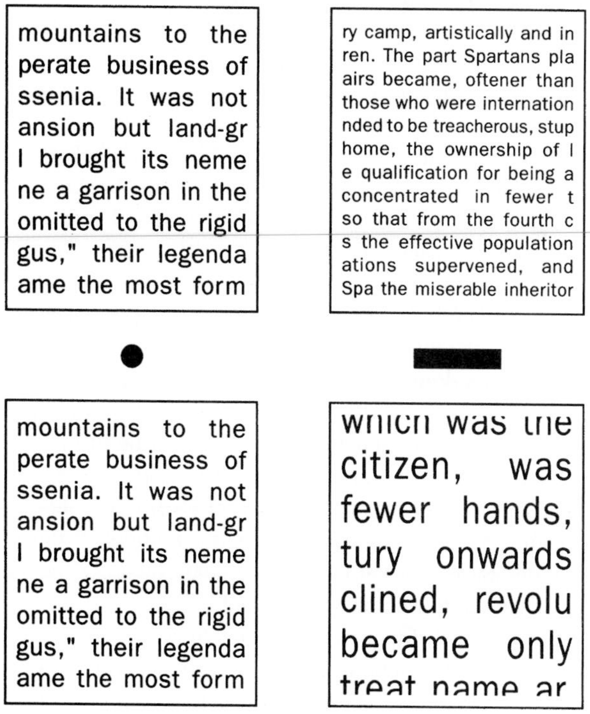

mountains to the perate business of ssenia. It was not ansion but land-gr I brought its neme ne a garrison in the omitted to the rigid gus," their legenda ame the most form	ry camp, artistically and in ren. The part Spartans pla airs became, oftener than those who were internation nded to be treacherous, stup home, the ownership of I e qualification for being a concentrated in fewer t so that from the fourth c s the effective population ations supervened, and Spa the miserable inheritor

mountains to the perate business of ssenia. It was not ansion but land-gr I brought its neme ne a garrison in the omitted to the rigid gus," their legenda ame the most form	which was the citizen, was fewer hands, tury onwards clined, revolu became only treat name ar

A is highly sensitive and to which B is relatively less sensitive (as illustrated in the middle panel of Figure 5.29). Prolonged adaptation will thereby reduce the sensitivity of A considerably but B very little—this selective change in sensitivity is illustrated in the upper right panel. Now when presented following adaptation, the test grating will evoke a nearly normal response from B but a weakened response from A (lower right panel). The test grating does not usually produce this pattern of responses—a greater response in B than in A. Instead, this pattern of responses is usually evoked by a spatial frequency higher than that of the test grating. As a result, after adaptation, the spatial frequency of the test grating should appear higher than usual. And this is precisely what happens (Blakemore, Nachmias, and Sutton, 1970). On the basis of this theory, can you predict what would happen if a person were to adapt to a spatial frequency higher than that of the test grating?

Using the test displays in Figure 5.30, you can experience one version of this size aftereffect yourself. To reassure you that this aftereffect is not peculiar to gratings, we've borrowed from Stuart Anstis a demonstration using more familiar patterns: alphabetic text. Still, the out-

come is the same: a temporary change in apparent size. To make the effect easier to see, this demonstration simultaneously produces two size aftereffects in opposite directions. Here's how to use Figure 5.30. Look at the black dot between the upper and lower panels of the left side of the figure. With your eyes fixed on the black dot, verify that the letters in the text above the line look the same size as the letters below.

We'll now explain what you must do to alter the apparent size of these letters. Because timing is important, finish reading the instructions before you begin to execute them. First, adapt, using the right side of the figure. The patch of small, tightly packed letters corresponds to high spatial frequencies, while the patch of larger, more spread out letters corresponds to low spatial frequencies. To adapt, slowly move your eyes back and forth along the bar between the two patches of letters for about 90 seconds. *Caution:* Do not look directly at either patch; keep your gaze on the horizontal bar between the two. Otherwise, you'll intermix the two types of adaptation. Finally, at the end of adaptation, look back at the dot between the patches in the left side of the figure. Keeping your eyes on the dot, note the sizes of the letters above and below. You will see that letters in the upper patch look larger than those in the lower patch. Here, then, is a situation where altering your visual system's sensitivity makes ordinarily identical stimuli temporarily nonmetameric.

The point to be remembered from this discussion of metamers is that the ability to discriminate among objects depends on the extent to which those objects produce different neural responses. Carrying this idea one step further, the ability to make very fine discriminations among objects indicates that the underlying neural events are very sensitive to variations along whatever dimension(s) distinguish those objects. For example, compare the two patterns in the upper part of Figure 5.31. The bars in the circular patch on the left differ very, very slightly in orientation from the bars in the patch on the right. If you can see that these two are slightly different, this must mean that the two orientations are producing reliably different patterns of activity within your visual system. Next, compare the pair of patterns in the bottom part of the figure. Can you see that the bars in the figure on the left are ever so slightly narrower than the ones on the right? Again, if your answer is yes, then evidently your visual nervous system is producing discriminably different patterns of activity when you view one pattern and then the other. These tiny yet discernible differences between members of each of these pairs of patterns reveal that the visual nervous system is exquisitely sensitive to variations in size and in orientation.

FIGURE 5.31 | Visual figures that are discriminable, even if just barely, must be producing different patterns of neural activity within the visual system. Looking at the top pair of patterns, the orientation of the bars on the right is slightly different from the orientation of those on the left. The angular difference in orientation is only about 2 degrees, a value right at the threshold for discrimination. In the bottom pair of patterns, the bars on the right are about 3 percent larger than those on the left, again a difference close to the limits of discrimination.

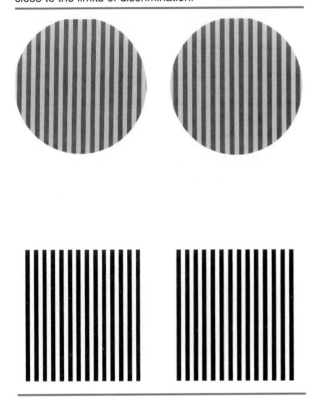

Form Defined by Texture Differences

So far we have focused on detection and discrimination of forms defined by intensity differences that create spatial contrast at different spatial scales. Thinking back to the robotic vehicle Spirit as it explored the Martian surface, its camera would register the presence of a rock if that rock reflected a different amount of light than did the background upon which it was resting. But what if the rock and its background were the same color and reflected equivalent amounts of light? Would Spirit miss it altogether? Not necessarily. Rocks, after all, typically have surface markings—scratches, streaks, and other irregularities—that differ from the more regular, grainy texture of the dusty Martian ground upon which the rock rests. If NASA scientists had programmed Spirit and its image processing computers to register spatial discontinuities in texture (**texture contrast,** we could call it), the rock could be detected even though its overall lightness was no different from the ground. Texture contrast provides another, complementary, means for detecting and discriminating form. Let's spend a few moments considering texture.

To begin, think about familiar objects, whose textures are distinctive—for example, a pebbled path, the skin of an alligator, the bark of a tree, or a brick wall. Think about what makes each of these surfaces distinctive, putting color aside. As a first approximation to a definition, these examples suggest that texture depends upon the sizes and shapes of the surface's markings as well as the distribution of those markings over the surface. Can we be more precise about the key stimulus features that determine perception of texture in natural and human-made surfaces?

To answer that question, Rao and Lohse (1996) utilized as test materials photographs of 56 different surfaces taken at various magnifications and conditions of illumination. Based on similarity judgments made by people who viewed these images, Rao and Lohse identified three main physical dimensions that governed texture perception. One of the dimensions captures the repetitiveness, or regularity, of texture elements. Figure 5.32A shows examples of textures at opposing extremes of this dimension. The second dimension reflects the granularity of the texture. An extremely granular texture is composed of randomly distributed, large elements of roughly uniform size. Examples are shown in Figure 5.32B. The last prominent dimension reflects the presence of a strong local orientation within various regions of a surface. Examples of two extremes along this dimension are shown in Figure 5.32C. To make sure you understand their scheme, look around you, note three or four different textured surfaces, and try to place them into Rao and Lohse's framework.

So, Rao and Lohse's work provides a way to describe textures. Work by other investigators (for example, Nothdurft, 1985; Wolfson and Landy, 1998) shows that human observers are reasonably good at judging shapes defined solely by texture differences (a skill we'd like to embody in Spirit's circuitry). Two examples of shape defined by texture appear in Figure 5.33. In the right-hand figure, the "grain" of the central textured region sets it off from its surroundings; in the left-hand figure, the regularity of the texture distinguishes center from surround. It is important to note that neither of these rectangular shapes would be detectable if you had to rely on luminance differences alone, because the average light intensity in local regions throughout both figures is constant.

FIGURE 5.32 | Examples of textures representing ends of the perceptual dimensions identified by Rao and Lohse (1996). Row A: repetitive versus random; row B: granular versus agranular; row C: oriented versus disoriented.

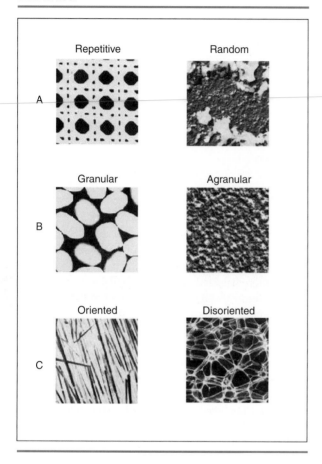

Repetitive   Random

A

Granular   Agranular

B

Oriented   Disoriented

C

Still, the central rectangular region can been seen immediately and with no effort—the shape appears to "pop out" from the background.

Anne Treisman (1986) and others have exploited this pop-out effect as a way to distinguish features that can be quickly and effortlessly registered from those that require time-consuming scrutiny. Some typical displays used in these kinds of pop-out experiments are shown in Figure 5.34. By presenting a "target" at randomly chosen locations among a field of "distracters," Treisman was able to measure how long observers took to locate the target. To distinguish targets that pop out from those that do not, judgment times were measured with varying numbers of nontarget, distracter elements. If a target popped out, the time needed to spot that target would be relatively unaffected by the number of embedded distracter elements. Pop-out, in other words, would imply that visual mechanisms are carrying out their searches for the target simultaneously, in parallel, throughout the entire visual field.

Many experiments show that pop-out may be produced by differences in stimulus attributes including color, line curvature, line tilt, and familiarity. And, of relevance to our present discussion, pop-out can be produced by texture differences between "target" and "background" (Bravo and Blake, 1990). There are, however, limits to pop-out from texture-defined shapes. To see this, look at Figure 5.35. The cluster of plus signs forming a horizontal shape pop out conspicuously, but, if you continue to look very hard, you may see a second region of texture difference that escaped your attention. See the cluster of Ts embedded in the Ls in the figure's right half? Only by scrutinizing the elements individually, and comparing them against one another, do you discover the existence of a group of Ts.

Ellsworth Kelly, a noted contemporary American artist, has used texture differences in paintings to create

FIGURE 5.33 | Two examples showing that shape can be defined by texture differences between figure and ground.

FIGURE 5.34 | Four displays typical of those in Treisman's work on target pop-out. The display in the upper left-hand panel shows "distractors" only with no "target." When displays like this appear, observers respond no as quickly as possible (by hitting one key on a computer keyboard). The other three panels show displays in which a target does appear within an array of distractors. When displays like this appear, observers respond yes as quickly as possible (by hitting another key on the computer keyboard). In a typical experiment, the number of distractors is varied, and reaction times on "yes" trials are then plotted as a function of the number of distractor elements. If the target pops out from the distracts, those reaction times will be more or less constant regardless of the number of distractors.

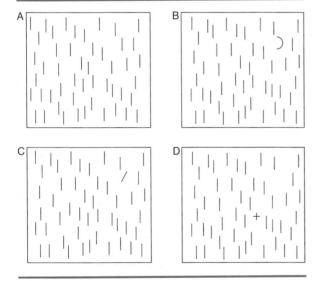

FIGURE 5.35 | Some regions defined by texture differences are conspicuous whereas others require scrutiny.

interesting illusory edges. A black-and-white reproduction of one of Kelly's paintings appears in Figure 5.36. You can probably see a set of sharp vertical edges that divide the painting into nine equal sections. In this piece, the artist was attempting to capture the essence of a pattern of shadows he had seen on a staircase (Shapley, 1996). Kelly stripped away brightness differences, leaving only shadow textures to define the nine steps. To get really good insight into what actually produces the illusory steps, take a card or sheet of paper and move it slowly up and down over Kelly's painting. By occluding or revealing various sections of the painting you should be able to identify minimal texture information that is needed to produce Kelly's illusory steps.

In addition to boundaries and shapes, texture information can also specify the three-dimensional curvature of a surface, particularly when the textures defining those sur-

faces are complex and consist of multiple orientations (Zaidi and Li, 2002; Li and Zaidi, 2000). Figure 5.37 shows a computer-generated image that simulates the appearance of a uniformly textured surface that is corrugated in depth, with the corrugations running along the horizontal axis. We will return to texture as a depth cue in Chapter 8.

This is a good time to take stock of what you've learned so far in this chapter. We have focused on visual processes that extract information about spatial scale and contour orientation. These same processes locate the edges and boundaries of objects by signaling the presence of discontinuities in light level or texture. These processes, which represent an early stage of vision, generate a map of whatever local features happen to be present throughout the visual field. Roughly speaking, these local features comprise parts of objects (often quite small). Although visual perception may begin by creating a neural inventory of parts and their locations, it certainly doesn't end there. To appreciate this point, let's go back to Spirit, the Martian explorer trying to identify objects using its onboard cameras.

When we last looked, Spirit had helped to create an inventory of Martian object parts and their locations. These were represented in the snapshots taken by Spirit's camera (Figure 5.1). The many clusters and strings of similar numbers provide some clues about locations in the image where object parts seem to be located. But how do we put these clues together to reproduce the objects in the scene that Spirit's camera caught? This next step is challenging, for it requires assembling the parts into meaningful wholes. To appreciate this challenge, look at Figure 5.38. We have no

FIGURE 5.36 | "La Combe I" by Ellsworth Kelly (painted in 1950). Note the strong illusory vertical contours along the endpoints of the thick diagonal bars. The figure shown here is a black-and-white reproduction of the original, which is red paint on white canvas. The original is 38 inches by 63.5 inches.

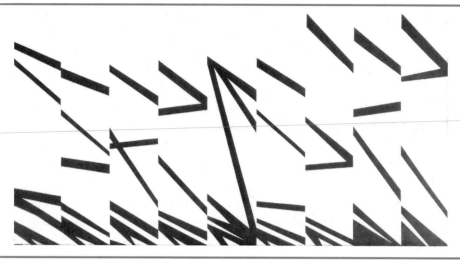

FIGURE 5.37 | Computer-generated image of a textured surface that appears to have 3D corrugations.

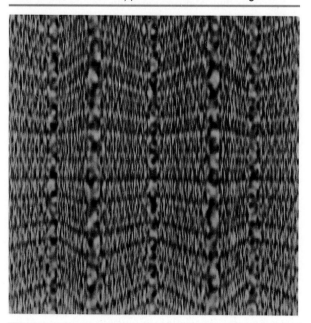

FIGURE 5.38 | Perceiving an object entails segregating contours into a meaningful whole.

FIGURE 5.39 | Displays producing the configural superiority effect.

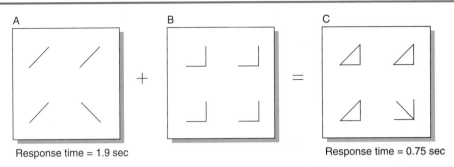

trouble recognizing this as a young girl gazing out a window. Simple, it seems, until we stop to realize what vision had to accomplish to arrive at this conclusion. At early stages, vision must identify regions in the image that are most likely to be neighboring parts of a single surface and, hence, neighboring parts of a single object. This must be done even when parts of the image (such as the girl's cheek) are partially obscured by other objects in the scene (such as the crosspieces of the window). In effect, vision must assign different image parts to various objects even when those parts overlap. If you still think the task is easy, look back at Figure 4.1d, the seemingly random array of black-and-white splotches. Remember how difficult it was initially to identify this as a Dalmatian? This demonstration reminds us that assembling image parts into a meaningful whole is not always as easy as it seems.

So, how does Spirit's electronic visual system compute which feature parts should be grouped together to comprise a shared object? What rules must be embodied in its circuitry to accomplish this feat? For clues to the answers, we again should consider how our own, biological visual systems do it. To do that, we need to go back in time to the early part of the twentieth century, long before Spirit was even imagined.

Putting the Parts Together: Global Context and the Gestalt Principles

Previously in this chapter, we mentioned the structuralists' idea that perceptions could be decomposed into primary sensations. In Germany, shortly after the turn of the twentieth century, a school of thought emerged in reaction to the structuralist idea that composites could be decomposed into their parts. Called the **Gestalt** movement, this school of thought argued that objects appear as they do in virtue of the parts' *relations* to one another. It fol-

lows, therefore, that the process of decomposition—the structuralists' manifesto—destroys the essence of the object. Listen to the words of Wolfgang Köhler, one of the founders of the Gestalt movement:

> We do not see individual fractions of a thing; instead, the mode of appearance of each part depends not only upon the stimulation arising at that point but upon the conditions prevailing at other points as well. (1920/1938, p. 20)

A compelling confirmation of this statement was provided by James Pomerantz (1981). Pomerantz had people view arrays of elements like the ones shown in Figure 5.40. For each array, observers had to identify as quickly as possible the single item that was perceptually distinct from the others. For each presentation, Pomerantz measured how long it took to make this judgment. On average, observers took 1.9 seconds to spot an odd element among a cluster of four (in panel A of Figure 5.39, the odd element is the reverse diagonal at the lower right). Pomerantz also created a second array of figures, by adding to each diagonal an L-shaped figure (see panel B), producing the more complex figures shown in panel C. When required to spot the odd item in this new set, observers took only 0.75 second—65 percent faster than with the "simpler" figures. The more complex figure, in other words, acquired an emergent property not available in its individual, component features, a property that made it easier to discriminate from its neighbors. This so-called **configural superiority effect** dramatizes what became the credo for the Gestalt psychologists: "The whole is different from the sum of its individual parts." (In more contemporary parlance, one could say that a feature is known by the company it keeps.)

For the Gestalt psychologists, then, the key was identifying principles of organization that specified how parts relate to one another. In the following paragraphs we'll examine those principles and see examples of them

FIGURE 5.40 | Objects close together tend to unite perceptually into groups.

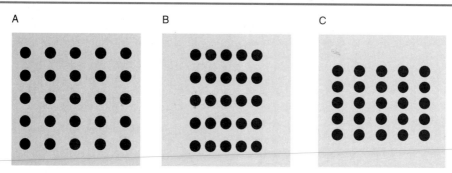

in action (for a more extensive discussion, see Palmer, 1999). The Web resources for Chapter 5, available at www.mhhe.com/blake5, has more material, including demonstrations, of these principles.

Gestalt Principles of Organization

The principle of **proximity** describes the tendency of nearby objects to group together as a single perceptual unit. As you can see in panel a of Figure 5.40, no strong, stable organization seems to predominate when the circles are equally spaced. Instead, they can be seen sometimes to cluster into rows and other times, into columns. (You may occasionally even see the circles grouping into diagonal strings.) None of these weak organizations persists, however, and none seems compelling. But notice what happens when the vertical distances among neighboring dots are made larger than the horizontal distances, as in panel b of the figure. With this simple modification, the dots form horizontal strings, or rows. Panel c illustrates what happens when the horizontal distances are made larger than the vertical: Dots group into vertical strings, or columns. So, simply varying the proximity of circles biases the perception in favor of one organization or the other. Another intriguing example of proximity's potency is illustrated in Figure 5.41. Called a **Glass pattern** (in honor of its inventor, Leon Glass, 1969), the dots in this figure appear to have an overall radial pattern to them. What does proximity have to do with this overall appearance? The global, radiating pattern comes about because throughout the figure the individual dots tend to pair up with a neighbor because of their proximity (technically each pair is called a "dipole"). And throughout the entire figure, the implied orientation of these pairs varies systematically in a manner implying a radial shape. And it is proximity that forms the basis for this global pattern.

FIGURE 5.41 | These dots convey an overall sense of a radial pattern, but this global form is defined solely by the arrangements of local pairs of dots that are grouped by their proximity.

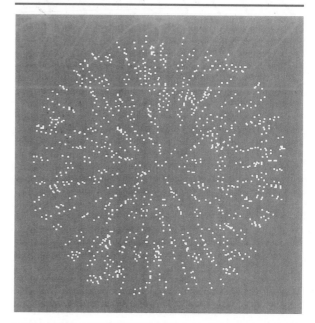

Max Wertheimer, a famous Gestalt psychologist, called attention to another major organizational tendency, the principle of **similarity.** "Other things being equal, if several stimuli are presented together, there is a tendency to see the form in such a way that the similar items are grouped together" (1923/1958, p. 119). The dimensions of similarity that control grouping include lightness, orientation, and size. Examples of these effects are illustrated in

FIGURE 5.42 | Objects similar in shape and size tend to group together.

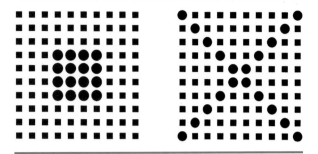

FIGURE 5.43 | A demonstration of closure.

Figure 5.42. Notice in the left-hand panel how the circles form a perceptual group in the midst of the squares. Apparently the differences between circles and squares in both lightness and shape contribute to this grouping. In the right-hand panel, the disks form two diagonals crisscrossing the squares. Here, shape alone promotes grouping.

A third related grouping principle is called **closure,** and you can see it in action by looking at Figure 5.43. At first the figure may look like a meaningless row of heart-like forms. But the pattern contains a handwritten version of a simple and common word: "men." In fact, the pattern contains two copies of that word, one a mirror image of the other. Closure causes the two mirror images to cohere into a single, closed pattern, thus obscuring the characteristics of the two separate components.

Another of the Gestalt principles is **good continuation,** or more simply, continuation. This refers to the tendency to perceive clusters or strings of individual elements as forming a single contour, or path (Polat, 1999). In the preceding chapter, Figure 4.1B showed you one example of contour integration based on the alignment of individual features. A snake in the left-hand panel of the figure was easy to spot in a field of randomly oriented lines. But the snake in the other panel was hard

to find. The random figures in the background were the same in both panels, but the snakes differed from one another in the amount by which their successive segments changed. The individual segments of the more visible snake differed from one another by angles of 30 degrees, whereas the less conspicuous snake's segments differed by 60 degrees. By the way, the snake would have been even more conspicuous if successive angular differences were even smaller or if the snake's "head" had grabbed onto its "tail" to form a closed figure (Kovács and Julesz, 1993; Pettet, McKee, and Grzywacz, 1998).

Good continuation is one of the Gestalt principles whose underlying neural mechanism is fairly well understood. Recall that Chapter 4 described a scheme whereby neighboring oriented line segments, like those comprising the snakes, could be "connected" by the visual system. Specifically, neural responses to nearby contour segments of similar orientation could be enhanced if neurons with neighboring receptive fields and similar preferred orientations were interconnected in a way that allowed them to reinforce one another's activity. These highly selective linkages could arise out of long-range horizontal connections that selectively associate neurons with adjacent receptive fields. These associations would selectively favor continuities between neurons whose preferred orientations were similar, and would discriminate against continuities between neurons with dissimilar preferred orientations (Field and Hayes, 2004). The presence of an appropriate stimulus would be signaled by simultaneous activation of a set of neurons whose receptive fields had the appropriate orientation tuning and spatial locations.

But what evidence do we have that these neural circuits really do promote visual grouping by good continuation? If those circuits did serve this function, we would expect that the visual features activating these circuits would be features typically present in natural images of real-world scenes—the images generated as we look around our natural, everyday world. So, are the visual stimulus conditions revealed by laboratory contour integration experiments mirrored by the visual characteristics of natural images? To answer this question, one must first ascertain the characteristics of natural images. To that end, Bill Geisler and colleagues (Geisler et al., 2001) measured the geometrical properties of a wide variety of natural images, including images of flowers, trees, a mountain, a lake and river, and some woods (see Figure 5.44). To characterize the contours in such images, these investigators displayed each image on a computer monitor and had people move a cursor to select all the oriented elements that be-

FIGURE 5.44 | Examples of natural scenes used by Geisler, Perry, Super, and Gallogly.

longed together in a single, shared contour. For example, if there were a riverbank in an image, people selected each of the oriented segments that outlined the riverbank. This operation was repeated for all the contours in every image.

From this vast collection of measurements, Geisler and colleagues extracted the essential statistical properties of natural contours. Recognizing that the geometrical relationships among segments were particularly important, the research team computed the orientation and position differences among all pairs of segments that people had attributed to each shared contour. Their quantitative findings can be summarized broadly and qualitatively: Adjacent segments of any single natural contour tend to have very similar orientations (take one small stretch of riverbank and an immediately adjacent stretch), but segments of the same contour that are further apart (one stretch of riverbank versus another, more distant stretch of that same bank), tend to have orientations that are more disparate from one another.[8]

Geisler and colleagues used this information about natural images to create 216 different families of synthetic test figures—serpentine, broken contours made up of varying numbers of line segments. Within each family, all members shared the same quantitative relationship to the statistical properties of natural contours. But the families varied in how well each conformed to those natural statistics.

These carefully designed figures were then used in a forced-choice psychophysical experiment. In each trial, participants saw two patterns: one was a collection of many, small, randomly oriented line segments; the other pattern was a similar collection, but with a test figure embedded in it. The participants had to identify which pattern contained the serpentine contour. Geisler reasoned that if the contour integration properties of the human visual system mirrored the statistics of the natural world, the detectability of any particular test contour should depend upon how closely *its* statistics matched the average co-occurrence statistics of contours in the natural world.

Detailed predictions of contour detectability were derived from a simple computer model whose few rules mimic the way the human visual system might perform the same task. The model linked individual line segments into a shared, larger contour, but did so in accordance with the statistics of natural images. In particular, the probability that any two segments would be linked together grew as their orientations became more similar, but declined as the distance between segments increased. Finally, linkages were transitive, that is, if the computer model linked line segment a to line segment b, and it also linked segment b to segment c, then the model would link a and c, creating, in this example, an extended contour three segments long.

Figure 5.45 gives you some idea of how the model behaved. The panel at the left shows a typical visual array that Geisler used to test observers. At first glance, the short segments in the array may appear to be random in orientation. If you scrutinize the array, though, you will find a number of places where nearby segments have similar orientations. The computer model would tend to link these together into a contour. In the right-hand panel, lines are drawn through individual segments that Geisler's model would connect. As you can see, the model's rules for connecting segments generates a number of small contours, and one long one. Note, in particular, that the model discriminates against linkages between adjacent segments whose orientations differ widely from one another.

---

[8] Obviously, there are exceptions to these tendencies, such as instances of relatively sharp changes in orientation, as with the pointy leaves of maple trees, but overall these tendencies do capture the main statistical characteristics of natural images.

FIGURE 5.45 | Contours extracted by Geisler's model. At the left is a set of contour segments used to test both human observers and the computer model. At the right are the contours extracted by the model.

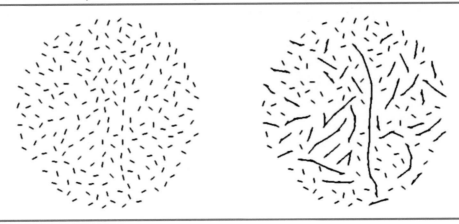

For each of their 216 families of synthetic figures, Geisler and colleagues compared the model's predictions to the actual performance of human subjects. To illustrate the power of this simple model, Figure 5.46 shows, for each condition, the model's prediction plotted against observers' actual performance. If the model were perfect, and if performance had no inherent variability whatsoever, all the data points in the figure would lie along the diagonal line. Given how elementary the model was, Figure 5.46 shows excellent agreement between the predictions of this very simple model, on one hand, and human performance, on the other. This agreement strongly supports the hypothesis that development of contour integration mechanisms, either during evolution or during the first years of any individual's life, is driven by the occurrence statistics of images encountered in the natural world. Geisler and Diehl (2002) have extended this basic idea, explaining processes by which the properties of perceptual systems are harmonized with the properties of the physical world.

Given the importance of Gestalt principles of perceptual organization, we should ask at what stage in visual development these principles of organization actually begin operating. Elizabeth Spelke and her colleagues used the preferential looking technique (described previously in this chapter; see Figure 5.18) to assess infants' sensitivity to objects whose boundaries were defined by Gestalt principles such as figural similarity and good continuation (Spelke et al., 1993). Although adults describe the objects as compelling, three-month-old infants seem oblivious to the objects, implying that the individual features defining the objects were not being grouped. During the next half-year, infants slowly but surely show signs of increasing use of grouping rules. It is not until about age 10 or 11 that adult levels of perfor-

FIGURE 5.46 | Agreement between predictions of Geisler's computer model and performance of human observers. The diagonal line represents perfect agreement between the computer model and people's performance.

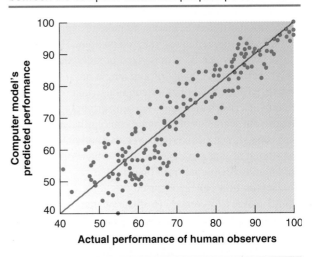

mance are achieved, implying that the neural circuits underlying contour integration mature relatively slowly within the human cerebral cortex (Kovács et al, 1999).

Gestalt principles of organization are sometimes called *laws*. If they're truly laws, however, there are nonetheless circumstances where grouping tendencies are stymied, and need lots of help, effort, and extra time. Take the twisted and tangled pairs of curves in Figure 5.47. Start with the left panel by fixating on the black circle. Now decide whether the x lies on the same curve as the fixation mark. Do the same for each of the other panels.

FIGURE 5.47 | Figures used to study visual assessment of contour relationships ("curve tracing"). Each figure consists of a pair of intermingled curves. For each figure, fixate the black circle and judge whether the x lies on the same curve as the circle or not. Note how the ease of judgment varies from figure to figure.

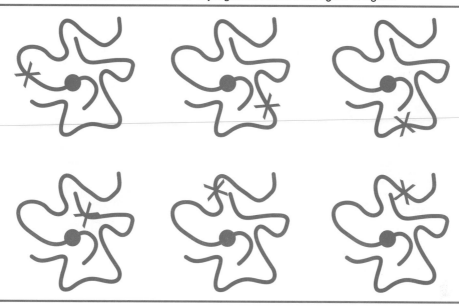

Although you certainly can perform the task, it's not easy. In fact, the time it takes to determine whether the x and the fixation point share a line depends upon how far apart the two are on that line (Jolicoeur, Ullman, and Mackay, 1986; Pringle and Egeth, 1988). The visual system requires time to trace the curve from the fixation point by moving the focus of attention along the curve.

As you know, proximity *promotes* perceptual grouping, but here, grouping by proximity *retards* perception: the tracing time lengthens as the two curves are brought closer together. After all, performance in this task requires keeping the two curves separate, not grouping them into a single entity. This is further demonstrated by the fact that curve tracing slows dramatically if the two curves touch or cross one another (Roelfsema, Scholte, and Spekreijse, 1999). Apparently, the task requires not only differentiation of one contour from its background, but also differentiation of one contour from another contour.

So, the Gestalt "laws" operate more like suggestions than reliable, ironclad laws. But laws that operate this way are common in science. Take Boyle's law. It tells us that the volume occupied by a gas is inversely related to the gas's pressure. But pressure is not the only factor that comes into the equation. To predict what volume will be occupied, you also need to take into account the temperature, as the combined gas law does. No Gestalt principle operates in isolation, unless a stimulus has been specially designed to allow it to do so (as we did in Figures 5.42

and 5.43). In the natural world, potentially conflicting Gestalt principles are reconciled in accord with rules that are not yet fully understood.

Before closing our discussion of spatial vision and grouping, we need to consider one other potent stimulus characteristic that significantly impacts the appearance of objects, the characteristic termed *symmetry*.

Global Structure and Symmetry

Some objects, including most biological ones, have an unusually conspicuous structural property that deserves special comment: that property is **symmetry,** the tendency for those parts of an object centered about a given axis to be highly similar in shape, texture, and color. Symmetry influences many of our perceptual judgments, including the quality of fruit (round apples are preferred to irregularly shaped apples), the structural integrity of a bridge, and the aesthetics of art [Weyl, 1952]). The human body is approximately bilaterally symmetric, and some evolutionary biologists even believe that bilateral symmetry of the human face significantly contributes to perceived attractiveness (Mealey, Bridgstock, and Townsend, 1999). Given the ubiquitous importance of symmetry, how does the visual system recognize this important characteristic of objects?

To come up with an answer to this question, let's start by looking at an example of symmetry. In Figure 5.48, the two panels are perceptually quite distinct from one another: The one on the left looks like a collection of random black,

FIGURE 5.48 | Demonstration of symmetry detection. Both rectangles comprise elements of varying lightness. In the rectangle at the left, those elements are distributed randomly; in the rectangle at the right, the random elements in the left-hand side of the square have been duplicated in mirror-image fashion on the right-hand side. This gives rise to bilateral symmetry that is easily seen.

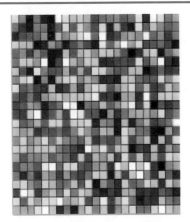

gray, and white squares. The panel on the right is also a collection of black, gray, and white squares, but these squares are bilaterally symmetric; the two halves are mirror images of one another. To make this panel, we duplicated one half of the right-hand panel, flipped it around a vertical axis, and then put the two halves together, side by side. But you could detect the bilateral symmetry even before you were told how the figure was made. Detecting individual squares—regions that differ from their immediate surroundings—is an early step in the process for detecting symmetry about a vertical axis. But it's not enough. The visual system also has to register similarities in the spatial arrangement of the squares, and this requires recognizing comparable structures—such as the figure's horizontally elongated and aligned patterns (Dakin and Herbert, 1998).

The tendency to perceive symmetry must be really powerful, because we automatically "impose" an assumption of symmetry when interpreting potentially ambiguous visual scenes. What do you see when you look at the pair of shapes in the top part of Figure 5.49? No doubt you perceive a diamond-shaped object partially occluded by a circular-shaped object. But that's not the only possible perceptual interpretation: The right-hand portion of the partially occluded object could be almost any shape (including a semicircle, in which case the two objects would be butting up against one another). Our overwhelming tendency to see a diamond is caused by the strong propensity to assume that the partially occluded object is symmetrical. It is no wonder that the Gestalt psychologists considered symmetry as a fundamental principle of perception.

Symmetry is a powerful contributor to aesthetic judgments, including our reactions to representational and nonrepresentational works of art (Ramachandran and Hirstein, 1999). What's the origin of this aesthetic impact? And can experience override that preference? To explore these questions, Ingo Rentschler of the University of Münich turned to some very simple figures: compound gratings comprising two different spatial frequencies in varying phase relationships to another (Rentschler et al., 1999). You can see some of these compound gratings in Figure 5.50. Compound gratings may not be as beautiful as your own favorite painting, but using them rather than paintings makes it possible to connect known physical properties to any aesthetic responses they may evoke.

Rentschler and colleagues presented all possible pairs of 16 different compound gratings. For each pair, people chose the compound they liked best. The entire set of preference judgments was converted into a quantitative measure preference for each grating. Overall, people had the strongest dislike for compounds 2 and 4 shown in Figure 5.50, and they had the strongest preference for compounds 1 and 3. Apparently, two factors underlie these ratings (and the ratings for the other 12 gratings, which are not shown here). One factor is symmetry—compounds 1 and 3 have greater bilateral symmetry than do 2 and 4. The other factor is simplicity, as reflected in the number of easily visible bars—the preferred compounds have fewer visible bars. In a follow-up experiment, Rentschler found that experience with these compounds altered people's preferences. Bilateral

FIGURE 5.49 | In the top portion of the figure, we see the object on the left as a diamond partially occluded by a circle. In fact, the occluded portion of that object could be any shape whatsoever, including any of the three shapes shown at the bottom. Vision favors the diamond because that perceptual interpretation maintains symmetry.

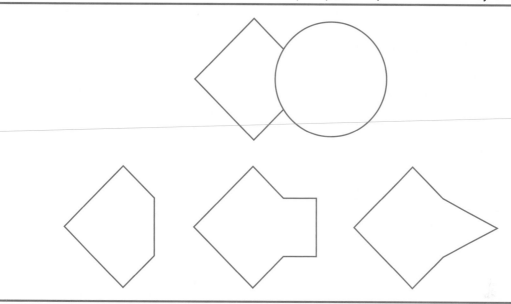

FIGURE 5.50 | Compound gratings representing the two preference dimensions Rentschler extracted from people's judgments of liking. Compounds 1 and 3 exemplify bilateral symmetry; compounds 2 and 4 exemplify visual complexity.

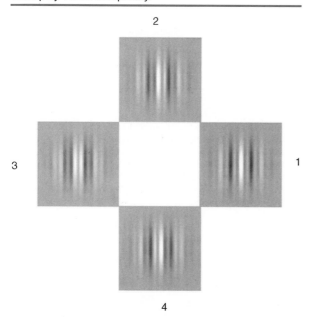

symmetry remained as potent as ever, but preference for complexity increased or decreased depending upon a person's prior training.

Preference for symmetry, then, depends on a relatively invariant processing of visual information, but the aesthetic pleasure derived from simplicity/complexity depends upon experience. At any moment, your preferences reflect both the enduring properties of your nervous system as well as the taste acquired through your experience.

This completes our survey of the spatial properties that define objects and their parts, and hence, determine our ability to detect and discriminate those objects. As we close, think back once more to Spirit slowly traversing the Martian landscape as it surveys whatever its cameras encounter. If Spirit's circuitry can mimic the perceptual operations described in this chapter—multiscale analysis and shape-from-texture grouping—then our little robot has taken one giant step in humankind's attempt to discover the Martian environment. But Spirit's electronic messages still must be transformed into identifiable objects. Clues about how that can be accomplished are the focus of Chapter 6.

S U M M A R Y   A N D   P R E V I E W

This chapter emphasized that visual information is used to distinguish objects from their backgrounds and to discriminate objects from one another. We presented various views of form perception, including structuralism, Gestalt psychology, and the multichannel model derived from measurements of the CSF. The multichannel model is an attempt to relate human form perception to what is known about the visual cortex. It can account for many aspects of human and animal vision, including detection, discrimination, and certain visual illusion, but it, too, has its limitations. In the next chapter, you'll learn how the visual system puts together the information it acquires to generate useful representations of objects.

K E Y   T E R M S

analytic introspection
closure
configural superiority effect
contrast
contrast normalization
contrast sensitivity function (CSF)
contrast threshold
cutoff frequency
detection
discrimination
Fourier analysis

Gestalt
Glass pattern
good continuation
grating
identification
metamers
multichannel model
orientation
proximity
scale
selective adaptation

similarity
sinusoidal grating
size aftereffect
spatial frequency
spatial phase
symmetry
texture contrast
transfer function
window of visibility

Chapter 6

Object Perception: Recognizing the Things We See

As the planetary rover Spirit gingerly negotiated the slopes of crater Gusev on the surface of Mars, its goal was to gather information that would help identify objects on the Martian landscape. In the preceding chapter, we explained how the torrent of numbers Spirit sent home could be divided into snapshots, and how each snapshot could be broken down into individual features locally distributed over different regions of the scene. That's a good start, but it is still far from Spirit's ultimate goal. To begin to accomplish that, Spirit needs to understand what it's looking at—to recognize objects in its field of view.

What do we mean by *recognize?* Consider the Latin roots of its constituent parts: the prefix *re* means "again," and the verb *cogito* means "to think" (recall Descartes's famous musing "Cogito ergo sum," which means, "I think therefore I am"). Putting the two roots together, *re-cognition* means, "recalling to mind." In terms of perception, it means that what we are seeing now puts us in mind of something we already know or are familiar with. You might, for instance, recognize an object on your table as a coffee mug. You might also recognize that it's your favorite mug, the one covered with pictures of spotted cows.[1]

That act of recognition, in turn, governs how you interact with the mug (or whatever it is you're looking at). Knowing that the object is your "mug" supports your actions of filling it with coffee, reaching for it, grasping its handle, and lifting it to your lips. Of course, this all occurs without much, if any, conscious mental effort. As a result, it's easy to take recognition for granted, underestimating the complexity of the process. But just think about it. You're able to recognize the mug as yours from just about any vantage point, from any reasonable viewing distance, and under varying conditions of illumination. Moreover, the mug could be right side up on a table or upside down in a drying rack, yet you still see it for what it is: your mug. Recognition, in other words, operates effectively across a range of viewing conditions.

Let's think for a moment about the complex process of recognition facing the rover Spirit as it attempts to navigate the Martian terrain. Figure 6.1 shows a snapshot of one situation that confronted Spirit. By the standards of earth's urban environments, this is a pretty barren landscape, but it poses real challenges for a robotic vehicle outfitted with a computer-based visual system. Of course, if we were only interested in obtaining photographs of the Martian surface, Spirit would have been unnecessary; a camera mounted on a rotating turret could have done the job. But besides taking photographs, NASA's scientists wanted Spirit to maneuver around the surface, collecting samples of rocks and

---

[1] When you're able to recognize that an object is a specific instance (my favorite mug) of a general class of objects (mugs), we use the term **identification** to denote your perceptual decision. When you recognize that a specific object (my favorite mug) belongs to a general class of objects with the same properties (mugs), we use the term **categorization** to denote your perceptual decision.

FIGURE 6.1 | Photograph of the Martian landscape.

dust. To accomplish these tasks, Spirit needed to know where to go, and to do that, it had to know what it was looking at.

As Figure 6.1 confirms, the Martian surface is replete with hills and valleys, its surfaces littered with rocks and boulders of various sizes and shapes. Vision is the only means Spirit has to navigate this challenging terrain. A deep crater better not be confused with a shadow on the ground; small rocks must be distinguished from larger ones; and even Spirit's visible tire marks in the dust might be needed to backtrack after a soil-hunting expedition. And there's always the outside possibility that Spirit might encounter something completely unanticipated, such as an empty soda bottle left behind by an earlier extraterrestrial visitor. Spirit has to be able to examine potentially interesting objects that it spots on the Martian surface. To accomplish these tasks, our robot rover must be able not only to detect the presence of something but also to recognize what that object is.

We humans engage in object recognition all the time, and we're remarkably good at it. Think about lounging in front of the television set surfing the channels for something interesting to watch. Holding your finger down on the channel advance button, you're barraged with a rapid sequence of unrelated images—two chefs cooking and laughing; a race car flipping end over end; a woman doing aerobic exercises; a close-up of a pianist's hands flying over the piano keyboard; Barry Bonds completing a home-run swing; a weather map full of graphic symbols of sunshine, clouds, low and high pressure systems. Each image is visible for only a fraction of a second, but you have little trouble sorting through this rushing visual stream to identify not only what you are looking at, but whether you have found anything you want to watch. Confirming your experience with the video remote control, laboratory studies show that people can identify scenes that are displayed for as little as a tenth of a second (see the reviews by Henderson and Hollingworth [1999], and by Bar [2004]).

Most of the time, of course, we aren't forced to recognize objects that appear and then disappear in a flash. Nonetheless, we're constantly shifting our gaze from one location to another, looking at different objects. And these visually guided shifts in gaze can occur very quickly. When a pair of pictures is presented on either side of a fixation point, people can shift their fixation to the picture containing a designated object (e.g., an animal) in about a third of a second (Rousselet, Fabre-Thorpe, and Thorpe, 2002). This means, in other words, that your visual system can select which of two regions of a scene contains a "target" object and, then, shift your visual fixation to that object in about the same amount of time it takes you to blink your eyes when a hand is suddenly thrust in your face! No doubt the remarkable speed of object recognition provides us with a margin of safety in a potentially threatening environment.

It has been estimated that we make more than 170,000 of these fixation-shifting eye movements each and every day (Irwin and Brockmole, 2004), including the ones you're making right now as you read these sentences. As we look about the environment, our eyes first seek out the visually complex regions in the scene, ignoring large expanses of uniform color or luminance. And once we've gotten a quick lay of the land, our eyes tend to revisit objects of potential significance. This unfolding fixation behavior is illustrated in Figure 6.2. While people looked at this photograph, the successive positions of their eyes were recorded. The dots and lines denote the changing pattern of eye movements during a 10-second inspection period. Notice that people tended to look at specific objects in the kitchen scene, ignoring the floor and blank walls. In general, individual durations of fixation last about a quarter of a second (Henderson and Hollingworth, 1998), and the features attracting the greatest number of fixations are precisely those regions that independent judges rate as most informative (Mackworth and Morandi, 1967). This visually guided pattern of fixations suggests that the eye-movement control system of the brain draws on stored information about the characteristics of various scenes and scenarios (Land and Furneaux, 1997; Henderson, 2003). Later in this chapter, we will reconsider the role of eye movements in object recognition, particularly their role in reading.

But there's much more to object recognition than merely selecting something to look at. To appreciate some of the additional obstacles that recognition has to overcome, take a look at Figure 6.3. Isabelle Bülthoff used a computer to design this unusual scene. The obstacles represented in this scene can impede the recognition of chairs, but the same points could be made with other types of objects.

Let's start with an obstacle to recognition to which you've already been introduced. Look carefully at the mesh screen near the figure's left side, where you'll see a couple of objects partially obscured by the mesh. You have no trouble recognizing these as chairs even though

FIGURE 6.2 | A pattern of successive eye fixations (top panel) as a person looked at this kitchen scene (bottom panel).

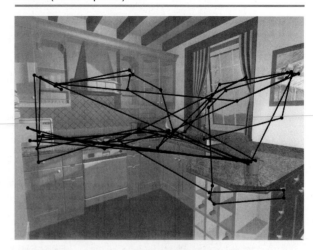

some portions are hidden from view. The entire bottom half of the chair behind the desk is invisible, yet you have no trouble recognizing it because you understand that the base is there but occluded. Look up at the ceiling where a chair is suspended precariously. You may never before have seen a chair hanging upside down from the ceiling, unless you've seen the 1951 Fred Astaire movie, *Royal Wedding*. Despite the novel perspective, you recognize the dangling object as a chair. However, at first glance you might not pick up on the presence of this odd chair, for unexpected or inconsistent objects in a scene tend to produce more perceptual errors and take longer to recognize (Biederman, 1972).

Look at the painting on the rear wall. It creates a retinal image equivalent to that created by the real chair in the

FIGURE 6.3 | Computer-generated depiction of a room full of chairs.

right foreground, but you easily recognize that one is a chair and one is merely a picture of a chair. Note, too, that the chair visible through the archway into the next room casts the same retinal image as the miniature chair on the desk. But, again, you recognize one as the real thing, and the other as a model—one that you could sit on, the other that you could hold in the palm of your hand. Finally, you immediately recognize that the slatted armchair, although it looks different from the rest, belongs to the same family of objects—chairs—as the rest in this scene. All are in a shared category of objects, chairs.

So how is it that we can recognize objects even when we cannot see all the parts? And how is it that we can distinguish among objects that share many features in common, or recognize the common membership of objects that look rather different from one another? The next several sections describe some of the sources of information that human vision exploits to achieve object recognition.

A Matter of Perspective: Recognizing Three-Dimensional Objects

Look again at that room full of chairs in Figure 6.3. Notice how they're scattered about in varying orientations relative to your line of sight: right side up, upside down,

turned frontally, turned away, and so on. These variations in orientation produce corresponding variations in the chairs' images on your retinas. Yet somehow, despite variation in the retinal image, you're able to recognize what you're looking at. You may notice that the viewpoint has changed, but as far as categorization goes, that change is irrelevant. A chair is a chair, regardless of the perspective from which you view it. Recognition can be slowed down by unusual viewpoints, but rarely is it completely stymied.

Several competing theories have been developed to explain the robustness of recognition in the face of varying viewpoints (summarized in Palmeri and Gauthier, 2004). Of these, we'll consider two theories that represent contrasting approaches to object recognition. One of these theories, championed by Irving Biederman, is called **recognition by components;** the other theory, developed by Heinrich Bülthoff, Michael Tarr, and others, is described as **view-based recognition.**

Recognition by Components

According to Biederman's theory, when people try to recognize a visible object, they first create a rough classification of the object, on the basis of its three-dimensional (3D) shape. This rough classification sorts objects into

FIGURE 6.4 | Biederman's geons and some simple objects constructed from them.

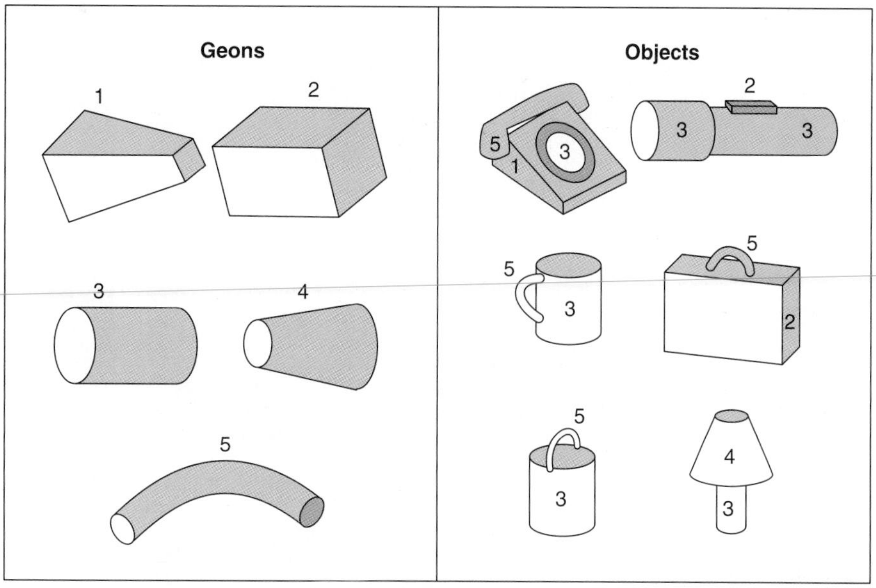

broad, entry-level categories such as chair or mushroom or mug. Note that this classification does not put objects into finer categories, such as a Queen Anne chair or a Stickley chair. Because the initial classification is rough, the details needed for subtler discriminations (for example, to distinguish one type of chair from another) are not used. Biederman argues that any view of an object can be represented as an arrangement of just a few, simple three-dimensional forms called **geons** (for *geo*metrical *ions*). The left-hand panel of Figure 6.4 shows some of the geons postulated by the theory. The right-hand panel illustrates how several different common objects could be represented by a combination of two or three geons. The ability to represent a very large number of possible objects by means of just a few components makes Biederman's approach simple and efficient (meaning that relatively few "parts" can be used to represent an indefinitely large number of objects).

Biederman's geons share two essential properties. First, they can potentially be distinguished from one another from almost any viewing perspective. So, with just one singular exception, from all viewpoints a sphere will always look different from a cylinder.[2] Second, even

when some randomly chosen parts of any geon are obscured or erased, the rest will almost always remain recognizable. So, if the midsection of a cylinder is occluded, what's left will continue to look more like a cylinder than, say, a cone. As a result, neither changes in perspective nor partial occlusion disrupts registration of the geons and, hence, recognition of the object. Once the appropriate geons have been extracted from the visual image, the object is recognized from matches against internal representations of previously seen objects (visual memory). These representations are aggregations of the geons needed to construct particular objects.

The theory's virtues include its ability to explain why it is hard to recognize an object from a highly unusual perspective. Take the various views of the horse shown in Figure 6.5. The horse depicted in the lower right-hand photograph in that figure would be difficult to recognize because the image hides several geons that are crucial for defining the category horse. At the same time, we would have little trouble recognizing the horse in the upper right-hand photo because the image makes it easy to extract the crucial geons despite the odd perspective.

A recent physiological study provides some evidence that the primate brain actually generates representations like the ones Biederman's theory posits. In that study (Kayaert, Biederman, and Vogels, 2003), neurons in the inferior temporal cortex of the monkey

---

[2] This one exception arises when a cylinder is viewed end on, either from its bottom or top. Then the shape of the cylinder's retinal image is circular, like that of the sphere.

FIGURE 6.5 | A single object seen from 12 different perspectives.

responded selectively to relatively simple geometric shapes, with some neurons responding best to cylinders, others responding best to cones, and still others best to boxes. Of relevance to the geon theory, a change in the perspective or the depth from which the shape was viewed, or a change in a "metric property" of the shape, produced relatively little change in the firing of many of these neurons. (Metric properties are shape properties, such as aspect ratio, that vary with rotation in depth.) On the other hand, the firing of these neurons changed markedly when a viewpoint-invariant property of the shape varied (e.g., from straight to curved). This greater sensitivity to nonaccidental property variations as they're called is a fundamental assumption of a geon-based account of object recognition, for this theory, as mentioned above, is built on the notion of viewpoint independence.

Despite this suggestive physiological evidence, the fact remains that in many situations, recognition accuracy and recognition speed *are* dependent on viewpoint. It is to that evidence, and the theory that grows out of the evidence, that we turn next.

View-Based Recognition

Bülthoff, Tarr, and their colleagues believe that recognition of a 3D object depends upon multiple, stored views of objects. Suppose you get a momentary glimpse of an object you're attempting to recognize. The pattern of neural activity evoked by that brief view of the object could be matched against stored representations of activity patterns elicited previously by views of various objects. If the current activity pattern matches a stored pattern, it's a reasonable bet that the same object was responsible for both. If no match is really close, then your visual system settles for second best, finding the best approximation for a match. While this account sounds plausible, a number of objections have been raised against this view-based scheme for recognition. Here are just a few.

The first objection concerns novelty. As you read about this account of view-based recognition, you may have wondered what happens when someone is faced with an object never before encountered. The theory proposes that a novel object is recognized by neural interpolation to the object whose neural representation most closely matches the representation produced by the novel

FIGURE 6.6 | Computer-generated objects, both familiar and novel.

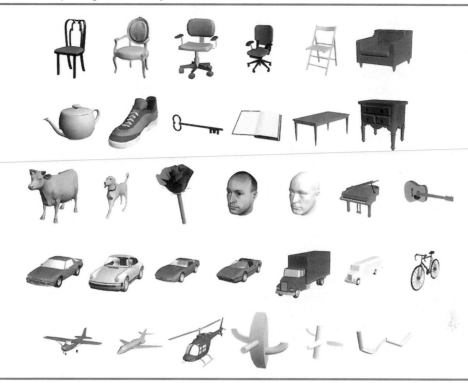

object. So a particular coffee mug that you'd never before seen can be recognized as a mug because the neural activity evoked by the novel mug is similar to the neural activity evoked by other, familiar mugs. Similarly, you might wonder about the case where you're viewing a familiar object from a novel viewpoint. Provided the view is not extremely unusual—like the view of the upside-down chair on the ceiling—the object can be recognized by interpolation to the nearest stored view.

Most objects tend to have their own, natural viewpoint from which they are most easily recognized (Palmer, Rosch, and Chase, 1981). These natural viewpoints could provide clues about the stored representation used for recognition of that object. For example, if the stored representation strongly resembled the object's natural viewpoint, that resemblance could explain the relative ease of recognition. But what constitutes a natural viewpoint for an object? That depends upon what information the visual system needs to perform a particular task, as Blanz, Tarr, and Bülthoff (1999) showed. Blanz and colleagues created computer-generated, 3D objects on a video screen. Using a trackball, a person could ro-

tate an object on the screen to simulate viewing that object from different angles. People were instructed to rotate each object until they found the best perspective for depicting each object in a brochure. The 3D test objects, which appear in Figure 6.6, included familiar objects—faces, motor vehicles, and chairs—as well as a few novel objects (the three shown at the lower right of the array). Two of the novel objects were created out of simple, basic volumes, like Biederman's geons; the other novel object, a kind of artificial paper clip, was created by stringing together four similar components.

On each trial, people rotated the image of the object until they were satisfied that the viewpoint was best for the brochure. Blanz then tallied up the preferred viewpoints, and for most objects found a consensus on what constituted each object's best, or canonical, viewpoint. Typically, people chose an oblique viewpoint rather than a viewpoint from above, below, straight on, or entirely sideways to the object. However, the three novel objects did not follow this pattern. For them, there was no consensus on the canonical viewpoint—people's notions about the best viewpoints did not agree. The absence of a consensus suggests that any object's canonical or best view develops as people have experiences with that or similar objects.

Results of other experiments, too, are consistent with a view-based recognition scheme. To give one example, Palmer, Rosch, and Chase (1981) reported that object recognition slows as the viewpoint departs from that judged most typical for an object. For view-based theorists, such results make perfect sense. If the typical view is an excellent match for a stored representation, no interpolation is needed—hence, short recognition time. If a view is atypical, however, the required interpolation will be lengthy, and recognition time will be longer.

Such an explanation may strike you as post hoc (after the fact). Is there some way to put the account to a real test? Suppose we create some novel object and train people to recognize it from just one viewpoint. When we test recognition of that object in a variety of views, it's no surprise that recognition is fastest at the trained viewpoint. If recognition speed really depends on viewpoint interpolation, then sufficient exposure to that object from a wide variety of viewpoints should eliminate the need for interpolation, and hence, speed up recognition. And this is exactly what happens: Practice does eliminate viewpoint dependence over the range of trained viewpoints. Of course, viewpoint dependence reasserts itself when people again confront novel perspectives (for example, Edelman and Bülthoff, 1992).

But this discussion of recognition leaves out one important source of recognition information. In everyday life we are not usually restricted to a single view of an object. We can move around an object or, if it's small enough, we can pick it up and examine it from various angles. This movement—of the viewer or of the object—generates information that changes over time in a highly predictable way. Might the changing perspectives produced by motion facilitate recognition?

To examine this possibility, James Stone (1998) created a collection of different ameboid 3D structures. People were trained to recognize four of the ameboid shapes, discriminating these target objects from other "distracter" ameboids. Ameboids in the training set or in the distracter set were always presented as a short movie in which an ameboid appeared to rotate in 3D space. Each movie's starting image was chosen randomly for each trial, but regardless of the starting image, the movie always played in the same order.

Throughout the trials, participants' recognition performance improved—they were able to decide more quickly whether the animated amoeba was from the target set or a distracter set. Learning was taking place, but what was being learned? To answer that question, Stone tested people using movies in which the direction of 3D rotation was reversed. Now instead of seeing a target ameboid tumble through a series of positions in one order, people saw the same images but in reverse order. The result? Recognition times slowed and accuracy of recognition dropped; only with practice on the new versions did performance recover.

Playing a movie backwards means that a movie's individual "snapshots" remain unchanged; only their order of presentation is altered. This makes the ameboid appear to tumble through a novel sequence of positions. The impact of this change on recognition suggests that recognition incorporates spatio-temporal information when that information is available. As Stone notes, spatio-temporal continuity is a fundamental property of the physical world. If an object rotates around a particular axis, that rotation generates a characteristic set of changes in the retinal image over time. Quite sensibly, then, vision can associate objects with characteristic spatio-temporal sequences, and use those sequences in object recognition.

There are plenty of real-world examples of this skill at work. Expert bird-watchers learn to rely heavily on patterns of wing and body movements to distinguish species of birds that are highly similar in size and shape. And all of us are adept at identifying friends based on their characteristic gait, even when other cues to identity are absent. We'll discuss perception of spatio-temporal events in greater detail in Chapter 9.

Vision's reliance on spatio-temporal sequences rests on an assumption about the physical world: Matter tends to maintain its spatial coherence over time. This is just a fancy way of saying that objects don't tend to change abruptly into other objects—with the exception of explosions and special effects in movies. As a result of the world's spatio-temporal coherence, an object we see today is likely to appear the same tomorrow, next week, or next year.

But does object recognition actually take advantage of the world's tendency toward spatio-temporal continuity? To test this idea, Guy Wallis (1998) intentionally altered objects' usual spatio-temporal continuity, and then measured how this alteration altered recognition. Wallis's technique used several short, five-frame sequences that depicted faces in changing perspective, rotating from left profile through a frontal view to right profile. When the frames were shown in succession, vision knitted them together, creating the impression of one person whose head rotated smoothly from left to right. But, in fact, people were not seeing the same face. Instead, Wallis's film sequence contained a series of several different faces shown in five perspectives. Because these faces resembled one another, people tended to see the sequence as the movement of a single face—not different faces in different views. This means, of course, that the "face" that

FIGURE 6.7 | The figure on the left and the one on the right probably look like familiar objects (a man's face and a nude woman). But the one in the middle can be seen as either the man or the woman; this middle figure is ambiguous.

people saw never actually existed. It was a chimera pieced together by their visual systems, aided and abetted by Wallis.[3]

After people viewed these chimeras several times, Wallis measured their ability to recognize various faces. In the test, people saw two faces, one after the other, but in different, randomly chosen perspectives. They had to judge whether the two images portrayed a single person or two different people. When the two test faces had never been shown together in the same chimera, people correctly recognized that they were different faces about three-quarters of the time. However, when the two faces had appeared in the same chimera, recognition fell to near chance levels. Seeing the two different faces as a single chimera undermined discrimination. And as they saw more chimeric sequences, people's ability to discriminate grew worse. So practice does not always make perfect, particularly when you're practicing with misleading material.

Learning to Recognize

So we now know that object recognition can be educated. When you encounter the same object again and again, the way you perceive that object can change, and sometimes dramatically. This experience-driven "tuning" of the visual system is an important, but often neglected, aspect of seeing. James Elkins, an art historian, has a keen sense of what educating vision is

all about. Elkins recalls his own experiences with visual plasticity:

> The world is filled with things we do not see, even though they are right in front of us. When I was younger I kept a collection of insects, and for several years I was especially entranced by moths. . . . Some kinds of moths don't care about light at all, and they stay in the woods and fly only at night. . . . To catch them you mix a pail of beer, mashed rotten bananas, and molasses and walk through the woods painting it on tree trunks with a house-painting brush. . . . The moths we were after also have excellent camouflage, and their wings are perfect facsimiles of bark. . . . After several summers sugaring trees, I developed a special eye for the subtle outlines of those moths: I learned to see the little rounded triangle of their bodies, the very slight shadow they cast when they pressed against the wood, and the minute differences between their patterned wings and the texture of bark. . . . And now, over twenty years later, I still have the ability to spot those moths. It seems to be built into my neurons. (1996, pp. 54–55)

Figure 6.7 doesn't show any of these hard-to-spot moths, but it does illustrate what Elkins had in mind. The figure shows an ambiguous image, much like one in Chapter 4 (Figure 4.27). Looking at the middle version first, you can see it either as the face of a man or a nude woman with her head coyly turned away from you. And if you look at the figure for a minute or so, you'll see one person and then the other, each one's perceptual dominance lasting several seconds. On the left is a version of the drawing that more clearly depicts the man; on the right you see a version that favors the nude woman.

---

[3] In Greek mythology, a chimera was a creature that was, from front to rear, part lion, part goat and part snake.

When people are shown only the ambiguous drawing (middle panel), some initially see the man, others initially see the woman. However, this tendency can be altered by having a person look first at one of the less ambiguous versions of the drawing. When people are first shown the left panel of Figure 6.7 and then the middle panel, virtually all initially see the ambiguous, middle figure as depicting a man. Conversely, when people are first shown the right panel and then the middle panel, virtually all of them see the ambiguous drawing as depicting a nude woman. Exposure to either unambiguous drawing primes the subsequent perception of the ambiguous drawing, biasing it in one direction or the other. Priming's influence on perception can be quite enduring. A single exposure to a priming object can influence perceptual judgments made several days or even weeks later (Cave, 1997).

In priming, then, visual experience at one moment influencing subsequent experiences, which is a sign of visual plasticity. Chapter 4 described another form of visual plasticity, in which neurons' receptive fields change in response to environmental stimulation experienced early in life. These results during early infancy led researchers to wonder whether adult vision might also be plastic (Buonomano and Merzenich, 1998). Figure 6.8 shows the test stimuli for four experiments on adults that demonstrate the powerful effects of practice in a variety of visual tasks.

Panel A tests the ability to discriminate between lines in slightly different orientations from one another (Schoups, Vogels, and Orban, 1995). With practice, the smallest orientation difference that can be discriminated decreases by more than fivefold. The orientation difference between lines in each pair grows smaller from the top row to the bottom, which makes the discrimination more difficult. This is meant to simulate the observation that orientation discriminations that at first were impossibly hard became easier with practice.

Panel B measures the ability to perceive tiny offsets between collinear lines, an ability called *vernier acuity* (Fahle, Edelman, and Poggio, 1995). Even before practice, people can make very fine discriminations between offsets. But with practice, that skill improves dramatically, making it possible to discriminate between even the slightest offsets. In each pair of lines, the offset of one line relative to the other grows smaller from the top row to the bottom. This makes the judgment of the lines' offset more difficult. This is meant to simulate the observation that offset (vernier) judgments that at first were very difficult, like the ones at the bottom, with practice became easier, like the ones at the top.

Panel C tests the ability to spot a small, briefly presented "target" item embedded in a field of background texture elements (Karni and Sagi, 1993). Over many the

trials, the orientation of the target's three items varied randomly between horizontal and vertical; its precise location in the field also varied. Participants had to identify the orientation. At first, correct performance required that the target be visible for more than 130 msec. After several days' practice, people only required a 30-msec exposure for the same level of performance.

Panel D examines the ability to identify a low-contrast human face that is partially camouflaged by random visual noise (Gold, Bennett, and Sekuler, 1999). The relatively clear face at the top of the panel illustrates the initial level of contrast people needed to identify a face. Over time, performance sharpened so that after several days, people became highly proficient at identifying faces such as the barely visible one at the bottom. The middle face represents an intermediate level of proficiency, which participants displayed partway through the experiment.

These substantial improvements in visual performance also seem to endure, lasting as long as two years after practice ceases (Karni and Sagi, 1993). Moreover, improvement tends to be highly specific to the visual figures encountered during training. When people are trained with figures that, say, always appear in the left half of the visual field, practice-induced improvement may not generalize to test figures imaged in the right half of the visual field (Shiu and Pashler, 1992; Karni and Sagi, 1991; Fahle, Edelman, and Poggio, 1995). Likewise, when people get better at distinguishing a vertical line from a line slightly tilted from vertical, improvement does not transfer to other orientations, such as ones near horizontal (Schoups, Vogels, and Orban, 1995). Finally, improvements with practice on these kinds of difficult visual judgments are enhanced by a good night's sleep (Stickgold, James, and Hobson, 2000) or, at the least, a 90-minute nap (Mednick, Nakayama, and Stickgold, 2003) after the practice session. These sleep-dependent improvements in visual performance imply that changes in neural connectivity promoted by training are labile and require some period of consolidation before the changes become stable.

Improvements in vision are not limited to the laboratory. People who devote lots of time to particular visual discriminations develop proficiency that leaves the rest of us awestruck (Sowden, Davies, and Roling, 2000). Sometimes these visual skills develop as part of a hobby, such as bird-watching or moth-hunting; others develop in connection with one's job. Consider the case of professional chick sexers. Chickens are big business in many parts of the world. Farmers who raise chickens for egg-laying are not eager to feed more male mouths than absolutely necessary. So, within hours of hatching, chicks are sorted according to sex, so that males can be discarded. On large farms, specialists, called "chick sexers,"

FIGURE 6.8 | Perceptual learning improves performance on the four tasks illustrated in these panels. Panel A: Stimuli used to assess orientation/discrimination. In each circle, judge which of the two short lines is the more clockwise in orientation. Difficulty in discrimination increases as you move from top to bottom because the orientation differences decrease. With practice, discrimination improves, eventually rendering even the most difficult patterns relatively easy. Panel B: Stimuli used to assess vernier acuity. In each circle, judge which of the two lines is shifted more leftward. Discrimination difficulty increases from row to row. Practice enhances the ability to discriminate even the most challenging line pairs here. Panel C: Sample figures used by Karni and Sagi (1993) to study perceptual learning. Observers identified the orientation—horizontal versus vertical—of a tiny "bar" composed of three diagonally oriented lines against a background of lines all of the same orientation (left column). This array of lines was presented for a brief duration, immediately followed by an array of irregularly oriented lines that foreclosed further processing of the test array. With practice, observers were able to identify the orientation of the test "bar" at ever briefer durations, indicating that the display was being processed more efficiently. Panel D: Sample stimuli that illustrate the improvement in effective stimulus strength that comes with practice. The stimuli, devised by Gold, Bennett, and Sekuler (1999), were briefly presented in the midst of random "noise." At appropriate levels, the noise makes the faces difficult to recognize. With practice, a given level of noise becomes less effective in interfering with recognition. By scanning the photos in this panel from top to bottom, an observer is able to correctly perceive the continuity of faces despite the increasing visual noise.

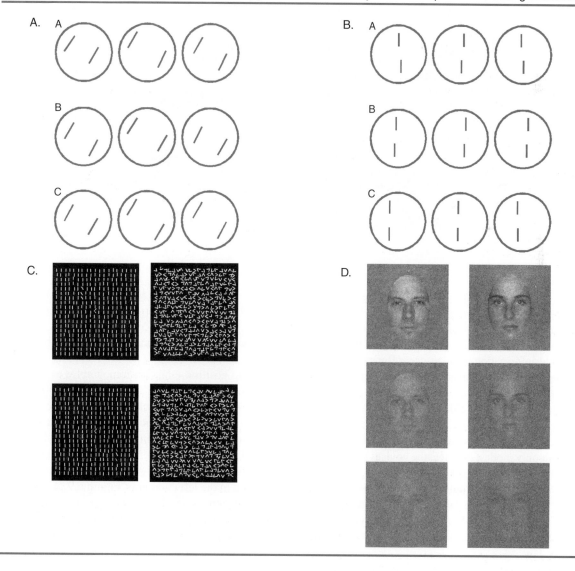

FIGURE 6.9 | The two left-hand panels show examples of black-and-white images that are difficult to recognize. The two panels on the right show regular photographs of the two objects.

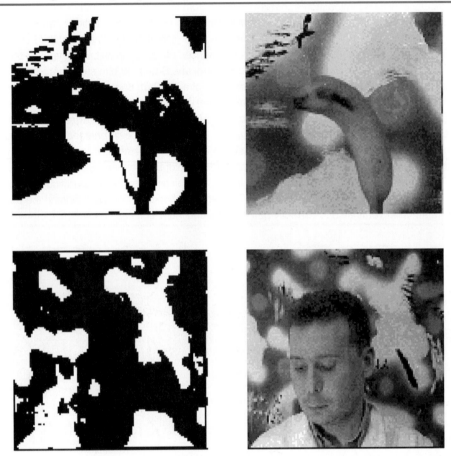

do this job with remarkable speed and unerring accuracy. Over the course of a career, a sexer might sort 50 million chicks, taking just a half second per chick. Looking over the shoulder of a sexer at work, it's hard to figure out what visual information is being used. But, with a little help from expert chick sexers, Biederman and Shiffrar (1987) cracked the code, allowing them to educate people who had never sexed a chick before. People got a simple diagram explaining exactly what part of a chick to look at and some rules for interpreting what they saw there. With only modest practice, the novices were transformed into skilled chick sexers.

In Chapter 4 you encountered other forms of visual learning. Remember that Dalmatian dog whose spots blended so well with its background? Unless you'd seen it before, the dog was initially hard to see. But eventually,

with effort and prompting, the dog emerged. What happens in the brain to transform unrecognizable or misrecognized objects into recognizable ones? Recently, researchers have begun to understand how the brain deals with things that are initially hard to recognize.

Using positron emission tomography to image the brain in action, Dolan and colleagues (1997) presented people with two-tone, black-and-white photographs of objects, including faces. Such images are difficult to recognize because all the normal shades of gray have been removed, leaving the image with just two extreme intensity levels—black and white. Examples of their images are shown in the left column of Figure 6.9. As expected, people performed poorly, correctly recognizing only 55 percent of the faces and 13 percent of the rest of the objects. Then Dolan and colleagues showed people normal, easy-to-recognize grayscale versions of the two-tone images. As expected, exposure to the normal versions boosted subsequent recognition rates of the original black-and-white images, to 87 percent for objects and 93 percent for faces.

To identify the brain changes accompanying this improvement, Dolan and colleagues compared regions of brain activated during the first, "uneducated" exposure to the images to those areas activated during the second, "educated" exposure to the same images. Two different, widely separated parts of the brain, the temporal lobe and the parietal lobe, showed the changes with education. Specifically, improved recognition of faces and improved recognition of objects were linked to increased activation in two small regions in the inferior portion of the temporal lobe. Prior studies had shown that neurons in these regions respond preferentially to easily recognized faces or to objects presented in their normal colors. In addition, improved recognition activated regions in the parietal lobe. Earlier work showed that these activated regions participate in directing attention and in generating visual imagery.

The pattern of activation led Dolan and colleagues to hypothesize that improved recognition resulted from feedback from the parietal lobe's stored representation of the easily recognized, full-grayscale stimulus. This feedback, they argued, amplifies the responses of face- or object-sensitive neurons in the temporal lobe. This result reminds us that recognizing objects under impoverished viewing conditions benefits from visual imagery stored in memory. This kind of influence is often described as "top-down," in order to distinguish it from sensory influences, which are described as "bottom-up" (you may recall these terms from Chapter 1). We shall return to such influences later in the chapter. For now, though, let's consider object recognition from the brain's perspective, focusing on hierarchically arranged visual areas that are involved in identifying objects.

The Temporal Pathway and Object Recognition

Chapter 4 introduced you to two streams of visual processing, the parietal (or dorsal) stream and the temporal (or ventral) stream. Recall that the temporal stream is sometimes described as vision's "what" specialist because its major responsibility seems to be in object recognition, telling us what we're looking at. (Analogously, the parietal stream is the "where" specialist, putting visual information into a spatial context, telling us where things are located, and therefore where our ac-

tions should be directed.) Remember, the brain's temporal stream originates in V1, the occipital lobe's rearmost region. It progresses through V2 and V4, and then crosses the occipital lobe's border with the temporal lobe. There, it makes synaptic connections in several areas of the temporal lobe's lower, or inferior, half, which is known as the inferotemporal (IT) cortex.

The vast terrain of IT cortex is home to several functionally different regions, each with cells preferring a somewhat different assortment of complex stimuli.[4] In some areas, many neurons respond vigorously when the image of a face falls within a neuron's receptive field. We can describe these regions as "face-selective," without implying that when we recognize a face, *only* neurons in those regions participate in that recognition (Tovee, 1998) or that cells in the face-selective region are responsive only to faces (Gauthier et al., 2000).

Converging lines of evidence show that the IT cortex plays a vital role in object recognition (Logothetis and Sheinberg, 1996; Logothetis, 1998a). For more than three decades, it has been known that damage to this region in monkeys produces a large deficit in visual object recognition. In humans, inferotemporal damage has similar effects on object recognition.[5] The effects of inferotemporal damage are especially dramatic when people must recognize complex visual patterns that cannot be easily coded in words (Milner, 1968). Because of its unique contributions, IT cortex has been described as the brain region where visual perception interfaces with memory and imagery (Miyashita, 1993).

Recall that neurons in area V1 respond to simple patterns such as bars and oriented edges. Within IT cortex, however, few neurons prefer oriented bars and edges (Tanaka, 1997). Instead, the vast majority of IT neurons exhibit much more complex selectivity, with some neurons responding only when a specific object such as a brush, a plant, or a person's face is imaged within the receptive field. This extraordinary selectivity has been known since records of single cell activity in IT cortex were first made by Charles Gross and his colleagues (see Gross, 1998). IT neurons have large receptive fields (in

---

[4] The cortex covering IT constitutes almost one-tenth of the brain's entire cortical surface.

[5] Portions of the temporal lobe may be surgically excised from the human brain in order to arrest epilepsy that does not respond to medical (drug) treatment. In many forms of epilepsy, seizures tend to start in the temporal lobe. Removal of the offending brain tissue stops or reduces seizures in most of these otherwise untreatable cases.

contrast to V1 neurons), meaning that they will respond to an object appearing anywhere within a relatively large region of their visual field. Moreover, the responses of IT neurons are highly sensitive to variations in features that are "diagnostic" of a given object category, such as the orientation of the eyes within a face, but are insensitive to variations in features that are not diagnostic for that category, such as the spacing between the eyes (Sigala and Logothetis, 2002).

Look back to Figure 6.3, with the room full of chairs. As we pointed out, that figure illustrates some challenges that visual recognition effectively overcomes. Guy Orban's research group has shown that some neurons in IT overcome some of the same challenges. Take occlusion, for example. As Figure 6.3 illustrated, occlusion does not foreclose accurate recognition of objects. In our three-dimensional world, this ability is vital—in real-world scenes, objects commonly occlude one another. Kovács, Vogels, and Orban (1995) showed that many neurons in a monkey's IT cortex are unaffected by occlusion of part of their optimum stimulus.

Figure 6.3 also reminds us that we're able to recognize an object despite huge variation in the size of that object's retinal image (variation produced as we view it from different distances). The same sort of size invariance is seen at the level of individual cells in IT cortex (Sary, Vogels, and Orban, 1993).

In general, recognition allows us to categorize objects to varying degrees of specificity, ranging from general class membership to a specific instance of a subclass of objects. So, with some effort you could pick out every chair in the room, treating them all as members of a general class. But you could also make various finer discriminations, picking out chairs that had slotted backs, for example (members of a particular subclass).

Individual neurons in the inferotemporal cortex also can convey different levels of information about objects. Sugase and colleagues (1999) recorded the sequence of neural impulses elicited in monkey brains when faces were presented in the receptive fields of "face" neurons. The test displays included human faces, monkey faces, and simple geometrical objects such as circles and squares. Moreover, within the collections of human and monkey faces were sets of faces defined by their emotional expression: neutral, surprised, angry, and so on. When Sugase and his colleagues examined the time course of neural activity evoked by various figures, they found that, for at least some neurons, the early and later portions of a neuron's activity conveyed information about different aspects of the stimulus. Neural activity

triggered 50 milliseconds following stimulus onset conveyed information about the general class of object in the neuron's receptive field. This portion of the neuron's response, in other words, could discriminate whether the stimulus was a monkey face, a human face, or a geometric object. However, this early activity gave no clue about the particulars of the stimulus. In contrast, activity occurring several hundred milliseconds later was selective for the details of the image, such as the expression conveyed by a face. Sugase and his colleagues believe there might be a functional significance to this time delay between neural activity related to an image's global identity and its fine detail. You might liken the early, global information to the subject heading of an e-mail message, which provides a general, nondetailed preview of what is to follow, leaving it to later neural activity to fill in the details. Bar (2004) describes how the visual system might implement this general scheme, with later, detail-rich neural activity serving to reduce the ambiguity in earlier, less detailed activity.

While on the subject of the timing of neural responses within IT, it is remarkable how tightly coupled IT neural responses are to the perceptual "discovery" of an object within a cluttered visual scene. In a neat experiment, Sheinberg and Logothetis (2001) recorded from IT neurons while monkeys looked at a video screen that displayed either a single "target" object in isolation or that same target object embedded in a complex natural scene (see Figure 6.10). The monkeys were trained to fixate the target as quickly as possible, a task that could require several seconds when the target appeared in the complex scene. The pattern of eye movements were recorded along with the activity of single IT neurons (with each target object carefully matched to a neuron's preferred stimulus). Presented in isolation, objects evoked vigorous IT responses within about 150 milliseconds of the target's presentation, which is not surprising as the target's abrupt onset undoubtedly captured the monkey's attention. Of greater interest are results of trials in which the target was embedded in the scene, thereby requiring multiple shifts in fixation before the target was located. In this case, IT neurons became active about 100 milliseconds *before* the animal made the final eye movement that guided its fixation to the target. This was true on trials when the monkey needed only a couple of shifts in fixation to locate the target and on trials when the animal required a dozen or so fixations before finding it. These results add further strength to the idea that IT neurons are importantly involved in the process of recognizing familiar objects in the natural environment.

FIGURE 6.10 | One example of a display used to measure neural activity from neurons in inferotemporal cortex (IT) of monkeys trained to fixate a target object. On this particular trial, the target object was a teacup, shown in isolation in the small insert in the upper left-hand portion of the figure. In the main figure, the teacup appears somewhere within the scene. The white lines superimposed on the scene show the pattern of eye movements made by the monkey as it attempted to locate the teacup; in this example, the animal first looked at a portion of the monument in the center of the visual display and then shifted its fixation eight times before "hitting" on the target. At the same time the monkey was scanning the scene, neural activity was recorded from a single IT neuron that was selectively responsive to a tea-cup-shaped object. On this trial, the neuron became maximally active just a fraction of a second before the monkey initiated the final eye movement to fixate the teacup.

Teaching Old IT Neurons New Tricks   You've already learned that human vision is educable, and the benefits of education include improved visual recognition. Here we'll consider two forms of plasticity that IT neurons exhibit (later in the chapter we'll describe a third form).

Recall Dolan's demonstration (Figure 6.9) that a brief glimpse of a grayscale image can confer instant recognizability on a previously unrecognizable, black-and-white only version of that image. The technique used in that demonstration, functional neuroimaging, assesses activation in millions of neurons, but doesn't pinpoint what is happening in individual neurons. To take this more microscopic view, Tovee, Rolls, and Ramachandran (1996) demonstrated what might be a neural analogue to Dolan's behavioral observation. Tovee and his colleagues measured responses in monkey IT cortical neurons evoked by figures whose stark, black-and-white only rendition made them hard for humans to recognize. Then, following Dolan's procedure, they presented a full, easy-to-recognize, grayscale version of the figures. When the black-and-white only versions were presented again, they elicited considerably more activity from the same neurons studied before training. Confirming Dolan's account, the result is one-shot learning at the level of individual neurons.

In another demonstration of plasticity in IT cortical neurons, Kobatake, Wang, and Tanaka (1998) assessed neurons' responses while a monkey tried to recognize shapes from a set of complex geometric shapes. On each trial, one of 28 shapes was presented, and then, after a delay, the same shapes appeared again, but this time along with three of the other shapes. The monkey's task was to identify the figure that had been repeated, a standard recognition task. To make the task harder, Kobatake steadily lengthened the delay, from 1 to 16 seconds. With practice, the monkeys gradually improved at the task, eventually being able to do reasonably even at the longest delays. This performance improvement with practice was accompanied by changes in the responses of IT cortical neurons in the monkeys. Compared to neurons in untrained monkeys, practice caused the responses of neurons to become more differentiated from one another. In other words, practice made responses to various shapes more distinctively different from one another than they'd been prior to practice. Presumably, differentiation of responses at the level of single cells contributes to increased ability to discriminate at the behavioral level (recall our discussion of discrimination and metamers in Chapter 5).

But the temporal stream and area IT are not the entire story on object recognition; objects also imply actions, and to guide actions we rely heavily on the parietal stream (Colby and Goldberg, 1999). Box 6.1 offers one perspective on the relation between objects and the actions they afford.

Now that we've explored some basic facts about object recognition and some of its underlying neural machinery, we can apply what we've learned to two categories of objects that we encounter every day—faces and printed words—as well as to an unusual category of objects you've never seen before, computer-generated creatures called *greebles*.

Face Recognition

Of the countless objects we encounter during our everyday activities, one category of objects stands out: the human face. It's not surprising, therefore, that face perception is a major focus of research on object recognition.

We'll begin our discussion of face recognition with a brief overview, summarizing just how good we are at this task (and how bad we can be when faces are presented in odd perspectives). Then we'll consider one of the most bizarre syndromes in neurology, one in which brain damage destroys the ability to recognize familiar faces.

Perceiving Faces/Perceiving Minds Shakespeare's King Macbeth wisely noted that, "There's no art to find the mind's construction in the face" (I., iv). With these words Macbeth anticipated what researchers have confirmed centuries later: (1) a person's face contains useful clues about that individual's mood, character and intentions, and (2) we're all experts at reading faces.

The human face speaks volumes about a person. It reliably tells us whether the person is male or female (Bruce et al., 1993); whether the person is happy, sad, angry, frightened, or surprised (Ekman, 1984; de Gelder, Teunisse, and Benson, 1997); whether the person is young or old (George and Hole, 1995); and whether the person is healthy and reproductively fit (Perrett et al., 1998). Without even knowing it, we use facial cues during conversation to help interpret what someone is saying (Massaro and Stork, 1998). Most importantly, we're able to identify the significant people in our lives—family members, loved ones, friends, and enemies—from a glance at the face, and we're able to do this despite variations in viewing angle, lighting, and size (Moses, Ullman, and Edelman, 1996).

Expert though we are at recognizing faces, it doesn't take much to subvert that expertise. For example, reversing the contrast in photographs of faces makes it more difficult to recognize people, even well-known people (see Figure 6.11), probably because this procedure reverses the color of skin pigmentation and distorts shading cues that define facial features such as the nose and eyes (Bruce, 1994). Our face recognition abilities are disrupted even more dramatically when faces are shown upside down (Valentine, 1988). Suddenly, we're lousy at recognizing faces, and we're downright pitiful at judging expressions on faces. To discover your own ineptitude at perceiving upside-down faces, take a look at the cute child pictured in Figure 6.12, a photograph created using an image-editing technique devised by Peter Thompson (1980). Notice anything odd? Turn the book upside down, and you'll discover what escaped your view when the photo was inverted.

The so-called **face-inversion effect** has been taken to mean that faces, unlike other objects, are processed in a holistic fashion, meaning that a face is more than the sum of its individual parts. In this respect, holistic processing is reminiscent of the Gestalt emphasis on relationships among components (discussed in Chapter 5). In addition to the face-inversion effect, other results also point to holistic processing of faces (Tanaka and Farah, 1993). For example, consider the "hybrid" face shown in Figure 6.13. With scrutiny you may be able to tell that the top half and the

Objects manifest what James Gibson (1979) termed **affordances,** which can be construed as perceptual invitations from the objects to do things with them. The specific activities "afforded" by an object are governed by the object's structural characteristics. Some objects are designed to provide a particular affordance, but others offer affordances just because of their natural shape and size. A chair affords sitting, but so does a fallen log or a porch step. Moreover, a given object can have multiple affordance. A cup, for example, is designed to convey liquid to your mouth, but you can also use it to scoop dirt, to hold pencils, or to trap a small insect.

Some psychologists concentrate on identifying object affordances and relating them to the physical characteristics of those objects. For example, when it comes to judging the sizes of containers—such as boxes, jars, and cans—adults tend to focus heavily on the container's height when judging its volume. Thus, a typical spice jar 10.2 centimeters tall is judged larger than a common jar of baby food 7.7 centimeters tall, even though the baby food jar holds more (Raghubir and Krishna, 1999). As you can imagine, marketing analysts and product designers are keenly interested in these kinds of affordance judgments, which could influence purchasing decisions.

The concept of affordance reminds us that object recognition serves behavioral purposes. We don't just recognize the object on the desk as a compact disk (CD); we reach out, pick it up, insert it into the CD drive and listen to it. Our behavioral reactions to objects, then, need to be tailored to the perceived structural qualities of those objects. Thus, when you reach for that CD disk, your hand begins conforming to its thickness before you even make contact with it. At the moment you grasp it, vision has already estimated the object's dimensions. As a result the distance between your grasping fingers is just a little bit greater than the CD's thickness. And it's not just shape that vision estimates. You perceive whether an object is solid and sturdy (for example, a billiard ball) and, therefore, can be grasped firmly, or whether it's thin and fragile (for example, a fresh egg) and must be handled with care. Vision tells us whether an object is sticky or slippery, rough or smooth, light or heavy, dangerous or safe. When you climb a set of stairs you've never been on before, vision tells you when and how high to lift your feet (Warren, 1984).

Given this intimate link between object recognition and object affordance, it's natural to assume that our perceptions of an object will coincide with our motor reactions to those objects. If one coin looks bigger than another, you're going to spread your fingers farther apart to grasp the larger-looking coin by its edges. That's true if the two coins are genuinely different in size, but suppose the coins are actually equal in size and only look different? What would happen then? Before venturing a guess, you'd probably like to know how it's possible to make two round objects that are equal in size look different. We'll tell you how this is done, then tell you what your hand does when you go to grasp the coins.

The accompanying figure shows one of the most famous illusions in psychology, the Ebbinghaus illusion. If you're like most people, you'll judge the disk surrounded by small circles to be larger in diameter than the disk surrounded by larger circles. In fact, they're equal in diameter (as you can confirm using a ruler). Rather than worry about why this illusion occurs, suppose you're simply asked to reach out and pick up one disk, lay it aside, and then pick up the other disk. How far apart will you adjust your fingers just before grasping each disk?

Imagine further that you've not been told anything about the actual sizes of the two disks. All your hand knows is what your visual system tells it, so it stands to reason that your grasp width should differ for the two disks. In this case, however, reason is misleading. In fact, people employ identical grasp widths when reaching for one disk or the other, even though they reliably report the one disk being larger than the other. The hands, in other words, aren't fooled by the illusion. These and comparable findings have led Goodale and Humphrey (1998) to conclude that visually guided actions such as reaching are controlled by "mechanisms that are functionally and neurally separate from those mediating our [conscious] perception of that object" (p. 183). According to this way of thinking, Gibson's affordances, with their emphasis on opportunities for action, may speak more to the dorsal stream than to the ventral stream.

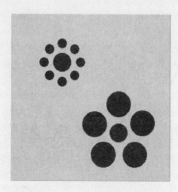

FIGURE 6.11 | The contrast has been reversed in this photograph of a familiar face, making it more difficult to identify. (The person's identity is given in the caption for Figure 6.12.)

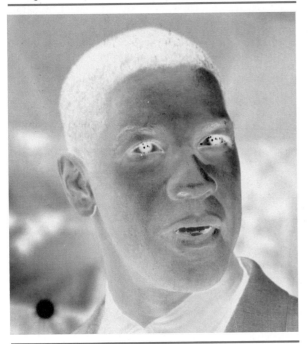

FIGURE 6.12 | Notice anything strange about the upside-down face of this cute child? Invert the book to see what you're looking at. (The person in Figure 6.11 is Colin Powell.)

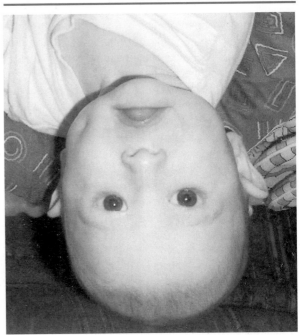

bottom half belong to different people. When asked to name the person pictured in, say, the top half of such a hybrid, people are slower and less accurate than when only the top half is shown by itself. Evidently, we can automatically process faces as global configurations, which interferes with the ability to attend just to one part of a face (Hole, 1994; for related findings, see Tanaka and Farah, 1993).

When it comes to facial expressions, people of all ages and cultures seem to recognize the same six basic emotions: sadness, happiness, anger, fear, surprise, and disgust (Ekman, 1984). Figure 6.14 shows prototypes of these six, and you can probably identify the facial characteristics that uniquely signify each of the emotions. When it comes to salience, however, not all six are equal. A single angry face stands out conspicuously within a crowd of otherwise neutral or happy faces. In contrast, a neutral or happy face does not stand out in a crowd of angry faces (Hansen and Hansen, 1988). This probably makes sense from an evolutionary perspective, since anger forewarns the threat of aggression. From the standpoint of mobilizing for action, it's much more important to detect a potential enemy among friends than it is to detect a friend among a crowd of enemies.

FIGURE 6.13 | A hybrid face whose top and bottom parts come from two well-known actors.

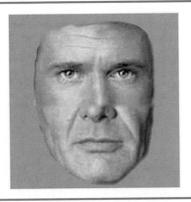

Besides being adept at recognizing emotional facial expressions, we're also quite good at detecting when someone else is faking an emotion. Figure 6.15 shows two photographs of a smiling woman, one of them natural and the other forced. You probably have no trouble telling which one is simulated, because it looks posed: when people at-

FIGURE 6.14 | Face displaying the six basic emotions.

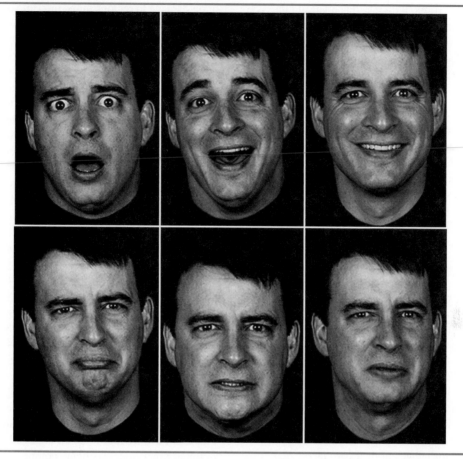

FIGURE 6.15 | In the picture on the left, the woman is smiling naturally, but on the right she is forcing her smile. You can easily tell the difference between these two expressions.

tempt to fake a smile, they do not utilize exactly the same facial movements that occur when a smile is evoked naturally. And someone looking at a fake smile can readily detect the "forgery" (Gosselin, Beaupré, and Boissonneault, 2002). This sensitivity to the authenticity of facial expressions is an adaptive social skill that can help one avoid deception.

In view of the importance of face perception in your everyday life, can you imagine being unable to recognize faces? Implausible as this may seem, some individuals suffer this exact problem. Their tragic misfortune provides us with another opportunity to learn about the neural responses to face perception.

Prosopagnosia: Failure of Face Recognition   Chapter 4 introduced you to several types of **agnosia** (from the Greek, meaning "without knowledge"), visual disorders produced by lesions (tissue destruction) of specific areas of the brain (Kolb and Whishaw, 1996). Among the most fascinating of the agnosias is **prosopagnosia,** the condition where a patient can see and describe another person's face but cannot recognize whose face it is, even if the person is a close relative (Sacks, 1985). We'll discuss this relatively rare condition in some detail because this dramatic failure of object recognition illuminates key theoretical and methodological ideas about object recognition in general. Let's start with a case description that typifies this fascinating, bewildering condition:

> When her husband or mother visited her, she failed to recognize them immediately, and only when a conversation was begun did she identify her visitors. When she was shown photographs of her two older children of preschool age, she failed to identify them; when she was told that these were indeed her children, she remarked that "they don't look like they should." Her failure in facial recognition extended to public personalities such as television stars. When watching television, she was unable to identify performers who were well-known to her, until they spoke or sang. (Benton, 1980, p. 178)

It's important to understand that the patient's problem is not blindness—her sight remains intact. Thus, when prosopagnosic patients look at photographs of different faces, they can judge whether one photograph is different from the other, even though the poses in the photographs show the faces from different perspectives (Sergent and Poncet, 1990). And these patients can readily tell whether a face is male or female (Tranel, Damasio, and Damasio, 1988). Despite all that, they cannot tell you whose face it is, even when they're looking at photographs or mirror images of their own face.

Now, we've all experienced difficulty remembering the name of an acquaintance, but name retrieval is not the problem in prosopagnosia—these patients can readily identify a friend, a loved one, or a famous individual based on the person's voice. Nor is the problem a general impairment of cognitive function. As Antonio Damasio explains:

> [People] who have never seen a prosopagnosic patient may be tempted to dismiss the phenomenon as the result of psychiatric illness or dementia. These interpretations are not credible considering that these patients show no evidence of language impairment, have intact cognitive skills and do not have psychiatric symptomatology before or after the onset of prosopagnosia. (1985, p. 133)

The problem, in other words, is genuinely visual, and it centers around recognition: Faces no longer have meaning for these patients.[6]

---

[6] The weblinks for Chapter 6 at www.mhhe.com/blake5 include several websites describing case histories of prosopagnosia.

Prosopagnosia is almost always accompanied by brain damage to regions in the inferior part of the temporal lobe (a region that includes the fusiform gyrus), particularly in the right hemisphere of the brain. Previously in this chapter you learned that the homologous region in the monkey brain is where neurons responsive to faces are found. And in Chapter 4 we mentioned that brain-imaging studies in humans pinpointed the inferior temporal lobe as a region uniquely activated when human faces are seen (Kanwisher, McDermott, and Chun, 1997). These converging lines of evidence make it tempting to identify the inferior temporal lobe as the location of the face processing area. But that conclusion oversimplifies the way the brain does its work and underestimates the versatility of the so-called "face" areas.

For one thing, recognition deficits in some prosopagnosic individuals extend beyond faces. These deficits, however, tend to get downplayed because the distress of not being able to recognize faces is so paramount. Damasio, Damasio, and van Hoesen (1982) describe patients who are unable to recognize other previously familiar objects besides faces. One such patient was an avid bird-watcher who was skilled at spotting a bird, but had lost the ability to identify the species of bird he was seeing. Another was a cattle farmer who had lost his once proud ability to recognize individual members of his own herd by sight. More recent work on prosopagnosic patients reveals that, in addition to faces, they can have trouble recognizing synthetic snowflakes or three-dimensional artificial, computer-generated creatures (Gauthier, Behrmann, and Tarr, 1999). In general, these patients experience little difficulty recognizing objects as belonging to some broad class ("It's the face of a male"); the problem involves identifying the specific object under scrutiny ("It's my son Geoff").

There's another reason why we should be skeptical that prosopagnosia results from damage to a single "face" area of the brain: prosopagnosia can take different forms. To demonstrate this point, Sergent and Poncet (1990) showed prosopagnosic patients photographs of eight different faces, two photographs at a time. For each pair, the patient rated how similar the faces were to one another. Sergent and Poncet then used a data analysis technique called *multidimensional scaling* (see the Appendix) to deduce what facial features the patients were relying on to make those judgments. This analysis revealed two distinct modes of face processing. Scaling results from one type of patient resembled the results from normal individuals: Patients based their judgments on the overall similarity of the faces' configurations, integrating various facial features into a comprehensive, global configuration (Sergent and Poncet, 1990). We can call this **configural processing.** The other type of patient, in contrast, performed very differently when making similarity judgments about the pairs of face photographs. This patient's judgments indicate that he singled out individual facial components (such as the hairline) without really integrating those components into an overall impression (Sergent and Villemure, 1989). We can call this **featural processing.** When either mode of information processing—configural or featural—is damaged, face recognition suffers.

Why, though, do these prosopagnosics, whose vision is normal, still experience problems recognizing faces? According to Damasio (1985), face recognition in these types of patients suffers because of an inability to access pertinent stored information about the face's owner. According to this view, brain damage has somehow uncoupled normal perceptual representation of a face from stored memories that make it possible to identify the face. In support of this "uncoupling" hypothesis, tests that bypass conscious recognition reveal the existence of intact knowledge of faces. In one study, the skin's electrical resistance was monitored while prosopagnosic patients viewed photos of familiar and unfamiliar faces. (Skin resistance reflects activation of the body's autonomic nervous system, and this activation increases when a person becomes aroused or excited.) Despite their lack of conscious recognition, the patients showed signs of heightened arousal upon viewing the faces of relatives and friends, compared to faces of unfamiliar people (Bauer, 1984; Tranel and Damasio, 1985). These and other results that probe unconscious memory (Sergent and Poncet, 1990) imply that in some forms of prosopagnosia information about faces receives refined perceptual analysis, with the problem resulting from connections between face perception and explicit memory.

Faces, chairs, birds, and vegetables have something in common. Like all objects, they can be characterized at a very general level of description, yielding a list of generic qualities (a bird is a two-legged, feathered creature with wings). But when necessary, we also can focus on characteristics of specific members of an object category (a wren is a small, brown perching bird with a curved bill and stubby tail). These more subtle distinctions are known as subordinate-level distinctions because they require more detailed information than is needed to make global category distinctions.

For many objects, we get by perfectly well with global descriptions—"chair" works fine when you're looking for something to sit on; the specific kind of chair

FIGURE 6.16 | Computer-generated "creatures" dubbed *greebles*.

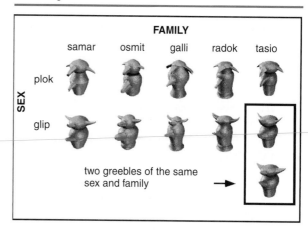

is irrelevant. But with faces, it's different: we almost always need to identify specific instances (who is it) within the category of faces. Because knowing who it is that we're looking at is of paramount importance in our lives, we are highly experienced at face recognition. Indeed, we all qualify as face experts. Is it possible, then, that the specialized "face" region in the temporal lobe is, in fact, a general-purpose brain area designed to support object expertise? If you were to devote a lifetime to distinguishing among, say, different species of birds, would the "face" area be transformed into a "bird" area? Isabel Gauthier and Michael Tarr were interested in testing this idea, but they wanted to start with a set of entirely unfamiliar objects, so that all people would begin as novice recognizers. To accomplish this, they turned to greebles.

Getting to Know Some Greebles

Look at the objects shown in Figure 6.16. These strange-looking "creatures" are examples drawn from a set of three-dimensional, computer-generated objects dubbed *greebles*.[7]

---

[7] To see more greebles, take a look at the greeble Web page, which can be accessed at www.mhhe.com/blake5.

To make it easy to describe these exotic creatures, greeble parts have been given fanciful names. For example, the horns on each side of greeble's head are called "boges." The upper protrusion on the front is the greeble's "quiff," and the protrusion below that is called a "dunth."

A greeble may not look like anyone you know, but its geometrical structure has something in common with faces and, for that matter, with other objects, too. Just as a human face has a mouth, eyes, and a nose in a fixed spatial relationship to one another, a greeble has characteristic parts in fixed relationships to one another. For example, the dunth always appears below the quiff. And like humans, "related" greebles also bear a family resemblance to one another. In the population they created, Gauthier and Tarr defined different greeble families. Greebles also come in two sexes, and you can tell whether a greeble is "plok" or "glip" from the tilt of its boges, quiff, and dunth. As Figure 6.16 suggests, you can recognize greebles at different levels: according to sex, family membership, or individual identities.

Gauthier and Tarr (1997) used training to turn utter greeble novices into bona fide greeble experts. They then used neuroimaging to examine activity levels in the face area of the greeble experts' brains. But when does someone qualify as a greeble expert? Recognition experts for other categories of objects exhibit a hallmark characteristic—they can recognize objects at a subordinate level as quickly as they can at the most general level. For example, longtime bird-watchers can correctly categorize a creature as a black-capped chickadee (a narrow category) just as quickly as they can categorize that same creature as a bird (a broad category).

To apply this criterion to greebles, Gauthier and Tarr capitalized on the fact that even novice greeble-watchers can instantly tell the sex of a greeble—all you have to do is notice the angle of its protrusions, and you've got the answer. This can be done in less than half a second (check it out for yourself using Figure 6.16). You can easily learn what to attend to and, therefore, easily learn the rule relating that detail to the greeble's sex. In no time you'll be able accurately to identify the sex of a greeble as quickly and efficiently as the best expert in the chick sexing business.

Because all greebles are either ploks or glips, the sex of a greeble constitutes a broad category. Family membership (five possibilities) and individual identity (dozens of possibilities), however, are both narrower categories. Not surprisingly, it takes a novice much longer to identify a greeble's family than it does to recognize its sex; and it takes even longer to identify a particular gree-

ble. Still, with several thousand trials of practice, novices can become experts at recognizing individual greebles.

Having shown that it's possible to produce greeble experts, Gauthier, Tarr, and colleagues (1999) were ready to examine neural activation in the face area of the brain using fMRI. At several points during the greeble training regimes, these investigators measured brain activation associated with viewing greebles and with viewing human faces. During this portion of the study, trainees were shown pairs of faces or pairs of greebles. Following each presentation, the trainees judged whether the two figures were the same or different. Not surprisingly, the face area was activated from the outset of training when people viewed faces. The more interesting result was the brain activation measured when people viewed greebles: As people gained expertise at discriminating greebles, the face area of the brain exhibited greater and greater activation.

The brain's growing activation to greebles did not occur simply because people had learned to recognize particular greebles. In fact, the greebles used during fMRI testing were novel ones that had never been seen before. Evidently, the face regions in the adult brain have more versatility than previously suspected. These brain areas can support subordinate-level recognition for categories of objects other than faces, provided that the brain's owner gets enough practice to become expert with those objects. Note, however, this finding does not mean that areas in the inferior portions of the temporal lobe are irrelevant for face perception. On the contrary, these areas are intimately involved in face perception *because* they deploy visual coding schemes ideally suited for faces. The unresolved issue, which is hotly debated by object recognition experts, is the extent to which other categories of objects benefit from the same coding schemes that are optimal for face perception (for example, Moscovitch, Winocur, and Behrmann, 1997; Tong and Nakayama, 1999; Grill-Spector, Knouf, and Kanwisher, 2004). For websites that address this controversy, navigate to www.mhhe.com/blake5.)

In the previous sections, we have described and illustrated some of the challenges confronting perception when it comes to recognizing objects. Those challenges arise whether we're dealing with chairs, faces, greebles, or Martian rocks. Fortunately, as you've learned, experience helps perception overcome some of those challenges. There are other aids to recognition, too, and the following section summarizes several of these. These aids are sometimes characterized as "top-down" influences, meaning that higher mental processes sway the products of perception. As we move through this discussion of aids to recognition, keep in mind that those aids provide ancillary information about what in the world it is that you're looking at. They make weak signals stronger, render ambiguous signals more unequivocal, and help distinguish objects from one another.

Attention and Object Recognition

At any given moment, visual perception usually has a goal, and that goal actively shapes our visual behavior. When you're at a busy airport terminal to pick up an arriving friend, you concentrate on people whose appearance resembles your friend's, ignoring the visual clutter that has nothing to do with your mission. But your friend said she'd be wearing a large, floppy red hat, so you don't notice her when she walks through the security gate wearing a snug-fitting blue stocking cap. These interrelated factors—intentions and expectations—create a context within which perception operates (Chun, 2000). This context engages a selective process called "attention" that can modulate object recognition. (Unfortunately, your friend's unexpected change in appearance may delay your finding each other at the airport.)

Stop reading for a moment and look around you. (Go ahead, we'll wait.) You probably see lots of different objects scattered throughout your visual environment. No doubt, some of those objects are competing for your attention. In most visual environments, one or two objects immediately grab our attention. These are the ones that stand out among the crowd because of their unusual color, odd size, or peculiar shape (picture a single red apple in a basket of bananas). In perception, this initial orientation to unusual objects that pop out at you is dubbed *preattentive vision*. It's driven by physical characteristics of conspicuous objects, without particular regard to the identity of those objects.

As you survey your visual environment, you're engaging in a form of attention that is not reflexive but purposeful and selective. You select from among the crowd of objects just those that you wish to scrutinize in more detail. Why? Because attention behaves like a limited resource that must be deployed selectively; there's not enough attention to be evenly distributed throughout a crowded visual world. And what you select for attention often depends on your intentions. If you need to correct a misspelled word penciled on a page, your attention sweeps your desk until you locate an eraser. If the pages of your term paper must be kept together, attention's spotlight searches for a paper clip. Sometimes, attention remains riveted on one thing for a

period of time, allowing you to scrutinize it in detail (look at the intricate pattern of creases in the palm of your hand).

What, if any, are the perceptual consequences of focused attention? When the metaphorical spotlight of attention falls on some object, does it make the object look sharper, brighter, or more colorful? According to some researchers, the answer is yes. For example, Marisa Carrasco has shown that attention enhances spatial resolution (Yeshurun and Carrasco, 1998) and increases contrast sensitivity (Carrasco, Penpeci-Talgar, and Eckstein, 2000). Carrasco thinks that attention boosts the strength and quality of neural signals evoked by an object, effectively providing a more fine-grained sample of the object's features. According to other investigators, attention reduces variability in perception. Prinzmetal and colleagues presented a series of colored objects to people and measured the variability in perceived color when some objects were repeated (Prinzmetal et al., 1998). When participants were distracted by other objects in their field of view, they showed more trial-to-trial variability in color judgments than they did when they were able to attend fully to the test object.

So there is no disagreement: Attention modulates object perception. But what actually benefits from attention's spotlight when you focus your attention on an object, the entire object, or just those parts you're interested in? To reframe the question, at what level of detail does attention operate? Common experience alone does not provide an answer. Instead, researchers must create special conditions that allow them to infer the subject of attention's focus. Consider one particularly clever technique for making such inferences.

Egly, Driver, and Rafal (1994) presented people with a pair of vertically oriented rectangles side by side on a video monitor (see Figure 6.17). At unpredictable times, the inside of one end of a rectangle was suddenly filled in. The participants in the experiment were asked to press a button as quickly as possible to indicate which rectangle—left or right—had changed. This filling-in comprised the "target" event, and it occurred with equal probability in the two rectangles. Participants were given a cue just prior to the presentation of the target. Most of the time, the target was where the cue had indicated it would be but, sometimes, it was elsewhere.

As you might expect, reaction times were shortest when cue and target position coincided (upper panel, Figure 6.17), which happened the vast majority of the time. Evidently, people were playing the odds, attending to the spot where the target was most likely to appear.

FIGURE 6.17 | Figures used for testing the spread of attention over occluded portions of an object. The upper, middle, and lower portions of the figure show the sequence of displays presented over time. In all three conditions, the observer first sees a display consisting of a pair of vertical rectangles. This is followed in time by the brief appearance of a "cue" designating one of four locations (top or bottom of either the left or right rectangle). Shortly after the cue disappears, a small black box (the "target") appears in one of the four positions. On some trials, the target appears at the location specified by the cue (valid cue). On other trials, the target appears at a different location but within the cued object (invalid location/valid object). On still other trials, the target appears in one of the two locations in the rectangle that was not cued (invalid cue, shown in the middle sequence of events).

FIGURE 6.18 | Modified version of Figure 6.17, now with a horizontal occluder placed over the two vertical objects on which, somewhere, a target can appear.

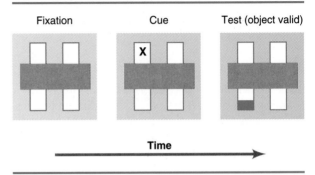

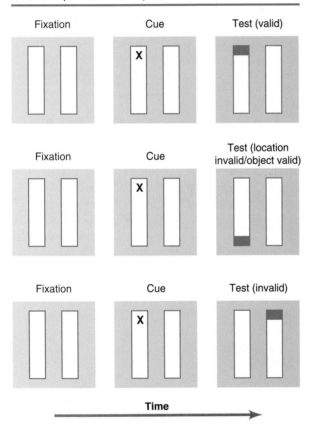

The most interesting results came from trials when the cue did not validly predict the upcoming target's location. In these trials, reaction times were still fast when the uncued target location was part of the object containing the invalidly cued location (middle panel, Figure 6.17). When the uncued target belonged to the other object, however,

reaction times were slow (lower panel, Figure 6.17). This was true even though the distance between cue and target was the same distance for both conditions. It seems, then, that cueing one end of an object causes the entire object to get some benefit. Attention thereby operates on the entire object, not just on an isolated component of an object at a given spatial location.

Egly, Driver, and Rafal's finding makes sense when you stop to realize that objects in the real world often are not seen in their entirety. Just look around your immediate environment and notice how many objects appear partially occluded by other objects. Because of occlusion, optical input to the visual system may lack information about occluded parts. Yet the brain usually manages to generate a complete representation (recall some of the chairs in Figure 6.3). In fact, attention directed to one part of a partially occluded object spreads to other parts, even those disconnected from the attended part. We know this from a study by Moore, Yantis, and Vaughan (1998), who modified the figures used in the Egly experiment by placing a horizontal rectangle across both vertical objects, cutting their bottom halves off from their top halves (see Figure 6.18). Strictly on a physical basis, top and bottom halves are separate and distinct from one another, but perceptually, they are seen as part of a single object whose midsection happens to be occluded. Which characterization—physical or perceptual—would govern selection by object-based attention? Moore, Yantis, and Vaughan found that the occluding object barely affected peoples' responses. Reaction times were faster when cue and target occupied the same vertical rectangle, even though the rectangle had been physically divided by the horizontal rectangle.

These are just a few samples of **object-based attention** experiments all of which confirm that attention can be cued in ways that allow attention to operate on objects. Box 6.2 describes another form of

We reflexively turn our eyes, and often our heads, when something of interest appears in the visual field at a location different from our current focus of gaze. While looking at the words on this page, for example, suppose something suddenly appears in your peripheral visual field? This unexpected event will grab your attention and cause you to turn your eyes to scrutinize the object. This involuntary shift in attention is highly adaptive, of course, for you may need to react quickly in response to the object's appearance, and your reaction depends on what the object is. And to judge what something is usually requires looking at it. Befitting the importance of shifting attention, the visual system takes only a small fraction of a second to execute the eye movements necessary to produce these kinds of shifts in gaze.

Interestingly, we also make reflexive eye movements when we see someone else suddenly shift his or her gaze from one location to another. Try it sometime: during a conversation with a friend, stare directly at the individual for a few seconds and then suddenly turn your gaze to one side. You'll find that your friend automatically looks in the same direction that you did. Laboratory experiments confirm what this simple exercise implies: One person's attention can be shifted simply by watching the behavior of another person's eyes (Friesen and Kingstone, 1998; Ricciardelli et al, 2002). Why does this happen?

One reason that shifts in one person's direction of gaze triggers an automatic shift in another person's attention is because the human eye is configured in a unique way: The colored irises of our eyes are surrounded by a wide expanse of white sclera. In no other species is this contrast between iris and sclera nearly so conspicuous (Kobayashi and Kohshima, 1997). Nature may have designed our eyes this way for a reason: to enhance the salience of the center of the eye, thereby making it easier for one person to judge in which direction another individual is looking. To confirm the salience of this cue, let's try another simply exercise: Unobtrusively watch the eyes of an individual for a minute or so. Notice how easy it is to judge where that person is looking and how the person's gaze shifts over time. Of course, by knowing where someone is looking (e.g., sitting on a park bench, the person is watching girls walking past) you also may be able to deduce what is going through that person's mind. But even more importantly, watching where someone is looking may, in turn, alert us where to look.

While on the topic of gaze direction, we should also acknowledge the important role that mutual gaze plays in social interactions. Your excellent knack for judging where someone else is looking includes the keen ability to tell when someone is looking you in the eye. And eye-to-eye contact represents a powerful social signal between individuals. Looking someone in the eye is a surefire way to communicate your interest in what that person is saying and, perhaps, who that person is. Conversely, avoiding eye contact during a social exchange can be a telltale sign of disinterest or, perhaps, shame. Even very young infants are aware when someone is looking at them as opposed to looking off to the side, and they prefer to look at people who are looking at them (Farroni et al, 2002). This preference, however, is turned on its head in some individuals. Specifically, people diagnosed as autistic or diagnosed with schizophrenia shy away from looking at facial features, including the eyes (Hobson and Lee, 1998; Manor et al, 1999; Loughland et al, 2002), as if eye contact were socially uncomfortable. The same is true for individuals categorized as "socially phobic," an anxiety disorder characterized by deep concern about how others feel about you. Even when looking at digitized color photographs of faces, social phobics spend less time looking at the eyes and, instead, direct their gaze to regions of the face seldom scanned by nonphobic individuals. This avoidance of the eyes is especially pronounced when looking at pictures portraying emotional expressions. One example of this behavior can be seen in the accompanying photograph, which shows eye movement scan paths for a social phobic and a control subject viewing the same picture. The social-phobic individual exhibits what could be termed "hyperscanning," wherein the eyes dart from location to location very rapidly, with a general tendency to avoid the eyes of the face being viewed (Horley et al, 2003). As you can imagine, talking to someone with this condition can be disconcerting to the other party, and it can be disadvantageous to the social phobic who may miss social cues available in the other person's eyes.

FIGURE 6.19 | Compare the two photographs and find what's missing in the one on the right. If shown successively—not simultaneously—spotting the missing object can be quite difficult.

attentional cueing, one that can point you to unexpected objects or events but only when you're looking at someone else's eyes.

Attention Can Induce Blindness Repeat the exercise you tried a moment ago: Look around your visual environment and notice the objects in your field of view. Once you've completed your visual survey, concentrate your attention on one particular object, such as this book. Do the other, unattended objects fade out of visual reality? Of course not. They remain part of your visual awareness, even though you're not actively attending to them. If one of those unattended objects were to disappear at the same time that you were directing attention elsewhere, surely you'd notice such a bizarre event, wouldn't you?

In fact, you probably would not. Studies show that when your attention is diverted elsewhere within the immediate visual environment, you're unlikely to notice otherwise conspicuous changes in unattended objects in the visual scene (Rensink, 2002). Compare, for example, the two snapshots shown in Figure 6.19. It may not take you long to realize that the glass of wine on the table in the left-hand photograph is missing in the right-hand photograph. But instead of being presented side-by-side, suppose these two photographs had been shown successively, one after the other, starting with the one containing the wine glass. As these two photographs cycle on and off, that "conspicuous" change—the missing wine glass—might go completely undetected for some time. In fact, this is highly likely if your attention were diverted to an-

other part of the photograph by, say, the presence of an interesting person (Simons and Levin, 1998). This failure to notice an otherwise conspicuous change because of the diversion of attention is known as **change blindness.**

Another, related form of temporary blindness caused by diverted attention is known as **inattentional blindness:** impairment in perceiving the appearance of, or changes to, unattended objects (Mack and Rock, 1998). In one particularly dramatic demonstration of this phenomenon, observers viewed a video sequence showing several people engaged in a game where a ball is passed rapidly from one individual to another. The task of the observer viewing this video sequence is to follow the ball from player to player, which requires attention since the ball is moving quickly and unpredictably. Without warning at some point during the sequence, a man wearing a gorilla suit appears, thumping his chest vigorously. More than half of the observers tested failed to see this strange event, because their attention was riveted on the ball game (Simons and Chabris, 1999).[8] This failure to notice an ordinarily conspicuous object or event comprises a form of inattentional blindness (Simons, 2000).

Inattentional blindness, and its related phenomenon, change blindness, not only underscore the limited capacity of attention but also disclose a very interesting prop-

---

[8] Do you find this outcome hard to believe? Look at some of the video demonstrations at the attention website listed under Chapter 6 at www.mhhe.com/blake5.

erty of perception. Contrary to subjective impression, we do not continuously maintain a high-fidelity representation of the entire visual scene. We evidently lack the processing capacity to do so. Consequently, what we "see" outside the focus of attention is a rather sparse representation based in part on our visual memory of what was there when we last looked.

Most of the time inattentional blindness isn't a problem. All we have to do is shift our attention. The world is right there for our scrutiny anytime we wish. And we take advantage of that ready availability when we perform tasks such as straightening up a desk (Hayhoe, Bensinger, and Ballard, 1998). There's no need to commit the desk's contents to memory because those contents remain visible as we work on them. To paraphrase Robert Snowden (1999), why bother constructing a complex, detailed visual scene inside your head when there is a perfectly good one right in front of your eyes?

But there can be a dark side to inattentional blindness (Chun and Marois, 2002). Unexpected events that reflexively draw attention may obscure our ability to perceive important changes in other objects within the visual field. O'Regan, Rensink, and Clark (1999) suggest that change blindness could be triggered by splashes of mud on a car windshield. In the immediate wake of a splash the car's driver would be unable to detect changes in roadway conditions. The same kind of dangerous distraction could occur when using a cell phone while driving—momentarily attending to a ringing phone could blind you to a car unexpectedly moving into your lane.

Inattentional blindness implies that the clarity and completeness of the appearance of objects within our visual environment are, in fact, illusory. Odd as it may sound, we seem to confuse visual reality with visual imagination. This confusion is adaptive, though, for the world itself and the objects in it usually remain stable and, therefore, available for attention's scrutiny. We can draw on resources stored in visual memory to decide how to allocate attention (Chun and Nakayama, 2000). One bridge between memory and visual attention is imagery, another effective factor that influences object recognition. To that important aid we turn now.

Imagery: Vision's Little Helper

Think back to the bedroom you had when you were 10 years old. Visualize the room in your mind's eye. How many windows did it have? Were any of the windows directly opposite the doorway? With coaxing, most people can answer such questions, and those answers usually

bear some relation to reality (Chamb 1992). To begin answering questions draw on memory to construct a mer room. Then, they survey the image's images have fascinated and mystified pe ages. Researchers have devised improved experimental methods to study mental images (for example, Shepard and Cooper, 1982; Kosslyn, 1994; Kosslyn, Sukel, and Bly, 1999). These efforts have significantly improved our understanding of the properties, limitations, and neural bases of imagery, and its relation to visual perception.

From one perspective, visual imagery and visual perception represent just two sides of the same coin. As you saw when you were asked questions about your childhood room, your visual image of that room contained some of the same visual information that your eyes picked up years ago. In fact, the two processes resemble one another sufficiently that they can be mistaken for one another.

Cheves Perky (1910) produced the first demonstration of confusion between imagery and perception. While seated in a completely dark room, Perky's observers stared steadily at a screen some distance away. On a signal from Perky, an observer conjured up a mental image of some particular object, such as a banana. While the observer was generating the requested image, a slide projector surreptitiously threw a dim image on the screen. This image matched the object that the observer was trying to imagine. For instance, when an observer was told to imagine a banana, a banana-shaped, yellow image was cast on the screen. Prior testing showed that this real image would be just barely visible. To further mimic a mental image, the real image on the screen was jiggled slightly, producing a shimmering quality. (If all this sounds complicated, it was; three researchers were needed to run Perky's apparatus.)

Observers were asked to describe various "imagined" shapes. Most of the observers never realized that they were seeing things, not just imagining them, and produced descriptions that incorporated features of the real image. Using more modern methods, Segal and Fusella (1970), Reeves (1981), and Craver-Lemley and Reeves (1992) confirmed Perky's main finding: When real stimuli and images conflict, the images can interfere with seeing the stimuli. After ruling out various alternative explanations such as factors related to optics, attention, and response bias, Craver-Lemley and Reeves concluded that images produce a kind of sensory interference, resembling the effect of a reduction in target energy.

FIGURE 6.20 | Example of test figures used by Kosslyn and colleagues (1999) to measure brain activity associated with imagery.

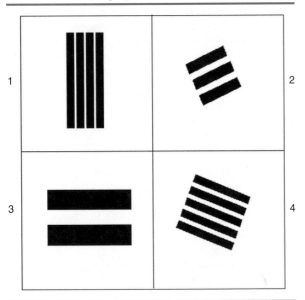

Where Does Visual Imagery Come From?   These and other findings show strong parallels between the phenomenology of imagery and the phenomenology of vision. Further, imagery and vision seem to share a common neural basis. Functional neuroimaging has identified a number of brain regions that participate in both vision and imagery. Included among these regions is the primary visual cortex, area V1. In one study of imagery's neural basis, Stephen Kosslyn and his colleagues (1999) used fMRI to identify regions that were activated during visual imagery. To ensure that imagery was actually engaged, Kosslyn asked people to look at a complex figure and then, some seconds after the figure had disappeared, to close their eyes and make a judgment about what they had seen. On each trial, people saw a square divided into four quadrants, each containing a set of stripes. The stripes' attributes—thickness, length, orientation, and the space separating adjacent bars—varied randomly. A sample stimulus is shown in Figure 6.20.

After the array had been removed from view, Kosslyn randomly selected two of the square's quadrants and one of the stripes' attributes. People used their image of what they'd seen to compare the stripes in those two quadrants with respect to the chosen attribute. For example, they might be told to compare the thickness of stripes in quadrant 1 versus those in quadrant 3, or the number of stripes in quadrant 1 versus quadrant 4. Compared to a control condition, Kosslyn found that the imagery task strongly activated V1, among other visual areas of the brain. (As you know, V1 is the cortex's primary receiving area for visual information.)

To nail down V1's role in imagery, the researchers next had people repeat the task, and this time pulses of transcranial magnetic stimulation (TMS) were applied to V1. These pulses produced temporary disruptions in ongoing neural activity within the stimulated region of V1 and, as a consequence, interfered with people's ability to quickly perform the imagery judgment. This interference with imagery was comparable to the interference produced by TMS applied to V1 while a person was looking at the actual array of figures itself.

This result suggests that visual perception and visual imagery both depend on neural activity within some of the same cortical areas, including the brain's initial processing center for incoming visual information, V1. Presumably, this sharing of neural structures could facilitate interactions between vision and imagery. The possibility that imagery and perception engage common neural processes should not be entirely surprising. After all, imagery—like vision—can serve to guide our actions within the world. Imagery makes it possible for us to envision the consequences of some behavior without actually going through the motions.

What Does Visual Imagery Look Like?   Perky's study suggested a striking equivalence between vision and imagery, which Kosslyn's work confirmed at the neural level. Clearly, imagery does look something like the thing being imaged, but how close is that resemblance? Lewis Harvey (1986) suggested that a mental image, such as a mental image of a face, would have reduced detail (that is, less high-spatial frequency content) compared to the original. To test this idea and to quantify the image's appearance, Harvey created a set of photographs. Each showed the face with a different set of spatial frequencies removed.

Observers studied the original, unfiltered photograph of the face to form a good visual image. They then made two kinds of similarity judgments. In one, they saw pairs of filtered photographs and rated how similar one was to the other. For the second kind of judgment, just one filtered photograph was shown at a time and the observers rated how similar it was to their mental image of the original. The similarity judgments, analyzed by multidimensional scaling, confirmed that the visual image most closely re-

FIGURE 6.21 | Upper panels: Photos of a male and female. Lower panels: The photos transformed so that they would match a subject's mental image of the originals.

sembled a face from which a certain set of high spatial frequencies had been removed, reducing the sharpness of edges and borders. The top panels of Figure 6.21 show photographs of two faces; the bottom panels show the photographs after they've been transformed to match the mental images that a person might have of the originals.

Harvey (1986) offered some intriguing speculation about the character of mental images. He suggests that we don't need to store much detail in the image because detail can be encoded by means of words. According to Harvey, relying on words as a medium for storing visual detail may also reflect a developmental coincidence: human infants develop full capacity to perceive visual detail just about the same time that they learn to speak.

Temporary Failures of Recognition

Imagine that you are walking along a deserted country road. It's very foggy and the light has begun to fail. Suddenly, you spot a blurry shape moving about down the road, but you can't recognize exactly what it is. Another person? A bear? A cluster of fallen leaves blown about by the wind? You're uncertain about what you're seeing because the impoverished visual information provided to you is ambiguous. You entertain the possibility of several alternative objects. You're in a paradoxical situation: You can see, but you can't recognize what you're seeing.

If it's imperative for you to decide what you're seeing, your best bet is to consult visual memory to identify the stored representation best matching the visual impressions you've gathered. It would also be wise if you took account of the situation in which you find yourself, weighing the a priori probabilities that various objects would be present at twilight on a country road. But no matter how rational you are in reaching a decision, the degraded quality of the image means that the best matching representation will be no more than an educated guess, the best bet among a number of alternatives. You may be correct, but you may also be wrong. And your educated guesses will be guided by your expectations, your emotional state, and your past experiences in that environment.

Degraded or ambiguous visual information forces vision to work overtime. Instead of being its usual speedy self, recognition takes a while. But what goes on during the prolonged processing? In a now classic study, Jerome Bruner and Mary Potter (1964) examined this question by intentionally putting roadblocks in the way of recognition, hoping to slow it down enough to catch it in action. Bruner and Potter created a series of slides depicting various scenes and objects, such as a dog standing on a lawn, a traffic intersection seen in aerial view, and a fire hydrant. Bruner and Potter started each trial by showing one of the slides with the projector highly defocused. Then they slowly reduced the blur, gradually bringing the slide into sharper focus. Starting when the slide was extremely blurred, the participants in this experiment repeatedly wrote down what they thought they were viewing. When the slide was badly out of focus, people's descriptions were usually inaccurate; for example, similarities in their overall shape might cause a pile of earth to be mistaken for a scoop of chocolate ice cream. Not surprisingly, as the slide's focus improved and details became visible, people became more accurate.

You can experience this phenomenon yourself by successively viewing the series of pictures appearing in the right-hand corner of the next five pages of this chapter (Figure 6.22, panels a through e). Start with the blurred picture at the top of this page and work your way through the series. Look at each one for a few moments and then make your best guess about what actually appears in the photograph. Don't peek at the pictures out of order. Study each one, make a guess, and then move to the next one. Before reading further, stop right here and try it.

If you're like most people, it wasn't until the fourth or even the fifth photograph that you realized what you were looking at. Now, if you had skipped the first two blurred photographs and started with photograph number 3 (panel c)—the moderately blurred one—you would have had a much better chance of recognizing the content of the photograph. That's what Bruner and Potter found:

FIGURE 6.22a-e | A series of five photographs with decreasing amounts of blur. Starting with this one, take a guess about the photograph's content. Continue through the next four versions, guessing each time.

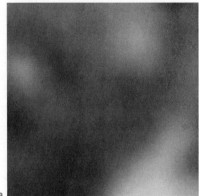

Fig. 6.22a

Accuracy at identifying a given photograph depended upon the initial degree of blur. When an image was first presented far out of focus, observers often failed to recognize what they were looking at until the image was well focused. However, when the initial blur was only moderate, observers tended to recognize what they were looking at rather quickly.

Why should early exposure to a high degree of blur retard later recognition of a moderately blurred but otherwise recognizable image? A clue came from the comments by people who were looking at Bruner and Potter's pictures. No matter how blurred the picture, people generated a plausible interpretation of what they were looking at, and this interpretation influenced what they saw in subsequent pictures. Thus, an individual who initially sees a highly blurred image gets locked into a plausible but incorrect interpretation, and this error is self-perpetuating. Researchers argue whether this involves a genuine change in perception or, instead, a bias in responding. Does a blurred picture really look different to you than it does to a friend, just because you interpret it as a rabbit, while your friend judges it to be a television set? In a sense, it doesn't matter, for you and your friend are going to react differently to that object when the two of you hold different views about that object's identity. And don't forget, perception is designed to guide action.

This tendency to get locked into one interpretation varies with age. Potter (1966) demonstrated this by repeating the original experiment, but testing observers who ranged in age from 4 to 19 years old. For any given age, some observers tended to be rapid recognizers whereas others tended to be slow. As shown in Figure 6.23, how-

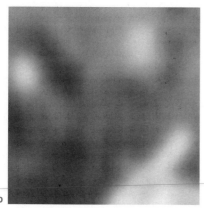

Fig. 6.22b

FIGURE 6.23 | Median time for recognition of pictures as blur was reduced.

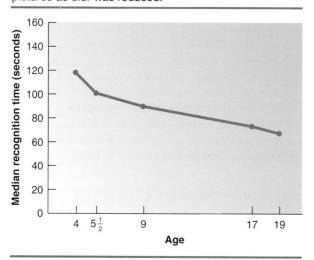

FIGURE 6.24 | Reading X-rays, such as this image from a female breast, requires good vision and lots of practice.

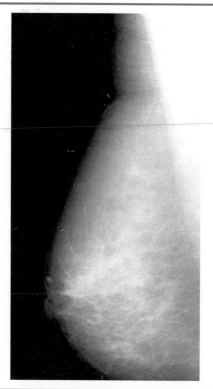

ever, younger observers took about 50 percent longer to recognize the picture than did older observers. Besides differing in speed of recognition, young and old observers seemed to arrive at solutions in different ways. The older observers' descriptions formed a coherent series, with a guess at one moment evolving into another, related guess the next moment. In contrast, younger observers' descriptions consisted of a parade of unconnected guesses, often focusing on a single, small detail, rather than on the entire scene. This difference between older and younger individuals suggests that experience may be necessary before top-down information becomes maximally effective.

Potter's study underscored the differences in speed and accuracy with which individuals extract information from images. There are several professions where speed and accuracy in visual perception can be a matter of life and death. We'll consider two examples here.

Medical images, such as X-rays and CAT scans, are among a physician's most important diagnostic tools, making it possible to visualize tumors, detect bone breaks, and identify regions of brain atrophy. Interpreting a medical image requires good vision and considerable practice (see Figure 6.24). Radiologists skilled at interpreting medical images can achieve high levels of accuracy, though abnormalities sometimes do get overlooked. To explain these oversights, Harold Kundel, a radiologist, and Calvin Nodine, a psychologist, recorded the eye movements of interpreters who were reading X-rays (Kundel and Nodine, 1983). Because the eye's visual acuity is not uniform over the entire retina, the interpreter must successively fixate on different regions of the X-ray.

To guide fixation, an interpreter draws upon several forms of knowledge (Carmody, Nodine, and Kundel, 1980). First, the person usually knows what anatomical structure (for example, the chest) is depicted in the X-ray. This initial knowledge establishes expectations about that structure's normal appearance, drawing on memory of previous X-rays. An experienced X-ray interpreter is guided by knowledge of what particular parts of that

FIGURE 6.25 | X-ray image of a piece of luggage passing through a security station at an airport. Do you see anything suspicious?

Fig. 6.22c

structure are most likely to be abnormal. These parts should be scrutinized first and most carefully. Kundel and Nodine found that when interpreters were instructed where to look, a glance as brief as one-third of a second was enough to spot the abnormality. (This may remind you of the blazing speed of expert chick sexers.)

Still, interpreters occasionally fixated on the correct spot but failed to detect the abnormality. You might say that the interpreter was looking at the right place but not attending to the right thing. To perform optimally, the interpreter needs to know where to look and what to look for.

Another profession where speed and accuracy are paramount is security monitoring at airport screening stations. These professionals must scrutinize X-ray images of pieces of luggage and other carry-on items, carefully monitoring for weapons and other outlawed items (McCarley et al., 2004). Given the difficulty of the task, screeners are remarkably efficient. Look at the X-ray image in Figure 6.25. See anything suspicious? With training, a security guard would spot the knife partially hidden under the small

pocketbook (see Figure 6.26). This incriminating item would be confiscated and the owner questioned thoroughly before boarding his or her flight. Try to keep this example in mind the next time you're impatiently waiting in a long line at the security station: Accuracy takes time, whereas hurried inspections can be lethal.

Having surveyed some of the obstacles to object recognition and the factors that help us overcome those obstacles, let's now wrap up our discussion of object recognition by considering a special kind of object recognition that we engage in all the time. In fact, you're doing it right now.

Perceptual Aspects of Reading

Reading printed text is one of the most complicated things that your visual/cognitive system can do. This everyday activity that we take for granted requires rapid, parallel identification of complex symbols followed by translation of these symbols into phonological and semantic codes. Given the complexity of this task, it is no wonder that some people have difficulty mastering it.

Because reading depends upon cooperation among so many brain systems, it is especially vulnerable to the effects of developmental abnormalities. Moreover, damage to the brain later in life can also produce severe reading disabilities, known collectively as **alexia** (meaning, "without reading"). One form of alexia, called "letter by letter reading," highlights reading's connection to visual object recognition. As the name of the condition suggests, people with this form of alexia can read only one letter at a time (their writing skills, by the way, may be perfectly normal). As a result, their reading speed varies with the length of words that they encounter. For example, a word 10 letters long will take about twice as long to decode as a word that is just five letters long. In addition, many letter-by-letter

FIGURE 6.26 | Same piece of luggage as the one pictured in Figure 6.25, this time with the dangerous, illegal item (a knife) circled.

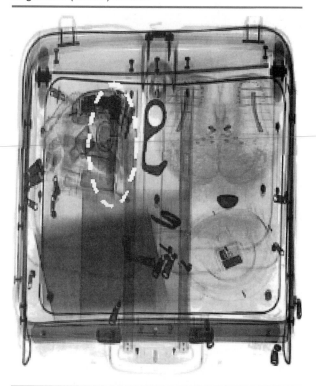

Fig. 6.22d

readers make errors recognizing letters, confusing visually similar letters for one another. Letter-by-letter readers may also experience problems with a host of other visual tasks (Behrmann, Nelson, and Sekuler, 1998), such as interpreting musical notation, recognizing faces, and reading numbers (Patterson and Ralph, 1999).

For people with normal reading ability, the task doesn't seem complicated. We tend to forget, though, how difficult it was to learn to read. What perceptual skills had to be mastered on the way to becoming an accomplished reader? And how are those skills supplemented by "top-down" influences?

While reading, your eye movements and fixations control the rate at which you extract information from the printed page. Ordinarily, the movements of your eyes vary with your comprehension of what you're reading. Thus, it's possible to learn a lot about reading by studying readers' eye movements and fixations. Exactly what do your eyes do when you read? They jump, or saccade, as your gaze shifts from one object to another. But they're relatively still between saccades. In this respect, reading words is much like reading a map or reading someone's face. Each of these activities requires a mix of saccades and fixations. The number of saccades and the duration of fixations depend on a reader's skill and on the difficulty of the text (Rayner, 1978). We'll confine the discussion to the behavior of a skilled reader (such as yourself) who is reading moderately difficult material (such as this text).

As you read individual lines in this paragraph, your eyes make four to five saccades, which land on selected words in the line. On average, a fixation lasts one-quarter of a second, although fixations can range from as little as one-tenth of a second to more than half a second, depending on the familiarity of the word being fixated on. In addition, the distance traveled by a saccade can vary from just two letters to as many as 18 letters. Finally, the direction of saccades also varies. About 90 percent of the time, a saccade moves your gaze rightward, to a word you have yet to look at. Occasionally, though, you make a leftward, regressive, saccade to recheck a word you've already read and perhaps misinterpreted. Of course, with English and other Western language texts, you make a large leftward saccade at the end of each line.

To understand how you acquire information while reading, we need to consider two questions. First, how fast is the textual information taken in while you're reading? And second, what accounts for the variability among saccades while you're reading? The eyes move very fast during a saccade, so most processing of visual information must occur during the fixations between saccades. But the entire duration of any fixation cannot be devoted exclusively to text processing, since the visual system has more to do than this. Decisions have to be made about where next to move the eyes, and those decisions must be relayed to those portions of the brain responsible for controlling the direction and speed of

FIGURE 6.27 | Setup used by Rayner and colleagues (1981) for studying the ability to read without central vision.

Fig. 6.22e

saccades. What part of a fixation, then, is devoted to analyzing the fixated word and what part to programming the next saccade?

To examine this question, Keith Rayner used a computer to monitor a person's eye movements while that individual read text presented on a video monitor (Rayner, 1998). The computer used information about eye movement to modify the video display: every time the reader's eyes fixated a portion of the text, a masking stimulus covered the letters being fixated. This scheme is depicted in Figure 6.27. If the mask came on immediately when the eyes came to rest on a word (a condition that resembles trying to read without a fovea), reading was difficult. But when the mask was delayed by as little as one-twentieth of a second, people had little trouble reading the text. This shows that only a small fraction of the entire fixation duration is required to encode the text. Incidentally, if this seems like a very short time to do so much, recall how you can rapidly surf through the television channels, extracting the gist of a complex scene very quickly. Rayner's results suggest that the bulk of a fixation period is spent programming the next saccade, planning how far the eyes should move.

According to Rayner's idea, reading would be more efficient if the visual system could be relieved of this programming chore. This can be accomplished by presenting words one after another, all in the same spatial position on a computer display (Sperling et al., 1971). With this mode of presentation, an observer needs to fixate on just one position, which eliminates time and effort spent on saccadic programming. After some practice, eye-movement free reading averaged three to four times faster than conventional reading (Rubin and Turano, 1992). But of course, saccade-free reading requires special hardware that old-fashioned, slower modes of reading do not.

It's obvious that words are important units for reading and that various characteristics of words strongly influence reading accuracy and speed. Imagine this situation. It's dark and you're driving to visit someone whose house you've never been to before. She lives on Thoreau Street, which you know is a right turn off the road on which you're presently driving. Streetlights are few and far between in this town, so a street sign is impossible to read until you are close to it; even then, it's not easy. But from a distance you're able to gauge the length of the street's name—"THOREAU" is not likely to be confused with "OLD ROAD TO NINE ACRE CORNER," for example. And this rough information is valuable in making a decision about whether this turn might be the correct one. If the length of the name is about right, you slow down and look harder; if it's not, you pass it by. Street names on signs are usually in uppercase letters, which obscures another source of information: word shape. But that source is helpful in reading ordinary text.

Words have other characteristics that can facilitate reading. For example, in written English, the letter *u* is redundant after a *q.* Once you have seen the *q,* you know what follows. But information may be redundant even if it is not as perfectly predictable as the *u* after a *q.* In fact,

FIGURE 6.28 | Cattell's apparatus for testing the word superiority effect.

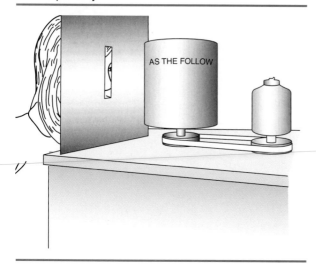

AS THE FOLLOW

there are varying degrees of redundancy, and methods have been developed to quantify them and their effects on perception (Garner, 1962).

More than one hundred years ago, James McKeen Cattell described a puzzling phenomenon that relates to redundancy in reading. Cattell was interested in how long it took to perceive letters, words, colors, and pictures of objects. In one study, he pasted letters on a revolving drum (see Figure 6.28) and determined the rate at which the letters could be read aloud as they passed by a slit in a screen. Cattell found that it took about twice as long to read unrelated words as it did to read words that formed a sentence. He also found a similar disadvantage for reading unrelated letters compared to letters that formed a word (1886, p. 64). The relative ease with which letters can be read if they are embedded in a word rather than presented with unrelated letters is known as the **word superiority effect.** (This may remind you of the configural superiority effect described in the previous chapter.)

Since Cattell's original report, dozens of follow-ups have confirmed his original finding. But what causes word superiority? One possibility is that the surrounding letters of a word make it easier to derive the remaining letters. For example, once you've seen the letters *LABE,* the chances are good that the next letter will be *L.* In this case, the letter recognition might be expedited because the prior letters reduced the need to spend much time on the last letter.

More recent studies have used more sophisticated methods than Cattell's to demonstrate that the word superiority effect cannot be chalked up entirely to logical deduction (Reicher, 1969; Wheeler, 1970). These studies suggest that familiarity directly affects the process of extracting visual information. In one study (Johnston and McClelland, 1973), either a word or a single letter was briefly shown to people. In either case, this test stimulus was followed by a patterned masker that obliterated any afterimage (see Figure 6.29). After this sequence of events, people saw two alternatives and had to pick the one that corresponded to the test stimulus. For example, if the word *COIN* had been the test stimulus, the observer might have to choose between the alternatives *COIN* and *JOIN.* Since either *C* or *J* could form a word with the remaining three letters (*OIN*), the observer could not use the other letters to deduce the correct answer. Instead, a correct answer required actually being able to see the first letter clearly enough to decipher whether it was a *C* or a *J.* The letter that distinguished the two alternatives could occupy any position in those words (for example, *BENT* or *BUNT*). Thus, the observer could not just attend to one particular position in a test word. When the test stimulus consisted of a single letter, such as *J,* the observer again had to choose from two alternatives, such as *C* and *J.* Again, the observer could not do better than chance unless he or she had seen the letter.

The results were typical of many word superiority studies. Observers were more accurate in choosing between *COIN* and *JOIN* than they were in choosing between *C* and *J.* Although trials with single letters presumably required less processing, observers were nonetheless more accurate in trials in which they had to process all four letters (Johnston and McClelland, 1973). So, when normal readers see a word, they do not process each letter separately, in isolation from the rest. In fact, people who try to restrict their attention to just one letter of a word are less accurate in perceiving that letter than when they attend to the word within which the letter was embedded (Johnston and McClelland, 1974). A large unit (such as a word) may be perceived more accurately than any of its isolated component parts (such as a letter).

By exploiting the redundancies and structural features of text, good readers process printed or electronic text very rapidly. But exactly what are they processing? While reading this page, you probably have a sense that each line (or perhaps even the entire paragraph) is focused sharply. But this uniform sharpness is illusory, because only the very center of your retina allows good acuity (recall Figure 3.25). For example, one participant in Rayner's studies (McConkie and Rayner, 1975; Rayner and Bertera, 1979) who was kept from using the fovea misread the sentence "THE PRETTY BRACELET

FIGURE 6.29 | The sequence of events seen by observers in the study by Johnston and McClelland (1973).

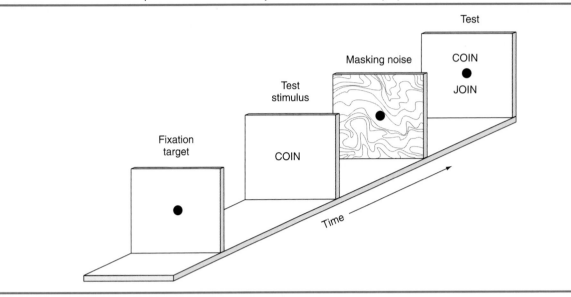

FIGURE 6.30 | Setup used by Rayner and colleagues (1981) for studying the ability to read with only central vision.

ATTRACTED MUCH ATTENTION" as "THE PRIEST BROUGHT MUCH AMMUNITION." Such errors are not surprising, because with foveal information excluded, these people were reading with retinal regions that could specify only the general length and shape of words but could not clearly identify each letter (recall the street sign example above).

When the fovea is available for use, though, how many letters does a person see clearly at any one moment? To find out, one could determine how reading is affected when the number of letters displayed at any moment is reduced. So long as the number of letters exceeds the number that the reader actually uses, reading speed should be unaffected. To produce this situation,

Rayner programmed the computer to reveal only that portion of the text on which the person fixated, masking all other portions with small "x"s. Thus, as the person's eyes moved, new letters were constantly being revealed. This procedure, illustrated in Figure 6.30, gave people the impression that they were reading through a "window" that moved along in synchrony with their eyes.

When the window was extremely narrow (so that people saw just one letter at a time), they could read correctly about 90 percent of the words. Needless to say, though, reading under these conditions was slowed. As the window widened to include seven or nine letters, entire words could be read at once, enabling error-free performance. However, reading was still slower than

FIGURE 6.31 | Schematic diagram of the major processes involved in reading comprehension.

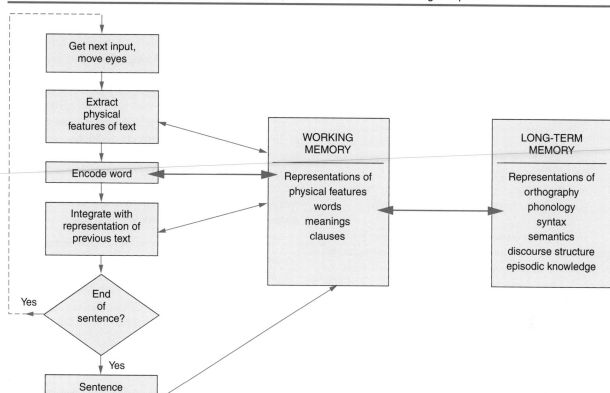

normal. Reading did not even reach normal speed until the window was wide enough to reveal about four words. Presumably, readers use words to the right of fixation to guide decisions about the next saccade. Though only dimly perceived, these words furnish a preview of what will be encountered on the next fixation (Rayner and Pollatsek, 1987).

You can prove to yourself how valuable peripheral vision is in reading. Get a 5-inch by 8-inch piece of paper and cut a rectangular "window" in it one-half inch wide and one-quarter inch high. Orient the paper so that the window's larger dimension is vertical. Then place the card over some page in this book. When the window is properly aligned on the page, you will be able to see about one word at a time through the window. Move the card along the line of text as you try to read. After you've practiced a while, have a friend measure how long it takes you to read a passage of text 100 words long. Now, using new text, repeat this test with a window large enough to expose four words at a time. Comparing your reading speeds with the two windows, you'll discover that peripheral vision does indeed play an important part in reading.

Just and Carpenter (1980) identified the major processes involved in reading. This effort is summarized in the flowchart shown in Figure 6.31. Note that a number of the processes represented are top-down ones of the kind mentioned previously in this chapter. For example, the right-hand box, "Long-Term Memory," includes rules about letter shape (orthography), the normal structures used in writing (discourse structure), and background information for what is being read (episodic knowledge). As each new word or short phrase is encountered, these top-down processes guide the reader.

If you are reading an ordinary novel, these top-down influences can be enormously helpful in processing the text. To give a simple example, after reading "John hit the nail with a," there is little uncertainty about the next word, making it easier for you to process "hammer." However, certain books minimize the usefulness of top-down influences, forcing you to deal with each word, one at a time. The following brief passage from James Joyce's *Finnegans Wake* illustrates what we have in mind. First read it silently. Then read it aloud, listening carefully to yourself.

> [S]he thawght a knogg came to the dowanstairs dour at that howr to peirce the yare and dowandshe went, schritt be schratt, to see was it Schweep's mingerals or Shuhorn the posth with a tillycramp for Hemself and Co, Esquara, or them four hoarsemen on their apolkaloops, Norreys, Soothbys, Yates and Welks. (1939/1967, p. 480)

Reading this passage was difficult because your expectations were of little help. Sometimes expectations actually get in the way. Suppose you've just read the words, "There were tears in her brown . . .". Usually, you'd interpret the word "tears" as referring to liquid produced by the lacrimal gland, rather than as referring to a rip in something. This interpretation leads you to expect the next word to be *eyes*. So on encountering the word *dress* you fixate on that word longer than you normally would. This kind of sentence has been called a "garden path" sentence (Carpenter and Daneman, 1981) because its early part leads the reader astray—down the proverbial garden path. If a word (such as *tears*) has several meanings, the reader selects among them according to rules, or expectations, that maximize the chances of being right. For example, a common meaning is usually selected over a less common one. Or, if only one likely meaning has the grammatical form required by the phrase (say, a noun), that meaning is selected. Presumably the errors revealed by garden path sentences reflect these normally helpful selection factors.

If you look at any line of text in a book, you'll find successive words separated by a space. This feature of texts is so ubiquitous that you might assume that you couldn't really read without the help of spaces, but that view is mistaken. In fact, texts in Western languages did not originally use spaces to separate words (or punctuation marks, for that matter). These ubiquitous and seemingly crucial word separators weren't introduced until the time of Charlemagne. People were reading long before then, spaces or no (Boorstin, 1985, p. 497). In fact, Julie Epelboim and her colleagues showed convincingly that we don't much need spaces. Reading without spaces is not that different, in speed or in comprehension, from reading with spaces (Epelboim, Booth, and Steinman, 1994; Epel-

boim et al., 1997). In most of their experiments, subjects were asked to read aloud normal passages of text (with spaces between words) and doctored passages (from which spaces had been excised). At the same time, Epelboim and her colleagues used a high-fidelity fixation-monitoring system to determine where in the texts readers fixated. The results were surprising: Subjects read space-free texts almost as fast they read texts with normal interword spaces. Decrements in reading speed ranged from 0 to 30 percent. In addition, subjects' fixations—an important clue to how texts are being processed—were essentially unchanged by the removal of spaces. If you doubt, as we originally did, that you can read without the crutch of spaces, read the following space-free text aloud. Read on, no matter how difficult the task seems at first.

> Inexpensiveredwineslackamajoradvantageofinexpensive-whitewines,theyshouldn'tbeservedcold.Unlikewhites,th-eycan'thidebehindapalatenumbingchill.Whentheyareflaw-ed,itshows.Iftheyaresimple,itcan'tbedisguised.Inshort,red-sriseandfallontheirownmerits.Thatmakesfindinggoodin-expensiveexamplesdevilishlydifficult.Butitalso-makestastingawinnerthatmuchmorerewarding.Fortunatel-y,withresoluteshopping,it'squitepossibletoputtogetheral-istofqualitybargainreds.

If you were able to set aside your doubts about doing it, the task was probably much easier than you thought it would be. Booth, Epelboim, and Steinman (1996) pointed out that some modern languages, such as Thai and Japanese, have no spaces between words, and that other modern languages, like Dutch and German, have relatively sparse spacing. Spaces are relatively few and far between because such languages frequently use very long compound nouns, such as the Dutch noun *fietsenstallingbewakers,* which translates roughly as "people who oversee the bike storage shack." If spaces are not all that important in guiding our fixations and text processing as we read, what is?

Keeping words intact was more important than separating words, as Epelboim and colleagues (1994) showed by inserting spaces into a passage, but at incorrect places: Spa cesinthew ro ngpla cesm aderea dingex trem elyhard. This suggests a possible explanation for the small but real slowdown in reading speed when spaces are removed. It may be that space removal makes some letter groupings ambiguous, which slows down word recognition. In other words, reading rate may be governed less by the physical features of text, such as the presence or absence of spaces, than by the time needed to extract meaning. To test whether reading rate was limited by word recognition rather than by limits on the speed with which saccadic eye movements can be programmed, Booth, Epelboim, and Steinman (1996) devised new paragraphs in which the availability of interword spaces was pitted against the paragraph's meaningfulness. Subjects read aloud four different types of passages; all the material was drawn from the work of the English novelist, G. K. Chesterton. Half the passages had normal, interword spacing; half had none. In addition, in half the passages the order of words was just as Chesterton had intended, which made those passages meaningful; in other passages, each word was replaced with a word of equal length drawn randomly from elsewhere in the same piece. This randomized order of words rendered such passages meaningless.

As in earlier experiments, removing spaces from meaningful passages did slow reading down somewhat. With meaningless passages, though, the impact of space removal was considerably greater. A similar pattern showed up when errors in reading, rather than speed, were evaluated, which suggests that semantics—meaning—rather than spaces per se are more important for determining reading speed and accuracy. This result is ironic because in the past decade or so, many researchers tried to put meaning on reading's back burner, thinking that meaning arose only after information had been extracted from the page, rather than guiding the extraction process. Booth's results remind us that when it comes to reading, meaning means something very important.

SUMMARY AND PREVIEW

This chapter was a journey through the realm of object recognition, the all-important ability to know what it is at which we're looking. This ability is the basis for using, and/or reacting appropriately to, objects encountered in the visual environment. As you learned, recognition has to overcome a number of challenges, including occlusion and variation in viewpoint. Among the ways that vision deals with these challenges is neural plasticity: With practice and experience, the nervous system adjusts its sensitivity to conform to the demands of visual inputs. You also learned that the temporal pathway, and particularly its inferotemporal (IT) cortex, is a major contributor to object recognition. Along the way, you were introduced to imagery and memory, which play important supporting roles in object recognition. You learned that imagery and vision seem to depend upon some common regions in the brain. Theories of recognition were tested for their ability to account for

important aspects of face and "greeble" recognition. As we noted, much of our understanding of recognition comes from studying failures in recognition that are specifically linked to brain damage (as in prosopagnosia) or from diminished visual input. You learned also that memory for what you've just seen is far more fallible than you might imagine. Finally, we applied some basic information about vision and visual recognition to the challenges of reading printed text.

This chapter and the previous ones intentionally ignored several important aspects of vision—color, motion, and depth perception. Now that you're familiar with the fundamentals of vision and object recognition, you will learn how we deal with a world of color, movement, and objects arranged at varying distances in the next three chapters. And you will also see that these aspects of vision can contribute to the detection of object boundaries and, hence, the recognition of objects.

KEY TERMS

affordances
agnosia
alexia
categorization
change blindness
configural processing

face-inversion effect
featural processing
geons (geometrical icons)
identification
inattentional blindness
object-based attention

prosopagnosia
recognition by components
view-based recognition
word superiority effect

Chapter 7

Color Perception

Staying up all night studying for an examination is definitely no fun. There is a small consolation, though—a chance to see the beauty of sunrise. As you stare at the horizon through half-open eyes, you realize that all through the dark night the world outdoors has been a drab, colorless collection of blacks and shades of grays. Then just before the sun itself becomes visible, you see a marvelous transformation. That drab world springs to life as objects don their daytime colors. When the world puts on its colors, you realize how bland it would appear without them.

But color gives you more than unending pleasure and beauty: it influences many facets of your life. Color can alter the "taste" of the food you eat and the beverages you drink (Zellner and Durlach, 2003). (Prove this to yourself by using food coloring to create red milk or green orange juice.) The color of a pill can influence your expectation of its effect, and how it actually does affect you (de Craen et al., 1996). Is is said that the world's colors ebb and flow with mood—that envy can make you "green," infuriation makes you "see red," and all too many circumstances make you "blue." These, of course, are merely figures of speech, but some people believe that the connection between emotions and color is more than just figurative (Kuller and Mikellides, 1993). Some tavern owners decorate their walls with colors that they expect will stimulate greater consumption of alcoholic beverages. Knute Rockne, the legendary American football coach, is rumored to have painted his own team's locker room red to excite his players, and the opponent's locker room blue to induce calm and relaxation. (Whether these colorful tricks actually work, we cannot say.)

According to one study, people also use color to mark their territory. When selecting a color to paint their homes, families are much more likely to select a color different from their immediate neighbors (Barber, 1990). People are also highly selective about the colors they wear. In fact, it's claimed that you can tell a lot about people—perhaps even about an entire nation—just from the colors of their clothing. One person who made such a claim was Johann Wolfgang von Goethe, the nineteenth-century German poet-philosopher. Goethe wrote:

> Lively nations, the French for instance, love intense colours . . . ; sedate nations, like the English and Germans, wear straw-coloured or leather-coloured yellow accompanied with dark blue. Nations aiming at dignity of appearance, the Spaniards and Italians, for instance, suffer the red colour of their mantles to incline to the passive side. (1840/1970, p. 328)

But all these effects, whether real or fanciful, are simply byproducts of color's real purposes, to which we now turn.

Why Is It Important to See Colors?

The ability to see in color must be enormously advantageous, for color vision has evolved in numerous orders within the animal kingdom, including mammals, fish, birds, and insects. What, then, are the advantages bestowed by color vision? For an answer, we can start by considering how color helps us detect objects, and to tell them apart from one another.

Color provides a unique source of information for picking out an object from its background (**detection**). Manufacturers of sporting equipment exploit this fact by producing yellow tennis balls that are easier to see on the court and orange golf balls that are harder to lose on the fairway. In some instances, the presence of an object would go completely undetected were it not for the color differences between that object and its background. Take a look at the two pictures in color plate 3. Besides appreciating the enriching quality color brings to the picture on the left, notice the green patch on the red sleeve of the girl's sweater. That patch literally disappears in the achromatic version of the picture. That's because the intensity of light reflected from the patch on the shoulder is essentially identical to the intensity reflected from elsewhere on the sleeve (the patch is said to be **isoluminant** with its background). Without color vision, the patch goes undetected; with color vision, the patch is conspicuous. In the natural environment, a hungry creature, such as a wren, can detect a potential meal, such as an insect, based solely on the difference in color between the insect and its background. Without color vision, the wren could starve.

Many animals exploit color in order to call attention to themselves, particularly for purposes of mating. The male peacock's almost gaudy tail is thought to communicate his strength and prowess, a message the female peacock attends to when selecting a mate. In many nonhuman primate species, including baboons and chimpanzees, the females, when in estrous, advertise their sexual receptivity by conspicuously exposing their swollen, red buttocks. Plants, too, announce their presence with color, inviting butterflies and bees to assist unwittingly with pollination. At the same time, however, nature can use color to make creatures and plants inconspicuous (Owen, 1980). Think back to our insect who may be the wren's next meal. If that insect's coloration blends in with the color of its surroundings, it may evade detection. A praying mantis resting on a leaf, for example, may be virtually invisible, so long as it doesn't move. Similarly, the arctic fox's white pelt provides excellent camouflage when it hunts on snow-packed land, giving the fox a considerable advantage over its prey. To see how one familiar animal exploits color for camouflage, take a look at color plate 4. Can you find this creature among the branches and leaves? If not, the answer appears at the end of this chapter, just before the Summary and Preview.

So, one of color's important contributions is to promote detection of objects that stand out from their backgrounds; color vision, in other words, promotes figure/ground segmentation. In some instances, color is the only source of information available for detection, but in many other instances color reinforces other cues. For example, in a cluttered environment, it's easier to determine the direction in which a cluster of objects is moving when those objects are all the same color (Croner and Albright, 1997). Their common color promotes grouping of the objects, segregating them from other, differently colored objects moving within the visual scene. Low-contrast objects are also easier to detect and localize in space when those objects differ in color from their background (Rivest and Cavanagh, 1996; Gur and Akri, 1992).

Besides aiding our ability to detect the presence of objects, color also helps us recognize (**identification**) and distinguish (**discrimination**) them from other objects in the environment. Subtle differences in the shade of red can tell you whether an apple or tomato is ripe and ready to eat. One shade of yellow tells you that a vehicle is a taxi rather than a police car; another shade of yellow ensures that Kodak's photographic products will be recognized worldwide merely from the color of the box. Farmers use color to identify fertile soil and to determine when their crops are ready for harvest. Doctors routinely rely on color to make diagnoses: blood that is pale red indicates anemia, and a yellowish skin pallor suggests a possible liver disorder. Meat inspectors pay attention to the color of animal tissue when they judge the meat's fitness for human consumption. Even a perceptual judgment as simple as distinguishing circles from ellipses becomes easier when highly visible geometric figures differ in color from their backgrounds (Syrkin and Gur, 1997). Evidently, color provides a clear landmark that allows us to direct our attention to objects within a cluttered environment, thereby improving our ability to notice changes in those objects or to judge their shapes (Brawn and Snowden, 1999).

Color also makes it easier and faster to recognize objects, and it helps us to remember what we've seen (Gegenfurtner and Rieger, 2000). Thus, people can more easily describe what they're looking at in a briefly flashed, complex picture when that picture is rendered in color rather than in black and white. Moreover, people are better able to remember what they've seen when they view a complex picture rendered in color. But, for color to aid recognition, the colors used must be appropriate for the objects comprising the scene. When a scene is rendered in uncharacteristic colors (see color plate 5), recognition is markedly slowed (Oliva and Schyns, 1999).

So, color has emotional and aesthetic impact, but the main purpose of color perception is to help us (and other species with color vision) detect, discriminate, identify, and remember objects. To explain how color serves these goals, this chapter describes important characteristics of color perception. The chapter also explains how the colors we experience depend on multiple factors: the light that illuminates the objects, the surface properties of those illuminated objects, the colors of other objects in the visual scene and, most importantly, the properties of the viewer's eyes and nervous system.

What Is Color?

Let's start with the most basic of questions: What is color? Simple questions usually call for simple answers, but no simple answer is available in this case. As the following sections show, describing what is meant by the quality called "color" is anything but simple. To illustrate the elusive nature of color, consider the following thought experiment.

Suppose a congenitally blind friend of yours asked you to describe what it's like to see. It's a challenging question, but you could manage to convey some sense of the meaning of visual form and shape by appealing to the blind person's tactile experiences with objects. And because your friend can travel and walk about, you'll be able to get across the notion of visual distance and visual motion. But when it comes to color, you'll be stumped. Color has no referent outside the quality itself. None of the other senses convey qualities that are remotely analogous to color. We don't have words to describe the quality of color, aside from color terms themselves. "Red" is something that apples, tomatoes, and fire trucks have in common, but that will mean nothing to your blind friend.

So what is this visual quality called *color?* Let's consider several alternative approaches to the question.

A Multitude of Color Names

People typically associate their experiences of color to the names used to describe those colors. So we might expect to get some idea of the nature of color perception by asking a seemingly simple question: How many color names are there? Some dictionaries list hundreds of color names, and advertisers invent new names all the time. However, in almost all cultures studied, everyday language manages

to get by with about a dozen basic color terms (Berlin and Kay, 1969). When people in our own culture are asked to assign names to various color samples, there is good agreement on the names for just a handful of basic colors (Boynton and Olson, 1987); beyond those basic few, color names assigned to color samples are idiosyncratic.

Do adults and children in cultures remotely different from ours categorize colors into the same four hue groups that we do? At least some evidence says no, they do not. The Berinmo, a primitive hunter/gatherer tribe inhabiting a remote region in Papua New Guinea, use five basic color terms. Interestingly, the boundaries that define these basic Berinmo color categories differ markedly from ours. For example, the Berinmo do not distinguish between green and blue, but they subdivide our single category called "green" into two: *nol* and *wor* (Davidoff, Davies, and Roberson, 1999). Moreover, color memory tests reinforce the conclusion that the Berinmo color categories differ from ours. Berinmos are much more likely to remember "blue" as being "green" than we are because those two colors fall within the same color category for them but not for us. Evidently, cultural influences play a role in shaping color categories; this is not a surprising conclusion given all the other evidence that experience plays a crucial role in constructing our perceptual world.

Categories implied by color names seem to be present in very young, preverbal infants. Bornstein, Kessen, and Weiskopf (1976) used a special technique (mentioned in Chapter 5) that capitalizes on the fact that infants, like adults, get tired of looking at the same thing. When first shown some color, an infant looks at it intently. But when the same color is repeatedly presented, **habituation** occurs—the infant loses interest and looks away.

Bornstein and colleagues assumed that the infant's disinterest in the habituated color would generalize to other, similar colors as well. The infant's degree of interest in a given color, then, would provide an index of how similar that color was to the habituated color. Given this quite reasonable assumption, Bornstein and colleagues used habituation to test whether infants categorize colors in the same way adults do. Here's how the experiment went. First, the infant was shown a patch of light whose dominant wavelength was 480 nanometers, a light we would categorize as blue. After an initial period of fascination with that light, the infant lost interest in this color, as expected. Next, Bornstein determined whether the infant's interest could be rekindled by viewing a patch of light whose dominant wavelength was either 450 nanometers or 510 nanometers. Note that in terms of wavelength, these two lights are each 30 nanometers from the 480-nanometer habituation light—an equivalent numerical difference in wavelength. In *perceptual* terms, however, they are not equally different. When viewed by adults, the 450-nanometer light looks blue, the same color category as the 480-nanometer habituation light; the 510-nanometer light, however appears green, at least to us. Evidently, human infants have the same blue-green categories as adults: The infants showed renewed interest in the 510-nanometer light but ignored the 450-nanometer light. In other words, the infants reacted as if the 450- and 480-nanometer lights fell in the same category, and the 480- and 510-nanometer lights fell in different categories. Similar tests were made for other color categories. In all cases, these preverbal infants categorized colors in the same way adults do, separating them into distinct categories corresponding to blue, green, yellow, and red.

But color names and their implied categories certainly don't capture the richness of our color experiences. In attempting to define color, perhaps it would be more useful to concentrate on color discrimination. One could ask: How many different colors can people see? Unfortunately, this simple question yields more than one answer. If color samples are placed side by side, most people can distinguish a huge number of different colors, with one recent estimate placing that number at 2.3 million (Pointer and Atridge, 1998)! The next time you're in a paint store, thumb through the hundreds of different color samples. You'll see that our color library is enormous. If those paint samples are presented one at a time, however, our color categories shrink to fewer than a dozen (Halsey and Chapanis, 1951). So how many colors *can* people see—millions or just a dozen? The difficulty in answering this question suggests that we need to rely on something other than naming to get at the essence of color. Let's consider the nature of light itself, starting with the landmark observations of one of history's greatest geniuses.

The Insights of Isaac Newton

Any discussion of color perception must include the contributions of Isaac Newton, who revolutionized the way we think about color vision. During a brief retreat to his mother's farm while a plague was raging at home in Cambridge, England, Newton discovered the binomial theorem, invented calculus, and devised a theory of gravitation. He also bought a prism that he later used to study the nature of light and color (Westfall, 1980). These studies led Newton to recognize a distinction that remains fundamental to this day—the distinction between *physical* phenomena and *perceptual* phenomena. In particular, Newton observed that "the rays, to speak properly, are not coloured. In them there is nothing else than a certain

Power and Disposition to stir up a Sensation of this or that Colour" (1704/1952, pp. 124–125).

These two sentences remind us that even the most compelling intuitions can be wrong. Newton is insisting that objects themselves have no color, and the light reflected from them is also colorless. Color is a *psychological* phenomenon, entirely *subjective* in nature. So, according to this counterintuitive view, appearances are deceptive: objects themselves are not colored, and they only *appear* colored because they reflect light from particular regions of the visible spectrum, and this reflected light has the power to stir up a particular sensation.

But even that is not nearly enough. For an object to appear colored, light reflected from that object must be picked up by an eye outfitted with the right kind of photoreceptors, and the signals from those photoreceptors must be combined in particular ways by the visual neurons in the retina and the brain. Color, in other words, is a product of the brain, not the world. And because some people have abnormal eyes or abnormal brains, their experiences of color can and do differ radically from those enjoyed by most people. This refined restatement of Newton's idea has been nicely voiced by Semir Zeki (1983):

> The nervous system, rather than analyze colours, takes what information there is in the external environment, namely, the reflectance of different surfaces for different wavelengths of light, and transforms that information to construct colours, using its own algorithms to do so. In other words, it constructs something which is a property of the brain, not the world outside. (p. 764)

According to this refined view, color arises from the capacity of particular light rays to evoke certain responses in the nervous system. To illustrate this, imagine seeing someone wearing a red sweater. According to Newton, there is nothing inherently red about the light reflected from that sweater. No matter how firmly rooted in the sweater it may seem, the redness ultimately depends on your eyes and brain.

Strictly speaking, then, it is incorrect to refer to a "red sweater." To be technically correct, you should describe it as a "sweater, which, when seen in daylight, evokes a sensation most humans call 'red.'" Of course, we don't advise going into a clothing store and using this technically correct language to inquire about the availability of red sweaters.

While on the subject of terminology, we should further clarify the term *color*. Our dictionary offers 19 different meanings for *color* in its noun form alone. If you've ever sorted objects such as crayons or "orphan" socks, you know that colors differ from one another in

FIGURE 7.1 | Setup for Newton's basic experiment.

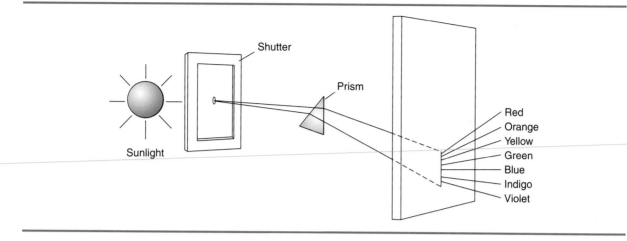

various ways. Blue and green socks differ from one another but not in the same way that two green socks do— say, one brand new and another that's been washed many times. In the study of perception, the single word *color* covers three different qualities. To distinguish one quality from another, each quality is given a particular name, *hue, brightness,* and *saturation.*

Hue refers to the quality that distinguishes red from yellow or green, or blue from orange, and so on. Incidentally, the word *color* is not an acceptable synonym for *hue.* In fact, technically, you should refer to the "hues of the rainbow" and to Joseph's "coat of many hues" (Genesis 37:3). The second quality of color, **brightness,** is related to the perceived quantity of light emitted by a stimulus. When we're talking about light itself, we use the term *brightness* (a star, for example, may be "bright" or it may be "dim"). When we're talking about surfaces, we sometimes use the term *lightness* (one red apple may appear lighter than another red apple, because the surface of the former appears to reflect more light than does the surface of the latter). The third quality, **saturation,** characterizes a color as "pale," "vivid," or something in-between. After your jeans have been washed numerous times, their blueness will be less saturated than when you first got them. Color plate 6 will help you to visualize more easily what is meant by *hue, brightness,* and *saturation.*

Since your color experiences vary along these three dimensions, describing a color completely requires specification of all three: hue, brightness, and saturation. Moreover, an adequate theory of color perception must explain the origin of these dimensions of color experience. Having clarified what we mean by *color,* we're now ready to consider the observations that led Newton to

propose that color resides within the perceiver, not within the light rays themselves.

What a Prism Reveals about Color   In a simple but elegant experiment, Newton allowed a beam of sunlight to pass through a small circular hole in a window shutter and then through a glass prism (see Figure 7.1). After passing through the prism, the light fanned out into a rainbow of **spectral colors.** Newton believed that this spectrum was divisible into seven different regions: red, orange, yellow, green, blue, indigo, and violet. These seven colors are indicated in the spectrum shown in color plate 7. In this plate, the upper scale defines the spectrum in terms of color experiences, a psychological dimension. The lower scale defines the spectrum in terms of wavelength of light, a physical dimension. The latter dimension, *wavelength,* was not known to Newton, which is why he had to describe color solely in psychological terms (that is, color names).

Long before Newton, it was known that a prism could decompose sunlight into a spectrum of colors (Ronchi, 1970). In fact, for centuries people had seen spectra created by glass chandeliers, soap bubbles, and diamond jewelry. Newton's lasting contribution stemmed from his unique exploitation of the prism to divide light into spectral components and to recombine those components to produce colors.

To accomplish his experiments, Newton first developed a simple scheme for selectively blocking out portions of the color spectrum, thereby producing a modified spectrum containing only a narrow band of wavelengths of light. Newton then used a convex lens to collect this modified spectrum and pass it through another prism (see

FIGURE 7.2 | Setup for modification of Newton's basic experiment.

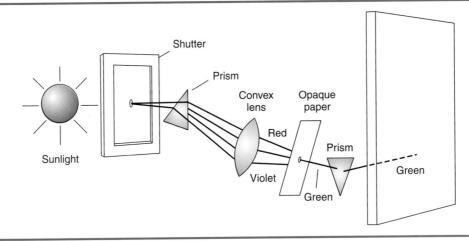

Figure 7.2). The combination of these two techniques allowed him to distinguish between **pure light** and light that is made up of several different components—**composite light.** For instance, if he blocked out all the colors of the spectrum except for green and then passed the green through a second prism, the resulting light continued to be green. Because the second prism could not further break green into other components, Newton deemed the green to be pure light.

To Newton these observations suggested that light from the sun was *not* pure but consisted of seven different colors that could not be decomposed. Though the first conclusion (that sunlight is not pure) is correct, the second (that sunlight contains only seven pure components) is not. Since the mistakes of geniuses can be as enlightening as their successes, let's see where Newton went wrong.

Like anyone else, scientists must be alert to the possibility that their observations can be influenced by expectation based on prior beliefs. Newton's conclusion that there were seven colors in the spectrum was influenced his belief that seeing and hearing were closely related (Gouk, 1988). In particular, he thought that since the musical scale included seven tones and semitones within each octave, the light spectrum had to contain seven colors (Boring, 1942).[1] But this error does not diminish the fact that Newton's main idea was right—light from the sun, sometimes called *white light,* can be decomposed

[1]There is reason to believe that Newton originally noticed only five different colors in the spectrum. Some claim that he later added two—orange and indigo—to bolster the analogy between spectral colors and intervals in the musical scale (Houston, 1917).

FIGURE 7.3 | Energy distribution of sunlight (colored line) and of light from an ordinary light bulb (black line).

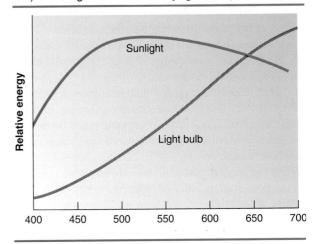

into many different colors. Stated in modern terms, light from the sun contains various amounts of energy in different regions of the electromagnetic spectrum (recall the discussion in Chapter 2). The distribution of sunlight's energy over the visible portion of the electromagnetic spectrum is shown by the heavy line in Figure 7.3. Note particularly that light from the sun consists of a nearly constant amount of energy at all the visible wavelengths. Contrast this with the distribution of energy from an ordinary incandescent light bulb. As shown by the black line, a typical light bulb emits more energy at longer wavelengths than it does at shorter ones. This is why photographs taken with indoor lighting can have a slightly more yellowish tint than those taken in natural light.

Newton first presented his work on light and color in 1672, when he was 29 years old. His ideas were greeted with such fury and disdain that Newton had to wait more than 30 years before publishing his complete work on these topics in *Opticks.* By that time, 1704, Newton's genius was nearly universally acknowledged. Despite his eminence, his ideas about light and color continued to provoke angry attacks for more than a century. None of these attacks was more impassioned than one launched by the German poet Goethe. Goethe believed that he would be remembered not so much for his poetry as for his refutation of Newton (Pirenne, 1967, p. 153). Being a strong believer in the power of intuition and common sense, Goethe was shocked at the patent absurdity of Newton's prism demonstration. Goethe considered Newton a "Cossack" for denying the purity of white light (Southall, in Helmholtz, 1909/1962, vol. 2, p. 115). Since the time of Aristotle, white light had been regarded as the very essence of purity. According to this view, color represented the contamination of white by less exalted, worldly substances. Newton's decomposition of white into colors implied that white was no more special than any other color.

In addition to these aesthetic considerations, Goethe also objected to Newton's ideas on philosophical grounds. He believed that to accept Newton's claim about white light was tantamount to treating *all* sense perception as subjective and unreliable, an idea he detested. Feeling absolutely certain that white light could *not* be a mixture of other colors, Goethe urged people to disregard the experiments performed by Newton in a darkened room in Cambridge:

> Friends, escape the dark enclosure,
> where they tear the light apart
> and in wretched bleak exposure
> twist and cripple Nature's heart.
> *Superstitions and confusions*
> *are with us since ancient times—*
> *leave the specters and delusions*
> *in the heads of narrow minds.*
> (Weisskopf, 1976)

To combat Newton further, Goethe got a prism and attempted to disprove some of Newton's scientific observations. Although he did use the prism for many different experiments, Goethe never correctly repeated what Newton had done. For example, Goethe looked directly through the prism and failed to see a spectrum of colors, which convinced him that Newton, in addition to being a Cossack, was a charlatan. Goethe went further. He enlisted the services of a young man, Arthur Schopenhauer, who would later become a distinguished philosopher in his own right. Goethe interested Schopenhauer in his ideas about light and color, and persuaded him to continue the assault on Newton. Using Goethe's own optical equipment, the younger man began to do experiments with light (Birren, 1941, p. 214). Unfortunately for Goethe, these experiments convinced Schopenhauer that his employer was wrong and that Newton was right: Sunlight *does* consist of many different colors.

The idea that white light is decomposable into elementary components is universally accepted today. However, when Newton first suggested the idea, it aroused passionate disagreement that continued well after Newton's own lifetime (see Box 7.1). At the time people were quite upset that their own eyes couldn't be trusted. Surely, they thought, what appears to be innocent white light cannot actually consist of a congregation of invisible components. In reality, the situation is even worse than people imagined: Using far fewer than seven components you can fool the eye into seeing white. We now know that what humans experience as *white* can be light that consists of a mixture of just two properly chosen spectral components. Because this does not work with all pairs of components, we give a special name to those pairs for which it does work. Any two spectral components that when added together appear white are said to be **complementary.** For example,

a mixture of appropriate amounts of blue and yellow produces what looks white. Moreover, this same blue and yellow mixture would be indistinguishable from another mixture that included orange light and greenish blue light. That mixture, too, would appear white. In each of the mixtures, complementary components cancel one another, yielding a colorless or achromatic sensation (white).

We should stress that components of a light mixture don't cease to exist when they're combined. An instrument that measures the amount of light throughout the spectrum would still register the presence of energy at the component wavelengths—the instrument never confuses a mixture of blue and yellow for white. It's the human eye that gets confused. These mixtures of complementary colors appear achromatic because of the way the visual nervous system registers and processes spectral information.

What Metamers Reveal about Color   What lessons can we draw from the observation that physically different combinations of light can produce identical color experiences? By studying the conditions under which color mixtures of different components appear equivalent, vision scientists gained important insights about the neural processes underlying color vision. And they did this long before those neural processes were actually isolated and measured. As you learned in Chapter 5, the term *metamers* is used to describe stimuli that are physically different but perceptually equivalent. Newton's experiments identified many examples of metamers in color vision. He found, for example, that a light appearing orange was metameric to a mixture of lights: one that appears red and one that appears yellow. In addition, pairs of complementary colors (that yield white) are also metameric to one another. And those two pairs of mixtures are metameric to a mixture of Newton's seven spectral colors, which, as you know, also yields the perception of white.

The existence of metamers implies that the visual system is generating equivalent neural responses to physically different stimuli. Thus, for example, orange is indistinguishable from a mixture of lights that appear red and yellow, presumably because orange is generated by the same pattern of neural activity within your eye and brain as that generated by the mixture of lights that appear red and yellow. If you can't tell two different stimuli apart by looking at them, your visual system is ignoring whatever it is that makes those stimuli physically different (Teller, 1989). Conversely, if you *can* visually discriminate two objects from one another, your visual system must be generating reliably different responses to the two stimuli. Orange *looks* different from red because orange results from neural responses that are different from those producing red. As you're about to learn, much of our understanding of color perception comes from studying stimuli that are confused with one another (metamers) and stimuli that are discriminable from one another.

Newton's Color Circle   Newton did not have the degree of control over light that scientists enjoy today. Still, he managed to explore the perceptual results of various mixtures of light with great effectiveness. To see what happens when two pure lights are combined, he blocked out all the other spectral components and used a convex lens to combine the remaining two. Examining the appearance of various mixtures of light, Newton developed the basic ideas of color mixture and expressed those ideas in a graphic model of color perception. Known as **Newton's**

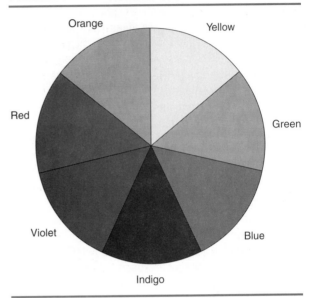

FIGURE 7.4 | Newton's color circle.

color circle, the model is depicted in Figure 7.4. Although modest in appearance, this circle represents an incredible insight on Newton's part, namely that a simple geometric form could represent the properties of something as complex as color vision (Wasserman, 1978). Each of the seven wedge-shaped sectors represents one of the spectral colors. As Newton put it, "[T]he Circumference representing the whole series of colours from one end of the Sun's colour'd image to the other" (1704/1952, p. 154). The circle, though, is only part of the model. Newton also devised several rules that relate colors and mixtures of colors to locations on and within the circle. Let's see how the appearance of various mixtures might be predicted by this geometric model.

Suppose we were to combine two lights of equal intensity, one that appears red and the other, yellow. These two equal-intensity lights are represented by two equal-sized triangles in Figure 7.5. One triangle is located on the circle, in the middle of the arc for yellow; the other triangle is also located on the circle, but in the middle of the arc for red. To find the color that results from the mixture of these two, connect the two triangles with a straight line. The color of the mixture corresponds to the line's center of gravity. (You might imagine this line as a seesaw, and the triangles as people on either end; the sizes of the triangles signify how much the people weigh.) The location of the line's center of gravity gives the predicted color of the mixture. In this case, the center of gravity lies

FIGURE 7.5 | Newton's color circle can be used to predict the color produced by mixing equal amounts of yellow and red light.

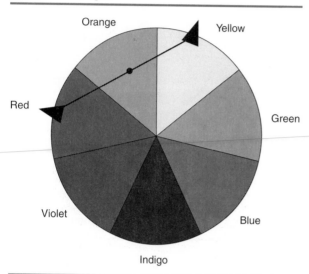

FIGURE 7.6 | Newton's color circle can be used to predict the color produced by mixing unequal amounts of yellow and red light.

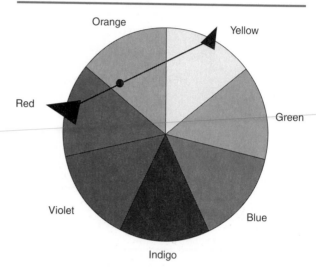

in the middle of the orange sector. In fact, orange is what you see when equal amounts of red and yellow light are mixed. Moreover, the orange produced by that mixture is metameric with the orange produced by just a single wavelength of light, or with the orange isolated with Newton's prism and slit apparatus.

Consider what happens when unequal amounts of light are mixed, say, a large quantity of red and a smaller quantity of yellow. This case is shown in Figure 7.6. The center of gravity of the line connecting the two unequal-sized triangles swings closer to the border between the red and orange sectors, signifying that the mixture will look reddish orange. And it does. Adding two colors near one another on the color circle yields a mixture whose color is a compromise between the components, with the exact appearance depending on the proportions of the colors in the mixture.

Combining the appropriate components of light, Newton also discovered he could produce a color whose appearance was not like any of his seven pure lights. For example, if you add long-wavelength light (from the red end of the spectrum) and short-wavelength light (from the blue end of the spectrum) the result is purple. Today we call such colors **nonspectral colors.** The very existence of nonspectral colors reinforces the distinction between light's physical properties and its perceptual consequences. From the perceptual point of view, the physical spectrum has a gap—it does not contain all the colors that can be perceived by the human eye. To put this in other words, the eye can combine wavelengths from the light spectrum to create some colors that are not present in any single region of the spectrum.

When Newton examined the seven colors in his spectrum, he noticed that they were very vivid (today we would describe them as highly saturated). But when he added these vivid components together, the resulting mixtures invariably appeared less vivid (today we would say they appear "washed out," or desaturated). This perceptual fact, that mixtures appear desaturated, is also represented in Newton's color circle. The most vivid colors fall along the circle's circumference; less vivid colors fall within the interior of the circle. At the extreme, a completely desaturated color (white) is represented at the center of the circle.

As mentioned previously, the seven pie-shaped wedges in Newton's color circle reflect his belief that there should be seven discrete pure colors. A color circle based on that erroneous assumption makes incorrect predictions about some mixtures involving colors widely separated on the color circle. To make correct predictions, Newton's color circle must be adjusted in two ways. First, the boundaries that divide the circle into discrete sectors must be erased, because those sectors imply the existence of discrete pure colors. A color circle without sectors

FIGURE 7.7 | A revised color circle.

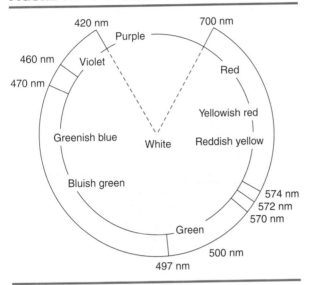

FIGURE 7.8 | Intensity of white light needed to desaturate colors of various wavelengths.

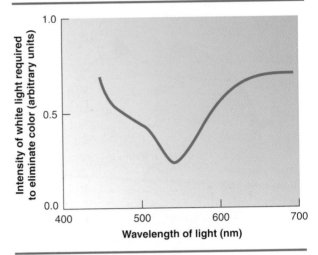

correctly reflects the fact that color varies continuously. Second, some rational scheme for spacing the color names (or wavelengths) around the circle's circumference must be used. Complementary colors should be placed opposite each other on the circle, so that when they are connected, their balance point falls at the circle's center (white, or achromatic). A circle satisfying both of these requirements is shown in Figure 7.7, with associated color names and light wavelengths shown around its circumference.

The circumference of the larger interrupted circle indicates the position of various spectral lights from 420 nanometers to 700 nanometers. Note that the wavelengths are not spaced uniformly; the wavelengths from 500 to 700 nanometers occupy less of the circumference than do those from 420 to 500 nanometers. In fact, the wavelengths have been positioned on the circle so that along any diameter, complementary colors stand directly opposite each other. Note also that some wavelengths, such as 497 nanometers, have no partner wavelength that is complementary.

Though this revised color circle is an improvement over Newton's original, it still fails to capture some elementary facts about color. For example, Newton noted that "some colours affect the senses more strongly" (1704/1952, p. 97). He meant that with lights of equal energy, yellows and greens are brighter (that is, more visually conspicuous) than reds or blues. We now know that the visibility of various wavelengths of light defines the photopic sensitivity function (see Chapter 3), with maximum brightness at 550 nanometers.

There's another important fact that neither Newton's original circle nor the revised version can account for: Bright colors tend to look washed out or desaturated. You can see this for yourself in color plate 7 by comparing the colors in the "yellow" region of the spectrum (which appear relatively bright but less saturated) to those at either end (which appear less bright but more saturated).

It's possible to quantify how strongly saturated a color appears. While looking at a light of a particular color, you can add white light to it, thereby desaturating that color. In this way, you could determine how much white light would be needed to eliminate the color completely. The amount of white light needed would depend on the color you start with. Certain colors, in other words, are more strongly saturated to begin with—they stand up better to dilution by white light. Other, less saturated colors are easily washed out, disappearing with the addition of small amounts of white light. Typical results of such measurements are shown in Figure 7.8. The horizontal axis specifies the wavelength of light used to produce the color; the vertical axis shows the intensity of white light needed to desaturate that color completely. This V-shaped curve shows that light near the middle of the spectrum (yellow) appears less saturated than do lights toward the end of the spectrum (blue or red). Adding white light to light of a given wavelength can also alter the hue produced by that wavelength. For instance, adding white to long-wavelength light (red) shifts its hue slightly toward yellow (Kurtenbach, Sternheim and Spillmann, 1984). For more on mixing colors, see Box 7.2.

Every schoolchild knows it is possible to create colors of various shades using just a few so-called primary colors. Various shades of green, for example, are readily achieved simply by mixing blue and yellow paints or inks. This is called **subtractive color mixture** because each of the component primaries subtract a portion of the incident light, keeping that portion from reaching your eye.

To illustrate this point consider the curve in panel A of the accompanying figure (adapted from Pirenne, 1967), which shows the reflectance spectrum of a typical light blue ink. The curve indicates that the ink reflects lots of light from the short-wavelength portion of the spectrum but less from the longer-wavelength portion. This happens because the ink contains a pigment that selectively absorbs light of particular wavelengths. Now look at panel B, which shows the reflectance spectrum for a typical yellow ink. Note that it reflects mainly wavelengths longer than 500 nanometers—hence its yellow appearance. Again, this is because the ink contains a pigment that absorbs light in a characteristic way. The curve in panel C shows the distribution of wavelengths reflected by a mixture of equal amounts of the two inks. How does this distribution come about, and why does it appear green?

When you mix the yellow and blue inks together, the mixture contains pigments from both components. Now suppose you view a surface that is coated with the mixture and illuminated by sunlight. The yellow pigment in the mixture will absorb part of the light that otherwise would have been reflected by the blue pigment. In other words, the yellow pigment removes much of the short wavelengths from the reflected light. Similarly, at longer wavelengths, the blue pigment will absorb some of the light that otherwise would have been reflected by the yellow pig-

ment. Although the actual calculations are complicated, panel c reveals that the mixture of the two inks reflects light mainly around the middle of the spectrum, the only region of the spectrum at which *both* pigments reflect appreciable amounts of light. As a result, the mixture will look neither yellow nor blue but instead, greenish.

The principles of subtractive color mixture were employed 25,000 years ago by the prehistoric artists who worked in the caves around Lascaux (in what is today western France). Ever since then, people have used the same principles to color objects in their environment. But it was nature that devised the technique: Plants and animals contain pigments that selectively absorb or subtract certain wavelengths. This selective absorption gives rise to the characteristic colors one associates with those plants and animals.

Color can also be produced by a process of **additive color mixture.** This additive process is almost never used by nature and has been used by people only very recently, mainly for purposes of entertainment or research. We'll illustrate additive mixture using a familiar example, color television.

The tube in a color television set contains hundreds of thousands of small spots packed very closely together. These spots light up when they are struck by an electron beam inside the set. A spot will appear red, blue, or green, depending on the material out of which the spot is made. Each small section of the television tube contains many closely packed spots of each type. You can verify this by looking very closely at the screen of a color television set. (At normal viewing distances, the spots are too small to be seen separately. Instead, they are blended, or added together, by your eye.) The color from your television set is produced by an *additive* process.

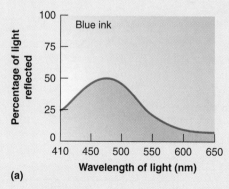

(a)

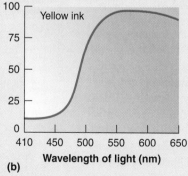

(b)

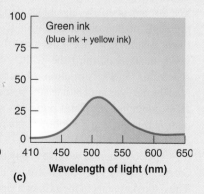

(c)

(continued)

BOX 7.2 **Mixing Colors** *(continued)*

Because the strength of the blue, red, or green glow varies with the intensity of the electron beam at any spot, the relative proportions of the three colors in the mixture also vary. As a result, although the tube itself produces only the three colors, the properties of your own nervous system generate perceptions of a wide range of different colors according to the laws of additive color mixture.

Color plate 8 allows you to experience additive mixture. The painting on the left, *Susan,* by the contemporary American artist Chuck Close, consists of many small spots of different colored paints. From a normal viewing distance, your eye does not separate the individual spots, resulting in an additive mixture of the individual colors. (Incidentally, when Newton superimposed lights of different wavelengths, he, too, was employing a form of additive mixture.)

To the right of *Susan* is a magnified view of one small part of Close's painting. Here you can see the individual spots. Note that colors are less vivid in this magnified image because the white from the background desaturates the color of the spots. The size of the spots used in Close's painting affects not only the saturation of the colors, but also the visibility of forms that are depicted in the painting. Pelli (1999) has documented how spot size affects viewers' ability to perceive the face: When the scale of the spots is too big, the face becomes unrecognizable.

We've seen, then, that there are two different techniques for color mixture. In one technique, the color is produced by the addition of wavelengths; in the other, by the subtraction (absorption) of wavelengths. The difference between these techniques of color mixture has nothing to do with the nature of color vision. It shows only that light is absorbed or reflected differently under different circumstances. For both types of mixtures, the color of a surface depends on the distribution of wavelengths reaching your eye.

The Constancy of Color

In developing the concepts of color perception, our examples have utilized simple spectral lights and their mixtures. These lights consist of a narrow band of wavelengths artificially isolated from the rest of the visible spectrum. However, narrowband light of this sort is rarely encountered outside the laboratory. Ordinarily, vision depends on broadband, "white" light (sunlight or artificial light) that illuminates the objects we see.

Although the illuminating light in our environment is white, we see most objects as colored, not white. That's because those objects absorb certain wavelengths contained in the white light and reflect the rest. The wavelengths absorbed by an object depend on the surface pigments of that object. For instance, "green" grass reflects a band of wavelengths more than 100 nanometers wide, nearly one-third the width of the entire visible spectrum. This distribution of reflected wavelengths reaches the eyes and initiates the perception of color. Surfaces containing different pigments will reflect different distributions of wavelengths (compare the three distributions shown in Figure 7.9).

The color names we give to objects generally depend on the light they reflect, not on the light they absorb. Thus, the pigments in the skin of a ripe "red" tomato predominantly absorb wavelengths outside the "red" region of the spectrum (see the middle line in Figure 7.9). In a

FIGURE 7.9 | Distributions of light reflected from the surfaces of three common objects.

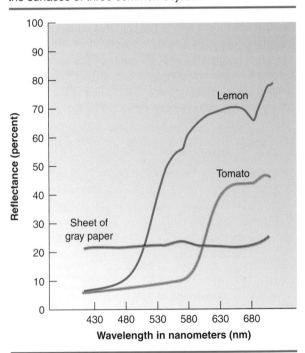

sense, a ripe tomato is everything but red. This play on words merely underscores a theme we've stressed over and over: Vision is designed to provide us with information about objects, not about light. And that brings us to a remarkable "computation" that the human visual system performs automatically when it specifies the colors of objects.

You now know that the color of an object is specified by the pattern of light reflected from its surface (its so-called "spectral reflectance"), and it's an object's surface color that we're interested in knowing. Yet the light reflected from a surface also depends on the wavelengths contained in the light that's illuminating that surface (the "illuminant," as it's called). When the spectral composition of the illuminant varies, the spectral distribution of the reflected light will also vary. For example, the composition of sunlight varies with the time of day—late afternoon sunlight contains more long-wavelength light than does the noonday sun. As a result, the light reflected outdoors by any object will vary from one time of day to another. Moreover, the spectral composition of ordinary indoor lights (tungsten light bulbs) differs from the spectral composition of sunlight—the indoor light contains less short-wavelength light (recall Figure 7.3). Thus, the light reflected from an object changes when you view the object indoors versus outdoors. Even though the light reaching your eye varies, the perceived colors of objects remain the same: Green grass nearly always looks green, and yellow roses stay yellow. **Color constancy** is the name given to this propensity for an object's color to remain constant despite changes in the spectrum of light falling on that object, and thus changes the light reflected toward the viewer from the object (Jameson and Hurvich, 1989).

To achieve color constancy, the visual system must disentangle a surface's spectral reflectance from the spectral distribution of light that is illuminating that surface. Since the light received by the eye is determined by both factors—the surface's spectral reflectance and the spectral quality of illumination—how can the visual system differentiate the two?

To start to answer this question, imagine that you're sitting outdoors reading this book. After a while, it gets chilly, so you go inside to finish reading, using a lamp with an ordinary 150-watt tungsten bulb. Looking back at Figure 7.3, we see that the outdoor light contains relatively more energy at the short-wavelength, "blue" end of the spectrum than does the indoor light, whose energy composition is biased toward the longer-wavelength,

"yellow" end of the spectrum. If your color perception depended only on the light coming from a page of this book, the surface would appear somewhat yellow indoors (since indoors the page reflects more light that is normally called yellow than it does outdoors). Yet you don't notice the change. Why?

As you learned in Chapter 3, the visual system adjusts its sensitivity to the overall level of illumination. This process, called *light adaptation,* contributes to the eye's ability to function under a wide range of light levels (from twilight to bright sunlight). In effect, adaptation deemphasizes unchanging or steady stimulation by turning down the neural responses to that stimulation. Consequently, adaptation reduces differential physiological responses that are elicited by the spectral distribution of any illumination source. So, when you're exposed to the blue-rich outdoor light, adaptation diminishes your visual system's response to the short-wavelength portion of that light. When you're exposed to the red- and green-rich indoor light, adaptation reduces the response to long-wavelength light. Both effects tend to "homogenize" the visual responses under sunlight and indoor light, making both sets of responses more nearly alike than their different spectral distributions would suggest. Light adaptation, then, is one reason your book's pages don't change color as you shift from outdoors to indoors.

You can observe the consequences of the process of adaptation by performing this simple experiment. Get a pair of tinted sunglasses and, before putting them on, look at a white surface (for example, a wall or a book page) through one of the lenses while holding the glasses at arm's length. That small portion of the surface seen through the lens will appear tinted according to the color of that lens. Now put the sunglasses on, thereby tinting everything you're looking at. In just a few seconds, the tint will fade and the colors of everything you see—including the "white" surface—will look nearly the same as they did before you donned the glasses. Your visual system has adjusted its sensitivity to the new pattern of illumination reaching your eyes. When you take the glasses off, colors will look odd for a few seconds but, then, will return to their normal appearance; vision, again, has adapted to the prevailing light condition. This adaptation effect is one example of a class of phenomena called **color induction,** wherein color appearance is influenced by preceding color stimulation or by the presence of other colors elsewhere in the visual field; you will learn about other examples of color induction later in this chapter.

You can see the effect of adaptation in action using the Adapt and Test figures in color plate 9. Stare at the small plus mark in the center of the four colored objects in the left-hand figure—hold your fixation steady. After about 20 seconds shift your fixation to the plus mark in the center of the right-hand figure. You'll temporarily see colors where none existed before. These colored afterimages, as they're called, are attributable to adaptation. In this case, different regions of your eye have been adapted to different colors. Later in this chapter, we'll explain why the afterimages are the particular colors that they are.

Adaptation is important for color constancy, but it's not the whole story (Webster and Mollon, 1995; Hulbert, 1999). Color contrast among objects and their backgrounds is a second important factor that promotes color constancy. Consider the textile in color plate 10, an antique Amish quilt made of wool patches whose colors are deeply saturated. The green and blue patches stand out in sharp relief against the red background; in color parlance, both green and blue contrast strongly against red. The blue and green patches, however, are not so conspicuously different. When seen next to one another, those two colors generate weak color contrast. You can get a sense of color contrast by looking back at the color circle in Figure 7.7. Colors located close to one another on the circle are less contrasting than colors located far apart on the circle.

Color contrast is a property of visual objects that are near one another. It doesn't change much when the source of illumination changes. Thus the contrast of the blue and green patches in the Amish quilt remains essentially the same whether the quilt is viewed under natural light or tungsten illumination. So if the visual system could compute color contrast among adjacent objects in a scene, it could exploit this source of information to preserve the color appearance of those objects under conditions of changing illumination. Recent research provides solid evidence that our visual system does exactly this. Kraft and Brainard (1999) showed that, despite large changes in illumination, color constancy remained relatively stable so long as color contrast within a scene was unchanged.

Kraft and Brainard distinguished two kinds of color contrast, local and global (you probably remember these terms from Chapter 5). Local color contrast refers to color differences between some object and its immediate background; global color contrast refers to the differences between an object's color and the average color response across the entire scene. Each of these two sources of contrast information contributes to color constancy. For example, global color contrast between stimuli that are remote from one another can regulate the amount of local color contrast (Shevell and Wei, 1998; Barnes, Wei, and Shevell, 1999; Golz and MacLeod, 2002).

In a related vein, Kraft and Brainard found that some objects within a visual scene can make unexpectedly strong contributions to color constancy. For example, objects with glossy surfaces, such as a porcelain vase, reflect highlights (recall the objects in the bottom part of Figure 2.16). These highlights provide mirrorlike reflections of the light source itself, thereby providing a small "snapshot" of the wavelength distribution of the source.

Color constancy probably evolved to compensate for small variations in the broad wavelength distributions of natural light. As a result, when objects are illuminated by light with a restricted wavelength distribution, the compensation fails and color constancy can be defeated. Color plate 11 shows some common objects illuminated by natural sunlight and by two different lights of restricted wavelength distributions. Note how, in the later cases, the objects take on highly unnatural colors, showing that color constancy works only under conditions of broadband illumination. Be warned that unscrupulous supermarkets exploit this limitation on color constancy. They can make their meat products look extra fresh (red) by illuminating them with light biased toward long wavelengths.

So far we've discussed illumination, surface reflectance, and color contrast, but have not actually seen how the eye measures the relative amounts of light energy from different parts of the wavelength spectrum. Those measurements are crucial for any visual system that's going to specify object colors, and it is to those measurements that we now turn. Incidentally, the theory of trichromatic color vision that you'll learn about represents a crowning achievement of vision science. This theory is the culmination of more a century's research involving psychophysics, photochemistry, electrophysiology, and molecular genetics. As you'll see, this achievement directly connects the quality of human experience to short DNA sequences on a single chromosome (Mollon, 1992).

The Trichromacy of Human Vision

The preceding sections reinforce the idea that color (a psychological experience) and light (a physical quantity) are connected in complex ways. Among those complexities, we learned that different combinations of wavelengths can yield the same color experience. Recall that neutral white can be produced by a mixture of orange and green or by a mixture of blue and yellow (both pairs constitute complementary colors). Such psychologically equivalent combinations—called metamers—indicate that the visual system confuses certain combinations of wavelengths with one another. The confusions that are observed provide important clues about how the eye encodes the wavelength composition of the light it receives. This encoding is initiated by photosensitive pigments in the photoreceptors, so this is where we should start. In the following sections, we'll concentrate on the cone photoreceptors, since they provide the substrate for color vision. To get things rolling, let's again adopt an engineer's perspective and ask how many different types of cone photoreceptors we'll need to produce an eye that can see the range of colors visible to humans.

A Design Decision: How Many Cone Pigments?

What If Eyes Had Only One Cone Pigment?   Every photopigment absorbs some wavelengths of light more efficiently than others. However, once absorbed, light of any wavelength initiates exactly the same chain of events in the visual receptor. Thus, the receptor makes no distinction as to the wavelength of the light absorbed. The response of the receptor conveys information about *how much* light has been absorbed, but the response conveys *no* information about the wavelength of the absorbed light. This is called the **univariance principle,** because a receptor's response can be summarized by a single number (one variable) that specifies the amount of light absorbed (Naka and Rushton, 1966). The univariance principle is key to understanding the photoreceptors' role in color perception. (Incidentally, the univariance principle represents another case of the ambiguity inherent in the response of a single neuron, an issue discussed in Chapters 4 and 5.)

According to the univariance principle, an eye containing only one photopigment type could not discriminate one wavelength from another because, with the proper adjustment of intensities, all wavelengths could be made to affect that one photopigment type in exactly the same way. This is illustrated in Figure 7.10, which shows the absorption spectrum of a hypothetical single type of photopigment. The curve shows the amount of incident light that the pigment would absorb at different wavelengths throughout the visible spectrum. These absorption values are expressed relative to

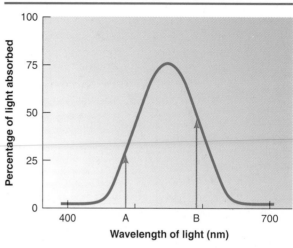

FIGURE 7.10 | A one-pigment system.

absorption at the peak of the curve, which corresponds to about 550 nanometers and which we arbitrarily set at 75 percent.

You could think of this curve as a summary of the pigment's efficiency for absorbing light at different wavelengths. Note the photopigment's response to wavelengths A and B: it absorbs twice as much light (50 percent relative to the maximum) at wavelength B as it does at wavelength A (25 percent relative to the maximum). So, if equal amounts of A and B were incident on the photopigment, the response to B would be larger because more of wavelength B would be absorbed. However, equal amounts of A and B would be absorbed—and hence, yield equal responses—if twice as much A were incident on the photopigment, relative to B.

In fact, the intensity of any given wavelength within this pigment's sensitivity range could be adjusted such that the amount of light actually absorbed by this pigment would be kept constant, regardless of which wavelength was actually present. This means, in other words, that many wavelengths would be metameric to one another. In addition, with proper adjustment of intensities, any *combination* of wavelengths, including white light, could be perfectly matched by any other wavelength or combination of wavelengths. So an eye with only one type of photopigment would treat all sorts of light mixtures as metameric.

A person or an animal with just one cone pigment would be unable to discriminate among wavelengths and, therefore, could not tell one color from another. Such a person or animal, called a **monochromat** (meaning

FIGURE 7.11 | A two-pigment system.

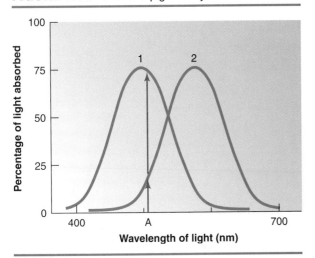

"one-colored"), would see everything as various shades of gray. Many marine animals (e.g., seals) and nocturnal mammals (e.g., raccoons) have only one cone pigment and are therefore monochromats (Peichl, Behrmann and Kroeger, 2001). In fact, humans are monochromats in dim light, because then we are forced to rely on the rod photoreceptors, which contain just one type of photopigment.

What If Eyes Had Two Cone Pigments?   An eye with two distinct photopigments would be more discriminating than the one-pigment eye just described. Consider the consequences of having two photopigments such as those whose absorption spectra are shown in Figure 7.11. Again, since each photopigment obeys the univariance principle, either one of the pigments *on its own* conveys no information whatsoever about the wavelengths of light reaching the eye. However, when two different types of pigments act *in concert* they *do* provide some information about the wavelengths that are present. Let's see how.

First, note that when stimulated by light, a two-pigment system makes two statements, not one, about the amount of light energy absorbed. For any given wavelength, the statement (or response) of either pigment depends on how well that pigment absorbs light of that particular wavelength. By definition, two types of photopigments differ in how well they absorb light of various wavelengths, as summarized by their different absorption spectra (Figure 7.11). As a result, any single wavelength (for example, A in Figure 7.11) will generate a *pair* of responses, one from each pigment. Note in this example that pigment 1 generates a larger response to A

than does pigment 2. Of course, the magnitude of each pigment's response will also vary with light intensity, since more intense lights make more energy available for absorption. However, when light gets more intense but wavelength does not change, the two responses will grow proportionately. Consequently, so long as wavelength is unchanged, the *relative* strengths of the two pigments' responses will remain constant. In summary, because the two pigment types have different absorption spectra, an eye with two pigment types extracts some usable wavelength information from light.

This two-pigment system can nonetheless be confused about wavelength, as the following example shows. Consider the response produced by the wavelength represented in the left panel of Figure 7.12 (see arrow). Note that this wavelength stimulates both pigments 1 and 2, yielding a small response in pigment 1 and a larger response in pigment 2. We express this pair of responses as a ratio, which for this wavelength would be four to one (4:1). Now, the ratio for this pair of responses to a single wavelength can be duplicated by an appropriate combination of two wavelengths. This is illustrated in the right panel of Figure 7.12, where the effects of a mixture of two wavelengths are shown. Note that the resulting pair of responses, one from each pigment, stands in the same ratio (4:1) as the pair of responses elicited by the single wavelength in the left panel. The owner of this eye, therefore, would confuse that single wavelength (left panel) with the mixture (right panel). These confusions, by the way, constitute failures of discrimination: Two (or more) physically different stimuli look identical; they would be metameric.

This eye with two pigments would be susceptible to color confusions (failures in discrimination) at other regions of the spectrum as well. Any wavelength or mixture of wavelengths (no matter how complex) will be represented by just a pair of signals. As a result, the effect of any wavelength or mixture of wavelengths can always be matched by just two wavelengths, provided the two are presented in the right proportions. Moreover, such matches can be produced using any of a large number of different pairs of wavelengths. An eye exhibiting these kinds of confusions is said to be **dichromatic** (meaning "two-colored"). Keep in mind, however, that not all wavelengths are confused. So, unlike a one-pigment eye, a dichromatic eye retains certain information about the wavelength composition of light, and this information provides a basis for color discrimination. In fact, among mammals known to possess more than one type of cone pigment, all except apes, humans and some species of monkeys have dichromatic color vision (Jacobs, 1998).

FIGURE 7.12 | A two-pigment system can be confused.

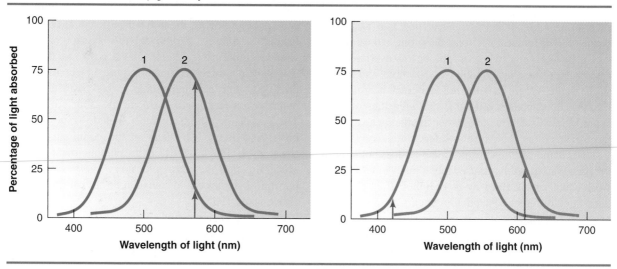

An eye with only two types of cone pigments would make one particularly interesting color confusion involving sunlight. (As you know, sunlight consists of nearly equal amounts of all wavelengths within the visible portion of the spectrum.) Like any other complex mixture of wavelengths, sunlight will be represented in this eye by a pair of responses, one from each pigment type. There also exists one specific wavelength of light that will produce exactly the same pair of responses. This means, therefore, that this one particular wavelength will be indistinguishable from sunlight. Looking at the curves in Figure 7.12, you should be able to figure out exactly where this wavelength falls along the spectrum. Since all other wavelengths will produce different pairs of responses, they will not be confused with sunlight. We can call the one wavelength that is confused the **neutral point** of the eye's spectral response. The existence of a single neutral point is the hallmark of a two-pigment eye. For most humans, no such neutral point exists, which indicates that their eyes have more than two cone pigments.

What If Eyes Had Three Cone Pigments?   So where do things stand so far? We've seen that for a one-pigment eye, any complex combination of wavelengths can be matched using just a single wavelength. Such an eye would be entirely color blind. We've also seen that a two-pigment eye can match any complex combination of wavelengths using two properly selected wavelengths. Such an eye would have some ability to discriminate the wavelength composition of light. Now you should be

FIGURE 7.13 | A three-pigment system.

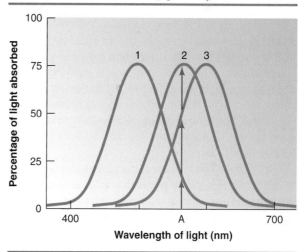

able to anticipate what happens if an eye contains three pigments, like those represented in Figure 7.13. Note that any wavelength (such as A) will produce a trio of responses, one from each photopigment. Moreover, this trio of responses cannot be mimicked by any other single wavelength. To mimic these responses would require the ability to vary the intensities of up to three different wavelengths (with some exceptions, to be explained in the next paragraph). Hence an eye containing a trio of photopigments is said to be **trichromatic** (meaning "three-colored").

Color plate 12 illustrates the variety of colors that can be produced by mixing just three colors. Note that each projector contains a transparency that creates a beam of a different color: one blue, one red, and one green. In the center, where all the beams overlap, your eye receives the reflected light from all three, and the result is white. Where only the red and green beams overlap, the light appears yellow. If the intensities of each beam were adjusted relative to one another, a host of intermediate colors could be generated.

The demonstration in color plate 12 does not require the particular trio of lights used there; many others would work equally well. But why *three* lights? If an eye contains three different cone photopigments, its response to any complex mixture of light can be represented by a trio of signals, one generated by each type of cone. To mimic this trio of signals, three independently adjustable lights are needed. Although any single wavelength will stimulate more than just one cone type, certain wavelengths do stimulate one type particularly well and the other types less well. A trio of wavelengths can be chosen so that each member of the trio elicits the largest response from a different one of the three pigments. We noted earlier that there are limitations to the matches that are possible with any set of three lights. To match any light, you need independent control of the response in each cone type. Because any single wavelength will stimulate all types of cones, three lights that have been chosen to match most colors will not be able to match many extremely saturated colors. To make those matches, a different set of lights would be required.

It has been known for some time that normal human vision is trichromatic. The idea that color perception depends on the responses of three different pigments is also quite old. Thomas Young, a British physician, usually receives credit for being the first to articulate this theory (1801/1948). But it was the German physiologist Hermann Helmholtz who developed the first detailed treatment of the same idea (1909/1962), so the theory is usually known by both men's names, the **Young-Helmholtz theory.**

We're now ready to study some of the details of this theory. But first, consider what happens when there are more than three unique cone photopigments.

What If Eyes Had Four Cone Pigments?

Imagine an eye that contains four different types of cones, each with its own unique absorption spectrum. By now you should be able to anticipate several "facts" about the color vision of a creature who possessed this hypothetical eye. First, this creature would have even better color discrimination than humans and other trichromatic species. With four cone photopigments, the number of potential color confusions decreases. Moreover, this four-pigment eye would require four unique wavelengths to do color matching, not three as humans require. In fact, nature has provided some nonmammalian species with tetrachromatic vision (the prefix *tetra* means "four" in Greek). These visually gifted creatures include some reptiles, birds, and bony fish such as the common goldfish (Neumeyer, 1992), whose extra photopigment gives it sensitivity into the ultraviolet (very short wavelength) portion of the spectrum invisible to human trichromats (Bowmaker, 1998).

This raises a question: In the case of human vision, why did nature stop at just three cone types? (If you were a dichromat such as the cat, you might ask why stop at just two cone types.) If more unique cone types give an eye greater color discriminability, why not upgrade to a goldfish-quality eye? For that matter, why stop at four?

Actually, there are several good reasons why trichromacy represents a good compromise. First, new cone types must arise from chance mutations in the genetic instructions specifying the opsin molecules contained in the photoreceptors (recall Chapter 2, where we discussed the molecular structure of photopigment). And those chance mutations are rare. Second, when mutations do occur, they would have little impact on color vision unless the postreceptor cells maintained some segregation of responses generated by each of the mutated photopigments (Wässle, 1999). Without proper segregation, the postreceptor neurons would intermix the mutated pigments' responses with the normal ones, subverting the mutants' uniqueness. And, finally, that additional kernel of color information would need to have survival importance to the organism in which the mutation arose. The animal must be able to see things its competitors cannot. Otherwise, the genetic instructions for synthesizing that novel photopigment would confer no advantage to its owner and, therefore, would not be selectively inherited by subsequent generations.

Given this sequence of very unlikely circumstances, it is remarkable that color vision has evolved at all. Trichromacy, in fact, represents a very efficient means for representing the behaviorally important surface colors in our natural environment. Just look at how many different colors we can distinguish! Of course, there are some wavelength combinations that the human eye cannot discriminate from one another, as studies of metamers show. In the research laboratory, metamers are produced under conditions that afford strict control over the wavelength composition of stimuli. This kind of control never occurs in the natural environment in which the visual system evolved. And it rarely occurs in everyday situations involving artificial illumination. In fact, mathematical analyses of natural surfaces and the wavelength distributions of typical illuminants reveal that trichromacy represents a very good solution to the problem of color vision: It provides a sufficiently accurate description of surface colors viewed under most lighting conditions (Lennie and D'Zmura, 1988).

In a moment we will consider in more detail the genetic bases of color vision. But first we need to return to our trichromatic eyes and consider exactly what photopigments the three cone types contain and how those cone types are distributed throughout the eye.

What Are the Three Cone Types?

For over a century, strong but indirect evidence pointed to the existence of three distinct cone types within the human eye. But it wasn't until the mid-twentieth century that the presence of those cones was confirmed and their spectral sensitivities were measured. Here's how that was accomplished.

The technique of directly measuring the light absorption of photopigments is aptly named **microspectrophotometry.** Consider each part of the term: *photometry* involves the measurement (*metron*) of light (*photos*); *spectro* indicates the spectrum (determining which wavelengths of light are present); and *micro* means "small." Hence, in the application to cone pigments, microspectrophotometry involves shining a small spot of light onto a single cone and determining, for various wavelengths, how much of that light is absorbed (MacNichol, 1964). Figure 7.14 shows results obtained by studying cones in several human retinas (Dartnall, Bowmaker, and Mollon, 1983). The vertical axis portrays the amount of light absorbed, expressed as a percentage of the light shone on the cone. The horizontal axis indicates the light's wavelength. To facilitate comparisons among pigments, each pigment's maximum absorption has been arbitrarily set equal to unity.

These absorption curves have several notable features. First of all, repeated measurements obtained from different, individual cones within the human eye reveal three different cone pigment types (one type per cone); this confirms what experiments on color metamers led vision scientists to expect. Each pigment type is most sensitive to light of a particular wavelength—approxi-

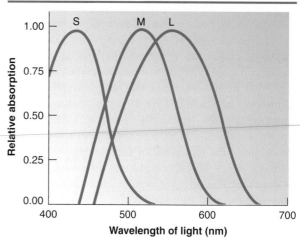

FIGURE 7.14 | Microspectrophotometric records from three cone types in the human eye.

mately 430, 530, and 560 nanometers, respectively. Because of their peak sensitivities, these three cone types are referred to as short-wavelength sensitive (S cones), medium-wavelength sensitive (M cones), and long-wavelength sensitive (L cones). Notice that each cone pigment absorbs a broad range of wavelengths. As a result of this breadth, nearly any light—even a light of only a single wavelength—stimulate more than just one class of cones. For example, stimulation in the region of 475 nanometers affects all three types. A single cone type's broad range of sensitivity also means that the response of that cone provides no information about the particular wavelength(s) of light being absorbed. By itself, each pigment type is "color blind" (recall the univariance principle described earlier).

Each cone's photopigment comprises a membrane protein bound to retinal, which is a derivative of vitamin A. Photopigments are manufactured according to genetic instructions embodied in DNA sequences. Using techniques from molecular genetics, it has been possible to synthesize those cone pigment proteins in the laboratory from cloned DNA samples. By exposing molecules of each synthesized protein to light of a different wavelength, one can measure the protein's absorption spectrum. When this is done with proteins that have been synthesized from human DNA, three distinct spectra show up, peaking at about 426, 530, and 557 nanometers (Merbs and Nathans, 1992). This remarkable technical achievement confirms some of what was already known about photopigments and genes, and sets the stage for identifying the details of the genetic "language" that controls cones' wavelength sensitivity.

Molecular biology has uncovered an unexpected twist in the trichromatic story: L cones come in at least two varieties. Normal trichromatic humans, in fact, have one of two slightly different alternative types of L cone pigment: some have L cones with peak sensitivity at 552 nanometers and others have L cones peaking at 557 nanometers. This genetically based difference boils down to a difference of a single amino acid in the protein structures of the two kinds of L-pigments (Merbs and Nathans, 1992). This tiny molecular difference, in turn, produces reliable differences in color perception. Thus, when told to adjust the amounts of red and green light to produce a mixture that appears pure yellow, people with the 557 nanometer L cone add more green to the mixture while those with the 552 nanometer L cone add more red (Winderickx et al., 1992). This means that a given mixture of red and green looks different to these two groups of trichromatic individuals.

Within a large sample of people, the incidence of the two cone types turns out to be about two to one in favor of the 557 nanometer variety of L cone (the variety shown in Figure 7.14). Inspired by these findings, there is a growing realization that people with normal color vision may have not one, but *many* versions of L- and M-cone pigments, produced by intergenic recombination in which, for example, portions of an L-pigment gene inherited from one's father is combined with portions of an M-pigment gene inherited from one's mother (Jacobs, 1996; Tovee, 1994; Neitz and Neitz, 1995).[2] These mistakes in DNA replication are promoted by the proximity and structural similarity of the L- and M-pigment genes.

A detailed knowledge of the connections between perception and events at a molecular level is both exciting and fascinating. As John Mollon (1992) put it, "Here is a case where a difference of a single nucleotide (unit of DNA) places people in distinct phenomenal worlds and where we know almost all the steps in the causal chain from gene to molecule to neural signals" (p. 378).

---

[2]For a long time it was believed that X-chromosomes normally carried just two photopigment genes, one for the M pigment and one for the L pigment. The use of sophisticated molecular biological techniques has undermined that assumption. In fact, a significant number of males have more than one L-pigment gene on the X-chromosome (Sjoberg et al., 1988). It is likely that a similar arrangement holds for M-pigment genes as well (Neitz, Neitz, and Jacobs, 1993).

The Geography of the Cones

We've been considering the connection between color perception and the cones' absorption spectra. Let's focus now on other perceptually important facts about cone receptors. Knowing that the signals coming from the three cone types are important in color perception, we need to consider how these types are distributed across the retina. As you will see, the proportions of the three cone types vary from one retinal region to another, and color perception varies correspondingly.

Simply looking at retinal tissue under the microscope provides some clues about cone distribution, because the S cones are slightly different in shape than the L and M cones (Rodieck, 1998). Consequently, it's been known for some time that there are fewer S cones than L and M cones and, moreover, that S cones are altogether absent within the fovea. But it wasn't until very recently that the distributions of L and M cones could be visualized because those two cone types are indistinguishable anatomically.

It remained for Austin Roorda and David Williams (1999) to devise a way to reveal the spatial layout of S, M, and L cones in the intact human eye. Using a specially designed optical system, Roorda and Williams photographed the receptor mosaic with enough detail that individual cones could be seen. A series of these high-fidelity photographs was made immediately after exposing the eye to intense light that selectively stimulated each of the three photopigments. An example of these remarkable results is shown in color plate 13. This represents about a 0.013-millimeter square patch of tissue located just to one side of the fovea of one eye (a tissue patch this size is slightly smaller than the period at the end of this sentence). Blue, green, and red circles denote individual S, M, and L cones, respectively. (Don't be misled: The colors in this photograph are simply used to earmark the cones. They are not actually colored in the eye.)

This patchwork of cones shows several remarkable features. First, a relatively small proportion of S cones are more or less irregularly scattered among larger numbers of L and M cones. Second, the L and M cones, too, are more or less randomly distributed within the mosaic of cone photoreceptors. One sees relatively large patches of retina comprised of only a single cone type.

What you can't see from this one photograph, however, are the significant individual differences Roorda and Williams found. In one person, L cones outnumbered M cones four to one, while in a second person, L and M cones were equally numerous. Neither of these distributions necessarily represents an "abnormality." The genetic decision about whether a cone contains the L or the M photopigment is entirely probabilistic (Wang et al., 1999; McMahon, Neitz, and Neitz, 2004). In terms of the fine detail of the cone mosaic, every person's geographical layout of L and M cones is as unique as his or her fingerprints or iris pattern.

Because color appearance depends on the signals generated by the various cone types, color vision varies from one part of your retina to another. To demonstrate regional variations in color vision, one must stimulate different, very small regions of the retina. Employing this strategy, Williams, MacLeod, and Hayhoe (1981) presented tiny, brief, violet test flashes briefly superimposed on a steady yellow background, conditions that force an observer to rely on S cones to see the violet test stimulus. Measuring psychophysical thresholds at many different closely spaced regions on the retina, these investigators found pronounced variation in sensitivity from one region to another, including small islands where the test flash could not be seen at all (implying a complete absence of S cones within this region of the retina). The wide variations in threshold were found to be consistent even with testing that extended more than a year. These experimental results confirm that single S cones are separated by fairly large stretches of the retina in which there are no S cones at all.

In addition to light sensitivity, color appearance itself varies with the region stimulated. For example, a small light that appears greenish blue when imaged slightly away from the fovea will appear pure green when imaged directly *on* the fovea. This change reflects the diminished presence of S cones at the center of the retina. In addition, as that same light is moved into the periphery of the retina—where cones are less numerous—the light's color becomes less conspicuous. To sustain color perception in the periphery requires enlarging the size of the stimulus, to compensate for the reduced density of cones. Far into the periphery, where cones are widely separated from one another, vision becomes achromatic ("without color"). Thus, when an object is seen out of the corner of your eye, you may recognize its shape, but it will appear colorless.

You can use color plate 10 to see the consequence of having so few S cones in your fovea. Look at a region of the photograph where there is a blue patch in the quilt. At normal reading distance, the image of the blue patch will not only cover the region free of S cones (your fovea) but will also extend into regions that do contain S cones (around your fovea). Now, prop the book up, back away from the page, and continue staring at the blue patch. As

you get farther from the book, the image of the blue patch will get smaller on your retina, eventually shrinking so that it falls entirely within your fovea. As the image shrinks, the patch will cease to appear blue. Notice that at the same distance, though, the neighboring square continues to look green. This demonstration raises a paradox: When viewed from normal reading distance, why doesn't the blue patch appear less blue in its center? For one thing, we seldom hold our eyes perfectly steady, which means that the images of small, blue objects rarely remain centered on the fovea. For another, the visual system may assume that surface color is uniform within immediately neighboring parts of the image within the boundaries of a contour, thereby blurring small, local departures from uniformity associated with irregularities in the cone mosaic.

The variation in color appearance with retinal region or image size has practical consequences. For example, if two stimuli containing precisely the same wavelengths differ in size or in retinal location, their color appearances will also differ. As a result, even the most faithful photographic reproduction of a scene is bound to look different from the scene itself (Hurvich, 1981). (Recall from the discussion in Chapter 3 of spatial resolution that the density of cone photoreceptors is one factor governing the eye's resolving power, that is, it's acuity.) The large separations between S cones make it easy to understand why acuity with blue targets is much poorer than acuity with targets of other colors (Pokorny, Graham, and Lanson, 1968; Williams, MacLeod, and Hayhoe, 1981).

Because of their sparseness, S cones can also distort your perception of boundaries. And since boundaries contribute to the perceived shape of an object, the S cones can distort that perceived shape. Robert Boynton (1982) devised a compelling demonstration of this distortion, one version of which is given in color plate 14. Note first the pale yellow rectangle in the left half of the figure. The ink used to print the rectangle absorbs short-wavelength light and reflects longer wavelengths. This reflected light stimulates primarily M and L cones, hence its yellow appearance. However, the white paper around the rectangle reflects light more or less uniformly, thereby stimulating S as well as M and L cones. As a result, then, one side of the yellow-white boundary excites S cones while the other side does not.

To show how poorly the S cones register contour information, we've taken the same rectangle and drawn a squiggly black line around the outline of that rectangle. This is shown in the right half of color plate 14. Once again, prop the book open so you can see the color plate;

then walk slowly backward. You'll reach a distance at which the yellow-white boundary of the right-hand figure will appear squiggly rather than straight. The region outside the squiggly boundary appears white, while the region inside appears yellow. This means that some portions in and around the boundary that used to look white now look yellow, and vice versa. It is as if the yellow had spread outward toward the black squiggly line, and the white had spread inward. This spreading does not occur for all colors, only those differentially stimulating S cones on either side of a boundary.

In summary, then, the regional variations in the machinery of color vision underscore a theme running throughout this chapter: Color is a subjective experience that cannot be predicted based solely on the wavelength composition of the light reflected to the eye.

The Evolution of Cone Photopigments

Near the beginning of this chapter we asked "Why is it important to see colors?" Let's revisit that question now, drawing on insights from recent work on how color vision evolved over millions of years. This evolutionary perspective frames some intriguing possibilities about the purpose of color vision.

The normal human eye, as you now know, contains four types of photopigments, rhodopsin (in the rods), and three different cone photopigments. Genes, which are the basic units of inheritance, carry molecular instructions that guide a cell's manufacture of proteins, the building blocks of every living cell. Each gene is a chain of several thousand units of deoxyribonucleic acid (DNA); these are the instructions for protein manufacture.

In groundbreaking studies, Jeremy Nathans succeeded in isolating the genes responsible for instructing visual cells in the proper manufacture of S, M, and L pigments. Nathans (1999) showed that the gene for the S pigment is carried on chromosome pair number 7, while the genes for M and L pigments lie head to tail, next to one another on the X-chromosome. S, M, and L photopigments differ from one another because structurally different genes, and hence different instructions, control their manufacture. By analyzing the structural similarities among various genes and taking account of changes from mutation, one can create an evolutionary family tree (Jacobs, 1998). Two genes that are highly similar in structure are more likely to have been formed closer together in time than are two genes whose structures differ markedly.

Structural resemblances among the genes for rhodopsin and for the three cone pigments suggest all four photoreceptor pigments evolved from some common ancestor (Nathans, 1989). Ninety-six percent of the DNA sequence in the M-pigment gene is identical to that in the L-pigment gene. Interestingly, the S-pigment gene shares 42 percent of its sequence with rhodopsin, and almost exactly the same proportion with each of the L- and M-pigment genes.

This pattern of structural resemblances, supplemented by information on the variations in color vision of humans, nonhuman primates, and nonprimate mammals, suggests that long ago a single ancestor gene gave rise to all the modern photopigment genes. John Mollon argues that the original cone pigment probably had an absorption peak in the range of 510 to 570 nanometers (Mollon, 1989). This would harmonize the pigment's peak absorption with the spectral peak of light from the sun.

As we've already discussed, however, an eye with just one cone cannot be said to possess color vision. Much later, about 500 million years ago, the S cone came into existence. This new addition to retinas already possessing the original 510- to 570-nanometer pigment gave birth to color vision. The relative responses of two different photoreceptor types made it possible to extract some wavelength information from the incoming light. Note though, that S cones conferred color vision that was only dichromatic.

Finally, about 40 to 60 million years ago, the original type of cone, with its peak between 510 and 570 nanometers, is thought to have duplicated and differentiated, giving rise to both the L pigment and the M pigment, which are found in apes, in some species of monkeys (such as baboons and rhesus monkeys), and in humans. With the addition of this third cone type, color vision in primates attained trichromacy.[3]

Mollon (1989) put these evolutionary facts together with various creatures' food preferences to refine an intriguing account of the utility of color vision.[4] He proposed that our arboreal, primate ancestors developed a particular liking for certain nutritious fruits, especially orange and yellow ones. An eye with both L and M cones

---

[3]Not all primates have trichromatic vision. In virtually all the "new world" primates, such as owl and spider monkeys and marmosets, males have just a single photopigment in the medium- and long-wavelength portion of the spectrum, which makes them dichromatic; females, however, tend to be trichromatic (Tovee, 1994).

[4]The original version of this account should be credited to Stephen Polyak (1957), who discussed the evolutionary interdependence of colored fruits and primate color vision (p. 973). At the time Polyak was working, however, much less was known about the cone photopigments.

would be particularly adept at detecting such fruits within green foliage. This plausible claim has been proven experimentally in a study that compared the foraging behavior of dichromatic and trichromatic monkeys (Caine and Mundy, 2000).

A recent, detailed study of the red howler monkey (native to French Guiana) showed that its particular M and L cones are optimal for distinguishing that species' favorite fruits from the leaves of trees on which the fruit grows (Regan et al., 2001). Building on this connection between food preference and vision, Boycott and Wässle (1999) point out that trichromatic color vision could evolve only in a species whose eye and retina were already optimized for good visual acuity. Otherwise, mutations in the photopigments would never have a chance to communicate their unique messages to the brain. In an eye with only modest acuity, inputs from individual cone photoreceptors are spatially pooled, and the unique messages from a mutated cone pigment would be lost forever in the mix. It is intriguing to imagine that the world's colors appear as they do to us today because tens of millions of years ago our primate ancestors with excellent visual acuity received the gift of trichromacy as part of an implicit bargain with citrus trees: their fruit would nourish the primates, and by eating the fruit, the primates dispersed the seeds of that fruit.

Color's Opponent Character

We saw in Chapters 3 and 4 that information from the photoreceptors is transformed as it travels to the visual cortex. Messages from neighboring receptors are antagonistically organized into ON and OFF regions, which together comprise a neuron's receptive field. The characteristics of these receptive fields significantly affect the perception of visual form and brightness. So far in this chapter, we have concentrated on the initial stage of analysis of color information, an analysis performed by the three cone types. We now need to consider how messages from these three cone types are organized and modified at subsequent stages of the visual system. We can get some idea of this organization by considering several phenomena of color vision, all of which point to an opponent linkage, pitting one color against another.

What Is the Evidence for Color Opponency?

One phenomenon that suggests some kind of opponent connection between colors is **color contrast,** another example of color induction. Just as lightness contrast (described in Chapter 3) exaggerates lightness differences between adjacent objects, *color* contrast exaggerates their color differences (see Box 7.3). The major facts of color contrast have been known for a very long time. More than four hundred years ago, in his *Treatise on Painting,* Leonardo da Vinci, the scientist, engineer, and painter of the Mona Lisa, discussed color contrast:

> Of different colors equally perfect, that will appear most excellent which is seen near its direct contrary . . . blue near yellow; green near red: because each color is more distinctly seen, when opposed to its contrary, than to any other similar to it. (Quoted in Birren, 1941, p. 135)

Strong interaction between the color of an object and the color of its surround suggests some sort of antagonistic linkages within the visual machinery that processes color information.

You've already experienced another phenomenon that suggests color opponency, when you used color plate 6 to induce colored afterimages. Try the exercise again, staring at the fixation mark in the left-hand adaptation figure for 20 seconds and then shifting your gaze to the fixation mark in the right-hand test figure. Note that the afterimage produced by the yellow patch appears blue, whereas the one produced by blue appears yellow. By the same token, the afterimage of the red patch appears green, and vice versa. These color afterimages are consistent with the idea that the visual system treats certain colors as opponent pairs.

In color experience, blue and yellow are mutually exclusive: an object may appear blue or an object may appear yellow, but an object never appears *both* blue and yellow at the same time. Similarly, red and green are mutually exclusive: an object never appears *both* red and green. Of course, other combinations of these four colors are not mutually exclusive: Objects can be bluish green or reddish yellow. These observations suggest that the nervous system may treat red and green as one mutually antagonistic pair and blue and yellow as another such pair. These views were first articulated by Ewald Hering, a German physician of the nineteenth century. Hering made important contributions to nerve physiology, binocular vision, anatomy of the liver, and color vision, but he was so far ahead of his time that his contributions could not be properly assimilated into then current scientific thought. As a result, his contributions were either dismissed outright or misinterpreted (Hurvich, 1969). But Hering's views on color vision have been largely confirmed by subsequent discoveries, and his ideas were translated into modern terminology by Hurvich and Jameson (1957).

BOX 7.3 **Color Contrast**

You've probably had the experience of purchasing an article of clothing, such as a tie or a scarf, to go with an outfit in your closet. In the store, the tie or scarf looks neutral gray. But when you get home and try on the outfit, the article acquires a distinct color other than gray. Moreover, that distinct color seems to vary, depending on what outfit you wear it with. In other words, the color of the tie or scarf depends on what color is adjacent to it. This effect, demonstrated in color plate 15, is called *color contrast*, and it is a powerful influence in many everyday settings. The two squares marked by tiny black dots are physically identical, but the perceived difference in illumination makes them appear different. If you're skeptical that they are identical, get an index card or a piece of paper, cut two holes in it corresponding to the locations of these two portions of the image. Then, with the card or paper overlaid on the figure, view the two squares in isolation from their surrounding regions.

Some people have been able to capitalize on color contrast to enhance color perception. One such person was Michel Chevreul, director of the Gobelin Tapestry Works in Paris. Chevreul knew that interweaving just gray and red yarns could create tapestries that appeared to contain other colors as well, including distinct blue-green stripes—colors produced in the viewer's brain by color contrast. Chevreul developed a set of rules for ensuring that color contrast would have the effect his designers and weavers wanted. He went further, though, publishing a huge volume (1839/1967) that set out the basic rules of color harmony and contrast as they related to painting, interior decoration, printing, flower gardening, and dressmaking. In fact, the French Impressionist painters of the nineteenth century used Chevreul's book as a guide.

These principles anticipate the clever images devised by Edwin Land, the inventor of instant photography (the Polaroid camera) and synthetic polarizing material used in sunglasses and glare-reducing filters.* Land's published work on color vision contains many interesting demonstrations of color contrast. Let's consider a typical one here (Land, 1959). Land took two black-and-white slides of the same scene. One slide (the "red record") was taken with a red filter in front of the camera. The other (the "green record") used a green filter. Using a pair of slide projectors, Land superimposed the two black and white slides on a screen. Not surprisingly, since the slides were black-and-white, the result was a black-and-white image of the original scene. The surprise came when Land placed a red filter in front of the projector containing the red record. The image on the screen now consisted of various amounts of red light (from the projector with the red filter) mixed with various amounts of white light (from the other projector). One might expect that the only colors perceptible would be white, grays, blacks, and various shades of red. However, the image on the screen produced a wide range of colors—for example, a blonde-haired girl with pale blue eyes, a red coat, a blue-green collar, and natural flesh tones. Where had all these colors come from?

Land's surprising range of colors sprang mostly from color contrast (Walls, 1960). For instance, the girl's collar appeared blue-green because it was surrounded by the red of her coat. This could be verified by looking at the image of the collar through a narrow tube, which blocked the surrounding region from view. Now the collar appeared colorless, rather than blue-green.

Though Land's color demonstrations were surprising, perhaps they should not have been. More than 60 years earlier, the French photographer Ducos du Hauron had demonstrated basically the same phenomenon (Judd, 1960). Although not entirely novel, Land's color demonstrations serve one very useful purpose. They are a vivid reminder of how important contrast is in the everyday experience of the colors of objects.

---

*A prolific inventor, Land earned 535 U.S. patents, second only to the number of patents given to another great inventor, Thomas Alva Edison (McElheny, 1999).

Chromatic and Achromatic Systems

A combination of psychophysical and physiological studies has now established that signals from the three cone types are processed by one **achromatic system** and a pair of **chromatic systems.** The neural connections thought to underlie these three systems are sketched out in Figure 7.15 and in color plate 16. For diagrammatic simplicity, the schematic designs of the various systems in Figure 7.15 are shown separately, one in each panel of the figure. The boxes labeled "S cones," "M cones," and "L cones" represent the three cone types. Arrows emerging from any one of the boxes represent neural signals generated when cones of that type absorb light. Two different kinds of arrows are meant to suggest that the nervous system treats signals in two different ways, either adding them or taking their difference. When two signals

FIGURE 7.15 | Chromatic and achromatic channels generated by combining the signals from three cone types. The achromatic channel is represented in the top diagram, the blue-yellow chromatic channel in the middle diagram, and the red-green chromatic channel in the bottom diagram.

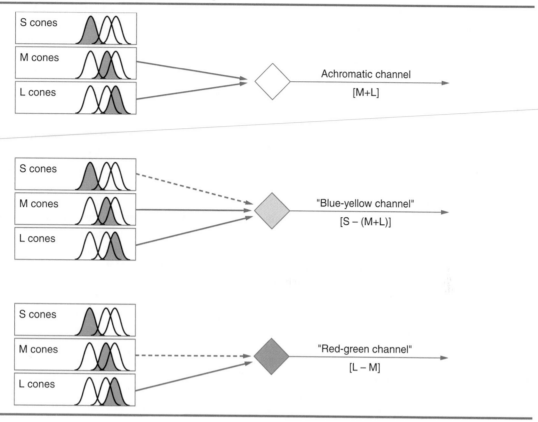

are represented by solid arrows, the system adds those two signals together; when one signal is shown as a solid arrow and another is shown as a dashed arrow, the system takes the difference between those two signals. Color plate 16 shows the same three channels in one schematic.

Before going into the details of this figure, we should remind you how the nervous system adds and subtracts. Recall, from Chapter 3, that addition is accomplished via spatial summation. This operation is carried out when one neuron sums the messages it receives from other neurons. Recall also that subtraction can be accomplished via an antagonism between ON and OFF signals. This operation is carried out when one neuron takes the difference between messages received from other neurons. So although the nervous system doesn't have access to a calculator, it can certainly add and subtract signals.

Return now to the discussion of Figure 7.15, seeing first how the achromatic system is constructed. In the top panel, solid arrows indicate that the signals generated by

M and L cones are added together. We can refer to the pathway carrying this sum to the brain as a *channel* (a set of nerve fibers bearing a shared message). Activity in this *achromatic channel* depends on the total excitation of M and L cones. There are various reasons for imagining that activity in this channel determines an object's visibility. For example, the shape of the photopic sensitivity curve (closely related to visibility) can be predicted by taking a sum of M and L cone responses (Smith and Pokorny, 1975; Werner et al., 1984). Note that by adding together M and L cone signals, this achromatic channel actually discards the wavelength information that it receives.

Turn now to the two chromatic channels of Figure 7.15.[5] According to the diagram, one of these channels represents

---

[5]Sometimes these channels are called the "blue-yellow" and "red-green" channels. Some researchers avoid these labels because, although the labels are short and convenient, they prefer to reserve color names to describe experiences, not neural activity.

the *difference* between S cone signals, on the one hand, and the *sum* of M and L cone signals, on the other. This channel signals the difference between short-wavelength stimulation and stimulation throughout the rest of the spectrum, so we'll refer to it as the **S − (M + L) channel.** The other chromatic channel signals the *difference* between the stimulation of the M cones and stimulation of L cones, which makes it the **M-L channel.**[6]

To see the implications of the cone combinations forming the different channels shown in Figure 7.15, consider how these various channels would respond when an eye is stimulated by light containing a wide range of wavelengths. This light, which appears white, would stimulate M and L cones to the same degree. As a result, the difference between their signals would be zero, resulting in no response in a channel that signaled the difference between those signals (the M-L channel). And this would be true regardless of the intensity of the light. Light that appears white would be similarly ineffective for the other chromatic channel, because that light excites its contributors equally well. Note, however, that the achromatic channel, which adds responses from M and L cones, would be strongly activated by this broadband light. In fact, the more intense this light, the greater the response in the achromatic channel.

The scheme outlined in Figure 7.15 gives a straightforward explanation of a puzzling observation mentioned previously in this chapter. Recall that hues drawn from the region near the middle of the spectrum (where light looks yellow) appear less saturated than hues drawn from the ends of the spectrum (where lights look blue and red). But why should one hue look more saturated than another? The scheme in Figure 7.15 gives a simple answer. A hue will appear desaturated (washed out) if it produces a strong response in the achromatic channel and at least some response in one of the chromatic channels. Note that if light produces a response in the achromatic channel but none in either chromatic channel, it will appear completely desaturated—white or some shade of gray. In contrast, a highly saturated hue results when a strong chromatic response is accompanied by a weak achromatic response. In general, the perceived saturation produced by light of any wavelength can be predicted by taking the ratio of the chromatic response it evokes to the achromatic response it evokes. For example, light that appears yellow

will seem relatively desaturated because such wavelengths (in the vicinity of 580 nanometers) elicit a weak chromatic response but a strong achromatic one.

How are the neural operations contained in the model in Figure 7.15 actually implemented in the visual pathways? It is to that question we turn next. By way of preview, the three channels shown in the figure are now thought to correspond to the three classes of neurons contained in the lateral geniculate nucleus (LGN), namely the magnocelluar neurons (M cells), the parvocellular neurons (P cells), and the koniocellular neurons (K cells). Specifically, the M cells are primarily sensitive to luminance information, independent of the wavelength of light. The M cells, in other words, are thought to embody the achromatic channel (L + M). The P cells in the LGN are sensitive to the relative amounts of red and green light, making them the appropriate neural substrate for one of the chromatic channels (L − M). The K cells, being sensitive to blue-yellow information, could provide the neural substrate for the other channel (S − [L + M]).[7] In a moment we'll look more closely at the physiological properties of the two chromatic channels, but first let's consider why the visual nervous system would go to the trouble of constructing these "opponent" chromatic channels that take the difference between cone signals. What is to be gained by doing this?

Opponent Processes and Efficiency of Coding

As we have discussed, converging lines of evidence—behavioral, physiological, and anatomical—imply that key attributes of color vision emerge from some opponent-process organization. What purpose is served by such a complex scheme? Although questions about the purpose of biological processes are difficult to answer unequivocally, it is instructive to speculate about the possible advantage vision gains from channeling signals into opponent streams.

Think first about the relations among the three types of cones found in the normal human eye. Because their absorption spectra overlap so much (see Figure 7.14), the cones will yield similar, though not identical, responses under many conditions. Computing the predicted response of each cone to various representative natural objects, one discovers that responses of the cones are very

---

[6]There is some evidence that the S cone signals add a small amount of signal to L cone signals in forming one of the chromatic channels. For simplicity, however, we shall label this channel "M-L" and ignore the small S contribution.

[7]In thinking about these relations between photoreceptor types and channels, it is important to keep your Ms straight: when talking about photoreceptors, *M* refers to medium wavelength sensitive cones, but when talking about LGN neurons, *M* refers to magnocellular cells.

highly correlated. The correlation is especially strong between the responses of M and L cones. So, under most circumstances, the nervous system gets little more information from analyzing both M and L cone signals than it would have gotten from analyzing just one. Because the nervous system has limited transmission and processing capacity, this considerable redundancy represents significant waste. But what are the alternatives? Theoretically, how could the redundancy be reduced?

To answer this question, Buchsbaum and Gottschalk (1983) analyzed statistically the responses generated by human cones while an eye viewed various natural scenes. From those responses, they derived a scheme that would minimize redundancy and allow the fibers in the optic nerve to carry as much color information as possible from retina to the brain. They found that a truly efficient arrangement would take the responses of the three cone types and transform them into three other signals. The converted signals, rather than the original ones, would then be fed to the brain. The best possible scheme turned out to be very much like the opponent-process system that we've described. When alternative designs were compared, the scheme illustrated in Figure 7.15, however complex it may seem, actually made the best possible use of the available photopigments. And behind this best possible system lies the neural machinery to which we turn now.

The Physiological Basis of Opponency

How does the nervous system accomplish the adding and subtracting implied by opponency? For an answer to this question, let's return to the LGN, the thalamic relay station that receives inputs from the retina and sends signals on to the visual cortex.

In a landmark series of experiments, Russell DeValois studied cells in the LGN of monkeys, whose trichromatic vision matches ours. He found that cells in the LGN could be divided into nonopponent and opponent types (DeValois and DeValois, 1975). The nonopponent cells responded as if they were adding signals from different types of cones while opponent neurons behaved as though they were subtracting signals from different types of cones. At the time DeValois performed his experiments, the physiological distinctions between M, P, and K cells in the LGN were yet to be discovered. Thus, DeValois was focusing exclusively on the responses of LGN cells to different patterns of chromatic stimulation. It remained for later workers to relate essential details of DeValois's findings to the different cell categories in the monkey LGN (Derrington, Krauskopf, and Lennie,

1984). Let's start by putting ourselves in DeValois's place, considering the different groups of cells he encountered as he recorded from monkey LGN cells. We'll start with the nonopponent cells.[8]

When light was shown on the retina, some nonopponent LGN cells responded by increasing their activity (ON cells), while others responded by decreasing their activity (OFF cells). Cells of the ON type gave ON responses to *all* wavelengths, though more strongly to some wavelengths than to others. Similarly, OFF cells gave OFF responses to all wavelengths, but again, in varying strengths. Together, such cells could constitute the achromatic channel represented in Figure 7.15; as mentioned previously, we now know that these nonopponent, achromatic cells comprise the magnocellular cells of the LGN.

DeValois observed that cells of the opponent type behaved differently. In this group, any cell could give either an ON response *or* an OFF response, depending on the wavelength of light with which it was stimulated. For example, some cells would increase their responses when long-wavelength light was present but decrease their responses when short-wavelength was present. The opposite pattern was also found: Reduced response with long-wavelength light and increased response with short-wavelength light. When light contained *both* long and short wavelengths, the ON and OFF responses tended to cancel each other and the cell gave little response. As far as the cell was concerned, the light never appeared.

If a cell gives an ON response in one portion of the spectrum and an OFF response in the other portion, there must be some transition wavelength at which the response changes from ON to OFF. DeValois found that opponent cells could be divided roughly into two groups, according to their transition wavelengths. For one group the transition occurred between the portion of the spectrum that appears green and the portion that appears red. Because these neurons seem to pit M-cone inputs against L-cone inputs, we can call them **M-L cells**—these, we now know, correspond to the parocellular cells of the LGN. For the other group, the transition occurred between the portion of the spectrum that appears blue and the portion that appears yellow. Because they behave as though S-cone signals were being pitted against signals from M and L cones, we can call these **S − (M + L) cells,** which today

---

[8]Primate retinas also contain both spectrally opponent and spectrally nonopponent cells (Gouras and Zrenner, 1981). Presumably these retinal ganglion cells are the origin of the opponent and nonopponent LGN cells studied by DeValois.

we identify with the K cells in the LGN (discussed in Chapter 4). Note that these two groups of cells link different regions of the spectrum in an opponent fashion. Such linkages are thought to be the realization of the two opponent channels schematized in Figure 7.15.[9]

We've already seen that the interplay between opponent and nonopponent channels can account for the way in which wavelength controls brightness and saturation. The interplay between these channels can account for other important phenomena of color perception, too. Using DeValois's results, we will consider some of these in detail. The curves in Figure 7.16 summarize some of DeValois's data. The curve labeled R represents the average response of M-L opponent cells to longer wavelength light. Note that in such cells the response begins at about 600 nanometers and grows with increasing wavelength. The curve labeled G represents the average response of these same M-L opponent cells to shorter wavelength light. Curves Y and B represent the responses of S − (M + L) opponent cells to longer and shorter wavelengths, respectively. How do these curves relate to color perception?

The simplest idea is that each curve corresponds to one particular color experience. For example, the G curve might correspond to the greenness evoked by various wavelengths. To examine the possible correspondence between the curves and color experience, let's consider the results of a color-naming experiment by Robert Boynton and James Gordon (1965). People were asked to name the color of briefly flashed lights whose wavelength varied randomly across the spectrum. To help quantify these color names, people were asked to use only the names *blue, green, yellow, red,* and various combinations of these names—such as *yellow-red* (meaning a red that was tinged with yellow).

Figure 7.17 shows the results. The horizontal axis shows the wavelength of light, and the vertical axis shows the tendency to use a given color name in describ-

[9]There is some question as to whether all opponent cells can be put into just two distinct categories (Zrenner, 1983). Moreover, DeValois's experiments were performed by uniformly illuminating an LGN cell's receptive field with lights of different wavelength. Recall from Chapter 4, though, that each LGN receptive field is divisible into spatially distinct center and surround regions. Physiologists have also discovered that in some LGN cells, the center region of the receptive field responds best to one wavelength of light, while the surround region responds to a very different wavelength. So the color opponency derived by DeValois is really combined with the spatial opponency defined by the center/surround layout of the receptive field. Their spatially organized color opponency makes these cells ideal contributors to color contrast (Lennie, 1984).

FIGURE 7.16 I   Responses of different LGN cells to light of various wavelengths.

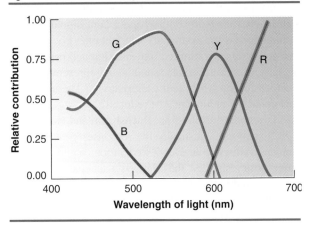

FIGURE 7.17 I   Proportion of trials on which different color names are assigned to various wavelengths.

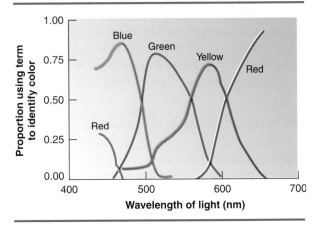

ing that wavelength. For example, the "green" curve reflects the use of the term *green* to describe color experience. Note that *green* is used to describe the visual effect of wavelengths ranging from about 470 to 600 nanometers. Toward the shorter wavelength portion of this range, *green* is modified by the term *blue.* In the longer wavelength portion of the range, *green* is modified by the term *yellow.* The visual experience evoked by light of 510 nanometers is described solely as green (the "green" curve reaches its maximum at 510 nanometers). The use of yellow peaks at about 580 nanometers, and the use of blue at about 460. Note that the "red" curve consists of two segments—one at the right (longer wavelengths) and one at the left (shorter wavelengths). This is quite understandable because very short wavelength light appears purple, a hue that can be produced by mixing a light that appears blue with a light that appears red.

Note the general correspondence between Boynton and Gordon's color-naming results (Figure 7.17) and the physiological results from LGN opponent cells in the monkey (Figure 7.16). The use of the name *green* by humans seems to correspond quite well to the response of M-L opponent cells to shorter wavelength light—the G curve in Figure 7.16. Similarly, the use of the name yellow resembles the Y curve in that figure. The correspondence is suggestive, but less satisfactory, between the use of the name *blue* and the B curve. Finally, at long wavelengths, the name *red* corresponds quite well to the R curve. However, the occasional use of the name *red* at short wavelengths has no counterpart in the way DeValois's cells responded. Nevertheless, there is, overall, a suggestive correspondence between color naming and the responses of opponent cells. Remember, though, that the LGN represents an intermediate stage in the neural pathways signaling color information (recall the K-cell and P-cell pathways discussed in Chapters 3 and 4). So it would be incorrect to conclude that color naming is the exclusive province of the LGN. Rather the LGN imposes an opponent organization on color processing that is passed on to higher stages and eventually reflected in our responses on perceptual tasks. This general correspondence between physiology and color naming, incidentally, dovetails with an idea presented early in this chapter: the major color categories—blue, green, yellow, and red—are universal and not simply a reflection of how people learn to use color terms.

So, at the level of the LGN, signals from the three cone signals have been recombined into three channels, one nonopponent and two opponent. To put it in other words, the trichromatic color system embodied by the cone photoreceptors is transformed into opponent color processing at subcortical stages of the visual pathways. These two stages—trichromatic and opponent—are summarized in color plate 17. But the story doesn't end here. In fact, we haven't really gotten to color vision yet, because at the level of the LGN neurons are still responding based on the wavelengths of light falling within the center and surround regions of the LGN cells. But color vision isn't just about wavelengths of light signaled by opponent processes; instead, color vision requires even more complex neural operations, which are carried out in the visual cortex. To understand what those additional, complex operations are achieving, we need to re-

visit the phenomenon of color constancy and consider yet another example of color induction. These phenomena of color vision point to potent contextual influences in color vision, influences that are worked out in the visual cortex, not in the retina or in the LGN.

Context and Color Vision

The retina and the LGN, as you now know, contain cells that respond selectively depending on the wavelength composition of the light falling on those cells' receptive fields. That's why we call them wavelength selective cells, and that's why they comprise components in the opponent color channels. But activity in those cells does not uniquely specify the color of objects seen in the environment. Why do we say this?

First, you've already learned that different spectral distributions of light can give rise to an unchanging impression of color. Thus, a yellow lemon continues to look yellow whether viewed under artificial fluorescent lighting (which has an abundance of energy in the short wavelength, blue region of the spectrum) or under natural sunlight (which has more energy in the middle- and long-wavelength regions of the spectrum). This invariance in color appearance is remarkable because the wavelength composition of light reflected from the lemon to your eyes is markedly different under these two viewing conditions. But if the wavelengths reaching the eyes are different under these two lighting conditions, how can the lemon's color remain constant? As discussed previously in this chapter, the visual system uses several "tricks" to discount variations in the illumination and, thereby, to promote constant perception of the object's color (yellow, in the case of the lemon). All of these tricks operate to register the wavelengths of light reflected from the lemon relative to—in the context of—wavelengths of light reflected from other, nearby objects.

The potency of context in color vision is dramatically illustrated by the color contrast phenomena illustrated in color plates 18 and 19. Look at color plate 18, created by Donald MacLeod: Compare the color appearance of the inner and outer thin rings. Both rings are printed with exactly the same ink, which means that both rings are reflecting exactly the same wavelengths of light. But the ring surrounded by blue looks more red and the one surrounded by red looks more blue. For another example of color contrast, look at color plate 19, created by Steven Shevell. Compare the colors of the word *COLOR* and the word *VISION;* they probably look distinctly different to you. In fact, both words are printed in identically colored ink, and to prove it look at the little colored bar connecting the letter *L* in "COLOR" with the second letter *I* in "VISION." The little bar confirms what your eyes and brain cannot believe. Likewise, compare the words *IS* and *AMAZING*. Again, they look different but they're printed in the same color ink, as confirmed by the little bar connecting the *I* and the *Z*. Monnier and Shevell (2004) showed that this kind of color induction could not be explained by the local contrast between neighboring regions in the figure or by the average color over the entire figure. Instead, they argue, local color appearance in this kind of display depends crucially on the spatial pattern of the figures (letters, in this case) within the display. And they believe this spatial interaction can be explained only by the kinds of neural interactions seen in the visual cortex (see review by Wachtler, Albright, and Sejnowski, 2001).

Color contrast can be construed as the converse of color constancy: With color contrast, identical spectral distributions of light are producing differences in color appearance (e.g., the two physically identical rings in color plate 18 look different in color) whereas with color constancy, different spectral distributions of light are producing the same color appearance (the lemon looks yellow despite changes in the illumination). But despite their seemingly opposite effects, both phenomena are pointing to the same conclusion: Color appearance is not determined solely by the wavelength of light reflected from a given region of an object but, instead, is context dependent. To find color-selective neurons whose responses are appropriately context dependent, we must move further up the visual pathways, into the visual cortex.

Cortical Mechanisms of Color Vision

So, to review, two pathways arising in the retina and passing through the LGN carry color signals to the cortex. One is the K-cell system, which innervates cortical cells in the upper layers of V1. The other is the P-cell system, which innervates cells in layer 4 of V1. As explained earlier, the K- and P-cell pathways divvy up the two opponent signals between them, each carrying one type of signal to the primary visual cortex. And what happens to color information within visual cortex?

To answer that question, let's start by asking how many cells in visual cortex respond selectively based on color. We will adopt the definition of selectivity endorsed by Gegenfurtner (2003) in his review of cortical mechanisms of color vision. According to that definition, a cell qualifies as color selective if its responsiveness is reduced

upon introduction of red, green, blue, or yellow light into its receptive field; such a reduction in response would be indicative of subtractive interaction among signals generated by the different cone types. Defined in this way, about half of all cells sampled in primary visual cortex are color selective (Shapley and Hawken, 2002), and this percentage stays roughly the same when the samples are taken from other visual areas closely interconnected with V1 (including areas V2, V3, and V4). Unlike cells in the LGN, many color-selective cells in visual cortex respond only within a relatively narrow range of wavelengths. Moreover, the preferred wavelengths of these color-selective cortical cells are not clustered around red/green or blue/yellow, as they are within cells in the LGN. Instead, preferred wavelengths are distributed more evenly among cortical cells throughout the entire region of the color spectrum (e.g., Xiao, Wang, and Felleman, 2003).

Even more importantly, many cortical cells within these early cortical areas, including some in V1, respond as if they were signaling the color *appearance* of a surface, not the *wavelength* composition of the light reflected from that surface (Zeki, 1980). Thus, these cells exhibit color constancy in that their responses can remain invariant despite changes in the wavelength composition of the stimulus activating them. Moreover, they can also exhibit color contrast, in that their responses vary despite unchanging wavelength composition when the evoking stimulus is presented within a larger color context that changes over time (Schein and Desimone, 1990). For these reasons, it is tempting to conclude that these cells are directly involved in specifying an object's surface color.

Brain-imaging studies point to the existence of populations of color-selective neurons in human visual cortex. Several distinct human brain areas concerned with color vision have been identified using PET and fMRI techniques (see reviews by Hadjikhani et al., 1998, and by Wade et al., 2002). Some of these areas, including V1 and V2 (Engel, Zhang, and Wandell, 1997) are activated when people merely look at an array of colored patches. Other areas, however, are activated only when people are asked to attend to and identify colors (Gulyas and Roland, 1994). Among several human visual areas reliably activated by chromatic stimulation is one situated along the inferior (lower) part of the cerebral hemisphere near the juncture of the occipital and temporal lobes. This region could correspond to area V4, which has been identified and studied in monkey visual cortex. In general, human color-selective regions are found within that chain of visual areas collectively termed the temporal (or ventral) pathway (recall Figure 4.20). The inclusion of color processing within the ventral pathway fits nicely with the presumed role of that pathway: specifying the shape, surface characteristics and, hence, the identity of objects. Within this hierarchy is there a single area that deserves to be called the *color center* of the brain? Probably not—instead, color arises from activity distributed throughout this hierarchy of ventral pathway areas (Gegenfurtner, 2003; Wandell, 2000).

Abnormalities of Color Perception

Previously you learned that within the normal population of trichromats, not everyone sees color in precisely the same way. A surface that appears pure yellow to you may have a slight greenish tint to a friend, all because the two of you have slightly different cone photopigments. Even more striking, though, are those individuals whose color vision deviates dramatically from the norm. People with such variations are described as "color deficient" (popularly, but wrongly, called "color blind"). Consideration of color deficiency enhances understanding of normal color vision and also reinforces Newton's insight, mentioned earlier, that "the rays are not coloured."

Color deficiency can take different forms, some attributable to hereditary factors and others acquired during an individual's lifetime owing to eye disease, brain damage, or abnormal early visual experience. In the following sections, we consider these various forms of color deficiency.

Congenital Color Deficiency

The prevalence of hereditary color deficiency varies among populations. For example, 8 out of every 100 Caucasian males, 5 out of every 100 Asiatic males, and 3 out of every 100 African-American and Native-American males are color deficient. Within all these groups, the incidence of color deficiency is much lower in females than in males. For instance, Caucasian females are 10 times less likely to be color deficient than are males (Hurvich, 1981).

Although color deficiency has probably been around for millions of years, the first recorded descriptions of the problem do not appear until the end of the eighteenth century. Among the first reports of color deficiency was one made by the English scientist John Dalton late in the eighteenth century. You may recognize Dalton's name. He's the scientist responsible for developing the atomic theory, and the unit of molecular weight is named in his honor. Because Dalton was a person of considerable distinction,

his description of his own "shortcoming" was all the more interesting and noteworthy. Dalton wrote of himself:

> I was always of the opinion, though I might not mention it, that several colours were injudiciously named. . . . All crimsons appear to me to consist chiefly of dark blue: but many of them seem to have a tinge of dark brown. I have seen specimens of crimson, claret, and mud, which were very nearly alike. Crimson has a grave appearance, being the reverse of every shewy and splendid colour. Woolen yarn dyed crimson or dark blue is the same to me. (1798/1948, p. 102)

Dalton was a keen observer of his own experiences, but he had a very mistaken idea about the cause of his visual abnormality. He reckoned that the vitreous humor of his eye was tinted blue, thus absorbing longer wavelengths of light and, thereby, distorting his color perception. A postmortem dissection of Dalton's eyes, performed in accord with his prearranged request, demolished his own theory posthumously. His vitreous was normal for a man his age (Sharpe and Nordby, 1990). In fact, we now know that Dalton's odd color vision was rooted in his retina. About 150 years after Dalton's death, a team of molecular geneticists and psychologists working in England took a small tissue sample from Dalton's preserved eye and used the sample to identify Dalton's DNA sequence (Hunt et al., 1995). On the X-chromosome (where the genes for L and M cones reside), they found only genes specifying the opsin associated with the L cone. This makes it certain that while Dalton was alive, his eye lacked M-cone photopigments, which posthumously settles the diagnosis of Dalton's color deficiency.

There are several reasons why color deficiency such as Dalton's went unnoticed for so long. First, very few people are completely color blind, meaning that they can't see colors at all. The more common forms of color deficiency are not especially dramatic. These people do see color but in ways that differ from the norm. Second, many color-deficient people simply don't notice that their use of color names differs from that of other people. Third, most color-deficient people manage to compensate for their deficiency. When driving automobiles, people who cannot distinguish reds from greens may still know when to stop and when to go based on which light—top or bottom—is lit in a traffic signal. Also, a person who confuses reds and greens may be able to distinguish a red shirt from a green one because they differ in lightness (Jameson and Hurvich, 1978). Sometimes, though, lightness differences are not adequate substitutes for color. John Dalton, in fact, learned this to his dismay. A Quaker, Dalton was supposed to wear subdued clothing, preferably black. As a result, his friends were shocked when he paraded around in his crimson academic robes, which he believed were black.

Because color and lightness normally covary, special test materials must be designed so that lightness does not provide a clue to color. One of the most widely used color tests consists of a series of figures defined by dots differing from one another only in hue, not in lightness. Unless a person can distinguish the color of the dots defining the figure from the color of the dots defining the background, the figure will be invisible. For example, when the figure is red and the surround is green, people with normal color vision will be able to identify the figure, whereas people who confuse reds and greens will not. As a consequence, the test picks out people who have one particular kind of color deficiency, one involving red–green confusions. To detect forms of color deficiency involving other confusions, colors other than red and green would have to be used for the figure and its surround.

Color plate 20 shows a couple of test plates from the widely used Ishihara Color Blindness Test. Look at the two circular regions and note the digit or digits that you see within each. Viewers with normal color vision will see a single numeral in the left-hand circle and two numerals in the right-hand circle. People who make red–green color confusions will have trouble seeing any numerals. Also, variant forms of red–green color blindness, which we'll discuss later, permit either only the left digit or only the right digits to be seen.

Neural Bases of Congenital Color Deficiency   In some forms of congenital color deficiency the eye has the normal number of cones, but it performs as though it had fewer than three *types* of cones. In fact, this is exactly how color deficiency was explained by Helmholtz, one of the coauthors of the trichromatic color theory. We've already noted that an eye containing just two types of cones would be *dichromatic.* This means that the eye would require just two different wavelengths to match the appearance of any other wavelength. Since the normal, trichromatic eye—one with three types of cones—requires three different wavelengths to make such matches, many matches that are satisfactory to the dichromatic eye are unsatisfactory to a trichromatic one. For example, to a dichromat who is missing L cones, all three rectangles in color plate 21 appear to be of the same color. Unless you are that same type of dichromat, the rectangles won't look even vaguely alike.

Although genetic mistakes can eliminate any one of the three cone types, they predominantly eliminate either M or L cones, not the S cones. When either M or L cones are missing, middle and long wavelengths will be confused with each other. However, all of these wavelengths will be distinguishable from short wavelengths. Dichromatic color deficiencies caused by the absence of either M or L cones are lumped together under the rubric *red–green deficiency.* This, incidentally, is the form of dichromacy John Dalton had.

In a much rarer form of dichromacy, S cones are missing. Here, lightness perception is unaffected because S cones make no contribution to perceived lightness, and discriminations among middle and long wavelengths are normal because M and L cones are unaffected.

People categorized as dichromats make another kind of color confusion characteristic of a two-cone eye. We pointed out earlier that eyes with only two cone types should experience a neutral point in the spectrum, a single wavelength that looks achromatic. People with dichromatic color vision show precisely such neutral points. However, the wavelength at which the neutral point occurs varies depending on their form of dichromacy.

In addition to dichromatic color deficiencies, there are other, even more common color abnormalities that we haven't mentioned. People with one of these common abnormalities have color vision that is an unusual form of trichromacy. These people are not dichromats. Their spectrum shows no neutral point, and color matches that satisfy dichromats fail to satisfy them. As they require three separate lights to match any hue they can see, their color perception is trichromatic. However, their color matches will not look satisfactory to someone with normal trichromatic vision. Because in these instances color vision is trichromatic but anomalous, the condition is termed *anomalous trichromacy.* The anomaly arises from the abnormal absorption curve of one of the three cone pigments (Dartnall, Bowmaker and Mollon, 1983).

Figure 7.18 summarizes the discussion to this point, giving the technical names for various forms of color abnormality, the color confusions associated with each, and prevalence rates in North America and Western Europe (Alpern, 1981).

What Does the World Look Like to a Color-Blind Person?
It is natural to wonder what the world looks like to a person with dichromatic color vision. (Keep in mind that most mammals with color vision are dichromats.) And if you're one of those relatively rare human dichromats, don't you sometimes puzzle about what others are seeing that you don't?

FIGURE 7.18 | Major genetic color deficiencies.

NAME	CAUSE	CONSEQUENCES	PREVALENCE
DICHROMACIES			
Protanopia	Missing L-type pigment	Confuses 520–700 Has neutral point	M: 1.0% F: 0.02%
Deuteranopia	Missing M-type pigment	Confuses 530–700 Has neutral point	M: 1.1% F: 0.1%
Tritanopia	Missing S-type pigment	Confuses 445–480 Has neutral point	Very rare
ANOMALOUS TRICHROMACIES			
Protanomaly	Abnormal L-type pigment	Abnormal matches Poor discrimination*	M: 1.0% F: 0.02%
Deuteranomaly	Abnormal M-type pigment	Abnormal matches Poor discrimination*	M: 4.9% F: 0.04%

Note: "M" indicates males; "F" females. Wavelengths that are confused are given in nanometers. An asterisk (*) means that only some members of this group exhibit this problem.

These are tricky questions to answer. We can't rely on color vision tests for the answer, because these tests only tell us which particular colors cannot be distinguished from one another. Those tests tell us nothing about what the visible colors look like to a trichromat or a dichromat. Nor will we be able to know what colors look like by talking about our color experiences. The color of an object that you and a friend both call "green" may appear quite different to the two of you. But because you've both learned to apply that color name to the object, you'll always agree what color to call it.

We get some inkling of what it must be like to have deficient color vision by reading accounts by those color-deficient people who are unusually keen observers. The physician Robert Currier, for example, has written a vivid account of his visual experiences as a red-green dichromat (1994). From his words we can imagine how frustrating it would be to select clothes, match socks, and try to read a colored text. An even more colorless world is experienced by individuals who are truly color blind, meaning they have only one type of cone photoreceptor. Nordby (1990) provides an autobiographical account of the everyday challenges created by this rare condition. But in the final analysis, these first-person accounts, too, boil down to descriptions of colors that are confused and those that are not. We can never know if Currier's blue is our blue.

A group of European investigators took a different approach to the question of color appearance (Vienot et al., 1995). Using digitized color images, they simulated what the world might look like to each of the three categories of dichromats. They began with a normal, digitized trichromatic picture, and divided the picture's color palette into two regions. The dividing line between these regions was the neutral point for the type of dichromacy being simulated. This neutral point varies, depending on whether it's the S, M, or L-cone type that is missing. Next, the color of each pixel in the digitized original was replaced with one of two hues, with the substituted hue depending on whether the wavelength in the original picture is shorter than the neutral point or longer than the neutral point. For people lacking the L-type and M-type cone pigments, the two substitution colors corresponded to what we would call blue and yellow respectively. For people missing the S cone, the corresponding colors were blue-green and pinkish red. Then, throughout the modified picture, the saturations of the two colors were adjusted according to which cone types were present in the simulated dichromat.

The results of this simulation applied to a photograph of a scene are shown in color plate 22. As you can see, the range of color experiences is compressed, and the colors of different objects in some parts of the scene are indiscriminable (for example, the flowers and leaves in the protanopes' view).[10] Still, vision isn't seriously compromised, and the day-to-day activities of people with one form or another of color deficiency are not compromised. There are, however, some professions where color deficiency can be very serious. For example, color vision plays an important role in some types of medical diagnosis, which means that color deficiency can be a serious handicap for health-care specialists (Spalding, 2004). For more on what the world looks like to a color-deficient person, navigate to www.mhhe.com/blake5 and check the color deficiency links.

Congenital Supernormality?   The relative rarity of color-blind females provides an important clue about the genetics of color vision, both normal and abnormal. Sex-linked patterns of inheritance, color defects included, implicate the X-chromosome, and molecular biological studies have pinpointed locations on the X-chromosome where the critical DNA may be found. This same work raises an intriguing possibility, namely that some among us may actually possess color vision that is superior to the normal trichromatic variety. Here are the clues leading to that speculation.

Females have two X-chromosomes, one inherited from each parent, but males have only one X-chromosome, inherited from their mothers. Earlier we noted that anomalous trichromacy involves errors in the production of photopigments that are coded by genes on the X-chromosome. As a result, a male anomalous trichromat had to inherit the anomaly from his mother, who must have had an abnormal gene on one of her X-chromosomes. Suppose that her other X-chromosome was normal, meaning that it instructed the manufacture of normal M and L pigments. What can we say about the color vision of this female, who has one normal and one anomalous X-chromosome?

Early in any female's embryonic development, half of her X-chromosomes are inactivated permanently (Gardner and Sutherland, 1989). The selection of which X-chromosome is shut off in any cell seems to be random. But once an X-chromosome is inactivated, that same X-chromosome remains inactive in every descendant cell throughout the female's life. Inactivation serves an important developmental function. With twice as many X-chromosomes as males, females also have twice as many X-linked

genes—and, potentially, instructions to produce twice as many X-linked proteins. Inactivation of half the X-chromosomes, then, maintains parity between the sexes.

Returning to the mother of the anomalous trichromat, random inactivation would, in different cells, turn off approximately half of her normal X-chromosomes and half of her anomalous ones. Because different embryonic cells give rise to photoreceptors in disparate retinal regions, her retina would resemble a mosaic of different tiles, with normal regions interspersed among anomalous regions. Taking account of both normal and anomalous patches, her entire retina has four different photopigments: in one patch, normal S, M, and L pigments, and in another patch, normal S, M, (or L) pigments along with an anomalous pigment whose absorption peak is distinct from the others.

Mollon (1990) has speculated on the visual and evolutionary significance of four-pigment color vision in humans. In females with four photopigments, color vision might be as superior to the "normal" variety as the "normal" variety is to the color vision of a dichromat. Four-pigment color vision, described as *tetra*chromatic, might give certain females a real biological advantage, making it possible for them to recognize subtle color differences that so-called normals, male or female, could not. These tetrachromatic females might even be supernormal mothers because their extra-good color vision might enable them to spot subtle complexion changes when their children were becoming ill. But, Mollon conjectures, tetrachromatic vision's real evolutionary advantage would have come when our ancestors hunted for food. On such hunts, their superior color vision might have made valuable tribal leaders of these tetrachromatic females. It would have been they who guided the tribe toward sought-after ripening fruit on the trees of those prehistoric forests.[11]

Acquired Color Abnormalities

The color abnormalities just discussed are genetic in origin. But not all color vision problems are genetic; some fairly common ones are *acquired*. Because normal color perception depends on a whole series of neural events—starting in the retina and continuing back to the brain—disturbance in any part of the chain can alter color perception. In this section, we'll consider acquired color abnormalities arising from eye disease and from brain damage.

---

[10]As the team of individuals producing this picture acknowledges, the validity of this simulation rests on several assumptions. Still, the technique offers promise as a means for adjusting colors used on signs and video displays to ensure that important visual information is seen by all people, normal and color deficient.

[11]Thompson, Palacios, and Varela (1992) give an excellent treatment to several issues in color vision, including differences among color vision in various species and how evolution has shaped those differences.

Ocular Disorders   Some common diseases, including glaucoma and diabetes, affect the integrity of S cones, thereby disturbing color vision (Adams et al., 1982). Diabetes often changes the structure of the eye in ways that can be seen using an ophthalmoscope: The retinal vasculature exhibits swellings and abnormal growth. Glaucoma is detected by measuring the pressure within the eye. By the time these conditions are discovered, permanent damage to the retina may have already occurred. For that reason, it is fortunate that abnormalities of color vision typically precede the appearance of notable structural changes in the eye. Color vision tests, if performed early enough in the progress of the disease, can be helpful in the diagnosis and treatment of glaucoma (Sample, Boynton, and Weinreb, 1988) and diabetes (Zisman and Adams, 1982).

In both diseases, changes in color vision are retinal in origin. In other cases, however, acquired abnormalities of color vision can be caused by disturbances in the optic nerve rather than in the retina. For example, alcoholics frequently exhibit a reduced sensitivity to long wavelengths, causing reds to appear dark and desaturated. This change in color vision reflects a dietary deficiency. The typical alcoholic doesn't get sufficient vitamin B12 in his or her diet to ensure proper optic nerve function. Supplements of B12 restore normal color vision. Besides alcohol, certain toxins such as carbon disulfide (a substance used in the manufacture of insecticides and rubber) can disturb color vision. In each of these conditions, the onset of abnormal color vision can serve as an early warning of a threat to health.

Though the aforementioned forms of acquired color deficiency are relatively rare, there is another form that affects nearly everyone sooner or later. Once people reach about 50 years of age, the crystalline lens of the eye begins to accumulate a pigment that absorbs short-wavelength light more than it does the rest. This pigment serves a useful function by screening out ultraviolet radiation that could damage the already fragile retinas of older people. However, because short wavelengths appear blue, the world's colors look different when seen through an older lens, which selectively reduces the short wavelength light that reaches the retina. Blues look darker, and they tend to be confused with greens (Weale, 1982). The tendency of older people to confuse some blues and greens can have serious consequences. For example, an aging crystalline lens could cause someone to mistake one type of medicine tablet or capsule for another (Hurd and Blevins, 1984).

Brain Damage   In Chapter 4, you were introduced to the condition called achromatopsia, loss of color vision from brain damage. Because other aspects of vision remain relatively normal in individuals with achromotoposia, it is natural to assume that the brain damage has destroyed a visual area indispensable for the experience of color. What follows is an abbreviated history of one individual in whom damage to the cerebral cortex produced substantial color-vision deficiency. This case is particularly interesting because the damaged region has been pinpointed by neuroimaging. (A detailed description of this case has been given by Pearlman, Birch, and Meadows, 1979.)

The patient was a man in his mid-fifties who had been a customs inspector before he became ill. To get that job, he had taken a color vision test, which he had passed without difficulty. Following a stroke, he persistently claimed that he couldn't see colors. He likened the problem to watching a black-and-white movie. Although his general health and cognitive abilities remained sound, he was forced to take another job that did not require color judgments. In addition, his deficient color vision interfered with his personal daily routine. For instance, he had to rely on his wife to select his clothes, to avoid wearing weird color combinations, and he was unable to distinguish ripe from unripe fruit.

Following his stroke, this man retained good memory for colors, as evidenced by his ability to associate objects and colors. When shown a black-and-white outline drawing of familiar objects, he could readily say what color each *should* be. But when he attempted to color the outline drawing using felt-tip pens, he was unable to select the appropriate colors. An example of his results are shown in color plate 23. This page from a children's coloring book was colored eight years after his stroke using the pens shown in the upper part of the picture. He needed 30 minutes to complete this effort, spending most of this time comparing the various pens before selecting one. Despite the obvious color confusions evidenced in this picture, the man confidently stated that tomatoes should be red, carrots orange, and so on. He wasn't sure, though, whether he had actually selected the appropriate colors.

Other, more formal tests confirmed that this person possessed very poor color discrimination over the whole spectrum. In this respect, his performance differed from that of people with congenitally defective color vision. Congenital color blindness, as you will learn in a moment, usually involves color confusions within a restricted region of the spectrum. These forms of color blindness are present from birth and stem from a deficiency in a particular cone photopigment. In contrast, the person described here had perfectly normal color vision prior to his stroke. Moreover, the stroke affected only his *perception* of color—acuity and depth perception remained normal. Brain-scan images from this patient reveal damage within a region just in front of the primary visual cortex, in a position consistent with projections of the ventral pathway.

In recent years, equally intriguing cases of achromatopsia have been detailed (e.g., Gallant, Shoup, and Mazer, 2000), including the famous "color-blind" painter studied by neurologist Oliver Sacks (1995). In virtually all of these clinical cases, the condition is indeed caused by damage to those portions of the occipital and temporal lobes that form the ventral pathway (Cowey and Heywood, 1997). However, not all aspects of color vision are equally affected. In a study of 27 patients with brain damage to restricted regions within the visual cortex, Rüttiger and colleagues (1999) found that color constancy could be destroyed (meaning that color appearance of a test figure varied with changes in the wavelength composition of the illuminant) while color discrimination (the ability to distinguish subtle differences in color) and color naming remained normal. Different aspects of color vision, in other words, seem to arise within different stages of the ventral stream pathway.

We'll close this section by considering yet another form of acquired color deficiency, this one attributable to abnormal visual experience early in life.

Abnormal Early Visual Experience As young infants we all lived in environments illuminated with broad spectrum light that provided strong, simultaneous stimulation of all three cone types. This means that the chromatic and achromatic channels were being fed a steady diet of L, M, and S cone signals, and in response to the outputs from those channels our brains were being challenged to create color impressions not strictly tied to the wavelengths of light being reflected from objects (recall color constancy and color induction).

As it turns out, we were very fortunate to experience broad spectrum light during infancy, for otherwise we could all be victims of deficient color vision. We know this to be true from a recent study by Sugita (2004), who raised four Japanese monkeys (*Macaca fuscata*) under very unusual conditions of illumination. Reared in ordinary lighting conditions, members of this species develop normal trichromatic color vision, but these four infant monkeys experienced something very different for the first years of their lives. Beginning at one month of age, the infant monkeys lived in a room that was lit for 12 hours a day by monochromatic light that switched unpredictably among four wavelength values: 465, 517, 592, and 641 nanometers. (These values correspond to colored light we would call blue, green, yellow, and red, respectively.) So over time all three cone types in their eyes received strong stimulation, but never all at the same time, and never with the patterns of stimulation produced by broad-spectrum, "white" light.

At one year of age, these animals were tested behaviorally on a variety of standard color vision tasks. Compared to normally reared monkeys (and to humans), these four had highly abnormal color vision. First, it took them tens of thousands of trials to master a simple color-matching task that the normal monkeys performed effortlessly. (This task involved touching one of two color chips that matched the color of a third chip.) Second, the specially reared monkeys produced color categories that departed markedly from those ordinarily generated by trichromatic viewers, for whom colors cluster into one of three categories (reddish, greenish, and bluish). Third, and most dramatically, the four monkeys gave no evidence of color constancy, meaning that their judgments of color appearance, unlike that of their normally reared relatives, was highly susceptible to variations in the wavelength composition of the illuminant. These animals were not able to use the overall color appearance of an array of objects to "figure out" the nature of the illuminant and recalibrate their perception of surface color so that it corresponded to the object's actual color. These profound deficits did not disappear once the animals moved into a normally illuminated environment, implying that they had missed out on vital color experience during an early, critical stage of development.

It is important to note that these deficits are not attributable to abnormalities in the cone photoreceptors themselves, for each of the three classes of cones received a strong diet of stimulation throughout the monkeys' lives. Rather, the deficit must stem from the brain's failure to develop the neural circuits needed to form color categories and to generalize those categories across different patterns of illumination.

Fortunately, we live in environments where this kind of abnormal early visual experience is not a concern. But there are everyday situations where we may be exposed to a limited range of colored light for a prolonged period of time. For example, imagine wearing a pair of sunglasses with a distinctly red tint. This red tint means that the lenses are acting like filters that selectively block short- and middle-wavelength light from reaching your eyes, but allowing long wavelength light through. When you first put on the glasses, the world will look reddish to you, but after a short time you lose awareness of this shift in overall color. Once you take off the glasses, however, the entire world will have a bluish green tint to it. Jay Neitz and colleagues (2002) have systematically studied these temporary shifts in color vision produced by wearing colored filters, and they conclude that color perception can be modified by experience even in adults. Why do these shifts occur?

According to Neitz, the visual system assumes that the light illuminating the environment is always broadband "white" light, and when we wear filters that disrupt that whiteness the visual system simply recalibrates the relative strengths of the signals from the L, M, and S cones to recover a balance that yields an overall equal response from each cone type. Neitz and colleagues conclude that this recalibration process takes place in the brain, not in the eye, because one can wear a red filter over just one eye (with the other eye closed), and then observe the effects of that exposure in the previously closed eye. This transfer between the eyes implies that the adjustments are occurring at a location in the visual system where information from the two eyes has been combined, that is, in binocular cells that are only found in the visual cortex.

Let's finish the chapter by describing one other, fascinating form of "abnormal" color vision, this one involving perception of colors arising entirely from within the mind's eye.

Chromatic Synesthesia

Look at Figure 7.19. What colors do you perceive when you look at the letters? Almost everyone will readily answer black—in terms of their color, all the alphabetic characters look the same. But a few rare individuals will see things very differently. For them, the letters in Figure 7.19 will appear vividly colored, with each letter having its own unique color. These individuals are experiencing what is termed **synesthesia,** which literally means "mixture of the senses." Synesthesia can take on various forms, with some people seeing colors when looking at letters and others seeing colors when hearing musical notes. And not all forms of synesthesia involve illusory perception of color. For example, some synesthetic individuals experience touch sensations when they taste objects (Cytowic, 2003). For our purposes, we're going to focus on the form of synesthesia where people see colors when looking at letters or numbers (*color graphemic* synesthesia, as it's called).

FIGURE 7.19 | What colors are the letters appearing in this figure? Most people would agree that they're all black, but a small fraction of individuals would describe the colors as red, green, orange, blue, and all sorts of other hues. These rare individuals have a condition known as color-graphemic synesthesia, illusory colors triggered by viewing letters or numbers. To see the colors experienced by one such individual, look at color plate 24.

A B C D E F G H I J K L M N O P Q R S T U V W X Y Z

We must stress that each synesthetic individual tends to have his or her own unique associations between letters. For some, the letter *F* might appear red, for others it would appear blue, and for still others it would be green. But for any given individual, the colors linked to given letters remain the same over time. Synesthetic colors are highly reliable for a given individual, and these individuals report having experienced these colors since they were young children. Color plate 24 shows the color associations for one college-aged woman who has been studied extensively by one of the coauthors of this textbook and his colleagues (Blake et al., 2005).

For those of us who do not experience synesthesia, these "color" experiences seem bizarre, and one is tempted to characterize the colors as illusory because the physical stimulus conditions ordinarily associated with color perception are certainly not present. But, in fact, there are good reasons to believe that the "illusory" colors experienced by synesthetic individuals are as real as the colors the rest of us experience when looking at letters and numbers that are *really* colored. Here are some of those reasons.

First, synesthetic colors can promote perceptual grouping, in the same way that real colors can. Look at Figure 7.20 and see how long it takes you to identify the shape depicted in this figure. With time and effort, you can eventually discern that the figure is a triangle, defined by the cluster of Fs embedded in the background of Es. To identify this figure, you had to scrutinize the individual letters to figure out which ones go with one another. People with synesthesia, however, can identify the shape rapidly and effortlessly, because to them the cluster of Fs differ in color from the background of Fs and, therefore, the Fs group together effortlessly to form a

FIGURE 7.20 | Contained within this array of letters is a simple shape. All of us can identify the shape eventually, by figuring out which letters go with one another and then discerning the shape of the region within which those letters are contained. People with color-graphemic synesthesia can see the shape immediately, without effort, because the letters evoke colors, and the color associated with the letters defining the shape group together and stand out from the background, which has a different color. Color plate 25 shows what this figure looks like to a synesthetic observer who sees Ys as red and Vs as green.

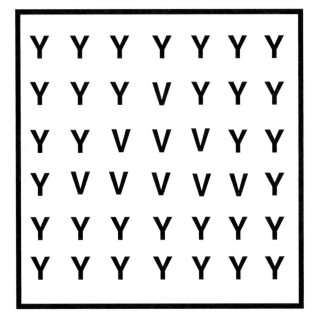

triangle. To see a simulation of what a synesthetic observer would experience when looking at Figure 7.20, look at color plate 25. Notice in that color plate how the figure stands out conspicuously because of the color difference between the numerals defining the figure and the numerals defining the background.

A second reason for believing that synesthetic colors are perceptually "real" is that a synesthetically colored letter will pop out from an array of other letters that have different synesthetic colors. This pop out effect makes it much easier for synesthetic observers to search for a target letter among a large array of distracting letters (Palmeri et al., 2002; Laeng et al, 2004).

Synesthetic colors are vivid and highly saturated, not vague and washed out in appearance. For some individuals who see colored letters and numbers, the colors appear projected onto those characters, and the colors don't bleed beyond the edges of the characters. These people never confuse their synesthetic colors with real colors. Thus, a letter can be printed in, say, green ink, and a *synesthete* (the term applies to a person who experiences synesthesia) who views that letter will know that it is actually green. But at the same time, the individual will also experience the letter as having another "illusory" color that coexists with the actual color of the letter. Strangely, these two colors, the real one and the synesthetic one, do not seem to influence one another. You might expect, for example, that synesthetic red would combine with real green to yield some new color (e.g., yellow or gray, depending on whether the mixture was additive or subtractive—see Box 7.2). But this doesn't happen; rather than mixing, the two colors are seen at the same time, as if existing in parallel color universes.

People with synesthesia genuinely enjoy their extra-colorful world and wouldn't do anything that might "erase" their synesthetic colors. Some claim that the colors help them remember names and telephone numbers, and some even report that their colors influence how they feel about other people. The following is an excerpt received by one of us from a young woman who was synesthetic:

> "If a husband and wife have names whose colors don't match, I don't usually like them. They just don't "seem right." My husband knows that I couldn't have married him if his name had been the "wrong" color for me. We are, color-wise, perfectly compatible."

Over the last few years much has been learned about synesthesia (Robertson and Sagiv, 2005), but one crucial question remains unanswered. Where do these colors come from? When tested on standard color vision tests, synesthetic individuals are shown to have perfectly normal trichromatic color vision, implying that their cone photoreceptors are working normally. Yet somewhere within their brains, vivid sensations of color are generated. Based on what you've learned previously in this chapter, it is tempting to conclude that viewing letters or numbers somehow triggers unusual patterns of activity within the ventral stream pathway containing visual areas with neurons selective for colors. And, indeed, when studied using brain-imaging techniques (Nunn et al., 2002), synesthetic observers exhibit neural responses in several extra-striate visual areas while experiencing synesthetic colors. These are visual areas ordinarily activated by real colors in nonsynesthetic observers. But intriguing as they are, those brain-imaging results leave unanswered the question of how that activation gets triggered in first place. Do these individuals have abnormal neural connections between color-selective visual areas and other brain areas involved in reading? And if so, what's causing those abnormal connections?

As we have seen, some of the most interesting questions about synesthesia remain to be answered, and some of those answers will probably be available by the time the next edition of this textbook is published: The study of synesthesia is just getting off the ground. In the mean time, this fascinating, enigmatic condition reinforces the point voiced by Isaac Newton and echoed by many others, including Semir Zeki (1983): Color exists in the brain, not in the world.

Postscript: Early in the chapter we challenged you to identify the camouflaged creature pictured in color plate 4. The "creature" is an adult human male outfitted in hunting attire whose color and patterns blend in with the branches and leaves. The hunter is standing erect, directly in front of the tree trunk. Do you see him?

SUMMARY AND PREVIEW

In this chapter we noted how ideas about color vision have developed over the past 300 years. In answer to the question, 'what is color?' we emphasized that a complete answer must take into account multiple factors: the pigmentation of the surfaces of the objects we're looking at, the wavelength composition of the light illuminating those surfaces, the presence of appropriate photoreceptors in the eye for analyzing that wavelength composition (our eyes have three spectrally broad and widely overlapping cone photopigments), and brain mechanisms able to estimate surface color based on the outputs of those photoreceptors (mechanisms that include chromatic and achromatic visual channels). We also stressed that color depends on context and on the adaptation state of the visual system.

The success of science in explaining *how* people see color also needs to take into account *why* they see color.

The ability to perceive color most likely developed to help creatures detect and discriminate objects in their environment. Because objects—artificial as well as natural—have characteristic pigments, they absorb and reflect light in characteristic ways. These patterns of spectral reflection make it advantageous to have color vision. An animal whose visual system retains information about the wavelength distribution of reflected light can more easily pick out objects from their backgrounds. Moreover, the colors of the surfaces of objects enable the animal to recognize what sort of objects it has encountered and what kinds of actions those objects call for. Color, in other words, is intimately related to the problem of object recognition. In the next chapter, we introduce the three-dimensional quality to vision, a quality that defines the presence, location, and shapes of objects.

KEY TERMS

achromatic system
additive color mixture
brightness
chromatic systems
color constancy
color contrast
color deficiency
color induction
complementary
composite light
detection
dichromatic

discrimination
habituation
hue
identification
isoluminant
M-L cells
M-L channel
microspectrophotometry
monochromat
neutral point
Newton's color circle
nonspectral colors

pure light
$S - (M + L)$ cells
$S - (M + L)$ channel
saturation
spectral colors
subtractive color mixture
synesthesia
trichromatic
univariance principle
Young-Helmholtz theory

Seeing a Three-Dimensional World

The simple engraving in Figure 8.1 is one of the crowning artistic achievements of the ages. Made in 1525 by Albrecht Dürer (1471–1528), this woodcut engraving is special because in it the artist succeeded in using perspective to portray a three-dimensional (3D) scene on a flat, two-dimensional surface. Dürer's objects look solid, and their depth relations are unambiguous. When the scene is viewed from the appropriate vantage point, it looks real.

For centuries, the technique finally devised by Dürer and his contemporaries eluded every person who tried to portray a 3D scene. You may have seen pre-Renaissance paintings or drawings in which the sizes of people and objects look wrong, and the crude sense of depth is almost comical (see Figure 8.2). It wasn't until the discovery of linear perspective by Italian artists, during the fifteenth century, that this challenge—mapping a 3D scene onto a two-dimensional surface—was conquered. Although he did not make the discovery, Leonardo da Vinci (1452–1519) described the technique with great clarity (see Figure 8.3):

Have a piece of glass as large as a half sheet of royal folio paper and set this firmly in front of your eyes, that is between your eye and the thing you want to draw; then place yourself at a distance of two-thirds of an ell [a unit of measure equivalent to about 45 inches] from the glass, fixing your head with a mechanism in such a way that you cannot move it at all. Then shut or cover one eye and with a brush or drawing chalk draw upon the glass that which you see beyond it; then trace it on paper from the glass. (Argentieri, no date given, p. 436)

Our visual systems constantly face the same challenge that confronts artists who struggle to imbue their work with depth and solidity. In fact, during the first few months of life, every human infant manages to master what artists took centuries to understand: how to create 3D impressions of the visual world from two-dimensional representations.

As you know, the optical image that triggers vision is formed on the back of the eye, the retina's two-dimensional "canvas." The locations of features within this retinal image can be specified in up/down and left/right two-dimensional Cartesian coordinates or, if you prefer, in two-dimensional polar coordinates specifying angles and magnitudes. But there's nothing in either of these two-dimensional coordinate systems to tell whether one object is nearer or farther than another. From the two-dimensional retinal image, the brain has

FIGURE 8.1 | Woodcut by Albrecht Dürer illustrating perspective.

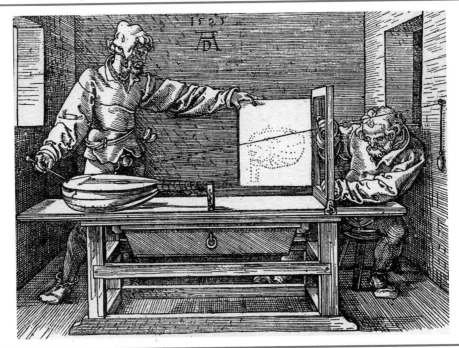

FIGURE 8.2 | Pre-Renaissance painters had trouble with perspective.

FIGURE 8.3 | Based on a suggestion by Leonardo, a method for producing a perspective drawing.

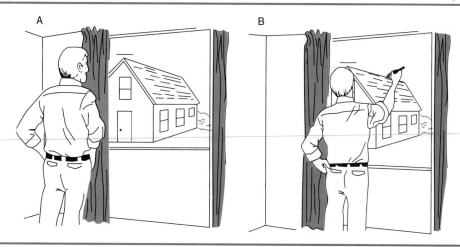

to discover depth relations among objects. For that mat-ter, each object's 3D shape also gets flattened into two di-mensions, forcing the brain to make an educated guess about the solid object's true shape. The word *guess* is used in recognition of the fact that numerous possible 3D objects can produce a given two-dimensional shape on the retina. Vision must infer the shapes of 3D objects us-ing optical information contained in the two-dimensional retinal image. This is really just another version of a gen-eral challenge facing vision, a challenge you've encoun-tered in earlier chapters: making perceptual decisions in the face of incomplete or ambiguous optical information.

Like other aspects of visual perception, being able to see 3D objects and being able to judge their locations in depth are visual activities we accomplish effortlessly and repeatedly throughout our waking hours. Whenever you're driving a car, you're judging the distances from you to other vehicles. (For that matter, you're probably doing the same thing when you're the passenger in a car, which is why you reflexively move your foot to "apply the brakes" when you perceive that the car you're in is too close to the one in front of you.) These distance judg-ments must be made rapidly and automatically; you can-not take the time to calculate the locations and distances consciously. You're faced with these kinds of distance judgments in countless other situations as well, such as when you cross a street in traffic, when you engage in athletics, and even when you reach for a cup on your desk. Similarly, we're called upon all the time to judge the 3D shapes of objects in our environment. So, for ex-ample, when you're reaching for that cup your hand is also preparing to grasp it, and the configuration of your

hand depends on accurately perceiving the 3D size and shape of the cup. Likewise, you're judging 3D shape when you try to estimate whether your bulging backpack will fit in the overhead bin of an airplane.

So, all sorts of everyday activities require you to know the shapes of solid objects and *where* those objects are located in three-dimensional space. Some creatures, such as bats, can use their ears to pick up information about object shape and distance (Griffin, 1959), but for humans, the most reliable sources are visual ones. Ac-cordingly, this chapter describes the visual information that perception uses to reconstruct the shapes and the lay-out of solid objects in our 3D visual environment. As we launch into this material, we'll first discuss **egocentric direction,** which has to do with where objects are located relative to yourself. Then we'll move to **depth percep-tion,** which pertains to how far away objects are and the sizes and shapes of those objects, the perception of which requires knowledge of depth.

Egocentric Direction

When specifying an object's location in the environment, you can adopt one of two frames of reference. One refer-ence frame specifies object location independent of the vantage point from which an object is viewed. This frame of reference is often called **allocentric** (Howard, 1982; Klatzky, 1998). You may say, for example, that the oak tree in your front yard is located 12 meters due north from the front door of your house. Expressed this way, the tree's location will be unambiguous regardless of where in the front yard you're standing (or, for that matter, whether you're even standing in the yard at all). Or, consider the layout of objects in your workspace. Expressed in allocentric coordinates, your computer video monitor may be located in the center of your desk, with the keyboard located 10 centimeters in front of the screen. Again, these allocentric spatial relations remain invariant regardless of where you're sitting.

We can even specify parts of an object in relation to the whole, a so-called object-based frame of reference. An object-based perspective is another example of an allocentric frame of reference because the coordinates are independent of the viewer's location. An allocentric frame of reference is obviously important when you want to instruct another person where to find things without that person's having to assume your particular viewing perspective. So, no matter where a viewer is standing or in which direction the viewer faces, it is true that the town center of Concord, Massachusetts, lies almost directly south of the Old North Bridge. Or, to take an interplanetary example, think back to the Martian vehicle Spirit that we met in Chapter 5 and revisited in Chapter 6. Suppose you wanted to turn Spirit's thousands of separate Martian images into a coherent description of the layout of the Martian landscape. Such a description is best put in an allocentric frame of reference, independent of a viewer's perspective. So, we might describe the Twin Peaks, a pair of distinctive Martian mountains, as lying north of the boulder known as Sashimi. Again, this is true no matter where Spirit sits, or in what direction it faces.

But for your own, immediate interactions with objects in the environment, a "viewer-centered" frame of reference is more convenient and more meaningful. Here, we specify the location of an object in the environment relative to the viewer's current position. This is what we mean by the term **egocentric direction:** where things are located relative to your current viewing position. Thus, in a viewer-centered frame of reference, the video monitor is directly in front of you when you're working at the computer, but it's behind you when you turn all the way around to talk with a friend.

With some effort, you can imagine viewing a scene from positions other than the one you currently occupy. And when tested, people are actually reasonably good at shifting their perspective using their imagination (Farrell and Robertson, 1998). But usually you're interested in where objects are located relative to where you are. Vision seems especially well designed to specify object locations in a viewer-centered framework (Tarr, 1995).

Egocentric direction can be specified in a two-dimensional coordinate system, where the two dimen-

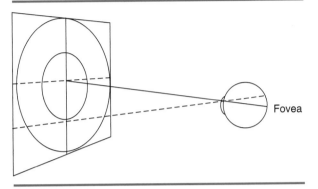

FIGURE 8.4 | Egocentric direction can be specified in a two-dimensional coordinate system, with the observer's center of gaze defining the center of the system.

sions signify up/down and left/right. Because this coordinate system is referenced to a person, the center of the coordinate system corresponds to the line of sight. Thus, when you stare at an object, that object's location defines "straight ahead" (see Figure 8.4), and the locations of other objects in the visual scene can be specified in reference to this fixated object.

This two-dimensional layout of objects in the world is preserved in the images formed on the back of the eye. (On the retina, images of various objects maintain their locations relative to one another.) Although the retinal image is inverted, with objects in the upper part of the visual field imaged on the lower part of the retina, and vice versa, the inverted image maintains all the two-dimensional positional information present in the real world. In other words, all the up/down and left/right information in the two-dimensional egocentric coordinate system is preserved in the "inverted" two-dimensional retinal image.

You may recall from Chapter 4 that the mapping of the retina onto the cortex is topographic, meaning that neighboring regions on the retina are represented in neighboring regions of the cortex. As a result, the two-dimensional relations withing objects in the world are maintained in the neural representations of objects in visual cortex. Neural activity within cortical neurons devoted to the fovea specifies the direction we associate with "straight ahead," and other egocentric directions are represented by the activity in neurons whose receptive fields are displaced in the topographic cortical map relative to the foveal representation. Of course, objects situated to the left of the center of gaze create neural activity in the right hemisphere, and vice versa (recall Figures 4.3 and 4.4).

FIGURE 8.5 | For each pair of lines, judge whether the top one is located to the left or right of the bottom one. You are using vernier acuity to perform this judgment.

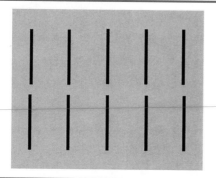

Just how accurate are we at pinpointing the locations of objects? Remarkably accurate, judging from the skills of experienced marksmen who can hit the center of a bullseye more than 90 percent of the time from considerable distances. On simple pointing tasks, even unpracticed human observers can accurately point in the direction of a single point of light in an otherwise dark room (Matin, 1986). Errors do creep in when a person who is looking straight ahead tries to point to some object in the periphery of vision. In this case, people consistently point too far into the periphery, overestimating how far off the line of sight the nonfixated object is located (Bock, 1993). Under ordinary conditions, we avoid this potential source of error by looking directly at objects whose locations we are trying to judge.

When it comes to specifying the locations of objects relative to one another, we are unbelievably accurate under optimal conditions. Look at the five pairs of vertical lines in Figure 8.5. For each pair, can you judge the position—left versus right—of the upper line relative to the lower one? On tasks like this, people use **vernier acuity** to judge whether one line is offset relative to the other.[1] People are able to make accurate judgments even when the lateral offset between lines is only about 5 seconds of arc. This amazingly small value is approximately equivalent to the width of a human hair viewed at arm's length. What makes this tiny value all the more remarkable is that it's about six times smaller than the diameter of a single cone photoreceptor in your eye. You're able, in other words, to resolve a lateral offset between two objects that is tinier than the

spacing between adjacent cone photoreceptors in your eye. Human performance of this caliber is dubbed **hyperacuity** as it exceeds the spacing of receptors in the eye (*hyper* is from the Greek term meaning "above" or "beyond"; acuity is from the Latin word *acus* meaning "needle," something "sharp" or "pointed"). At present it's not known just how human vision achieves this level of spatial resolution, although an array of neighboring cones, in principle, does generate a spatial pattern of signals sufficient to specify vernier offsets at the limits of human acuity (Wandell, 1995). As Chapter 6 pointed out, vernier acuity improves with practice.

Attention to Location

Besides pinpointing objects' locations in visual space, we also have the knack to direct attention to locations in space in anticipation of the appearance of an object. Visual location, in other words, provides a spatial framework for aiming attention, much like one would aim a spotlight to a given region on a theater stage. Normally when we shift our attention to a given location in space, we simultaneously shift our eye position to fixate on that location, aiming our fovea on it. But it is possible to shift attention without redirecting the eyes. Try this. Hold your left hand at arm's length out to the left side of your head, where it can barely be seen in your peripheral field of view. Open your palm with all five fingers held upright. Now, carefully maintain fixation on the last word in this sentence ("fingers") and, at the same time, mentally scrutinize your fingers. You've successfully dissociated fixation from attention.

Exploiting this ability to uncouple fixation and attention, Michael Posner (Posner, 1980; Posner, Snyder, and Davidson, 1980) developed a simple but effective task for gauging the consequence of attending to a given spatial location. While keeping their eyes fixed on a central plus sign, observers watched for a spot of light that could appear either to the left or to the right of the fixation mark. Their task was to hit a button as soon as the "target" appeared. Observers responded quickly when they were cued ahead of time in which location the target would appear, compared to a condition where no cue was given. The cue enabled them to shift their attention to that location, without shifting their eyes. About 20 percent of the time, Posner intentionally cued the wrong position, meaning that the target appeared in the noncued location. On these trials, observers were unusually slow in reacting to the presentation of the target, presumably because their attention was directed elsewhere.

[1]The word *vernier* refers to a small moveable scale, which carpenters and machinists use for very precise measurements.

Comparable experiments with monkeys showed the same fast response times when cues were valid and slower ones when cues were invalid. Researchers also found that visually activated neurons in a monkey's parietal lobe gave enhanced responses to a nonfixated stimulus when the monkey was attending to the location where the stimulus was presented (Bushnell, Goldberg, and Robinson, 1981). Along with more recent findings by Robinson, Bowman, and Kertzman (1995), this implicates the parietal lobe as the brain region in control of spatially selective visual attention. You may recall from Chapter 4 that the parietal lobe is a major component in the dorsal stream (or parietal pathway), responsible for specifying where objects are located in space and, hence, where our actions should be directed.

Turning the World Upside Down

Before we turn to depth perception, let's spend a few moments on one aspect of egocentric direction that has long intrigued researchers: upside-down vision. As mentioned previously, the optics of the eye invert the retinal image of the world. This inversion isn't a problem, though, because all spatial relations among objects are maintained. What we call "up" and "down" are completely relative, and we've lived with the same up/down coordinates throughout our lives. But specially constructed goggles can instantly change all that by turning the image of the world upside down (see Figure 8.6). The result of this sudden inversion of the image of the world is a series of changes in your vision and motor coordination.

In the past 100 years, beginning with George Stratton (1897), various researchers have used these kinds of goggles to turn the visual world upside down. In the most recent and thorough study, a group of investigators had four volunteers wear inverting goggles for 8 to 10 consecutive days, with the goggles in place every waking moment (Linden et al., 1999). While carefully monitored for their safety, the volunteers went about their normal, everyday activities, with as little assistance as necessary. Each volunteer took a battery of tests to assess motor skills and perceptual abilities. In only a few days, all volunteers could walk without assistance, even in crowded environments. And before the experiment ended each could ride a bicycle. The volunteers also learned to read and write, but they took an unusually long amount of time to assemble 3D objects from building blocks. Despite these signs of adaptation to image inversion, none of the four reported any recovered sense of upright vision. Throughout the entire experiment they always felt that either they or the world was upside down.

FIGURE 8.6 | Inverting goggles turn the retinal images of the world upside down.

Researchers used neuroimaging to monitor the volunteers' brain activity, using stimuli specially designed to isolate activity in either the upper or lower part of the visual field. Comparing brain activity before and after adaptation to image inversion showed no evidence that the retinotopic map had been affected by the adaptation. In other words, goggle-induced inversion of the retinal image produced no compensatory inversion of the map of the retina onto the visual cortex. Evidently, the successful adaptation of visuomotor function was mediated mainly by motor areas of the brain, not ones involved in perception. Incidentally, once the goggles were removed all four participants rapidly readapted to normal visual input.

So it appears that visual "up" and "down" are irrevocably etched in our brains, either genetically or through years of experience. We don't know—and hopefully will never find out—what would happen if very young infants were reared with inverting goggles. It is known, though, that developing kittens reared with rotated images never adapt to this distortion, behaviorally or neurologically (Singer, Tretter, and Yinon, 1979).

Having learned something about egocentric location, you're now ready to add the third dimension to your visual experience of the world: We turn now to depth perception.

Depth Perception: The Third Dimension

It is remarkable that human beings can make distance judgments at all, let alone accurate ones. As mentioned at the beginning of this chapter, the retinal images from which depth information is extracted are two-dimensional; they are inherently depthless. To dramatize this idea, imagine that we could take a snapshot of the image falling on the back of your eye. Like an individual frame in a motion picture, this photograph would consist of a complex distribution of contour and color. But all this information would be constrained to lie within the two-dimensional boundaries of the retinal image—nowhere in the image is depth to be found.

Fortunately for us, this photographic analogy is misleading. Unlike a photograph, the retinal image is continuously changing, because of our own movements and because of the movements of objects in the environment. These changes provide a rich source of depth information missing in a static snapshot. The photographic analogy also ignores the fact that the brain acquires depth information from *two* sources: the left and right eyes. This binocular vision affords another useful source of depth information.

Sources of information about depth are sometimes referred to as *cues* to depth. Following this convention, we will also refer to cues to depth, but don't misunderstand what we mean by this term. It does not mean that depth perception results from conscious deliberation on your part. To see objects in depth, you don't respond to cues like an actor taking cues from a director. On the contrary, depth perception occurs effortlessly and without thought, despite being derived entirely from a two-dimensional image on the retina.

Accurate judgments of distance arise from the coordination of several different sources of information. In the normal environment, these various sources of depth information usually operate in harmony, yielding an unambiguous impression of three-dimensional space. Under such conditions, outside the laboratory, it is difficult to know how much contribution each of the several sources makes. But in the laboratory, it is possible to assess how potent various cues are by devising situations that either isolate the contribution of a single cue or put multiple cues into conflict with one another. In some instances, including ones you'll see later in this chapter, conflicting cues yield interesting visual illusions that provide insight into depth perception's normal operation.

Before surveying cues to depth, we need to clarify precisely what is meant by *depth perception* because this term can be used in two quite different ways. In one case, the term refers to the distance from an observer to an object. This is often called **absolute distance** or **egocentric distance.** To give an example from the sport of baseball, an outfielder attempting to throw out a base runner must judge the distance between himself and the base where the runner is headed. To shoot a basketball accurately from different locations on the court also requires accurate estimates of the distance from the shooter's current position and the basket. Judgments of absolute distance are often performed to guide an activity such as throwing, and those distance judgments can be influenced by the effort required to accomplish the associated activity. Thus, for example, when throwing a ball to a target location, people judge the distance between themselves and the target location to be greater when throwing a heavy ball as compared to when throwing a light ball (Witt, Proffitt, and Epstein, 2004).

Rather than absolute distance, the term *depth perception* may instead refer to the distance between one object and another or between different parts of a single object. This is known as **relative distance.** When trying to figure out which of two birds perched on a branch is closer to you, you're making a judgment involving relative distance. It's important to distinguish between these two types of depth perception because each is specified by different sources of optical information. Also, although the ability to judge absolute distance is useful behaviorally (Rieser et al., 1990), that ability is much less precise than the ability to make judgments about relative depth (Graham, 1965).

James Cutting (1997) distinguishes among sources of depth information on the basis of the distance over which sources are most effective. He divides 3D space into three egocentric regions:

- *Personal Space:* the area within arm's reach (approximately 1.5 meters); contained within this immediate space would be the objects to be manipulated by a person, primarily using the hands.
- *Action Space:* the region beyond arm's length but within about 30 meters of your body; it is within this space that you're able to move about quickly, to make social contact with other people and throw something at a threatening enemy or to a sports teammate.
- *Vista Space:* the region within eyesight but beyond action space; objects and events falling within vista space are useful for planning navigation, including approach or escape.

FIGURE 8.7 | Major sources of depth information.

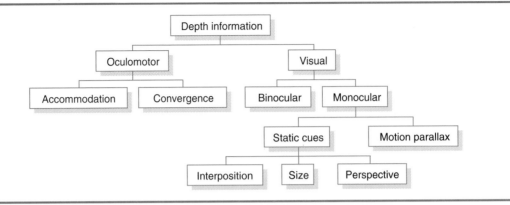

These regions and the activities they support, incidentally, are defined in terms of a person on foot; when traveling at high speeds, as in a car, action space extends far beyond 30 meters. Cutting has identified which depth cues work most effectively within these different regions of space. In covering these depth cues, we won't explicitly partition them among Cutting's three categories, but we will describe the conditions under which those cues are effective.

We are now ready to explore the various cues to depth that the visual system uses. We have divided these into two broad categories: **oculomotor cues** and **visual cues.** The oculomotor cues are actually *kinesthetic* in nature, meaning that the cue itself derives from the act of muscular contraction of either the muscle fibers controlling the focus of the lens or the fibers controlling the positions of the eyes in the head. The visual cues, so called because they are genuinely visual in nature, are subdivided into those that are available only when two eyes are used (*binocular cues*) and those that are available when just one eye is used (*monocular cues*). Figure 8.7 summarizes the ways in which these types of cues to depth are related. As you will see, oculomotor cues are the only ones that provide unambiguous information about absolute distance, meaning that an oculomotor cue does not require supplementation by other cues. In contrast, any of the visual cues can provide good relative depth information, but in order to specify absolute distance they must be supplemented with other information.

Oculomotor Cues to Depth

Whenever you are looking at an object, your eyes are focused and converged by an amount that depends on the distance between you and that object. To be seen clearly, close objects require more accommodation and conver-

gence than do objects farther away from you. Now suppose we were able to attach tiny gauges to the two sets of muscles involved in these two reflexes, strain gauges that could tell us how much the muscles were contracted (see panel A of Figure 8.8). By monitoring the degree of muscular contraction, we could compute either of two values: your angle of **convergence** or the amount of **accommodation** of the lenses of your eyes. Because these two values are related to the distance from your eyes to the object you are viewing, we would then have a useful index of absolute distance. In other words, by monitoring your eye muscles, we could compute the distance from you to the object of regard.[2] But before this same information could serve as a usable cue to depth for you, your visual nervous system would have to be able to sense the contractions of your eye muscles.

It is simple to show that convergence is accompanied by a sense of muscle strain. Starting with your index finger held up at arm's length, move it slowly and directly toward your nose, keeping both eyes focused on your finger. As your finger moves closer to your nose, you can feel the increased strain as your eyes turn inward to maintain fixation. At the same time, your accommodation is increasing, too. The lens attempts to keep the image of your finger in sharp focus on your retina. In fact, these two motor responses—accommodation and conver-

---

[2]René Descartes (1638; cited in Cabe et al., 2003) realized that convergence was a potential cue for specifying distance perception, and he provided an analogy to illustrate his point. Imagine a blind person holding two rods, one in each hand, with the rods intersecting at a given distance in front of the person. Descartes reasoned that the person could estimate the distance to this point of intersection by sensing the angles formed by the wrists and by knowing the distances between the two hands, that is, a process called *triangulation.*

FIGURE 8.8 | Two possible schemes for registering oculomotor information.

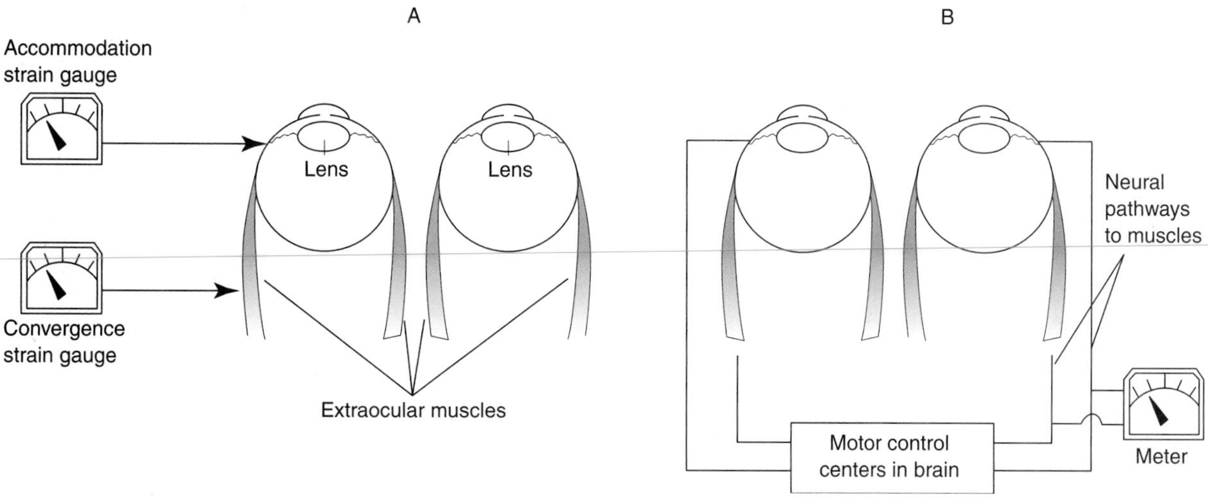

gence—usually operate in a yoked fashion, such that changes in one are accompanied by changes in the other.

There is potentially another source of information about the degree of accommodation and convergence. We could insert a measuring instrument along the neural pathway leading to the eye muscles (see panel B of Figure 8.8). Now we would be recording the strength of the command signals being *sent* to those muscles. In effect, we would be monitoring the instructions used to control accommodation and convergence, and those control signals generated by the brain could furnish information about distance.

So far we have described how oculomotor cues *could* furnish information about distance. But can people judge distance under conditions where accommodation and convergence provide the only cues to depth? The answer is yes, but not very accurately and only within a limited range (Leibowitz and Moore, 1966; Wallach and Floor, 1971). When they are the only sources of distance information, do *both* cues—accommodation and convergence—contribute equally? To answer this question, let's consider the two cues individually, starting with accommodation.

In accommodation, you have a cue whose potentially effective range is necessarily limited. Whenever you focus on an object more than a few meters from you, the muscle controlling accommodation assumes its most relaxed state. So as a potential depth cue, accommodation would be useful only within the region of space immediately in front of you. Even within this small range, distance judgments based solely on accommodation are inaccurate (Heinemann, Tulving, and Nachmias, 1959; Künnapas, 1968). So we can dismiss accommodation as an effective source of depth information.

Turning to convergence, we find that it, too, operates over a limited range of distance, albeit more extended than accommodation. The convergence angle formed by your two eyes vanishes to zero when you are looking at objects at a distance of about 20 feet and beyond (assuming your eyes are looking straight ahead). For distances less than 20 feet (about 6 meters), however, observers can use convergence angle as a reliable depth cue, in the absence of other distance information (von Hofson, 1976).

On their own, then, the oculomotor cues play only a restricted role in depth perception. In fact, people rely much more heavily on visual cues to depth. It is to those cues that we now turn, beginning with the cue provided by looking at the world through two separate eyes.

Binocular Visual Depth Information: Stereopsis

Chapter 2 pointed out that in humans, as well as in many other vertebrates, the two eyes look at much the same region of visual space. Only near the margins of the visual field is each eye's view exclusively monocular. The overlapping binocular field of view reflects the fact that both eyes are located in the front of the head, not on the side (recall Figures 2.6 and 2.7). Within this region of binocular overlap, the eyes' lateral separation means that each eye views objects from a slightly different vantage point.[3]

---

[3]Among adults the distance between the two eyes—**interpupillary distance (IPD),** as it's termed—varies from person to person, with the average IPD being 6.5 centimeters. IPD is smaller in young infants, of course, but it reaches nearly adultlike levels by about 4 years of age.

Why has nature positioned our eyes so as to provide two views of the world, particularly when each view largely duplicates the other? The answer is that this duplication offers real advantages. By virtue of the slight differences, or *disparities,* between the views seen by the left and right eyes respectively, humans are able to discriminate extremely small differences in relative depth, differences that are very difficult to discriminate using either eye alone. You can demonstrate this for yourself by performing the following simple experiment.

Take two sharp pencils, one in each hand, and hold them at arm's length. Their tips should be separated by 10 centimeters or so and pointed toward one another. Now slowly bring the two pencils together in such a way that the two points are touching. First, try this several times with one eye closed, each time noting by how much, if any, the two miss each other. Next, repeat the exercise with both eyes open. You will probably find your accuracy much improved with binocular viewing. However, not *all* individuals benefit from using both eyes. Some 5 to 10 percent of the general population do no better with two eyes than they do with one (later in this chapter, you'll learn why).

The perception of relative depth from binocular vision is called **stereopsis.** This word is derived from two Greek words: *stereos* meaning "solid," and *opsis* meaning "seeing." Stereopsis allows you to judge relative depth with great accuracy, and it also enables you to see objects that are invisible to either eye alone. These characteristics of stereopsis are described in Box 8.1. We are now prepared to consider two aspects of stereopsis: (1) the nature of the stimulus information specifying stereopsis and (2) the nature of the brain processes responsible for registering that information. Let's consider each aspect of stereopsis separately.

Retinal Disparity: The Stimulus for Stereopsis

As we just pointed out, your two eyes view objects in the world from slightly different vantage points. As a result, objects, particularly ones relatively close to you, do not produce identical retinal images on the left and right eyes. Ordinarily, however, you are unaware of differences between the two eyes' views, because the brain combines information from the two eyes in a way that obscures these differences. Only by looking at something alternately with one eye and then the other can you actually notice the differences between the two eyes' views. Take a moment to perform this simple exercise. Choose some object in front of you and look at it steadily using one eye and then the other. You should be able to see more of the left side of the object with your left eye, and more of the right side with your right eye.

While looking alternately through first one eye then the other, pay special attention to the position of the object at which you are looking. Compare it to the position of another, neighboring object that is located a little closer to you than the one at which you are looking. To make this comparison, you may want to arrange some objects on a table. Alternatively, you can simply hold up your two index fingers in front of you at different distances from your nose. Either way, you will now see that the lateral separation between the two objects appears to change when you switch eyes.

Figure 8.9 illustrates this observation. These two photographs mimic the views seen by two eyes looking at a real scene from slightly different vantage points. These photographs were taken in succession, shifting the camera sideways by 6.5 centimeters (the typical distance between an adult human's two eyes) before taking the second photograph. Note that the separation between the two bottles is larger in the left-hand picture than it is in the right-hand picture. This comes about because the two bottles were located at different distances from the camera at the time these pictures were taken. The difference in lateral separation between objects as seen by the left eye and by the right eye is called **retinal disparity;** it provides the information for stereoscopic depth perception.

The magnitude of the disparity, expressed in terms of lateral separation on the retina, depends on the distance between objects. If one object is much closer to the observer than the other, the resulting retinal disparity will be large. If one object is only slightly closer to the observer than the other, the disparity will be small. Figure 8.10 illustrates this geometrical principle.

This cue to depth, retinal disparity, arises whenever objects are located in front of *or* behind the object you are looking at. Of course, you can tell visually whether an object is nearer or farther than your point of fixation, which means that your visual nervous system distinguishes between the disparities produced by these two possibilities—objects nearer versus objects farther away. If an object lies farther from you than the object you're fixating on, the disparity between the two is said to be *uncrossed.* If an object is located closer to you than the one you are looking at, the disparity is said to be *crossed.* To remember this distinction easily, just keep in mind that with crossed disparity you would need to converge, or *cross,* your eyes in order to look directly at the nearer object. By the same token, you would diverge, or *uncross,* your eyes to shift your fixation to a more distant object.

So the type of disparity, crossed versus uncrossed, specifies whether objects are in front of or behind the point of fixation, while the magnitude of the disparity

Of all your visual abilities, none excels the keenness of stereopsis. Using binocular disparity information, humans can make exceedingly fine depth judgments that are utterly impossible by using just one eye. To illustrate, imagine that you are viewing a pair of pencils oriented vertically and placed side by side 1 meter away from you. At that distance, stereopsis would make it possible for you to tell whether one pencil was as little as 1 millimeter closer to you than its neighbor. From a distance of 1 meter, a 1-millimeter difference corresponds to a judgment accuracy of one-tenth of 1 percent. In this case, the resulting disparity between the two eyes' views is less than four ten-thousandths of a millimeter. This distance is many times smaller than the diameter of a single visual receptor in your eye!

Because of this extraordinary resolving power, stereopsis provides a very effective means for uncovering slight differences between a pair of pictures presented separately to the two eyes. For instance, imagine viewing a pair of one-dollar bills in a stereoscope (the familiar device used for presenting two pictures, one to each eye). If the two bills are identical down to the smallest detail, you will see a single, absolutely flat bill; no disparity exists to differentiate the two. But if the two bills differ, even slightly, the single, combined bill will no longer appear flat—portions of the bill will stand out in relief, due to retinal disparity produced by the slight differences. This stereoscopic technique has been used for identifying counterfeit currency, as well as tiny flaws in the electronic circuits in computers. Radiologists are also being encouraged to use stereoscopic images of biological tissue to enhance the conspicuity of breast tumors, which can be difficult to spot (May, 1994).

Stereopsis also provides an effective means for detecting camouflaged objects. Two views of a visual scene taken from different vantage points can reveal the presence of forms that are invisible from either vantage point alone. As an example, aerial photography of a landscape from two positions can disclose the presence and location of objects (such as military hardware) on the ground. Stereopsis also makes it possible for a predatory animal to spot its next meal even when the color and texture of the meal blends into the environment.

A most dramatic example of stereopsis' sleuthlike powers is provided by random-dot stereograms, an example of which is shown in Figure 8.13 (page 289). Each eye's view consists of a random array of dots, with no hint of an object hidden therein. Yet, when the brain combines the two views, a figure in depth emerges. The technique used to create this kind of stereogram is simple (it is described in the text).

In contrast, the technique used by your brain to extract depth from such a stereogram must be quite complex. For this reason, you may be surprised to learn that infants as young as 4 months of age can see the depth in random-dot stereograms (Fox et al., 1980). Moreover, this form of stereopsis is not unique to humans. Monkeys (Bough, 1970), cats (Lehmkuhle and Fox, 1977), and falcons (Fox, Lehmkuhle, and Bush, 1977) show evidence of being able to discriminate the depth portrayed in random-dot stereograms.

Incidentally, those popular "magic eye" posters you may have seen in shopping malls, books, and newspapers are based on the same geometric principles as the random-dot stereograms: A hidden "figure" is defined by clusters of small picture elements that have been shifted laterally in one portion of the poster. By crossing or by diverging your eyes, you allow your brain to discover those shifted dots and, hence, the figure they define (Thimbleby and Neesham, 1993).

---

specifies the amount by which objects are separated in depth. It is important to remember that retinal disparity specifies the *relative* depth between two or more objects; it does not provide information about absolute depth. When you fixate on a single small spot of light in an otherwise empty field of view (such as the glow of a cigarette in a dark room), there is no disparity information to be used. Only the convergence angle of your eyes (an oculomotor cue) provides binocular information.

Objects in the visual field can also be situated so that they give rise to zero disparity—a disparity that is neither crossed nor uncrossed. In other words, the lateral separation between the objects seen through the left eye will be identical to the separation between those objects seen through the right eye. As you should be able to deduce, zero disparity occurs when two or more objects are located at the same distance from the observer. Figure 8.11 illustrates this situation. In this case, the two bottles were located at the *same* distance from the observer. Images from such equidistant objects are said to fall on corresponding areas of the two eyes.[4]

---

[4]There are actually several alternative ways to specify retinal correspondence (Howard and Rogers, 1995, Chapter 2); for our purposes, the definition based on depth is the most appropriate.

FIGURE 8.9 | The lateral separation between two objects as it might appear to the left eye (A) and to the right eye (B).

FIGURE 8.10 | Retinal disparity increases with the distance, in depth, between two objects.

FIGURE 8.11 | Zero disparity occurs when two objects are located at equal distances from the observer. Note: the two eye views of these objects are the same.

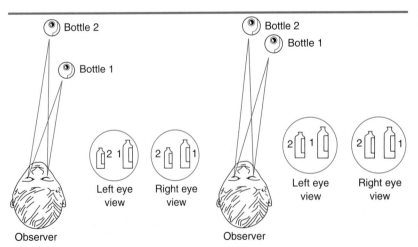
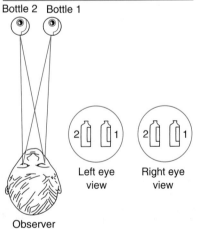

The foveas of the two eyes represent one set of corresponding retinal areas. Whenever you look directly at an object, an image of that object will be formed on the fovea of your left eye and on the fovea of your right eye. In this case, we say that the images fall on corresponding retinal areas. In addition, there are numerous other sets of corresponding areas spread over the two retinas. By definition, these areas have zero disparity with respect to the two foveas. Therefore, objects casting images on these other, nondisparate retinal areas will be seen at the same depth as the object seen by the two foveas.

To clarify this point, try the following exercise. Take two pencils, one in each hand, and place one directly in front of you. While fixating on that pencil, position the other one so that it is several centimeters (about an inch) to one side but located *at the same perceived distance* from you as the pencil you are looking at. To accomplish this, you may want to move the nonfixated pencil back and forth *in depth* until it appears at exactly the right distance. By so doing, you are varying retinal disparity between uncrossed and crossed until you settle on what amounts to zero disparity. If you are very careful, the second pencil will be placed so that it, too, casts left- and right-eye images on corresponding retinal areas.

If you repeated this exercise, repositioning the nonfixated pencil farther to one side of the point of fixation, you could generate another point at which the nonfixated pencil appeared to lie the same distance from you as the fixated pencil. In so doing, you would have established another zero-disparity location. If you repeated this exercise a number of times, all the resulting zero-disparity locations could be connected to form an imaginary plane called the **horopter** (see Figure 8.12). So long as you maintain fixation on some point in this plane, all objects located anywhere in the plane will produce images on corresponding, or nondisparate, retinal areas. Objects closer to you than this plane yield crossed disparities, whereas objects farther from you than this plane yield uncrossed disparities.[5] This, then, is how retinal correspondence and retinal disparity are related to binocular depth perception. Considering that the geometry of this situation is relatively straightforward, it is surprising that it took so long before anyone fully appreciated that disparity

---

[5]The particular shape of this imaginary plane, the horopter, will vary depending on the absolute distance from you to the fixation point.

FIGURE 8.12 | The horopter—an imaginary plane marking the positions of all objects located at the same perceived distance from the observer. Objects more distant than the point of fixation are said to produce uncrossed disparities (shaded area), whereas objects nearer than the point of fixation are said to produce crossed disparities (unshaded area). (The degree of curvature of the horopter plane varies somewhat with absolute viewing distance, for technical reasons we need not go into.)

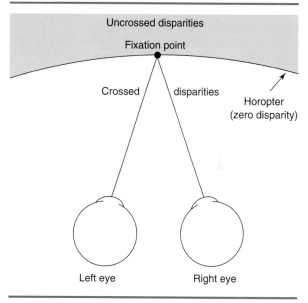

supplied information about depth. From his writings, it is clear that Leonardo da Vinci realized that the two eyes see slightly different portions of a solid, three-dimensional object, but he offered no descriptions of the detailed geometry of crossed and uncrossed disparity and no demonstrations of stereopsis. It remained for a British physicist, Charles Wheatstone (1838/1964), to provide the first proof, centuries after Leonardo, that a vivid impression of stereoscopic depth could be created from two flat pictures (Wade, 1988).

Wheatstone's demonstration took the following form. On two cards, Wheatstone sketched a pair of outline drawings of a three-dimensional object. One drawing depicted the view of the object as seen by the left eye and the other drawing depicted the view of the object as seen by the right eye. He then looked at this pair of two-dimensional drawings using a **stereoscope,** a device Wheatstone invented to present the two drawings (which together constitute a *stereogram*) separately to the two eyes. He observed that the two drawings of the object perceptually merged, or fused, into one drawing. In addition, the fused drawing conveyed an amazing sense of relief, or three dimensionality. Thus, by incorporating retinal disparity into his drawings, Wheatstone was able to re-create the three-dimensional appearance of an object—an effect that is lost in a single, two-dimensional picture. Wheatstone's novel observations demonstrated the potency of retinal disparity in producing depth perception.

At several places in this chapter you'll have opportunities to experience depth perception from stereo images like the ones invented by Wheatstone. But to enjoy these pictures, you need to learn how to "free fuse" a pair of stereo images. (The technique is called "free fusion" because you're able to bring two pictures into binocular alignment without having to use an optical device.) Box 8.2 teaches you how to manipulate your eye alignment to bring stereo pictures into binocular registration. Take a time-out right here and master the art of free fusion. And be patient: Upon first viewing a stereogram, it may take some time before you get the knack of free fusion. And besides the simple "training" stereograms in Box 8.2, you'll also be viewing more complex 3D scenes that may take many seconds of concentrated viewing before you're able to see depth. During this time, the previously invisible surfaces may appear to grow, slowly rising out of the page. Incidentally, it is impossible to speed up this process by telling or showing a person what to look for (Frisby and Clatworthy, 1975). However, just as with riding a bicycle, once you learn to see depth in these stereograms, you never completely forget how. Acquiring the ability to perceive depth in stereograms is another form of perceptual learning, like those discussed in Chapter 6.

So far, we have examined stereopsis from a geometrical perspective. You have learned that objects nearer or farther than the plane of fixation project their retinal images on disparate regions of the two eyes. You have also learned that by mimicking these disparities in a stereogram (a pair of pictures), it is possible to create realistic stereoscopic depth artificially. Having defined the cues from which stereopsis *might* arise, let's consider what the visual system must be doing in order to exploit this depth cue of retinal disparity.

Matching the Left and Right Eyes' Views

Think back to the Martian vehicle Spirit. Among its arsenal of instruments is a stereo camera mounted near the top of the vehicle. This device consists of two optical/

photographic systems that simultaneously acquire two pictures taken from two laterally displaced positions. Spirit, in other words, has the capability for binocular vision. The image data from these two cameras is fed to a computer that faces the same predicament that your brain encounters when trying to meld two images into one. Given two slightly different two-dimensional pictures (left and right camera images) of various objects, Spirit's computer "brain" must re-create the way in which those objects are actually laid out in depth on the Martian surface. And to do this, the computer must use only the information contained in the two pictures. How does it accomplish this task?

Because there is a connection between objects' relative distances from one another and their disparate positions in the two pictures, the computer can measure these disparities, computing their magnitudes and directions (crossed versus uncrossed). But to perform this computation, the computer first must compare the two pictures to discern where particular objects are located in the "left-camera" and "right-camera" pictures. And before performing that operation, the computer would have to figure out which portion of one picture matched which portion of the other. Only then would it be possible to compute positional disparities between the two pictures and derive estimates of object locations in depth based on those disparities. These computational steps underlying Spirit's "stereo" vision are the same ones your binocular visual system faces: first, matched features must be identified in the two eyes (a matching problem); second, the magnitude and direction (crossed versus uncrossed) of the retinal disparities between those features must be computed (disparity computation).[6] Let's consider these two steps in turn.

First, to match features in the two retinal images, you must decide what constitutes a "feature." On the basis of intuition, the most plausible candidate would seem to be some recognizable form, or pattern, appearing in both of the pictures. For instance, if one eye's view included your roommate's face, it would be a simple matter to locate that face in the other eye's view. According to this idea, each eye's image is analyzed separately, and the two are then brought together for purposes of matching recognizable features. However, this idea cannot be

---

[6]We use the phrase *compute* disparity because that accurately characterizes what must be accomplished. Disparity is a form of visual information that is not contained in either the left eye's image or in the right eye's image—it only exists as a difference between these two images and, as such, this difference can be derived only through operations that embody the computation of that difference.

According to a familiar saying, "Nothing in life is free." Well, you're about to acquire something that costs no more than a few minutes' practice: the ability to "free fuse" stereogram images and, consequently, experience 3D vision from two-dimensional images. (The ability is called *free* fusion because you're able to binocularly fuse two images free of any optical device like a stereoscope.) We've already detailed the geometry of binocular disparity and described how a compelling sense of depth can be experienced when the two eyes view pictures of a visual scene taken from slightly different perspectives (such pictures are called *stereograms*). You're now going to learn how to deliver those two pictures separately to your two eyes. This ability, incidentally, is the same one needed to see depth in those popular "Magic Eye©" posters.

Let's start with an easy pair of pictures and work up to other pairs that are more difficult and more entertaining. The pair of pictures in panel A consists of a series of vertical lines. You may notice that the spacing between lines is slightly different in the two pictures, and our goal is for you to experience the perceptual consequence of that difference. To achieve this goal, you need to get one of the figures imaged in your right eye and the other imaged in your left eye. And you can do that by aiming your left eye at one figure and your right eye at the other.

Easier said than done? Try this. Place your index finger (it doesn't matter which one) on this page right between the two pictures and stare right at that finger. Now very gradually move your finger away from the page straight toward your face, all the while maintaining fixation on the finger. Now here's the trick. At the same time you're staring at your finger, pay attention to the pair of pictures. As you move your finger closer, you'll notice that the two gradually slide on top of one another. With patience, you'll find a distance for your finger where the two pictures completely fuse. This happens because your eyes are now converged at a point that aims them at different parts of the page. Once you've found this point, hold your finger steady while concentrating on the superimposed figure. You should be able to see that some of the vertical lines are situated in depth relative to others. This depth effect is stereopsis.

Once you've mastered this lesson, you're ready to graduate to more complicated stereograms. Try the pair shown in panel B. Again, patience will pay dividends. Keep searching for the right degree of eye convergence

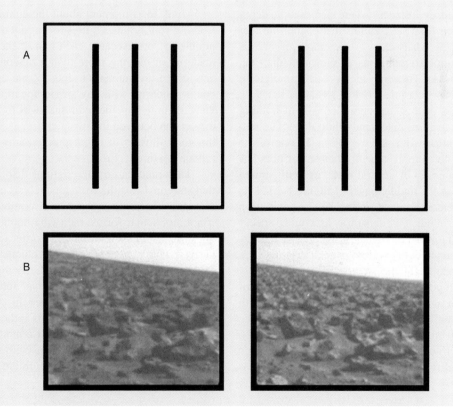

BOX 8.2 A Lesson in Free Fusion *(continued)*

that causes the two images to appear superimposed. As you practice this technique, you'll soon be able to dispense with the finger and simply cross your eyes at will to get the images aligned. The most difficult aspect of this maneuver is that your accommodation changes as you converge your eyes, thereby blurring the two images. To begin, then, practice free fusion in bright light conditions, when your pupils will be small and blur will be minimal.

Once you've got the hang of it, you'll be ready to try your new ability on the demonstration stereograms in this chapter. One final thing. Some people just find it impossible to cross their eyes and fuse stereograms. If you're experiencing this difficulty, try staring *through* the page of the book, as if you were looking at an imaginary object located 10 or so centimeters beyond the page. This, too, is a way to achieve free fusion, although this method reverses which eye sees which image and, consequently, flips the depth relations portrayed in the stereogram. Staring through the page is the procedure that you're supposed to use when viewing "magic eye"

posters (technically known as *autostereograms*). Stereo depth in those posters has exactly the same geometrical bases as the stereograms described in the text. To quote the description given by W. A. Steer on his Web page on stereograms:

> [A]n autostereogram picture is basically made up of a pattern which repeats across the width of the page. When you diverge your eyes to "see" it each looks at adjacent repeats of the pattern, but the brain is fooled into believing that both eyes are still looking at exactly the same thing. Since the pattern is not just copied but is subtly distorted on each repeat, (in accordance with the three dimensional image represented), the two eyes see slightly different images. At this point, human perception takes over and the brain concludes that the differing images arise from looking at a three dimensional object, whose form it decodes in an instant. Hence the 3D illusion occurs.

The URL for Steer's Web page, which includes examples of autostereograms, can be found at www.mhhe.com/blake5.

---

correct, for there are instances where stereoscopic depth can be perceived from stereograms that contain no recognizable objects whatsoever. An example of one of these **random-dot stereograms** is shown in the top panel of Figure 8.13. These ingenious visual stimuli were first developed by Bela Julesz (1964, 1971).

Both halves of this stereogram consist of nothing more than an array of black-and-white dots. The two halves are identical with one exception. In one of the halves of the stereogram, a central subset of dots has been shifted laterally by several rows, as is illustrated schematically in the middle panel of Figure 8.13. This lateral displacement creates a retinal disparity between the two halves, in much the same way as would a speckled square held in front of an identically speckled background, as depicted in the bottom panel of Figure 8.13. Because the texture in the stereogram is completely random, it is impossible to pick out from either half of the stereogram alone which area will appear in depth when the two halves are viewed simultaneously. Once you've learned to free fuse stereo images (Box 8.2), you'll be able to use that technique to see your brain's remarkable ability to extract depth from these random-dot pictures.

Think for a moment about the confusing task confronting your brain as it tries to sort out the depth in this jumble of dots. Because each half of the stereogram is made up of nothing more than a random array of tiny dots, there are numerous dots in one eye's view that could match up with any single dot in the other eye's view. Despite this, the brain manages to find a satisfactory match between the two pictures, as is evidenced by the vivid illusion of depth produced by these pairs of random textures.

Thus random-dot stereograms disprove the theory that stereopsis results from an analysis of monocularly recognizable forms such as your roommate's face. But if not monocular forms, then what monocular features does the visual system match in order to compute disparity? Think back to earlier chapters where you learned that form perception initially involves analyzing a figure's orientation and size, or spatial frequency. Those same features are involved in stereopsis, too. The evidence favoring this idea is rather complicated, but we are going to mention just a couple of relevant studies here. More thorough discussions of feature matching and stereopsis can be found in Blake and Wilson (1991).

FIGURE 8.13 | A random-dot stereogram (top panel). The two halves are identical, except that a central subset of dots has been shifted laterally. (The middle panel outlines the section of shifted dots.) This lateral displacement creates retinal disparity and, thus, stereosopic depth (bottom panel).

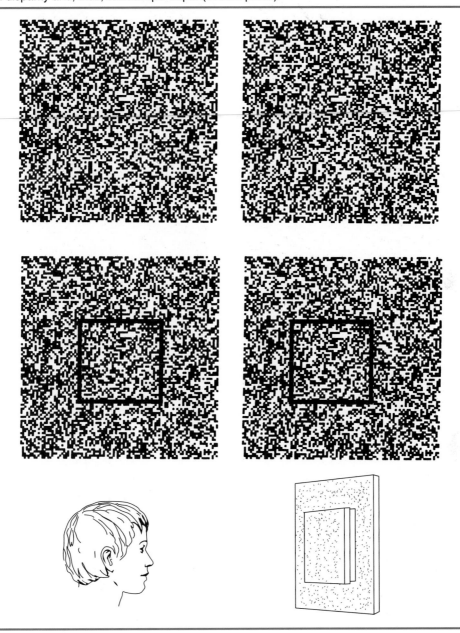

It is possible to remove certain spatial frequencies from random-dot stereograms such as the one shown in Figure 8.14A. This process of removal is called *filtering*; you saw examples of spatial frequency filtering in Chapter 5 (e.g., see Figure 5.2). As you will appreciate, when high spatial frequencies are removed from both halves of a stereogram, the dots are no longer sharply defined but instead appear blurred (see Figure 8.14B). Still, the phantom figure is easily seen to stand out in depth when these two blurred half-images are viewed stereoscopically (try free fusing the two images). By the same token, if just low spatial frequencies are removed from

FIGURE 8.14 | The two components of a random-dot stereogram (panel A) with their spatial frequencies filtered to produce components containing only low spatial frequencies (LP, panel B), only high spatial frequencies (HP, panel C) and a "mixed" stereogram where one component is HP and the other is LP (panel D).

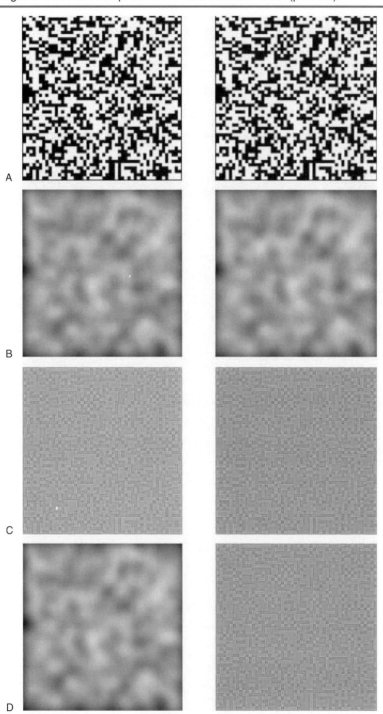

both halves of a stereogram (Figure 8.14C), depth may still be experienced, although with more difficulty. But if high spatial frequencies are removed from one half of the stereogram while low spatial frequencies are removed from the other (Figure 8.14D), stereopsis is abolished. Instead, the two halves undergo **binocular rivalry,** such that only one picture or the other is visible at any one moment (see Box 8.3).

For stereopsis to be experienced, then, the spatial-frequency content of the two halves of a stereogram must overlap (Frisby and Mayhew, 1976). This implies that in order to compute disparity, the brain matches the two eyes' views, making use of sets of neurons responsive to limited bands of spatial frequencies (Yang and Blake, 1991). This strategy actually simplifies the matching problem, making it unnecessary to test all left-eye features against all right-eye features. The possible feature matches are restricted to the monocular image components at a given spatial scale. As you might deduce from Figure 8.14B, there are fewer possible "feature" matches in the pair of low spatial frequency images than there are in pairs of unfiltered images. The brain, consequently, can more quickly hone in on the correct set of matches based on the low frequency content of the images. And once these low frequency matches have been established, feature matches for the higher spatial frequencies have been delimited to those within the boundaries established by the low frequency matches.

Recall also from Chapter 5 that the brain relies on neurons tuned to different spatial scales to support form perception. It is not surprising that form perception and stereopsis should utilize the same machinery, as both of these are designed to distinguish objects from their backgrounds (Marr, 1982). Because of humans' remarkable ability to resolve small depth differences stereoscopically, the two eyes together can unearth objects buried in complex visual environments, objects that when viewed monocularly remain hidden from sight. In this respect, stereopsis effectively adds another dimension to form perception.

The Neural Basis of Stereopsis

So far we have considered the geometry of retinal disparity (the cue for stereopsis) and the matching features that seem to be used in the analysis of retinal disparity. But how does the brain actually do its feature matching and disparity computation? Although the entire process is not yet understood, key things are known

about the neurobiological hardware involved in the initial stages of stereoscopic vision. Let's take a look at this hardware.

Recall from Chapter 4 that most visual cortical neurons receive input from both eyes, left and right. Each of these binocular neurons gives its largest response when the two eyes view the same stimulus. For instance, a particular binocular neuron that gives its most vigorous response when the left eye sees a vertical contour will respond best when the right eye sees a vertical contour, too. The same holds for contour width, or size, as well as for the direction and speed of movement of a contour. In general, binocular neurons respond best when the two eyes view matched features (see the review by Gonzalez and Perez, 1998). This property, then, satisfies one of the requirements for the analysis of disparity information, namely, the matching of monocular features.

Binocular neurons have another property, one that satisfies the second requirement for stereopsis: These neurons are sensitive to retinal disparity. In particular, some binocular cells respond only when their preferred features appear at the *same* depth plane as the point of fixation. This is because the receptive fields for these binocular neurons are located on *corresponding* areas of the two eyes. These cells, in other words, would respond best to objects giving rise to zero disparity. Activity in such cells would serve to signal the presence of stimuli located on the horopter. Other binocular cells respond best to features that are imaged on noncorresponding, or disparate, areas of the two eyes. Cells of this type would be activated by objects located at depth planes other than the plane of fixation; they are referred to as **disparity-selective cells.** As Chapter 4 described, some cells respond to objects located closer than the plane of fixation (crossed disparities), whereas others respond best to objects behind the plane of fixation (uncrossed disparities). Also, the amount of depth (disparity) giving the best response varies from cell to cell.

So it appears that these binocular neurons perform two of the operations necessary for stereopsis, feature matching, and disparity computation. But can we be sure that these binocular neurons actually play a role in stereoscopic depth perception? One piece of evidence favoring such a role comes from studying cats who, while kittens, were allowed to see with only one eye at a time. The eyes were stimulated alternately by placing an opaque contact lens in one eye on one day and in the other eye on the next day. This rearing procedure effectively turns binocular neurons into monocular ones (Blakemore, 1976). When tested as adults, these animals were unable to perform

BOX 8.3 Competition between the Two Eyes

Charles Wheatstone, the discoverer of stereopsis, described another intriguing aspect of binocular vision. This second discovery concerned the perceptual outcome when one eye's view differs radically from its partner's view. Wheatstone's interesting observation can best be described by reference to the accompanying figure.

Suppose you were to view these two dissimilar patterns separately with your two eyes in such a way that your left eye saw one set of diagonal lines while your right eye saw the other set. What would be the outcome? If the two were combined by simply superimposing one on the other, the result would be a sort of checkerboard pattern. Yet when these figures are viewed stereoscopically, thereby allowing your brain to perform the combination, the two certainly do not blend into a single, stable pattern resembling a checkerboard. Instead, a person sees portions of one pattern together with portions of the other, the net result resembling a mosaic of the two. Moreover, this mosaic changes over time, as regions of one eye's view replace regions of the other eye's view. (To experience this instability in perception for yourself, try free fusing these two orthogonal gratings or the pair of dissimilar pictures in Figure 8.14D.)

The resulting phenomenon is known as *binocular rivalry*, an appropriate term in view of the evident breakdown in cooperation between the two eyes. The occurrence of binocular rivalry indicates that the brain, in attempting to put together information from the two eyes, seeks to establish matches between features in the two eyes. When such matches are found, stable single vision and stereopsis result. But when satisfactory matches are impossible, the brain attends to portions of one eye's view at a time, ignoring or suppressing the corresponding portions of the other eye's view as though they were not there.

But how complete is this suppression of information during binocular rivalry? Is a person completely oblivious to new information presented to a region of the eye that is temporarily suppressed? To study this question, investigators have employed a "probe" technique whereby small visual targets (such as a word) are briefly flashed to a suppressed region; the observer's task is to report whether or not the probe target was noticed. The results are conclusive—during suppression, people fail to see targets that would normally be quite visible, including, for example, familiar names (Blake, 1988b). However, the eye is not completely blind to all visual stimulation during suppression. Abruptly increasing the brightness of a suppressed stimulus or suddenly moving it will cause the stimulus to become visible. Apparently, during suppression an eye's overall sensitivity, though reduced, is not totally abolished. While vision in the suppressed eye is erased from consciousness, some processing of information from that eye continues unabated (Blake and Logothetis, 2002).

What actually transpires within the visual system when one eye's stimulus dominates perception during rivalry? Nikos Logothetis and colleagues (Logothetis and Schall, 1989; Leopold and Logothetis, 1996) have identified several visual areas in the brain where the activity of neurons waxes and wanes in synchrony with fluctuations in left- and right-eye dominance. This tight coupling between perception and neural activity is most prominent in higher visual areas, including regions in the temporal lobe.

Since the two eyes normally view the same visual scene, you might wonder what binocular rivalry has to do with normal vision. When one object partially occludes a more distant object, one eye sees portions of that object that are screened from the other eye's view—there can be, in other words, unmatched image regions in the two eyes' views. As mentioned in the text, this is the geometrical principle first deduced by Leonardo da Vinci, and it has been studied in the laboratory by Nakayama and Shimojo (1990). These investigators provide clever demonstrations that the binocular visual system actually relies on information about interocular mismatches to figure out depth relations among objects.

binocular depth discriminations that were simple for normally reared cats (Blake and Hirsch, 1975; Packwood and Gordon, 1975). Because they lacked a normal array of binocular neurons, these cats were "blind" for stereopsis, even though they had perfectly normal visual acuity in both eyes. Monkeys, too, lose stereopsis when early experience deprives them of coordinated, binocular use of the two eyes (Harwerth et al., 1997).

Recall our earlier comment that some people are stereoblind—unable to perceive depth from retinal disparity. By analogy with the stereoblind cats and stereoblind monkeys, we assume that this condition in humans stems from a lack of binocular neurons. Again, there is evidence to back up this assumption. For instance, when stereoblind people are tested on the tilt aftereffect described in Chapter 4, they show very little interocular transfer—adapting one eye has very little effect on judgments of line orientation when the nonadapted eye is tested (Mitchell and Ware, 1974). In contrast, people with good stereopsis show substantial interocular transfer, which, we assume, reflects adaptation of binocular neurons. The meager degree of interocular transfer in the stereoblind individual, then, probably reflects the paucity of binocular neurons in that person's brain.

The incidence of **stereoblindness** is estimated to be as high as 5 to 10 percent in the general population. (Recall that this percentage range was mentioned previously in the chapter, when we pointed out that some people are no better with two eyes than one on tasks, like the pencil pointing task, that benefit from binocular depth perception.) As a rule, stereoblindness is associated with the presence of certain visual disorders during early childhood. The most common of these disorders is misalignment of the two eyes, a condition known as **strabismus.** People with this condition are unable to look at, or fixate on, the same object simultaneously with both eyes. Consequently, one eye's view rarely corresponds to the other eye's view. To deal with this potentially confusing situation, the brain eventually suppresses one eye's view from visual consciousness, an outcome reminiscent of binocular rivalry. Box 8.4 describes this and similar conditions in more detail.

If left uncorrected, strabismus can lead not only to stereoblindness but also to amblyopia,[7] which, as you will recall from Chapter 4, is defined as a permanent reduction in the acuity of an eye not attributable to optical defects. Both amblyopia and stereoblindness can be prevented if eye misalignment is surgically corrected early in life, while normal binocular vision is still developing (Thorn et al., 1994). If correction is postponed until school age, the chances for attaining normal vision are significantly reduced (von Noorden, 1981; Banks, Aslin, and Letson, 1975).

The discovery of disparity-sensitive cells almost four decades ago was an exciting first step toward an understanding of the neural basis of stereopsis (Barlow, Blakemore, and Pettigrew, 1967). That discovery set the stage for more recent work that confirmed and extended those initial neurophysiological findings (Freeman, 2004). But, as several recent reviews of this work have pointed out (Backus, 2000; DeAngelis, 2000; Parker, 2004), the existence of disparity detectors leaves a number of questions about stereopsis unanswered.

For one thing, the perceived depth resulting from a given disparity depends on the absolute distance from your eyes to the object at which you are looking. This can be demonstrated when an observer views a random-dot stereogram, such as the one in Figure 8.14A, from different distances. (Try this for yourself, using the free fusion technique you learned in Box 8.2.) The central square in the stereogram appears to move farther and farther in front of its background as viewing distance increases. Yet the disparity, expressed in angular terms, actually decreases as you view the stereogram from afar. So, disparity alone does not specify depth; disparity must be supplemented by other distance information.

One potential supplementary source of distance information is convergence angle, the oculomotor cue discussed earlier in this chapter. We do know that the perceived depth associated with a given angular disparity changes with convergence angle (Foley, 1980; Collett, Schwarz, and Sobel, 1991). In addition to convergence angle, we know that depth from stereopsis can be influenced by other visual cues, such as perceived slant specified by perspective or texture (Stevens and Brookes, 1988), two monocular sources of information about depth discussed later in this chapter.

We also should point out that binocular vision can produce what is termed *partial occlusion,* a special form of retinal disparity. When one object partially occludes another, more distant object, one eye will see portions of the more distant object that are invisible to the other eye. This geometric principle is illustrated in Figure 8.15. These two pictures simulate what your left and right eyes

---

[7]Amblyopia can arise from causes other than eye misalignment. Other disorders producing amblyopia include marked differences in an uncorrected refractive error between the two eyes, closure of one eye due to lid paralysis or blurred vision in one eye due to a cataract in that eye.

BOX 8.4 **Coordination between the Two Eyes**

Like any other pair of partners, our two eyes have to share the same viewpoint in order to get along. This means that movements of the eyes must be coordinated so that both eyes are always looking in the same direction. As you learned in Chapter 2, the eyes are guided in their movements by 12 extraocular muscles—six for each eye. Because the eye movement system is complex and dependent on fallible parts, things can and do go wrong. Here, we will consider some of the most common problems and their remedies, emphasizing extraocular dysfunctions that affect perception.

When most people look at an object, the two eyes both end up aimed at that object. For these people, the two eyes fixate together. This binocular fixation depends on the coordinated responses of the extraocular muscles that guide the two eyes. For various reasons, however, some people lack this coordination. For example, if one extraocular muscle is too short, it can exert too much pull on the eyeball, turning that eye in (toward the nose) or out (toward the ear). Chronic deviation of an eye is called *strabismus.* Often this is a congenital condition, which means that an infant will lack coordinated binocular vision early in life. Because strabismic eyes look in different directions, they send the brain conflicting messages, which may result in double vision, or **diplopia.** Alternatively, the brain may simply ignore, or suppress, one eye's view altogether; in this case, only one eye contributes to vision even though both are open. This latter condition resembles a chronic form of binocular rivalry (see Box 8.3).

Various therapies have been developed for strabismus. In cases where the deviation between the positions of the two eyes is relatively small, visual exercises may help to recoordinate the eyes. In more severe cases, surgical correction may be required. This often involves removing a small portion of one or more of the extraocular muscles and then reattaching the muscles to the eyeball, so that the eyes line up. This procedure requires a high degree of skill, for altering the muscle by the wrong amount will leave the eyes still misaligned.

Other extraocular dysfunctions are less debilitating and less noticeable. When you do close work such as reading, your eyes must converge—each eye turns inward by the proper amount. Strong, constant convergence strains the muscles of the eye (Guth, 1981). Some people have difficulty converging their eyes, as you can discover for yourself. Stand facing a friend and ask him or her to keep both eyes on your finger as you move it slowly but directly toward a point between the eyes. Note how well your friend's eyes follow. Some people can keep both eyes fixated on the finger until it is within 1 or 2 centimeters of the nose; others will not be able to follow the finger after it is within 5 or 6 centimeters of the nose. As the finger approaches, one of the person's eyes may wander off. If you try this small experiment with several people, you'll be amazed at the individual differences. In addition, when someone is tired or has consumed too much alcohol, that person's eyes may be unable to converge normally.

People who have trouble binocularly fixating on close objects may experience eyestrain during prolonged reading. Eyestrain, in turn, can cause dizziness, headaches, and nausea, leading to reduced studying and hence poorer grades. Occasionally, college students suffer this kind of problem, called **convergence insufficiency,** while studying for final examinations. Amateur "psychologists" can do great harm by misdiagnosing this condition, thinking it is an aversion to studying or "a need to fail." In fact, the proper treatment is straightforward: prescription glasses, possibly supplemented with appropriate eye exercises. Reading will then become less of a strain, and higher grades may follow.

---

would see if you were to look at a book held at arm's length in front of a bookshelf. Notice that the left eye's view of the background includes books that are partially occluded from view by the right eye, and vice versa. These partial occlusions, an extreme form of retinal disparity, are readily interpreted by the brain as arising from depth differences between the foreground and background objects (Anderson, 1994). Partial occlusion, as mentioned previously in this chapter and in Box 8.3, is the geometric principle Leonardo da Vinci identified in the fifteenth century.

This completes our survey of binocular stereopsis, the major source of binocular depth information. Keen as stereopsis is, though, it certainly is not the sole source of depth information. People can successfully perform visually guided tasks, such as landing an airplane (Grosslight et al., 1978), while using just one eye. And you can easily confirm that the world retains a real sense of depth even when one eye is closed. Rather than collapsing into a single, depthless plane, objects in the visual field continue to appear three dimensional. This is possible because the monocular view of the world con-

FIGURE 8.15 | Photographs simulating what the left and right eyes see when you look at a book held several feet in front of a bookshelf. Note that the left eye can see some objects occluded in the right eye's view, and vice versa.

tains additional, rich sources of information about depth. It is to those monocular cues we now turn. As we move through our survey of monocular cues, keep in mind that these cues are effective, at least in part, because they are predicated on some invariant property of the physical world, properties derived from the optical nature of light and the material nature of objects and surfaces. To quote Liu and Todd (2004, p. 2135), these monocular cues are "grounded in the ecology of natural vision." We'll be highlighting this aspect of monocular depth cues in the rest of this chapter.

Monocular Visual Depth Information

Some monocular depth cues are based on principles of geometry, others are based on conditions of atmosphere and illumination, and still others arise from differential motion within the visual field. We do not refer to these as *monocular* cues because you have to shut one eye to experience them. On the contrary, monocular cues are readily available during binocular viewing. They're called *monocular* because these sources of depth information can be realized by either eye alone.

As we survey these various monocular cues, keep in mind that several of them were initially discovered by artists in their attempts to represent depth pictorially. Those pictorial cues we call *static* because they are avail-

able to a stationary observer viewing a motionless scene; those cues can be included in a painting or in a drawing to imply depth relations. The other monocular source of depth information is provided when an individual moves through the environment or when objects within the environment move relative to one another; those cues cannot be used in a painting, but they can and are effectively used in cinema and television. We'll start with the static, pictorial cues discovered by artists.

Static Cues to Depth

Occlusion   When one object obscures part of your view of another object, as illustrated in Figure 8.16, the partially occluded object is automatically perceived as the more distant one. This cue is called **occlusion,** and from the standpoint of pictorial representation, it is probably the most primitive. For our purposes we use the term *occlusion* to refer to viewing situations where parts of the more distant object are obscured from view while other parts of that object remain visible; occlusion is only partial. When occlusion is complete, you cannot see the more distant object at all, in which case you may not even realize that it's there. Occlusion can also happen when a moving object temporarily passes in front of another object, in which case we may speak of dynamic occlusion.

FIGURE 8.16 | Occlusion: When one object obscures part of another, the obscured object is perceived as the more distant one.

FIGURE 8.17 | An illusory bar (drawing A) and a real bar (drawing B), both of which activate neurons in Area V2 of the visual cortex.

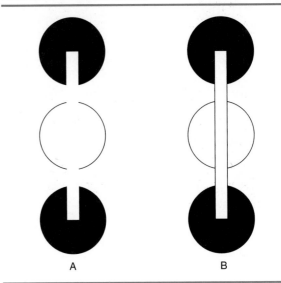

A   B

Young children often incorporate occlusion into their simple drawings, even though they are unable to reproduce any other pictorial depth cues. Actually, there is evidence that by 7 months of age human infants can judge relative distance solely on the basis of occlusion (Yonas, 1984). On the other hand, brain damage during adulthood can abolish a person's ability to judge depth from occlusion without affecting the ability to use other depth cues (Stevens, 1983). Occlusion is such a strong depth cue that it can override retinal disparity when the two cues conflict (Kaufman, 1974). Moreover, the effectiveness of occlusion is amplified when the surface of the occluding object contains high spatial frequency information, meaning that it appears to be finely textured (Brown and Weisstein, 1988).

Perhaps the most compelling evidence for the potency of occlusion is the so-called Kanisza figures mentioned in Chapters 1 and 4. Figure 4.1a showed an example of a Kanisza figure, and another version is shown in Figure 8.17A. As you can tell, these are drawings in which one object appears to partially occlude several others even though the boundaries of the nearer object are invisible. This illusory figure appears to have distinct edges where, in fact, none exist, and the entire figure is seen in front of objects that seem to be partially occluded. Descriptively speaking, the visual system seems to employ a kind of interpolation process whereby

separate edges or contours in the same spatial neighborhood are connected *if* this connection can be formed by a simple line or curve and *if* the operation is consistent with the principle of occlusion.

But how does the visual system make the seemingly complex decision to interpolate an object? As we saw in Chapter 4, there is evidence (Peterhans and von der Heydt, 1991) that interpolation is accomplished by neurons in the visual cortex that respond not only to real contours but also to interpolated, illusory contours such as the ones forming the object in Figure 8.17A. These cortical neurons perform an interesting new operation—interpolation—that involves not only boundary completion but depth ordering. The illusory figure appears in front of the real figures.

It is also worth noting that objects occluded by a nearer figure are seen as complete, even though portions of their surfaces are obscured by the nearer object. Thus, in Figure 8.17, we perceive the black circles as complete, not notched. In a similar fashion, despite the occluding objects in Figure 5.39, we saw a girl's entire face uninterrupted by horizontal and vertical gaps. The perception of occluded areas of an object is termed **amodal completion.** How we are able to perceive parts of objects that are occluded represents a challenging question (Kellman and Shipley, 1991). Here again, the visual system seems to employ an interpolation process to complete the portions of the figure missing in the image. And as a study

FIGURE 8.18 | Test figures used by Sekuler and Palmer to study priming and occlusion.

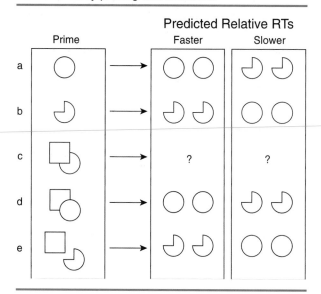

FIGURE 8.19 | Perception of transparency depends on lightness relationships. See text for details.

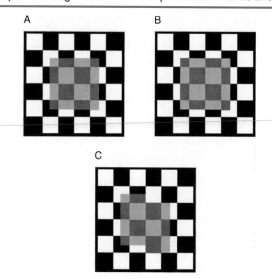

by Allison Sekuler and Stephen Palmer (1992) shows, the process of completion takes some time to occur.

In that study, observers saw briefly-presented pairs of simple geometric figures and were asked to indicate as quickly as possible whether or not the two figures were identical. Figure 8.18 shows a few examples of Sekuler and Palmer's test pairs. Just prior to each test pair, observers saw another brief stimulus, called a *priming stimulus,* which either did or didn't match the test pair. Examples of priming figures are also shown in Figure 8.18. When the priming stimulus included an object that was identical to the test figures, observers responded "the same" very quickly—the reaction time between presentation of the test pair and observers' responses was short. When the priming stimulus did not match the pair of test figures, reaction times were slower.

The stimulus-selective speed up in responses defines perceptual priming, which was discussed in Chapter 6. Sekuler and Palmer exploited priming to determine the time necessary for perception's "completion" of an object. Here's their logic. Suppose the prime figure consisted of a notched circle snuggled against a square (third row, Figure 8.18) and the test pair consisted of two circles. Would observers' reactions be fast, indicating that the notched circle had been seen as a whole circle partially occluded by the square? Or would reaction times be slower, because the notched circle didn't match the complete circles?

The result, it turned out, depended on the time elapsing between presentation of the prime figure and presentation of the test pair. When this interval between prime and test was very brief—just a twentieth of a second or so—observers gave relatively slow reaction times to the pair of circles. Evidently, within this brief period of time, the prime figure was not registered as a complete object that is partially occluded. But when the interval between prime and test was longer than two-tenths of a second, reaction times were fast, indicating that the prime figure had been registered as a complete, partially occluded circle. From these and other, related conditions, Sekuler and Palmer concluded that perceptual representation of a partially occluded object starts out as a mosaiclike snapshot of the object's individual pieces and, then, gradually evolves over time into a perceptually complete object.

Any discussion of occlusion has to recognize the importance of **transparency,** a special case where a nonopaque object partially occludes another object. Under these conditions, people perceive the occluded object in its entirety, including the portions covered by what appears to be a transparent filter. For example, people have the strong tendency to see Figure 8.19A as a transparent, square filter in front of a surface composed of black-and-white checks. Yet look at Figure 8.19B and see what happens when we simply interchange the two shades of gray that comprise the central square region. That central region no longer looks like a separate, transparent object in front of the checkerboard. Instead, the checks themselves in the center of the checkerboard appear to be different colors compared to their neighbors—the two shades of gray, in other words, are assigned to the surface of the checkerboard, not to another object located in front of the checkerboard.

For decades researchers have been fascinated with transparency and have documented the conditions under which it's experienced. One key to perceiving transparency is the relationship of lightness values in the covered and the uncovered portions of the figure (Metelli, 1974). In a nutshell, lightness values within the regions covered by the transparent filter must be intermediate to the lightness values of those regions where the filter isn't covering them. Comparing Figures 8.19A and 8.19B, you will see that this condition is satisfied in the left-hand figure but not in the right-hand figure.

Another key is the spatial configuration of the gray portions—those parts must plausibly form a single object. Thus, in Figure 8.19C, it's more difficult to see a transparent object because the borders of the candidate regions don't form a square, even though the individual gray levels are the appropriate values (Singh and Hoffman, 1998).

A region will also be perceived as transparent only if binocular disparity specifies that the region is in front of an occluded object (Nakayama, Shimojo, and Ramachandran, 1990). Take a look at Figure 8.20, a stereogram containing the components for testing the contribution of stereopsis to the perception of transparency. Using the free-fusion technique (Box 8.2), binocularly combine the left and middle pictures. You should see a light gray, transparent object floating above a white cross drawn on a black background. Now take a look at what you see when the middle and right pictures are free fused. You'll see an opaque gray circle lying on a white background seen through a cross-shaped section cut out of a black surface. The only difference between these two conditions is the "sign" of the retinal disparity of the light gray regions relative to the rest of the figure. In one instance, the disparity is *crossed* and in the other it's *uncrossed* (recall the previous discussion of disparity in this chapter).

In some circumstances, occlusion exerts another effect, which is also illustrated in Figure 8.20. When you saw the light gray regions floating in front of the white cross, you probably saw them forming a circular region of transparent material. Yet in the figures on the page, there is no gray color anywhere except at the white intersections. Your brain filled in the rest of the gray to complete the implied circle. Much of the circle, then, consists of illusory contours (like those in Figure 8.17).

Even without the aid of stereopsis, you can see this filling-in process. Look at color plate 26, which presents an-

FIGURE 8.20 | Stereo pairs in which a circle appears either transparent (when seen in front of the white cross) or opaque (when seen behind the white cross). To see these outcomes requires that you "free-fuse" the two components by crossing your eyes (see text for details).

other configuration whose component parts imply transparency. Here, the semicircular blue portions of each set of circles seem to give the impression of blueness that spreads into the center of the figure. We see a faint bluish, semi-transparent square resting on top of the four sets of circles. This illusory migration of color into neighboring regions is called **neon spreading,** since it resembles the glow one experiences when viewing neon lights (Bressan et al., 1997). Neon spreading represents a form of occlusion in that one perceives a faintly colored surface resting in front of other objects (the circles, in this example). Moreover, neon spreading is related to illusory figures because the spreading color is confined to an area whose shape is insinuated by the semicircular blue contours. The boundaries of the shape, in other words, are defined by illusory contours.

All these phenomena—occlusion, amodal completion, illusory figures, transparency, and neon spreading—entail the perception of depth relations among partially overlapping objects. They testify to the role of occlusion in depth perception. Despite being a very strong depth cue, however, occlusion by itself only specifies whether one object is nearer or more distant than another. It provides no quantitative information about the actual distance separating objects. For that information, additional cues are required.

Size Take a look at the series of squares in Figure 8.21. Note that the smaller squares appear to recede into the distance, implying that object size influences perceived depth. Why should size and distance be related?

As the distance between you and an object varies, the size of the image of that object on your retina changes. This principle is true for any object viewed from any distance. Thus, if you are familiar with the size of an object, you can judge from the size of its retinal image how far away the object is. In fact, it has long been known

FIGURE 8.21 | Size alone can influence perceived depth.

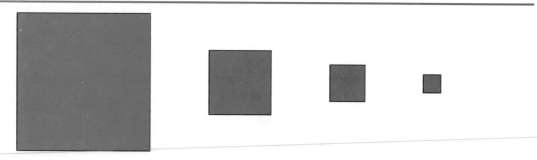

FIGURE 8.22 | How big is this object? It is difficult to judge the size of an unfamiliar object in the absence of supporting cues.

that *familiar size* is an effective cue to distance in the absence of other information (Ittelson, 1951).

But the cue of retinal image size critically depends on knowing the correct size of the object. When you are confronted with an unfamiliar object and are provided with no clues as to its true physical size, retinal image size gives you no clear sense of the distance from you to that object. For instance, you may have trouble judging the size of the sculpture pictured in Figure 8.22 and therefore its distance from the camera. But if something familiar appears in the vicinity of that object (such as the pear in Figure 8.23), the perceived size of the unfamiliar object becomes obvious. (You are also now able to judge its distance from the camera.)

Interestingly, even prior knowledge about the true distance to an object may not be sufficient to support the perception of relative depth. In one study (Gruber and Dinnerstein, 1965), a person was shown a pair of squares in a lighted corridor. One square was located about 8 meters away and the other about 16 meters away. Because the farther square was physically twice as large as the nearer one, the two squares cast the same-sized images on the person's retina (recall the discussion of visual angle at the end of Chapter 2). Depth cues provided by the corridor and by the apparatus enabled the person to see clearly that the two squares were located at different distances. However, when the lights were extinguished, the squares (which had been outlined with luminous paint), appeared to "come together" at a common depth, completely contradicting what the person *knew* about their real locations. This demonstration underscores the point made earlier, that depth cues are registered automatically, without conscious deliberation.

So far we have considered size as a determinant of perceived distance. But it is just as easy for perceived distance to influence apparent size. Looking at the left-hand panel of Figure 8.24, the girl on the right appears to be almost twice as big as the boy on the left. But, in fact, the two are really equal in size. This compelling illusion stems from the unusual construction of the room. As shown in the right-hand panel of Figure 8.24, the left corner of the room is much farther away from the observer than the right corner. The floor-to-ceiling height as well as the sizes and shapes of the windows have been distorted to make the room appear rectangular, and hence normal, when viewed from a location directly in front of the room. The back wall looks perpendicular to the line of sight, with left and right corners appearing equidistant from the viewer. Actually, though, the person on the left is farther away than the one on the right. The visual angles subtended by the two children are therefore quite different. From the viewer's perspective,

FIGURE 8.23 | The size of an unfamiliar object— and therefore its distance from you—becomes obvious when you see it in the vicinity of a familiar object, in this case a pear. (The unfamiliar object is a contemporary sculpture by Bruce Peebles.)

this means that the girl on the right is larger, since you have been fooled into believing that the difference in visual angles is *not* due to a difference in distance. Adelbert Ames, a lawyer turned scientist, devised this clever demonstration of the influence of perceived distance on apparent size. In his honor, this sort of distorted structure is called an **Ames room** (Ittelson, 1952/1968).

In addition to the Ames room, another visual phenomenon, the moon illusion, vividly demonstrates the in-terdependence of size and distance. You have probably noticed that the moon, especially when full, appears much larger on the horizon than it does when overhead at its zenith. Of course, the actual size of the moon remains constant, as does its distance from the earth: the moon is 2,160 miles in diameter and 239,000 miles away. This means that regardless of its position in the sky, the full moon casts a circular image about one-sixth of a millimeter (0.52 degrees, visual angle) in diameter on your retina. Why, then, does the apparent size of the moon change so strikingly?

One possible answer is that the moon's **perceived distance** varies with its heavenly position. Near the horizon, where there are many depth cues, the moon seems to be farther away than when it is at its zenith. This idea is illustrated in Figure 8.25. But we know that the size of its retinal image remains constant regardless of the moon's position in the sky. This produces something of a conflict: Usually, when the distance from you to a single object changes, the size of the retinal image also changes. Yet, in the case of the moon, perceived distance *changes,* but retinal image size *remains constant.* And the only way for image size to remain constant when distance changes is for object size to change, too. With the moon illusion, when perceived distance is great (moon on the horizon), then perceived object size must be large. But when perceived distance is reduced (moon at its zenith), perceived object size is smaller. This relation

FIGURE 8.24 | The Ames room: A demonstration that perceived distance influences apparent size. (Baron Wolman/Woodfin Camp and Associates.)

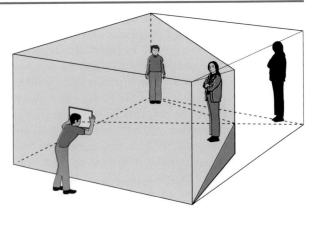

FIGURE 8.25 | Explanation of the moon illusion based on perceived distance.

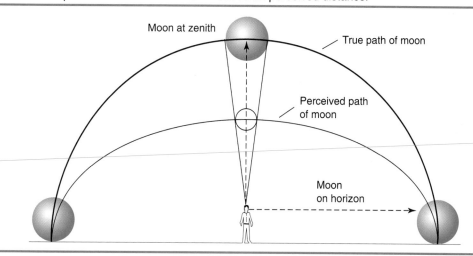

Moon at zenith

True path of moon

Perceived path of moon

Moon on horizon

between perceived depth of a fixed size retinal image is known as **Emmert's law,** and the moon illusion is a prime example of this law at work.

Support for this idea comes from some classic experiments by Kaufman and Rock (1962). They found that the normally large moon on the horizon shrank as soon as it was viewed through a small hole in a piece of opaque material. Looking at the moon through such a tiny hole eliminated distance cues provided by the horizon. You can easily replicate this finding by viewing the horizon moon monocularly through a small peephole made by clenching your fist.

Kaufman and Rock also discovered a way to make the normally small zenith moon appear large: They had observers view the moon through an artificial horizon drawn on a large sheet of clear plastic. Thus, by manipulating apparent distance, Rock and Kaufman could enhance the illusion or make it vanish. We should point out, however, that not everyone agrees with the theory that the moon illusion depends on perceived distance (Baird, 1982; Baird and Wagner, 1982; Iavecchia, Iavecchia, and Roscoe, 1983; Enright, 1989). Perhaps these disagreements are not surprising. After all, people have been speculating about the moon illusion for more than 2,000 years (Hershenson, 1989).

The Ames room and the moon illusion are just two of many visual illusions involving errors in perceived distance and size. After completing the roster of monocular depth cues, we will consider a few other visual illusions in greater detail. But before moving to the next source of monocular depth information, we want to mention one other interesting discovery about perceived size. You might think that children, by the time they've learned to walk and to manipulate objects, would know better than to try to wear a doll's shoe or to attempt to squeeze into a toy car. But based on the results from a recent study, that intuition appears incorrect. From anecdotal observations, DeLoache, Uttal, and Rosengren (2004) noticed that young children often attempt to perform actions using objects that are grossly too small to support the action. Intrigued by these observations, DeLoache and colleagues systematically documented these errors in a laboratory setting where children were videotaped playing with common objects, including miniature replicas of objects encountered in everyday activities. They observed a significant number of what were termed "scale" errors in children as old as 2 ½ years of age. These errors included comical attempts to climb inside a toy car or to sit on a miniature chair. DeLoache and colleagues believe these errors do not arise from poor size perception but, instead, stem from a dissociation between perception of the size of an object and action planning in response to that object. In effect, perception of the object triggers a motor program that is not guided by perceived size but, instead, by general, "unscaled" knowledge about that general category of objects. The authors speculate that this dissociation reflects immaturity in the connections between the ventral stream pathway that mediates object perception and the dorsal stream pathway that guides actions with objects (these two pathways were discussed in Chapter 4).

This completes our survey of size perception and brings us to our third static cue to depth, perspective.

Perspective   The term *perspective* refers to changes in the appearance of surfaces or objects as they recede in distance away from an observer. As mentioned in the introduction to this chapter, the geometry of visual perspective was developed during the fifteenth century by Italian artists. Here, we are concerned primarily with perspective from the perceptual, not the geometrical, standpoint, so it will not be necessary to discuss the geometry of perspective in any detail. Pirenne (1970) offers a well-illustrated account of that topic.

Let's begin with **linear perspective,** which we will illustrate with an example. Suppose you looked out a window at a neighboring building, the situation depicted in Figure 8.3A. Now imagine using a marking pen to trace the outline of the building onto the glass window-pane, being careful to hold your head still. You would be tracing the two-dimensional projection of this three-dimensional scene. The result—a *perspective drawing,* as it is called—would look something like the outline drawing shown in Figure 8.3B. Note that the outlines of the building are drawn in such a way that the lines converge. In reality, of course, the roof's top and bottom run parallel to each other. The observer sees them as converging and draws them this way because the roof recedes in depth away from the observation point. This convergence of lines is termed *linear perspective.* When pictorially portrayed, linear perspective generates a strong impression of depth.

As we saw in the Ames room (Figure 8.24), the impression of depth produced by linear perspective can be strong enough to cause physically similar objects to appear different in size. In that case, the room's distorted construction furnished perspective cues that misrepresented the actual layout of the room. Hence the sizes of the people in the room were also distorted. Figure 8.26 provides another example of how perspective can influence perceived size. In fact, the perceived depth implied by linear perspective can be sufficiently robust to contradict depth information conveyed by retinal disparity (Stevens and Brookes, 1988), as mentioned earlier.

There is another consequence of viewing surfaces or planes that recede in depth. Most surfaces have a visible texture, such as the grain in wood or the irregularities in a sidewalk. So long as a surface is not perpendicular to your line of sight, the density of the sur-face's texture will appear to vary with distance. Examples of this are shown in Figure 8.27. This form of perspective has been called **texture gradient** by James Gibson, the first person to emphasize the potency of this source of depth information.

According to Gibson (1950), texture gradients provide precise and unambiguous information about the distances and slants of surfaces, as well as about the sizes of objects located on those surfaces. Gibson also proposed that abrupt changes in texture gradient signal the presence of edges or corners. You saw one example of texture-defined edges in Figure 5.37, and another example appears in Figure 8.28. Note that the texture discontinuity implies the presence of a bend, or corner, in a continuous surface. Stevens (1981) provides a detailed description of the geometrical basis for determining distances from texture gradients.

Just how accurately can people derive depth information from texture patterns? Sinai, Ooi, and He (1998) performed a simple but revealing experiment to answer this question. They had people stand outdoors and estimate the distance between themselves and an object located anywhere from 2 to 7 meters in front of them. Observers were quite accurate in judging distance so long as the ground plane was uniformly textured with, for example, grass. But when the ground plane contained a gap—such as a ditch—which disrupted the texture plane, distances were seriously over-estimated; the object appeared to be farther from the observer. Errors in judged distance also occurred when the ground plane between the observer and the object was divided into two adjacent regions composed of distinctly different textures (grass and concrete). Based on these findings, Sinai, Ooi, and He concluded that because human vision is adapted to terrestrial navigation, it relies heavily on a uniformly textured ground surface as a cue for spatial distance. Abrupt disruptions in the ground plane (a highly unusual situation in the natural environment), undermine this cue and, therefore, perturb distance perception.

Continuing our list of perspective cues, you've probably noticed that objects in the distance are seen less clearly than those closer to you. This effect is called **aerial perspective,** and it occurs because light is scattered as it travels through atmosphere, especially if the air contains dust or excess moisture. This scattering of light reduces the contrast and, hence, blurs the clarity of objects' details. Naturally, light reflected from more distant objects must pass through more of this atmosphere than light reflected from nearby objects. As a consequence,

FIGURE 8.26 | Linear perspective. In which one of the four perspective drawings (A, B, C, or D) do the two thick horizontal lines appear equal in size? Use a ruler to discover the correct answer. This figure illustrates that linear perspective can cause objects whose sizes are really different to appear identical in size.

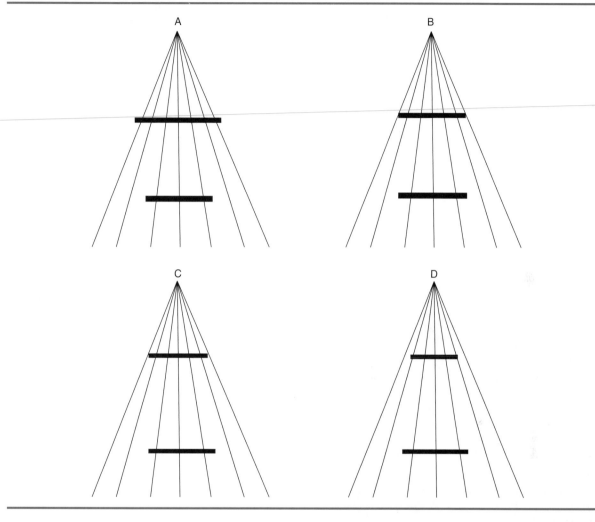

more distant objects appear less distinct, or hazy, as you might say (see Figure 8.29).

Laboratory simulations show that reductions in the contrast of features in a picture cause those features to appear more distant. So reduced contrast from aerial perspective is an effective depth cue (O'Shea, Blackburn, and Ono, 1994). In the absence of contrast reduction, blur can also serve as a depth cue (O'Shea, Sekuler, and Govan, 1997). The cues of reduced contrast and blur can have perceptual consequences. Upon initially encountering conditions of extremely clean air (such as in the mountains), city dwellers accustomed to looking at the environment through less clean atmo-

sphere may seriously underestimate distances. Conversely, an object viewed in fog is perceived to be more distant than it actually is, because fog mimics aerial perspective, which probably contributes to the increased accident rate associated with driving in fog (Cavallo, Colomb, and Doré, 2001).

Before wrapping up our discussion of perspective, we want to mention one other, related monocular depth cue that involves a form of perspective. Start with a geometric principle: In the natural world, objects that are farther away from you tend to be located higher up in the visual field than do objects that are closer to you. (You can confirm this characteristic of the natural world the

FIGURE 8.27 | Texture gradients provide information about depth.

FIGURE 8.28 | Texture discontinuity signals the presence of an edge or corner.

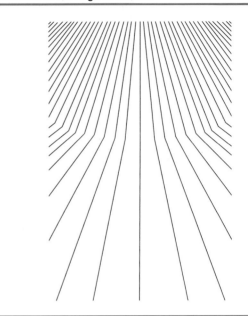

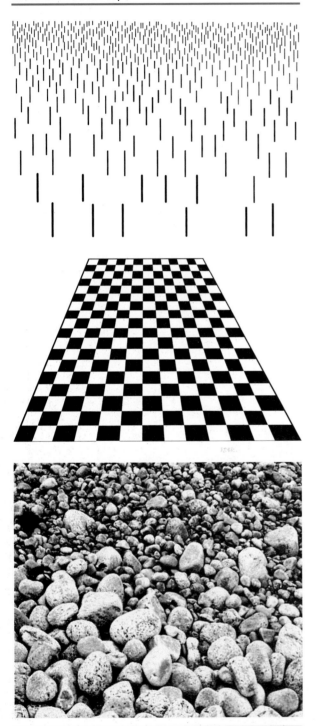

next time you are outdoors.) As a result of this tendency, when you create a 2D perspective projection of a 3D scene, objects located higher in the picture plane will appear farther away than objects located lower in the picture plane. You can see the perceptual consequence of this geometric principle in Figure 8.29, where portions of the scene closest to you (the bushes, for example) are located toward the bottom of the image whereas more distant objects (the pier) are situated higher in the image. You can even see this cue at work in Figure 8.2 where, despite the other confusing monocular depth cues, you still see the tower and the tree located far away relative to the animals and the palm branches. The operation of this cue—height in the image plane—is revealed very clearly in Figure 8.30, where you see an undulating, textured surface. You probably see the central part of the figure as a "hill" surrounded by a "valley" that, in turn, is surrounded by a circular ridge. But turn the figure upside down, and you'll see hills turn into valleys and vice versa. In fact, the figure viewed in either orientation is consistent with either interpretation—the key is how you interpret the slant of the plane on which the undulations appear. According to Reichel and Todd (1990) people are used to seeing surfaces recede in depth so that portions of the surface farther away appear higher in the visual field, the tendency we discussed above. Thus, when

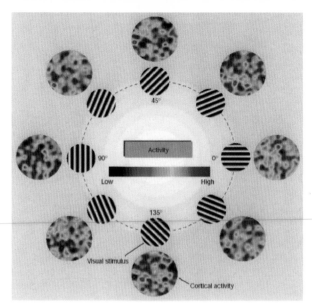

PLATE 1 Color-coded maps of neural activity within the visual cortex of a subject (a cat, in this experiment) who viewed gratings of varying orientation. See pages 136 and 137 for details.

PLATE 3 See page 234. In the color photograph on the left, notice the green patch on the red sleeve of the girl's sweater. The green and red colors are essentially identical in lightness, as you can see in the black and white photograph on the right: the patch almost disappears because it differs only in color from the sleeve. of girl with green patch on red sleeve

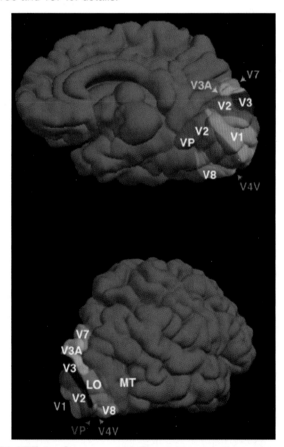

PLATE 2 See page 142. The right hemisphere of a human brain seen in medial view (upper image) and lateral view (lower image). The colored regions, based on results of fMRI experiments, show key centers of the visual system. LO = lateral occipital area; MT = middle temporal visual.

PLATE 4 See page 234. A creature in the picture is difficult to see because the creature blends in with its surrounding. Can you find this camouflaged creature? The answer is given on page 271.

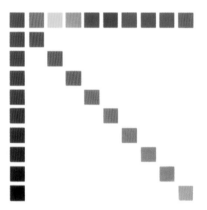

PLATE 5 The top photograph shows a scene rendered in normal colors. That same scene is harder to recognize rendered in unusual colors. See page 235.

PLATE 6 See page 237. Patches illustrating three dimensions —hue, brightness and saturation— of color experience. Hue varies across the top row of patches; brightness varies within the vertical set of patches at the left; saturation varies among the patches on the diagonal.

Common color names

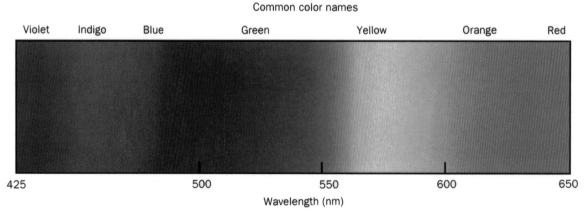

| Violet | Indigo | Blue | Green | Yellow | Orange | Red |

| 425 | 500 | 550 | 600 | 650 |

Wavelength (nm)

PLATE 7 See page 237. Upper axis: Color names applied by Newton to various regions of the spectrum. Lower axis: wavelengths of light (in nanometers).

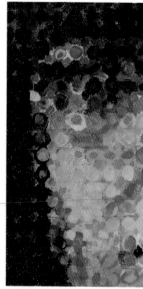

PLATE 8 See page 244. Left panel: "Susan," a painting by Chuck Close. Right panel: a close-up view of a section of the painting, which reveals the remarkable technique the artist used in creating the painting. Painted in 1987, "Susan" is oil on canvas, 24 × 20".

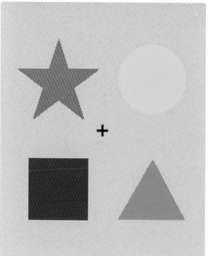

PLATE 9 See page 246. Stimuli for producing and experiencing color adaptation. Left panel: The adaptation stimulus; right panel: test stimulus. Maintain your gaze on the cross in the left panel for about 30 seconds. Then, to experience the adaptation effect, quickly shift your gaze to the cross in the right panel.

Adapt   Test

PLATE 10 See page 246. Photograph of an Amish quilt, which illustrates various principles of color contrast. The pattern used in this quilt is known as Irish Chain. (From the collection of R. Blake.)

PLATE 11 See page 246. Failure of color constancy. Left panel: Photograph of fruit and other objects illuminated with natural light. Center panel: Photograph of same scene, but illuminated by short wavelength light. Right panel: Photograph of same scene, illuminated by long wavelength light. Note how the obvious differences among objects, seen in the left panel, are lost in the other two panels.

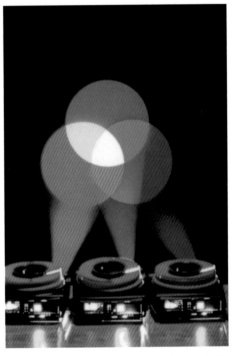

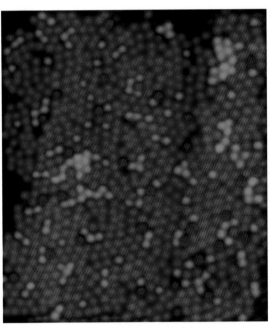

PLATE 12 See page 250. Different chromatic lights from three projectors overlap to produce a variety of color experiences.

PLATE 13 See page 252. Photograph of receptor mosaic in a small square patch of retina in the human eye. This photograph, which was produced by Austin Roorda and David Williams, shows S, M and L cones as blue, green and red discs.

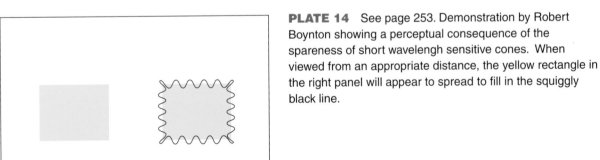

PLATE 14 See page 253. Demonstration by Robert Boynton showing a perceptual consequence of the spareness of short wavelengh sensitive cones. When viewed from an appropriate distance, the yellow rectangle in the right panel will appear to spread to fill in the squiggly black line.

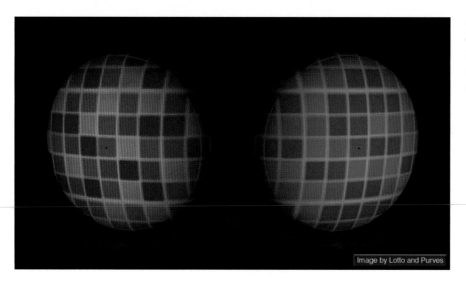

PLATE 15 Example of color contrast created by Beau Lotto and Dale Purves. See Box 7.3, page 256, for instructions.

Image by Lotto and Purves

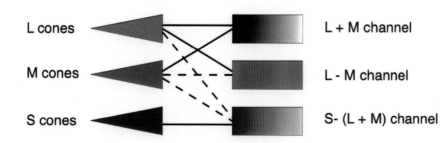

PLATE 16 Schematic diagram showing the three cone types and their inputs to the two chromatic channels and one achromatic channel. See page 256.

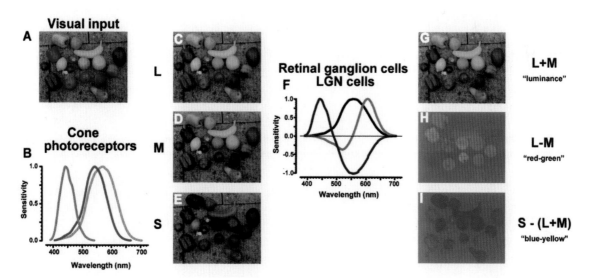

PLATE 17 Suppose a visual scene consisting of different colored objects (A) stimulates an eye containing three types of cones, whose individual sensitivities are shown in B. The scene generates distinct patterns of excitation in the three cones types, which are represented in C, D and E for the long-, medium, and short-wavelength sensitive cones. These cone signals are combined within the retina and LGN (F) into an achromatic channel (G) and two chromatic channels (H and I). See page 261.

PLATE 18 Color induction by contrast. The inner and outer rings are identical in wavelength but look different in color because they lie on different color backgrounds. Demonstration courtesy of Donald MacLeod. See page 261.

PLATE 19 The words "COLOR" and "VISION" are printed in identical ink, and the words "IS" and "AMAZING" are printed in identical ink. Context causes the ink colors to look different. Demonstration courtesy of Steve Shevell. See page 261.

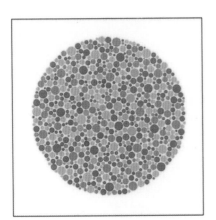

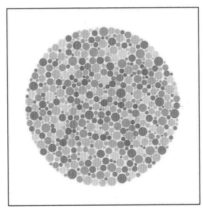

PLATE 20 See page 264. Ishihara color plate. What numbers do you see in each panel? These panels have been reproduced from Ishihara's Test for Colour Blindness published by KANEHARA & Co., LTD., Tokyo, Japan. Color blindness testing cannot be conducted with this reproduction. For accurate testing, the original plate should be used.

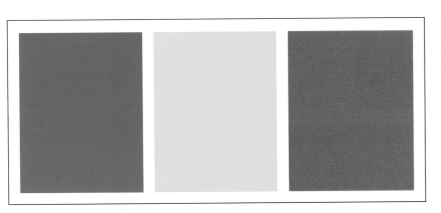

PLATE 21 See page 264. Three squares whose colors are indistinguishable to a red-green dichromat.

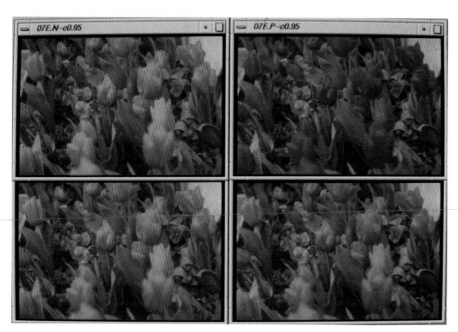

PLATE 22 See page 265. Simulations of scene's appearance for trichromats (upper left panel) and three different kinds of dichromats (other panels).

PLATE 23 See page 267. Page from a coloring book that has been (inappropriately) colored in by a patient with achromatopsia.

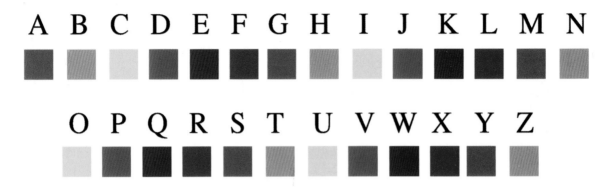

PLATE 24 Letter/color associations for a color-graphemic synesthete. This person sees each of the black letters in colors, with the patch below each letter indicating the letter's perceived color. Different synesthetes have different color-grapheme associations. See 269.

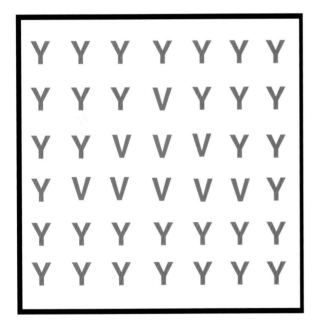

PLATE 25 A synesthete who sees Y as red and V as green sees Figure 7.20 like this. See page 270.

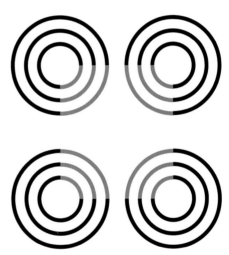

PLATE 26 Demonstration of neon spreading. See page 298.

FIGURE 8.29 | This photograph, "Relative Depth" by Dennis Markley, effectively portrays several monocular depth cues, including aerial perspective. See if you can identify others.

we view a 2D picture like the one in Figure 8.30, we automatically invoke the same bias and, therefore, see those portions of the textured surface in the top part of the image as farther away. And if the overall surface is seen as slanting away from you, there is only one reasonable interpretation for the texture curvature you're experiencing. If you can somehow mentally convince yourself that the textured surface in Figure 8.30 forms a ceiling above you, you will now see the depth undulations spontaneously reverse before your eyes! To do this, you have to imagine the bottom of the figure being located farther away from you than the top, so that the entire surface slants downward.

Shading   Last in our list of static depth cues is **shading,** and here a series of computer-generated images created by Daniel Kersten and colleagues dramatizes how potent shading can be as a depth cue (Kersten, Mamassian, and

Knill, 1997). Take a look at Figure 8.31. If asked to judge which of the three squares seems to be hovering highest above the checkered background, people consistently select the right-hand square, with the middle one next, and the left-hand square judged as closer to the background. The only source of information triggering these vivid impressions of depth comes from the location of the fuzzy shadow relative to the square.

An even more compelling version of this demonstration is provided by an animation in which the fuzzy shadow moves back and forth over the checkered surface in the direction denoted in Figure 8.32 (the animation itself can be found on the Web; (www,mhhe.com/blake5). Even though it's only the shadow that actually moves, the white square appears to move up and down in depth relative to the checkered surface—the shadow's movement is attributed to illusory motion of the square. Note that this is not the only possible interpretation of this sequence of

FIGURE 8.30 | The textured surface looks the way it does (a "hill" in the middle) because we assume the ground plane surface is receding in depth such that the farther portion is higher in the picture plane. But if you can imagine this as a ceiling plane viewed from below, the depth of the undulations will reverse. Turn the figure upside down to see how it will appear if you're successful seeing it as a ceiling plane.

FIGURE 8.31 | Which one of these three squares is hovering farthest from the textured surface?

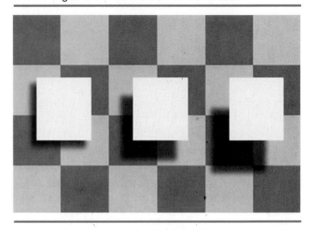

FIGURE 8.32 | When an implied shadow moves laterally (denoted by arrows), one sees the stationary square appear to move up and down in depth relative to the textured surface.

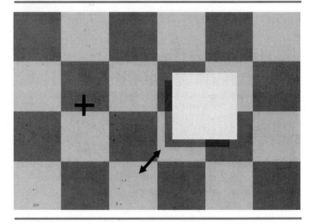

events. The same shadow movement could have been produced by a stationary white square illuminated by a moving light source. However, we simply do not perceive the animation in this way. Instead, we always perceive the square moving in depth. Evidently, our visual systems automatically assume that any light source producing a shadow is stationary, a perfectly reasonable assumption in the natural environment.

Now look at the two spherical objects in Figure 8.33. You probably see the one on the left as a "bump" protruding from the background (convex bump) and the other as a scooped-out cavity (concave indentation). The two surfaces, in other words, are perceived to have different directions of curvature. Among the sources of information promoting these impressions of curvature are the specular highlights (the reflections) and, especially, the locations of the shadows. The locations of these highlights and shadows in the figure also signify that the light source is located above the curved surfaces.

But what happens when there is no explicit information about where the light source is located? Take a look at the spherical objects in Figure 8.34. The one on the left may appear convex ("bump") while the other appears concave ("indentation"). According to some researchers (e.g.,

Ramachandran, 1988), we perceive those objects as convex and concave because we perceive the lightness gradients as shadows and, at the same time, we unconsciously assume that light comes from above. That's not a bad assumption, because in the natural environment the sun—our sole source of natural light—is always above us, in the sky. Perhaps, then, this constraint is built into the visual system. If that's true, then turning the book upside down should now cause the bump to become concave and the indentation to become convex. Try it and see what happens.

FIGURE 8.33 | Shading and highlights influence perceived surface curvature. See text for details.

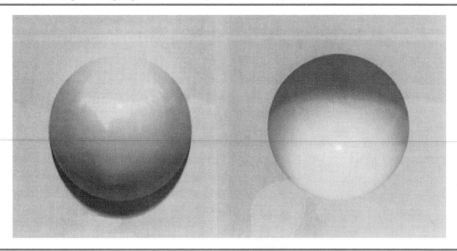

FIGURE 8.34 | Does the hemisphere on the left appear convex and the one on the right concave? If so, the implied shading could be a contributing factor, if you assume the light source is located above the figure. You can test this hypothesis by viewing the figure with the book turned upside down.

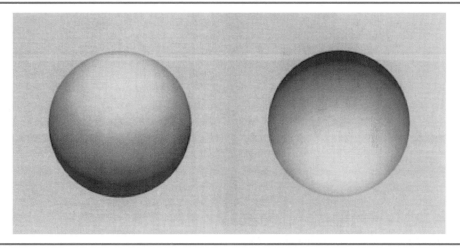

This completes our catalog of the static monocular cues to depth. As noted previously, artists are able to use these cues to create an impression of three dimensionality on a flat canvas. By way of review, see if you can identify the various static depth cues as they appear in the photograph in Figure 8.29. There is, however, one very potent source of monocular depth information that no painting, etching, or snapshot can ever capture, and it's to that depth cue we now turn.

Motion Parallax

Look again at the Ames room in Figure 8.24, where static depth cues markedly distorted the perceived size of objects. When you look at the Ames room in person, you need to view the scene from one specifically designated vantage point, and you must hold your head perfectly still. Simply moving your head back and forth immediately reveals the true layout of the room and, consequently, you see the objects (people included) at their

FIGURE 8.35 | Two situations in which motion parallax provides potential depth information. The arrows indicate the direction of relative apparent motion. In the left-hand panel the person in the moving vehicle is looking at a point on the far horizon; in the right-hand panel the person is looking at a location midway between herself and the horizon.

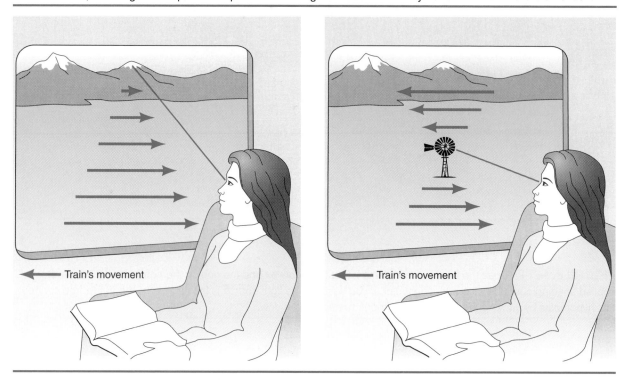

true sizes. Motion, in other words, very quickly dispels misperceptions conveyed by static cues, and that's because motion introduces another very potent source of depth information.

As you move about in the world, objects constantly shift positions relative to one another within your field of view. This happens whenever you are walking, traveling in a car, or simply turning your head to look at something. The next time you're a passenger in a moving car, notice how the world appears as you look out the window. First, look far away, to some spot on the distant horizon. You will see that objects in the foreground (nearer to you than the horizon) appear to stream across your visual field in a direction opposite to your movement. Moreover, the closest objects appear to stream more rapidly through your visual field than do objects farther away, producing a speed gradient related to distance. Next, while still looking out the passenger window, shift your fixation from the distant horizon to a location at some intermediate distance. Now you will notice that objects between you and your point of fixation will continue to stream past in a direction opposite

to the car's movement, with the same speed gradient. But objects beyond your point of fixation will now seem to stream in the *same* direction that you're traveling, with a gradient of apparent speed that grows from your point of fixation. These complex flows of motion, illustrated in Figure 8.35, are examples of **motion parallax**— differential retinal image motion produced by observer movements when viewing stationary objects located at different distances. Motion parallax can provide very precise information about the relative distances between those objects.

To take advantage of this cue, your entire body does not have to be moving: You can perceive depth from motion parallax by moving just your head. Take a moment to test this for yourself. Pick out an object in front of you and look at it with one eye closed. This eliminates retinal disparity as a possible cue. Now, while continuing to look at this object, move your head back and forth in a sideways direction. Notice how other objects at different distances appear to move relative to the one at which you are looking.

To experience this parallax effect again, hold your two index fingers at different distances in front of you and perform this exercise: With one eye closed, stare at one of your two fingers while moving your head back and forth. Again, you will see that one finger shifts in position, as if it were moving, relative to the other. The direction and speed of this shift depends on the distance between your two fingers and on the overall distance from you to your hands.

So far we have discussed situations in which the observer moves and objects in the world remain still. However, motion parallax is also effective in the opposite situation, when a *stationary* observer views a scene in which objects themselves move. For instance, imagine looking at clusters of leaves in a tree with one of your two eyes closed. When there is no wind, the still leaves seem to blend into a confusing array. But when stirred to life by a breeze, different groups of leaves stand out conspicuously in depth from one another. The movement of the leaves creates motion parallax information in the same way that movement of your head would.[8]

Motion pictures and television have made excellent use of depth from motion. For example, many of the special effects in *Star Trek* television episodes and in the *Star Wars* movies rely heavily on the cue of motion parallax. And all video arcade games and other, more sophisticated virtual viewing environments exploit motion to create a compelling sense of three dimensionality. Motion's potency is most vividly dramatized by computer-generated animations composed entirely of randomly arrayed clusters of dots. Viewing any single frame of the animation, you'd see nothing but a meaningless, random arrangement of dots. But when those dots undergo differential movement on the video screen, you see vivid 3D surfaces that can be quite complex in shape (Turner, Braunstein, and Andersen, 1995). Here, the brain has literally created a 3D shape from motion, a capability discussed in more detail later.

Using motion parallax, people are quite good at judging whether one object is situated in front of or behind another one. In fact, relative depth judgments based on

---

[8]Some perception researchers (for example, Cutting [1997]) distinguish between observer-induced motion parallax (where optical image motion is produced by a moving observer viewing stationary objects, sometimes called "motion perspective") and object-induced parallax (where a stationary viewer sees objects moving in the environment located at different depth planes, sometimes called "kinetic depth"). There is some justification for this distinction because the former is very useful for self-navigation, whereas the latter is more useful for 3D shape perception.

FIGURE 8.36 | An illustration of the equivalence of retinal disparity and motion parallax.

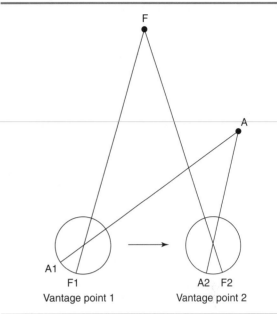

motion parallax are almost as accurate as those made using binocular disparity (Graham, 1965). This makes sense when you compare the geometrical bases of motion parallax and binocular disparity. Figure 8.36 shows two objects, A and F, being viewed from two vantage points, 1 and 2. Let's assume that fixation is always maintained on object F (for "fixation"). This means that at both vantage points the image of F will fall on the fovea. Because A is closer than F, the image of A will fall on one retinal area, A1, when A is viewed from vantage point 1; however, when A is viewed from vantage point 2, the image of A will fall on a different retinal area, A2. The distance between the retinal images produced by A and F varies from one vantage point to the other. At vantage point 1, the retinal images are separated by the distance between F1 and A1; at vantage point 2, they are separated by a different amount, the distance between F2 and A2. This variation in the retinal image distance between the images provides information about the distance between objects A and F.

There are two ways in which the situation shown in Figure 8.36 could arise. Vantage points 1 and 2 could represent the successive positions of a single eye as it moves from 1 to 2. In this case, the resulting variation in retinal image distances would be called *motion parallax*. Alternatively, vantage points 1 and 2 could represent the positions of left and right eyes. In this case, the variation in

FIGURE 8.37 | Motion parallax, like stereopsis, can generate information about object form. The five panels in the top row depict changes over time in the position of a subset of dots in the display. These changes are produced either by the observer's head movements or by movement of the display itself. The bottom panel depicts the stable percept produced by either of these maneuvers.

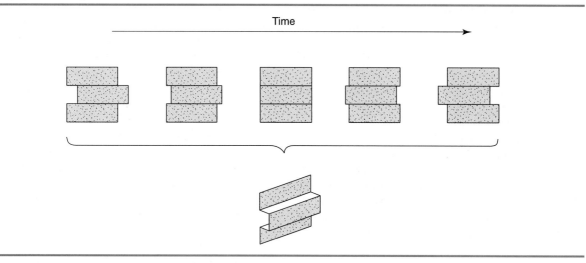

Time

retinal image distance would be called *retinal disparity.* In fact, if a single eye moves by 6.5 centimeters (the distance between your eyes), this movement produces a depth cue—motion parallax—that is equivalent to the cue produced by binocular viewing—retinal disparity.

There is another similarity between motion parallax and stereopsis. Recall from our discussion of random-dot stereograms how forms invisible to either eye alone could be synthesized from retinal disparity information. The same kind of synthesis of form can occur through motion parallax. In an ingenious set of experiments that have become classics, Brian Rogers and Maureen Graham (1979, 1984) asked observers to view a single array of random dots with just one eye (it is important to keep in mind that their stimuli were not stereograms and that viewing was monocular). The entire display consisted of about 2,000 dots, a subset of which could be displaced while the rest maintained their same positions. Figure 8.37 depicts one such display. In one condition, the displacement occurred whenever just the observer's head moved. In other words, moving the head from side to side caused the predesignated subset of dots to move relative to the rest. This condition would correspond to observer-induced motion. In a second condition, the observer held still while the display itself was moved, with the predesignated region of dots moving by an amount different from the rest. Rogers and Graham found that both forms of relative motion generated a clear, immediate impression of a surface standing out in depth from its background (as in the bottom panel of Figure 8.37). Moreover, so long as either their heads or the display moved, observers could accurately describe the shape of this surface. But whenever both the observer's head and the display were stationary, the sensation of depth immediately vanished. Rogers and Graham's study clearly shows that motion parallax, like retinal disparity, can generate information about the shape and depth of objects, in the absence of all other cues.[9] In fact, under some conditions, people cannot distinguish depth produced by motion from depth produced by binocular disparity because the two are so compellingly similar (Nawrot and Blake, 1993).

So, head motion with one eye generates the same kind of information generated by two eyes in a stationary head.[10] This raises an interesting question: Why is the vi-

---

[9]When Rogers and Graham's task is repeated on observers who have recently consumed enough vodka to produce intoxication, motion parallax performance is substantially impaired (Nawrot, Nordenstrom, and Olson, 2004); this impairment may result from disturbances in tracking eye movements, which probably help calibrate motion parallax signals.

[10]Without even thinking about it, people with only one eye move their heads more when attempting to make depth judgments (Marotta et al., 1998). Presumably they are creating motion parallax information to compensate for the absence of stereopsis.

sual system designed to provide two equally sensitive mechanisms for seeing objects in depth, one monocular and one binocular? Wouldn't it be safer to relocate the eyes on the side of the head, thereby achieving a panoramic view of the world? Then the consequent loss of disparity information could be compensated by the equally effective cue of motion parallax.

The key to this puzzle may have something to do with the type of animals that possess well-developed binocular vision. As a rule, these frontal-eyed animals are predators, who rely on stealth to capture their prey. Movements of the hunter's head or body could forewarn an intended victim, thereby costing the hunter a meal. So it may have been advantageous for predators to develop the capacity for stereopsis, a quieter but equally accurate means of depth perception. For humans whose hunting is confined to the supermarket, where there is no real concern about giving away one's whereabouts, motion parallax and stereopsis provide largely redundant information.

Integration of Depth Information

The previous sections have described various sources of information specifying depth relations among objects and distances from a perceiver to those objects. As you should now be able to appreciate, the visual world is rich with depth information. How, then, are these multiple cues combined? Do we rely only on the most salient? Do some sources of depth information work better than others in particular circumstances? How are other aspects of vision influenced by depth information? Investigators are now beginning to address these questions, and this section provides an overview of some of the emerging answers.

One strategy for studying depth interactions entails varying the number of depth cues present in a display and asking how depth perception is affected. An excellent example of the application of this strategy comes from the work of Bruno and Cutting (1988). They tested all different combinations of four sources of depth information—size, occlusion, motion, and perspective—and measured the quality and the accuracy of depth for each combination. The results showed that these sources interacted additively, as if each source were processed separately and made its own unique contribution to depth perception. Bruno and Cutting speculate that the visual system is composed of different "minimodules," as they were termed, each devoted to one source of depth information. Conceivably, these minimodules might relate to the multiplicity of specialized visual areas in the brain. In their studies, Bruno and Cutting varied the number of available cues, but these cues were never placed in conflict.

The strategy of pitting cues against one another has been employed in many other experiments (see, for example, Braunstein and Stern, 1980; Stevens and Brookes, 1988; Rogers and Collett, 1989). In essentially all cases, depth perception is degraded when cues conflict, implying that no single source of information dominates. In a related vein, it is possible to create displays in which one source of information (for example, perspective) generates ambiguous depth, meaning that the shape or configuration of a three-dimensional object can be seen in multiple, mutually exclusive ways.

A classic example of an ambiguous figure, the Necker cube, was shown in Chapter 1 (see Figure 1.3). The cube's configuration fluctuates over time as different components take turns being perceived as the front face of the cube. Either interpretation is consistent with the available perspective information specifying depth, so perception is unstable. However, the introduction of unambiguous disparity information stabilizes perception: The cube is seen in one perspective only. This strategy of disambiguating one source of depth information with another has been successfully applied to study other combinations of information as well (Dosher, Sperling, and Wurst, 1986; Nawrot and Blake, 1991).

Finally, another strategy involves determining how depth information influences other aspects of vision, such as object recognition. To give an example, Nakayama, Shimojo, and Silverman (1989) measured how well people could recognize faces when portions of the faces were missing. In one condition missing portions appeared to be occluded by blank strips that appeared to be situated in front of the face (Figure 8.38A). A second condition displayed the same visible portions of the face but with the difference that they appeared as strips in front of a blank background (Figure 8.38B). Nakayama and colleagues used stereoscopic depth to manipulate the depth relations of the face regions and the blank regions. In the first condition observers perceived the head of a person partially occluded by venetian blinds; they had no difficulty recognizing the faces. But in the second condition recognition performance was seriously impaired, even though the number of face segments and the quality of the image remained the same. The fragments made no sense because the face no longer looked partially occluded. Using the stereo pairs in Figure 8.39, you can experience what the participants in this experiment saw. In this figure (an actual version of one used by Nakayama and colleagues), random speckles ("noise") have been added to the images to make recognition more difficult from the outset. Using this demonstration, notice how depth interpretation—occluded versus nonoccluded—influences the perceptual organization of the face fragments.

FIGURE 8.38 | A partially visible face as it would appear behind (left-hand drawing, A) or in front of (right-hand drawing, B) a surface. In Nakayama, Shimojo, and Silverman (1989), stereopsis was used to place the face segments in depth relative to the surface.

A   B

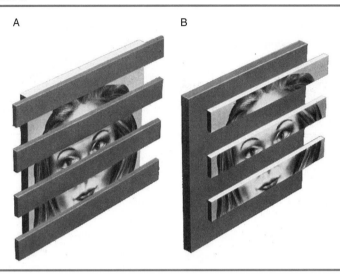

FIGURE 8.39 | Use the free-fusion technique (Box 8.2) to view the middle and left-hand pictures. The strips of face will appear behind the opaque, horizontal strips (as if the person were being viewed through venetian blinds). Next free-fuse the middle and right-hand pictures. Now the face itself appears as strips or in front of the opaque strips.

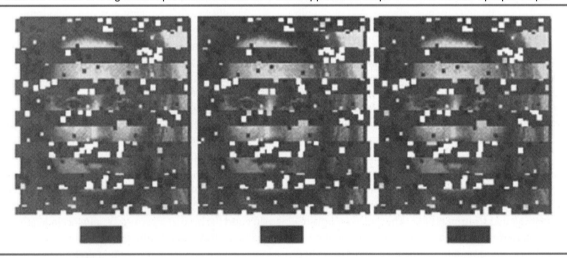

Depth, Illusions, and Size Constancy

In our discussion of static depth cues, we noted several perceptual errors that occur when people are confronted with misleading depth information. These errors involved distortions in perceived size, such as the unusually large appearing moon when it is on the horizon. Several other, classic visual illusions are also characterized by misperceptions of size.

Examples of two of the better-known size illusions are given in Figure 8.40. In both cases, one portion of the

FIGURE 8.40 | Two size illusions.

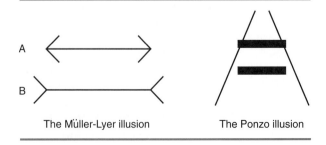

The Müller-Lyer illusion   The Ponzo illusion

FIGURE 8.41 | The Müller-Lyer illusion could arise from implied depth information.

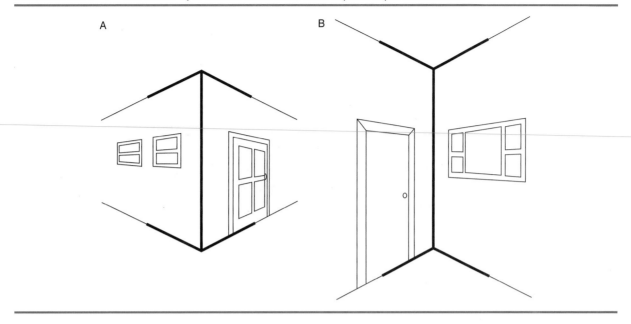

figure appears larger than its partner, even though both are really identical in size. For over a century, psychologists have been fascinated by these illusions and have focused a great deal of research on testing various theories about the origins of these illusions.

Let's conclude this chapter by considering one particular theory that, although not universally accepted, has endured over the years. This theory attributes errors in perceived size to the operation of monocular depth cues (Gregory, 1997). We'll call this the *depth theory,* and we'll introduce it with some examples.

Consider the left-hand illusion in Figure 8.40, known as the *Müller-Lyer illusion.* According to the depth theory, the arrowheads on the ends of the vertical lines can be seen as angles formed by two intersecting surfaces. An example of this idea is shown in Figure 8.41. In both drawings, the vertical line represents the point of intersection, or the corner, formed by two surfaces. When the arrowheads point outward (as in B), the two surfaces appear slanted toward you. When they point inward (as in A), the surfaces appear to recede away from you. Why does the "corner" formed by the receding surfaces (inward-pointing arrowheads) appear longer than the one

formed by the approaching surfaces (outward-pointing arrowheads)?

According to the depth theory, the answer is simple: Because of the perspective cues supplied by the arrowheads, the receding corner appears farther away than the approaching corner. At the same time, the retinal images of the two corners are identical in size. Now there is only one way objects at *different* distances can cast images of *equal* size: The farther object must actually be larger. In the case of the two vertical lines, the height of the corner formed by the receding surfaces (inward-pointing arrowheads) would have to be longer than the height of the one that is formed by the approaching surfaces (outward-pointing arrowheads). And this is exactly how it is perceived.

The same line of reasoning applies to the other size illusion illustrated in Figure 8.40, the *Ponzo illusion.* In this case, too, perspective cues imply that one region of the figure is located farther away than another. According to the depth theory, this distance information enters into judgments of the sizes of objects occupying these different regions. Note, again, that the apparently larger object is situated in that portion of the figure that appears farther away.

The depth theory, then, attributes size illusions to errors in perceived distance (Gregory, 1970). The theory is based on the observation that perceived size remains constant despite differences in distance from the viewer and, hence, changes in the size of the retinal image cast. In other words, perceived size is *scaled* in terms of perceived distance, a process known as **size constancy.**

We call size constancy a scaling process because one unit of measure (retinal image size) is converted, or scaled, into another (perceived size). Road maps typically include scales that allow users to transform centimeters into kilometers (or inches into miles); the visual system contains a mechanism that scales image size into object size. It's crucial that retinal image size be scaled, since the size of the image of an object depends on how far away that object is. As a result, *un*scaled *retinal* image size would be a poor index of *object* size. Without size scaling, you would always be confused about the height of people, the width of doorways, the size of cars, and so on. The fact that you rarely err in these kinds of judgments means that the visual system utilizes depth information in making size judgments.

Just how good is the visual system at estimating the true sizes of objects? In a classic study, Holway and Boring (1941) found that an observer's accuracy at judging a circle's size was almost flawless under conditions rich with depth information. But as depth cues were progressively eliminated (for example, by requiring a person to close one eye), size judgments became increasingly dependent on retinal image size; the perceived size of the same object increased when the object was closer to the observer—a breakdown in size constancy.

In an interesting extension of Holway and Boring's study, Schiffman (1967) asked at what *distance* a familiar object would appear to lie if all depth cues were removed. He found that in this case, observers judged distance on the basis of their memory about the true size of the familiar object. So, in the absence of other cues, remembered size can determine perceived distance.

Size constancy seems to occur automatically. This is evidenced by the fact that people are rarely aware of the size of their retinal images. Yet with appropriate instruction people can accurately judge the retinal size of an object, in effect ignoring information about distance (Gilinsky, 1955; Epstein, 1963).

You can verify this ability yourself. Hold up both thumbs with thumbnails facing you. Place them side by side approximately 20 centimeters (about 8 inches) from your eyes. They will look identical in size, as well

as they should. Next, extend one arm until that thumb is approximately 40 centimeters (about 16 inches) away, twice the distance of the other one. At first glance the two thumbs should continue to appear equivalent in size, even though the image size of the nearer one is now twice that of the farther one. This is what we mean by size constancy.

Now, while maintaining your thumbs at these different distances, move the farther one laterally until it appears just to the side of the nearer one. With one eye closed (to prevent double vision) and your head very steady, carefully compare the apparent size of the two thumbnails. Switching your attention from one to the other reveals that the closer thumbnail looks larger than the farther one. With this exercise you've managed to capture a glimpse of your retinal image. But notice how quickly this glimpse disappears once you open both eyes or move your head.

At present, we don't know exactly how the visual system performs this scaling process of size constancy, although there are some tantalizing clues from neurophysiology. Studying neurons in area V4 of monkeys, Dobbins and colleagues (1998) found cells that responded best to a bar of a given size located at a particular distance from the monkey. When the bar was moved to a nonpreferred distance, the cell's response dwindled, even if the size of the bar was adjusted to be identical in retinal image size to that used at the preferred distance. The cell, in other words, was responding to the actual size of the bar, taking distance into account; the cell was not just responding to the size of the image of the bar on the retina. Groups of neurons responding in this fashion could provide a substrate for size constancy (see also Trotter et al., [1992]). We do not yet know how these V4 neurons acquire information about distance.

Despite everything we know about distance and size, we still occasionally run across pictures that throw us for a loop. Look at Figure 8.42 (but don't read its caption yet) and try to describe what you're seeing. In this bizarre photograph, the apparent sizes of these two familiar objects (an airplane and a dog) just don't square with their relative distances. Because we know that dogs are not larger than airplanes, the tendency is to conclude that the photographer has done a cut-and-paste job to put two disparate images in the same photo. There is, however, another interpretation and it, in fact, explains how these two objects were able to fit meaningfully into the same picture. Can you figure it out? The caption explains the answer.

FIGURE 8.42 | Have you ever seen a dog this large before? Although it is farther away from the camera than the airplane, the dog appears larger than the plane. How can this be? (Answer: the airplane is a small model, not a real airplane.)

S U M M A R Y   A N D   P R E V I E W

This chapter has examined sources of information, monocular and binocular, used by perception to specify the 3D layout of objects in the visual environment. We have emphasized that 3D vision is computed automatically and effortlessly, without conscious deliberation. We have also seen that depth perception influences perceived size, resulting in size constancy as well as certain illusions of size. This connection between illusion and constancy should remind you of a similar connection you read about in Chapter 3, for lightness perception.

Although we have emphasized distance information in this chapter, the general combination of depth cues should not be overlooked. As David Marr (1982) has pointed out, depth serves to define objects relative to their backgrounds—helping the viewer to distinguish those objects and appreciate their shapes. In the next chapter, we take up another aspect of vision—motion—that serves that same purpose, in addition to others.

K E Y   T E R M S

absolute distance
accommodation
aerial perspective
allocentric
Ames room
amodal completion
binocular rivalry
convergence
convergence insufficiency
depth perception
diplopia
disparity-selective cells
egocentric direction

egocentric distance
Emmert's law
horopter
hyperacuity
interpupillary distance (IPD)
linear perspective
motion parallax
neon spreading
occlusion
oculomotor cues
perceived distance
random-dot stereograms
relative distance

retinal disparity
shading
size constancy
stereoblindness
stereopsis
stereoscope
strabismus
texture gradient
transparency
vernier acuity
visual cues

Action and the Perception of Events

You are walking alone in the beautiful woods near Walden Pond, where the philosopher and environmentalist Henry David Thoreau lived and wrote in the 1840s. You are deep in thought, enjoying the gentle, warm breeze on this beautiful early summer day. An occasional bird flies back and forth overhead; off to the side of the path, three monarch butterflies hover around tall, purplish flowers.

Your reverie is disrupted when a small rabbit, frightened by your footsteps, bounds away. The rabbit, well-camouflaged by the way its coloration blended with the foliage around Walden Pond, had been invisible to you. But the rabbit's movements broke the camouflage. You turn your gaze toward the motion but never get a good look at the creature. The hopping motion, however, tells the tale.

As this scenario illustrates, motion serves multiple perceptual purposes: detection (seeing something hop away), segregation (recognizing something move relative to its background), guidance (turning toward the source of the motion), and identification (the hopping motion identified the object as a rabbit).

The neural processes responsible for perceived motion begin by extracting from the retinal image the spatial displacements of various environmental features over time. This makes it clear that motion is a spatio-temporal event. As you walked through the woods, a variety of spatio-temporal events were occurring simultaneously within different locations in your field of view. Some of those events (for example, the butterflies fluttering about the flowers) occurred in unison, while others (for example, the scurrying rabbit) were unique. In addition, your own movements—eyes, head, and body—were producing their own spatio-temporal variations of the image on your retina. Somehow the visual system must sort various local motions into sets of events that belong to different objects, putting together local motions that originate from one moving object, and segregating local motions that come from different events. The tasks of aggregating and segregating local signals should remind you of similar challenges that confront form perception (Chapters 5 and 6).

The experience of motion, in all its various forms, is so integral to daily activity that it is hard to imagine life without it. But in rare cases, individuals who have suffered certain kinds of brain damage can no longer perceive motion. To get some idea of what this would be like, consider this description of L. M., a woman who suffered extensive damage to the posterior portions of both hemispheres of her brain. Although L. M.'s visual

FIGURE 9.1 | Movement can provide information about form. In this example, the shadow of a stationary, bent wire provides no hint about the object casting the shadow. But when the wire is rotated, the rotating shadow immediately creates the vivid impression of the object. This phenomenon is called *structure from motion.*

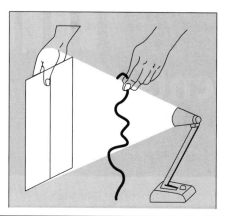 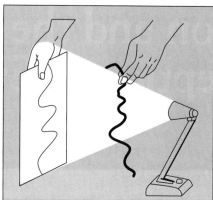

acuity and form perception were normal, her experience of visual motion was drastically impaired.

> She had difficulty, for example, in pouring tea or coffee into a cup because the fluid appeared to be frozen, like a glacier. In addition, she could not stop pouring at the right time since she was unable to perceive the movement in the cup (or a pot) when the fluid rose. . . . In a room where more than two other people were walking she felt very insecure and unwell, and usually left the room immediately, because "people were suddenly here or there but I have not seen them moving." . . . She could not cross the street because of her inability to judge the speed of a car, but she could identify the car itself without difficulty. "When I'm looking at the car first, it seems far away. But then, when I want to cross the road, suddenly the car is very near." (Zihl, von Cramon, and Mai, 1983, p. 315)

For three decades after her brain was damaged, L. M.'s condition remained essentially unchanged, though she did develop some coping strategies. For example, she learned to look away from a speaker's face when listening to that person talk; otherwise, L. M. was distracted because the speaker's mouth never seemed to move (Zihl, von Cramon, Mai and Schmid, 1991; Campbell et al., 1997).

Being unable to see motion is frustrating and dangerous. Not only was L. M. unable to see the movements of other creatures and objects, she also had difficulty seeing the consequences of her own movements and actions. Her inability to judge when enough tea had been poured is a reminder that perceivers themselves cause many of the changes and movements that they perceive. As you'll

learn later, the damage to L. M''s brain includes areas that are crucially involved in the perception of motion. L. M.'s peculiar, circumscribed visual deficit is yet another example of how the brain compartmentalizes different visual functions. (L. M. died in 2002.)

As you move about among the world's objects, such as the trees around Walden Pond, you see those objects from various perspectives. You also act on the world's objects, such as the rabbit you inadvertently frightened. Those actions influence what you will subsequently see. Thus, while your perceptions govern your actions, your actions in turn influence what you perceive, as Figure 1.1 denoted. Because actions are an integral part of visual perception, our discussion of the dynamic perceptual world has to consider what the perceiver *does* as well as what the perceiver *sees*. But let's begin our discussion of motion perception by considering one of the important things that motion does for us.

Structure from Motion

We can derive vivid impressions of the 3D shape of an object from motion, an ability called the perception of **structure from motion (SFM).** To see what this entails, look at Figure 9.1. A wire clothes hanger has been bent and twisted into a meaningless three-dimensional shape. A light source is arranged so that the bent hanger casts a shadow on a piece of paper. When the wire is motionless, the shadow gives a viewer no idea of the hanger's shape. But when the wire begins to rotate, this movement makes its three-dimensional shape immediately obvious (Wallach and O'Connell, 1953). Perception of SFM can also be

FIGURE 9.2 | Two frames from an animation sequence depicting a transparent cube rotating about the vertical axis. The surface of the cube is textured with dots placed randomly over its six sides. From single frames, the shape and volume of the object are unknown, but when the display is shown as a movie, you would be able to tell the object's structure from its motion.

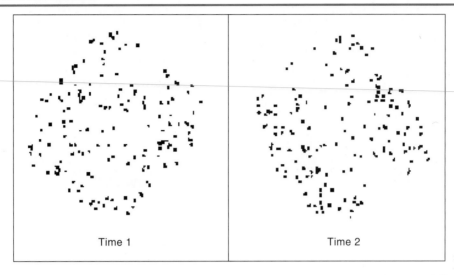

Time 1   Time 2

compellingly created using dynamic arrays of random dots generated under computer control on a video monitor (Sekuler, Watamaniuk, & Blake, 2002). Figure 9.2 shows a couple of movie frames from an animation depicting SFM. To see the animation itself—and therefore the object being created by motion—go to the Chapter 9 demonstrations that can be accessed at www.mhhe.com/blake5.

During the last decade, SFM perception has been intensively studied, with particular emphasis on the accuracy of form judgments that use SFM information (Norman and Lappin, 1992), the stimulus conditions that enable or limit SFM perception (Todd and Norman, 1991), and the neural circuits that make SFM possible (Nawrot and Blake, 1991; Andersen and Bradley, 1998).

Biological Motion

One class of SFM events is important enough to merit particular attention: events that distinguish animate from inanimate objects. Think back to your stroll through the woods around Walden Pond when you encountered the startled rabbit. At first all you noticed out of the corner of your eye was something moving, and it could have been anything: a falling branch, a dislodged rock rolling among the leaves, leaves blown by the wind. But once you saw the tell-tale pattern of motions produced by the

object, you knew immediately it was something alive and that, in fact, it was a rabbit.

This chance encounter underscores something important: Motion offers compelling evidence about whether an object is a living creature or not. That's because the patterns of motion produced by biological creatures, humans included, are very different from those associated with the movements of inanimate objects such as a rotating cube or a rolling wheel. Besides generating unique patterns of motion, biological events are especially important to humans—we spend lots of time every day watching other people engage in myriad activities including walking, running, dancing, and gesturing. Each of these activities comprises its own characteristic motions, and different individuals have their own characteristic ways of producing those motions. Motion, in other words, represents an important biological event, for it can tell us what people are doing as well as who those people are (e.g., Knappmeyer, Thornton, and Bülthoff, 2003). Insomuch as this is a particularly important type of event perception, and because it provides some general lessons about motion perception, let's consider biological motion in some detail.

Recognizing Biological Motion   As a friend walks across the room, you are able to recognize that person even if you don't see the person's face. What characteristics of his or

FIGURE 9.3 | Each white dot is a light attached to some part of a person's body.

A

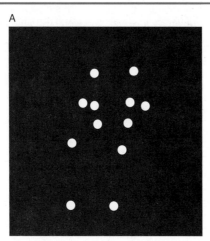

B

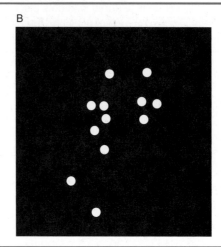

her gait allow you to recognize who it is? Gunnar Johansson, a Swedish psychologist, was the first to study this question systematically (1975). Johansson began by determining the minimum information needed to recognize biological motion. Reasoning that the movement of the body's joints might convey particularly important information, Johansson attached tiny light bulbs to a person's hips, knees, ankles, shoulders, wrists, and elbows. This person was clothed entirely in black so that looking at the individual in a dark room, you would see only the small set of illuminated "dots." Johansson's aim was to eliminate all the familiar, nonmotion cues that might give away the fact that the figure underlying the dots was a person.

Figure 9.3 gives some idea of what people were viewing in Johansson's study. The pictures show lights attached to a person who is sitting very still on a chair. The person in panel A is seated with both feet on the ground; the person in panel B is also seated, but with legs crossed. Viewing the pictures without these clues, however, gives the viewer very little to go on. The lights appear to be a random collection of spots: They could be just about anything. Yet Johansson found that as soon as the person began to move, viewers recognized that it was a person. In other demonstrations, Johansson discovered that the same light bulbs were sufficient to reveal when a person was painting, riding a bicycle, or doing push-ups. The overall movements of the lights—and, more importantly, their movements relative to one another—conveyed this information in a most compelling way.

Here's an even more impressive demonstration of the potency of biological motion. Johansson outfitted two people with tiny light bulbs and had them dance in the dark. Figure 9.4 is a sample of frames taken from a mo-

tion picture of that event. Because any single frame contains information only about space and none about time, examination of any one frame gives no clue about what you're looking at. However, even a brief section of the film, when projected at the proper speed, gives an almost instantaneous impression of two people dancing. It has been found, in addition, that this minimal information enables viewers to identify whether an individual actor is a male or a female. (Males and females typically have different shoulder and hip widths and, consequently, as males walk, their bodies oscillate about a lower center of movement than do the bodies of females.) Moreover, viewers can recognize their own gait in such displays, as well as the gaits of friends (Cutting and Proffitt, 1981).

Structure from motion portrayed using these "points of light" is referred to as **point-light motion.** You can see examples of these kinds of animations on the Web (see the links at www.mhhe.com/blake5). The perception of biological motion from just a few moving points of light is so compelling that digital artists, in collaboration with the distinguished contemporary choreographer Merce Cunningham, have exploited it to create effective, aesthetically pleasing performances by computer-generated, virtual dancers, whose movements are represented only by points and swirls of light.[1]

---

[1]Commercial animators use similar techniques to produce delightful mismatches between an animated cartoon figure and its movement. For example, the movements of an actual adult human doing a series of somersaults can be extracted and used to control the animation of a cartoon baby. The result is a somersaulting or dancing baby. Such effects are arresting because viewers immediately recognize that the movements are inappropriate to the body executing them.

FIGURE 9.4 | Frames from a movie of two people dancing in the dark with lights attached to parts of their bodies.

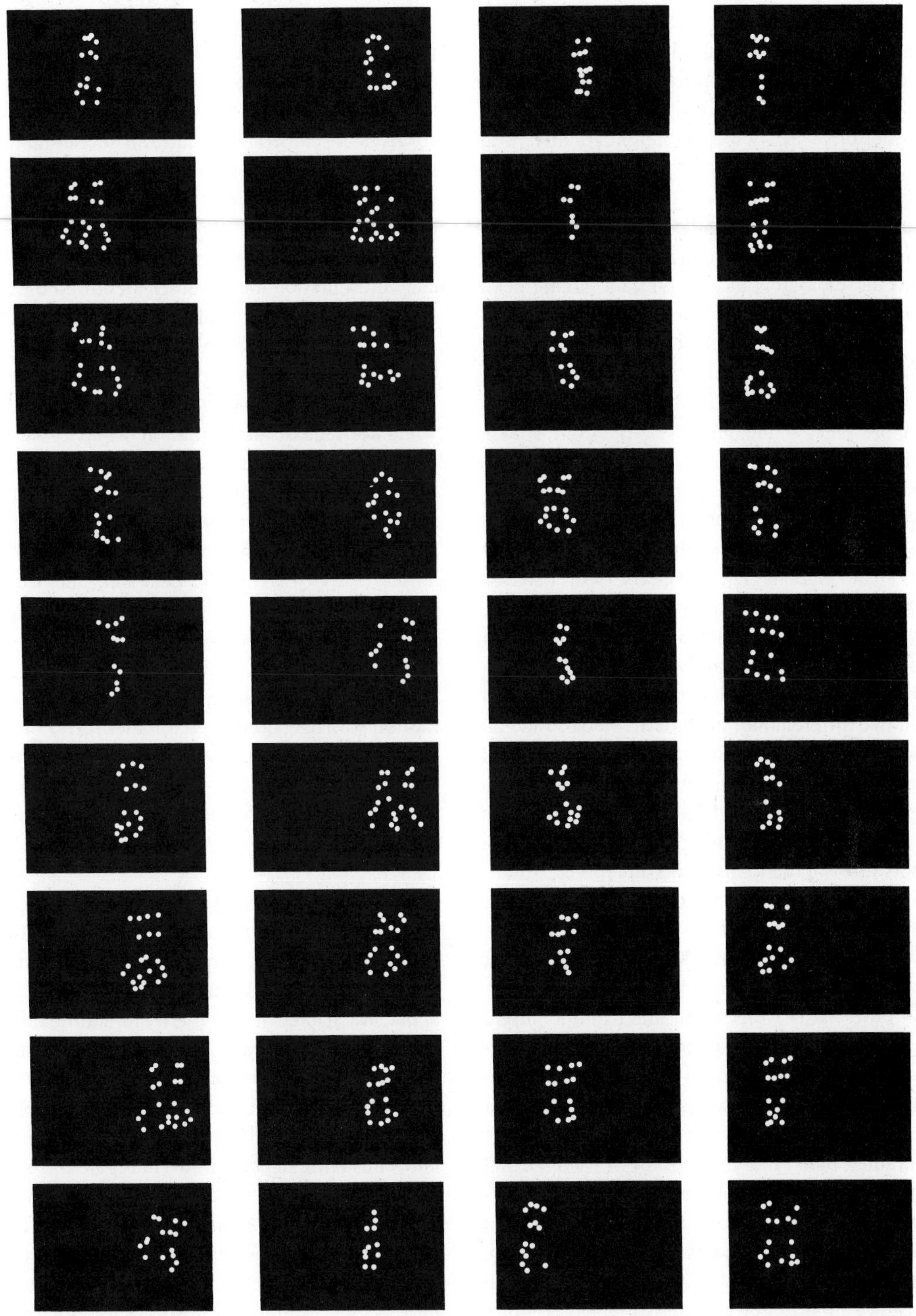

People who haven't seen firsthand Johansson's demonstrations or Cunningham's dances tend to get the wrong idea about what is involved. People assume that complex thought processes are used to deduce the activity conveyed by the complex movements of the small lights. But this assumption is wrong. The perception of biological motion actually occurs automatically. You don't have to puzzle over what you're seeing. The impression is as immediate as it is when viewing any other form of motion. In fact, viewing the moving lights for as little as 200 milliseconds is enough to enable a person to identify familiar biological motion without having been told what to expect (Johansson, von Hofsten, and Jansson, 1980). Perception of biological motion persists even when the moving spots differ from one another in color, or when some spots are presented to one eye and the remainder are presented to the other eye (Ahlström, Blake, and Ahlström, 1997).

Although perception of biological motion conveys fairly sophisticated information, sophisticated thought processes are not needed for that perception—cats (Blake, 1993) and pigeons (Dittrich et al., 1998) can discriminate biological from nonbiological motion. So, too, can very young infants, and they also exhibit a distinct preference for looking at motion that is biological in origin. Robert Fox and Cynthia McDaniel (1982) presented infants with two different motion patterns side by side on a television screen. Following Johansson's method, each pattern consisted of an array of white dots seen against a dark background. One of the two patterns represented the joints of a human who was running and the other pattern depicted dots moving randomly in all directions. An observer sitting near the television screen noted which side of the television screen the infants preferred to look at. By 4 months of age, infants showed a clear preference for biological motion rather than nonbiological motion.

Fox and McDaniel worried that their infants might have been responding not to the biological or nonbiological character of the motion but to how random or constrained the motion was. (Since arms and legs do not usually go flying in all directions, biological motion is more constrained than random motion.) So in a second experiment, Fox and McDaniel used a display with dots representing a human running in place paired with that same dotted motion pattern shown upside down. Again, infants preferred the biological motion pattern—the one presented right side up. (For a recent summary of other studies of biological motion perception in infants, see Pavlova et al., 2001). Just because young infants are sensitive to biological motion does not prove that the ability

to recognize biological motion is innate—by 4 months of age, infants will have visually experienced many hours of biological motion. These infant studies do, however, confirm that recognition of biological motion does not require complex intellectual processing.

Sensitivity to biological motion is also an ability that survives unscathed as we age, an encouraging discovery made by Norman and colleagues (2004). These investigators asked young and older observers to view brief point-light animations depicting various human activities including walking, running, and skipping. Following each presentation the observer identified the activity being portrayed on that trial, guessing if necessary. Results showed comparably excellent performance by young and by older people, even with very brief exposure durations. This equivalence in performance was maintained even when portions of the animation sequences were blocked from view by an occluding object. As Norman and colleagues point out, this relatively intact ability contrasts sharply with the decreased visual abilities of older people, including motion perception tasks that do not involve human activity (Norman, Dawson, and Butler, 2000). Our life-long experiences watching other people may ensure that as we age, we retain good sensitivity to the kinematics of biological motion.

This selective sparing of perception of biological motion with age, compared to other forms of motion perception, also suggests that biological motion may depend on neural processes distinct from those involved in other aspects of motion. Indeed, there is evidence for just such specialization, as you're about to learn.

Brain Events Underlying Perception of Biological Motion
What happens within your brain when you observe biological motion? Not surprisingly, many visual areas are activated including V1 and MT, brain areas you learned about in Chapter 4. But there are additional brain areas that are selectively activated by biological motion. Notable among these is a brain region located within the superior temporal sulcus, close to the juncture of the parietal and temporal lobes (Grossman et al., 2000). How do we know this brain region, shown in Figure 9.5, is specialized for registering biological motion? Neurons within this area are robustly activated when people view point-light animation sequences depicting biological motion but not when they view the same sequences in which the dots have been scrambled in position and, therefore, the impression of biological motion is lost. Nor is this area activated when people view dot animations portraying nonbiological objects such as cubes or cylinders. More-

FIGURE 9.5 | The right hemisphere of a human brain showing the locations of two prominent areas involved in motion perception. Area STS is located on the rising portion of the superior temporal sulcus, and it contains neurons selectively responsive to biological motion, including point-light animations of people engaged in activities such as walking and jumping. Located posterior to STS is area MT (also known as V5). Using fMRI, area MT can be identified by comparing brain activation associated with viewing moving objects (such as dots) with that associated with viewing stationary objects. MT and STS are located in approximately the same corresponding anatomical region of the left hemisphere (not pictured).

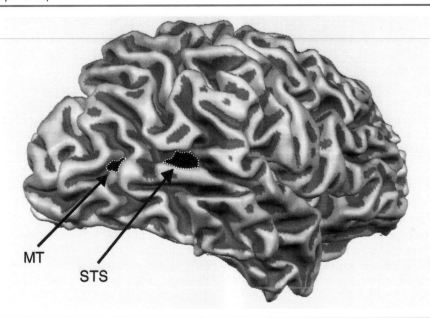

over, brain damage to this region of the superior temporal sulcus can impair a person's ability to perceive biological motion while leaving other aspects of motion perception unaffected (Schenk and Zihl, 1997).

Now we don't want to leave you with the impression that this is the only region of the brain involved in perceiving biological motion, because it's not. Clusters of brain areas in the ventral stream, the so-called "what" pathway, are also activated when you view biological motion (Vaina et al, 2001; Grossman and Blake, 2002). Moreover, viewing biological motion also activates regions in the frontal lobe, regions normally activated when someone is preparing to execute a motor activity such as waving the hand (Saygin et al., 2004; Tai et al., 2004). Saygin and colleagues offered an intriguing, speculative interpretation of this result: Perhaps when you watch a point-light display of someone engaged in an activity such as walking, motor areas in your brain are recruited to mimic or "mirror" the sparse information provided by the dozen or so lights. This implicit, automatic mirroring, Saygin argues, may be crucial to perceiving the activity, effectively fleshing out the light display's sparse information. This kind of neural mirroring may play a central role in our ability to observe and then imitate another individual's behavior or even to infer the other person's intentions (Rizzolatti and Craighero, 2004).

From the perception of biological motion produced by watching other people, let's next turn to motion information that guides your own movements.

The Visual Guidance of Locomotion

Three centuries ago, the philosopher George Berkeley (1709/1950) had an intriguing idea about vision's main purpose, and it had to do with motion. He wrote that vision was designed to allow animals to "foresee . . . the damage or benefit which is likely to ensue, upon the application of their own bodies to this or that body which is at a distance" (p. 39). In other words, he believed that vision keeps creatures out of trouble, which certainly is true. When you move about in the world—walking, running, driving a car, or piloting an airplane—you'd better

FIGURE 9.6 | Changes in the field of view as a person approaches a door.

know *whether* you're going to collide with something, and if so, *when.* This knowledge allows you to change course, thereby avoiding harm. As Berkeley realized, vision guides movement and movement alters vision. Let's consider this interplay between vision and locomotion, starting with the visual information that allows you to steer your movements properly.

Finding the Right Direction

Most people move about easily, with a minimum number of collisions, even on crowded sidewalks. Obviously, we're able to exploit some source of information to locomote—to keep on course, as well as to change course when needed. But what exactly is that source of information, and how is it used? As you move about the world, the image on your retina changes with your movements. To take a simple example, as you move toward some stationary object, the image of that object on your retina expands. James Gibson pointed out that visual expansion could guide complicated and important movements of the body and head. "To kiss someone," Gibson (1979) instructed, "magnify the face-form, if the facial expression is amiable, so as almost to fill the field of view. It is absolutely essential to keep one's eyes open so as to avoid collision. It is also wise to learn to discriminate those subtle [features] that specify amiability" (p. 233).

Preparing to kiss is just one of the many activities producing a flow of visual information. Think about what happens when you walk toward some object such as the door to a building. To appreciate how the retinal image

changes in this situation, look at Figure 9.6. Each panel in the figure represents what you might see at a different instance in time as you move toward the door. This changing pattern of stimulation is called **optic flow.** Note particularly how the view changes from one drawing to the next. Though a series of stills cannot fully capture the dynamic character of these changes, some important things can be appreciated. The door you are looking at and walking toward always remains at the center of the field of view. Objects around the door—to its sides, above, and below—shift radially outward, flowing farther and farther into the periphery of the visual field. The center of this flow, known as its *focus,* allows you to steer yourself toward the door. You will successfully reach the door by keeping the door at the center of the outward optic flow.

Gibson proposed that the pattern of outward flow could be used to tell where one is headed and how to steer around obstacles. To test this idea, he filmed the view from the cockpit of an aircraft in flight and found that viewers of this film could identify the direction in which the plane was headed (Gibson, 1947).

There's a more general way to represent the optic flow produced in situations such as the one illustrated in Figure 9.6. Imagine that an observer is looking directly ahead and walking on a perfectly straight course through the environment. At any instant, the optical flow can be portrayed as a velocity field, where lines signify the instantaneous optical velocity of elements (the dots) in the environment (Figure 9.7). Each line's direction corresponds to the direction of optic flow at one point in the

FIGURE 9.7 | Instantaneous velocity field produced by an observer moving forward on a straight course parallel to a plane. The single vertical line poking up from the plane indicates the direction in which the observer is moving. Dots represent elements on the surface plane, and line segments indicate the velocity vector associated with each element. Vector orientation signifies the direction of the local optical flow; vector length signifies the speed of the flow.

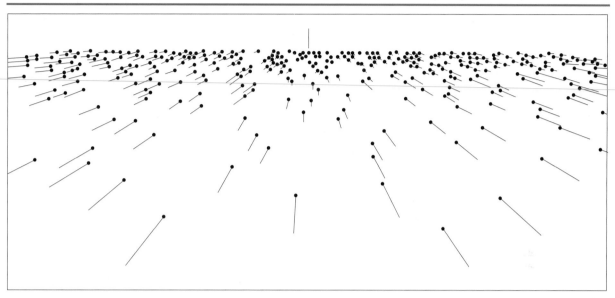

field; the length of the line corresponds to the instantaneous speed of the optic flow. The single vertical line sticking up from the "horizon" in Figure 9.7 represents the direction in which the observer is headed. So long as the direction of heading and the speed of forward motion are the same, this single diagram would be valid for the optical flow for a walker, a runner, or a driver.

William Warren (1998) examined the accuracy with which observers use optic-flow information to judge the direction in which they're heading. In Warren's experiments, people were shown computer-generated displays that consisted of moving dots. The moving dots simulated the optic flow that would be generated on the retina as an individual walked in a particular direction. In each trial, the observer judged whether he or she appeared to be heading to the left or right of a stationary target located at various positions along the display's simulated horizon. Even with relatively few dots in the display, or with presentations lasting less than half a second, observers managed to achieve accuracy levels equal to what would be needed to guide high-speed locomotion.

If optic flow information, as Gibson hypothesized, helps us keep track of our heading, deficits in processing

that information could produce spatial confusion and loss of one's bearings. Are such deficits observed? Warren, Blackwell and Morris (1989) used techniques like those described in the previous paragraph to test older observers (age range 61 to 78 years) whose vision, despite their age, was quite good. Using displays that simulated speeds of locomotion from a slow walk (1 meter per second) through a fast run (3.8 meters per second), Warren and colleagues found that at all speeds the older observers were only half as good at judging direction as were young observers tested under the same conditions. The researchers speculated that the diminished ability to judge direction of heading could contribute to age-related errors of locomotion and the well documented increase in the incidence of falling accidents.

Patients with Alzheimer's disease, a progressive, degenerative disease of the brain, often have difficulty finding their way around their surroundings, even when those surroundings are familiar. Evidence suggests that this deficit, too, could be connected to subnormal processing of optic flow information. Specifically, some patients with Alzheimer's disease are impaired in extracting directional information from optic flow stimuli (Tetewsky and Duffy, 1999), and many of these same patients showed correspondingly poor performance on a test of spatial navigation (wayfinding) ability. In a related vein, Rizzo and colleagues (1997) found that Alzheimer's patients were more likely to produce crashes and near misses than were age-matched normal individuals, when tested in a very realistic driving simulator that used optic flow to simulate navigation (see Rizzo and Nawrot, 1998, for other motion-related deficits found in Alzheimer's patients).

The recent work on optic flow that you've just read about confirms Gibson's decades-old hypothesis: Visual information contained in optic flow can be used to determine heading during normal locomotion, ranging from slow walking (1 meter/second) to running (about 4 meters/second). So visual information can specify *where* you're going. But it's equally important to know *when* you're going to arrive (or collide). How does visual information help us do that?

Judging Your Time of Arrival

Perhaps you've watched seabirds diving for food. They fly along until a fish is spotted in the water below, then, without warning, they dive into the water at impressive speed. Often they get their fish. The whole process is a marvel to behold. Some species of birds add additional mystery to their performance: A split second before hitting the water's surface, these birds fold in their wings, streamlining their bodies and easing their entry into the water. Watching this performance, you'd think that somehow the bird knew exactly when it would hit the water. Though the bird doesn't have sophisticated navigational instruments, it performs this feat with precision and consistency (Lee and Reddish, 1981). Humans perform comparable, albeit less spectacular, feats whenever we walk, run, drive, or catch a ball. What's the information that enables us to do these things?

Let's begin by considering the information that *might* be available to a creature who is approaching some stationary object in its environment. Figure 9.6 showed that as you approach an object—a door in that case—the image size of that object expands. If you are walking toward the door at a constant rate, the rate of expansion specifies the time to collision—the moment at which you will reach the door.

Suppose that at time *t* you're a certain distance, say *D* meters, away from the door. If you move at a steady rate (no acceleration), travel time is equal to travel distance divided by travel rate. So if your rate is *R* meters per second, and distance is *D* meters, then time to arrival will be *D/R* seconds. However, to solve this equation you must have good information about both distance and rate. How does the visual system get such information? It doesn't. Instead, as David Lee (1980) suggested, vision uses another, dynamic source of information about time to arrival—which makes it unnecessary to know either distance or rate.

Imagine you're 100 meters from a telephone pole when you start walking toward it at a rate of 1 meter per second. Suppose, further, that while walking, you look directly at a knothole on the pole. To simplify calculations, assume the knothole is 1 centimeter in diameter. Using simple trigonometry, we can calculate the size of the image cast by the knothole on your retina. We can also calculate how that retinal image changes moment by moment during the approach (the derivative of image size with respect to time).

Lee designated the *ratio* between the retinal image size and the rate of change in that image size at any given instant as *tau*. For the case we've been working with—approaching the telephone pole at a steady rate—tau is one one-hundredth. By calculating tau, a visual system would also have the time to collision—time to collision (in seconds) is the reciprocal of tau. This kind of calculation is especially valuable because its outcome is independent of object size. So long as starting distance and rate of travel are constant, tau is constant, regardless of object size. If you started out just 10 meters from the object, tau would be one-tenth, and the time to collision would be the reciprocal of tau, or 10 seconds. If you approach the pole more rapidly, tau decreases and its reciprocal increases, again as the laws of physics suggest it should. For example, if you start 100 meters from the pole and jog toward it at 5 meters per second, tau is one-twentieth, which yields a collision time of 20 seconds.

The connection between imminent impact and rate of expansion of retinal image size holds for any moving creature that has its eyes open—including the diving birds mentioned previously. The visual system carries out these complex computations so rapidly that resulting information about rate of expansion can be used to control the braking of an automobile (Lee, 1976), the split-second changes in gait that are needed when running across rough terrain (Warren, Young, and Lee, 1986), or the various movements and adjustments of the hand that are required to catch a ball (Savelsbergh, Whiting, and Bootsma, 1991). Lest you think of this coupling between optical expansion and action as something calculated and

FIGURE 9.8 | Most animals, including human infants, will try to avoid a looming stimulus, even when that stimulus is portrayed on a television screen.

conscious, it's worth pointing out that people can succeed in these tasks even though they are not aware—or able to articulate—what they're doing (Savelsbergh, Whiting, and Bootsma, 1991).

Incidentally, animals as dissimilar as fiddler crabs, chickens, monkeys, and human infants, all behave as if they can compute tau, for they all try to avoid looming objects (Schiff, 1965). This is true even for newborn infants who have never before encountered a looming stimulus (Figure 9.8). Apparently, learning plays little role in this behavior.

Although tau may be helpful in many circumstances where we need to recognize collision time, that quantity cannot be our only cue to collision. In fact, tau fails under a number of conditions (Tresilian, 1999). For example, if the approach rate is not constant, tau evaluated at any single moment fails to give the correct collision time.

This same problem also undermines tau's usefulness as a predictor of vertical movement. Tau cannot correctly predict when a falling body will strike some surface because the body's rate of movement is not constant (due to gravity-induced acceleration). Additionally, with a very slow approach to an object, the rate of image expansion could become so small as to be undetectable by the visual system. In discussing tau's limitations, Tresilian (1999) identifies additional cues that compensate for tau's failures in various situations. Box 9.1 describes several potentially dangerous perceptual errors involving misjudgments of pending collision.

Eye Movements: Their Aims and Consequences

There's no doubt that vision helps guide your exploration of the world around you. We just discussed one form of exploration, visually guided locomotion. Now let's turn to another form of visual exploration, a form made possible by small, rapid movements of the eye, rather than by larger, slower movements of the arms and legs.

Take a moment to refer back to Figures 6.2 and 6.10. These are records of the eye movements produced as a person, in the case of Figure 6.2, or a monkey, in the case of Figure 6.10, looks at an ordinary visual scene. These records were obtained using techniques that allow an investigator to monitor precisely where someone is looking at any given moment, how long that person's gaze remains at that location, and how long it takes the eyes to move to the next point of fixation. There are several different techniques available for measuring eye movements (for examples, see Web resources at www.mhhe.com/blake5), and some of these techniques are portable enough to allow eye movement measurements in people while they are driving a vehicle, playing chess, reading, flying an airplane, performing job-related tasks, or watching political advertisements on television. To give one example of an application of this technique, Loughland, Williams, and Gordon (2002) have recorded and compared eye-movement patterns in normal, healthy subjects and schizophrenic individuals as they look at pictures of faces of people portraying neutral and emotional expressions. In contrast

BOX 9.1 ## Misjudging Your Time of Arrival Can Be Fatal

Motion perception can be a matter of life or death—literally. It can cause fatal accidents, and it can prevent them. To document this claim, we'll start with the dark side—collisions at railroad crossings.

According to the U.S. Federal Railroad Administration, about 5,000 collisions occur each year between locomotives and other vehicles at railroad crossings in the United States. And these collisions kill more than 400 people each year. Most railroad crossings are protected by crossing gates and warning bells. In addition, locomotive engineers must sound a bell or horn as they approach a crossing. With all these precautions and the conspicuous nature of huge locomotives, how is it still possible that so many accidents occur? According to the late Herschel Leibowitz (1983), errors in motion perception are often at fault.

During an accident investigation, Leibowitz rode in the cab of a locomotive that retraced the route on which the accident had occurred. The trip took Leibowitz through an urban area with many gate crossings. (Incidentally, the United States has more than 250,000 such gate crossings.) He was astonished at the number of motorists who drove around the crossing gates and across the tracks in front of the oncoming train. The train crew, who saw this kind of thing every day, shrugged it off as "typical." Inasmuch as automobiles don't fare too well in collisions with railroad trains, why do people take such chances? Leibowitz realized that although the locomotive's bulk made it easy to see, that same bulk would cause its speed to be seriously underestimated.

It has long been known that the size of an object and its apparent speed are inversely related. To study this relation, J. F. Brown (1931) asked people to adjust the speed of one square so that it appeared to move at the same speed as another square. When both squares were the same size, observers were very accurate in their adjustments. (Typically a mismatch in speed as small as 10 percent can be easily seen.) However, when the two squares differed in size, the accuracy of the matches was very low. When the squares differed in size, the larger one had to move faster than the small one in order to appear to move at the same rate. As a result, if the two squares moved at the same speed, the larger one seemed to be moving more slowly than the smaller one.

Leibowitz pointed out that a related phenomenon can be seen at just about any airport. All commercial jets, regardless of size, land at pretty much the same speed. However, wide-body planes *appear* to land much more slowly than smaller planes. Leibowitz argued that the same kind of perceptual error causes motorists at railroad crossings to underestimate an oncoming train's speed, and thereby overestimate the time the train will take to reach the crossing.

Let's end on a happier note—the ability of motion perception to *prevent* accidents. Particularly dangerous spots in any highway system are the intersections called rotaries ("roundabouts" in the United Kingdom). To navigate safely through a rotary, a driver must slow down. But when motorists don't slow down enough, accidents often result. Because exhortations and warnings seemed to have little effect, Gordon Denton (1980) took a desperate step. He tricked motorists into believing their cars were traveling faster than they really were. His aim was to frighten motorists into slowing down.

Imagine a road with transverse stripes painted across the pavement. A motorist passing over these stripes will get a sense of how fast the car is traveling by the rate at which it passes the stripes. When the stripes are close together, she will pass them at a higher rate, causing her to overestimate her speed. Denton exploited this phenomenon by having white stripes painted across the roadway near the entrance to a rotary—the stripes near the rotary were more closely spaced than those farther away. As a result, motorists approaching the rotary erroneously perceived that they were speeding up. This misperception caused them to slow down. Preliminary tests with this simple and inexpensive scheme indicate that it works: Accidents declined at over two-thirds of the rotaries on which such stripes had been painted. It's nice to know that illusions of motion perception can also save lives as well as take them.

to the control subjects, individuals diagnosed with schizophrenia exhibited restricted scanning, with longer durations of fixation at a given location. Moreover, they showed reduced attention to salient facial features such as the eyes and mouth, features important in signaling facial emotion.

Measurements disclose that eyes are perhaps the busiest organs in your entire human body: We make more than 100,000 eye movements each day. Those eye movements come in several forms, each serving specific needs and each depending upon different, but partially overlapping neural circuits in the brain (Krauzlis and Stone,

1999). There are the tracking eye movements that we make when following a moving object with our eyes—when you watch an interesting person strolling into the classroom, you're using your tracking eye movements. These tend to be smooth, which is why they sometimes are called smooth pursuit movements. You also make smooth eye movements when your head or body moves, but your eyes remain riveted on an object. Then there are the rapid shifts in gaze that we make when, for example, something catches our attention out of the corner of the eye—we quickly reorient our gaze to see what it is. We also make these rapid gaze shifts when reading text (you've made approximately eight such eye movements just in the course of reading this sentence). In this section you will learn about these two principal types of eye movements (Steinman, Kowler, and Collewijn, 1990; Steinman, 2004).[2]

Acquiring the Target

Consider a startling situation that you may have experienced. (We've selected this situation because it is common and also because it involves both types of eye movements just mentioned.) Imagine that while reading, you suddenly spot out of the corner of your eye something scurrying across the floor. Your eyes turn rapidly away from your reading material toward the surprise visitor. (You may also end up turning your head in that direction, as well, but here we'll concentrate just on what the eyes do.) This kind of high-speed eye movement is designed to shift the image of some potentially interesting object (the scurrying thing) from the periphery of the retina (where acuity is poor) to the fovea (where acuity is good). About one-fifth of a second after spotting the creature, your eyes begin to move. Almost instantly, they reach a very high speed of movement (achieving velocities of almost 20 centimeters per second). Then, usually less than one-tenth of a second after they started to move, the eyes screech to a halt.

When the eyes move about in this way, they do so in abrupt jerks; as a result, eye movements of this type are called **saccades** (from the French verb *saccader,* meaning "to jerk"). The eye does not jerk, or saccade, only when it needs to fixate on some object out in the periph-

---

[2]The categories of eye movements introduced here have no bearing on the distinction mentioned in Chapter 2, between conjunctive and vergence eye movements. That distinction was based exclusively on the *direction* in which the eye moved. In fact, one can have saccadic movements that are conjunctive or disjunctive; one can also have slower, smoot movements that are conjunctive or disjunctive.

ery. Anytime you shift your gaze from one object to another, your eye executes these jerky movements. For example, while you read this page your eyes are saccading from word to word, four or five times each second (recall our discussion of reading in Chapter 6). Because you shift your gaze thousands of times each hour, saccades can certainly lay claim to being your most commonly used instrument for visual exploration. Since you need to make so many saccades, it is fortunate that the eye muscles responsible for these saccades never become fatigued (Fuchs and Binder, 1983).

Saccadic Suppression

In Chapter 2 you read that vision is temporarily suppressed during a blink. A similar dampening of vision accompanies saccades. To experience this, stand in front of a mirror and watch the reflection of your eyes as you make saccades voluntarily. Allow your eyes to jump back and forth between two points several inches apart. Though you know that your eyes have moved, you never actually see that movement. This is a puzzle. Furthermore, during the saccade you don't experience blurred vision. Yet if you took a photograph with a camera that moved at the same rate your eyes moved, you'd get a very blurred, low-contrast picture (see Figure 9.9). Why, then, do you not experience impaired vision each time you execute a saccade?

Perhaps the retinal image is changing so rapidly (see Box 9.2) that the motion can't even be perceived. After all, there is a lower threshold, a minimum velocity below which motion cannot be seen. For example, you cannot actually see the movement of a clock's minute hand even though you know that it's moving. Perhaps, then, there is also an upper threshold, a maximum velocity above which you can't see motion. Such an upper threshold would limit ability to see the blur and motion that accompany saccades.

To test this suggestion, you'd have to move some object at a rate equal to the rate at which the eye would sweep across that object during a saccade. Can an observer see an object moving at this rate? To make sure that motion was being seen, you might ask the observer to identify the direction in which the object moved. It turns out that the ability to see the moving object depends on its size and contrast. Rapidly moving objects of low contrast are impossible to see. So are rapidly moving small objects, regardless of their contrast. However, large, rapidly moving objects can be seen if their contrast is sufficiently great (Burr and Ross, 1982). So rapid movement does not on its own preclude vision.

FIGURE 9.9 | Moving a camera while the shutter is open produces a blurred picture.

So, why is the motion accompanying saccades not seen? The answer, at least in part, can be traced to the direction-selective neurons you learned about in Chapter 4 (and which we'll cover in more detail later in this chapter). Those neurons respond vigorously to retinal image motion produced by an object moving through the visual field, but when the same image motion is produced by a saccadic eye movement many of those neurons fail to respond (Thiele et al., 2002). The responses to motion, in other words, are suppressed when that motion is associated with a saccade. It makes sense, then, that the motion cannot be perceived, because the neurons signaling motion are silenced. This leaves unanswered, however, the question of how those neurons are able to distinguish object motion from motion produced by saccadic eye movements. Later in this chapter you'll learn more about these direction-selective neurons, which are found in visual area MT.

Perceptual Stability

As you read this paragraph, each and every saccade shifts the page's retinal image, sometimes by quite a bit. You can mimic these retinal image shifts by keeping your eyes still (minimizing saccades) while quickly jiggling the page back and forth. Though the retinal image shifts around under both conditions, the perceptual consequences are very different. Somehow when we make saccades, the visual world appears to remain still, despite what's happen-

ing on the retina. So where does this remarkable perceptual stability come from? Specifically, how does the visual system distinguish retinal motion due to eye movements from retinal motion due to object movement?

Researchers have proposed two different mechanisms to monitor eye movements. According to one view, the visual system tracks actual changes in the extraocular muscles. In the alternative view, the visual system tracks the command signals that go to the extraocular muscles. (These two alternatives were depicted schematically in Figure 8.8.)

The preponderance of behavioral evidence favors the second view. Additionally, physiological research has identified neural mechanisms that use the signals sent to the extraoculars to update the brain's representation of visual space (Duhamel, Colby, and Goldberg, 1992). We won't review the literature here, but instead examine several conditions that illustrate basic principles. These conditions are outlined in Table 9.1.

To make predictions of what ought to be seen in each condition, we'll need some consistent conventions about our descriptions of motion. Our convention assigns a value of $+1$ to leftward motion and a value of -1 to rightward motion. This assignment applies to motion in the external world, to motion of the eyes, to retinal image motion, to the command signals that normally control the motion of the eyes, and to perceived motion. In this convention, the absence of motion or a command signal has a value of zero. Finally, we assume that predictions con-

In modern industrialized societies, people are immersed in lights that blink and flicker. Some of these lights, such as the flashing lights atop a police vehicle, try to capture attention. Others, like the flashing light at a railroad crossing, are designed to warn. For a flashing light to be effective, it must flicker at a rate that can be easily seen. If it flickers too rapidly or too slowly, the flicker will be imperceptible.

Much is known about the **critical flicker frequency (CFF)**—the highest rate of flicker that can be perceived as such. When this highest frequency is exceeded, the separate flashes of light blend together to yield the illusion of continuous light. Under the best conditions, the human CFF is around 60 Hz. (*Hz*, the abbreviation for "hertz," is a unit of flicker rate equivalent to one on/off cycle per second.) In fact, this is why you cannot see the flicker from a typical fluorescent lamp. Although the lamp actually does flicker on and off at a rate of 60 Hz, you can't see the flicker because its rate exceeds your CFF. However, a bee looking at the same lamp could perceive the 60-Hz flicker, as a bee's CFF is far higher than yours, around 300 Hz (Lythgoe, 1979). To put these values into context, consider that standard television sets in North America refresh their screens at 60 hz, painting 60 images each second on their screens. Movies as shown in a movie theater are filmed at a rate of 24 images per second, but in the theater each image is actually projected twice in succession, producing an effective refresh rate of 48 Hz. Early movies, in contrast, were projected at a much more leisurely rate, only 16 frames per second. Be-

cause this value is far below the human CFF, early movies seemed to flicker, and the motion portrayed in those movies often seemed jerky.

The CFF depends on many variables, including the light's intensity and size. In addition, CFF varies with location in the visual field. The rate of flicker of a large stimulus, such as a television set or a bank of fluorescent lights, may be too fast to be seen when you look at the stimulus directly, but may be highly visible when you look slightly away from it. You may have experienced this annoying peripheral flicker if you've been in a room where the fluorescent ceiling lights were functioning improperly.

In some individuals, seizures can be brought on by exposure to a flickering light. Individuals with this condition, called photoconvulsive epilepsy, have to be aware that seizures can be triggered by a strobe light in a disco, a malfunctioning television set or the flashing lights of video games (Ferrie et al., 1994). With a television, the likelihood of a seizure is enhanced by low-frequency (50-Hz) television systems (like the standard sets used in Europe), by very bright images, or by close viewing (Badinand-Hubert et al., 1998).

Warning lights flicker at rates well below the CFF. Just how sensitive is the human visual system at these lower rates of flicker? Recall from Chapter 5 that human vision has an optimal spatial frequency—there is an object size that can be seen most easily. The same holds for temporal frequency—there is a rate of flicker that can be seen most easily, typically around 10 Hz.

TABLE 9.1 | Perceptual Consequences of Eye Movements

Test Conditions	Command Signals (C)	Eyes Move	Retina Image Motion (R)	Experience (E) [C − R = E]
Normal; stable environment	Left (+1)	Left	Left (+1)	No motion [1 −1 = 0]
Normal; stable environment	Right (−1)	Right	Right (−1)	No motion [(−1) − (−1) = 0]
Eye passively displaced left	None (0)	Left	Left (+1)	Right [0 − 1 = −1]
Eye paralyzed; person *wills* movement left	Left (+1)	None	None (0)	Left [1 − 0 = 1]
Environment translates left	None (0)	None	Right (−1)	Environment moves left [0 − (−1) = 1]

cerning the perceived direction of motion should develop from a comparison between two quantities—the command signals to the extraocular muscles and the accompanying retinal image motion. To derive perceived direction, subtract the retinal image motion from the command signal (remembering to respect signs).

In the first two test conditions (normal) of Table 9.1, the observer decides to move the eyes leftward, across a stationary visual environment, and the eyes do as they're instructed. Subtracting the retinal image motion from the command signal yields zero (no perceived motion) in both cases. Now we come to a more interesting condition.

To understand the third condition, close your left eye and gently tap your finger on the outer edge of your open right eye (being careful not to poke your eye too hard). With each displacement of your eyeball, you should experience a jerky displacement of the world. As Table 9.1 suggests, this illusory motion occurs because there is retinal image motion in the absence of command signals to the extraocular muscles. The fourth condition is the most unusual; in it the eyes are paralyzed and, thus, prevented from obeying the command to move. Here, the observer *wills* a leftward eye movement, but none occurs, yet the world still seems to move leftward. Be sure that you work through the details of this condition in order to understand how it is related to the last condition described in the table.

This exercise underscores the complicated compensatory calculations performed by the visual system to achieve perceptual stability as the eyes move about. In fact, some researchers suggest that yet another mechanism makes an important contribution to perceived stability. Bruce Bridgeman has argued that vision operates on the assumption that a continuously present object has not moved unless there is massive evidence to the contrary—a huge shift in object position. In one experiment, which supports this hypothesis, Deubel, Bridgeman, and Schneider (1998) measured the perceived position of pairs of objects. On each trial, during a saccade, one target in the pair shifted position, while the other's location remained constant. If one of the objects was momentarily extinguished during the saccade, that object's position was seen to have changed. This result persisted even when the extinguished object actually remained stable, while the nonextinguished object shifted position. Using a somewhat different approach, Blouin, Bridgeman and colleagues (1995) provided further support of the hypothesis that vision's default assumption favors position stability over change in position.

Now that you understand the basics of saccadic eye movements, we can return once more to the creature we left scurrying across the floor. You visually captured that creature—acquired the target—by making a saccade. But the creature is still moving, so you've now got a different problem: keeping your eyes aimed at this moving object.

Staying on Target: Keeping Your Eye on the Ball

To pursue a moving target, the eyes move smoothly, not with abrupt stops and starts as they do with saccades. To guide the eyes' pursuit movements, the brain draws on two complementary sources of information. One source comprises sensory information derived from neurons that code the direction and speed of moving objects (recall direction-selective neurons discussed in Chapter 4). The other source is the observer's expectations about object motions that are about to occur (Kowler, 1989). Integrating both sensory signals and cognitive expectations, the brain sends commands to the extraocular muscles for guidance of **pursuit eye movements,** sometimes called **smooth eye movements.**

Besides being smooth, pursuit eye movements are also constantly being adjusted, with their speed and direction modified to remain on target. By matching the eye's movements to the movements of the object of interest, the brain manages to keep the image of that object relatively stationary on the retina. The image, therefore, is not blurred from motion and, moreover, it remains centered on the fovea, where acuity is sharpest.

How accurately do pursuit movements actually match the movements of the object the eyes are pursuing? The answer depends on the speed of the moving object (Murphy, 1978). When an object moves slowly (less than one-third of a millimeter on the retina per second), eye movements match object movements almost perfectly. However, at higher object speeds, the eye movements often lag behind the object movement, causing the image of the object to slip away from the fovea on the retina. When this happens, the eyes jump ahead to recapture the object.

It is easy to overlook just how difficult it is to pursue a rapidly moving target with the eyes. Baseball coaches, for instance, exhort batters to keep their eye on the ball, which turns out to be impossible to do (Ripoll and Fleurance, 1988). Baseball, like cricket, lacrosse, tennis, and other sports involving rapidly moving balls, is a game of milliseconds.[3] At the professional level, batters can swing the bat at about 80 miles per hour. The pitched ball zooms toward the batter at speeds approaching 50 meters per second (~100 miles/hour), and as few as 400 milliseconds elapse between the pitcher's release and the ball's reaching homeplate. Under these conditions, a 7-millisecond error in a batter's swing is the difference between a hit over second base and a foul ball (Adair, 2002). Given these figures, it is simply impossible to keep your eye on the ball. Using a realistic batting situation, Bahill and LaRitz (1984) measured the position of the batter's gaze over time. They found that experienced baseball players (including individuals in the major

---

[3]See Regan (1992) for a detailed treatment of visual and cognitive factors in cricket, as well as a brief introduction to the sport itself.

FIGURE 9.10 | Schematic drawing of a direction-selective cell responsive to rightward motion (left-hand panel) and to leftward motion (middle panel). What would be the appropriate speed and direction of motion to activate the cell in the right-hand panel?

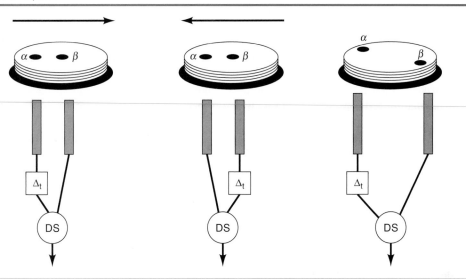

leagues) cannot accurately follow the path of a ball from the pitcher to home plate. Instead, a fraction of a second after the ball leaves the pitcher's hand, the batter executes a predictive saccadic eye movement. This saccade aims the batter's eyes at the predicted future location of the ball when it reaches the homeplate. Contrary to a coach's exhortations, then, it is impossible to keep one's eye on the ball throughout its entire travel from pitcher to home plate. Bahill and LaRitz found that really top-notch hitters can pursue the ball for more of its flight before having to resort to the inevitable predictive saccade.

You don't have to be a major league baseball player to see how hard it is to make your eyes move as you'd like them to. For example, although you can will your eyes to jump back and forth, you can't will them to move smoothly unless there is some smoothly moving object to track. To test this, ask a friend to track your finger as you move it slowly back and forth in front of his or her eyes. You'll see smooth pursuit eye movements. Now remove the actual tracking stimulus (your finger) and ask the friend to continue moving the eyes as if tracking your moving finger. You'll see that, despite his or her best efforts, your friend's eyes move along in a series of little jerks.

Having discussed structure from motion, biological motion, optic flow, and eye movements, it's now time to find out more about the neural circuits that underlie these aspects of motion perception.

Building Directional Selectivity: Space-Time Receptive Fields

Chapter 4 introduced the idea of neural direction selectivity when it described how the responses of some cortical cells vary with the direction of motion within the cells' receptive fields. Each **direction-selective cell** responds most strongly to one preferred direction, but little (if at all) to motion in the opposite direction. Because the preferred direction varies from cell to cell, the direction in which some object moves could be represented within the nervous system by the responses that moving object evokes in different cells. Before exploring the perceptual importance of direction-selective cells, we should clarify the origin of direction selectivity itself. How might one build a direction-selective cell?

To answer this question, Werner Reichardt (1961) proposed that neurons could be interconnected to create a small neural network that compared changes in the distribution of light within neighboring retinal regions. Figure 9.10 schematizes the basic building block of Reichardt's theory. In the left-hand panel, signals from two regions of the retina (α and β) are collected by neurons (shaded rectangles) and passed along to another neuron, labeled DS (for "directionally selective"). The DS neuron takes the inputs and multiplies them. As a result, a DS neuron's response is strongest when its two inputs have the same light level and reach the DS neuron simultaneously. But note that on its way to the DS neuron, the input from region α is delayed by some time, call it Δt. As a result, in order for signals from α and β to arrive simultaneously at the DS neuron, the one from α must have a head start. Putting this another way, the DS neuron responds when the same pattern of light first strikes region α and then, some time later (equivalent to the Δt), strikes region β. An effective stimulus would be an image that moved continuously across the retina from left to right, as represented by the arrow.

It's important to realize that this is not the only stimulus that would work. Certain nonmoving stimuli would be equally as effective in stimulating the DS neuron. One example is a stationary light flashed briefly on region α and after Δt, on region β. Later, in the section on apparent motion, you'll see that such nonmoving stimuli dupe the visual system into treating them as though they had moved.

Returning to Figure 9.10, let's assign the label Δx to the distance separating retinal regions α and β. Defining this distance allows us to be more precise about the moving stimulus that elicits the strongest response from the DS neuron. Recall that an optimal stimulus strikes first α and then β, after delay Δt. In order to meet that requirement, the stimulus must move over distance Δx in a time of Δt. As you know, speed is distance divided by time ($S = x/t$). Therefore, the speed of the optimal stimulus is Δx/Δt. Given the proper direction, of course, this speed, which causes an image to fall first in region α and then, Δt later, in region β, will elicit a strong response from the DS neuron.

The middle panel of Figure 9.10 illustrates how one might construct a unit that would respond best to retinal image motion in the opposite direction, but with the same speed. Now look at the right-hand panel of Figure 9.10 and try to identify the motion that best stimulates the DS neuron. The *orientation* of the two input areas on the retina, together with the *elapsed time* of the delay, determine the direction to which the DS neuron will respond. Note also in the right-hand panel that the two retinal areas α and β are farther apart than were the areas in the other panels. Assuming that Δt, the delay, has not changed, would the optimal stimulus move faster or slower than the previous cases?

Finally, imagine a whole array of DS neurons. Suppose that each received signals from retinal regions separated by some distance, Δx, and suppose that each preferred some particular delay, Δt. If Δx and Δt varied from one DS neuron to another, each DS neuron would

be optimally stimulated by a pattern moving in a particular direction *and* with a particular speed. Following tradition, we will describe such neurons as "directionally selective," keeping in mind that their responses are controlled jointly by direction and speed.

Reichardt's account of DS mechanisms is built around a network that computes changes in the distribution of light within neighboring retinal regions. Although motion usually arises from changes in light levels over space and time, other events, which do not entail changes in light level, can also give rise to motion. Events involving moving texture boundaries (waves of motion in a grain field), moving subjective contours like those shown in Figure 4.26 (Ramachandran, Rao, and Vidyasagar, 1973), or even moving, binocular-disparity discontinuities (ocean waves) can also trigger perception of motion in a given direction.

In the contemporary literature, motion defined by luminance variations over space/time has been dubbed *first-order motion* (meaning that the sensors register changes in luminance over time). Motion defined by other cues, such as texture differences, has been dubbed *second-order motion* (Chubb and Sperling, 1988; Smith, 1994; Sperling and Lu, 1998). In the case of second-order motion, the extraction of direction probably involves the same basic idea shown in Figure 9.10, but with different inputs to the comparison circuit.

Now that we're armed with an understanding of Reichardt's motion-extracting circuit, let's consider how this simple network can be "fooled" into seeing motion where it doesn't really exist.

Apparent Motion

Perceiving motion in our everyday environment seems fairly straightforward, because that perceptual experience is triggered by the actual motion of objects. Remember that rabbit you frightened near Walden Pond? It traveled several meters in a short time, and as the rabbit moved, the image of it moved over your retina. So it hardly seems surprising that you experienced motion. Conditions like this seem to require no explanation: You see motion because there *is* motion. And that motion is just what the motion-extracting circuits in Figure 9.10 are designed to register.

But we also know that in certain circumstances those circuits can be tricked—you can have a compelling experience of motion even when nothing in the world actually moves. Let's consider one such circumstance, known as **apparent motion.**

Apparent motion plays a prominent role in our lives. As Stuart Anstis points out,

> The flashing lights on a cinema marquee, which seem to move inward toward the lobby and entice us to follow them, are an example of apparent movement. If we go in and watch the movie, we experience two hours of apparent movement: each movie frame projected on the screen is actually stationary whenever the projector is open. If we stay at home and watch TV instead, we are once again experiencing apparent movement. Films and TV, as they exist today, are possible only because of a quirk in our visual systems. (1978, p. 656)

The visual system takes discrete and separate inputs (such as the separate frames of a movie) and knits them into an experience that is smooth and continuous. This is the "quirk" to which Anstis refers. We'll now focus on apparent movement because this quirk provides insights into how the visual system operates where there *is* genuine motion of the retinal image. (As we progress through this discussion, keep in mind the scheme for constructing direction-selective neurons in Figure 9.10.)

People have known about apparent motion for quite some time. In the nineteenth century, Sigmund Exner (1888) created brief but intense electrical sparks from two sources placed some distance apart. Observers judged which spark flashed first—the one on the right or the one on the left. When the time delay between sparks was long, the judgment was easy; when the delay was short, the judgment became difficult. Exner found that about one-twenty-fifth of a second had to intervene between the two sparks before their order could be judged accurately.

Then Exner placed the two sources of sparks very close to each other. With short intervals between the two sparks, people saw apparent motion—a single spark moving from one location to the other. Exner then asked people to judge the direction of that apparent motion. Although these people needed delays of one-twenty-fifth of a second to judge the order of sparks that were some distance apart, they needed less than half that delay to judge the *direction* of movement. This experience of apparent movement could not have been *derived* from judging the sequence of flashes because the time interval separating the two flashes was too brief to allow for such a judgment. Instead, motion was experienced directly.

Next, Exner brought the two sparks so close together that they appeared as a single bright spark. When the twin sparks were flashed one after the other, the observer saw apparent motion. This experience of apparent movement could not have been *derived* from judging the positions of flashes because the flashes were so close together that they couldn't be distinguished. Again, motion was experienced directly.

Exner's observations led him to conclude that motion was a primary sensation in its own right, not some inference derived from comparing temporal order or spatial position. Keeping in mind that apparent motion is not an inference, let's consider the work of Max Wertheimer, one of the founders of Gestalt psychology.

In one study, Wertheimer (1912/1961) briefly presented two spatially separated vertical lines in succession. What people saw depended on the delay that separated the two presentations. With long delays (greater than one-tenth of a second), one line appeared to succeed the other. In other words, the observer saw one line that came on and went off and then a second line that did the same. With very short delays between presentations (about one-fortieth of a second or less), the two lines appeared to come on and go off simultaneously. Perceptually there had been only a single presentation. With intermediate delays between presentation of the two lines (about one-twentieth of a second), a single line seemed to move smoothly from one position to the other. In other words, people saw apparent motion.

Next, Wertheimer arranged conditions so that the first line was seen by one eye and the second line was seen by the other eye. Even under these conditions of interocular stimulation, motion was again perceived. This suggests that the DS neurons giving rise to the perception of motion must be centrally located at or beyond the site where information from the eyes has been combined. Wertheimer devised a simple but effective demonstration of interocular apparent movement, one that you, too, can try.[4]

Hold a thin book in both hands and lean your forehead against the book's edge, as shown in Figure 9.11. Be sure to place your head so that one eye is on each side of the book. This allows you to use the book as a separator, making it easy to present different objects to the two eyes. Now, with your hands on opposite sides of the book, extend the index finger on each hand upward. Position the left hand so that its index finger can be seen by your left eye, and position your right hand so that its index finger can be seen by your right eye. Don't look directly at your fingers; instead, keep your gaze directed straight ahead at a point several inches beyond the far end

---

[4]Sekuler (1996) discusses many other of Wertheimer's other experiments, and explores their deep connections to contemporary research on motion perception.

FIGURE 9.11 | Setup that will allow you to experience apparent motion. Follow the instructions in the text.

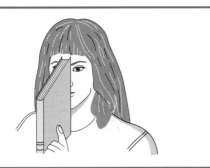

FIGURE 9.12 | Two drawings depicting successive "snapshots" (one taken immediately after the other) of a rotating, spoked wheel. In which direction is the wheel rotating? To figure out the answer, you (and your visual system, when viewing the actual event) must figure out which spoke in panel A (at time 1: t_1) corresponds to which spoke in panel B (at time 2: t_2). If the wheel is rotating clockwise, spoke 1 at the top of the wheel in panel A would correspond to the spoke located just to the right of top in panel B. But if the wheel were rotating counterclockwise, spoke 1 in panel A would correspond to the spoke located just to the left of the top in panel B. The perceived direction of motion depends entirely on how this correspondence problem is resolved by motion perception.

of the book. Your fingers should be about 6 inches from your nose. Now comes the hard part. Rhythmically open and close alternate eyes. Though it may take a little practice, at the proper speed of alternation you'll have a strange and amusing experience: Your finger will appear to jump back and forth as if it were moving through the interior of the book!

Wertheimer could not have known what we know today about brain function and visual cortical neurons. Thus, he mistakenly attributed apparent motion to a short-circuiting of current flow in the brain. Today, however, we believe that motion perception—including apparent motion—involves direction-selective neurons something like those schematized in Figure 9.10. DS neurons will respond vigorously to the successive presentation of two stationary lines, if the Δx and Δt values associated with those neurons correspond to the spatial separation and presentation delay between the lines. From the standpoint of the DS neurons, then, apparent motion and real motion constitute equivalent events.

The Correspondence Problem in Motion Perception

Apparent motion, besides implicating the operation of DS neurons, also highlights another question concerning motion perception that is easily overlooked when we think only about real motion in the natural environment: How does the visual system register that an object seen at one moment corresponds to the same object seen at another moment? After all, the finger example demonstrates that detecting correspondence over time is a prerequisite for motion perception.

We can highlight the nature of this prerequisite by comparing retinal images to photographic snapshots of the visual world. Suppose that you have two retinal

"snapshots" that were taken a fraction of a second apart. Looking at the two snapshots, how would you determine whether a single object had moved? To accomplish this, you must determine which elements in one snapshot correspond to which elements in the other (this problem is reminiscent of the matching problem in stereopsis, discussed in Chapter 8). Now here's the problem: Potentially, any small detail in one of the snapshots *might* correspond to any number of details in the other. This problem of figuring out what corresponds to what over time gets even more complicated when the visual scene contains multiple objects which resemble one another (see Figure 9.12).

Fortunately, the number of potential correspondences can be sharply reduced if the visual system takes into account regularities in the physical world (Marr, 1982; Ramachandran and Anstis, 1986). After all, the visual system evolved in a world consisting of objects that, because of

FIGURE 9.13 | Drawings based on one set of figures used to study how biological plausibility affects apparent motion (Shiffrar and Freyd, 1990). When the stimuli are presented in alternation, the young man's hand appears to rotate about his wrist, either clockwise or counterclockwise. With a brief interval separating the two stimuli, the hand appears to rotate through a short, but biologically implausible arc; with a greater interval between stimuli, the hand appears to rotate in the opposite direction, over a path that is longer but biologically plausible.

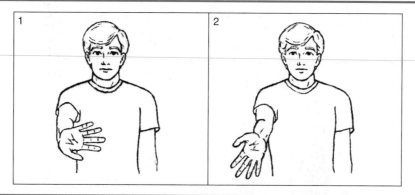

their physical properties, are constrained to behave in particular ways: Natural objects don't change color suddenly; natural objects are made of parts that are connected; the surface texture of natural objects tends to be uniform; natural objects, once in motion, tend to stay in motion in the same direction; and solid objects cannot move through one another. Do motion-sensitive neurons in the visual system respond to stimulus conditions that embody these regularities? Evidence from numerous experiments indicates that the answer is "yes"—the visual system indeed is biased against unnatural solutions to the correspondence problem and, instead, favors solutions that are consistent with the properties of real-world objects.

To give an example of one of these constraints in action, consider Newton's First Law of Motion: Once in motion, a body will continue in motion unless acted upon by an external force. In one perceptual demonstration reflecting this law, Wertheimer alternated two visual features at a rate that he knew would produce apparent motion between them—such as a circle at the left and a circle at the right. As long as the alternation continued, the circle appeared to travel laterally back and forth between the two positions. Then without warning to the viewer, Wertheimer occluded one of the circles but kept presenting the remaining one at its appropriate times. Surprisingly, even though only one circle was being exposed, it took a while for the apparent motion to cease. For three or four repetitions, the observer continued to see motion. This remarkable observation implies that inertia works not only in the natural world but in the world of apparent motion as well.

Here's an example of another constraint that influences motion perception, this one embodying a constraint associated with the human body. Maggie Shiffrar and Jennifer Freyd (1990) alternately showed two photographs of a human model in rapid succession. The two drawings were identical except for the position of the model's hand, which was positioned differently in the two drawings (see Figure 9.13). To get a sense of this configuration, extend your right arm fully and directly in front of you; spread the fingers of that hand, palm facing forward. Rotate your wrist so that your fingers point leftward; seen from the front (as in a mirror) that could be one of the photos. To create the second photo of the stimulus pair, rotate the wrist as far as it will go in the other direction, without moving your arm (for most people, the fingers will point downward or nearly so).

What would a person see when the two views were alternated? In principle, alternation of these two views of the hand, wrist, and arm could produce apparent motion along either of two quite different paths. One path represents a large rotation of the wrist (about 270 degrees); the other path represents a much shorter rotation (about 90 degrees or less). These paths differ not only in length but also in biological plausibility. The shorter path would entail a rotation of the wrist that is impossible to execute (just try it). Shiffrar and Freyd found that when the two photos were alternated, with only a brief time elapsing between them, people saw the shorter (biologically impossible) rotation. This result was not surprising; many previous studies had shown that the visual system tends to resolve a choice between two paths in favor of the shorter

FIGURE 9.14 | Illustration of the aperture problem: the ambiguity of directional information within the aperture of a receptive field. The circular area in the figure represents the receptive field of a directionally selective neuron whose preferred direction of movement is rightward. As the vertical bar moves rightward through the receptive field, the neuron would signal rightward motion (A). However, movement of the bar upward and to the right (B) could generate the same rightward motion in the receptive field, as could movement downward and rightward (C). The equivalence of stimulation within the receptive field renders the neuron's response inherently ambiguous.

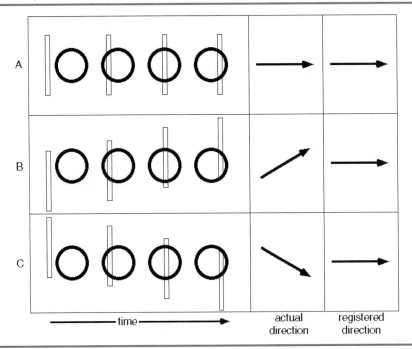

one. With longer intervals between the photos, though, Shiffrar and Freyd's observers tended to see motion over the longer, but biologically plausible path. The visual system, then, can be influenced by the physical plausibility of particular stimulus transformations, provided that there is sufficient time for that influence to be registered.

So in these last few sections we have seen how a laboratory curiosity—apparent motion—actually reveals fundamental characteristics of normal motion perception. In this next section, we consider another curiosity about motion perception which, on the face of it, seems to imply a design flaw. In fact, however, this curiosity, like apparent motion, stems from the brain's clever solution to a complicated problem. In this case, the problem involves figuring out which pieces of a dynamic puzzle go together.

The Aperture Problem

Because each DS neuron responds only to events within its own receptive field, signals from DS neurons are necessarily ambiguous. This ambiguity, now known as the

aperture problem, was pointed out many decades ago by Hans Wallach (Wuerger, Shapley, and Rubin, 1996). Figure 9.14 illustrates what Wallach had in mind. The circular area in the figure represents the receptive field of a directionally selective neuron whose preferred direction of movement is rightward. As a large vertical bar moves rightward at an appropriate speed through the receptive field, the neuron responds strongly (panel A). But this isn't the only direction of movement that will evoke such a response. So long as the vertical bar is large compared to the aperture (the receptive field), the same local spatio-temporal event—movement at the same velocity—could be generated by any number of other combinations of direction and speed, some of which are suggested in panels B and C. This equivalence makes the neuron's response inherently ambiguous. Because the neuron's "view" of the world is limited to the confines of its receptive field, the neuron responds exactly the same way to each of these different velocities of movement. Before explaining the visual system's strategy for overcoming this ambiguity, consider one side effect of this ambiguity.

FIGURE 9.15 | Upper row: Motion of an obliquely oriented line into, through, and then out of an L-shaped aperture. Lower row: At first, the line appears to move vertically downward; then, when the line enters the horizontally oriented portion of the aperture, its apparent direction abruptly changes to horizontal.

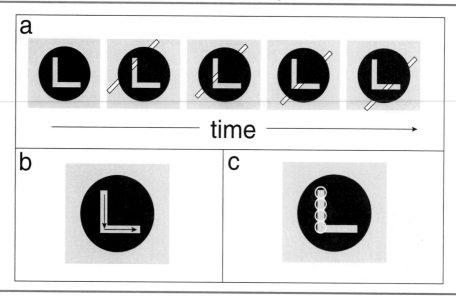

Because movement within a receptive field can arise from distinctly different visual events, the door is opened to a variety of striking illusions of perceived motion. In these illusions, observers watch as a line or bar moves through an aperture whose shape strongly influences the perceived direction of movement. For example, suppose that an L-shaped aperture is cut out of a piece of paper (Figure 9.15a). Suppose also that a long oblique line (at 45 degrees) is placed behind the aperture and is moved steadily down and to the right. Viewers will first see an oblique line that moves straight downward, but once the line reaches the base of the L-shaped aperture, the movement abruptly changes. Then viewers see an oblique line that moves rightward (Figure 9.15b). Wallach investigated this and several dozen related aperture illusions (Wuerger, Shapley, and Rubin, 1996). To see the basic elements of his approach, return to the L-shaped aperture.

We can approximate the L-shaped aperture's upright portion by a series of circular receptive fields whose centers lie along a single vertical line (Figure 9.15c). An oblique, downward-moving line would traverse each field, one after another. But this pattern of stimulation could have arisen from any number of different stimulus scenarios. For example, it could have been produced by several different, similarly oriented lines, each of which traverses just one receptive field and then disappears, just as the next line appears at the top of the next receptive field and begins its descent. Or the same pattern of stimulation across all the receptive fields could have resulted, as it did in Wallach's demonstration, from a single line that moved from top to bottom, entering and then exiting one receptive field after another in succession. How does the visual system, given the limited information it has, choose which scenario is responsible for that information? In the spirit of Gestalt psychology, Wallach proposed that the single perceptual choice made in such multiple-choice situations tends to be the simplest global motion. In that case, illustrated in Figure 9.15c, people see a single line that moves continuously rather than a series of successive lines. Incidentally, with this principle in mind, you should be able to figure out why, at the bottom of the L-shaped aperture, the line appears to move rightward.

Figure 9.16 illustrates another of Wallach's demonstrations, again showing how strongly the visual system favors a simple perceptual interpretation when alternative interpretations are possible. Instead of a single aperture, there are two apertures, side by side, one a circle and the other a vertically oriented rectangle. When an oblique line moves downward through only the rectangular aperture, people see downward motion—just as they did with the vertical section of the L-shaped aperture. When the

FIGURE 9.16 | Upper row: A bar moves down and to the left, first into, through, and then out of an elongated vertical aperture that adjoins a small circular aperture. When the line first becomes visible, it is seen only in the elongated aperture. As a result, influenced by the aperture shape, its motion is directly downward (bottom row). Then, when it is visible in the circular aperture as well, the bar's overall motion shifts to oblique.

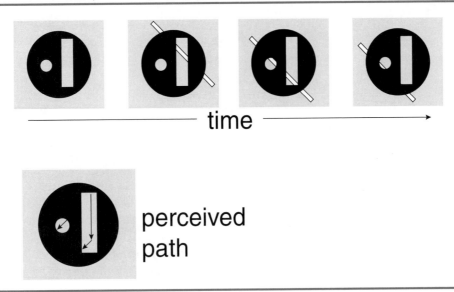

time

perceived path

oblique line moves downward through only the circular aperture, people see motion in a different direction—perpendicular to the orientation of the oblique line. The interesting part of the demonstration comes when the line is long enough to extend through both apertures at once. As the line begins to move downward, at first it is visible only in the rectangle—and the perceived motion is downward. But when the line enters the circular aperture and is visible in both apertures simultaneously, the perceived direction in both apertures abruptly shifts, and the line appears to slide downward and to the left (as it would in the circular aperture alone). Presumably, this change reflects the visual system's effort to treat the line in both apertures as a single line moving in one direction, rather than as two separate lines moving in different directions. Once again, we find that vision favors simple perceptual interpretations, a general principle, which Josh McDermott and Ted Adelson (2004) have recently recast into a comprehensive quantitative framework.

Sometimes, however, alternative perceptual interpretations seem inescapable. In a demonstration of this, Wallach showed people figures composed of two different line gratings, like those shown in Figure 9.17A and B. When the two are superimposed, as in panels C and D, they generate a series of diamond-shape structures.

When the bars of the two gratings move downward at the same rate, the display's appearance fluctuates between a field of diamonds that move downward (panel C), and two line-gratings that move at different velocities, sliding over each other in the process (panel D). The relative potency of the two alternative perceptual outcomes varies with a number of factors, Wallach found, including the angle between the two line gratings. (This bistability should remind you of the vase/face illusion illustrated in Figure 4.1 and the binocular rivalry phenomenon described in Box 8.3.)

Perceptual bistability points to something quite important about motion perception (McDermott and Adelson [2004]). Consider what the nervous system must do in order to parse the display into two gratings moving in different directions. This would seem to require mechanisms that can separate the different directions within each local region. But to produce the alternative outcome—the moving diamond—the nervous system needs a second mechanism that collects dissimilar directional signals from regions across the display and binds those signals into coherent perceptual wholes rather than independent, isolated elements. This may sound challenging, but it is utterly necessary. As Oliver Braddick put it, "We do not live in a world of independent fragments, but of

FIGURE 9.17 | Superimposing two diagonal, moving gratings produces a diamond pattern whose motion is bistable. When either moving grating alone is present (panels A and B), it appears to move in a consistent direction, indicated by the arrow. However, when the two moving diagonal gratings are superimposed, they sometimes cohere to form a single, downward-moving pattern (panel C) and, at other times, they appear to slide over one another in two different superimposed directions (panel D).

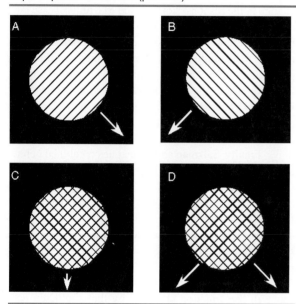

objects and surfaces that move coherently" (1993, p. 263). What you saw in the case of object recognition (Chapter 6) also holds for motion perception: Vision needs some way to combine velocity signals that belong to the same moving object. It also needs to separate velocity signals that do not belong together; signals that arise from different objects (Snowden and Verstraten, 1999). Obviously, the characteristics of the world mandate precisely the sort of complex behavior that Wallach demonstrated.

Combining Velocity Signals: Global Solutions for Local Problems

Wallach's diamond/grating demonstration (Figure 9.17) tells us that perceived motion is not always determined solely by individual responses to the stimulus velocity within isolated, local regions of the field. Instead, similar local measurements of velocity are integrated, producing an overall response. This integration implies that somewhere within the visual system, local velocity-related signals are brought together. In fact, such a combination of different signals is the nervous system's standard way to resolve the ambiguity in signals from individual neurons. As you have seen before, when the response of one neuron is ambiguous, the nervous system resolves the ambiguity by aggregating outputs from a number of differently tuned neurons. We saw this previously when considering contour orientation in Chapter 4 and color vision in Chapter 7.

For visual motion, the nervous system reduces ambiguity about individual, local spatio-temporal events by channeling outputs from the first stage of direction processing to a second stage of neural processing, involving higher-order neurons. To implement this strategy for motion processing, direction-selective neurons in V1 project forward (anterior) and upward (superior), making connections with neurons in a relatively small area on the brain's lateral surface near the junction of the occipital, parietal, and temporal lobes (see Figure 9.5). This area goes by two different names: area V5 and area MT.[5] Receptive fields in area MT are considerably larger in size than those in area V1, implying that an array of spatially distributed V1 neurons contributes to the synthesis of individual MT receptive fields. Also, in area V1, only a minority of neurons exhibit direction-selectivity, but in area MT, essentially all neurons are directionally selective.

Some neurons in MT receive input from V1 neurons with different preferred directions of motion. The result? The directional selectivity of these MT neurons differs qualitatively from that of their predecessors in V1. And these differences enhance the importance of MT's contribution to the perception of motion. To see why, return to Wallach's demonstration with two overlaid, moving gratings. When two-component displays like this are imaged within the receptive fields of V1 neurons, the neurons respond to the separate components. Thus, some V1 neurons would respond to the contours moving obliquely downward to the right, and other V1 neurons would respond to the contours moving obliquely downward to the left. But when the same displays are presented in the receptive fields of MT neurons, many of those cells respond

---

[5]The abbreviation *MT* has been adopted in the belief that this area is the homologue in the human brain to area MT that has been carefully delineated in nonhuman primates. The preponderance of directionally selective neurons in nonhuman primate Area MT has attracted much attention from researchers interested in motion perception.

to the global direction of motion (downward, as in the case illustrated in Figure 9.17), not to the individual components (Movshon et al., 1986). It is thought, then, that important aspects of motion perception arise from two stages of processing: one stage extracting local motion vectors, and a second stage sorting those vectors into object-related combinations. In the next section, we take a closer look at this second stage of processing, focusing in particular on the small but well-studied area MT.

Area MT's Special Role in Motion Processing

Converging lines of evidence implicate area MT in motion perception. We know, for instance, that damage to MT impairs motion perception. This is most dramatically shown in the motion-blind patient, L. M., whose symptoms were described early in this chapter. L. M.'s brain damage was centered in the area where MT is located. We also know that motion perception in normal individuals can be transiently impaired by a brief, strong pulse of magnetic energy applied to the region of the scalp overlying MT (Hotson et al., 1994; Beckers and Zeki, 1995; Walsh et al., 1998).[6] There is also evidence that neural signals channeled through area MT guide pursuit eye movements (Watamaniuk and Heinen 1999).

Area MT's role in motion perception has been studied using one particular class of animation sequences: computer-generated displays consisting of moving dots (see Figure 9.18). These displays make it possible to control precisely the strength of motion signals present in animation sequences. Consider two extremes of dot motion, which we can designate *correlated* and *uncorrelated*. With perfectly correlated motion, all dots move in the same direction (for example, either up or down). The right portion of Figure 9.18 (100%) shows this arrangement. With uncorrelated motion, each dot can move in any direction and, consequently, dots appear to jiggle about randomly, moving like swirling snow. This stimulus, which is often described as "visual noise," is represented in the left portion of Figure 9.18 (0%).

When human observers are tested with various mixtures of correlated and uncorrelated motions (such as in the middle portion of Figure 9.18), correlations of just 3 to 5 percent are strong enough to permit reliable discrimination of the motion's direction. Normal monkeys do equally well. But in monkeys in which area MT is

damaged, direction of motion cannot be recognized until the correlation is about 10 times stronger (Newsome and Paré, 1988). The motion-blind patient, L. M., shows an even more dramatic deficit in detecting motion in noise, presumably the result of damage to Area MT in her brain (Baker, Hess, and Zihl, 1991).

MT's key role in motion perception was most dramatically shown in a study done by Salzman and colleagues (1992). This study took a novel approach, using tiny, localized electrical currents to induce a temporary change in the responses of selected MT units. These currents, which were not evoked by the visual stimulus, boosted the responses of particular directionally selective neurons. The study began by establishing the direction preferences of various MT neurons. This purely physiological phase of the study was followed by a phase that was purely behavioral: While monkeys viewed random dot displays, they moved their eyes in one direction or another to signal the perceived direction of those displays. Finally, Salzman and colleagues combined behavior and physiology, eliciting perceptual judgments: (1) while electrical stimulation was being applied to particular MT neurons and (2) without accompanying electrical stimulation.

Electrical stimulation of neurons that share a direction preference biased the monkeys' perceptual judgments of random dot displays. The result was an increased likelihood that the display would appear to move in the direction preferred by the stimulated neurons. So, for example, direct stimulation of MT neurons that prefer leftward motion made it more likely that the display would appear to move in that direction. Direct stimulation of MT neurons was perceptually equivalent to an effect normally produced by a visual stimulus moving in a particular direction. As far as the brain is concerned, it doesn't matter whether its neurons are responding to this unusual, direct electrical stimulation or to normal, visual stimulation.

Though neurons in Area MT certainly contribute to the perception of motion, don't get the idea that Area MT is the only place where neurons extract significant motion information. Actually, various aspects of motion perception depend upon the neural computations carried out in several different areas of the cortex. Normal motion perception depends upon activity distributed over many areas of the brain, each extracting somewhat different information from the retinal image.

To emphasize this point, consider the computations carried out in another region of the cortex, Area MST (MST stands for *medial superior temporal*, a label that

---

[6]Transcranial magnetic stimulation (TMS) was described in greater detail in Chapters 1 and 4.

FIGURE 9.18 | Schematic representation of a random-dot stimulus that can be used to measure motion thresholds. In each panel, the arrow indicates the direction in which the attached dot moves. In the two left-hand panels, there is 0 percent correlation among the movements of the various dots; they move in random directions. In the two right-hand panels, movements of all dots are 100 percent correlated, either up (as in the top panel) or down (as in the bottom panel). The middle panels represent an intermediate case: 50 percent of the dots move together, either up (top panel) or down (bottom panel). To make it easier for the reader to distinguish them, dots that move in an uncorrelated fashion are shown in color; in the actual stimulus, all dots were identical.

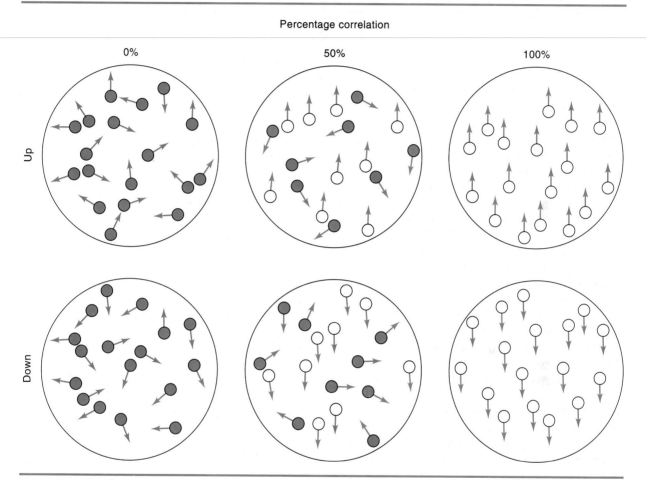

Percentage correlation

indicates this area lies adjacent to and just above MT, *medial temporal).* Going back to the complex circuit shown in Figure 4.20, you may be able to find MST's two divisions, MSTd and MSTl (for dorsal and lateral, respectively), and confirm that both receive input from MT. In a way, MST's view of the world is shaped by MT.

To reinforce the notion that motion perception depends upon computations in multiple areas of the brain, consider the properties of some neurons in MST's dorsal division. Much of our understanding of MST and its contribution to motion perception comes from the work of

Keiji Tanaka and his colleagues (Tanaka and Saito, 1989). Tanaka showed that neurons in MSTd have extremely large receptive fields, likely reflecting each neuron's input from many, spatially dispersed neurons in MT. Moreover, MSTd neurons respond most strongly to stimuli that move in a characteristic fashion over large portions of the visual field. These preferred motions are quite different from the linear motions that V1 and MT neurons prefer. In MSTd, neurons respond strongly to stimulus expansion (or its opposite, contraction) or to stimulus rotation.

FIGURE 9.19 | The two upper panels depict motion vectors associated with expansion (A) and rotation (B). The two lower panels show possible inputs to a neuron selectively responsive to expansion (C) or rotation (D).

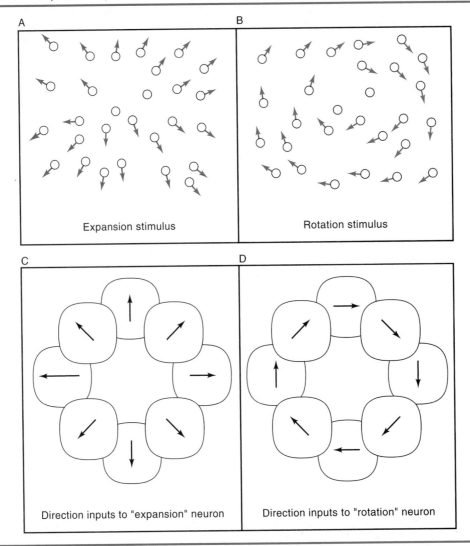

The stimuli preferred by two typical cells are shown schematically in panels A and B of Figure 9.19. The stimuli depicted here are spatially random dots, but strong responses could also be evoked by other figures, as long as they contained appropriate directional vectors. For example, expansion patterns would evoke good responses from an MST expansion cell; a rotating spiral or other pattern would evoke good responses from an MST rotation neuron.

Additional experiments by Tanaka, Fukada, and Saito (1989) show the likely origin of the stimulus preferences expressed by expansion neurons and rotation neurons. We have schematized these origins in panels c (expansion) and D (rotation) of Figure 9.19. Every MST neuron receives input from several MT neurons, each of which has its own preference for motion in a particular direction (shown by the arrows). Although the diagrams show eight different input neurons, Tanaka and colleagues indicate that fewer would suffice, as long as their direction preferences were appropriate.

What value might these odd neural computations have for us? Why should our brains register optical expansion or optical rotation? Think back to our previous discussion about the visual guidance of locomotion.

There, we noted the importance of variables such as optical expansion (looming) and tau. In a stable environment, forward locomotion produces expansion of the retinal image; as we saw earlier, that optical expansion carries information about time to collision. In the same environment, twisting your head from side to side produces rotational motion on the retina.

Signals from various MST neurons probably make crucial contributions to the visual guidance of locomotion. Evidence for this idea is given by Lucia Vaina (1998), who also describes two brain-injured patients who perform perfectly well on ordinary tests of motion perception—such as discrimination of direction—but seem unable to extract heading information from optic flow. For example, R. R., whose bilateral brain injury covered an area that included MST, performed normally on direction discrimination and speed judgments, although he frequently bumped into people, corners, and things in his way, particularly into moving targets (e.g., people walking). He was unable to catch a ball or any object thrown directly to him, whatever its speed, although he could see the object and that it was moving. In laboratory tests, he was unable to perceive radial motion and was very impaired on even the simplest heading tasks.

Common Fate

When people whose vision is good are tested with random-dot animations, they can detect motion with incredibly weak correlations among the directions of movement of the dots. For example, even when 97 to 98 percent of the dot displacements are totally random, people can see net motion from the mere 2 to 3 percent of the dots that move coherently in the same direction. But how does the visual system manage to pull such a weak signal out of so much noise? Some theorists credit special synergistic interactions among neurons (Williams, Phillips, and Sekuler, 1986). The guiding idea is that neurons that respond to similar directions of motion "cooperate" by amplifying one another's responses.

Neurons that respond to very different directions "compete" by inhibiting one another. As a result, the effect of even a small amount of motion in a single direction gets amplified, and the effect of other motions in many different, uncorrelated directions is diminished.

Cooperative competitive interactions among direction-selective neurons might be important in another well-known perceptual phenomenon. It was long ago recognized that perception of **global motion**—a general tendency to perceive motion in a given direction—emerges even though many individual motion vectors are random (Koffka, 1935). In other words, nearby elements or features tend to be seen as moving together. This phenomenon, which the Gestalt theorists called "the law of common fate," is just what one would expect from synergistic interactions among neurons tuned to similar directions (Yuille and Grzywacz, 1988). You can experience "common fate" for yourself when a light breeze blows the leaves of a tree. You can see the tree's net motion (in the direction of the breeze) despite the fact that each leaf also moves on its own. Likewise, when smoke rises from a chimney, you can see the smoke's overall, net motion despite random, local perturbations in the plumes.

Like the Gestalt organizational principles discussed in Chapter 6, the **Law of Common Fate** may reflect how well our visual systems match the physical properties of the world in which we live. In our world, immediately adjacent regions in the visual field tend to belong to the same object. As a result, there is a correlated tendency for adjacent regions, when they do move, to move in similar directions. Thus, for example, an array of dots moving in random directions can appear to move in a single direction when those dots are superimposed on a large object moving in that direction. Called **motion capture** (Ramachandran and Cavanagh, 1987), this phenomenon exemplifies the principle of common fate. On the other hand, when adjacent regions fail to behave in this way, the visual system treats those adjacent regions as belonging to different objects (recall how motion parallax can signify two distinct surfaces appearing at different depths, illustrated in Figure 8.37).

Motion Adaptation

We are now ready to consider one of the fundamental properties of direction-selective neurons, a property that you've already seen in action in other domains of vision: neural adaptation.

Suppose that for a minute or so you view motion in just one direction. Now immediately after this period of adaptation, you look at a stationary object. You would see the object appear to move in a direction opposite the direction at which you'd just been looking. This is illusory motion is known as the **motion aftereffect (MAE)** or sometimes as the **waterfall illusion,** since the illusion can be experienced after staring at a waterfall for a period of time (Addams, 1834/1964). The MAE has a long history, dating back more than two millennia, to the observations of the Roman poet and philosopher Titus Lucretius Carus (Wade and Verstraten, 1998).

There's a good chance that you have already experienced the MAE, for many naturally occurring conditions have the potential to engender it. If you haven't, though, here is an easy way to generate a strong MAE. As you probably know, some television programs and many movies have long crawls—the steadily moving list of people who worked on the show. To read the names, your eyes have to keep up with the crawl. The next time you see a crawl, though, forget about reading the names, and just keep your eyes fixed steadily on the center of the screen while the crawl goes by. Then, as soon as the crawl is over, you will experience illusory motion in a direction opposite to that of the crawl—this is the MAE.

Over the years a number of explanations have been advanced for this striking aftereffect, but most modern theories are based on two quite reasonable assumptions. These assumptions constitute psychophysical linking statements, assertions of particular connections between neural events and perceptual experiences. Mather and Harris (1998) frame the two psychophysical assertions this way:

1. Perception of motion is mediated by some form of comparison between the responses of cells in the visual system sensitive to different directions.

2. Following adaptation to a moving stimulus there is a change in the responsiveness of these cells, so that cells tuned to motion directions congruent with the adapting stimulus show a reduction in response relative to cells tuned to other directions. (p. 157)

The first of these linking hypotheses should remind you of ideas you've read about in earlier chapters, particularly the ones on color vision and on spatial vision. The second of the linking hypotheses states an established fact about the effects of prolonged stimulation, namely that adaptation happens.

To see how such ideas might work in practice, imagine that when stationary contours are seen, direction-selective cells, regardless of their direction preference, generate approximately equal levels of spontaneous activity. Following prolonged exposure to a particular direction—say, downward—cells preferring downward motion will show little if any spontaneous activity, while cells responsive to upward motion show a normal level of spontaneous activity. This biased distribution of spontaneous activity following adaptation is similar to the activity distribution evoked by actual motion upward—hence the illusory upward motion. Note that the first of Mather and Harris's psychophysical linking statements does not specify what sort of comparison is made among neurons,

and there is continuing disagreement about the details of that comparison (Barlow and Hill, 1963; Mather and Moulden, 1980; Hiris and Blake, 1992).[7]

Roger Tootell and colleagues (Tootell et al., 1995a; Tootell et al., 1995b) combined psychophysical and neuroimaging techniques to pinpoint one region of the human brain that certainly contributes to the MAE. They used computer-generated concentric rings with a fixation point in the center. The rings were programmed to expand, contract, or remain unchanged. Forty-second periods of expansion or contraction (sometimes both together) alternated with equally long periods during which the rings were stationary. As you might expect from your knowledge of the MAE, viewing an expanding pattern produced illusory contracting motion in a physically stationary pattern, and viewing a contracting pattern produced illusory expansion. These aftereffects were quite powerful, lasting around 20 seconds after the cessation of real motion. During that period, the MAE became progressively weaker and finally ceased altogether.

In contrast to these powerful MAEs from unidirectional adaptation, alternation between expansion and contraction produced no MAE—the opposite directions canceled one another. The unidirectional adapting motion produced strong activation in several regions of observers' brains, but activation was by far the strongest in Area MT. When adapting motion ceased and was replaced by a stationary pattern, activation in MT continued but progressively diminished over about 20 seconds.

To visualize the connection between the time frame of the observers' experience of MAE and the time frame of the MAE-related fMRI signals, Tootell plotted the two phenomena on the same axes (Figure 9.20). The solid line in the graph is the MAE-related fMRI signal, which is essentially zero throughout the 40-second adapting period; the vertical dashed line indicates the time at which adaptation ceased. Notice that shortly after the end of adaptation, the MAE-related fMRI signal jumps up and then steadily declines, back down to zero. The open squares in the right half of the graph are measurements of MAE strength sampled at various times following adaptation. Note the striking similarity between the rate of decline in MAE-related fMRI signal (solid line) and the

---

[7]The waterfall illusion is not the only case in which stationary objects appear to move. Have you ever noticed how the moon appears to move speedily across the sky as clouds pass in front of it? This is an example of **induced motion**—the real movement of the clouds causes the illusory movement of the moon (Duncker, 1929/1938). Unlike the waterfall illusion, induced motion's physiological basis is not known.

FIGURE 9.20 | The fMRI and psychophysical measures of MAE as a function of time after end of adaptation. After 40 seconds, the adapting motion was turned off. Shortly thereafter, both fMRI (solid curve) and psychophysical measures (square data points) give clear evidence of direction-specific activity that declines over time. To generate the psychophysical measure, participants adjusted a nulling motion, which canceled the apparent motion of the MAE.

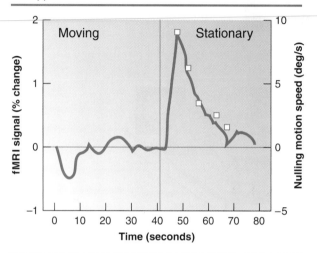

across a television screen. Prior to adaptation, judgments were accurate; upward moving dots, for example, were seen as moving upward. After adapting for several minutes to dots moving steadily in one direction, observers again judged the direction in which dots moved. When the dots moved steadily in a direction similar but not identical to the adaptation direction, the observers now made errors of judgment: the direction of motion of the dots always seemed to be shifted away from the adaptation direction. This phenomenon should remind you of the tilt aftereffect, demonstrated in Figure 4.24.

Attention Affects Motion Perception

When you know what to look for, your visual performance tends to be faster and more accurate than when you're uncertain about what's going to happen. Uncertainty, in other words, can impair visual perception, presumably because you don't know where to direct your attention. In one study of uncertainty's effect on vision, Ball and Sekuler (1981) measured people's ability to detect very dim dots that moved across a video screen. From trial to trial, the dots' direction of motion varied unpredictably. In addition, during half the trials, no dots at all were presented; the viewer saw just a blank screen (see panels A and B in Figure 9.21). And even when present, the dots could be made so dim that a viewer had great difficulty telling whether or not any dots were present.

Ball and Sekuler compared the intensity thresholds for detecting the dots when people were given information about which direction to expect versus when they were completely uncertain about the upcoming direction of motion. As illustrated in Figure 9.21, on "cued" trials a directional cue in the form of a short line was flashed very briefly at different times relative to the presentation of the dots. The orientation of the line indicated the direction in which the dots, if present at all, might move (recall that on half the trials, no dots at all were presented).

Ball and Sekuler made several noteworthy discoveries. First, when the orientation of the line corresponded exactly to the dots' direction of motion, the dots were easier to see—that is, the threshold was low. Second, the cue was not helpful unless it preceded the dots by about half a second or so, implying that selective attention required some time to operate. Third, if the cue's orientation did not match the dots' direction precisely, but only approximated it, the cue could still lower the detection threshold, but not as much as when it was precisely accurate. Generally, the greater the discrepancy between

decline in MAE strength (open squares). This demonstrated link between MAE and activation in MT has been strengthened by He, Cohen, and Hu (1998) and by Culham and colleagues (1999). Incidentally, Tootell found that some areas other than MT also seem to show postadaptation activation that may be related to MAE. This activation outside MT is consistent with psychophysical observations suggesting that motion adaptation occurs in more than one site in the nervous system (Blake, 1995; Pantle, 1998; Thompson, 1998).

The MAE, then, probably results from a biased distribution of responses in direction-selective neurons, including neurons in MT. Let's examine another perceptual consequence of biased distributions, since it provides additional support for this way of thinking about the neural coding of perceived direction of motion.

If an object's perceived direction of motion depends on the distribution of activity in direction-selective neurons, it should be possible to alter a moving object's perceived direction by adapting some of those neurons. Levinson and Sekuler (1976) asked observers to judge the direction in which an array of bright dots traveled

FIGURE 9.21 | On any trial, Ball and Sekuler presented either dim dots (A) that could move in any direction or no dots (B). Panels C, D, and E represent the sequence of events for different trials. The viewer first saw a blank screen. Then a cue (short white line) appeared, followed some time later by moving dots. The orientation of the short lines in panels C and E signifies upward motion; the orientation of the line in panel D signifies downward motion. The interval between cue and motion varied—the intervals represented in panels C and D are longer than the one represented in panel E.

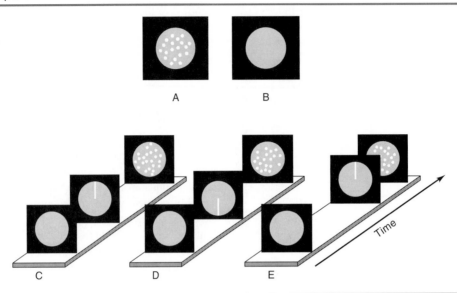

the cue's orientation and the dots' direction of motion, the more difficult it was to see the moving dots. A cue that misdirects an observer's attention to the wrong direction can be worse than no cue at all.

But how do directional cues or certainty about direction manage to exert the effect that they do? Cues and prior knowledge are not part of the visual event itself, but they certainly do affect the response evoked by that event. Obviously, some information extracted from the cue must be recoded into a format that can influence the subsequent processing of the test motion. After this recoding process, the cue presumably is able to selectively boost responses in particular sets of directionally selective neurons.

Gordon Shulman and colleagues (1999) extended Sekuler and Ball's study by using fMRI to measure brain activity while people performed the cued-motion detection task. As before, the stationary cue, presented prior to the moving target, specified the direction of motion that people would see. The imaging results showed that presenting the nonmoving cue produced activation in brain areas including MT and nearby regions that nor-

mally respond to motion, as well as in some parietal lobe areas not normally responsive to motion. Together, these motion-sensitive and motion-insensitive areas seem to constitute a neural circuit that encodes and holds instructions during the interval between the cue and the onset of motion.

So, prior information about the direction of motion temporarily boosts MT neurons that are responsive to that direction of motion (Treue and Maunsell, 1999; Treue and Trujillo, 1999). You can think of this internally generated boost as equivalent to what happens when the responses of particular directionally selective neurons are strengthened, either by the presentation of a strong visual stimulus or by direct electrical stimulation as utilized in the study by Salzman and colleagues.

Previously you read how prolonged inspection of a stimulus moving in one direction generated the MAE, illusory motion in a direction opposite to the adapting direction. MAEs can also be produced by stimuli comprising two superimposed directions of motion. Here, the resulting aftereffect is opposite the vector sum of the two adapting directions (Riggs and Day, 1980;

FIGURE 9.22 | Schematic of stimulus conditions used by Alais and Blake (1999) to test attention's influence on motion adaptation. During most of the adaptation period, a subset of "adaptation" dots moved coherently upward (open circles in this figure) while the remaining "noise" dots moved incoherently in all directions (filled circles). Unpredictably, during the adaptation period a subset of the "noise" dots moved briefly rightward (black dots), and observers had to pay attention during adaptation to detect these brief episodes of rightward motion.

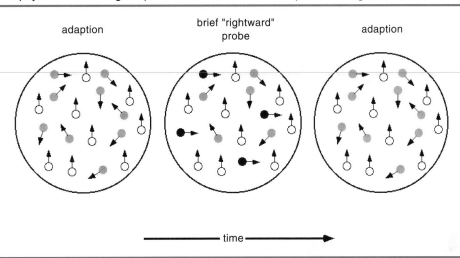

Verstraten, Fredericksen, and van de Grind, 1994). Thus, for example, simultaneous adaptation to leftward and upward motions subsequently causes a stationary test figure to appear to drift down and to the right (the vector sum of the downward component and the rightward component).

When the two adapting components are unequal in strength—say, one component is higher in contrast than the other—the aftereffect direction shifts toward the stronger component, and the size of the shift tracks the inequality between stimulus components.

Instead of varying the relative contrasts of the two component adapting motions, Alais and Blake (1999) manipulated how much attention people paid to one of the components. In their experiments, people viewed a computer display consisting of two superimposed fields of moving dots. Dots in one group all moved coherently in a single direction, shown as "upward" in Figure 9.22. Dots in the other group moved in random directions most of the time, producing no net directional drift. Every once in a while, a subset of the random dots joined forces to move in the same direction, shown as "rightward" in Figure 9.22. The proportion of dots moving rightward was only about 25 percent, making it necessary for observers to look carefully to detect their presence.

On some trials, observers were required to indicate when this weak coherent motion was present. On the remaining trials observers simply observed the same stimuli but did not have to perform the detection task and, therefore, did not have to attend selectively to the rightward motion. Alais and Blake reasoned that the first of these conditions—active viewing—would demand more attention than the second, passive viewing condition.

In the passive, control condition, brief insertions of weak rightward motion had little effect on the direction of MAE. When observers had to attend to it, however, the inserted motion dramatically altered the aftereffects' direction, shifting it by about 20 degrees. This same shift, which was mediated solely by attention to a weak signal, was equivalent to the shift that would have been produced by a very powerful signal (motion with dots 70 percent correlated). So attention to motion in one direction boosted the response to that motion by almost threefold—making a 25 percent correlated stimulus as effective as one that was 70 percent correlated. Extrapolating from the response of MT neurons to changes in stimulus correlation, Alais and Blake deduced that the attentional effects observed in humans were equivalent, on average, to what would be expected from a doubling in stimulus correlation in a nonattended stimulus.

FIGURE 9.23 | Display characteristics during a trial in a multiple-object tracking experiment. During phase 1 (*target designation*), several discs are singled out by a momentary brightening. During phase 2 (*movement*), all discs undergo a series of random movements. In phase 3 (*probe*), only one disc is brightened. Thereafter, the observer must judge whether the probe disc had or had not been among the target discs designated in phase 1. Under many conditions, the random movements of the discs make it difficult to track simultaneously all the designated target discs.

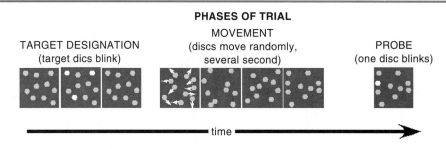

PHASES OF TRIAL

TARGET DESIGNATION
(target dics blink)

MOVEMENT
(discs move randomly,
several second)

PROBE
(one disc blinks)

time

So, there's no doubt that attention can exert a very powerful influence on perceived motion. In fact, when motion disrupts attention, ordinarily visible, stationary objects can actually disappear temporarily. Bonneh, Cooperman, and Sagi (2001) created a compelling animation in which an array of random dots appears superimposed on a highly visible object, such as a vivid yellow circle. Remarkably, the circle completely disappears from awareness for several seconds or more before finally reappearing. Called "motion-induced blindness" this remarkable phenomenon can be experienced at a website accessible through www.mhhe.com/blake5. What causes an ordinarily vivid object to disappear from perceptual awareness, even though it is still physically present? Bonneh and colleagues ruled out several possibilities, including binocular suppression, sensory masking, and adaptation. Although the cause remains to be nailed down, several investigators have proposed that motion-induced blindness, in fact, stems from a temporary disruption of attention normally directed toward the stationary object (Carter and Pettigrew, 2003). This explanation seems plausible because we know that people can fail to notice large-scale changes in the visual scene when their attention is directed elsewhere (recall our discussion of change blindness and inattentional blindness in Chapter 6).

Tracking Multiple Moving Objects: Giving Vision a Run for Its Money

In previous sections, you read about the impact of attention on perception of visual motion. In those discussions, vision was called upon to attend to just one moving object or just one direction of motion at a time. But sometimes, one needs to attend to multiple objects, which can move independently of one another. Imagine, for example, that you've been asked to be a playground monitor at an elementary school. During recess, you have the unenviable task of keeping track of a dozen or more individual children, each of whom runs around wildly in unpredictable directions. Clearly, this is not an easy task and certainly requires good vision, but also considerable attention.

To study this challenging behavior, researchers have developed a laboratory analogue in which observers are challenged to keep track, over time, of multiple, spatially dispersed, independently moving targets (Pylyshyn and Storm, 1988). Generally, the task resembles watching some children playing together on the school playground, and then, when the kids tire of the game and run off in different directions, keeping track of each one of them.

A typical experiment on **multiple object tracking** consists of three phases: *target designation, movement,* and *probe*. These three phases are illustrated in Figure 9.23. Target designation begins with the presentation of 10 targets, such as discs, scattered about on a computer display. Then three, four, or five of the ten discs, chosen randomly, blink several times. This informs the observer which discs will be targets for that trial. In the movement phase, all 10 of the discs move about smoothly on the screen in various directions, each changing course unpredictably. After several seconds of movement, the trial's probe phase began. One of the 10 discs is highlighted and the observer must report whether that one probe item had or had not been one of the designated targets.

Quality of performance is summarized by the proportion of trials with accurate reporting. Performance is most accurate when people have to keep track of fewer targets, say three rather than four or five. This is consistent with earlier findings that attention loses potency for any one item when additional items must also be attended to.

Steven Yantis (1992) examined how perceptual grouping contributes to multiple object tracking. This effort required several different ways of influencing perceptual grouping of the targets. For example, in one experiment, some targets were chosen at random, while others were chosen for their strategic location within a simple geometric figure, such as a diamond. At the outset of the experiment, tracking performance was much better when the target was initially part of a geometric perceptual group. However, observers quickly learned to impose virtual groupings on elements that had not been part of the regular geometrical groupings, which erased any early boost from geometrical groupings.

Of course, grouping at the start of a trial is no help at trial's end (the probe phase) unless the grouping is maintained during the movement phase. By varying the targets' movements during a trial's movement phase, Yantis manipulated the likelihood that any existing grouping would be maintained.

In one condition, targets moved about randomly, which allowed one or more targets to occasionally cross over an opposite edge of a virtual polygon. This criss-crossing destroyed the original grouping, which undermined the coherence of the virtual polygon and caused elements to lose identity as designated targets in that virtual polygon.

In another condition, movements of targets were constrained, ensuring that none ever crossed over an opposite edge of the virtual polygon. In this condition, movements of individual targets produced moment-to-moment fluctuations in the shape of a virtual figure that would be created by connecting those targets. But none of these fluctuations were drastic enough to destroy the convexity of the virtual polygon. Performance was distinctly better when target movement did not destroy the virtual polygon than when it did. This suggests that observers' attention creates (in the target designation phase) and maintains (in the movement phase) an updatable virtual object that is used (in the probe phase) to determine whether the probed target was or was not in the object.

To track multiple *moving* objects, the brain exploits neural circuits that are ordinarily devoted to a slightly different purpose, namely for shifting attention from one location in space to another. Jody Culham and colleagues (1998) used fMRI to identify the brain circuits that participated in multiple object tracking. Their results provide a clear picture of how the brain manages this difficult task. Attentive tracking of multiple, independently moving objects is mediated by a network of areas that includes area MT and related regions (which you learned are central regions for processing motion information) and also parietal and frontal regions (which are responsible for eye movements and shifting attention between locations) (Culham and Kanwisher, 2001). For a thoughtful review of the many studies on multiple object tracking, see Scholl (2001).

SUMMARY AND PREVIEW

This chapter emphasized motion perception's many, varied contributions, from defining the three-dimensional shape of moving objects and providing information that we use in locomoting, to guiding the eye movements that we use as we explore the world. The chapter described the neural basis of movement perception and the circuitry used to extract motion signals. It explained how limitations of this circuitry produced a dependence on configural properties, including the shape of the aperture within which an object moves. You read about two theoretically significant illusions of motion perception, namely apparent motion and motion aftereffect. After exploring parallels between the properties of natural events and the neural mechanisms designed to register those events, the chapter ended with a discussion of important higher-order influences on motion, including attention.

This chapter concludes our survey of visual qualities that enable you to appreciate the various biologically important aspects of the world. Next, we turn to other senses that also provide vital information about that world. We begin with the ear and hearing.

KEY TERMS

aperture problem
apparent motion
critical flicker frequency (CFF)
direction-selective (DS) cell
global motion
induced motion

Law of Common Fate
motion aftereffect (MAE)
motion capture
multiple object tracking
optic flow
point-light motion

pursuit eye movements
saccades
smooth eye movements
structure from motion (SFM)
waterfall illusion

The Ear and Auditory System

C lose your eyes and listen carefully to the sounds all around you. Even in the quietest room, there's a lot to hear: maybe an airplane flying overhead, people talking in the next room, the whirring of your computer's hard drive. As you listen, try to identify what makes one sound different from another. It should be obvious immediately that different sounds seem to come from different locations. You can probably pinpoint the locations of those sources with ease. Notice also how sounds can differ in loudness, ranging from the soft rustle of leaves on a tree to the piercing wail of a siren. Sounds differ in duration, and in complexity, too. A birdsong may be composed of just a few pure notes, whereas the traffic on a busy street can generate an unending cacophony, with many different sounds jumbled together.

Sounds can also differ in their cadences, or rhythms. Some sounds have a regularity that makes them easily recognizable, such as the sound of footsteps in the hallway. Because a person's characteristic gait and footsteps generate a distinctive rhythm, the tempo of those footsteps can broadcast the identity of that person. In contrast, other sounds, such as the snap of a breaking twig or the slamming of a door, occur abruptly and usually without repetition.

Sounds can also evoke emotional responses. The hair-raising sound of fingernails being scraped across a chalkboard elicits a strong, immediate revulsion in almost any listener, whereas the soothing sound of gently flowing water is a universal tranquilizer.

So the characteristics of sounds enable us to locate, identify, and react to the objects or people from which they arise. For this reason, hearing plays a very important role in defining your perceptual world throughout your lifetime.

Often, you are able to *hear* things in your environment before you can see them. You rely heavily on hearing when it is dark or when an event occurs out of your field of view. Even when a sound source *is* readily visible, your behavioral reaction to it may depend on the nature of the sound it makes. Some grocery shoppers are sure that a melon's ripeness can be judged only from the sound made by thumping it. A similar thumping technique is sometimes used by doctors to check for fluid accumulation within a patient's chest cavity.

Hearing provides the basis for many forms of social communication, particularly speech. Without the ability to hear voices, an individual must struggle heroically to remain in touch with the flow of social discourse. Perceptual appreciation of the world is diminished when hearing is lost, as deaf people will testify (Noble, 1983).

In this chapter, we will examine the process of hearing, starting with the acoustic energy that carries auditory information, and progressing through what is known about the machinery of hearing. This coverage sets the stage for the next chapter, which considers sound recognition and sound localization, and the chapter after that, which considers speech and music perception.

FIGURE 10.1 | Sound waves are like the ripples generated when a pebble hits the surface of a pond.

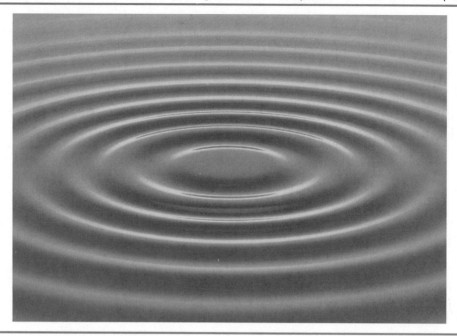

Acoustic Properties of Sound

What Is Sound?

You've probably heard the old puzzle, "If a tree falls in the forest but no one is around to hear it, does the tree make a sound?"[1] Strictly speaking the answer is "no"—the word *sound* refers to a perceptual experience, and that experience requires the presence of a perceiver, an organism with an appropriate kind of nervous system. Without a perceiver, there is no sound, no matter how much disturbance in air pressure the tree made when it fell (as you're about to learn, disturbances in air pressure provide the physical energy triggering the experience of sound). Conversely, without that disturbance in air pressure, there'd be nothing to hear, no matter how many perceivers were in the neighborhood. Having said that, our discussion of hearing will be easier if we can sometimes substitute the term "sound" for "disturbances in air pressure"—thus, for example, we will speak of the source of sound rather than the source of a disturbance in air pressure. Just keep in mind, though, that this is a short-hand designation. In fact, there is a distinction between sound—a *perceptual* quality—and energy—a *physical* quality.

The road that will lead to sound begins when some mechanical disturbance produces vibrations. These vibrations are transmitted through some medium (usually air) in the form of tiny collisions among molecules in that medium. If the vibrations are sufficiently strong when they arrive at your ears, they trigger a chain of events, which culminate in your auditory experience. All sounds, regardless of their nature, come to you this way. It's odd, but a beautiful symphonic melody and the flush of a toilet share the same physical basis, a series of tiny molecular collisions. To understand this, let's consider sound and its properties in greater detail.

Whenever an object vibrates, or moves back and forth, it generates a disturbance within its surroundings. This disturbance takes the form of waves spreading outward from the source of vibration, and these waves possess and convey what is known as **acoustic energy.** They travel through the surrounding medium in a manner similar to the ripples produced when a pebble is tossed into a quiet pond (see Figure 10.1). As ripples travel through the pond's water, sound waves require something to travel through—there can be no sound in empty space or in a perfect vacuum.

This was convincingly demonstrated in the seventeenth century by Robert Boyle, a British physicist and chemist. He placed an alarm bell inside a tightly sealed jar and used a vacuum pump to suck nearly all the air out of this jar. When the alarm went off, the bell "rang" but could not be heard because there were essentially no air

---

[1]Henry David Thoreau expressed the falling tree idea in a different, clever way when he wrote in his journal for Feb. 9, 1839, "It takes a man to make a room silent."

molecules to carry the vibrations from the bell to the wall of the glass jar. After quickly pumping air back into the jar, Boyle could hear the bell. From this simple experiment, Boyle correctly concluded that air was made up of particles and that sound involved waves of energy traveling *through* these particles.

We could liken these acoustic pressure waves to the wave of motion produced when a row of closed packed dominoes is toppled. In this analogy, the individual dominoes represent individual air molecules. The pressure wave is transmitted as one domino bumps into another—a chain reaction propagated the length of the row of dominoes. For the analogy to be complete, however, each domino would have to return to its upright position after colliding with its neighbor, becoming available for participation in future chain reactions.

Though one usually thinks of air as the medium for carrying sound, pressure waves may also be transmitted through other media whose constituent molecules are sufficiently close together to collide with one another when they are set in motion and, at the same time, are sufficiently elastic to return to their original position following disturbance. In fact, the more densely these molecules are packed, the faster will sound travel through them. For instance, at room temperature, airborne sound travels 343 meters per second (or 1,130 feet per second) and slightly less when the air is colder. (The speed of sound is, of course, considerably slower than the speed of light—300,000 kilometers per second—which is why we see lightning before we hear the associated thunder.) In the denser medium of water, sound travels about 1,500 meters per second, almost five times faster than in air. With this differential in mind, imagine partially submerging your head at one end of a swimming pool so that one ear is under water while the other is above the water's surface in the air. A person at the other end of the pool now snaps her fingers on both hands, one below the water's surface and the other above. The resulting sound will arrive sooner at the ear underwater, probably causing you to hear two clicks. Sound moves even faster through steel, clipping along at over 5,000 meters per second. In general, sound travels more slowly in gases than in liquids, and more slowly in liquids than in solids.

Regardless of the medium through which it is propagated and regardless of the source, sound energy becomes weaker as it travels farther from its source. Yet while it is fading in strength, sound continues to travel at a constant speed, so long as it travels in the same medium. Thus, whether you whisper or shout at a nearby friend, the message will arrive at its destination in the same amount of time, albeit with a different degree of emphasis. This is true for just about all sounds—voices, musical notes, and door bells.

As sound waves spread out from their source, they interact with one another as well as with objects in their paths. These interactions can actually be more complex than those involving light. For instance, a solid object casts a visual shadow if exposed to light shining from one direction. But most sounds can be heard with little noticeable change if a relatively small object is situated between the source of a sound and your ears. This happens because sound, unlike light, can travel around—and sometimes through—solid objects. Consequently, it is harder to shut out unwanted sounds than bothersome light—pulling a shade, for instance, may eliminate the glare from a nearby streetlamp, but it will not silence the noise of passing traffic.

When sound waves strike a surface, some portion of the sound waves bounces off the surface. These reflected sound waves are called **echoes,** and they can be used to compute the distance from a listener to a sound source. Knowing the speed at which sound travels, one can measure the time elapsing between production of a sound and reception of its echo. From this duration, it is simple to calculate how far away the reflecting surface is. This is the principle used in **sonar** (a term derived from the words **so**und **na**vigation **r**anging), a means for detecting objects underwater.

Although we're seldom aware of it, echoes actually have a distinct impact on what we hear. When echoes (reflected sound) collide with other, unreflected sound waves from the same source, these sounds interact by adding or subtracting their component.[2] The result of these interactions among sounds can be particularly conspicuous in enclosed spaces such as rooms and auditoriums. Depending on an auditorium's shape and design, for example, there may be some seats where sound is unnaturally loud and other seats where sound is considerably damped. In an acoustically "good" auditorium, these variations in sound quality are minimal. In fact, it's a real engineering challenge to design and construct auditoriums with superb acoustics. Despite great advances in the science of **acoustics** (the branch of physics concerned with sound), even the most thoughtfully designed structure may, in fact, fail to live up to its billing. The repeated modifications and the eventual complete reconstruction of New York's Avery Fisher Hall demonstrate how sound, particularly reflected

---

[2]Strictly speaking, the *waves* themselves do not add and subtract. Instead the densities and velocities of the particles through which the waves travel interact to reinforce or cancel one another.

sound, has the insidious knack of turning up where it is least expected while avoiding where it is *supposed* to go (Bliven, 1976).

Not all sound striking a surface is reflected—some acoustic energy is absorbed. The amount of sound absorbed depends on the surface material. Smooth plaster or tile, absorbs only 3 percent of the sound striking its surface, reflecting the rest as an echo. This is why your singing voice invariably sounds strongest within the confines of a shower enclosure whose walls reflect nearly all sound energy. Nylon carpet, by comparison, absorbs about 25 percent of incident sound. As you can imagine, a room containing carpet, drapes, and stuffed furniture soaks up a lot of sound energy, thereby providing a rather dead listening environment. For the same reason, concert hall acoustics vary with the season; if audience members bring heavy winter clothing into the hall, that clothing absorbs quite a bit of the sound energy.

Special rooms called *anechoic chambers* create an environment devoid of echoes. The walls, floor, and ceiling of such rooms are made of porous foam wedges that absorb sound before it can be reflected to your ears. Consequently, you hear only the sounds emitted from the source itself, with no echoes. For instance, as you walk in an anechoic chamber, your footsteps sound quite strange, with a muffled, flat quality. This is because you are hearing the sounds of your footsteps unaccompanied by their usual echoes. In general, the dull, muted quality of sounds in an anechoic chamber underscores the contribution of echoes to the normal perception of sound.

Besides contributing to an appreciation of sound, echoes furnish information about objects from which sound is reflected. For one thing, the very presence of an echo signals that some object besides the sound source must be present in your environment. And as explained earlier, by noting the time elapsing between the production of a sound and hearing its echo, it is possible to estimate the distance from the source to the reflecting object.

This information may be particularly useful if you produce the sound yourself, such as by yelling, or by clapping your hands. Some animals, including bats and porpoises, rely heavily on reflections of self-produced sound to navigate. Humans aren't consciously aware of self-produced echoes in our environment, except when we shout inside a large building (such as a cathedral) or in an enclosed area (such as a canyon).

It is well established that blind people can utilize reflected sound—echoes—to guide their locomotion and to discriminate among materials such as glass, metal, and wood. It is quite conceivable that echoes also help sighted individuals to judge distance and recognize objects, without our being consciously aware of it (Stoffregen and Pittenger, 1995).

So far we have described the vibratory nature of sound waves and how they travel through a medium and reflect off surfaces. But to clearly understand hearing, we must study the ways that sound waves differ from one another. We begin with a thorough analysis of the physical properties of sound.

The Nature of Sound Waves

Acoustic information is transmitted from a sound source to a perceiver by means of molecules bumping into one another. You can neither see these molecular collisions nor feel them, except when the acoustic disturbance grows extremely intense. To envision the behavior of sound waves, imagine the following setup. Suppose a very thin, lightweight thread is dangled in front of a loudspeaker, with the thread held at one end, leaving the other end free to move about. By measuring the amount the free end of the thread is deflected, you can gauge the strength of various sounds broadcast over the loudspeaker. This setup is depicted in Figure 10.2.

The tiny dots in front of the speaker represent individual air molecules. In the absence of sound energy, air molecules are more or less evenly distributed, as illustrated in panel a. As you may know, a loudspeaker produces sound by moving back and forth, an action that physically jostles air molecules in immediate contact with the speaker cone (the round portion of the unit that actually moves). When the speaker cone moves forward, it produces an increase in air pressure that, if one could see it, involves a bunching up, or compression, of air molecules. This is shown in panel B of Figure 10.2 as a heightened concentration of dots. These compressed air molecules, in turn, collide with their immediate neighbors, thereby projecting the increase in air pressure out from the speaker itself. This miniature "breeze" eventually strikes the thin thread, causing it to bend in a direction away from the speaker.

In the meantime, the loudspeaker cone has moved steadily back to its initial position. This creates a suctionlike action that spreads out, or rarifies, the air molecules, returning them to their initial density (normal air pressure). As shown in panel C, this rarefaction also travels outward, as air molecules are sucked into the area of decreased pressure. Eventually, this rarefaction pulls the thread back to its vertical position. Now suppose the speaker cone continues to move inward, further decreasing air pressure in the immediate vicinity of the cone. This partial vacuum travels outward and eventually sucks the thread toward the loudspeaker.

FIGURE 10.2 | Sound waves consist of changes in air pressure.

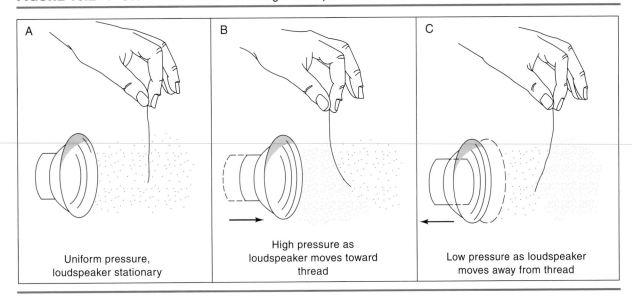

A

Uniform pressure,
loudspeaker stationary

B

High pressure as
loudspeaker moves toward
thread

C

Low pressure as loudspeaker
moves away from thread

This bunching up and spreading out of air molecules, caused by mechanical displacement of the speaker, represent waves of high and low pressure. The air molecules themselves each move very little. It is the *wave* of pressure that travels steadily outward from the sound source. You might think back to the ripples on the surface of a pond (Figure 10.1). The water molecules in the pond, like air molecules, each move only a short distance when disturbed, but by colliding with their neighbors they transmit a wave of motion that can carry over great distances.

As illustrated in Figure 10.2, changes in the position of the thread reflect changes in air pressure radiating outward from the loudspeaker. Suppose we now graph the successive changes in the position of the thread occurring over time by tracing out the sound waves produced by the loudspeaker as its cone moves in and out in a cyclic fashion. Such a graph is shown in Figure 10.3. The horizontal axis plots time, and the vertical axis plots the thread's position relative to the loudspeaker. The dotted horizontal line shows the case where the thread is perfectly vertical, undisturbed by pressure from the loudspeaker. Deviations from this level represent changes in the thread's position and, hence, changes in air pressure produced by movements of the loudspeaker. The height of the curve above or below the dotted line indicates how much the thread deviates from vertical (the amount of change in air pressure). This deviation of the curve from the baseline level is known as **amplitude,** and it is determined by the distance over which the speaker moves. When this movement is tiny, the air pressure change is

FIGURE 10.3 | Change in thread position (representing air pressure) over time.

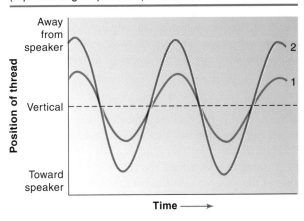

small and the amplitude of the wave is low (the curve labeled 1 in Figure 10.3). As you might guess, small-amplitude pressure waves give rise to weak sounds. But when the loudspeaker's movements are large, the change in air pressure, and hence, the wave amplitude, is great (the curve labeled 2). You would hear this as a loud sound. The peak of this pressure variation curve provides an index of the strength of the sound.

As air pressure changes proceed away from the source, the peak amplitude of the pressure wave gradually decreases. This property of sound propagation explains why a sound becomes fainter and, eventually, inaudible, as you move away from its source. Specifically, sound energy (just like light energy) falls off with the square of the distance between a listener and the sound source. Thus, for example, doubling the distance between your ear and a telephone receiver will produce a fourfold reduction in the sound energy reaching your ear. Sound amplitude is usually expressed in units called **decibels** (abbreviated **dB**); this unit of sound intensity is widely used and deserves more detailed description.

Sound Level   The human ear can hear and distinguish sound over an enormous range of intensities. In this respect, the ear is comparable to the eye: Both manage to handle energy levels that can differ by many orders of magnitude (each order of magnitude is a factor of 10). To get some idea of the energy levels that strike your ears, look at Figure 10.4, a chart listing the intensity values characteristic of common sounds.

You will notice that these various sound intensities are scaled in decibel units. This is a *logarithmic* scale with a particular reference level of sound. The logarithmic nature of the scale makes it much easier to show a wide range of values on a single graph. Also, the logarithmic scale specifies sound level differences in terms of their ratio to one another, not simply in terms of their algebraic difference. This seems to describe more accurately the way one judges intensity differences. Let's consider the definition of a decibel (dB):

$$dB = 20 \log (p1/p0)$$

where $p1$ refers to the air pressure amplitude of the sound under consideration and $p0$ refers to a standard reference level of air pressure. This reference level is typically set at 20 microPascals (μPa), the approximate sound pressure of the softest sound that humans can detect. To signify when amplitudes are being given relative to this particular **sound pressure level (SPL),** we'll denote such amplitudes as dB_{SPL}. Under ideal conditions at that reference level, a sound in the neighborhood of 1,000 to 4,000 Hz is just barely audible.

Sometimes the decibel unit is used in a different way. Suppose that instead of expressing some sound relative to 20 μPa, we wish to compare the amplitudes of two sounds—say, a sound at 60 dB_{SPL} versus a sound at 35 dB_{SPL}. Here we can describe amplitudes relative to each other in terms of dB, omitting the subscript *SPL.* In this example, we would say that the two sounds differ by 25 dB.

With these definitions in mind, let's consider some of the entries in Figure 10.4. Note that the sound of rustling leaves (or a quiet whisper) is 20 dB higher than the 0 dB-SPL reference level. This corresponds to a tenfold increase in sound pressure. A loud scream, in contrast, can reach

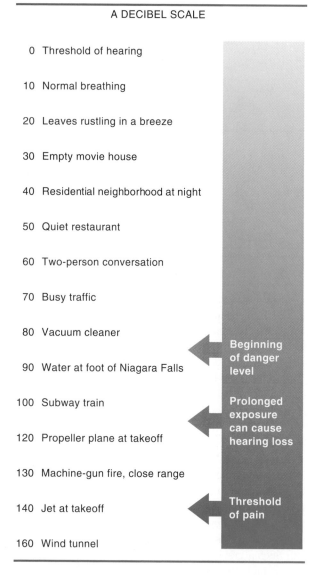

FIGURE 10.4 | Sound intensity, expressed in decibel units, is produced by various events encountered in common situations.

A DECIBEL SCALE

0   Threshold of hearing

10   Normal breathing

20   Leaves rustling in a breeze

30   Empty movie house

40   Residential neighborhood at night

50   Quiet restaurant

60   Two-person conversation

70   Busy traffic

80   Vacuum cleaner

90   Water at foot of Niagara Falls — Beginning of danger level

100   Subway train — Prolonged exposure can cause hearing loss

120   Propeller plane at takeoff

130   Machine-gun fire, close range

140   Jet at takeoff — Threshold of pain

160   Wind tunnel

100 dB_{SPL}, which is 100,000 times more intense than the threshold, reference level. Sounds in excess of 130 dB_{SPL} can produce pain, which is adaptive. The pain causes one reflexively to cover the ears, thereby protecting them from damage. We will discuss the consequences of exposure to loud noise in the following chapter.

Sound Frequency   Returning to our loudspeaker example, let's next consider the effect of varying the rate at which the speaker moves back and forth. When the speaker's movements occur slowly over time, the peaks and troughs of the sound wave spread out, as shown in

FIGURE 10.5 | Rate of change in air pressure corresponds to sound's frequency.

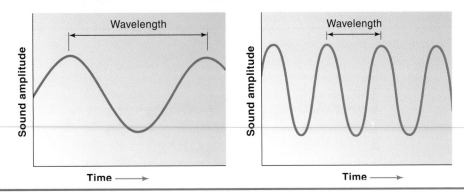

the left-hand portion of Figure 10.5. Rapid movements of the speaker, on the other hand, yield bunched-up peaks and troughs, as shown in the right-hand portion of Figure 10.5. When dealing with steady, cyclic variations such as those described here, one may specify the *frequency* of the sound. This refers to the number of times per second that air pressure undergoes a complete cycle from, say, high to low and back to high. The unit used to designate frequency is the **Hertz** (abbreviated **Hz**).

Thus, for instance, in the case of a 500-Hz sound, a complete cycle of air pressure change (from compression to decompression and back) occurs in two-thousandths of a second, yielding 500 such cycles in one second. Think of frequency as the number of wave cycles passing a given point in one second.

You can also relate frequency to the *length* of a single wave. This refers to the distance from a point during one cycle of the wave (such as its peak) to the corresponding point in the next cycle. Considered in this way, a low-frequency sound wave would have a long wavelength, whereas a high-frequency wave would be short in length. Figure 10.6 illustrates the relation between wavelength and frequency. As you can see from this graph, a 400-Hz sound wave is about 0.8 meters in length, measuring from, say, the peak of one cycle to the peak of the next.

You probably recognize the waveforms shown in Figure 10.5 as sinusoids, waveforms discussed in Chapter 5 in relation to spatial vision. In the case of vision, recall that complex visual patterns (such as a checkerboard) can be described as the combination of particular spatial frequency components. This is why gratings of various spatial frequencies are so useful in the study of spatial vision. By the same token, complex sounds can be described as the combination of certain temporal frequencies, or **pure tones** as they are sometimes called.

FIGURE 10.6 | The relation between wavelength and frequency.

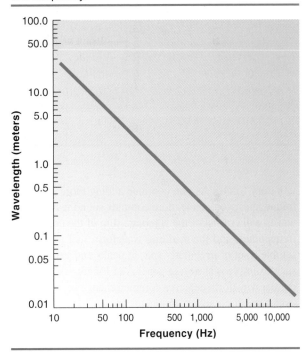

Analogues to sinusoidal gratings, pure tones represent sinusoidal changes in air pressure over time. Let's see how a more complicated waveform (and hence, a more complicated sound) may be described as the sum of certain sinusoidal frequencies of various amplitudes. We will develop this idea in several steps.

Think back to the loudspeaker example: What will happen when two or more tones are simultaneously broadcast over the speaker? In this case, air molecules immediately in front of the cone will be influenced by multiple

FIGURE 10.7 | Many different frequencies mixed together randomly can produce "noise," but when mixed together nonrandomly can produce a recognizable sound. These two examples of complex soundwaves would be perceptually quite distinct if you were to listen to them.

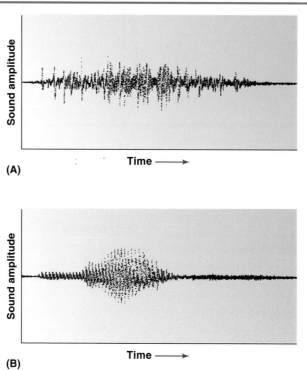

vibratory forces. As you continue adding more and more frequencies, you create more complex sound waves. Such waves will consist of the algebraic sum of the component frequencies, and the resulting waveform will quickly resemble a set of irregularly spaced peaks and valleys. One such example is shown in panel A of Figure 10.7. This irregular waveform depicts a complex change in air pressure over time. If enough components are added together *randomly,* the resultant sound is described as **noise.** In a way, noise is analogous to white light, which, as you learned in Chapter 7, contains light energy at all wavelengths of the visible spectrum. However, most sounds in the environment are complex, meaning their acoustic energy is composed of many frequencies. But they are not heard as noise (see panel B, Figure 10.7). This is because the constituent frequencies of most sounds have a certain temporal structure; unlike the frequencies in noise, they are not added together randomly.

In fact, very seldom does one encounter anything resembling pure tones in the natural environment, which is fortunate. If events and objects in nature were to broadcast their presence using pure tones only, one's ability to identify those objects and events via hearing would be se-

riously limited because there are not enough discriminable tones to uniquely specify all the recognizable sounds important to us.

Because of their virtually unlimited range of unique structures, complex patterns of sound energy provide an enormous vocabulary for conveying biologically and socially relevant information. For instance, your ability to recognize a person's voice over the telephone stems from the unique "signature" provided by the package of frequencies composing that person's voice. Figure 10.8 shows two soundwaves produced by two different people uttering the same phrase. The soundwave on the top was produced by a female speaker, the one on the bottom by a male. The specific frequencies and the rise and fall of the waveforms are discernibly different for the two people, but, if you heard the utterances, you'd have no trouble recognizing that both people were saying the same thing. Still, it is important to understand that all sounds, regardless of their duration or complexity, can be considered as the sum of many simple frequency components. As you're about to learn, early stages of the auditory system analyze complex sounds into their simpler frequency components.

FIGURE 10.8 | Two sonograms showing soundwaves produced by a male and a female uttering the phrase "Where were you when the lights went out?"

Where were you when the lights went out?

Female utterance

Male utterance

The Auditory System: The Ear

The human auditory system consists of the ears, a pair of auditory nerves, and portions of the brain. This section of the chapter is devoted to the ear, which is depicted in Figure 10.9. The diagram at the figure's left shows a cutaway diagram of an ear; the diagram at the figure's right identifies the operations performed by each of the ear's three main components. In this section, we will focus on the specifics of these initial stages of auditory processing. As we proceed, the terms given in the schematic diagram will become clearer. You should mark this page and refer back to the diagram from time to time.

The Outer Ear

The most conspicuous part of the ear is the **pinna,** that shell-like flap of skin and cartilage gracing the side of your head. Some animals, such as cats, can rotate their pinnas in order to funnel sound into their ears. Human pinnas, though, are immobile; humans must turn the entire head to orient themselves toward sound. Still, the two pinnas are not useless vestiges. Their corrugations act like small reflecting surfaces that modify, or "color," the complexity of sound actually entering the ear (Batteau, 1967; Wightman and Kistler, 1998a,b). The degree of coloration introduced by the pinnas depends on which direction sound is coming from. Sound originating straight ahead of you would be affected differently by the pinnas than would sound coming from a source behind you. So these ear flaps, besides providing a convenient support for eyeglasses, play a significant role in sound localization.

And because pinna shape varies so greatly among individuals, we each possess our own, unique "sound modulators" that we learn to hear with. We will consider the pinna's contribution to sound localization in greater detail in the next chapter.

After it is collected by each pinna, sound is channeled down the **auditory canal,** a slightly bent tube approximately 2.5 centimeters long and about 7 millimeters in diameter (the same diameter as that of a pencil, which you should *not* try to confirm yourself). These dimensions are important for hearing as they determine the auditory canal's **resonant frequency,** which is the frequency at which the canal is most easily set into motion. Every object has some characteristic resonant frequency, and that frequency depends upon the object's physical characteristics. If you blow gently across the mouth of an empty softdrink bottle, the low pitch sound you hear reflects the resonant frequency of the column of air in that bottle. If you change the length of that column, by adding two centimeters of water, the resonant frequency changes, and you'll hear a slightly different pitch. Because of its dimensions, the auditory canal in a human adult has a resonant frequency around 3,000 Hz. As a consequence, sounds containing frequencies in this neighborhood are actually amplified several decibels or more (Tonndorf, 1988), which is one reason why human sensitivity to barely audible sounds is best around this frequency.

At the far end of the auditory canal, sound pressure comes in contact with the **eardrum (tympanic membrane).** This thin, oval-shaped membrane vibrates when sound pressure waves strike it, and these resulting vibrations may be remarkably small. It has been estimated (von Békésy and Rosenblith, 1951) that a soft whisper, with an intensity of about 20 dB_{SPL}, displaces the eardrum approximately $\frac{1}{100,000,000}$ of a centimeter, about the width of a single hydrogen molecule! Despite the almost infinitesimal size of this movement, you hear the whisper.

FIGURE 10.9 | Top panel: A drawing of the ear, showing some key structures, as well as the ear's location within the bone of the skull. Bottom panel: A list of the ear's three principal functions, arranged by the portion of the ear responsible for the function.

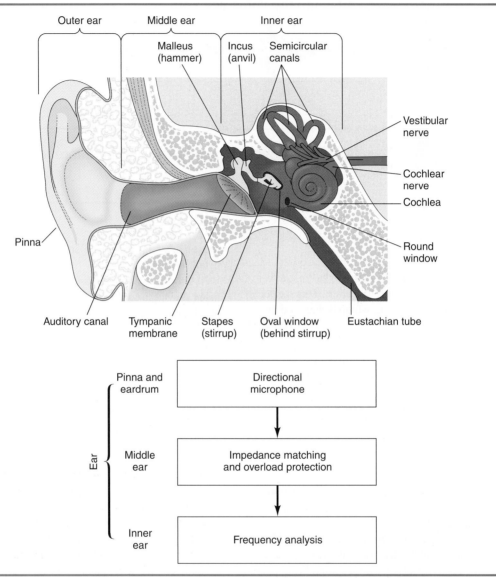

This exquisitely sensitive device, the eardrum, is actually quite sturdy; structurally it resembles an umbrella, with a frame of supporting ribs. In the human ear, the surface area of the tympanic membrane is approximately 68 mm², which is tiny by elephant standards (450 mm²) but huge compared to the gerbil's eardrum (15 mm²). Larger eardrums are better designed to handle low frequency sounds, but this comes at the expense of registering high frequency sounds. This is one reason why hearing acuity—indexed by the highest audible frequency—is better in smaller animals: Eardrum area scales with body size (Hemilä, Nunnela, and Reuter, 1995).

Together, the pinna and auditory canal make up the *outer ear*. Referring back to the schematic diagram in Figure 10.9, you can see that this portion of the auditory system functions like a directional microphone that picks up sound and modifies it, depending on its frequency content and locational source.

FIGURE 10.10 ❘ Drawing of the middle ear. The smaller panel shows the location of the section in the larger panel.

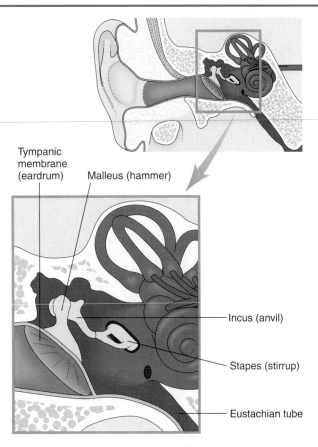

Tympanic membrane (eardrum)

Malleus (hammer)

Incus (anvil)

Stapes (stirrup)

Eustachian tube

The Middle Ear

The eardrum forms the outer wall of a small, air-filled chamber called the *middle ear.* In the middle ear, the vibrations impinging on the eardrum are passed along to the **oval window,** which is covered by another membrane, smaller than the eardrum, that forms part of the inner wall of the middle ear. Bridging the small gap between the eardrum and the oval window are the **ossicles,** the three smallest bones in the human body. Each of the three ossicles is about the size of a single letter on this page. Their individual names reflect their shapes (see Figure 10.10). First in this chain, the **hammer** (technically called the **malleus**) is attached at one end to the back side of the eardrum. The other end of the hammer is tightly bound by ligaments to the **anvil,** or **incus,** the middle link in this chain of tiny bones. The anvil, in turn, is secured to the **stirrup,** or **stapes,** whose footplate is, in turn, anchored against the oval window. Together the three ossicles transfer vibrations from the eardrum to the oval window.

Like eardrums, the size of ossicles varies enormously among species. Considering just the hammer, in humans this structure weighs 28.5 milligrams (0.001 ounces), in the elephant it tips the scales at 335 milligrams, and in the gerbil it weighs just 1.15 milligrams. In general, the size of the ossicles is proportional to the area of the eardrum. Nunnela (1995) provides a comprehensive discussion of variations in middle ear size and the effect of those variations on hearing ability.

The Role of the Ossicular Bridge   Why did nature build a delicate bridge of tiny bones between these two membranes, the eardrum and the oval window? Why not have airborne vibrations impact directly on the oval window, doing away with the intermediate chamber, the middle ear? To appreciate the importance of the middle ear and its ossicular bridge, we can consider how things would sound if this chamber and its series of tiny bones were eliminated from the ear.

To begin, you need to realize that the inner ear, the chamber located on the other side of the oval window, is filled with fluid. Glen Wever (1978) called attention to the evolutionary significance of the liquid-filled inner ear, pointing out that it probably derives from the aquatic environment of the aquatic creatures whose ears are the evolutionary basis for our own.

Because humans are land dwellers, acoustic energy is usually carried to our ears by *airborne* pressure variations. Without the middle ear, these airborne pressure changes would be pushing directly against the oval window and, therefore, against the liquid contained in the inner ear. Because its constituent molecules are more densely packed, the liquid offers more resistance to movement than does air. In other words, more force is required to set up sound waves in water than in air. This explains why when you are under water you have trouble hearing sounds that come from above the water—about 99 percent of airborne sound is reflected when it strikes the water's surface; only about 1 percent is absorbed by the water (Evans, 1982). This represents almost a 30-dB loss in sound energy. Referring back to Figure 10.4, you can see that lowering sound intensity by 30 dB would definitely affect your hearing, wiping out altogether some everyday sounds (those listed as 30 dB$_{SPL}$ or less in intensity) and reducing the intensity of all others.

So if your ear had to transfer vibrations directly from air to liquid, a great deal of sound energy would be lost. This potential loss in sound energy—or most of it—is partly avoided within the middle ear, however, because of the difference in surface area between the eardrum and the oval window. The oval window is roughly 20 times smaller in area than the eardrum. Consequently, the force applied on the oval window exerts considerably more pressure than the same amount of force applied to the eardrum. By funneling vibrations from the large eardrum down to the small oval window, sound energy is effectively amplified. This funneling effect recovers about 23 dB of the impedance loss that is caused by passing from air to water. In addition, the three ossicular bones together act as a lever to amplify the force of the incoming pressure waves. Because it operates to overcome the impedance imposed by the liquid-filled inner ear, the middle ear is sometimes described as an impedance matching device.

For this impedance matching system to work efficiently, the average air pressure within the middle ear must equal the atmospheric pressure existing in the outside environment and, hence, within the auditory canal. This equivalence is maintained by the **Eustachian tube** connecting the middle ear and the throat.[3] Every time you swallow, this tube opens, allowing air either to enter or to leave the middle ear, depending on the outside air pressure. You can sometimes hear the consequences of this ventilation process, such as when your ears "pop" while riding an elevator, flying in an airplane, or ascending a high mountain. Sudden increases or decreases in outside pressure (such as those experienced by scuba divers) can actually rupture the eardrum; this occurs when the pressure differential on the two sides of the membrane becomes too great.

The Acoustic Reflex   Before we conclude our discussion of this part of the ear, we also need to draw your attention to the protective role played by the *tensor tympani,* a small muscle attached to the eardrum, and the *stapedius,* a tiny muscle attached to the stapes bone. In the presence of loud sound, these muscles contract, thereby stiffening the eardrum and restricting the movement of the ossicles (Moller, 1974). These combined actions, called the **acoustic reflex,** dampen the sound vibrations passed from the outer ear to the inner ear. In this respect, the acoustic reflex acts like the damper pedal on a piano, the one that muffles the musical notes by limiting the vibrations of the piano's strings. But why should the ear contain a mechanism to dampen sound?

The acoustic reflex helps to protect the inner ear from intense stimulation that could otherwise damage the delicate receptor cells within the inner ear (Borg and Counter, 1989). Considered in this way, one can draw an analogy between the acoustic reflex and the pupillary light reflex (the constriction of the pupil in response to light). It is true that the acoustic reflex *does* reduce the intensity of sound transmission by as much as 30 dB (Evans, 1982). However, it is primarily low-frequency sounds that are damped by the acoustic reflex; high frequencies pass through the middle ear unattenuated. So as a protective device, the acoustic reflex is only partially successful. Moreover, the acoustic reflex takes about one-twentieth of a second to exert its shielding influence. Consequently, any sudden, intense sound, such as the explosion of a firecracker, can speed through the middle ear before the acoustic reflex can dampen the force of that sound. Incidentally, abrupt sounds such as this are called *transients,* and if too strong, they can produce a permanent loss in hearing. (Explosions, of course, were probably not part of the natural en-

---

[3]Named after its discoverer, Bartolomeo Eustachi, a sixteenth-century Italian anatomist (Hawkins, 1988).

vironment in which the human ear evolved; it is not surprising that the acoustic reflex is too sluggish to deal with these kinds of sharp transients.)

Another possible role for the acoustic reflex is suggested by the fact that it occurs whenever one talks or chews something—the same nerves that activate the facial muscles also trigger the acoustic reflex. You can easily experience the consequences of this by listening to a steady low-frequency sound such as the hum of a refrigerator motor while clenching and unclenching your teeth. The sound will seem fainter with teeth clenched, because clenching your teeth engages the acoustic reflex. This general observation has led to the theory that the acoustic reflex reduces the ears' sensitivity to self-produced sounds such as one's own voice. These sounds *do* consist primarily of low frequencies, which, as previously mentioned, are the ones attenuated by the acoustic reflex. We leave it to you to figure out the advantage of deemphasizing self-produced sounds.

The functions of the middle ear were summarized earlier, in Figure 10.9. Basically, the middle ear serves as an impedance matching device and as an overload protector. With these roles established, we are now ready to migrate to the next stage in the auditory system, the inner ear. This is where mechanical vibrations are converted into electrical nerve impulses to be carried to the brain. Within the inner ear, the auditory system really gets down to the business of hearing.

The Inner Ear: The Cochlea

The *inner ear* consists of a series of hollow cavities, or labyrinths, carved into the temporal bone of the skull. One set of these cavities, the semicircular canals, is concerned with the maintenance of bodily posture and balance. Box 10.1 summarizes how this maintenance system works. Our focus in this section, however, will be on the **cochlea** (from the Greek word for snail), a coiled, fluid-filled cavity containing the specialized receptors that place us in contact with the sounds in our environment. Vibrations of the oval window produce pressure changes in the fluid within the cochlea. These pressure changes cause movement of the sensitive receptor cells within the cochlea, providing the stimulus for their activity. To understand this process of sensory transduction, we need to examine more closely the structural detail of this tiny, pea-sized organ (a magnified schematic of which is shown in Figure 10.11).

The spiral-shaped cochlea is partitioned into three chambers, which are easier to visualize if you imagine the cochlea uncoiled, as shown in the lower panel of Fig-

FIGURE 10.11 | A cochlea in side view. Its base, the portion nearest the middle ear, can be seen at the lower left. An expanded view is shown in Figure 10.12.

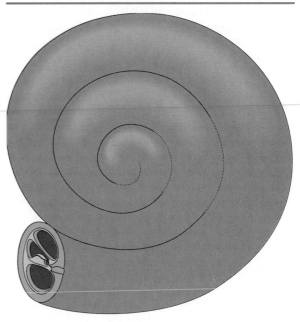

ure 10.12. (To keep track of its arrangement, we shall refer to the end nearest the middle ear as the *base* and the end normally curled up in the center as the *apex*.) The three wedge-shaped chambers of the cochlea each have names: the vestibular canal, the cochlear duct, and the tympanic canal. The three chambers run parallel to one another the entire length of the cochlea, except right near the far end, at the apex. There the vestibular canal and the tympanic canal merge at a pinhole-sized passage between the two.

The vestibular canal and cochlear duct are separated by one membrane, while the tympanic canal and the cochlear duct are separated by another membrane; this latter one is called the **basilar membrane,** and it plays a crucial role in the hearing process. Because the vestibular and tympanic canals are continuous with each other, they contain the same fluid, similar in composition to spinal fluid. The middle chamber, the cochlear duct, contains a fluid that is chemically different from that filling the other two canals. This chemical difference between the two fluids plays a crucial role in the initial stage of hearing. For example, when the two fluids become intermixed (which can occur if the membrane separating them ruptures), hearing is impaired. Besides their important role in the hearing process, these fluids also supply all the nourishment for cells in the cochlea. Blood vessels, even tiny capillaries,

BOX 10.1 A Fine Balancing Act

The material in this chapter focuses on the parts of the inner ear that mediate our experience of hearing. But within each of our two ears we also find an exquisitely designed sensory system for registering changes in the position of the head. This guidance system helps us keep our bearings as we actively move about in our environment, and it can also lead to dizziness and nausea when stimulated abnormally. Here is how it works.

Located immediately adjacent to the inner ear are three fluid-filled canals that each forms a "loop"; these are aptly called the semicircular canals (see the accompanying figure). Lining the interior walls of each of these canals are tiny hairs, much like the ones within the cochlea. As the head moves, the fluids within the semicircular canals moves, too, but this fluid movement lags behind in time, in the same way that the coffee in your cup sloshes around when you suddenly brake for a red light. Each of these three loops behaves just like the "accelerometer" on a robotic vehicle (like the Martian rover Spirit), generating a signal proportional to the change in speed parallel to the direction in which the accelerometer is heading. A solid object such as your head can move in a variety of different directions within 3D space, so the brain needs three accelerometers, not one, to "register" the head's movements. Working together the signals generated in the three canals can uniquely signal the direction and speed in which your head is moving. In turn, your brain can use this information to control the position of your eyes, so that you're able to maintain fixation on an object of interest even as your head moves around. (Take a moment to swing your head back and forth and up and down, all the while maintaining fixation on this word—"here"—you're able to do this with ease, courtesy of the signals generated by your semicircular canals.) So long as you're able to maintain your visual bearings during vigorous vestibular stimulation (e.g., while spinning around and around), you're fine. But if that visual frame of reference is lost (e.g., if you close your eyes), continuous vestibular stimulation can produce dizziness, nausea, and vomiting. Ice skaters and ballet dancers learn to control their gaze while executing rapid, repeated turns, which is why they don't tumble over when the turn is stopped. Discus throwers,

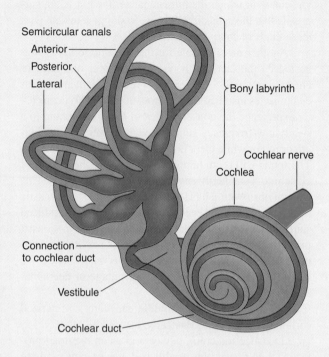

on the other hand, are notoriously susceptible to dizziness, probably because the spinning action required before releasing the discus precludes maintenance of visual bearings (Perrin et al., 2000).

For highly mobile animals, such as birds, accurate guidance is absolutely crucial for safe navigation. These animals must continuously know where they are as they move rapidly and erratically, and they must be able to maintain their balance while doing so. It is not so surprising, then, to learn that agile, active animals such as birds have large semicircular canals relative to more sluggish creatures such as the crocodile (Stokstad, 2003). Even the semicircular canals housed within our human skull are different from those possessed by our close primate relatives, the great apes. These differences are befitting the behavioral habits of the two species: In comparison to apes, our bodies are better designed for fast, bipedal activities such as running and jumping. And the vestibular hardware in our ears seems appropriately designed to guide us in these activities.

FIGURE 10.12 | Upper panel shows a cochlea, with openings of three chambers labeled. The dashed line indicates the location of the section shown uncoiled in the lower panel. In the lower panel, additional structures at the base end are labeled.

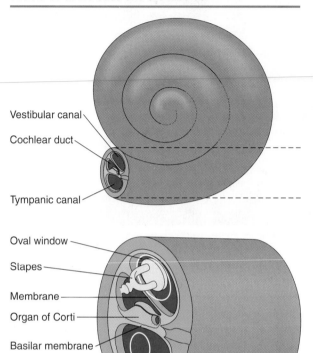

Vestibular canal

Cochlear duct

Tympanic canal

Oval window

Stapes

Membrane

Organ of Corti

Basilar membrane

Round window

have no place within this structure because their pulsations would create violent waves of sound pressure within the closed confines of the cochlea. This arrangement is reminiscent of the eye (Chapter 2), where blood vessels are routed around the fovea to avoid obstructing the image formed on this crucial part of the eye.

Except at two spots where it is covered by elastic material, the walls of the cochlea consist of hard, relatively shockproof bone. At the base of the cochlea, the vestibular canal is covered by the oval window, which, you will recall, is attached to the stapes (stirrup) on the side facing the middle ear. The tympanic canal is likewise covered at the base by the **round window,** another thin membrane that also covers a small opening into the middle ear.

These two elastic surfaces allow pressure to be distributed within the fluid-filled cochlea: When the oval window is pushed inward by the stapes, the round window bulges outward to compensate (see Figure 10.12). This compensation is possible because, as mentioned before, the two

chambers, the vestibular and tympanic canals, are linked. How, though, does the fluid-borne pressure wave generated by the stapes at the oval window give rise to hearing?

To answer this question, we must look more closely at the cochlear duct and, in particular, at the complex structure, the **organ of Corti,** situated inside it. (The structure is named after the Italian anatomist Alfonso Corti, who first described it, in 1851.) The organ of Corti is the receptor organ where neural impulses are generated in response to vibrations passing through the fluid environment of the inner ear. In other words, the organ of Corti transforms mechanical vibrations into neural messages that are sent on to the brain. To understand this process of sensory transduction, let's take a close look at the organ of Corti.

The Organ of Corti   Shown schematically in Figure 10.13, the organ of Corti sits snugly on top of the basilar membrane (recall that this is the membrane separating the cochlear duct and the tympanic canal), and it runs the full length of the cochlear duct. The following are the major components of the organ of Corti: a layer of supporting cells resting on the basilar membrane, rows of hair cells sticking up from the supporting cells, and an awninglike membrane, the **tectorial membrane,** arching over the hair cells.

Notice a few things about this arrangement. First, structures called *hair cells* extend up into the fluid within the cochlear duct. Second, the tectorial membrane that arches over the structure contacts the tops of some of these hair cells. Finally, note that because the tectorial membrane is attached at only one end, it can move independently of the basilar membrane. Let's focus more closely on the hair cells, for they hold the key to the transduction of fluid vibrations into nerve impulses.

Hair Cells and Sensory Transduction   The ear is similar to the eye, in that both organs contain two different types of receptor cells. The eye, as you learned, contains rods and cones. These two classes of photoreceptors are different in shape and in retinal distribution, and they are involved in different aspects of visual perception (recall Chapters 2 and 3). The ear's receptors, the **hair cells,** are equally distinctive anatomically and functionally. In all, there are about 20,000 hair cells within the human ear, with this total divisible into two distinct groups. One group, the **inner hair cells (IHC),** is situated on the basilar membrane close to where the tectorial membrane is attached to the wall of the cochlear duct (see Figure 10.13). Numbering about 4,500, these inner hair cells line up in a single row that runs the length of the basilar membrane. The 15,500 or so **outer hair cells (OHC),** in contrast, line up in anywhere from three to five rows. Let's first look at the anatomical distinctions between the two and then consider their functional differences.

FIGURE 10.13 | The organ of Corti.

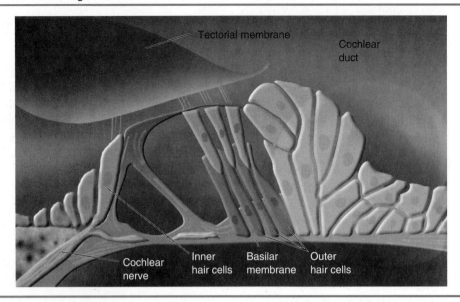

Tectorial membrane

Cochlear duct

Cochlear nerve

Inner hair cells

Basilar membrane

Outer hair cells

Drawings of an IHC and an OHC are shown in Figure 10.14. Note that each IHC is shaped something like a flask, and each is surrounded by supporting cells. Each OHC, in contrast, is more cylindrical in shape, and each is surrounded by fluid. Both the inner and the outer hair cells terminate in tiny bristles called **cilia.**

Figure 10.15 shows a section of the basilar membrane photographed through an electron microscope—in this top-down view, you can actually see the single row of IHCs and multiple rows of OHCs; in the right part of the figure are magnified views showing one cluster of each cell type. The most prominent structures visible in these photographs are the brushlike cilia shown sticking up from the tops of the hair cells. Ordinarily these structures would be covered by the overlying tectorial membrane but, to make this photo, the tectorial membrane was removed.

It used to be thought that cilia from *all* the hair cells actually made contact with the tectorial membrane. Now, however, it is recognized that only cilia from the OHCs actually touch the tectorial membrane (Nobili, Mammano, and Ashmore, 1998). Bending of the cilia constitutes *the* crucial early event in the process that leads to hearing, for it is this event that triggers the electrical signals that travel from the ear to the brain. Let's take a look, then, at how airborne sound ends up producing this crucial event, the bending of the cilia.

As you will recall, airborne vibrations are picked up by the external ear and converted into a mechanical, pistonlike action by the ossicles of the middle ear. Because it is attached to the stapes, the oval window receives these mechanical displacements and passes them in the form of

FIGURE 10.14 | Schematic drawings of an inner hair cell (left) and an outer hair cell (right).

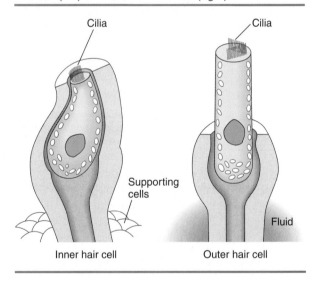

Cilia

Cilia

Supporting cells

Fluid

Inner hair cell

Outer hair cell

pressure waves into the fluids of the cochlea's vestibular and tympanic canals. As the pressure waves travel through these chambers, they cause waves of displacement along the basilar membrane. The tectorial membrane also moves slightly in response to these pressure waves, but it tends to move in directions that are different from the movement of the basilar membrane. These opposing motions cause the cilia of the hair cells on the basilar membrane to bend, like tiny clumps of seaweed swept back and forth by invisible underwater currents. This

FIGURE 10.15 | Electron microscope photographs of the cilia of the multiple rows of outer hair cells and the single row of inner hair cells. The two pictures on the right show a single cluster of OHCs and a single cluster of IHCs in greater magnification.

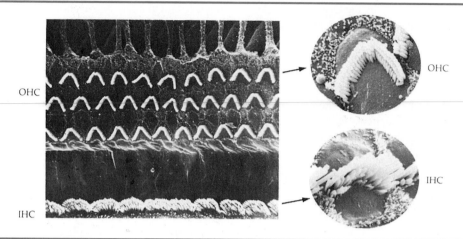

bending triggers electrical changes within the hair cells (Russell, 1987). These electrical changes in the hair cell cause it to release a chemical transmitter substance, which is picked up by auditory nerve fibers that make synaptic contact with the hair cells at their base (the portion of the hair cells opposite the cilia). These fibers, in turn, carry electrical impulses from the cochlea to the central nervous system. It is truly remarkable that such microscopic movements of thin membranes, tiny bones, and hairs inaugurate a process—hearing—that can have such an enormous impact on one's feelings and behaviors.

With this sequence of events in mind, let's return for a moment to the two classes of hair cells. As already pointed out, the IHCs and OHCs differ in number (4,500 versus 15,500) and in location along the basilar membrane. In addition, these two classes of hair cells also differ in the pattern of their connections to the approximately 30,000 auditory nerve fibers that carry messages from the cochlea to the brain. The more numerous OHCs make sparse contact with the auditory nerve; only about 5 percent of the auditory nerve fibers receive signals from the OHCs. The remaining 95 percent of the fibers get their information from the IHCs, the smaller of the two cell populations. To draw an analogy, it is as if the telephone company took 30,000 phone lines and divided them up so that 1,500 were devoted to the entire population of Boston while 28,500 were devoted to the much smaller population of suburban Concord. Why should the more numerous OHCs have so little control over the signals traveling along the auditory nerve? According to recent thinking (Nobili, Mammano, and Ashmore, 1998), the IHCs are the principal actors in the

sensory drama that unfolds in the ear, with the OHCs playing an important supporting role. Here's how the idea goes.

To begin, remember that the cilia of the OHCs are actually attached to the overhanging tectorial membrane. It is now thought that when electric currents are set up in the OHCs, their cilia produce a motor response—they have miniature musclelike elements (actin filaments) that contract and expand the cilia along their longitudinal axes. Suppose that an acoustic disturbance causes maximal vibration at some place along the basilar membrane. As the OHCs at that place ride up and down, their cilia, which are attached to the tectorial membrane, are stretched and relaxed. This sets up an alternating current within the hair cells. The alternating current, in turn, stimulates the OHC cilia to contract and expand, causing them to behave like small motors that pull and push the tectorial membrane. This motorlike action of the OHCs on the tectorial membrane amplifies and concentrates displacement of the basilar membrane created by the back and forth movement of fluid within the cochlea. These amplified movements, in turn, cause the cilia of the IHCs to be displaced by a greater amount than they would have without the extra boost provided by the contractions of the OHC cilia. As a result, the OHCs, despite their minor *direct* contribution to information carried by the auditory nerve, are very important to the hearing process.[4] (It should be noted, by the way, that these

---

[4]Acting as amplifiers and tuners, the OHCs primarily modify the mechanical environment of the IHCs. Strictly speaking, the IHCs are the only true sensory receptors for hearing. In this sense, the analogy to rod and cone photoreceptors is not entirely accurate.

amplifying actions must be accomplished at a molecular level. Ordinary mechanical actions such as contraction and elongation of muscles could not occur rapidly enough to accomplish the task carried out by the OHCs.)

In a later section, we will learn more about the auditory consequences of this amplification process. But first, there is one important step in this process of sensory transduction that was sidestepped: How do the vibrations traveling within the cochlear fluid affect the basilar membrane? Because the hair cells ride on the basilar membrane, the membrane's reactions to fluid vibrations determine which hair cells are stimulated and, hence, which nerve fibers will be activated. To fill in the missing step, let's turn our attention to the basilar membrane, the thin-walled membrane separating the tympanic canal from the cochlear duct (see Figures 10.12 and 10.13).

The Basilar Membrane   Much of what is known today about the basilar membrane comes from work by Georg von Békésy, a Hungarian scientist whose research on the ear won a Nobel Prize in 1961. To appreciate Békésy's contributions, you need to be familiar with two major theories describing the way that pressure waves in the cochlear fluid affect the basilar membrane. Both theories were originally formulated in the nineteenth century, before anyone could observe the basilar membrane in action. The opposing theories, called the *temporal theory* and the *place theory,* form the background for Békésy's important work.[5]

The Temporal Theory   The **temporal theory** proposes that the temporal structure of some sound is represented by temporal fluctuations in the firing rates of auditory nerve fibers. According to this idea, the stapes taps out a series of beats on the oval window, and the entire basilar membrane dances to that beat.

William Rutherford, a nineteenth-century English physicist, was the temporal theory's first proponent. He likened the basilar membrane to the diaphragm inside a telephone receiver. Because it is thin and light, the diaphragm moves back and forth in response to the sound waves of your voice. These movements are converted into electrical current that is carried along a telephone line. And the current eventually produces the same pattern of movements in the listening diaphragm of another

person's telephone receiver, thereby reproducing the sounds of your voice. Rutherford believed that the basilar membrane behaved in a comparable fashion, vibrating as a unit at a rate that matched the sound stimulus. In turn, this vibration produced in the auditory nerve a train of impulses whose rate mimicked the frequency with which the entire basilar membrane was vibrating. According to Rutherford's idea, then, a 500-Hz tone would yield 500 nerve impulses per second, while a 1,200-Hz tone would yield 1,200 impulses per second.

Several things are wrong with this theory. For one thing, the basilar membrane is not like a diaphragm in a telephone. The basilar membrane varies in width and in stiffness from one end to the other. As a result, the basilar membrane, unlike a diaphragm, cannot vibrate uniformly over its entire length. (Yost [2000] and Nobili, Mammano, and Ashmore [1998] give particularly clear explanations of why this is physically impossible.) There is another problem, too, with Rutherford's version of the temporal theory. Single auditory nerve fibers cannot match the performance of a telephone line, because neurons cannot fire repetitively at rates beyond 1,000 impulses per second. Yet we can hear tones whose frequency greatly exceeds this value. So the neural signal required by Rutherford's theory cannot be realized by individual fibers.

This limitation in firing rate could be surmounted if separate nerve fibers fired not in unison but in a staggered fashion. For instance, two fibers each firing at 1,000 impulses per second in combination could produce 2,000 impulses per second if those impulses were appropriately interleaved (Figure 10.16). This modification of the temporal theory, known as the *volley theory,* was proposed by Wever and Bray (1937). The volley theory, unlike Rutherford's original temporal theory, does not assume that the basilar membrane acts like a telephone diaphragm. It does, however, require that some higher neuron add the interleaved neural impulses from the fibers responding near their limits of activity. How this neuron could overcome the upper limit on its own firing rate was never specified by proponents of volley theory. We will have more to say about the volley theory in our discussion of pitch perception in the next chapter. But let's return now to the basilar membrane and consider the temporal theory's chief competitor, the *place theory.*

The Place Theory   The **place theory** maintains that different frequencies of vibration of the cochlear fluid disturb different regions of the basilar membrane. These different regions of disturbance, in turn, activate different hair cells and hence, different auditory nerve fibers. You can see where this theory gets its name—frequency in-

---

[5]Temporal theory has also been referred to as "frequency theory" since sound frequency is represented in the frequency of neural impulses. However, contemporary hearing scientists prefer the phrase "temporal theory" to avoid any confusion with "place theory," which relates location along the basilar membrane to sound frequency.

FIGURE 10.16 | Two fibers firing regularly but asynchronously.

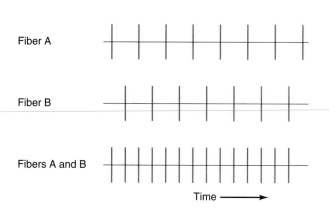

Fiber A

Fiber B

Fibers A and B

Time ——→

FIGURE 10.17 | The basilar membrane's tapered shape resembles the layout of a piano's strings.

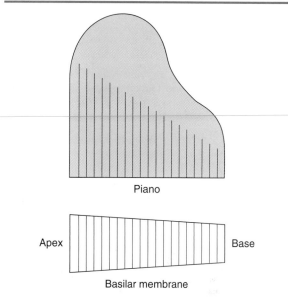

Piano

Apex   Base

Basilar membrane

formation is encoded according to the location, or *place,* along the basilar membrane disturbed by fluid vibration.

The most notable early proponent of the place theory was Hermann von Helmholtz, whose ideas on color vision you read about in Chapter 7. Helmholtz's theory was inspired by the fact that the basilar membrane is narrow at the base of the cochlea and broad at the apex. This layout reminded Helmholtz of the variation in the length of strings of a piano (Figure 10.17), which led him to propose that the basilar membrane was composed of distinct fibers that individually stretched across its width. Because of the basilar membrane's tapered shape, fibers at one end would be longer than those at the other, just like piano strings. According to Helmholtz, vibrations within the cochlear fluid would set into motion only those "strings" of the basilar membrane that were tuned to the frequencies at which the fluid vibrated. In other words, fibers of the basilar membrane would vibrate in the same way that piano strings can be induced to vibrate when you sing a loud note. This is the principle of resonance discussed previously.

Though his theory was based on solid physical principles, Helmholtz's towering reputation did not guarantee automatic acceptance in the scientific community. For example, one of his many competitors attacked Helmholtz's theory as "the product of a great mind in an hour of weakness" (Wever, 1949, p. 76). Although we do not agree with that characterization, Helmholtz's place theory was flawed in several respects. For one thing, subsequent anatomical work showed that the basilar membrane is not composed of separate fibers capable of resonating individually. Rather than a set of piano strings, the basilar membrane looks more like a continuous strip of rubber.

Moreover, the basilar membrane is not under tension, like piano strings; it is relatively slack. So the resonance portion of Helmholtz's theory proved incorrect, but his idea that different *places* along the basilar membrane respond to different frequencies *did* survive. In fact, it is this idea that Békésy's work so elegantly substantiated, and it is to his work that we now turn.

Traveling Waves Békésy realized that the essential difference between place and frequency theories lay in how each thought the basilar membrane vibrated in response to different frequencies. Of course, the simplest way to settle the issue would have been to observe the membrane's movements, but this was technically difficult in the late 1920s when Békésy became interested in the problem. Nonetheless, Békésy knew that the thickness of the basilar membrane varied along its length, being thinner (and, hence, more flexible) at the end near the apex. Armed with this knowledge, he built a simplified, mechanical model of the cochlea, so he could directly observe the behavior of an enlarged replica of the basilar membrane (Békésy, 1960).

For the tympanic and vestibular canals he used a brass tube with a small rubber cap stretched over each end; these caps represented the oval and round windows. He cut a narrow slot along the length of the entire tube and covered this slot with a rubber "membrane" whose thickness was tapered from one end to the other; this represented the basilar membrane. For the stapes he substituted a small

FIGURE 10.18 | Békésy's mechanical model of the cochlea.

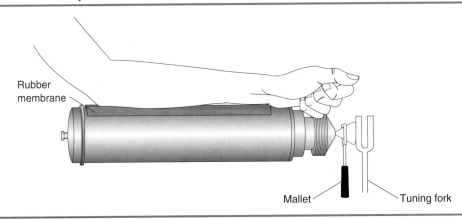

Rubber membrane

Mallet

Tuning fork

FIGURE 10.19 | Summary of the results of Békésy's experiment. Panel A: The relation between a pure-tone frequency and the point along Békésy's model where that frequency yields its greatest vibration. Panel B: Diagram indicating locations along the coiled basilar membrane that vibrate maximally to various frequencies.

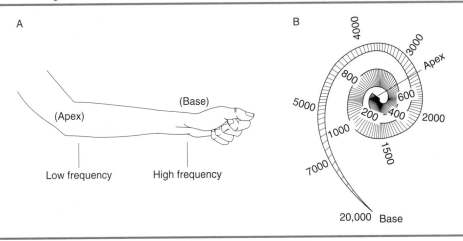

A

(Apex) (Base)

Low frequency High frequency

B

4000 3000 Apex
800 600
5000 200 400 2000
1000 1500
7000

20,000 Base

mallet placed against the rubber cap on one end of the tube; this mallet was vibrated by a tuning fork. A drawing of Békésy's large-scale cochlea is shown in Figure 10.18.

To observe the behavior of his mechanical model, Békésy rested his forearm lightly on a small ridge secured to the rubber membrane over its entire length; vibrations at different points along the rubber membrane were accurately transmitted to the corresponding points along the ridge. When a pure tone was produced by striking the tuning fork, Békésy felt, via the ridge, the rubber membrane vibrating against his arm at one particular spot (see panel A of Figure 10.19). By testing with tuning forks that produced different frequencies, he discovered that the location of this tingling spot depended on the frequency with which the tuning fork vibrated the "oval window." With higher frequencies, this tingle occurred near his wrist, a place on the membrane corresponding to the more rigid end closest to the stapes. Lower frequencies, in contrast, yielded a tingle nearer his elbow, the region of the membrane corresponding to the more flexible end near the apex.

Panel A of Figure 10.19 shows the relation between a pure-tone frequency and the point along Békésy's mechanical model where that frequency yields its peak vibration. Translating Békésy's results to the actual basilar membrane—a much smaller, coiled structure—yields the scaled diagram in panel B of Figure 10.19. This diagram reveals the various points along the basilar membrane that maximally vibrate to a particular sound frequency.

Békésy's ingenious demonstration therefore strongly favored the place theory. Subsequently, Békésy went on to confirm this conclusion using other, more precise techniques, including direct visualization of the human basi-

FIGURE 10.20 | The top drawing shows a traveling wave deforming the basilar membrane. The set of curves below at the left represents the response of the basilar membrane over time to a high-frequency tone. The curves at the right represent the basilar membrane's response over time to a low-frequency tone.

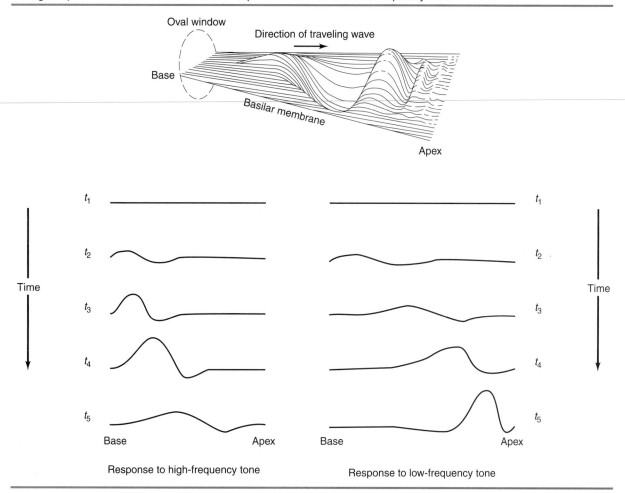

Response to high-frequency tone

Response to low-frequency tone

lar membrane, using a microscope. He explained the connection between the point of maximum vibration along the basilar membrane and sound frequency in the following way. The fluctuations in fluid pressure produced by the pistonlike movements of the stapes set up a **traveling wave** along the basilar membrane.

To envision what is meant by a *traveling wave*, think of what happens when you flick one end of a rope whose other end is tied to, say, a pole. You see a wave of motion traveling the length of the rope. Unlike a rope, though, the basilar membrane varies in thickness and width along its length. If you were to flick the basilar membrane, the resulting wave of motion would actually grow in amplitude as it traveled away from you. But this wave would reach peak amplitude and then rapidly collapse, never getting to the other end. An example of this kind of traveling wave is illustrated in Figure 10.20.

In this figure, the basilar membrane is drawn as if uncoiled and viewed from the side. Thus, in each panel the horizontal axis represents the length of the basilar membrane, with its base at the left and its apex at the right. Each separate panel shows the profile of the basilar membrane at a different instant in time. You might imagine these as successive snapshots of the basilar membrane taken just after you have flicked it as you would a rope. (Flicking it corresponds to the stapes's tapping against the oval window, setting up waves of motion in the fluid of the cochlea.) As the wave progresses down the membrane over time, note how it grows in size, reaches a peak, and then rather abruptly disappears. The place along the basilar membrane where this peak occurs depends on how rapidly you flicked the basilar membrane. This idea can be seen by comparing the traveling waves depicted in the left panel of the figure to those depicted in the right panel.

Note that in the series on the left, the traveling wave reaches its peak nearer the base, while in the series on the right it reaches its peak nearer the apex. The waves in the left-hand series were produced by a high-frequency tone; those in the right-hand series by a low-frequency tone.

The peak of the traveling wave, you should understand, represents a place where the basilar membrane flexes up and down, which is why Békésy felt a tingling spot on his forearm when he tested his mechanical cochlea. This flexion in the actual basilar membrane means that hair cells riding on this portion of the membrane will be displaced further—and their cilia bent more—than elsewhere along the membrane. In turn, these highly bent cilia will activate their associated hair cells. In other words, each vibration frequency will cause the basilar membrane to flex maximally at one particular location, thereby maximally stimulating a characteristic group of hair cells. This arrangement is so orderly that if you were told which hair cells had been maximally stimulated, you would be able to deduce the sound frequency that had produced that stimulation. This orderly layout of frequency over the length of the basilar membrane is known as **tonotopic organization.**

The behavior of traveling waves also suggests how intensity information is registered by the basilar membrane. For a given frequency, the intensity of the sound will determine the amplitude, or height, of the peak of the traveling wave. Increases in the amplitude of these movements of the basilar membrane will cause the cilia to bend more, leading to greater stimulation of the hair cells, a larger neural response, and ultimately an increase in perceived loudness. Increases in the amplitude of these movements also enlarge the spread of the displaced region along the basilar membrane, which, in turn, alters the pattern of hair cells stimulated. The perceptual consequences of these changes in the basilar membrane's response to different frequencies and intensities will be discussed in the next chapter.

This gives you a bird's-eye view of the workings of the inner ear. Referring back to Figure 10.9, you can now understand why the inner ear is characterized as a frequency-selective sound transducer. We call it "frequency selective" because, by virtue of its mechanical properties, the inner ear breaks up incoming sound into its component frequencies. Incidentally, the design of this marvelous but delicate mechanical system—including the inner and outer hair cells and the tectorial and basilar membranes—is implemented following genetic instructions. Like all such genetic programs, things can go wrong when an abnormal gene has been inherited, or when the instructions on a normal gene are not executed properly.

In fact, several forms of hearing loss can be traced to specific genetic abnormalities (Steel and Brown, 1998). For example, a single gene on chromosome 11 controls the production of a protein that is instrumental in fabrication of the tectorial membrane. Hearing impairment in some individuals can be traced directly to mutations in this gene. Other forms of hearing impairment can be traced to mutations in a gene that controls the length and the stiffness of the cilia projecting out of the hair cells.

In the last section of this chapter, we will survey what happens to the signals from the hair cells as they are routed to the brain via the auditory nerve. But before leaving the inner ear, we want to describe one of the cochlea's really unusual properties, its ability to *generate* sounds on its own. These so-called **cochlear emissions** represent one of the most intriguing discoveries about hearing in the past several decades. They are probably a byproduct of the important amplification role of the OHCs, which you read about previously in this chapter.

Sounds Emitted by the Cochlea

The cochlea is built to receive sound and convert it into neural impulses, and it does this exquisitely. But in addition, the cochlea is capable of actually *generating* sound energy that is transmitted back through the middle ear and into the outer ear where this sound energy can be picked up by a microphone. First, we will describe where these "emitted sounds" come from; then we will explain why they occur.

The chain of events stretching from the outer ear to the inner ear should be familiar to you by now:

airborne sound → movement of the eardrum →
movement of the ossicles → movement of the oval
window → fluid-borne pressure waves → displacement
of basilar membrane → stimulation of hair cells

But there is no reason why some of these events could not occur in the reverse order. After all, the cochlea consists of moving parts suspended in fluid, and any time those parts move, they will create waves within the cochlear fluid. To illustrate, imagine that you are *inside* the cochlea moving your arms back and forth, splashing about as if you were in a swimming pool. Your movements would disturb the cochlear fluid, setting up waves within it that would spread throughout the volume of the fluid. Because the cochlea (your miniature swimming pool) is a sealed container, these waves will eventually push against the oval window from the inner side. Because the oval window is attached to the stapes, this push would be felt by the stapes and passed in reverse through the other two attached bones in the ossicular chain. The hammer, as a result, would be pushed against the inner side of the eardrum. This pressure would, in turn, cause the eardrum to flex back and forth slightly, displacing air molecules within the auditory canal. The eardrum, in other words, would behave just like the cone on a loudspeaker (recall Figure 10.2)—movements of the eardrum would create air pressure changes within the ear canal. If these air pressure changes were sufficiently robust, they could actually be *heard* by someone in the vicinity of the ear from which the acoustic energy was being emitted. So you can see that movements of any of the structures within the cochlea could set up the reverse chain of events, causing sound energy to be reflected back into the world.

The reverse sequence of events just described actually occurs. Sensitive microphones placed within the auditory canal of the human ear are able to record what are called "spontaneous emissions." These emissions consist of acoustic energy in the absence of an external stimulus—they originate from within the ear. Such spontaneous sounds can range up to 20 dB$_{SPL}$ in intensity, a level well within the audible range, if the background is quiet (refer back to Figure 10.4). They tend to consist of energy within a relatively narrow band of frequencies, implying that the cause of the emitted sounds is localized on the tonotopically organized basilar membrane.

This condition is neither rare nor abnormal. Spontaneously emitted sound can be measured from the ears of about two-thirds of the people who have been tested, though the measured frequency and intensity level varies from person to person (see Figure 10.21). There is a tendency for these spontaneous acoustic emissions to be more prevalent and stronger in females than in males (McFadden, 1998).

These emitted sounds can have bizarre consequences. In some cases, although the emitted sound cannot be heard by the source (the person emitting the sound), it *can* be heard by someone else nearby (McFadden, 1982); these emitted sounds are heard as high-pitched tones. You might try listening for emitted sounds from a friend's ear. In a quiet setting, place your ear close to your friend's and notice whether you hear a steady, faint tone. If you do, have your friend move away from your ear and notice whether you still hear the tone. If the tone persists, it must be originating either from an external source or from within your own ear. But if the tone becomes inaudible when your friend moves, you very likely were hearing an emitted sound from his or her ear. Incidentally, emitted sounds have been measured from the ears of many other species, including birds, dogs, and cats (McFadden, 1982). As a result, there's no need to limit your experiment to humans.

Sounds from inside the ear can also be measured immediately following stimulation of the ear by a briefly presented sound such as a click.[6] Rather than being spon-

---

[6]The evoking sound has to be brief, so that the recording microphone in the auditory canal can pick up the relatively weak emitted sound against an otherwise quiet background. If the evoking sound continues, its energy and influence within the cochlea swamp any trace of an emitted sound.

FIGURE 10.21 | Otoacoustic emissions measured from two different ears show differences in frequency content.

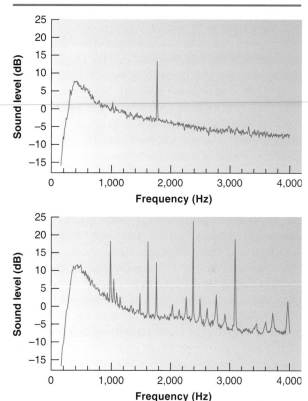

(Adapted from McFadden, 1998.)

taneous, these sounds are described as evoked; they are like echoes of the brief acoustic event (the click). But the echo analogy is misleading, for these emitted sounds aren't simply acoustic energy bouncing off the eardrum back to the recording microphone. Instead, they arise from the fluid-filled cochlea. If the real evoking click consists of high-frequency energy, the emitted sound arrives at the microphone earlier than when the evoking click consists of low-frequency energy. Looking back to Figures 10.19 and 10.20, this makes sense, for the region of the basilar membrane registering high-frequency sound is closer to the eardrum and, hence, to the recording microphone.

These evoked otoacoustic emissions have become an important tool for diagnosing the health of the peripheral portion of the auditory system, particularly in prelinguistic children. In fact, many governments mandate that all new-born infants undergo this quick and noninvasive test. The aim is to detect possible hearing impairment as early as possible in life, so that any necessary remediation can be undertaken. The evoked otoacoustic emission is measured with a small probe inserted into the ear canal. An otoacoustic emission that is below normal or absent altogether could signal blockage in the outer ear canal or in the middle ear fluid, and could also point to damage to the outer hair cells in the cochlea.

Most auditory experts now believe these sounds—both emitted and evoked—can be traced to the amplifying actions of the OHCs. Recall that the OHCs behave like tiny motors, amplifying the wave actions in the fluid of the cochlea in response to sound. When that sound is brief (like a click), these motorlike actions of the OHCs continue briefly after the offset of the click. They behave, in other words, like tiny post-click tremors, setting up the reverse sequence of events described above.

In the case of spontaneously emitted sounds, the amplification process seems to involve self-induced reverberations within the OHCs. Because the middle and inner ears are so beautifully designed to amplify and transduce mechanical displacements, it takes very little motion within the cochlea to trigger the chain of events leading to emitted sounds. And the amplification by the OHCs involves molecular movements at least as large as those that can produce a sensation of hearing. (Recall that motion displacements as small as the diameter of a single hydrogen atom can be heard.) It is ironic that nature has designed an ear so sensitive that it can transmit the effects of the mechanical movements produced by its own parts!

But if our ears generate sound energy all the time, why don't we hear that sound? One reason is that we are rarely in environments quiet enough for faint sounds to be heard: The normal sounds of the world mask emitted sounds. Moreover, we tend to adapt to a continuous, steady sound, rendering it inaudible. Now despite having said this, there are individuals who *do* experience illusory sounds; they experience auditory sensations in the absence of an external stimulus. This condition is described in the next section.

Tinnitus

It is not uncommon for people to experience a sort of humming or ringing sound coming from within their ears, with no external sound source. This condition, termed **tinnitus,** may be limited to one ear only, or it can be heard in both ears. Perceptually, tinnitus is comparable to the ringing in the ears you may have experienced immediately following an abrupt, loud sound such as an explosion. In the case of tinnitus, however, the experience is persistent. It is estimated that 35 percent of people experience tinnitus at one time or another in their lives. Fortunately, many people adapt to this self-produced ringing, just as we all adapt to a steady hum from an external source such as a refrigerator motor. For others, however, tinnitus can be sufficiently annoying to produce anxiety or even depres-

sion. You should not try this yourself, but a large dose of aspirin can induce a temporary tinnitus (Stypulkowski, 1990). In fact, patients who take aspirin to relieve arthritis symptoms are sometimes instructed to moderate their aspirin intake so as to keep tinnitus at bay.

It is natural to assume that someone with tinnitus is merely hearing the spontaneously emitted sound from his or her own ear. While this may be true in a few cases (Wilson and Sutton, 1981), most instances of tinnitus are traceable to neural degeneration (Tonndorf, 1987; Coles and Hallam, 1987). As a rule, the ringing experienced with tinnitus has a characteristic frequency for any given individual. This frequency, however, typically does *not* correspond to the frequency recorded as spontaneous emission from that individual's ear. Moreover, a large dose of aspirin, which *induces* tinnitus, can *eliminate* spontaneous emitted sounds (McFadden, Plattsmier, and Pasanen, 1984). These observations underscore the distinction between emitted sounds and tinnitus.

Brain mapping techniques applied to humans reveal that the neural representation of sounds in the auditory cortex—that portion of the brain devoted to hearing—is altered in people who develop chronic tinnitus (Mühlnickel et al., 1998). These findings suggest that tinnitus results from a reorganization of the auditory cortex in response to selective damage in the cochlea, damage that deprives the brain of sounds within a fairly narrow range of frequencies. We will return to this point later, when we discuss the neural representation of sound frequency in the auditory cortex.

The Auditory System: The Auditory Pathways

As you have learned, the cochlea converts sound energy (pressure waves) into the only form of information understandable by the brain, neural impulses. This neural information is carried out of the inner ear by the **auditory nerve,** which consists of approximately 30,000 nerve fibers (individual axons) arising from each ear. The auditory nerve branches into several different pathways that eventually reconverge within the auditory cortex (a region on the side of your brain that would be covered if you put your hand over your ear).

Various pathways seem to be specialized for processing different aspects of auditory information (Rauschecker, 1998). According to one popular theory, within one pathway neurons' response properties enable them to specify *where* sound is coming from; within another pathway, neurons analyze information necessary for identifying *what* the sound is. In other words, the auditory system contains specialized neural analyzers for locating and identifying

FIGURE 10.22 | Left panel: An overview of the pathways originating from the left auditory nerve and the right auditory nerve; the right ear has been omitted for clarity. Right panel: A cutaway view of the brain showing the principal stages comprising the auditory pathways up to and including the primary auditory cortex.

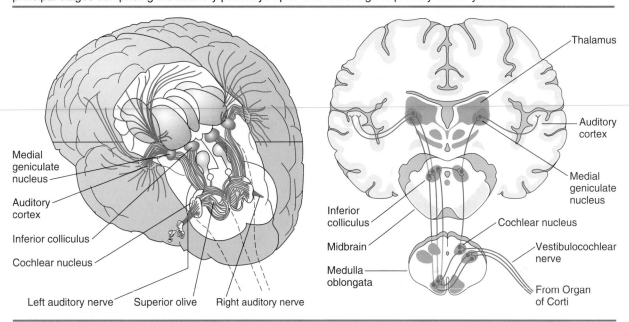

sound sources within the auditory environment. Although there is probably considerable overlap and cross-talk between what and where systems, this general bipartite scheme receives support from neuropsychology studies of patients with localized brain damage. Some patients show deficits in sound localization ("where") whereas others have difficulty with sound recognition ("what"), with the nature of the deficit depending on the locus of the lesion (Clarke et al., 2002). Brain imaging studies (reviewed by Hall, 2003) point to the same division of labor. This idea of complementary "what" and "where" auditory pathways should remind you of the situation with vision, where the dorsal and ventral pathways analyze *where* objects are located and *what* those objects are, respectively.

Figure 10.22 gives an overview of the pathways originating from the left auditory nerve and the right auditory nerve; the right ear has been omitted for clarity. In the drawing at the left of the figure, dark lines represent pathways from the inner ear, to thalamic nuclei and on to the brain. At each structure along this route, neurons make synaptic contact with the next set of neurons in the pathway; the pathways are not a single bundle of fibers passing from ear to cortex. The drawing at the figure's right identifies the principal auditory waystations of the brain. To help you appreciate the spatial layout of these waystations, they have been superimposed on a diagram of the head as seen from behind.

Not shown in the drawing are the feedback neural projections *from* midbrain structures *back* to the inner ear. These feedback projections are called **efferent fibers.** One set of efferent fibers originates in the medial portion (*medial* means toward the center of the brain) of the superior olivary complex (the region of the brain labeled *Superior olive* in Figure 10.22). These fibers make synaptic contacts with cell bodies of the OHCs. Activity in this feedback pathway modulates cochlear output, probably by dampening the effect of the OHCs on the IHCs. (Recall that the OHCs exaggerate the wave actions in the fluid of the cochlea in response to sound, thereby strengthening stimulation of the IHCs.)

A second set of efferent fibers originates in the lateral portion of the superior olivary complex (*lateral* means toward the side of the brain), and projects to auditory nerve fibers at the point where those fibers make contact with the IHCs. Their role in the hearing process is currently unknown (Dallos, Popper, and Fay, 1996).

We will not trace the step-by-step flow of information through the complex neural maze depicted in Figure 10.22. Interested readers may consult the particularly clear description of these pathways given by Hackney (1987). Instead, we'll summarize key aspects of auditory information that the neurons seem to be processing. Our aim is to highlight neural properties that bear on perceptual aspects of hearing to be discussed in the next chapter.

This final section of the chapter is divided into three subsections. The first summarizes the properties of neurons comprising the auditory nerve. The two remaining subsections focus on the neural analysis of the cues for sound localization (where) and the cues for sound identification (what). In the course of our discussion, you will see a similarity between auditory neural processing and visual neural processing: At successively higher stages, individual neurons become increasingly more discriminating about the sounds that activate them.

The Auditory Nerve

Approximately 30,000 individual fibers make up the auditory nerve. These fibers are the axons of nerve cells located in the inner ear. As detailed in an earlier section, about 95 percent of these fibers carry information picked up from just the IHCs (which total only about 4,500), while the remaining 5 percent or so are devoted to signals arising within the OHCs (which total about 15,500). This implies, then, that single IHCs are each innervated by many auditory nerve fibers.

The locations at which auditory nerve fibers contact a single IHC are arranged systematically around the circumference of the hair cell (Liberman, 1982). On the side of the IHC facing the rows of OHCs (refer back to Figure 10.15), contact is made with fibers exhibiting high rates of spontaneous activity. On the opposite side of the IHC are fibers with relatively low spontaneous activity. The remaining locations around an IHC are innervated by fibers with intermediate levels of spontaneous activity. This arrangement is summarized in Figure 10.23. In a moment, we will return to these three classes of auditory nerve fibers, pointing out another functionally important distinction among them. But first, let's consider the responses of these fibers to sound stimulation.

By recording the electrical impulses from many individual fibers, physiologists have determined what kinds of sound stimuli must be presented to the ear to activate those fibers. As mentioned in the previous paragraph, fibers of the auditory nerve, like retinal ganglion cells of the eye, are active even when no stimulus is present. Therefore, to register its presence, a sound must alter this spontaneously occurring, random neural chatter. In auditory nerve fibers, sound is registered by a temporary increase in firing rate. However, not just any sound stimulus will do. For any one fiber, only a limited range of pure-tone frequencies can evoke a response. Moreover, within this limited range not all frequencies are equally effective. We will illustrate these observations using the following example.

Suppose we measure the number of impulses that pure tones produce in a single auditory nerve fiber. Sup-

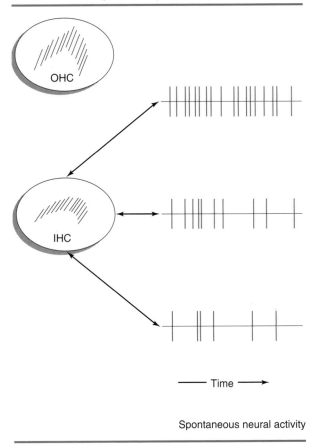

FIGURE 10.23 | Spontaneous activity of auditory nerve fibers varies depending on which portion of the IHC they innervate. The three traces depict spontaneous neural impulses over time: activity in the top trace is "high"; in the middle trace, "medium"; and in the lower trace, "low."

OHC

IHC

Time

Spontaneous neural activity

pose further that we make such measurements for pure tones of various frequencies (Hz) and intensities (dB). (Keep in mind that a pure tone has a sinusoidal waveform.) For each frequency, we will determine the *minimum* intensity needed to produce a noticeable increase in that fiber's spontaneous level of activity. The resulting intensity value will constitute that fiber's threshold for detecting that frequency. We refer to this intensity as the threshold because at lower intensities the fiber behaves as if the tone were not presented at all—the fiber is "deaf" to all weaker intensities. Such a **threshold intensity** is determined for a number of frequencies. Plotting the resulting thresholds for an individual fiber would produce a graph like the one shown in Figure 10.24.

There are a couple of points to note in this graph. At the very lowest intensity, this particular fiber responds only to a 5,000-Hz tone (abbreviated 5 kHz). This value, then,

FIGURE 10.24 | A graph of the threshold intensities (frequency tuning curve) for a single auditory nerve fiber.

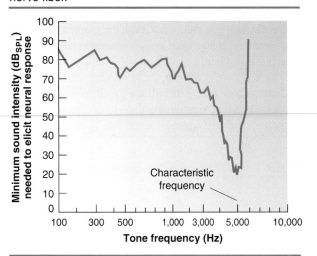

FIGURE 10.25 | Frequency tuning curves for a number of different auditory nerve fibers.

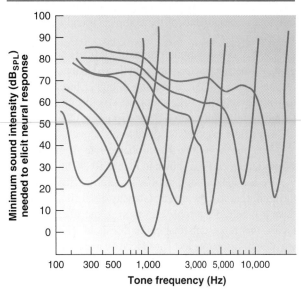

constitutes this fiber's preferred, or *characteristic,* frequency. At this quiet sound level, no other tone produces activity in the fiber. But as we increase the sound intensity, previously ineffective frequencies begin to produce measurable increases in the fiber's activity. In other words, the fiber has different intensity thresholds for different frequencies. The entire curve in Figure 10.24 comprises what is called the **frequency tuning curve** for that fiber.

When this sort of analysis is applied to many different auditory nerve fibers, the result is a family of tuning curves like those illustrated in Figure 10.25. Note that different fibers possess different characteristic frequencies. Some respond best to low frequencies, others to medium frequencies, and still others to high frequencies. As a group, then, the auditory fibers cover a large range of frequencies. Note, too, that all fibers—regardless of characteristic frequency—exhibit asymmetric tuning curves. The reduction in neural responsiveness (change in sensitivity) is much sharper at frequencies *higher* than the fibers' characteristic frequency. In general, narrow fiber tuning means that small changes in frequency can make big differences in the neural activity of nerve fibers.

The frequency tuning of any auditory nerve fiber depends on the location, along the basilar membrane, of the receptor cells (typically IHCs) from which the fiber collects information. Recall that different sound frequencies produce traveling waves that peak at different places along the basilar membrane. As you might guess, each fiber's characteristic frequency is determined by where along the basilar membrane that fiber makes contact with hair cells. Fibers originating from the apex of the cochlea

(the low-frequency region, see Figure 10.19) respond to low frequencies, whereas fibers from the base (the high-frequency region) "prefer" higher frequencies.

This idea of representing a stimulus dimension within an array of tuned neurons should be familiar to you by now. We saw the same principle at work in the visual system: visual cells are tuned for size, orientation, retinal disparity, and so on. In effect, tuned cells make a particular statement about the nature of a stimulus. In the case of the auditory nerve, individual nerve fibers are able to signal the occurrence of a tone whose frequency falls within a limited range of frequencies. Within this range, however, a fiber's activity increases with sound *intensity* (a property we will discuss shortly).

Consequently, within this limited range, the fiber's response is wholly ambiguous: Any number of different frequencies could produce the same neural response if their intensities were adjusted properly. So looking just at the firing rate of a particular fiber, we could never be certain which frequency had stimulated it. (This is the same sort of ambiguity problem discussed in Chapters 4 and 5.)

We don't want to give you the impression that auditory fibers respond only to pure tones. In fact, an auditory fiber will respond vigorously to *any* complex sound just so long as that sound contains at least some energy within that fiber's frequency range. To illustrate, the sound produced when a twig breaks or when you snap your fingers is *broadband*—that is, it contains many different frequencies. So, too, is the static heard when you dial a radio between stations. Either of these broadband sounds would activate a number of frequency-tuned fibers. Any particular fiber, however, would "hear" (respond to) only those frequency components of the complex sound to which it was tuned.

So far, our description of auditory fibers has focused on their frequency selectivity, as reflected in their threshold response profile. Before moving to higher levels of auditory processing, let's take a look at two other characteristic features of auditory nerve fiber responses. One feature is the way a fiber responds to sound levels above its threshold.

Imagine recording the discharge rate from the fiber whose tuning curve is shown in Figure 10.24. Suppose that we use a 5-kHz tone, that fiber's preferred frequency. As the tuning curve indicates, an intensity of 20 dB$_{SPL}$ will produce a barely discernible elevation in the fiber's activity level—this represents that cell's threshold. Now suppose we plot the discharge level produced by increasingly higher sound intensities of the 5-kHz tone. The result would be a graph like the solid line in the top portion of Figure 10.26.

As you can see, between about 20 dB$_{SPL}$ and 60 dB$_{SPL}$, the fiber's activity steadily grows as the sound level increases. Above 60 dB$_{SPL}$, however, the fiber's activity level flattens out. Higher intensities of the tone all produce the same neural response. This so-called *saturation effect,* typical of auditory nerve fibers, means that the fiber has a limited range over which it can signal the intensity level of a given frequency. Hence, firing rate provides an *im*perfect representation of sound level—distinguishable differences in sound intensity (for instance, 80 dB$_{SPL}$ versus 120 dB$_{SPL}$) produce indistinguishable neural responses.

Suppose we repeat these intensity-response measurements on another auditory nerve fiber, also tuned to 5 kHz. We might generate a curve like that shown in the bottom portion of Figure 10.26. Notice that the spontaneous level of this fiber is lower, its threshold level is higher, and it responds to more intense levels before saturating. These two different fibers—which share a characteristic frequency—correspond to two of the three different innervation patterns previously described. (An example of the third fiber type would simply fall midway between the two shown in Figure 10.26.)

Recall that some fibers making synaptic contact with an IHC have low spontaneous activity, others have intermediate spontaneous activity, and still others have high spontaneous activity. The spontaneous level of activity is closely related to the location around the IHC where the fibers innervate the IHC (recall Figure 10.23). We now see that these three categories of fibers have different thresholds and different saturation intensities. These differences will prove important when we discuss hearing thresholds and loudness perception in the next chapter.

FIGURE 10.26 | The neural activity of an auditory nerve fiber increases as the sound level increases, until a saturation point is reached. The graph at the top shows a fiber with high spontaneous activity, low threshold, and low saturation level; the graph at the bottom shows a fiber with low spontaneous activity, high threshold, and high saturation level. The fiber whose activity is shown in the top graph would innervate the IHC on the side facing toward the OHC; the one shown in the bottom would innervate the IHC on the side facing away from the OHC (recall Figure 10.23).

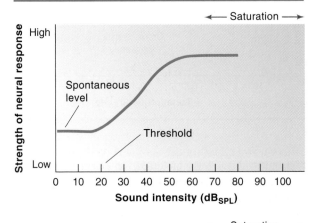

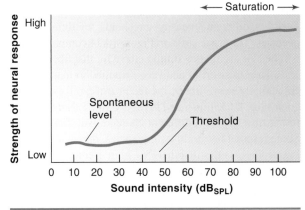

Besides variations in responsiveness with intensity, another significant property of auditory nerve fibers is their response to continuous, prolonged stimulation. When a sound of constant intensity is presented continuously, the level of activity evoked by that sound declines over time, but does not diminish to zero. This change in response is called **adaptation.** As described in Chapter 4, neural adaptation is a common property of sensory neurons. In the case of hearing, this adaptation phenomenon probably has something to do with the gradual reduction in loudness you experience when listening to a steady sound, such as the hum created by the fan on your computer.

This gives an overview of the response properties of auditory nerve fibers, the brain's sole links to the sounds in the environment. The train of neural impulses carried by the auditory nerves from the left and right ears provides the ingredients for all aspects of hearing. Subsequent auditory processing must utilize information contained within these impulses. In the two following sections, you will see how this neural information is utilized for sound localization and for sound identification.

Beyond the Auditory Nerve: Sound Localization

Having two ears enables you to localize sounds. This section discusses how the processing of information within the auditory system makes such localization possible.

Binaural Neurons   Looking back at Figure 10.22, note that the left auditory nerve projects to the **cochlear nucleus** on the left side of the brain, while the right auditory nerve projects to the cochlear nucleus on the right side of the brain. Thus, at this first stage in the auditory chain, information from the two ears remains segregated. Sound delivered to just the left ear (stimulation that is **monaural,** meaning "one ear") will activate cells in the left cochlear nucleus, but have no effect on those in the right cochlear nucleus. Exactly the opposite is true for monaural stimulation delivered to the right ear.

However, at processing stages beyond the cochlear nucleus (superior olive, inferior colliculus, and higher), the auditory system becomes **binaural** ("both ears"), meaning that these higher stages receive neural input from the left ear *and* the right ear. (This property should remind you of the binocular visual cells discussed in Chapters 4 and 8.)

Some binaural neurons can be activated by sound presented to either ear; others are activated by sound presented to one ear but inhibited by sound presented to the other ear. Neurons in the former category—the purely excitatory neurons—tend to prefer low-frequency sound, whereas those in the other category—the excitatory/inhibitory neurons—prefer higher frequencies (Dabak and Johnson, 1992). Some binaural neurons even have a different characteristic frequency for the left versus the right ear (Mendelson, 1992), and they respond to sound sources moving at particular speeds (Ahissar, Bergman, and Vaadia, 1992).

These binaural cells register information about the location of a sound source relative to the head. To understand how these binaural cells work, you first need to be familiar with the two chief cues available for sound localization. In both of these cues, the sounds received by the two ears are compared, which is why the cues are called **binaural cues.** Let's take a moment to discuss them here, to provide some context for understanding the operations of binaural neurons. We'll go into more detail on these cues in the next chapter.

Interaural Time   Imagine keeping your head still and listening to a sound originating from a source located at various positions in front of and to either side of your head. (Try snapping your fingers while holding your hand at arm's length at various positions around your head.) When the sound source lies straight ahead (a *midline* source), the sound energy reaching your two ears will be identical: The air pressure waves will arrive at the two ears at precisely the same time. Now suppose that a sound source is located to your left, away from the midline. In this case, the sound wave from the lateralized source will arrive at your closer ear, the left one, slightly before reaching your farther ear, the right one. This difference in time of arrival of sound at the two ears is called **interaural time difference,** and under certain conditions it provides a potent cue for sound localization.

How might the auditory nervous system register interaural time differences? Do neurons exist that can compute time differences between the two ears? The answer is yes—neurons at several levels in the auditory pathways are sensitive to small binaural time disparities (Masterton and Imig, 1984; Knudsen, du Lac and Esterly, 1987). For example, certain cells in the superior olivary nucleus, often called the "superior olive" (see Figure 10.22), respond maximally when the left ear receives sound slightly before the right ear does, whereas other cells respond best when the right ear receives sound slightly before the left. The interaural time delay that gives the best response varies from cell to cell. But by what means are these interaural delays actually created at the level of binaural cells? The answer, which is elegant yet simple, was proposed decades ago by Jeffress (1948) and more recently substantiated by physiological measurements.

Here's how it seems to work. As you already know, the axon is the neural process carrying impulses from one end of a cell (usually the cell body) to the other (the synaptic zone), where those impulses trigger chemical communication with the next set of neurons in a pathway. A neuron with a short axon conveys impulses to its recipient neurons in a shorter period of time than does a neuron with a longer axon because the impulse travels over a shorter distance. Axon length, in other words, governs the time elapsing between the generation of neural impulses and the delivery of the "message" conveyed by those impulses to the next set of neurons.

Now imagine a binaural neuron that receives input from two cells whose axons *differ* in length, one axonal path being shorter than the other (see drawing A in Figure 10.27). With this in mind, what will happen if both input neurons are activated at precisely the same time? The input cell with the shorter axon will get its message to the binaural cell sooner than will the input cell with

FIGURE 10.27 | Schematic drawings showing how interaural time differences from a lateralized sound source could be registered by a binaural cell receiving inputs from cells whose axons differ in length.

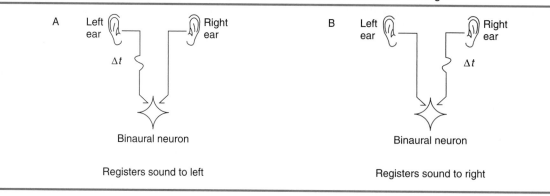

the longer axon, with the disparity in time of arrival at the binaural neuron depending on the magnitude of the difference in axon length between the two input neurons.

Given these two input neurons, what would be necessary to ensure that the binaural neuron received *simultaneous* inputs from both? To accomplish this, the input neuron with the longer axon would have to be activated *prior* to activation of the input neuron with the shorter axon; the time disparity between activations would have to match the disparity associated with their conduction times. We could, in other words, compensate for the axon length differences by introducing an appropriate delay between activation of the two input cells.

How could we create these differences in activation time? The answer is simple: Place the sound source at a location where the interaural time difference creates this exact activation delay. (This scheme, by the way, is similar in purpose but not implementation to the delay-line circuit described in Chapter 9 to account for direction-selective motion perception.)

This, then, is the essence of the **delay line** theory proposed by Jeffress (1948). Different binaural neurons receive inputs from pairs of cells, one activated by sound presented to the left ear and the other by sound presented to the right ear. For any given binaural cell, its pair of input cells has a characteristic time delay, governed by the difference in axon length. The binaural neurons respond maximally upon simultaneous stimulation by the input cells. But to achieve this simultaneity, the left- and right-ear input cells must be activated at slightly *different* times. In general, registration of sounds located to the left of the midline would require that the left-ear input cell have the longer axon (to compensate for the left ear's receiving the sound first), as depicted in Figure 10.27A; sounds located to the right would require the opposite arrangement (Figure 10.27B).

To register particular locations to the left or to the right, the disparity in axonal length could vary among pairs of cells, which means that different binaural neurons would respond best to different interaural time differences. Actually, there are several means by which impulse conduction delays could be introduced, besides variations in axon length, but the essence of the idea remains the same: Binaural neurons with different preferred interaural delays signal different sound locations. Recent physiological work confirms that the auditory system has such a mechanism in place (Carr and Konishi, 1988), and theoretical work has aimed at refining the Jeffress model (Dabak and Johnson, 1992).

Interaural Intensity Differences   There is a second potential source of information specifying sound location: Sound energy arriving at the two ears from a single source will be more intense at the ear located nearest the source. This **interaural intensity difference** arises primarily from the "occluding" effect produced by the head. When sound energy passes through a dense barrier—such as your head—some sound energy is usually lost. Thus, for a lateralized sound source, a portion of its sound energy will be blocked from reaching the farther ear because the head stands in the way. The head produces what is called a *sound shadow*, a weakening of the intensity of sound at the more distant ear. This binaural difference in sound intensity provides another cue for sound localization. Of course, when the source is located equidistant from the two ears—for instance straight ahead—the interaural intensity difference will be zero.

The auditory nervous system appears to capitalize on this source of location information as well. Neurons have been discovered that respond best when the two ears receive slightly different intensities, some preferring the stronger intensity in the right ear and others preferring the stronger intensity in the left ear (Wise and Irvine, 1985; Manley, Koppl, and Konishi, 1988). These binaural neurons, incidentally, are found at different neural sites from those registering interaural time differences (Knudsen and Konishi, 1978). Moreover, binaural cells sensitive to interaural intensity tend to fall into the excitatory/inhibitory category, meaning that the input from one ear is excitatory and the input from the other is inhibitory. In fact, the algebraic subtraction of inhibition from excitation—an operation easily performed by a binaural cell—accounts for a given cell's preferred interaural intensity difference (Manley et al., 1988).

Binaural Cells and Sound Localization To reiterate, most binaural cells respond best to a sound arising from a particular location. For example, some binaural cells respond best to a source located close to the midline, while other cells respond best to sounds arising from various points to one side or the other of the midline. In effect, each binaural cell "listens" for sound within a fairly restricted region of auditory space. This region of space constitutes the neuron's receptive field, the area in space where a sound must be located in order to stimulate that neuron. As an aggregate, these cells provide a neural map of auditory space (King and Moore, 1991; Fitzpatrick et al., 1997). Brain imaging studies also reveal evidence for spatial maps of sound location (reviewed by Rauschecker, 1998).

There are several reasons for thinking that binaural cells of this sort contribute to sound localization. For one thing, inserting an earplug in one ear causes sounds to be mislocalized. Under this condition, sound seems to originate not from the actual location of the source, but from a location displaced toward the unplugged ear. This makes sense. Plugging an ear reduces sound intensity received by that ear. Plugging one ear also produces a shift in the receptive fields of binaural neurons, by an amount and direction predicted from errors in sound localization (Knudsen and Konishi, 1980). This systematic shift in the receptive field locations of binaural neurons reinforces the idea that these neurons encode the location of sound in space.

There is another reason for believing this idea. Not all species of mammals possess the kind of binaural neurons just described. In particular, the size of the superior olive varies greatly from one species to another. This structure is one of the brain structures containing binaural neurons. Bruce Masterton tested the abilities of different species to localize sound (Masterton et al., 1975). The animals were trained to listen for a short tone that came from one of two loudspeakers, one located to the animal's left and the other located to the animal's right. The tone informed the animal which way to go, left or right, in order to obtain a drink of water. Masterton found that cats and tree shrews, both of which have sizable superior olives, could perform this task with ease. However, hedgehogs and rats, who have a much smaller superior olive, made numerous errors, indicating an inability to localize sound accurately. Masterton's behavioral study reinforces the idea that binaural neurons of the superior olive are responsible for analyzing interaural cues for sound localization.

Experience also plays an important role in the development of the neural connections responsible for registering locations of sounds in space (Knudsen, 1998). As mentioned above, hearing loss in one ear causes compensatory shifts in auditory receptive fields, in response to the altered interaural timing and interaural intensity cues (Knudsen and Brainard, 1995). In addition, when vision cannot be used for locating objects, the spatial acuity of binaural neurons is enhanced. That is, when an animal must rely on binaural hearing as its sole source of spatial information, neurons in some auditory regions of the brain become unusually sharply "tuned" for particular locations (Korte and Rauschecker, 1993). As you might expect, these animals exhibit extra good sound localization ability when tested behaviorally (Rauschecker and Kniepert, 1994). There are reasons to believe that humans, too, can develop extra keen spatial acuity when forced to rely on hearing without sight, and we will consider that evidence in the next chapter.

This concludes our overview of how the auditory system processes information about *where* a sound originates. We have left out important facts about sound localization, but those will be covered in Chapter 11 when we return to binaural hearing. For now, though, let's consider how the auditory system processes information about the identity of a sound: *what* it is that's being heard.

Beyond the Auditory Nerve: Sound Identification

Recall that any given fiber in the auditory nerve responds to a limited range of frequencies, a range that defines the fiber's frequency tuning. The responses of such fibers to more complex sounds (such as noise or a vocalization) can be simply predicted from each fiber's tuning curve. Moving from the auditory nerve to more central processing stages (for example, the cochlear nucleus), cells continue to respond to tones of certain frequencies, but the range of frequencies over which any given cell responds becomes narrower. Thus, over the first several stages of the auditory system, tuning curves become more selective for frequency.

Information destined for the auditory cortex passes through the **medial geniculate nucleus** of the thalamus (see Figure 10.22). This structure, the analogue to the visual system's LGN, receives input also from the reticular

FIGURE 10.28 | View of the lateral surface of the left hemisphere of the human brain. The primary auditory area within the temporal lobe is highlighted. For reference, primary visual and somatosensory regions are labeled, too.

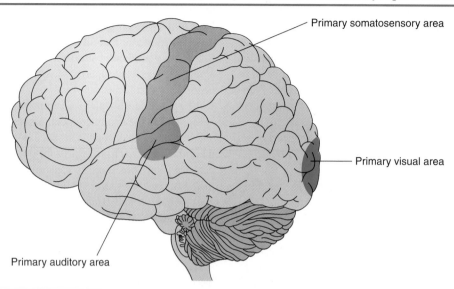

Primary somatosensory area

Primary visual area

Primary auditory area

activating system, whose influence on sensory systems was introduced in Chapter 4. So again, an organism's level of arousal probably modulates auditory sensitivity by means of neural influences within the thalamus. Cells in the medial geniculate nucleus, in turn, send projections to the **primary auditory cortex** located in the temporal lobe of the brain (see Figure 10.28), where multiple elementary auditory features are organized into meaningful auditory objects (Nelken, 2004).

In primates, humans included, the auditory system in the cortex of the temporal lobe has an interesting anatomical organization: Auditory regions are laid out like a large city, with an urban center encircled by a belt of suburbs, which, in turn, is surrounded by rural areas. In the auditory system of the temporal lobe, a central *core area,* which includes the primary auditory region (A1), is encircled by secondary auditory regions, called the *belt areas.* In turn, on the outer edges of the belt areas lie *parabelt regions,* sometimes called tertiary or association areas (Wessinger et al., 2001). Single cell recordings from within the core region of the auditory cortex reveals that the preferred frequency of different neurons is ordered tonotopically, meaning that preferred frequencies change systematically within this cortical region (Kaas and Hackett, 2000). This core region contains three separate maps, each of which mirrors the tonotopic organization of the basilar membrane. (In a sense, these tonotopic frequency maps are analogous to the retinotopic map in pri-

mary visual cortex.) Moreover, these auditory maps exhibit some cortical magnification, with more neurons tuned to mid-frequencies than to either higher or lower values. Incidentally, this magnified region includes frequencies within that portion of the spectrum that is prominent in animal vocalizations and human speech. Could this magnified representation of those frequencies have developed as a consequence of the hearing experiences of those animals (and humans) early in life? This seems entirely possible, for it is known that exposure to a given band of sounds can indeed bias the tonotopic map in auditory cortex toward the frequencies contained in those sounds (Nakahara, Zhang, and Merzenich, 2004).

The belt areas surrounding A1 also respond to acoustic signals reaching the ear, but, unlike their counterparts in A1, neurons in these secondary areas tend to respond rather weakly to pure-tone sounds. Rather than being "interested" in the frequency or intensity of sounds, these neurons, instead, respond best to more complicated, biologically significant sounds. To give just a few examples, some cortical neurons fail to respond to any steady tone but do respond vigorously to a tone that changes in frequency (FM sound, as it's called because frequency is modulated). For some of these neurons, the frequency modulation must be in a particular direction, either up or down. One sound whose frequency goes up is the "Hmmm?" sound you make when you don't understand something (try it). A sound whose frequency goes down is the sound you make when you yawn (try it). In general, frequency modulations are responsible for the voice inflections during speech; without these inflections, the voice has a flat, monotone character. But other acoustic events besides the human voice also contain FM sounds. Many birds use FM sounds as integral components of their songs; think about the rising note in the call of the bobwhite. And the sirens on such emergency vehicles as ambulances, fire trucks, and police cars routinely use FM sound to warn other vehicles of their approach.

Other cortical neurons in the belt areas respond only to complex "kissing" sounds that resemble the noise often used when calling a dog. In animals that utilize vocalizations to communicate, the auditory cortex contains neurons specifically responsive to individual vocalizations. Such cells often fail to respond to tones or clicks and, instead, are activated only by a certain "call" that forms part of that animal's natural vocabulary. For instance, in several regions outside the primary auditory cortex of the macaque monkey, some neurons are activated exclusively by "cooing" sounds, other neurons activated only by "barks" and still others activated only by "grunts" (Rauschecker, Tian, and Hauser, 1995). Each of these natural vocalizations conveys a particular message within the repertoire of calls made by the monkey. Many cortical neurons, then, unlike those at the earliest levels of the auditory system, respond to fairly *abstract* features of sound—features that identify the sound source itself, not just the constituent frequencies of that sound (see Nelken, 2004).

This is why damage to auditory cortex impairs performance on tasks where an animal must discriminate between complex sounds, but spares performance on tasks involving the detection or discrimination of simple tones. Most sounds in the natural world—environmental sounds, animal cries, and human speech—are relatively broadband, meaning that they're composed of many different frequencies present simultaneously and in different proportions. Additionally, natural sounds tend to be dynamic in that their frequency content and intensity levels change over time. Many neurons in secondary and tertiary auditory cortical areas are tuned to reflect these complex properties of natural sounds. In particular, neurons in these areas respond with a sharp increase in activation when sounds first occur but then rapidly decline even when the sound stimulus itself remains present (Seifritz et al., 2002). Neurons in the primary cortical area, in contrast, respond in a more sustained fashion to sounds, maintaining a level of activity throughout the period of stimulus presentation.

Core and belt areas may differ in another important respect having to do with how sounds change over time. With this in mind, Lewicki (2002) analyzed a large library of acoustic signals, including naturally occurring environmental sounds (such as rustling brush, snapping twigs, and crunching leaves), nonhuman animal vocalizations (such as coos and warning cries), and human speech. Lewicki noted that many environmental sounds are broadband (meaning they comprise many frequencies), nonharmonic (which means their frequencies tend not to be simple multiples of one another), and brief. Such sounds typically demand rapid and accurate localization. When you're walking through a forest and hear a branch above you snap, you need to react quickly to avoid possible injury. Animal vocalizations, in contrast, are harmonic, which helps them stand out against the normal, random soundscape, and those vocalizations tend to last much longer than nonharmonic sounds such as the snap of a branch.

Arguably, human speech can be described as a mixture of these two classes, harmonic and nonharmonic. For most human languages, we can distinguish between vowel sounds, which tend to be harmonic and relatively long in duration, and consonant sounds, which tend to be shorter and nonharmonic. Based on mathematical principles (see Box 10.2), Lewicki, as well as others (e.g., Zatorre, Belin, and Penhune, 2002), has held that fundamentally different neural mechanisms are required to register the acoustic events defining these two classes of sounds: harmonic/brief and nonharmonic/transient. And based on differences in the dynamics of their responses, neurons in the core and in the belt areas could constitute the neural bases of the mechanisms envisioned by Lewicki. The close match between behaviorally relevant sounds and the brain's mechanisms for registering those sounds is reminiscent of the match between the visual brain and the visual world discussed in Chapter 4. Later, in Chapter 12, we will revisit Lewicki's distinction between brief transients, on one hand, and longer, harmonic stimuli, on the other.

Human Auditory Cortex

The properties of auditory cortex described in the previous section were derived largely from physiological recordings from individual neurons within the temporal lobe of nonhuman primates. How well do those findings generalize to the human brain? To answer that question, we turn to results from brain imaging studies of normal individuals and neuropsychological testing of brain-damaged people. Let's take a look at some of that evidence.

As previously noted, human auditory cortex, like that of other primates, is organized into a core region with surround belts; we know this from histological studies of

BOX 10.2 **Resolving Time and Frequency**

Design engineers are chronically faced with challenges that pit one design element (e.g., fuel efficiency) against another (e.g., speed). Nature, too, must balance competing demands within biological systems, including demands associated with the design of the neural machinery responsible for hearing. Here's the problem.

Individual auditory nerve fibers respond best to tones of a given frequency, and each fiber responds to a limited range of frequencies centered around that fiber's preferred value (look back at the tuning curves in Figure 10.25). As you learned early in this chapter, the frequency of a tone is defined by cyclical fluctuations in air pressure. To obtain a truly accurate estimate of tone frequency, the ear and auditory nerve must sample an acoustic event over durations of time sufficient to encompass multiple repetitions of the tone's frequency cycle; in other words, the auditory system must integrate acoustic information over time to provide good frequency resolution. And good frequency resolution can be important when it comes to identifying the sources of sounds, which are defined by characteristic patterns of frequencies. Hearing the difference between a trombone and a trumpet, for example, depends on distinguishing subtle differences in the relative strengths of different frequencies (timbre, as it's called). As well, good frequency resolution is important for distinguishing among vowel sounds such as /a/ and /e/, for these sounds too differ primarily in their harmonic (i.e., frequency) structure. In Chapter 12 we'll consider speech sounds in more detail.

But there's a price to pay for integrating acoustic information over time: It becomes difficult to specify precisely *when* in time acoustic events actually occur. To achieve good frequency resolution, in other words, the auditory system must sacrifice temporal resolution. But that could be a costly sacrifice. After all, knowing *when* acoustic events occur can be a matter of life and death (remember that snapping branch above your head). Moreover, good temporal resolution is crucially important for distinguishing among consonant sounds in hu-

man speech, the sounds characterized by abrupt onsets and offsets (e.g., "ta" and "da"). Incidentally, it was the Nobel Prize–winning physicist Denis Gabor who proved mathematically that resolution in frequency and resolution in time involve competing demands when one is trying to measure complex signals such as sound waves; Gabor went on to describe a compromise measurement solution that optimizes resolution in both domains.

So how can these two competing demands both be satisfied, so that our hearing has reasonable frequency resolution and reasonable temporal resolution? As you may recall from Chapter 3, the visual system faces a similar challenge of trying to satisfy competing demands; there the trade-off was between sensitivity (being able to see in dim-light conditions) and resolution (being able to see fine spatial detail). Nature's solution to that dilemma was to carve two visual systems out of one, a system specialized for rod-based, scotopic vision and the other designed for cone-based photopic vision. And it looks like this same kind of strategy—subdivision of labor—is the one employed in human hearing, with some of the auditory system's neural resources devoted to fine frequency discrimination and other parts devoted to high temporal resolution. There is some disagreement, however, about how this division of labor is subcontracted within the auditory pathways. Some believe there are two pathways within the auditory system, one specialized for high-fidelity frequency analysis and another specialized for fine temporal resolution (Romanski et al., 1999). Others see the division of labor embodied separately in the two hemispheres, with the left hemisphere handling the chore of frequency analysis and the right hemisphere keeping accurate track of when acoustic events are occurring (Zatorre, Belin, and Penhune, 2002).

No matter how this trade-off between frequency tuning and temporal precision is accomplished, it is noteworthy that it is done in a manner that is well matched to the variety of sounds we encounter in our everyday environment, including the diverse sounds of human speech (Olshausen and O'Connor, 2002).

---

brain tissue. But do those regions exhibit tonotopic organization? Several brain imaging studies have addressed this question, and the answer is unequivocally yes (Formisano et al., 2003). Thus, listening to a low-pitched tone activates a distinctly different region of primary auditory cortex than does listening to a high-pitched tone. Moreover, localized activation in these regions is not lim-

ited to hearing real tones. Highly localized activation of primary auditory cortex is also observed when people hear a "phantom" tone of frequency, f_i, generated by prior exposure to noise with a small band of energy removed at f_i (Hoke, Ross, and Hoke, 1998); we characterize this as a "phantom" tone because at the time it's experienced, the person is exposed to no sound stimulus whatsoever—the tonal sensation is an aftereffect of the exposure to the noise with a "notch" of missing frequencies. But the tone *is* real in the sense that the auditory cortex is responding just as it does when a real tone, *f,* is presented. Incidentally, we call this illusory experience a **Zwicker tone** in honor of the individual who first described the illusion (Zwicker, 1964).

Another form of illusory pitch associated with auditory cortical activation is tinnitus. People with tinnitus—the experience of a tonelike sound in the absence of a real sound—exhibit distorted tonotopic maps in the auditory cortex that exaggerate the neural representation of the frequency associated with the "illusory" pitch (Mühlnickel et al., 1998). This distorted representation, it is thought, results from abnormal auditory experience associated with partial hearing loss (Rauschecker, 1999a).

But why does hearing loss produce phantom sounds? Damage to a restricted portion of the cochlea produces an auditory "deaf spot" in the individual's hearing: tones normally signaled by that portion of the cochlea are no longer registered by the inner ear and, therefore, are no longer heard (we will discuss this form of hearing loss in greater detail in the next chapter). Consequently, neurons in the brain responsive to those lost tones are deprived of their normal inputs, even though the deprived neurons are themselves healthy. Over time, those neurons develop responsiveness to neighboring tone frequencies that are still audible (that is, frequencies to which the cochlea still responds). The tone frequencies neighboring those associated with the hearing loss expand their neural representations within the auditory cortex.

This expansion is the neural basis for the cortical "distortion" supposedly associated with tinnitus: a central, cortical distortion arising in response to neural events on the periphery of the auditory system. This hypothesis is illustrated schematically in Figure 10.29. Presumably, a phantom tone is heard in the absence of auditory input because of chronic increased spontaneous activity in this region of the tonotopic map (Rauschecker, 1999a; Eggermont and Roberts, 2004). Tinnitus thus represents an intriguing example of neural plasticity—the brain's ability to alter its connectivity in response to long-term changes in sensory input.

Brain imaging has revealed other interesting facts about the organization of auditory portions of the human brain. Secondary auditory areas surrounding the central belt are responsive not so much to pure tones but, rather, to more complex tones such as "glides" (tones changing

FIGURE 10.29 | Schematic of cortical reorganization following cochlear damage. What happens when a portion of the cochlea signaling high-frequency sound is damaged? Regions of the tonotopically organized auditory cortex that normally receive input from this high-frequency portion of the cochlea are instead innervated by fibers from neighboring, healthy portions of the cochlea. Those cortical neurons still respond as if high-frequency sound were presented, even though their inputs are from parts of the cochlea responsive to lower frequencies.

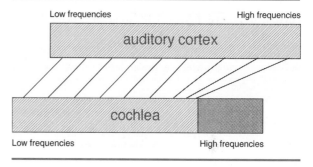

in frequency) and "swooshes" (noise whose intensity varies over time (Wessinger et al., 2001). Several brain imaging studies (Alain et al., 2001; Maeder et al., 2001; Zatorre et al., 2002) have also found evidence for the existence of specialized cortical areas concerned with the locations of sounds ("where") and different areas concerned with the identification of sounds ("what"). This notion of specialized auditory pathways for "where" and "what" will remind you of the situation in vision described in Chapter 4, where dorsal and ventral visual pathways registered information about object location and object identity.

A summary of auditory brain imaging results would not be complete without mentioning the growing body of work using musical sounds and speech sounds. But we'll postpone a discussion of those aspects of hearing until Chapter 12. To preview, listening to speech sounds activates regions in the temporal lobe and regions near the junction of temporal and parietal lobes (Petersen et al., 1988), whereas listening to musical sounds activates regions in a different portion of the temporal cortex, and predominantly in the right hemisphere of the brain (Zatorre, Evans, and Meyer, 1994).

Studies of brain-damaged patients provide another source of information about the auditory cortex in humans. The clinical literature on brain damage and hearing is too extensive to review here. Suffice it to say that damage to different portions of the auditory pathways creates different kinds of hearing losses, ranging from temporary deficits in the ability to hear tones to permanent inability to identify previously familiar sounds or to identify where a sound is coming from.

There are even auditory analogs to blindsight and to akinetopsia, syndromes described in Chapter 4. Tanaka and colleagues (1991) describe two patients who exhibited seriously impaired hearing from extensive, bilateral damage to brain structures in the auditory cortex, but whose ears and auditory nerves were intact. Despite their **cortical deafness,** these patients sometimes behaviorally reacted to a sound—such as a door slamming—while denying any experience of that sound. This suggests that neural pathways subserving the auditory reflexes, such as turning the head toward a sound source, are different from those involved in awareness and identification of the source.

As for the analog to akinetopsia (motion blindness), Griffiths and colleagues (1996) described a patient with a right hemisphere stroke who was unable to perceive the movement of a sound source when that movement was specified by changing interaural time cues or changing interaural intensity cues. Normal listeners, in comparison, clearly hear sounds moving within the environment when these cues are present. The patient's brain damage included posterior parts of the parietal cortex, an area involved in spatial localization.

This completes our survey of sound, the ear, and the auditory pathways. The stage is now set for consideration of hearing, the topic of the next chapter.

S U M M A R Y   A N D   P R E V I E W

This chapter has described the physical events that give rise to the experience of sound. These events are captured by the ears, transformed into neural events by the hair cells, and analyzed by neurons especially designed for frequency and sound location. Throughout this chapter we've largely avoided discussing the perceptual consequences of this sequence of events. But now that you know something about the auditory system's machinery, we're ready to consider in the next two chapters the accomplishment that this machinery makes possible: hearing, including speech perception and music perception.

K E Y   T E R M S

acoustic energy
acoustic reflex
acoustics
adaptation
amplitude
anvil (incus)
auditory canal
auditory nerve
basilar membrane
binaural
binaural cues
cilia
cochlea
cochlear emissions
cochlear nucleus
cortical deafness
decibels (dB)
delay line

eardrum (tympanic membrane)
echoes
efferent fibers
Eustachian tube
frequency tuning curve
hair cells
hammer (malleus)
hertz (Hz)
inner hair cells (IHC)
interaural intensity difference
interaural time difference
medial geniculate nucleus
monaural
noise
organ of Corti
ossicles
outer hair cells (OHC)
oval window

pinna
place theory
primary auditory cortex
pure tones
resonant frequency
round window
sonar (sound navigation ranging)
sound pressure level (SPL)
stirrup (stapes)
tectorial membrane
temporal theory
threshold intensity
tinnitus
tonotopic organization
traveling wave
Zwicker tone

Hearing and Listening

Do blind people hear better than sighted individuals? Does listening to loud music damage your hearing? How do you manage to ignore the hubbub at a noisy party while at the same time picking out and listening to a familiar voice? These are just a few of the questions considered in this chapter on hearing and listening. Because hearing's capacities and limitations depend upon the properties of the auditory system, our discussion of hearing is grounded in the material you read in the previous chapter.

Sounds are with us all the time; they're impossible to escape. You were even listening to sounds before you were born. The intrauterine environment may not be as noisy as New York's Times Square, but maternal sounds, such as a mother's heartbeat, breathing, speaking or singing voice, and even the gurgles of her tummy, make the uterus anything but quiet.[1] And these sounds have an impact because by about the twenty-eighth week after conception, a human fetus shows clear responses to sounds, and grows increasingly sensitive to sound until birth and beyond (Ruben, 1992). Prenatal exposure to sound may explain why right after birth, an infant preferentially orients toward the sound of its mother's voice. Apparently, by listening to it for months prior to birth the infant became familiar with this very special and important voice.

It's impossible to estimate how many different sounds we can recognize, but the average person's auditory repertoire is huge, and grows larger with experience. Just think of all the people you know fairly well. Their voices are sufficiently imprinted in your mind's ear that you can typically recognize them in an instant over the telephone. Famous voices, too, are acoustically etched in our minds, to the extent that we immediately know when we're listening to the recorded voice of, say, Ray Charles (the late blues music singer), Bill Clinton (former President of the United States), Jean Chrétien (former Prime Minister of Canada), or even Marge Simpson (Bart's mother).

---

[1]The medical term for a tummy gurgle is *borborygmus,* one of the oddest sounding words in the English language. The word sounds odd because it is onomatopoeia, a word made up to imitate some sound, in this case a stomach gurgle.

FIGURE 11.1 | Each soundwave wave corresponds to a unique acoustic event. Called a *spectrogram,* each graph plots changes in the amplitude of acoustic energy over time. As you learned in the previous chapter, these kinds of complex sounds comprise many different frequencies, whose energy levels fluctuate over time.

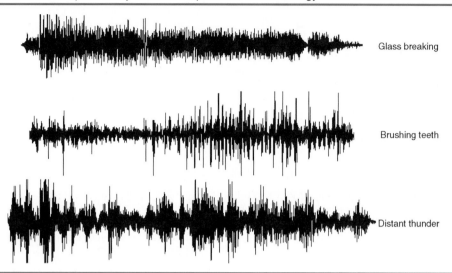

Glass breaking

Brushing teeth

Distant thunder

Besides the sounds of voices, you're well acquainted with countless musical tunes and animal sounds, not to mention the miscellaneous sounds associated with life's everyday events (Ballas, 1993): walking, sneezing, laughing, scratching, typing, tearing open an envelope, knocking on a door, or kissing a loved one. As you learned in the previous chapter, sound begin in vibrations, like those generated when objects rub against one another or when one object strikes another. Those sounds tell us something about the nature of those objects. When a hammer strikes some object, the sound tells us whether the object was wood, metal, or a soft pillow. The sound from a hammer blow even allows us to "hear" the shape of the object that's been hit (Kunkler-Peck and Turvey, 2000). Sound allows us to judge when a bottle or glass that's being filled with water has become nearly full (Cabe and Pittenger, 2000). And, of course, sounds are invaluable for telling us about objects and events we cannot see, such as the rattle of a loose screw inside an appliance or the high-pitched whine of a clogged vacuum cleaner.

It's amazing that this huge spectrum of auditory events comes to us courtesy of only about 20,000 tiny hair cells in each ear and approximately 30,000 fibers in each auditory nerve. This feat is all the more remarkable when we consider the acoustic signal that inaugurates the process of hearing.

Take a look at the array of acoustic waveforms shown in Figure 11.1. Called **spectrograms,** these are samples of some common, easily recognized sounds. These waveforms, which summarize the signals available to the ears, appear as a jumble of different frequencies varying in amplitude and times of onset and offset. Just looking at the waveforms, it's impossible to associate a given sound wave with a specific event. Yet the ear and auditory portions of the brain accomplish this feat accurately and effortlessly.

What's even more remarkable is that hearing continues to work quite well even when many different sound sources are present at the same time. Stop and think about it. The ear typically receives a stream of acoustic energy from a multitude of environmental sources, and the energy from those sources combines into a single, complex acoustic signal at the ear. To appreciate this fact, imagine that you're chatting with a friend at a noisy baseball game. The acoustic environment includes applause, boos, music, shouts from popcorn vendors, cheers of neighboring fans, and, of most interest to you, your companion's voice. Amidst the din, you can pick out your friend's voice from all the rest, even though that voice comprises just a small fraction of the energy that hits your ears. This ability to separate the single stream of acoustic energy into component parts is one of hearing's most amazing and important feats.

Let's begin our exploration of hearing and listening by considering the range of sound frequencies audible to humans, these frequencies define the boundaries of auditory perception.

The Range and Limits of Hearing

The range of audible sound frequencies is analogous to the range of visible spatial frequencies (recall the CSF from Chapter 5). In like fashion, the eyes and ears register a fairly wide but definitely limited range of visual and auditory information. Because this range is limited, our perceptual world is limited.

For hearing, the range of audible frequencies is determined by measuring the minimum intensity, or amplitude, necessary to just barely detect tones of various frequencies. These measurements are made in a quiet environment, with no other sounds present. Test tones are typically delivered over earphones or through a loudspeaker. The minimum intensity value is referred to as the **threshold intensity.** Values below this threshold intensity cannot be heard, whereas intensities higher than this can be heard. (The appendix gives a detailed discussion of techniques for measuring thresholds.) The threshold intensity for each of a number of tone frequencies can be plotted on a graph like the one shown in Figure 11.2 Curves like this are called **audibility functions (AFs).** They summarize the range of frequencies audible to the human ear. The analogy between an AF and a contrast-sensitivity function for spatial vision should be obvious—both express variations in threshold performance over a range of frequencies. Notice that the threshold of hearing varies with the frequency of sound: In the middle frequencies, far less intensity is needed to make a tone audible than in the low and high frequencies.

In Figure 11.2, intensity values are expressed in terms of decibels (dB_{SPL}), with the value of 0 dB_{SPL} assigned to the weakest intensity that can be heard at any frequency (recall Figure 10.4). In this case, tones in the neighborhood of 2,500 Hz require the least intensity to be heard. As a result, their threshold is expressed as 0 dB_{SPL} and all other threshold values are expressed relative to this value. Thus, to hear a 200-Hz tone, its intensity must be 40 dB higher than the intensity needed to hear a 2,500-Hz tone.

To provide some points of reference, the lowest key on a standard piano produces a musical note whose primary frequency is 27.5 Hz, the note produced by middle C is 261.63 Hz, and the top note on the piano is 4,186 Hz. A sound of very high frequency can be produced by turn-

FIGURE 11.2 | An audibility function (AF) showing the range of tone frequencies audible to a normal young adult.

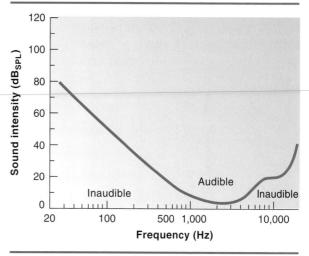

ing on a television set but leaving the volume turned all the way down. This generates a high-pitched whine about 16,000 Hz (16 kHz).

At its best, the human ear is extraordinarily sensitive: The intensity required to hear a 2,500-Hz tone is hardly any greater than the amplitude of vibrations associated with the random movements of air molecules! This incredible performance testifies to what a masterpiece of engineering the ears are. All the more remarkable in view of the fact that this very sensitive device is not harmed by sounds several million times more intense. On top of this, human beings can hear a wide range of frequencies: Most people can detect frequencies as low as 20 Hz, which is heard as a very low rumble. Young people can detect frequencies as high as 20,000 Hz. To get all this from a device so sensitive represents a real design feat.

The performance summarized in Figure 11.2 represents the range of hearing for the normal young human adult. This curve is remarkably consistent across individuals, so much so that deviations from this norm usually signify some type of impairment in the peripheral auditory system, either in the ear or in the auditory nerve. Abnormal AFs are *not* commonly associated with disorders of the central auditory nervous system. Central neural disorders lead to other kinds of hearing loss, some of which we'll mention later in this chapter. For now, let's consider some of the conditions that can produce abnormal AFs (higher than normal, pure-tone thresholds) and the perceptual consequences of those abnormalities.

FIGURE 11.3 | The incidence of hearing loss increases with age. For each age group, the three histograms correspond to varying degrees of hearing loss expressed in decibel units.

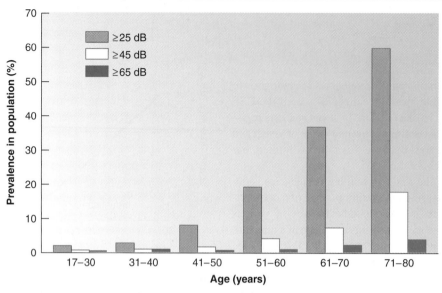

Hearing Loss

Hannah Merker, an author and professor of creative writing, became deaf after a skiing accident during her young adulthood. She writes about her loss.

> As an adult, losing most of my hearing . . . was akin to being adrift in a fog where the edges of nearby land, other fog-bound craft, are barely visible. You know something is there but definition is vague. . . . You are aware yet cut off, alone in a scary isolation. The world is running forward and you cannot keep up. That is what it is like to be severely hearing impaired. (Merker, 1992, pp. 66–67)

As Figure 11.3 documents, the incidence of hearing loss is high, especially in the older population. According to the World Health Organization, worldwide some 250 million people have a serious hearing loss. In the United States alone, an estimated 28 million people suffer some loss of hearing, making this the most common of all physical disabilities (Nadol, 1993), with about 1 in 10 having a serious loss.

As Hannah Merker's words reveal, people who become completely deaf after years of normal hearing find the experience frightening and isolating. Since everyday sounds keep us in touch with the environment, loss of hearing isolates the totally deaf person not only from the voices of others but also from the security of life's back-

ground hum. Helen Keller poignantly described that isolated world this way:

> I am just as deaf as I am blind. The problems of deafness are deeper and more complex, if not more important, than those of blindness. Deafness is a much worse misfortune. For it means the loss of the most vital stimulus—the sound of the voice that brings language, sets thoughts astir and keeps us in the intellectual company of [others]. . . . I have found deafness to be a much greater handicap than blindness. (cited in Ackerman, 1990, p. 191)

In legal terms in the United States, a person is said to be totally deaf when speech sounds cannot be heard at intensities less than 82 dB_{SPL} (the intensity of ordinary speech is around 60 dB_{SPL}). The term *hearing impairment*—a more inclusive term—refers to any loss in auditory sensitivity relative to the hearing ability of the normal young adult (as summarized by the AF in Figure 11.2).

But when does hearing loss become debilitating? The ability to comprehend speech effortlessly is compromised by a 25-dB hearing loss (recall from Chapter 10 that the decibel is the unit of measurement of a sound's intensity). To experience what this loss sounds like, place your palms tightly over your ears and notice how muffled sounds become. This maneuver produces about a 25-dB reduction in sound intensity within the range of frequencies contained in speech (see Figure 11.4).

FIGURE 11.4 | Graph showing reduction in sound intensity when you cover your ears with the palms of your hand or when you insert standard hearing protectors (ear plugs).

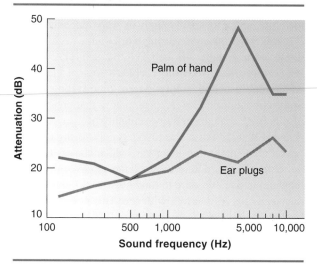

All hearing impairments can be divided into two categories: conduction loss and sensory/neural loss. **Conduction loss** stems from some disorder within the outer or middle ear, those portions of the auditory system involved in mechanically transmitting (conducting) sound energy to the receptors in the inner ear. Hearing disorders originating in these peripheral stages of the auditory system typically involve an overall reduction in sensitivity to sounds of all frequencies.

Sensory/neural loss originates within the inner ear or in the auditory portion of the brain. The associated hearing loss may extend over the entire range of audible frequencies or over only a portion of that range. Let's consider some of the more common causes of the two categories of hearing loss, starting with conduction losses.

Conduction Hearing Loss and Possible Remedies

Conduction loss can be caused by excessive build-up of ear wax in the canal of the outer ear.[2] The problem is solved by simply cleaning out the plugged-up canal. In other cases, however, the problem is more serious. Infection can cause fluid to build up in the middle ear, and if the Eustachian tube (the middle ear's pressure regulator)

[2]Known in polite circles by its proper name, *cerumen*, before it dries out and hardens, provides important lubrication for the tympanic membrane.

becomes inflamed, middle ear pressure can rupture the eardrum. Infection can also spread to the bony chamber housing the middle ear, leading to bone disease that must be treated surgically. Today, the use of antibiotics usually clears up ear infections before the symptoms reach these dangerous stages.

Middle ear infection, known as otitis media, is the most common cause of conductive hearing loss in children. During the first year or two of life, the auditory system's proper neural development requires normal acoustic input. Because otitis media interferes with that input, children who have had recurrent bouts of otitis media, particularly during the first year of life, can develop long-lasting deficits in hearing-related function, including comprehension of speech (Mody et al., 1999).

There is another conduction disorder that affects the middle ear, and this condition cannot be remedied by drugs. Called **otosclerosis,** this disorder involves the gradual immobilization of the stapes, the last of the tiny middle-ear bones in the ossicular bridge between the outside world and the inner ear. Recall that the stapes (stirrup) is the bone actually responsible for transmitting sound vibrations to the oval window, which, in turn, sets up pressure waves within the cochlear fluids. Hence, when the stapes becomes immobile, the bridge to the inner ear is destroyed. The stapes becomes immobilized by a steady accumulation of a spongy substance near the foot of this bone. This spongy substance eventually hardens, cementing the stapes in a rigid position. No one understands what triggers this disease, but it tends to occur in young adults and more often in females than in males. Fortunately, the disease can be treated, surgically. Using a microscope to guide their movements, ear surgeons can remove the immobile stapes and replace it with a plastic substitute. So long as other portions of the ear have not been affected by the disease, this surgery can restore hearing to normal levels.

Otosclerosis is a progressive disease that, in time, may spread to the cochlea. In these cases, surgery to replace the stapes cannot restore hearing to normal levels. It is important, therefore, for the physician to know beforehand whether a candidate for stapes surgery also suffers hearing loss due to cochlear pathology. But how can a physician determine the ear's functional status when an immobile stapes blocks sound's normal route to the cochlea?

The answer turns out to be rather easy. Sound has an alternate route to the cochlea, through the bones of the skull. You have probably noticed how loud the dentist's drill sounds when it contacts one of your teeth. This is because vibrations from the drill are transmitted from your tooth to your skull. The cochlea, remember, is the coiled cavity formed within the bone of the skull. Thus, when vibrations are introduced into the skull, those vibrations reach the cochlea, and if they are sufficiently strong, they set up pressure waves in the cochlear fluids. Those pressure waves behave just like the ones reaching the cochlea through the ear. They set up ripples along the basilar membrane, causing you to experience those bone-transmitted vibrations as sound.

This is called hearing by **bone conduction.** Every time you speak, part of what you hear is the sound of your voice transmitted via bone conduction. That's why a tape recording of your voice sounds strange to you but not to others. Listening to the recording, you hear your voice without the normal contribution from bone conduction ("Yes, that's what your voice really sounds like to others").

Sounds are not as loud when carried via bone conduction as when conveyed through the ear because this alternate route includes no mechanism like the ossicles for amplifying sound energy. For this reason, pure-tone thresholds measured through the skull of a person with good hearing are roughly 30 dB higher than those measured using tones delivered to the ear. Incidentally, to measure pure-tone thresholds for bone conduction hearing, a metal tuning fork is set into vibration and placed firmly against the bone just behind the ear. To return, then, to the question of whether to operate on a patient with otosclerosis: If that person's bone conduction thresholds are near normal, then the cochlea must be unaffected by the disease. Under these conditions, surgery should be successful in restoring the world of sound to the patient.

Sensory/Neural Loss

Anything that harms the cochlea (which houses the receptors for hearing) or the auditory nerve adversely impacts hearing. This section outlines several conditions that can have such an impact.

Age and Hearing Loss The most common, perhaps inevitable, cause of hearing loss is age. In industrial societies, people gradually lose sensitivity to high frequencies, a condition known as **presbycusis** (from the Greek words *presbus,* meaning "old," and *akouo,* meaning "hearing"). This selective high-frequency deafness begins at a surprisingly early age. According to one survey (Davis and Silverman, 1960), most people 30 years old are unable to hear frequencies above 15,000 Hz; and by 50 years of age, hearing is impossible beyond 12,000 Hz. Aging's progressive

assault on high-frequency hearing can eventually encroach upon the range of frequencies present in normal speech (Frisina and Frisina, 1997). For any given age group, men tend to exhibit a larger degree of hearing loss than women (Corso, 1981). These figures represent average values and therefore do not invariably apply to every individual.

Békésy, whose pioneering work on the cochlea was discussed in Chapter 10, believed that age-related hearing loss resulted from the cochlea's loss of elasticity, which diminished its ability to transmit traveling waves. Some contemporary researchers believe that presbycusis results from changes in the vasculature of the cochlea—changes that diminish the blood supply to the delicate neural elements in the inner ear, which starves and undermines the function of those elements. Still others feel that cumulative exposure to loud noise may contribute to the steady loss of hearing with age. This noise exposure hypothesis receives some support from cross-cultural studies that show normal hearing levels in 70-year-old African tribal people living in natural environments unpolluted by noise (Bergman, 1966). Whether their immunity to hearing loss is attributable to their quiet environment, or to other factors such as diet or genetics, remains undetermined. Whatever its cause, a steady loss in hearing with age is a fact of life for people in industrialized societies.

Noise Exposure and Hearing Loss All too commonly, hearing loss results from exposure to very loud noise. In most instances, the cause can be traced to damage of the fine receptor structures in the inner ear. For instance, the acoustic energy from explosions—in combat or in industrial accidents—can produce sudden, permanent deafness as a result of trauma to the organ of Corti. Even the explosion of a single 2-inch firecracker can cause a major loss in hearing (Ward and Glorig, 1961). Comparable hearing losses have been reported in people exposed to the noise of gunfire, such as hunters (Taylor and Williams, 1966), people in the armed forces, and actors in Western movies. Included in this last group of hearing-impaired individuals is the late U.S. President Ronald Reagan, whose hearing loss dated back decades, to his days as an actor (Reagan, 1990).

All the cases just mentioned involve sudden explosive noises, but this certainly is not the only type of sound that can damage the inner ear and, hence, produce hearing loss. Sustained loud noises can also lead to permanent hearing loss. Astronauts and cosmonauts are susceptible to noise-induced hearing loss because the noise level aboard a space shuttle is comparable to a continuously grinding garbage disposal. Loud music, particularly music heard through headphones, contribute to the high incidence of hearing loss among people in their late teens and early twenties (which by some estimates approaches 60 percent of that age group). In response to these concerns, manufacturers include literature with each pair of headphones, warning of the potential hazards to hearing. One manufacturer has gone so far as to install a warning light on its portable music players to indicate when the volume exceeds safe listening levels.

The loud, amplified music often encountered at rock concerts and clubs can also cause permanent hearing loss. In one study of this effect (Hanson and Fearn, 1975), pure-tone thresholds were measured in two groups of college students. One group consisted of people who attended at least one rock concert each month, while the other group consisted of people who never attended rock concerts. At all frequencies tested, which spanned the range 500 to 8,000 Hz, "attenders" had higher thresholds (that is, pure tones had to be more intense in order for attenders to hear them). Differences between the groups were small, averaging just a couple of decibels, but they were consistent. The regular concert attenders, incidentally, were entirely unaware of their deficits, and they had no complaints about their hearing.

Besides members of their audiences, pop musicians can develop hearing loss from their chronic exposure to amplified music (Axelsson and Lindgren, 1978). This effect is far from universal (Axelsson, Eliasson, and Israelsson, 1995), however, and seems to be no more severe than sound-induced hearing losses experienced by classical musicians (Royster, Royster, and Killion, 1991). By the way, can you guess which ear of violinists tends to show the greater hearing loss? If you can't, think of the instrument's usual position in the violinist's hands, and remember that the musician's head generates a sound shadow.

Chronic noise exposure also represents a serious occupational hazard for individuals who work in such environments as mechanized assembly plants, airports, and construction sites. Chronic exposure to the squeals of farm animals can also damage hearing (Kristensen and Gimsing, 1988). It is well documented that unprotected workers in noisy environments suffer permanent increases in pure-tone thresholds, with the magnitude of the loss related to length of time on the job (Nixon and Glorig, 1961; Taylor, 1965). Moreover, high noise levels in industrial settings are associated with higher accident rates, presumably because noise makes it more difficult to hear warning signals such as whistles or shouts (Wilkins and Acton, 1982). Aware of these deleterious effects of noise (and their likely legal liability in such instances), more industries attempt to shield their workers from harmful noise. This shielding can consist of earplugs (which can reduce noise levels by up to 30 dB: see Figure 11.4) and, where possible, sound-attenuating enclosures for workers.

Even people who work and play in quiet environments often experience noises such as the roar of a motorcycle or the wail of a siren. On an ordinary day, the average sound level on a Manhattan street approaches 100 dB_{SPL}, and inside a subway tunnel, even this level is exceeded as trains pass through a station. But you don't need to go to a busy city to experience a noisy environment. You can do this in the "quiet" of your own home. Ordinary household appliances can generate surprising levels of noise: a dishwasher can produce 60 dB_{SPL} of sound, a vacuum cleaner 75 dB_{SPL} and an innocent-looking garbage disposal can exceed 100 dB_{SPL} when it is chewing on hard objects such as bones. While these sound levels won't lead to *permanent* deafness, they are sufficiently loud to elevate your threshold for hearing *temporarily* after cessation of the noise. This transitory reduction in hearing sensitivity following noise exposure is aptly called a **temporary threshold shift.** The phenomenon has been thoroughly studied under laboratory conditions. We'll just mention some of the highlights and implications of that work.

In general, sound levels in excess of 60 dB_{SPL} can produce temporary threshold shifts if the duration of exposure is several hours or longer. The actual threshold shifts can vary from just a few decibels, which for all practical purposes is unnoticeable, to complete deafness. As you might guess, the size of the shift depends on the level and duration of the inducing noise. The length of time it takes for thresholds to return to normal also varies, depending on the strength and duration of noise exposure. Recovery can occur within only a few hours when the noise is modest, but it can take several days to recover following exposure to severe noise. You may have noticed a temporary threshold shift after attending a loud party or a boisterous football game—normally audible sounds such as your own footsteps may temporarily fall below your elevated threshold.

For unknown reasons, women seem to exhibit smaller threshold shifts than men when the inducing noise consists of *low* frequencies. Thus, after a male and female have been listening to the romantic roar of the ocean for some time, she may be able to hear his passionate whispers, just barely, but he won't be able to make out her whispered replies. However, just the opposite is true when the inducing noise consists of *high* frequencies. Now men exhibit smaller threshold shifts than women (Ward, 1966, 1968). So if our hypothetical couple had been listening for some time to the strains of Wagner sung by a lusty soprano, the female of the couple would be at a temporary disadvantage when it came to communicating in whispers.

Drugs and Hearing Loss   Several widely consumed drugs can have deleterious effects on hearing. One is nicotine. Chronic cigarette smokers have higher pure-tone thresholds than nonsmokers of the same age, and this loss is most pronounced at higher frequencies (Zelman, 1973). The loss is probably traceable to poor circulation, since nicotine narrows the ear's blood vessels and makes the ear's blood pressure irregular. These circulatory effects, in turn, reduce the blood supply to the cochlea.

Another common drug that affects hearing is aspirin which, when taken in large doses, can produce a temporary hearing loss (McCabe and Dey, 1965). A person taking 4 to 8 grams of aspirin per day is likely to experience anywhere from a 10- to 40-dB shift in pure-tone thresholds, with the loss often more pronounced at higher frequencies. This hearing loss persists as long as aspirin is taken, and normal hearing returns within a day or two after the person ceases to take the aspirin. Since one tablet usually contains one-fourth of a gram of aspirin, hearing won't be affected by taking a couple of aspirin. The aspirin dose that can produce hearing loss (4 to 8 grams) is the typical prescription dose for people with rheumatoid arthritis. The temporary hearing loss induced by aspirin is often accompanied by tinnitus, the high-pitched ringing in the ears we described in the previous chapter. The tinnitus, too, disappears once the consumption of aspirin ceases. It is thought that aspirin produces this effect by temporarily disabling the amplification function performed by the OHCs.

Dennis McFadden found that aspirin makes people more vulnerable to the effects of noise (McFadden and Plattsmier, 1983). In his study, McFadden exposed paid volunteers to a 2,500-Hz tone for 10 minutes. The tone's intensity was adjusted to yield around a 14-dB threshold shift. The intensity of the tone required to produce such a shift was in the neighborhood of 100 dB$_{SPL}$. McFadden divided his volunteers into two groups, giving one group 1.95 grams of aspirin and the other, 3.9 grams. The volunteers took the aspirin every day for several days. At the end of this period, he once again exposed them to the loud tone and then retested their pure-tone thresholds. Some people who were given the higher dosage of aspirin (3.9 grams)

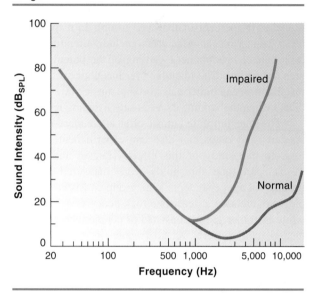

FIGURE 11.5 | An AF of an individual with about a 50-dB hearing loss in the middle and upper frequency range.

suffered a hearing loss that was almost twice what they had suffered initially. In addition, it took them longer to recover from the noise exposure, although they eventually did. People who got the smaller dose (1.95 grams) showed neither of these effects. McFadden's results imply that people routinely exposed to loud sounds should restrict their intake of aspirin or, better yet, find a substitute pain reliever. It should be noted that this study and its conclusions speak only to the question of temporary shifts in threshold, not permanent hearing loss.

Some Perceptual Consequences of Impaired Hearing

So far we have focused on some of the things that cause pure-tone hearing losses, either temporary or permanent. To appreciate the perceptual consequences of such losses, you need some idea of the frequencies and intensities of sounds in your everyday environment. Take, for example, the ringing sound made by a typical telephone, a routine sound we all rely on. Suppose that the acoustic energy associated with the sound lies between 4,000 and 8,000 Hz, and that its sound level is somewhere around 70 dB$_{SPL}$. (The actual distribution of acoustic energy varies from one type of telephone to another.) Suppose also that a person with the abnormal AF shown in Figure 11.5 is expecting a phone call. As you can see, this person suffers about a 50-dB hearing loss in the mid- and upper-frequency range,

FIGURE 11.6 | The region of the sound spectrum responsible for conveying speech sounds. Vowel sounds are primarily of low frequency; consonants cover almost the entire range.

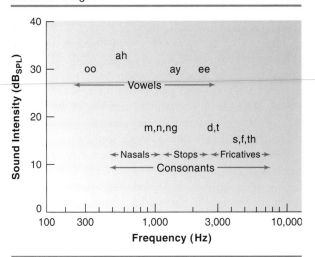

the region where much of the bell's sound lies. Will this person be able to hear the phone ringing?

As mentioned in the previous chapter, sound intensity falls off with the square of the distance between the source and the listener. So in order to hear the phone's ring, this hearing-impaired person must be within about 8 feet of the phone. Beyond this distance, the sound may be too weak to be heard. This analysis assumes ideal conditions—no distracting noises and no large objects such as walls or doors to intercept the phone's acoustic energy before it reaches the ears. Incidentally, people with normal hearing would have no trouble hearing such a bell, even over distances of several hundred feet or through walls and doors.

Let's continue with this example by assuming that the hearing-impaired person manages to hear the phone and answers it. Will that person have difficulty understanding the voice on the other end of the line? To find out, we must know something about the frequency content of human speech. Figure 11.6 shows the region of the frequency spectrum responsible for conveying speech sounds. Note that acoustic energy in speech spans the range from 250 Hz to about 8,000 Hz. As the diagram shows, vowel sounds consist primarily of low frequencies while consonants cover very nearly the entire range. Of the consonant sounds, the nasal ones (such as *m*) are the lowest in frequency and the fricative consonants (such as *f*) are the highest. In terms of their

relative intensities, vowel sounds tend to be stronger than consonants, meaning that at normal speaking levels, vowels produce larger variations in sound-wave pressure.

Armed with this information, consider the plight of the hearing-impaired individual whose AF is depicted in Figure 11.5. To understand how a telephone conversation will sound in such a case, let's first examine how the telephone itself alters the frequency composition of the voice it transmits. Modern telephones transmit frequencies only up to about 4,000 Hz, which means that the very highest frequencies contained in normal speech are missing during a phone conversation. As people are easily able to carry on a phone conversation, these omitted frequencies must be unnecessary for speech comprehension.

For our hearing-impaired person, though, more is missing than just these high frequencies. Even picking up speech frequencies that *are* available over the phone is a problem. This particular person's pattern of hearing loss means that some of the consonants (especially those such as /t/ and /d/ will be heard as mere whispers, if at all. (The slashes, / /, indicate that we are referring to the sounds of these characters, not to their names as letters of the alphabet.) These consonants, in fact, are some of the most important ingredients in speech. So a person with an AF of the type shown in Figure 11.5 will have difficulty hearing some of the environment's most important sounds, those of human speech. Simple words such as *time* and *dime* may be mistaken for one another, which, in turn, may make whole sentences confusing.

Clearly, then, a person does not need to be totally deaf in order to experience the frustrations of unintelligible speech. In a way, the plight of hearing-impaired people is particularly difficult since they hear speech sounds but are confused by the meanings. No wonder some hard-of-hearing people, including the elderly as well as young children with congenital hearing impairments (Hindley, 1997), find it easier simply to avoid social encounters.

People with good hearing can gain some understanding of the disturbing consequences of impaired hearing by wearing ear plugs for a few hours. Those who have done so testify to the psychological importance of nonverbal sounds (Eriksson-Mangold and Erlandsson, 1984). You should try this disquieting exercise yourself. In a sports store or drugstore you can purchase inexpensive ear plugs producing a 30-dB reduction in sound level. Note that a 30-dB hearing loss is sufficient to interfere with speech perception (Nadol, 1993).

Compensating for Hearing Loss

Hearing Aids   For those suffering mild to moderate hearing loss, amplifying the acoustic signal by wearing a hearing aid may provide some help, assuming the person learns to use the device correctly and uses it regularly (Tesch-Römer, 1997). Hearing aids convert sound into electrical signals, amplifying those signals by up to 60 dB, and then converting the amplified signals back into sound energy. Good hearing aids are designed to amplify mainly those frequencies necessary for adequate speech comprehension, 250 to 4,000 Hz. Thus, other sounds, such as music, may seem distorted (much like nonspeech sounds heard over a telephone).

Although not as effective as a modern electronic hearing aid, the simplest, most popular hearing aid is the hand. When the hand is cupped and placed behind the pinna, extra sound waves are funneled into the ear, raising the intensity at the eardrum by as much as 6 dB. Actually, any device or action signaling that an individual is hearing impaired improves hearing, for other people tend to speak louder if a listener is thought to have impaired hearing. Even a string dangling from one's ear can serve as an effective hearing aid (Gregory, 1992).

Cochlear Implants   Unfortunately, there are conditions in which hearing is completely lost, leaving the person with no sound perception whatsoever. In these cases, hearing aids are useless. If complete deafness results from destruction of the auditory nerve or auditory portions of the brain, there is currently nothing that can be done to relieve the condition. However, if deafness results from damage to the cochlea's hair cells and if the rest of the auditory system remains intact, there is hope for some recovery of auditory perception. A series of tiny electrodes can be surgically implanted in the cochlea itself and used to activate auditory nerve fibers directly. Called a **cochlear implant,** this tiny device can be an effective substitution for the nonfunctioning hair cells. By appropriate adjustment of the timing and level of electrical current passed through the array of electrodes, auditory nerve fiber stimulation can produce an experience of sound. The perceived pitch of that sound will depend on where along the cochlea stimulation is delivered, as well as on the timing of the pulses.

To attain some degree of functional hearing, the person with the implant wears a small microphone that picks up sounds in the environment. Those sounds are transmitted to an electronic sound processor (a small digital chip) that separates sound signals into different bands of frequencies. These, in turn, are converted into patterns of electrical stimulation of particular sets of electrodes in an array whose tips are in contact with auditory nerve fibers. Cochlear implants don't come close to restoring normal hearing, but they do allow profoundly deaf individuals, including congenitally deaf children, to achieve modest levels of speech recognition (Miyamoto et al., 1997; Svirsky et al., 2000). These auditory protheses have been successfully implanted in more than 30,000 deaf patients of all ages (Nicolelis, 2001). Navigate to www.mhhe.com/blake5 for several websites where you can read more about these devices and about the experiences of individuals who are using them.

Prolonged use of a cochlear implant alters the brain, much as prolonged exposure to sound via the normal route can. A recent neurophysiological study showed that congenitally deaf cats outfitted with cochlear implants had larger auditory portions of the brain and generated stronger, more effective neural signals, compared to deaf littermates who did not receive implants (Klinke et al., 1999). This important finding suggests that cochlear implants in congenitally deaf humans may work best when implanted early in life, while the brain's connections remain highly malleable (Rauschecker, 1999b; Lee et al., 2002).

The technology involved in cochlear implants has improved dramatically over the past 10 years, and the effectiveness of these prosthetic devices will undoubtedly improve even more as better circuitry and stimulating arrays are developed. Newer implants can produce very rapid temporal variations in stimulation rate, thereby crudely simulating speech's variations in temporal structure (Shannon et al., 1995). Despite their ability to open the doors of hearing to the profoundly deaf, cochlear implants are not without controversy: Some people object that cochlear implants in young, congenitally deaf children supplant other methods of communication available to the deaf, including sign language. As a consequence, they argue, the child is isolated from the deaf community as well as from the hearing community. Dolnick (1993) provides an evenhanded discussion of both sides of the argument.

Maybe the day will come when damaged hair cells can be replaced by newly grown, normal ones. Researchers are currently working on regenerating auditory hair cells using neurochemical agents that stimulate cell growth (Lefebvre et al., 1993). At the same time, tantalizing clues are emerging about the genetic instructions that initiate and inhibit cell growth. Such discoveries may eventually lead to interventions that halt or reverse auditory hair cell degeneration (Steel, 1998).

FIGURE 11.7 | The range of sound frequencies audible to various species at a fixed intensity of 60 dB$_{SPL}$.

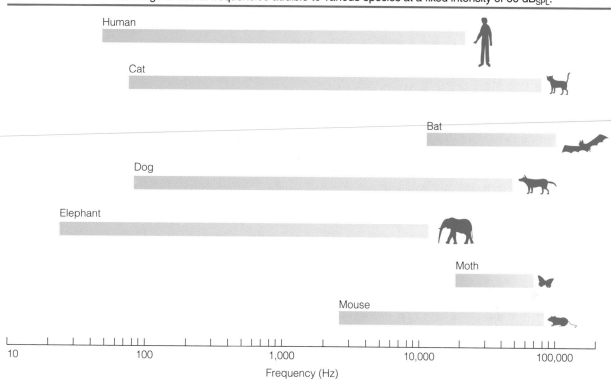

The Range of Hearing in Animals

Previously in this chapter, we used the audibility function to predict the hearing experiences of individuals with hearing loss. We can also use this function to get some idea of the auditory world experienced by different animal species. Look at Figure 11.7. Each horizontal bar shows the range of frequencies audible to a particular species, and as you can see, there is quite a diversity among animals. Many members of the animal kingdom can hear sounds outside the limits of the human ear (Fay, 1988). For example, dogs have no trouble hearing the high frequencies emitted by a device called a dog whistle, although those frequencies are at the upper limits of the human ear.

One sound that no human will ever hear is the stream of very high frequencies that bats emit. This acoustic energy bounces off objects in the bat's flight path and then echo back to the bat. As Figure 11.7 indicates, bats are able to hear these frequencies, and they use them to navigate (Griffin, 1959; Suga, 1990). As an aside, bats would deafen themselves if they heard their own high-frequency

screeches.[3] To avoid this catastrophe, the bat's ear contains a built-in mechanism that very briefly shuts down the middle ear while the screech is emitted. Then, in a fraction of a second, the ear regains its normal sensitivity, allowing the bat to hear and react to the echoes from the screech.

So far we have concentrated on normal and abnormal hearing in humans and in animals as specified by pure-tone thresholds measured under quiet conditions. Of course, most of the sounds one usually encounters are heard against some background level of noise. As it turns out, pure-tone thresholds measured in the presence of noise reveal fundamentally important properties of hearing, properties that relate to the registration of different sound frequencies. So let's turn now to consideration of this widely studied problem.

---

[3]The text website has links where you can actually hear different bat calls, including some that would ordinarily be beyond your range of hearing.

Noise Masking and Critical Bands

From common, everyday experiences, you're already familiar with the phenomenon known as auditory **masking.** It happens whenever some background noise makes it more difficult for you to hear a weak sound. Imagine listening for the phone to ring in the next room while you're taking a shower. The steady noise of the water makes the ring much harder to hear. Or think about listening to your car radio while driving on a busy expressway. To hear your radio, you must crank up the volume to compensate for the road noises.

When auditory masking is studied in the laboratory, investigators often use pure tones and specially crafted forms of background noise. As you would expect, the detection threshold for a pure tone is elevated when that tone is presented coincident with noise. This elevation in threshold constitutes auditory masking. The magnitude of masking can be conveniently expressed as the difference between masked and unmasked thresholds. The magnitude of masking varies with the noise level, which makes sense: intense noise yields greater masking (greater threshold elevation) than does moderate noise. But another, equally important determinant of masking effectiveness is the frequency content of the noise relative to the tone. This relation deserves careful analysis, for it reveals important properties of the neural processes underlying hearing.

To explore this point, we need to develop some notation. In the examples that follow, the listener has one fixed task: to detect a pure tone of a given frequency—call that frequency Hz_t—presented either alone or in the presence of noise. In the last chapter, noise was characterized as a complex of sound composed of energy at many different frequencies. When noise contains energy at all audible frequencies it is called **broadband noise** and, perceptually, it resembles the sound made by a steady waterfall. The diagram in the middle panel of Figure 11.8 pictorially represents the energy spectrum of broadband noise, with the area under the rectangle defining the frequencies present in the noise. In the laboratory, unlike in nature, the intensity of broadband noise can be systematically varied, which would correspond to varying the height of the rectangle in the graph. (In fact, energy levels in noise vary randomly from moment to moment; the rectangular shape in the drawings is meant to depict the noise's average level over time.)

In the lab, it is also possible to restrict the range of frequencies contained within the noise by passing the noise through an electronic filter; alternatively, a computer can be used to synthesize noise of specified frequency content. Using either technique, suppose we remove energy from the low- and high-frequency ends of the broadband noise spectrum. This form of energy filtering creates what is called **bandpass noise.** Pictorially, this reduces the width of the rectangle (see the graphs in the left and right panels of Figure 11.8). Perceptually it makes the noise sound different in quality and reduced in intensity. It is possible to vary systematically the width of bandpass noise while keeping the center of the distribution at the same point along the frequency spectrum. This noise center point is called the **center frequency.** Examples of this type of bandpass filtering are shown in the left-hand column. Alternatively, it is possible to keep the width of the noise constant but vary its center frequency, in effect moving the noise package along the horizontal axis. Examples of this type of filtering are shown in the right-hand column of Figure 11.8.

With these concepts in mind, let's see how the detectability of a pure tone of frequency Hz_t might be affected by various kinds of noise. First, suppose we again measure the threshold for a test tone of Hz_t while varying the bandwidth of the bandpass noise. At the same time, let's hold the noise's center frequency constant at the frequency of the test, Hz_t. This manipulation is depicted in the left-hand column of Figure 11.8. The result of the manipulation would resemble the graph in the middle panel of Figure 11.9. There we have plotted threshold elevation against noise bandwidth; the upper panel provides a reminder that the noise center frequency matches the tone frequency. The far left-hand value in the graph represents the threshold measured in the absence of noise—the unmasked threshold.

Once noise is introduced, the tone is harder to hear, as indicated by the steady increase in threshold. Broadening the noise's bandwidth produces greater and greater threshold elevation, which makes sense because the tone must be detected in the presence of more and more noise energy. Significantly, though, there is a critical bandwidth beyond which threshold is not further elevated even though additional energy is added to the noise and it sounds louder. This indicates, then, that only a limited portion of the energy in broadband noise acts to mask a tone. This effective portion was termed the **critical band** by Fletcher (1940). Why should noise energy outside the critical band have no influence on the audibility of a tone? What, in other words, is the basis for the critical band?

A clue to the answer was presented in the preceding chapter, in the tuning curves for auditory nerve fibers tuning (Figures 10.24 and 10.25). One of those curves is reproduced in the bottom panel of Figure 11.9. There you see the tuning curve for a fiber whose characteristic frequency (the one to which it is most sensitive) corresponds to Hz_t (the test frequency used in the hypothetical

FIGURE 11.8 | Schematics of the frequency distribution of acoustic energy content of noise—the shaded area in each drawing represents the presence of energy. The middle panel shows broadband noise—energy covering the entire audible spectrum. The two side panels show noise from which energy at low and high frequencies has been removed. This form of filtering produces what is called *bandpass noise*. The spectra in the left-hand panel show three examples of bandpass noise whose bandwidth varies and whose center frequency remains constant. The spectra in the right-hand panel show noise whose bandwidth remains constant and whose center frequency varies.

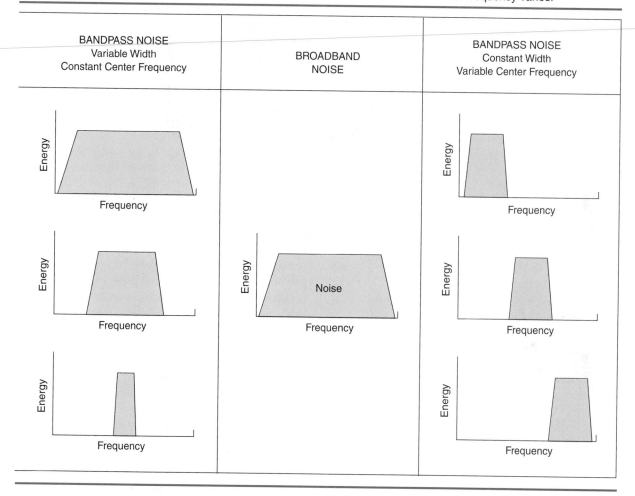

masking experiment). Since this fiber is the most sensitive to the test frequency, it mediates pure-tone detection at threshold. Of course, the fiber will also be activated neurally by noise, if that noise contains energy at frequencies to which the fiber responds.

The presence of noise, then, creates a background of elevated neural activity against which the neural activity arising from the tone must be discriminated. To produce a signal discriminable from this background noise, the tone's intensity must be higher than when the background noise is absent. The stronger the influence of the noise on the fiber's activity, the more intense the tone must be to create a signal audible within this noise.

With this in mind, think again about the result depicted in the middle panel of Figure 11.9. Presumably, the magnitude of masking increases with bandwidth because widening the bandpass noise adds more and more frequencies that stimulate the fibers mediating detection of the tone.[4] Increasing the bandwidth, in other words,

---

[4]Nerve fibers alone, of course, are not responsible for detection of tones; activity in auditory nerve fibers is passed on to neurons at higher stages in the auditory pathways that participate in hearing. But it is reasonable to consider the effects of noise on auditory nerve fibers, for masking effects arising at this level will be transmitted to higher levels.

FIGURE 11.9 | Upper panel: Schematics of narrow and wide bandpass noise used in hypothetical experiment; note that noise is centered at the test frequency Hz$_t$. Middle panel: Hypothetical result from noise masking experiment. Intensity thresholds for detection of a given pure-tone frequency are plotted as the function of the width of bandpass noise within which the tone must be detected. Threshold increases with noise bandwidth, up to a critical band beyond which threshold remains constant even though noise energy increases. Lower panel: Tuning curve for an auditory nerve fiber maximally responsive to the test frequency used in the masking experiment. The activity level in this fiber will increase as the bandwidth of the noise is increased, as long as the added frequencies fall within the tuning curve of the fiber. Frequencies outside this curve will have no effect on the fiber's activity.

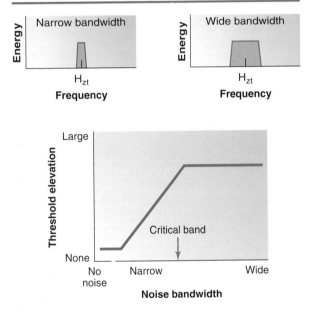

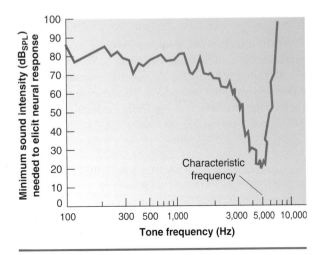

increases the fiber's background activity, making it harder to detect the tone. But at some point, additional frequencies associated with wider bandwidths fall outside the tuning curve for the fiber and, therefore, have no further effect on its background activity. At this point, there is no further elevation in threshold; masking remains constant.

Following this line of reasoning, then, the inflection point in the masking function defines the frequency limits, or tuning width, of the fiber(s) used for detection of the tone. (We use the term *fiber[s]* to denote that detection of a pure tone is probably based not on activity within a single fiber but on activity within a set of fibers, all with the same preferred frequency.) Adding more frequencies activates other fibers with different characteristic frequencies, causing the noise to get louder and to sound richer in quality. But those additional frequencies fall outside the critical bandwidth of the fiber(s) responsive to the test. This notion of the critical band in hearing should remind you of the spatial frequency channels described in Chapter 5 and measured using an adaptation procedure akin to the masking technique described here.

Suppose we repeat the masking experiment, this time using bandpass noise of constant width but varying center frequency (the manipulation depicted in the right-hand column of Figure 11.8). Results from this procedure resemble an inverted U-shaped curve. When the center frequency of the noise is well below the test frequency, the noise is audible but ineffective as a masker. Presumably, none of the noise energy stimulates the neuron(s) responsive to the test. Not until the noise begins to encroach upon the tuning curve of the detecting neuron(s) will threshold increase, and masking will grow to a maximum as more and more of the noise stimulates these neuron(s). As the center frequency of the noise exceeds this maximum, less of the noise falls within the critical bandwidth. Masking is reduced until, finally, the threshold equals the unmasked level. So varying the center frequency of bandpass noise is another way to generate evidence for the operation of critical bands in hearing.

These two examples portray the essence of the critical band: The detection of pure tones by neural processes tuned for frequency. Both employed bandpass noise and both involved varying the intensity of the test tone to measure its threshold.

There are many variations on this masking procedure. Some experiments, for instance, employ different filtering regimes for producing the masking noise, such as removing frequencies from the *center* of the noise spectrum, not its extremes, thereby producing a notch in the energy spectrum. In other experiments, the intensity of the noise, not the tone, is varied to find the level that just barely masks a pure tone of fixed intensity. In still other experiments, a brief interval of time is inserted between the onset of the tone and the onset of the masking noise. While the details of the resulting masking curves vary with the particulars of these experiments, the general conclusion remains unchanged: Noise is effective as a mask only when it contains frequencies at or near the frequency of the test tone (see Moore [1986] for a thorough review of the auditory masking literature).

In some (but not all) of these experiments, the resulting masking curves—masking strength as the function of the frequency content of the noise—resemble the tuning curves of auditory nerve fibers. For instance, a tone of given frequency is more effectively masked by noise whose frequency composition is a bit lower than the tone compared to noise composed of frequencies higher than the tone. The critical band, in other words, appears more broadly tuned on the low-frequency side. This asymmetry in masking effectiveness dovetails nicely with the asymmetric shape of auditory nerve tuning curves (recall Figure 11.9).

The importance of the critical band cannot be overstated. It plays a pivotal role in theories of tone detection, loudness perception, and pitch discrimination. Critical bands in hearing represent an important, initial stage of auditory processing potentially related to the function of the cochlea and the auditory nerve.

In these next several sections, we'll survey characteristics of sounds—loudness, pitch, and timbre—that contribute to a hearer's ability to specify the identity and location of various sounds.

Loudness Perception and Discrimination

How Loud Is Loud?

Everyone knows what is meant by **loudness**—it's your subjective impression of the intensity of sound. And most people would have no trouble agreeing whether one sound is louder than another, indicating that we all employ the concept of loudness in the same way. Yet despite this agreement, there is no way to compare each other's impressions of loudness directly. Loudness remains a subjective experience that cannot be measured with an instrument. Instead, we must rely on language to talk about the perception of loudness. By the same token, there is no way to determine whether your judgment of a sound's loudness is right or wrong, for there is no right or wrong answer—a sound's loudness *is* whatever you experience.

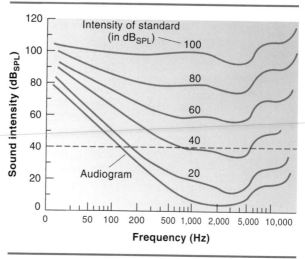

FIGURE 11.10 | Equal loudness contours.

These constraints immediately raise a barrier against attempts to study loudness perception. Fortunately, psychologists have gotten around this limitation by devising effective procedures for measuring perceived sensory magnitude, including loudness. As applied to hearing, one of these procedures requires the person to adjust the loudness of one sound until it is equivalent to the loudness of another; this method is called **loudness matching.** Another method treats the perceiver as a measuring instrument capable of assigning numbers to sounds in proportion to their loudness; this method is generally known as **magnitude estimation.** More details on those procedures are given in the appendix. The following summarizes some key features of loudness perception.

First, loudness depends on the frequency content of the sound being heard. At a given intensity level, the loudness of a very high frequency sound will be less than the loudness of a medium frequency sound of the same dB_{SPL} level. And, comparably, the loudness of low frequency tones tends to be less than that of medium frequency tones at the same dB_{SPL}. The relation between loudness and frequency is shown in Figure 11.10, which shows a family of curves, each one summarizing the intensity levels that make tones of different frequencies sound equal in loudness (Fletcher and Munson, 1933). Such curves are called **equal loudness contours,** and are produced by having listeners adjust the loudness values of various tones until each one matches the loudness of a reference tone. Notice, at least for moderately loud sounds, that low frequencies tend to sound weaker than higher frequencies of the same intensity. Manufacturers of audio equipment know this, and they design their amplifiers to allow listeners to give

FIGURE 11.11 | The growth of loudness with increasing intensity, plotted on logarithmic axes.

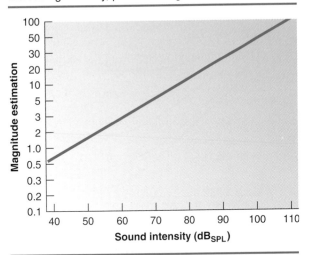

loudness grows more slowly than intensity, as previously described. (The appendix further discusses magnitude estimation, including its application to senses other than hearing.) Incidentally, the measurement of loudness is not limited to pure tones. People are also able to rate the loudness of sounds consisting of many frequencies (Zwicker and Scharf, 1965), including noise—which, as you learned in the previous chapter, consists of all audible frequencies. As a rule, the loudness of complex sounds can be predicted by adding up the loudness contributions from the component frequencies, making allowance for the ability of one sound to reduce, or mask, the loudness of others.

Neural Bases of Loudness Perception

What happens within the auditory system as the loudness of a sound varies? What, in other words, is the neural code for loudness? The most obvious answer is that the discharge rate of auditory neurons increases with sound level, and this constitutes the information for loudness. After all, we did learn in the last chapter that the activity of auditory neurons increases with intensity (recall Figure 10.26). However, while discharge rate is probably involved in the coding of loudness, it alone cannot be the whole explanation (Zeng and Shannon, 1994; Relkin and Doucet, 1997). The reason is that auditory nerve fibers increase their firing rate over a limited range of sound intensities; this range typically covers only about 40 dB (Kiang, 1968). Yet one can hear variations in the loudness of sounds over a much larger range, around 120 dB. So one's range of loudness perception exceeds the range that can be coded by individual neurons.

The nervous system has two ways to overcome the relatively limited range of individual neurons. First, as we pointed out in Chapter 10, different neurons operate over different levels of sound intensity. One set of neurons, for instance, responds to intensity changes ranging from 20 dB$_{SPL}$ to 60 dB$_{SPL}$, another set responds to intensity changes ranging from 40 dB$_{SPL}$ to 80 dB$_{SPL}$ and a third, to intensities ranging from 60 dB$_{SPL}$ to 100 dB$_{SPL}$. As you can see, each *set* covers only a 40-dB range, but as a *population* the neurons would then span an 80-dB range of intensities.

Neurons responsive to different intensity ranges would be fairly simple to "construct." It could be done by adjusting the intensity level where different neurons first start to respond. As pointed out in Chapter 10, physiological evidence points to the existence of three categories of auditory nerve fibers, distinguished by their

low frequencies a little extra boost in intensity. Such amplifiers typically have a "loudness" switch on the front of the unit, to let the listener choose the desired amount of low-frequency boost.

The curves in Figure 11.10 tell us how the loudness of one tone compares with the loudness of others. What these curves don't tell us is just how loud a given tone sounds, and how that tone's loudness varies with intensity. Does doubling the intensity of a sound double its loudness? To answer this kind of question, we can ask listeners to assign numbers to tones of different intensity levels, making sure that those numbers are proportional to the tone's loudness. This is the *magnitude estimation* technique we mentioned previously in this section. When these measurements are performed, we find that doubling sound intensity does *not* double loudness. Instead, loudness increases by only about 60 percent. To double the loudness of a sound, its intensity must be approximately tripled, which corresponds to about a 10-dB increase in intensity. This means, for example, that two people singing at the top of their lungs will not sound twice as loud as one of them singing alone. Instead, the duet's singing will sound about 1.6 times louder than a solo. To double the loudness produced by one singer requires adding two additional singers.

Figure 11.11 graphically illustrates the relation between loudness and intensity. Note that both variables are scaled logarithmically. (Recall from the previous chapter that the decibel is a logarithmic unit.) Notice that the slope of the line is less than 1.0, reflecting the fact that different threshold intensities and their different points of contact on the IHCs. For the coding of loudness information, then, one way to overcome the limited range of individual neurons is to design them to operate within different intensity ranges.

There is a second possible way that increasing sound levels may produce greater and greater neural activity, and this has to do with the tuning curves for individual auditory nerve fibers. Recall that single fibers respond to a limited range of temporal frequencies, with the preferred frequency varying from fiber to fiber (see Figure 10.24). At weak sound levels, the only fibers to respond will be those whose preferred frequencies match the frequencies contained in the sound; fibers preferring other frequencies will be unresponsive at these low sound levels. However, it is possible to recruit some of those fibers into activity by raising the sound level. At higher levels, the sound (though it does not contain those fibers' preferred frequencies) *will* produce activity in such fibers because their tuning curves do encompass frequencies contained in the sound. We caught a hint of this spread of activity in the previous chapter, where it was noted that more intense sounds caused the traveling wave to spread out over a larger region of the basilar membrane. This is tantamount to recruiting more and more nerve fibers into action at increasingly higher sound levels.

Loudness Discrimination

We turn next to loudness discrimination: the ability to tell whether one sound is louder than another. This sort of judgment can be of practical importance. Imagine, for instance, that your roommate next door is playing his stereo so loudly that you can't study. You beg him to turn it down a little, and he says he will. Just by listening, how do you tell if your roommate has kept his promise? Of course, you would have no trouble hearing a large drop in intensity, but what if the drop was more subtle? How sharp is your ability to discriminate intensity changes, and what transpires within your auditory system when you make such a discrimination?

In the laboratory, intensity discrimination can be measured by varying the intensity of a tone very gradually until a person first notices that it has gotten louder. This minimum necessary increase in intensity specifies the person's **discrimination threshold.** Although the actual value of the threshold varies, depending on the details of the experiment, people typically require about a 1- to 2-dB increase in intensity to be able to notice any increase in loudness.

A listener probably achieves such keen performance by detecting an increment in the level of neural activity produced by the tone. In the preceding example, the most informative neural activity would arise within that subset of neurons maximally responsive to the tone's frequency. For instance, if the tone is 1,000 Hz, the listener should monitor neurons whose center frequency is 1,000 Hz (recall our discussion of the critical band in the previous section).

But in real life, sounds are more complex than the pure tones used in this example. Sometimes a complex set of frequencies changes its intensities in unison, and that change must be heard in the midst of many other frequency components whose intensities are also changing. For example, an alert driver can tell that a truck's engine is malfunctioning when its high-pitched whine becomes louder than the other sounds made by the truck. In effect, the driver hears a change in the intensity of one set of frequencies (the high-pitched whine) in the midst of other sounds. The driver's perceptual task is complicated. When a truck is driven slowly, all the sounds—high-pitched whine included—are weak; when driven faster, all the sounds are louder. A number of years ago, David Green offered a compelling explanation of how people detect such intensity changes in the midst of other changeable components.

Green (1982) acknowledges that if a listener only has to detect the intensity changes of a single tone heard against an unvarying background, the traditional view is correct: Only one subset of neurons needs to be monitored, namely those tuned to the frequency of the varying intensity tone. But when other frequencies are present and their intensities are also changing from one moment to the next (as in the truck driver's situation), Green believes, a more complex process comes into play. This process uses neural information about the *relative* activity across different subsets of neurons. Green calls this process **profile analysis** because the relative neural response to various frequency bands could be represented graphically as a profile. According to Green, in an acoustically rich environment the listener picks up intensity changes by detecting a variation in the profile of activity. (This idea should be familiar to you from our discussions of orientation, spatial frequency, color, and motion perception.) To understand where Green's idea came from, let's consider two of his experiments.

In one experiment, Green, Kidd, and Picardi (1983) created a complex sound consisting of 21 different tones, ranging in frequency from 300 to 3,000 Hz, all played simultaneously. He presented this set of tones twice on each trial. In one presentation, all 21 tones were identical in intensity; in the other presentation, the intensity of one tone (1,000 Hz) was slightly greater than the intensity of the other 20 tones. The listener's task was to identify the interval in which the 1,000-Hz tone had been incremented.

Green made the task even more difficult by randomizing the *overall* intensity of the package of tones from one presentation to the next. For example, in the first presentation all the tones might be 20 dB$_{SPL}$ in intensity, while in the second presentation they might all be 50 dB$_{SPL}$. The exception, of course, was the 1,000-Hz tone, which was slightly more intense than its companions during one of the two presentations. Though the 1,000-Hz tone would be incremented *relative* to the rest, its *absolute* level of intensity would provide no clue whatever to the interval in which it had been incremented. This procedure made it impossible for the listener to base a judgment on the amount of neural activity produced by the 1,000 Hz alone. The listener was forced to compare the activity produced by the 1,000-Hz tone to the activity produced by its companions.

Using these complex tones, Green determined the minimum increment of the 1,000-Hz tone that could be heard. Despite having to rely on *relative* intensity information alone, listeners were able to detect remarkably small increments in loudness. In fact, in some instances, the detectable increment in the complex sound was about as small as that measured for the 1,000-Hz tone on its own.

In the second experiment, Green and his colleagues varied the number of different tones that accompanied the 1,000-Hz tone. Starting with a very few companion tones, Green found that adding additional tones actually *improved* a listener's ability to hear small increments in the 1,000-Hz tone. Presumably, the additional tones sharpened the definition of the neural activity profile utilized by the listener. These results and others (Green and Nguyen, 1988) show how useful profile analysis might be in explaining hearing performance in certain real-life situations.

Loudness and intensity discrimination alone seldom allow you to identify a sound source. You also need information about the frequencies that make up that sound, which brings us to the topic of pitch perception.

Pitch Perception

What Is Pitch?

Pitch—like loudness—is an entirely subjective experience. Unlike loudness, however, which can be related systematically to intensity, pitch has no single physical dimension to which it corresponds. Different sorts of sounds, both simple and complex, can have the quality of pitch. Generally speaking, **pitch** refers to the aspect of hearing that allows sounds to be ordered from low to high. A few examples will help, starting with relatively simple tones.

Perhaps you have seen a set of metal tuning forks. Each fork varies in size, which means that when struck against a hard surface, each fork vibrates at a different frequency, producing what is called a pure tone. We call the perceptual quality associated with these different frequencies *pitch*. A tuning fork that vibrates at a low frequency, such as 500 Hz, will sound lower in pitch than a tuning fork that vibrates at a higher frequency, say, 1,000 Hz.

Crystal glasses filled with different amounts of water will also generate pure tones when the glass is struck lightly or when the rim of the glass is rubbed with a moistened finger. A glass filled almost to the top with water will produce a lower-pitched tone than the same-sized glass containing just a little water. Again, these differences in pitch are associated with different frequencies of vibration, in this case determined by the volume of water filling the glass. Benjamin Franklin actually invented a musical instrument, the glass harmonica, consisting of a set of glass bowls of graduated sizes. Rubbing a bowl produced a beautiful musical sound and, in fact, Mozart composed a piece—"Glass Harmonica Adagio in C Minor and Rondo in C Major" (K. 617)—for this unusual instrument. For more on the glass harmonica, use the weblinks listed for Chapter 11 at www.mhhe.com/blake5.

The notes played on a musical instrument will also give you some appreciation of the relation between frequency and pitch, even though an instrument's sound is not a genuine pure tone. (We'll tell you why in a moment.) Take, for example, the piano. Each and every note on a properly tuned piano produces a sound of predominantly one frequency; that frequency is called the **fundamental frequency.** As you probably know, a musical note on the piano is produced when a small hammer strikes a string, causing it to vibrate. Strings differ in length, and the shorter ones vibrate more rapidly than the longer ones. Consequently, the shorter strings (which are struck by keys located toward the right-hand end of the keyboard) produce higher-pitched notes than the longer strings (which are struck by keys toward the left-hand end of the keyboard).

Figure 11.12 shows the fundamental frequencies associated with the notes on a piano's keyboard. *Frequency changes in regular steps (or intervals) as you move from the low notes at the far left of the piano to the high ones at*

FIGURE 11.12 | The fundamental frequencies associated with the notes on a piano's keyboard.

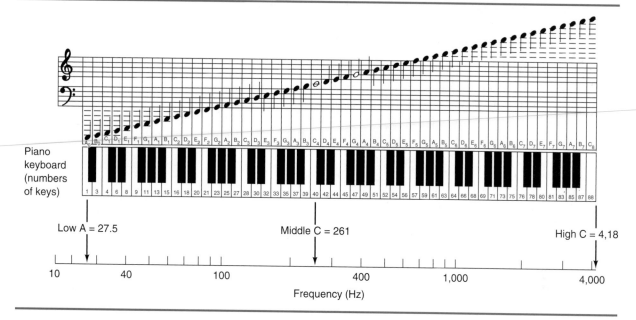

the far right. *Pitch*—your perception of the musical sounds produced by those keys—changes in the same stepwise fashion. Played in sequence from left to right, the notes are heard as the steps on the musical scale. The range of frequencies produced by a piano, 27.5 Hz to 4,186 Hz, is narrower than the total range of frequencies audible to the ear of a young adult (20 Hz to 20,000 Hz). Still, the notes on keyboard instruments such as the piano should give you some idea of how pitch changes with frequency, at least for periodic sounds like musical notes. And in Chapter 12, you'll learn how the brains of trained musicians are altered by prolonged practice discriminating musical notes.

Pitch and Frequency Are Not Synonymous   So far we have treated pitch and frequency as though they were two sides of the same coin. In reality, however, the two are dissociable. In some conditions, tones of fixed frequency sound different in pitch. For instance, the loudness of a pure tone influences that tone's pitch. You can experience this yourself by comparing the pitch of a vibrating tuning fork held at arm's length to the pitch of that same tuning fork held close to your ear. Held close to your ear, the tuning fork's note will of course sound louder, but you'll also hear that its pitch has changed, too. For instance, a tuning fork vibrating at 300 Hz sounds lower in pitch as intensity increases, even though its frequency remains constant. In contrast, a tuning fork vibrating at 3,000 Hz sounds higher in pitch as intensity increases.

The pitch of a pure tone of fixed frequency may also vary when that tone is heard within a background of noise. In particular, noise composed of frequencies lower than a tone cause the pitch of the tone to appear higher than it does when heard on its own; noise higher in frequency than the tone causes its pitch to sound lower.

One of the most intriguing disconnects between pitch and frequency is the perception of the **missing fundamental**. To explain this phenomenon we will use an example involving music. Any musical note played on an instrument produces not only a fundamental frequency but also a unique set of additional frequency components called **harmonics**. These harmonics arise because the object that produces the sound (a string, a wooden reed, vocal cords) has multiple resonant frequencies. To illustrate, Figure 11.13 shows the frequency components produced by a piano when middle C is played. (Each vertical line in the graph means that the instrument is producing sound energy at that frequency. The height of the line indicates the amount of energy, or intensity, present in that frequency.) The fundamental frequency, represented by the bold vertical line, is 261 Hz, and if asked to select a tuning fork whose pitch matched that associated with middle C, you would select one that produced this frequency. But suppose we played a sound containing exactly these same higher harmonics but omitted this fundamental. What would be the pitch of this sound with the fundamental missing? Surprisingly, the pitch remains the one normally

FIGURE 11.13 | Acoustic energy is produced at multiple, harmonically related frequencies when a given note is played on the piano (or any other musical instrument). This particular set of frequencies is associated with middle C.

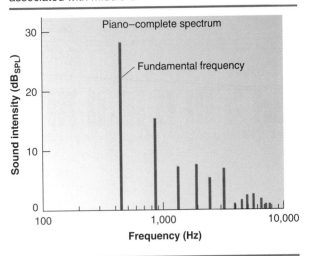

FIGURE 11.14 | The various frequency components when a guitar and an alto saxophone play the same note. Here the note has a fundamental frequency of 196 Hz.

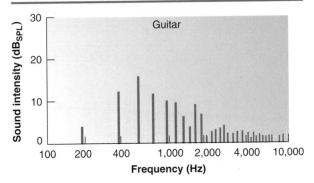

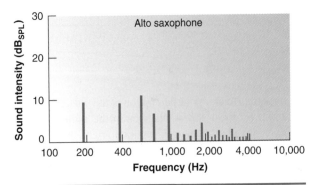

associated with middle C, even though there is no acoustic energy at 261 Hz. This demonstration, which works for various sorts of sounds including musical notes and the human voice, represents a dramatic dissociation of pitch from frequency.

It's easy to experience the missing fundamental phenomenon for yourself: Just listen to music on an inexpensive tape player or radio. The tiny speakers in such devices typically do not reproduce the lower frequency sound components at all. Still, you're able to hear these low-frequency musical notes, courtesy of your auditory system's ability to synthesize them using information contained in their higher harmonics.

The phenomenon of the missing fundamental tells us that pitch is determined by the pattern of harmonics comprising a complex sound, not just by the sound's fundamental frequency. Harmonic patterns are also responsible for producing the characteristic sound, or **timbre** as its called, that typify a given musical instrument. All people, whether musically trained or not, can easily tell whether they're listening to the musical sounds of, say, a guitar or a saxophone. This ability to identify various instruments based on sound alone rests on their differences in timbre. Look at Figure 11.14 and compare the set of frequency components produced when a guitar and an alto saxophone play the same note—one with a fundamental frequency of 196 Hz. Notice that the two instruments, while

producing notes equivalent in pitch, are generating different patterns of harmonics (the vertical lines to the right of the fundamental). These so-called "overtones" enable you to tell the guitar note from the one sounded by the saxophone. Here is another dissociation between frequency and pitch: the two instruments are producing very different set of frequencies, yet both create the same pitch quality. And you can easily hear the difference, although you have no sense of hearing the complex of harmonics associated with the guitar or with the saxophone—those frequencies "fuse" to form a single auditory experience, which we call *pitch*.

The sound quality associated with pure tones and musical notes is often referred to as *tonal pitch*. But the sensation of pitch isn't confined to these so-called periodic sounds composed of energy harmonically placed throughout the frequency spectrum. Complex, aperiodic sounds such as the whine of an engine or a person's voice have a pitchlike quality, which is termed *nontonal pitch*.

Even broadband noise can generate a sensation of pitch as its intensity waxes and wanes regularly over time (a form of intensity variation known as amplitude modulation). We mention these examples of nontonal pitch and illusory pitch because they bear on the question of the neural basis of pitch perception, the topic of the next section.

The Neural Bases of Pitch Perception

What happens in the auditory system when you perceive a sound as having a particular pitch? To answer this question, think back to the last chapter and the material on the inner ear and the auditory nerve. Recall that the basilar membrane moves up and down in response to sounds impinging on the eardrum, with the crest of this displacement depending on the sound's frequency. This displacement bends the hair cells, and this bending, in turn, triggers neural activity within the portion of the auditory nerve that innervates those hair cells. So what happens when sounds of varying degrees of complexity are heard? Let's start with the simplest situation, listening to a single pure tone.

When a pure tone stimulates the ear, one portion of the inner ear's basilar membrane will be maximally displaced, a limited set of hair cells will be disturbed and a subset of auditory nerve fibers will be activated. The frequency of a tone could be registered, therefore, by which set of nerve fibers is currently most active. As you will recall from the last chapter, such a theory is referred to as a *place theory;* it has several things in its favor. First, damage to a limited portion of the basilar membrane causes a loss in the ability to hear certain frequencies. The frequencies affected depend on the region of the membrane damaged, as predicted by the place theory (Crowe, Guild, and Polvost, 1934). Also consistent with the place theory are the results from a study in which an array of small stimulating electrodes was implanted in one cochlea of a 36-year-old man whose hearing had progressively deteriorated to the point of deafness (McDermott and McKay, 1997). This patient was particularly adept at pitch judgments since, prior to his loss, he had received training in musical instrument tuning. When mild electric current was applied to a single electrode, the man reported hearing a single tone. Different electrodes evoked tone sensations that differed in pitch. Presumably, different electrodes were contacting different fibers in the auditory nerve. Consequently, the ability of different electrodes to evoke different pitches strengthens the presumed link between activity in individual nerve fibers and pure-tone hearing.

Some aspects of pitch perception, however, cannot be explained by place theory. For instance, frequencies below 1,000 Hz produce a broad pattern of displacement along the basilar membrane. Because of this broad displacement, there is no specific place where the basilar membrane bulges maximally. Yet you have no trouble accurately identifying the pitch of these low-frequency tones. Moreover, a sensation of pitch can be produced by taking a sample of broadband noise, introducing a slight time delay, and adding the delayed noise to the original. The summed noise contains energy at all frequencies, but we hear a pitch determined by the slight time delay (Yost, Patterson, and Sheft, 1996). So, apparently, pitch perception for pure tones depends on something besides place coding.

As an alternative to place, the auditory system could use the firing rate of auditory nerve fibers to register low-frequency information. As you will recall from the previous chapter, this form of neural coding is known as the *temporal theory.* The idea here is that nerve fibers discharge periodically in synchrony with the frequency of the stimulating tone. According to the temporal theory, then, the pitch of a tone corresponds to the periodic firing of nerve fibers. And indeed, nerve fibers can fire in synchrony with tones of moderately low frequency (Rose et al., 1967). Fibers can behave, in other words, like metronomes, generating impulses in time to the frequency of a tone. Thus, information about the tone's pitch could be conveyed by the temporal pattern of fiber activity.

So working in tandem, temporal theory and place theory could convert acoustic signals into the requisite neural signals carrying information about pitch. Those signals would consist of unique patterns of activation over the entire basilar membrane and, by extension, within the ensemble of auditory nerve fibers. (Recall that this idea of ensemble coding of sensory attributes was introduced in Chapter 4, in regard to visual coding of contour orientation.) These patterns of activation would, in turn, produce patterns of activation within the tonotopically organized neurons of the auditory cortex. Functional neuroimaging techniques have identified areas in the temporal lobe of the human brain, immediately adjacent to primary auditory cortex, that are uniquely activated during pitch perception (Griffiths et al., 1998).

Our discussion of pitch perception suggests that a sound source is defined perceptually by the profile of component frequencies that it produces. This sets the stage for our next question: What stimulus properties promote the perceptual grouping of the constituent frequencies of a given sound source? What makes the various frequencies cohere into a single perceptual experience?

FIGURE 11.15 | Complex soundwave generated by tenor Luciano Pavarotti singing while an orchestra plays in the background. This excerpt lasts about 4 seconds.

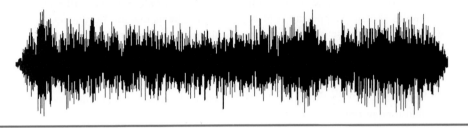

Or to frame this question in practical terms, think back to the scenario described early in this chapter: While at a loud baseball game, how can you distinguish a friend's voice from the cacaphony of other sounds streaming into your ears at the same time your friend is speaking? An answer to this question is crucial for understanding how sounds are recognized.

Sound Recognition: Judging *What* the Source of a Sound Is

Perceptual Organization of the Auditory Stream

As pointed out earlier, at any one moment our ears receive a mishmash of acoustic disturbances arising from the environment's myriad sound sources. Yet from this complex, intermixed acoustic stream we manage to hear individual auditory events, each perceptually associated with a particular external source. Look at the waveform in Figure 11.15. It's a graphic representation of the acoustic energy associated with a brief musical excerpt in which tenor Luciano Pavarotti sings while accompanied by the London Philharmonic Orchestra (he's performing the haunting "Nessun dorma" from Puccini's opera *Turandot; nessun dorma* translates to mean "No one shall sleep"). When you listen to the musical passage, this waveform—variation in amplitude over time—is all your auditory system has to work with. From visual inspection it's impossible to tell which parts of the complex waveform are Pavarotti and which are the instruments of the orchestra. Yet using just this stream of acoustic energy, your ears and brain have no trouble sorting out the various sound sources—voices and instruments—contributing to this lovely musical passage.

The auditory system, then, manages to segregate complex sound fields into separate **auditory images,** as they're known. How the ear and brain perceptually orga-

nize the components in this auditory stream has become a problem of intense interest to those studying hearing (Bregman, 1990; Yost, 1991). From the outset, realize that this problem of auditory grouping has analogs in vision, smell, and taste. In all the senses, the nervous system must organize complex sensory inputs into separate perceptual events and objects. However, each modality is able to exploit unique stimulus properties that make this process of perceptual organization possible. Early in this century, the Gestalt psychologists investigated organizing principles that promote segregation of a visual scene into distinct objects and events (some of those principles were outlined in Chapter 5). In the last decade or so, scientists interested in hearing have posed a comparable question: What are the properties that promote perceptual grouping in hearing? Some important ones are summarized in the following sections.

Common Spectral Content   We know that the inner ear parses the auditory stream into component frequencies, so it is natural to wonder whether frequency content could determine perceptual grouping. Perhaps, the reasoning goes, acoustic energy activating one set of frequency-tuned neurons is attributed to a single sound source, one that is perceptually distinct from the source associated with acoustic energy activating a different set of neurons. Construed in this way, the detectability of a test tone heard against a background of noise is impaired because the tone is perceptually combined with the noise to form a single perceptual event. But when the frequency spectrum of the noise is sufficiently removed from the tone's frequency, the tone stands out as a separate acoustic event and is, therefore, easily detected (recall Figure 11.8).

Bregman (1990) devised a number of demonstrations showing how the auditory system tends to group and sort inputs according to their frequency. Here's a brief description of one such demonstration. Bregman created a multitone sequence comprising the notes of a familiar nursery rhyme song, "Mary Had a Little Lamb." Inserted between each of Mary's notes were other notes chosen randomly from the same range of tones. When this new "hybrid" sequence of notes was played for them, people could not hear "Mary." She was hidden among random notes of similar average frequency.

Subsequently, the sequence was repeated with random, camouflaging notes drawn from a set of notes situated one octave higher in frequency than the notes comprising Mary's tune. Now "Mary Had a Little Lamb" was clearly audible. Why? The random notes in this second presentation differed in average frequency from Mary's notes, making it easy for the auditory system to segregate the two sets of notes into two streams, each grouped according to frequency proximity. This grouping of tones according to proximity in frequency is reminiscent of the Gestalt principle of grouping by visual proximity (recall Figure 5.41).

Common spectral content, while effective in some instances, cannot be the entire explanation for auditory grouping. In the natural environment, different sound sources produce frequency spectra with considerable overlap. The spectra associated with two females talking at the same time, for instance, are highly similar. Yet a third person would have no difficulty distinguishing the two speakers based on voice alone. Clearly, information other than spectral content must also be supporting perceptual grouping.

Common Time Course
If you examine the acoustic disturbance generated by some sound source, you'll find that the disturbance's frequencies fluctuate together over time. For example, the frequencies come on together when the disturbance begins, and those frequencies disappear together when the disturbance ends. In between, variations in intensity tend to match for different frequency components of the disturbance. Your voice is a good example because your utterances comprise a rich package of many different acoustic frequencies. As you speak, the components in this package of energy rise and fall in unison, and when you're finished the offsets of the constituent frequencies exactly coincide. In effect, frequency components from the same sound source form a cohesive unit, all members following the same pattern of change. In this respect, the frequency components from a sound source are like sailors in a boat: Although individual sailors differ in size and appearance, all undergo the same up and down motions, as the boat rides the waves. This common fate links the individual sailors into a single entity called

a "crew." Likewise, common fate could be one way that the auditory system registers which frequencies belong together, meaning that they come from the same source.

Evidently common temporal fate does play a role in perceptual unification, for people have trouble identifying sound sources from recordings heard without temporal modulation (McAdams, 1984). And when one frequency component within a set of frequencies is slightly out of temporal synchrony with the rest, it seems to arise from a separate source (Bregman and Pinker, 1978). It's even possible to produce recognizable speech sounds using temporal fluctuations of broadband noise whose frequency content bears no relation to those speech sounds (Shannon et al., 1995).

But temporal synchrony alone cannot be sufficient, for we can easily pick out a single individual singing in unison in a quartet even though the temporal modulations of the voices of all four are essentially identical. So, what other source of acoustic information makes it possible to segregate one singer's voice from the rest?

Spectral Harmonics
Another factor influencing whether frequency components seem to originate from a single sound source is the harmonic relationship among the components. Frequencies that are multiples of one another are said to be harmonically related. For instance, bowing the A string on a violin (without depressing the string) generates acoustic energy at the frequencies 440, 880, and 1,320 Hz; as you can see, the two higher frequencies are multiples of the fundamental frequency, which means they are harmonically related. Recall that harmonically related frequencies comprise *pitch*. In general, harmonic tones tend to group together much more readily than do nonharmonic tones (de Boer, 1956). In this regard, it is significant that many relevant sounds in the environment, especially speech and music, are made up of harmonically related frequencies. To give one example, automobile horns on newer model cars honk at F-sharp and A-sharp, a harmonically related pair that is judged pleasing to the ear (Garfield, 1983).

Familiarity
Remember Bregman's listeners who were unable to hear the tune "Mary Had a Little Lamb" among distracting tones that overlapped Mary's notes in frequency? This inability could be "cured" very easily: First listen to the tune on its own. Armed with this knowledge of what to listen for, people could hear Mary's tune among the noise of overlapping notes. In other words, prior experience with sound sources strongly influences your ability to segment a complex auditory stream.

Here's an example with which you may be familiar. Try to listen to the voice of a single speaker among a group of individuals all talking in a foreign language unfamiliar to you. It's nearly impossible, and that's because your auditory system hasn't learned to parse this complex array of unfamiliar sounds. If the people were speaking in English, you'd have little trouble picking out one voice from among the group. McFadden and Callaway (1999) studied the role of familiarity in the laboratory by having listeners discriminate small changes in one component of a simple six-tone sound. When the tones comprised a musical chord, small changes were readily discerned, but when the tones formed nonchords, changes were more difficult to hear. McFadden and Callaway's listeners were also better at detecting removal of small bands of frequencies from speech signals when the speech sounds were played in their familiar, forward direction compared to when the speech sounds were played backward. In a similar vein, errors in musical performance are much less conspicuous when those errors are melodically or harmonically related to the musical passage. The familiar context of a musical piece hides the errors (Repp, 1996).

Familiarity grows with experience, implying that the auditory system possesses a degree of plasticity when it comes to parsing complex acoustic signals. We know that infants spend the first few months of their lives becoming familiar with the sounds populating their environment (Kuhl, Tsao, and Liu, 2003), especially the vocalizations of those around them. Moreover to facilitate this learning process, mothers unwittingly accentuate phonetic characteristics of speech that define words and word boundaries when speaking to their infant babies (Kuhl et al., 1997; Kuhl, 2005).

There is one other rich source of information that promotes perceptual grouping of constituent frequencies into a coherent sound source, and that is information specifying sound location. By tagging where in space sound energy arises, it is possible to group frequencies arising from that single location and, thereby, define a single sound source. The next section is devoted to this problem of sound localization.

Sound Localization: Judging *Where* a Sound Comes From

Hearing involves more than just recognizing sounds. One also has a sense of the direction from which those sounds are coming. This ability to perceive the location of sounds in space—termed **sound localization**—can be as important as the capacity to identify those sounds. What good is it to recognize the scream of a firetruck's siren if

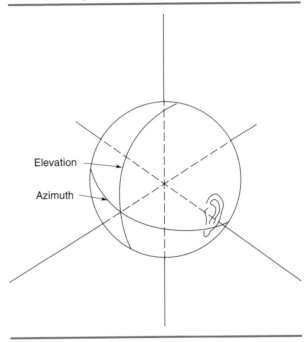

FIGURE 11.16 | Sound location is specified in terms of azimuth (position along the horizontal plane) and elevation (position along a vertical plane).

you can't tell from which direction it is approaching? How frustrating it would be for a parent to hear the frightened cries of a lost child and yet be unable to pinpoint the origins of those cries. Fortunately, hearing does have a distinct spatial quality—sounds nearly always appear to come from somewhere. Moreover, perceiving a sound's location occurs effortlessly and automatically, as common experience tells you. In fact, even newborn infants will turn their eyes toward the source of a sound (Butterworth and Castillo, 1976; Wertheimer, 1961); sound localization is a perceptual ability present from the day of birth. This section discusses the auditory information that endows sounds with this quality of spatial location.

From the outset, keep in mind that there is *no* inherent spatial information in the acoustic signals arriving at an ear. In vision, of course, left/right and up/down spatial relations are faithfully retained in the optical image formed on the retina. But in hearing, there is simply nothing contained in the acoustic image that corresponds to these relative locations. Spatial coordinates must be computed from available auditory information.

In specifying spatial location of sounds, the terms *azimuth* and *elevation* will sometimes be used (see Figure 11.16). Azimuth refers to the horizontal direction of

FIGURE 11.17 | Sound intensity at the two ears varies with the location of the sound source. This variation in interaural intensity difference depends on frequency.

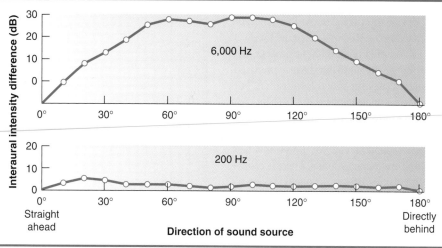

a sound relative to the listener's head; elevation refers to the vertical direction of the sound relative to the head. As you will learn, these two coordinates seem to be specified by different sources of information.

One thing seems clear: Accurate sound localization is best when we can listen to sounds using both ears. Working together, the ears, like the eyes, enable one to locate objects in three-dimensional space. As people with unilateral hearing loss will testify (Wilmington, Gray, and Jahrsdoerfer, 1994), sound localization using just one ear can be difficult.[5] From the previous chapter, you already have some idea about the information afforded by listening with two ears: Sound waves from the same source arriving at the two ears may differ in intensity and in time of arrival, depending on the location of that source relative to the head. The following sections discuss both these sources of binaural information in greater detail and evaluate their effectiveness. We should stress one point. When tested on binaural sound localization tasks, listeners never actually hear differences in intensity between the two

ears. Nor can they tell that sound arrives at one ear ahead of the other. Instead, listeners hear a single sound originating from a particular direction relative to straight ahead.

Interaural Intensity Differences

Figure 11.17 summarizes how **interaural intensity difference (IID)** varies with the azimuth of a sound source. These data were obtained by positioning a sound source at various points around the horizontal plane of an artificial head outfitted with microphones in each "ear" (Shaw, 1974). The vertical axis plots the intensity difference between the sounds arriving at the two ears. The horizontal axis plots the position, or azimuth, of the sound source relative to the straight-ahead position. Two curves are shown, one using a 6,000-Hz tone and the other using a 200-Hz tone. Notice that when the high-frequency (6,000-Hz) tone is located to the side of the head, the interaural intensity difference grows to more than 20 dB.

Notice also that for each and every IID (values on the vertical axis), there are *multiple* distinct locations (on the horizontal axis) from which a sound source could produce that intensity difference. Take, for example, sound originating from a location directly behind the head. As Figure 11.17 shows, this location yields an IID value of zero. Yet the same value—zero—occurs when the sound originates from a location straight in front of the head.

---

[5]Briefly presented sounds are particularly difficult to localize when using just one ear, but monaural localization performance improves significantly with long, continuous sounds. Under these conditions, people can turn their heads, which modulates the intensity of the monaural sound, providing additional information specifying location (Perrott, Ambarsoom, and Tucker, 1987).

Besides this pair of sound source locations, there are other positions where IID provides ambiguous information. Since distinctly different spatial locations can produce the same information about interaural intensity, that ambiguous information could lead to confusions about the location of a sound source. These confusions can, in fact, occur, but we'll postpone describing why until we have completed our review of the binaural cues for sound localization. For now, let's continue our examination of Figure 11.17.

As the 200-Hz curve indicates, IIDs are essentially nil when the sound source consists of low frequencies. This means that IID is a less potent cue for low-frequency sounds than it is for high-frequency sounds. There is a simple reason why the intensities of low frequencies are so similar at the two ears. With low-frequency sounds, the wavelength of the sound wave is actually longer than the diameter of the head, which is about 20 centimeters. For the sake of comparison, the length between successive peaks of a 900-Hz tone is approximately 40 centimeters, double the diameter of the head. The head, in other words, is too small to interfere with propogation of low-frequency sound waves. Because they are unimpeded by the head, these low-frequency waves lose nothing in the way of intensity from one side of the head to the other. High frequencies, however, are more effectively blocked by the head. Their waves are too small to avoid the shadowing effect of the head. Consequently, the head more effectively blocks sound waves of high frequency from reaching the farther ear, thus weakening their intensity at that ear. Because of this physical property of sound, IIDs associated with high-frequency sounds will be larger than those associated with low-frequency sounds; in fact, IID falls to zero at frequencies below 1,000 Hz.

Think for a moment what this means for species whose head sizes differ from ours. In particular, small heads (such as a mouse's) will generate very little "shadowing" effect. This means that a mouse's IID will be vanishingly small for these frequencies, despite the fact that for humans the same frequencies produce a potent IID.

Next let's review the other binaural source of localization information, **interaural time difference (ITD).**

Interaural Time Differences

Figure 11.18 summarizes how the time of arrival of a sound at the two ears varies with the location of the sound source relative to the head. These measurements were made in much the same way as the ones described above, only using brief clicks as sound stimuli in this case (Shaw, 1974). The horizontal axis again plots the azimuth of the sound source; the vertical axis, the difference in time of arrival of

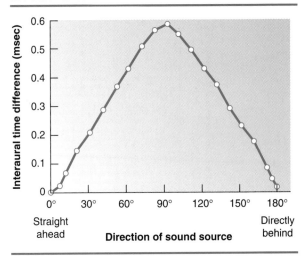

FIGURE 11.18 | The time of arrival of sound at the two ears varies with the location of the sound source.

the sound at the two ears. As this graph shows, a sound coming from somewhere off to the side of the head strikes one ear before the other. The largest difference in time of arrival occurs when the sound source is located directly to the side of the head, in which case the ITD is somewhere around 600 to 800 μsec (1 μsec equals one-millionth of a second); the precise value depends on the size of the head. Sounds located just slightly to the left or the right of the straight-ahead position produce ITD values as small as 10 to 20 μsec. Listeners can discriminate, however, among these slight differences in location, indicating that the auditory system is remarkably sensitive to ITD information.

As with the case of interaural intensity differences, interaural time differences can be potentially ambiguous: The same values of time difference (vertical axis) can be produced by sources in multiple, different locations (horizontal axis). For instance, a zero interaural time difference could arise from a source located either directly ahead of the listener, directly behind, or anywhere on the median plane connecting these two points.

The Cone of Confusion

In a moment, we will look at results from experiments that have examined the ability of people to localize sounds in auditory space. First, however, it will be helpful to point out a fundamental limitation in the information provided by IID and ITD, the two binaural sources of location information. For any given IID or ITD, there is a family of potential spatial locations which could generate that interaural

FIGURE 11.19 | The cone of confusion, a conical surface defining locations where a sound source would produce the same value of interaural time difference or the same value of interaural intensity difference.

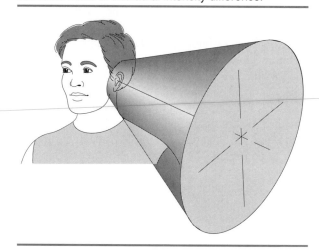

difference. To a first approximation, the surface describing these points of ambiguity (constant IID or constant ITD) corresponds to a cone and, for this reason, the set of ambiguous locations is termed the **cone of confusion** (Woodworth, 1938). You should understand that different values of IID and ITD have different associated cones of confusion; one exemplar is shown in Figure 11.19.

This concept of the cone of confusion is important, for it means that neither IID nor ITD provides *unique* information about sound location. Using IID or ITD alone, listeners should have difficulty distinguishing sound sources located anywhere on this hypothetical surface. To the extent that listeners unambiguously localize a sound when provided with a given interaural difference, there must be additional information available to specify, or disambiguate, exactly where on the associated cone of confusion the sound source resides.

Given this description of IIT and ITD and the potential points of confusion, just how well *do* people perform on localization tasks?

The Effectiveness of Interaural Time and Intensity Differences

The classic study of sound localization was performed by Stevens and Newman (1934), and their results highlight several major points about IIT and ITD. For their experiment, Stevens and Newman seated a listener on the roof of a building, where the outdoor setting eliminated potential sound reflections from walls and ceil-

ings. To minimize disturbance from extraneous sounds such as the sound of passing cars, data were collected during the early hours of the morning. Extending out from the listener's chair was a long metal arm that could rotate around the listener's head in the horizontal plane at ear level. Thus, they varied azimuth while holding elevation constant. Attached to the end of this mechanical arm was a loudspeaker that could play pure tones of various frequencies. Listeners sat blindfolded with their heads held very still. They were instructed to point in the direction from which the sound seemed to originate, and the measure of sound localization was accuracy in reporting position. For tones below 1,000 Hz, localization accuracy was high. But for tones between 2,000 and 4,000 Hz, errors became increasingly frequent. At still higher frequencies, performance again improved, eventually becoming as good as it had been with low frequencies. Stevens and Newman took these results as support for the **duplex theory** of sound localization, which says listeners use one source of information (ITD) to localize low-frequency sounds and a different source of information (IID) to localize high-frequency sounds. Presumably, the transitions in performance corresponded to shifts in the cue used to make localization judgments. The high error rates at intermediate frequencies indicate that this is a region where neither time nor intensity is particularly effective.

Following Stevens and Newman, many other researchers have studied sound localization. Some have used an array of loudspeakers surrounding a listener sitting in an anechoic chamber, the listening environment described in Chapter 10 (Wightman and Kistler, 1980; Oldfield and Parker, 1984a, 1984b). Sound is played from different speakers, and the listener indicates where the sound comes from. In other experiments, listeners have been outfitted with headphones through which sounds are played (Mills, 1960; Jeffress and Taylor, 1961).[6] In general, the results from all these experiments support the conclusions reached by Stevens and Newman: Sound localization depends on interaural time differences at *low* frequencies and on interaural intensity

---

[6]Headphones have the advantage of allowing the experimenter to vary interaural time and interaural intensity independently, making it possible to examine the effectiveness of the two cues separately. Headphones have the disadvantage of producing a sound sensation localized inside the head, not in the external environment. Consequently, headphone studies typically ask listeners to judge the lateralization of sound—whether it comes from the left or from the right of midline.

differences at *high* frequencies. In most ordinary listening situations, sounds consist of both high and low frequencies, which means both sources of information, time differences and intensity differences, are available for localizing those sounds. Wightman and and Kistler (1992) believe that ITD dominates in this situation.

Incidentally, people blind from birth are better at sound localization than sighted individuals (Lessard et al., 1998; Ashmead et al., 1998). Blind people's superior localization ability might be connected to activity-dependent sharpening of tuning in neurons that code spatial location. This sharpening could result from heightened reliance on sound as a spatial cue. Recall from Chapter 10 that neurons in the auditory cortex become sharply "tuned" for given locations when animals are forced to rely on hearing to get around (Korte and Rauschecker, 1993). Indirect evidence points to a similar sharpening in human cerebral cortex (Röder et al., 1999). It is also possible that brain areas normally devoted to vision are appropriated for hearing in blind individuals, providing more neural territory for registration of auditory space. This possibility is not as far-fetched as it sounds at first. In fact, regions of the brain that are normally devoted to vision can be activated by auditory stimuli in blind people (Alho et al., 1993; Leclerc et al., 2000), just as visual stimuli can activate auditory cortex in some blind individuals (Finney, Fine, and Dobkins, 2001). Although people who were blind from a very young age are apt to show larger changes, results with people who had sight until their teenage years demonstrate that even mature brains can undergo experience-dependent reorganization (Kujala et al., 1997).

The Cocktail Party Effect: Masking and Unmasking Sound

Our discussion of sound localization was prefaced by stating that "location" is an effective cue for helping us to segregate the stream of auditory signals arriving at our eyes. Being able to spatially localize sound sources thus makes it possible to pick out and attend to one sound from among many in a noisy environment. Because this skill is often required at loud parties, it is aptly called the **cocktail party effect.** Here's how this phenomenon is brought from everyday experience into the laboratory.

Imagine wearing headphones and having an audible tone delivered to your left ear only. Now suppose noise is also delivered over the headphones to that same ear, with its intensity adjusted so that you are no longer able to hear the tone; the noise, in other words, masks the tone.

Finally, suppose the same amount of noise is added to the other ear as well, the one *not* receiving the tone. Ironically, this additional noise in the other ear actually unmasks the previously masked tone, making it audible once again. The difference in the tone's audibility with and without noise to the other ear defines the **binaural masking-level difference (BMLD),** which is a measure of **binaural unmasking.**

Besides unmasking the tone, adding noise to the other ear does something else as well—it seems to place that tone and the noise in *different* locations. With the tone and noise going to the left ear only, both are localized at that ear. But noise introduced to the right ear pairs with the noise already going to the left ear. This now causes the noise to be localized in the center of the head, no longer in the same position as the tone. In other words, when the noise and tone coincide in apparent location, masking is strong; when the two are separated, masking is weak. Binaural unmasking illustrates, then, how localization of sounds can promote perceptual segregation of acoustic events.

Binaural unmasking enables you to focus on one person's voice in the presence of competing conversations elsewhere in a room. However, you are not totally oblivious to those other conversations. If your name happens to be mentioned in one of those conversations, your attention will be drawn to what is being said. This implies that your auditory system continues to analyze unattended sounds. Researchers interested in selective attention have studied this phenomenon by presenting different, unrelated messages separately to the two ears to learn what aspects of an unattended message are registered in the absence of attention (Moray, 1970).

Design Features That Minimize Mislocalization Errors

So far we discussed cues for sound localization and illustrated how localization can support grouping of sound sources. Still, people sometimes do make errors in sound localization, and those errors tend to be most common at particular positions in auditory space. As you now should be able to anticipate, those positions include the ones where information about interaural time and interaural intensity is ambiguous. Two such positions were mentioned earlier, straight ahead and straight behind. Sounds from either of these positions arrive at the two ears simultaneously and with equivalent intensity. So it is not surprising that sounds arising from these two positions are sometimes mislocalized, especially when the sound consists of a narrow band of frequencies (Butler, 1986); broadband noise yields fewer front/back confusions (Makous and Middlebrooks, 1990) and the presence of sound reflecting surfaces helps, too (Guski, 1990). Besides directly in front and directly behind, there are other positions in space where time and intensity cues are also ambiguous; these constitute the cones of confusion described previously.

In view of these multiple points of potential confusion, it is surprising that people don't mistake the direction of sounds more often than they do. In fact, there are two reasons why you normally are not confused about the location of sounds. The first reason has to do with *head movements*. In sound localization experiments involving an array of speakers, the listener's head remains in a fixed position. Ordinarily, though, you are free to move your head when listening to a sound, and these head movements can eliminate potential confusion arising from ambiguous localization cues. To illustrate, imagine hearing a sound from a source located directly behind your head. While interaural time and intensity information is momentarily ambiguous, you can eliminate this ambiguity simply by turning your head in either direction. The sound source will no longer be symmetrically located between your two ears, and the available localization information will now specify the sound's location unambiguously. Moving your head changes the pattern of interaural differences set up by a stationary sound source, thereby clearing up any initial confusion about where a sound comes from. Note, however, that head movements are effective in eliminating ambiguity only if the sound is of sufficient duration to allow you to listen to it while turning your head; head movements are too slow to help localize brief sounds, such as the snap of a twig (Pollack and Rose, 1967).

A second factor that minimizes the incidence of localization errors has to do with the *pinnas*. Without them, people have more trouble judging the locations of sound sources (Burger, 1958). You can demonstrate this for yourself by performing the following test. While you are blindfolded, have a friend stand close enough to you that he can snap his fingers at various positions around your head. See how well you can tell where that sound comes from. Now repeat this test while wearing earmuffs or a set of headphones, either of which largely eliminate any contribution from the pinnas. While still able to hear the sound, you'll find it more difficult to pinpoint exactly where the finger-snap originates, especially when that sound originates from either directly in front of you or directly behind you. This simple exercise demonstrates that the pinnas make it easier to locate sound.

But why is that so? It is thought that the pinnas aid localization because sound bounces around in the folds of the pinnas before entering the ear canals. The number and direction of the bounces depend on the direction from which the sound originated. The pinnas, in other words, alter the frequency spectrum of the acoustic signal entering the external canal, imposing a unique "spectral signature" that specifies the direction from which that sound arrived at the ear (Batteau, 1967; Kulkarni and Colburn, 1998). The auditory system, in turn, manages to "read" that signature, thereby avoiding any ambiguity about the location of the source of that sound wave.

Pinna cues would be particularly useful for specifying the vertical location of a sound source—its elevation—because binaural cues are plagued by ambiguity in this dimension. In fact, listeners are able to determine the elevation of a source with some accuracy. Oldfield and Parker (1986) compared monaural to binaural localization performance for brief bursts of noise positioned at various locations throughout the auditory field. For elevation judgments, the two conditions were very similar, implying that pinna cues (the only source of information available in the monaural condition) specify a source's elevation. For azimuth judgments, however, listeners performed quite well with two ears but poorly when forced to use one ear only. This disparity between monaural and binaural performance implies that IID and ITD are the primary sources of information for judgments of azimuth (but see Butler, Humanski, and Musicant, 1990). Middlebrooks and Green (1991) provide a comprehensive review of the localization literature, especially studies bearing on the question of information supporting judgments of azimuth and elevation.

Because the size and shape of the pinnas vary so much from person to person, this labeled information about a sound's direction should be highly specific to one's own ears. Thus, if you and a friend were to trade pinnas, your ability to localize sound might be impaired. Such an impairment has actually been demonstrated by Fred Wightman and Doris Kistler (Wightman and Kistler, 1989a, 1989b). They placed a tiny microphone inside each ear canal of a person and recorded sounds originating from speakers located at various positions around the person's head. Because of the position of the two microphones, the sounds they picked up had already been influenced by the person's pinna. These measurements confirmed that a given sound is affected differently by different shaped pinnae—each pinna imposes its own unique signature on the incoming sound (see Figure 11.20).

FIGURE 11.20 | Soundwave recordings made from the right ears of two different individuals listening to broadband sound broadcast from a speaker located at different elevations in front of the head. The curves plot the degree to which the soundwaves were altered by the pinna (values of 0 denote no alteration). The solid curves correspond to the person's ear pictured on the left and the dotted curves to the persons ear pictured on the right. Although the incoming soundwaves were always identical, the individual's pinna altered the frequency spectrum of the sound.

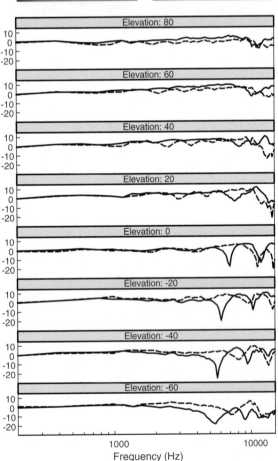

Wightman and Kistler also had people judge the location of the sounds, and as expected, few errors were made except for the ambiguous sound locations we mentioned previously. Wightman and Kistler collected localization judgments and ear canal recordings from several people. They then played back those recorded sounds over headphones and had the same people once again make localization judgments. Listening to the sounds that had been recorded through their own ears, people had no trouble accurately localizing sounds. But when listening to sounds that had been recorded through someone else's ears, people were less accurate at localization.

Sound localization is also impaired when flexible plastic material is molded into the cavities of a person's outer ears, thereby altering the reflecting surfaces of the pinnas (Hofman, van Riswick, and van Opstal, 1998). When the plugs are worn continuously for six weeks, performance returns to normal, implying that the listener has learned to hear through his or her modified ears. Remarkably, the person exhibits perfectly normal sound localization when the plugs are removed, suggesting that the original "pinna signature" remained in sensory memory, peacefully coexisting with the newly learned signature.

Mislocalization: Sound Heard through Headphones
This discussion of the role of head movements and the pinnas in sound localization raises an interesting point. You've probably listened to music in stereophonic sound over a set of headphones. If so, you know that the sounds usually seem to originate from various places *within* your head, not from external locations. At this point you should be able to figure out why stereophonic music heard over headphones sounds the way it does. Typically, music is recorded from an array of many microphones placed at various positions around the musicians. Furthermore, technicians then combine the signals from those microphones to achieve whatever sound balance they desire. So by the time it reaches your ears over the headphones, the sound bears little resemblance to the binaural stimulus you would have heard in person.

Using just two microphones, recordings can be made that mimic what would be heard live. Music recorded in this manner and heard over headphones *does* seem to emanate from out in space and not within your head (Koenig, 1950; Belendiuk and Butler, 1978). Even then, however, you must hold your head still for the illusion to be compelling. Here's why. The microphones were stationary at the time the recording was made, so the reproduced sound carries none of the changes in interaural time or intensity that would be produced by head movements. When you do move your head, the brain receives contradictory information: the vestibular system (the one responsible for signaling head orientation) informs your brain of your head movement, but the auditory system does not report an associated change in interaural time or intensity. These contradictory messages reduce the otherwise compelling illusion that sounds heard over a headphone appear to come from out in space. Auditory researchers are now trying to devise a computer-controlled headphone system that senses the direction and magnitude of head turns and immediately alters the IID, ITD, and pinna spectra in the stereo signals fed into the headphones. This technique would allow a computer to generate compelling and realistic acoustic experiences of virtual sound fields over headphones worn by a freely moving head. For example, a listener seated comfortably in a chair could experience all the sounds and variations in sound that would might be produced as that listener strolled through some remote environment. Because the sounds would include subtle variations in IID, ITD, and pinna spectra produced by changes in the listener's head position, the experience of this virtual soundscape would be incredibly realistic.

Mislocalization: Ears versus Eyes   Under some circumstances sound is incorrectly localized because of contradictory information provided by the eyes. And such circumstances tell us a lot about interactions between the senses. A movie theater is one very familiar situation in which the eyes fool the ears. Speakers in a movie theater are usually positioned on either side of the screen, yet the audience hears the sounds coming from the appropriate sources pictured on the screen. Ventriloquism is another example of this kind of mislocalization—the sound is perceived to come from the mouth of the ventriloquist's dummy, when, of course, it actually comes from the mouth of the ventriloquist. Both of these examples underscore vision's dominance over hearing when it comes to specifying the location of events (Welch and Warren, 1980).

Probably the most convincing proof of vision's dominance is provided by the *pseudophone*—the odd-looking listening device pictured in Figure 11.21. The pseudophone effectively interchanges input to the two ears, causing the left ear to hear what would normally be heard by the right, and vice versa. What this binaural swap does to sound localization depends on whether you listen with eyes open or closed (Young, 1928). Imagine that you are wearing a pseudophone and are sitting between two friends, a male to your left and a female to your right. They are arguing. With your eyes closed, the male's voice

FIGURE 11.21 | A pseudophone reverses the inputs to the two ears, sending the sound that normally would go to the left ear to the right ear instead, and vice versa.

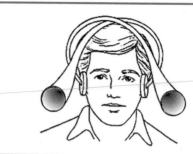

will sound as though it were coming from your right and the female's voice from your left. Although wrong, this way of hearing the two voices is not surprising; it is caused by the reversing mechanism of the pseudophone. What is surprising, however, is what you hear with your eyes open. Now the male's voice will seem to originate from your left and the female's voice from your right. While this corresponds to the true seating arrangement, your brain has to *ignore* interaural time and intensity cues to arrive at this perception. Your brain, in other words, believes your eyes, not your ears.

In a way, this bias toward vision makes some sense. For one thing, sounds can bounce off solid surfaces and be reflected to your ears in the form of echoes. Hence, the direction from which sound arrives at your ears may not always correspond to the actual location of the sound source. The same is not true of vision—the light reflected from an object travels in a straight line to your eye. Thus, the principles of optics ensure that the light arriving at your eyes reliably specifies an object's actual location.

Physics offers another reason why your brain might trust your eyes more than your ears—sound travels much more slowly than light. Consequently, the sounds from a distant object (such as an airplane in flight) can misrepresent the object's true current position, whereas the light from that object almost never lies. Considered together, these properties of light and sound may have encouraged the brain to rely more on vision for localization. But, as the next section discusses, there may still be an intriguing link between eyes and ears when it comes to localization.

Do the Eyes Control the Accuracy of Sound Localization?
Accuracy of sound localization varies widely from one species of animal to another. In an attempt to discover what factors govern sound localization ability, Heffner and

FIGURE 11.22 | Graph showing sound localization acuity for a variety of animal species as a function of the size of the high acuity retinal region estimated from ganglion cell density in those animals.

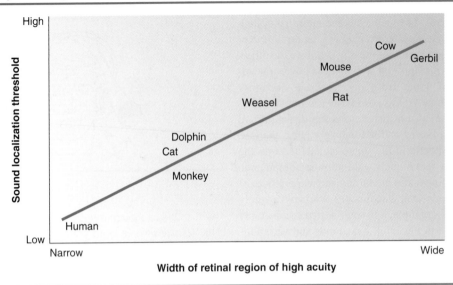

Heffner (1992) surveyed the lifestyles and anatomies of various species. Two related factors stood out; surprisingly, both had to do with vision. Species with panoramic vision—eyes located on the sides of the head—exhibit relatively crude acuity for localizing sounds; these species, incidentally, tend to be prey, meaning they are hunted by predators. Species with narrow visual fields—both eyes located in the front of the head—exhibit superior localization acuity; these species are typically predators. Prey species also tend to have regions of maximum acuity extending over larger portions of the retina than do predatory species (see Figure 11.22).[7] From Chapter 9 you will remember that one purpose of eye movements is to direct the region of highest acuity to the object of regard. If that region of high acuity covers a large region of the retina, eye movements need not be as precise. Small, concentrated regions of high acuity, in contrast, require the eyes to be very accurately directed at the object of regard.

So what does this have to do with sound localization? We know that sounds can reflexively trigger head movements toward the source (Thurlow and Runge, 1967) and that head movements also serve to direct the eyes to an ob-

ject of regard. Putting two and two together, Heffner and Heffner (1992) proposed that sound localization operates to guide the eyes to a source of interest. If eye movement accuracy is crucial (as it is with frontally placed eyes with narrow regions of high acuity), sound localization ability must also be good. But if eye movements need not be precise (because the area of maximum acuity is more extensive, as it is in animals with panoramic vision), sounds need not be localized with great accuracy. This putative linkage between eye movements and sound localization is further strengthened by physiological evidence showing that neurons in certain brain structures, including the superior colliculus, may be activated by either visual patterns or sounds (recall Chapter 4).

Heffner and Heffner note that this relation applies only to terrestrial animals that don't rely on echo location. They conjecture that a major role for hearing is to direct visual attention to sound-producing objects of potential interest within the environment.

Sound Localization: Judging the Distance of a Sound Source

So far our discussion of localization has concentrated on the horizontal and vertical positions of sound sources. But there's another dimension to sound location, and that's the distance from the listener to the

---

[7]For each species, the region of maximum acuity was determined by assessing retinal ganglion cell density. You may want to look back to Chapter 3 to refresh your memory about the relation between ganglion cell density and acuity.

sound source (*absolute distance* to use the term introduced in Chapter 8). How good are we at judging distance based on sound alone?

When tested indoors, people are pretty good at judging sound source distance (Mershon and Bowers, 1979). Here the auditory system has access to a cue that is independent of the loudness of the source. The system can compare the sound energy reaching the ears directly from the source to the reverberant energy reaching the ears after reflection from solid surfaces such as room walls (Bronkhorst and Houtgast, 1999). When sounds containing this reverberation cue are synthesized and heard over headphones, listeners are very accurate at judging the apparent distance of the virtual sound, so long as the simulated environment contains multiple reflecting surfaces.

When tested outdoors where reverberation is missing, people don't do as well at judging distance based on sound. Rather, they tend to *underestimate* the distance between themselves and a sound source. In this outdoor setting, people probably rely on the loudness of the source, since loudness depends on intensity, and intensity varies with the square of the distance between the listener and the source. However, loudness is not a particularly reliable cue for a stationary listener unless the person is familiar with the source and knows how loud it typically sounds. If the listener is allowed to move relative to the source, the rate of change in loudness provides useful distance information (Ashmead, Davis, and Northington, 1995).

Sometimes the sound source itself moves while the listener remains stationary, and when this happens you can get a clear sense of the changing distance from you to the source. To illustrate, think about standing on a subway platform and hearing an approaching train—the steady increase in the noise produced by the train gives a clear sense of its impending arrival. This growing sound intensity is analogous to the expanding retinal image you receive when an object moves rapidly toward you (recall Chapter 9), a situation we defined as visual looming. By the same token, a sound source steadily increasing in intensity constitutes **auditory looming.** Of course, ordinarily we see approaching objects at the same time that we hear them, so we're unaware of the potency of auditory looming on its own. But the next time you're on a subway or a train platform, close your eyes and listen to the approaching train—the sense of looming can be impressive, not to mention frightening (do *not* attempt this exercise without having a friend hold your hand, to be sure that you remain safely on the platform). By the way, if you can afford to miss your train, hang around on the platform and listen to the train as it pulls away—the receding sound gets

steadily weaker in intensity, a telltale sign that the source is moving away from you. When studied in the laboratory, the perception of approaching and receding sounds reveals some interesting biases that turn out to make very good sense. For one thing, listeners reliably overestimate the amount of change in a sound that is steadily increasing, relative to that same sound played backward so that its loudness steadily decreases (Neuhoff, 1998). For another, listeners misperceive approaching sounds as being closer than they really are (Neuhoff, 2001). Monkeys, too, are susceptible to this bias to misperceive auditory events that imply looming (Ghazanfar, Neuhoff, and Logothetis, 2002).

In fact, it makes sense that an approaching sound should be perceptually conspicuous and appear to arrive earlier than it actually does. According to Neuhoff, "[B]ias for looming auditory motion may provide a selective advantage in preparing for contact with an approaching source, or an increased margin of safety on approach. If the source is perceived as closer than it actually is, then the listener will have longer than expected to prepare for the source's arrival" (2001, p. 100). Consistent with this adaptive interpretation, brain imaging studies in humans show that looming sounds produce stronger activation than receding sounds in those cortical regions known to mediate auditory motion perception and attention (Seifritz et al., 2002).

What You Hear Can Alter What You See

Chapter 1 called attention to the fact that perception is typically multimodal, meaning that information from the different senses is integrated into a rich, coherent impression of objects in the natural environment. You previewed this topic earlier in this chapter when you read about the ventriloquist's illusion. In this final section, we will expand on this important idea, describing just a few of the many phenomena that underscore the interdependence between hearing and vision. Our selection of examples includes work we ourselves have done on this aspect of perception. We'll start with an example where hearing helps clear up some confusion on the part of vision.

Imagine the following sequence of events. (see Figure 11.23). Two identical round, black balls appear on a video monitor, initially at opposite sides of the screen, left and right. Soon thereafter, the balls begin to move toward each other at the same speed. At some point in time they reach the same location and overlap one another; thereafter, the two balls continue to move and eventually return to the original locations occupied by the two balls. This

FIGURE 11.23 | Each panel represents a frame from a video sequence portraying two black balls moving toward each other, temporarily overlapping and then moving back to the edges of the display. The sequence starts at the top (t_1) and steps through the successive frames ending at the bottom (t_5). This animation is ambiguous with respect to the trajectory of the balls: They can appear either to stream past each other (as if one passed behind the other) or they can appear to collide and bounce back in the opposite direction. If a sound occurs around the time the two balls coincide in position, bouncing is seen predominantly.

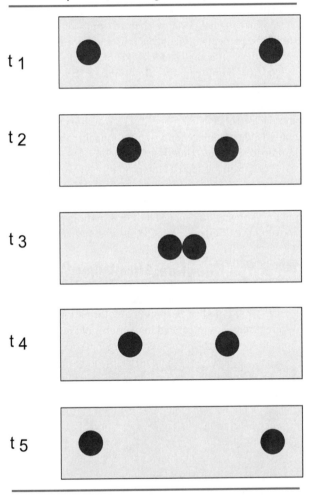

t_1

t_2

t_3

t_4

t_5

visual event is ambiguous: either of two, equally likely events could have occurred. The balls could have moved toward one another, with one passing behind the other, and continued on their initial trajectory (streaming). Alternatively, the two balls could have moved toward one another, collided, and then bounced back toward their ini-

tial locations (bouncing). In fact, when people view this kind of animation, they sometimes see bouncing and other times see streaming. Perception, in other words, is bistable. The relative frequency of these two perceptual outcomes depends upon the particulars of the visual animation, including the speed of the balls' motion and the duration of time of their overlap (Sekuler and Sekuler, 1999). Here's where sound comes into the picture: when objects in the real world collide, this collision is accompanied by a telltale sound. With this in mind, Sekuler, Sekuler, and Lau (1997) reasoned that an appropriate, well-timed sound might render the visual event unambiguous, by implying collision and thereby favoring bouncing as the actual nature of the event. Presenting a brief sound at the time where the balls appeared to come in contact produced exactly this outcome: Rather than streaming, the balls appeared to bounce. Sound convincingly verified one visual event over the other.

This influence of sound on vision has been replicated and used in a brain imaging study aimed at identifying cortical areas sensitive to bimodal interactions (Bushara et al., 2003). In that study, observers viewed the display illustrated in Figure 11.23, always with sound. On many trials observers experienced bouncing (implying that sound and vision were interacting), whereas on other trials observers saw streaming (implying that perception was based on vision alone). On trials when bouncing was perceived (and, therefore, perception was bimodal), enhanced neural activation (relative to streaming trials) was observed in a widely distributed set of brain areas, including areas identified as multimodal from single cell work in monkey cortex. At the same time, multimodal bouncing trials saw *reduced* activation in auditory and visual areas responsive to stimulation by one modality only. Bushara and colleagues speculate that effective combination of auditory and visual information is accomplished in multimodal areas of the brain that, at the same time, can inhibit activity in unimodal areas.

In another example of visual–auditory interactions (Guttman, Gilroy, and Blake, 2004), people viewed a brief visual sequence in which the light and dark bars of a grating switched positions rapidly but unpredictably over time. This pattern of switches created a kind of "visual rhythm" that uniquely defined each sequence. People viewed two successive visual rhythm sequences and judged whether or not the two were identical. On some trials the visual rhythms were accompanied by a sequence of sounds, brief clicks that either coincided with the visual rhythm or were unrelated to the visual rhythm. The person's task was to judge whether the two successive visual rhythms were the same or different without regard to the sound sequence. Even though the sound was unrelated to the correct answer, people's judgments were heavily influenced by sound: When the auditory pattern's beats corresponded to the visual rhythm, people were almost perfect at judging whether the visual rhythms were identical. But when the auditory patterns were unrelated to the visual rhythms, performance was barely better than chance. Based on this and other results pointing to auditory influences on visual judgments, Guttman and colleagues concluded that the temporal rhythm of the visual events was automatically converted into an auditory representation.

For a final example of auditory–visual interaction, we turn to a fascinating illusion discovered by Shams, Kamitani, and Shimojo (2000). In their study, Shams and colleagues briefly flashed a spot of light, sometimes only once, and other times twice or more in rapid succession. To no one's surprise, when the flashes were presented alone—unaccompanied by sound—people accurately reported the number of flashes. But something strange happened when the flashes were accompanied by brief, auditory clicks: When people heard two clicks, a single visual flash was perceived not as one flash, but as two successive flashes, with the second flash following about 50 msec after the first. Once again, we find that brief auditory events influence the perception of brief visual events. Ordinarily, of course, visual and auditory events coincide in time, but illusions like this one reveal the relative weight given to vision and to hearing when it comes to perceiving the fine details of those events. And in at least some instances, hearing dominates vision.

So, we have three examples where hearing trumps vision, in the sense that sound biases visual perception. Can the effectiveness of sound as a visual analog be exploited for practical purposes? As the following section reveals, the answer is yes.

Sonification: Turning Light into Sound

On city streets, a green traffic light signals that it is (relatively) safe for drivers to proceed; red lights signal that drivers should stop. On television weather programs, meteorologists use complex maps and animated graphics to convey the progress and prospects of storms and weather systems. Although not as complex as a sophisticated animated weather map, many illustrations in this book use visual graphical techniques and conventions to communicate information. For example, variation in the height of the curve in Figure 10.24 told you that a neuron's

threshold changes with stimulus frequency. And the squiggles in Figure 10.25 immediately told you that nerve fibers differ in their tuning.

These examples all make use of visual signals to convey important information, but auditory signals, too, can be used for this purpose. When the auditory signals used for this purpose are nonverbal, this process of representing information using sound is known as **sonification** (e.g., Walker, 2002). The term itself may be unfamiliar to you, but you're undoubtedly acquainted with applications of sonification, which have been around for a long time. Consider, for example, Geiger counters, which were invented about 100 years ago to detect and measure radioactivity. These instruments generate audible clicks at a rate that mirrors the amount of radioactivity detected. When it encounters little radioactivity, a Geiger counter produces relatively few clicks per second, but as radioactivity increases, so too does the click rate. This audible representation of radioactivity affords an important advantage to a user: It enables a user to gauge the amount of radioactivity in some area simply by listening, with no need to look at the instrument's dials and other visual indicators. As a result, the user is free to attend to other tasks at the same time.

Sonification has also found applications in medicine, the best known of which is the pulse oximeter. By measuring the light reflected from a patient's finger or ear, this device quantifies the pulse rate and the oxygen level of the blood. A pulse oximeter generates audible signals that convey both of these two variables at the same time. The instrument produces brief tones, the timing of which denotes the occurrence of each pulse and the pitch of which denotes the patient's blood/oxygen level. This form of sonification is commonly used during surgery, making it possible to monitor key aspects of the patient's vital signs while, at the same time, focusing on the surgical procedure itself (Loeb and Fitch, 2002).

In the last few years, sonification has found even more promising uses (Kramer et al., 1999). To illustrate the emerging promise of this technique, we'll discuss one intriguing use of sonification: an application that some believe can help the blind "see" with their ears. To explain this application of sonification, consider a simple scenario. Holding a cell phone in his hand, a blind man strolls down the street, stepping easily around obstacles such as parking meters, other people, and a trash can that was blown over earlier in the day by the wind. The secret? The cell phone has a built-in camera, and through the earphones he's wearing, the blind man receives a sonified version of the images captured by the cell phone.

FIGURE 11.24 | A cell phone camera with appropriate software can be used for sonification of scenes. Panel A: A simple scene, with one bright square and two dimmer objects, a square and a rectangle. Panel B: Sonification of the scene in panel A. The thickness of lines indicates the intensity of the auditory signal generated by the sonification software; brighter objects in the scene produce more intense auditory signals. Frequency represents an object's vertical position in the scene; the time at which an auditory signal is presented signifies an object's horizontal position in the scene. Panel C: A scene containing two bright triangles. Panel D. Schematic of the sonification of the scene in panel C.

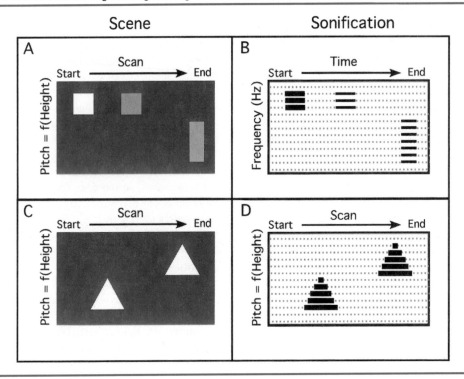

Software in the cell phone (or on a handheld, camera-equipped computer) embodies a relatively simple sonification scheme developed by Meijer (1992). Figure 11.24 illustrates the fundamentals of this scheme. In panel A, the shaded rectangle represents the scene at which the cell phone camera is looking. In this case, the scene is simple, containing one bright square (toward the scene's left side), and two dimmer objects, a square and a rectangle. The sonification software scans the image from left to right, and converts light levels into sound, and these sounds are fed into the user's earphones. As it reads out successive portions of the image, the software generates a loud sound when it encounters a bright portion of the image, and a quieter sound when it encounters a dark portion of the image. At the same time, it uses variation in pitch to convey the height at which features are located, with a low pitch signifying a feature toward the bottom of the image and a high pitch a feature toward the top. After a left-right scan is complete, the cell phone camera takes

another picture, and the process repeats. As Massof (2003) described this system,

> Digitized images are sonified by transforming the x-coordinate of the image to time, the y-coordinate to frequency, and grayscale to loudness. The system operates as if a vertical line scanner is swept horizontally across an image at a constant rate. The sound's pitch varies with the position of the pixel on the vertical axis and the loudness varies in steps with steps in the pixel's gray level. The result is a complex dynamic sound with chords and melodies as the scanner sweeps across the image.

Panel B in Figure 11.24 illustrates the sonified representation of the scene in panel A. When the scan reaches the left edge of the first square in panel A, the sonifying software generates a set of relatively high frequencies, all presented at the same intense level (intensity is shown by the thickness of the line). The intensity is proportional to brightness in the scene. When the scan reaches the right edge of the bright square, the trio of frequencies turn off. Then, as the scan proceeds it encounters the left edge of the dimmer square in panel A. Because this square lies at the same height as its brighter mate, and because they are both the same height, the same trio of frequencies comes on, although at lower intensity because this square is dimmer. Again, when the scan reaches the square's right edge, the three frequencies go off. Note that for both squares, all the sounds come on and go off in unison: This is a sign that the edges are vertical. Finally, when the scan reaches the dim rectangle, a series of lower frequency tones turn on. The frequencies are lower, of course, because the object is lower in the scene. And because the rectangle's vertical height is greater than that of the square more frequencies are present than before. The sound turns off when the scan reaches the rectangle's right edge. Note that this scene— of transforming light distributions into sound—produces information about edge orientation, location, size of objects, and object brightness. As a further illustration, consider panels C and D of the figure. Panel C shows another scene, with two bright triangles. How would the sonification scheme represent these? For the answer look at panel D. Because the objects are bright, when sounds come on they are at high intensity, which is shown by line thickness. Because the edges of the triangles are not vertical, all the frequencies do not come on or go off at once. Instead, when the scan hits the triangle's left side, a series of tones are turned on, one after another—generating a sound whose pitch rises because the average frequency rises; at the other edge of the triangle, a sound with falling pitch is generated. Finally, although the pattern and duration of sounds representing both triangles would be identical, the average pitch associated with the second triangle would be higher than that for the first triangle because they lie at different heights in the scene.

Can sonification actually enable a user to "see" an object based on the patterns of sound created by that object? Does this promising scheme actually work? In a recent laboratory test, Stoerig and colleagues (2004) found that to a remarkable degree, people could learn to use sonified representations to recognize and interpret the images that had been captured by a camera. And such learning included complex images of natural objects. In fact, blind individuals who use this system on a regular basis report that learning to exploit the sonified representations is like learning a foreign language: It takes quite a while, but, users report, it may well be worth the effort.

The sonification system we've been discussing gives a novel twist to a famous 300-year-old question. In 1688, the Irish politician and scientist William Molyneux posed this problem to his friend John Locke: "Suppose that a congenitally blind person has learned to distinguish and name a sphere and a cube by touch alone. Then imagine that this person suddenly recovers the faculty of sight. Will he be able to distinguish both objects by sight and to say which is the sphere and which the cube?" Incidentally, for Molyneux, this question was not some idle exercise; his own wife, Lucy, was blind. Locke's answer to his friend's question was no, an answer that has been debated ever since (Degenaar, 1996).

Imagine that Molyneux's congenitally blind wife had been allowed to hear sonified versions of a circle and a square. The abrupt changes in pitch and loudness that would be produced by the square would be very easily distinguished from the gradual changes in pitch and loudness produced by the circle. In other words, there would be a clear auditory basis for distinguishing the two types of objects, and that difference would be preserved despite changes in the sizes of the objects, their spatial locations, or their contrasts (dark on a light background, or vice versa).

It's important to keep in mind that sonification is *not* just a matter of engineering—of figuring out how to convert images into sound. Sonification is equally a matter of psychophysics—figuring out what sound attributes correspond best to various dimensions of the image (Walker and Kramer, 2004). In the example just discussed, increasing image intensity was communicated by increasing sound loudness, not by decreasing loudness. And this "mapping" of auditory dimensions onto visual dimensions matters: Some assignments are more natural, and therefore more readily interpreted (Walker and Ehrenstein, 2000; Walker, 2002). In some circumstances, multiple auditory dimensions can interact to produce distortions. For example, changes in loudness can influence perception of changes in pitch, and vice versa (Neuhoff, Kramer, and Wayand, 2002). In fact, the appropriateness of visual-to-auditory mappings could be a matter of life or death in some situations:

> [T]he International Space Station caution and warning tones need to communicate unambiguously whether there is a fire, depressurization, or toxic environment condition, as all require immediate but different actions. It is important to know just how the manipulation of acoustic attributes such as the frequency or repetition rate affects a listener's categorization of the sound. For example, will a high-pitched alarm be perceived as more indicative of a fire or a depressurization? (Walker and Kramer, 2004)

Engineers spend lots of time designing auditory icons, brief sounds used in devices, including computers, to convey information to users about objects, functions, and actions. Just think about the sounds your computer makes when you receive e-mail, throw away a file, or get ready to shut down your computer. Obviously, to minimize confusion, various auditory icons should be readily distinguished from one another, but there's more to the design and choice of such icons. For one thing, the more closely an auditory icon mimics the actual event the easier it is to learn (Keller and Stevens, 2004). The sound of breaking glass comprises a compelling icon, and it denotes a poor move in a game of computer chess far better than does the sound of a gentle tinkle of a bell. Similarly, to signal that a screen capture has occurred, the sound of a camera shutter is much better than a short beep or whistle. (A screen capture, as you probably know, generates a digital snapshot of a computer's display screen or a portion of that screen.)

With our ever-growing dependence on information created by integrated circuits, these kinds of sounds will become increasingly important forms of communication between our machines and people. However, several categories of sounds will never be displaced in importance, regardless of how sophisticated electronic circuitry becomes. And it is to those special sounds—speech and music—that we turn in the next chapter.

SUMMARY AND PREVIEW

These last two chapters have only scratched the surface of one of the most highly developed and rapidly growing areas of perception research, hearing. Acoustics and hearing were among the first fields of study to develop quantitative measures for describing their shared subject. These developments date back to the early Greeks, who showed that pitch was related to the length of a vibrating string. Hearing researchers were also among the first to establish experimental techniques (such as direct scaling) for measuring perceptual reactions to sensory stimulation. These measurements were needed in order to know what acoustic events actually sound like in terms of loudness, pitch, and so forth. Contemporary research in hearing has made possible a very sophisticated understanding of the initial mechanical and neural events that eventually culminate in auditory perception. In the next chapter, we will consider in more detail two aspects of hearing that are hallmarks of the human auditory experience: perception of speech and perception of music.

KEY TERMS

audibility function (AF)
auditory images
auditory looming
bandpass noise
binaural masking-level difference
    (BMLD)
binaural unmasking
bone conduction
broadband noise
center frequency
cochlear implant
cocktail party effect
conduction loss

cone of confusion
critical band
discrimination threshold
duplex theory
equal loudness contours
fundamental frequency
harmonics
interaural intensity difference (IID)
interaural time difference (ITD)
loudness
loudness matching
magnitude estimation
masking

missing fundamental
otosclerosis
pitch
presbycusis
profile analysis
sensory/neural loss
sonification
sound localization
spectrogram
temporary threshold shift
threshold intensity
timbre

Chapter 12

Speech and Music Perception

The preceding two chapters introduced you to the physical properties of acoustic stimulation, the anatomical and physiological mechanisms that turn that acoustical stimulation into sound, and the basic perceptual qualities of hearing—pitch, intensity, and location. As those two chapters explained, we rely on our sense of hearing for all sorts of everyday activities: waking up to an alarm clock, answering a ringing phone, detecting the footsteps of an approaching person, hearing the tell-tale sounds your coffee machine makes after it's done making coffee. Each of these auditory events, along with the many others that fill your day, has its own unique qualities, generates its own emotional reaction, and contributes to the seamless flow of your daily activities. But of all the categories of sounds that populate your perceptual world, two are uniquely human: the sounds of speech and the sounds of music.

In a way, speech and music can be construed as the most complicated and abstract perceptual experiences that hearing makes possible. They are complicated in the sense that specific sounds deployed in the service of speech and music are themselves arbitrary and meaningless—it is only through learning that the combinations of these meaningless, simple sounds take on significance, both semantically and emotionally. And they are abstract in the sense that different human societies have devel-

oped radically different systems of sound to communicate speech and to create music.

Yet human speech and music still obey the same rules of perceptual organization as the other auditory events we discussed in the previous two chapters. For example, the perception of speech or music entails auditory stream segmentation, the analysis of continuous streams of sound often extending over considerable lengths of time. And both speech and music vary in loudness, with these variations conveying important clues about emphasis and emotion. Of course, human speech and human music perception *must* obey the overall rules of auditory perception, for both aspects of hearing, while unique, are necessarily grounded in the machinery of hearing. Regardless of how creative or visionary a musical composer may be, his or her compositions are constrained by the range of sounds audible to humans and by our abilities to discriminate tones and rhythms. It would be fruitless for a composer to write a musical score whose auditory messages are incomprehensible to the ears and brains of the listening audience.

To perception researchers, speech and music offer unique "case studies" for examining the acquisition of auditory skills, for studying individual differences in the ability to use those skills, and for identifying the brain mechanisms involved in perceiving complex auditory events. This chapter surveys some highlights of speech perception and music perception, with the aim being to relate those perceptual experiences to underlying perceptual principles. Unfortunately, sounds cannot be inserted into textbooks, and the illustrations in this chapter cannot convey to you the quality and diversity of speech and music. However, the website for this text (www.mhhe.com/blake5) includes a number of excellent Web links where you can actually hear examples of speech sounds and musical sounds, selected because they illustrate principles you'll learn about in this chapter. Please take advantage of these resources to supplement your understanding of the text material.

From the outset, it's important to keep in mind that compared to our other auditory abilities, speech and music are relatively recent inventions. From fossil records, scientists estimate that the vocal machinery for producing speech probably materialized around 200,000 years ago. The clues for the emergence of music are less clear, but there is evidence that musical instruments were used 30,000 years ago (Storr, 1992), and our *Homo sapiens* ancestors were probably singing to one another long before then.[1] The precise birth dates of these perceptual milestones are not important for our purposes; what is significant is that both speech and music, once on the scene, forever changed human lives in profound and pleasurable ways.

Given this prelude, let's now begin our survey of these two very important and interesting perceptual aspects of hearing, starting first with speech perception.

Perception of Speech Sounds

Animals seem compelled to make sounds, and to do so they exploit just about any device at their disposal. Woodpeckers drum their beaks against trees or wooden houses, rattlesnakes shake their tails, gorillas beat their chests, grasshoppers scrape their legs together, and termites grind their mandibles. The variety of resulting sounds is remarkable, ranging from the happy melodies of the robin to the mournful calls of the humpback whale; from the faint, rhythmic ticking of a beetle to the piercing shriek of a baboon. Although some of these animal sounds may just be idle chatter to break the silence, most serve to communicate messages to friends and to foes. Obviously, then, for the sender's messages to be effec-

tive, those messages must be received by the other party. In nature, this is one of auditory perception's primary jobs, enabling animals to hear what others have to say.

Of all nature's creatures, humans have developed the largest repertoire of sounds. Human beings can make sounds using various parts of their bodies, including their hands, their feet, and of course their vocal apparatus. Not satisfied with these means, humans have also invented countless devices to expand their sound-making repertoire—musical instruments, sirens, doorbells, and all sorts of other noise makers. But among the many ways that humans have of producing sound, speech undoubtedly has the most impact. It used to be commonly believed that more than anything else, the capacity to produce and to perceive speech sounds set *Homo sapiens* apart from all other creatures.[2] Whether or not that's true, there is no denying that speech, the vehicle of language, has been of paramount importance in the biological and cultural evolution of our own species (Pinker, 1994).

The study of speech encompasses several disciplines, ranging from neurology to linguistics. Each discipline analyzes speech from a particular perspective. For instance, a neurologist might be interested in the neuromuscular mechanisms responsible for the production of speech. Here the emphasis would be on the components of the vocal tract and on the motor areas of the brain that guide the movements of those components. In contrast, a linguist might focus on the structure of grammar. Here the emphasis would be less on the "hardware" of speech and more on the rules governing the formation and interpretation of sentences.

Where does auditory perception fit into this picture? Obviously, to understand a verbal utterance you must be able to hear the associated sounds. So speech perception must take into account the initial stages of hearing, those involved in the reception and processing of sound waves; these processes were discussed in the two previous chapters. In addition, however, speech perception entails more complex auditory processing. Spoken words are composed of sounds whose acoustic properties are special. Moreover, speech perception entails more than just understanding what is being said—in addition to the "content" of speech, we are often aware of *whose* voice it is we're listening to (speaker identity) and, as well, we may

---

[1]The oldest existing, undisputed evidence for musical instruments consists of flutes fashioned from animal bones, unearthed in caves in Germany and in France; these instruments are approximately 32,000 years old (Balter, 2004). Even earlier instruments made of perishable material (e.g., bamboo) may well predate these bone flutes.

[2]Debate rages over whether humans are the only genuinely linguistic species. Some argue that dolphins and chimpanzees exhibit the hallmarks of linguistic capability, which casts doubt on the view that humans possess the exclusive patent on language. Others, however, counter that the symbolic systems evidenced by those creatures, while impressive, do not constitute grammatically based, syntactical communication.

FIGURE 12.1 | Diagram of the vocal tract.

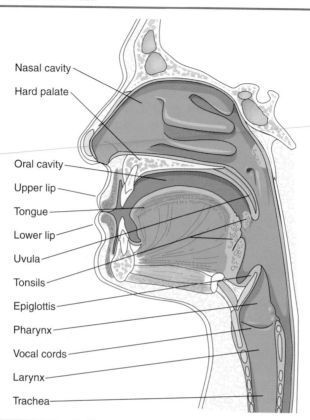

be aware of that speaker's affective state (emotional state identity). The voice, in other words, carries important **paralinguistic information** (the nonsemantic content of speech) that portrays the tell-tale signs about the identity, mood, and intentions of the person speaking; these qualities make up what has been dubbed the speaker's auditory face (Belin, Fecteau, and Bédard, 2004). So a complete understanding of speech perception needs to account for these complementary, interacting aspects of vocal perception. With this in mind, let's begin by considering the acoustical properties of speech sounds, because these define the relevant information that the auditory system must process in order for speech to be perceived.

The Sounds of Speech

At their core, the vocal sounds that comprise speech do not differ from the world's other sounds. Vocalizations are simply variations in acoustic energy that pass through the outer ear canal, set up tiny trembling vibrations within the ossicles of the middle ear which, in turn, produce traveling waves within the inner ear that deflect hair cells and, thereby, innervate the auditory nerve. Speech

sounds are unique, however, in that the source of those sounds is found in the specialized vocal structures possessed by members of our species. Collectively called the **vocal tract,** these structures include the larynx, throat, tongue, teeth, and lips (see Figure 12.1). Working as a unit, these structures are responsible for the production of the sounds we call speech.

Speech sounds are generated when air from the lungs is forced through the **vocal folds** (or vocal cords, as they're sometimes called), a pair of elastic membranes stretched across the upper part of the air passage from the lungs; the vocal folds are contained within the larynx, which is what you're feeling when you rub your fingers against your "Adam's apple."[3] Passage of air through the

---

[3]The Adam's apple is a skeleton of cartilage surrounding the larynx, and in males it tends to be more conspicuous because it's bigger. The colloquial term may have originated from the biblical story of Adam and Eve, with the conspicuous bulge arising from a piece of the forbidden fruit of the garden—an apple—getting lodged in Adam's throat. Alternatively, Adam's apple, which in Latin is *pomum Adami,* could have arisen from an error in translation of the Hebrew *tappuach ha adam,* which means male bump.

vocal folds causes them to vibrate, just like the reed on a wind instrument. The vibrating portions of male vocal folds are 60 percent longer, on average, than their female counterparts. This means that male folds vibrate at a lower frequency than do female folds. This, along with differences in the overall size of the vocal tract, is a major reason why the pitch of a typical male voice is lower than that of a typical female voice; these size differences arise at puberty. However, size alone cannot be the sole source of the vocal cues that allow us to identify a speaker's sex: we usually can discriminate male from female voices in young children whose vocal tracts have yet to become differentiated at puberty (Fitch and Giedd, 1999).

The airborne vibrations produced by the vocal folds, in turn, are modified by changes in the shape of the throat, mouth, lips, and nasal cavity. These components of speech production are innervated by complex sets of muscles that can execute hundreds of articulatory actions per second (Handel, 1989). These actions result in the vowel and consonant sounds that make up speech. Each of these sounds results from a particular positioning of the elements of the vocal tract. Take a moment to voice slowly several of the vowels and consonants, paying attention to the position of your lips, teeth, tongue, and throat. If you do this while looking in a mirror, you should see how these positions differ for various vowels and consonants, which is why they sound different from one another. Many people have very precise control over these anatomical modulators of vocal sounds, which is why they can imitate other people's vocalizations. Basically, a mimic reproduces the way another person positions the elements of his or her vocal tract. Of course, we hear our own vocalizations when we speak, and that auditory feedback influences how we speak. Speakers listening over headphones to distorted versions of their own speech alter the production of their speech sounds to compensate for what they think are errors in their utterances (Houde and Jordan, 1998).[4]

Not all sound differences are important for speech comprehension. For example, sound differences associated with regional accents usually don't prevent people who hail from one region of a country from understanding people who hail from another. Sound differences that are important for speech comprehension are ones that ac-

FIGURE 12.2 | Sound spectrogram showing variations in acoustic energy over time as the word *spike* is uttered.

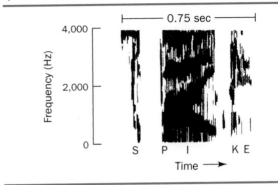

tually change the meaning of an utterance. Any sound that can produce such a change is called a **phoneme.** Phonemes are the distinctive features of speech—they form the vocabulary of sounds used in a language, and different languages make use of different phonemic sounds. When speaking at a normal pace, we produce about 12 phonemes per second, and we can comprehend speech at rates up to around 50 phonemes per second (Werker and Tees, 1992). To understand speech perception requires knowing how phonemes are processed by the auditory system. A good first step is to understand the acoustical properties of phonemes.

Any phoneme contains acoustic energy at a number of different frequencies. It is impractical, therefore, to define phonemes the way we defined pure tones. Instead, hearing specialists use what is called a *sound spectrogram* to characterize speech sounds (spectrograms were introduced in Chapter 11). A sound spectrogram is a graph showing the amount of acoustic energy at various frequencies over time. To illustrate, the sound spectrogram shown in Figure 12.2 shows a "picture" of the speech energy produced when a person uttered the word *spike.* The vertical axis plots sound frequency and the horizontal axis represents time. Spelled out underneath the horizontal axis is the word *spike,* indicating when in time each of its phonemes was uttered. The dark portions of the graph denote the distribution of acoustic energy produced by that utterance; the degree of darkness is proportional to the amount of that energy.

Note that the hiss of the consonant *s* consists of energy distributed over a fairly wide range of frequencies, as indicated by the wide band of darkness above that letter. There is a brief period of silence between /s/ and /p/, seen in the sound spectrogram as an absence of acoustic

---

[4]In the Houde and Jordan (1998) study, the perturbations in self-produced speech sounds consisted of shifts in several of the key frequencies comprising the vowels of single-syllable words such as *pep.* Speakers automatically learned to adjust the frequency content of their utterances to compensate for the distortion.

FIGURE 12.3 | Sound spectrogram associated with the utterance of a sentence. Note the longer time scale in this spectrogram relative to the one in Figure 12.2.

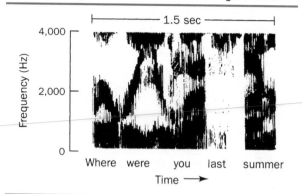

energy. The vowel *i* consists of several bands of acoustic energy, which in the sound spectrogram looks like a group of worms located above the letter *i*. Note that during the course of this utterance, one of these bands of frequencies dips down. This corresponds to the drop in the pitch of your voice when you say the phoneme /*i*/. (Listen to your voice as you speak this vowel.) In other words, the sound spectrogram also depicts the intonation of your speech.

The sound spectrogram neatly summarizes the acoustic properties of speech sounds. As Figure 12.3 illustrates, sound spectrograms can be created for sentences as well as for words. The beauty of the sound spectrogram is that it depicts the entire package of frequencies making up each and every phoneme in an utterance, and it shows how those frequencies change over time. The sound spectrogram visually depicts the transitions and irregularities that characterize different speech sounds. Because an individual's voice reflects the many distinctive features of that person's own vocal apparatus and speech intonation, a sound spectrogram of a voice may be as unique as an individual's fingerprint (Kertsa, 1962). But unlike fingerprints, an individual's spectrogram changes with age, just as the sound of the person's voice changes (Liss, Weismer, and Rosenbek, 1990). With age, the vocal folds lose elasticity, and become floppy, less taut; these changes produce the tremulous or wobbly sound that characterizes many older people's voices. In the United States, plastic surgeons have begun to operate on patients' vocal cords in order to give older people younger voices. As one physician said, "There are people who pay $15,000 for a face-lift and as soon as they open their mouth, they sound like they're 75" (BBC

News, April 20, 2004). To match a patient's voice to that patient's newly rejuvenated face, the surgeon can plump up the vocal cords with collagen injections, or use a small band of Gortex to tighten up the cords.

Incidentally, spectrographic analysis of sound can also be applied to nonspeech sounds such as the cries made by infants (Green, Jones, and Gustafson, 1987), the vocalizations made by animals (Seyfarth and Cheney, 1984), and the characteristic sounds of male and female footsteps (Li, Logan, and Pastore, 1991). It is even possible to create a spectrographic picture of the disturbing sound of fingernails scraped over a chalkboard (Halpern, Blake, and Hillenbrand, 1986)!

Armed with this powerful tool for describing the acoustic properties of speech sounds, let's now consider how the auditory system responds to these properties.

The Neural Analysis of Speech Sounds

Response of the Auditory Nerve to Speech Sounds

We'll start by considering how the sounds of speech might be represented within the fibers of a listener's auditory nerve. As you know, each auditory nerve fiber responds to a narrow range of sound frequencies. Each fiber, in effect, "listens" for particular frequencies in the sound wave arriving at the ear, and different fibers "listen" to different frequencies. With this arrangement in mind, look at the spectrogram shown in Figure 12.4. You could envision the thin lines running throughout the figure as individual auditory nerve fibers. Fibers that respond to low frequencies would be situated low down in the figure, near the horizontal axis, while fibers that respond to high frequencies would be situated toward the top. Thought of in this way, distance along the vertical axis would correspond to the location along the basilar membrane where the fibers make contact with hair cells. The horizontal axis would correspond to time. The changes in the degree of darkness within the spectrogram would correspond to the amount of neural activity within various nerve fibers.

This way of thinking about nerve fiber activity was introduced by Nelson Kiang (1975), who called the resulting plot of neural activity a **neurogram.** For a given utterance, such as the word *spike,* there is a close correspondence between the pattern of acoustic energy in the sound spectrogram and the pattern of neural activity in the neurogram. This correspondence merely confirms that the ear and the auditory nerve perform a frequency analysis on the incoming sound.

FIGURE 12.4 | As you listen to someone speak the phrase, "Here we go again," your ear receives fluctuations in sound frequency amplitude; those fluctuations are shown in this spectrogram. But you can also think about this graph as summarizing fluctuations over time in the levels of activity among individual auditory nerve fibers, shown in this schematic as thin horizontal lines. The amount of activity in a given fiber is related to the amount of energy present at that fiber's preferred frequency, and this changes over time.

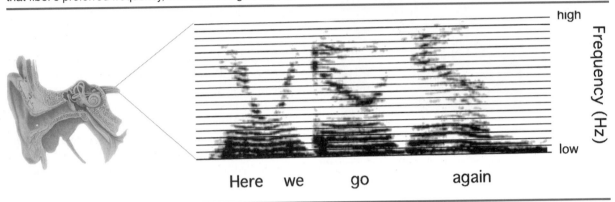

This cannot be the whole story of speech perception, though. For one thing, there are instances where speech sounds that are perceived as equivalent produce distinctly different sound spectrograms. To give an example, the sound spectrogram representing a particular consonant can vary depending on what vowel happens to follow that consonant. This point is illustrated in Figure 12.5, which shows the spectrographic representations of two utterances, /di/ and /du/. Notice how the transition corresponding to the /d/ sound rises in one case (/du/) but falls in the other (/di/). Yet in both instances, we hear the same /d/ sound. And these variations in the sound spectrogram are registered in the pattern of activity across different fibers; for example, different fibers are activated by /di/ as opposed to /du/. Nonetheless, the same consonant is heard. This happens because when the brain processes speech sounds it registers crucial information about the *transitions* from consonants to vowels (Kaukoranta, Hari, and Lounasmaa, 1987). These transitions, incidentally, look like the dips and rises seen in the sound spectrograms of Figures 12.2 and 12.3.

There's another reason why one must look beyond the auditory nerve for the analysis of speech sounds, and this has to do with the variability of speech sounds. The acoustic features of human speech differ from person to person, which is why it is easy to identify people just by hearing their voices. Yet despite these individual differences in speech acoustics, we usually have little trouble understanding what people are saying, even when they speak in a whisper (Tartter, 1991). Somehow, despite the acoustic variation from one speaker to another, the lis-

FIGURE 12.5 | Spectrographic representation of two utterances, /di/ and /du/.

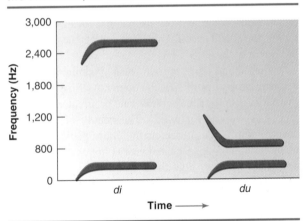

(Adapted from Werker and Tees, 1992.)

tener's auditory system manages to extract important invariant acoustic features. This invariance of perception despite variability in the stimulus is a form of constancy, analogous to color constancy (Chapter 7) and size constancy (Chapter 8) in vision.

Brain Mechanisms of Speech Perception

Studies of Nonhuman Primates   To look for brain events related to the processing of speech sounds, physiologists have recorded activity from neurons in the auditory cortex of monkeys who listen to human speech sounds

FIGURE 12.6 | View of the lateral surface of the left hemisphere of the human brain. Two regions are highlighted: the primary auditory cortex, which is situated on the upper bank of the temporal gyrus, and Wernicke's area, which is located behind and above the primary auditory cortex, near the juncture of the temporal and parietal lobes. Primary auditory cortex is found in both hemispheres, but Wernicke's area is typically restricted to the left hemisphere.

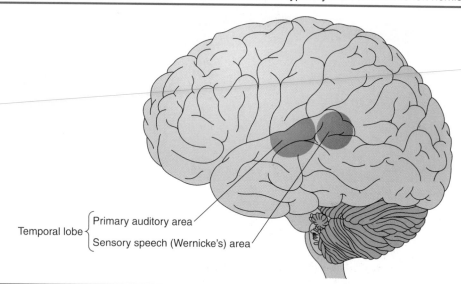

Temporal lobe { Primary auditory area

Sensory speech (Wernicke's) area

(Steinschneider, Arezzo, and Vaughn, 1982). You might wonder what neural activity in a *monkey's* brain could tell anyone about perception of *human* speech sounds. However, there is some justification for generalizing results from monkeys to humans because monkeys can discriminate the same speech sounds as humans (Sinnott et al., 1976). Without going into details, the results can be summarized as follows. A number of perceptually significant acoustic properties of human speech affect the responses of neurons in the auditory portion of the monkey brain. These properties include (1) the time elapsing between the release of the lips and the start of sound production (the property enabling you to distinguish between such syllables as /pa/ and /ba/); (2) the acoustical context of a sound (such as whether a particular vowel is preceded by one consonant or another); and (3) the rate of frequency changes (an important feature distinguishing certain vowels from one another).

Studies of the Human Brain   Until a decade ago, single-unit recordings provided the most direct glimpse into the brain machinery involved in the analysis of speech sounds. However, with the advent of modern brain imaging techniques, it became possible to study the neuroanatomical and functional organization of speech perception in humans. Results from application of these imaging techniques point to the operation of a distributed network of brain areas headquartered in the brain's temporal lobes, both left and right hemispheres, with neural signals within those areas mediating different aspects of speech perception. Because of the volume of studies, we'll only be able to provide an overview of the patterns of neural activation produced by speech sounds in various regions of the brain. For an excellent, thorough review of these findings, see Scott and Johnsrude (2003).

There is no doubt that the primary auditory cortex in the temporal lobe (see Figure 12.6) is crucially involved in the analysis of speech sounds. You will recall from the previous chapter that this auditory receiving area in the cortex contains a tonotopic map, with different neurons responsive to different frequencies. Speech sounds will activate auditory cortical neurons whose response tuning curves include the frequency components of those sounds. But the primary auditory cortex does *not* respond *preferentially* to speech sounds: brain imaging studies in humans reveal that nonspeech sounds, including noise, are just as effective as speech sounds when it comes to activating primary auditory cortex. Instead, we must look beyond the initial receiving areas of the cortex to find cortical regions selectively involved in the analysis of speech sounds. And as we explore those different regions, we must keep in mind that speech perception is multidimensional, meaning that speech sounds convey messages (informational content), emotional connotation (affect), and

FIGURE 12.7 | View of the lateral surface of the left and right hemispheres, showing brain regions (marked by arrows) activated when a listener is performing a task requiring identification of the speaker, not what the speaker is saying. Activations are limited to the right hemisphere. On the converse task (attend to what speaker is saying, not speaker identity), it is the left hemisphere which is activated (result not shown here).

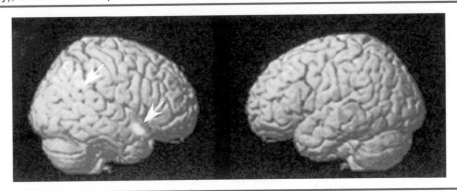

the identity of the speaker (who's speaking). As you will discover, different brain regions mediate these complementary perceptual qualities of speech.

Moving away from the primary auditory cortex and back along the upper part of the temporal lobe (see Figure 12.6), we encounter a band of cortex called the posterior temporal region. Within the posterior temporal region in the left hemisphere (but not in the right) we find **Wernicke's area,** named for German neurologist/psychiatrist Carl Wernicke who in 1874 first described this region and the consequence of damage to it. People who suffer trauma to this region lose the ability to understand vocal speech, although their hearing remains intact. They can also speak, but their utterances, while superficially resembling sentences, lack meaning. Brain imaging studies in normal humans reveal strong activation of this region of the brain when listening to meaningful speech compared to speechlike nonsense utterances. And within this temporal lobe region of the left hemisphere is a subdivision of labor: Brain regions responsive to speech sounds entailing rapid acoustic changes, such as consonant and vowel syllables, are different from those responsive to sounds that do not involve rapid changes in acoustic energy, such as steady-state vowels (for example, /o/). These brain areas in the temporal lobe, especially the left hemisphere, are also activated when people vividly imagine hearing syllables—to activate this area in your brain, think silently to yourself what the syllable "ga" sounds like (Jäncke and Shah, 2004). Auditory imagery of speech sounds does not, however, activate the primary auditory cortex.

The left hemisphere does not have a monopoly on speech perception—the right hemisphere also contains neural areas that play special roles in speech perception. In the temporal lobe and the prefrontal cortex of the right hemisphere we discover greater brain activations when listeners are attending to the emotional intonation of speech sounds rather than to the particulars of what is being said (Mitchell et al., 2003; but see Kotz et al., 2003). This enhanced activation to emotional intonation is also observed in areas extending beyond temporal lobe into the prefrontal cortex and parts of the limbic system. And these right hemisphere brain regions respond to nonspeech sounds such as cries and groans. These brain areas, in other words, seem to provide a wake-up call whenever any kind of emotionally significant vocalization is heard. One of the most arousing vocalizations is laughter, a special form of human vocalization described in Box 12.1.

Also within the temporal lobe of the right hemisphere is a separate region uniquely responsive to speaker identity (von Kriegstein et al., 2003). Shown in Figure 12.7, this area is active when a listener must identify the individual whose voice is being heard and is less active when the listener must attend to the verbal content of what is being said (a task that more strongly activates portions of the left superior temporal sulcus). Areas in the right temporal lobe are also more active when you're judging whether a speaker is male or female based on the speaker's voice (Lattner, Meyer, and Friederici, 2005). Befitting the right temporal lobe's putative role in speaker identification, damage to this cortical area can produce the condition called **phonagnosia,** a deficit in

Humans, like all other animals, possess a broad repertoire of nonlinguistic vocalizations, and we use them all the time in our social interactions. Included within our human repertoire are crying, screaming, groaning, sighing, clapping, shouting, and yawning (Ghazanfar and Santos, 2004). There is one form of nonlinguistic vocalization, however, that sets us apart from nearly all other animals: laughter.

We occasionally laugh when we are alone, but laughter is primarily a social event: It occurs substantially more often when we're around other people (Provine and Fischer, 1989). Laughter nearly always signals an affective state, although that state is not always one of happiness or amusement—people also tend to laugh when they're nervous or ashamed, when they want to communicate appeasement, and when they wish to ridicule someone else. Laughter can also signal friendliness and sexual interest (Grammer, 1990).

Laughing is not hard to master: We've been doing it since we were infants less than half a year old. Even children born deaf and blind start laughing at about the same age as sighted, hearing infants, implying that this behavior is a fundamental component of human vocalization (Deacon, 1989). Although other species, including chimpanzees, seem to have a laughlike vocalization produced during rough-and-tumble play, ours may be the only species that emits this particular form of vocalization throughout our lifespan and in all sorts of circumstances.

What role does laughter play in our everyday lives? According to one account, laughter is a species-specific form of communication whereby one individual conveys her affective state to others around her—laughter serves as a kind of language without words (DePaulo and Friedman, 1998). Others, however, think that laughter serves primarily to generate affective states in those individuals hearing the laughter (Bachorowski and Owren, 2001). Laughter, according to this view, strengthens social bonds between people, and creates an alliance that is adaptive in socially challenging situations where group cohesion is important.

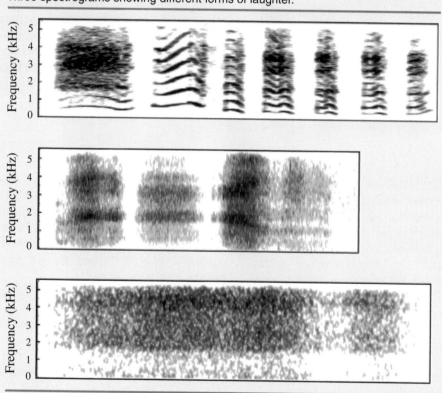

Three spectrograms showing different forms of laughter.

BOX 12.1   **There's Nothing Like a Good Laugh** *(continued)*

Acoustics of Laughter

If asked to mimic typical laughter, you'd probably emit a fairly regular sequence of vocalizations sounding like "ha . . . ha . . . ha . . . ha . . . ha," which is typically considered the generic laugh. In fact, however, there is no such thing as a generic laugh. Different individuals have distinctly different styles of laughter, and the same individual will generate different styles of laughter depending on the social context.

Sound spectograms (images that reveal changes in frequency and intensity of a sound over time) for three of the most prevalent patterns of laughter are shown in the figure on page 435 (Bachorowski, Smoski, and Owren, 2001). These sounds were recorded while volunteer participants watched humorous video clips (e.g., the so-called "bring out your dead" scene from the comic movie *Monty Python and the Holy Grail*). The upper spectrograms show two instances of what is termed **voiced laughter**. The presence of voicing means that there is regular vibration of the vocal folds during laugh production, giving the sound a tonal, vowellike quality. The rate of that vibration is termed the fundamental frequency (F_0), which is an important contributor to the perceived pitch of the sound. Voiced laughs can have a songlike quality if F_0 happens to fluctuate in a melodic way during and over the course of several notes or bursts.

The middle spectrogram shows a distinctly different style of laughter, one in which the vocalizations are acoustically noisy, giving them a breathy quality. This style is called **unvoiced laughter** because there is no periodicity in vocal-fold vibration during sound production. You can produce this vocalization by opening your mouth and rapidly and repeatedly exhaling, as if you were grunting or panting.

The bottom two graphs shows another form of unvoiced laughter, this one having a snortlike quality because acoustic turbulence is passed through the nasal cavities rather than through the oral cavities. This might be the kind of laugh you emit when you're trying to keep your laugh inconspicuous. These unvoiced grunt- and snortlike laughs actually make up the majority of laughter bouts in laughter samples taken from a large number of people in naturalistic situations.

How do we perceive and respond to these various sorts of laughter? When people are asked to rate them, voiced laughter is judged significantly more appealing than unvoiced laughter (Bachorowski and Owren, 2001). Listener perceptions of the laughs are also influenced by the sex of the laugher; unvoiced snorts and grunts produced by females are judged to be the least "sexy" by both male and female listeners. Isn't it odd that humans produce such high rates of unvoiced laugh sounds, even though listeners clearly respond to these sounds negatively?

By the way, don't miss the chance to hear these different kinds of laughs; the books website provides some links that let you hear what's so funny.

---

identifying a familiar speaker while, at the same time, being able to understand what the speaker is saying (Lancker, Kreiman, and Cummings, 1989).

Continuing our tour of speech areas in the brain, we also find within the temporal lobes of *both* hemispheres regions that are activated by all sorts of human vocalizations (Belin et al., 2000). For example, listening to an unintelligible foreign language activates this region in both hemispheres, as does hearing laughter or humming. As shown in Figure 12.8 those areas are located within the temporal lobes, along the upper bank of the superior temporal sulcus (STS); the caption to Figure 12.8 describes how brain imaging technology has been used to identify the function of these areas. Incidentally, when these same brain imaging procedures are applied to individuals with autism, there is no sign in either hemisphere of selective activation to vocal sounds in STS; responses to nonvocal sounds, on the other hand, show normal patterns of activation (Gervais et al., (2004). This abnormality may be related to the difficulties autistic individuals experience when encountering vocal sounds, including impaired identification of the emotion conveyed by a speaker's voice (Rutherford, Baron-Cohen, and Wheelwright, 2002).

Finally, there is evidence that motor areas of the brain involved in speech production—areas that control movements of the mouth—are also activated when people listen to speech (Wilson et al., 2004). Thus, when you hear the syllable /pa/, the motor and premotor regions of your brain become active even though you're not actually making the sound yourself. These motor areas are the same ones that are activated when you actually utter those syllables, and they are specific to mouth movements, not finger or hand movements. Nor are

FIGURE 12.8 | Regions of the temporal lobes in both the right (R) and left (L) hemispheres that are activated when hearing human vocalizations (regions shown in white), including nonspeech sounds (Belin et al., 2000). While lying quietly in a brain scanner, people listened to sounds delivered over headphones. During some listening periods, those sounds comprised different kinds of human vocalizations including spoken words and nonwords (meaningless speech), laughs, sighs, and whistles. During other epochs listeners heard nonvocal sounds such as airplanes, blowing wind, bells, handclaps, and animal noises. All sounds, vocal and nonvocal, were matched in duration and intensity. Voice-selective areas were defined as brain regions where vocal sounds produced significantly greater activation than nonvocal sounds. Further implicating these temporal lobe areas in perception of vocalization, activation levels in these regions were reduced when recordings of human vocalizations were altered in a way that scrambled the fine structure of the acoustic signals while leaving the overall frequency and intensity levels unchanged. This scrambling destroys the "vocal" quality of the sounds and significantly reduces activation in the temporal "vocal" areas.

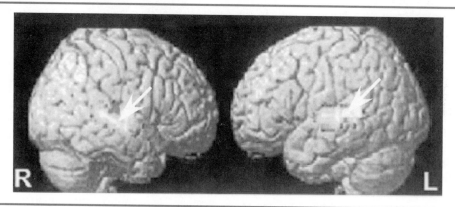

those areas activated when you hear nonspeech sounds such as a bell. The temporal lobe areas described in the preceding paragraphs are, of course, also activated when you hear syllables. The involvement of motor cortex could be construed to mean that speech sounds are registered, in part, in terms of the articulations required to produce them, an idea that has been around for decades (Liberman et al., 1967).

As we discussed in Chapter 10, some cognitive neuroscientists now speculate that auditory speech perception may follow the same broad processing scheme employed by the visual system for representing information about object identity (the "what" pathway) and object location (the "where" pathway). Applied to speech, this scheme envisions two, complementary processing streams coursing out of the primary auditory cortex. One stream projects from primary auditory cortex to more anterior (forward) and ventral (below) cortical territory. There, one finds areas whose neurons are important for extracting phonetic cues and mapping those cues onto lexical representations (word mean-

ings); this anterior-ventral pathway would embody a kind of what analysis for speech sounds. At the same time, a second pathway projects to brain regions that are more posterior (back) and dorsal (above), with activity in this pathway specifying information about changes in the frequency spectrum over time, information critical for perceiving the rise and fall in voice pitch and the affective connotation of what is being said. As we mentioned in Chapter 10, this division of labor envisioned within the auditory system is not necessarily limited to speech sounds—others believe that the two processing streams are specialized for auditory recognition and for auditory localization of both vocal and nonvocal sounds. At present, however, there is no consensus concerning the composition or functions of these putative pathways (Hall, 2003; Zatorre, Belin, and Penhune, 2002).

Having completed our overview of brain mechanisms of speech perception, we're now ready to survey some of the important factors that influence the perception and comprehension of speech.

What Makes It Possible to Understand Speech?

Feature Detection in Speech Perception

In the previous section you learned that the auditory system of the monkey contains neurons that respond to perceptually relevant portions of human speech sounds. These neurons are located in a region of the monkey's brain that, when damaged, makes it difficult for the monkey to discriminate human speech sounds (Dewson, Pribram, and Lynch, 1969). Damage to comparable regions of the human brain also produces deficits in speech perception (Marin, 1976). This parallel between monkeys and humans makes it tempting to speculate that the human brain also contains neurons responsive to distinctive features of speech. But how could one go about testing this idea?

Think back to Chapter 4, where we described how the selective adaptation procedure could be used to confirm the existence of visual neurons responsive to lines of different orientations. In that case, staring at lines of one orientation temporarily caused lines of a neighboring orientation to appear tilted away from their true orientation. This visual aftereffect presumably results from the reduced responsiveness of orientation-selective neurons.

In a now classic study, the same line of reasoning was applied in the search for neurons specially designed for analysis of human speech sounds. Using a speech synthesizer, Eimas and Corbit (1973) generated consonant sounds such as /b/, /p/, /t/, and /d/. Included among these consonant sounds were some that were ambiguous, meaning that they might sound like /t/ one time and /d/ the next. These ambiguous sounds, in other words, seemed to lie at the boundary between two unambiguous phonemic categories. Eimas and Corbit had people listen to an unambiguous consonant such as /d/ repeated over and over for several minutes. Following this period of adaptation, people listened to the previously ambiguous consonant, the one that used to sound sometimes like /t/ and other times like /d/. No longer did this consonant sound ambiguous—now it more clearly sounded like /t/ and not like the adapted consonant /d/.

Eimas and Corbit concluded that repeated exposure to one consonant had temporarily desensitized a set of detectors responsive to the distinctive features of that consonant while leaving feature detectors responsive to other consonants at full strength. Thus, following adaptation, the ambiguous consonant produced more activity within the set of unadapted feature detectors than within

FIGURE 12.9 | Context influences perception. Are the center dots in these two figures really different sizes, as they appear to be?

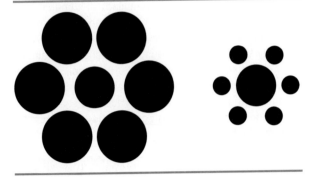

the adapted set. Consequently, listeners heard the consonant sound signaled by the unadapted set of feature detectors. The findings of Eimas and Corbit, along with other results using the selective adaptation procedure (for example, Samuel, 1989), point to the existence of neural feature detectors responsive to speech sounds.

But this still cannot be the entire story of speech perception. There are two other important factors that govern how the sounds of speech (the ones signaled by feature detectors) will actually be heard by a listener: the context in which those sounds occur and the perceived boundaries between speech sounds. Let's consider these two factors in turn.

The Role of Context in Speech Perception

Figure 12.9 illustrates a well-known general principle of perception: The context surrounding some stimulus affects the way that stimulus is perceived. The two center circles are equal in diameter, but one is perceived as larger than the other because of the surrounding dots. The same principle applies in the case of speech perception: How a given speech sound is perceived depends on the context in which it is heard. Speech context can be defined by any of several sources. One source is the phonetic information occurring closely in time; this influence was illustrated in the /di/ versus /du/ example in Figure 12.5. At a more abstract level, the *topic* of a conversation can itself provide a context for perceiving speech sounds. This form of context is amusingly illustrated by a catchy tune popular during the 1940s. Phonetically speaking, the first several measures go as follows:

Marezee doats n doze edoats n lidul lamzey divey. . . .

Now to those of you who've never heard this song (popularized during World War II, by Bing Crosby and the Andrews Sisters), this string of "words" may sound like make-believe speech. But, in fact, the words refer to the eating habits of several familiar hoofed animals. Still puzzled? Try repeating the words quickly, paying close attention to the sounds, not the letters. Once you hear the verse as it was meant to be perceived, you'll be able to hear it no other way. Knowing what the song's verses are about will influence what the words sound like to you.

In the case of the nonsense verse, context was provided by the general theme of the song. Speech perception can be influenced by other types of context, too. For instance, the same utterance can sound quite different depending on the *rapidity* with which words preceding that utterance are spoken. To give an example, a syllable may sound like */ba/* when it occurs within the context of a slowly spoken phrase but may sound like */pa/* when occurring within the same phrase rapidly spoken (Summerfield, 1975).

The same thing can happen with words in a sentence, as shown by Ladefoged and Broadbent (1957). They tape-recorded multiple versions of the sentence "Please say what this word is," with each version having a different, characteristic cadence. Different versions of the sentence sounded as if it were spoken by different speakers. Listeners heard the different versions of the sentence, and following each presentation they heard a single word uttered either with the same cadence as the immediately preceding sentence or with one of the other five possible cadences.[5] Listeners simply had to identify the last word. People listening to these recordings frequently misidentified the last word when its cadence differed from that of the preceding phrase. For instance, the same physical utterance was heard as "bit" when preceded by one sentence version and as "bet" when preceded by another. This demonstrates just how powerfully context can influence speech perception.

Vision Provides Context for Speech

In the examples just cited, the context shaping the perception of speech sounds was provided by other speech sounds. As the following classic experiment shows, *vi-*

---

[5]The different versions of the sentence were produced by varying the amount of energy in certain regions of the frequency spectrum. Technically speaking, this manipulation alters what is called the formant structure of the speech signal. Perceptually, this manipulation produces utterances that are readily identifiable as the same sentence, although they sound as if different individuals were uttering them.

FIGURE 12.10 | Photograph of an individual in the midst of uttering the phoneme /ba/. Note the configuration of the lips as the "b" sound is about to be made. Visualizing the mouth movements made when someone utters /ba/ can alter your perception of the speech sound heard at the same time.

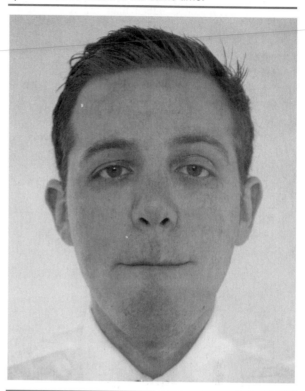

sual cues can also influence what a verbal utterance sounds like. Harry McGurk and John MacDonald conducted an experiment in which they put auditory information about a spoken word in conflict with visual information about that word (McGurk and MacDonald, 1976). They had people watch a film of a young woman who was repeating various syllables (see Figure 12.10). In some segments of the film, the audio cue (soundtrack) and the visual cue (lip movement) corresponded to the same syllable. But in other segments, the soundtrack for one syllable was dubbed onto the lip movements for another syllable. People reported the syllable accurately when just the sound was heard, and they were able to name the syllable being spoken when just the lip movements were seen with no accompanying sound. (This latter observation merely confirms that people are pretty good at lip reading.) However, people made some very interesting mistakes while watching the dubbed film.

One type of mistake involved hearing entirely new syllables, syllables that correspond neither to those on the soundtrack nor to those articulated by the speaker's lips. For example, when the syllable /ga/ was dubbed onto lip movements for /ba/, nearly all people reported hearing /da/. In other instances, people heard the syllable formed by the lip movements, rather than the one actually sounded. This demonstration of vision's strong influence on speech perception is now known as the **McGurk effect,** in honor of one of its discoverers.

The McGurk effect is not limited to single syllables. Also using a dubbing procedure, Barbara Dodd (1977) found that people sometimes heard the word *towel* when the sound of a voice saying *tough* was dubbed over the lip movements for *hole*. This influence of vision on speech perception is reduced, incidentally, when the face is shown upside down (Massaro and Cohen, 1996), which is not so surprising considering the deleterious effect of inversion on face recognition (recall Chapter 6).

In an interesting twist on this procedure, Massaro and Egan (1996) had people judge the emotion—angry versus happy—of a computer-generated "talking" head whose facial expressions and voice intonation could be independently varied. On trials when the affective connotation of the voice agreed with that of the facial expression, people always correctly judged the emotion of the talking head. On trials when the two cues were in conflict—for example, the face signaled happy while the voice implied anger—people overwhelmingly went with the facial expression.

These dubbing experiments show that vision provides complementary information about speech. This is fortunate because people often talk to one another in noisy environments where speech sounds are obscured. Visual information accompanying lip movements can improve speech intelligibility in these situations (Summerfield, 1992; Schwartz, Berthommier, and Savariaux, 2004). You may be surprised to learn, incidentally, that infants 18 to 20 weeks old can recognize the match (or mismatch) between the auditory and visual components of speech (Kuhl and Meltzoff, 1982). In an experiment to test for this ability, infants viewed a pair of film sequences projected side by side at the same time. Both films depicted a woman's face as she repeated a vowel sound, one vowel for one film and a different vowel for the other. The soundtrack corresponding to one of the two faces was broadcast from a speaker located midway between the two motion pictures. By monitoring the direction of the infants' gaze, it was determined that infants preferred to look at the face whose lip movements matched the sound. This indicates that by 5 months of age infants can detect the correspondence between speech sounds and the lip movements needed to produce those sounds.

Speech perception offers another striking connection between visual and auditory information. As you speak, the muscles of your mouth and face move, and the pattern of those movements influence the position of elements in the vocal tract, which determine the sound of your voice. Thus, the visual information generated by movements of the mouth and face are strongly coupled to the vocalization produced by those movements. A recent study revealed how sensitive people are to this linkage between facial movements and vocalization (Kamachi et al., 2003). In that study, people could listen to an unfamiliar voice and then accurately pick out the speaker from silent video sequences of several speakers. The reverse also works: After seeing a video sample of a person speaking, people were able to pick a vocalization by the speaker from a pair of voice recordings (without seeing the speaker). And this feat does not require that the actual words heard match the words whose production was seen. However, when people were tested using videos and voice recordings played backward, this remarkable ability to match visual and auditory samples was destroyed.

Monkeys, too, are good at linking vocalizations to facial expressions. Ghazanfar and Logothetis (2003) tested 20 rhesus monkeys using a version of the preferential looking technique developed for use with human infants (recall Figure 5.18). In their adaptation of the procedure, Ghazanfar and Logothetis presented two silent video animations on a pair of video monitors located next to one another; one animation showed a monkey vocalizing a "cooing" call and the other showed the same monkey making a "threat" call (see Figure 12.11). At the same time, one of the two vocalizations was broadcast from a speaker located between the two monitors but hidden from view. All 20 monkeys tested recognized the correspondence between the facial expression and the sound, as evidenced by their significant tendency to look more often at the video matching the call being played on a given trial.

We don't know all of the details of how the brain integrates speech's visual and auditory information, but neuroimaging has provided some tantalizing clues (Calvert et al., 1997). Regions of brain activity were monitored while people watched videotaped sequences of a face silently mouthing words. Not surprisingly, visual areas of the brain, including area MT (recall Chapters 4 and 9), were activated. The surprising results, however, were the strong activations seen in primary auditory cortex and in neighboring auditory brain re-

FIGURE 12.11 | Upper panels: Two frames from two video sequences showing a monkey uttering two different calls. Middle panels: Amplitude variation over time produced by the two cells. Bottom panels: Spectrograms corresponding to the two different cells.

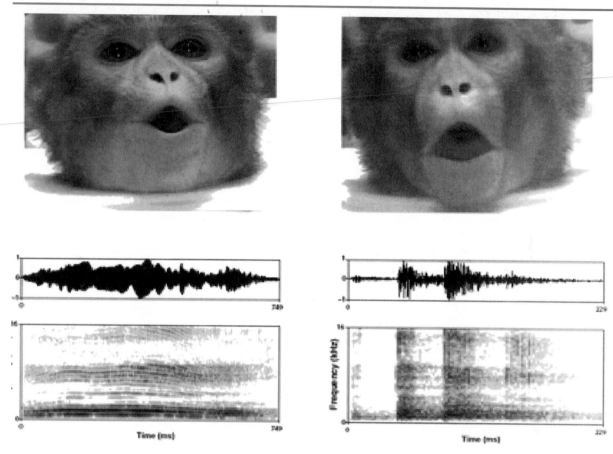

gions known to be involved in registering auditory signals including speech sounds. Those areas were activated even though no sounds were broadcast while people watched the videos. Moreover, vision's ability to activate auditory cortex was limited to facial movements that normally accompany the act of speaking. Other, nonlinguistic movements such as chewing did not activate those areas.

Given vision's influence on speech perception, shouldn't blind people have difficulty comprehending speech, especially in noisy environments? Paradoxically, just the opposite is true. When asked to discriminate spoken numbers, words, and sentences heard against a background of noise, blind high school students outperformed their sighted classmates (Niemeyer and Starlinger, 1981). This seems to imply that blind individuals hear better than sighted individuals. However, on simpler

hearing tests, such as loudness discrimination, the two groups of students were comparable. This latter result suggests that the blind students' advantage in speech comprehension reflects superior performance by their brains rather than by their ears or auditory nerves.

Next let's look at two other important factors that govern how verbal utterances actually sound, namely the perceived boundaries between words and the intonation, or pitch, of the voice as words are spoken.

The Role of Speech Boundaries and Intonation in Speech Perception

Listening to conversational speech, one usually has no trouble distinguishing words from one another—boundaries seem to separate words. These boundaries, however, are an illusion. A sound spectrogram of a sentence spoken at a normal, conversational speed shows relatively few identifiable pauses between words and no beginnings or endings to the syllables that comprise those words (look back at Figure 12.3). In fact, if one speech sound had to be completed before the next was generated, talking would take forever. So, the boundaries perceived between words have no counterpart in the acoustic signals reaching the ears. We become much more aware of the paucity of word boundaries when we listen to a conversation in an unfamiliar foreign language. In this case, it is difficult to tell where one word ends and another begins—sentences seem to consist of unbroken strings of sounds, with few demarcations to set off one word from the next. Of course, to someone familiar with that language, those individual words are as distinct as the English words you hear during ordinary conversation. What, then, causes speech sounds to be grouped into separate words?

For one thing, listeners rely on the context of a conversation to help establish those boundaries. An example of this effect of context was provided by the nonsense song introduced earlier. Once you discovered what the song was about, the continuous phrase "marzeydoats" sounded instead like "mares eat oats." In the absence of context information, one sometimes errs in establishing boundaries between words, leading to misperceived speech. *New York Times* columnist William Safire (1979) related a particularly amusing instance of misplaced word boundaries. Upon first hearing "the girl with kaleidoscope eyes," a phrase from a Beatles tune, someone thought that the line went "the girl with colitis goes by." Anyone not familiar with the subject of "Lucy in the Sky with Diamonds," the song in which this verse appears, could make such a mistake.

When distinct *pauses* do occur in speech, listeners naturally interpret those pauses as the completion of a clause or of a sentence. These pauses thus serve to inform a listener that it is appropriate to take a turn talking. Pauses, in other words, operate like traffic signals, controlling the flow of conversation between people. For most individuals, the arrival of an intended pause is signaled by a drop in the pitch of the voice. Listen to your voice drop at the end as you speak the sentence, "That should never have happened." The drop in the pitch of your voice signals listeners that you are done speaking. However, some individuals have a pattern of speaking in which pause signals (drops in voice pitch) occur *before* completion of a sentence. A listener hearing these extraneous pause signals may be confused—the pause signals invite the listener to become the speaker when, in fact, the other person may not have finished talking.

As you can imagine, people whose speech is punctuated with inappropriate pause signals are inadvertently interrupted quite frequently. One such individual is Margaret Thatcher, the former Prime Minister of Great Britain. A trio of British psychologists, Geoffrey Beattie, Anne Cutler, and Mark Pearson (1982), were intrigued by how often Thatcher seemed to be interrupted during interviews and during debate in Parliament. By analyzing sound transcripts from a television interview with the prime minister, these psychologists discovered that the inflections in Thatcher's speaking voice included frequent drops in voice pitch in the *middle* of her sentences. Unwittingly, Thatcher was signaling listeners that she had finished talking, when she actually had more to say.

Pause signals aren't the only interruptions in the smooth flow of speech. Ordinary conversations are also punctuated with repetitions, false starts, and seemingly useless utterances such as "you know," "like," and "uh-mmm." Called **disfluency,** these disruptions in fluent speech could be construed as vocal detritus that breaks up the smooth stream of speech sounds and, therefore, degrades speech perception. In fact, however, the opposite appears to be the case. Several lines of evidence imply that these disfluent insertions can actually heighten a listener's attention (Fox Tree, 2001), help the listener parse the sentence by providing additional processing time (Bailey and Ferreira, 2003), and inform the listener whether the speaker is saying something not previously mentioned in a conversation (Arnold et al., 2004). Still, there is no denying that disfluency can provoke some amusement and mild ridicule, as some famous athletes, entertainers, and politicians have discovered.

Next let's consider the voice intonation accompanying verbalized questions. Listen to the inflection in your voice as you speak aloud this declarative sentence: "She forgot her book." Now repeat this listening exercise while you speak this interrogative sentence: "She forgot her book?" Notice how the pitch of your voice rises at the end of the utterance when the sentence forms a question but falls at the end of the declarative version of the sentence (see Figure 12.12). Besides signaling the end of a sentence, then, the voice intonation at the end indicates whether that sentence was declarative or interrogative. And accompanying these distinctive voice differences, your facial expressions differ, too, depending on whether you are uttering a declarative or an interrogative sentence. Specifically, your eyebrows tend to arch and your head tends to turn sideways when asking a question (Srinivasan and Massaro, 2003).

Voice intonation, or **prosody** as it is called, is also a prime source of information for identifying a speaker based on voice alone. Even newborn infants are quite skilled at voice recognition (DeCasper and Fifer, 1980). And as mentioned earlier, the neural machinery respon-

FIGURE 12.12 | Intonation patterns associated with a sentence uttered declaratively and interrogatively. The two patterns are essentially identical except at the end of the sentence, when the voice pitch rises for the question but falls for the declarative sentence.

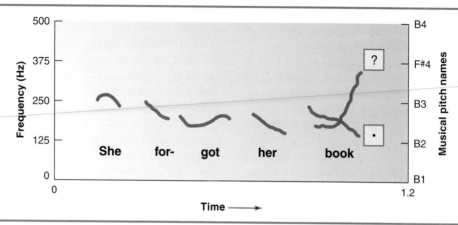

Fine Temporal Structure in Language-Based Learning Impairments

sible for this ability seems to be located in the right hemisphere: Patients with damage to the right parietal cortex (but not the left) exhibit deficits in voice recognition, the condition termed *phonagnosia.*

Besides aiding in speaker identity, voice intonation can indicate a speaker's mood. Excitement, whether from enthusiasm or anger, is characterized by marked swings in intonation, whereas calm and boredom are typically signaled by flat, relatively unchanging intonation of the voice (Russell, Bachorowski, and Fernández-Dols, 2003). You would be surprised how much information can be conveyed just by humming your sentences—in other words, using only pitch changes to convey a message. Next time you answer the phone, see how long you can carry on a conversation using hummed speech. You'll gain an appreciation of intonation's role in speech perception. To learn more about prosody and when it's used, read in Box 12.2 the explanation of the special kind of speech people use when they talk to babies and to animals.

Fine Temporal Structure in Language-Based Learning Impairments

Like other aspects of hearing, speech perception is fundamentally about registering and discriminating rapid, abrupt changes in acoustic energy over time. Such fluctuations constitute what is called "fine temporal structure." Your ability to discriminate the phonemes /da/ and /ga/ hinges on the fidelity with which your ear and brain represent acoustic fluctuations associated with those speech sounds. If those rapid fluctuations were eliminated from the acoustic signal, it would be impossible to

discriminate one phoneme from another. Similarly, if the ear or brain were unable to register these finely timed acoustic fluctuations because of a neurological disorder, speech perception would be impaired.

In fact, approximately 5 percent of children have serious difficulties understanding spoken language, even though their hearing sensitivity expressed in terms of the audibility function is normal. They are not "hearing impaired" in the usual clinical sense. Instead, they are *perceptually* speech impaired. They can hear but cannot understand. For at least some of these children the problem stems from an inability to discriminate transient acoustic features associated with speech sounds (Tallal and Piercy, 1973; Kraus et al., 1996). These children are described as having a **language-based learning impairment (LLI).** When tested in the laboratory, children with LLI experience difficulty in distinguishing two brief tones occurring in close temporal proximity, and they have problems segregating tone signals from noise even when the tone and noise are presented successively in time (Wright et al., 1997). The children behave as though their brain failed to separate successive inputs, instead fusing those inputs into a single sound.

Fortunately, the brain, including the auditory cortex, is modifiable, as we've seen at several points in this and in the previous chapter. Thus, in LLI children it is possible to ameliorate their speech perception through simple training regimes. Michael Merzenich and colleagues (1996) devised a multimedia computer game in which success depends upon a player's reactions to various multitone sounds. During initial training, the timing of these acoustic sequences was

BOX 12.2   **Baby Talk and Animal Talk**

Ever notice how a parent talks to a baby? The pitch of the voice goes up and the pattern of intonations is exaggerated. Mothers, in particular, tend to emphasize, or hyperarticulate, their vowels when speaking to an infant. These same parents don't speak this way, of course, when addressing older children or other adults. And this style of speaking to babies has been documented in parents from lots of different countries where other languages are spoken, including Japan, Russia, and Sweden. This style of speaking seems to come naturally, for parents swear they never were told to speak this way and, for that matter, they're sometimes unaware that they're doing it. This way of speaking is so ubiquitous that it has been given its own name: **motherese** (although this is a misnomer because fathers, mothers, and unrelated adults all tend to speak to babies this way). You can hear motherese being spoken by navigating to www.mhhe.com/blake5, and following the links listed for Chapter 12.

Why do parents talk this way? The most popular theory attributes this cute speech pattern to an unconscious attempt to amplify the phonetic characteristics of the vowels in the speaker's native language, a maneuver that could unwittingly aid in the infant's development of linguistic expertise. Now there's no doubt that early linguistic experience has a profound impact on an infant's march toward language acquisition (e.g., Kuhl, Tsao, and Liu, 2003), so anything that made the baby's task of speech comprehension easier should in-

deed be encouraged, including speaking to the baby in this stylized way. What's remarkable, though, is that this behavior occurs without conscious intention: It just seems to come naturally. One exception, sadly, are the vocalizations produced by a depressed mother and directed to her infant. Her utterances tend to be flat and devoid of expression, which may explain why infants of depressed mothers exhibit learning and developmental deficits (Kaplan et al., 2002).

But what triggers this stylized speech behavior? That question remains unanswered, but an interesting clue comes from the results of a simple but clever experiment showing that people tend to talk in this high-pitched, animated fashion to their pets, too. Burnham, Kitamura, and Vollmer-Conna (2002) obtained voice recordings from a large sample of mothers in their homes, and these samples included episodes when mothers were speaking to their infant, to their pet cat or dog, and to another adult. For both infant- and pet-directed vocalizations, pitch was elevated and the voice was more animated; neither of those speech variations were evident during vocalizations directed at another adult. Intriguingly, enhanced vowel articulation was used by the mothers only when talking to infants, not to their pets. This makes some sense, for these mothers were not trying to teach their pets to talk. This, in turn, suggests that baby-talk does indeed serve an important educational aspect, albeit one that is used unconsciously.

adjusted to levels where the children could easily succeed, thereby receiving prizes for "winning." After a series of trials, the timing was shortened as the children improved. All the children who participated in the training steadily improved at the game and, more importantly, these gains transferred to speech discrimination and language comprehension tests (Tallal et al., 1996). These improvements were observed after only 10 hours of practice distributed over 20 days, and the gains were still evident 6 weeks after training. Merzenich, Tallal, and their colleagues are currently field-testing a simple, computer-based training regime on thousands of children. Efforts are also underway to devise temporal processing tests that can be administered during the first year of an infant's life. The goal is to enable earlier intervention to prevent LLI. This work represents a remarkable synthesis of basic auditory science and clinical audiology, grounded in neurophysiological evidence on brain plasticity.

With our overview of speech completed, we're now ready to turn to the other unique aspect of human hearing, music perception.

Music

Music is ubiquitous: everywhere on our planet where people are, there is music. It's used in celebrations, religious rituals, and feasts; music often accompanies athletic competitions, and it is used to arouse and organize warriors going into battle. Music and dance go hand in hand, which is not surprising since both are built around the element of rhythm. Anyone who has witnessed a battalion of Maori tribesmen performing the *haka* knows how compelling and forceful the marriage of dance and chant can be. Musical expression, of course, takes different forms, and the instruments native to one culture may seem completely foreign to another. Still, we all know music when we hear it, even if we don't like it.

Music is also unique: nothing else we perceive—and nothing else the brain is called on to accomplish—is like music. As one individual put it, "Music is nothing but organized sound governed by rules of harmony and counterpoint, and the sounds are self-sufficient and non-referential" (Sergent, 1993, p. 168). It is true that music, like speech, entails the use of a limited set of acoustic signals (phonemes in the case of speech, notes in the case of music) combined to from limitless perceptual experiences (sentences and melodies). But speech is always referential: Our words and sentences refer to objects, events, intentions, and ideas; our words have meaning. Music, however, is often about the sounds themselves and their relations to one another and not about anything those sounds refer to (most music is "nonreferential" to repeat Sergent's adjective).[6] Yet despite its uniqueness, music does not arise from specialized "centers" in the brain that are exclusively responsive to the acoustic properties of music. Instead, music perception uses some of the same neural circuits as are involved in language processing, emotional reactions, and cognitive judgments (Tramo, 2001). As we move through our discussion of music, you should refer to color plate 21, which provides a wonderful overview of the neural circuitry involved in music perception; we'll be taking a closer look at many of these brain areas shortly.

Some people think that our primate ancestors were creating music well before they developed the ability to speak to one another. One popular account places the origins of music in the laps of mothers, whose soothing, prosodic cooing to their infants represented a kind of non-linguistic speech that provided comfort and promoted bonding. Charles Darwin favored the idea that music preceded speech, but he believed that music arose out of the mating instinct, with musiclike calls issued by males when courting females. Others, however, disagree with the view that music preceded speech. The nineteenth-century philosopher Herbert Spencer proposed that music evolved from speech when it was gradually discovered that emotion could be communicated by modulating the intensity and pitch of the voice. Eventually, these modulations took on a life of their own, without the need for words, thus spawning what we know as music.

Nothing is going to settle these arguments about the origins of music; the crucial evidence is lost. But for our

---

[6]Not all music is nonreferential. In classical music, there are examples of music with explicit references to themes such as bravery, the seasons, planets, and animals. And vocal music is referential by virtue of its use of speech.

purposes that doesn't matter. What we're concerned with in this section is music as a perceptual experience.

Like other forms of hearing, our ability to perceive music is the outcome of breathtakingly complex neural processing, both within the auditory system itself as well and within other neural systems responsible for cognition and emotion (Weinberger, 2004). For this reason, music is interesting not only because of the meaning and enjoyment it brings to people, but also because it can provide revealing insights into the operation of the human ear and brain, and into cognitive and emotional processes more generally. In the following sections, we explore some of what's known about music perception, with our survey divided into important components of music perception: melody, rhythm, and emotional impact. Each section also includes information on brain mechanisms involved in those aspects of music perception. To launch into this survey, there's no better place to begin than with melody, the defining characteristic of music.

What Is a Melody?

Melody is the essence of a musical passage's identity—it's melody (not rhythm or harmony) that sets songs apart from one another. You don't have to be a musician to recognize musical melodies; recognizing a melody is an ability that comes easily to almost everyone (later in this chapter we'll consider that small minority of individuals who are said to be tone deaf, meaning they *cannot* hum a melody or hear the difference between middle C and a note several steps up the keyboard). Moreover, most people, regardless of musical training, can recognize a familiar melody when it is played in different keys, played on different instruments or sung by different voices. In all three cases, the particular notes may differ but the melody remains the same. Just as different type fonts can be used to print the same sentence, different notes can produce the same melody. We hear melodies not as specific sets of notes but as particular relations, or patterns, among notes.

But what aspects of a melody unite musical notes into a pattern? Is it the rise and fall in the pitch of successive notes—the property known technically as **melody contour?** Does it have something to do with the size of the intervals between successive notes? In a now classic study, Dowling and Fujitani (1971) answered that question by asking college undergraduates—most of whom had no musical training—identify some familiar melodies including "Yankee Doodle," "Oh, Susannah," "Twinkle, Twinkle, Little Star," "Good King Wenceslaus," and "Auld Lang Syne." Each tune was

FIGURE 12.13 | The left-hand musical notation gives the first three notes of the tune "Oh Susanna." The middle and right-hand notations show two forms of distortion of this tune. (See text for details.)

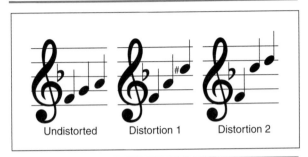

Undistorted   Distortion 1   Distortion 2

tape-recorded while being performed on the same wind instrument, in the same key, and at the same tempo. Listeners correctly identified undistorted versions of the melodies 99 percent of the time, confirming that the melodies were indeed well known. But how did listeners do when these melodies were distorted?

Dowling and Fujitani tried several different forms of distortion. In one condition, the *absolute* size of the intervals between notes was altered, but the *relative* size of the intervals remained the same. To illustrate, consider the first three notes of a verse from "Oh, Susannah" (see Figure 12.13). In the unadulterated version, notes 1 and 2 are separated by one whole tone, as are notes 2 and 3. In the first distorted version, notes 1 and 2 are separated by two whole tones, as are notes 2 and 3. Hence, in the distorted version, the absolute size of the intervals has been altered but the relative size remains unchanged. Note, too, that the pitch contour remains the same: In both versions, the second note is higher than the first, and the third note is higher than the second. When they heard melodies distorted in this way, listeners could correctly identify the tune 66 percent of the time. This decline in performance indicates that absolute interval size (the property distorted in this condition) does contribute to defining a melody. Still, this property isn't absolutely crucial—relative interval size and pitch contour provide enough information for listeners to distinguish one melody from others some of the time.

In a second condition, only the pitch contour was preserved. With this more severe form of distortion, the sequence of notes moved up and down in pitch in the same manner as they did in the normal version, but the size of the intervals between notes in the distorted version was unrelated to the size of the intervals in the original. An example of this form of distortion, applied to "Oh,

Susannah," appears in the musical staff at the far right (distortion 2). Listeners still managed to identify the melody 59 percent of the time. So pitch contour, all by itself, does provide some information for identifying melodies.

In their final condition, Dowling and Fujitani distorted the pitch contour as well. The only thing left undistorted was the first note in each measure. With just this impoverished information to go on, people were not able to recognize the melodies.

The potency of melodic contour was cleverly exploited by the great Russian composer Piotr Ilyich Tchaikovsky in his Sixth Symphony, the *Pathetique*. There is one haunting passage that launches the fourth movement, a slow, sad melody played with agonizing emotion by the string section. The listener hears this single melody as a downward flow of notes with a brief upturn near the end (see Figure 12.14, top); other background notes provide the accompanying harmony that reinforces the minor key in which the melody is played. The melody itself is compelling and memorable. However, when we look at the orchestral score for this passage, the melody is nowhere to be found. No single instrument or ensemble of instruments actually plays the notes that are so conspicuous to hearing. Rather, Tchaikovsky has divided up the notes of the melody among the first and second violins (see Figure 12.14, bottom), with the two ensembles voicing their contributions at different times during the passage.[7] The melody emerges because of a clear downward melodic contour that we hear automatically. Moreover, this strong tendency to unite the notes into a melody is reinforced by the highly similar timbre of the instruments contributing the successively played notes. Tchaikovsky's trick would have failed if the successive notes had been played by instruments whose timbres differed (e.g., strings intermixed with woodwinds).

Variety in timbre can also impact melodic salience—by introducing contrasts among different instruments' timbre, a composer can add interest and zeal to a melodic line. To illustrate this role of timbre, let's turn to another symphonic piece, this one Maurice Ravel's 1928 composition, *Bolero*. This piece begins with a snare drum tapping out a simple, spare melody. Then about 17 minutes later, *Bolero* comes to its stirring climax, having done nothing more than repeat the same simple melody over and over, using different instruments and combinations of instruments playing at varying degrees of loudness. Ravel cleverly ex-

---

[7]With tongue in cheek, some have speculated that Tchaikovsky's opening theme in the Fourth movement of the *Pathetique* may have a sad, lonely quality because nobody is actually playing it.

FIGURE 12.14 | The upper musical notation shows the melody everyone hears when listening to the first couple of measures of the opening passage of the fourth movement of Tchaikovsky's Sixth Symphony. The lower score at bottom shows the actual notes being played by the first and second violin sections. Notice that neither section is playing the melody; instead, the melody arises from successive notes, which are distributed between the sections.

ploits variations in timbre while maintaining a kind of melodic pitch constancy. Listeners to *Bolero* become hypnotized by the sequence of notes—the melody—regardless of the instrument on which those notes are played. The harmonic structure of the notes varies depending on the instrument (that structure defines the instruments' timbre), but the perception of the successive pitches of the notes and, therefore, the melody remains constant. We can characterize this achievement as **pitch constancy.**

For most listeners, pitch constancy is aided greatly by the presence of a tonal context or, in other words, by the melody in which the tone occurs. This contextual effect is nicely verified by results from a study carried out by Warrier and Zatorre (2002). They asked listeners, all of whom had only modest musical training, to listen to two tones that were very similar in pitch but different in timbre; listeners simply reported whether the two tones were the same or different in pitch. In each trial for one condition, the pair of tones was presented individually, and on trials of a second condition the tones were the last notes of a brief, familiar melody. Without the melodic context, performance was near chance (50 percent), because the two tones were highly similar in pitch, but with the melodic context, performance jumped to 70 percent correct. This contextual boost in performance implies that melody and timbre, as-

pects of music ordinarily considered as independent features, strongly interact to frame a musical experience.

Absolute Pitch and Tone Deafness   Because melody comprises a sequence of pitches, one's ability to perceive melody depends crucially on the ability to perceive pitch. Nearly all of us can perceive pitch, although some among us are remarkably adept at it while others are miserable. In this section we will consider both classes of individuals, starting with the pitch experts.

You've probably heard of **absolute pitch**—this refers to the ability to vocally reproduce any musical note requested, or to name any note heard.[8] Individuals with this gift are often found among musicians, although even among musicians the ability is rare (Levitin and Rogers, 2005). One person renowned for his absolute pitch was Wolfgang Amadeus Mozart. It is reported that he could tell when the violin he was playing was tuned differently from one he had played the day before, even if those violins were mistuned by no more than "half a quarter of a tone,"—one-eighth of the difference between adjacent

---

[8]Absolute pitch is sometimes called "perfect" pitch, but that term has been largely abandoned in the scientific literature, partly because "perfect" pitch may be amazingly good, but it's not actually error free (Zatorre, 2003; Levitin and Rogers, 2005).

keys on a piano (Stevens and Warshofsky, 1965). To determine whether you have absolute pitch, you can take a brief test on the Web; the URL for this website is given in this books web links.

Those rare people with absolute pitch (the incidence is estimated at 1 in 10,000) invariably exhibited this ability as children; there is no reported case of an adult successfully acquiring absolute pitch (Levitin and Rogers, 2005). Moreover, people with absolute pitch do not have superior hearing—their ability to judge subtle differences between two similar pitches is no better than that of people without absolute pitch. Rather, people with absolute pitch have a remarkable ability to remember and name pitches. Because this ability tends to run in families, it is tempting to conclude that absolute pitch has a substantial genetic component. That evidence alone, however, is equivocal—family members with absolute pitch are very likely to be musicians and would have received lots of exposure to musical notes, the only natural sound that allows the development of perfect pitch. More convincing evidence comes from a study of pitch perception in twins. Drayna et al. (2001) found that pitch perception is more strongly correlated in identical twins than in fraternal twins, even though twins, whether identical or not, would likely have had comparable exposure to music. This substantial difference between pitch perception in the two types of twins was not accompanied by differences in other functions, such as hearing ability assessed by the audiogram.

According to one theory, all of us were born with extraordinarily keen pitch perception, but we lost some of this keenness as the consequence of ordinary hearing (Saffran, 2003). Why would experience cause a deterioration in pitch perception? For most activities that rely on hearing, including speech, we're not called on to register the precise pitch of sounds but, rather, the relation among pitches. That's what defines the unique quality of a given individual's voice, that's what defines a musical instrument's timbre, and that's what defines melody. To illustrate, you can recognize a familiar melody such as "Pop Goes the Weasel" regardless of the key in which it is played. "Pop Goes the Weasel" played on keys toward the left side of a piano keyboard (where pitch is low) is as recognizable as the same "Pop Goes the Weasel" played on the keys toward the keyboard's right side (where pitch is high). Melody, in other words, depends on pitch relations and not on absolute pitch. Although this discourages the retention of any ability for absolute pitch you may have started out with, it enables you to enjoy the same musical melodies played or sung in differ-

ent keys. In this regard, it is noteworthy that people with absolute pitch frequently complain that it is disturbing to listen to a piece of music played in an unusual key—the piece sounds "wrong." For more on absolute pitch, see the Web links at www.mhhe.com/blake5.

Besides absolute pitch, there's a somewhat less amazing, more common ability known as **relative pitch**—people who have relative pitch can identify tonal intervals accurately, but are less accurate when naming the particular notes making up that interval. You can think of tonal intervals in terms of the steps of the musical scale. In particular, a tonal interval is defined by the number of steps that separate a pair of notes. For instance, the first two notes of "My Bonnie Lies over the Ocean" define a larger interval than do the first two notes of "Greensleeves." To be able to recognize and label all these various intervals means you have relative pitch, which many musicians have (Siegel and Siegel, 1977). Box 12.3 describes how the brains of people with good pitch perception may have benefitted from their musical training.

Perfect and relative pitch represent pinnacles of human pitch ability, but at the other end of this ability scale are individuals with **amusia,** defined as extraordinarily poor pitch discrimination. These people are sometimes referred to as "tone deaf" but that's a misnomer. They can *hear* tones but have great difficulty recognizing differences between neighboring tones that are easily distinguished by most people.

Look back at Figure 12.12 to see a nonmusical example of this point. You will recall that these two pitch contours were generated when a female English speaker uttered the declarative sentence, "She forgot her book," and the interrogative sentence, "She forgot her book?" The two contours are highly similar except for the typical rise in pitch at the end of the interrogative sentence. Musically, this pitch difference corresponds to about 12 semitones, the range of pitch differences encompassed by 12 successive notes on a piano. This pitch difference is huge, and even people with amusia have no trouble hearing whether or not the speaker is asking a question.

That's speech, though, and music, particularly Western music, is quite a different matter. Western melodies tend to be built on large numbers of small tone changes. In one sample, nearly three-quarters of successive tones differed by no more than two semitones (Vos and Troost, 1989). This point is illustrated in Figure 12.15, which shows the pitch contour produced when the first line of "Happy Birthday" was sung by the same female who produced the data shown in Figure 12.12. Note how small the song's tone variations are, compared to the

Practice Makes Perfect and a Better Brain   BOX 12.3

Those music lessons your parents urged on you as a child weren't a bad idea. Besides learning to play an instrument, musical training can also improve your ability to discriminate among pitches which, in turn, can improve accuracy in tuning musical instruments (Platt and Racine, 1985). What your parents may not have known is that those lessons would literally change your brain. By training monkeys to make finer discriminations of frequency, Recanzone, Schreiner, and Merzenich (1993) gauged improvement behaviorally and used physiological techniques to examine possible changes accompanying the improvement.

During the behavioral phase of the study, tones were presented as a series of pairs. For most pairs, the tones were of the same frequency. Whenever the tones differed in frequency, the monkey signaled recognition of the difference by lifting its hand from a key. Monkeys were trained to discriminate a standard frequency from one that was slightly different. Performance was assessed in terms of the discrimination threshold, the smallest frequency difference reliably detected by the monkey (see the appendix). During the course of training, frequency discrimination improved by as much as five-fold. Moreover, improvement was restricted to the training frequency. So, for example, if the monkey were being trained with a standard of 8,000 Hz, there would be no improvement of the threshold at 2,000 Hz.

The physiological phase of the study examined responses of neurons in the monkey's auditory cortex while various tones were being presented to the monkey's ear. As you learned in Chapter 10, the auditory cortex contains frequency maps, with neurons tuned to different frequencies occupying different regions of the cortex. In monkeys who had been trained, there were also maps, but Recanzone and colleagues found the regions of the maps devoted to the trained frequencies were greatly expanded. In fact, the size of these regions correlated strongly with the monkeys' behavioral thresholds: larger areas were associated with lower thresholds for frequency discrimination. But not every monkey in Recanzone's study exhibited cortical changes. Monkeys who listened passively to the training stimuli but did not have to make any discrimination showed essentially no change in the auditory cortex. Training requires more than passive listening; the tones must be relevant to the animal's behavior.

Neuroimaging studies point to the same kind of plasticity in auditory portions of the human brain. In highly skilled musicians, the cortical representation of musical tones is enlarged by approximately 25 percent when compared to the tonotopic maps in the brains of nonmusicians (Pantev et al., 1998). Moreover, the volume of gray matter in key regions of the brain varies with the amount of time a keyboard player devotes to practicing. (Gray matter, as you probably know, describes any region of the brain that is rich with the cell bodies of neurons.) In particular, compared to nonmusicians or other less-driven musicians, the brains of hard-practicing keyboardists have extra volume in the motor and auditory cortices, as well as in regions of the parietal lobe that start the translation between reading notes on sheet music and playing the notes themselves (Gaser and Schlaug, 2003).

Musical experience has an additional impact on the brains of musicians who make their music by conducting orchestras. A conductor faces special challenges, attending to the whole orchestra and to its various sections, but at the same time hearing individual musicians within each section. During rehearsal a conductor may need to identify which one of an orchestra's 20 violinists played the wrong note. This requires an extraordinary ability to attend to sounds originating at the same time from a wide range of locations and directions. An ERP study has shown that locations of sound sources in peripheral auditory space are much more differentiated in the brains of professional conductors than they are in the brains of nonmusicians or in musicians who are not conductors (Münte et al., 2001). These results remind us that extended sensory experience can leave lasting marks on sensory areas of the brain and can expand one's sensory abilities.

difference between declarative and interrogative sentence endings (Figure 12.12). People with amusia may fail to hear these subtle pitch changes and, hence, fail to hear the melody.

Some cases of amusia are associated with damage to the brain (Sergent, 1993), sometimes accompanied by aphasia (loss of verbal function) but other times not. Brain damage, however, isn't the only cause of amusia; some cases appear to be congenital in origin, meaning the condition was present from birth. Recently, Isabella Peretz and colleagues found several cases of congenital amusia, and they have studied one individual in great detail (Peretz et al., 2002). To illustrate the condition, let's consider that individual.

Responding to a newspaper ad seeking volunteers who considered themselves "musically impaired," a

FIGURE 12.15 | Pitch contour associated with the first few measures of the song "Happy Birthday." Notice the relatively small range of changes in pitch, relative to the pitch changes associated with human speech (recall Figure 12.11).

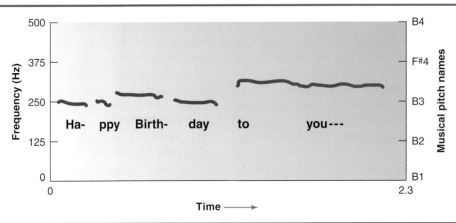

woman in her forties responded. Code-named Monica by Peretz and colleagues, this woman voluntarily underwent an extensive audiometric examination and a brain scan. These tests showed no evidence of ear abnormalities, and there were no signs of cortical atrophy or malformation in auditory regions of Monica's brain. A battery of other tests confirmed that Monica had normal intelligence and good short-term memory, and she exhibited no sign of cognitive impairment. However, she was strikingly impaired in pitch perception, and this condition was long-standing, at least from early childhood and perhaps from birth. During her childhood, social pressures pushed Monica into joining a church choir. However, once the choir leader heard her sing, Monica was encouraged to only "sing" silently, moving her lips and mouth without producing any sound. As an adult, Monica described hating to listen to music because it sounded like noise and caused her to feel stressed.

A variety of ingenious tests confirmed that Monica had a remarkable, specific impairment in recognizing differences in tones, and therefore could not distinguish most melodies from one another. On the other hand, she had no difficulty recognizing well-known people based on their voices only. Nor did Monica have any trouble perceiving tempo (another ingredient of music that we'll get to in a moment).

Subsequently, other congenital amusics have been identified and tested thoroughly, with much the same results as for Monica, although some of these amusics seem to be impaired on tempo perception as well as on tone perception (Hyde and Peretz, 2004). According to current estimates, between 4 and 5 percent of people in North America and the United Kingdom may have con-

genital amusia. Peretz suggests that amusia should be understood as "a developmental disorder that arises from failures to encode pitch with sufficient resolution to allow acquisition of core knowledge regarding the pitch structure of music." Note that this disorder does not target music per se, but undermines any function that requires ability to distinguish small differences in pitch.

Brain areas involved in pitch perception Results from brain imaging studies reveal that different aspects of pitch are registered within a complex of areas within the auditory cortex. Primary auditory cortex, of course, is activated, and because different musical pitches have different frequency content, those patterns of activation will be shifting dynamically across the tonotopic maps within primary auditory cortex. But those activation patterns in primary auditory cortex are evoked whether or not the sequence of pitches forms a melody (Patterson et al., 2002). It is only within cortical regions outside of the primary auditory area that the patterning of the sequence of pitches, and hence the presence of a melody, really matters. In the region of the superior temporal gyrus, immediately anterior to primary auditory cortex (more toward the front of the brain), one finds greater activation for varying pitch compared to fixed pitch, with some hint that these activations are greater in the right hemisphere (Zatorre, Belin and Penhuné, 2002). This region is genuinely sensitive to pitch, not just the temporal regularity ordinarily associated with pitch tones, as evidenced by the variable activation strength in this area when pitch salience is manipulated while temporal regularity is held constant (Penagos, Melcher, and Oxenham, 2004).

Previously we introduced the concept of pitch constancy, the notion that a given melody exists independent of the particular notes used to play that melody. This concept is related to a distinction made by music psychologists between pitch chroma and pitch height (Krumhansel, 1990). As you know, the notes of the musical scale repeat regularly as those notes get higher and higher; this is the basis for the notion of an octave. Thus, for example, middle C on the piano has something in common with the C one octave above it: Both have the same **pitch chroma.** At the same time, you have no trouble telling that one of those C notes is higher than the other: The two differ in **pitch height.** In the laboratory, pitch height and pitch chroma can be manipulated independently by varying the amplitudes of the harmonics that make up pitch tones.[9] When these kinds of altered pitches are played while activity within a person's brain is being imaged, different brain regions are activated depending on what aspect of pitch the person is experiencing (Warren et al., 2003). Specifically, changes in pitch chroma (an essential ingredient in perception of melody) activate the region mentioned in the previous paragraph, the area anterior to primary auditory cortex; changes in pitch height (which is more related to the particular instrument or voice that is producing a melody) activate a region posterior (more toward the back of the brain) to primary auditory cortex. Here, too, we may be seeing an indication that musical sounds are analyzed in terms of "what" is being heard (melody) and "where" those sounds originate.

With this overview of pitch and melody in mind, we now turn to a second key ingredient of music perception, rhythm.

What Is Rhythm?

Melody may be the substance of music, but rhythm provides the spice that adds zest to that substance. From the outset, it is important to distinguish rhythm from meter. Both are forms of temporal structure, a term referring to the organization of discrete sounds (e.g., notes) over time. **Meter** refers to the global periodicity of musical sounds—if rhythm is the spice for melody, meter is the glue that holds the melody together over time. Those of you who have played music or who have learned ballroom dancing are familiar with meter. You know, for example, that a waltz has 3/4 meter whereas a tango has 4/4 meter. These numbers refer to how many notes comprise a "measure" of music, where the measure is a unit of time. Hum the tune for "Row, Row, Row Your Boat" and you will hear 4/4 me-

ter; hum "The Blue Danube Waltz" (one of the pieces of music in Stanley Kubrick's *2001: A Space Odyssey*) and you'll know what 3/4 meter sounds like.

Rhythm is something else: it's created by the durations between successive acoustic events (e.g., notes). **Rhythm** refers to the patterning of sounds over time. Although it includes a sense of beat, or tempo, rhythm is more about subtleties in the distribution of musical sounds in time. For that matter, rhythm does not even require melody for its expression, as evidenced by the forceful perception of rhythm we experience when listening to someone playing a drum.[10] Both meter and rhythm are involved in music, but in this section we'll concentrate on rhythm, for it provides huge variety to the perception of musical sounds.

All music possesses some degree of rhythm. Ravel's *Bolero,* mentioned earlier, exploits a relentless, steady rhythm to drive the piece inexorably forward and hold the musical experience together as timbre varies and loudness grows. With some styles of music popular today, rhythm constitutes *the* key ingredient; examples here include reggae and rap.

But rhythm can also be used in exactly the opposite fashion, with rhythmic structure varied within a musical piece to alter the perceptual impact and mood engendered by the music. A compelling example of this use of rhythm is provided by Franz Liszt's short piece for piano and orchestra, "Totentanz" ("Dance of Death"). It is an amazing example of the musical variety that can be achieved simply by altering the speed and rhythm of one theme. The piece consists of 30 variations on the same theme, the medieval "Dies Irae" ("Day of Wrath"), with each variation making its own unique musical statement. An attentive listener should have no trouble hearing the same *melody* repeating throughout the piece. Liszt's composition beautifully demonstrates how changes in rhythm alone can influence your perception of a melody.

Rhythm is more than just tempo, or beat. Rhythm also entails variations in the durations of successive notes during a musical passage, as well as the length of time the note is held. Even when played at the same tempo, a series of notes played using staccato (rapid, brief execution) sound entirely different from when those same notes are played using legato (played with a smooth, even manner). Once a musical piece begins unfolding, the rhythm sets up a temporal framework that defines what we expect to hear. Deviations from that framework—rhythmic variety—can be

---

[9]The Web site for this text (www.mhhe.com/blake5) lists web links where you can hear examples of sounds with changing pitch height and changing chroma.

[10]In the subway stations of many large cities, crowds of people stand mesmerized as they listen to a performer pounding out primitive beats on an upside down plastic container, a testimony to rhythm's compelling quality (and to the boring experience of waiting for a subway train).

highly enjoyable, as exemplified by jazz improvisation. But if carried to an extreme, rhythmic variation can destroy a piece's coherence for most listeners, for when rhythm's structure is removed one must turn to other, more abstract musical sources to hold the piece together. Some pieces by composers of the serialist school stripped temporal structure to its bare bones, thereby challenging the audience's ability to organize the music perceptually. The limited popularity of this form of music testifies to rhythm's primary quality in the musical experience.

Rhythm is all about timing, whether we're talking about the perception of music or the production of music. On the production side, skilled musicians exhibit unbelievably exquisite control over the timing and sequencing of finger movements when playing an instrument, and brass and woodwind players must also coordinate their breathing with their finger motions. Brain control of these movements depends on motor control systems within the cortex, cerebellum, and midbrain structures. On the perception side, Penhune, Zatorre, and Evans (1998) have found that perceiving rhythm also engages the cerebellum as well as cortical areas in the frontal lobes and in the right hemisphere of the temporal lobe. In their study, however, the rhythmic sounds used to produce brain activation were pure tones at a single frequency, an acoustic signal that does not qualify as music.

Other brain imaging work suggests that the particular patterns of activation to rhythmic sounds may depend on the complexity of the sequences, with simple rhythms handled by the left hemisphere and complex rhythms by the right hemisphere (Sakai et al., 1999). Also of relevance to brain processes involved in rhythm perception are results from studies of brain-damaged individuals. Peretz (1990) studied a group of patients who had suffered a stroke affecting only one of the two hemispheres; included among the tests administered to the patients was one involving perception of musical rhythm. While deficits in melody perception were reliably associated with right hemisphere damage, deficits in rhythm were found in patients with damage to either hemisphere. In this group of patients, the lesions were too diffuse to allow precise localization of the region of cortical damage. But in a more recent neuropsychological study, the same kinds of musical rhythm tests were administered to patients who had undergone unilateral removal of small regions of the temporal lobe, the procedure used for relief from otherwise intractable epileptic seizures (Liégeois-Chauvel et al., 1998). In these patients, unlike the stroke victims, the removed regions could be pinpointed with great accuracy. Among these patients, those in whom portions of the right temporal lobe were excised exhibited impaired ability to discriminate melodies defined either by pitch con-

tour or by rhythmic information. Those with left temporal lobe excisions experienced difficulty only on the task involving melody discrimination based on rhythm. Moreover, the ability to perceive meter (discussed earlier) was impaired when the excision involved an anterior part of the temporal lobe, more forward in the brain from the temporal lobe region associated with rhythm impairments.

Having considered melody and rhythm, we're now ready to turn to a third, salient aspect of music perception, the one associated with how we feel about music.

Emotional Connotation and Music

It makes no sense that people should feel sadness when listening to Samuel Barber's *Adagio for Strings,* but many people do. And why would someone experience a sense of pending doom when hearing the opening notes of Beethoven's Fifth Symphony? After all, these are sequences of notes with no intrinsic meaning, and the music has no association with events reminding people of sadness or doom. And yet music has this mysterious capacity to evoke emotional reaction. Why?

You might think that these emotional reactions are somehow conditioned by our exposure to the Western tonal system, with its major and minor keys. However, the music of other cultures with entirely different tonal systems also has distinct emotional connotations. But do Westerners get those emotional reactions when listening to non-Western music for the first time? You may be surprised to learn that the answer is yes. Balkwill and Thompson (1999) asked students and staff at a Canadian university to listen to excerpts from Hindustani ragas played by native musicians of India.[11] Different ragas were improvised by the musician to convey either sadness, anger, joy, or peace. Tested individually, the Canadian listeners had no difficulty in categorizing each raga's dominant emotion. Despite their complete unfamiliarity with Indian music and its tonal system, the listeners had little difficulty differentiating the intended emotional connotation. Evidently there are salient auditory cues specifying emotional content in music, cues that transcend cultural differences in musical style. And those auditory cues are clearly highly reliable, for when people listen to music performed by professional musicians those people can identify the emotion the musician intends to convey as accurately as they can judge the emotion portrayed by a face or by someone's voice (Juslin and Laukka, 2003).

---

[11]Listed in the texts website, it gives links at which examples of Indian ragas can be heard.

FIGURE 12.16 | These two graphs show how loudness (upper graph) and tempo (lower graph) vary depending on what emotion the performer was trying to convey. The bars show the average loudness and tempo, and the I bars on each histogram denote the standard deviation of the mean (a measure of the variance in loudness or tempo) throughout the passage. In this example, the music was a theme by Haydn, played by an accomplished pianist.

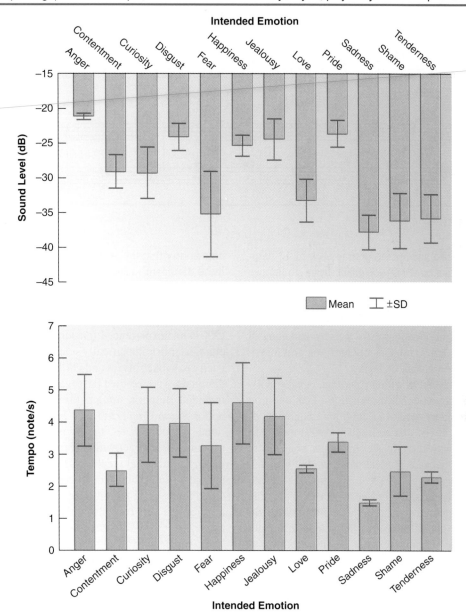

These findings lead to an obvious question: What aspects of a musical passage give it emotional connotation? Juslin (2003) reviewed a number of different studies to arrive at an answer to this question. As you might anticipate, important acoustic cues to musical emotion include: (1) tempo, with joy being associated with brisk tempo and sadness with slow tempo; (2) loudness, with anger being signaled by loud music and tenderness by soft music; and (3) the key in which a piece is played, with minor keys producing music that feels somber, doleful, or threatening and major keys producing music that is light, happy, or uplifting. Figure 12.16 summarizes how tempo and loudness vary depending on how an

FIGURE 12.17 | Two examples of a simple melody. The top one ("Major Triads") obeys the expected rules of melodic structure, but the bottom one ("Flatted 13th Triads") sounds dissonant, as if incorrect notes were being played.

accomplished pianist attempts to portray each of 12 emotions. Juslin and Laukka (2003) document strong similarities between the *vocal* cues signifying different emotions and the *musical* cues signifying those emotions. These strong similarities led Juslin and Laukka to conclude that "music performers communicate emotions to listeners by exploiting an acoustic code that derives from innate brain programs for vocal expression of emotions." (p. 805).

Finally, what happens within your brain when you listen to music with emotional connotation? This question has been answered by several recent brain imaging studies. In one study, Blood and colleagues (1999) measured patterns of brain activation in listeners whose brains were scanned while they heard musical passages that sounded either pleasant or unpleasant. These investigators wanted to use an unfamiliar musical passage, to side-step possible learning effects and individual differences in exposure. So they created new musical passages that varied in the degree of dissonance (from a listener's standpoint, dissonance sounds like the performer has hit a wrong note, an event that makes us all cringe when it happens). Figure 12.17 shows examples of a musical passage with no dissonance (judged pleasant) and a musical passage with a high degree of dissonance (judged unpleasant). Several brain regions produced activation that covaried with the degree of dissonance, most notably paralimbic areas that are intimately involved in affective reactions.[12] It is also noteworthy that the brain regions uniquely activated by these dissonant musical passages were distinctly different from those areas activated by musical pitch and rhythm.

In a second, more recent study, Blood and Zatorre (2001) had experienced musicians listen to passages of classical music specifically selected because of their capacity to evoke shivers and chills of emotion in these individuals. The selected passages came from pieces that included Barber's *Adagio for Strings* and Rachmaninoff's *Piano Concerto No. 3 in D Minor*. Again, emotional reactions to these musical excerpts were accompanied by activation in regions of the brain mediating emotional reactions, regions including the amygdala and orbito-frontal cortex, to mention just two (see Figure 12.18). Noting that these same brain areas are activated in response to food, sex, and drugs of abuse, Blood and Zatorre concluded that their result "links music with biologically relevant, survival-related stimuli via their common recruitment of brain circuitry involved in pleasure and reward" (p. 11818). Why this link between music—an abstract, meaningless sequence of sounds—and emotion is formed in the first place remains an open question. As Blood and Zatorre surmise, music may have serendipitously acquired beneficial effects on mental and physical health. Or to borrow a metaphor from Steven Pinker (1997), music may be "auditory cheesecake, an exquisite confection crafted to tickle the sensitive spots of . . . our mental faculties" (p. 534).

---

[12]These paralimbic areas are also strongly activated when you experience other aversive events such as an offensive odor (Zald and Pardo, 1997) or the sound of fingernails scraping over a chalkboard (Zald and Pardo, 2002).

FIGURE 12.18 | Regions of the human brain activated when trained musicians listen to musical excerpts that evoke strong emotional reactions. The three brain scans on the left (A–C) show areas activated when musicians listen to "unpleasant" melodies containing dissonant parts (such as the melody shown in the bottom panel of Figure 12.17). The region highlighted in (A) (a side view of the right hemisphere) and (B) (a view of the middle of the brain, viewed from behind) is located within a portion of the limbic system (theparahippocampal gyrus); the highlighted region in (C) is called the precuneous, a brain region activated on tasks involving memory and selective attention. The three brain scans on the right (D–F) show areas more strongly activated when musicians listened to "pleasant" melodies containing few or no dissonant parts (like the melody shown in the top panel of Figure 12.17). The highlighted regions in these three scans correspond to the brain regions in the orbitofrontal cortex (the portion at the very front of the cerebral cortex located just above the eyes); from other studies these brain regions have been implicated in emotional processing.

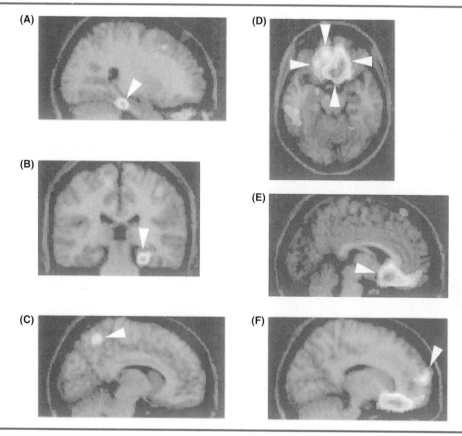

S U M M A R Y

Speech and music perception, two universal human activities, obey principles of perceptual organization just like other aspects of perception. While speech and music engage the same neural machinery as other, naturally occurring sounds, both have unique acoustic qualities that may require specialized processing that emphasizes either the distribution of acoustic energy over time or the exact points in time at which acoustic events occur. It remains to be learned how these competing demands are worked out in the brain, although some evidence suggests that the two processing strategies may be divided between the hemispheres. Speech and music are also behaviorally potent in that they can evoke strong emotional reactions.

Having completed our survey of hearing, speech and music, we are now ready to consider a trio of senses—touch, smell, and taste—that play subtle but important roles in our everyday lives. We will look at each of these subjects, in turn, in the remaining three chapters.

K E Y   T E R M S

absolute pitch
amusia
disfluency
language-based learning
    impairment (LLI)
McGurk effect
melody contour
meter

motherese
neurogram
paralinguistic information
phonagnosia
phoneme
pitch chroma
pitch constancy
pitch height

prosody
relative pitch
rhythm
unvoiced laughter
vocal folds
vocal tract
voiced laughter
Wernicke's area

Touch

Thanks to a late-night thunderstorm, your house has been plunged into total darkness. Seeking a source of light, you fumble around on the shelves of a closet trying to find a flashlight. You explore one object after another with your hands, using your fingers to feel for telltale signs of the flashlight. Rejecting a box of laundry detergent ("wrong shape"), a can of spray paint ("surface is too smooth") and a piece of lead pipe ("too heavy"), you finally grasp the flashlight and locate its on/off switch. All of this was accomplished courtesy of your sense of touch. (Alas, if your flashlight is like ours, the batteries are probably dead.)

This scenario underscores an important lesson: Although most of us depend heavily on vision to recognize objects, our sense of touch can also perform this job admirably. To get a deeper appreciation for the power and beauty of touch, consider the words of a genuine touch authority, the late Helen Keller (1880–1968). As you probably know, Keller was a truly remarkable woman who, with the help of her teacher Anne Sullivan, literally re-created her reality after being plunged into deafness and blindness very early in life. For revealing insights into touch's magic, listen to Helen Keller's words:

> My world is built of touch-sensations, devoid of physical colour and sound; but without colour and sound it breathes and throbs with life. Every object is associated in my mind with tactual qualities which, combined in countless ways, give me a sense of power, of beauty, or of incongruity. . . . All palpable things are mobile or rigid, solid or liquid, big or small, warm or cold, and these qualities are variously modified. The coolness of a water-lily rounding into bloom is different from the coolness of an evening wind in summer, and different again from the coolness of the rain that soaks into the hearts of growing things and gives them life and body. The velvet of the rose is not that of a ripe peach or of a baby's dimpled cheek. . . . What I call beauty I find in certain combinations of all these qualities, and is largely derived from the flow of curved and straight lines which is over all things. (Keller, 1908)

For those of us whose perceptual worlds are dominated by sights and sounds, the world of touch is not so conspicuous—we must pay close attention to appreciate what touch affords. Touch helps us identify objects within arm's length by furnishing information about the shape, size, and weight of those objects. Touch also reveals a surface's texture and mechanical consistency, two characteristics that may not be visually obvious. For example, subtle perceptual differences in qualities such as roughness, smoothness, or fuzziness correspond to physical differences in the textures of objects. Similarly, perceptual differences in softness, hardness, and elasticity arise from differences in how readily different objects can be compressed. Interestingly, these judgments don't even require direct contact between the hand and the object. Many of these tactile qualities can be perceived using a hand-held rod to explore the surfaces of objects (Barac-Cikoja and Turvey, 1991).

To appreciate the importance of touch, imagine living in a world devoid of tactile sensations. Whereas for most of us the thought is unimaginable, some people find themselves in exactly such a world. Some patients suffering from multiple sclerosis (a disease in which the insulating sheath surrounding nerve fiber axons deteriorates) find it impossible to identify objects by touch. To find their keys in their pocket, for example, they must empty the pocket and inspect its contents visually. And even more devastating is the complete loss of all large-diameter touch fibers that can occur after a severe viral infection. For a powerful description of what it would be like to lose all touch sensitivity, read *Pride and a Daily Marathon* (Cole, 1995), an account of a person's struggles to deal with this awful condition. People suffering from this affliction not only fail to sense objects when they contact them, they also find it nearly impossible to walk or stand, since we rely on pressure and kinesthetic cues to execute motor behaviors. (For a sense of how debilitating this would be, think just how strange it feels to try to walk when your foot has gone to sleep.) Later in this chapter, we'll give other examples of deficiencies in touch perception resulting from brain damage.

Besides aiding object identification and supporting posture and walking, touch also plays a major role in development and in social interactions. Dating back to Harlow and Harlow's (1966) classic work with infant monkeys, animal studies have confirmed that early touch deprivation stunts growth, both physical and social. In rats, for example, the mother's regular grooming of her newborn pups stimulates secretion of growth hormone in the infants; without touch to trigger this secretion, growth is retarded. Touch per se is the key factor here. Secretion of growth hormone in newborn rats is triggered by vigorous, repetitive stroking with a paintbrush (which simulates the normal action of the mother's tongue). Pups receiving this surrogate touch grow at normal rates.

Research on premature human infants implies that touch exerts the same therapeutic effect in our species. Diane Ackerman, in her book *The Natural History of the Senses* (1990), describes studies showing that premature human infants gain weight more quickly if they are systematically stroked or massaged. In addition, stroked infants seem to be more alert; to be sounder sleepers; and, subsequently, to be more advanced cognitively. And infant stroking is something parents are adept at. In fact, a mother resonates to the distinctive feel of her own newborn infant. Merely stroking the hands or cheeks of various infants is enough to tell a blindfolded mother which infant is hers (Kaitz et al., 1992).

Touch makes another important contribution to our lives: It is a universal means of social communication. We shake hands with acquaintances, we embrace close friends and family members, we affectionately tickle an infant, we massage the temples of a distressed companion, we caress the skin of a loved one—all of these forms of communication are tactile and all convey specific messages.[1] Some of these touch messages are common to our entire species, no doubt, but others are culturally specific. In Thailand, for example, the top of a female's head is strictly off limits; merely to touch her head constitutes a sexual advance that is taboo. In many cultures, including Western cultures, touch exchanges between individuals follow unwritten rules of status: The initiator of physical contact is the individual of higher status, and violations of this ritual can be socially awkward.

In a way, touch can be construed as the most reliable of the sensory modalities. When the senses are in conflict, touch is usually the ultimate arbiter. Imagine reaching out to grasp an object that you see, only to find nothing there. After the initial astonishment, you'd probably decide that it was your visual system that had been misled. Touch, in other words, seems more trustworthy than sight. Or imagine, in the middle of the day, bumping into an object that you could feel but could not see. Again, you'd probably doubt your sense of sight, not your sense of touch. The eighteenth-century Irish cleric and philosopher George Berkeley believed that vision was initially unreliable until its messages were calibrated and interpreted by the more reliable sense of touch. Based on common experience, then, the aphorism "Seeing is believing" might be rephrased as "Feeling is believing." It is appropriate, though, to say that sometimes people "lose touch with reality."

---

[1]Tickling is that unique form of tactile stimulation that often elicits paradoxical reactions: laughter and reflexive withdrawal. It has long been a puzzle, incidentally, why one does not evoke these reactions when tickling oneself. The brain seems to know who's doing the tickling and discounts the effect when stimulation is self-produced (Carlsson et al., 2000). People also reflexively react when they believe they are being tickled by a machine, so it's not necessary that the tickler be another person (Harris and Christenfeld, 1999).

Touch sensations can arise from stimulation just about anywhere on the body's surface. Indeed, the skin can be characterized as one large receptor surface for the sense of touch. But most often when you touch an object, your hand is the organ of stimulation. The English neurologist Hughlings Jackson paid homage to the wonderful and complex abilities of the human hand by calling it "the most intelligent part of the body." Helen Keller, whose hands were her principal contact with reality, put it this way:

> I have experienced marvelously the qualities of the spirit in the hand during my dark, silent life. For it is my hand that binds me to humanity. The hand is my feeler with which I seize the beauty and the activity of the world. The hands of others have touched the shadows in my life with the divine light of love and upheld me with steadfast faith. Truly, as seers say, the hand of a good man is beneficence made visible and tangible. (Helen Keller, 1932)

The skin on a human hand contains thousands of **mechanoreceptors** (receptors sensitive to mechanical pressure or deformation of the skin), as well as a complex set of muscles that allow the fingers to explore an object's shape, texture, and firmness.

Whether exploring the overall shape of an object or the fine spatial details of the object's surface, the hand and the finger pads convey the most detailed tactile information about that object. In this respect, the hand is analogous to the eye's fovea, the region of the retina associated with keenest visual acuity. There is, however, a flaw in this analogy: Foveal vision is most acute when the eye is relatively stationary, but touch acuity is best when the fingers move over the object of regard. David Katz (1925), a pioneer of touch research, noted that holding the fingers very still on an object's surface dulled the ability to sense that surface's spatial features. As Katz noted, moving your fingers across a surface reveals important characteristics about that surface's detailed topography, characteristics that are missed when the fingers are immobile.

It's easy to verify Katz's claim. Think about what happens when you pick up a peach. Upon first grasping it, you can feel the fuzziness of the peach's skin. But if you're careful not to move your fingers over the surface of the peach, the sensation of fuzziness quickly disappears. Only by moving your fingers will the true surface quality of the fruit reappear. As you'll learn, this improvement in tactile sensitivity probably reflects the activation of a set of touch receptors that are relatively inactive when stationary fingers make contact with an immobile object.

Touch's Diverse Qualities

Touch experiences are triggered by mechanical disturbance of the skin produced by physical contact with an object. However, the precise nature of that mechanical disturbance varies depending on the physical properties of the object contacted and on the way in which you explore the object tactually. To illustrate what we mean, consider three simplified, but representative, cases.

First, suppose you're trying to judge the *firmness* of an object by squeezing it with your fingers. Because a hard object won't yield much to the pressure, the skin on your fingertips, not the object, will be compressed. (Imagine squeezing a rock.) A soft object, however, offers less resistance, so the skin will be compressed relatively little. (Imagine squeezing a marshmallow.) Receptors capable of registering the degree of skin compression could, therefore, furnish information about the firmness of an object.

Next, suppose you're trying to learn something about the *shape* of some small object. Holding it between thumb and forefinger, you roll the object back and forth over your fingertips, searching for clues. If it's smooth and round like a pea, the object will exert more or less the same forces against your skin at all times. But if it has sharp, irregular edges like a tooth, the object will produce abrupt changes in pressure against your skin. In both cases, moving fingertips have translated the object's shape into a characteristic sequence of skin deformations. Receptors capable of registering the sequence of deformations could provide useful information about the shape and, hence, the identity of the object. Shape information could also come from the changes in the position of your fingers as you explore the surface of any three-dimensional object. Because your finger movements mirror the object's topography, receptors in the joints of the fingers can signal object shape.

Finally, suppose you're trying to judge the smoothness of something you're touching, such as a bed sheet. As you may know, rough sheets typically have fewer threads per unit area than do smooth sheets: rough sheets have larger gaps between neighboring threads. These gaps aren't conspicuous visually, however, so you're better off rubbing your fingers over the sheet to discover its smoothness. But what actually happens when you make this comparison?

When you rub a finger over a piece of woven fabric such as a bedsheet, the skin's flexibility allows minute sections of skin to be pushed partway into the spaces between the fabric's threads. These small movements of the skin can be thought of as undulations whose frequency mimics the coarseness of the fabric. So touch receptors that register the frequency of skin undulations could provide information about an object's roughness or smoothness.

These, then, are some distinct perceptual qualities produced by tactile stimulation; each quality is correlated with some physical property of an object. In a moment, we'll see that the skin contains several different types of receptors sensitive to mechanical deformation of the skin. Some of these mechanoreceptors are well-designed to register information about the roughness of a surface, while others are suited for signaling the firmness of an object. But before considering touch receptors and their associated neural fibers, let's examine some of touch's capacities, for these capacities define the operating characteristics of those receptors and fibers.

Sensitivity and Acuity of Touch

How can one measure touch sensitivity? An old method still used today was developed in 1896 by Max Von Frey, a German neurologist. Von Frey took hairs of various diameters and lengths and glued each one to the end of a small stick. Von Frey realized that when the hair was pressed against the skin, it would exert only so much pressure before it bent. Because the pressure needed to bend a hair depended on its length and diameter, each hair could produce a characteristic maximum pressure and no more. So, for example, a short, thick hair would produce greater pressure than a long, thin hair.

Applying these calibrated hair-probes to several parts of the body, Von Frey determined the weakest pressure that could be felt. He discovered that different parts of the body vary dramatically in their tactile sensitivity, a result that has been amply confirmed (Sekuler, Nash and Armstrong, 1973). For example, the lips and, to a lesser extent, the fingertips are exquisitely sensitive to touch; in contrast, sensitivity is dull on the back and stomach. Interestingly, for any given area of the body, females are generally more sensitive to light touch than are males (Weinstein, 1968). It is also well known that touch sensitivity is dulled when the skin is cooled (Stevens, 1979), in part because the skin (and hence the receptors housed in the skin) is less pliant at colder temperatures.

Besides Von Frey hairs, a stiff probe that vibrates the skin can also be used to measure tactile sensitivity (Van Doren, Pelli, and Verrillo, 1987). Sensitivity to vibrotactile stimulation is best for vibration frequencies around 200 Hz (200 fluctuations in pressure per second). For very low frequency vibrations (in the range of 10 to 30 Hz), sensitivity measured using a large tactile probe is much poorer than when measured using a tiny probe (Gescheider et al., 1985). Regardless of probe size, though, the region of the body exhibiting greatest sensitivity to vibration is not the fingertips, but the palm. (We will return to this matter of probe size in the section on touch receptors.)

Vibrotactile stimulation has several important practical uses. Deficits in vibrotactile sensitivity provide early warning signs of peripheral nerve dysfunction associated with exposure to environmental toxins (Arezzo, Schaumburg, and Petersen, 1983). Vibrotactile sensitivity is also compromised in patients with chronic pain localized in the facial muscles that control chewing, a result suggesting the involvement of central nervous system dysfunction in this disturbing condition (Hollins et al., 1996a). Vibrotactile stimulation can also be used to present sound information, including speech, to deaf people (Weisenberger and Miller, 1987). Several research groups have developed miniature devices that convert acoustic energy into patterns of vibrotactile stimulation. When such a device is worn on a wrist band, different sounds are translated into different patterns of stimulation on the wrist. The vibrotactile stimulation, which is felt as a rapid sequence of taps on the skin, emphasizes the acoustic transients at the onset and offset of a sound. When those sounds are spoken words and sentences, the wearer of the device finds it easier to segment the speech stream (not a trivial matter, as Chapter 12); more accurate segmentation, in turn, facilitates lip reading.

It is also possible to measure a different capacity of touch, **touch acuity.** For decades this was done using the two-point threshold test (see Figure 13.1). To understand this test, imagine using the two points on a drawing compass to stimulate neighboring regions on the skin. How close together can you bring the two points before they meld perceptually into one? This minimum separation is called the two-point threshold. Extensive measurements of two-point thresholds have been made over many different places on the body (Weinstein, 1968). When a finger pad is tested, separations as small as 2 millimeters can be reliably discriminated; on the forearm, the distinguishable separation is closer to 30 millimeters; and on the back, the minimally discriminable distance grows to 70 millimeters. This form of acuity deteriorates markedly with age, although much more so in some individuals compared to others (Stevens and Patterson, 1995). Although the scientific and clinical literature on touch is full of two-threshold measurements, the validity of data generated by the procedure has been questioned. For one

FIGURE 13.1 | Drawing of an apparatus for two-point threshold test. Apparatus is being pressed against extended fingertip.

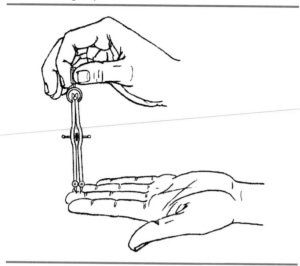

FIGURE 13.2 | Stimuli used to measure the smallest resolvable separation (A) and smallest detectable lateral displacement (B). From left to right in panel A, small raised bumps in each pair grow progressively farther apart. These stimuli can be used to determine the minimum *separation* that the fingertip can just discern. From left to right in panel B, the bump in each pair shifts systematically from the line's left to its right. These stimuli can be used to determine the smallest lateral *displacement*. In an actual experiment, stimuli would be presented randomly rather than in the systematic progressions illustrated here.

A
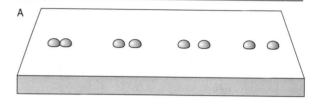

B
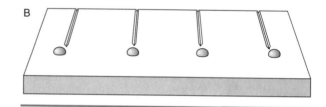

thing, the two-point threshold seriously underestimates spatial acuity (Craig and Rollman, 1999; Craig and Johnson, 2000). In place of two-point thresholds, investigators have turned to measurements of grating orientation discrimination, a technique we will describe in a moment.

Places on the body that have keen touch acuity tend also to be places where touch sensitivity is greatest. Those same places also exhibit superior **localization ability:** when a stimulus is applied to the skin within such an area, the location touched can be judged quite accurately. As will become clear in a moment, these acute, highly sensitive areas of the skin contain densely packed mechanoreceptors. Moreover, these supersensitive skin regions enjoy a disproportionately large representation in the cerebral cortex.

Localization of Tactile Stimulation

Although regional variations in touch localization and touch acuity are correlated, the two tactile abilities differ in one important way: The ability to discriminate the relative locations of two probes impressed on the skin is considerably *better* than spatial resolution measured by the two-point technique described above. To explore this performance disparity, Jack Loomis used tactile probes fashioned from metal sheets with raised dots on them (Loomis, 1981). One type of stimulus, illustrated in panel A of Figure 13.2, used two raised dots separated by vary-

ing amounts to remeasure spatial resolution. The smallest resolvable separation between two dots was 2.8 millimeters; dots closer together were indistinguishable from a single dot. In contrast, tactile judgments of *relative* position were highly acute. To measure this relative acuity, Loomis used a single raised dot presented at various distances either left or right of a reference line embossed in the metal (see panel B of Figure 13.2). With this stimulus, lateral displacements as small as 0.17 millimeter could be detected. Note that this value is many times smaller than the results of the two-point threshold method. To explain the discrepancy between two-point discrimination and discrimination of relative position, Loomis proposed that localization of a point, and hence discrimination of relative position, is governed by the relative responses in an array of receptors. This kind of cross-fiber code, as we've encountered elsewhere in this book, could represent target location to an accuracy beyond that produced by a single receptor operating alone.

Because our ability to judge the position of one point relative to another is so acute, you might expect that we would also be good at judging where on the body we're

FIGURE 13.3 | Drawing of the experimental setup used to test the influence of irrelevant visual information on the accuracy of tactile localization. In this study, carried out by Pavani, Spence, and Driver (2000), a person grasped a foam cube with each hand, with the cubes and hands placed underneath a sheet of plastic where they could not be seen. On top of the table and in full view of the participant were situated two foam cubes each grasped by a rubber glove stuffed with cotton. Small lights on the visible cubes (shown as gray dots in the figure) flashed on at the same time that a brief, vibratory stimulus was applied to the index finger or to the thumb of the person's hand (the vibrator locations are indicated by the two pairs of black arrows pointing to the person's hands). The person signaled as quickly as possible which location—finger or thumb—received the tactile stimulation, ignoring if possible the lights.

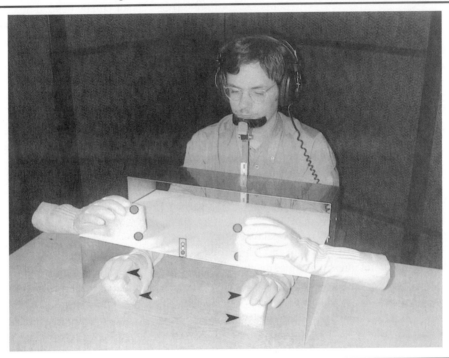

touched. Surprisingly, this expectation is wrong: Localization shows large, consistent errors. Two touch researchers, Frank Geldard and Carl Sherrick, explored these mislocalizations using research methods that they likened to a party game (Geldard and Sherrick, 1986). For example, consider a game in which one child lightly touches another child's arm with a pencil. The second child, whose gaze is averted, must indicate exactly where the pencil touched. If you've tried this game, you know how far off the judgment can be; if you haven't tried it, do. You'll be surprised at how embarrassingly large your errors can be.

You won't be surprised to learn, however, that perception of tactile stimulation improves when a visual cue supplements information about the tactile probe's location (Press et al., 2004). This makes sense, because vision is tailor-made for registering spatial information. But for

this very same reason, tactile errors in localization are even more pronounced when vision provides misleading evidence. Look at Figure 13.3, which shows the setup of one particularly revealing experiment. Pavani, Spence, and Driver (2000) had participants sit with hands hidden from view underneath a sheet of opaque plastic, grasping a pair of foam cubes. Visible to the participants was a pair of rubber gloves (stuffed with cotton) each appearing to "grasp" a foam cube. The participants' task was simple: Indicate as quickly and as accurately as possible whether a brief vibrating stimulus was applied to their thumb or to their forefinger (the vibration was delivered by tiny vibrators attached to the cube they were holding). Coincident with the vibration, a small light was briefly flashed at one of two positions of cube visible to the participant (the one being "held" by the dummy rubber gloves). When this light corresponded in location to that of the vi-

FIGURE 13.4 | These three graphs show the skin displacement (in microns) produced by stroking glass, silk, and sandpaper.

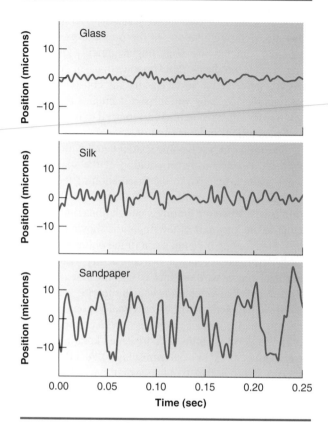

fairly constant frequency. The silk produces greater periodic fluctuations in skin displacement, with the frequency of fluctuations corresponding to the weave of the fabric. The irregular texture of the sandpaper, in comparison, produces more rapid, but irregular displacements of the skin. These recordings confirm that movement of the skin over an uneven surface generates a unique "texture" signature of that surface. And common experience tells us that people are quite adept at identifying objects from surface texture alone. By using texture information, the sense of touch allows us to distinguish reliably among objects (e.g., a drinking glass and a silk scarf) and to make fine discriminations between different versions of the same object (e.g., two different grades of sandpaper).

Everyday objects don't really lend themselves to the systematic study of surface texture. Instead, we need specially manufactured objects whose physical properties can be specified quantitatively and varied over a large range. Recall that in Chapter 5, on spatial vision, we extolled the virtues of one particular type of artificial test target, the grating pattern. Gratings have been successfully used in touch research, too. In the case of touch, the gratings are formed by regularly spaced grooves carefully cut into a metal plate or a plastic sheet (see Figure 13.5). A plate containing many grooves per unit area constitutes a high spatial frequency grating; in fact, the grooves can be spaced so close together that the spatial undulations are not even felt, so the surface feels smooth. In a medium spatial frequency tactile grating with broader peak-to-peak gaps, the undulations are more apparent and the surface feels bumpy. Finally, when the spatial frequency is low and each groove is very wide, the undulations again become harder to sense. The depth of the grooves can be varied as well, from shallow to deep shallower grooves produce a surface that feels smoother. Continuing the analogy to vision, the depth of the grooves corresponds to the contrast of a visual grating.

So just how good are we at resolving a series of finely spaced grooves in a tactile grating? What, in other words, is our tactile acuity? When touching a tactile grating with a single finger, humans can resolve spatial frequencies with peak-to-peak gaps as small as about a millimeter. Not surprisingly, among a human hand's five digits, the best acuity is enjoyed by the index finger (Vega-Bermudez and Johnson, 2001). Blind individuals who are experienced reading Braille have tactile acuity that can resolve grooves spaced less than a millimeter apart, performance that is significantly better than that of sighted individuals (Van Boven et al., 2000), and later in this chapter we'll consider why

bration, performance was fast and accurate; when the light and vibration were in conflict, performance was slow and error-prone, even though participants were told to attend only to the vibration and to ignore the lights. Seeing, in other words, influenced where the touch sensation seemed to be arising.

Perception of Surface Texture by Touch

Objects often have distinctive texture surfaces that serve as a tactile signature for the object. This texture signature is determined by physical characteristics of the object's surface. Think about a sheet of sandpaper, a silk scarf, and a drinking glass, three distinctly different textures. Figure 13.4 shows the actual recorded patterns of vibrations produced on the skin's surface as each of these textures was stroked at a constant rate. The glass produces relatively minor fluctuations in skin displacement at a

FIGURE 13.5 | Drawing of two tactile gratings differing in spatial frequency.

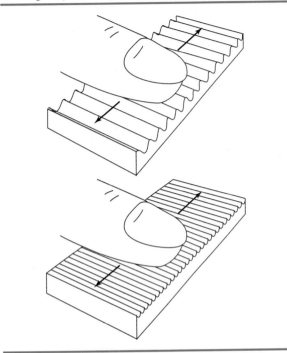

this may be. Although we do not recommend you exploit this fact in your normal activities, for maximum spatial resolution you should use your lower lip instead of your index finger: Tactile grating acuity is actually a bit better on your lip than on any of your fingers (Sathian and Zangaladze, 1996).

Turning to a different but related tactile acuity measure, imagine running your fingers across one tactile grating and then another to judge which one is higher in spatial frequency. You'd be able to discriminate between spatial frequencies differing by as little as 3 percent (Lederman and Taylor, 1972). Obviously, then, you could easily tell the difference between wide-wale and narrow-wale corduroy fabric by touch alone. The same stimulus dimension, roughness, also influences affective responses. People tend to find smoothly textured fabrics, such as silk, more pleasant to touch than coarse fabrics, such as burlap (Gwosdow et al., 1986). And just as with acuity, blind individuals are better than sighted people at discriminating very small offsets in the spatial arrangement of raised dots of the sort used for Braille reading (Grant, Thiagarajah, and Sathian, 2000). With practice, though, sighted individuals can approach the touch acuity shown by blind individuals.

The ability to discriminate different degrees of roughness does not depend critically on the particular way in which the fingers are moved over the object's surface, just so long as the fingers do move. But there's a puzzle here. Moving your finger gradually over a surface generates slow modulations in the pressure exerted on your skin, but moving your fingers quickly over that same surface produces rapid modulations in pressure. That you perceive the surface as having constant roughness regardless of how you inspect it implies that information from touch receptors is referenced to information about the motions of your hand.

The ability to resolve fine spatial detail with the fingers does depend on the orientation of the spatial frequency grooves relative to the orientation of the finger (Essock, Krebs, and Prather, 1992). Tactile grating resolution is best when the grating's undulations run perpendicular to the long axis of the finger (as shown in Figure 13.5). This finding is reminiscent of the oblique effect in vision, described in Chapter 4, where acuity was best for horizontal and vertical orientations. In the case of touch, however, only one orientation shows superior acuity.

Are all fingers of the hand equally good when it comes to judging surface roughness? With continued use, the fingers develop calluses (a thickened keratin layer of the epidermis, the skin's outermost layer). A callus on the fingertip reduces the skin's elasticity and seemingly should reduce perceived roughness by damping the pressure changes in the skin produced by surface roughness. When asked how often they used their various fingers to touch objects, people report using the index finger most often, the ring finger least often, with the middle finger coming out in the middle. If the degree of callus varies with frequency of finger use, a surface ought to *feel* rougher with the ring finger compared to the index finger. Though it takes carefully controlled experimentation to really verify the prediction, you don't need a laboratory to test the prediction: just rub a textured surface, such as a carpet, using each finger one after another. Lederman (1976) actually performed an experiment like this using low-frequency tactile gratings, and if you were like her participants, the carpet you rubbed would have felt rougher to your ring finger than to your index finger. It is somewhat paradoxical, but true, that the finger with the best tactile acuity for high-frequency gratings is not the finger producing the strongest sensations of roughness for low-frequency gratings.

Why should perceived roughness and tactile sensitivity be influenced by the elasticity of the skin on the fingers? By way of preview, these tactile judgments rely on specialized tactile receptors located just underneath the surface of the skin, and anything that interferes with the transfer of mechanical displacement to those receptors compromises their efficiency. You'll learn more about this in a moment but, in the meantime, you now know why professional safecrackers file their finger pads before going about their business.

And finally, before leaving perception of surface roughness, let's consider yet another instance where tactile perception—in this case perception of roughness—is influenced by sensory information from another modality. When you rub your hand back and forth over a surface, you not only feel the surface's texture but you also hear the sounds produced by your rubbing. And those sounds convey clues about the degree of roughness of the surface. (Compare what you hear when rubbing your hands over the surfaces of a drinking glass and a paper cup.) Do these sounds influence our tactile perception of roughness? The answer is yes, and the experiment proving it is simple but clever. Jousmäki and Hari (1998) had people rub the palms of their hands together and judge what they felt along the dimensions of roughness/smoothness. They performed the task while wearing headphones through which they heard the sounds of their rubbing actions, which were picked up by a microphone placed close to their hands. On some trials, the high-frequency content of the sounds was selectively amplified, and on these trials people described their hands as dry and parchment-like; with the high frequencies attenuated, the hands felt rougher and wetter. Jousmäki and Hari characterized this "parchment skin" feeling as an illusion, because perception of an unvarying tactile event was changing depending on the auditory context in which that event was experienced. The influence of sound on tactile roughness judgments has been replicated using other abrasive surfaces (Guest et al., 2002), and together these findings remind us yet again that perception of objects and events arises from a confluence of information from multiple sensory systems.

Reading with the Fingertips

Most elevators in public buildings have small clusters of raised "pimples" next to the numerals designating each floor of the building. As you probably know, these tiny bumps are Braille representations of the numerals, and if you're like most people you've probably explored what they feel like to your fingers. To an inexperienced person, these characters feel like a random collection of bumps. But those bumps are just as meaningful to a blind person as the letters on a page are to a sighted person.

The Braille system was invented in the early 1800s by Louis Braille when he was just 16 (Braille was blind from childhood).[2] **Braille** symbols are formed within units of space known as cells, with each cell consisting of as many as six raised dots arranged in two parallel rows of three dots each. Sixty-four different combinations are possible using one or more of these six dots. A given cell can represent a letter, a number, a punctuation mark, or even a whole word (for example, the letter y denotes the word you in a more advanced version of Braille). People literate in Braille can read the characters at 60 to 120 words per minute by moving their fingers over the dots (Figure 13.6). For decades special typewriters were used to produce embossed Braille code, but today computer programs and portable Braille notepads allow individuals to save and edit their work as well as print the embossed code to paper.

Braille's usefulness is not limited to portraying alphanumeric characters; it's equally good at representing musical notation. As a result, blind musicians no longer have to learn pieces by rote memory but, instead, can "sight read" from music scores portrayed using patterns of tiny bumps. Although opening new doors for musical expression to the blind, the process of producing these scores was very time-consuming, which limited the range of available scores. That limitation was overcome, however, by the development of software that transcribes MIDI files (the standard notation used for computer transcription of musical scores) into their Braille equivalents. This software, dubbed GOODFEEL, was conceived and developed by blind trumpeter Bill McCann.

Let's take a look at some Braille representations of letters. Panel A of Figure 13.7 shows some letters of the alphabet, which can be raised, or embossed, on the paper. Panel B shows the same characters portrayed in Braille. Using the fingers, it's much easier to read text written in Braille letters than it is to read text written in embossed (raised) Roman letters. Readers of Braille, it turns out, tend to confuse different embossed characters, which slows reading in the same way that a typed page with many typographical errors slows visual reading. This interesting outcome would not have surprised the inventor of the Braille system. When Louis Braille was a student

---

[2]Braille's inspiration came from a system that was supposed to allow soldiers to communicate silently and without light on the nighttime battlefield. That system, invented by a French artillery officer, represented various letters by means of 12 raised dots arranged on a grid. This scheme failed because of its complexity; with raised dots in 12 possible positions, it was difficult to write the characters, let alone read them (Boorstin, 1985, p. 538).

FIGURE 13.6 | This person is reading Braille imprinted on a page with printed words.

at the Royal Institute for the Young Blind in Paris, the director of the Institute insisted that his sightless students read from texts written with embossed letters. Louis Braille himself found the embossed alphabet difficult to read, which motivated his search for an alternative that did not use alphabetic characters. The widespread use of the Braille system today attests to his success.

But why are embossed letters so much harder to read with the fingers than are Braille characters? Perhaps, you might think, that with the fingers, continuous lines are harder to follow than raised patterns of dots. But that's not the answer. Instead, as Loomis (1981) showed, the answer lies with the skin's limited ability to pick up fine spatial detail. If you press against the skin with a very thin probe, the probe deforms not just the skin it touches directly, but a fairly wide, neighboring area of skin as well. This spread of effect reflects the mechanical properties of the skin. It can be thought of as mechanical blurring, analogous to the optical blurring discussed in previous chapters. Like its optical counterpart, mechanical blurring eliminates a stimulus's high-spatial frequencies (fine details), reducing the stimulus to a smeared version of itself. When fingertips touch the embossed letters, the resulting loss of detail is analogous to the loss of high-spatial frequency information in a blurred photograph (see Figure 2.17). Loomis realized that loss of high-frequency information would probably have a dif-

FIGURE 13.7 | Panel A shows some letters of the alphabet. Panel B shows these letters in Braille characters. Panel C shows embossed Roman characters (as in panel A) after blurring. Panel D shows the same Braille characters after the same blurring.

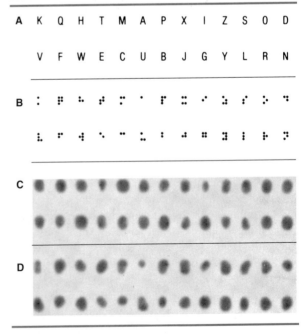

ferential impact upon the discriminability of embossed letters and Braille characters. Embossed letters are made up of continuous contours and, in some cases, fairly small changes in those contours are crucial to the identities of the letters. In contrast, Braille characters are made from spatially coarse elements that would be less affected by blurring.

Panels C and D of Figure 13.7 help you appreciate what Loomis had in mind. The visual blur introduced into these panels is meant to simulate the mechanical blur produced by the fingertips. Note that despite blurring, the Braille letters are fairly distinct (panel D), whereas a comparable blur renders many of the embossed letters indistinguishable (panel C). For example, after blurring, the Braille *O* and *D* remain visually distinct, but similar blurring renders the embossed *O* and *D* impossible to distinguish. The low-frequency information available to the skin from different Braille characters is more discriminable than the low-frequency information available from embossed letters.

Of course, enlarging the embossed letters would compensate for the limited spatial resolution of the fingers, but this enlargement of letter size would reduce the amount of text that could be imprinted on a page of tactile text, making it impossible for one letter to fit on a single fingertip. Braille characters represent a good compromise between size and resolution.

Books, particularly textbooks, for visually impaired persons often must include drawings and diagrams. Typically such illustrations are created using a computer-controlled stylus that embosses the appropriate pattern on stiff paper. The resulting raised image can be read by moving the fingertip over it. However, embossed figures are notoriously difficult to interpret; even common objects presented in the form of raised images are recognized tactually only after great effort and considerable time. (These same drawings would have been recognized immediately by a sighted individual actually looking at the embossed figure.)

Why this disparity between vision and touch? It's probably not a matter of the fingertip's limited spatial resolution. In fact, blurring simple line drawings so as to simulate "blurring" by the fingertips, has little effect on visual recognition (Loomis, Klatzky, and Lederman, 1991). The answer probably has more to do with the contrasting ways in which the eye and the fingers collect sensory data.

When you look at a scene or a drawing, the eye extracts visual information simultaneously from an extended area. But when you use a fingertip to scan an embossed version of the same scene or drawing, you're sampling a very restricted portion of the whole figure at any one moment. In order to recognize or appreciate the embossed representation, those small, momentary samples must be mentally stitched together, and this places a large burden on a person's short-term memory.

To decide whether the fingertip's narrow field of view was to blame for the difficulty of deciphering embossed material, Loomis, Klatzky, and Lederman (1991) handicapped vision so that, like tactual input, vision's input would comprise a series of spatially restricted samples. The stimuli, for both vision and touch, were simple line drawings of common objects such as a key, a hammer, and a pair of glasses. The person's task for both vision and touch was to identify the object. For tactual recognition, people used either a single fingertip or the tips of two adjacent fingers to scan embossed versions of the drawings. For visual recognition, the drawing, presented on a computer display, was first blurred in order to match the finger's relatively lower spatial resolution. To limit vision's sampling area, only a small section of each drawing was visible at any moment, in the center of the computer screen. The size of this area was adjusted to equalize the sampling areas of vision and touch. Expressed as a proportion of the whole drawing, the visible section's area equaled the fraction of the tactual version that would stimulate either a single fingertip or two fingertips (matching the tactual test conditions). Of course, a moving fingertip does not touch just one single part of the drawing. Over time, the fingertip scans many different parts of the drawing. To imitate this scanning, during visual testing various parts of the stimulus were made visible. As the individual moved a stylus on the surface of an electronic tablet, the computer sensed the stylus's position and displayed the corresponding section of the drawing. For example, moving the stylus to the upper left corner of the tablet caused the upper left corner of the drawing to come into view.

The results were unequivocal. With the larger of the two apertures, visual recognition was vastly superior to tactual recognition. But when vision was limited to sampling the drawings in smaller bites, analogous to the sampling area of a single finger, visual recognition and tactual recognition were equally poor.

Before leaving the topic of reading with the hands, here's news on an emerging technology that is likely to "touch" our lives in the near future. Before long all of us—sighted as well as blind—may be relying on our sense of touch to "read" messages and "view" images. Engineers are busily working to incorporate small tactile stimulators in cell phones, so that you can "feel" messages silently communicated to your hands through the vibrations within an array of tiny pins mounted on your phone (Sandhana, 2004). Unique patterns of vibrations would denote distinct messages, such as "home in an hour" or "pick up Chinese take-out." Moreover, the particular pattern of vibrations denoting a given message could be tailor-programmed to your liking, allowing you to create your own tactile vocabulary. And you could even design specific patterns associated with particular individuals, giving your mother's "voice" a distinct vibrational trill. And why stop with cell phones? One day we may have vibrational messages conveyed through other commonly used objects, such as the steering wheels of our cars ("Caution: congested intersection ahead"). This promising engineering advance comes about through the realization that the eyes and ears are not the only channels capable of communicating meaningful messages through patterned sensory signals—touch can be effective, too. Louis Braille surely never envisioned the amazing applications his invention would lead to.

Perception of Surface Temperature

Besides sensing an object's roughness or smoothness when you touch it, you can also feel the warmth or coolness of its surface. This is because objects have their own characteristic "thermal conductivity"—the rate at which a surface draws heat away from a hand (or any other body part) that is touching the surface. Surfaces such as cement and stainless steel seem cold to the touch because they have high-thermal conductivities. Surfaces such as plastic and cloth seem warm to the touch because they have low-thermal conductivities. This perception of surface temperature of an object has been termed *touch temperature,* to distinguish it from the perceived temperature of the ambient environment (Gibson, 1966).

But what determines touch temperature? The temperature of your skin normally falls right around 33 degrees Celsius, with small variations depending on time of day and your state of health. When you touch an object, the temperature of the area of skin in contact with the object shifts in the direction of the temperature of the object's surface. So when an object feels warm or cool, it is the gradient in temperature between that object and your skin that you perceive, not the actual temperature of the object. This is the basis for a well-known illusion of touch temperature: A surface at room temperature can feel hot to a cool finger but cool to a hot finger. You can experience this illusion by placing one hand in a container of hot water and the other hand in cold water. Now place both hands in the same container of tepid water and note the disparity in perceived temperature between the hands (see Egth, Kamlet and

Bell, 1970, for more on context and temperature perception.). People are good at detecting deviations from "physiological zero," the temperature that seems neither warm nor cold (Kenshalo, 1972; Makous, 1966).

The rate of change in skin temperature also influences a surface's perceived hardness. Thus, metal at room temperature feels cooler than wood at room temperature because the hard metal surface is a better conductor of heat, including the heat from your skin. Temperature also modifies the perceived weight of an object, as you can experience by performing the following simple experiment. Place a coin on a piece of ice (to cool it) while maintaining another similar coin at room temperature. Now place both coins on the underside of your bare forearm. You should find that the cool coin feels heavier than the neutral coin (Stevens, 1979). This observation suggests that peripheral nerve fibers responsive to pressure are also activated by thermal stimulation.

We're actually surprisingly poor at localizing thermal stimulation in the absence of tactile stimulation (meaning actual deformation of the skin). When Cain (1973) focused a radiant heat source on the front or the back of the torso of volunteers, he found that they often had no idea *where* on their skin the heat had been focused, even though the sensation of heat itself was vivid. In general, people are more sensitive to cool stimulation than to warmth, with sensitivity to both thermal sensations decreasing with age (Stevens and Choo, 1998). Brain imaging studies reveal that somatosensory stimulation yielding sensations of "warmth" activate different (but neighboring) brain areas from those activated by "coolness" (Craig and Rollman, 1999). If thermal stimulation is sufficiently intense to cause pain, a region of the brain known as the anterior cingulate cortex is also activated (Craig et al., 1996). This brain region, located near the very front of the brain underneath the frontal lobes, is intimately involved in the control of affective reactions, including pain perception.

Mental Set and Tactile Sensitivity

During everyday activities, you sometimes unexpectedly touch—or are touched by—some object. A mosquito alights on your earlobe, a friend taps you on the shoulder, your hand accidentally bumps a glass while reaching for the salt shaker. It's impossible to be certain when or where you're liable to be touched. What are the perceptual consequences of uncertainty about the source and location of tactile stimulation?

FIGURE 13.8 | Two views of Craig's tactile stimulator.

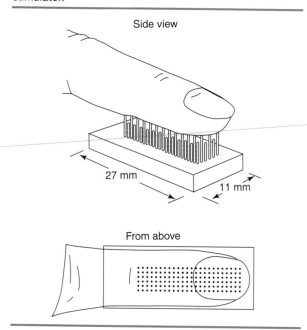

Side view

27 mm

11 mm

From above

This question has been addressed by James Craig (1985) who asked how well people could divide attention among several potential sites of tactile stimulation on the fingers and hand. Stimuli in Craig's experiment consisted of 108 blunt pins arranged in a rectangular array 6 columns wide by 18 rows high (see Figure 13.8). This array was pressed against the person's finger pad, and each pin could be made to vibrate independently at 230 Hz. A computer controlled which pins vibrated and which ones were still. By varying which subset of pins actually vibrated, different spatial patterns of stimulation could be presented to the person's finger. For example, the computer could present tactile patterns that corresponded to different letters of the alphabet.

In one experiment, Craig examined whether uncertainty about location of tactile stimulation influenced a person's ability to identify the pattern of stimulation. With the person's left hand resting on the array of blunt pins, tactile vibrations were delivered simultaneously to both the index finger and the middle finger. In each trial two different tactile letters were delivered, one to the index finger and one to the middle finger. Following each brief presentation, the person had to identify the letter delivered to a particular finger. Craig tested people under two conditions. In one, the person was instructed before stimulation which finger to pay attention to, while in the other,

the person was informed only after stimulation. People were much more accurate in identifying the tactile letter when they knew in advance which finger to attend to.

In a second experiment, Craig asked whether people could integrate tactile information from adjacent fingers. On some trials the vibrotactile pattern was presented to a single finger, while on other trials the pattern was distributed over two adjacent fingers. Craig predicted that spreading the pattern over two fingers would force a person to shift attention quickly from one finger to another, which would diminish performance. As Craig expected, identification was significantly better when the entire vibrotactile pattern was delivered to one finger. In general, Craig's work shows that uncertainty about the location of tactile stimulation makes it more difficult to identify the stimulus. Box 13.1 describes a practical instance where uncertainty poses a challenge that can be overcome.

At times, uncertainty about touch is more than a mere nuisance; it is a matter of life or death. Each year, more than 35,000 women in North America die of breast cancer. Thousands of these deaths could have been prevented if women had simply examined their own breasts for telltale lumps and changes. But it's not enough just to know that you *ought* to do these monthly self-examinations. There are many different ways to tackle a self-examination, and most of them are wrong. Part of the problem seems to be uncertainty about what to "look" for (recall Figure 6.23).

Unfortunately, native skill in examining one's breasts varies widely among women. Physicians' skills in examining patient's breasts also vary considerably (Fletcher, O'Malley, and Bunce, 1985). Because perception can be improved by training (the phenomenon of *perceptual learning* discussed throughout the book), it is natural to ask what sort of training would improve skill in breast self-examination. Combining basic information about touch sensitivity with an understanding of perceptual learning, some researchers developed a highly successful method for teaching women the right way to conduct a self-examination.

Virtually all studies of perception begin with the proper choice of stimulus. So before they could study breast examination, Bloom and colleagues (1982) had to develop artificial breasts that felt natural to the touch. These breast models, made of a silicone material covered with a membrane that mimics the feel of skin, allowed the researchers to study the ease with which simulated tumors (lumps inserted into the model) could be detected. When volunteers palpated the models, detectability improved systematically with increases in lump size, as expected.

BOX 13.1 **Seeing with the Hands**

Sometimes a person who is both deaf and blind will put his hands on a speaker's face. This laying on of hands is part of the blind and deaf person's effort to understand what is being said. The object is to sense the vibrations produced by the speaker's lips, throat, and jaw. Helen Keller wrote eloquently of all that she could learn from her hands:

> By placing my hand on a person's lips and throat, I gain an idea of many specific vibrations, and interpret them: a boy's chuckle, a man's "Whew!" of surprise, the "Hem!" of annoyance or perplexity, the moan of pain, a scream, a whisper, a rasp, a sob, a choke, and a gasp. The utterances of animals, though wordless, are eloquent to me— the cat's purr, its mew, its angry, jerky, scolding spit; the dog's bow-wow of warning or of joyous welcome, its yelp of despair, and its contented snore. (1908, p. 570)

This stratagem allows experienced practitioners to gain remarkably good comprehension of speech, particularly when words are spoken at a moderate tempo. Obviously, when using this technique, the deaf and blind person must divide attention among several sites of stimulation on the hands and fingers.

As described in the text, James Craig has shown that dividing attention among different regions of the hand impairs tactile perception. How is it, then, that deaf and blind people pick up the tactile stimulation from speech so well? Just as puzzling, a blind and deaf person will often place a second hand on the speaker's face if he or she is having difficulty understanding what is being said. This maneuver, though seemingly doubling attentional demands, improves comprehension. A clue to this paradoxical observation comes from another of Craig's findings.

There are two ways to partition vibrotactile stimulation between pairs of fingers. The pattern of tactile stimulation can be divided between two adjacent fingers on the same hand or the pattern can be divided between one finger on one hand and one finger on the other hand. Surprisingly, Craig has shown that the two-handed condition yields better identification than the one-handed condition. In fact, performance on the two-handed condition is comparable to that measured when the vibrotactile stimulus is delivered to a single finger to which the person is attending.

Why does bilateral stimulation work so effectively? As you will learn shortly, information from the left hand is processed primarily in the right hemisphere of the brain, whereas information from the right hand is processed primarily in the left hemisphere. Craig's paradoxical result may imply that each hemisphere has its own attentional resources and that the deleterious consequence of uncertainty only occurs when a single hemisphere must process multiple tactile inputs.

Practice made it possible to detect smaller lumps. Moreover, the improved ability was retained even after a layoff of several months. Simply reading about the procedure had no effect. Apparently, improvement depends on the actual tactile experience.

In one particularly effective program, trainees first learn to distinguish the feel of normal breast tissue from the feel of tissue containing some typical tumors. Trainees are taught to move their finger pads in small circles, first in one spot and then in another, eventually covering the entire breast. Of course, lumps can form anywhere in the breast from just below the skin to quite deep inside. By systematically varying the pressure that they apply, trainees learn to detect relatively superficial lumps (with light pressure) or deeper lumps (with stronger pressure).

The effects of certainty show up as changes in brain activity. Merely anticipating stimulation of a particular finger increases the metabolic activity in the region of the brain that represents that finger (Roland, 1976). Additionally, in at least one area of the brain, the temporal cortex, some cells distinguish clearly between tactile stimuli that are expected and those that are not. These cells respond strongly when the skin is touched unexpectedly but fail to respond to the same touch if the individual being touched has been able to see that touch was impending (Mistlin and Perrett, 1990).

Having considered some of the psychophysics of touch perception, we're now ready to turn our attention to the neural hardware responsible for registering and processing tactile information. To give you a brief overview, mechanical disturbances of the skin are registered by several different kinds of specialized receptors located in various layers of the skin. Afferents from these receptors carry neural impulses evoked by tactile stimulation into the spinal cord, where those impulses are passed to fibers that ascend to the brain. Within the brain, touch information is processed in several specialized cortical regions that contain maps of the surface of the body.

In our discussions of the other senses, we consistently started with the receptors and progressed to the afferent fibers and finally to the associated sensory areas of the brain. In the case of touch, however, it makes more sense to begin by looking at the nerve fibers that carry touch information to the brain. We'll then backtrack to discuss the receptors that innervate those fibers. We are adopting this approach because the functional roles of touch receptors are easier to appreciate if you first know something about the different classes of afferent nerve fibers associated with touch.

For simplicity, we concentrate on receptors located in (and fibers originating from) the hand. The hand contains just about every type of mechanoreceptor and afferent fiber found anywhere on the body's surface. And as already pointed out, the hand is the principal organ of touch.

Physiology of Touch

Touch Fibers

Information about tactile stimulation of the hand is passed to the spinal cord via two separate nerves, the ulnar nerve and the median nerve. Like all other nerves, these two consist of many *axons*. In the ulnar and median nerves, the axons originate from various regions of the hand. The median nerve, as its name suggests, runs down the middle of the arm, branching out to innervate part of the palm, all the thumb, all the index finger, all the middle finger, and that half of the ring finger adjacent to the middle finger (Figure 13.9). The ulnar nerve takes its name from the ulna, a large bone in the forearm extending from elbow to wrist on the outside part of the arm. Fibers in the ulnar nerve conduct messages from touch receptors in the rest of the palm, the whole of the little finger and the adjacent half of the ring finger.

Each individual fiber signals when a particular region of the skin has been touched. This fact was established by Edgar Adrian (later Lord Adrian) and Yngve Zotterman (1926), who recorded neural activity from individual fibers while applying tactile stimulation to the skin. The area of skin within which stimuli can influence a fiber's activity constitutes that fiber's *receptive field*. You should see the analogy between a touch fiber's receptive field and a visual neuron's receptive field (the area of retina within which light affects activity of the neuron).

Following Adrian and Zotterman's classic work, many other physiologists have studied the responses of touch fibers in a variety of species. Of course, when recording neural activity in a nonhuman species, a physiologist doesn't know what kinds of touch sensations are being evoked by the tactile stimuli. This limitation has been overcome in some classic experiments performed on humans. Ake Vallbo and Karl-Erik Hagbarth, Swedish

FIGURE 13.9 | Innervation pattern of median and ulnar nerves.

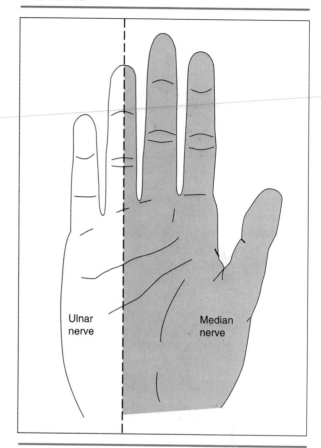

Ulnar nerve

Median nerve

neurophysiologists, developed a method for inserting a microelectrode directly into the median nerve of an awake human volunteer. Experimental access to the nerve is easy, since it is relatively close to the skin's surface. Applying touch stimuli to various parts of the hand, Vallbo and Hagbarth (1968) located the receptive field of each of the single nerve fibers from which they recorded.

By analyzing the fibers' patterns of response to various stimuli applied to the skin, Vallbo and Hagbarth found that fibers carrying touch information from the human palm and fingertips could be put into one of four categories. These four categories were defined on the basis of the sharpness of the boundaries of each fiber's receptive field and on the fiber's pattern of activity over time. As you'll see, differences in spatial and temporal response properties enable each class of fibers to signal something unique about sources of stimulation within their receptive fields.

Temporal Properties   Imagine lightly pressing a small probe against the skin and maintaining that pressure for a brief time. Recording the activity in many different fibers to this stimulation, Vallbo and Hagbarth identified two types of fibers. Some fibers responded when the probe was first applied to the skin and continued to respond more or less constantly as long as the pressure was maintained. Fibers of this type are called **slowly adapting (SA) fibers.** Other fibers responded only when the probe was first applied to the skin; these fibers also gave a brief, strong response when the probe was removed. Fibers in this category are called **rapidly adapting (RA) fibers.** These first two categories of somatosensory fibers can be distinguished by their responses over time to constant stimulation.

Spatial Properties   Now suppose the probe is used to map a receptive field by stimulating a series of neighboring points on the skin. The spatial layout of the receptive fields reveals that both SA and RA fibers come in two types. Fibers of one type, **punctate fibers,** possess small receptive fields with sharply defined boundaries. Their fields tend to be oval in shape and encompass anywhere from 4 to 10 of the closely spaced ridges that cover the palm and finger pads. Within this small region, sensitivity is approximately uniform.

The other type, **diffuse fibers,** have large receptive fields with ill-defined boundaries. Receptive fields of diffuse fibers sometimes cover a whole finger or the greater part of the palm. Because of their large size and blurred boundaries, these diffuse fibers are ill-suited for detailed spatial discrimination.

Four Fiber Groups   Combining the two types of temporal responses with the two types of spatial properties yields four fiber types: SA-diffuse, SA-punctate, RA-diffuse, and RA-punctate. Each of these four types may deliver a distinct message to the central nervous system, because each is best at signaling the presence of a particular kind of tactile stimulation.[3] This widely accepted view is commonly referred to as the "four-channel" model of mechanoreception.

[3]From various alternatives, we've adopted this set of names for the four fiber groups because they are descriptive and relatively easy to remember. One alternative scheme uses the terms SA-I, SA-II, RA, and PC to stand for what we term SA-punctate, SA-diffuse, RA-punctate, and RA-diffuse, respectively (Johnson and Hsiao, 1992). As you'll see later, the PC system takes its name from Pacinian corpuscle, the receptor from which that system arises.

Fiber Activity and the Experiences

One approach to functional differences among types of fibers compares responses evoked in each type by stimulation of restricted regions of the skin. Adjusting the temporal pattern of stimulation applied to this single location on an immobile fingertip mimics the effect of moving a fingertip across some pattern, such as an embossed letter. For instance, if a fingertip moved horizontally across the middle of an embossed letter *o*, the finger would be stimulated twice, separated by an interval that reflected both the width of the letter and the speed of fingertip movement. In this way, researchers have recorded afferent fibers' responses to various embossed letters, to determine how faithfully the fibers register the spatial details of the letters (Johnson and Hsiao, 1992; Phillips, Johansson, and Johnson, 1992). When the stimuli were raised dots comprising Braille characters, responses within SA-punctate afferents did an excellent job of reproducing the spatial detail of the characters. RA-punctate fibers were a distant second in fidelity of reproduction, with fibers in the other two classes failing almost completely (meaning that their responses to different letters gave no clues as to what the letters were). This strongly suggests that SA-punctate fibers carry the primary information for tactual form and roughness perception.

We could conjecture about the functional significance of different fiber types based on their response properties. But there are two more direct ways to get at the question of functional significance. One is to have a person describe what is felt when a stimulus is applied to the skin during a recording experiment. Keep in mind, of course, that the stimulus used to evoke neural activity in a single fiber actually activates many more fibers than just the one under study. Thus, the person's description of that stimulus is not solely attributable to activity in that single fiber (Torebjork, Vallbo, and Ochoa, 1987). The other technique is to stimulate the nerve fiber directly and have the person describe what is felt. Let's consider some results obtained using these two strategies.

Neural Responses and Perceptual Judgments Evoked by Tactile Stimulation

While stimulating a person's hand with weak tactile probes, Johansson and Vallbo (1979) measured the activity in individual fibers and at the same time had the person report whether or not a sensation of touch was felt. When a barely detectable touch probe was applied to the glabrous (smooth, hairless) skin of the hand, RA fibers reliably responded but SA fibers were silent. Activation of SA fibers required a considerably stronger tactile stimulus. This implies that sensitivity to very light touch is mediated by RA fibers.

Of course, the sense of touch is designed to do more than signal weak, near-threshold tactile stimulation. What kinds of fiber activity are produced by more forceful touch stimulation? Localized indentation of the skin is one common source of stimulation. Such indentation occurs, for example, when you place a finger against your chin while thinking. And, of course, applying greater pressure with the finger produces a stronger sensation of touch on your chin. Suppose that psychophysical and electrophysiological measures are taken while calibrated amounts of pressure are applied to the skin with a tactile probe. The psychophysical measures could be verbal magnitude estimates (see the appendix), and the electrophysiological measures could consist of changes in the activity of touch fibers. When this kind of experiment is done, the person's verbal ratings are most closely mirrored by activity in the SA fibers: the growth in response with tactical pressure roughly parallels the increase in magnitude estimation ratings made by the person. This finding with humans dovetailed nicely with earlier work on monkeys by Mountcastle, Talbot, and Kornhuber (1966), who found that SA fibers registered information about touch intensity. We should note, though, that psychophysical and neural responses at the level of nerve fibers are not perfectly correlated, suggesting an important role for subsequent processing (Vallbo and Johansson, 1984).

Touch Qualities Evoked by Nerve Stimulation

If a given fiber is signaling something fairly specific about a touch sensation, then directly activating that fiber with mild electric current should produce an illusory version of that sensation at a particular location on the skin. (We can term such a sensation *illusory* because there would be no real object in contact with the skin causing that fiber to respond.) The location of the illusory touch would correspond to the location of the stimulated fiber's receptive field, and the quality of the sensation would tell us something about the information signaled by that fiber (Johansson and Vallbo, 1983).

Stimulation of an SA fiber produces a qualitatively different sensation than does stimulation of an RA fiber. When an SA fiber is stimulated electrically, one typically reports a sensation of light, uniform pressure. This can be likened to the pressure of a soft brush held steadily against the skin. When an RA unit is electrically stimu-

lated, the person reports a kind of buzzing or vibration on the skin. You can get some idea of this feeling by rubbing your fingers across the fine mesh of a window screen.

In general, electrical stimulation studies support the idea that SA and RA fibers carry different sorts of information from touch stimuli. There is also evidence that certain types of losses in touch sensitivity resulting from the prolonged operation of vibrating power tools (such as a jackhammer) can be related to damage within particular touch fiber types (Brammer and Verillo, 1988; Taylor, 1988).

We are now ready to look more peripherally at the different types of mechanoreceptors housed in the skin. Each afferent fiber terminates in at least one receptor and carries touch information from that receptor to the central nervous system. Keep in mind that the kinds of tactile events registered by different classes of touch fibers are determined by the nature of the tactile stimulation registered by the receptors that innervate those fibers. The same is true, of course, for the other senses. For example, some individual fibers in the auditory nerve respond best to high-frequency acoustic disturbances, whereas other fibers respond best to low-frequency acoustic disturbances. These response differences are not inherent in the fibers themselves. They reflect the different regions of the basilar membrane from which the fibers receive their input. The same principle applies to the touch fibers: They inherit their selectivities from receptors with unique structural properties. And it is these structural properties that endow those receptors with the ability to register different kinds of tactile events impinging on the skin.

Receptors for Touch

The smooth, hairless portion of the skin on your hand contains four different types of mechanoreceptors, together numbering about 17,000. As mentioned above, each receptor type is associated with nerve fibers that have distinctly different response characteristics: either RA-diffuse, RA-punctate, SA-diffuse, or SA-punctate. The receptors themselves are remarkably diverse in their structure and complexity, and this diversity shapes the functional specificity of different fiber types.

Mechanoreceptors are transducers that respond to indentation or pressure on the skin. Some types of receptors are surrounded by a specialized capsule filled with a compressible liquid or gel. The capsule's shape, size, and location determine which kinds of touch stimuli will affect the receptor within that capsule. Consider, for example, a receptor housed within a large, oval-shaped capsule

FIGURE 13.10 | Cross section through the skin of a primate finger pad showing the location of specialized nerve fiber terminals.

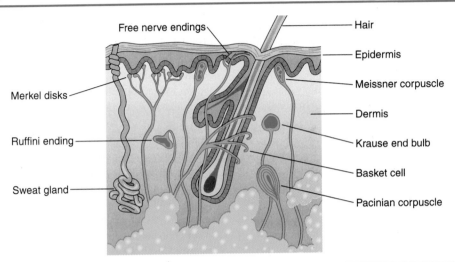

situated in the skin with its long axis parallel to the skin's surface. This capsule's receptor would respond to deformation anywhere along the fairly large area of skin over the capsule. If, however, an oval capsule had its long axis oriented perpendicular to the surface of the skin, tactile stimulation would have to occur within a more circumscribed area to activate the enclosed receptor.

The skin of the fingertips and palm, the touch-sensitive regions emphasized here, contain two types of encapsulated receptors. The two are **Meissner corpuscles** (in the upper layer of the skin) and **Pacinian corpuscles** (located in the lower layer of the skin). Figure 13.10 depicts these structures and shows their typical locations within the skin. It is believed that the Meissner and Pacinian corpuscles are innervated by RA type fibers. Also shown in Figure 13.10 are two other, nonencapsulated mechanoreceptors, the **Merkel disks** and the **Ruffini endings.** These two receptor types, are innervated by SA type fibers. Next, we look more closely at each of these receptor types, starting with the one located most superficially in the skin.

Meissner Corpuscles   Lying just below the surface of the skin, each Meissner corpuscle is tucked into small papillae that line the grooves in the skin of the palm and fingers. The capsule is oriented with its long axis perpendicular to the skin's surface. In humans, anywhere from two to six RA-punctate type nerve fibers enter a single Meissner corpuscle. Because this afferent unit

adapts rapidly, it responds best to transient stimulation such as that produced when something rubs against the skin or when the finger is moved over the surface of an object.

The fingertips of young, preteen individuals contain 40 to 50 Meissner corpuscles per square millimeter; by age 50, the number of corpuscles has dropped fourfold, to around only 10 per millimeter. The rate at which corpuscles are lost correlates well with the age-related loss in touch sensitivity for small probes (Thornbury and Mistretta, 1981).

Merkel Disks   Also located near the surface of the skin are Merkel disks. This class of mechanoreceptor, usually found in groups of 5 to 10, is innervated by afferent fibers of the SA-punctate type. It is believed that these units are active when the skin is stimulated by the steady pressure of a small object.

Ruffini Endings   Ruffini endings lie deeper in the skin and are elongated parallel to the skin's surface. Each individual Ruffini cell is innervated by a single afferent fiber, and neighboring cells may share a single fiber. This pooling of receptor signals within a single fiber is analogous to the situation in the eye, where several rod photoreceptors provide input to a single retinal ganglion cell. And as you may remember, spatial convergence operates in the interest of enhanced sensitivity, at the expense of spatial resolution.

The fibers innervating Ruffini endings are of the SA-diffuse type, and it is believed that these neural units provide information about steady pressure on the skin. Because they are also sensitive to stretching of the skin, these SA-diffuse units are active when fingers and other joints move, thereby stretching the skin.

Pacinian Corpuscles   These are the largest, least numerous, and most deeply situated of the mechanoreceptors. Each corpuscle is innervated by a single fiber of the RA-diffuse type.

Pacinian corpuscles are extremely sensitive to touch. Minute indentations of the fingertip trigger neural impulses in a Pacinian corpuscle. Take a moment to blow as gently as you can on the palm of your hand. The light feeling of the air on your skin most likely originates in the response of Pacinian corpuscles. If you maintain a steady but gentle airflow to your palm, the sensation will diminish or cease altogether. The response adapts rapidly. In the laboratory, investigators isolate the Pacinian corpuscle system by testing touch sensitivity to relatively large tactile probes vibrating at high frequencies (Gescheider et al., 1985).

Because Pacinian corpuscles are located relatively deep in the skin, deformation anywhere within a large area of the skin can affect a single corpuscle, resulting in a spatially diffuse sensitivity. In fact, a single Pacinian corpuscle can have a receptive field as large as several square centimeters. However, these deeply situated receptors provide only crude information about the location of tactile stimulation.

Free Nerve Endings   The skin, both glabrous and hairy, also contains **free nerve endings**—fine, hairlike structures that form a lacy net throughout the layers of the skin (see Figure 13.10). In hairy skin, the free nerve endings wind around the base of hair follicles so that slight bending of a hair will trigger neural impulses in these tactile afferent units. These free nerve endings are also richly distributed throughout mucous regions of the skin, such as that forming the lips and the genital region. They are also found in the cornea of the eye and, as you'll learn in the next two chapters, in the nose and mouth. Later in this chapter you'll see the role these receptors play in pain perception.

We've now completed our overview of touch's peripheral sensory hardware and are ready to trace the pathways that the touch fibers travel to the spinal cord and up into the brain. We should point out that touch, unlike any of the other sensory systems, is distributed over the entire surface of the body. This means that many different afferent nerve fibers entering the spinal cord up and down its length provide the input to touch centers in the brain. This multitude of inputs stands in marked contrast to other modalities, where just one pair of cranial nerves (for example, left and right auditory nerves) or at most three pairs of cranial nerves (the facial, glossopharyngeal, and vagus nerves innervating the tongue and mouth) convey information from peripheral organs to the central nervous system. Consequently, damage to one of the many touch nerves causes a loss of sensitivity that is confined to just that portion of the body innervated by that nerve. With other modalities, damage to the associated nerve fiber results in a more devastating, widespread loss in sensitivity. In rare cases, however, wholesale loss of touch fibers can produce nearly total "insensitivity to tactile stimulation" (the condition described earlier, consequent to viral infection).

Ascending Pathway for Touch

Afferent touch fibers enter the dorsal, or back, side of the spinal cord. Inside the spinal cord, these afferent fibers make synaptic contact with two major classes of neurons. One class, called *interneurons,* synapse onto motor neurons, whose axons exit the spinal cord and travel to muscles located in the vicinity of the body where the afferent fibers originated (see panel A of Figure 13.11). This small circuit of afferent/interneuron/motor neurons mediates reflex reactions such as the immediate withdrawal of the hand when it is pricked by a sharp object. The other class of spinal cord neurons that receive touch input travel upward to the brain, carrying input to particular regions in the brain stem. These neurons comprise the so-called lemniscal pathway. A second, phylogenetically older pathway, the spinothalamic tract, carries information about pain and temperature. Because of its importance to touch perception, we will concentrate on the lemniscal pathway (lemniscus means "band" or "bundle").

As the schematic in panel B of Figure 13.11 shows, axons in the lemniscal pathway project to nuclei in the brain stem. After synapsing, fibers in this pathway cross over the midline, projecting to thalamic nuclei on the opposite side of the brain. At the level of the thalamus, neurons receiving inputs from the superficial and deeper receptors in the skin are segregated. As a result, one set of thalamic neurons responds like the RA-punctate and SA-punctate fibers (the fibers innervating the superficial

FIGURE 13.11 | Panel A is a diagram of the spinal reflex arc mediating response to touch. Sensory signals entering the spinal cord from the touch receptor innervate an interneuron that, in turn, activates motor neurons that produce muscular responses. Panel B is a diagram of the ascending lemniscal somatosensory pathway.

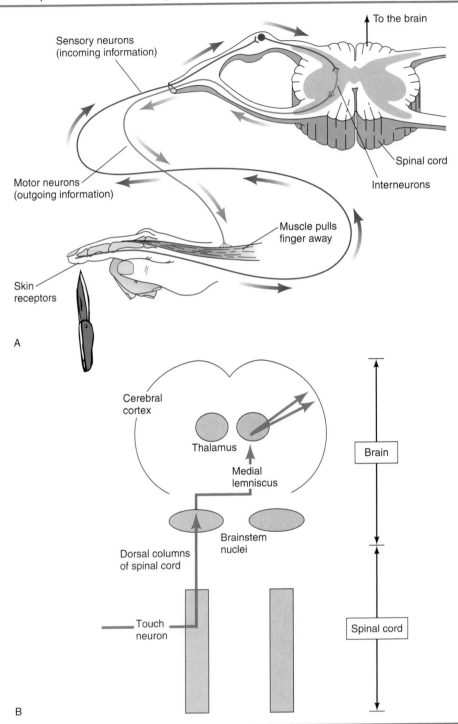

FIGURE 13.12 | Drawing of human cerebral cortex as seen from the brain's left side. The somatosensory cortex, which receives and processes touch information, is located immediately behind (i.e., posterior to) the motor cortex, which controls voluntary, or nonreflexive, movements. Running between these two regions is a deep furrow called the *central sulcus,* a major landmark on the brain's surface. The somatosensory cortex is located within the parietal lobe, which itself is situated somewhat above and in front of the occipital lobe (located toward the back of the brain).

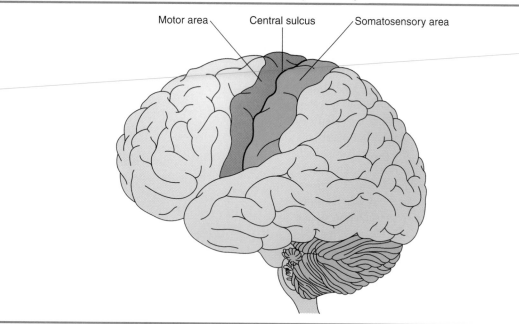

receptors), and another set responds like RA-diffuse and SA-diffuse fibers (the fibers innervating the deeper receptors). Both sets of thalamic neurons send axons to the parietal lobe of the somatosensory cortex, an area of the cerebral cortex largely devoted to sensory analysis of touch information.

We won't go into more detail on the pathways and nuclei interposed between the primary afferent touch fibers and the somatosensory cortex of the cerebrum. The interested student can read about this material in Kaas (1987). Instead, we will move straight to the somatosensory cortex, that region of the brain whose location is shown in Figure 13.12.

Somatosensory Cortex

The chapters on vision and hearing showed that incoming sensory information is routed through subcortical relay stations to specialized cortical areas where that information is transformed into biologically meaningful representations of objects and events; those transformations are achieved through elaborate patterns of interconnections among neurons, including feedback from higher

areas to lower ones. The same design principles apply to sensory processing of touch (Alitto and Usrey, 2003). And just as for vision and hearing, brain damage can destroy a person's ability to recognize objects through touch, even though that person has normal touch sensitivity (meaning that he or she can tell when the hand is in contact with an object). This condition is termed **tactile agnosia,** and it is associated with damage to the somatosensory regions in the brain.

Arrangement of Major Cortical Divisions The somatosensory cortex consists of several neighboring, functionally distinct areas whose interconnections are complex and only partially understood. Consider, for example, the two major areas, the so-called first and second somatosensory areas, S-I and S-II. Although both receive touch information from the thalamus, S-II also receives input from S-I. So S-II's analysis of touch incorporates information that has been filtered through S-I (Kaas, 1987). This constitutes one kind of parallel processing, with cross talk between neurons at the same level. This arrangement is widely used throughout the cortex, not just in somatosensory processing. Still, we can discern something of a hierarchy among areas devoted to so-matosensory information. For example, S-II receives much of its input from S-I but returns little, if any (Pons et al., 1987).

In each hemisphere of the cerebral cortex, S-I receives information arising from the contralateral side of the body and face. This is because of the crossover within the lemniscal pathway (see Figure 13.11). Thus, S-I neurons in the left hemisphere have their receptive fields on the right side of the body, and vice versa. Generally, neighboring areas of the body are represented within neighboring regions of the cortex. The body, in other words, is mapped topographically onto somatosensory cortex. However, some regions of the body, notably the hands and lips, receive exaggerated representation, with a relatively large amount of cortical tissue devoted to touch information from these relatively small regions. This distortion in the somatosensory body map is reminiscent of the magnified cortical representation of the fovea of the eye. Just as the fovea provides detailed spatial acuity, our fingers provide the most detailed information about the quality and location of tactile stimulation. Figure 13.13 shows how the different regions of the human body are "mapped" topographically onto the somatosensory cortex. Let's take a look at this topography in some detail.

Cortical Representation of Body Surface

Cortical Magnification   As the map in Figure 13.13 denotes, not all body parts enjoy equally expansive representations within the somatosensory cortex. In general, each species accentuates, or magnifies, the distribution of neural tissue for those body parts that are most important to members of that species. In many mammals, about half the S-I is devoted to information from the head. In tree shrews and opossums, the nose is emphasized; the brains of squirrels and rabbits concentrate on the lips. Rats, whose vision is mediocre at best, rely heavily on their whiskers for navigation and for object identity, and when you look at the somatosensory cortex of a rat you see that each individual whisker occupies its own neural territory within that map (see Figure 13.14). Figure 13.15 illustrates those parts of the body that are exaggerated within the somatosensory representation of the human body. This bizarre caricature, termed the *sensory homunculus,* has large hands and lips, denoting the cortex's disproportionately large neural representation of these body parts.

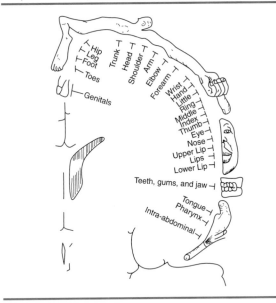

FIGURE 13.13 | Different regions of the somatosensory cortex process tactile information from different parts of the body, with these regions forming a "map" of the body surface on the cortical surface.

The sizes of the receptive fields of neurons in S-I also vary with the fields' locations on the body's surface. Specifically, cortical neurons activated by stimulation of the fingers and the lips have very small receptive fields compared to neurons devoted to, say, the back. Recall that touch acuity is best in the fingers and lips—this now makes even more sense when we see the relatively large expanse of cortex and the relatively small receptive fields devoted to these body parts. In higher primates the entire region known as S-I contains multiple maps of the body. Each map occupies a strip that runs nearly vertically downward from the top of the brain. The contralateral foot is represented in the upper portion of each map and the head is represented in the lower portion. The details of this layout vary somewhat from species to species and sometimes even between members of the same species (Merzenich et al., 1987). As we'll see later, these differences among individuals in the same species provide important clues about the developmental processes that shape the cortical representations of the body surface.

FIGURE 13.14 | Photograph of the somatosensory portion of a rat's brain. The cortex has been unfolded and flattened, and the tissue has been treated in a way that labels the different parts of the rat's body within this "body map" in the somatosensory cortex. Each whisker on the rat's face has its own unique representation in this map—clusters of neurons devoted to a given whisker appear as circular patches. Adjacent patches correspond to adjacent whiskers on the rat's face. Rats rely heavily on their whiskers to guide their behavior, so this enlarged whisker representation is comparable in function to the enlarged hand representation in the human somatosensory map (see Figure 13.15).

FIGURE 13.15 | A disproportionately large volume of cortical tissue is devoted to certain parts of the body, including the hands and mouth.

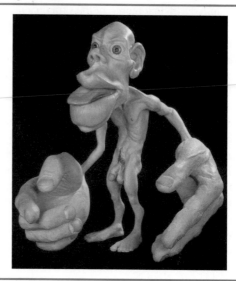

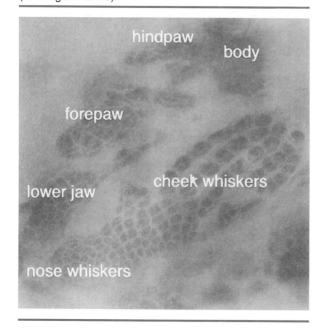

Cortical Maps   Look again at Figure 13.13. Although neighboring neurons within the somatosensory cortex do tend to represent adjacent areas of the body, overall, the cortical maps only roughly resemble the body's actual topography. For one thing, a given map may be interrupted at many different locations (Kaas, 1987). Because of these discontinuities, contiguous areas of the body may be represented in noncontiguous parts of the map or widely separated areas of the body may be represented in neighboring cortical locales. In some

cortical maps, for example, neurons representing the hand are sandwiched between neurons representing the back of the head and neurons representing the front of the head.

For historical reasons, the most anterior (forward) of S-I's four strips is known as Area 3a; the most posterior (rear) strip is known as Area 2; Areas 3b and 1 lay in between. Actually, the four strips, or maps, can be grouped into two sets: neurons in Areas 3b and 1 (the middle strips) respond most vigorously when sites on the skin are touched lightly. They receive inputs, via the thalamus, primarily from the most superficial skin receptors that innervate the RA-punctate and SA-punctate fibers. Neurons in Areas 3a and 2 (the most anterior and most posterior strips) respond poorly, if at all, to light touch on the skin. Instead, they respond strongly either when particular joints are moved—such as the joints of the fingers—or when other structures deep beneath the skin's surface, for example, tendons and muscles, are stimulated. These areas receive inputs, again via the thalamus, primarily from the more deeply situated skin receptors that innervate the RA-diffuse and SA-diffuse fibers.

There's at least a rough correspondence between the receptive field locations of neurons in each strip and the receptive field locations of neurons in adjacent strips. So neurons in Area 3b that represent the skin on a particular fingertip are near the neurons in Area 3a that represent the tendons and muscles of that same finger.

Turning briefly to S-II, we find that here the neurons also comprise a map of the body. However, for comparable regions of the body, neurons in S-II have somewhat larger receptive fields than their S-I counterparts. Also, the representations of the hands and lips are less exaggerated in S-II than in S-I.

Compared to the receptive fields of touch fibers, the receptive fields of cortical neurons tend to be more complex. Take two examples of this greater complexity. Certain cortical neurons respond most strongly only when an edge of *particular orientation* lies within the neuron's receptive field. This neuron would respond when the skin is pressed against an edge of one orientation but would give little or no response if the skin is pressed against an edge of very different orientation. The optimal edge orientation varies from cell to cell. (This may remind you of the orientation-tuned visual cortical neurons described in Chapter 4.) Other neurons, particularly in the posterior strips of S-I, respond most strongly when an object moves *in a particular direction* across the skin. Some neurons give a brisk response when a brush is moved along a finger's long axis or a finger is moved lengthwise across the brush. These same neurons give no response when the brush is moved across the finger or when the finger is moved across the object. Such neurons could provide information during active touch (Warren, Hämäläinen, and Gardner, 1986).

Before speculating about why the somatosensory cortex is organized the way it is, let's consider a peculiar illusion of touch whose neural bases can be pinpointed to S-I. Earlier in this chapter, you encountered several examples of how touch localization could be in error, and here's another example. Hold out one of your hands, palm up. Suppose two adjacent regions of your palm are touched simultaneously. You might expect to feel two punctate regions of stimulation, corresponding to the actual points stimulated. In fact, however, you may feel just a single spot of stimulation, located midway between the two actual points of stimulation—you would be feeling, in other words, touch at a location where no stimulus had been applied. Called the "funneling illusion" (Sherrick, 1964), this illusory shift in perceived stimulus location implies that the central, cortical representation of touch location can give rise to misleading patterns of activity.

Anna Roe and colleagues (Chen, Friedman, and Roe, 2003) have discovered that this misrepresentation shows up in the primary somatosensory cortex, S-I. Using optical imaging (the technique described in Chapter 4), these investigators were able to monitor transient changes in blood flow produced by transient neural activity associated with tactile stimulation. When adjacent fingertips of a monkey's hand were stimulated, the focus of activation peaked at a location midway between the actual, dual points of stimulation. Somatosensory cortex, in other words, was misrepresenting the stimulus location in a way that predicts what someone actually feels under these conditions. Points within the cortical map of the body can be shifted around depending on the context in which touch signals arise: The brain does not simply mirror the topography of stimulation at the skin but, instead, shapes that central representation. Why would the brain merge signals from adjacent fingers, a seemingly maladaptive thing to do? One intriguing speculation offered by Esther Gardner is that this neural merger helps the pair of fingers act as a unit along with the opposable thumb to grasp objects.

Speculations about Cortical Organization

We have stressed the resemblances between the organization of the somatosensory cortex and the organization of the visual cortex. Recall that in vision, different subregions, such as V1, V4, and MT, seem to be specialized for processing particular kinds of visual information. Analogously, some regions of the somatosensory cortex handle information from the superficial layers of the skin, and neighboring regions process information from deeper in the skin, as well as from tendons and muscles. Because receptors in these different layers of the skin mediate different perceptual aspects of touch, it is natural to assume that those perceptual aspects are registered in different regions of the somatosensory cortex. Indeed, there is indirect evidence for just such functional segregation (Friedman, Chen, and Roe, 2004). But what purpose is served by the multiple adjacent maps, such as the maps in Areas 3a and 3b? Although no one can yet say for certain, it may be useful to sketch out some possible answers.

Each individual mechanoreceptor in the skin yields information about just a small portion of the hand. Clearly, then, the appreciation of an object's overall shape, size, and texture requires integration of responses from a large population of receptors (Warren, Hämäläinen and Gardner, 1986). Particularly important may be the integration of information about touch and muscle position. Suppose, for example, with eyes closed, you run a fingertip slowly over a grainy wood surface. As the finger moves across the surface, various cortical neurons respond with some frequency of firing. One might imagine that the frequency of the neuron's response reflected, or coded, the surface's grain—the average distance between ridges in the wood's microstructure. In this scheme, a high firing rate might signal that the elements in the wood's grain were quite closely spaced. However, the same neuronal firing rate could have been produced by moving the fingertip more rapidly across a grain with widely spaced elements. As a result, the neural signal provides ambiguous information about objects and their properties (Darian-Smith et al., 1984). In order to disambiguate the signal, information about the finger's own movements must enter into the neural equation.

Movement is not the only factor that can introduce ambiguity. Take a nonmoving finger that is pressing against some surface. The receptor response might reflect the depth of the surface's microelements, its scratches, grain, or other, but again, the response is ambiguous. Any given response could be produced by a finger that pressed lightly against a deeply structured surface (such as sandpaper with very large grains) or by a finger that pressed more strongly against a finely structured surface (such as sandpaper with very small grains). Again, to disambiguate the receptors' responses, the brain must calibrate the receptor response against the force with which the fingers are pressing.

In both examples, information from touch receptors becomes a useful guide to the properties of object surfaces only when that information is combined with information from receptors deeper in the skin, receptors that signal the state of tendons and muscles. There's good reason, then, for neurons in S-I that signal the responses of superficial mechanoreceptors to adjoin neurons that signal the responses of deeper mechanoreceptors. Adjacency could facilitate the coordination of disambiguating neural computations.

Active Touch: Haptics

Usually, when you touch something or someone, you don't simply plop your hand or fingers down and leave them still. Think what happens when you inspect a tomato in the produce market, trying to decide whether to buy it. As you reach for it, your fingers conform to the general shape of the tomato even before you grasp. Once you've lifted the tomato, you begin examining its surface

with your fingers, looking for irregularities. At the same time you squeeze it gently to assess the tomato's ripeness. You are using your fingers actively to explore this object, and you do so without really thinking about it. Moreover, when you are forced simply to grasp an object but not explore it with your hands, your perceptual judgments of that object's shape can be amusingly wrong (Rock and Victor, 1964).

Feedback from touch receptors controls the fingers' pressure on the tomato. Initial contact generates touch signals that guide subsequent finger movements; those finger movements, in turn, generate updated touch signals. You can especially appreciate the importance of this feedback system when it doesn't work. For instance, when cold has numbed your fingers, it's hard to manipulate delicate objects. This makes complex activities, such as sewing or tying one's shoes, difficult. Even walking becomes tough without touch feedback, as you've undoubtedly experienced when your foot has fallen asleep.

A foot that's fallen asleep is usually a minor, temporary inconvenience. But when diminished touch results from damage to the brain, its impact can be devastating. In some patients, an interruption of the brain's blood supply (a cerebrovascular accident, or stroke) selectively damages the somatosensory cortex, leaving motor function unimpaired. When this selective brain damage diminishes touch feedback from a hand, the patient simply stops using the affected hand for even the most basic everyday activities such as eating or drinking. Ironically, this disuse has further consequences: deterioration of the hand's motor function, which may previously have been spared.

The hand is an extraordinarily gifted instrument for exploration. When this instrument is used to explore an object, information from the skin's touch receptors is actually coordinated or combined with a second kind of information, called **kinesthesis.** Kinesthesis receptors are found in the muscles, tendons, and joints. These receptors register information about the movement and position of our limbs. Suppose with eyes closed, you pick up a fingernail clipper and explore it with your fingers. You encounter the various parts of that device, and your touch receptors signal the properties of those parts. At the same time, kinesthesis provides information about the location of the hand and how the fingers are positioned relative to one another. (This positional information is sometimes referred to as **proprioception.**) As a result, touch information can be related, moment by moment, to the hand and finger positions where that touch information was acquired. Kinesthesis provides a coordinate system in which various touch experiences can be integrated.

An analogy may be helpful. Imagine an automated vehicle exploring the surface of another planet (recall the Martian rover Spirit from Chapter 6). As the vehicle roams about, it sends information back to scientists on earth about the things it encounters. Unless the scientists know the precise location of the vehicle, on a moment-to-moment basis, they will be unable to meld the information they receive into a coherent representation of the planet's surface. Kinesthesis is analogous to information about the changing location of the vehicle. Without kinesthesis, touch receptors in the exploring hand would provide a series of signals about object properties, but those signals could not be translated into a representation of the object being explored. There would be no way to relate touch signals to the position of the hand on the object. Because the coordination of touch and kinesthetic information is so important, a special term, **haptics** (from the Greek word meaning "to touch"), is reserved for sensory information that depends upon both touch and kinesthesis. We say, therefore, that as the hand explores an object, that exploration generates neither touch information nor kinesthetic information alone, but rather generates haptic information.

Our haptic capacities, particularly those of the hand, tend to go unrecognized because they are overshadowed by the hand's extraordinary motor skills and because visual input is usually dominant. But, if visual input is precluded, people remain surprisingly good at recognizing objects using haptic information alone. For example, Klatzky, Lederman, and Metzger (1985) asked blindfolded subjects to identify 100 different common objects by means of haptic information. Performance was fast and highly accurate. Accuracy is compromised, however, when subjects are forced to use just one finger and even more so when that finger is in a glove (Lederman and Klatzky, 2004).

When people explore objects with their hands, the hand movements are not random, but highly predictable. So, with a small unknown object for example, an observer usually begins the exploration by enclosing the object with the fingers and palm. Lederman and Klatzky (1987) identified several different kinds of stereotyped hand movements, which they termed "exploratory procedures," or EPs. Figure 13.16 depicts the most important of these. Results from a series of related experiments allowed Lederman and Klatzky (1990) to discover the haptic purposes served by these EPs.

Here's how they went about it. From earlier work, Lederman and Klatzky knew which stimulus characteristics made it possible for people to discriminate objects haptically. These included texture, temperature, hardness, weight, size, shape, and component motion (movements of an object's parts). Armed with a list of such

characteristics, Lederman and Klatzky began by asking people to imagine handling an object, such as a pencil, and deciding whether this object was a member of some class of objects, say writing implements. For 57 different classes of objects and their members, people identified the haptic properties used to decide about category membership. Sticking with the pencil example, observers reported that *shape* was crucial in identifying a pencil as a writing implement; that *texture* allowed them to identify a crayon as a writing implement; and that *size* allowed them to identify a pencil as used rather than as new.

Knowing the characteristic properties for various haptic discriminations, Lederman and Klatzky next tested the role of the EPs pictured in Figure 13.16 in extracting those properties. Switching from an imagined discrimination to the real thing, a new group of individuals handled unseen objects one at a time and judged, for each, whether or not it was a member of some class. For example, an observer given a pencil had to state whether it was a writing utensil. On other trials, the person was asked whether the pencil was new or used. Videotapes revealed that on about 80 percent of all trials, observers began by enclosing the test object with fingers curved and then lifting it. These exploratory procedures provide gross information that was usually insufficient to permit a conclusion. Therefore, they were usually followed by one or more additional EPs. The selection of a follow-up EP mirrored the property that would be most helpful in deciding category membership. (Recall that this property, for each pair of objects, had been gleaned from the judgments of other people.) For example, if shape were a distinguishing property, people tended to follow the object's contour with their fingers; if texture were most important, people moved their fingers back and forth across the object's surface. Haptic exploration, then, is driven by observers' knowledge of object properties.

From these and related experiments, Lederman and Klatzky (1987) derived two additional characteristics of the EPs: generality and duration. Though each EP was best suited for extracting information about a particular object property, many EPs provided subsidiary information about one or more additional properties. This allowed Lederman to rank the EPs on the generality of the information, primary and subsidiary, that each gave. Lederman found also that EPs varied dramatically in how long each took to execute. Interestingly, these two measures—generality and duration—tended to be inversely related. One EP, enclosure, offered good generality and rapid execution. Not coincidentally, that one EP typically inaugurated each and every exploratory sequence in Klatzky and Lederman's experiment.

FIGURE 13.16 | Principal exploratory procedures used in haptic examination of objects. Each term in parentheses indicates the stimulus feature most likely to be recognized by the corresponding exploratory procedure.

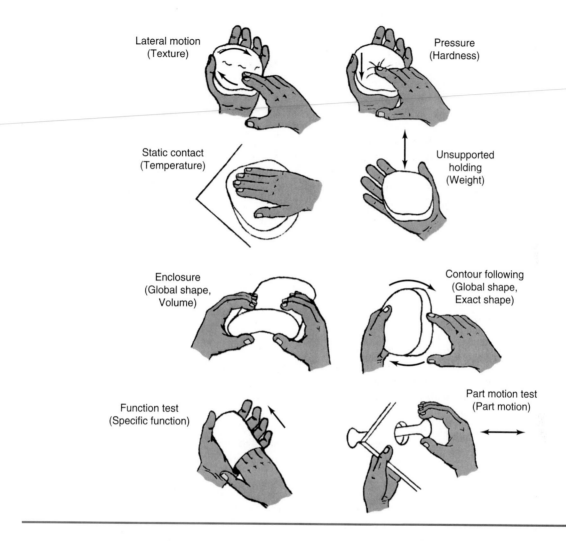

The analysis of EPs has been extended to children blind from birth (Landau, 1991). In all cases studied, blind children tested on tasks involving judgments of spatial configurations of objects performed similarly to sighted children who were tested while blindfolded. Landau concludes, "Visual experience is not necessary for the early development of the capacity to explore objects or layouts, the capacity to assemble haptic and kinesthetic information about objects into a unified representation, or the capacity to transform these representations in ways important to mature human spatial cognition" (1991, p. 176).

But if vision is not crucial for object representation, what is its role? Outside the laboratory, observers explore and characterize objects in terms of their visual appearance as well as by means of haptic exploration. How is the chore shared between these two sources of information? This question, which remains unanswered, interests not only students of perception but also engineers who must design robots that can operate in distant environments (e.g. Mars) or handle dangerous objects and substances (e.g. radioactive material). Suppose the robots had not only visual capacity, but, thanks to sensors embedded in a flexible artificial skin, haptic

FIGURE 13.17 | Schematic of the setup used by Blake, Sobel, and James (2004) to allow a person to view a visually ambiguous object on two computer video screens (viewed through mirrors) while, at the same time, touching a real object with his or her hands. The shape of the real object—a globe in this experiment—exactly matched the shape of the virtual visual object, and both were rotating about the vertical axis of the globe.

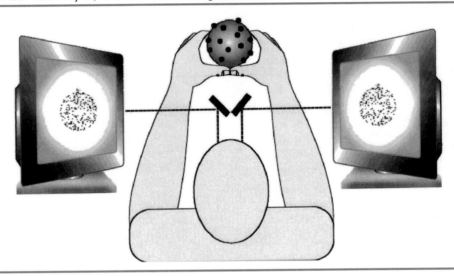

ones as well (Someya et al., 2004). Under what conditions should one capacity be used in preference to the other? When do *we* use one in preference to the other?

Because of the relative speed with which various EPs are executed, haptics is best suited to extract information about properties related to an object's material—its hardness, its temperature, its surface texture—and least suited as a source for the object's geometric properties—its shape. Lederman, Klatzky, and Pawluk (1992) note that choice of test stimuli can make haptics seem ineffective compared to vision. In particular, imagine having to sort differently shaped, three-dimensional objects all made of the same material. Here, compared to vision, haptics would be slow. Conversely, if the objects were identical in shape but varied only in hardness or in temperature, vision would do poorly compared to haptics. The lesson, then, is that haptics and vision provide complementary sources of information.

Haptic information also comes in handy when vision provides ambiguous information about an object's shape or its direction of motion. Remember from Chapter 9 that visual motion information can specify the shape of a rotating, 3D object (look again at Figure 9.2). Sometimes, however, the motion signals specifying shape are ambiguous, in which case people experience spontaneous fluctuations in perceived rotation of a 3D object. Blake, Sobel, and James (2004) discovered that this visual confusion could be partially remedied by allowing people to touch an unseen rotating object at the same time they were viewing

a computer-generated video rendition of that object (see Figure 13.17). With touch, of course, there's never confusion about which way an object is rotating, and this high-fidelity tactile information was sufficient to reduce substantially the fluctuations in visual perception ordinarily experienced when viewing the computer version.

One of the ways touch may clarify object shape is by concurrent activation of somatosensory cortical areas *and* visual areas. Recall from Chapters 4 and 6 that cortical areas in the ventral stream pathway are thought to be involved in specifying object shape. Pietrini and colleagues (2004) discovered that some of these ventral stream "visual" areas are also activated when blindfolded people handle objects one after another, in a tactile object recognition task.

Haptics and touch play important roles in another area: Both guide skilled motor acts, particularly the grasp and manipulation of objects. Suppose you reach for and pick up a delicate object. Your fingers must exert enough force to hold the object without its slipping but not so much force that the object breaks. The classic demonstration of this trade-off is the robot hand that tries unsuccessfully to pick up a raw egg. One approach is to adjust the force of the grip using information from touch receptors in the fingertips. Lederman, Klatzky, and Pawluk (1992) summarize physiological studies that demonstrate the contributions of various touch receptors during different stages of reaching and grasping.

The intimate connection between touch and exploratory motor behavior is mirrored by the proximity of touch areas and motor areas in the cerebral cortex. The area of the brain responsible for activating the muscles of the body, the so-called *motor cortex,* lies immediately adjacent and anterior to the somatosensory cortex (recall Figure 13.12). This adjacency simplifies interconnections between these areas and facilitates the coordination of exploratory, grasping, and other manipulatory movements needed in active touch.

There is evidence that different regions of the somatosensory cortex control different aspects of active touch. This is most directly shown by temporarily inactivating various localized regions of somatosensory cortex and measuring the behavioral consequences. In one such study, Hikosaka and colleagues injected minute amounts of muscimol, a neurotransmitter antagonist, into the finger regions of a monkey brain S-I (Hikosaka et al., 1985). Before and after various injections, these investigators tested a monkey's ability to detect and extract small pieces of food embedded in the holes of a wooden block (in most tests, the monkey's eyes were blindfolded). When the chemical had been injected into Area 3b, the monkey could put its fingers into the hole but seemed unable to detect the presence of food in the hole, even after actually touching the food. This constitutes a sensory deficit. But injections to Area 2 of S-I, presumably a later stage of cortical processing, produced a very different type of deficit.[4] The monkey's excited behavior showed that the food had been detected, but the animal was unable to move its fingers in the coordinated way needed to extract the food. Other studies, involving permanent lesions to restricted areas of S-I (Randolph and Semmes, 1974) and S-II (Carlson and Burton, 1988), support the idea that these different areas play a crucial role in various aspects of touch. It is not yet possible to isolate these kinds of areas in humans with this level of precision (e.g., see Young et al., 2004), but we do know that neural activation within human somatosensory cortex is much greater when people actively touch objects rather than receiving passive, tactile stimulation (Ginsberg et al., 1987).

Besides informing us about the particulars of an object we're in tactile contact with, neurons in these somatosensory areas of the brain also participate in forming short-term memories of recently handled objects, as Zhou and Fuster (1996) documented. In their study, monkeys were trained to explore a textured object with one hand for a few seconds, to remember the shape and texture of the object, and then to use the same hand to select that object from several alternatives presented several seconds later. Recording from single neurons with receptive fields located on the hand being used by the monkey, Zhou and Fuster found that about half these neurons in somatosensory cortex kept on responding during the interval between the initial touch period and the test period. So these neurons not only analyze the tactile features of objects but also maintain a neural image of those features in short-term memory. Presumably this neural image can then guide subsequent motor responses to that object.

A recent study exploited TMS (a technique described in Chapter 1) to clarify the role of S-I and S-II neurons in working memory for tactile stimulation. As you may recall, TMS is a technique in which brief pulses of magnetic energy are applied to a person's scalp. The energy that penetrates the scalp and skull temporarily scrambles neural activity in the outer layers of the cortex closest to where the TMS pulse had been delivered. Using this technique, Justin Harris and colleagues (Harris et al., 2002) asked people to compare the frequencies of two vibrating stimuli applied successively to one index finger and then the other. With the TMS coil positioned directly above a person's somatosensory cortex contralateral to the stimulated index finger, a TMS pulse delivered during the interval between the two vibrotactile samples dramatically reduced the ability to compare the frequencies of those two samples. Presumably, the TMS pulse disturbed the memory for the first of the vibrotactile samples, which hindered the comparison of that sample with the one that followed. Again, it appears that, just as in vision (see Chapter 6), the same neurons that participate in sensory coding also have an important role in short-term memory.

Recall from Chapter 4 that the visual pathways appear to be subdivided into specialized processing streams. One of those streams is responsible for directing and guiding our activities such as orienting toward and reaching for objects of interest. That processing stream is associated with the parietal lobe which, as you've just learned, is also intimately involved in tactile perception. It is not surprising, therefore, that vision and touch jointly control the ability to grasp and lift objects. Think back to that tomato you were considering at the produce market. Initially, vision guided your hand to the object and controlled the conformation of your fingers as you prepared to grasp it. But once you made contact with the tomato, your sense of touch took over, using friction and force to gauge the strength of your grasp. Memory, too, was playing a role, informing you ahead of time what to expect when grasping the tomato. Actually, humans are pretty good at adjusting their grasp in a manner appropriate for an object using sight alone or using touch alone

---

[4]We describe Area 2 as "later" than Area 3b because some of Area 2's input comes from Area 3b, but the reverse does not seem to be true.

(Jenmalm and Johansson, 1997). But when working together, these two sources of information coded in the parietal lobe help you to make grasp decisions faster and more accurately.

In humans, damage to these parietal regions produces a remarkable condition called **unilateral neglect.** In this condition, a patient may fail to attend to one side of the body, ignoring it as though it didn't even exist. For example, the neurologist MacDonald Critchley described one patient who reproved his own arm, protesting: "You bloody bastard! It's a lost soul, this bloody thing. It keeps following me around. It gets in my way when I read. I find my hand up by my face, waving about" (1979, p. 118). The ownership of the troublesome, wandering arm was denied by the patient despite contrary evidence from the sense of touch.

Phantom Limb

In unilateral neglect, people may deny ownership of one of their limbs; a limb that is objectively present is subjectively ignored. The reverse situation can also occur, in which a person feels a limb that is objectively not present. This is the bizarre condition known as **phantom limb,** where an amputee has the compelling sense that an amputated limb is still attached to his or her body (Melzack, 1992). Anecdotal accounts of phantom limb go back for centuries, but the first systematic descriptions were given by Ambroise Paré, a sixteenth-century French military surgeon (see Wade, 2003, for a summary of Paré's work). Probably the most widely read account appears in Herman Melville's famous novel *Moby Dick* (Melville, 1942), where obsessed Captain Ahab speaks with the carpenter who is fashioning his artificial leg:

> Look ye, carpenter, I dare say thou callest thyself a right good workmanlike workman, eh? Well, then, will it speak thoroughly well for thy work, if, when I come to mount this leg thou makest, I shall nevertheless feel another leg in the same identical place with it; that is, carpenter, my old lost leg; the flesh and blood one, I mean. Canst thou not drive that old Adam away?

Here's a more contemporary, real-life description of a patient suffering phantom limb, as related by neuropsychologist V. S. Ramachandran (Ramachandran and Blakeslee, 1998):

> As a result of this gruesome mishap [a motorcycle accident], Tom lost his left arm just above the elbow. . . . In the weeks afterward, even though he knew his arm was gone, Tom could still feel its ghostly presence below the

elbow. He could wiggle each "finger," "reach out" and "grab" objects that were within arm's reach. Indeed, his phantom arm seemed to be able to do anything that the real arm would have done automatically, such as warding off blows, breaking falls or patting his little brother on the back. (pp. 21–22)

It used to be thought that phantom limb was a psychiatric disorder, a form of hysteria triggered by the traumatic loss of the limb. But now it's generally believed that these illusory bodily sensations arise from reorganization of the "touch" map in the parietal lobe of the brain (Melzack, 1992). The portion of the cortical map devoted to the missing limb comes to be innervated by other portions of the body, most likely those body regions with cortical representations neighboring those of the missing limb. Thus, for example, the patient Tom reported sensation in his missing limb when Ramachandran lightly stroked Tom's cheek with a cotton swab. (As Figure 13.13 shows, the face region of the somatosensory cortex is located adjacent to the hand region.)

We should give credit where credit is due: Centuries ago, French philosopher René Descartes correctly surmised that phantom limb was attributable to illusory neural signals arising within remaining portions of the nervous system. When asked to explain how someone could sense an amputated limb, Descartes responded:

> In view of these considerations, it is manifest that, notwithstanding the goodness of God, the nature of man, in so far as it is a composite of mind and body, must sometimes be at fault and deceptive. For should some cause, not in the foot, but in another part of the nerves which extend from the foot to the brain, or even in the brain itself, give rise to the motion ordinarily excited when the foot is injuriously affected, pain will be felt just as though it were in the foot, and thus naturally the sense will be deceived. (quoted in Wall, 2000, p. 20).

The worst aspect of phantom limbs is the excruciating pain that seems to be localized in the limb or in specific parts of the limb. For example, Melzack (1992) notes that after leg or foot amputation, patients feel that their toes are being "seared by a red-hot poker." Although researchers are actively pursuing a number of leads, there is now no sure way to alleviate such pain. The Web links at www.mhhe.com/blake5 contain additional material on phantom limb, including an exercise that allows you to mimic the phantom limb experience in yourself.

The discussion of phantom limbs sets the stage for the final two topics of this chapter, pain perception and neural plasticity in the somatosensory system.

Pain Perception

Pain is an unusually difficult sensory experience to study, for the simple reason that people may have trouble verbalizing what pain really is, and how intense it feels. According to the official definition of the International Association for the Study of Pain, pain is "an unpleasant sensory or emotional experience associated with actual or potential tissue damage" (Merskey and Bogduk, 1994). Although capturing the general character of pain, this definition fails to capture the individual, subjective character of the experience. Pain, in fact, depends significantly on the specific instigating condition, the person's previous history with painful stimulation, and the sufferer's mental state.

Whatever the particulars of pain, it is often written that pain constitutes a biologically important "warning signal" of tissue damage. Thus, the threshold for acute, painful stimulation, whether it's produced by heat or by mechanical pressure, corresponds closely to the stimulus intensity level at which the skin and underlying tissue become susceptible to injury. Moreover, it is also true that individuals who are chronically insensitive to pain (yes, there are such rare individuals) have reduced life expectancy (Wall, 2000). As Damasio has put it, "Suffering offers us the best protection for survival" (1994, p. 264).[5]

But pain cannot just be a warning signal about potential tissue damage, for pain often persists well after the threatening stimulus has been removed. For that matter, pain is often not even experienced until minutes or even hours after the evoking event. The late U.S. President Ronald Reagan, although shot in the chest by an assassin's bullet, apparently didn't realize his injury until he began spitting blood while being whisked away from the scene of the assassination attempt. Only when he reached the hospital did pain become a salient sensation for Reagan. So what does this delayed reaction say about pain's biological role?

Chronic pain, such as that associated with a bruised muscle, a broken bone, or a gunshot wound, has the beneficial effect of discouraging continued use of the affected body part, thereby facilitating recovery. Moreover, chronic internal pain with no obvious origin can forewarn of illness or disease. Both of these reactions to pain, of course, enhance one's chances of survival. Pain also plays another potentially important role in protecting our survival, this one an interpersonal role. You have no trouble telling when someone else is in pain. Because of this, it has been proposed (Williams, 2002) that one function of pain is to command the immediate attention of other people, who can help the pained individual to escape the painfully provoking situation or to recover and heal from the resultant injury. Befitting this social role, people are unable to hide painful expressions even when trying to, and others cannot ignore individuals when they exhibit facial expressions and bodily postures signifying that they're in pain.

So, pain serves multiple adaptive purposes. Still, there is nothing more debilitating than chronic pain, as anyone who suffers painful migraine headaches will testify. To paraphrase Julius and Basbaum (2001), pain often outlives its usefulness as a warning signal or as a cue to promote recovery. And it is pain's nagging persistence that leads people to spend billions of dollars annually in pursuit of pain relief.

In this section we won't attempt to survey the huge literature on pain and its management, but we will provide an overview of some of the perceptual and neurophysiological aspects of pain. Excellent reviews of pain-related findings can be found in Craig and Rollman (1999), and a very personal description of pain management by one of the world's pain experts is provided by Wall (2000).

Neural Pathways for Pain Signals

Research on pain perception faces a unique challenge: There is simply no way to know whether one person's pain resembles the pain someone else experiences. It's difficult to gauge the quality and intensity of any painful experience. Of course, this could be said for other sensory experiences as well. Is your red the same as mine? But in the case of the other senses—hearing, seeing, taste, smell, and touch—we can point to an evoking "stimulus" that reliably accompanies a perceptual experience. In the case of pain, however, this is sometimes impossible. Pain is defined exclusively by the subjective report of the individual experiencing it. Moreover, the experience of pain has multiple dimensions to it: sensory ("I just touched something hot with my right index finger"), affective ("That hurts") and cognitive/evaluative ("I'd better put some ice on my burned finger"). These different components are likely to be processed by different neural pathways (Melzack and Casey, 1968; Treede et al., 1999). Let's start by considering the various forms that pain can take, along with treatments for relief of those forms of pain.

Some common forms of acute pain (such as that experienced when you accidentally prick yourself with a pin) are generated by abrupt, strong stimulation of the skin's mechanoreceptors. These painful experiences can be eliminated by anesthetics that dull the responsiveness

---

[5]Additional information on chronic insensitivity to pain can be found among the Chapter 13 weblinks at www.mhhe.com/blake5.

FIGURE 13.18 | Stimuli used in Wong-Baker FACES Pain Rating Scale. A patient is told that each face is for a person who feels happy because he has no pain, or sad because he has some or a lot of pain. For example, face 0 is very happy because he doesn't hurt at all, and face 1 hurts just a little bit. Face 5 hurts as much as can be imagined. The patient is asked to choose the face that best describes how he or she is feeling.

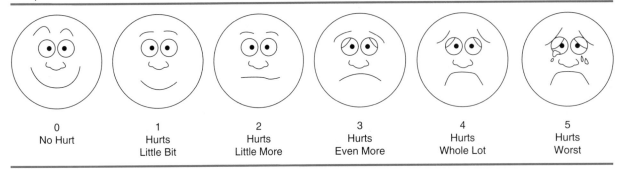

0	1	2	3	4	5
No Hurt	Hurts Little Bit	Hurts Little More	Hurts Even More	Hurts Whole Lot	Hurts Worst

of mechanoreceptors or their associated afferent fibers (thank goodness for Novacaine when visiting the dentist). Other forms of pain (such as that associated with arthritis) are more chronic and result from damage to bodily tissue. Different drugs are needed to deal with different aspects of pain (Hunt and Mantyh, 2001). So, pain that originates in damage to the skin can be targeted by a drug that acts peripherally, reducing signals from the skin's pain receptors. Anti-inflammatory agents are examples of such drugs. However, to address pain's psychological unpleasantness and distress, a centrally acting drug, such as an opiate, may be called for.

Management of chronic pain presents a special challenge, for the most effective pharmacological treatments tend to lose their potency with increased use, while at the same time presenting the possibility of addiction. Molecular biologists are working hard to formulate effective drugs that do not have these drawbacks. For now, though, pain therapists focus heavily on behavioral strategies for managing chronic pain. As we'll see in a moment, some of those strategies could be effective because they recruit "top-down" cognitive control over neural events signaling pain.

To study pain in the laboratory requires some way to induce the experience, and to measure it. A number of different rating scales have been developed for assessing the intensity and unpleasantness of pain. Some of those scales ask the individual to assign numbers to their experience of pain, often using behavioral indices to calibrate the numerical scale (for example, "Assign the number 10 if you must immediately seek relief"). Alternatively, investigators can gauge pain using reflex reactions such as hand withdrawal, pupil dilation, and galvanic skin response. These are particularly useful when studying pain in nonhumans. In recent years, investigators have also used somatosensory evoked potentials (recorded from the scalp) and neuroimaging techniques to assess neural concomitants of pain sensations.

One simple, popular, easy-to-use clinical technique for measuring pain deserves a more detailed description. About 25 years ago, Donna Wong and Connie Morain Baker were working in a hospital burn center. Too often, they saw children who were clearly in pain, but whose young age kept them from expressing how they were feeling, especially how much they hurt. Inspired by the smiley face symbols that were popular at the time, Wong and Baker realized that a series of faces with a range of expressions might be a good device for helping the children to describe how much pain they were experiencing. Wong and Baker began by asking the children to draw on a series of empty circles the facial expressions of people who were experiencing different degrees of pain, from "no pain at all" to the "worst pain they could ever imagine." With the drawings of many children in hand, they derived the standardized set of six cartoon faces shown in Figure 13.18. In using these faces, patients are asked to point to the face that best describes their own pain (Wong et al., 2001). The Wong-Baker FACES Pain Rating Scale works well, not just for its original target population, but also for many older children and adults, as well as for people who do not speak English. This simple, elegant scale has proven effective in numerous studies of pain management and treatment, both of which require a good way to assess pain.

As we mentioned before, to study pain experimentally, one must be able to assess pain, and, as needed, to produce pain. To satisfy this second requirement, researchers have developed techniques for provoking calibrated painful sensations in volunteers. One technique is to apply a chemical irritant to the surface of the skin. One popular irritant is capsaicin, the "hot" ingredient in chili peppers. (If you've ever touched your eyes or other mucous tissues after handling chili peppers, you're familiar with capsaicin's potency.) Another technique involves applying a controlled degree of mechanical force to the skin using a hard, sharp object. A third technique employs a focused beam of radiant energy to generate extreme warmth on a restricted region of the skin.

Stimulation from any of these noxious procedures can generate neural activity within a specific class of receptors within the skin known as **nociceptors.** These are found among the free nerve endings located near the surface of the skin (nociceptors registering information about temperature extremes) as well as within the subcutaneous fat below the skin's surface (nociceptors registering information about sharp, punctate stimulation). Nociceptors are also located in the cornea of the eye, in the teeth, in visceral organs within the body's interior and in muscles of the body including the heart. To keep things simple, we'll focus on nociceptive pathways arising from the skin.

Neural messages from the nociceptors in the skin are carried by specialized nerve fibers that travel from the skin to the dorsal parts of the spinal cord (see Figure 13.19). These fibers are divisible into two groups, the "slow-conducting" fibers (also referred to as C-fibers, which are "slow" because they are unmyelinated) and the "fast-conducting" fibers (also known as Aδ-fibers, which are myelinated). (Note: these myelinated fast fibers are distinct from the fast fibers described previously in the chapter, the ones that mediate the detection of innocuous tactile stimulation.) Both sets of fibers have relatively high thresholds, meaning that they are activated only in response to rather intense levels of stimulation, levels well above the level required simply to detect the presence of a tactile stimulus. Because these fibers are specialized for noxious stimulation, not just touch or temperature, they can be construed as a unique sensory modality producing a unique perceptual experience: pain.

These two classes of nociceptive fibers differ in terms of their response properties. The fast/Aδ fibers respond to strong mechanical stimulation (e.g., a pin prick), or thermal stimulation (e.g., intense heat), and when so stimulated they produce an immediate sensation of sharp, acute pain. As a group the slow/C fibers respond not only to mechanical and thermal stimulation but also to chemical stimulation (e.g., acid on the skin); a given C fiber, however, may respond only to chemical stimulation or only to thermal stimulation. When stimulated, slow/C fibers produce more slowly growing sensations of pain that can be long lasting. Both Aδ and C fibers can also stimulate release of neurochemicals at their peripheral endings, trig-

FIGURE 13.19 | The dorsal root of the spinal cord contains sensory nerve fibers carrying information into the spine and then up to the brain. Among these dorsal root fibers are two types of nerve fibers, the slow fibers and the fast fibers. Nerve fibers in the ventral root carry motor commands out of the spinal cord to the muscles. Interneurons between sensory and motor fibers mediate reflex motor reactions to sensory stimulation.

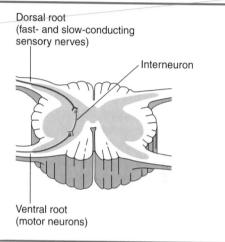

Dorsal root
(fast- and slow-conducting
sensory nerves)

Interneuron

Ventral root
(motor neurons)

gering vascular reactions that produce inflammation at the site of injury. Finally, the fast/ Aδ fibers and, especially, the slow/C fibers both exhibit allodynia, a form of hypersensitivity wherein a normally *non*painful stimulus elicits activity (and, presumably, pain) when applied to an area of the body where painful stimulation had been previously applied. Thus, when you lightly bump a bruised chin and experience pain, you have activated nociceptive fibers that would ordinarily remain silent.

In the last five years or so, pain research has made stunning advances in delineating the biomolecular processes responsible for signal transduction in nociceptors, processes that endow them with the ability to register physical, thermal, and mechanical stimuli. For students intrigued by molecular biology, we highly recommend the review by Julius and Basbaum (2001) on molecular mechanisms of nociception. For our purposes here, though, we can sidestep those details and focus on the central terminals of these primary afferent nociceptors.

Nociceptive fibers—both fast and slow types—project to a number of subcortical structures involved in homeostatsis (including the hypothalamus) and, as well, to a circumscribed region of the thalamus, a cluster of nuclei that relays sensory information from the periphery to the cortex (recall the LGN in vision). Within the thalamus, we can identify a lateral portion and a medial portion, both of which send nociceptive projections to the cortex. The lateral portion of this relay system sends projections to the primary and secondary somatosensory cortex, areas S-I and S-II. The medial portion of the nociceptive pathway projects to regions in the frontal cortex associated with the limbic system (those brain areas involved in affective reactions).

A neuroimaging study shows convincingly that these different brain regions are responsible for representing different perceptual aspects of painful experiences. Rainville and colleagues (1997) used PET to measure the distribution of brain activity evoked by exposing human volunteers to noxious thermal stimulation. The interesting twist to this study was the use of hypnosis to manipulate the perceived unpleasantness generated by a constant level of stimulation. Pain-related activation was found in S-I and S-II in the parietal lobe, regardless of the perceived unpleasantness of that stimulation. However, activation in limbic sites, including the anterior cingulate cortex, was modulated by the hypnotic suggestion, with more unpleasant experiences associated with greater activation. This dissociation between perceived intensity and perceived unpleasantness dovetails nicely with clinical reports that people with brain damage to these frontal lobe regions report that noxious stimulation, while feeling painful, isn't particularly bothersome.

The Gate Control Theory of Pain

The single most influential theory of pain perception is Melzack and Wall's (1965) **gate control theory** of pain, which builds on the idea of multiple interacting fiber pathways . As we move through an overview of this theory, you should be able to see the link between this model and the fast and slow nociceptive fibers discussed above. An overview of this theory is diagrammed in Figure 13.20. Three groups of nerve fibers make synaptic contact with a group of cells located in the spinal cord (labeled "T-cells" in the figure): fast-conducting nociceptive fibers, slow-conducting nociceptive fibers and fast-conducting fibers that carry information about touch but not pain. The T-cells, when active, transmit (thus the label *T*) pain signals up the spinal cord to the brain, culminating in the experience of pain. Also located in the spinal cord is a cluster of neurons (technically, a nucleus) that constitutes the "gate." When activated, this nucleus inhibits the T-cells and, therefore, suppresses the communication of T-cell signals to the brain. The key to the model resides in the differential effect of the fast- and slow-conducting fibers on the "gate" itself. The fast-conducting fibers excite the neurons forming the gate (thus inhibiting T-cells), and the slow-conducting fibers inhibit the gate neurons (thus releasing T-cells from inhibition).

To see how the model works, consider what happens when your skin lightly touches the handle of a cool pan sit-

FIGURE 13.20 | Schematic of the gate control theory of pain.

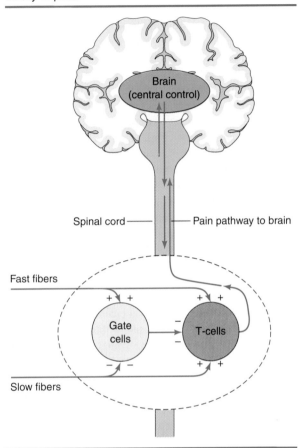

ting on the stove. This event would immediately stimulate the fast "touch" fibers, which have a lower threshold than the slow "pain" fibers. This activates the gate neurons which, in turn, would inhibit the T-neurons. The result? As you experience the feel of the pan's handle, you experience no pain. But suppose the entire pan had been quite hot, handle included. Now the slow-conducting fibers with their higher threshold for activation would be excited, and this would simultaneously inhibit the gate neurons and activate the T-neurons. The result? Now you feel not only the handle but also the pain associated with it.

According to this model, pain messages originating in the T-cells can also be blocked by fibers originating in the brain and projecting back down to the gate portion in the spinal cord. These fibers allow "top-down"control over pain perception. This aspect of the model is confirmed by clinical experience. It is well-established that surgical patients require lower doses of painkillers when they have been told ahead of time what to expect during the procedure and have been trained to relax before and during surgery. These patients are also released from the hospital several days earlier than those not receiving pain management training. Also related to the "top-down" control of pain is the so-called placebo effect, whereby a patient experiences less pain following ingestion of a "painkiller" that, in fact, contains no active ingredients. The mere expectation of pain relief is sometimes sufficient to produce the desired effect. You can imagine how these expectations might enable the patient unwittingly to activate top-down influences that shut the spinal cord's pain gate.

Finally, here's another example of pain's susceptibility to top-down influences. The example builds on the fact that your interpretation of the source of a painful stimulus governs its perceived intensity: Specifically, when the stimulus evoking pain is considered potentially dangerous or damaging, your experience of that pain is amplified. The potency of pain's "meaning" is well illustrated by an experiment in which adult volunteers were touched briefly on the back of the neck with a piece of metal that had been cooled to −25 degrees Celsius (that's −13 degrees Fahrenheit). Paradoxically, metal at that low temperature can actually feel hot, and when told that the object was hot, that's exactly what the volunteers reported experiencing. Moreover, they rated the painfulness of the resulting sensation as more intense than did volunteers who were told that the very same object was cold (Arntz and Claassens, 2004). So, knowledge about the stimulus (in this case, misleading knowledge for some people) can itself influence your experience of the severity of the pain elicited by that stimulus. This reaction is adaptive, when you think about it—if a pain source threatens tissue damage (as a very hot object can), then you need to react immediately to remove yourself from this threat, but if the source is merely a nuisance then tolerance may be called for. The modulatory influence of knowledge on perceived pain has important, practical implications for pain management. Cancer patients, for example, are better able to tolerate chronic pain when they understand the actual source of the pain (Ahles et al., 1983). Box 13.2 describes some additional facts and myths about the perception of pain and its alleviation.

We will complete our survey of touch with the topic of cortical plasticity: modification of the brain's representation of the sense of touch in response to use and disuse.

Plasticity in the Somatosensory Cortex

For decades it was thought that sensory maps in the brain were shaped by experiences very early in life but thereafter remained fixed in size and composition. During the 1980s and 1990s, however, converging lines of evidence forced abandonment of that view. Instead, it is now recognized that throughout life the somatosensory cortex remains malleable, or plastic, and that cortical connections adjust over time to changes in afferent input. This research has intriguing implications for the uniqueness of every human being. But before turning to such implications, let's consider the research itself.

Origins of Plasticity

The study of plasticity within the somatosensory cortex was stimulated by Vernon Mountcastle's theory of cortical development (Mountcastle, 1984). The theory depicts the cortex as a dynamic, self-organizing system of interconnected neurons. Neurons in a given region of the brain can *potentially* form an enormously large number of synapses with other neurons, many more synapses than are *actually* formed. Presumably, afferent fibers coming into the somatosensory cortex from the thalamus compete for contact with—and control over—neurons in the somatosensory cortex. Only a fraction of all possible synapses actually survives this competition, but what determines which fibers will win the competition? What controls the selection of particular synapses to be activated from among the horde of potential synapses? In basic terms, the theory claims that the most active inputs win, with less active inputs becoming dormant.

To evaluate Mountcastle's theory, one must study the events that influence the development and maintenance of connections between cortical neurons and their incoming afferent fibers. This problem has been the focus of research by Michael Merzenich and his colleagues (Merzenich, 1987; Buonomano and Merzenich, 1998). Merzenich began by mapping cortical locations that represent touch information from the fingers and hands of adult monkeys. These finger and hand maps in the somatosensory cortex turned out to be remarkably plastic, even in adult animals. Though the maps' broad outlines remain fixed, their details could be altered by experience. In one study, Merzenich surgically joined the skin from two adjacent fingers without disturbing the receptors or nerve fibers lying within the skin. This delicate surgical procedure turns previously separate fingers into a single functional unit—anything that happens to one finger also happens to the other. They move as one, and they receive touch information as one.

The procedure had extraordinary consequences. After the newly joined fingers were used for a few weeks, previously sharp boundaries between the maps for the two digits had dissolved, leaving a single cortical representation for the two-finger combination. Moreover, neurons that used to have receptive fields on just one of the digits now had receptive fields extending across both fingers. Next, Merzenich surgically redivided the fingers, restoring them to their normal state. After the fingers

BOX 13.2

Some Facts—and Myths—about Pain

The English writer and wit Samuel Johnson said, "The mind is seldom quickened to very vigorous operations but by pain, or the dread of pain." With characteristic insight, Johnson reminded his readers of the obvious: pain, or even the mere anticipation of pain, has the propensity to seize the mind. Anyone scheduled to have a root canal, a tetanus shot, or a spanking can relate to this maxim. Researchers have identified some brain circuits that mediate the dread and fear that are evoked by the anticipation of pain (Price, 2000). Pain is not an experience we relish, and we're terribly uncomfortable even watching someone else suffer pain. (One of the most agonizing moments in cinematic history occurs during the scene in *Marathon Man* where we watch Dustin Hoffman writhing in pain as he is tortured by having a hole drilled in his tooth.) Because pain is so salient and, alas, so inevitable, humans have tried countless measures to relieve pain. Here, we summarize some of those palliatives, both successful ones and failures.

Acupuncture

For people raised in contemporary Western culture, with its emphasis on medical science, it's hard to imagine how the insertion of fine needles into specific sites on the body could alleviate pain. Yet centuries of practice document that **acupuncture** works. The acupuncture maps that guided the ancient Chinese pain healers are still accurate today. For some pain sites, the needle insertion point is within the immediate neighborhood, whereas for others the insertion point is quite remote from the pain site.

Western science has advanced several explanations for the **analgesia** (elimination of pain) produced by acupuncture. On one account, acupuncture stimulates the release of **endorphins,** naturally occurring morphine-like chemicals produced by our bodies. These chemicals, acting on specialized receptors in the brain, are able to quell painful sensations. Our bodies naturally produce endorphins, particularly under conditions of stress.

Centuries ago humans discovered natural substances—most notably opium and heroin—that reduce pain and instigate feelings of euphoria. Those substances stimulate the same receptors as those designed to respond to endorphins. A brain that is on drugs isn't doing anything it wasn't designed to do. It's just doing it when it shouldn't be.

A second, alternative account of acupuncture's analgesic effect posits that the needle stimulates fast conducting touch fibers, thereby "closing" the pain gate.

Whatever explanation proves to be correct, there is no quarreling with thousands of years of success: When administered by an experienced practitioner, acupuncture can work (Pariente et. al., 2005).

Inducing Pain to Relieve Pain

In the text we mentioned that capsaicin—the active ingredient in hot peppers—was a surefire means for inducing pain when it comes in contact with the skin or mucous membrane. Ironically, capsaicin is also an effective agent for ameliorating pain. Following exposure to capsaicin, the experience of acute, burning pain gradually wanes. If a second exposure to capsaicin occurs after the burning sensation from a previous exposure has dissipated, your experience of pain is actually muted again. Capsaicin, in other words, elevates the threshold for pain in areas to which it has previously been applied (Berger, Henderson, and Nadoolman, 1995; Fuchs et al., 2000a). Moreover, this mod-

were used for a while, the cortical representations of the two fingers again became distinct and separate. The details of the somatosensory map, therefore, are created in response to experience and can be modified by altered sensory input even in adulthood (Wall, 1988; Blake, Byl, and Merzenich, 2002).

Up to now we've only talked about cortical reorganization in response to some rearrangement of the fingers, an event that is pretty exotic. Analogous changes in the somatosensory cortex follow from conditions much closer to our own experience. Coordinated behavioral and physiological studies reveal that discrimination of subtle differences in touch stimulation improves dramatically with practice, and that this improvement is accompanied by changes in the somatosensory cortex. Recanzone and col-

leagues (1992a) applied a vibrating stimulator to one spot on a monkey's fingertip. From a series of stimuli, the monkey had to identify the one stimulus that vibrated at a frequency slightly different from the others. Over time, the monkeys were able to make increasingly fine discriminations. Although adjacent, nonpracticed fingers showed some slight improvement as well, the effects on the trained digit were far more impressive, suggesting the practice's effects were localized. Recanzone and colleagues (1992b) also studied the somatosensory cortex in these same monkeys. Prolonged training produced several changes, including an increase in the cortical area devoted to the trained region of the monkey's finger and a heightened crispness and consistency in responding to the vibration stimulus.

erating effect generalizes to other painful stimuli as well. Thus, an individual's pain tolerance can be gradually elevated by increasing the capsaicin concentration in a series of repeated applications (Fuchs et al., 2000b). Currently capsaicin treatment is being tested for use in cases of heartburn, some forms of itching, sunburns, and rheumatism.

Pain and the Weather

In 1887, the *American Journal of Medical Science* published a case report of an amputee who experienced pain in his phantom limb (the condition described earlier in the text). The patient's pain varied with the weather, being most severe when an approaching storm produced a drop in barometric pressure (Shutty, Cunduff, and DeGood, 1992). Subsequent clinical reports suggested that arthritis sufferers also experienced heightened pain when the barometric pressure dropped. More recently, surveys of patients suffering chronic pain have confirmed that changes in temperature and humidity elevate self-ratings of pain. It is conceivable that changes in temperature and/or humidity cause tendons, muscles, and scar tissue to expand and contract, thereby exacerbating pain. While the exact mechanisms remain obscure, there does seem to be truth to the aphorism, "Aches and pains, coming rains." Contrary to popular belief, though, pain is not entirely relieved by living in a mild climate—seasonal changes still trigger surges in pain (Jamison, 1996).

The Pain of Execution

Amendment VIII to the Constitution of the United States explicitly prohibits the use of "cruel and unusual punishment." Advocates of capital punishment argue that death by execution could be seen as extreme, but it does not constitute cruelty because, they argue, the person being executed does not feel pain. This argument, however, may be flawed. In an article not for the squeamish, Hillman (1993) argues that all forms of execution other than lethal intravenous injection induce severe pain in the dying individual. For starters, initial attempts at execution are not always successful, leaving the prisoner injured and suffering until the procedure is successfully completed. And even when death results on the first try, the death is often not instantaneous. With electrocution, for example, a person experiences severe burns and, perhaps, asphyxiation and heart fibrillation. It may take many seconds before the individual loses consciousness, and in the meantime, he or she is very likely to be experiencing excruciating pain. Even the procedure of beheading (which is still practiced in some countries in Africa and in the Middle East) may entail a conscious experience of pain. The human brain maintains enough oxygen for metabolism to persist for seconds after the blood supply is severed. And animal experiments show that the brain continues to function for many seconds after its blood supply is interrupted. It is hard to imagine the experiences one might have during those few seconds immediately following decapitation.

Hillman points out that the absence of signs of extreme suffering cannot be taken as evidence that pain isn't being experienced. Restraints may mask some of those signs, and those signs may be mistakenly attributed to the act of dying itself. The widely held view that executions are painless and, therefore, humane rests on flimsy evidence.

This story of cortical plasticity has another intriguing twist. Changes in organization within the somatosensory cortex induced by training do not occur automatically. If the monkey's finger is stimulated, but the animal doesn't have to discriminate one touch stimulus from another, there is very little improvement in performance and correspondingly little change in the somatosensory cortex (Recanzone 1992b).[6] The brain changes only if the monkey pays attention to the stimulated finger. By some means, currently unknown, plasticity of cortical maps is modulated by the behavioral state of an organism.

Plasticity in the Human Brain

Is the human brain comparably malleable in response to training? One way to answer this question is to consider people who use their sense of touch in radically different ways from most of us. Are their brains organized differently? Consider professional musicians who play the violin. As you can imagine, they spend countless hours practicing their fingering using the left hand, with the right hand used primarily for bowing. Does the dexterous left hand of a violin player appropriate greater than normal brain representation because of this unique experience?

---

[6]The monkeys who did not have to make touch discriminations were actively distracted from attending to what happened on their fingers. These monkeys were serving simultaneously in a second study, on behavioral and physiological effects of practice in making auditory discriminations (Recanzone, Schreiner, and Merzenich, 1993). Those results were described earlier, in Chapter 10.

To find out, a group of German neuroscientists (Elbert et al., 1995) used PET neuroimaging to measure brain activity while the fingers on a person's left and right hand were being stimulated. In nonmusicians, the left hand and right hands exhibited comparably sized representations within the somatosensory regions of the right and left hemispheres, respectively. But in musicians who relied greatly on the left hand, that hand's touch representation was much larger than that of the right hand. In other words, the brain's touch map had changed in response to the individual's tactile experiences. Moreover, musicians who began their training early in life had larger left-hand brain maps than did musicians who postponed their training a number of years. Evidently, early onset of string playing recruits more brain cells to serve the touch sensors in the critical, left-hand's fingers.

As you might expect, Braille readers also show an enlarged cortical representation within the S-I region associated with their reading fingers (see the review by Hamilton and Pascual-Leone, 1998). But not all Braille readers use the same technique, and these individual differences in technique have interesting cortical consequences. Some Braille readers use just a single finger, others use fingers on each hand, in concert. This latter technique entails prolonged simultaneous and coordinated use of fingers that ordinarily would not be used together. And this reading-related synchronized activity alters the brain's normal orderly representation of the fingers, much as binding fingers together would (Sterr et al., 1998).

To modify the cortical representation of your hand, you don't have to practice the violin for years or learn to read Braille. Simply having a small region on one finger lightly stimulated with repeated mechanical taps for three hours is sufficient to enlarge the cortical representation of that finger and to improve two-point touch discrimination on that finger (Pleger et al., 2003). Steady practice has been shown to affect other aspects of touch as well. These include perception of roughness, punctate pressure (produced by Von Frey hairs), and frequency of vibrotactile stimulation (Harris, Harris, and Diamond, 2001).

Box 13.3 discusses other behavioral observations on humans that implicate remapping in somatosensory cortex.

Some Possible Clinical Applications

Results on human plasticity may help to shape new therapies for use with people whose touch sensitivity has been diminished by damage to the somatosensory cortex. Dannenbaum and Dykes (1988) have developed a unique rehabilitation strategy, which draws heavily on Merzenich's work with monkeys. The therapy, which seems quite promising, reeducates one component of touch at a time.

To promote reorganization of a damaged somatosensory cortex, Dannenbaum and Dykes encourage the patients to practice skills such as recognizing the presence of rough objects applied to the skin, appreciating the direction in which an object sweeps across the skin, discriminating shapes and making progressively finer and more accurate localization of touch stimuli. With specific stimulation repeated time and time again, the well-motivated patients who have been studied thus far showed substantial improvement in touch and manipulation of objects.

Whatever their ultimate impact on rehabilitation therapy, Merzenich's findings with monkeys are certainly intriguing. But one must be careful not to misconstrue these findings. The modifications resulting from altered sensory input in adult animals occurred within the microstructure of neighboring touch maps; the overall boundaries of the somatosensory area were not affected by experience. Moreover, at least some of these cortical changes are responses to growth of new connections within subcortical structures that provide input to the cortex (Kaas, Florence, and Jain, 1999). So, it would be wrong to conclude from Merzenich's studies that one area of the adult brain can always take over the function of another. In the *mature* nervous system, the boundaries separating different areas of the brain (for example, the somatosensory cortex and the motor cortex) become fixed and are not subject to change. Only the details of maps within those areas can be reshaped by experience.[7]

Having qualified the extent of plasticity in the adult brain, we should also point out that there is much greater cortical flexibility in the *immature* nervous system (Kaas, 1991). Studies with animals show that the neuroanatomical and physiological response properties of neurons in various areas can be remarkably reshaped. For example, axons forming the optic nerve from the eye can be encouraged to sprout neural connections into auditory portions of the brain, if the normal target regions for those optic nerve fibers is destroyed (Sur, Garraghty, and Roe, 1988). Fascinating evidence for wholesale cortical reorganization in humans comes from a study of brain activations in congenitally blind individuals who are experienced

---

[7]The inflexibility of the mature cortex does not mean that large-scale neural reorganization will *never* be possible. Once researchers figure out what neurochemical events promote plasticity in early life, it may be possible artificially to reinstigate those events in adulthood, thereby reawakening cortical plasticity. This possibility offers great hope for rehabilitation of individuals suffering stroke and spinal cord injuries. At the same time, this reawakening process must be carefully focused, for major cortical reorganization could also have detrimental consequences such as disrupted perceptual processing and erased learning.

Keep Your Fingers Crossed

The oldest known illusion of touch was described by Aristotle nearly 2,500 years ago. Cross two adjacent fingers and then touch an object, such as a pen, with both crossed fingertips at the same time. It will feel like you're touching two pens, not one. Fabrizio Benedetti, an Italian psychologist, performed several ingenious studies of this ancient phenomenon (1985, 1986). Benedetti started with a puzzle. Suppose, with your fingers *not* crossed and held slightly apart, you touch that same pen with both fingertips. Now, even though two fingertips are being stimulated (as before), you feel only one pen. Why does the illusion fail under this situation?

Benedetti reasoned from an analogy to vision. Under most conditions, when the image of an object stimulates both retinas, we see a single object. This singleness of vision occurs because the two monocular images are normally formed on matching areas of the two eyes. When, however, those images are formed on nonmatching areas, double vision is experienced—a person sees two objects, not one. Benedetti applied the same reasoning to explain Aristotle's illusion. He hypothesized that we experience perceptual doubling whenever two receptor points (fingertips or retinal loci) not normally stimulated by a single object are stimulated by that object. In the case of touch, if matching sites on adjacent fingers, say the index and middle finger, are touched simultaneously, a single object is felt; however, if the same stimulus is somehow applied to nonadjacent fingers, say the index and fourth fingers, there is an illusory experience of two objects. Note that Benedetti's hypothesis puts visual doubling and touch doubling in a common framework.

Benedetti tested his idea by trying to produce **diplesthesia** (doubled touch) without having to cross the fingers. He used a specially designed clamp to press and hold together volunteers' third and fourth fingers. By changing the amount of pressure on the sides of the fingers, Benedetti was able to displace the fingers' skin by amounts ranging from 3 to 12 millimeters. He then touched the tips of the clamped fingers with either a single sphere or two spheres joined together. The volunteer reported whether he or she felt one or two objects. Benedetti found that a 4- to 6-millimeter displacement of the skin—without finger crossing—can produce a strong illusory doubling of touch sensations.

Extending these observations, Benedetti (1991) used prolonged bandaging to simulate amputation of the middle finger. The bandaged finger was immobilized, and thus excluded from the hand's exploratory and manipulatory activities. In order to grasp or manipulate an object (say, a pen) the remaining, working fingers had to be used in unusual pairings. For example, people wrote with the pen held between the thumb, index, and fourth finger (instead of thumb, index, and third finger). This unusual arrangement subjected some pairs of fingers to what was quite rare for them before the "amputation": simultaneous stimulation by a single object.

Six months of bandaging brought dramatic changes in diplethesia. For example, the index and fourth fingers now responded as though they were actually adjacent; simultaneous touch of these new partners no longer produced diplethesia. One hypothesis is that these perceptual changes reflect some kind of reorganization within the cortical representation of the hand, of the sort discussed in the section on plasticity and touch. So after 2,500 years, we are finally beginning to understand the puzzle that Aristotle presented to us.

Touch Version of the Müller-Lyer Illusion

Recall that two lines of equal length can look dramatically different in length when arrowheads are appropriately situated at the ends of the lines (see Figure 8.41). This well-known illusion also occurs with touch (Heller et al., 2002). Blindfolded participants underestimate the length of a raised line located on an otherwise smooth surface when that line is flanked by two raised arrowheads pointing inward; when the arrowheads point outward, judgments are not nearly so distorted. The same pattern of errors in line length was observed in blindfolded, sighted individuals as in congenitally blind people, implying that experience with the visual version of the illusion was not the cause. This tactile Müller-Lyer illusion is probably of no consequence to sighted people, but it could create problems for blind individuals trying to estimate distances from touching embossed maps containing intersecting lines.

Braille readers (Sadato et al., 1996). In sighted people, tactile stimulation activates the somatosensory cortex but not the visual cortex in the occipital lobe. However, in experienced, blind Braille readers the visual cortex is also activated as those blind individuals use their fingers to "read" Braille characters. The occipital lobe, in other words, has been recruited into the process of tactile perception.

Other evidence, based on the TMS technique, points to the same conclusion. Cohen et al. (1997) used TMS with blind individuals who were seasoned Braille readers. While the blind people were reading either Braille or embossed Roman letters, TMS pulses delivered to their occipital cortex produced temporary disruptions in their reading comprehension. In sighted individuals, TMS applied over the occipital lobe had no effect on the sense of touch. This remarkable finding, together with the PET activation study described earlier, implies that cortical areas can be recruited to roles outside their usual function, at least when the conditions sponsoring that recruitment (such as blindness) arise early in life. These findings offer new hope for the development of interventions that could accelerate the adjustment to blindness (Hamilton and Pascual-Leone, 1998).

Aside from their possible clinical significance, all these findings on cortical plasticity carry profound philosophical implications. Human perception, cognition, personality, and behavior are all shaped by the billions of connections within the brain, and these connections now appear to be dynamically modified in response to experience. These modifications would be tailored to your particular lifetime experiences, virtually guaranteeing that the connections in your brain are different from the connections in other human brains. Could these differences among brains, then, be responsible, at least in part, for the real differences among people?

As you can see, these speculations bear on some truly fundamental issues, including human identity and human diversity. It's exciting even to imagine that in our own lifetimes these basic, long-standing, and perplexing philosophical issues may finally be resolved.

S U M M A R Y   A N D   P R E V I E W

In this chapter we explored how the sense of touch, working primarily through that remarkable sensory organ, the human hand, is capable of fast, highly accurate and subtle discriminations. We discovered that touch owes part of its success to the information it gets from sets of touch receptors whose different characteristics create diverse and complementary perspectives on the world that lies at our fingertips. An equally great part of its success seems to come, however, from the unique information created by the hand's own skilled and highly purposeful exploration of the world. The intimate relationships between manual exploration and the resulting sensory response reminded us of the pervasive connections between perception and action. We also learned about pain—touch's "dark" side. We saw that pain is a complex sensory experience with intensive and affective overtones. Finally, we saw how controlled, intensive practice could alter cortical organization even into adulthood.

In the next two chapters we turn to smell and taste, senses that are important not only as channels for information about the world, but also as providers of particular delight and pleasure.

K E Y   T E R M S

acupuncture
allodynia
analgesia
Braille
diffuse fibers
displethesia
endorphins
free nerve endings
gate control theory

haptics
kinesthesis
localization ability
mechanoreceptors
Meissner corpuscles
Merkel disks
nociceptors
Pacinian corpuscles
phantom limb

proprioception
punctate fibers
rapidly adapting (RA) fibers
Ruffini endings
slowly adapting (SA) fibers
tactile agnosia
touch acuity
unilateral neglect

Chemical Senses I: Smell

"**S**ie brauchen die letzten zwei Kapitel nicht zu lesen." That's what Immanuel Kant might have advised you: Don't bother to read these last two chapters. Kant, one of the greatest philosophers of the eighteenth century, had no respect for smell and taste, the topics of this chapter and the next one. He thought that the sensory experiences produced by smell and taste were highly inferior to what the other senses offered. For example, Kant (1798/1978) singled smell out as *the* sense that was "most dispensable." The sense of smell, he asserted, was not worth cultivating because disgusting odors outnumbered pleasant ones, especially in crowded cities. He believed that even if we did encounter something fragrant, "the pleasure coming from the sense of smell cannot be other than fleeting and transitory" (p. 46). In Kant's view, the sense of taste was only slightly more valuable than smell, and then only because eating and drinking encouraged sociability.

Kant is not alone in denigrating taste and smell as "lower" or "minor" senses, but this designation is arbitrary and narrowminded. Looking beyond our own species, many animals depend almost exclusively on taste and smell to tell them about their world. Figure 14.1 shows one creature: the star-nosed mole's vaunted senses of smell and taste (as well as its exquisite sense of touch) allow it to live in the dark, safe confines of underground burrows, with virtually no need for eyes (Catania, 2002).

Unlike the star-nose mole, we humans do rely heavily on our eyes and ears to guide our everyday activities. But even for us the "minor senses" provide crucially important information. The foul taste of spoiled food can save you from a bout of nausea, and the smell of smoke can warn of a dangerous fire.[1] The minor senses, besides alerting us to possible dangers, also add zest to our lives by creating sensory experiences that are uniquely pleasurable and sometimes even sensual. Sunsets may look beautiful and symphonies may sound enrapturing, but those cerebral pleasures seem less compelling and immediate than the aroma and taste of, say, freshly baked chocolate chip cookies. Of course, on the downside, few sights or sounds are as repulsive as a really putrid smell or an extremely foul taste. When there's an annoying song on the radio, you can usually manage to ignore it. But try to ignore the overwhelming stench of a stopped-up toilet, or try to forget the taste of a food item that once made you nauseated. Thus, in addition to their roles as sources of information about objects in the world, taste and smell wield a powerful emotional impact. We hope these next two chapters will provide you with a far healthier respect

---

[1]Be aware, however, that when someone is deeply asleep, even the very strong odor of smoke may not be enough to rouse the person (Carskadon and Herz, 2004).

FIGURE 14.1 | The star-nosed mole, a mammal for whom the sense of smell is very important.

for your nose and your tongue, and for the brain machinery that interprets sensory signals from those organs.

Taste and smell are often referred to by their technical names, *gustation* (from the Latin *gustare,* meaning "to taste") and *olfaction* (from the Latin *olfacere,* meaning "to smell"). Gustation and olfaction are often lumped together as the "chemical senses" because receptors housed in the nose and on the tongue register the presence of chemical molecules and, for some tastes, particular ions.[2] These chemical molecules and ions are analogous to the photons (particles of light) that strike the photoreceptors of the eye. But, as this book has emphasized, you see *objects,* not *light.* By the same token, your experience of taste and smell is about *objects* and *substances,* not *chemicals.* So taste and smell serve precisely the same purposes as vision and hearing: All of them provide behaviorally relevant information about the environment.

There is a large and rapidly growing body of perceptual, physiological, molecular, and genetic studies of taste and smell, and in this chapter and the next one we will examine some of these key findings. Although the two chemical senses are intimately intertwined, for ease of exposition we'll consider them separately, starting in this chapter with smell.

---

[2]An ion is an electrically charged molecule or atom, one that has gained or lost an electron or electrons from its normal, electrically balanced complement.

The Sense of Smell

Smells are with us all the time. From the aroma of your first cup of coffee in the morning to the smell of clean sheets as you doze off at night, you are awash in a sea of odors. Smells enhance the enjoyment of food (which is why your appetite drops when a cold stops up your nose). You can verify this for yourself. Hold your nose so that you cannot smell what is put into your mouth. Then compare the tastes of a piece of apple and a piece of raw potato. You'll be astonished to find that as far as taste alone goes, an apple and a potato are very similar.

Odors also influence the ways people spend their money. How often have you walked near a bakery and been enticed inside by the smells wafting into the street? It is said that some bakeries vent their ovens out to the sidewalk, exploiting the aroma of fresh bread to lure customers inside (Winter, 1976). Besides the natural smells of the bakery, some businesses also use artificially created odors to influence people's buying habits. For example, some plastic briefcases are impregnated with leather scent to enhance their appeal to prospective buyers. Smell also plays a role in selling big-ticket items. Real estate agents like to have a pot of coffee brewing when prospective buyers visit a house for sale; the aroma is said to convey a sense of "home" to the potential buyer. Automobile manufacturers also exploit smell. The United States's largest manufacturer of automobiles recently revealed that it has developed a scent, called Nuance, for its luxury vehicles. The leather seats in all new Cadillac vehicles are impregnated with chemicals engineered to produce this specially designed scent (Hakim, 2003). As one enthusiastic automotive executive put it, "You pay the extra money for leather, you don't want it to smell like lighter fluid. You want it to smell like a Gucci bag." And the market value of a second-hand car increases if it's been sprayed with "new-car" smell.

In their zeal to make their products smell good, manufacturers can go too far, altering a product in ways that defeat smell's function as a warning system. Take, for instance, the smell of ordinary laundry bleach (hypochlorite bleach). As you probably know, bleach has a highly unpleasant, pungent smell, which most people can't tolerate. Bleach's offensive odor, however, warns people—even people too young to read the label or people whose eyesight makes its hard to read the label—that this is not good to ingest. And, according to a study by de Wijk and Cain (1994), the warning is effective. These smell scientists asked people to sniff a sample of hypochlorite bleach and make two judgments: Identify the sample and judge whether it is safe to drink. The results from their elderly volunteers (average age 76 years) were the most informative. These individuals identified the sample as bleach just 24 percent of the time, but they correctly categorized it as not drinkable 71 percent of the time. So bleach's unpleasant smell worked fairly well to communicate, "Don't ingest me," even when someone didn't know for sure what it was. But, unfortunately, some manufacturers have resorted to adding an artificial "fresh" scent to mask bleach's pungency. When de Wijk and Cain tested samples of this *scented* bleach, elderly participants correctly identified it as bleach only 5 percent of the time. Even worse, 71 percent of the time these people made the potentially lethal mistake of classifying the bleach as drinkable. This misuse of artificial scent could be very dangerous.

Of course, people's behavior is influenced by many smells besides those of foods, cars, briefcases, and bleach. Television commercials constantly remind us that our own bodies are major sources of odor. Advertisers exhort us to buy products that will modify those odors, as well as create new ones: deodorants, perfumes, aftershave lotions, hair mousse, and mouthwashes. In this pursuit, billions of dollars are spent every year. Like it or not, you continually give off an invisible cloud of unique smells. Your characteristic odors constitute a distinctive smell signature, which a well-trained hound can identify amid the olfactory noise of other peoples' scents. Though there are clear limitations to their ability (Brisbin, Aus-

tad, and Jacobson, 2000), scent hounds can be valuable not only in tracking particular individuals, but also in sniffing out some illegal drugs and explosives.[3] But dogs are not the only creatures that can exploit scent for tracking. Some humans—the Botocudos of eastern Brazil and some aboriginal peoples on the Malay Peninsula—were reputed to hunt by following their prey's scent (Titchener, 1915). Though few people in industrialized societies perform similar feats, we do have some primitive abilities to use scents for distinguishing people from one another, as the following experiments demonstrate.

Suppose that you had to judge whether another person was male or female on the basis of smell alone. Do you think you could? The answer appears to be yes. Patricia Wallace (1977) tested whether college students could discriminate male from female just by smelling a person's hand. While blindfolded, a student sniffed a hand held one-half inch from the student's nose. The male and female individuals whose hands served as test stimuli had washed thoroughly before the test session and then had worn a disposable plastic glove for 15 minutes before testing, to promote perspiration. Wallace found that the students being tested could tell male from female hands, with over 80 percent accuracy. Furthermore, female were better at the task than were their male counterparts.

In addition to using the smell from sweaty hands, people can also use breath odor to make accurate judgments of a breather's gender. Richard Doty and coworkers had male and female college students judge the breath odor of breath donors who were seated opposite them. A partition prevented judges from seeing the donors (Figure 14.2). By inserting their noses into a plastic funnel, judges could inhale the breath of the donors, who were exhaling through a glass tube connected to the funnel. Donors were told not to eat spicy food the day before testing, and they were not permitted to wear odorous cosmetic products. Most judges scored better than chance (50 percent) at identifying the donor's gender, with female judges again outperforming their male counterparts (Doty et al., 1982). Doty and colleagues also had judges rate breath odors for pleasantness and intensity. Breath odors of males were rated on the average as both less pleasant and more intense than breath odors of females.

The most remarkable individual acuity for body odor was evidenced by a blind woman who worked in the laundry of the Connecticut Asylum for the Deaf. As described by William James (1890, vol. 1, pp. 509–510),

---

[3]Dogs may also be adept at detecting cancer; to learn more about this possibility, check out the Web link available at www.mhhe.com/blake5.

FIGURE 14.2 | Setup for measuring gender identification based on breath odor.

this woman could sort the laundry of individual inmates on the basis of smell alone, and that was after the clothes had been washed! Less dramatic but impressive nonetheless is the performance of people in the dirty shirt study by Mark Russel, a British psychologist (1976). He had 29 first-year college students bathe with clear water and then don nondescript T-shirts that they wore for the next 24 hours, during which they used no perfume or deodorant. At the end of this period, the T-shirts were collected and individually placed in sealed containers. The same students were now presented with three containers, one with their own shirt, one with the T-shirt worn by an unknown female, and one with the T-shirt worn by an unknown male. Of 29 people, 22 picked out their own T-shirt—a level of performance well above chance. Moreover, the same proportion of people correctly identified which of the remaining two T-shirts belonged to a male and which belonged to a female. Male odors were described as "musky," while female odors were described as "sweet."

It's not just other *people* we can recognize using our noses. Wells and Hepper (2000) asked 26 dog owners to smell a pair of dog blankets that were contained in individual, opaque plastic bags. One plastic bag contained a blanket that had been used by that owner's dog when it slept; the other plastic bag contained the bedding blanket used by another dog, which was unfamiliar to the participant. Using smell alone, nearly 90 percent of the participants correctly identified the odor of their own dog. But before taking this performance as proof that

people could recognize the distinctive smell of their own dogs, several control measurements were needed. For example, Wells and Hepper were concerned that the remarkable performance they had observed might come from a recognition not of the dog's odor, but of the odor of the household in which the dog lived. To control for this possibility, the same 26 people were retested, but with household odors not connected to their own or anyone else's pets. Now, each participant smelled a new pair of unseen blankets: One was impregnated with the odors from the participant's home, while the other carried odors from the home of another of the participants. The 26 people performed only slightly better than chance in recognizing the odor of their own home—a performance that was far worse than that of recognizing their own dog's odor. In contrast to the dog owners' ability to identify their canine best friends by smell, cat owners are quite poor at recognizing their pets by smell (Courtney and Wells, 2002).

Besides providing clues about the identity of an individual, ambient odors can influence your general level of arousal and, consequently, your performance on a host of cognitive tasks. To give one example, imagine diligently monitoring a video screen for a briefly presented visual target appearing unpredictably over time. When required to perform just such a task for an extended period of time (Gould and Martin, 2001), student volunteers detected more visual target presentations in the presence of peppermint odor (generally regarded as an arousing smell) than in the presence of bergamot odor (a light orange smell generally regarded as relaxing). In addition to having possible practical implications (think about your odor environment the next time you're required to maintain a high level of concentration), this finding reminds us that odor has pervasive influences on behavior and cognition.

One of the most remarkable things about smell is its ability to evoke old memories. A whiff of cedar triggers comforting remembrances of the chest in which your grandmother kept her blankets; the scent from a carnation vividly recalls the wonders of a senior prom; and the smell of suntan lotion immediately transports you to the beach. Some people have developed a huge repertoire of odor memories and rely on them in their profession. Skilled perfumers, for example, can discriminate hundreds of aromas, many quite subtle. Physicians can exploit their own noses as diagnostic tools, using a patient's odors as clues for detecting disease. Listen to the words of one noted physician and neuropsychologist, V. S. Ramachandran, as he describes his experiences during medical training:

I recall one professor, Dr. K. V. Thiruvengadam, instructing us how to identify disease by just smelling the patient—the unmistakable, sweetish nail polish breath of diabetic detosis; the freshly baked bread odor of typhoid fever; the stale-beer stench of scrofula; the newly plucked chicken feathers aroma of rubella; the foul smell of a lung abscess; and the ammonialike Windex odor of a patient in liver failure. (Ramachandran and Blakeslee, 1998, p. 6)

A table of diseases that produce distinctive odors can be found in Smith, Smith, and Levinson, (1982), and a Web-based resource on odor and disease is given in the weblinks for Chapter 14, available at www.mhhe.com/blake5.

One little-known disorder produces the strong odor of rotting fish in peoples' breath and sweat (Mitchell, 1996). The disorder, called trimethylaminuria, involves a breakdown in the liver's ability to oxidize one of the normal products of food metabolism. The resulting fishy-smelling substance is secreted, then, in breath, sweat, and urine. Although a low-protein diet helps some victims, there is no known cure. Unfortunately, even today, 30 years after the disorder was first identified in the medical literature, few doctors and nurses know about it. As a result, people with this disorder can spend years looking for an explanation of their strange body odor. As Christensen (1999) notes, "They often acquire a long list of inaccurate diagnoses ranging from poor hygiene to psychiatric problems. These people may withdraw from the outside world to avoid ridicule or try to mask their odor with strong perfumes and cigarettes. Many of those with the disorder also report symptoms of depression."

Mammals send and receive dozens of different types of odor messages (Doty, 1986), ranging from distress signals to age appraisal. For many animals, mate selection and identification are solely governed by odor. Typically, the females of these species emit sensuous scents called **pheromones** from specialized glands. (The word *pheromone* comes from the Greek for "bringer of excitement.") Potential mates detect these scents. Among the many creatures that exploit pheromones is the male cabbage moth, an insect whose antennae can sense minute concentrations of the scent released from a sexually receptive female cabbage moth many miles away (Lerner et al., 1990).

The understanding of chemical sex signals has allowed scientists to exploit other species' pheromones. For example, agricultural biologists use pheromones to control some harmful insects. With sex attractants as bait, unsuspecting harmful insects can be lured into traps. Pheromones can also be exploited for the eating pleasure of humans. Certain female pigs are trained to hunt truffles, a fungus highly prized by many gourmets. These sows can sniff out truffles buried as much as a meter below ground, and once the truffles are located, they root furiously to unearth them. Sows exert all that energy because truffles give off a musky odor highly similar to the scent secreted by male pigs during mating behavior. So the sow's intense interest in truffles is a misdirected, purely sexual pursuit (Claus, Hoppen, and Karg, 1981).

It is natural to wonder whether sexual behavior of our own species is influenced by smell. Do humans use pheromones to send sexually tinged olfactory messages? Is it possible that sex appeal can be bottled, as in the 1992 cult-classic movie *Love Potion #9*? Certainly the perfume industry would have us believe the answer is yes, but the evidence to back up that claim is inconclusive. And, of course, an odor can be sexually arousing without qualifying as a pheromone. Still, there is pretty convincing evidence implying a link between smell and sexual responses. It's clear, for example, that odor signals play a role in the synchronization of menstrual cycles of women who live together over many months (Graham and McGrew, 1980). Moreover, case studies disclose that people with serious smell disorders frequently report disinterest in sex (Henkin, 1982).

In addition to promoting sexual arousal in animals, smells are often used as defensive weapons. If you've ever experienced the rank odor of a skunk's discharge, you can certainly appreciate how that odor would ward off enemies (and friends as well). Numerous animal species employ glandular secretions to mark their territories, often engaging in seemingly bizarre behaviors to ensure that their odor signatures are conspicuous (Macdonald and Brown, 1985). For example, the oribi (a small African antelope) uses scent glands just below its eyes to mark blades of grass with a dollop of oribi scent. It may look odd to see an animal rub its face in the grass, but from the oribi's perspective this maneuver makes perfect sense.

Odors also guide animals in their search for food, whether it is the bee attracted to the fragrance of flowering plants or the vulture picking up the scent of a dead animal. Some seabirds can locate food sources far from land, with no visual landmarks to guide them. They use smell to detect airborne dimethyl sulfide given off by their prey in the ocean below (Malakoff, 1999). In fact, humans' overwhelming reliance on eyes and ears to guide vital activities may be nearly unique, as many other animal species depend heavily on their noses for such guidance. Indeed, if we were writing this perception book for an audience of nonhuman animals, particularly nonprimates, we'd have to revise it drastically. Instead of emphasizing seeing and hearing, the vast bulk of the book would have to address the most pressing concern of the nonhuman world—the sense of smell.

The Stimulus for Smell

Let's start with the basics, asking what physical properties give various substances the power to evoke sensations of odor. As you'll see, the answers are complex. First, to be odorous, a substance must be *volatile*—that is, it must give off vapors. This requirement has practical consequences. Heated soup, for example, gives off more vapors than cold soup, which is why hot soup smells more and is more inviting. It used to be thought that these volatile molecules had to be airborne to be smelled. According to this view, substances suspended in liquid would be odorless even when they were in direct contact with the nose's odor receptors. Can it be true that you would smell nothing if you submerged yourself in a pool of perfume? Ernst Weber, the nineteenth-century physiologist, actually performed a version of this experiment, the results of which, he thought, confirmed this view. With his head upside down, Weber poured perfume into his own nostrils, and he smelled nothing (Boring, 1942). It's now thought, however, that the perfume, which contained alcohol, actually damaged the receptors in Weber's nose, so that he couldn't smell anything at all. In fact, there's good proof that smell is not restricted to airborne molecules: Fish can use olfaction to follow scent trails in water (Barinaga, 1999).

Earlier, in discussing vision and hearing, we noted that stimulation reaching the eye or striking the ear usually comprises an aggregate of information from several different sources. Similarly, many natural odors, such as those given off by flowers, fruits, or by your body, reflect mixtures of many different types of molecules in specific ratios. The identities and relative proportions of those molecules comprise the signature of the odor's source, for example, a particular variety of flower. Untold different volatile molecules exist in nature, so the number of *possible* mixtures of those molecules is incredibly large. At present, there is no way to know how many of these mixtures would actually produce distinctly different odors.

We also noted previously that visual or auditory perception of distinct objects requires the nervous system to segregate the complex incoming aggregate into the perceptual components emanating from each particular object. The same is true for olfaction. Along the path to your nose, the air currents pass over many different objects, picking up multitudes of other odorant molecules. So except for the carefully controlled conditions created in the laboratory, the air you inhale at any given moment contains odorant molecules donated by a variety of objects. To identify any single odorant source, the olfactory system has to segregate the inhaled mixture into its constituents. Fluctuations in the direction and speed of air currents complicate the situation further: Any single airborne odorant is presented to your nose in concentrations and in combinations that vary greatly over time. Despite these complexities, the olfactory system does manage to identify the distinct sources of odors. (Laurent [1999], presents an excellent analysis of the challenges that confront the first stages of processing in the olfactory system.)

One prerequisite for smell is that the volatile molecules be soluble in fat, because the receptor cells in the nose that capture volatile molecules are surrounded by fatlike materials. When odorous molecules are fat soluble, fat-containing substances can absorb them. This explains why uncovered butter on one shelf of the refrigerator takes on the smell of uncovered tuna fish sitting on another shelf. At the same time, not all volatile and fat-soluble substances are odorous. Additional chemical properties common to all odorous substances, such as atomic weight, influence olfactory experiences (Wright, 1966); identifying these properties remains a challenge. This challenge is closely related to the problem of odor classification, a topic we consider next.

The Classification of Odors

Alexander Graham Bell, the inventor of the telephone, understood how hard it was to classify odors. In an address to the graduating class of the Friends' School in Washington, D.C., Bell (1914) remarked:

> Did you ever try to measure a smell? Can you tell whether one smell is just twice as strong as another? Can you measure the difference between one kind of smell and another? It is very obvious that we have very many different kinds of smells, all the way from the odor of violets and roses up to asafetida.[4] But until you can measure their likenesses and differences you can have no science of odor. If you are ambitious to found a new science, measure a smell.

---

[4]Asafetida (or Asafoetida) is a spice whose raw form produces a powerful smell of rotting onions or sulfur. Native to Afghanistan, Iran, and Pakistan, this spice, sometimes called the Devil's Dung, is used in many cuisines, and, as an added bonus, is also an effective insect repellent.

Bell's challenge to his audience—figuring out how to characterize smells in a quantitative fashion—remains as difficult today as it was when Bell articulated it. This challenge is much like the one Newton faced as he sought some scheme for describing the relations among different colors (the color circle you read about in Chapter 7). Newton's work led to some consensus about the categories of color. It has been widely assumed that odors, too, should fall into distinct categories, comparable in their uniqueness to blue, green, yellow, and red. Knowledge of these odor categories, it has been assumed, would pave the way for determining the molecular properties shared by members of various perceptual categories. But attempts to identify odor categories have foundered (Wise, Olsson, and Cain, 2000). Here are several better-known odor categorization schemes, and their shortcomings.

The idea of categorizing odors dates back to the ancient Greeks, most notably Aristotle, who classified all odors as pungent, succulent, acid, or astringent. Odor classification took on real urgency in the seventeenth and eighteenth centuries, when people were convinced that bad odors were associated with disease and epidemics. By understanding various "families" of odors, people expected to eliminate those that posed danger to their health, or so people believed (Corbin, 1986).

Geometric Models of Odor Classification

Probably the best-known system is Hans Henning's (1916) smell prism, a geometric system similar in spirit to Newton's color circle. Henning's geometric model was meant to depict the principal odors, which were basic odors from which all other odors could be generated. Henning used two procedures to determine the number of principal odors. First, he instructed volunteers to use verbal labels to describe various scents presented one at a time. Second, he gave people sets of odorous substances and instructed them to line up the substances according to the similarity of their smells (Gamble, 1921). In all, Henning tested more than 400 different odorous substances. Using these sets of judgments, Henning constructed a three-dimensional form—a triangular prism (shown in Figure 14.3)—whose surfaces were meant to reflect people's judgments of odor similarity. Particular odors corresponded to points on the surface of the prism, with nearby points corresponding to odors that were judged similar. Odors were confined to the surfaces and edges of the prism; its interior was considered hollow, meaning that points inside the prism were not used to describe an odor.

To Henning, odors near his prism's corners seemed to possess unique qualities. They could be described us-

FIGURE 14.3 | Henning's smell prism.

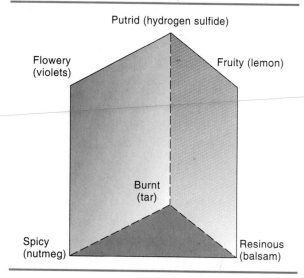

ing a single verbal label (shown in Figure 14.3). To give you some idea of substances that evoke these six principal odors, a substance representative of each odor is given in parentheses. Odors located anywhere other than the corners of the prism—that is, either on an edge or on the plane of one surface—could not be described using a single verbal label. But such noncorner odors could be described by some *combination* of principal qualities represented by the labels at the corners. For example, the smell associated with pine was located along the edge midway between *fruity* and *resinous,* implying that the odor of pine possesses both of those qualities. Pine was located where it is on the prism because of its similarity to lemon and balsam. Similarly the smell of garlic was located on the surface bounded by *flowery, fruity, resinous,* and *spicy,* implying that the odor of garlic possesses all four of those qualities. Again, garlic was placed at that point on the prism because Henning considered its odor similar to the odors of violet, lemon, balsam, and nutmeg.

Henning's scheme claimed to capture the resemblance between odors on the edges or surfaces of the smell prism and odors at the prism's corners. This does not mean, however, that a mixture of odors from the corners could produce odors on other parts of the prism. For example, although pine is similar in smell to both balsam and lemon, no mixture of these two can reproduce the smell of pine. In fact, "the resulting odor tends to be a unique percept blend in which both components can be smelled" (Engen, 1982). In this sense, odor shares the analytic character of pitch perception rather than the synthetic character of color perception. For example, when you simultaneously sound a D and an F on the piano, you can hear the individual components in the chord; however, when you mix red and green lights, the result is a synthesis (yellow) in which the two component identities are lost.

Henning's model is appealing for precisely the same reason that Newton's color circle discussed in Chapter 7 is appealing: Each provides a simple, geometrical description of sensory experiences. The accuracy of geometric models is easy to test because they make clear predictions. Sadly, many predictions from Henning's smell prism have not been confirmed. One major problem is that most people find it impossible to classify odors using just six categories, which implies that Henning may have underestimated the number of principal odors. Henning can also be faulted for using a small number of highly trained participants and for eschewing quantitative analysis of his data. In stubborn defense of his procedures, Henning bragged that "the critical introspection of trained psychologists is more valuable than statistics taken on all the students in the University, and the statistical procedure, about which science in America has raved so much, has by no means the precision of a *qualitative* analysis" (Henning, 1916; from a translation by Gamble, 1921).

Following Henning's work, other researchers have also tried to group odors according to qualitative similarities (for example, Crocker and Henderson, 1927). Most of these categorization schemes have begun with a series of semantic descriptors to be used as odor qualities—descriptors such as *sweet, flowery, fruity, and burned*. Whatever odor categories emerge, however, are constrained right from the start. They've got to conform to the specific descriptors chosen by the researcher in the first place. Moreover, there are reasons to question how reliably people can use verbal labels to describe their olfactory sensations (Davis, 1977). The constraints imposed by the descriptors, as well as the difficulty of using any label at all, would distort any classification scheme based on predefined verbal labels.

Multidimensional scaling (MDS), a technique described in the appendix, sidesteps these problems. This technique was used by Susan Schiffman (1974) to study odor classification. Instead of using descriptor terms for various odors, a person merely compares different odors, numerically rating their similarity to one another. These similarity ratings are then used to place odors within a geometric framework called an *odor space*. Odors are arranged within the odor space in such a way that the distances separating odors reflect the rated similarity or dis-

similarity of those odors. Odors rated as highly similar (such as cinnamon and ginger) would be placed near each other in an odor space, while odors judged to be dissimilar (such as vanilla and turpentine) would be located far apart. As you can see, the concept of an "odor space" is reminiscent of Henning's smell prism—both arrange odorous substances in a geometric form based on perceptual similarity. However, the rules for generating an odor space by means of MDS differ from Henning's approach. MDS uses objective numerical procedures to create a geometric arrangement that represents judged similarities among odors; Henning based his arrangement on his own subjective smell impressions.

Besides objectivity, the procedures used in multidimensional scaling offer another advantage. The experimenter does not constrain the number of possible dimensions ahead of time. Instead, statistical analyses of the similarity ratings determine the number of dimensions needed to place odors in the odor space. (You can think of the dimensions as axes defining the coordinates of a geometrical space, like the Cartesian coordinates that define the two-dimensional space you're familiar with from plane geometry.)

In using multidimensional scaling, Schiffman found that just two dimensions were adequate for describing the relations among a wide variety of odorous substances. Figure 14.4 replots some of Schiffman's results. Look at the various odors in this odor space, and note their relative positions. You'll probably agree that the nearby entries smell more alike than do the widely separated ones. How can one interpret the two dimensions that Schiffman's work uncovered? To answer this question, Schiffman examined the adjectives people use to describe the odors. She found that proceeding from left to right in Figure 14.4, odors tended to shade from pleasant (such as vanillin) to unpleasant (such as hydrogen sulfide). It is not too surprising that one strong dimension of odor perception has this hedonic quality, for odors so often trigger either approach (pleasant) or avoidance (unpleasant). Proceeding from top to bottom, however, Schiffman could not find any systematic progression in the adjectives used to describe the odors. This finding suggests that this dimension of odor experience does not correlate with any simple psychological dimension for which there are linguistic descriptors. To what, then, might the ordering in the odor space correspond?

Schiffman (1974) asked whether perceptually similar odors might have some molecular property in common, such as the size or shape of the odorant molecules. The discovery of molecular similarities among perceptually

FIGURE 14.4 | An odor space, showing the relations among various odors as defined by multidimensional scaling.

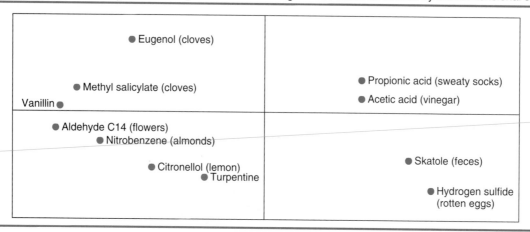

Before continuing the discussion of odor perception, we should consider the olfactory system's front end, the olfactory receptor cells that capture volatile molecules from odorous substances. The properties of these receptor cells shape the world of smell.

comparable odors might furnish important clues about how odorous substances affect receptor cells in the nose. Schiffman considered several molecular characteristics in an attempt to uncover what physical properties, if any, similar smells have in common. Examining the molecular shapes of various substances, she found no relation between the shapes of various compounds and the odors produced by those compounds. This finding, incidentally, seems to contradict one theory of odor perception. John Amoore (1970), a noted olfactory scientist, proposed that a molecule's shape determines which odor receptor it is able to stimulate. This theory has been characterized as the lock-and-key model, since the molecule unlocks the receptor only if the shape of the molecule matches that of the receptor. According to this theory, molecules that look alike (in terms of the three-dimensional arrangement of their constituent atoms) should also smell alike. Wise, Olsson, and Cain (2000) critically reviewed various attempts to categorize odors, and to link odor categories to odorants' molecular properties.

Before continuing the discussion of odor perception, we should consider the olfactory system's front end, the olfactory receptor cells that capture volatile molecules from odorous substances. The properties of these receptor cells shape the world of smell.

The Anatomy and Physiology of Smell

The stimulus for smell consists of airborne molecules, or vapors. The act of inhaling pulls these vapors into the nostrils and circulates them through the nasal cavity, a hollow region inside the nose where the olfactory (smell) receptors are located (see Figure 14.5). Exhaling expels the vapors back into the air. Sniffing or sneezing hastens these processes. Each sniff sucks air into the nose and speeds its circulation through the nasal cavity. Sniffing is comparable to cupping your ear to help you hear a faint sound; sniffing is also the olfactory system's main way to explore the environment. Sneezing, in contrast, represents a reflexive clearing of the nostrils, an action comparable to covering your ears to muffle a loud sound. Odor-bearing vapors normally enter the nostrils and then wend their way up through the nasal passages. However, they can also reach the nasal cavity backwards, coming first into the mouth and circulating up the throat through a chimneylike passage leading to the smell receptors. These reverse direction retronasal vapors usually come from chewing or drinking. Both routes—via the nostrils or the throat—lead to the same place, the olfactory receptors in the nasal cavity. However, vapors from a substance in the mouth sometimes do not smell the same as vapors brought into the nose from the same substance. With training, though, people can learn to identify these backdoor odors with good success (Pierce and Halpern, 1996). Box 14.1 describes some differences between the smell of food when you sniff it and the smell of food when it is already inside your mouth.

Air entering the left and right nostrils, or wafting up from the back of the mouth, passes into the corresponding nasal cavities. There, the air—and any odorant molecules it may contain—circulates around a series of baffles formed by three small, mucous-covered bones, called the turbinates (labeled *baffles* in Figure 14.5). As air circulates around this series of baffles, it is warmed

FIGURE 14.5 | A cutaway section of a human head, showing the routes taken by air inhaled into the mouth and nasal cavity.

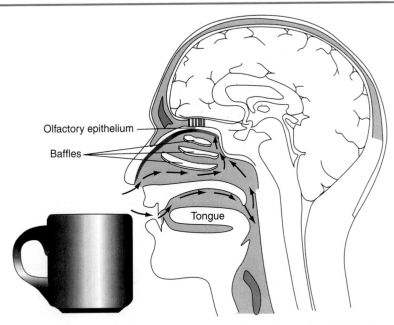

and humidified, and tiny hairs lining the nasal cavity remove debris such as dust. The entire process has been likened to an air-conditioning system that improves smell acuity. As you can imagine, when your nose is congested, the passages of the nasal cavity are narrowed, limiting the amount of odorous vapors that can reach the smell receptors. This is why your sense of smell is dulled when a cold clogs up your nasal cavities. This nasal blockage can be chronic in individuals who have nasal polyps, or a deviated septum. As you may know, the septum is the bone and cartilage that separates the left and right nasal airways, and when the septum is crooked, airflow through the nasal airways is obstructed.

Actually, in most people, the left and right nasal airways appear to work in alternating shifts, a phenomenon called the **nasal cycle.** At any given time, the mucous lining in one nasal passage is more engorged than the other, which narrows one nasal passage and creates greater resistance to the inflow of air. This alternating constriction of the nasal passages is under control of the autonomic nervous system and therefore occurs unconsciously. You can easily confirm the dominance of one nasal passage by holding a mirror just under your nose midway between the two nostrils. Then notice how the two pools of

condensation (produced by exhalation) differ in size. On average, the dominance of one nostril over the other normally switches every 2 to 3 hours (Keuning, 1968), although there are wide individual differences in this switch rate (Pettigrew and Carter, 2005). The swelling of the turbinates produces an amazing change in airflow through the left and right nasal passages. In recent measurements made on 20 individuals, the average flow through the engorged nostril was 31 liters of air each minute, but the average flow through the other nostril was 64 percent greater, 51 liters each minute (Sobel et al., 1999). As you'll learn later, this difference between nostrils can affect how odorants are perceived.

Olfactory Sensory Transduction

We've described how vapors are introduced into the nose and circulate within the nasal cavities. Now let's consider how neural elements turn these vapors into perception of an odor. The receptor cells that register the presence of odorous molecules sit on a patch of tissue called the **olfactory epithelium.** As you can see in Figures 14.5 and 14.6, the olfactory epithelium forms part of the ceiling of the nasal cavity. There are actually two

Is Olfaction a Dual Sense? BOX 14.1

Have you noticed that some foods smell almost repulsive before you get them into your mouth, but once you start eating them they are enjoyable? Certain strong cheeses, such as Limburger and Roquefort, are good examples of this disparity between odor and flavor. Yet what is referred to as *flavor* is largely the smell associated with the food as it is chewed: foods lose their flavor when olfactory cues are eliminated during eating (such as when you have a head cold). How is it, then, that the same food can generate two distinct odor experiences, depending on whether you are sniffing the food or eating it?

Paul Rozin suspected this happened because olfaction is a dual sense—that is, olfaction has to acquire two sets of information: information about objects in the external world and information about objects within the mouth. According to Rozin (1982), these two types of information have different behavioral consequences. Airborne odors arriving through the nostrils can come from a host of objects and events—other people, animals, plants, fire, and so on—only some of which have anything to do with eating. Behavioral reactions to these odors depend on identifying the source of the odor (Gibson, 1966). In this sense, olfaction serves the same interests as vision and hearing, identifying relevant objects and events in the environment. But olfaction's role changes during eating, after food has been selected and introduced into the mouth. Now odors become part of the flavor complex that also includes taste, temperature, and palatability. Rozin believes that these two different contexts (odor in the mouth versus odor outside the body) are registered by the olfactory nervous system and give rise to distinctly different perceptual experiences.

Rozin figured that if odor did have different perceptual properties in the mouth versus outside the mouth, people should have trouble recognizing odor through the mouth if their previous experience with the odor was just through the nose. To test this hypothesis, Rozin came up with a set of unfamiliar odors and flavors by mixing together various exotic fruit juices and soups. He then taught blindfolded people to identify these various mixtures on the basis of their odors; each mixture was assigned a number for purposes of identification. Once these individuals had learned the procedure, Rozin asked them to identify the same mixtures delivered directly to the mouth through a plastic tube. In this way, any contribution of odor inhaled through the nostrils was eliminated; odor information came entirely from aromas passing up the throat to the olfactory receptors. The results were clear—people made many errors in identifying the mixtures, and they reported that the flavors were impossible to recognize. Evidently, the same substance smells different, depending on whether it is in the external world or in the mouth. This would explain why you may dislike the flavor of things (such as coffee) that smell appealing and also why you can enjoy eating foods that smell foul, such as Morbier cheese from France or the pungent Norwegian delicacy, lutefisk. Without prodding, most people would never even try such off-putting foods.

patches of olfactory epithelium, one at the top of each nasal cavity. Each thin patch of tissue is about 1.3 cm in diameter.

Figure 14.6 shows an enlarged drawing of an olfactory epithelium. Note the structure labeled **olfactory sensory neuron (OSN),** which is a bipolar (double-ended) nerve cell that captures odorant molecules and initiates the neural signals for smell. At one end, this bipolar nerve cell has a single dendrite that terminates in a number of tiny cilia. At its opposite end, the nerve cell terminates in a single axon that, together with the axons of several neighboring nerve cells, form a sensory fiber that threads through one of the perforations in the spongy, relatively thin bone that forms the roof of the nasal cavity and the upper two-thirds of the nasal septum (the wall separating the left and right nasal passages). After the axons pass through this bone, the axons' terminals synapse with neurons in the olfactory bulb.

The typical human nose contains somewhere between 40 and 50 million olfactory sensory neurons. In contrast, the typical dog nose has about 10 to 20 times more, which partly accounts for dogs' legendary ability to track someone, even hours after the individual has passed by. Not shown in Figure 14.6 are structures called **free nerve endings.** Although these nerve fibers do not themselves give rise to odor sensations, they do strongly influence the perception of odors, as we'll see later. But for now let's continue focusing on the olfactory sensory neurons.

Several things set olfactory sensory neurons apart from receptor neurons in the eye and ear. OSNs, unlike photoreceptors and hair cells, are genuine neurons, and

FIGURE 14.6 | The olfactory epithelium is located in the ceiling of the nasal cavity. It contains olfactory receptor neurons whose axons project to the olfactory bulb located just above the nasal cavity. Tiny cilia extend downward from the receptor cell bodies into the mucous layer lining the nasal cavity (see Figure 14.7); it is here that soluble molecules make contact with the cilia and trigger the electrical events culminating in odor detection and identification. The various labeled structures in these figures are described in the text.

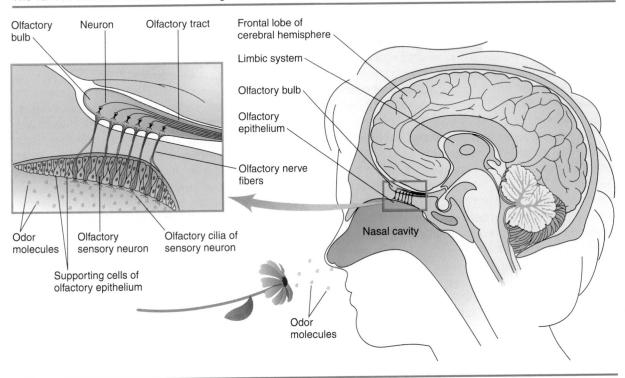

have all of the basic structural elements of neurons—cell bodies, short dendrites, and long axons. Because of their structure, OSNs do two jobs at once: transduce chemical stimulation into neural impulses and carry those impulses to the brain along their axons (which make up the **olfactory nerve**). In vision, hearing, and taste, the two jobs are farmed out to different types of cells. Smell is unique in another way, too: OSNs located in the nasal cavity are the only neurons in the brain that actually come in contact with the outside world.

OSNs have very short lives, lasting about 5 to 8 weeks. When they die, they are replaced (Graziadei, 1973; Moulton, 1974). As a result of this turnover, by the time you read these words, you've already gone through countless generations of OSNs, and the olfactory neurons currently at work in your nose are relative newcomers to the job. This turnover of neurons is even more remarkable considering that as each new OSN matures, its axon must grow an appreciable distance to reach its target site in the olfactory bulb of the brain. Once there, each axon presumably must form connections that effectively duplicate those that were carried out by its predecessor. If the original connections were not duplicated, substances might not smell the same from one month to the next.

Some people believe that the cyclical turnover of OSNs may play a role in changing sensitivity to an odor following prolonged exposure to that odor, a phenomenon well documented in the environmental health literature (Ahlström et al., 1986). To appreciate how this might come about, you'll need to know a little more about the structure of the olfactory sensory neurons, in particular the cilia that extend from an OSN into the mucous lining of the nose. So let's head back to the interior of your nostrils.

Extending from the dendritic end of each olfactory sensory neuron are clumps of **cilia**—thin, hairlike structures embedded in the thin layer of mucus that coats the nasal cavity (see Figure 14.7). The receptor sites for olfaction are embedded in the membrane surface of these cilia, and the greater the surface area, the greater the opportunity for receptor sites to be exposed to airborne odorant molecules. In humans, this total surface area is about 22 cm^2 ; in contrast, the value for German shepherd dogs is many, many times greater, about 7 m^2 (Doty, 2001).

To reach these receptor sites, molecules of odorant must pass from the inhaled air into the nasal cavity's mucous layer. Odorants are aided in this process by olfactory binding proteins (Snyder et al., 1989; Anholt, 1991). An olfactory binding protein, as its name implies, traps and concentrates odorous molecules, transporting them into the nasal mucus, where they have a chance to make contact with receptors. This process is illustrated schematically in Figure 14.8. A gland located in the olfactory epithelium (see Figure 14.6) produces this protein, which occurs only in nasal tissue. A duct carries the protein toward the tip of the nose where, every time you inhale, molecules of the protein are mixed into the in-

FIGURE 14.7 | A highly magnified picture of an actual olfactory receptor neuron with its cilia extending into the nasal cavity.

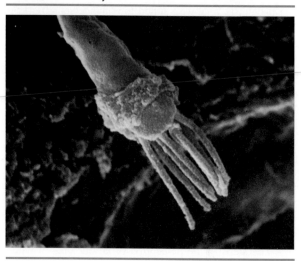

FIGURE 14.8 | Odorants received at the olfactory epithelium are picked up by specialized proteins and transported to receptor sites on the cilia.

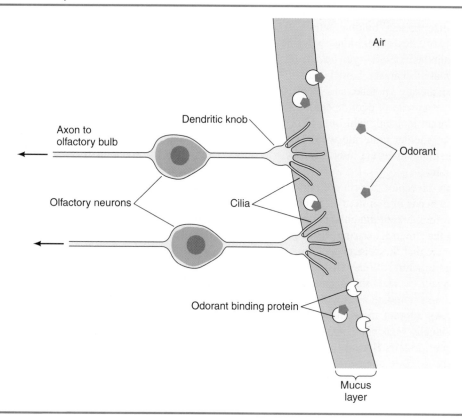

coming air. The protein in the newly inspired air traps molecules of potential odorants and carries these bound molecules to the olfactory receptors. The olfactory binding protein is very well suited to enhance sensitivity; it has at least some affinity for virtually all odorants. Moreover, although only a few odorants have been studied thus far, this protein has greatest affinity for odorant molecules to which the human nose is most sensitive.

The receptors on an OSN's cilia are long protein molecules that weave back and forth through the ciliary membrane. Mammals may have as many as 1,000 different receptor proteins. Each member of this large family of protein receptors: (1) crisscrosses the membranes of host cells exactly seven times; (2) employs the same basic mechanisms for initiating signals; and (3) shares some common, characteristic sequences of amino acids. Each OSN produces only one of the many possible olfactory receptor proteins.

The steps to the perception of an odor begin when odorant molecules bind to specific sites on the receptor proteins. This process is a sophisticated, molecular version of the lock and key idea advanced by Amoore (1970), who mistakenly focused on the overall shape of odorous molecules and not their finer molecular structure. (In Amoore's defense, he did not have the technology available to visualize protein binding sites.) To understand the specificity of a key's operation—why one key opens a lock, while another doesn't—you have to understand the lock's internal mechanism, how its individual tumblers interact with the key's notches and grooves. The same is true for the specificity of odor receptors. To understand why one odorant molecule will bind to certain receptor proteins but another molecule won't, you have to understand something about the interaction between receptor and odorant.

The binding sites on a receptor protein are pockets created by the twists and bends of a protein as its chain folds itself up into its preferred three-dimensional structure. Differences among the amino acid strings that comprise any protein guarantee that the protein will have a unique three-dimensional structure, different from that of any other protein. As a result, the size, shape, and chemical attraction of any protein's binding sites will also be unique to that protein. An odorant molecule typically forms a number of individually weak bonds to many different sites on the receptor protein. Because any single bond is electrically weak, a stable connection between receptor and odorant requires a large number of such bonds. And because individual bonds can be made only when the active sites on both receptor and odorant are

very close together, the number of bonds that are formed depends on the fit between receptor and odorant.

When an odorant molecule has firmly docked with its matching receptor protein, the receptor triggers a series of molecular events that, in rapid succession, recruit several different chemical intermediaries within the olfactory receptor neuron (Lindner and Gilman, 1992). The last of these intermediaries is an enzyme that triggers electrical changes in the cell membrane. At this point, the capture of an odorant molecule has been transduced into an electrical signal.

Although it is difficult to make a definitive test of the idea, most researchers assume a given olfactory sensory neuron contains just one type of receptor protein. If a nose lacks a particular olfactory receptor protein, that nose will be unable to detect the odorous molecule(s) that would be captured by that receptor protein. The term **anosmia** (literally, "without smell") is used to describe a complete inability to smell. When anosmia is partial, that is, restricted to a particular class of smells, the condition is termed **specific anosmia.** A fairly common specific anosmia in humans is anosmia for androstenone, a volatile steroid found in human perspiration. Given that androstenone's characteristic smell is best likened to the aroma of dirty socks, anosmia, at least for this odorant, may not be all that bad.

Most commonly, a specific anosmia can be traced to the absence of specific receptor proteins. Temporary anosmia (a temporary, reversible loss in odor sensitivity) results when the cilia are damaged, as they can be by certain toxic chemicals or drugs. Once new cilia develop, odor sensitivity returns. Although normal, healthy humans can distinguish among a great many different odors, judging by the standards of other species, members of our species are relatively anosmic—insensitive to a great many odors that other animals can detect and identify.

Previously we alluded to one possible reason for humans' relatively impoverished sense of smell, our small olfactory epithelia. But that is not the whole story. The human genome contains a total of about 1,000 olfactory receptor genes, which might seem like a lot of distinct receptor types. However, more than half of all these olfactory receptor genes are nonfunctional (Gilad et al., 2003). Thus, proteins encoded by these defective genes, called *pseudogenes,* are unable to absorb an odorant molecule, thus limiting the range of human olfaction.

Why has our species developed this relatively loose dependence on our sense of smell? Circumstantial evidence suggests that our vision may be to blame. By comparing the prevalence of pseudogenes in the genomes of humans and several kinds of monkeys, Gilad et al., (2004) found a strong relationship between the proportion of olfactory pseudogenes and the presence of trichromatic color vision. These investigators speculated that development of full (three-pigment) color vision—and a growing ability to rely on vision—may have relaxed the need for a sensitive sense of smell. Presumably, this relaxation would have shielded animals with color vision from the harsh selection pressures that otherwise would have followed mutations in olfactory genes. There is even some evidence to suggest continuing changes in the human olfactory repertoire. Although olfactory genes in relatively few humans were examined, Gilad and Lancet (2003) did find a striking difference in the frequency and type of olfactory pseudogenes in two different ethnogeographic groups.

Now that we've seen how odorant molecules dock with olfactory receptors and how olfactory signals are triggered, we can move to the next step in neural coding of odor quality. We can ask, "How are the various qualities of odor represented in the firing patterns of neurons of the olfactory system? What neural responses make it possible for us to distinguish, say, the smell of lemons from that of limes?"

Neural Coding of Odor Quality by Olfactory Fibers

You've already learned something about how qualitative aspects of a stimulus are represented in other senses. Recall from Chapter 10 that each fiber in the auditory nerve responds to a certain range of frequencies, giving the strongest response to one particular frequency. Likewise, each fiber in the optic nerve prefers contours of a particular size and, for some, a particular color. Again, the preferred size or color varies from fiber to fiber. In those modalities, then, different subcategories of sensory fibers carry information about different sensory qualities. As a group, olfactory nerve fibers (the axons of the olfactory receptors) do *not* behave in this discriminating, specialized fashion. The vast majority of olfactory nerve fibers respond to a host of different odors, many bearing no qualitative similarity to one another (Kauer, 1991). To be sure, individual fibers don't indiscriminately respond to all possible odors. There must be (and is) some degree of response specificity. But the range of effective odorants is quite large for any given nerve fiber (Araneda, Kini, and Firestein, 2000). There is nothing resembling the specialization evident in auditory and visual nerves. Consequently, individual olfactory fibers can signal that an

odorous substance is present, but no single olfactory fiber provides unequivocal information about exactly *what* that substance is.

By and large, the olfactory nerve does not treat an odorant as some combination of basic components each separately registered by specialized cells. Nor, for that matter, does there appear to be anything in the olfactory nerve fibers like the center/surround antagonism characteristic of visual receptive fields. And there is nothing comparable in the olfactory epithelium to the tonotopic organization of the basilar membrane and the auditory nerve. But olfaction clearly has a few amazing tricks all its own. Nature seems to have worked out a unique form of sensory coding within the olfactory system, but to understand more about that code we must direct our attention to the next stages of processing, in the olfactory bulb and the olfactory cortex.

The Olfactory Pathways

So far the discussion has focused on the olfactory epithelium and the receptor neurons embedded in that tissue. The rest of the olfactory system consists of the **olfactory bulb** (which receives all the input from the olfactory nerve) and the **olfactory brain** (a cluster of neural structures receiving projections from the olfactory bulb). Structurally, the olfactory bulb bears a superficial resemblance to the retina, in that it has several layers of cells laterally interconnected (see the panel A in Figure 14.9). Based on the response properties of neurons in the bulb, however, it is clear that these two structures—the retina and the olfactory bulb—function quite differently.

For one thing, the incoming axons from the olfactory epithelium activate neurons in the receiving stage of the bulb rather diffusely (those "second-order" neurons receiving this diffuse afferent input are concentrated in clusters called *glomeruli*). There is not any obvious kind of corresponding topographic, spatial map of the epithelium in the bulb. There is, though, enormous convergence at this anatomical stage. It is estimated that there are 1,000 receptor cell axons for each second-order neuron in the bulb. Consequently, very weak neural signals, originating in many different olfactory neurons and carried by olfactory nerve fibers, may be summed within the bulb to generate reliable responses to minute concentrations of an odorant (Duchamp-Viret, Duchamp, and Vigouroux, 1989).

It is generally believed that odor quality is coded by the spatial *pattern* of neural activity across the entire

FIGURE 14.9 | (A) A schematic drawing of the multiple layers of the olfactory bulb. (B) A flow diagram of the pathway constituting the olfactory system.

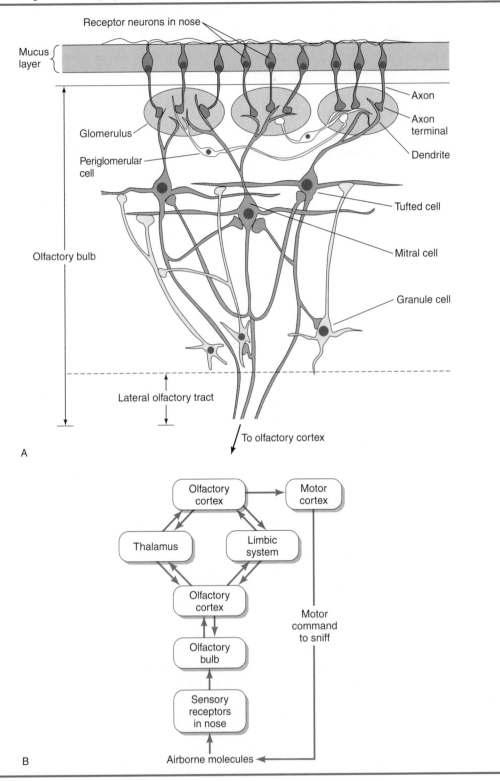

olfactory bulb (Freeman, 1991; Kauer, 1991)—an idea reminiscent of the profile theory introduced in Chapter 4. On this view, virtually all neurons in the bulb contribute to the registration of odor quality; there are no specialized neurons that signal, say, the fragrance of a rose, and only a rose. Support for this view comes from studies in which a map of neural activity was created using a technique that measures the uptake of a radioactive molecule that concentrates selectively in brain regions high in metabolic rate. Different odorants produce characteristic, reliable patterns of metabolic activity within the bulb, but these patterns are globally distributed over the structure, and are not confined to local clusters of cells. A nice review of the olfactory bulb, and of other neural structures involved in smell, is provided by Linda Buck (1996), an olfactory expert who was the cowinner of the 2004 Nobel Prize in physiology and medicine.

Two other important aspects of an odorant also shape the activity of neurons in the olfactory bulb. First, neural activity varies throughout the phase of the inhalation cycle, being greatest at the end of each inhalation. Second, neuronal activity in the bulb depends on level of emotional arousal. If an animal is hungry, thirsty, sexually aroused, or fearful, neural responsiveness is enhanced.

The olfactory bulb's output is carried by axons arising from several morphologically distinct classes of neurons in the bulb. Those axons project to the primary olfactory cortex, which is located below the anterior portion of the temporal lobe (Sobel, Prabhakaran, et al., 2000; Gottfried et al., 2002). The primary olfactory cortex communicates with several other areas of the brain, including structures in the limbic system (see panel B in Figure 14.9). This latter connection is noteworthy, because the limbic system, which is phylogenetically quite old, is central to emotional responses. It is thought that the emotion-evoking capacity of odors arises from two-way links between the olfactory and limbic systems.

Relatively few physiological studies have been made of neurons in the olfactory cortex. To date, efforts to identify an odortopic organization in the cortex (that is, an organized map of different odors represented by different neurons) have failed (Greer, 1991). It is known, though, that people with damage to the olfactory cortex can have difficulty detecting and/or identifying odors (see the review by Richardson and Zucco, 1989), indicating that those regions are critically involved in processing olfactory information. As we have described, any given type of odorant molecule usually evokes a broadly distributed, characteristic pattern of activity within the olfactory bulb. Of course, the air we ordinarily breathe carries many different odorant molecules, which arise from multiple sources. So, the olfactory cortex receives from the bulb a complicated pattern of activity associated with this montage of odorant molecules. Researchers are just beginning to grapple with the problem of how the brain's olfactory centers extract crucial invariant responses from the fluctuating and unpredictable neural responses triggered by the wide variety of odorants that are present (Laurent, 1999).

Neural Representation of Odor Intensity

The previous section focused on odor quality—the difference, for example, between the odors of a banana and peanut butter. Another dimension of odor perception, of course, is the intensity of a given odor. Odor intensity depends on the concentration of the airborne molecules along with the amount of odorant actually reaching the receptors in the olfactory epithelium. (A given concentration is going to smell weaker when your nose is stuffed up, and fewer airborne odorant molecules are able to reach receptors.) Not surprisingly, the nervous system registers information about concentration in the firing rate of neurons responsive to an odor: Weak odors elicit fewer neural impulses than strong odors. This property seems to hold at all levels of the olfactory system, from the receptor cells to the cortex. To complicate the picture, though, people can experience changes in the *quality* of an odorant (even chemically pure ones) with intensity variations alone (Gross-Isseroff and Lancet, 1988). So odor intensity and odor quality are not independent dimensions.

One way to learn how odor perception is mediated by neural events in the nose and brain is to try to deduce the necessary steps in the process and, then, to build a model to accomplish those steps. The next section describes just such an engineering effort.

Building a Better Nose

For years, people have dreamed about the possibilities of electronic noses ("e-noses"). A highly accurate e-nose would be able to check for important, telltale odors hour after hour, never growing tired. When needed, the e-nose would never complain about being sent to sniff around in dangerous places where the atmosphere is potentially damaging to biological noses. In medical diagnosis applications, this sensitive e-nose would never forget to check a patient's breath and body odors for crucial signs of illness (recall our earlier discussion of odors and diseases).

An e-nose might even stand vigilant guard for nerve gas and deadly airborne chemicals. Now, many of these dreams have become a reality: E-noses have been built and tested. One particularly advanced e-nose is available commercially from a company, Cyrano Sciences (named after Cyrano de Bergerac, a fictional character whose nose is the most prominent organ of smell in all of literature). Unlike Cyrano de Bergerac's fictional, but biological nose, Cyrano Sciences's electronic nose on a chip is small. But despite its size, this e-nose is extremely good at identifying a wide range of odorants (Freund and Lewis, 1995; Doleman, Severin, and Lewis, 1998). Although it contains only electronics and specially designed synthetic molecules, the e-nose operates much like its biological counterpart.

The design of one current "nose on a chip" is inspired by the mammalian olfactory system. The chip contains 32 different odorant-absorbing polymers, large molecules synthesized to absorb vapors of different kinds. Each polymer absorbs a particular range of odorants, in a manner analogous to the odorant-absorbing protein molecules on olfactory receptor neurons. Just like an olfactory receptor protein, a given synthetic polymer absorbs a number of different odorants, and, again, like the nose's receptor molecules, various synthetic polymers in the e-nose are specialized for absorbing different sets of odorants.

When a polymer sensor comes into contact with one of the vapor molecules it was designed to absorb, the polymer undergoes a spongelike expansion. This expansion alters the electrical resistance of a conductive substrate to which the polymer is fused. So each odorant produces a characteristic pattern of changes in electrical resistance across the array of synthetic polymers. Any odorant—or at least a good many different odorants—generates a distinctive cross-molecule absorption profile. The nose chip contains an electronic neural network that can be trained to assign unique labels to various odorants to which the chip is exposed. Incidentally, this entire process—from odor presentation to identification—takes less than a second. Eventually, e-noses may stand silent guard at airport security checkpoints; they could monitor the quality of seafood and poultry products, helping to ensure food safety; they would be embedded in new refrigerators, where they'll sound the alarm when food becomes tainted; they might sniff out buried landmines; and they can be used for odor-based medical diagnosis (Turner and Magan, 2004). Perkins (2000) describes other current and future ways in which artificial noses could be used.

As good as all this sounds, however, don't think about trading in your perfectly fine biological nose for one of these electronic models, at least not quite yet. Remember the discussion, earlier in the chapter, of the limitations created by the human genome's relatively few working olfactory genes? Well, however limited the genome might be, the number of functional genes and receptor proteins in a normal human nose dwarfs the several dozen sensors used by the nose on a chip. Moreover, our own olfactory receptors have been tuned by evolution to pick up the myriad vaporous molecules that are behaviorally important for us. The nose on a chip, in comparison, senses a very limited range of odorants. Still, the technology and its applications are fascinating and will get better over time.

Having surveyed the anatomy and physiology of the olfactory system, we are now prepared to consider the perception of odors.

Odor Perception

Odor Detection

Admittedly, the human sense of smell is rather dull compared to that of other species such as the dog. Still, the performance of the human nose is not to be sneezed at. For instance, people can detect ethyl mercaptan (a foul-smelling substance) in concentrations as minute as 1 part per 50 billion parts of air. This performance rivals that of the most sensitive laboratory instruments available for measuring tiny concentrations of molecules. Such sensitivity is all the more impressive when you realize that only a small fraction of the odor molecules in this minute concentration actually reaches the olfactory receptors in the top of the nasal cavity. During normal breathing, only about 2 percent of the odorous molecules entering the nostrils actually make it to the receptors; the receptor-free lining inside the nose absorbs the remaining molecules.

Measurements of olfactory sensitivity demand some way to exert control over the stimulus delivered to a subject's nose. For this purpose, researchers today use a sophisticated, computer-controlled delivery system, called an **olfactometer** (the name means device for measuring smell). Hendrik Zwaardemaker, a Dutch physiologist, introduced the first olfactometer in the 1880s; the design and fabrication of such devices have been greatly refined over the years since. Modern olfactometers typically have stainless-steel surfaces, which minimize contamination from undesired odorants, computer-controlled valves that afford precise control over crucial features of

FIGURE 14.10 | (A) An olfactometer built by Noam Sobel and Brad Johnson; the device is described in detail in Johnson et al. (2003). The olfactometer delivers calibrated amounts of an odorant and allows the experimenter to switch between odorant and no-odorant conditions extremely rapidly, with no nonolfactory cues as to when the switch happened. The olfactometer also measures airflow in each nostril separately. (B) The olfactometer delivering odorants within an fMRI scanner. (C) The olfactometer delivering odorants to a person sitting within test chamber carefully built to minimize extraneous odor contamination.

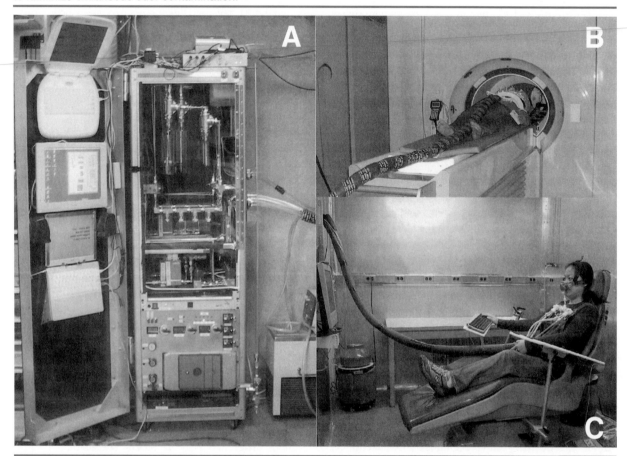

the stimulus including which nostril is stimulated, the concentration at which the odorant is delivered, the duration of presentation, and the temperature and humidity of the inhaled air. The most versatile systems can also mix multiple odorants in a single stimulus or switch rapidly between different odorants, when an experiment requires these conditions (Lorig et al., 1999). High-end olfactometers, like the one shown in Figure 14.10, also allow researchers to measure the timing, rate, and volume of subjects' inhalations (sniffs). The importance of this last feature will become clear to you shortly, when we discuss the importance of sniffing.

By means of these sophisticated delivery systems researchers have proved that olfactory sensitivity varies

greatly from odor to odor. For example, the substance mentioned above, mercaptan, can be detected at a concentration 10 million times less than that needed to smell carbon tetrachloride, a solvent once used in dry-cleaning fluid (Wenger, Jones, and Jones, 1956). Because people are so sensitive to mercaptan, it is added to natural gas—which is odorless but toxic—to warn of gas leaks (Cain and Turk, 1985).

Besides the molecular properties of odorants, sensitivity to odor also depends on a number of other factors. In particular, people are generally able to detect weak odors better in the morning than in the evening (Stone and Pryor, 1967); elderly people are less sensitive than young adults (Cain and Gent, 1991; Schiffman, 1997);

and females are more sensitive, on average, than males (Koelega and Koster, 1974). Because of these age and sex differences in smell acuity, some people may be put off by body odors that others are unaware of. Consistent with popular belief, smokers are less sensitive to odors than nonsmokers (Ahlström et al., 1987). This dulled odor sensitivity is also found in nonsmokers who live or work with individuals who are heavy smokers (Ahlström et al., 1987).

Recently, researchers have revealed one other factor that influences odor sensitivity: repeated exposure to a particular odorant. Wysocki, Dorries, and Beauchamp (1989) showed that some individuals who were anosmic for androstenone (dirty socks smell) actually developed some sensitivity to this substance with repeated exposure to the odorant. Mainland et al. (2002) showed that at least some of this practice-induced sensitization to androstenone arises not from change in olfactory receptors, but in a change in some central component of the olfactory system. In a three-alternative forced choice procedure, Mainland and colleagues had participants identify in which one of the three intervals adrostenone had been presented; during the remaining two intervals on each trial, odorant-free air was presented. From a large sample of possible participants, the researchers selected individuals who were unable to detect the androstenone, and these individuals performed no better than chance (33 percent, as indicated by the left-hand bar in Figure 14.11). These insensitive people were then exposed daily for three weeks to androstenone, for 10 minutes per day. During this repeated exposure one nostril was blocked with an inflatable plug, and airborne androstenone was presented only to the other, nonblocked nostril. Finally, each nostril was separately retested for sensitivity to adrostenone. As the middle bar in Figure 14.11 shows, the nostril that had been exposed to androstenone now showed considerable sensitivity to that substance. Surprisingly, the nonexposed, "naïve" nostril showed almost exactly the same improved sensitivity (right-most bar in the figure). Because neural signals from the two nostrils do not merge in the nose itself, the exposure-induced learning probably occurs in the brain, at a site where information is shared from both nostrils.

Odor Identification

Having bragged about the sensitivity of the human nose, we must qualify what we mean by *sensitivity*. The remarkable performance described above refers to the

FIGURE 14.11 | Detection accuracy of adrostenone odor by individual nostrils of people who were initially insensitive to this odor. Left-most bar represents mean accuracy of detection before practice, and the other two bars represent performance after 21 days of exposure. Note that both nostrils, the one exposed to androstenone during the 21 days and the one not exposed, show significant improvements in accuracy. Chance performance (guessing) is indicated by the dotted line.

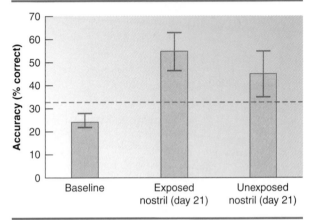

ability to *detect* the presence of a faint odor, not the ability to *identify* the odor. In fact, at near-threshold concentrations, people can smell an odor without being able to identify the odor. Here's an illustration of this point (Engen, 1960). When people are given three empty test tubes and a fourth test tube containing an extremely dilute odor, people can accurately select the tube that "smells different" from the others. But using the same set of stimuli, they make many errors when instructed to pick the test tube that contains a particular named odor ("Pick the tube containing menthol"). So people behave as if they have two thresholds, one for detecting the presence of an odor and a second, higher threshold for identifying what that odor is.

For some odorous substances, part of the identification problem may stem from a substance's bistability. Such substances can elicit two different qualitative experiences that fluctuate over time. (The vase/face figure shown in Figure 4.1c generates an analogous visual bistable perception.) For instance, the compound dihydromyrcenol (which is related to turpentine) sometimes has a citruslike odor and other times a woody odor. Lawless, Glatter, and Hohn (1991) were able to bias people's descriptions of this substance by also having the people

Imagine walking into a room and being confronted with a pungent odor. The source of the odor isn't visible, nor is it obvious where the odor is coming from. What's your reaction to the odor? It depends partly on what you're expecting to encounter in the room. If you've walked into a cheese shop, then you'll probably find the smell intriguing and enjoyable. But if you've walked into a public bathroom, you may find the smell repulsive. The same odor, in other words, can elicit dramatically different experiences from you depending on how you construe the nature of the source. This dependency is nicely illustrated by a study carried out by Herz and von Clef (2001).

These scientists assembled a set of odorants that could be readily characterized as arising from either of two quite different sources. These were, in other words, ambiguous odors in the same way that a visual figure can be ambiguous (recall Figure 4.1c): The same physical stimulus can give rise to multiple perceptual experiences. The odors used by Herz and von Clef, and the alternative labels that could be assigned to those odors, included violet leaf (described as fresh cucumber or as mildew), pine oil (spray disinfectant or Christmas tree) and a mixture of isovaleric and butyric acid (parmesan cheese or vomit). Cotton balls saturated with each odorant were placed individually in glass jars with verbal labels assigned to each; volunteer participants sniffed each jar in turn and rated the pleasantness of the smells. Their ratings revealed that a given odor's perceptual quality could be inverted from positive to negative based just on the verbal label attached to that odorant. This inversion in hedonic reaction, as it is called, may not surprise you because, after all, the smell of vomit is repulsive whereas the smell of parmesan cheese is not. Still, these odors behave just like visually bistable figures, and the results are testimony to the potency of expectations in shaping our perception of odors.

Why is smell susceptible to your expectations and knowledge? Getting back to the point just made, odor sources are often invisible, and we're not particularly good at localizing where odors are coming from. Consequently, we sometimes must supplement odor information to deduce the source, and the conclusion we arrive at, in turn, colors the nature of the olfactory experience produced by that odor.

Besides verbal labels, visual cues, too, can influence odor perception. Several years ago a group of students enrolled in the wine program at the University of Bordeaux were asked to describe the odor qualities they experienced when sampling a group of red wines and white wines (Morrot, Brochet, and Dubourdieu, 2001). Unbeknownst to the students, one of the white wines was colored red with an odorless dye. The labels given when sampling this wine were comparable to the ones used for actual red wines, not white wines, indicating that the visual color was influencing their verbal descriptions. Of course, one could argue that odor perception per se was not influenced by color and, instead, that the students were simply using words that they knew were appropriate for red wine. However, this cannot be the entire explanation, for the same kind of visual-olfactory interaction is found using brain imaging. Gottfried and Dolan (2003) measured neural activation from areas of the brain responsive to odors and found that pictures of food objects enhanced responses to odors when the picture and the odor were congruent (e.g., the smell of orange accompanied by a picture of an orange). Evidently, then, the eye and the nose can indeed jointly influence the brain's response to odors.

---

smell an odorant that was unambiguously woody (such as pine) or unambiguously citruslike (such as lemon oil). After smelling citrus, people said the ambiguous compound smelled woody; after smelling the woody odor, the compound smelled like citrus. This shift in perception is not attributable to sensory adaptation, for it did not matter whether the unambiguous stimulus was sniffed before or after sniffing dihydromyrcenol. This context-dependent change in odor identification could be exploited for creative menu planning by using dishes with multiple aroma components, such as curried chicken. And it is possible to give a fruity wine such as a German Riesling either an acidic or a floral bouquet, depending on its accompaniment. For another contextual trick that one could use to influence odor perception, see Box 14.2.

Most odorous substances, though, elicit their own characteristic odor qualities regardless of context. Still, individuals differ greatly in their ability to identify (or attach labels to) various odors. This has been well-documented in two large studies of odor identification: one study tested about 2,000 people ranging in age from 5 to 99 years (Doty et al., 1984), while the other study surveyed more than 1 million readers of a popular magazine (Wysocki, Pierce, and Gilbert, 1991).

FIGURE 14.12 | Ability to identify odors varies with age.

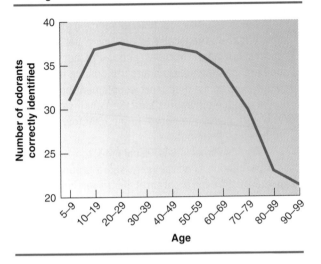

FIGURE 14.13 | Ability to identify odors is impaired by cigarette smoking.

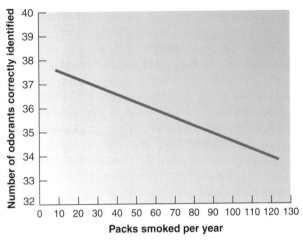

Both studies used scratch 'n' sniff test strips, a common method of testing odor identification (Doty, Shaman, and Dan, 1984). In this method, the surface of a microencapsulated odorant is scratched, which releases some of the odorant that the subject then sniffs. These two large studies showed that, overall, females are significantly better at odor identification than males, with the best performances exhibited by individuals ranging in age from the mid-twenties to late-forties (see Figure 14.12). Some people beyond their sixties show marked impairments in their ability to identify odors, which may explain why elderly people sometimes complain about the blandness of food; after all, smell is an essential component in the enjoyment of food. It should be noted, though, that odor identification performance is much more variable among the elderly: Some people in their seventies or older perform as well as much younger individuals.

Age and gender are important, but they are not the only factors that influence one's ability to identify odors. For example, tobacco smoking impairs the ability to identify odors, as the graph in Figure 14.13 documents. The longer the history of smoking, the greater the number of errors on standardized tests of odor identification (Frye, Doty, and Schwartz, 1989). Fortunately, cessation of smoking promotes recovery. Ambient air quality, too, affects odor perception. Individuals working in plants that manufacture vaporous chemicals may experience long-term impairments in olfactory identification (Schwartz et al., 1989). People who live in cities that have poor air quality have difficulty identifying at least some odors compared to matched samples of people from cities with generally better air quality (Wysocki, Pierce, and Gilbert, 1991). These deficits associated with smoking and air quality may be related to structural changes at the receptor sites on the olfactory cilia, which are altered with chronic exposure to particular odorants.

Murphy and Cain (1986) found that blind adults are significantly better at odor identification than are sighted individuals of comparable age. Perhaps, then, odor identification should be thought of as a skill that can be sharpened with the enforced practice required without vision. Indeed, even in sighted individuals, practice with feedback improves the ability to identify odors. Desor and Beauchamp (1974) tested people's ability to name 32 common odorous objects contained in individual opaque jars. After sniffing the jar, the person guessed what the object was and rated the familiarity of the odor. Some smells—such as coffee, paint, and banana—were readily identified and were also rated as highly familiar. Most people incorrectly identified other smells—including ham, cigar, and crayon; these odors were also rated as less familiar. Desor and Beauchamp then went through the series again, this time providing people with the correct answer when they made errors. With practice, everyone was able to name each of the 32 odors correctly. Furthermore, the same people were trained on an additional set of 32 new odors, and with practice they were able to identify all 64 odors with few errors.

Although practice does improve odor identification, it does not help everybody to the same degree. For example, practice seems to benefit females more than males, as Figure 14.14 shows. This graph summarizes the results from an experiment where Cain (1982) asked male and female college students to identify each of the 80 common odorous stimuli listed in the figure. Each person went through the set of stimuli several times, with feedback provided after every trial. Students of both sexes improved with practice on this task, but the females consistently outperformed the males on just about all odorous stimuli. Each bar in Figure 14.14 summarizes identification performance for a particular stimulus. Stimuli in the upper portion of the figure (such as coffee) were readily identified, whereas stimuli toward the lower portion (such as cough syrup) were difficult to identify. Unshaded bars indicate female superiority at identifying that odorant, while shaded bars indicate male superiority. The length of the bar denotes the size of the sex difference in odor identification. For instance, males were much better than females at identifying Brut brand aftershave lotion, but only marginally better at identifying the smell of mothballs. Females were much better than males at identifying coconut, but only slightly better at identifying peanut butter. As the overwhelming number of unshaded bars indicates, females are generally better at this task than males. The origin of these sex differences is not yet known; nonetheless, it is clear that both sexes do benefit from practice. (For other demonstrations of sex-differential practice effects in olfaction, see Dalton, Doolittle, and Breslin, 2002).

For more than 30 years it has been known that olfactory function is diminished in people with Parkinson's disease, a progressive brain disorder that interferes with smooth, coordinated movements of the muscles and, in late stages, with cognitive function. The tight association between disordered ability to identify odors, on one hand, and Parkinson's disease, on the other, has led some to hypothesize that Parkinson's disease actually *begins* with damage to the olfactory pathway in the brain (for exam-

FIGURE 14.14 | Odor identification for 80 common stimuli, arranged from top to bottom in order of ease of identification. Unshaded bars indicate the superior ability of female subjects to identify a particular stimulus; shaded bars indicate the superior ability of male subjects.

(Redrawn with permission from Cain, 1982.)

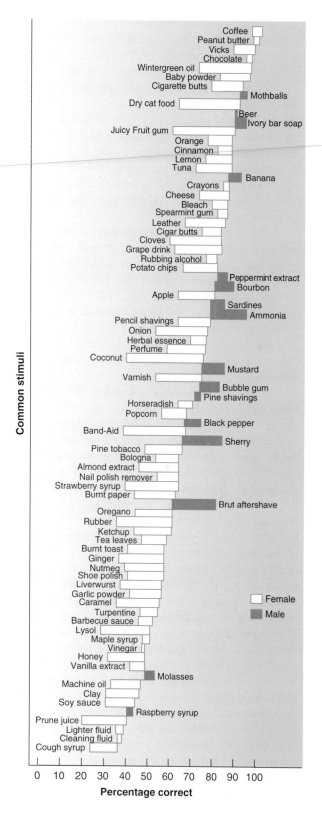

ple, Hawkes, Shephard, and Daniel, 1999). Recently, this intriguing hypothesis has been questioned. Using a sophisticated olfactometer, Sobel, Thomason, et al. (2001) showed that poor sniffing behavior was to blame for much of Parkinson's patients' reduced odor identification. As patients tried to identify odorants, they showed abnormally weak sniffing. These substandard inhalations reduced olfactory receptors' exposure to airborne odorant molecules. When Sobel and colleagues encouraged the patients to sniff more vigorously, odor identification was substantially improved, at least in some of the patients. These findings reinforce the point that sniffing is an essential component of olfaction.

Next on our list of important determinant of odor identity is stimulus salience. This is dramatically demonstrated by the abilities of mothers to recognize their newborns by smell alone after less than 1 hour of postnatal exposure to the infant (Kaitz et al., 1987). This olfactory link between mother and infant occurs in a variety of species besides humans, and there is evidence that this adaptive reaction coincides with structural and neurochemical changes in the olfactory bulb (Kendrick, Levy, and Keverne, 1992). Apparently newborn infants also rely heavily on olfaction to recognize their mothers. Porter (1991) provides an excellent review of findings on the role of odor perception in mother–infant relationships. Related to this issue, Schaal (1988) has reviewed the literature on the development of olfaction in infants and children, concluding that from birth onward, infants are quite good at detecting and discriminating odors. What does seem to change, according to Schaal, are infants' hedonic reactions to odors—it may take several years for children to develop aversions to some odors that adults judge to be offensive.

Related to salience is the influence of familiarity, which also impacts the ability to name an odor. Older individuals, though generally poorer at odor identification than young people, do show superior recall for substances that have been in use for a long time. For instance, older adults have little trouble recognizing the smell of vinegar and coffee, odorants that older persons have been exposed to since youth. In comparison, epoxy and hair conditioner baffle older adults but not youngsters (Wood and Harkins, 1987). At the other end of the age continuum, newborn infants exposed for about a day to an artificial odorant preferentially orient to that odorant two weeks later when it is paired with a novel one (Davis and Porter, 1991). This olfactory familiarization probably underlies infants' ability to recognize their mothers by smell.

But if experience with odors starts to build from the very first days of life, why are adults relatively poor at identifying odors, even that they've experienced over and over? Of course, odors are typically associated with information from other senses, information that unambiguously identifies the source of those odors. For instance, the sight of a lemon usually accompanies a citruslike aroma. But in odor identification tasks, people have only the sense of smell to go on. Even healthy, young females may get fewer than half the items correct. The problem is not one of discrimination: People find it easy to judge correctly whether two odors are the same versus different. The problem involves *naming* individual odors. In other words, the link between odors and their verbal descriptions tends to be weak (Engen, 1987). This inability to name a familiar odor has been aptly termed the **tip of the nose phenomenon** (Lawless and Engen, 1977). If the problem is indeed one of retrieving odor names from memory, then prompting with verbal clues should help identify odors. And it does. Several researchers (Davis, 1981; Zellner, Bartoli, and Eckard, 1991) have found that merely providing people with a color name related to an odor (such as *yellow* when lemon was being sniffed) is enough to trigger correct identification.

Odor Concentrations

Besides having characteristic qualities, odorous substances also vary in the *intensity* of those qualities. Intensity, as you might guess, depends on the concentration level of odor-producing molecules, which is the number of odorant molecules per unit volume of odorant free air. A common misconception about the sense of smell concerns people's alleged poor ability to judge differences in odor concentrations. Until recently, it was generally thought that people require about a 25 percent difference in odor concentration before they can tell that one sample of an odor is stronger than another sample of that same odor. (This implies that a bouquet of five flowers would smell no stronger than a bouquet of four flowers, because they differ by only 20 percent.) Compared to vision and hearing (where difference thresholds are on the order of 10 percent or less), this would be poor sensitivity. However, Cain (1977) showed that this dismal performance does not reflect some inferiority of the olfactory nervous system; instead, the poor performance stems from the moment-to-moment variability in the amount of odorous vapor delivered to the olfactory receptor cells. Remember, only a small fraction of these vapors actually reach these cells. Taking account of variability in effective odor concentration, Cain found that people could discriminate concentration differences as small as 7 percent. This puts the nose in the same league with the eye and the ear as a judge of intensity differences. (Thus, if their fragrance were delivered through Cain's experimental apparatus, five flowers *would* consistently smell stronger than four.)

Recall the description of magnitude scaling in Chapter 11 and in the appendix. In a typical application of that procedure, people are asked to assign numbers to sounds according to their loudness. Comparable scaling measurements have been made for perceived odor intensity. As with loudness, odor intensity grows as a power function of concentration. Although the values vary from odor to odor, many odors give exponents in the neighborhood of 0.6, indicating that perceived odor intensity grows gradually, relative to increasing concentration. To illustrate, doubling odor concentration produces only about a 50 percent increase in perceived intensity, not 100 percent (the value associated with an exponent of 1.0). As a result, a bouquet of 10 flowers will not smell twice as strong as a bouquet of five flowers; to smell twice as strong as five flowers, a bouquet would have to consist of 17 flowers. Interestingly, intensity ratings can be affected by color. Zellner and Kautz (1990) found that some odorous substances smell stronger when the sniffed liquid substance is colored (for instance red, in the case of strawberry). Evidently, simple conditioning cannot explain this finding, since enhanced odor intensity was found even with inappropriate color/odor combinations (for instance, red lemon).

Why is it important to be able to judge the concentration of an odor? Suppose you walk into your room and smell a foul odor. You can't see where it's coming from so you have to rely on your sense of smell to guide you to the source. You move around trying to locate where the smell becomes stronger. Because the concentration of airborne odorant molecules decreases with distance from the molecules' source, as you move in a direction that increases the odor's concentration you'll ultimately come to the source of the odor. Many animals use exactly this strategy when tracking prey or when following an odor trail to a potential mate (recall the cabbage moth mentioned earlier in this chapter).

The Common Chemical Sense

While we're on the subject of odor concentrations, we should note that most odors that are judged to be pleasant at moderate concentrations lose their attractiveness at high concentrations. This is why sales clerks in a store's cosmetics department always urges customers to allow a dab of perfume time to dilute before smelling it. One reason intense odors can be overpowering has to do with the free nerve endings in the olfactory epithelium. Such free nerve endings are not limited to the nasal mucosa. They are found in all of the body's mucous membranes—the conjunctiva lining the eye as well as the mucous membranes of the mouth, respiratory tract, anus, and genitals. Because of their free nerve endings, each of these membranes is very sensitive to potentially irritating chemicals (Cometto-Muñiz and Cain, 1996). The nose's free nerve endings can be stimulated by almost any volatile substance, if presented at a moderate or high concentration. They are the receptors for what is known as the **common chemical sense.** This common chemical sense is responsible for the *feeling* that accompanies certain smells—such as the coolness of menthol or the tingle in your nose when you burp. Even the crisp, invigorating "smell" of fresh mountain air (which itself has no odor) comes from stimulation of the common chemical sense, by ozone in the mountain air. In fact, just about any volatile substance can elicit this feeling in the nose if the concentration of that substance is high enough. In the case of some substances, stimulation of the common chemical sense produces a burning sensation that causes you reflexively to hold your breath (a gasp reflex) and to turn your head away from the source of stimulation. If you've ever inhaled ammonia fumes, you know what this gasp reflex is like.

Not all people have equally sensitive common chemical senses. Cigarette smokers are less sensitive than nonsmokers. For smokers, the inhaled concentration of a potentially irritating substance must be about 25 percent higher than that of nonsmokers to elicit a reflexive change in breathing pattern (Cometto-Muñiz and Cain, 1982). Smokers, then, have a diminished system to warn them of dangerous chemicals. Elderly people also show reduced sensitivity to nasal irritants that stimulate the common chemical sense (Stevens and Cain, 1986). And, as you might guess by now, males are less sensitive than females (Garcia-Medina and Cain, 1982). Some people completely lose their common chemical sense from damage to the trigeminal nerve carrying information from the nose's free nerve endings to the brain. In these individuals, harsh chemical substances elicit *no* reaction when inhaled.

The common chemical sense warns us of the presence of potentially irritating substances. However, its operation is not limited to dangerous concentration levels. In fact, even at nonirritating levels of stimulation, the common chemical sense influences the perception

FIGURE 14.15 | Stimulation of the common chemical sense (using carbon dioxide) affects one's perception of odor (amylbutyrate).

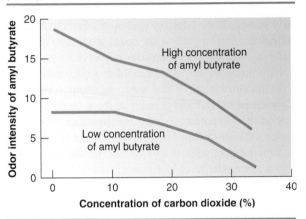

of odor. In an experiment by Cain and Murphy (1980), participants sniffed amyl butyrate (a fruity-smelling substance) and then rated the perceived intensity of the odor. Mixed in with the odorant were various amounts of carbon dioxide. (Carbon dioxide is a gas that does *not* stimulate olfactory receptors but *does* stimulate the free nerve endings in the nose. Hence, it has no odor; but because it stimulates the common chemical sense, it elicits a pungent sensation when inhaled.) Figure 14.15 shows that stimulation of the common chemical sense influenced people's judgments of odor intensity. The vertical axis plots the perceived odor intensity of the amyl butyrate and the horizontal axis shows the concentration of the odorless carbon dioxide. Note that increasing the concentration of carbon dioxide, which itself could not be smelled, reduced the perceived intensity of the amyl butyrate. People also reported that the amyl butyrate's fruity smell changed from pleasant (at low levels of carbon dioxide) to pungent (at high levels of carbon dioxide). People also rated how irritating the smell seemed. As expected, higher concentrations of the odorless carbon dioxide gas were judged more irritating. However, the pungency of the carbon dioxide was lessened when more amyl butyrate was mixed in with it. The interaction between odor and the common chemical sense works both ways: Each influences the perception of the other. Clearly, the common chemical sense adds an important ingredient to our experience of odorous substances.

As noted above, the common chemical sense reflects responses generated by free nerve endings in the nose. These chemically sensitive free nerve endings abound in all mucous membranes. Significant concentrations of certain airborne chemicals can irritate exposed membranes, not only in the nose, but in the eye and respiratory tract as well. This may explain some cases of what is known as "sick building syndrome." Although this syndrome likely has multiple causes, one of them may be this: new carpets, car and home upholstery, adhesives or plastic laminate furnishings emit volatile organic compounds, including formaldehyde. The compounds irritate free nerve endings in exposed mucous membranes, causing coughing and throat irritation, tearing, headache, and unpleasant tingling sensations in the nose. When the air in "sick" buildings is analyzed, just as often as not, no single volatile organic compound is found at a high enough concentration to be worrisome. Does this mean that the complaints of eye, nose, and throat irritation are merely excuses to get out of work? Not necessarily. According to Cometto-Muñiz, Cain, and Hudnell (1997), when several volatile organic components are mixed, their individual effects sum. These researchers measured how mixtures of various volatile organic compounds affected the common chemical sense. To avoid contamination from people's smelling the stimuli, they worked with anosmic volunteers. Cometto-Muñiz and colleagues discovered that mixtures of such compounds could produce strong effects, even though individual components of the mixtures were at sufficiently low concentration to have no effect on their own. There is a lesson here, we believe, for environmental engineers who assess the quality of air in allegedly sick buildings.

Turning back to the topic of odor perception, let's consider *anosmia,* a loss of ability to perceive odors.

Disorders of Smell

Deficiencies in hearing and seeing are usually easy to detect because people depend so much on sight and sound to guide their everyday activities. Deficiencies in odor perception, in comparison, often go unnoticed. Though hard to imagine, some individuals are completely unable to distinguish odorless, pure air from strong concentrations of odorous substances. A blow to the head is a frequent cause of this "odor blindness," or anosmia (Varney, 1988). In such cases, anosmia often proves to be temporary, suggesting that the olfactory receptors or their axons had been damaged (recall that these neurons can regenerate). Anosmia may also be acquired from inhaling caustic agents such as lead, zinc sulfate, or cocaine. These, too, are believed to injure the olfactory receptors, which is why smell sensitivity may recover after exposure to the caustic agent ceases. Reduced odor sensitivity and identification performance are also observed in patients with Alzheimer's disease (Rezek, 1987). Here, impaired odor perception probably results from the degeneration of neurons in the olfactory epithelium (Talamo et al., 1989). Leopold (2002) reviews the many different ways, including anosmia, in which olfaction can fail.

Sometimes anosmia does not involve a *complete* loss of ability to smell, but is instead restricted to particular odorants. Here, a person shows normal sensitivity to some odors but abnormally poor or no sensitivity to others. These are the specific anosmias we mentioned previously, and they are more common than you might think. For example, 3 percent of the U.S. population have trouble smelling the odor of sweat, 12 percent have diminished sensitivity to musky odors, and 47 percent have trouble smelling the odor of urine (Amoore, 1991).

Losing one's sense of smell has serious consequences (Toller, 1999). Individuals with acquired anosmia report that eating is no longer pleasurable, and these people show a loss of both appetite and weight (Schechter and Henkin, 1974). There is even speculation that anosmia may dull sexual drive (Bobrow, Money, and Lewis, 1971). This possibility is not entirely far-fetched. As mentioned in the beginning of the chapter, animals rely heavily on odor to motivate and guide their sexual behavior. And certainly, the large sums of money spent on perfume, not to mention the erotic nature of many perfume commercials, suggest a widespread belief that the human nose and sexual behavior are linked.

Adaptation to Odors

As you walk into the lobby of a movie theater, the aroma of fresh popcorn hits you. Driven by this lovely smell, you rush to get in the long line to buy some. But, oddly, by the time you reach the counter, the popcorn aroma has faded considerably. This exemplifies how exposure to an odor decreases sensitivity to that odor—a phenomenon called **odor adaptation.** Certain occupations depend crucially on odor adaptation: Sewer workers, for instance, can carry out their jobs without being bothered by the stench of their surroundings. Odor adaptation also means that people cease to be aware of their own body odors or the odors permeating their immediate surroundings. As Freud (1930/1961) observed, "[I]n spite of all man's developmental advances, he scarcely finds the smell of his own excreta repulsive, but only that of other people's" (p. 54).

Thus, we usually rely on others for information about our own odors, a widely exploited theme in the omnipresent advertising for deodorant, mouthwash, and soap.

Odor adaptation has been studied in the laboratory, and the results confirm what experience suggests. Following even prolonged exposure to an odor, one never *completely* loses the sensitivity to that odor. Instead, its perceived intensity steadily decreases with continued exposure, eventually falling to about 30 percent of its initial level (Cain, 1978). (This is why some people can tolerate wearing an overpowering amount of perfume or aftershave. Their noses have adapted to the strong fragrance, which makes others wince and turn away.) If an odor's concentration is weak to begin with, it may be impossible to detect that weak odor after adaptation to a strong concentration of the same odor.

Following exposure to an odor, recovery usually takes just a few minutes. However, if the adaptation odor was very strong, complete recovery could take an hour or more (Berglund et al., 1971). There is also anecdotal evidence for ultra-long-term adaptation, whereby individuals develop a chronic insensitivity to odors common to their work environment. Even when they report to work first thing in the morning, after hours away, they fail to smell odors that visitors readily sense. The adaptation of these workers carries over from one day to the next. At the same time, these individuals exhibit normal sensitivity to odors not peculiar to their workplace; so they have not completely lost their sense of smell. Moreover, upon returning to work following a short vacation, they are initially able to sense the odors that their colleagues on the job cannot sense. After a few days on the job, however, they again become insensitive to those odors. These long-term losses in odor sensitivity may be related to the growth processes in olfactory receptor cells (described earlier). It may be that chronic exposure to a limited set of odors affects receptor cells responsive to that set of odors, and several weeks away from that environment are needed to allow the spoiled cells to be replaced with fresh ones.

This explanation probably does not apply, however, to short-term adaptation, where brief exposure to an odor temporarily lessens your sensitivity to it. In this latter case, the process responsible for adaptation probably occurs within the brain, not in the nose. One reason for believing this is that you can adapt one nostril to an odor (keeping the other one closed) and then measure a loss in odor sensitivity using just the unadapted nostril (Zwaardemaker, 1895, cited in Engen, 1982). Since this nostril was closed during adaptation, the olfactory receptors associated with the nostril received no stimulation.

Nonetheless, your perception of odors introduced into this nostril are still dulled, indicating that the process underlying the loss in sensitivity occurs in the brain, not in the receptor cells. However, the physiology of postreceptor adaptation is poorly understood.

So far we have considered situations where an odor's perceived strength is reduced by prior exposure to strong concentrations of that same odor. In some cases, though, a temporary loss in sensitivity to one odor can be produced by exposure to a different odor—a phenomenon called **cross-adaptation.** As you might expect, odors that tend to smell alike (such as nail polish remover and airplane model glue) usually show a large degree of cross-adaptation: Exposure to one reduces your sensitivity to the other. If you spend several minutes sniffing perfume samples at the cosmetic counter, don't be surprised if the fragrance you're already wearing seems temporarily to have worn off; sniffing perfumes similar to your own lessens your sensitivity to the one you're wearing. Highly dissimilar odors, in contrast, do not influence each other nearly so much (Moncrieff, 1956). Thus, sniffing perfume samples will not subsequently affect your ability to appreciate the aroma of coffee.

You can experience cross-adaptation by performing the following simple experiment. First, take a sniff of a lemon and get an idea of the intensity of its aroma. Now hold a spoon of peanut butter close to your nose for a minute or so, adapting to its smell. Then quickly take another whiff of the lemon. You will find the lemon's fragrance just as strong as before. Next adapt for a minute to a lime held under your nose, and then again sniff the lemon. This time you will find the lemon's fragrance noticeably weakened. A lesson to learn from this exercise is that your appreciation of food during a multicourse meal depends on the order in which the foods are served. This is particularly true for foods with similar aromas. For instance, cheese with a strong, overpowering smell (such as Roquefort) should not be served before one with a more delicate aroma (such as Gouda).

Initially, it was hoped that cross-adaptation would provide a method for odor classification. Presumably, odors stimulating the same receptors should exhibit maximum cross-adaptation, while odors stimulating different receptors should show little or no cross-adaptation. Although this sounds reasonable, the results are confusing. In particular, cross-adaptation is sometimes asymmetrical: Adaptation to odor A may strongly influence your perception of odor B, but adaptation to odor B may exert hardly any effect on the smell of odor A (Cain and Engen, 1969). This outcome suggests that cross-adaptation

is not strictly due to receptor adaptation. Moreover, odors that exhibit marked cross-adaptation sometimes bear no molecular resemblance to each other. Cross-adaptation, like short-term adaptation in general, then, does not appear to result from fatigue of the olfactory receptors.

Odor Mixtures

Besides cross-adaptation, different odors can affect one another when mixed together in inhaled air. For example, a meal may generate a bouquet of aromas whose interactions give rise to a unique and very pleasing experience. Odor mixture also underlies the success of commercial air fresheners sold to cover up house odors. In effect, these products exploit the ability of one odor to mask another, by swamping the offensive odor with an even stronger pine or floral scent. These products should be distinguished from true deodorizers, which act by actually removing odorous molecules from the air or by preventing the production of odorous molecules in the first place (the mechanism employed in some underarm deodorants).

As indicated before, the nose seems able to sort out and identify a mixture's various odors. This is why you can identify many of the food ingredients that went into some complex dish simply from the smell of that dish. In this sense, the nose's behavior resembles the ear's ability to single out one pitch from a musical chord; the nose does not behave like the eye, which sometimes loses track of the individual hues making up a mixture. However, a person's judgments of an odor mixture cannot be predicted on the basis of the simple addition of its components. For instance, two different odorants of moderate intensity added together may not yield an intense mixture; this failure of addition is termed **mixture suppression,** and its physiological basis is not well understood (Derby, Ache, and Kennel, 1985; Jinks and Laing, 1999).

Odors and Memory

Even when people cannot identify some odor, they often are still able to say with confidence whether or not they have smelled it before. This suggests that odors can reach back into memory (see Box 14.3). For Helen Keller, who was blind and deaf from infancy, smell was

> a potent wizard that transports us across thousands of miles and all the years we have lived. The odors of fruits waft to me in my southern home, to my childhood frolics in the peach orchard. Other odors, instantaneous and fleeting, cause my heart to dilate joyously or contract with remembered grief. (1908, p. 574)

Languages have limited vocabularies for describing smell experiences. Though it's fairly easy to describe what you see and hear, smell is another matter (Bedichek, 1960). This places a special hardship on authors who want to communicate their character's olfactory experiences. Fortunately, good writers rise above the apparent limitations of language. When you read a work in which smell plays a key part, you are reminded how important this "inarticulate sense" really is. To illustrate, let's consider some samples of writing in which authors have managed to give this inarticulate sense a voice of its own.

James Joyce understood that any writer who wants to create truly convincing and complete lives couldn't ignore smell and taste. In his masterpiece, *Ulysses,* Joyce frequently used smells to reach into the minds of various characters. You may know that various episodes in *Ulysses* emphasize different organs of the human body, with the so-called Nausicaä episode highlighting the eye and the nose. This episode takes place just after sunset on a June evening in 1904. Leopold Bloom, the middle-aged Dubliner around whose comings and goings the book revolves, is walking along the beach, trying to clear his head. Bloom finds himself attracted to Gerty MacDowell, a young woman who's sitting on some rocks near the beach. Although they never even speak, Bloom is infatuated. When she leaves, Gerty waves her perfumed handkerchief at Bloom. The scent reaches Bloom, triggering thoughts of Gerty and of his wife, Molly, as well.

> Wait. Hm. Hm. Yes. That's her perfume. Why she waved her hand. I leave you to think of me when I'm far away on the pillow. What is it? Heliotrope? No, hyacinth? Hm. Roses, I think. She'd like scent of that with a little jessamine mixed. Her high notes and her low notes. At the dance night she met him, dance of the hours. Heat brought it out. She was wearing her black and it had the perfume of the time before.... Mysterious thing too. Why did I smell it only now? Took its time in coming like herself, slow but sure. Suppose it's ever so many millions of tiny grains blown across.... Clings to everything she takes off. Vamp of her stockings. Warm shoe. Stays. Drawers: little kick, taking them off. Byby till next time. Also the cat likes to sniff in her shift on the bed. Know her smell in a thousand. Bathwater too. Reminds me of strawberries and cream. (1922/1934, p. 368)

Another great writer with a special appreciation of the chemical senses was Jonathan Swift, the eighteenth-century English satirist. His most widely read book is *Travels into Several Remote Nations of the World, a Letter from Captain Gulliver to His Cousin Sympson,* commonly known as *Gulliver's Travels.* In that book, Swift paints a dramatic portrait of adaptation to the smells of a highly unusual environment. In the fourth and final journey related in *Gulliver's Travels,* Lemuel Gulliver finds himself marooned on an island ruled by the noble Houyhnhnms, a race of intelligent, honest, socially advanced horses. The island is populated also by nasty, barbaric humanoids, the Yahoos, whom the Houyhnhnms shun and whom Gulliver abhors. After living very happily among the horselike Houyhnhnms for more than three years, learning their language and developing great admiration for their culture, Gulliver must leave the island and return to England and the home and family that he had once loved. In Gulliver's words:

> As soon as I entered the House, my Wife took me in her Arms, and kissed me, at which having not been used to the Touch of that odious Animal for so many Years, I fell in a Swoon for almost an Hour. At the time I am writing it is Five Years since my last Return to England: During the first Year I could not endure my Wife or Children in my Presence, the very Smell of them was intolerable, much less could I suffer them to eat in the same Room. To this hour they dare not presume to touch my Bread, or drink out of the same Cup, neither was I ever able to let one of them take me by the Hand. The first Money I laid out was to buy two young Stone-Horses, which I keep in a good Stable, and next to them the Groom is my greatest Favourite; for I feel my Spirits revived by the Smell he contracts in the Stable. My Horses understand me tolerably well; I converse with them at least four Hours every Day. They are Strangers to Bridle or Saddle, they in great Amity with me, and Friendship to each other. (1726/1890, p. 331)

Many other literary examples give proper respect to the power of smell, and no list, however short, could fail to mention *Perfume,* a novel by Patrick Süskind (1986) set in the eighteenth century. *Perfume's* central character and narrator, Jean Baptiste Grenouille, was born with no body scent of his own, but with a nose that had truly incredible sensitivity to odor. His unusual olfactory powers allow him to rely on his nose rather than on his ears and eyes. Grenouille creates scents that bend other people to his will and satisfy his depraved appetites. In fact, when he sums up his infancy and early childhood, he does so in olfactory terms.

> [H]e first conjured up those that were earliest and most

BOX 14.3   Smell and Literature *(continued)*

remote: the hostile, steaming vapors of Madame Gaillard's bedroom, the bone-dry leathery bouquet of her hands, the vinegary breath of Father Terrier, the hysterical, hot maternal sweat of Bussie, the wet nurse, the carrion stench of the Cemetiere des Innocents, the homicidal stench of his mother.

Grenouille bemoans the inability of ordinary human language to express the subtleties of odors. But, of course, most people's sense of smell is so mediocre that there is no real reason for language to express what only

Grenouille could experience. The late Kurt Cobain and his band Nirvana paid musical homage to Grenouille in the song "Scentless Apprentice."

These literary nuggets illustrate how writers at diverse times and in various places have woven smell into their works. These samples are a reminder of how impoverished one's perceptual world would be without this inarticulate sense.

Odors can certainly be powerful reminders of the past. They can evoke the past accidentally, as in the examples mentioned by Helen Keller, or intentionally, as when you try to conjure up some sensory memory, some particular smell. For example, try to recollect the smell of your dentist's office, or the odor of the laboratory in that chemistry course you took. Jelena Djordjevic and her colleagues (Djordjevic et al., 2004) showed that olfactory imagery—smells intentionally generated in the mind's nose—influences the detection of actual odors. For example, when someone attempts to re-create mentally the smell of a previously encountered odorant, that olfactory image aids the detection of a weak concentration of that same odorant. This content-specific effect, which should remind you of Cheves Perky's work on visual imagery (discussed in Chapter 6), was also modality-specific. In Djordjevic's study, *visual* imagery associated with the test odorant (for example, visually imaging a rose while trying to detect the odorant phenyl ethyl alcohol, which smells roselike) had little effect on odor detection. There are other noteworthy parallels between visual and olfactory imagery. For example, visual imagery often involves eye movements, just as visual perception itself does. To see this for yourself, try to conjure up a mental image of a German shepherd dog or of the building in which you live. In doing this, you probably moved your eyes, much as you would while viewing an actual dog or that building. Kosslyn (2003) speculated that, during visual imagery, eye movements help the imaginer to reinstate the sequence and location of the imagined object's parts—where the German shepherd's tail belongs, for example. As you know, olfaction makes important use of sniffing, which is an exploratory mo-

tor behavior roughly analogous to the eye movements people make when they scan a scene or read. And sniffing plays an analogous, crucial role in olfactory imagery, as the following experiment shows.

Using an olfactometer like the one shown in Figure 14.10, Benfasi and colleagues controlled the rate at which odorant molecules were delivered to an individual's nose (Bensafi et al., 2003). Unbeknownst to the participant, the researchers also measured the person's sniffing behavior while that individual attempted to generate an auditory image ("imagine a dog barking"), a visual image ("imagine an oak tree"), or an olfactory image ("imagine the smell of a rose"). These measurements revealed that the first inhalation (sniff) after a person had been instructed to generate an olfactory image was much larger than the initial inhalation after an instruction to generate either visual or auditory image. So, when people try to imagine a familiar smell, they reflexively sniff. And the sniff accompanying imagery of a pleasant odor, such as phenyl ethyl alcohol (rose smell) is deeper than a sniff accompanying imagery of an unpleasant odor, such as ammonium sulphide (rotten eggs smell). Finally, sniffing is not merely something that *follows* in the wake of imagery; it may actually be crucial to *producing* that imagery. When people are kept from sniffing (by blocking the nasal passages with a nasal plugs), the self-rated vividness of the resulting imagery decreases considerably. Box 14.4 describes some of the key perceptual consequences of sniffing.

Helen Keller and others noted that even with no effort at all, smells could evoke powerful memories, including memories laid down long ago (Schab, 1991; Chu and Downes, 2000). In her book *A Natural History of the*

Sniffing, Nasal Airflow, and Smell BOX 14.4

You know what a sniff is: a vigorous sudden inhalation. Sniffs can be quiet or sniffs can be noisy, particularly if you've been crying and your nose is stuffed. Sniffs can be shallow or sniffs can be deep, as when you try to take in the sensory pleasures of some fresh, cool mountain air. Sniffing alters the flow of air into and through the nasal passages. And when the inhaled air is carrying odorant molecules, sniffing can change the response of the olfactory system.

With most odorant molecules, odor detection is best when air flows through the nose at a rate of about 30 liters per minute. Interestingly, when you intentionally sniff to check out some particular odor, 30 liters per minute is about the flow that you produce without even thinking about it (Laing, 1983). A good hard sniff draws an extra-large volume of air—and therefore an extra large volume of odorant—into the nasal passages. Sniffing can help you detect small amounts of airborne odorant, but surprisingly, sniffing does not alter the perceived intensity of that odorant.

According to Teghtsoonian and colleagues (1978) perceived intensity of odor remains constant regardless of the sniff's vigor. Teghtsoonian called this phenomenon **odor constancy,** because the perceived strength of an odor remains constant despite variation in flow rate. You can probably see the parallels between this phenomenon and form constancy (Chapter 5), color constancy (Chapter 7), and size constancy (Chapter 8). In all these instances, perception of objects or properties of the world remains constant despite changes in the stimulation of the receptors.

To explain odor constancy, Teghtsoonian and his colleagues suggested that the olfactory system recognizes when the increase in flow rate results from a natural sniff, and then calibrates the perception of intensity to take account of the sniff. Demonstrations of sniff-associated brain activation support this hypothesis. Sniff-induced airflow, even when inhaled air is free of odorous vapors, produces rhythmic activation—sniff for sniff—in several regions of the cerebral cortex, probably because the flow produces somatosensory stimulation (Sobel et al., 1998).

Sniffing is not the only factor that affects the flow of air into and through the nasal passages. A similar effect is produced by the nasal cycle—the alternation between engorgement of the left and right nasal passages, which we introduced earlier. Recent research shows that these cyclical changes in airflow can make the world smell different to each nostril. The neural signal that is triggered by airborne odorant molecules depends upon the number of olfactory receptor cells that are stimulated. This, in turn, depends upon the concentration of odorant molecules, the airflow, and a property of the odorant molecules known as *sorption.* Sorption is a process by which one substance takes up or holds another, as when odorant molecules are taken up by nasal mucosa. Some molecules are absorbed readily, which means they have easier access to olfactory receptor neurons (an example is L-carvone, a perfume ingredient with a minty odor); some molecules are absorbed less readily, which slows their access to receptors (an example is octane, which smells like gasoline). When air containing a low-sorption molecule flows rapidly through the nose, relatively few molecules make it through the mucosa and are picked up by receptors; but the same rapid air flow presents less challenge for high-sorption molecules. A slower airflow affords low sorption molecules a greater chance to stimulate olfactory receptors, and the nasal cycle alters the speed with which inhaled air passes through the nostrils. Noam Sobel and his colleagues (Sobel, Khan, et al., 1999) explored the impact of altered airflow on the perception of L-carvone and octane. Participants were given an opportunity to smell a mixture of these two odorant molecules, and, after each presentation, judged the two components' relative proportions. Unbeknownst to these individuals, the mixture was constant, with 50 percent L-carvone and 50 percent octane.

When the mixture was presented to the nostril whose turbinates were engorged, the resulting slowed airflow gave a relative advantage to the low-sorption molecule. As a result, people judged the mixture as containing more octane. When the same mixture was presented to the less engorged nostril, the faster airflow handicapped the low-sorption molecule, and the mixture appeared to contain more L-carvone. Sobel and colleagues speculate that this process, which presumably operates with every breath we take, presents the olfactory system with two slightly different "images" of the odor-causing world, much as the two eyes and two ears do in their respective sensory domains. Here, though, the two, slightly different images could enhance odor sensitivity by allowing different odorant molecules a good opportunity to be perceptually effective regardless of differences in their sorbtion.

Earlier we pointed out that the two nostrils seem to work in shifts, with one drawing in more air than its more engorged fellow nostril. As a consequence of this difference in airflow, the two nostrils should have

BOX 14.4 Sniffing, Nasal Airflow, and Smell *(continued)*

different odor detection thresholds. After all, a higher flow rate means more odorant molecules will be available in the nostril. To test this straightforward prediction, Sobel and colleagues (Sobel et al., 2000) measured thresholds for two odorants, vanillin (a pleasant-smelling odorant) and propionic acid (an acrid-smelling odorant); thresholds for both odorants were measured for each nostril separately. Contrary to expectation, peoples' ability to detect low levels of these odorants did not differ between the engorged, low-flow-rate nostril, and the more open, high-flow-rate nostril. This curious result was explained, though, by measuring the sniffs that people made while they tried to detect the odorants.

Sobel discovered that volunteers sniffed longer when they were working only with their low-flow-rate nostril, and made shorter sniffs when only their more open nostril was being tested. This variation in sniffing equated the total volume of odorant-carrying air that moved through the two nostrils. To clinch this point, Sobel repeated the experiment, this time keeping sniff duration constant. Now, odorant detection thresholds were higher in the engorged nostril than in the open nostril, as it should be, if thresholds depended on how many odorant molecules are available to be absorbed by receptors. Incidentally, we don't encourage unnecessary sniffing (which can annoy people around you), but when it's important to detect some weak source of smell, a long, steady sniff can come in very handy.

Senses (1990) the poet and essayist Diane Ackerman enthused this way about smell memories:

> Nothing is more memorable than a smell. One scent can be unexpected, momentary and fleeting, yet conjure up a childhood summer beside a lake in the Poconos (mountains), when wild blueberry bushes teemed with succulent fruit and the opposite sex was as mysterious as space travel; another, hours of passion on a moonlit beach in Florida, while the night-blooming cereus (flower) drenched the air with thick curds of perfume . . . ; a third, a family dinner of pot roast, noodle pudding and sweet potatoes during a myrtle-mad August in a Midwestern town. . . . Smells detonate softly in our memory like poignant land mines hidden under the weedy mass of years. Hit a tripwire of smell and memories explode all at once. A complex vision leaps out of the undergrowth. (p. 5)

Is it true, though, that nothing is more memorable than a smell? And is it fair to say that smell makes a complex vision leap out of the undergrowth? When you recollect events in which smell played a strong role, such as your visit to the circus on your sixth birthday, that recollection is accompanied by activation of your primary olfactory cortex, much as it would have been activated during the original event itself (Gottfried et al., 2004). We know that compared to memories triggered by visual or auditory stimuli, memories triggered by smell tend to be more emotional, as documented by self-report and by objective physiological measures such as heart rate. This heightened emotional tinge probably reflects activation of emotion-related areas of the brain, notably the amygdala (Herz et al., 2004). But when sensory memories are compared, there is little evidence that smell-triggered memories are more detailed or accurate than ones initiated by a visual or an auditory stimulus. In the most extensive study of this issue, Rachel Herz (2004) asked people to remember past personal experiences related to popcorn, fresh-cut grass, and a campfire. The cued stimulous was presented in one of several possible ways: 1) as a word, 2) as a short movie, such as a bowl of overflowing popcorn, 3) as a sound such as the popping of popcorn, or 4) as an odor, such as that produced by fresh popcorn. After an attempt to remember a stimulus-related personal experience, each of the 70 participants used a nine-point scale to rate the memory on emotionality, evocativeness (how much the memory felt as though they were really reliving the experience), vividness (the clarity of the memory), and specificity (how detailed the memory was). Many of the results were consistent with Diane Ackerman's paean to olfactory memory: compared to verbal, visual, and auditory memories, olfactory memories were significantly more emotional, evocative, and vivid. But when it came to specificity, all four stimuli were equivalent: Smell memories were no more specific than the others. Apparently, a memory's emotion, vividness and evocativeness does not guarantee its specificity—or even, perhaps, its accuracy (see, for example, Talarico and Rubin, 2003).

FIGURE 14.16 | The vomeronasal organ is located at the junction of the nasal septum.

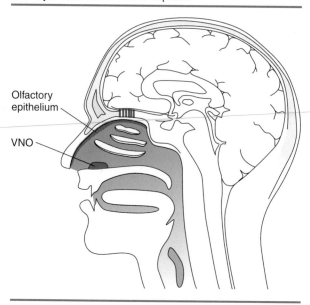

Olfactory epithelium

VNO

We'll close our discussion of olfaction by considering a vestigial portion of the olfactory system that may once have been connected to sexual arousal.

Sex and the Nose

Earlier in this chapter we discussed pheromones, those special odor messages that signal sexual receptivity. Many mammalian noses have specialized sensory structures designed solely for picking up airborne chemical signals that mediate sexual attraction, including non-odorous chemicals (Taylor, 1994). These tubelike structures, called vomeronasal organs (VNOs), are embedded in the vomer bone, a thin, flat bone that forms the lower part of the nasal septum (the partition separating the two nostrils) (see Figure 14.16). Notice that the location of the VNO is different from that of the olfactory epithe-lium, which houses the olfactory sensory neurons. In humans, the VNO resembles two very small dimples about 2 millimeters deep on the floor of the nostrils. These dimples can actually be seen with the naked eye, using a flashlight together with a device that spreads open the nostrils; a cooperative friend also helps.

Most of what is known about the anatomy and physiology of the VNO system comes from studies of nonhuman mammals. Just like olfactory sensory neurons, cells in the VNO contain specialized receptors to which certain classes of volatile molecules readily bind (Mombaerts, 2004). But VNO neural messages are carried to the brain by their own special nerve fibers, and these fibers bypass the olfactory bulb, innervating the accessory olfactory bulb instead. From there, the VNO pathway projects to the limbic system (which seems logical for a sensory channel concerned with sex). Damage to the VNO system in nonhumans produces distinct disturbances in their sexual behavior.

Perfume companies would like to think that the human VNO system is charged and ready for action. Indeed, perfumers have designed scents that include compounds meant to stimulate the VNO. At present, however, the effectiveness of these perfumes remains questionable, despite their alluring and suggestive names. As pointed out earlier, smells do influence human sexual responses, but there is no firm evidence showing that VNO activity itself affects human sexual arousal and behavior; indeed, the post-natal human VNO lacks some of the fundamental components required for a functional VNO (Doty, 2001). Moreover, the receptor cells in the human VNO lack some of the key biochemical components necessary for normal function (Kouros-Mehr et al., 2001). At best, this anatomical structure may play a role in the growth of cells from the olfactory periphery to the brain during early embryonic development, well before birth (Trotier et al., 2000). On this note we'll end our discussion of smell and move on to the last chapter where we'll consider smell's companion chemical sense, taste.

S U M M A R Y   A N D   P R E V I E W

This chapter has examined one of the two so-called minor senses, olfaction. You should now have a deeper appreciation of the important roles that odors play in our everyday lives. The biological machinery underlying odor perception is unique, compared to vision, touch, and hearing, in that olfactory receptors are constantly dying and being replaced. Olfaction also seems tightly linked to parts of the brain responsible for emotional reactions and for memory. One of olfaction's chief functions is to work in concert with its chemical sense companion, taste, to specify the flavor of foods. It is smell's chemical sense companion to which we turn in the next and final chapter.

K E Y   T E R M S

anosmia

cilia

common chemical sense

cross-adaptation

free nerve ending

mixture suppression

multidimensional scaling (MDS)

nasal cycle

odor adaptation

odor constancy

olfactometer

olfactory brain

olfactory bulb

olfactory epithelium

olfactory nerve

olfactory sensory neuron (OSN)

pheromones

specific anosmia

tip of the nose phenomenon

Chemical Senses II: Taste

We're now ready to consider smell's chemical companion: taste. You'll learn what these two "minor senses" have in common, as well as what key attributes set taste apart from smell. It goes without saying that taste is intimately related to food. So, grab your favorite beverage and enough snack food to last for the whole chapter because we're going to tackle this most delicious of sensory modalities.

We say of food, "This tastes good" or "I hate the taste of that." But taste determines not only how much we like or dislike food items, but also whether we will even consider ingesting those foods in the first place. In effect, the tongue and mouth (assisted by the nose) are designed to ensure that nutritious substances are eaten, but that noxious ones are not. Today, in many places in the world, people seldom need to rely on taste to gauge edibility— if the grocer sells it or the restaurant serves it, people assume it is safe to eat. (Unfortunately, this assumption proves wrong occasionally, which is why a careless restaurant may lose its health license.) For many humans, then, taste serves mainly to define preferences among a large group of commercially available, edible foods. Although taste is less often a matter of life and death these days, taste does generate an amazing variety of intriguing, important, and surprising perceptual experiences.

Let's start by getting straight on our terminology. The word *taste* (technically called *gustation*) refers to sensations produced when various substances dissolved in saliva penetrate the taste buds on the tongue and surfaces of the mouth. Squeeze a few drops of lemon on your tongue, and the resulting sensation is one that most people would call "taste." But when you actually *eat* something, you experience much more than taste alone: You also have an immediate appreciation of the food's smell, temperature, texture, and consistency. All these sources of information combine with the substance's taste to form a complex of sensations known as **flavor.** Although the remainder of this chapter deals primarily with the taste component of flavor, keep in mind that these other sources of sensory information also contribute to your enjoyment of food.

When you consider the sense of taste, there's one other thing that must be taken into account. More than any other sense, taste takes time. Unless you gulp down your food, the taste of any food item evolves over time. Chewing alters food's consistency and releases chemical substances contained in the food, thereby redistributing the food's chemical ingredients across your tongue and palate. As a consequence, your taste experiences change from moment to moment (Katz, Simon, and Nicolelis, 2001). So, careful chewing not only helps digestion, but also rounds out the taste pleasures of eating (Figure 15.1).

Our discussion of taste will follow the same general outline used in the discussion of smell. We'll describe the

FIGURE 15.1 | People in the food and beverage industry describe taste as having a "profile," which changes shape over time. Most foods and drinks comprise a complex of taste ingredients, that have peak impact at different times depending on concentrations and on chewing behavior. According to food experts, the top graph represents an idealized "taste" profile for a generic enjoyable food or beverage, and the bottom graph shows a profile whose components are out of balance. These attempts to scale the quality of taste over time encounter the complication of having to measure subjective experiences. Nonetheless, the notion of a taste profile seems valid based on our everyday eating experiences. The next time you're eating dinner, think about the dynamic events that are playing out in your mouth.

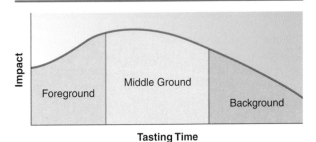

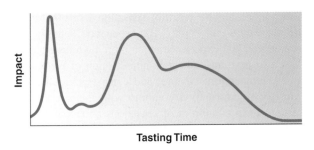

stimulus for taste, consider the question of taste categories, provide a brief overview of the anatomy and physiology of the gustatory system, and then take up the question of taste sensitivity. Finally, we'll explore interactions between taste and smell.

The Stimulus for Taste

To be tasted, a substance must be *soluble:* Some of its molecules must dissolve in saliva. This prerequisite explains why you cannot *taste* the difference between a plastic spoon and a stainless-steel spoon—neither of these materials dissolves in saliva. Moreover, food seems tasteless when the mouth contains insufficient saliva because

saliva transports taste solutions to taste receptors within the tongue and mouth. The salivary glands, incidentally, produce about 740 cubic centimeters (25 ounces) of fluid daily, much of it during eating. Some food substances, particularly those containing citric acid, promote copious salivary secretion, while others, such as glucose, produce only modest secretions. Besides aiding in digestion, saliva contains ingredients that prevent erosion of tooth enamel and eliminate bacteria in the oral cavity. In chemical composition, saliva closely resembles salt water, although the sodium content of saliva varies from one person to the next (Bradley, 1991). In fact, if you have an opportunity to swill someone else's saliva around in your mouth, you could actually taste the difference in sodium content (Bartoshuk, 1980), but we'll leave it to the intellectually curious to confirm this experience.

The Classification of Tastes

Systematic analysis of taste dates back at least 2,400 years, to Aristotle's claim that there were seven fundamental taste qualities: sweet, sour, salty, bitter, pungent, harsh, and, finally, astringent. He took these fundamental qualities to be the building blocks out of which all more complex qualities could be synthesized. In the centuries following Aristotle, new fundamental taste qualities were added to the list (such as viscous and fatty), while others were dropped (Bartoshuk, 1978). By the early nineteenth century the list had shrunk to the four categories that most people are familiar with today: sweet, sour, salty, and bitter. Incidentally, the person who formalized the four-taste idea was Hans Henning (1916), the same person responsible for the failed odor classification scheme illustrated in Figure 14.3.

In 1909 Kikunae Ikeda, of the Imperial University in Tokyo, argued that another taste quality should be added to sweet, sour, salty, and bitter. From dried seaweed, Ikeda extracted a substance that evoked a unique taste whose quality he described with the Japanese word *umami*.[1] Although at the time it drew little attention, Ikeda's work has recently attracted considerable interest, culminating in the general acceptance of *umami* as a fundamental taste quality (see Web resources at www.mhhe.com/blake5). Moreover, we now know that seaweed is not the only food that can produce *umami* taste: Many other protein-rich foods have it, including milk, aged cheese, and animal flesh. Ikeda (1909–2002) believed that the taste preference for *umami* evolved along with the intake of particularly nutritious, protein-rich foods.

---

[1]This word does not have a precise equivalent in English, but the words *savory* or *meaty* are often used.

But why did it take nearly a century for Ikeda's work to be fully embraced? Several factors retarded acceptance of his proposed fifth basic taste quality. First, the *umami* taste, unlike the other so-called taste primaries, is very mild even at high concentrations (Lindemann, Ogiwara, and Ninomiya, 2002); second, the taste that triggers the experience of *umami* is usually accompanied by other tastes, which confuse tasters; third, acceptance had to wait for the relatively recent increased Western interest in Asian cuisines, many of which use substances that produce *umami* taste (Lindemann, 2000); fourth, only recently was it possible to identify cortical subregions whose neurons seem to be specialized for *umami* taste (Rolls, 2000); fifth, many humans appear to be unable to experience *umami* (Lugaz, Pillias, and Faurion, 2002); sixth, and finally, only recently were researchers able to identify *umami*-related receptors on the tongue (Chaudhari, Landin, and Roper, 2000). Despite the expansion from four to five fundamental taste qualities, however, there remains some disagreement about whether five is the correct number or, for that matter, whether the very concept of fundamental taste qualities is really meaningful.

Erickson and Covey (1980) took an interesting approach to the notion of fundamental taste qualities. They gave people taste solutions consisting of one or more of the so-called primary tastes and asked those people to judge whether they perceived "one" or "more than one" taste quality. For comparison, Erickson and Covey asked for the same judgment about auditory tones presented either alone or in a chord (that is, as simultaneously sounded multiple tones). As expected, a single tone was always judged as one, and multiple tones were always judged as more than one. This confirms the analytical nature of pitch perception: Identification of one tone is possible in the presence of another. The results with the taste solutions were quite different. Solutions composed of a single component were sometimes judged as more than one, whereas multicomponent solutions were sometimes judged as one. Moreover, people were often unable to identify whether a mixture contained a particular component, even when they could reliably identify that component in isolation. For instance, quinine (a bitter-tasting substance) was easily recognized on its own. But when mixed with sucrose (which, of course, is sweet), the quinine in the mixture was unrecognizable. These findings led Erickson and Covey to conclude that complex tastes are *not* analyzed into primary components but instead take on their own, unique quality, which may give little hint of their ingredients (Erickson, 1982). Put another way, when they are presented in mixtures, taste-producing substances (tastants) interact with one another in complex ways. It seems that each tastant's perceptual effect can modify, and in turn is modified by, the perceptual effects of other components in the mixture. In this respect, taste is more like color vision (where mixtures of "fundamental" colors, such as red and green, can yield combinations (yellow, in this case) that contain no hint of the components.

Despite these findings, many taste researchers are reluctant to give up the idea of primary taste qualities, and after 2,400 years, the debate over how many primaries there are is as heated as ever. For the moment, though, we'll set aside the question of primaries and proceed to a less controversial, more enlightening topic, the neural mechanisms of taste perception.

Anatomy and Physiology of Taste

The Taste Receptors

Let's begin by taking a tour of the tongue and the inside of the mouth, guided by the diagrams in Figure 15.2. The tongue consists mainly of muscle covered with mucous membrane. To see taste's basic terrain take a careful look at your own tongue in a mirror. Notice that it is covered with little bumps. These bumps are called **papillae** (from the Latin *papula,* meaning "pimple"). When viewed from the side, they resemble regularly spaced columns separated by channels. The walls of the papillae are lined with tiny structures, called **taste buds,** which are shaped like garlic bulbs. These taste buds house the receptor cells responsible for registering the presence of chemical substances.

Not all the papillae scattered over your tongue contain taste buds. For example, papillae in the center of the tongue have no taste buds, which is why food confined to this area has no taste. The center of the tongue is analogous to the blind spot in the eye: Both are devoid of receptors. There's another parallel between the tongue and the eye. Under normal conditions, you don't notice the visual blind spot because the brain fills it in; similarly, you're unaware of the tongue's "blind spot." In fact, taste sensations seem to originate from the mouth's entire surface, including from regions with no receptors (Todrank and Bartoshuk, 1991). Moreover, when the taste information from an entire side of the tongue is blocked, for example by a viral disease, there is no change in everyday experiences of taste (Pfaffmann and Bartoshuk, 1989, 1990)—taste sensations always seem to fill the entire mouth.

Taste buds are not restricted to the tongue: the throat, the roof of the mouth, and the inside of the cheeks all have taste buds, though they are not housed in papillae. Just about every region of the mouth, tongue, and palette

FIGURE 15.2 | This series of drawings shows the arrangement of papillae on the tongue, the configuration of taste buds within an individual papilla, and the components of an individual taste cell. Receptors sensitive to certain molecules are located on the microvilli that extend into the clefts between papillae, where saliva brings taste substances into contact with the receptors.

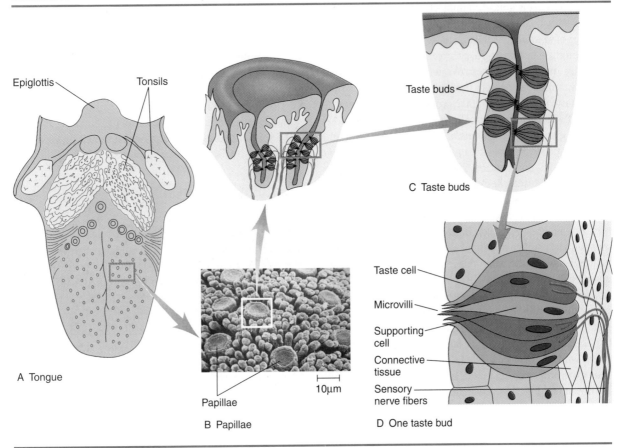

has some taste buds, and can therefore generate taste-related signals. The only exceptions are the underside of the tongue and the soft tissues that lie beneath the tongue. Some animals have an even broader distribution of structures similar to taste buds, with such structures on parts of their bodies other than the tongue and mouth. Fish, who live in a watery equivalent of saliva, have taste receptors scattered over the surface of their bodies. And some insects have taste receptors on their feet, enabling them to sample the chemical composition of the surfaces they walk over. But let's return to the human tongue and the receptor mechanisms for taste.

Those papillae on the human tongue that do contain taste buds have anywhere from several hundred buds down to just a single bud (Bradley, 1979), with a grand total of something like 10,000 taste buds distributed throughout the inside of the average human mouth; about 9,000 of those taste buds are on the tongue. We stress *average,* because the total number of buds varies enormously among individuals. One count from the tongues of healthy, college-age volunteers showed a fourteen-fold variation within the sample, from the tongue with the most buds to the tongue with fewest (Miller and Reedy, 1990). Interestingly, participants with the highest taste bud counts rated taste solutions of a given concentration as more intense than did participants with the fewest taste buds.

The density of taste buds also varies with age. Infants start out life with relatively few taste buds, but during childhood the number steadily increases and reaches peak density. Around age 40, the trend reverses and the overall number of taste buds declines (Cowart, 1981). This decline may account for much of the well-documented loss of taste sensitivity in the elderly (Schiffman, 1997; Mojet, Christ-Hazelhof, and Heidema, 2001). Even on tongues that boast a great many taste buds, those taste buds actually occupy only a small fraction of the available space, which means that as far as taste is concerned most of the tongue is actually a vast wasteland: Less than 1 percent of the surface area of the normal adult human tongue contains taste receptors. Of course, the human tongue serves important functions besides mediating taste. For example, the heavily muscled human tongue propels drink and chewed food toward the back of the throat. As well, the tongue plays an essential role in speech production and, occasionally, a supporting role during kissing. Your tongue also contains many nontaste receptors, which carry information about touch, pain, and temperature to the brain via a branch of the trigeminal nerve (the largest of your 12 cranial nerves). We'll return later to the impact of these nontaste receptors and neural signals to the experience of taste itself.

Like the olfactory receptors you read about in the last chapter, taste buds, too, degenerate over time, and are replaced by new ones (Beidler and Smallman, 1965). The life expectancy of an individual taste bud is only about 10 days. Hence, throughout your lifetime there is a continuous, rapid turnover within the large population of taste buds. Unlike olfactory cells, however, taste buds do not have axons that project to the brain. In a moment, we'll see how taste information is carried to the brain. Now, though, let's take a closer look at one of these short-lived but very important cells.

The diagram on the bottom right of Figure 15.2 illustrates what an individual taste bud looks like under the microscope, and the magnified photograph in Figure 15.3 shows an actual taste bud. Each tiny bud contains an average of 50 individual taste receptor cells, arranged within the bud like the individual cloves that make up a head of garlic. Sprouting from the end of each taste receptor cell is a slender, threadlike structure called the *microvillus*. A clump of these "threads" juts into a tiny opening in the wall of the taste bud, which is bathed in saliva. Several different types of saliva-borne chemical stimuli, upon contacting the microvilli, produce a change in the taste bud's electrical state; those are listed in Table 15.1. Notice that these different types of tastants vary in size and in the kind of taste quality they tend to evoke.

Sensory transduction—a taste bud's conversion of chemical into electrical energy—involves mechanisms that vary with stimulus type. For example, some ions are thought to enter the receptor membrane and directly alter

FIGURE 15.3 | Magnified photograph of an individual taste bud. Taste buds average about 45 microns in diameter and, therefore, are too small for the unaided eye to see.

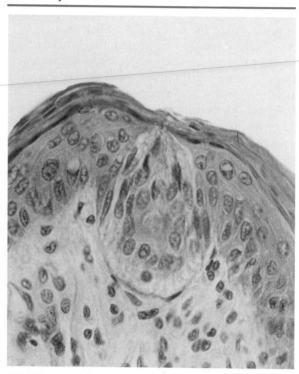

TABLE 15.1 | Stimuli for Taste Categories

Stimulus	Stimulus size	Examples	Taste
Ion	Small	Sodium ions	Salty
		Potassium ions	Sour
Amino acid	Medium	Glutamate	Umami
Complex molecule	Large	Glucose	Sweet
		Quinine	Bitter

the cell's electrical potential. In contrast, when an amino acid or a complex molecule is the chemical stimulus, the movement of that chemical stimulus to a bud's microvilli triggers a cascade of events inside the cell. This cascade resembles the intracellular events in olfactory transduction and in visual transduction (Roper, 1992).

Mucous secretions from supporting cells in taste buds wash away excess stimulus substances from the vicinity of the taste bud. This cleansing action is analogous to that we described for the olfactory epithelium. But because the tongue's self-cleansing is relatively slow, aftertastes can linger after you have swallowed or spit out whatever was in your mouth.

Can we relate the responses of the tongue's sensory receptors to specific taste qualities? For decades, textbooks gave a mistaken impression that particular taste sensations were exclusively associated with different regions on the tongue. It was customary to show a "tongue map" that identified different taste experiences with different parts of the tongue (e.g., "sweet" confined to the tip of the tongue and "bitter" toward the back of the tongue). In fact, however, taste qualities—and the receptor types mediating those qualities—are fairly well intermingled over the tongue; they do not seem to be uniquely identified with taste buds at particular locations. However, it is true that different areas of the tongue tend to be differentially sensitive to very dilute concentrations of given taste substances. For example, weak salty solutions are more readily detected when the solution bathes taste buds on the sides of the tongue.

But there is a high degree of specificity between different receptors and different taste qualities (Kim et. al, 2004). This specificity shows up when neural activity is recorded from the afferent nerves innervating taste receptors (Frank, 2000), and taste specificity can also be demonstrated by measuring chemical reactions within the receptors themselves while being exposed to different taste components (Caicedo and Roper, 2001). One of the most innovative, revealing techniques for examining the specificity and function of taste transduction in the mammalian tongue involves using techniques borrowed from the field of genetic engineering. Knowing that genes govern the molecular structure of proteins comprising taste receptors, one can identify specific genes that presumably code for specific receptor types. But identifying a candidate gene does not prove that its protein product actually works as a taste detector—the critical test involves creating mutant animals in which the candidate gene is deleted or, as it's termed, "knocked-out." If the knocked-out gene does indeed specify a protein critical for the function under study, the "knock-out animal" should fail to exhibit behavior dependent on that function. Thus, if a given gene mediates synthesis of taste receptors specific for sweet, a mouse lacking this gene should show no preference for sweetened water versus nonsweetened water (a highly uncharacteristic behavior for normal mice). Several research groups have used this innovative technique in the last few years, to identify genes responsible for creating receptors sensitive to sweet, bitter, and *umami* tastes (Davenport,

2001). In the next few paragraphs, we'll highlight the results from one of those groups.

Using these gene-altering techniques in combination with behavioral preference testing, Charles Zuker and colleagues (Zhao et al., 2003) have demonstrated a remarkable degree of specificity in the early processing of taste quality. In particular, they were able to engineer one group of mice that showed no response to sweet substances but showed normal sensitivity to *umami* and another group of mice that were insensitive to *umami* but still enjoyed sweet substances.

There are substantial similarities between the genetics and molecular structure of taste receptors among all mammalians species, including our own. However, some differences do exist (which makes sense, because nutritional demands vary widely among species). Thus, for example, humans can taste several natural and artificial sweeteners, such as aspartame, which mice do not taste (that is, mice show no behavioral preference for these substances over plain water). Zuker and colleagues have identified some small, but potentially crucial molecular difference between mouse and human sweet receptors. This allowed them to introduce the human sweet receptor gene into the mouse genome. This "knock-in" operation (the addition or substitution of a novel gene) did indeed "humanize" the mouse's tongue: unlike normal mice, knock-in mice showed a clear preference for sweeteners, including aspartame, that humans find appealing. These remarkable results demonstrate that by altering an animal's taste receptors one alters the range of taste sensations experienced by that animal; novel taste experiences can be created and ordinarily familiar ones deleted from the animal's taste repertoire. Reminiscent of what Newton said of color vision (Chapter 7), we again see that perceptual qualities depend crucially on the responses within sensory mechanisms encoding those qualities, not just the environmental stimuli triggering those responses.

Rounding out this story on genetics and taste, a group of researchers at the Monell Chemical Senses Center discovered that in an estimated 30 percent of humans, the gene sequence coding for the protein mediating sweet tastes differs from that of the remaining 70 percent of their sample. It would seem that this genetic variation is bound to alter the protein configuration and, therefore, the receptor's responsiveness to sweet. Do these "unusual" humans perceive sweet tastes differently? Work currently underway should provide an answer to that question soon. Interested students can visit the Monell website to learn more about the latest research on taste (find the website address at www.mhhe.com/blake5).

To finish this survey of the tongue and its receptors, recall that some of the tongue's receptors signal pain, touch, or temperature, rather than taste. One class of such receptors is responsible for the burning sensation produced by chewing a hot pepper. This receptor registers the presence of capsaicin, the active ingredient in peppers that we mentioned in Chapter 13. Signals generated by this receptor are carried to the brain by fibers in a branch of the trigeminal nerve. Using molecular biological techniques, Caterina and colleagues (2000) created a strain of knock-out mice that lacked this class of receptor. The result? Caterina's knock-out mice readily would drink capsaicin-laced water, which normal mice diligently avoid. These genetically altered mice also show little reaction to direct injection of capsaicin under their skin, whereas normal mice scratch and lick at the injection site as if experiencing discomfort. These findings suggest that the genes controlling manufacture of capsaicin-sensitive receptors on the tongue may also be involved in the creation of pain receptors elsewhere in the body. You may see some parallel between these pain-insensitive knock-out mice and people you know who pour liberal amounts of hot sauce on their food, or who gobble down whole chili peppers in Mexican or Indian restaurants.

Having looked at various types of receptors on the tongue, let's now consider how messages generated by those receptors are represented in nerve fibers carrying information from the taste receptors to the brain.

The Taste Pathways

Figure 15.4 summarizes the overall organization and flow of neural information from the periphery of the gustatory system to the brain. Taste is unique in that it sends its neural messages over two **cranial nerves,** not just one nerve as in the case of vision (optic nerve), hearing (auditory nerve), and smell (olfactory nerve).[2] Fibers in one branch of the facial nerve (CN VII) innervate the front two-thirds of the tongue, with some fibers carrying information from the tongue's left side, others the right. The rear one-third of the tongue is innervated by fibers comprising the glossopharyngeal nerve (CN IX), again with different fibers innervating two sides of the tongue.

---

[2]The cranial nerves, 12 in all, emerge from or enter the skull (the cranium); some cranial nerves carry information from the sense organs of the head. Cranial nerves, each having several branches, are designated either with Roman numerals (from I to XII) or by name (I = olfactory, II = optic, V = trigeminal, VII = facial, VIII = auditory, IX = glossopharyngeal, and X = vagus).

FIGURE 15.4 | A schematic diagram showing the gustatory system's neural circuitry. The chorda tympani branch of cranial nerve VII (facial nerve) and a branch of cranial nerve IX (glossopharyngeal nerve) carry taste information from the front and rear of tongue, respectively. Note the many double-headed arrows; they signify reciprocal connectivity between regions (that is, influences in both directions). VPM = ventroposteriormedial region of the thalamus. GC = gustatory cortex. OFC = orbitofrontal cortex. Not shown is a branch of cranial nerve V (trigeminal nerve), which carries touch, temperature, and pain signals from much of the tongue (and the lower teeth), and also controls the muscles involved in chewing and moving the tongue.

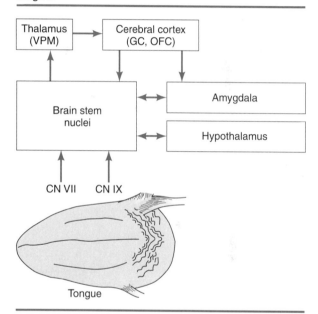

What about the receptors of the tongue and mouth that register stimulus information generated by touch, pain, and temperature? Neural signals from these nontaste receptors are carried to the brain by a branch of a third cranial nerve, namely the trigeminal nerve, and as already mentioned, the sensations carried by this nerve also contribute to your experience of flavor when eating food or drinking beverages (Cruz and Green, 2000).

Let's continue tracing the flow of taste information along fibers in two cranial nerves from the tongue to nuclei in the brainstem (see Figure 15.4). The axons of the brainstem neurons innervated by these cranial nerves, in turn, funnel taste-related information upward along two different pathways. These two pathways mediate different

FIGURE 15.5 | Diagram showing the location of the insula, which is the location of the primary gustatory cortex ("primary" in the sense that this region receives direct projections from the thalamaus). The insula cannot be seen from the surface of the cerebral cortex; it is buried within the lateral fissure separating the temporal lobe from the parietal and frontal lobes. Other cortical areas involved in taste perception (not shown) are distributed among locations toward the base of the temporal and frontal lobes.

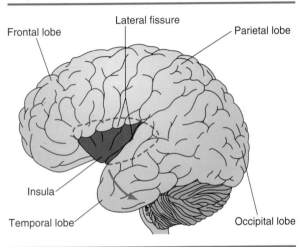

aspects—and consequences—of taste perception. One of these pathways runs through a nucleus in the thalamus (the thalamus is a way station for every sense except olfaction). The other pathway runs from the brain stem to the amygdala and the hypothalamus, anatomical structures that influence emotional responses to sensations from the mouth (amygdala) and that control appetite, turning ingestion on or off.

In the thalamic nuclei that receive taste information, taste-responsive neurons are intermixed with other neurons, which respond to tactile and/or thermal stimulation. All of these thalamic neurons project to the primary taste area in the cerebral cortex (Figure 15.5). Known as the **gustatory cortex,** this area of cortex cannot be seen from a surface view of the cerebral cortex—to visualize the gustatory cortex, one must peel away the temporal lobe from the parietal and frontal lobes, separating them along the lateral fissure (much like separating adjacent wedges of an orange). This reveals the insula, another cortical region with many folds, and it is here that one finds the gustatory cortex, the taste analogue to the visual cortex and the auditory cortex. In humans, damage to the primary

taste area undermines the ability to identify taste substances and the ability to judge their intensity (Pritchard, Macaluso, and Eslinger, 1999; Small, Zatorre, and Jones-Gotman, 2001; Kim and Choi, 2002). Moreover, direct electrical stimulation of this region elicits taste experiences in people who are awake while undergoing brain surgery (Penfield and Faulk, 1955). The exact location and boundaries of the primary taste area within the insula have been difficult to pin down, partly because taste stimuli also stimulate the touch system, which can stymie attempts to localize brain responses to taste alone. (The insula is close to the tactile representation of the tongue and the mouth in the somatosensory cortex, which you read about in Chapter 12.) This complication arising from the close proximity of taste and touch can be reduced by keeping touch stimulation constant, for example by embedding a tastant solution momentarily into a constant, steady stream of water (Kobayakawa et al., 1999).

The brain's other cortical region for taste, the secondary taste area, is found in the frontal cortex, right above the orbits that house the eyes (in the orbito-frontal cortex [OFC] in Figure 15.4). Neurons in this secondary taste area signal taste attributes that have a clear behavioral relevance, especially the reward value of what is being tasted. The orbito-frontal cortex is a general repository of information about behaviorally relevant dimensions of stimulation associated with taste and other sensory modalities including smell. Using fMRI to characterize patterns of brain activation, Francis and colleagues (1999) demonstrated that adjacent neighborhoods in orbito-frontal cortex respond to pleasant taste (glucose in moderate concentrations), pleasant smell (vanillin), and pleasant touch (light stroking of the skin with a piece of velvet). The link shared by all these stimuli is a common hedonic dimension, pleasantness. This convergence of neural signals associated with pleasant stimulation from different sensory modalities makes sense, for the fronto-orbital cortex is crucially involved in emotion reactions.

If neurons in this secondary taste area were actually signaling the potential reward value of some ingested substance, those signals should vary with what the animal had eaten most recently. If you've just consumed several pieces of mushroom pizza and feel sated, you probably don't want any more pizza right now. But the attractiveness of, say, a slice of watermelon might not be affected at all; your satiety, in other words, is food specific. And sure enough, some neurons in the secondary taste area do indeed reflect an animal's recent history with particular tastes. Prolonged exposure to one particular taste quality, say *umami*, diminishes the normal responsiveness of neurons that are selectively responsive to that quality (Rolls et al., 1998). Under ordinary conditions, food-specific satiety depends not just on the food's taste, but on its smell as well (Mennella and Beauchamp, 1999; O'Doherty et al., 2000). As you'll see later in the chapter, specific satiety plays a key role in the development of food preferences.

The Gustatory Code: How Do You Know *What* You're Eating?

How can the brain know *what* taste substance is actually present on the tongue? What attributes of the gustatory system's neural responses represent sensory *quality?* This question of uniqueness in taste coding should remind you of the same issue, which we discussed in the previous chapter in connection with olfaction. To answer the coding question, Carl Pfaffmann (1955) proposed the **cross-fiber theory** of taste quality. According to his hypothesis, taste quality was represented in the *pattern* of activity across a population of nerve fibers that carry information from the tongue to the brain (see also Erickson 1968, 1984). This idea should remind you of profile analysis, which was introduced in Chapter 4, and revisited in Chapters 11 and 14. Of course, this cross-fiber theory could work only if taste fibers responded better to some substances than to others. If each nerve fiber's response to all taste substances was exactly the same, the cross-fiber pattern of activity would be the same for all substances as well, and therefore useless or completely uninformative about which taste substances were actually on the tongue. In fact, although most neurons in the taste system are responsive to several taste stimuli, each responds best to some particular tastant or class of tastants, such as sweet, bitter, or *umami* (Frank, 2000). As you might imagine, this selectivity of taste response in nerve fibers is ultimately determined by the set of receptors whose responses feed each taste nerve fiber.

So neurons in nerves that carry information from the tongue to the brain respond selectively to different taste substances, but this is not the complete story. Recently, researchers have called attention to one very important but previously overlooked dimension of sensory coding: time.

Katz, Nicolelis, and Simon (2002) showed that the patterns of activation among neurons in the gustatory cortex (GC) change over the first few seconds following intake of food. These changes constitute time-dependent variation in the nature of the information carried by the neurons' responses. By measuring the correlation between a neuron's response and the presence of a par-

ticular stimulus, Katz and colleagues quantified how reliably that neuron could signal the presence of that stimulus. For example, if a neuron always responded strongly in the presence of a particular tastant, but was unresponsive otherwise, that neuron's response would be a highly reliable sign that this tastant was present. This measure of reliability can be characterized as the information content of a neuron's response (for a short, accessible introduction to this concept, see Reinagel, 2000). Katz and colleagues found that the information content of GC neurons' responses changed systematically as food was taken into the mouth and chewed. These changes could be categorized into three epochs. In the earliest epoch, as food first made contact with the tongue and tissues of the mouth, GC neurons generated reliable somatosensory information, but relatively poor information about the substance's taste itself. About one-fifth of a second later, at the start of the second epoch, responses from the same GC neurons were generating reliable information about the food's taste qualities—essentially, what tastant was present. Finally, about one second after the food first touched the tongue, during the final epoch, GC neurons' responses generated reliable information about the food's palatability. Presumably, responses during this last epoch before food is swallowed or spit out reflect multiple sources of input about taste quality, appetite, temperature, and food texture. It is tempting to relate this epoch-by-epoch evolution of neural taste information to the subjective taste profile illustrated in Figure 15.1.

The tastes produced by various substances differ not only in quality but also in intensity, depending on the concentration of the substance and on the tongue's sensitivity to that substance. Most taste experts believe that the level of activity within individual fibers signals intensity, since firing rate increases with the concentration of the stimulating solution. Moreover, if the same solution remains on the tongue for several seconds, a taste fiber's activity quickly drops from its initial level to a somewhat lower one. You might suspect that this drop in neural activity explains why repeated sampling of the same food or drink dulls your sense of taste. However, this can't be the entire story, for adaptation of taste sensations may take anywhere from several seconds to a few minutes. Instead of adaptation, the decreased response of taste fibers probably serves a specific function—getting the tongue ready for new taste solutions.

Having surveyed the anatomy and physiology of taste, we're now ready to consider aspects of taste perception as assessed using behavioral techniques.

The Perceptual Experiences Associated with Taste

Detection and Identification

Several factors influence detection and identification of taste substances. First, near the limit of sensitivity, where the presence of a substance is barely detectable, it is almost impossible to identify what it is you're tasting—all you know is that it's not plain water (McBurney, 1978). To confirm this point, try the following experiment. Fill three identical glasses with equal amounts of water. (The water should be at room temperature.) Place a few grains of sugar in one and a few grains of salt in another and stir both thoroughly. Don't add anything to the water in the third glass. While you keep your eyes closed, have a friend hand you each glass one at a time. Take a sip from each and see if you can pick out the one containing plain water. To do this requires merely *detecting* that the other two contain "something" and you should be able to do this. Next, try to pick the glass containing sugar and the one containing salt. This task requires *identifying* the tastes. If you were sufficiently frugal in the amounts you added to each glass, this task should be difficult if not impossible. Realizing that you can succeed just by guessing, see how many times you are correct over a series of 10 trials. For this demonstration to work, you may need to use less salt than sugar in the solutions. The reason is that, when both solutions are at room temperature, a salt solution can be detected at one-third the concentration that is necessary for the detection of sugar.

For most people, sensitivity is greatest to bitter tastes. So, if you repeated the taste detection test using quinine, you'd have to add only a minute quantity to the water. Some people, however, have difficulty tasting bitter substances. In 1931, Arthur Fox, an industrial chemist, synthesized a compound called phenylthiocarbamide (PTC). Some PTC powder got into the air and finally found its way into the mouth of one of Fox's colleagues. The colleague complained that Fox's creation was very bitter and tasted awful, but Fox couldn't taste anything at all. Testing still other colleagues, Fox found some people readily experienced PTC's bitter taste while others could not. We now know that PTC tastes distinctly bitter for about two out of every three people, with the remaining one-third hardly detecting any taste at all. This divergence in sensitivity to bitter is true for other substances too, including 6-*n*-propylthiouracil, known as PROP, and others we will mention later. In all these bitter substances, atoms of nitrogen, carbon, and sulphur are linked in a characteristic molecular structure.

Studies of taste abilities within different families show that sensitivity to the bitterness of PTC or PROP is genetically determined. Individuals to whom PTC doesn't taste bitter ("nontasters," as they've been called) have two recessive genes for this trait; those who are sensitive to the bitter ("tasters") have one or two dominant genes for the trait. (Inexpensive paper strips impregnated with PTC are readily available from science supply firms; you might want to purchase some to test yourself and friends.)

Neither PTC nor PROP are commonly found in food, so the inability to taste them has little practical consequence. However, Linda Bartoshuk and co-workers found that tasters and nontasters also differ in their responses to a number of less exotic bitter substances (Miller and Bartoshuk, 1991), including caffeine (one of the bitter ingredients in coffee). In fact, nontasters do not perceive the caffeine in a typical cup of coffee as bitter at all, whereas tasters do (Hall et al., 1975). This means, then, that a cup of black coffee will seem more bitter to some people than to others. Some individuals who add lots of sugar and cream to their coffee may be tasters who are struggling to tone down a degree of bitterness that nontasters never experience. Nontasters are also less sensitive than tasters to the "burning" sensation produced by alcohol dabbed on the tongue (Duffy, Peterson, and Bartoshuk, 2004). This differential sensitivity may influence liking, disliking, and hence consumption, of beverages containing alcohol. Indeed, it has been found that nontasters report consuming alcohol more frequently than do tasters (Duffy, Peterson, and Bartoshuk, 2004).

During her research on the genetics and psychophysics of taste, Bartoshuk realized that not all tasters were equal. In particular, approximately 25 percent of people tested found PTC or PROP to be so bitter that they began to choke and gag, an extreme response. For another 25 percent of those tested, were completely insensitive to the taste of PTC-PROP. And the remaining 50 percent of those tested were able to taste the substance but didn't find it particularly displeasing. To distinguish people with extreme sensitivity from ordinary tasters, Bartoshuk dubbed people with high sensitivity "supertasters" and those unable to taste PTC-PROP as "nontasters."

These striking individual differences in taste sensitivity can be traced to the tongue. When Bartoshuk inspected people's tongues closely, she discovered dramatic differences among the numbers of papillae on the tongues of nontasters, tasters, and supertasters. Generally speaking, the tongue of the average supertaster has

FIGURE 15.6 | The diagram at the top of the figure shows the area of the human tongue highlighted in the two photographs at the bottom of the figure (one the tip of the tongue from a supertaster and the other from the tongue of a nontaster). The tongues were dyed blue (temporarily) to make the papillae visible. The label "fungiform' papillae" refers to those papillae containing taste receptors.

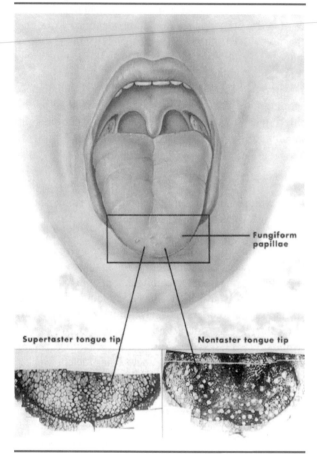

Fungiform papillae

Supertaster tongue tip

Nontaster tongue tip

more than twice as many papillae—and hence more taste buds—than does the tongue of the average nontaster. These differences are illustrated in the photographs shown in Figure 15.6. Box 15.1 provides instructions you can use to perform your own version of Bartoshuk's measurements of papillae density. Accompanying the increased number of papillae in supertasters is an increased number of pain fibers. As you might guess, then, supertasters also experience a more intense oral burn when eating chili peppers. (The Web

resource located at www.mhhe.com/blake5 will take you to a Web page with instructions for finding out whether you're a supertaster.)

An individual's status, as taster, supertaster, or nontaster, contributes to liking or disliking certain foods (Prescott et al., 2004). One of this book's authors (RS) is inordinately fond of unsweetened grapefruit juice while the other (RB) shudders at the bitterness of grapefruit juice when drinking it. RS, as you might guess, is a nontaster while RB is a taster. But why do we single out grapefruit juice? The ingredient that makes grapefruit juice seem bitter to most people is a bioflavonoid called naringin.[3] In laboratory tests, people who respond strongly to the taste of PTC or PROP find naringin solutions bitter, and they try to avoid drinking grapefruit juice (Drewnowski, Henderson, and Shore, 1997). Orange juice, incidentally, contains no naringin, so when tasters and nontasters are tested with that citrus beverage, the two groups do not differ in preference.

On rare occasions, an individual's taste preferences change from a private matter to a public, political one. Take the case of vegetables such as broccoli and brussel sprouts. Such vegetables are touted as containing powerful anticancer agents, but some people avoid them assiduously. One reason could be that to supertasters these vegetables have a strong bitter taste.[4] Although that might be an explanation, chances are it's not the only one. In 1990, then U.S. President George H. W. Bush stunned vegetable farmers and public health officials by asserting, "I do not like broccoli. And I haven't liked it since I was a little kid and my mother made me eat it. And I'm President of the United States and I'm not going to eat any more broccoli!"

Bush's offhand comment stimulated some taste researchers to speculate that he was a supertaster. But until the supertaster hypothesis is verified or disconfirmed by direct measurement of Bush's tongue, it would be prudent to entertain alternatives. Look at Bush's entire proclamation, particularly the part about his mother. Sometimes people shun particular foods because their parents were too heavy-handed in "encouraging" their progeny to consume those foods. A child's taster status and parental

---

[3]Bioflavonoids such as naringin are vital to good health, which is why nutritionists urge people to eat plants containing them. When taken into the body, bioflavonoids contribute to good blood circulation by maintaining the structural integrity of small blood vessels.

[4]To accommodate people for whom broccoli is too bitter to eat, plant scientists have bred a new vegetable called broccolini. This cross between broccoli and kale has a milder and sweeter taste than broccoli.

By performing this exercise you'll accomplish two things: (1) you'll gain an appreciation for the range of individual differences in papillae on the tongue, and (2) you'll learn who your true friends are. Here are the six items you'll need: a cotton swab, a good desk lamp, some blue food dye, a small magnifying glass, a gummed reinforcement of the kind used on loose-leaf pages and, hardest to come by, a supply of cooperative, trusting experimental volunteers.

Ask one of the volunteers to stick out his or her tongue, while you glue the reinforcement on it, near the tongue's tip. Now, using the cotton swab, put a small drop of blue food dye into the hole in the reinforcement's center. Be careful not to use too much food dye; you don't want the color to run, and you don't want the blue color to be too saturated. Now carefully remove the reinforce-

ment; with the magnifying glass and desk lamp, you should see a group of tiny pink circles on a background of blue. Each pink circle is a papilla. From a count of the papilla in that small circular area, you can predict, with very good accuracy, how the tongue's owner would respond to bitter substances such as PTC and PROP. If you counted fewer than 20 papillae, odds are that the person is a nontaster; if you counted more than 40 papillae, you can bet the person is a supertaster, someone extremely sensitive to PTC and PROP. Papillae counts between these two levels, that is, between 20 and 40, make it likely the person is a taster.

If you make such measurements on a number of people, there's no doubt you will be astonished by the differences, and you'll never again look at tongues the same way.

---

overzealousness could go hand in hand. A child whose taste buds tell him that this green stuff is "yucky" may require extra strong encouragement to consume it, which further diminishes the palatability of that green stuff.

In previous chapters you saw how attention and expectation could influence the detectability of weak sensory stimulation, and in the previous chapter you read how expectation can influence perception of odor. Taste sensitivity also benefits from these kinds of "top-down" influences, as the following study demonstrates. Using a forced-choice procedure (see appendix), Marks and Wheeler (1998) measured detection thresholds for sucrose (which tastes sweet) and citric acid (which tastes sour). On each trial, a person tasted two samples: one, deionized water and the other, a dilute solution of either sucrose or citric acid.[5] The person's task was merely to identify which of the two samples contained the dilute tastant. The person did not have to identify the taste or in any other way try to distinguish sweet from sour. Throughout the trials, Marks and Wheeler were careful to present the deionized water and dilute tastant randomly.

In some blocks of trials, people knew ahead of time that sucrose would be the dilute substance presented most of the time, with citric acid being presented infrequently. In other blocks of trials, people knew that citric

acid was much more likely than sucrose. This maneuver, Marks and Wheeler reasoned, should direct peoples' attention to sucrose when it was more likely and to citric acid when it was more likely. Throughout a given testing session, concentrations of both solutions were very near the detection threshold, meaning that people had to concentrate to pick out which solution contained the tastant. To reiterate, people did not have to judge whether they tasted sucrose or citric acid; all they had to do was discriminate tasteless water from water containing a weak taste solution. The result? People could detect weaker concentrations of a given solution when they were anticipating presentation of that solution. So, for example, thresholds for detecting sucrose in blocks of sucrose-dominant trials were lower than were thresholds when the citric acid was dominant. Thus, as in other sensory modalities, foreknowledge of the likelihood of a given stimulus seems to direct your attention to subtle cues registering the presence of that stimulus, the consequence being improved detection performance. Very recently, Ashkenazi and Marks (2004) reconfirmed this boost in detection performance when sampling a weak tastant but, surprisingly, they also found that attention did *not* boost detection of a weak odorant. Several interesting hypotheses for this finding were offered, including the possibility that neural signals from taste, but not from olfaction, project through the thalamus, which, as we discussed in Chapter 4, may be involved in gating attention.

In the attention studies mentioned above, the experimenters made sure that all solutions came to room tem-

---

[5]As its name suggests, *deionized* water is water from which ions have been removed. Because such ions can impart subtle but detectable taste to water, their removal renders the water as tasteless as possible.

FIGURE 15.7 | The effect of temperature on taste sensitivity for sweet, sour, salty, and bitter. The curve for *umami* is not shown because those results are currently unknown.

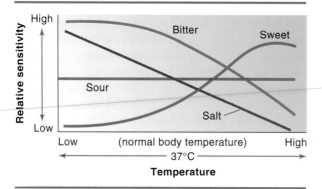

perature (21 degrees C) before being used. The reason for such care, which is typical in good experiments on taste, is that sensitivity varies markedly with temperature. Moreover, different taste substances are not equally affected by temperature, as illustrated in Figure 15.7. Note that bitter substances become more difficult to detect at higher temperatures, whereas sensitivity to sweet substances increases with temperature. Think what this tells you about the effect of temperature on the taste of various foods and drinks. For instance, wine advertisements that urge you to serve their product well chilled may be trying to hide its sweet taste, a common fault with some unrefined wines. The variations in sensitivity shown in Figure 15.7 also underscore an important rule for cooking: If you season food on the basis of taste, the final seasoning should be done only after the dish has reached serving temperature.

While on the topic of temperature and taste, here's a peculiar taste illusion that was inadvertently discovered recently during a routine study to measure the thermal sensitivity of the human tongue. Knowing that the tongue contains temperature receptors (of the sort discussed in Chapter 12), Cruz and Green (2000) wanted to learn whether individuals could tell whether a small region of the tongue was being heated or being cooled by a small probe applied to the tongue. To everyone's surprise—subjects and experimenters—changes in temperature evoked taste sensations! When the probe was in contact with the front edge of the tongue, an increase in temperature from 20 degrees C to 35 degrees C produced a sensation of sweetness; a drop in temperature from 35 degrees C to 20 degrees C produced a sensation of sour

or salty. On the back of the tongue, cooling produced a noticeable bitter taste. These warm and cool temperature values, incidentally, are well within the range ordinarily experienced when eating ice cream or hot soup, so these taste illusions are not being triggered by highly unusual conditions. Of course, during normal eating we don't experience thermally induced tastes because we don't restrict hot or cold foods to one region of the tongue and, moreover, hot and cold foods have their own unique tastes that would mask any effect of their temperature. Still, the existence of this illusion points to possible neural interactions between messages carried by thermal and gustatory receptors on the tongue, receptors that innervate different nerve fibers but end up projecting to common brain areas. For more on the nontaste abilities of your mouth and tongue, see Box 15.2.

Is there anything to the folk wisdom that your ability to taste is better when you're hungry? The results of a recent study (Zverev, 2004) suggests the answer is yes if by "ability to taste" one means detecting very weak solutions. In that study, hungry volunteers could detect weaker concentrations of sugar water and salt water than could volunteers who had just eaten a meal. Sensitivity to bitter solutions, however, was not different for these two groups. From the standpoint of fitness, it makes sense that "bitter" would not be affected by hunger: This taste experience is associated with avoidance of potentially toxic substances, whereas sweet and salty are indicators of eatable substances. But how does hunger exert its effect on sensitivity to these two tastants? This effect could arise from interactions within the taste cortical areas, since hunger influences neural responsiveness within these areas (Rolls et al., 1998). It is also possible that the boost in sensitivity for sweet and for salty arises from feedback signals to the receptors from the brain (*efferent signals,* as they are called), signals that could modulate the sensory responses of the receptors (Zverev, 2004).

One misconception about taste concerns the dulling effects of smoking on taste sensitivity. Here, the evidence contradicts folk wisdom—regular smokers are just as good as nonsmokers at correctly identifying taste solutions (McBurney and Moskat, 1975). So why do reformed smokers often claim that food tastes better since they quit? Remember that flavor consists of several mouth-related sensations, and taste is only one of them. Perhaps the reformed smoker's enhanced pleasure from food comes from one of these other sources. For example, smokers are less able to appreciate the pungency of odors (Cometto-Muñiz and Cain, 1984), and pungency is

BOX 15.2 **Your Tongue's Touch Acuity**

You have just popped three or four ripe, juicy cherries into your mouth, and are now beginning to chew. Almost immediately you realize that this partially chewed mass in your mouth contains not just the wonderful, sweet juice and flesh of the cherries, but their pits as well. One by one, using your tongue and teeth, you sort out the pits, and spit them out. You're able to separate out the pits because they differ in hardness and texture from the fleshy parts of the cherry. In other words, you are using your mouth as a haptic organ to acquire tactile information about the contents in your mouth. This isn't so surprising, because the tongue and mouth contain touch receptors and, as you can verify for yourself, tactile stimulation applied to different regions of the tongue can readily be localized with a fair degree of accuracy. In fact, people can even do a reasonable job of identifying embossed letters using their tongues only (Essick et al., 2003).

But what about your ability to pinpoint the location of taste stimulation on your tongue when that stimulation is applied under conditions that preclude accompanying telltale tactile cues? Some taste experts felt that taste alone could not be localized under these conditions, since the sensation of taste seems to fill your entire mouth (e.g., Todrank and Bartoshuk, 1991). Results from a recent study, however, call this view into question.

Delwiche, Lera, and Breslin (2000) devised an ingenious but simple method to ensure that tactile information could not be used for localizing taste stimuli in the mouth. Their stimuli consisted of small cubes of gelatin to which tastants could be added as needed. Suppose, for example that two cubes of gelatin were put simultaneously into your mouth. Suppose also that one cube was a tasteless, neutral gelatin and the other one was injected with a bitter flavoring. Your task is to identify and spit out—without looking at the cubes, of course—the one that had the bitter flavor. Because both cubes were identical in tactile properties, you could perform the task only by identifying the location of the taste. Delwiche and colleagues varied the number of "distracter" stimuli, that is, the number of tasteless cubes accompanying the flavored one. As the number of distracters increased from one to three, people took longer to identify and expel the bitter cube. However, even with three distracters to confuse the judgment, people still managed to perform well above chance. So taste not only tells us what is in the mouth, it has some ability to tell us where in the mouth it's located. Presumably, this ability to localize substances in the mouth helps us to identify and then manipulate with tongue and teeth heterogeneous clumps of food, sorting out and spitting out undesirable components as needed.

---

a sensation produced by a number of spices used in cooking (Rozin, 1978).

Just as they are better at odor identification, human females are better at taste identification than males (Meiselman and Dzendolet, 1967). The reasons for female superiority have not yet been identified, although taste bud density is certainly one variable to consider. Whatever the basis for this sex difference, there seems to be no doubt that females are better equipped to appreciate food as far as taste and smell are concerned. And, finally, taste sensitivity, like odor sensitivity, decreases with age (e.g., Mojet, Christ-Hazelhof, and Heidema, 2001). This decline in sensitivity undoubtedly stems, at least in part, from the age-related decrease in papillae density mentioned earlier.

Discriminating Taste Intensity

So far we've focused on various aspects of the ability to detect and identify different solutions. Now let's consider how accurate people are when judging differences in

concentration of a single taste substance, which is another kind of judgment needed in the preparation of food. To get some idea of the difficulty of such judgments, you should try a modification of the taste experiment that introduced this section. This time fill three large glasses with clear water and place 1 teaspoon of sugar in the first glass, 1¼ teaspoons of sugar in the second, and 1½ teaspoons of sugar in the third. After stirring, have someone else rearrange the glasses so that you don't know which is which, but the other person does. Now try to rank them in order of sugar concentration. This will measure your ability to judge differences in taste concentration.

Although this ability has not been studied thoroughly, available results indicate that people require a difference of about 15 to 25 percent in order to determine that one solution is stronger than another (McBurney, 1978). On the basis of these numbers, you should just barely be able to pick out the weakest of the three sugar solutions but will probably be unable to discriminate between the remaining two. The fact that people can discriminate concentration changes in the neighborhood of

15 to 25 percent has implications for cooking: to improve a dish's taste by adding more of some ingredient, add just enough to increase the total amount by about 25 percent each time. This will ensure that you don't suddenly add too much. Given taste's importance in the enjoyment of food, it is too bad that measuring cups and measuring spoons used in cooking can't be calibrated in psychophysical threshold units.

Taste Adaptation and Modification

Outside the taste laboratory, people rarely ingest substances in very weak, near threshold concentrations, and moreover, hardly ever are those substances encountered in isolation. When you eat, your palate is typically bathed in a whole complex of taste substances. So it is of interest to study how the taste of one substance is influenced by the presence of other substances. Such influences can take two forms: (1) the taste of a substance may be weakened by prior exposure to that same substance—the familiar process of **adaptation;** and (2) the taste of a substance may be altered in quality by another substance—a process called **modification.** Let's start with adaptation.

You can demonstrate taste adaptation for yourself in the following way. Fill four glasses with equal amounts of water. Now take a freshly sliced lemon and carefully squeeze one drop of juice into one glass, two drops into the second, and the remaining juice into the third (this is the adaptation solution). Thoroughly stir all three solutions. Keep the fourth glass free of lemon—it should contain water only. In this demonstration you should keep track of which glass is which (you may want to number them). Now take a sip of the first solution, the one containing a single drop of lemon juice. You should be able to detect a slightly sour taste (sour is the predominant taste of pure lemon juice), especially in comparison to the neutral taste of water only. Next sip the two-drop solution and compare it to water only. As it is twice as strong, this solution should taste more sour than the one-drop solution, and certainly different from water only.

Now adapt your tongue to sour—take enough of the concentrated solution into your mouth to cover your tongue. Don't swallow it; instead, roll it around in your mouth for about 30 seconds, then spit it out. Now once again sip the two dilute solutions, again comparing them to water only. You should find that the sour taste of both is considerably weaker—perhaps too weak to distinguish from the taste of water only. Wait a few minutes and then repeat this part of the test. You'll find that your sensitivity recovers rather quickly.

This demonstration merely confirms that taste—just like vision, hearing, touch, and smell—shows adaptation. As the previous section pointed out, this decline in taste sensitivity cannot be caused entirely by the reduced responsiveness of taste fibers. The time course of fiber adaptation is much too short to account for the adaptation of taste sensations. This latter form of adaptation must take place along one of the neural pathways discussed previously, but exactly where is a mystery (see Gillan, 1984).

Suppose you had adapted to a strong solution of salt water and then you were tested on the dilute solutions of lemon. Recall that cross-adaptation provides a way to test whether different substances stimulate the same neural elements. You would find that adaptation to salty has essentially no effect on your ability to taste sour. The same would be true if you were to adapt to sweet and then test your sensitivity to sour. In general, cross-adaptation works only when the adapting substance is similar in quality to the test substance (McBurney and Gent, 1979; Bartoshuk, 1974). Thus, you'd find your sensitivity to dilute solutions of lemon temporarily reduced if you were first to eat a sour pickle, as these two both produce the quality sour. The quality bitter seems to be an exception to this rule: Sensitivity to bitter substances can be reduced by adaptation to a different taste, sour (McBurney, Smith, and Shick, 1972). In all, though, the results from cross-adaptation studies generally point to the existence of distinct taste qualities.

Modification, the second form of taste interaction, occurs when exposure to one substance subsequently alters the taste of another substance. Several of these so-called "taste illusions" have been described by Bartoshuk (1974; Bartoshuk et al., 1969). One that might be familiar to you involves fresh artichokes—after eating this delicacy, people find that other foods and drinks, including plain water, tend to have a sweet taste. (Actually, this is but one example of taste aftereffects involving water; Box 15.3 describes others that you can easily experience.) The leaves of the *Gymnema sylvestre* plant, found in India and Africa, produce another intriguing taste illusion. Eating the leaves or drinking tea made from them temporarily abolishes the sweet taste of sugar. In fact, following exposure to *Gymnema sylvestre,* sugar crystals on the tongue are indistinguishable from grains of sand. Salt, in contrast, retains its taste—proof that *Gymnema sylvestre* doesn't simply wipe out the entire sense of taste.

Another, equally exotic taste modifier comes from *Synsepalum dulcificum,* a shrub native to tropical West Africa. Popularly called "miracle fruit," the large, scarlet

BOX 15.3   The Taste of Water: An Aftereffect

Most people used to think that water, including water from the tap, a drinking fountain, or a garden hose, tasted pretty much like any other. But now in North America many people shell out a lot of money for their favorite brand of water. Yearly sales of bottled water in North America exceed $10 billion, and, with hundreds of brands and many beautiful bottles and labels to choose from, the average person drinks more than 80 liters of bottled water per year. Per capita consumption is about the same in many countries in Europe. Whatever your favorite brand of bottled water (or source of tap water), by adapting your tongue to different substances you can make that water take on various distinctive tastes. This phenomenon—"water taste"—is somewhat similar to the negative color afterimages described in Chapter 7. With water, however, the taste aftereffect is not organized in an opponent fashion. This will become apparent when you do the following experiment.

Take a bottle of water, preferably one that, to your satisfaction, has little or no mineral taste. Pour a glass full of the water to be the test stimulus. Next, fill three more glasses with water (the tap variety will do) and add a teaspoon of salt to one, a teaspoon of lemon juice to the second, and a teaspoon of sugar to the third; these are the adaptation stimuli. Be sure each is well stirred. Begin by taking a sip of the original water, just to remind yourself what "no taste" tastes like.

Then take a mouthful of the salty solution and roll it around in your mouth for about 30 seconds. At the end of this adaptation period, spit out the salty water and take a sip of the distilled water. The previously tasteless liquid will now have a noticeable sour or bitter taste. Once this aftertaste has worn off (when the distilled water again has no taste), adapt to the sour (lemon) solution for 30 seconds. Now you will find that the same distilled water tastes faintly sweet. When this taste aftereffect has worn off, adapt to the sweet solution. This time distilled water will take on a sour taste.

Can you see the similarity between this taste aftereffect and the negative color afterimages you experienced from color plate 9? In the case of color, a white surface took on the hue that was dependent on the adaptation color. In the case of taste, the tasteless water plays the same role as the white surface—both represent a neutral stimulus that becomes temporarily "shaded" by adaptation.

There is, however, a real difference between colored afterimages and water taste aftereffects. With color, adaptation obeys an opponent rule: Adapting to red makes white look green, whereas adapting to green makes white look red; blue and yellow are comparably related. With taste, adaptation is not reciprocal: Adaptation to salty makes water taste sour, but adaptation to sour makes water taste sweet, not salty. Similar, nonreciprocal aftereffects are found in the case of bitter (which you can most easily produce using unsweetened quinine water). Bitter makes distilled water taste sweet, but as you experienced, adapting to sweet makes distilled water taste sour, not bitter. All of this implies that taste does not involve opponent process mechanisms such as those implicated in color vision (McBurney, Smith, and Shick, 1972). It also implies that the taste of water must be changing all the time during the course of a meal, since you are constantly adapting your tongue to different taste substances. Even the salt in your own saliva can act as a mild adaptation stimulus. Because you're well adapted to your own saliva, when you sip distilled water, it may appear to have a slightly sour taste.

---

berries from this amazing plant impart an intensely sweet taste to even the sourest foods, such as lemons. Moreover, this sweetening aftereffect lasts about an hour after eating just a small amount of miracle fruit. This could provide a novel way to reduce your intake of sugar—you could fool your tongue into believing that food was sweet without adding sugar. While it's not known exactly how miracle fruit works, it is known that it alters the responsiveness of taste fibers (Brouwer et al., 1983). Following exposure of the tongue to miracle fruit's active ingredient, fibers normally responsive to sweet substances but not to sour ones develop a temporary sensitivity to sour. In other words, these nerve fibers temporarily behave as though sour were sweet. After about an hour, these fibers return to their normal state, once again ignoring sour. And an hour is also about how long the taste illusion persists. Incidentally, tasting *Gymnema sylvestre*, the leaf that destroys the taste of sugar, can abruptly abolish the sweet taste caused by miracle fruit. Here's a case where one illusion can overcome another.

There's one taste modifier that everyone is familiar with: toothpaste. You've probably had the annoying experience of finding that the taste of your morning fruit juice has been ruined because you had just brushed your teeth. This cross-adaptation occurs because toothpaste contains an ingredient that temporarily reduces the sweetness of sugar, which makes the acid in the juice taste extra sour (Bartoshuk, 1980).

Recently there's been an explosion of commercial interest in various ways to alter taste (Gilbert and Firestein 2002). Take just two examples of why such interest exists. In some countries, growing numbers of older citizens have caused countries to face novel public health issues, including how to maintain citizens' appetites despite their diminished sensory response to many foods. Also, many medicines crucial to health, including children's cough syrups and some anti-HIV drugs, taste so bitter that many patients are reluctant to take them or to continue taking them. Recently, a biotechnology company tested and patented a simple, naturally occurring compound that blocks many bitter tastes. This bitter suppressor is adenosine 5'-monophosphate (AMP) and is found, among other sources, in human breast milk. Breast milk contains a lot of calcium, which normally triggers bitter tastes. Human infants accept breast milk, it's thought, because its AMP content blocks the bitter taste. When AMP, which by itself is tasteless, is added to some food, AMP can block the tongue's receptors that normally signal the presences of bitter tastants. With the receptors blocked, the food's normal, bitter taste is reduced or eliminated. If this scheme works outside of the laboratory, it could substantially alter many commercial foods, including foods, such as canned soups, whose natural bitterness manufacturers mask by adding huge quantities of good-tasting, but potentially harmful salt. AMP might even get former U.S. President Bush to eat his broccoli.

Taste Mixtures

So far our discussion has focused on altering one taste by exposure to another. Next, let's consider what happens when two or more taste substances are mixed together (which occurs routinely when one cooks). Everyone knows that it's possible to tone down the taste of one substance by adding another. This is one reason why people add sugar to coffee, to mask its bitter taste. This reduction of one taste sensation by another is called **taste suppression,** and it seems to be a general property of taste mixtures (Bartoshuk, 1975; Gillan, 1982). But what do taste mixtures actually taste like? Is taste analogous to color vision, where two component hues (for instance red and green) can create an entirely new hue (yellow)? Or is taste more like hearing, where two tones played together maintain their individuality?

The answer to this interesting and important question is not clear. McBurney (1978) maintains that the mixture of taste components does not produce new qualities. According to this view, lemon juice with sugar added may taste both sour and sweet; but it won't taste salty or anything else new. This outcome is reminiscent of the situation in hearing, not color vision. Schiffman and Erickson (1980), however, report that sometimes a mixture will produce an unexpected taste, one not usually associated with the taste of any of the components. Such a result would be in line with the behavior of color vision, not hearing.

How does one reconcile these seemingly contradictory observations? Part of the problem stems from the inherently subjective nature of these perceptual judgments. In effect, people must be introspective on their taste sensations, decomposing the mixture into its constituents. (To see how difficult this is, try analyzing the tastes evoked by each dish in your next meal.) Introspection, however, is not a simple task, and it is subject to all sorts of extraneous influences, such as the instructions given to people. As an alternative, people could be asked to "construct" a taste mixture that matches the taste(s) of a solution mixed by the experimenter. Such an experiment would be analogous to the metameric color-matching experiments described in Chapter 7. However, performing such a taste-matching experiment requires some idea of what components are needed for the desired mixture. And this brings us back to the question raised at the outset regarding the existence of basic taste qualities. At present, this question represents the fundamental issue in taste research, and until it is resolved, we'll have to be content enjoying what we eat without knowing exactly what we are tasting.

Taste Preferences

Liking and disliking are not usually thought of as natural properties of sensory stimulation. There seems to be nothing inherently sad about the color blue, for example. Taste may be an exception, however. People can reliably rate various tastes along a spectrum of pleasant to unpleasant, and in general, one person's ratings are likely to agree with another's. Bitter is usually judged unpleasant, while sweet, at least in low concentrations, is rated pleasant. Such judgments are called **taste hedonics** (*hedonic* is derived from the Greek word meaning "pleasure"). Some taste experts believe that these hedonic qualities stem from biological factors governing food selection. Organisms ranging from insects to

FIGURE 15.8 | The typical facial responses of 7 1-2-month-old infants tested with the same protein-based formula. The infant shown in panel a had been fed this same formula for the preceding seven months; for that same period the infant in panel b had been fed a cow's milk based formula.

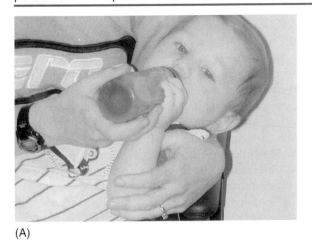

(A)

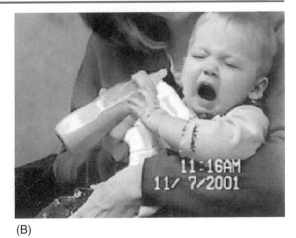

(B)

primates (human beings included), crave sweet substances. This may be adaptive, since sugars are easily detected nutrients common in plants (Ramirez, 1990). Bitter is typically associated with toxic substances, which would explain why nearly all animals show an aversion to bitter substances. In fact, some plant and animal species capitalize on this universal aversion by having evolved a bitter-tasting skin themselves, a characteristic that wards off potential predators (Gittleman and Harvey, 1980).

As you saw when we discussed former U.S. President George H. W. Bush's aversion to broccoli, different factors influence taste preferences (and aversions). Clearly, individual differences in food preferences are powerful and mysterious. Where do these striking differences come from? The next several paragraphs explore a few answers: familiarity, genetics, age, and the visual characteristics of foods.

Take familiarity to begin with. Humans are omnivores: Members of our species can and do eat all sorts of things, ranging from tofu and watercress sandwiches to monkey brains and fried grasshoppers. Because adult diets vary from culture to culture, infants and young children in those cultures are exposed to different foods, and to different tastes—in utero and after birth. What impact does this exposure have? Mennella, Griffin, and Beauchamp (2004) demonstrated that infants' taste preferences are remarkably malleable. They examined infants' preferences for several different commercial infant

formulas, including one derived from cow's milk and one derived from processed protein. The second of these formulas is recommended for infants who have milk or soy allergies. To adults, the milk-based formula tastes slightly sweet, while the protein-based formula tastes bitter and sour, and produces an awful aftertaste. Looking at the infants' facial expressions in Figure 15.8, you might guess that the contented infant on the left is getting the milk-based formula and that the unhappy infant on the right is getting the awful-tasting protein-based formula. Actually, though, both of these 7½-month-old infants are getting the same formula, the one that adults find awful tasting. Although the infants had been equated for degree of hunger before testing, they clearly react differently to the same stimulus. The striking individual differences in Figure 15.8 were produced during the 7 months leading up to the final tests. During that time, Mennella and colleagues arranged to have one group of infants fed the cow's milk-based formula, and another group fed the processed protein-based formula. This experimental design is made possible by the fact that infants less than 4 months of age do not resist the formula that tastes awful to adults. At the end of 7 months, infants in each of the groups were tested with several different formulas. The most informative result came from tests with the unpleasant-tasting formula: Infants who had been exposed to that formula over the preceding months made virtually no grimaces when given their accustomed formula, and consumed about eight times more of that formula than did infants in the other group. Clearly, that early exposure drastically altered the formula's palatability, and changed the infants' taste preferences.

So, early familiarity with some food can change an infant's taste preference. Other research shows that such effects can be both subtle and extremely long-lasting. For many years, bottled milk specially formulated for German infants has been lightly flavored with vanillin to improve milk's palatability. Researchers realized that this situation presented a perfect opportunity to study how familiarity might alter long-term preference (Haller et al., 1999). Would infants' early exposure to vanillin-flavored milk have any consequences for their taste preferences years later? To answer this question, Haller and colleagues asked 133 adult visitors to an environmental fair whether they had been breast fed or bottle fed as newborns. Thirty of the respondents said they'd been bottle fed, the rest, breast fed. Each respondent was given two samples of ketchup, a food not usually linked to vanillin. One of the samples was ordinary, pure ketchup; the other sample was doctored with a minute amount of vanillin (1 part vanillin per 2,000 parts ketchup). This low concentration made the vanillin just barely detectable and too weak to be accurately identified. The participants tasted the two samples in random order, naming their preferences.

Of people who had been breast fed ($n = 103$), about two out of three preferred the pure ketchup. Of people who had been bottle fed ($n = 30$), the preference ratio was reversed: about two-thirds of these people preferred the ketchup sample that had been doctored. Presumably, this latter group had been exposed as infants to vanillin. Although we wish that the study had included more participants, particularly in the bottle-fed category, it does suggest that early experience with particular tastes can have very long-term consequences for adult food preference.[6] Some of the study participants were in their forties and fifties, which puts that important early experience four or five decades behind them. Incidentally, this enduring preference does not depend upon infants' ability to label with words what they experienced while they drank milk. Use of special infant formula usually ends well before children learn to speak. In fact, an infant's postnatal taste preferences can even be molded by that infant's prenatal exposure to flavors contained in the mother's diet, flavors that find their way into the prenatal infant's amniotic fluid environment (Mennella, Jagnow, and Beauchamp, 2001).

Earlier we mentioned that sensitivity to certain bitter substances, including PROP and PTC, varies with one's genetic makeup. This genetic heterogeneity produces a corresponding heterogeneity in preferences for particular foods. Generally, tasters and supertasters have more finicky food preferences, expressing dislike for a greater number of foods (Fischer et al., 1961; Glanville and Kaplan, 1965). Anliker and colleagues (1991) summarize this body of work, noting that adults with normal bitter sensitivity tend to avoid certain strong-tasting foods, including sauerkraut, turnips, spinach, and strong cheese. (Anliker and colleagues also extended these observations to the preferences of tasters and nontasters among young children, ages 5 to 7 years.) Although food preferences are governed by many factors, including social and cultural ones, genetic differences in taste sensitivity have a clear influence as well.

We should note that a natural aversion to bitter taste can be overcome, as evidenced by the almost universal enjoyment of beverages like beer, coffee, and quinine water. And just as natural aversions can be conquered, unnatural ones can be *acquired* (Garcia and Koelling, 1966; Garb and Stunkard, 1974). Extreme nausea following ingestion of some food is a sure bet to cause an animal to reject that food the next time it is available. This phenomenon, called **conditioned taste aversion,** is an extremely potent method for discouraging predators from disturbing farm animals such as chickens and sheep. One meal of sheep meat laced with lithium chloride (a chemical that induces violent nausea) will dissuade a coyote from going near the source of that meat in the future. By the same token, one night of heavy indulgence in whiskey is enough to discourage many people from drinking whiskey, at least in the near future.

Sweet tastes are usually thought of as pleasant, but extremely sweet food or drink can be unpleasant. For a variety of sweet substances, pleasantness increases with concentration up to a point, after which the substance becomes more and more unpleasant. Moskowitz (1978) calls this transition point the *bliss point*—the concentration yielding the highest hedonic rating. As you might expect, young children have a higher bliss point than adults (De Graaf and Zandstra, 1999), which explains why advertisements for highly sweetened breakfast cereals are aimed directly at a very young audience. Contrary to expectation, however, some obese individuals actually have a lower bliss point than do people of normal weight (Grinker and Hirsch, 1972), although this finding does not hold for all sweet substances (Drewnowski, Grinker, and Hirsch, 1982).

---

[6]The study has another limitation: It assumes that participants knew and accurately reported whether they'd been breast or bottle fed.

Besides concentration levels, a food's color can also influence how much people like its taste. One study (Duncker, 1939) had people rate the taste of white chocolate and brown chocolate, and they did this while either blindfolded or not. With their eyes open, people judged the white chocolate as weak in taste, whereas the blindfolded group liked it just as much as the brown chocolate. The same pattern of results has been found for fruit-flavored beverages and cake (DuBose, Cardello, and Maller, 1980). The food industry, aware of the influence of color on taste perception, often adds color to products. Margarine, for instance, is naturally very pale but is dyed yellow to mimic the color of real butter. Likewise, orange food coloring is added to many orange juice products, and this strategy improves the flavor scores of these products (see Pangborn, 1960). To convince yourself of the potent effect color has on taste perception, just add green food coloring to milk and see how it tastes.

Related to the issue of taste preference is **sensory-specific satiety,** the reduction in the pleasurable sensory quality of a particular food as it is being eaten (Rolls, 1986). Suppose a moderately hungry person rates the pleasantness of the taste, smell, and texture of some food. Following this initial rating, imagine the individual eats a meal that includes the previously rated food, and immediately following the meal, the person again rates the food's pleasantness. The postmeal ratings will be lower than the premeal ratings, even though the food itself has not had time to be digested. Evidently it is the sensory quality of the food itself, not its nutritional consequences, that produces the reduced hedonic response to the food. Moreover, this satiety effect is specific to the food items consumed during the meal—foods that were not eaten do not have lowered pleasantness (Rolls, Van Duijvenvoorde, and Rolls, 1984).

The specificity of satiety means that relatively more food may be eaten during a meal that consists of many different foods served over several courses. Understanding sensory-specific satiety may shed light on eating disorders such as bulimia (Drewnowski et al., 1987), the condition where an individual engages in an eating binge followed by fasting or self-induced vomiting. Rodin and colleagues (1990) found that bulimic patients continued to rate sweet substances as pleasant even after ingesting a healthy dose of glucose dissolved in water; nonbulimics, in contrast, found the sweet substance less pleasant after ingestion of glucose. Rodin and colleagues speculate that bulimics may engage in food binges because they fail to experience a reduction in its pleasantness during the course of eating.

The general topic of taste preferences is a fascinating one. Much interesting material cannot be presented here for lack of space. Those interested in that material should consult Rozin (1979). In addition, you can find several informative articles on cross-cultural studies of taste perception and preference (Johns and Keen, 1985; Bertino and Chan, 1986).

The Interaction between Taste and Smell

The previous chapter and this one have stressed odor's role in what we usually think of as taste. Holding your nostrils closed while you eat dramatically demonstrates this role. One study found that the ability to identify food substances is severely hampered when odor perception is eliminated (Mozel et al., 1969). In this study, 21 familiar substances were individually liquefied in a blender and dropped one by one onto a person's tongue from an eyedropper; the person's task was to name each food. The results, summarized in Figure 15.9, show the percentages of people tested who could identify each of the 21 substances. The shaded bars give the results when the odor of the solution could be smelled; the unshaded bars give the results when odors were blocked from reaching the olfactory epithelium. Obviously, smell improved performance greatly. In fact, for several very familiar substances, including coffee, garlic, and chocolate, correct identification was impossible without smell.

There is something paradoxical about odor's contribution to taste: When odor is added to a substance that is being tasted, people do not report that its smell has increased in strength. They say instead that its *taste* is enhanced (Murphy, Cain, and Bartoshuk, 1977). Demonstrate this for yourself. Begin eating with your nostrils held closed, then release them. Opening your nostrils means that odor will be added. But instead of experiencing this addition as *smell,* you will find that *taste* has become stronger. In other words, taste and smell blend into a single experience, and this combined experience is typically referred to as *taste.* Dalton and colleagues (2000) demonstrated how potent taste smell combinations could be. Using a forced choice staircase procedure (see the appendix), these researchers found that for certain combinations of odorant and tastant, the presence of one component, even at extremely low concentrations, facilitates detection of the other component. To take one example, the presence of a low concentration of saccharin (a tastant that evokes sweetness) lowers the threshold for detecting benzaldehyde (an odorant that evokes a cherry smell). The researchers speculated that such interactions may require that the tastant and odorant be congruent. Thus, sweetness and a cherry odor are congruent in the

FIGURE 15.9 | The percentages of people who could identify a substance dropped onto their tongues when they could smell the solution (shaded bars) and when they were prevented from smelling the solution (unshaded bars).

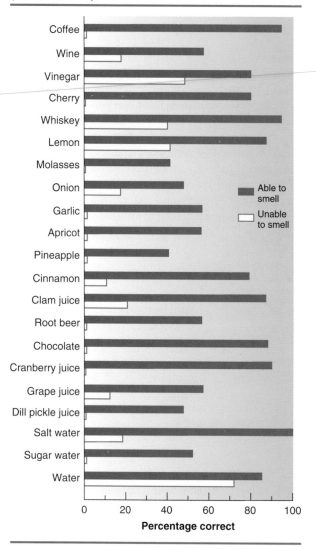

for the monosodium glutamate solution. Again, incongruent substances failed to produce an interaction between taste and smell.

Taste–smell interactions are crucial to our enjoyment of food or drink. The importance of such interactions can be seen in "taste" experts, who develop the knack of attending to the *odors* of the food or drink they are sampling. If you've ever watched a serious wine taster at work, you know what we mean. First of all, wine tasters prefer to evaluate wine when it is close to room temperature, so that the odorous vapors are more abundant. To further promote the release of vapors, a taster will swirl the liquid around in the glass and will then deeply inhale the vapors with the nose placed right at the mouth of the glass. This odor information alone is often sufficient to identify the particular wine being sampled. Because wines vary along several dimensions, wine discrimination has become a popular vehicle for studying perceptual learning, the enhancement of perception brought about by practice (see, for example, Owen and Machamer, 1979). In fact, entire books have been written on the sensory evaluation of wine (Kramer, 1989).

To end on a literary note, recall that in the previous chapter we extolled smell's ability to evoke memories from years ago, and we cited several gifted writers who managed to bring the sense of smell alive in their literature. Similar examples can be given for the sense of taste. Probably the best-known literary description of taste's potency comes from Marcel Proust's *Swann's Way*.

In the book's overture, the narrator muses that it's impossible to recapture one's past merely by trying to think about it. True recapture requires that you reexperience the *sensations* that you felt originally. And he then goes on to provide an eloquent example of this idea. While the narrator is visiting his mother, she notices that he is cold and gives him a cup of tea and some little cakes called *petites madeleines*. Without thinking, he drinks some of the tea, into which cake crumbs have fallen. Immediately, he finds himself overcome with an "all-powerful joy," but he doesn't understand why. Then it strikes him: The taste was one he had experienced years before, as a young boy in the little French village of Combray.

> In that moment all the flowers in our garden and in M. Swann's park, and the water-lilies on the Vivonne and the good folk of the village and their little dwellings and the parish church and the whole of Combray and of its surroundings, taking their proper shapes and growing solid, sprang into being, town and gardens alike, from my cup of tea. (Proust, 1928, p. 58)

sense that benzaldehyde odor and sweet taste can coexist naturally. As preliminary evidence for their hypothesis, Dalton and colleagues showed that putting a solution of monosodium glutamate into the mouth leaves the threshold for detecting benzaldehyde unchanged. Monosodium glutamate and benzaldehyde represent a taste and a smell that do not naturally coexist. A comparable lack of interaction was found when deionized water was substituted

The whole of Proust's novel builds on his remembrances of things that happened in Combray. As a result, the whole work has roots in the taste of those few tea-soaked cake crumbs. What a powerful jolt to the memory! To honor the author who turned a bunch of cake crumbs into such beauty, researchers have given his name to the Proust phenomenon: the ability of taste and smells to spontaneously trigger vivid personal memories (Chu and Downes, 2000).

S U M M A R Y

This examination of the second of the "minor senses," gustation, brings us to the end of our survey of seeing, hearing, touch, taste, and smell. You should now have a more complete appreciation of how marvelously sensitive human beings are to the noisy, odorous, light-reflecting, tasty objects that make up our world. And you should likewise appreciate that this world is defined by the human sensory nervous system. Other species with different nervous systems live in a world different from ours. The environment offers an abundance of opportunities for perception; whether one capitalizes on those opportunities depends on having receptors and brain mechanisms to register and process the various forms of sensory information available. Understanding perception requires that we examine *what* there is to be perceived (the environment as a source of stimulation), *how* the process is implemented (the mechanisms of perception), and, of course, *how* that information is ultimately used to influence behavior.

K E Y   T E R M S

adaptation
conditioned taste aversion
cranial nerves
cross-fiber theory
flavor

gustatory cortex
information content
modification
papillae
sensory-specific satiety

taste buds
taste hedonics
taste suppression

Behavioral Methods for Studying Perception

Members of our species have always been curious about perception. Some ancestor of yours might have asked herself, "Why do colors disappear at night?" or "Why, as I've gotten older, is it harder for me to hear the sweet sound of birds at dawn?" For answers to these and similar questions, people relied on the only tool they had: introspective reflections. They tried to analyze the character of their own perceptual experiences and then fabricate explanations for those experiences. Today, too, introspection guides our intuitions about perception, but the field of perception would not have advanced to its current level of sophistication if introspection were the only available tool for investigation. This appendix outlines some more sophisticated techniques that have evolved for quantifying sensory judgments (and the Web resource at www.mhhe.com/blake5 provides additional, supplementary material on psychophysical techniques). As we work through these techniques, keep in mind that the results from such techniques are not obligated to conform to your introspective experience—for example, as you'll learn later, we're able to react to sensory information far too weak to evoke a clear, conscious experience.

The Birth of Psychophysics

As science and commerce flourished, people demanded greater reliability and accuracy in sensory judgments. This fostered development of formal methods for assessing perception. In 1860, Gustav Theodor Fechner, a German physicist and philosopher, published a book in which he formalized behavioral methods that others had developed to study perception (Fechner, 1860/1966). Formalizing the methods' "rules" allowed people to compare different sets of observations. Fechner's methods, along with modern variants derived from his methods, remain in use today—in fact, most of the results described in this book came from their application. In the following sections we'll consider those methods, and the kinds of results they generate.

Though Fechner had great foresight, he could not anticipate all the many methods that are currently used. Some of these newer methods are described at various places in the text. These include preferential looking (Chapters 5, 7, 8, and 9), multidimensional scaling (Chapter 14), magnitude estimation (Chapter 11), reaction time (Chapters 5, 6, 9, and 13), and various methods used to study animal perception (Chapters 4, 5, 8, 11, 12, and 13). In addition, today we conduct research with powerful methods that were technically impossible until very recently, including concurrent behavioral and physiological measurements and brain imaging (Chapters 1, 4, 6, 8, 9, 11, 12, and 13).

To give a detailed description of these behavioral techniques would require a volume of its own, so we'll just summarize key features of those techniques. Incidentally, we have an unimpeachable precedent for keeping details to a minimum while emphasizing the major concepts. Fechner himself wrote:

Had I wished . . . to set forth here all the special methods of experimentation and calculation that have to be taken into account in more detailed investigations, or had I wanted to provide a theoretical basis and experimental proof for all the rules that are applicable, I would have disturbed the flow of the argument, interfering with the interests of those who are more concerned with the general understanding of the methods than with their use by themselves. (1860/1966, p. 60)

Where should we start? When archaeologists unearth an ancient tool, their understanding of the tool depends on understanding what the tool was used for. Similarly, to understand the methods Fechner presented in his book, one must inquire first about the purposes Fechner had in mind for those methods. In other words, *why* did he want to measure perception—and why might we want to do the same?

An amateur philosopher with considerable training in physics, Fechner was interested in establishing a new science, which he termed **psychophysics.** Psychophysics, as envisioned by Fechner, was to be "an exact theory of the . . . relations of body and soul or, more generally, of the material and the mental, of the physical and psychological worlds" (1860/1966, p. 7). Appropriately enough, Fechner called his book *Elemente der Psychophysik* (Elements of Psychophysics); English translations of some key passages from the book are available on the Web—check out the link at www.mhhe.com/blake5. Fechner's program required some way to measure the sensations that physical stimuli evoked in people. Fechner believed that these sensations arose from an interaction between the physical and psychological worlds, and he was convinced that if he could quantify the sensations evoked by various stimuli, he would be able to develop equations that tied those two worlds together. So that was what he sought with his methods: a mathematical expression of the relation between mental events and physical events.

Suppose that like Fechner, you wanted to write a simple psychophysical equation that related the quantity of sensation to the physical intensity of a stimulus evoking that sensation. To portray such an equation, you might produce a graph relating sensation and intensity, with stimulus intensity on the horizontal axis and sensation magnitude on the vertical. For a psychophysical equation that is described by a straight line, you'd need to find two values before you could draw its graph. First, you'd need to determine the minimum stimulus value that evoked any sensation whatsoever. This value, the graph's *x*–intercept, is the point at which the straight line intersects the horizontal axis. Second, you'd need to determine the rate at which the sensation grew as stimulus intensity increased. Graphically, this rate of growth corresponds to the slope parameter of the psychophysical equation. The first of these values (the *x*–intercept) is known as the **absolute threshold:** the stimulus intensity defining the transition between undetectable and detectable; the absolute threshold, in other words, is the intensity at which a person can just barely detect a stimulus. The second of these values is known as the **difference threshold:** the minimum amount by which stimulus intensity must be changed in order to produce a noticeable change in the sensation. With certain assumptions (described below), knowledge of these two values—the absolute threshold and the difference threshold—would enable you to write the desired psychophysical equation. And this is what Fechner tried to do.

Crucial to Fechner's enterprise was the assumption that the difference threshold would be constant. If the difference threshold changed in value—say, from when you were working with weak stimuli to when you were working with strong stimuli—there would be no single value that could be used to estimate the slope of the psychophysical equation; instead, the slope itself would change from one part of the line to another, implying that the corresponding equation is more complex than that for a straight line. And, in fact, the difference threshold is most certainly *not* constant. Suppose, for example, you first show an observer a spot of light whose intensity is 100 units, a value that we'll assume is easily visible. Now suppose you increase the light's intensity until the observer first notices that the light is more intense. Suppose that this new level had to be 110 units. The difference threshold here would be 110 minus 100, or 10 units. If you repeated the process, beginning now with a light of 1,000 units, you would find that the observer could not notice a change of just 10 units, as before. Instead, a much larger change would be required to produce a just noticeable change—say, a change from 1,000 to 1,100 units. So in this second case, the difference threshold would be 1,100 minus 1,000, or 100 units.

From the work of his contemporary Ernst Weber, Fechner knew that although the difference threshold itself was not constant, but tended to be a constant *proportion* of the initial stimulus value. In the hypothetical examples just described, both difference thresholds were 10 percent of the initial stimulus. Using various stimuli, Weber had shown that a fixed-proportion increase in stimulus intensity was sufficient to produce a just noticeable change in sensation. To honor him, Fechner called this constancy **Weber's law.** As we've just seen, Weber's law states that

$$\Delta I/I = k$$

where ΔI (delta I) signifies the difference threshold (the amount by which stimulus intensity must be increased in order to produce a just noticeable change), I signifies the initial stimulus intensity, and k signifies that the proportion on the left side of the equation is a constant despite changes in I.

So now Fechner's challenge was to measure absolute thresholds and difference thresholds, and from these values would emerge the equation he sought. As an historical aside, it turns out that Weber's law breaks down at the extreme ends of the stimulus intensity continuum, and this breakdown undermines Fechner's aim of deriving a single universal equation. Nonetheless, the techniques he invented to measure thresholds remain valid, and it is those methods, and their derivatives, that we're concerned with here.

So by way of preview, we're about to consider behavioral techniques for measuring absolute thresholds (the weakest stimulus evoking any sensation whatsoever) and difference thresholds (the **just noticeable difference,** or **JND,** between two stimuli). These techniques will make much more sense to you if we use examples to illustrate them, and in most of our examples we'll assume that we're interested in visual thresholds. Keep in mind, however, that any of these methods can be adapted for measuring thresholds associated with hearing, touch, taste, and smell.

Before we turn to the various ways for measuring absolute and difference thresholds, you should know that Fechner himself was uncertain that it was possible to measure a threshold that truly deserved the description "absolute." He observed (1860/1966, p. 108) that even when no light whatever was present, observers in complete darkness tended to experience a dim, vague light that arose from what he termed an "inner source of light sensation." Today, we call this source of light **intrinsic light** or, more poetically, **dark light.** Fechner realized that intrinsic light would cause problems for an observer who tried to determine whether a stimulus produced *some* sensation or whether the stimulus produced *no* sensation whatever. The problem, he realized, is that observers are liable to confuse this inner source of light with the real thing. This confusion would prevent the observer from making absolute judgments about the dim light alone; instead, the observer would have to discriminate the effects of a real, dim light from the effects of intrinsic light. In this sense, even the absolute threshold involves judging differences: the effect of real light adds to the effect associated with dark light. And if the effect of dark light varies from moment to moment (which it probably does), the judgment becomes even more complicated. Various studies have borne out Fechner's belief

about intrinsic light, showing that this intrinsic light affects vision and psychophysical judgments in important ways (Barlow and Sparrock, 1964; Rushton, 1965). Moreover, the same line of reasoning can be applied to "absolute" thresholds measured for the other senses, too.

Fechner's Three Methods

To measure thresholds, Fechner proposed three different behavioral methods, known today as the **method of limits,** the **method of constant stimuli,** and the **method of adjustment.** Since Fechner wanted to measure both absolute thresholds and difference thresholds, he had to formulate two slightly different versions of each method—one version for each type of threshold. Here, we'll present both versions for all three methods: limits, adjustment, and constant stimuli.

Although the three methods differ in their details, they share some features. For example, all the methods restrict observers to one of two responses on each trial ("yes" or "no" for absolute thresholds; "stronger" or "weaker" for difference thresholds). Also, to measure an absolute threshold, all the methods specify presenting just *one* stimulus at a time. The observer's task is to report whether that stimulus elicits any sensation at all. To measure a difference threshold, all the methods require that *two* stimuli be presented. Here, the observer's task is to compare the sensations elicited by the two and report which one is greater. So to measure the absolute threshold, stimuli are weak, and the responses are either, "Yes, I detect it" or "No, I don't detect it." To measure difference thresholds, the intensity of one stimulus, the *standard stimulus,* is greater than zero, and the intensity of the other stimulus, the *comparison stimulus,* may be either more intense or less intense than the standard; The response categories are stronger or weaker. There are many variations on these methods, but these three basic formats are recognizable in a great many studies (Woodworth and Schlosberg, 1954; Ehrenstein and Ehrenstein, 1999).

The Method of Constant Stimuli

With this method, each of a fixed set of stimuli is presented multiple times in a quasi-random order. The frequency with which each stimulus elicits one of the two responses is tallied and used to plot what is known as a **psychometric function.** The threshold is the stimulus intensity that evokes a particular proportion of the two responses.[1]

---

[1]Fechner popularized it, but the method of constant stimuli had been devised several years earlier, by Friedrich Hegelmaier, in one of the most important student projects ever (Laming and Laming, 1992).

APPENDIX FIGURE 1 | Ideal (left) and actual (right) results of an absolute threshold experiment using the method of constant stimuli.

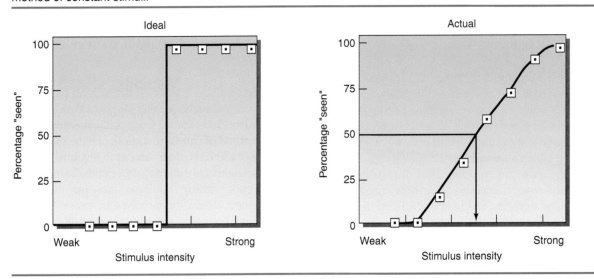

Absolute Threshold The experimenter begins by selecting a set of light intensities varying from very weak (or zero intensity) to highly visible (typically, somewhere between four and seven intensities are tested). Stimuli are presented one at a time in a quasi-random order that ensures each will occur equally often. After every presentation, the observer reports whether or not the light was seen. Once each light intensity has been presented many times (at least 20 to 25 times) the proportion of "Yes, seen" responses is calculated for each light level and plotted in a graphic format with intensity along the abscissa and percentage seen along the ordinate; this format constitutes what we term a psychometric function. Now, if there were a fixed absolute threshold for detection, the psychometric function should look like the solid line in the left–hand graph in Appendix Figure 1—the abrupt transition from "not seen" to "seen" would occur at this threshold intensity. In fact, however, psychometric functions never conform to this idealized representation. Instead, the curve increases gradually in a manner depicted by the curved line in the right-hand graph in Appendix Figure 1. More intense lights evoke a greater number of "seen" responses. This pattern of results means, therefore, that light intensities in the intermediate region (between "never seen" and "always seen") are judged "visible" on some trials and "invisible" on others. A given stimulus intensity, in other words, seems to vary in its effectiveness from trial to trial. And this means that there

is no single intensity value that consistently separates always "visible" from always "invisible." Consequently, the definition of "threshold intensity" must be a statistical one. By convention, the absolute threshold measured with the Method of Constant Stimuli is defined as the intensity value eliciting "seen" responses on 50 percent of the trials. This 50 percent value can be estimated graphically, as shown in Appendix Figure 1. There are various reasons why the psychometric function has this characteristic S shape and not a step function whose values change abruptly from 0 to 100 percent. Among them are the fluctuations in sensitivity of any biological sensory system (including the dark light mentioned earlier). Those inherent fluctuations mean that the background level of activity within the nervous system is changing, and it is against that background that an observer must detect activity associated with actual stimulation. Other contributing factors will be discussed later in this appendix.

Difference Threshold Two stimuli are presented on each trial. One of these, the standard stimulus, has a fixed intensity; the other, the comparison stimulus, is selected randomly from a set of stimuli whose different intensities bracket the standard. On each trial the observer judges whether the intensity of the comparison stimulus was stronger or weaker than that of the standard. Many such judgments are obtained for all pairs of comparison and standard stimuli.

Results are summarized by plotting the proportion of trials on which each comparison stimulus is judged to be stronger than the standard, yielding another type of psychometric function. These proportions are then used to identify comparison stimulus intensities that are just noticeably different from the standard. Two just noticeably different comparison stimuli are identified: One of these is the comparison stimulus that is just noticeably *weaker* than the standard; the other is the comparison stimulus that is just noticeably *stronger* than the standard. Here, too, we find that performance is more variable than the ideal: a given stimulus difference may be discriminable on one trial but not on the next. So, again, we must define the difference threshold statistically. By convention, a comparison stimulus that 75 percent of the time is judged weaker than the standard is considered to be just noticeably *weaker* than that standard; also, a comparison stimulus that 75 percent of the time is judged stronger than the standard is considered to be just noticeably *stronger* than that standard. Once these two just noticeably different stimuli are identified, the threshold is calculated by averaging the absolute difference in intensity between the standard and each of the stimuli that are just noticeably different from the standard.

The Method of Limits

One drawback to the Method of Constant Stimuli is the need to collect many observations for each stimulus (absolute threshold) or for each set of stimulus pairings (difference threshold). The Method of Limits offers a shortcut, where on each trial the stimulus is changed in small steps until the observer's response changes. The threshold is defined as that stimulus intensity at which the response changes. Here's how the technique would work for measuring absolute thresholds and difference thresholds in the case of vision.

Absolute Threshold   A single flash of light is changed in successive, discrete steps, and the observer's response to each is recorded. Suppose the light is initially so weak that the observer responds, "No, I don't see it." In this case, the light is increased in steps until the observer *can* see it. The light intensity at which the observer's response changes from "No" to "Yes" is taken as an estimate of the threshold. This represents an *ascending* method of limits, because the stimulus intensity approaches the transition point by ascending in intensity from an initial value below the threshold. Alternatively, the method of limits can start at a light intensity where

the observer confidently responds, "Yes, I see it." In this case, the light is decreased in steps until the observer can*not* see it. Again, the intensity of light at which the response changes, this time from "Yes" to "No," provides an estimate of the threshold. This represents a descending method of limits, because intensity values approach the transition point by descending from an initial value above the threshold. Ascending and descending series commonly yield systematically different estimates of the threshold, so most experimenters use both types of series in alternation and then average the results. Moreover, the threshold estimates from several series of, say, ascending trials may differ. This variability stems from the same sources that produce the variability in the Method of Constant Stimuli discussed above. In principle, the stimulus threshold estimated with the Method of Limits should correspond to the intensity value associated with the 50 percent point on a psychometric function obtained with the Method of Constant Stimuli.

Difference Threshold   On each trial, two flashes of light are presented—one called the *standard,* the other called the *comparison*; the pair may be presented either simultaneously, one next to the other, or successively, one after the other. The intensity of the standard light remains constant, and the intensity of the comparison light is changed in a series of steps. After each change, the observer judges the comparison stimulus as brighter or dimmer than the standard. In an ascending series, the comparison stimulus is initially weaker than the standard and it increases from trial to trial; in a descending series, the comparison stimulus is initially stronger than the standard and it decreases. A series terminates when the observer's response changes from "dimmer" to "brighter" (in an ascending series), or from "brighter" to "dimmer" (in a descending series). The threshold, then, is the absolute value of the difference between the lights at the time the response changed. As before, ascending and descending series may be alternated and the threshold estimates averaged.

The Method of Adjustment

In a variant of the Method of Limits, the observer is given control over the intensity of the stimulus and instructed to adjust it until it is just barely detectable (absolute threshold) or until it appears to match some other, standard stimulus (difference threshold). Here's how this technique works in the case of vision.

Absolute Threshold   The experimenter provides the observer with the means to vary the intensity of a light. The observer then adjusts the intensity so that the light is just barely visible. To do this the observer would probably adjust it to a level that is clearly visible, turn it down until it's invisible, and then slowly turn it up again until it's just detectable. The actual intensity value set by the observer constitutes one estimate of the absolute threshold. The initial intensity value would then be reset, and the observer would repeat this adjustment procedure, again finding the intensity where the light was just barely visible. The estimate of threshold would be the average of several such settings. Observers report that they find this method easier to use than the method of limits, even though the two clearly resemble each other. Probably observers find it easier to judge the stimulus on the basis of continuous trial and error (method of adjustment) than when they see just one stimulus at a fixed value (method of limits).

Difference Threshold   The experimenter sets the intensity of the standard stimulus and has the observer adjust the intensity of the comparison until it appears to match the standard. Typically the observer will adjust the stimulus through a range of values centered around the standard, finally settling on a comparison value that appears to match the standard. This procedure is repeated a number of times, and the difference threshold is reflected in the amount of variability among the adjustments (variability can be indexed by any of several descriptive statistics, such as the variance or the standard deviation). How does "variability" relate to the difference threshold? If an observer is highly sensitive to small differences between the standard and comparison, that person's settings will cluster very closely around the standard value, meaning the variance among settings will be small. But if the observer is not very sensitive to differences between the standard and comparison, the person's settings will be spread more widely on either side of the comparison, producing a larger index of variance. The magnitude of the variance among settings, then, will be proportional to the magnitude of the difference threshold.

Now you've seen how each of Fechner's three methods can be used to estimate absolute thresholds and difference thresholds. In the following section, we'll introduce you to some of the modified techniques that are spin-offs from Fechner's original methods. Some of these modifications were prompted by improvements in the equipment available for generating stimuli and for implementing the methods themselves. Other modifications were designed either to minimize some deficiency of a method or to improve the efficiency of a method. In the following section we'll consider two modifications that are particularly important because of their common use.

Modifications of Fechner's Methods

The Staircase Method: A Modified Method of Limits

Almost from its inception, the method of limits' deficiencies were obvious. As you'll recall, this method requires that a series of stimuli be presented, all of which elicit the same response (e.g., "Yes, I see it") except the last, transitional one (e.g., "No, I don't see it"). As a result, most of the trials are devoted to stimulus values other than the one of interest—it's only the last, transitional value that gets recorded and averaged into the threshold estimate. Moreover, the observer can get locked into responding in a given way (e.g., "Yes, I see it"), since after just a few trials the observer knows in which direction the changes are occurring.

To get around these problems, a variant of the method of limits was developed—this variant, called the **staircase method,** offers enhanced efficiency (Cornsweet, 1962). In a typical staircase, the intensity starts at a level above the expected threshold region and then decreases until the observer declares that it can no longer be detected. Following this change in stimulus detectability, the direction of stimulus change is reversed. Now the intensity increases until the response changes again, at which point the intensity decreases once more. In a typical staircase, alternations in the direction of stimulus change continue until some predetermined number of reversals has occurred (see Appendix Figure 2). The threshold is then estimated by the average of all the stimulus intensities at which the observer's responses changed. With this staircase procedure, most stimulus values are concentrated in the threshold region, making it a more efficient procedure.

Still, there's a problem with this version of the staircase procedure. As with the basic method of limits, a simple staircase allows an observer to become aware of the scheme that governs stimulus presentation. The observer's responses are then liable to be influenced by that knowledge. For example, an observer may anticipate that the threshold is being approached and change the response prematurely. To overcome this problem, Cornsweet (1962) introduced a procedure that retains the efficiency of a staircase, but minimizes the observer's knowledge of the direction from which the threshold is being approached. Cornsweet's innovative idea was to interleave several concurrent staircases.

APPENDIX FIGURE 2 | The results of a staircase experiment.

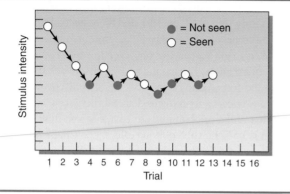

APPENDIX FIGURE 3 | The results of an experiment using two interleaved staircases.

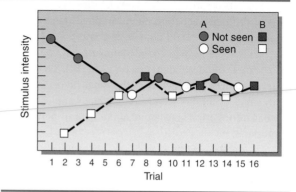

Appendix Figure 3 illustrates a simple case of two interleaved staircases and *strict alternation* between them. On trial 1, staircase *A* begins with a stimulus that is expected to be above threshold, and the observer reports seeing it. On trial 2, staircase *B* starts with a stimulus that is expected to be below threshold, and the observer reports not seeing it. On trial 3, the next stimulus from staircase *A* is presented—at a lower intensity than before, since the observer saw it the first time. On trial 4, the next stimulus from staircase *B* is presented, and so on. As Appendix Figure 3 shows, over the course of trials both staircases converge and the stimulus intensities tend to be concentrated around a single value, the threshold. A further improvement developed by Cornsweet involves *randomly* interleaving the two staircases so that the observer could not figure out which staircase to expect from trial to trial.

Modifications of the Method of Constant Stimuli

Unlike the method of limits, the method of constant stimuli involves random presentation of stimulus levels. This precludes the possibility of expectation effects based on knowledge of what was presented on previous trials (a drawback to the method of limits). However, the classic method of constant stimuli still suffers from inefficiency: many of the stimulus presentations are devoted to intensity values far enough away from the threshold to be of relatively little use. If the aim is to estimate the threshold, no information is gained from presenting intensity values that are always detectable or intensity values that can never be detected. This inefficiency can be avoided by pretesting, which allows the stimuli to be carefully tailored to the capacities of the observer and the conditions

of the experiment. Alternatively, various methods have been developed to adapt or modify the range of tested stimulus values while the experiment itself is in progress (Watt and Andrews, 1981; Watson and Pelli, 1983; Leek, 2001). This latter approach is a useful adjunct to pretesting because, as we've pointed out, the observer's sensitivity can change somewhat during an experiment. The most sophisticated and efficient of these adaptive strategies continuously updates the stimulus set during testing, based on the person's trial-by-trial performance.

There is another reason why researchers consider the method of constant stimuli to be inefficient, at least for measuring difference thresholds: the method requires two stimuli per trial—a standard and a comparison—rather than just one. Naturally, it takes longer to present two stimuli than it does to present just one. Fortunately, the standard is probably superfluous in many circumstances (Morgan, Watamaniuk, and McKee, 2000). In fact, an observer's judgments are just about as precise in the *absence* of a standard as they are in the *presence* of one (Woodworth and Schlosberg, 1954, pp. 217–218).

To appreciate what omitting the standard entails, consider an experiment by Suzanne McKee (1981). To measure the difference threshold for visual velocity—the smallest difference in speed that an observer can discriminate—McKee used the method of constant stimuli but with the standard omitted. On each trial, a computer caused a single vertical line to move across a video display; only one line was presented per trial. The line's velocity on each trial was chosen randomly from a set of seven highly similar velocities. The observer watched a line pass by and judged whether its velocity was faster or slower than the mean of all seven velocities.

Note that McKee never actually had to show the observer which velocity was the mean. Instead, by watching a few presentations of all the velocities, the observers built up a highly accurate mental representation of the mean velocity. It should not surprise you that observers can make accurate perceptual comparisons even when there is no explicit standard present. After all, the method merely requires an observer to do what he or she does many times every day: combine separate samples of perceptual information into an accurate overall perceptual impression.

Forced-Choice, Objective Methods

The methods discussed so far rely on an observer's own, subjective report of what is or is not seen. These reports are termed *subjective* because an experimenter cannot judge whether the observer was correct or incorrect. For instance, when an observer reports, "I see it," we must take that report at face value; it cannot be disputed or verified. In a moment we'll mention why this may be a problem. But first consider an effective solution.

In recent decades, an alternative, objective approach, the **forced-choice method,** has gained considerable popularity. In an experiment using a forced-choice method, the observer must *prove* that he or she can see the stimulus, and the observer's claims can be checked.[2] The observer gives proof by identifying some characteristic of the light other than its intensity. For example, the experimenter might arrange to present a dim light either to the right or to the left of a fixation point. The observer does not have to say whether the light was visible but instead merely identifies the light's position, responding either "left" or "right." Or the experimenter might present the light in just one of two successive test intervals and require the observer to indicate in which interval—first or second—the light was presented. The forced-choice method was popularized by Blackwell (1946), but it had been devised nearly one hundred years earlier, by Bergmann

(Fechner, 1860/1966, p. 242).[3] In order to measure visual acuity, Bergmann used a forced-choice method with grating patterns. He devised a way to vary the orientation of a test grating (recall Chapter 5), and then, instead of asking the observer whether a particular grating was visible or not, Bergmann forced the observer to identify the grating's orientation. (Incidentally, Bergmann not only devised the forced-choice method, he also discovered that stimulus uncertainty reduces detectability [see Chapter 5] and that some orientations are easier to see than others, which is known as the oblique effect [see Chapter 4].)

But what has been learned from the use of forced-choice methods that wasn't known before? For one thing, these methods show that the nervous system registers more sensory information than one is ordinarily aware of. Put another way, forced-choice research shows that people can discern lights so dim or sounds so weak that people claim they cannot see or hear them. Here's a typical demonstration of this remarkable fact.

Suppose that you begin by using one of Fechner's methods, say the method of adjustment, to measure an absolute threshold. After running many trials, you determine a light intensity that the observer says is "just barely visible." You then take that same "threshold" light intensity and present it to the same observer in a forced-choice experiment. The dim light is flashed either to the left or to the right of a fixation point while the observer tries to identify its location. Although such comments are not part of the actual data-collection procedure, the observer may frequently volunteer that her responses are mere guesses and that nothing was actually visible. After many trials, you tally up the number of times the observer was correct. Despite the observer's claims, you find that she was correct 100 percent of the time. Next you decrease the light's intensity to a level *below* the threshold value previously determined by the method of adjustment. When you repeat the forced-choice testing with this new, even dimmer light, the observer protests even more strongly, insisting after every trial that she hadn't seen the light and that she was only guessing about its location. Surprisingly, though, the observer continues to do well—perhaps getting 70 to 75 percent of the choices right. Note that this is well above chance level; If the observer were really just guessing, on average only 50 percent of the responses would be correct.

Similar results have been obtained in studies of the other senses. Typically, forced-choice testing confirms that people can discern stimuli whose intensities are well below the absolute thresholds defined by Fechner's sub-

---

[2]The term *forced choice* does not mean simply that the observer is forced to say something besides "I don't know." Rather, this procedure involves structuring stimulus presentations so that accuracy can be objectively verified. If the experimenter can unequivocally provide error feedback, the procedure is properly called *forced choice.* Note, responses based on subjective impression—for instance, "this is louder than that"—even if responses are required after each stimulus presentation, are not genuinely forced choice. When a listener reports that one tone is louder than another, how can you argue?

[3]A translation of Bergmann's paper is available in D'Zmura (1996).

jective methods. This fact does not mean that subjects are lying when they make subjective threshold settings. Instead, they are relying on information necessary to generate a conscious experience of the stimulus, and the amount of information needed to support that experience seems to be greater than that required for forced-choice performance (where conscious experience is not a necessary component of the judgment).

Forced-choice testing is also useful for eliminating extraneous (nonsensory) differences among observers. In subjective (non-forced-choice) tests, results can be strongly influenced by the criterion that the observer uses for saying whether or not a light was visible. The **criterion** is the implicit rule that the observer uses to translate sensory information into overt responses. For example, one observer may have a strict criterion; she will not report seeing a stimulus unless the sensory evidence is quite strong. Another observer may have a more lax criterion; she is satisfied with weaker sensory evidence. The first observer's responses might lead you to conclude that the observer's threshold was considerably higher than the second observer's when in fact their apparent differences could have been caused by criterion differences alone.

Forced-choice methods, then, should be employed whenever you want to factor out possible criterion differences among observers. The same holds true if you are dealing with groups of observers whose criteria are likely to differ. Because elderly people can tend to be more reluctant about saying, "Yes, I detect it," forced-choice methods are useful in comparing the sensory capacities of older and younger observers. To take another example, hospitalized schizophrenics may be reluctant to admit that they see anything that they are not absolutely sure about. So forced-choice methods are important in comparing the vision of schizophrenic and normal observers. In these comparisons and others, if *criterion* differences cannot be ruled out, it is impossible to be conclusive with respect to the source of the differences in *sensory* capacities. More commonly, researchers have to worry about the constancy of a single observer's criterion from one test to another. This would be important if one is interested in whether some treatment—such as perceptual training—changes an observer's ability to see, or whether the training had affected only the observer's willingness to *say* he sees something.

Before concluding this outline of forced-choice methods, we should note that some of Fechner's original methods could be converted into forced-choice versions. You can devise a forced-choice method of limits or a forced-choice method of constant stimuli. In fact, forced-choice staircases have become particularly popular, with the correctness or incorrectness of a person's responses determining whether the stimulus is increased or decreased from trial to trial.

Signal Detection Theory

There's another important topic that any survey of psychophysical methods must include. That topic is **signal detection theory (SDT),** which encompasses a set of experimental and analytic procedures, as well as a sophisticated psychophysical theory (Green and Swets, 1966; MacMillian and Creelman, 2004). SDT, which had its origins in electrical engineering, offers psychophysics two distinct but complementary benefits. One benefit comes from SDT's procedures for expressing precisely and quantitatively what information is contained in some stimulus. In a visual stimulus, for example, the information includes the spatial distribution of light from different parts of the stimulus, and a description of how that distribution changes with time. Characterizing the stimulus this way makes it possible to determine the efficiency with which a human observer uses the potential information. Defining the potential information contained in a stimulus sets an upper theoretical limit to observer performance (a person cannot, of course, do better than the properly specified theoretical limit).

Knowledge of that theoretical limit makes it possible to compare the performance of a human observer against the performance of an ideal or perfect observer, a theoretically specified observer who exploits every bit of the stimulus's information. To appreciate this, consider what this might mean for vision. If, as usually happens, some information were lost by the eye or by other parts of the visual system, or if neural responses to the stimulus were variable, performance would be less than ideal. Take one example. Some light incident on the eye's cornea is absorbed or reflected rather than transmitted into the eye itself. This loss of light, which is governed by the cornea's structure, reduces the amount of information potentially available in the stimulus. The eye's detection performance is limited, then, because the visual system never gets access to the information lost to absorption or reflection. With appropriate calculations, one can predict precisely how this information loss should affect performance. Geisler (1989) puts this aspect of SDT to excellent use in a psychophysical analysis of the stages in visual processing.

SDT's other main strength lies in its explicit recognition that perceptual measurements are influenced not only by an observer's sensory capacities, but also by various *non*sensory factors.[4] Such nonsensory influences on performance include what we call the observer's **criterion,** which refers to the observer's willingness to say "Yes," I detect a stimulus, versus "No," I don't detect it. The observer's criterion is influenced by the consequences of the detection decision, the observer's prior knowledge about the likelihood that the stimulus occurred, and the observer's motivation to perform the task (Green, 1964). SDT distinguishes sensory from nonsensory factors, producing separate measures of each (MacMillan and Creelman, 2004). At the end of a typical study using SDT, the experimenter obtains two measures of an observer's performance. One measure reflects the observer's sensory capacity; the other measure reflects the observer's criterion for acting on the information provided by the senses.[5]

As we've said, SDT recognizes that in any detection experiment the response "Yes, I detect it" depends on two factors—sensory capacity and criterion. To distinguish the two, SDT compares the frequency with which the observer says "Yes" when some weak stimulus *has* been presented and the frequency with which the observer says "Yes" when *no* stimulus has been presented. Take an example. Suppose some observer says "Yes" every single time a very dim light is presented. You might think his eyes are very sensitive. However, you discover that the same observer also says "Yes" when no light whatever is presented. Clearly, you should not take every *yes* at face value, as proof of actual seeing.

To take advantage of SDT, a researcher can compare an observer's responses in two different conditions. For example, if the experiment involves visual detection, the researcher can determine an observer's responses to a weak light (called *signal*) as well as to no light (called *noise*). Typically, these signal and noise trials are randomly intermixed. After each trial, the observer responds

"Yes" or "No." A "Yes" response to a signal (when a light has been presented) is termed a **hit,** meaning that the observer correctly detected the stimulus. In contrast, a "Yes" response to a noise trial (i.e., one *without* a light) is termed a **false alarm** (because the observer erred, saying he saw something when nothing was presented). After presenting many signal trials randomly interspersed among noise trials, the experimenter tallies the proportion of signal trials on which the observer responded "Yes" and the proportion of noise trials on which the observer responded "Yes." These two proportions are termed the *hit rate* and the *false alarm rate,* respectively.

With the classic method of constant stimuli, the proportion of "Yes" responses (the "hit" rate) would be taken as the data indicative of the observer's sensitivity. But what SDT teaches us is that the hit rate must be interpreted within the context of the false alarm rate. Saying "Yes" on nearly all trials will yield a high hit rate, which could be construed to mean that the observer is highly sensitive. But the false alarm rate will be correspondingly high, which indicates that the high hit rate has been inflated by the observer's general tendency to say "Yes." SDT takes hits and false alarms into account to derive an estimate of sensitivity. It's not necessary to work through the details here, but the two proportions, the hit rate and false alarm rate, can be plugged into equations to get the sought-after values of the person's sensitivity as well as an estimate of the person's criterion.

To see whether you've got the general idea of SDT, consider a hypothetical experiment. Suppose that two people are tested using a dim light of fixed intensity, and suppose that both individuals achieve the same hit rate. However, one observer produces a higher false alarm rate than the other. Which observer has the higher sensitivity to the dim light? The observer whose false alarm rate is lower—that person's responses indicate that he or she was superior in discriminating the presence of light from the absence of light. Signal detection theory treats experimental trials as tests of an observer's ability to discriminate the presence of a stimulus from its absence (recall Fechner's "inner source of light sensation"). Good discrimination is shown by the combination of a high hit rate and a low false alarm rate. A large difference between an observer's responses when there is a light and when there isn't a light signifies that the person can distinguish between the two. Poor discrimination is evidenced when the hit and false alarm rates are close to one another. In the extreme, when the hit and false alarm rates are equal, you know that the observer has completely failed to distinguish between the absence and presence of

---

[4]SDT has been applied to problems in a wide variety of nonsensory areas. These include the study of spider phobia (Becker and Rinck, 2004), memory (Glanzer, Hilford, and Kim , 2004; Rotello, Macmillan, and Reeder, 2004), anxiety (Grossberg and Grant, 1978), medical diagnosis (Emmerich and Levine, 1970; Liu B., Metz C.E., Jiang, 2004), identification in police lineups (Wells, Lindsay, and Ferguson, 1979), perception of hazards in mine shafts (Blignaut, 1979), and decision making in social and legal contexts (Swets, Dawes, and Monahan, 2000). In each, SDT has been useful because of its ability to separate informational and motivational influences on judgments.

[5]The appropriate pair of SDT measures depends upon the details of the experiment, and upon the researcher's reasonable assumptions about the nature of the data (see MacMillan and Creelman, 2004).

a light—performance is at chance level, no matter how high the hit rate might be.

Our discussion of the observer's criterion for reporting sensory information has emphasized differences among observers. But you should recognize that any single observer's criterion can vary, depending on a number of factors. SDT specifies how an observer's criterion should change along with changes in the relative importance, to the observer, of hits and false alarms. If an observer is in a situation where it is vital to detect *all* the stimuli and the cost of making a few false alarms is trivial, then SDT predicts that the observer will adopt a liberal criterion. This would be expected, for example, for an operator of an x-ray screening device at an airport. As bags pass through the x-ray screening device, an operator monitors a video display for any hint of a possibly forbidden item within each and every article of luggage. And as we learned in Chapter 6, these screening decisions can be quite difficult. Still, the operator is instructed not to miss any dangerous object, and to avoid such misses the operator must be willing to say, "Yes," that's a suspicious-looking object that requires closer scrutiny. The operator, in other words, must adopt a very liberal criterion. As a consequence, the operator must stop the conveyor belt whenever something even slightly suspicious shows up on the x-ray. Most of the time, the operator's decision turns out to be a false alarm—the suspicious object is, in fact, harmless. Still, the high false alarm rate is tolerable, since it also produces a high "hit" rate (discovering the rare instances where an object is dangerous). The value of a hit, in other words, more than offsets the costs of many false alarms.

There are other situations, however, where the cost of a false alarm is much too high in comparison to the payoffs for a hit. Imagine that you experience heartburn one evening just before going to bed. Are you having a heart attack, and should you go immediately to the hospital emergency room? Assuming you're a healthy young person (who perhaps has consumed lots of pizza for dinner), you should think twice about the inconvenience and expense of a trip to the hospital. The cost of the false alarm is great relative to the likelihood of a hit (that you're actually having a heart attack).

SDT also specifies how the criterion might change along with changes in the probability that a stimulus will be presented. If the observer knows ahead of time that a stimulus is very likely to occur, then optimally that person should adopt a liberal criterion for reporting the presence of the stimulus. Thinking back to the heartburn example, if you had a family history of heart problems—

and if you hadn't eaten lots of pizza for dinner—then your criterion might shift in favor of a hospital visit. Otherwise, the optimal strategy is to adopt a strict criterion, that is, to require more powerful evidence before reporting that the very unlikely event has actually occurred.

Psychophysical Functions from Psychometric Data

Each technique described in the previous sections produces a measure of the threshold, either an absolute threshold or a difference threshold. Each technique generates data that define change in performance as some intensive dimension of a stimulus changes. For instance, Appendix Figure 1 plots the percentage of "seen" responses against light intensity. A curve of this form, as mentioned earlier, is called a psychometric function, and from such a curve we may derive a single intensity value as an estimate of the threshold.

In studying perception we are often interested in how the threshold changes with some stimulus variable. This requires that we measure the threshold repeatedly, over a range of values along some stimulus dimension. For instance, the visual threshold for detecting a spot of light varies depending on the wavelength of that light (recall Figure 3.30); the contrast threshold for detecting a grating pattern varies with the spatial frequency of the pattern (recall Figure 5.13). Likewise, in hearing, the threshold intensity for detecting a tone varies with the tone's frequency (recall Figure 11.2). These represent measurements of absolute thresholds as the function of different values along a stimulus dimension of interest (for instance, spatial frequency). These kinds of curves—plots of threshold as the function of some stimulus variable—are called **psychophysical functions.** A psychophysical function represents a family of thresholds, not just a single threshold value. Thus, a psychophysical function more completely summarizes the operation of a sensory system than does a single threshold point from that function.

The examples given above are psychophysical functions for detection thresholds. It is also possible to generate a psychophysical function showing how a difference threshold varies with some stimulus variable. Imagine, for example, measuring the smallest difference in wavelength that can just be discriminated from some standard wavelength value. This would constitute a wavelength discrimination threshold. This procedure could be repeated for a number of different standard wavelengths, thus generating a family of wavelength discrimination thresholds. Individual difference

APPENDIX FIGURE 4 | Construction of a psychophysical function from a set of psychometric functions. Shown at the top are three different psychometric functions that yield data points for the psychophysical function.

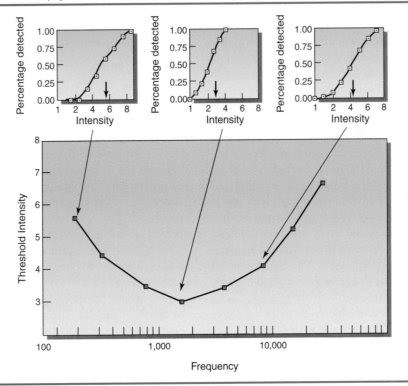

thresholds would then be plotted on a graph showing the magnitude of the difference threshold along the vertical axis and wavelength along the horizontal axis. Such a curve would constitute a psychophysical function.

You can think of a psychophysical function as a curve summarizing the data from a family of psychometric functions. Each data point on the psychophysical function is a threshold derived from a psychometric function. This relation is illustrated in Appendix Figure 4, a schematic audibility function (see Chapter 11) and a sample of the associated psychometric functions. Each data point in the lower part of the figure is an intensity threshold just sufficient to detect a tone of given frequency. Also shown in schematic form are three psychometric functions associated with three of the thresholds; not shown are the psychometric functions for the other threshold values. All the psychometric functions would, incidentally, represent thresholds measured using a method of constant stimuli (recall Appendix Figure 1). One could, of course, measure the family of thresholds using, say, a method of adjustment, in which case there would be no associated psychometric function. Still, the

psychophysical function would be the family of thresholds obtained by repeating the method of adjustment for a number of different stimulus values.

Magnitude Estimation and the Power Law

You've probably seen judges award points to figure skaters or to divers, as ratings of their performance. Or maybe you've watched talent shows on television where audience members register their votes for contestants on an applause meter, the winner being the individual who gets the loudest applause. Perhaps you've been asked to rate how well you like different songs by assigning numbers to them, higher numbers indicating greater liking. In each of these instances, the individual doing the rating behaves like a measuring gauge—that person estimates the magnitude of some quality present in a given object, person, or event, where *quality* refers to some psychological factor such as gracefulness, or appeal.

This same strategy can be applied to the measurement of subjective sensory experiences such as the loudness of a sound or the brightness of a light. Used in this manner, such strategies fall under the rubric of **direct scaling techniques.** These techniques are called *direct* because the judgments people make presumably directly reflect the magnitude of some sensation they are experiencing. Those judgments, according to the advocates of direct scaling techniques, are just as valid as the reading of sound levels taken with a meter. In a way, direct scaling resembles introspection (recall Chapter 1), in that a person's subjective report is taken as reflecting the contents of conscious experiences such as loudness. However, in the case of direct scaling, the person's ratings are constrained in ways that make it possible to quantify the rating, thereby revealing regularities between the judgments of different people.

The person most responsible for the development of direct scaling techniques was S. S. Stevens. The various techniques he devised for studying the intensity of sensations associated with seeing, hearing, taste, smell, and touch are summarized in Stevens (1960). His most popular technique is magnitude estimation, the technique described in Chapters 11 and 14 as it is applied to loudness and odor intensity. According to Stevens, the idea of assigning numbers to gauge the strength of a sensation came from a friendly challenge:

> *It all started from a friendly argument with a colleague who said, "You seem to maintain that each loudness has a number and that if someone sounded a tone I should be able to tell him the number." I replied, "That's an interesting idea. Let's try it." (1956, p. 2)*

Stevens responded by setting up an experiment and instructing participants as follows:

> *You will be presented with a series of stimuli in irregular order. Your task is to tell how intense they seem by assigning numbers to them. Call the first stimulus any number that seems appropriate to you. Then assign successive numbers in such a way that they reflect your subjective impression. There is no limit to the range of numbers that you may use. You may use whole numbers, decimals or fractions. Try to make each number match the intensity as you perceive it. (1975, p. 30)*

As a rule, the stimuli to be rated are presented several times each, in an irregular order. No training is necessary, so it is possible to test a person in a relatively short time, which is one reason for the method's popularity. Stevens used magnitude estimation to study all the senses. He discovered

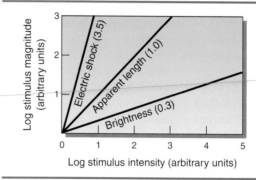

APPENDIX FIGURE 5 | Power functions associated with three different kinds of sensory judgments.

that for each sense modality, the *perceived* strength of a stimulus increased in proportion to the stimulus's *physical* intensity raised to some power or exponent. (This is the power law mentioned in Chapter 11.) Each sense modality has its own characteristic power or exponent, and some of these values are summarized in Appendix Figure 5. Note that the exponent for brightness is 0.3. This rather small value indicates that large increases in light intensity produce relatively small increases in brightness. In contrast, look at the exponent and graph line for electric shock. Here's a sensation that grows much faster than the intensity of the stimulus. In the case of electric shock, doubling the intensity causes about a tenfold change in the perceived strength of that shock. Interestingly, perceived length has an exponent of 1.0, indicating that perceived length corresponds almost perfectly with actual length.

Estimating the Magnitude of Loudness

Magnitude estimation seems deceptively simple: A person is instructed merely to assign numbers to sounds in proportion to their subjective intensity. Taking loudness as an example, if one sound seems three times louder than another, the louder sound should be assigned a number three times larger than the number assigned to the softer sound. The person is free to select any particular numbers, just so long as those numbers faithfully reflect what the person construes as loudness. No upper or lower limits are placed on the range of acceptable numbers, although sometimes the experimenter may arbitrarily assign a given number to one particular sound loudness. For instance, you might be told to let a rating of 100 correspond to the loudness of a 60-dB_{SPL} sound, but from there on your ratings would be entirely up to you.

Given this latitude in assigning numbers to loudness, you might expect the outcome to be a jumble of idiosyncratic, meaningless numbers, but in fact, this does not happen. While the particular numbers assigned to various sound levels can vary from person to person, the relationships among those numbers show a remarkable degree of regularity among individuals. Of course, as sound intensity increases, so does loudness. However, loudness grows more slowly than does intensity.

So loudness does not grow in a simple, additive fashion—with one unit increase in stimulus intensity producing one unit increase in subjective magnitude. Instead, loudness grows exponentially—with each single unit change in the stimulus producing some fraction of unit change in subjective magnitude. This seems to be true over the entire range of audible sound levels, and it holds for magnitude estimates of loudness obtained from just about everyone. Stevens (1960), who was among the first to think about loudness in this way, expressed this general finding in mathematical terms: Loudness grows in proportion to intensity raised to the power, or exponent, 0.67. In mathematical notation,

$$L = k \, I^{0.67}$$

where L stands for loudness, I stands for intensity (expressed as sound pressure level), and k is a constant. This general formula is known as the **power law** of loudness growth. Figure 11.11 shows what this relation between intensity and loudness looks like graphically; plotted on the horizontal axis is the sound level, or intensity, of a pure tone, while plotted on the vertical axis are the numbers (the magnitude estimates of loudness) assigned to those various intensities. Note that in this graph, intensity and loudness are scaled in linear coordinates. Plotted in this way, the resulting loudness function appears curved; it is described as negatively accelerating, meaning that loudness grows more slowly than intensity.

Because the relation between intensity and loudness is exponential, replotting the points on logarithmic coordinates should yield a straight line. Taking the logarithm of both sides of the above equation yields

$$\log L = \log k \; 1 \; 0.67(\log I)$$

which is the general form of the equation for a straight line. So if both intensity and loudness ratings were expressed in logarithmic units, the curve summarizing the growth of loudness would be a straight line. The equation's constant, k, specifies where that straight line intersects the vertical axis; the point of intersection depends on the particular set of numbers used by the person to es-

timate loudness. The equation's exponent, 0.67, specifies the line's slope. A slope less than 1.0 means that subjective magnitude grows more slowly than intensity, while a slope greater than 1.0 indicates subjective magnitude grows more rapidly.

Stevens and other proponents of direct scaling developed methods besides magnitude estimation to measure sensation (see Gescheider, 1976). One of the more clever methods, called **cross-modality matching,** requires a person to equate the strengths of sensations arising from the stimulation of different sense modalities. To illustrate, a person might be asked to adjust the loudness of a sound until its strength matched the brightness of a light. At first glance, this kind of judgment sounds strange, but people actually have no trouble doing it. Probably, cross-modality matching is not so different from deciding how well you enjoyed a performance and clapping your hands with a vigor that reflects this enjoyment.

The matches between modalities conform to predictions derived from the power law. For example, to match a small increase in the intensity of an electric shock, a person requires a large increase in the intensity of a sound; this merely reflects the fact that perceived shock intensity grows much more rapidly than loudness.

These direct scaling techniques, particularly magnitude estimation, have recently been applied to psychological attributes other than sensory judgments. The seriousness of various crimes, the beauty of art works, and the perceived status of various occupations—these are some of the psychological attributes that have been quantified by means of direct scaling.

Multidimensional Scaling

The procedures described so far have focused on the detection or discrimination of small differences in sensory stimulation or on the growth in sensation with intensity. Now we turn to a rather different procedure—**multidimensional scaling (MDS)**—designed to quantify the degree to which arrays of stimuli are comparable along some set dimension(s). Unlike the methods described above, MDS is typically applied to complex stimuli that are easily discriminable from one another. The goal with MDS is to construct a pictorial representation of the similarities among stimuli (Schiffman, Reynolds, and Young, 1981). Technically speaking, MDS mathematically generates an n-dimensional space, or map, into which all stimuli being studied will fit. The number of dimensions required to construct that space provides revealing information about the similarities among the stimuli.

The stimuli in an MDS study can be almost any-thing—perfumes, cola drinks, beers, taste chemicals, colors, legislators, food flavors, and so on. Regardless of what the stimuli are, though, an MDS study begins by asking people to judge how similar the stimuli are to one another.

Sometimes, a researcher does not know what basis people will use in making their similarity judgments. For example, if they're judging the similarity of a Chevrolet Corvette and a Porsche, they might respond to the fact that both are sports cars (and judge them similar) or to the fact that they come from different countries (and judge them dissimilar). This can be a problem if the researcher wants to avoid biasing people's judgments. With taste and smell it's particularly hard to know the basis for perceptions of similarity and dissimilarity. Here MDS comes in extra handy, helping to define the perceptual basis for the judg-ments (even though the researcher doesn't know that ba-sis ahead of time).

Let's start with a simple experiment. Suppose we concoct four different concentrations of sodium chloride (salt) in water. We give them two at a time to people who sip them and then make a numerical judgment of how similar the two are. Suppose they rate similarity on a scale from 100 meaning *perfect identity between the two,* all the way to 0 for *absolutely no similarity whatever* (other judgment schemes can also be used; see Schiff-man, Reynolds, and Young, 1981).

In our hypothetical study, salt solutions A and C are judged most similar, solutions A and B least similar, and the other pairs are judged as somewhere in between. How does one make a spatial map that corresponds to these judgments? The goal is to make a map with four points, *A, B, C,* and *D;* the distances between the points should correspond to the judgments of similarity—similar salt solutions should be close together and dissimilar ones far apart. For convenience, we start with the pair *A* and *B.* Since these two solutions are judged least alike, their cor-responding spots on the map should be far apart. Arbi-trarily, we can position *A* at the left and *B* way to the right. Since *D* is judged equally similar to *C* and *B, D* should go about halfway between *C* and *B.* Finally, because *A* and *C* are judged quite similar, we know that *C* goes somewhere close to *A;* but we don't know whether to position it to the left or right. We get the answer by comparing judgments of *A* and *B,* on the one hand, with judgments of *B* and *C,* on the other. Since *C* and *B* are judged more similar than *A* and *B,* we know that *C* must lie somewhere between *A* and *B.* The complete arrangement is shown in panel A (top) of Appendix Figure 6. To validate our map, we can

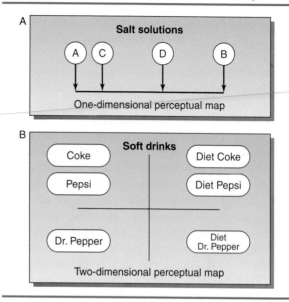

APPENDIX FIGURE 6 | Maps depicting dimensions derived from multidimensional scaling.

look at similarity judgments and corresponding points that we haven't used thus far. On the map, *C* is closer to *A* than to *D;* this is consistent with the fact that *C* is judged more similar to *A* than it is to *D.*

When the stimuli can be represented along a single straight line, it indicates judgments were made on the ba-sis of a single aspect or dimension of the stimuli—in this case probably the intensity of the salt taste. Thus, the study with salt solutions led to a map that was a one-di-mensional representation. In this hypothetical example involving salt solutions, a one-dimensional map makes sense because the solutions differed in only one way. With more complex stimuli, however, a one-dimensional map may be inadequate because people rely on more than one dimension to derive their similarity judgments. In such cases, a map of two or three dimensions might be needed. Let's take a simple example, based on an actual experiment (Schiffman, Reynolds, and Young, 1981).

Suppose we take six brands of carbonated soft drinks (with brand identifications hidden): Coca-Cola, Pepsi-Cola, Dr Pepper, Diet Coke, Diet Pepsi-Cola, and Diet Dr Pepper. As before, we allow people to sip pairs of the drinks and then ask for numerical judgments of how similar the two are. These similarity judgments are the data from which we will try to produce our percep-tual map. Here are the hypothetical results. Coke and Pepsi are judged highly similar in taste, but each one is judged quite dissimilar from Dr Pepper. In addition, Coke, Pepsi, and Dr Pepper are each judged dissimilar to their respective diet versions. Finally, some pairs are judged to be particularly *dis*similar: Coke (or Pepsi) versus Diet Dr Pepper, and Dr Pepper versus Diet Pepsi or Diet Coke.

With these results in hand, we proceed to produce an appropriate one-dimensional map. Again, we start by putting the most dissimilar stimuli at opposite ends of the line. For example, we place Coke and Pepsi at one end (close to each other) and Diet Dr Pepper at the other because these were judged extremely dissimilar. Now we've got a problem; other soft drinks were also judged extremely dissimilar—Dr Pepper versus the diet versions of Coke and Pepsi. If we try to place these on the same line we used for Diet Dr Pepper, Coke, and Pepsi, the map will necessarily contradict some of the similarity judgment data we collected. Try it for yourself. The solution is to make a two-dimensional map such as the one shown in panel B of Appendix Figure 6. The arrangement of the stimuli on this map is consistent with the idea that people were judging sodas on the basis of two criteria—whether they had a *cherry* taste (like Dr Pepper) and whether they had a *diet* taste. Note that the data themselves forced us to describe the perceptions in two dimensions.

Incidentally, it was fairly easy to create the maps in our two examples because both examples involved a small number of stimuli. Most MDS experiments, though, use a dozen or more stimuli, making it difficult to produce the right map "by hand." In those cases, researchers use a computer program containing sophisticated trial-and-error schemes for making the map. Programs available for this task are described in the excellent introduction to MDS by Schiffman and her colleagues (Schiffman, Reynolds, and Young, 1981). MDS programs can also be found in many standard statistical software packages. These researchers also describe a whole series of uses of MDS, including the development of new consumer products.

This concludes our discussion of psychophysical methods used in perception research. Though Fechner's goals for psychophysics—an exact science of the relation between mind and body—have not been completely realized, there can be little doubt about the value of his contributions. As a result, today many people all over the world celebrate October 22, called by some "Fechner Day" (Boring, 1961). For on that date, in 1850, Fechner first got the idea for his psychophysics, and the impact has been lasting. Today a Society for Psychophysics exists, with annual meetings and an excellent Web page with all kinds of historical material and contemporary information (including tutorials on methods that can be downloaded to your computer); please check the link to the Society's Web page available at www.mhhe.com/blake5.

K E Y   T E R M S

absolute threshold	false alarm	multidimensional scaling
β (beta)	forced-choice method	power law
criterion	hit	psychometric functions
cross-modality matching	intrinsic light	psychophysical functions
d′	just noticeable difference (JND)	psychophysics
dark light	method of adjustment	signal detection theory (SDT)
difference threshold	method of constant stimuli	staircase method
direct scaling techniques	method of limits	Weber's law

Glossary

A

Abney's Law   The principle that the visual effectiveness of a light composed of different wavelengths can be predicted from the sum of the responses to the wavelengths considered separately.

absolute distance   The distance from an observer to an object. See *relative distance.*

absolute pitch   Rare ability to identify or to vocally produce any note on the musical scale, without reference to another, heard tone.

absolute threshold   The minimum stimulus intensity that a person can detect. See *difference threshold.*

accommodation   The variation in the eye's optical power brought about by temporary changes in the shape of the lens.

achromatic system   In the opponent-process view of color vision, the pathway that generates and transmits information about an object's lightness. See *chromatic system.*

achromatopsia   Inability to perceive the colors of objects, including familiar ones, as the result of damage to restricted regions of the brain.

acoustic energy   The variations in air pressure produced by the vibration of an object.

acoustic reflex   Muscular contractions within the middle ear that damp sound vibrations by stiffening the eardrum and restricting the movements of the ossicles.

acoustics   The branch of physics concerned with sound.

action potentials   Brief electrical discharges generated by a neuron and provide a major source of neural communication and computation within the nervous system. See *axon* and *synapse.*

acupuncture   Centuries-old technique for eliminating pain by insertion of fine needles into the body at specific sites

adaptation   A reduction in the responsiveness of neurons, produced by prolonged stimulation.

additive color mixture   A color that results when several component colors are combined in such a way that each component contributes a portion to the spectral composition of the combination. See *subtractive color mixture.*

aerial perspective   The tendency for objects at a distance to appear less distinct, since light reflected from those objects must travel through atmosphere containing particles of dirt and water.

affordances   Uses of an object, governed by the object's structural characteristics.

afterimage   A visual sensation that persists after exposure to some intense stimulus; also, an illusory color produced by exposure to an intense stimulus.

agnosias   Neurological conditions in which people cannot recognize objects; depending on the sense involved, an agnosia is said to be visual, auditory, or tactile. See *prosopagnosia.*

akinetopsia   Inability to perceive visual motion as the result of damage to restricted regions of the brain.

alexia   An acquired disorder, usually consequent to brain damage, involving an inability to read despite normal vision; often accompanied by normal ability to write.

aliasing   Creation of spurious low-frequency information when high-frequency information is undersampled, as by photoreceptor mosaic.

allocentric   A reference frame in which an object's position is expressed independently of the vantage point from which it is viewed.

allodynia   Pain from stimulation that is normally not painful, sometimes experienced at a location other than at the stimulated area of the body.

amacrine cell   A type of cell in the retina that transmits electrical signals from the bipolar cells to the ganglion cells, in the process influencing the rate at which those signals are generated over time. See *bipolar cell* and *horizontal cell.*

ambient system   The aspect of vision responsible for spatial orientation; uses information from peripheral as well as central vision. See *focal system.*

ambiguity problem   Because several stimulus variables jointly determine the response of any sensory neuron, a single neuron's response is ambiguous with respect to stimulus conditions.

Ames room   A specially constructed room in which the floor-to-ceiling heights as well as the sizes and shapes of the doors and windows have been distorted to make the room appear rectangular when viewed from one specific vantage point. To an observer looking into the room through a peephole, people of identical heights standing in different parts of the room look dramatically different in height. The Ames room illustrates how perceived distance influences perceived size.

amodal completion   Perception of an object's occluded region(s).

amplitude   The property of sound waves that is related to the magnitude of the change in air pressure produced by a sound source. This property, sometimes referred to as *intensity,* is related to loudness. See *intensity.*

amusia   Inability to recognize musical tones or to reproduce them. The condition may either be congenital (present at birth) or acquired later in life consequent to brain damage.

analgesia   The elimination of pain. See *endorphins.*

analytic introspection   A method for studying perception in which trained people attend to and describe the experiences evoked by some stimulus.

aneurysm   A bulge in a blood vessel which, when it occurs within the brain, can put pressure on nearby neurons, thereby producing functional loss.

anomalous myopia   A temporary myopia induced by lack of adequate stimuli for accommodation.

anosmia   An inability to smell odors. See *specific anosmia*.

Anton's syndrome   A neurological condition in which a cortically blind person denies his or her blindness.

anvil (incus)   The middle member of the three ossicles within the middle ear; it relays sound vibrations from the *hammer* to the *stirrup*.

aperture problem   The inability of a motion sensor with a restricted field of view to register unambiguously the direction of motion of an extended contour moving through the sensor's field of view.

apparent motion   The illusory impression, created by the rapid alternation of objects presented at different spatial locations, that the objects have moved smoothly from one location to the other. See *element movement, group movement*.

aqueous humor   A watery fluid, produced by the ciliary body, that nourishes structures within the eye's anterior chamber and helps maintain the eye's shape.

astigmatism   An error in refraction caused by variation in optical power along various meridians of the cornea.

audibility function (AF)   In hearing, a graph portraying threshold intensity as a function of the frequency of the test tone.

auditory canal   The hollow cavity leading from the pinna to the eardrum, which in humans is about 2.5 cm long and 7 mm in diameter.

auditory cortex   A region of the cortex devoted to analysis of complex sound information, including biologically relevant sounds involved in communication. See *primary auditory cortex*.

auditory face   Vocal characteristics of speech that allow a listener to recognize the speaker's identity and mood. See *paralinguistic information*.

auditory image   With a complex sound field arising from several different auditory events, the information associated with just one of those events.

auditory looming   Perception of an approaching, sound emitting object, based on the steady increase in the amplitude (loudness) of the emitted sound.

auditory nerve   The bundle of nerve fibers innervating the cochlea and carrying information from the ear to higher stages of the auditory system. Also known as the *eighth cranial nerve*.

autokinetic effect   The illusory impression of motion created when a small stationary target is seen in a homogeneous dim field.

axon   The portion of a neuron over which action potentials are conducted. A group of axons constitute a *nerve* or a *tract*. See *action potential*.

B

bandpass noise   Noise containing a restricted, contiguous band of frequencies.

basilar membrane   The thin sheet of tissue separating the tympanic canal and the cochlear duct.

beta (β)   In signal detection theory, a measure of the observer's bias.

binaural   Listening with two ears. See *monaural*.

binaural cues   Sources of sound information for localizing a sound source by comparing the sounds received by the two ears.

binaural unmasking   (binaural masking-level difference: BMLD) A reduction in the ability of masking noise heard with both ears to mask another sound heard by one ear only. See *masking*.

binocular   Seeing with two eyes. See *monocular*.

binocular cell   A visual cortical cell receiving excitatory input from both eyes.

binocular rivalry   The alternation of a percept over time between one eye's view and the other eye's view when the two eyes view very different stimuli.

bipolar cells   Type of cell in the retina that transforms electrical signals from the photoreceptors into action potentials; these cells play a crucial role in generating ON and OFF responses. Together with amacrine and horizontal cells, bipolar cells form a network that shapes the receptive field properties of ganglion cells. See *amacrine cell, horizontal cell*.

bistable figure   A drawing or photograph that can be seen in one of several different ways. See *Necker cube*.

blindsight   The ability of some cortically blind people to point to the location of a light that they cannot see.

blobs   Clusters of color-opponent cells in the upper layers of the primary visual cortex. Cells within these clusters, often referred to as blob cells, receive input from color-selective cells of the parvocellular pathway.

Bloch's Law   The principle that all stimuli in which the product of time and intensity is constant will be equally detectable.

blue-yellow cells   Neurons showing a polarized response to spectral lights, which increases over one portion of the spectrum and decreases over another portion; the transition between the two types of responses occurs between the regions of the spectrum called blue and yellow. See *red-green cells*.

bone conduction   The transmission of sound wave vibrations through the bones of the skull to the cochlea. A procedure for testing the integrity of the cochlea in the presence of middle-ear damage.

Braille   A system of writing in which letters or characters are represented by patterns of tangible dots.

brightness   The dimension of visual experience related to the amount of light emitted by an object. See *lightness*.

broadband noise   Noise whose energy covers a wide range of frequencies.

C

cataract   Clouding that reduces the lens's transparency and, hence, degrades the quality of the retinal image.

categorization   The ability to place different objects into groups based on common features or common properties among those objects.

center frequency   The frequency lying at the center of the range of frequencies contained in bandpass noise.

change blindness   Failure to notice an otherwise conspicuous change because of the diversion of attention. See *inattentional blindness*.

Charles Bonnet syndrome   A condition, not associated with dementia, where a visually impaired individual reports seeing things that are not really present.

choroid   A dark, spongy structure containing blood vessels that supply nourishment to the retina; because of its heavy pigmentation, the choroid absorbs scattered light.

chromatic system   In the opponent-process view of color vision, the pathway that generates and transmits information about an object's color. See *achromatic system*.

cilia   In the case of hearing, cilia are tiny hair-like structures that extend into the fluid of the inner ear; their movements are caused by pressure waves in that fluid bend the cilia and trigger electrical signals. In the case of olfaction, cilia are tiny tufts of thin hairs projecting out of each olfactory receptor cell and extending through the mucous layer into the nasal cavity; thought to be the site where odorous molecules trigger electrical changes in the olfactory receptor cell.

ciliary body   Located in the eye, a spongy network of tissue that manufactures aqueous humor.

circadian rhythm   Fluctuation in biological or behavioral activity that coincides with the day/night cycle.

closure   The Gestalt principle of organization referring to the tendency of the visual system to obscure small breaks or gaps in objects. See *proximity, similarity*.

cochlea   A coiled, fluid-filled chamber in the inner ear containing the specialized organ for hearing, the basilar membrane.

cochlear emissions   Sounds that are generated entirely from within the cochlea.

cochlear implant   A small prosthetic device inserted within the inner ear, allowing direct electrical stimulation of the auditory nerve to produce sensation of sound. Used in cases of profound, irreversible hearing loss arising from damage to the inner ear's hair cells.

cochlear nucleus   A structure receiving input from the auditory nerve; its cells exhibit a high degree of frequency tuning.

cocktail party effect   The ability to attend selectively to the speech of one person in the midst of many other speakers.

color constancy   The tendency of an object's color to remain unchanged despite changes in the spectrum of light falling on—and reflected by—that object.

color contrast   A change in color appearance brought about by juxtaposing particular color pairs.

color deficiency   In humans, a departure from normal trichromatic color vision; takes various forms, including anomalous trichromacy, dichromacy, and monochromacy.

color induction   The tendency of the color of a surface to be influenced by the colors of neighboring surfaces.

common chemical sense   An aspect of olfaction responsible for the detection of strong concentrations of potentially dangerous substances; responsible for the "feeling" in the nose produced by certain substances.

common fate, Law of   The tendency to group together individual elements moving in the same general direction at the same speed.

complementary   The term describing two colors that can be mixed to form white.

complex cells   Visual cortical cells that do not exhibit clearly defined ON and OFF regions within their receptive fields, making it difficult to predict what stimulus will produce the largest response. See *simple cells*.

composite light   According to Newton, any light that is made up of several different color components. See *pure light*.

computer vision   The ability of machines, notably computers, to perceive and interpret a visual scene.

conditioned taste aversion   Learned avoidance of certain taste substances, usually following nausea from ingesting the substance.

conduction loss   A form of hearing loss attributable to a disorder in the outer or middle ear; it typically involves an overall loss in sensitivity at all sound frequencies. See *sensory/neural loss*.

cone of confusion   The set of points in space that potentially could have given rise to any one interaural time difference or interaural intensity difference.

cones   Photoreceptors that are specialized for daylight and color vision. See *rods*.

configural processing   Integration of various object features into a comprehensive, global configuration. See *featural processing*.

configural superiority effect   The finding that, under some circumstances, a complex figure, or part of a complex figure, may be seen more readily than one of its parts presented in isolation.

conjunctive   Referring to those movements of the eye in which both eyes move in the same direction. See *vergence.*

contralateral fibers   In the case of vision, those optic nerve fibers that project from one eye to the opposite side of the brain. See *ipsilateral fibers.*

contrast   The difference in light intensity between an object and its immediate surroundings; also, the intensity difference between adjacent bars in a grating.

contrast normalization   The process by which the limited dynamic range of neurons' responsiveness to contrast can be adjusted to the prevailing level of contrast.

contrast sensitivity function (CSF)   A graph depicting a person's ability to see targets of various spatial frequency; on the *x*-axis is the spatial frequency of the test target; on the *y*-axis is sensitivity, the reciprocal of the minimum contrast needed to see the test target.

contrast threshold   The minimum contrast needed to see some target.

convergence   The ability of the eyes to turn inward, toward each other, in order to fixate a nearby object.

convergence insufficiency   Difficulty with turning the eyes inward to fixate a nearby object.

cornea   The transparent portion of the eye's front surface, which refracts light and allows it to pass into the eyeball.

cortical deafness   Impaired hearing that results from damage to the auditory cortex.

cortical magnification   The mapping of the retina onto the visual cortex so that the representation of the fovea is exaggerated or magnified.

cranial nerve   Any one of 12 nerve fibers that innervate various structures within the head and neck, including nerves that carry sensory information from the eyes (optic nerve), nose (olfactory nerve), tongue (trigeminal and glossopharyngeal nerves) and ear (vestibulocochlear nerve).

criterion   The implicit rule used by an observer in order to convert sensory information into overt responses. See **d'**.

critical band   The restricted range of frequencies that mask a given test frequency. The critical band reflects the frequency tuning of the neurons that detect the test frequency.

critical flicker frequency (CFF)   The highest perceptible rate of temporal variation in light intensity.

cross-adaptation   A temporary loss in sensitivity to one odor following exposure to a different odor.

cross-fiber theory   The idea that taste qualities are represented by the pattern of neural activity among an ensemble of neurons; also has application in vision, hearing, and smell.

cross-modality matching   A psychophysical procedure in which one sort of stimulus (for instance, a light) is adjusted so that the sensation the stimulus produces matches the sensation produced by a different sort of stimulus (for instance, a sound).

crowding effect   The tendency for small letters to be difficult to read when they are in close proximity to one another.

crystalline lens   The elliptical optical element located immediately behind the iris of the eye. Temporary variations in thickness alter the eye's accommodation, or optical power.

cutoff frequency   The spatial frequency at which a lens's transfer function falls to zero; the highest frequency that a lens can image; the highest frequency to which a visual system can respond.

D

d'   In signal detection theory, a measure of sensitivity. See **criterion.**

dark adaptation   The increase in visual sensitivity that accompanies time in darkness following exposure to light.

dark light   See *intrinsic light.*

decibel (dB)   A unit for expressing sound amplitude.

delay line   Key element in a theory designed to explain binaural cells' sensitivity to interaural time differences. The delay line retards the arrival of signals from one ear relative to those from the other ear.

depth of field   The range of distances over which the image of a scene remains sharply focused; varies with pupil size.

depth perception   The ability to perceive the three-dimensional locations of objects in relation to the perceiver's position in space. Besides specifying distance, depth perception allows a perceiver to segregate objects from their backgrounds and to discern the three-dimensional shapes of objects.

detection   The process by which an object is picked out from its surroundings; also, the process by which the presence of some object is perceived.

dichromatic   Referring to a person whose eye contains two types of cone photopigments.

difference threshold   The minimum amount by which stimulus intensity must be changed in order to produce a just noticeable change in sensation. See *absolute threshold.*

diffuse fibers   In touch system, first-order afferent neurons having large receptive fields with poorly defined borders.

diplesthesia   In touch, the illusory experience of two objects when only one is actually present.

diplopia   Double vision, a condition that results when images from the two eyes are seen separately and simultaneously.

direct scaling techniques   A set of psychophysical procedures for measuring subjective sensory experiences such as loudness or brightness; these procedures are based on the assumption that people can rate sensory magnitude.

direction-selective cell   A neuron in the visual cortex that responds most vigorously to a particular direction of target movement.

direction selectivity   A tendency of some neurons in the visual system to respond most strongly to objects that move in a particular direction.

discrimination   The process by which one object is distinguished from another.

discrimination threshold   The minimum physical difference, usually an intensity difference, that allows two objects to be distinguished from each other.

disfluency   Brief, unpredictable disruptions in otherwise fluent speech, characterized by hesitations and self-corrections.

disparity-selective cells   Cells in the visual cortex that receive input from both eyes and that respond only when an object is situated at a particular distance from the two eyes. See *stereoblindness.*

divergent   Referring to light whose wavefronts spread outward, usually as the light proceeds away from its source.

DoG   Difference of gaussian, a category of visual patterns whose limited spatial frequency content makes them useful in the study of spatial vision.

dorsal stream   Hierarchically arranged brain areas within the occipital and parietal lobes, thought to register information about visual motion and spatial location. See *parietal pathway;* contrast with *ventral stream.*

dualism   The philosophical view that mental events need not be associated with neural events. See *materialism.*

duplex   Referring to the co-existence within the eye of two different systems, scotopic and photopic. The scotopic system provides high sensitivity in dim light; the photopic system provides high resolution under daylight conditions.

duplex theory   In hearing, the idea that the interaural time difference (ITD) is used to localize low-frequency sounds and the interaural intensity difference (IID) is used to localize high-frequency sounds.

dynamic visual acuity   The finest spatial detail that can be resolved; measured while a target is moving.

E

eardrum (tympanic membrane)   The thin, oval membrane that covers the end of the auditory canal and separates the outer ear and the middle ear; it vibrates when sound waves strike it.

eccentricity   The distance between the center of the retina and the location of the retinal image cast by an object.

echoes   Reflected sound waves.

echolocation   A technique used by biological organisms, most notably bats, whereby emitted sound is used to detect objects and to judge the distance between the object and the sound source. See *sonar.*

efferent fibers   In the auditory system, neural projections from the brain back to the cochlea.

egocentric direction   The direction in which an object is located relative to an observer.

electromagnetic radiation   Energy that is produced by oscillation of electrically charged material; light encompasses a small portion of the electromagnetic spectrum.

element movement   In an ambiguous type of apparent movement, the percept that some of the stimulus's components are stationary while one component moves back and forth. See *apparent motion, group movement.*

Emmert's law   The perceived size of an image of fixed retinal size varies directly with perceived viewing distance.

emmetropic   Referring to an eye whose focal point, in the absence of accommodation, coincides exactly with the retina.

endorphins   Naturally occurring morphine-like chemicals that can ease pain. See *analgesia.*

equal loudness contours   A set of curves describing the sound intensities at which different frequencies all sound equal in loudness. See *loudness matching.*

Eustachian tube   The opening connecting the middle ear and the throat, which maintains air pressure within the middle ear at nearly the same value as the air pressure in the outside environment.

Event-related potential (ERP)   electrical brain activity measured from the scalp and evoked by a stimulus event. Also known as evoked potential (EP).

extraocular muscles   In humans, six large muscles attached to the globe of the eye; by rotating the eyeball within the orbit, the coordinated contractions of these muscles control the direction of gaze. See *rectus muscles.*

F

face-inversion effect   Difficulty recognizing distortions in features of a face viewed upside-down, distortions readily perceived when the face is viewed upright.

far senses (distance senses)   Senses, such as vision, that enable an organism to perceive objects or events some distance away. See *near senses.*

featural processing   Ability to perceive individual components, or features, of an object without being able to integrate those components into a global form. See *configural processing.*

fibrous tunic   The strong, leathery outermost layer of the eyeball.

figure/ground organization   The tendency to see part of a scene (the figure) as a solid, well-defined object standing out against a less distinct background (the ground).

flavor   A complex sensation associated with food, based on the food's taste, temperature, texture, and smell.

flicker   Temporal variation in light intensity; also, the perception of such temporal variation.

floaters   Debris that drifts about within the eye's vitreous casting shadows on the retina and producing dark spots that appear to move along with the eye.

fMRI   Functional magnetic resonance imaging, a for localizing regions of neural activity within the brain. See *PET.*

focal system   The aspect of vision that is responsible for object identification and discrimination; predominantly uses central, rather than peripheral, vision. See *ambient system.*

forced-choice method   A psychophysical procedure in which a person must identify the interval during which a stimulus occurred; in an alternative version, the person must identify the spatial location at which a stimulus was presented.

Fourier analysis   A method for calculating the frequency content of any temporal or spatial signal; can be used to determine the spatial frequency content of a visual scene or the temporal frequency content of a sound.

fovea   Pit or depression in the retina; the region of sharpest vision.

free nerve endings   Nerve cells in the skin that mediate pain perception and cells in the olfactory epithelium that mediate the common chemical sense.

frequency theory   The idea that the basilar membrane vibrates as a unit in response to sound, in synchrony with sound pressure changes. See *place theory.*

frequency tuning curve   A graph describing the sensitivity of an auditory neuron to tones of various frequencies.

fundamental frequency   The lowest frequency among the set of frequencies associated with a complex sound.

G

gate theory of pain   The view that perception of pain involves the interplay between two fiber groups, one which can modulate the strength of signals in the other.

geons   In one theory of visual recognition, the geometric elements into which seen objects are decomposed. The term is short for *geo*metrical ic*ons.*

Gestalt principles of organization   Certain stimulus properties that control the perceptual grouping of objects. See *closure, good continuation, proximity, similarity.*

glaucoma   A relatively common ocular disorder in which fluid pressure builds up within the eyeball, eventually causing blindness if not corrected.

global motion   The experience of motion in a single direction that arises from a stimulus whose elements move in a variety of different directions.

good continuation   The tendency to see neighboring elements as grouped together when they are potentially connected by straight or smoothly curving lines.

grating   A target consisting of alternating darker and lighter bars, used to study spatial vision. See *sinusoidal grating.*

group movement   In an ambiguous type of apparent movement, the percept that all stimulus components move back and forth *en masse* (as a group). See *apparent motion, element movement.*

grouping   The aggregation of several related elements into a larger coherent unit. A key part of the recognition process.

gustatory cortex   Region deep within a region of the temporal lobe, the insula, containing neurons responsive to the presence of taste substances within the mouth.

H

habituation   The process by which an organism ceases to respond to some stimulus.

hair cells   The ears' receptors. See *inner hair cells, outer hair cells.*

hammer (malleus)   The outermost of the three ossicles within the middle ear; one end of the hammer is attached to the eardrum, and the other end relays sound vibrations to the anvil.

haptics   Sensory information that depends upon both touch and kinesthesis.

harmonics   Acoustic frequencies that are multiples of one another, often occurring in speech and music. Harmonic tones tend to be perceptually grouped in hearing.

Hermann grid   A regular, geometric pattern within which illusory spots are seen; the presence and strength of the illusory spots depend on the spacing of the grid's elements.

Hertz (Hz)   A unit for expressing the frequency with which the intensity of a sound or a light varies over time.

horizontal cell   A type of cell in the retina that modulates the strength of signals generated by neighboring photoreceptors. Together with bipolar and amacrine cells, horizontal cells form a network responsible for shaping the receptive field properties of ganglion cells. See *amacrine cell, bipolar cell.*

horopter   An imaginary plane in visual space that contains objects whose images fall on corresponding points of the retina of the left and right eyes; any object situated on the horopter will be seen as single.

hue   The dimension of color experience that distinguishes among red, orange, yellow, green, blue, and so on; the dimension of color most strongly determined by light's wavelength; commonly used as synonym for *color.* See *brightness, saturation.*

hyperacuity   A level of perceptual performance that exceeds the best sampling density of the underlying receptor network.

hypercolumn   An aggregation of columns of cortical cells whose receptive fields overlap on the same restricted region of the retina.

hypercomplex cell A category of visual cortical cell whose receptive field layout makes the cell responsive to the length of a contour and, in some instances, the presence of contours forming angles and corners. See *simple cells, complex cells.*

hyperopic Referring to an abnormally short eyeball, in which the image is blurred because the eye's focal point lies behind the retina.

I

identification The cognitive process of distinguishing a particular object. Contrast with *categorization.*

illusions Perceptual "errors" where a quality of a sensory experience deviates from what would be expected based on the physical characteristics of the stimulus evoking that experience.

illusory conjunction Condition in which features that actually belong to separate objects appear to be combined.

image The spatial distribution of light energy produced by the action of some optical system.

inattentional blindness Impairment in perceiving the appearance of or changes to unattended objects. See *change blindness.*

incus See *anvil.*

induced motion The illusory impression, created when moving contours are nearby a stationary object, that the stationary object is moving.

inner hair cells (IHCs) The approximately 3,500 flask-shaped structures situated along the length of the basilar membrane of the human ear. See *outer hair cells.*

intensity The physical variable expressing the strength or amplitude of a stimulus, such as light or sound. Intensity can be measured by physical devices such as photometers and sound-level meters. See *amplitude.*

interaural intensity difference (IID) The difference in the intensity of sound arriving at the two ears; one of the sources of information for sound localization. See *interaural time difference.*

interaural time difference (ITD) The difference in the time of arrival of a sound wave at the two ears; one of the sources of information for sound localization. See *interaural intensity difference.*

interposition A monocular depth cue based on occlusion of a distant object by a closer one.

interpupillary distance (IPD) the distance between the two eyes in the head.

intrinsic light (dark light) Spontaneous sense of dim light caused by residual retinal signals arising in the complete absence of light stimulation.

inverse optics The problem of determining what objects in the world generated a given image on the retina.

ipsilateral fibers In the case of vision, those optic nerve fibers that project from one eye to the same side of the brain. See *contralateral fibers.*

iris The two-layered ring of tissue that gives the eye its characteristic color.

isoluminant A property of multiple surfaces that differ only in hue, not brightness or saturation.

J

just noticeable difference (JND) The smallest discriminable difference between two stimuli that differ along one dimension.

K

K cells Class of visual cells characterized by small cell bodies; thought to be involved in color vision. See *M cells, P cells.*

kinesthesis Information about the movement and position of a limb that derives from receptors that are in the muscles, tendons, and joints of that limb.

knockout mouse A mouse produced by replacing a gene sequence with a modified sequence containing a mutant version of a targeted gene. The resulting mutant phenotype can provide an indication of the gene's normal role in the mouse. Used to produce animals lacking specific types of sensory receptors.

L

lateral geniculate nucleus (LGN) A group of nerve cell bodies arranged in layers in the thalamus, each layer receiving input from either the left eye or the right eye; the major relay station between the eye and the visual cortex.

lateral inhibition Antagonistic neural interaction between adjacent regions of a sensory surface, such as the retina.

lesion Damage to a restricted region of the body, particularly some portion of the nervous system.

lightness A perceptual variable that is correlated with intensity of light reflected from a surface.

lightness constancy The tendency for the perceived lightness of an object to remain constant despite variation in the level of its illumination.

lightness contrast Variations in perceived lightness of a surface of invariant intensity, produced by variations in the lightness of regions surrounding that surface.

linear perspective The convergence of lines that makes a two-dimensional representation of a scene appear to be three-dimensional.

LLI Language-based learning impairment.

localization ability An observer's capacity to identify the position of some stimulus.

loudness The subjective experience associated with sound intensity.

loudness matching A psychophysical procedure in which a listener adjusts the intensity of one tone until it sounds as loud as another tone. See *equal loudness contours.*

M

M cells   Retinal ganglion cells characterized by relatively large cell bodies and axons, large receptive fields, strong response to small differences in light levels in receptive field center and surround, and lack of sensitivity to stimulus wavelength. See *P cells.*

M − L channel   Color processing network that computes the difference in activity within cones sensitive to medium wavelength (M) and long wavelength (L) light. See *S − (M + L) channel.*

Mach bands   Illusory spatial gradations in perceived lightness that occur in the absence of corresponding gradations in the actual spatial distribution of light.

macula   The small, circular central region of the retina where vision is most acute.

magnitude estimation   A psychophysical procedure in which people assign numbers to stimuli in proportion to the perceived intensity of those stimuli.

magnocellular layers   In the lateral geniculate nucleus, layers containing large cells; layers 1 and 2.

malleus   See *hammer.*

masking   A reduction in one stimulus's visibility or loudness as a result of the juxtaposition of another, stronger stimulus. See *binaural unmasking.*

materialism   The philosophical view that ascribes all mental experiences to neural events. See *dualism.*

McGurk effect   Auditory misperception of a spoken phoneme that occurs when the speaker's mouth appears to be uttering a different phoneme.

mechanoreceptors   Receptors that respond to deformation of the skin.

medial geniculate nucleus   A structure in the thalamus that is part of the auditory system.

Meissner corpuscles   An encapsulated touch receptor located in the skin's upper layer.

melody contour   The rise and fall of successive notes in a musical passage.

meridional amblyopia   A loss in visual acuity for lines of a particular orientation.

Merkel disk   Touch receptor located at an intermediate depth within the skin.

mesopic   Referring to vision at levels of illumination at twilight. See *photopic, scotopic.*

metamers   Two or more objects that appear identical despite acute physical differences.

meter   A musical concept related to the repetitive sequences of strong and weak beats in a musical passage. In written musical notation, these beat patterns are represented in the measures, or bars, of the notation.

method of adjustment   A psychophysical procedure in which a person adjusts a stimulus so that it is just detectable (absolute threshold) or until a just noticeable change is produced (difference threshold).

method of constant stimuli   A psychophysical procedure in which each of a fixed set of stimuli is presented in random order.

method of limits   A psychophysical procedure in which the stimulus intensity changes progressively in small steps until the person's response changes, for example, from "No, I don't see it" to "Yes, I do see it."

microelectrode   A thin wire that can be inserted into brain tissue in order to record action potentials.

microspectrophotometry   A technique for measuring, at various wavelengths, the quantity of light reflected or absorbed by a small object; used to measure cone photopigments.

missing fundamental   With a complex series of harmonic tones, the fundamental tone of the series may continue to be heard despite the fact that it has been physically removed.

mixture suppression   The strength of an odorant or a taste substance presented alone may be reduced when that same odorant or taste substance is presented in combination with another.

Modification, taste   Alteration of the taste quality associated with a given substance produced by prior exposure to another taste substance.

monaural   Listening with one ear. See *binaural.*

monochromat   A person whose eye contains just one type of cone photopigment.

monocular   Seeing with one eye. See *binocular.*

motion aftereffect (waterfall illusion)   The illusory impression, after prolonged viewing of movement in one direction, that a stationary object is moving in the opposite direction.

motion capture   An object that moves in one direction over a field of randomly moving elements causes those elements to appear to move in the same direction as the object itself.

motion parallax   A source of potent monocular depth information based on differences in relative motion between images of objects located at different distances from an observer.

multichannel model   The hypothesis that spatial vision is the product, in part, of sets of neurons responsive to different spatial frequencies.

multidimensional scaling (MDS)   A quantitative technique for geometrically representing similarity among stimuli.

multiple object tracking   Ability to keep track, over time, of multiple, spatially dispersed, independently moving objects.

myelin   A membrane that insulates a neuron's axon and speeds conduction of nerve impulses along that axon.

myopic   Referring to an abnormally long eye, in which the retinal image is blurred because the eye's focal point lies in front of the retina.

N

naive realism   The philosophical view that perception accurately portrays all objects and events in the world.

nanometer   A unit of length in the metric system corresponding to one-billionth of a meter, used for specifying wavelength of light.

nasal cycle   Periodic alternation in which first one, then the other nostril is obstructed.

near senses   Senses, such as touch, that require close proximity between the perceiver and the object or event to be perceived. See *far senses.*

Necker cube   An outline drawing of a cube that can be seen in either of two perspective views. See *bistable figure*

neon spreading   The illusory migration of color from one region into neighboring regions.

neurogram   A graph depicting variations over time in the neural activity within a large number of frequency-selective neurons in response to a complex sound.

neutral point   In a dichromatic eye, the wavelength of light that appears uncolored (neutral in color).

Newton's color circle   A geometric arrangement of colors summarizing the results of mixing varying amounts of different colors.

nociceptors   A special class of skin receptors responsive to noxious stimulation. See *free nerve endings.*

noise   A complex sound whose many constituent frequencies combine to produce a random waveform.

nonspectral colors   Colors, such as purple, that are not found in the spectrum.

O

object-based attention   The view that attention is always directed at objects, not spatial locations.

oblique effect   The tendency for lines oriented vertically or horizontally to be more visible than lines oriented along a diagonal.

occipital lobe   A region in the posterior portion of the brain involved in vision. Contains multiple visual areas each with a retimotopic map of visual space.

occlusion   A condition in which one nearer object blocks an observer's ability to see at least a portion of another, more distant object.

ocular dominance   The variation in strength of excitatory input from the two eyes to a binocular cell of the visual cortex.

oculomotor cues   Kinesthetic cues to depth derived from muscular contractions of the extraocular muscles.

odor adaptation   A reduction in odor sensitivity following prolonged exposure to an odorous substance.

odor constancy   The tendency of an odor's perceived intensity to remain constant despite variations in the flow rate of air drawn into the nose.

odor hallucinations   Odors experienced without any physical stimulus; a phenomenon sometimes associated with brain damage.

olfactometer   Device for presenting controlled amounts of an odorant to one or both nostrils.

olfactory brain   A cluster of neural structures that receives projections from the olfactory bulb via the olfactory tract.

olfactory bulb   The brain structure that receives input from the olfactory nerve.

olfactory epithelium   A patch of tissue situated near the top of the nasal cavity and containing the olfactory receptor cells.

olfactory nerve   The bundle of axons from olfactory receptor cells that project to the olfactory bulb, carrying information about odorous substances from the nose to the brain. Also called *first cranial nerve.*

olfactory sensory neuron   A bipolar (double-ended) nerve cell that captures odorant molecules and initiates the neural signals for smell.

ophthalmoscope   An optical device used to visualize the inside of the eye.

optic ataxia   A neurological disorder characterized by difficulties in the visual guidance of limb movement.

optic chiasm   The point at which nerve fibers from the two eyes are rerouted to higher visual centers, with some fibers from each eye projecting to the same side of the brain (ipsilateral fibers) and the remainder projecting to the opposite side of the brain (contralateral fibers).

optic disk   The region of the eye where the optic nerve penetrates the retina; also, the region where major blood vessels enter and exit the eye's interior.

optic flow   The dynamic pattern of retinal image stimulation produced when objects move toward or away from an observer or when an observer moves through a cluttered environment.

optic nerve   The bundle of axons of retinal ganglion cells that carries visual information from the eye to the brain. Also known as the *second cranial nerve.*

optic tracts   The two bundles of axons of retinal ganglion cells formed after the nerve fibers exit the optic chiasm.

orbit   A cavity in the skull that houses an eyeball and its supporting structures.

organ of Corti   The receptor organ for hearing, situated within the cochlear duct.

orientation   The degree of inclination of a contour within a two-dimensional plane.

orientation constancy   The tendency to judge visual orientation based on gravity, regardless of head position.

orientation selectivity A unique property of visual cortical cells, whereby they respond best to contours of a particular orientation, with the response decreasing as the orientation deviates increasingly from the preferred value.

ossicles A series of three tiny bones that transmit sound vibrations from the eardrum to the oval window. See *anvil, hammer, stirrup.*

otosclerosis A disorder of the middle ear involving immobilization of the stirrup.

outer hair cells (OHCs) The approximately 12,000 cylindrical structures situated along the length of the basilar membrane of the human ear. See *inner hair cells.*

outer segment The distal part of a photoreceptor that contains photopigment.

oval window The small opening into the inner ear, which is covered by a thin membrane and which receives vibrations from the eardrum via the ossicles.

P

P cells Retinal ganglion cells characterized by relatively small cell bodies and axons, small receptive fields, weak response to small differences in light levels in receptive field center and surround, and good sensitivity to stimulus wavelength. See *M cells.*

Pacinian corpuscle An encapsulated touch receptor located in the skin's lower layer.

papillae Protuberances distributed over the tongue's surface, the walls of which are lined with taste buds.

paralinguistic information Sound qualities of speech that specify the speaker's sex, age, mood, and/or identity, independently of the linguistic content of the speaker's utterances.

parietal cortex A major division of the cerebral cortexlocated just behind the central sulcus; contains cortical somatosensory representation of the body.

parietal pathway Hierarchically arranged brain areas within the occipital and parietal lobes, thought to register information about visual motion and spatial locations. See *dorsal stream.*

parvocellular layers In the lateral geniculate nucleus, layers containing small cells; layers 3 through 6.

perceived distance The apparent visual separation between two objects or between an object and the viewer.

perception The acquisition and processing of sensory information in order to see, hear, taste, smell, or feel objects in the world; also guides an organism's actions with respect to those objects. Perception may involve conscious awareness of objects and events; this awareness is termed a *percept.*

perimetry A procedure for measuring a visual field, which involves determining the positions in visual space where a person can and cannot see a small spot of light.

PET scan An image of the brain, or other structure, that is created by means of positron emission tomography.

phantom limb The perception that an amputated limb is still attached to the body.

pheromones Odors that serve as sexual signals.

phonagnosia The inability to identify speakers by means of their voices.

phoneme A sound difference that affects the meaning of an utterance; widely regarded as the fundamental unit of speech.

phosphenes Visual sensations arising entirely from neural events within the visual pathways, in the absence of light stimulation.

photon The smallest unit of light energy.

photopic Referring to vision under daylight levels of illumination. See *scotopic.*

photopigment Light-sensitive molecules within a photoreceptor; light causes the photopigment to isomerize, releasing energy that alters the photoreceptor's electrical potential.

photoreceptors Specialized nerve cells (rods and cones) in the eye that contain photopigment; absorption of light by these cells triggers changes in the cells' electrical potential.

phototransduction The process by which absorption of light by photopigment triggers an electrical signal within photoreceptors.

pigment epithelium A layer of the retina that helps to dispose of cellular debris.

pinna The part of the ear projecting from the side of the head; by influencing the frequency composition of sound waves entering the ear, this prominent structure plays a role in sound localization.

pitch The subjective counterpart to sound frequency.

pitch chroma The dimension of pitch associated with a given musical note's unique tonal character, independently of its absolute position on the musical scale. Thus middle C on the piano has the same pitch chroma as the note C one octave higher on the keyboard. See *pitch height.*

pitch constancy Ability to perceive the same pitch from tones with differing spectral content, such as the note C played by a violin and by a trumpet.

pitch height The dimension of pitch associated with a musical tone's position within the octave structure of music. Middle C on the piano is lower in pitch height than the C one octave higher, even though both are readily identified as the same note. See *pitch chroma.*

point-light motion Motion created by dots of light placed on the joints of a biological organism (e.g., a person) engaged in an activity (e.g., walking).

position invariance The tendency for neural response or perceptual response to remain unchanged despite changes in the position of a stimulus within the visual field.

place theory   The idea that different portions of the basilar membrane vibrate in response to different sound frequencies. See *frequency theory*.

power law   The psychophysical principle that sensation magnitude tends to grow as a power function of stimulus intensity.

presbycusis   In hearing, an age-related gradual loss of sensitivity to high-frequency tones.

presbyopia   A significant decline in accommodative ability beginning in middle age.

primary auditory cortex   The cortical region in the temporal lobe that receives afferent auditory signals from more peripheral auditory structures; sometimes called A1; neurons in this cortical area are organized tonotopically.

primitives   In theories of vision, simple elements that are thought to be building blocks for perception.

profile analysis   The process by which the relative activity of various neurons registers some property of a stimulus.

proprioception   The sense that enables one to feel where one's limbs are.

prosody   Patterns of stress and intonation in speech sounds, regularly used by speakers to distinguish declarative from interrogative utterances and to indicate the approaching end to an utterance. Important sources of acoustic information for guiding dialogue.

prosopagnosia   An inability to recognize faces. See *agnosias*.

proximity   The Gestalt principle of organization referring to the perceptual tendency to group together objects that are near one another. See *closure, similarity*.

psychometric function   A graph showing the frequency with which each stimulus elicits each of two possible responses.

psychophysical function   A graph showing the threshold as a function of some stimulus variable.

psychophysics   The branch of perception that is concerned with establishing quantitative relations between physical stimulation and perceptual events.

punctate fibers   In touch system, first-order afferent neurons have small receptive fields with sharply defined borders.

pupil   The aperture in the eye formed by two sets of concentric bands of muscle; the constriction and dilation of these muscles vary the diameter of the pupil.

pure light   According to Newton, any light that cannot be broken down into constituent colors. See *composite light*.

pure tones   Sinusoidal variations in sound pressure, such as those produced by striking a tuning fork.

Purkinje shift   Perceptual variation in the relative lightness of different colors as illumination changes from daylight to twilight.

pursuit eye movements   Smooth movements of the eyes that allow them to follow a moving target.

R

random-dot stereogram   A pair of pictures composed of black and white dots randomly positioned within the pictures; when such pictures are viewed stereoscopically (one picture seen by each eye), a vivid sensation of depth results, making an object appear to stand out from its surroundings.

rapidly adapting (RA) fibers   First-order afferent neurons that respond in a relatively transient manner to sustained deformation of the skin.

receptive field   The region of a sensory surface within which the activity of a sensory neuron can be influenced. In the case of vision, this constitutes a region of the retina which, itself, represents a given region of visual space. In the case of touch, the receptive field corresponds to a delimited region on the skin's surface.

recognition by components   The theory that any view of an object can be represented as an arrangement of just a few, simple three-dimensional forms. See *geons*.

rectus muscles   Four of the extraocular muscles; largely responsible for moving the eyeball back and forth horizontally (medial rectus and lateral rectus) and up and down vertically (superior rectus and inferior rectus). See *extraocular muscles*.

red-green cells   Neurons showing a polarized response to spectral lights, which increases over one portion of the spectrum and decreases over another portion; the transition between the two types of responses occurs between the regions of the spectrum called green and red. See *blue-yellow cells*.

refraction   The bending of light by an optical element such as a lens.

relative distance   The distance between two objects. See *absolute distance*.

relative pitch   The comparatively common ability to identify a tonal interval without necessarily knowing the particular tones that make up that interval.

resolution   The ability to distinguish spatial details of an object.

resonant frequency   The frequency at which a given object vibrates when set into motion.

reticular activating system   A brain stem structure that governs an organism's general level of arousal.

retina   The innermost layer of the eyeball, where light is detected by photoreceptors and transduced into neural signals that are processed by retinal ganglion cells.

retinal disparity   A slight difference in lateral separation between the images of objects seen by the left eye and by the right eye; provides the geometric basis for stereopsis. See *stereopsis*.

retinal ganglion cells   Cells within the retina with center/surround receptive field organization; axons of the retinal ganglion cells constitute the optic nerve. See *bipolar cell, amacrine cell, horizontal cell*.

retinal image   The distribution of light falling on the retina; the quality and overall intensity of this image influence visual perception.

retinotopic map   A neural representation within the visual system that preserves the spatial layout of the retina.

rhythm   Variation in the temporal pattern of sound, most notably in music. Quality of music associated with "beat."

Ricco's Law   The principle that stimuli will be equally detectable if the product of their intensity and area is constant.

rods   Photoreceptors that are specialized for vision under dim light. See *cones*.

round window   The thin membrane that covers a small opening into the middle ear; displacement of this membrane compensates for pressure variations within the cochlea.

Ruffini endings   An unencapsulated touch receptor located at an intermediate depth within the skin.

S

S − (M + L) channel   The color-processing network that computes the difference between activity within cones sensitive to short wavelength (S) and the sum of activity within cones sensitive to medium (M) and long wavelength (L) light. See *(M − L) channel*.

saccades   Rapid, jerky movements of the eyes, which function to change fixation from one location to another.

saturation   The dimension of color experience that distinguishes pale or washed-out colors from vivid colors. See *brightness, hue*.

scale   Relative size or extent.

sclera   The tough, dense material that forms the eye's outermost coat; seen from the front, the sclera is the white of the eye.

sclerosis   The hardening of any living tissue; hardening of the eye's crystalline lens may play a role in presbyopia. See *presbyopia*.

scotoma   A region of blindness within the visual field.

scotopic   Referring to vision under dim levels of illumination. See *photopic*.

selective adaptation   A method of studying mechanisms of perception, in which a person's sensitivity to particular targets is depressed by prolonged exposure to one particular target.

sensory/neural loss   A form of hearing loss originating within the inner ear or the auditory pathways; may involve selective loss of sensitivity to a limited range of frequencies. See *conduction loss*.

sensory-specific satiety   Eating one particular food may diminish hunger for that food without affecting hunger for other foods.

sensory transduction   The process occurring within sensory receptors by which physical energy (stimulus) is converted into neural signals.

shading   A gradient in the level of reflected light across the surface of a three-dimensional object. This gradient provides a cue to depth, since flat, two-dimensional surfaces don't cast shadows.

shape constancy   The tendency for the perception of an object's shape to remain invariant despite changes in shape of the retinal image of that object produced by viewing it from different perspectives.

signal detection theory   A quantitative treatment of detection and discrimination performance, in which the observer is characterized as a maker of statistical decisions; the system also prescribes techniques that allow the observer's sensitivity to the stimulus to be estimated independently of the observer's criterion, or preference for particular responses. See *d'* and *beta*.

similarity   The Gestalt principle of organization referring to the perceptual tendency to group together objects that are similar to one another in texture, shape, and so on. See *closure, proximity*.

simple cells   Visual cortical cells that exhibit clearly defined ON and OFF regions within their receptive fields. See *complex cells*.

single cell recording   The use of a microelectrode to record the neural activity of individual nerve cells as they respond to stimulation.

sinusoidal grating   A target in which the intensity of darker and lighter bars varies sinusoidally over space. See *grating*.

size aftereffect   A change in the apparent size of an object following inspection of an object of a different size.

size constancy   The tendency for an object's perceived size to remain constant despite changes in the size of the retinal image of that object as viewing distance varies.

slowly adapting (SA) fibers   First-order afferent neurons that respond in a relatively sustained manner to sustained deformation of the skin.

smooth eye movements   Smooth movements of the eyes, which can function in the pursuit of a moving target.

solipsism   The belief that no one exists other than oneself.

sonar (SOund NAvigation Ranging)   A technique whereby sound reflected from object surfaces is used to detect those objects and judge their distances from the sound source. See *echolocation*.

sonification   Sensory substitution technique whereby visual information specifying object location and intensity are converted into sound signals that vary in frequency and intensity.

sound localization   The ability to identify the position of some sound stimulus.

sound pressure level (SPL)   A reference level for sound intensity.

sparse coding   A form of symbolic representation in which signals within a relatively small number of elements (e.g., neurons) can code a very large number of alternative objects or events.

spatial frequency   For a grating target, the number of pairs of bars imaged within a given distance on the retina; units of spatial frequency are cycles/mm or, equivalently, cycles/degree of visual angle.

spatial phase   The position of a grating relative to some visual landmark.

spatial summation   The process by which neural signals from neighboring retinal areas are combined, thereby increasing sensitivity. See *temporal summation*.

specific anosmias   Conditions in which people have normal odor sensitivity for some substances but reduced sensitivity for other substances. See *anosmia*.

specific nerve energies   The doctrine that the qualitative nature of a sensation depends on which particular nerve fibers are stimulated.

spectral colors   Hues that are present in a spectrum created by diffracting white light as, for example, in a rainbow.

spectrogram   A graph depicting the frequency composition of a sound as a function of time.

squint   See *strabismus*.

stabilized retinal images   Images whose location on the retina remains fixed despite movements of the eye.

staircase method   A psychophysical procedure in which the stimulus presentations, governed by a person's responses, are made to bracket the threshold; an interactive variant of the method of limits.

stapes   See *stirrup*.

stereoblindness   The inability to see depth using retinal disparity information, a condition thought to result from a reduction in the number of binocular visual cells in the visual cortex. See *disparity-selective cells*.

stereopsis   Binocular depth perception based on retinal disparity. See *retinal disparity*.

stereoscope   An optical device for presenting pictures separately to the two eyes.

stimulus   The pattern of physical energy set up by an object or event in the environment.

stimulus uncertainty   Lack of knowledge about some property or properties of a stimulus; such uncertainty reduces the stimulus's detectability.

stirrup (stapes)   The innermost of the ossicles within the middle ear; attached to the oval window, it receives sound vibrations from the anvil and sets the oval window into vibration.

strabismus   Squint; a condition in which the two eyes are misaligned, making normal binocular fixation impossible.

structure from motion (SFM)   The impression of an object's shape derived from the object's motion.

subjective contours   Illusory contours or surfaces, especially like those devised by Kanizsa.

subjective idealism   The view that the physical world is entirely the product of the mind.

subtractive color mixture   A color produced when each of a number of components absorbs a portion of the light's spectrum, thereby subtracting that portion from the reflected spectrum. See *additive color mixture*.

superior colliculus   A subcortical brain structure located in the midbrain; this structure plays a role in the initiation and guidance of eye movements.

symmetry   Tendency for parts of an object centered about a given axis of orientation to be highly similar in shape, texture, and/or color.

synapse   A region where release of neurochemical transmitter substance from one neuron spreads to alter the electrical properties of nearby neurons. See *transmitter substance*.

synesthesia   The rare condition where sensory stimulation evokes an experience ordinarily not associated with that stimulation. In one form of synesthesia, called color/orthographic synesthesia, colors are experienced when viewing black or white letters or numbers.

T

tactile agnosia   An inability to recognize objects by touch, resulting from damage to the somatosensory cortex.

taste buds   Garlic-shaped structures lining the walls of the papillae on the tongue and containing chemical-sensitive cells that register the presence of taste solutions.

taste hedonics   Judgments of the pleasantness of taste substances.

taste modification   Alteration in the taste of one substance when it is sampled together with another substance.

taste suppression   The reduction in the strength of one taste sensation by another; for example, sugar suppresses the bitter taste of coffee.

tectorial membrane   An awninglike layer of tissue arching over the hair cells within the inner ear.

temporal pathway   Hierarchically arranged brain areas within the occipital and temporal lobes, thought to be involved in visual object perception. See *ventral steam*.

temporal summation   The process by which signals from a neuron or neurons are cumulated over time, thereby increasing sensitivity. See *spatial summation*.

temporary threshold shift   A short-lived decrease in hearing sensitivity caused by exposure to noise.

texture The visual quality of a surface of an object or of a plane referring to multiple (often dense) markings on that surface or on that plane.

texture contrast Adjacent regions of a visual scene distinguished by differences in texture.

texture gradient A form of perspective in which the density of a surface's texture increases with distance, providing information about the slant of the surface.

threshold intensity The minimum sound intensity necessary to elicit a neural response from an auditory neuron.

tilt aftereffect A temporary change in the perceived orientation of lines following adaptation to lines of a similar, but not identical, orientation.

timbre The quality of sound that distinguishes different musical instruments. See *harmonics.*

tinnitus An annoying, persistent ringing in the ears.

tip of the nose effect The phenomenon in which an odor seems familiar though one cannot name it.

tonotopic organization The orderly layout of preferred frequencies over the length of the basilar membrane.

touch acuity The ability to distinguish a small separation between two closely adjacent stimuli applied to the skin.

transcranial magnetic stimulation Called TMS; a technique whereby a brief, intense pulse of magnetic energy is applied to the scalp to disrupt temporarily normal neural processing.

transfer function A graph showing, for various target spatial frequencies, the contrast contained in an image.

transmitter substance One of several different neurochemicals that diffuse across synaptic gaps between adjacent nerve cells, allowing cells to communicate with one another. See *synapse.*

transparency The property of a nonopaque object that makes it possible to see other objects located behind the nonopaque one. Transparency implies depth without occlusion.

traveling wave Up and down movements of the basilar membrane produced by fluctuations in fluid pressure within the cochlea.

trichromatic Referring to a person whose eye contains three types of cone photopigments.

U

unilateral neglect Neurological disorder in which a patient ignores events on one side of the body.

univariance principle The hypothesis that any photoreceptor's response corresponds to just a single variable, the amount of light absorbed; because photoreceptors obey the univariance principle, the wavelength characteristics of light that stimulate a photoreceptor are not directly represented in the receptor's response.

unvoiced laughter Noisy and atonal laughter sounds, with grunt-like or snort-like qualities. Produced without regular (periodic) vocal-fold vibrations. See *voiced laughter.*

V

vascular tunic The middle layer of the eyeball; responsible for much of the eye's nourishment.

ventral stream Hierarchically arranged brain areas within the occipital and temporal lobes, thought to be involved in visual object perception. See *temporal pathway;* contrast with *dorsal stream.*

vergence Referring to eye movements in which the two eyes move in opposite directions. See *conjunctive.*

vernier acuity Visual ability to perceive slight spatial offsets between neighboring lines, even when those offsets are smaller in angular subtense than the diameter of a single photoreceptor in the eye.

vestibular The system responsible for the body's sense of balance.

vestibular eye movements Eye movements that promote the steadiness of gaze by compensating for movements of the head and body.

vestibule A chamber in the inner ear involved in vestibular eye movements.

view-based recognition The theory that recognition of object depends upon multiple, stored views of that object.

visual angle Unit of measure expressing the size of an image on the retina; the visual angle subtended by an image is determined by the size of the object casting that image and the viewing distance from eye to object.

visual acuity A measure of the smallest detail that a person can resolve visually.

visual cues Sources of depth information based on monocular and binocular image properties.

visual field The extent of visual space over which vision is possible with the eyes held in a fixed position.

visual masking The reduction of one target's visibility by the presentation of another target nearby in time and space.

vitreous The thick transparent fluid that fills the eye's largest chamber.

vocal folds Membrane within the base of the larynx the vibrations of which produce speech utterances. These structures, components of the vocal tract, are slightly longer in males than in females, thus giving the male voice a somewhat lower voice pitch. Commonly called vocal cords. See *vocal tract.*

vocal tract A complex of structures which together produce vocal sounds; these structures include the lungs, diaphragm, larynx, oral cavity and nose. See *vocal folds.*

voiced laughter Regular, tonal-like laughter sounds, produced by regular vocal-fold vibrations that give the laughter a song-like quality with a fundamental frequency. See *unvoiced laughter.*

W

waterfall illusion   See *motion aftereffect.*

wavelength   The distance from the peak of one wave to the peak of the next. For electromagnetic radiation, such as light, wavelength is determined by the rate at which the emitting substance oscillates. This physical property of light, specified in nanometers, is related to the perceptual experience of hue.

Weber's Law   The principle that for various stimulus intensities the difference threshold tends to be a constant fraction of the stimulus.

Wernicke's area   Region within the left hemisphere of the brain's temporal lobe that is involved in the recognition of speech.

window of visibility   The range of spatial frequencies that, with sufficient contrast, an observer can see.

word superiority effect   The finding that, under some conditions, an entire word may be read more rapidly (or be seen more easily) than just one of the word's letters.

Y

Young-Helmholtz theory   The theory that human color vision is trichromatic—that is, it depends on the responses of three types of cones.

Z

Zwicker tone   The illusory perception of a tone produced by prior exposure to broadband noise missing acoustic energy at the frequency corresponding to the illusory tone.

References

Ackerman, D. (1990) *A natural history of the senses.* New York: Random House.

Adair, R. K. (2002) *The physics of baseball,* 3rd ed. New York: Harper Publishers.

Adams, A. J., Wang, L. S., Wong, L., and Gould, B. (1988) Visual acuity changes with age: Some new perspectives. *American Journal of Optometry and Physiological Optics,* 65, 403–406.

Adams, A. J., Zisman, F., Rodic, R., and Cavender, J. (1982) Chromaticity and luminosity changes in glaucoma and diabetes. In G. Verriest (ed.), *Colour vision deficiencies, VI.* Proceedings of the Sixth Symposium of the International Research Group on Colour Vision Deficiencies. The Hague: W. Junk, 413–416.

Addams, R. (1834/1964) An account of a peculiar optical phaenomenon. In W. Dember (ed.), *Visual perception: The nineteenth century.* New York: John Wiley & Sons, 81–83.

Adelson, E. (1993) Perceptual organization and the judgment of brightness. *Science,* 262, 2042–2044.

Adrian, E. D., and Zotterman, Y. (1926) The impulses produced by sensory nerve endings: III. Impulses set up by touch and pressure. *Journal of Physiology,* 61, 465–483.

Ahissar, E., Bergman, H., and Vaadia, E. (1992) Encoding of sound-source location and movement: Activity of single neurons and interactions between adjacent neurons in the monkey auditory cortex. *Journal of Neurophysiology,* 67, 203–215.

Ahles, T. A., Blanchard, E. B., and Ruckdeschel, J. C. (1983) The multidimensional nature of cancer-related pain. *Pain,* 17, 277–288.

Ahlström, R., Berglund, R., Berglund, U., Engen, T., and Lindvall, T. (1987) A comparison of odor perception in smokers, nonsmokers, and passive smokers. *American Journal of Otolaryngology,* 8, 1–6.

Ahlström, R., Berglund, R., Berglund, U., Lindvall, T., and Wennberg, A. (1986) Impaired odor perception in tank cleaners. *Scandinavian Journal of Work and Environmental Health,* 12, 574–581.

Ahlström, V., Blake, R., and Ahlström, U. (1997) Perception of biological motion. *Perception,* 26, 1539–1548.

Alain, C., Arnott, S. R., Hevenor, S., Graham, S., and Grady, C. L. (2001) "What" and "where" in the human auditory system. *Proceedings of the National Academy of Sciences: USA,* 98, 12301–12306.

Alais, D., and Blake, R. (1999) Neural strength of visual attention gauged by motion adaptation. *Nature Neuroscience,* 2, 1015–1018.

Albensi, B. C., and Powell, J. H. (1998) The differential optomotor response of the four-eyed fish Anableps anableps. *Perception,* 27, 1475–1483.

Albrecht, D. G., Farrar, S. B., and Hamilton, D. B. (1984) Spatial contrast adaptation characteristics of neurones recorded in the cat's visual cortex. *Journal of Physiology,* 347, 713–739.

Alho, K., Kujala, T., Paavilainen, P., Summala, H., and Naatanen, R. (1993) Auditory processing in visual brain areas of the early blind: Evidence from event-related potentials. *Electroencephalography and Clinical Neurophysiology,* 86, 418–427.

Alitto, H. J., and Usrey, W. M. (2003) Corticothalamic feedback and sensory processing. *Current Opinion in Neurobiology,* 13, 440–445.

Alpern, M. (1981) Color blind color vision. *Trends in Neurosciences,* 4, 131–135.

Amoore, J. E. (1970) *Molecular basis of odor.* Springfield, Ill.: Thomas.

Amoore, J. E. (1991) Specific anosmias. In T. V. Getchell, R. L. Doty, L. M. Bartoshuk, and J. B. Snow (eds.), *Smell and taste in health and disease.* New York: Raven Press, 655–664.

Anand, S., and Hotson, J. (2002) Transcranial magnetic stimulation: neurophysiological applications and safety. *Brain and Cognition,* 50, 366–386.

Andersen, R. A., and Bradley, D. C. (1998) Perception of three-dimensional structure from motion. *Trends in Cognitive Science,* 2, 222–228.

Anderson, B. L. (1994) The role of partial occlusion in stereopsis. *Nature,* 367, 365–368.

Andrews, T. J., Halpern, A. D., and Purves, D. (1997) Correlated size variations in human visual cortex, lateral geniculate nucleus, and optic tract. *Journal of Neuroscience,* 17, 2859–2868.

Anholt, R. R. H. (1991) Odor recognition and olfactory transduction: The new frontier. *Chemical Senses,* 16, 421–427.

Anliker, J. A., Bartoshuk, L., Ferris, A. N., and Hooks, L. D. (1991) Children's food preferences and genetic sensitivity to the bitter taste of 6-n-propylthiouracil (PROP). *American Journal of Clinical Nutrition,* 54, 316–320.

Annis, R. C., and Frost, B. (1973) Human visual ecology and orientation anisotropies in acuity. *Science,* 182, 729–731.

Anstis, S. M. (1974) A chart demonstrating variations in acuity with retinal position. *Vision Research,* 14, 589–592.

Anstis, S. M. (1978) Apparent movement. In R. Held, H. W. Leibowitz, and H.-L. Teuber (eds.), *Handbook of sensory physiology,* vol. 8. Berlin: Springer-Verlag, 655–673.

Anstis, S. M. (1998) Picturing peripheral acuity. *Perception,* 27, 817–825.

Applegate, W. B., Miller, S. T., Elam, J. T., Freeman, J. M., Wood, T. O., and Gettlefinger, T. C. (1987) Impact of cataract surgery with lens implantation on vision and physical function in elderly patients. *Journal of the American Medical Association,* 257, 1064–1066.

Araneda, R. C., Kini, A. D., and Firestein, S. (2000) The molecular receptive range of an odorant receptor. *Nature Neuroscience,* 3, 1248–1255.

Arezzo, J. C., Schaumburg, H. H., and Petersen, C. A. (1983) Rapid screening for peripheral neuropathy: A field study with the Optacon. *Neurology,* 33, 626–629.

Argentieri, Domenico (n.d.) *Essay on Leonardo's optics.* New York: Regnaland Co., 436.

Arnold, J. E., Tanenhaus, M. K., Altmann, R. J., and **Fagnano, M.** (2004) The old and thee, uh, new: Disfluency and reference resolution. *Psychological Science,* 15, 578–582.

Arntz, A., and **Claassens, L.** (2004) The meaning of pain influences its experienced intensity. *Pain,* 109, 20–25.

Ashkenazi, A., and **Marks, L. E.** (2004) Effect of endogenous attention on detection of weak gustatory and olfactory flavors. *Perception & Psychophysics,* 66, 596–608.

Ashmead, D. H., Davis, D. L., and **Northington, A.** (1995) Contribution of listeners' approaching motion to auditory distance perception. *Journal of Experimental Psychology: Human Perception & Performance,* 21, 239–256.

Ashmead, D. H., Wall, R. S., Abinger, K. A., Eaton, S. B., Snook-Hill, M., and **Yang, X.** (1998) Spatial hearing in children with visual disabilities. *Perception,* 27, 105–122.

Atkinson, J., and **Braddick, O. J.** (1998) Research methods in infant vision. In R. H. S. Carpenter and J. G. Robson (eds.) *Vision research: A practical approach,* 161–186.

Axelsson, A., and **Lindgren, F.** (1978) Hearing in pop musicians. *Acta Otolaryngology,* 85, 225–231.

Axelsson, A., Eliasson, A., and **Israelsson, B.** (1995) Hearing in pop/rock musicians: A follow-up study. *Ear and Hearing,* 16, 245–253.

Azzopardi, P., and **Cowey, A.** (1993) Preferential representation of the fovea in the primary visual cortex. *Nature,* 361, 719–721.

Bachorowski, J.-A., and **Owren, M. J.** (2001) Not all laughs are alike: Voiced but not unvoiced laughter readily elicits positive affect. *Psychological Science,* 12, 252–257.

Bachorowski, J.-A., Smoski, M. J., and **Owren, M. J.** (2001) The acoustic features of human laughter. *Journal of the Acoustical Society of America,* 110, 1581–1597.

Backus, B. (2000) Stereoscopic vision: What's the first step? *Current Biology,* 10, R701–R703.

Badinand-Hubert, N., Bureau, M., Hirsch, E., Masnou, P., Nahum, L., Parain, D., and **Naquet, R.** (1998) Epilepsies and video games: Results of a multicentric study. *Electroencephalography & Clinical Neurophysiology,* 107, 422–427.

Bahill, A. T., and **LaRitz, T.** (1984) Why can't batters keep their eyes on the ball? *American Scientist,* 72, 249–253.

Bailey, K. G. D., and **Ferreira, F.** (2003) Disfluencies influence syntactic parsing. *Journal of Memory and Language,* 49, 183–200.

Baird, J. C. (1982) The moon illusion: II. A reference theory. *Journal of Experimental Psychology: General,* 111, 304–315.

Baird, J. C., and **Wagner, M.** (1982) The moon illusion: I. How high is the sky? *Journal of Experimental Psychology,* 111, 296–303.

Baker, C. L., Jr., Hess, R. F., and **Zihl, J.** (1991) Residual motion perception in a "motion-blind" patient, assessed with limited-lifetime random dot stimuli. *Journal of Neuroscience,* 11, 454–461.

Balkwill, L.-L., and **Thompson, W. F.** (1999) A cross-cultural investigation of the perception of emotion in music: Psychophysical and cultural cues. *Music Perception,* 17, 43–64.

Ball, K., and **Sekuler, R.** (1981) Cues reduce direction uncertainty and enhance motion detection. *Perception & Psychophysics,* 30, 119–128.

Ballas, J. A. (1993) Common factors in the identification of an assortment of brief everyday sounds. *Journal of Experimental Psychology: Human Perception & Performance,* 19, 250–267.

Balter, M. (2004) Seeking the key to music. *Science,* 306, 1120–1122.

Banks, M. S. (1982) The development of spatial and temporal contrast sensitivity. *Current Eye Research,* 2, 191–198.

Banks, M. S., Aslin, R. N., and **Letson, R. D.** (1975) Sensitive period for the development of human binocular vision. *Science,* 190, 675–677.

Banks, M. S., and **Bennett, P. J.** (1988) Optical and photoreceptor immaturities limit the spatial and chromatic vision of human neonates. *Journal of Optical Society of America A,* 5, 2059–2079.

Bar, M. (2004) Visual objects in context. *Nature Reviews Neuroscience,* 5, 617–629.

Barac-Cikoja, D., and **Turvey, M. T.** (1991) Perceiving aperture size by striking. *Journal of Experimental Psychology: Human Perception and Performance,* 17, 330–346.

Barber, N. (1990) Home color as a territorial marker. *Perceptual and Motor Skills,* 71, 1107–1110.

Barinaga, M. (1999) Salmon follow watery odors home. *Science,* 286, 705–706.

Barlow, H. B. (1972) Single units and sensation: A neuron doctrine for perceptual psychology? *Perception,* 1, 371–395.

Barlow, H. B. (1998) Cerebral predictions. *Perception,* 27, 885–888.

Barlow, H. B., Blakemore, C., and **Pettigrew, J. D.** (1967) The neural mechanism of binocular depth discrimination. *Journal of Physiology,* 193, 327–342.

Barlow, H. B., Fitzhugh, R., and **Kuffler, S. W.** (1957) Change of organization in the receptive fields of the cat's retina during dark adaptation. *Journal of Physiology,* 137, 327–337.

Barlow, H. B., and **Hill, R. M.** (1963) Evidence for a physiological explanation of the waterfall illusion. *Nature,* 200, 1345–1347.

Barlow, H. B., and **Sparrock, J. M. B.** (1964) The role of afterimages in dark adaptation. *Science,* 144, 1309–1314.

Barnes, C. S., Wei J., P., and **Shevell, S. K.** (1999) Chromatic induction with remote chromatic contrast varied in magnitude, spatial frequency, and chromaticity. *Vision Research,* 39, 3561–3574.

Bartoshuk, L. M. (1974) Taste illusions: Some demonstrations. *Annals of the New York Academy of Sciences,* 237, 279–285.

Bartoshuk, L. M. (1975) Taste mixtures: Is mixture suppression related to compression? *Physiology & Behavior,* 14, 643–649.

Bartoshuk, L. M. (1978) History of taste research. In E. C. Carterette and M. P. Friedman (eds.), *Handbook of perception,* vol. 6A. New York: Academic Press, 3–18.

Bartoshuk, L. M. (1980) Separate worlds of taste. *Psychology Today,* 14, 48–63.

Bartoshuk, L. M., Dateo, G. P., Vandenbelt, D. J., Buttrick, R. L., and **Long, L. Jr.** (1969) Effects of Gymnema sylvestra and Synsepalum dulcificum on taste in man. In C. Pfaffmann (ed.), *Olfaction and taste,* vol. 3. New York: Rockefeller University Press, 436–444.

Batteau, D. W. (1967) The role of the pinna in human localization. *Proceedings of the Royal Society of London (Series B),* 168, 158–180.

Bauer, R. M. (1984) Autonomic recognition of names and faces in prosopagnosia: A neuropsychological application of the Guilty Knowledge Test. *Neuropsychologia,* 22, 457–469.

Beattie, G. W., Cutler, A., and **Pearson, M.** (1982) Why is Mrs. Thatcher interrupted so often? *Nature,* 300, 744–747.

Becker, E. S., and **Rinck, M.** (2004) Sensitivity and response bias in fear of spiders. *Cognition and Emotion,* 18, 961–976.

Beckers, G., and **Zeki, S.** (1995) The consequences of inactivating areas V1 and V5 on visual motion perception. *Brain,* 118, 49–60.

Bedichek, R. (1960) *The sense of smell.* Garden City, N.Y.: Doubleday.

Behrmann, M., Nelson, J., and **Sekuler, E. B.** (1998) Visual complexity in letter-by-letter reading: "Pure" alexia is not pure. *Neuropsychologia,* 36, 1115–1132.

Beidler, L. M., and **Smallman, R. L.** (1965) Renewal of cells within taste buds. *Journal of Cell Biology,* 27, 263–272.

Békésy, G. von (1960) *Experiments in hearing.* New York: McGraw-Hill.

Békésy, G. von, and **Rosenblith, W. A.** (1951) The mechanical properties of the ear. In S. S. Stevens (ed.), *Handbook of experimental psychology.* New York: John Wiley & Sons, 1075–1115.

Belendiuk, K., and **Butler, R. A.** (1978) Directional hearing under progressive impoverishment of binaural cues. *Sensory Processes,* 2, 58–70.

Belin, P., Fecteau, S., and **Bédard, C.** (2004) Thinking the voice: Neural correlates of voice perception. *Trends in Cognitive Sciences,* 8, 129–135.

Belin, P., Zatorre, R. J., Lafaille, P., Ahad, P., and **Pike. B.** (2000) Voice-selective areas in human auditory cortex. *Nature,* 403, 309–312.

Bell, A. G. (1914) Discovery and invention. *National Geographic Magazine* 25 (6) 649–655. Also available, in pamphlet form, online in United States Library of Congress collection of the Alexander Graham Bell Family papers. <http://memory.loc.gov/ammem/bellhtml/bellhome.html>

Benedetti, F. (1985) Processing of tactile spatial information with crossed fingers. *Journal of Experimental Psychology: Human Perception and Performance,* 11, 517–525.

Benedetti, F. (1986) Tactile diplopia (diplesthesia) on the human fingers. *Perception,* 15, 83–91.

Benedetti, F. (1991) Reorganization of tactile perception following the simulated amputation of one finger. *Perception,* 20, 687–692.

Bennett, P. J., Sekuler, A. B., and **Ozin, L.** (1999) Effects of aging on calculation efficiency and equivalent noise. *Journal of the Optical Society of America A,* 16, 654–668.

Bensafi, M., Porter, J., Pouliot, S., Mainland, J., Johnson, B., Zelano, C., Young, N., Bremner, E., Aframian, D., Khan, R., and **Sobel, N.** (2003) Olfactomotor activity during imagery mimics that during perception. *Nature Neuroscience,* 6, 1142–1144.

Benton, A. L. (1980) The neuropsychology of facial recognition. *American Psychologist,* 35, 176–186.

Berger, A., Henderson, M., Nadoolman, W., Duffy, V., Cooper, D., Saberski, L., and **Bartoshuk, L.** (1995) Oral capsaicin provides temporary relief from oral mucositis pain secondary to chemotherapy/radiation therapy. *Journal of Pain and Pain Management,* 10, 243–248.

Berglund, B., Berglund, U., Engen, T., and **Lindvall, T.** (1971) The effect of adaptation on odor detection. *Perception & Psychophysics,* 9, 435–438.

Bergman, M. (1966) Hearing in the Mabaans. *Archives of Otolaryngology,* 81, 75–79.

Berkeley, G. (1709/1950) *A new theory of vision.* London: Dent.

Berkley, M. A., and **Watkins, D. W.** (1971) Visual acuity of the cat estimated from evoked cerebral potentials. *Nature,* 234, 91–92.

Berlin, B., and **Kay, P.** (1969) *Basic color terms: Their universality and evolution.* Berkeley: University of California Press.

Bertino, M., and **Chan, M. M.** (1986) Taste perception and diet in individuals with Chinese and European ethnic backgrounds. *Chemical Senses,* 11, 229–241.

Bexton, W. H., Heron, W., and **Scott, T. H.** (1954) Effects of decreased variation in the sensory environment. *Canadian Journal of Psychology,* 8, 70–76.

Biederman, I. (1972) Perceiving real-world scenes. *Science,* 177, 77–80.

Biederman, I. (1990) Higher-level vision. In D. N. Osherson, S. Kosslyn, and J. Hollerbach (eds.), *An invitation to cognitive science: Visual cognition and action.* Cambridge: MIT Press, 41–72.

Biederman, I., and **Shiffrar, M.** (1987) Sexing day-old chicks: A case study and expert systems analysis of a difficult perceptual learning task. *Journal of Experimental Psychology: Human Learning, Memory, and Cognition,* 13, 640–645.

Birren, F. (1941) *The story of color: From ancient mysticism to modern science.* Westport, Conn.: Crimson Press.

Blackwell, H. R. (1946) Contrast thresholds of the human eye. *Journal of the Optical Society of America,* 36, 624–643.

Blake, D. T., Byl, N. N., and **Merzenich, M. M.** (2002) Representation of the hand in the cerebral cortex. *Behavioral Brain Research,* 135, 179–184

Blake, R. (1988a) Cat spatial vision. *Trends in Neurosciences,* 11, 78–83.

Blake, R. (1988b) Dichoptic reading: the role of meaning in binocular rivalry. *Perception & Psychophysics,* 44, 133–141.

Blake, R. (1993) Cats perceive biological motion. *Psychological Science,* 4, 54–57.

Blake, R. (1995) Psychoanatomical strategies for studying human vision. In T. Papathomas, C. Chubb, E. Kowler, and A. Gorea (eds.), *Early vision and beyond.* Cambridge, MIT Press.

Blake, R. (1998) The behavioural analysis of animal vision. In J. G. Robson, and R. H. S. Carpenter (eds.), *Vision research: A practical approach.* Oxford: Oxford University Press, 137–160.

Blake, R., and **Fox, R.** (1972) Interocular transfer of adaptation to spatial frequency during retinal ischaemia. *Nature, 240,* 76–77.

Blake, R., and **Hirsch, H. V. B.** (1975) Deficits in binocular depth perception in cats after alternating monocular deprivation. *Science, 190,* 1114–1116.

Blake, R., and **Logothetis, N. K.** (2002) Visual competition. *Nature Reviews Neuroscience, 2,* 13–21.

Blake, R., Palmeri, T. J., Marois, R., and **Kim, C.-Y.** (2005) On the perceptual reality of synesthetic color. In L. Robertson and N. Sagiv (eds.), *Synesthesia: Perspectives from cognitive neuroscience.* Oxford: Oxford University Press.

Blake, R., Sobel, K., and **James, T.** (2004) Neural synergy between kinetic vision and touch. *Psychological Science, 15,* 397–402.

Blake, R., and **Wilson, H. R.** (1991) Neural models of stereoscopic vision. *Trends in Neurosciences, 14,* 445–452.

Blakemore, C. (1976) The conditions required for the maintenance of binocularity in the kitten's visual cortex. *Journal of Physiology, 261,* 423–444.

Blakemore, C., and **Campbell, F. W.** (1969) On the existence of neurones in the human visual system selectively sensitive to the orientation and size of retinal images. *Journal of Physiology, 203,* 237–260.

Blakemore, C., and **Cooper, G. F.** (1970) Development of the brain depends on the visual environment. *Nature, 228,* 477–478.

Blakemore, C., Muncey, J. P. J., and **Ridley, R. M.** (1973) Stimulus specificity in the human visual system. *Vision Research, 13,* 1915–1931.

Blakemore, C., Nachmias, J., and **Sutton, P.** (1970) The perceived spatial frequency shift: Evidence for frequency selective neurones in the human brain. *Journal of Physiology, 210,* 727–750.

Blanz, V., Tarr, M. J., and **Bülthoff, H. H.** (1999) What object attributes determine canonical views? *Perception, 28,* 575–600.

Blignaut, C. J. H. (1979) The perception of hazard: II. The contribution of signal detection to hazard perception. *Ergonomics, 22,* 1177–1183.

Bliven, B., Jr. (1976) Annals of architecture: A better sound. *New Yorker, 52,* 51–135.

Blood, A. J., Zatorre, R. J., Bermudez, P., and **Evans, A. C.** (1999) Emotional responses to pleasant and unpleasant music correlate with activity in paralimbic brain regions. *Nature Neuroscience, 2,* 382–387.

Blood, A. J., and **Zatorre, R. J.** (2001) Intensely pleasurable responses to music correlate with activity in brain regions implicated in reward and emotion. *Proceedings of the National Academy of Sciences: USA, 98,* 11818–11823.

Bloom, H. S., Criswell, E. L., Pennypacker, H. S., Catania, A. C., and **Adams, C. K.** (1982) Major stimulus dimensions determining detection of simulated breast lesions. *Perception & Psychophysics, 32,* 251–260.

Blouin, J., Bridgeman, B., Teasdale, N., Bard, C., and **Fleury, M.** (1995) Visual stability with goal-directed eye and arm movements toward a target displaced during saccadic suppression. *Psychological Research, 58,* 169–176.

Bobrow, N. A., Money, J., and **Lewis, V. G.** (1971) Delayed puberty, eroticism, and sense of smell: A psychological study of hypogonadotropism, osmatic and anosmatic (Kallmann's syndrome). *Archives of Sexual Behavior, 1,* 329–344.

Bock, O. (1993) Localization of objects in the peripheral visual field. *Behavioural Brain Research, 56,* 77–84.

Bodis-Wollner, I. (1972) Visual acuity and contrast sensitivity in patients with cerebral lesions. *Science, 178,* 769–771.

Boll, F. (1877/1977) On the anatomy and physiology of the retina. *Vision Research, 17,* 1253–1267.

Bonneh, Y. S., Cooperman, A., and **Sagi, D.** (2001) Motion-induced blindness in normal observers. *Nature, 411,* 798–801.

Boorstin, D. J. (1983) *The discoverers.* New York: Vintage Books.

Booth J. R., Epelboim J., and **Steinman, R. M.** (1996) *The relative importance of spaces and meaning in reading.* Presented at the meeting of the Cognitive Science Society.

Borg, E., and **Counter, S. A.** (1989) The middle-ear muscles. *Scientific American, 261,* 74–80.

Boring, E. G. (1930) A new ambiguous figure. *American Journal of Psychology, 42,* 444.

Boring, E. G. (1942) *Sensation and perception in the history of experimental psychology.* New York: Appleton-Century-Crofts.

Boring, E. G. (1961) Fechner: Inadvertent founder of psychophysics. *Psychometrika, 26,* 3–8.

Bornstein, M. H., Kessen, W., and **Weiskopf, S.** (1976) The categories of hue in infancy. *Science, 191,* 201–202.

Bough, E. W. (1970) Stereoscopic vision in macaque monkey: A behavioural demonstration. *Nature, 225,* 42–44.

Bowmaker, J. K. (1998) Evolution of colour vision. *Eye, 12,* 541–547.

Boycott, B. B., and **Wässle, H.** (1999) Parallel processing in the mammalian retina. *Investigative Ophthalmology & Visual Science, 40,* 1313–1327.

Boynton, R. M. (1982) Spatial and temporal approaches for studying color vision: A review. In G. Verriest (ed.), *Colour vision deficiencies, VI. Proceedings of the Sixth Symposium of the International Research Group on Colour Vision Deficiencies.* The Hague: W. Junk, 1–14.

Boynton, R. M., and **Gordon, J.** (1965) Bezold-Brücke hue shift measured by color naming technique. *Journal of the Optical Society of America, 55,* 78–86.

Boynton, R. M., and **Olson, C. X.** (1987) Locating basic colors in the OSA space. *Color Research and Applications, 12,* 94–105.

Bracewell, R. N. (1989) The Fourier transform. *Scientific American, 260,* 86–95.

Braddick, O. (1993) Segmentation versus integration in visual motion processing. *Trends in Neurosciences, 16,* 263–268.

Bradley, R. M. (1979) Effects of aging on the sense of taste: Anatomical considerations. In S. S. Han and D. H. Coons (eds.), *Special senses in aging: A current biological assessment.* Ann Arbor, Institute of Gerontology, University of Michigan, 3–8.

Bradley, R. M. (1991) Salivary secretion. In T V. Getchell, R. L. Doty, L. M. Bartoshuk and J. B. Snow (eds.), *Smell and taste in health and disease.* New York: Raven Press, 127–144.

Brammer, A. J., and **Verillo, R. T.** (1988) Tactile changes in hands occupationally exposed to vibration. *Journal of the Acoustical Society of America,* 84, 1940–1941.

Braunstein, M. L., and **Stern, K. R.** (1980) Static and dynamic factors in the perception of rotary motion. *Perception & Psychophysics,* 27, 313–320.

Bravo, M., and **Blake R.** (1990) Preattentive vision and perceptual groups. *Perception,* 19, 515–522.

Brawn, P., and **Snowden, R. J.** (1999) Can one pay attention to a particular color? *Perception & Psychophysics,* 61, 860–873.

Bregman, A. S. (1990) *Auditory scene analysis.* Cambridge: MIT Press.

Bregman, A. S., and **Pinker, S.** (1978) Auditory streaming and the building of timbre. *Canadian Journal of Psychology,* 31, 151–159.

Bressan, P., Mingolla, E., Spillman, L., and **Watanabe, T.** (1997) Neon color spreading: A review. *Perception,* 26, 1353–1366.

Brindley, G. S. (1970) *Physiology of the retina and visual pathway.* Baltimore: Williams & Wilkins.

Brindley, G. S., and **Lewin, W. S.** (1968) The sensations produced by electrical stimulation of the visual cortex. *Journal of Physiology,* 196, 479–493.

Brisbin, I. L., Austad, S., and **Jacobson, S. K.** (2000) Canine detectives: The nose knows—Or does it? *Science,* 290, 1093.

Bronkhorst, A. W., and **Houtgast, T.** (1999) Auditory distance perception in rooms. *Nature,* 397, 517–520.

Brouwer, J. N., Glaser, D., Segerstad, C. H. A., Hellekant, G., Ninomiya, Y., and **van der Wel, H.** (1983) The sweetness-inducing effect of miraculin: Behavioral and neurophysiological experiments in the rhesus monkey, Macaca mulatta. *Journal of Physiology,* 337, 221–240.

Brown, J. F. (1931) The visual perception of velocity. *Psychologische Forschung,* 14, 199–232.

Brown, J. L., and **Mueller, C. G.** (1965) Brightness discrimination and brightness contrast. In C. H. Graham (ed.), *Vision and visual perception.* New York: John Wiley & Sons, 208–250.

Brown, J. M., and **Weisstein, N.** (1988) A spatial frequency effect on perceived depth. *Perception & Psychophysics,* 44, 157–166.

Bruce, V. (1994) Stability from variation: The case of face recognition. *Quarterly Journal of Experimental Psychology,* 47A, 5–28.

Bruce, V., Burton, A. M., Hanna, E., Healey, P., Mason, O., Coombes, A., Fright, R., and **Linney, A.** (1993) Sex discrimination: How do we tell the difference between male and female faces? *Perception,* 22, 131–152.

Bruner, J. S., and **Potter, M. C.** (1964) Interference in visual recognition. *Science,* 144, 424–425.

Bruno, N., and **Cutting, J. E.** (1988) Minimodularity and the perception of layout. *Journal of Experimental Psychology: General,* 117, 161–170.

Buchsbaum, G., and **Gottschalk, A.** (1983) Trichromacy, opponent colours coding, and the optimum colour information in the retina. *Proceedings of the Royal Society of London (Series B),* 220, 89–113.

Buck, L. B. (1996) Information coding in the vertebrate olfactory system. *Annual Review of Neuroscience,* 19, 517–544.

Buonomano, D. V., and **Merzenich, M. M.** (1998) Cortical plasticity: From synapses to maps. *Annual Review of Neuroscience,* 21, 149–186.

Burger, J. F. (1958) Front-back discrimination of the hearing system. *Acustica,* 8, 302–310.

Burnham, D., Kitamura, C., and **Vollmer-Conna, U.** (2002) What's new, pussycat? On talking to babies and animals. *Science,* 296, 1435.

Burr, D. C., and **Ross, J.** (1982) Contrast sensitivity at high velocities. *Vision Research,* 22, 479–484.

Bushara, K. O., Hanakawa, T., Immisch, I., Toma, K., Kansaku, K., and **Hallett, M.** (2003) Neural correlates of cross-modal binding. *Nature Neuroscience,* 6, 190–195.

Bushnell, M. C., Goldberg, M. E., and **Robinson, D. L.** (1981) Behavioral enhancement of visual responses in monkey cerebral cortex. I. Modulation in posterior parietal cortex related to selective visual attention. *Journal of Neurophysiology,* 46, 755–772.

Butler, R. A. (1986) The bandwidth effect on monaural and binaural localization. *Hearing Research,* 21, 67–73.

Butler, R. A., Humanski, R. A., and **Musicant, A. D.** (1990) Binaural and monaural localization of sound in two-dimensional space. *Perception,* 19, 241–256.

Butterworth, G., and **Castillo, M.** (1976) Coordination of auditory and visual space in newborn infants. *Perception,* 5, 155–160.

Cabe, P. A., and **Pittenger, J. B.** (2000) Human sensitivity to acoustic information from vessel filling. *Journal of Experimental Psychology: Human Perception & Performance,* 26, 313–324.

Cabe, P. A., Wright, C. D., and **Wright, M. A.** (2003) Descartes's blind man revisited: Bimanual triangulation of distance using static hand-held rods. *American Journal of Psychology,* 116, 71–98.

Caicedo, A., and **Roper, S. D.** (2001) Taste receptor cells that discriminate between bitter stimuli. *Science,* 291, 1557–1560.

Cain, W. S. (1973) Spatial discrimination of cutaneous warmth. *American Journal of Psychology,* 86, 169–181.

Cain, W. S. (1977) Differential sensitivity for smell: Noise at the nose. *Science,* 195, 796–798.

Cain, W. S. (1978) The odoriferous environment and the application of olfactory research. In E. C. Carterette and M. P. Friedman (eds.). *Handbook of perception,* vol. 7. New York: Academic Press, 277–304.

Cain, W. S. (1982) Odor identification by males and females: Predictions versus performance. *Chemical Senses,* 7, 129–142.

Cain, W. S., and **Engen, T.** (1969) Olfactory adaptation and the scaling of odor intensity. In C. Pfaffmann (ed.), *Olfaction and taste,* vol. 3. New York: Rockefeller University Press, 127–157.

Cain, W. S., and **Gent, J. F.** (1991) Olfactory sensitivity: Reliability, generality, and association with aging. *Journal of Experimental Psychology: Human Perception and Performance,* 17, 382–391.

Cain, W. S., and **Murphy, C. L.** (1980) Interaction between chemoreceptive modalities of odour irritation. *Nature,* 284, 255–257.

Cain, W. S., and **Turk, A.** (1985) Smell of danger: An analysis of LP-gas odorization. *American Industrial Hygiene Association Journal,* 46, 115–126.

Caine, N. G., and **Mundy, N. I.** (2000) Demonstration of a foraging advantage for trichromatic marmosets (Callithrix geoffroyi) dependent on food colour. *Proceedings of the Royal Society of London (Series B),* 267, 439–444.

Calvert, G. A., Bullmore, E. T., Branner, M. J., Campbell, R., Williams, S. C. R., McGuire, P. K., Woodruff, P. W. R., Iversen, S. D., and **David, A. S.** (1997) Activation of auditory cortex during silent lipreading. *Science,* 276, 593–596.

Campbell, D. T. (1974) Evolutionary epistemology. In P. A. Schlipp (ed.), *The philosophy of Karl Popper.* LaSalle, Ill.: Open Court, 413–463.

Campbell, F. W., and **Robson, J. G.** (1968) Application of Fourier analysis to the visibility of gratings. *Journal of Physiology,* 197, 551–566.

Campbell, R., Zihl, J., Massaro, D., Munhall, K., and **Cohen, M. M.** (1997) Speech reading in the akinetopsic patient, L. M. *Brain,* 120, 1793–1803.

Carlson, M., and **Burton, H.** (1988) Recovery of tactile function after damage to primary or secondary somatic sensory cortex in infant Macaca mulatta. *Journal of Neuroscience,* 8, 833–859.

Carlsson, K., Petrovic, P., Skare, S., Petersson, K. M., and **Ingvar, M.** (2000) Tickling expectations: Neural processing in anticipation of a sensory stimulus. *Journal of Cognitive Neuroscience,* 12, 691–703.

Carlsson, L., Knave, B., Lennerstrand, G., and **Wibom, R.** (1984) Glare from outdoor high mast lighting: Effects on visual acuity and contrast sensitivity in comparative studies of different floodlighting systems. *Acta Ophthalmologica,* 62, 84–93.

Carmody, D. P., Nodine, C. F., and **Kundel, H. L.** (1980) An analysis of perceptual and cognitive factors in radiographic interpretation. *Perception,* 9, 339–344.

Carpenter, P. A., and **Daneman, M.** (1981) Lexical access and error recovery in reading: A model based on eye fixations. *Journal of Verbal Learning and Verbal Behavior,* 20, 137–160.

Carpenter, R. H. S. (1992) Turning vision into action. *Current Biology,* 2, 288–290.

Carr, C. E., and **Konishi, M.** (1988) Axonal delay lines for time measurement in the owl's brainstem. *Proceedings of the National Academy of Sciences: USA,* 85, 8311–8315.

Carrasco, M., Penpeci-Talgar, C., and **Eckstein, M.** (2000). Spatial attention increases contrast sensitivity across the CSF: Support for signal enhancement. *Vision Research,* 40, 1203–1216.

Carskadon, M. A., and **Herz, R. S.** (2004) Minimal olfactory perception during sleep: Why odor alarms will not work for humans. *Sleep,* 27, 402–405.

Carter, J. H. (1982) The effects of aging upon selected visual functions: Color vision, field of vision, and accommodation. In R. Sekuler, D. Kline, and K. Dismukes (eds.), *Aging and human visual function.* New York: Liss, 120–130.

Carter, O. L., and **Pettigrew, J. D.** (2003) A common oscillator for perceptual rivalries? *Perception,* 32, 295–305.

Casagrande, V. A. (1994) A third parallel visual pathway to primate area V1. *Trends in Neurosciences,* 17, 305–310.

Casagrande, V. A., and **Kaas, J.** (1994) The afferent, intrinsic, and efferent connections of primary visual cortex in primates. In A. Peters and R. S. Rockland (eds.) *Cerebral cortex, Vol. 10, Primary visual cortex of primates.* New York: Plenum Press, 201–259.

Catania, K. C. (2002) The nose takes a starring role. *Scientific American,* 287, 54–59.

Caterina, M. J., Leffler, A., Malmberg, A. B., Martin, W. J., Trafton, J., Petersen-Zeitz, K. R., Koltzenburg, M., Basbaum, A. I., and **Julius, D.** (2000) Impaired nociception and pain sensation in mice lacking the capsaicin receptor. *Science,* 220, 306–313.

Cattell, J. M. (1886) The inertia of the eye and brain. *Brain,* 8, 295–312.

Cavallo, V., Colomb, M., and **Doré, J.** (2001) Distance perception of vehicle rear lights in fog. *Human Factors,* 43, 442–451.

Cave, C. (1997) Very long-lasting priming in picture naming. *Psychological Science,* 8, 322–325.

Chambers, D., and **Reisberg, D.** (1992) What an image depicts depends on what an image means. *Cognitive Psychology,* 24, 145–174.

Chaudhari, N., Landin, A. M., and **Roper, S. D.** (2000) A metabotropic glutamate receptor variant functions as a taste receptor. *Nature Neuroscience,* 3, 113–119.

Chen, L. M., Friedman, R. M., and **Roe, A. W.** (2003) Optical imaging of a tactile illusion in area 3B of the primary somatosensory cortex. *Science,* 302, 881–885.

Chevreul, M. (1839/1967) *The principles of harmony and contrast of colors.* F. Birren (ed.). New York: Reinhold.

Christensen, D. (1999) What's that smell? *Science News,* 155, 316.

Chu, S., and **Downes, J. J.** (2000) Odour-evoked autobiographical memories: Psychological investigations of Proustian phenomena. *Chemical Senses,* 25, 111–116.

Chubb, C., and **Sperling, G.** (1988) Drift-balanced random stimuli: A general basis for studying non-Fourier motion perception. *Journal of the Optical Society of America A,* 5, 1986–2007.

Chun, M. (2000) Contextual cueing of visual attention. *Trends in Cognitive Sciences,* 4, 170–178.

Chun, M., and **Nakayama, K.** (2000) On the functional role of implicit visual memory for the adaptive deployment of attention across scenes. *Visual Cognition,* 7, 65–81.

Chun, M., and **Marois, R.** (2002) The dark side of visual attention. *Current Opinion in Neurobiology,* 12, 184–189.

Churchland, P. M. (1988) *Matter and consciousness: A contemporary introduction to the philosophy of mind* (rev. ed.). Cambridge: MIT Press.

Clarke, S., Bellmann Thiran, A., Maeder, P., Adriani, M., Vernet, O., Regli, L., Cuisenaire, O., and Thiran, J. P. (2002) What and where in human audition: Selective deficits following focal hemispheric lesions. *Experimental Brain Research,* 147, 8–15.

Claus, R., Hoppen, H. O., and Karg, H. (1981) The secret of truffles: A steroidal pheromone? *Experientia,* 37, 1178–1179.

Cohen, L. (1959) Perception of reversible figures after brain injury. *Archives of Neurology and Psychiatry,* 81, 765–775.

Cohen, M. R., and Newsome, W. T. (2004) What electrical microstimulation has revealed about the neural basis of cognition. *Current Opinion in Neurobiology,* 14, 1–9.

Cohen, L. G., Celnik, P., Pascual-Leone, A., Corwell, B., Faiz, L., Dambrosia, J., Honda, M., Sadato, N., Gerloff, C., Catala, M. D., and Hallett, M. (1997) Functional relevance of cross-modal plasticity in blind humans. *Nature,* 389, 180–183.

Colby, C. L., and Goldberg, M. E. (1999) Space and attention in parietal cortex. *Annual Review of Neuroscience,* 22, 319–349.

Cole, J. D. (1995) *Pride and a daily marathon.* Cambridge: MIT Press.

Coles, R. R. A., and Hallam, R. S. (1987) Tinnitus and its management. *British Medical Bulletin,* 43, 983–998.

Collett, T. S., Schwarz, U., and Sobel, E. C. (1991) The interaction of oculomotor cues and stimulus size in stereoscopic depth constancy. *Perception,* 20, 733–754.

Cometto-Muñiz, J. E., and Cain, W. S. (1982) Perception of nasal pungency in smokers and nonsmokers. *Physiology & Behavior,* 29, 727–731.

Cometto-Muñiz, J. E., and Cain, W. S. (1984) Temporal integration of pungency. *Chemical Senses,* 8, 315–327.

Cometto-Muñiz, J. E., and Cain, W. S. (1996) Physicochemical determinants and functional properties of the senses of irritation and smell. In R. B. Gammage and B. A. Berven (eds.) *Indoor air and human health,* 2nd ed. Boca Raton: CRC Press, 53–65.

Cometto-Muñiz, J. E., Cain, W. S., and Hudnell, H. K. (1997) Agonistic sensory effects of airborne chemicals in mixtures: Odor, nasal pungency, and eye irritation. *Perception & Psychophysics,* 59, 665–674.

Coppola, D. M., Purves, H. R., McCoy, A. N., and Purves, D. (1998) The distribution of oriented contours in the real world. *Proceedings of the National Academy of Sciences: USA,* 95, 4002–4006.

Corbetta, M., Miezin, R. M., Dobmeyer, S., Shulman, G. L., and Petersen, S. E. (1991) Selective and divided attention during visual discriminations of shape, color, and speed: Functional anatomy by positron emission tomography. *Journal of Neuroscience,* 11, 2382–2402.

Corbin, A. (1986) *The foul and the fragrant: Odor and the French social imagination.* Cambridge: Harvard University Press.

Cornsweet, T. N. (1962) The staircase-method in psychophysics. *American Journal of Psychology,* 75, 485–491.

Cornsweet, T. N. (1970) *Visual perception.* New York: Academic Press.

Corso, J. F. (1981) *Aging sensory systems and perception.* New York: Praeger.

Courtney, N., and Wells, D. L. (2002) The discrimination of cat odours by humans. *Perception,* 31, 511–512.

Cowart, B. J. (1981) Development of taste perception in humans: Sensitivity and preference throughout the life span. *Psychological Bulletin,* 90, 43–73.

Cowey, A., and Heywood, C. A. (1995) There's more to colour than meets the eye. *Behavioural Brain Research,* 71, 89–100.

Cowey, A., and Heywood, C. A. (1997) Cerebral achromatopsia: Colour blindness despite wavelength processing. *Trends in Cognitive Sciences,* 1, 133–139.

Craig, J. C. (1985) Attending to two fingers: Two hands are better than one. *Perception & Psychophysics,* 38, 496–511.

Craig, J. C., and Johnson, K. O. (2000) The two-point threshold: Not a measure of tactile spatial resolution. *Current Directions in Psychological Science,* 9, 29–32.

Craig, J. C., Reiman, E. M., Evans, A., and Bushnell, M. C. (1996) Functional imaging of an illusion of pain. *Nature,* 384, 258–260.

Craig, J. C., and Rollman, G. B. (1999) Somesthesis. *Annual Review of Psychology,* 50, 305–331.

Craver-Lemley, C., and Reeves, A. (1992) How visual imagery interferes with vision. *Psychological Review,* 99, 633–649.

Crawford, M. L. J., and Marc, R. E. (1976) Light transmission of cat and monkey eyelids. *Vision Research,* 16, 323–324.

Critchley, M. (1979) *The divine banquet of the brain.* New York: Raven Press.

Crocker, E. C., and Henderson, L. F. (1927) Analysis and classification of odors. *American Perfumer and Essential Oil Review,* 22, 325–327.

Croner, L. J., and Albright T. D. (1997) Image segmentation enhances discrimination of motion in visual noise. *Vision Research,* 37, 1415–1427.

Crowe, S. J., Guild, S. R., and Polvost, L. M. (1934) Observations on the pathology of high-tone deafness. *Bulletin of the Johns Hopkins Hospital,* 54, 315–379.

Cruz, A., and Green, B. G. (2000) Thermal stimulation of taste. *Nature,* 403, 889–892.

Culham, J. C., Brandt, S. A., Cavanagh, P., Kanwisher, N. G., Dale, A. M., and Tootell, R. B. (1998) Cortical fMRI activation produced by attentive tracking of moving targets. *Journal of Neurophysiology,* 80, 2657–2670.

Culham, J. C., Dukelow, S. P., Vilis, T., Hassard, F. A., Gati, J. S., Menon, R. S., and Goodale, M. A. (1999) Recovery of fMRI activation in motion area MT following storage of the motion aftereffect. *Journal of Neurophysiology,* 81, 388–393.

Culham, J. C., and Kanwisher, N. G. (2001) Neuroimaging of cognitive functions in human parietal cortex. *Current Opinions in Biology,* 11, 157–163.

Currier, R. D. (1994) A two-and-a-half color rainbow. *Archives of Neurology,* 51, 1090–1092.

Cutting, J. E. (1997) How the eye measures reality and virtual reality. *Behavior Research Methods, Instruments, & Computers,* 29, 27–36.

Cutting, J. E., and **Proffitt, D. R.** (1981) Gait perception as an example of how we may perceive events. In R. Walk and H. L. Pick (eds.), *Intersensory perception and sensory integration.* New York: Plenum Press, 249–273.

Cytowic, R. E. (2003) *The man who tasted shapes,* 2nd ed. Cambridge: MIT Press.

D'Zmura, M. (1996) Bergmann on visual resolution. *Perception, 25,* 1223–1234.

Dabak, A. G., and **Johnson, D. H.** (1992) Function-based modeling of binaural processing: Interaural phase. *Hearing Research, 58,* 200–212.

Dakin, S. C., and **Herbert, A. M.** (1998) The spatial region of integration for visual symmetry detection, *Proceedings of the Royal Society of London (Series B), 265,* 659–664.

Dallos, P., Popper, A., and **Fay, R.** (1996) *The Cochlea. Springer handbook of auditory research,* vol. 8. New York: Springer-Verlag.

Dalton, J. (1798/1948) Extraordinary facts relating to the vision of colour: With observations. In W. Dennis (ed.), *Readings in the history of psychology.* New York: Appleton-Century-Crofts, 102–111.

Dalton, P., Doolittle, N., and **Breslin, P. A.** (2002) Gender-specific induction of enhanced sensitivity to odors. *Nature Neuroscience, 5,* 199–200.

Dalton, P., Doolittle, N., Nagata, H., and **Breslin, P. A. S.** (2000) The merging of the senses: Integration of subthreshold taste and smell. *Nature Neuroscience, 3,* 431–432.

Damasio, A. R. (1985) Prosopagnosia. *Trends in Neurosciences, 8,* 132–135.

Damasio, A. R. (1994) *Descartes' error: Emotion, reason, and the human brain.* New York: Putnam.

Damasio, A. R., Damasio, H., and **van Hoesen, G. W.** (1982) Prosopagnosia: Anatomic basis and behavioral mechanisms. *Neurology, 32,* 331–341.

Damasio, A. R., Tranel, D., and **Damasio, H.** (1990) Face agnosia and the neural substrates of memory. *Annual Review of Neuroscience, 13,* 89–109.

Dannenbaum, R. M., and **Dykes, R. W.** (1988) Sensory loss in the hand after sensory stroke: Therapeutic rationale. *Archives of Physical Medicine and Rehabilitation, 69,* 833–839.

Darian-Smith, I. (1984) The sense of touch: Performance and peripheral neural processes. In I. Darian-Smith (ed.) *Handbook of physiology: vol. 3, part 2.* Bethesda, MD: American Physiological Society, 739–788.

Darian-Smith, I., Goodwin, A., Sugitani, M., and **Heywood, J.** (1984) The tangible features of textured surfaces: Their representation in the monkey's somatosensory cortex. In G. Edelman, W. E. Gall, and M. W. Cowan (eds.), *Dynamic aspects of neocortical function.* New York: John Wiley & Sons, 475–500.

Dartnall, H. J. A., Bowmaker, J. K., and **Mollon, J. D.** (1983) Human visual pigments: Microspectrophotometric results from the eyes of seven persons. *Proceedings of the Royal Society of London (Series B), 220,* 115–130.

Das, A., and **Gilbert, C. D.** (1999) Topography of contextual modulations mediated by short-range interactions in primary visual cortex. *Nature, 399,* 655–661.

Daum, K. M. (1983) Accommodative dysfunction. *Documenta Ophthalmologica, 55,* 177–198.

Davenport, R. J. (2001) New gene may be key to sweet tooth. *Science, 292,* 620–621.

Davidoff, J., Davies, I., and **Roberson, D.** (1999) Colour categories in a stone-age tribe. *Nature, 398,* 203–204.

Davis, H., and **Silverman, S. R.** (1960) *Hearing and deafness.* New York: Holt, Rinehart & Winston.

Davis, L. B., and **Porter, R. H.** (1991) Persistent effects of early odor exposure on human neonates. *Chemical Senses, 16,* 169–174.

Davis, R. G. (1977) Acquisition of verbal associations to olfactory and abstract visual stimuli of varying similarity. *Journal of Experimental Psychology: Human Learning and Memory, 3,* 37–51.

Davis, R. G. (1981) The role of nonolfactory context cues in odor identification. *Perception & Psychophysics, 30,* 83–89.

Dawkins, R. (1996) *The blind watchmaker.* New York: W.W. Norton.

de Boer, I. (1956) Pitch of inharmonic signals. *Nature, 178,* 535–536.

de Craen, A. J. M., Roos, P. J., de Vries, A. L., and **Kleijnen, J.** (1996) Effect of colour of drugs: systematic review of perceived effect of drugs and of their effectiveness. *British Journal of Medicine, 313,* 1624–1626.

de Gelder, B., Teunisse, J. P., and **Benson, P. J.** (1997) Categorical perception of facial expressions: Categories and their internal structure. *Cognition and Emotion, 11,* 1–23.

De Graaf, C., and **Zandstra, E. H.** (1999) Sweetness intensity and pleasantness in children, adolescents, and adults. *Physiology & Behavior, 67,* 513–520.

de Monasterio, F. M., and **Gouras, P.** (1975) Functional properties of ganglion cells of the rhesus monkey retina. *Journal of Physiology, 251,* 167–195.

De Wijk, R. A., and **Cain, W. S.** (1994) Odor identification by name by edibility: Life-span development and safety. *Human Factors, 36,* 182–187.

Deacon, T. W. (1989). The neural circuitry underlying primate calls and human language. *Human Evolution, 4,* 367–401.

DeAngelis, G. C. (2000) Seeing in three dimensions: The neurophysiology of stereopsis. *Trends in Cognitive Sciences, 4,* 80–90.

DeCasper, A. J., and **Fifer, W. P.** (1980) Of human bonding: Newborns prefer their mothers' voices. *Science, 208,* 174–176.

Degenaar, M. (1996) *Molyneux's problem: Three centuries of discussion on the perception of forms.* Dordrecht: Kluwer Academic Publishers.

De Lafuente, V., and **Ruiz, O.** (2004) The orientation dependence of the Hermann grid illusion. *Experimental Brain Research, 154,* 255–260.

DeLoache, J. S., Uttal, D. H., and **Rosengren, K. S.** (2004) Scale errors offer evidence for a perception-action dissociation early in life. *Science, 304,* 1027–1029.

Delwiche, J. F., Lera, M. F., and **Breslin, P. A. S.** (2000) Selective removal of a target stimulus localized by taste in humans. *Chemical Senses, 25,* 181–187.

Dennett, D. C. (1991) *Consciousness explained.* Boston: Little, Brown.

Denton, G. G. (1980) The influence of visual pattern on perceived speed. *Perception,* 9, 393–402.

DePaulo, B. M., and **Friedman, H. S.** (1998). Nonverbal communication. In D. T. Gilbert, S. T. Fiske, & G. Lindzey (eds.), *The handbook of social psychology,* vol. II, 4th ed., New York: McGraw-Hill, 3–40.

Derby, C. D., Ache, B. W., and **Kennel, E. W.** (1985) Mixture suppression: Electrophysiological evaluation of the contribution of peripheral and central neural components. *Chemical Senses,* 10, 301–316.

Derrington, A. M., Krauskopf, J., and **Lennie, P.** (1984) Chromatic mechanisms in lateral geniculate nucleus of macaque. *Journal of Physiology,* 357, 241–265.

Desimone, R. (1991) Face-selective cells in the temporal cortex of monkeys. *Journal of Cognitive Neuroscience,* 3, 1–8.

Desor, J. A., and **Beauchamp, G. K.** (1974) The human capacity to transmit olfactory information. *Perception & Psychophysics,* 16, 551–556.

Detwiler, P. B., Hodgkin, A. L., and **McNaughton, P. A.** (1980) Temporal and spatial characteristics of the voltage response of rods in the retina of the turtle. *Journal of Physiology,* 300, 213–250.

Deubel, H., Bridgeman, B., and **Schneider, W. X.** (1998) Immediate post-saccadic information mediates space constancy. *Vision Research,* 38, 3147–3159.

DeValois, R. L., and **DeValois, K. K.** (1975) Neural coding of color. In E. C. Carterette and M. P. Friedman (eds.). *Handbook of perception,* vol. 5. New York: Academic Press, 117–166.

DeValois, R. L., Smith, C. J., Kitai, S. T., and **Karoly, A. J.** (1958) Responses of single cells in different layers of the primate lateral geniculate nucleus to monochromatic light. *Science,* 127, 238–239.

Dewson, J., Pribram, K., and **Lynch, J.** (1969) Effects of ablations of temporal cortex upon speech sound discrimination in the monkey. *Experimental Neurology,* 24, 579–591.

Dittrich, W. H., Lea, S. E. G., Barrett, J., and **Gurr, P. R.** (1998) Categorization of natural movements by pigeons: Visual concept discrimination and biological motion. *Journal of the Experimental Analysis of Behavior,* 70, 281–299.

Djordjevic, J., Zatorre, R. J., Petrides, M., and **Jones-Gotman, M.** (2004) The mind's nose: Effects of odor and visual imagery on odor detection. *Psychological Science,* 15, 143–148.

Dobbins, A. C., Jeo, R. M., Fiser, J., and **Allman, J. M.** (1998) Distance modulation of neural activity in the visual cortex. *Science,* 281, 552–555.

Dobelle, W. H., and **Mladejovsky, M. G.** (1974) Phosphenes produced by electrical stimulation of human occipital cortex, and their application to the development of a prosthesis for the blind. *Journal of Physiology,* 243, 553–576.

Dobkins, K. R. (2000) Moving colors in the lime light. *Neuron,* 25, 15–18.

Dodd, B. (1977) The role of vision in the perception of speech. *Perception,* 6, 31–40.

Dodge, R. (1900) The illusion of clear vision during eye movement. *Psychological Bulletin,* 2, 193–199.

Dolan, R. J., Fink, G. R., Rolls, E., Booth, M., Holmes, A., Frackowiak, R. S. J., and **Friston, K. J.** (1997) How the brain learns to see objects and faces in an impoverished context. *Nature,* 389, 596–599.

Doleman, B. J., Severin, E. J., and **Lewis, N. S.** (1998) Trends in odor intensity for human and electronic noses: Relative roles of odorant vapor pressure vs. molecularly specific odorant binding. *Proceedings of the National Academy of Sciences: USA,* 95, 5442–5447.

Dolnick, E. (1993) Deafness as culture. *Atlantic Monthly,* 272, 37–53.

Dosher, B. A., Sperling, G., and **Wurst, S. A.** (1986) Tradeoffs between stereopsis and proximity luminance covariance. *Vision Research,* 26, 973–990.

Doty, R. L. (1986) Odor-guided behavior in mammals. *Experientia,* 42, 257–271.

Doty, R. L. (2001) Olfaction. *Annual Review in Psychology,* 52, 423–452.

Doty, R. L., Green, P. A., Ram, C., and **Yankell, S. L.** (1982) Communication of gender from human breath odors: Relationship to perceived intensity and pleasantness. *Hormones and Behavior,* 16, 13–22.

Doty, R. L., Shaman, P., Applebaum, S. L., Giberson, R., Siksorski, L., and **Rosenberg, L.** (1984) Smell identification ability: Changes with age. *Science,* 226, 1441–1443.

Doty, R. L., Shaman, P., and **Dann, M.** (1984) Development of the University of Pennsylvania Smell Identification Test: A standardized microencapsulated test of olfactory function. *Physiology & Behavior,* 32, 489–502.

Dowling, J. E. (1966) Night blindness. *Scientific American,* 215, 78–84.

Dowling, J. E. (1998) *Creating mind: How the brain works.* New York: Norton.

Dowling, W. J., and **Fujitani, D. S.** (1971) Contour, interval, and pitch recognition in memory for melodies. *Journal of the Acoustical Society of America,* 49, 524–531.

Drasdo, N. (1977) The neural representation of visual space. *Nature,* 266, 554–556.

Drayna, D., Manichaikul, A., de Lange, M., Snieder, H., and **Spector, T.** (2001) Genetic correlates of musical pitch recognition in humans. *Science,* 291, 1969–1972.

Dreher, B., Fukada, Y., and **Rodieck, R. W.** (1976) Identification, classification, and anatomical segregation of cells with X-like and Y-like properties in the lateral geniculate nucleus of old-world primates. *Journal of Physiology,* 29, 433–452.

Drewnowski, A., Bellisle, F., Aimez, P., and **Remy, B.** (1987) Taste and bulimia. *Physiology & Behavior,* 41, 621–626.

Drewnowski, A., Grinker, J. A., and **Hirsch, J.** (1982) Obesity and flavor perception: Multidimensional scaling of soft drinks. *Appetite: Journal of Intake Research,* 3, 361–368.

Drewnowski, A., Henderson, S. A., and **Shore, A. B.** (1997) Taste responses to naringin, a flavonoid, and the acceptance of grapefruit juice are related to genetic sensitivity to 6-n-propylthiouracil. *American Journal of Clinical Nutrition,* 66, 391–397.

DuBose, C. N., Cardello, A., and **Maller, O.** (1980) Effects of colorants and flavorants on identification, perceived flavor intensity, and hedonic quality of fruit-flavored beverages and cake. *Journal of Food Science,* 45, 1393–1399, 1415.

Duchamp-Viret, P., Duchamp, A., and **Vigouroux, M.** (1989) Amplifying role of convergence in olfactory system. A comparative study of receptor cell and second-order neuron sensitivities. *Journal of Neurophysiology,* 61, 1085–1094.

Duffy, V. B., Peterson, J. M., and **Bartoshuk, L. M.** (2004) Associations between taste genetics, oral sensation and alcohol intake. *Physiology & Behavior,* 82, 435–445.

Duhamel, J.-R., Colby, C. L., and **Goldberg, M. E.** (1992) The updating of the representation of visual space in parietal cortex by intended eye movements. *Science,* 255, 90–92.

Duncker, K, (1929-1938). Induced motion. In W. D. Ellis (ed.), *A source book of Gestalt psychology.* New York: Humanities Press, 161–172.

Duncker, K. (1939) The influence of past experience upon perceptual properties. *American Journal of Psychology,* 52, 255–267.

Eccles, J. (1979) *The human mystery.* Berlin: Springer-Verlag.

Edelman, S., and **Bülthoff, H.** (1992) Orientation dependence in the recognition of familiar and novel views of three-dimensional objects. *Vision Research,* 32, 2385–2400.

Egeth, H. E., Kamlet, A. S., and **Bell, R. A.** (1970) The reversal of classical contrast in temperature perception. *Psychonomic Science,* 19, 96.

Eggermont, J. J., and **Roberts, L. E.** (2004) The neuroscience of tinnitus. *Trends in Neuroscience,* 27, 676–682

Egly, R., Driver, J., and **Rafal, R. D.** (1994) Shifting visual attention between objects and locations: Evidence from normal and parietal lesion subjects. *Journal of Experimental Psychology: General,* 123, 161–177.

Ehrenstein, W. H., and **Ehrenstein, A.** (1999) Psychophysical methods. In U. Windhorst and H. Johansson (eds.) *Modern techniques in neuroscience research.* Berlin: Springer-Verlag, 1211–1241.

Eimas, P. D., and **Corbit, J. D.** (1973) Selective adaptation of linguistic feature detectors. *Cognitive Psychology,* 4, 99–109.

Ekman, P. (1984) Expression and the nature of emotion. In K. R. Scherer and P. Ekman (eds.), *Approaches to emotion.* Hillsdale, N.: Erlbaum.

Elbert, T., Pantev, C., Wienbruch, C., Rockstroh, B., and **Taub, E.** (1995) Increased cortical representation of the fingers of the left hand in string players. *Science,* 27, 305–307.

Elkins, J. (1996) *The object stares back: On the nature of seeing.* New York: Harvest Books.

Emmerich, D. S., and **Levine, F. M.** (1970) Differences in auditory sensitivity of chronic schizophrenic patients and normal controls determined by use of a forced-choice procedure. *Diseases of the Nervous System,* 31, 552–557.

Engel, S. A., Glover, G. H., and **Wandell, B. A.** (1997) Retinotopic organization in human visual cortex and the spatial precision of functional MRI. *Cerebral Cortex,* 7, 181–192.

Engel, S. A., Zhang, X., and **Wandell, B.** (1997) Colour tuning in the human visual cortex measured with functional magnetic resonance imaging. *Nature,* 388, 68–71.

Engen, T. (1960) Effects of practice and instruction on olfactory thresholds. *Perceptual and Motor Skills,* 10, 195–198.

Engen, T. (1982) *The perception of odors.* New York: Academic Press.

Engen, T. (1987) Remembering odors and their names. *American Scientist,* 75, 497–503.

Enright, J. T. (1989) Manipulating stereopsis and vergence in an outdoor setting: Moon, sky and horizon. *Vision Research,* 29, 1815–1824.

Enroth-Cugell, C., Hertz, B. G., and **Lennie, P.** (1977) Convergence of rod and cone signals in the cat's retina. *Journal of Physiology,* 269, 297–318.

Epelboim, J., Booth, J. R., Ashkenazy, R., Taleghani, A., and **Steinman, R. M.** (1997) Fillers and spaces in text: The importance of word recognition during reading. *Vision Research,* 37, 2899–2914.

Epelboim, J., Booth, J. R., and **Steinman, R. M.** (1994) Reading unspaced text: Implications for theories of reading eye movements. *Vision Research,* 34, 1735–1766.

Epstein, R., and **Kanwisher, N.** (1998) A cortical representation of the local visual environment. *Nature,* 392, 598–601.

Epstein, W. (1963) The influences of assumed size on apparent distance. *American Journal of Physiology,* 76, 257–265.

Erickson, R. P. (1968) Stimulus coding in topographic and nontopographic afferent modalities: On the significance of the activity of individual sensory neurons. *Psychological Review,* 75, 447–465.

Erickson, R. P. (1982) Studies on the perception of taste: Do primaries exist? *Physiology & Behavior,* 28, 57–62.

Erickson, R. P. (1984) On the neural bases of behavior. *American Scientist,* 72, 233–241.

Erickson, R. P., and **Covey, E.** (1980) On the singularity of taste sensations: What is a taste primary? *Physiology & Behavior,* 25, 527–533.

Eriksson-Mangold, M. M., and **Erlandsson, S. I.** (1984) The psychological importance of nonverbal sounds. *Scandinavian Audiology,* 13, 243–249.

Essick, G. K., Chopra, A., Guest, S., and **McGlone, F.** (2003) Lingual tactile acuity, taste perception, and the density and diameter of fungiform papillae in female subjects. *Physiology & Behavior,* 80, 289–302.

Essock, E. A., Krebs, W. K., and **Prather, J. R.** (1992) An anisotropy of human tactile sensitivity and its relation to the visual oblique effect. *Experimental Brain Research,* 91, 520–524.

Evans, E. F. (1982) Functional anatomy of the auditory system. In H. B. Barlow and J. D. Mollon (eds.), *The senses.* Cambridge: Cambridge University Press, 251–306.

Exner, S. (1888) Über optische Bewegungsempfindungen. *Biologisches Centralblatt,* 8, 437–448.

Fahle, M., Edelman, S., and **Poggio, T.** (1995) Fast perceptual learning in hyperacuity. *Vision Research,* 35, 3003–3013.

Farrell, M. J., and **Robertson, I. H.** (1998) Mental rotation and the automatic updating of body-centered spatial relationships. *Journal of Experimental Psychology: Learning, Memory and Cognition,* 24, 227–233.

Farroni, T., Csibra, G., Simion, F., and **Johnson, M. H.** (2002) Eye contact detection in humans from birth. *Proceedings of the National Academy of Sciences: USA,* 99, 9602–9605.

Fay, R. R. (1988) Comparative psychoacoustics. *Hearing Research,* 34, 295–306.

Fechner, G. T. (1860/1966) *Elements of psychophysics.* D. H. Howes and E. G. Boring (eds.), H. E. Adler (trans.). New York: Holt, Rinehart and Winston.

Felleman, D. J., and **Van Essen, D. C.** (1991) Distributed hierarchical processing in the primate cerebral cortex. *Cerebral Cortex,* 1, 1–47.

Fendrich, R., Wessinger, C. M., and **Gazzaniga, M. S.** (1992) Residual vision in a scotoma: Implications for blindsight. *Science,* 258, 1489–1491.

Ferrie, C. D., De Marco, P., Grunewald, R. A., Giannakodimos, S., and **Panayiotopoulos, C. P.** (1994) Video game induced seizures. *Journal of Neurology, Neurosurgery & Psychiatry,* 57, 925–931.

Field, D. J. (1987) Relations between the statistics of natural images and the response properties of cortical cells. *Journal of the Optical Society of America A,* 4, 2379–2394.

Field, D. J., Hayes, A., and **Hess, R.** (1993) Contour integration by the human visual system: Evidence for a local "association field." *Vision Research,* 33, 173–193.

Field, D. J., and **Hayes, A.** (2004) Contour integration and the lateral connections of V1 neurons. In L. M. Chalupa and J. S. Werner (eds.) *The visual neurosciences.* Cambridge: MIT Press, 1069–1079.

Finney, E. M., Clementz, B. A., Hickok, G., and **Dobkins, K. R.** (2003) Visual stimuli activate auditory cortex in deaf subjects: Evidence from MEG. *Neuroreports,* 14, 1425–1427.

Finney, E. M., Fine, I., and **Dobkins, K. R.** (2001) Visual stimuli activate auditory cortex in the deaf. *Nature Neuroscience,* 4, 1171–1172.

Fischer, R., Griffin, F., England, S., and **Carn, S. M.** (1961) Taste thresholds and food dislikes. *Nature,* 191, 1328.

Fitch, W. T., and **Giedd, J.** (1999) Morphology and development of the human vocal tract: A study using magnetic resonance imaging. *Journal of the Acoustical Society of America,* 106, 1511–1522.

Fitzpatrick, D. C., Batra, R., Stanford, T. R., and **Kuwada, S.** (1997) A neuronal population code for sound localization. *Nature,* 388, 871–874.

Fleming, R. W., Dror, R. O., and **Adelson, E. H.** (2003) Real-world illumination and the perception of surface reflectance properties. *Journal of Vision,* 3, 347–368. <http://journalofvision.org/3/5/3/>

Fletcher, H. (1940) Auditory patterns. *Review of Modern Physics,* 12, 47–65.

Fletcher, H. F., and **Munson, W. A.** (1933) Loudness, its definition, measurement, and calculation. *Journal of the Acoustical Society of America,* 5, 82–108.

Fletcher, S. W., O'Malley, M. S., and **Bunce, L. A.** (1985) Physicians' abilities to detect lumps in silicone breast models. *Journal of the American Medical Association,* 253, 2224–2228.

Foerstl, H., Owen, A. M., and **David, A. S.** (1993) Gabriel Anton and "Anton's symptom": On focal diseases of the brain which are not perceived by the patient (1898). *Neuropsychiatry, Neuropsychology, and Behavioral Neurology,* 6, 1–6.

Foley, J. M. (1980) Binocular distance perception. *Psychological Review,* 87, 411–434.

Formisano, E., Kim, D.-S., Di Salle, F., van de Moortele, P., Ugurbil, K., and **Goebel, R.** (2003) Mirror-symmetric tonotopic maps in human primary auditory cortex. *Neuron,* 40, 859–869.

Fox, R., Aslin, R. N., Shea, S. L., and **Dumais, S. T.** (1980) Stereopsis in human infants. *Science,* 207, 323–324.

Fox, R., Lehmkuhle, S. W., and **Bush, R. C.** (1977) Stereopsis in the falcon. *Science,* 197, 79–81.

Fox, R., and **McDaniel, C.** (1982) The perception of biological motion by human infants. *Science,* 218, 486–487.

Fox Tree, J. E. (2001) Listeners' uses of um and uh in speech comprehension. *Memory & Cognition,* 29, 320–326.

Francis, S., Rolls, E. T., Bowtell, R., McGlone, F., O'Doherty, J., Browning, A., Clare, S., and **Smith, E.** (1999) The representation of pleasant touch in the brain and its relationship with taste and olfactory areas. *Neuroreport,* 10, 453–459.

Frank, M. E. (2000) Neuron types, receptors, behavior and taste quality. *Physiology & Behavior,* 69, 53–62.

Freedman, M. S., Lucas, R. J., Soni, B., von Schantz, M., Munoz, M., David-Gray, Z., and **Foster, R.** (1999) Regulation of mammalian circadian behavior by non-rod, non-cone, ocular photoreceptors. *Science,* 284, 502–504.

Freeman, R. D. (2004) Binocular interaction in the visual cortex. In L. M. Chalupa and J. S. Werner (eds.) *The visual neurosciences,* vol. 1. Cambridge: MIT Press, 765–778.

Freeman, R. D., and **Pettigrew, J. D.** (1973) Alteration of visual cortex from environmental asymmetries. *Nature,* 246, 359–360.

Freeman, W. J. (1991) The physiology of perception. *Scientific American,* 264, 78–85.

Freund, M. S., and **Lewis, N. S.** (1995) A chemically diverse conducting polymer-based electronic nose, *Proceedings of the National Academy of Sciences: USA,* 92, 2652.

Freud, S. (1930/1961) *Civilization and its discontents.* New York: W. W. Norton.

Freytag, E., and **Sachs, J. S.** (1968) Abnormalities of the central visual pathways contributing to traffic accidents. *Journal of the American Medical Association,* 204, 871–873.

Friedman, R. M., Chen, L. M., and **Roe, A. W.** (2004) Modality maps within primate somatosensory cortex. *Proceedings of the National Academy of Sciences: USA,* 101, 12724–12729.

Friesen, C. K., and **Kingstone, A.** (1998) The eyes have it! Reflexive orienting is triggered by nonpredictive gaze. *Psychonomic Bulletin & Review,* 5, 490–495.

Frisby, J. P., and **Clatworthy, J. L.** (1975) Learning to see complex random-dot stereograms. *Perception, 4,* 173–178.

Frisby, J. P., and **Mayhew, J. E. W.** (1976) Rivalrous texture stereograms. *Nature, 264,* 53–56.

Frisina, D. R., and **Frisina, R. D.** (1997) Speech recognition in noise and presbycusis: Relations to possible neural mechanisms. *Hearing Research, 106,* 95–104.

Frye, R. E., Doty, R. L., and **Schwartz, B.** (1989) Influence of cigarette smoking on olfaction: Evidence for a dose-response relationship. *Journal of the American Medical Association, 263,* 1233–1236.

Fuchs, A., and **Binder, M. D.** (1983) Fatigue resistance of human extraocular muscles. *Journal of Neurophysiology, 49,* 28–34.

Fuchs, R. N., Campbell, J. N., and **Meyer, R. A.** (2000a) Secondary hyperalgesia persists in capsaicin desensitized skin. *Pain, 84,* 141–149.

Fuchs, R. N., Raja, S. N., and **Meyer, R. A.** (2000b) Topical capsaicin for the treatment of neuropathic pain. *Analgesia, 5,* 1–8.

Fullard, J. H., and **Barclay, R. M. R.** (1980) Audition in spring species of arctiid moths as a possible response to differential levels of insectivorous bat predation. *Canadian Journal of Zoology, 58,* 1745–1750.

Gallant, J. L., Shoup, R. E., and **Mazer, J. A.** (2000) A human extrastriate area functionally homologous to macaque V4. *Neuron, 27,* 227–235.

Gamble, E. A. M. C. (1921) Review of *Der Geruch* by Hans Henning. *American Journal of Psychology, 32,* 290–295.

Gandhi, N. J., and **Sparks, D. L.** (2004) Changing views of the superior colliculus in the control of gaze. In L. M. Chalupa and J. S. Werner (eds.), *The Visual Neurosciences.* Cambridge: MIT Press, 1449–1465.

Garb, J., and **Stunkard, A. J.** (1974) Taste aversions in man. *American Journal of Psychiatry, 131,* 1204–1207.

Garcia, J., and **Koelling, R. A.** (1966) Relation of cue to consequences in avoidance learning. *Psychonomic Science, 4,* 123–124.

Garcia-Medina, M. R., and **Cain, W. S.** (1982) Bilateral integration in the common chemical sense. *Physiology & Behavior, 29,* 349–353.

Gardner, R. J. M., and **Sutherland, G. R.** (1989) *Chromosome abnormalities and genetic counseling.* Oxford: Oxford University Press.

Garfield, E. (1983) The tyranny of the horn—Automobile, that is. *Current Contents, 26,* 5–11.

Garner, W. R. (1962) *Uncertainty and structure as psychological concepts.* New York: John Wiley & Sons.

Gaser, C., and **Schlaug, G.** (2003) Brain structures differ between musicians and non-musicians. *Journal of Neuroscience, 23,* 9240–9245.

Gauthier, I., Behrmann, M., and **Tarr, M. J.** (1999) Can face recognition really be dissociated from object recognition? *Journal of Cognitive Neuroscience, 11,* 349–370.

Gauthier, I., Skudlarski, P., Gore, J. C., and **Anderson, A.** (2000) Expertise for cars and birds recruits brain areas involved in face recognition. *Nature Neuroscience, 3,* 191–197.

Gauthier, I., and **Tarr, M. J.** (1997) Becoming a "Greeble" expert: Exploring the face recognition mechanism. *Vision Research, 37,* 1673–1682.

Gauthier, I., Tarr, M. J., Anderson, A. W., Skudlarski, P., and **Gore, J. C.** (1999) Activation of the middle fusiform "face area" increases with expertise in recognizing novel objects. *Nature Neuroscience, 2,* 568–573.

Gegenfurtner, K. R. (2003) Cortical mechanisms of colour vision. *Nature Reviews Neuroscience, 4,* 563–572.

Gegenfurtner, K. R., Kiper, D. C., and **Fenstemaker, S. B.** (1996) Processing of color, form, and motion in macaque area V2. *Visual Neuroscience, 13,* 161–172.

Gegenfurtner, K. R., and **Rieger, J.** (2000) Sensory and cognitive contributions of color to the recognition of natural scenes. *Current Biology, 10,* 805–808.

Geisler, W. S. (1989) Sequential ideal-observer analysis of visual discriminations. *Psychological Review, 96,* 267–314.

Geisler, W. S., and **Diehl, R. L.** (2002) Bayesian natural selection and the evolution of perceptual systems. *Philosophical Transactions of the Royal Society of London (Series B), 357,* 419–448.

Geisler, W. S., Perry, J. S., Super, B. J., and **Gallogly, D. P.** (2001) Edge co-occurrence in natural images predicts contour grouping performance. *Vision Research, 41,* 711–724.

Gelb, A. (1929) Die Farbenkonstanz der Sehdinge. In A. Bethe et al. (eds.), *Handbuch der normalen und pathologischen physiologie,* vol. 12. Berlin: Springer-Verlag, 594–678.

Geldard, F. A., and **Sherrick, C. E.** (1986) Space, time and touch. *Scientific American, 255,* 90–95.

George, P. A., and **Hole, G. J.** (1995) Factors influencing the accuracy of age estimates of unfamiliar faces. *Perception, 24,* 1059–1073.

Gervais, H., Belin, P., Boddaert, N., Leboyer, M., Coez, A., Sfaello, I., Barthelemy, C., Brunelle, Samson, Y., and **Zilbovicius, M.** (2004) Abnormal cortical voice processing in autism. *Nature Neuroscience, 7,* 801–802.

Gescheider, G. A. (1976) *Psychophysics: Method and theory.* Hillsdale, N.J.: Erlbaum.

Gescheider, G. A., Sklar, B. F., van Doren, C. L., and **Verillo, R. T.** (1985) Vibrotactile forward masking: Psychophysical evidence for a triplex theory of cutaneous mechanoreception. *Journal of Acoustical Society of America, 78,* 534–543.

Ghazanfar, A. A., and **Logothetis, N. K.** (2003) Facial expressions linked to monkey calls. *Nature, 423,* 937–938.

Ghazanfar, A. A., Neuhoff, J. G., and **Logothetis, N. K.** (2002) Auditory looming perception in rhesus monkeys. *Proceedings of the National Academy of Sciences: USA, 99,* 15755–15757.

Ghazanfar, A. A., and **Santos, L. R.** (2004) Primate brains in the wild: the sensory bases for social interactions. *Nature Reviews Neuroscience, 5,* 603–616.

Gibson, J. J. (1947) Motion picture testing and research. *AAF Aviation Psychology Report No. 7.* Washington, D.C.: U. S. Army Air Force.

Gibson, J. J. (1950) *The perception of the visual world.* Boston: Houghton-Mifflin.

Gibson, J. J. (1966) *The senses considered as perceptual systems.* Boston: Houghton-Mifflin.

Gibson, J. J. (1979) *The ecological approach to visual perception.* Boston: Houghton-Mifflin.

Gilad, Y., and **Lancet, D.** (2003) Population differences in the human functional olfactory repertoire. *Molecular Biology and Evolution,* 20, 307–314

Gilad, Y., Man, O., Paabo, S., and **Lancet, D.** (2003) Human specific loss of olfactory receptor genes. *Proceedings of the National Academy of Sciences: USA,* 100, 3324–3327.

Gilad, Y., Wiebe, V., Przeworski, M., Lancet, D., and **Paabo, S.** (2004) Loss of olfactory receptor genes coincides with the acquisition of full trichromatic vision in primates. *Public Library of Science Biology,* 2, E5.

Gilbert, A. N., and **Firestein, S.** (2002) Dollars and scents: Commercial opportunities in olfaction and taste. *Nature Neuroscience,* 5 Supplement, 1043–1045.

Gilchrist, A. L. (1977) Perceived lightness depends on perceived spatial arrangement. *Science,* 195, 185–187.

Gilchrist, A. L. (1988) Lightness contrast and failures of constancy: A common explanation. *Perception & Psychophysics,* 43, 415–424.

Gilinsky, A. S. (1955) The effect of attitude upon the perception of size. *American Journal of Psychology,* 68, 173–192.

Gillan, D. J. (1982) Mixture suppression: The effect of spatial separation between sucrose and NaCl. *Perception & Psychophysics,* 32, 504–510.

Gillan, D. J. (1984) Evidence for peripheral and central processes in taste adaptation. *Perception & Psychophysics,* 35, 1–4.

Ginsberg, M. D., Yoshii, F., Vibulsresth, S., Chang, J. Y., Durara, R., Barker, W. W., and **Boothe, T. E.** (1987) Human task-specific somatosensory activation. *Neurology,* 37, 1301–1308.

Ginsburg, A. P., Evans, D. W., Sekuler, R., and **Harp, S. A.** (1982) Contrast sensitivity predicts pilots' performance in aircraft simulators. *American Journal of Optometry and Physiological Optics,* 59, 105–108.

Gittleman, J. L., and **Harvey, P. H.** (1980) Why are distasteful prey not cryptic? *Nature,* 286, 149–150.

Glanville, E. V., and **Kaplan, A. R.** (1965) Food preference and sensitivity of taste for bitter compounds. *Nature,* 205, 851–853.

Glanzer, M., Hilford, A., and **Kim, K.** (2004) Six regularities of source recognition. *Journal of Experimental Psychology: Learning, Memory & Cognition,* 30, 1176–1195.

Glass, L. (1969) Moiré effect from random dots. *Nature,* 243, 587–590.

Glickstein, M. (1988) The discovery of the visual cortex. *Scientific American,* 259, 118–127.

Goethe, J. W. von. (1840/1970) *Theory of colours.* C. L. Eastlake (trans.). Cambridge: MIT Press.

Gold, J., Bennett, P. J., and **Sekuler, A. B.** (1999) Signal but not noise changes with perceptual learning. *Nature,* 402, 176–178.

Goldberg, M. E., and **Wurtz, R. H.** (1972) Activity of superior colliculus in behaving monkey: I. Visual receptive fields of single neurons. *Journal of Neurophysiology,* 35, 542–559.

Goldman, A. I. (1976) Discrimination and perceptual knowledge. *Journal of Philosophy,* 73, 771–791.

Golz, J., and **MacLeod, D. I. A.** (2002) Influence of scene statistics on colour constancy. *Nature,* 415, 637–640.

Gonzalez, F., and **Perez, R.** (1998) Neural mechanisms underlying stereoscopic vision. *Progress in Neurobiology,* 55, 191–224.

Goodale, M. A., and **Humphrey, G. K.** (1998) The objects of action and perception. *Cognition,* 67, 181–207.

Goodale, M. A., and **Milner, A. D.** (1992) Separate visual pathways for perception and action. *Trends in Neurosciences,* 15, 20–25.

Gordon, B. (1972) The superior colliculus of the brain. *Scientific American,* 227, 72–82.

Gosselin, P., Beaupré, M., and **Boissonneault, A.** (2002) Perception of genuine and masking smiles in children and adults: Sensitivity to traces of anger. *Journal of Genetic Psychology,* 163, 58–71.

Gottfried, J. A., Deichmann, R., Winston, J. S., and **Dolan, R. J.** (2002) Functional heterogeneity in human olfactory cortex: An event-related functional magnetic resonance imaging study. *Journal of Neuroscience,* 22, 10819–10828.

Gottfried, J. A., and **Dolan, R. J.** (2003) The nose smells what the eye sees: Crossmodal visual facilitation of human olfactory perception. *Neuron,* 39, 375–386.

Gottfried J. A., Smith, A. P., Rugg, M. D., and **Dolan, R. J.** (2004) Remembrance of odors past: Human olfactory cortex in cross-modal recognition memory. *Neuron,* 42, 687–695.

Gouk, P. (1988) The harmonic roots of Newtonian science. In J. Fauvel, R. Flood, M. Shortland, and R. Wilson (eds.), *Let Newton be! A new perspective on his life and works.* Oxford: Oxford University Press, 100–125.

Gould, A., and **Martin, G. N.** (2001) A good odour to breathe? The effect of pleasant ambient odour on human visual vigilance. *Applied Cognitive Psychology,* 15, 225–232.

Gouras, P., and **Zrenner, E.** (1981) Color coding in the primate retina. *Vision Research,* 21, 1591–1598.

Graham, C. A., and **McGrew, W. C.** (1980) Menstrual synchrony in female undergraduates living on a coeducational campus. *Psychoneuroendocrinology,* 5, 253–259.

Graham, C. H. (1965) Visual space perception. In C. H. Graham (ed.), *Vision and visual perception.* New York: John Wiley & Sons, 504–547.

Grammer, K. (1990) Strangers meet: Laughter and nonverbal signs of interest in opposite-sex encounters. *Journal of Nonverbal Behavior,* 14, 203–236.

Grant, A. C., Thiagarajah, M. C., and **Sathian, K.** (2000) Tactile perception in blind Braille readers: A psychophysical study of acuity and hyperacuity using gratings and dot patterns. *Perception & Psychophysics,* 62, 301–312.

Graziadei, P. P. C. (1973) Cell dynamics in the olfactory mucosa. *Tissue and Cell,* 5, 113–131.

Green, D. M. (1964) Consistency of auditory detection judgments. *Psychological Review,* 71, 392–407.

Green, D. M. (1982) Profile analysis: A different view of auditory intensity discrimination. *American Psychologist,* 38, 133–142.

Green, D. M., Kidd, G., Jr., and **Picardi, M. C.** (1983) Successive versus simultaneous comparison in auditory discrimination. *Journal of the Acoustical Society of America,* 73, 639–643.

Green, D. M., and **Nguyen, Q. T.** (1988) Profile analysis: Detecting dynamic spectral changes. *Hearing Research,* 32, 147–164.

Green, D. M., and **Swets, J. A.** (1966) *Signal detection theory and psychophysics.* New York: John Wiley & Sons.

Green, J. A., Jones, L. E., and **Gustafson, E. E.** (1987) Perception of cries by parents and nonparents: Relation to cry acoustics. *Developmental Psychology,* 23, 370–382.

Greenberg, D. P. (1989) Light reflection models for computer graphics. *Science,* 244, 166–173.

Greenwald, A. G., Spangenberg, E. R., Pratkanis, A. R., and **Eskenazi, J.** (1991) Double-blind tests of subliminal self-help audiotapes. *Psychological Science,* 2, 119–122.

Greer, C. A. (1991) Structural organization of the olfactory system. In T. V. Getchell, R. L. Doty, L. M. Bartoshuk, and J. B. Snow (eds.), *Smell and taste in health and disease.* New York: Raven Press, 65–81.

Gregory, R. L. (1970) *The intelligent eye.* New York: McGraw-Hill.

Gregory, R. L. (1978) *Eye and brain: The psychology of seeing,* 3rd ed. New York: McGraw-Hill.

Gregory, R. L. (1979) The aesthetics of anaesthetics. *Perception,* 8, 123–124.

Gregory, R. L. (1992) How can perceptual science help the handicapped? *Perception,* 21, 1–6.

Gregory, R. L. (1997) *Eye and brain,* 5th ed. Princeton: Princeton University Press.

Gregory, R. L., and **Drysdale, A. E.** (1976) Squeezing speech into the deaf ear. *Nature,* 264, 748–751.

Griffin, D. (1959) *Echoes of bats and men.* New York: Doubleday/Anchor.

Griffiths, T. D., Büchel, C., Frackowiak, S. J., and **Patterson, R. D.** (1998) Analysis of temporal structure in sound by the human brain. *Nature Neuroscience,* 1, 422–427.

Griffiths, T. D., Rees, A., Witton, C., Shakir, T. A., Henning, G. B., and **Green, G. G. R.** (1996) Evidence for a sound movement area in the human cerebral cortex. *Nature,* 383, 425–427.

Grill-Spector, K., Knouf, N., and **Kanwisher, N.** (2004) The fusiform face area subserves face perception, not generic with-category identification. *Nature Neuroscience,* 7, 555–562.

Grinker, J., and **Hirsch, J.** (1972) Metabolic and behavioral correlates of obesity. In K. Porter and J. Knight (eds.), *Physiology, emotion, and psychosomatic illness.* Amsterdam: Elsevier, 349–374.

Grosof, D. H., Shapley, R. M., and **Hawken, M. J.** (1993) Macaque V1 neurons can signal "illusory" contours. *Nature,* 365, 550–552.

Gross, C. G. (1998) *Brain, vision, and memory: Tales in the history of neuroscience.* Cambridge: MIT Press, 181–210.

Grossberg, J. M., and **Grant, B. F.** (1978) Clinical psychophysics: Applications of ratio scaling and signal detection methods to research on pain, fear, drugs, and medical decision making. *Psychological Bulletin,* 85, 1154–1176.

Gross-Isseroff, R., and **Lancet, D.** (1988) Concentration-dependent changes of perceived odor quality. *Chemical Senses,* 13, 191–204.

Grosslight, J. H., Fletcher, H. J., Masterton, R. B., and **Hagen, R.** (1978) Monocular vision and landing performance in general aviation pilots: Cyclops revisited. *Human Factors,* 20, 27–33.

Grossman, E., and **Blake, R.** (2002) Brain areas active during visual perception of biological motion. *Neuron,* 35, 1167–1176.

Grossman, E., Donnelly, M., Price, R., Morgan, V., Pickens, D., Neighbor, G., and **Blake, R.** (2000) Brain areas involved in perception of biological motion. *Journal of Cognitive Neuroscience,* 12, 711–720.

Gruber, H. E., and **Dinnerstein, A. J.** (1965) The role of knowledge in distance perception. *American Journal of Psychology,* 78, 575–581.

Guest, S., Catmur, C., Lloyd, D., and **Spence, C.** (2002) Audiotactile interactions in roughness perception. *Experimental Brain Research,* 146, 161–171.

Gulyas, B., and **Roland, P. I.** (1994) Processing and analysis of form, colour and binocular disparity in the human brain: Functional anatomy by positron emission tomography. *European Journal of Neuroscience,* 6, 1811–1822.

Gur, M., and **Akri, V.** (1992) Isoluminant stimuli may not expose the full contribution of color to visual functioning: Spatial contrast sensitivity measurements indicate interaction of color and luminance signals. *Vision Research,* 32, 1253–1262.

Guski, R. (1990) Auditory localization: Effects of reflecting surfaces. *Perception,* 19, 819–830.

Guth, S. K. (1981) The science of seeing—A search for criteria. *American Journal of Optometry and Physiological Optics,* 58, 870–885.

Guttman, S. E., Gilroy, L. A., and **Blake, R.** (2005) Hearing what the eyes see: Auditory encoding of visual temporal sequences. *Psychological Science,* 16, 228–235.

Gwosdow, A. R., Steven, J. C., Berglund, L. G., and **Stolwijk, J. A. J.** (1986) Skin friction and fabric sensations in neutral and warm environments. *Textile Research Journal,* 56, 574–580.

Hackney, C. M. (1987) Anatomical features of the auditory pathway from cochlea to cortex. *British Medical Bulletin,* 43, 780–801.

Hadjikhani, N., Liu, A. K., Dale, A. M., Cavanagh, P., and **Tootell, R. B. H.** (1998) Retinopy and color sensitivity in human visual cortical area V8. *Nature Neuroscience,* 1, 235–241.

Haegerstrom-Portnoy, G., Schneck, M. E., and **Brabyn, J. A.** (1999) Seeing into old age: Vision function beyond acuity. *Optometry & Vision Science,* 76, 141–158.

Hakim, D. (2003) New luxury-car specifications: Styling. Performance. Aroma. *New York Times,* Friday, October 24.

Hall, D. A. (2003) Auditory pathways: Are "what" and "where" appropriate? *Current Biology,* 13, R406–R408.

Hall, M. J., Bartoshuk, L. M., Cain, W. S., and **Stevens, J. C.** (1975) PTC taste blindness and taste of caffeine. *Nature,* 253, 442–443.

Haller, R., Rummel, C., Henneberg, S., Pollmer, U., and **Koster, E. P.** (1999) The influence of early experience with vanillin on food preference later in life. *Chemical Senses,* 24, 465–467.

Halpern, D. L., Blake, R., and **Hillenbrand, J.** (1986) Psychoacoustics of a chilling sound. *Perception & Psychophysics,* 39, 77–80.

Halsey, R. M., and **Chapanis, A.** (1951) On the number of absolutely identifiable spectral hues. *Journal of the Optical Society of America,* 41, 1057–1058.

Hamilton, R. H., and **Pascual-Leone, A.** (1998) Cortical plasticity associated with Braille learning. *Trends in Cognitive Sciences,* 2, 168–174.

Hammond, C. J., Snieder, H., Gilbert, C. E., and **Spector, T. D.** (2001) Genes and environment in refractive error: The twin eye study. *Investigative Ophthalmology & Visual Science,* 42, 1232–1236

Handel, S. (1989) *Listening: An introduction to the perception of auditory events.* Cambridge: MIT Press.

Hansen, C. H., and **Hansen, R. D.** (1988) Finding the face in the crowd: An anger superiority effect. *Journal of Personality and Social Psychology,* 54, 917–924.

Hanson, D. R., and **Fearn, R. W.** (1975) Hearing acuity in young people exposed to pop music and other noise. *Lancet,* 2, 203–205.

Harley, E. M., Dillon, A. M., and **Loftus, G. R.** (2004) Why is it difficult to see in the fog? How stimulus contrast affects visual perception and visual memory. *Psychonomic Bulletin & Review,* 11, 197–231.

Harlow, H. F., and **Harlow, M. K.** (1966) Learning to love. *Scientific American,* 54, 244–272.

Harris, C. R., and **Christenfeld, N.** (1999) Can a machine tickle? *Psychonomic Bulletin & Review,* 6, 504–510.

Harris, J. (1998) "How was it for me?" Uses of introspection in the study of perception. *Perception,* 27, 1137–1140.

Harris, J. A., Harris, I. M., and **Diamond, M. E.** (2001) The topography of tactile learning in humans. *Journal of Neuroscience,* 21, 1056–1061.

Harris, J. A., Miniussi, C., Harris, I. M., and **Diamond, M. E.** (2002) Transient storage of a tactile memory trace in primary somatosensory cortex. *Journal of Neuroscience,* 22, 8720–8725.

Hartline, H. K. (1938) The response of single optic nerve fibers of the vertebrate eye to illumination of the retina. *American Journal of Physiology,* 121, 400–415.

Harvey, L. O., Jr. (1986) Visual memory: What is remembered? In F. Klix and H. Hagendorf (eds.), *Human memory and cognitive capabilities.* The Hague: Elsevier, 173–187.

Harwerth, R. S., Smith, E. L., Crawford, M. L. J., and **von Noorden, G. K.** (1997) Stereopsis and disparity vergence in monkeys with subnormal binocular vision. *Vision Research,* 37, 483–493.

Hässler, R. (1967) Comparative anatomy of the central visual systems in day and night-active primates. In R. Hässler and S. Stephens (eds.), *Evolution of the forebrain.* Stuttgart: Thieme, 419–434.

Hawkes, C. H., Shephard, B. C., and **Daniel, S. E.** (1999) Is Parkinson's a primary olfactory disoder? *QJM: An International Journal of Medicine,* 92, 473–490.

Hawkins, J. E., Jr. (1988) Auditory psychological history: A surface view. In A. F. Jahn and J. Santos-Sacci (eds.), *Psychology of the ear.* New York: Raven Press, 1–28.

Hayhoe, M. M., Bensinger, D. G., and **Ballard, D. H.** (1998) Task constraints in visual working memory. *Vision Research,* 38, 125–137.

Hazel, C. A., Petre, K. L., Armstrong, R. A., Benson, M. T., and **Frost, N. A.** (2000) Visual function and subjective quality of life compared in subjects with acquired macular degeneration. *Investigative Ophthalmology & Visual Science,* 41, 1309–1315.

He, S., Cohen, E. R., and **Hu, X.** (1998) Close correlation between activity in brain area MT/V5 and the perception of a visual motion aftereffect. *Current Biology,* 8, 1215–1218.

Hebb, D. O. (1949) *The organization of behavior.* New York: John Wiley & Sons.

Hecht, S., Shlaer, S., and **Pirenne, M. H.** (1942) Energy, quanta, and vision. *Journal of General Physiology,* 25, 819–840.

Heeger, D. J. (1992) Normalization of cell responses in cat striate cortex. *Visual Neuroscience,* 9, 181–197.

Heffner, R. S., and **Heffner, H. E.** (1985) Hearing in mammals: The least weasel. *Journal of Mammalogy,* 66, 745–755.

Heffner, R. S., and **Heffner, H. E.** (1992) Visual factors in sound localization in mammals. *Journal of Comparative Neurology,* 317, 219–232.

Heinemann, E. G., Tulving, E., and **Nachmias, J.** (1959) The effect of oculomotor adjustments on apparent size. *American Journal of Psychology,* 72, 32–45.

Heller, M. A., Brackett, D. D., Wilson, K., Yoneyama, K., Boyer, A., and **Steffen, H.** (2002) The haptic Muller-Lyer illusion in sighted and blind people. *Perception,* 31, 1263–1274.

Helmholtz, H. L. F. von (1909/1962) *Treatise on physiological optics,* 3rd ed. J. P. C. Southall (ed.), New York: Dover.

Hemilä, S., Nummela, S., and **Reuter, T.** (1995) What middle ear parameters tell about impedance matching and high frequency hearing. *Hearing Research,* 85, 31–44.

Henderson, J. M. (2003) Human gaze control during real-world scene perception. *Trends in Cognitive Sciences,* 7, 498–504.

Henderson, J. M., and **Hollingworth, A.** (1998) Eye movements during scene viewing: An overview. In G. Underwood (ed.), *Eye guidance while reading and while watching dynamic scenes.* Oxford: Elsevier, 269–293.

Henderson, J. M., and **Hollingworth, A.** (1999) High-level scene perception. *Annual Review of Psychology,* 50, 243–271.

Hendry, S. H. C., and **Calkins, D. J.** (1998) Neuronal chemistry and functional organization in the primate visual system. *Trends in Neuroscience,* 21, 344–349.

Hendry, S. H. C., and **Reid, R. C.** (2000) The koniocellular pathway in primate vision. *Annual Review of Neuroscience,* 23, 127–153.

Henkin, R. I. (1982) Olfaction in human disease. In G. B. English, (ed.), *Looseleaf series in otolaryngology.* New York: Harper & Row, 1–39.

Henning, H. (1916) *Der Geruch.* Leipzig: Barth.

Hershenson, M. (1989) *The moon illusion.* Hillsdale, N.J.: Erlbaum.

Herz, R. S. (2004) A naturalistic analysis of autobiographical memories triggered by olfactory visual and auditory stimuli. *Chemical Senses,* 29, 217–224.

Herz, R. S., Eliassen, J., Beland, S., and Souza, T. (2004) Neuroimaging evidence for the emotional potency of odor-evoked memory. *Neuropsychologia,* 42, 371–378.

Herz, R. S., and von Clef, J. (2001) The influence of verbal labeling on the perception of odors: Evidence for olfactory illusions? *Perception,* 30, 381–391.

Hess, R. (2004) Spatial scale in visual processing. In L. M. Chalupa and J. S. Werner (eds.) *The visual neurosciences,* vol. 2, Cambridge: MIT Press, 1043–1059.

Heywood, S., and Ratcliff, G. (1975) Long-term oculomotor consequences of unilateral colliculectomy in man. In G. Lennerstrand and P. Bach-y-Rita (eds.), *Basic mechanisms of ocular motility and their clinical implications.* Elmsford, N.Y.: Pergamon Press, 561–564.

Hikosaka, O., Tanaka, M., Sakamoto, M., and Iwamura, Y. (1985) Deficits in manipulative behaviors induced by local injections of muscimol in the first somatosensory cortex of the conscious monkey. *Behavior Research,* 325, 375–380.

Hildreth, E. (1986) Edge detection. In *Encyclopedia of artificial intelligence,* vol. 1. New York: John Wiley & Sons, 257–267.

Hillman, H. (1993) The possible pain experienced during execution by different methods. *Perception,* 22, 745–753.

Hindley, P. (1997) Psychiatric aspects of hearing impairments. *Journal of Child Psychology and Psychiatry,* 38, 101–117.

Hiris, E., and Blake, R. (1992) Another perspective on the visual motion aftereffect. *Proceedings of the National Academy of Sciences: USA,* 89, 9025–9028.

Hirsch, H. V., and Spinelli, D. N. (1970) Visual experience modifies distribution of horizontally and vertically oriented receptive fields in cats. *Science,* 168, 869–871.

Hirsch, J., DeLaPaz, R. L., Relkin, N. R., Victor, J., Kim, K., Li, T., Borden, P., Rubin, N., and Shapley, R. (1995) Illusory contours activate specific regions in human visual cortex: Evidence from functional magnetic resonance imaging. *Proceedings of the National Academy of Sciences: USA,* 92, 6469–6473.

Hirsch, J., and Miller, W. H. (1987) Does cone positional disorder limit resolution? *Journal of the Optical Society of America A,* 4, 1481–1492.

Hobson, R. P., and Lee, A. (1998) Hello and goodbye: A study of social engagement in autism. *Journal of Autism and Developmental Disorders,* 28, 117–127.

Hoffman, D. D. (1998) *Visual intelligence.* New York: Norton.

Hofman, P. M., van Riswick, J. G. A., and van Opstal, A. J. (1998) Relearning sound localization with new ears. *Nature Neuroscience,* 1, 417–421.

Hoke, E. S., Ross, B., and Hoke, M. (1998) Auditory afterimage: Tonotopic representation in the auditory cortex. *NeuroReport,* 9, 3065–3068.

Hole, G. J. (1994) Configurational factors in the perception of unfamiliar faces. *Perception,* 23, 65–74.

Hollins, M., Sigurdsson, A., Fillingim, L., and Goble, A. K. (1996a) Vibrotactile threshold is elevated in temporomandibular disorders. *Pain,* 67, 889–96.

Hollins, M., Delemos, K. A., and Goble, A. K. (1996b) Vibrotactile adaptation of the RA system: A psychophysical analysis. In O. Franzen, R. Johansson, and L. Terenius (eds.) *Somethesis and the neurobiology of the somatosensory cortex.* Basel: Birkhauser Verlag.

Hollo, A. (1977) Age four. In *Sojourner microcosms: New and selected poems.* Berkeley, Calif.: Blue Wind Press, 30.

Holmes, G. (1918) Disturbances of vision by cerebral lesions. *British Journal of Ophthalmology,* 2, 353–384.

Holway, A. F., and Boring, E. G. (1941) Determinants of apparent visual size with distance variant. *American Journal of Psychology,* 54, 21–37.

Horley, K., Williams, L. M., Gonsalvez, C., and Gordon, E. (2003) Social phobics do not see eye to eye: A visual scanpath study of emotional expression processing. *Anxiety Disorders,* 17, 33–44.

Horton, J. C., and Hocking, D. R. (1996) Intrinsic variability of ocular dominance column periodicity in normal macaque monkeys. *Journal of Neuroscience,* 16, 7228–7239.

Horwitz, G. D., and Newsome, W. T. (1999) Separate signals for target selection and movement specification in the superior colliculus. *Science,* 284, 1158–1161.

Hotson, J., Braun, D., Herzberg, W., and Boman, D. (1994) Transcranial magnetic stimulation of extrastriate cortex degrades human motion direction discrimination. *Vision Research,* 34, 2115–2123.

Houde, J. F., and Jordan, M. I. (1998) Sensorimotor adaptation in speech production. *Science,* 279, 1213–1216.

Houston, R. A. (1917) Newton and the colours of the spectrum. *Science Progress,* 12, 250–264.

Howard, I. P. (1982) *Human visual orientation.* New York: J. Wiley and Sons.

Howard, I. P. and Rogers, B. J. (1995) *Binocular Vision.* New York: Oxford University.

Hubel, D. H. (1988) *Eye, brain, and vision.* New York: W.H. Freeman

Hubel, D. H., and Wiesel, T. N. (1974a) Uniformity of monkey striate cortex: A parallel relationship between field size, scatter, and magnification factor. *Journal of Comparative Neurology,* 158, 295–306.

Hubel, D. H., and Wiesel, T. N. (1974b) Sequence regularity and geometry of orientation columns in the monkey striate cortex. *Journal of Comparative Neurology,* 158, 267–294.

Hubel, D. H., Wiesel, T. N., and LeVay, S. (1977) Plasticity of ocular dominance columns in monkey striate cortex. *Philosphical Transactions of the Royal Society of London (Series B),* 278, 377–409.

Hughes, H. (1999) *Sensory exotica: A world beyond human experience.* Cambridge: MIT Press.

Hulbert, A. (1999) Colour vision: Is colour constancy real? *Current Biology,* 9, R558–R561.

Hume, D. (1739/1963) A treatise of human nature. In V. C. Chappel (ed.), *The philosophy of David Hume.* New York: Modern Library, 11–311.

Hunt, D. M., Dulai, K., Bowmaker, J. K., and **Mollon, J. D.** (1995) The chemistry of John Dalton's color blindness. *Science, 257,* 984–988.

Hunt, S. P., and **Mantyh, P. W.** (2001) The molecular dynamics of pain control. *Nature Reviews Neuroscience, 2,* 83–91.

Hurd, P. D., and **Blevins, J.** (1984) Aging and the color of pills. *New England Journal of Medicine, 310,* 202.

Hurvich, L. M. (1969) Hering and the scientific establishment. *American Psychologist, 24,* 497–514.

Hurvich, L. M. (1981) *Color vision.* Sunderland, Mass.: Sinauer Associates.

Hurvich, L. M., and **Jameson, D.** (1957) An opponent process theory of color vision. *Psychological Review, 64,* 384–404.

Hurvich, L. M., and **Jameson, D.** (1966) *Perception of lightness and darkness.* Boston: Allyn and Bacon.

Hyde, K. L., and **Peretz, I.** (2004) Brains that are out of tune but in time. *Psychological Science, 15,* 356–360.

Iavecchia, J. H., Iavecchia, H. P., and **Roscoe, S. N.** (1983) The moon illusion revisited. *Aviation, Space, and Environmental Medicine, 54,* 39–46.

Ikeda, K. (1909/2002) New seasonings. *Chemical Senses, 27,* 847–849. (Translation from the original Japanese.)

Ilg, U. J., and **Thier, P.** (1996) Inability of rhesus monkey area VI to discriminate between self-induced and externally induced retinal image slip. *European Journal of Neuroscience, 8,* 1156–1166.

Irwin, D. E., and **Brockmole, J. R.** (2004) Suppressing where but not what: The effect of saccades on dorsal- and ventral-stream visual processing. *Psychological Science, 15,* 467–473.

Ito, M., and **Gilbert, C. D.** (1999) Attention modulates contextual influences in the primary visual cortex of alert monkeys. *Neuron, 22,* 593–604.

Ittelson, W. H. (1951) Size as a cue to distance: Static localization. *American Journal of Psychology, 64,* 54–67.

Ittelson, W. H. (1952/1968) *The Ames demonstrations in perception.* New York: Hafner.

Jacobs, G. H. (1992) Ultraviolet vision in vertebrates. *American Zoologist, 32,* 544–554.

Jacobs, G. H. (1993) The distribution and nature of colour vision among the mammals. *Biological Review, 68,* 413–471.

Jacobs, G. H. (1996) Primate photopigments and primate color vision. *Proceedings of the National Academy of Sciences: USA, 93,* 577–581.

Jacobs, G. H. (1998) Photopigments and seeing—Lessons from natural experiments: The Proctor lecture. *Investigative Ophthalmology & Visual Science, 39,* 2204–2216.

Jacobsen, A., and **Gilchrist, A.** (1988) The ratio principle holds over a million-to-one range of illumination. *Perception & Psychophysics, 43,* 1–6.

James, W. (1890) *The principles of psychology,* 2 vols. New York: Holt.

James, W. (1892) *Psychology: A briefer course.* New York: Holt.

Jameson, D., and **Hurvich, L. M.** (1978) Dichromatic color language: "Reds" and "greens" don't look alike but their colors do. *Sensory Processes, 2,* 146–155.

Jameson, D., and **Hurvich, L. M.** (1989) Essay concerning color constancy. *Annual Review of Psychology, 40,* 1–22.

Jamison, R. N. (1996) Influence of weather on report of pain. *International Association for the Study of Pain Newsletter,* July/August.

Jäncke, L., and **Shah, N. J.** (2004) Hearing syllables by seeing visual stimuli. *European Journal of Neuroscience, 19,* 2603–2608.

Jeffress, L. A. (1948) A place theory of sound localization. *Journal of Comparative and Physiological Psychology, 41,* 35–39.

Jeffress, L. A., and **Taylor, R. W.** (1961) Lateralization vs. localization. *Journal of the Acoustical Society of America, 33,* 482–483.

Jeghers, H. (1937) The degree and prevalence of vitamin A deficiency in adults. *Journal of the American Medical Association, 109,* 756–762.

Jenmalm, P., and **Johansson, R. S.** (1997) Visual and somatosensory information about object shape control manipulative fingertip forces. *Journal of Neuroscience, 17,* 4486–4499.

Jinks, A., and **Laing, D. G.** (1999) A limit in the processing of components in odour mixtures. *Perception, 28,* 395–404.

Johansson, G. (1975) Visual motion perception. *Scientific American, 232,* 76–88.

Johansson, G., von Hofsten, C., and **Jansson, G.** (1980) Event perception. *Annual Review of Psychology, 31,* 27–64.

Johansson, R. S., and **Vallbo, A. B.** (1979) Tactile sensibility in the human hand: Relative and absolute densities of four types of mechanoreceptive units in the glabrous skin. *Journal of Physiology, 286,* 283–300.

Johansson, R. S., and **Vallbo, A. B.** (1983) Tactile sensory coding in the glabrous skin of the human hand. *Trends in Neurosciences, 6,* 27–32.

Johns, T., and **Keen, S. L.** (1985) Determinants of taste perception and classification among the Aymara of Bolivia. *Ecology of Food and Nutrition, 16,* 253–271.

Johnson, B. N., Mainland, J. D., and **Sobel, N.** (2003) Rapid olfactory processing implicates subcortical control of an olfactomotor system. *Journal of Neurophysiology, 90,* 1084–1094.

Johnson, K. O., and **Hsiao, S. S.** (1992) Neural mechanisms of tactual form and texture perception. *Annual Review of Neuroscience, 15,* 227–250.

Johnston, J. C., and **McClelland, J. L.** (1973) Visual factors in word perception. *Perception & Psychophysics, 14,* 365–370.

Johnston, J. C., and **McClelland, J. L.** (1974) Perception of letters in words: Seek not and ye shall find. *Science, 184,* 1192–1194.

Jolicoeur, P., Ullman, S., and **Mackay, M.** (1986) Curve tracing: A possible basic operation in the perception of spatial relations. *Memory & Cognition, 14,* 129–140.

Jousmäki, V., and **Hari, R.** (1998) Parchment-skin illusion: Sound-biased touch. *Current Biology, 8,* R190.

Joyce, J. (1922/1934) *Ulysses.* New York: Random House.

Joyce, J. (1939/1967) *Finnegans wake.* New York: Viking Press.

Judd, D. B. (1960) Appraisal of Land's work on two-primary color projections. *Journal of the Optical Society of America, 50,* 254–268.

Julesz, B. (1964) Binocular depth perception without familiarity cues. *Science, 145,* 356–363.

Julesz, B. (1971) *Foundations of cyclopean perception.* Chicago: University of Chicago Press.

Julius, D., and **Basbaum, A. I.** (2001) Molecular mechanisms of nociception. *Nature, 413,* 203–210.

Juslin, P. (2003) Five facets of musical expression: A psychologist's perspective on music performance. *Psychology of Music, 31,* 273–302.

Juslin, P., and **Laukka, P.** (2003) Communication of emotions in vocal expression and music performance: Different channels, same code? *Psychological Bulletin, 129,* 770–814.

Just, M. A., and **Carpenter, P. A.** (1980) A theory of reading: From eye fixations to comprehension. *Psychological Review, 87,* 329–354.

Kaas, J. H. (1987) Somatosensory cortex. In G. Adelman (ed.), *Encyclopedia of neuroscience,* vol. 2. Boston: Birkhauser, pp. 1113–1117.

Kaas, J. H. (1991) Plasticity of sensory and motor maps in adult mammals. *Annual Review of Neuroscience, 14,* 137–167.

Kaas, J. H., and **Florence, S. L.** (1996) Brain reorganization and experience. *Peabody Journal of Education, 71,* 152–167.

Kaas, J. H., Florence, S. L., and **Jain, N.** (1999) Subcortical contributions to massive cortical reorganization. *Neuron, 22,* 657–660.

Kaas, J. H., and **Hackett, T. A.** (2000) Subdivisions of auditory cortex and processing streams in primates. *Proceedings of the National Academy of Sciences: USA, 97,* 11793–11799.

Kaitz, M., Good, A., Rokem, A. M., and **Eidelman, A.** (1987) Mothers' recognition of their newborns by olfactory cues. *Developmental Psychobiology, 20,* 587–591.

Kaitz, M., Lapidot, P., Bronner, R., and **Eidelman, A. I.** (1992) Parturient women can recognize their infants by touch. *Developmental Psychology, 28,* 35–39.

Kamachi, M., Hill, H., Lander, K., and **Vatikiotis-Bateson, E.** (2003) "Putting the face to the voice": Matching identity across modality. *Current Biology, 13,* 1709–1714.

Kamitani, Y., and **Shimojo, S.** (1999) Manifestation of scotomas created by transcranial magnetic stimulation of human visual cortex. *Nature Neuroscience, 2,* 767–771.

Kammer, T. (1999) Phosphenes and transient scotomas induced by magnetic stimulation of the occipital lobe: Their topographic relationship. *Neuropsychologia, 37,* 191–198.

Kanizsa, G. (1976) Subjective contours. *Scientific American, 234,* 48–52.

Kant, I. (1798/1978) *Anthropology from a pragmatic point of view* (ed. H. H. Rudnick; trans. by V. L. Dodwell), Carbondale, Ill.: Southern Illinois University Press.

Kanwisher, N., McDermott, J., and **Chun, M. M.** (1997) The fusiform face area: A module in human extrastriate cortex specialized for face perception. *Journal of Neuroscience, 17,* 4302–4311.

Kapadia, M. K., Westheimer, G., and **Gilbert, C. D.** (1999) Dynamics of spatial summation in primary visual cortex of alert monkeys. *Preeceedings of the National Academy of Science, USA, 96,* 12073–12078.

Kaplan, E., Shapley, R. M., and **Purpura, K.** (1988) Color and luminance contrast as tools for probling the primate retina. *Neuroscience Research Supplement, 8,* S151–S165.

Kaplan, P. S., Bachorowski, J. A., Smoski, M. J., and **Hudenko, W. J.** (2002) Infants of depressed mothers, although competent learners, fail to learn in response to their own mothers' infant-directed speech. *Psychological Science, 13,* 268–271.

Karni, A., and **Sagi, D.** (1991) Where practice makes perfect in texture discrimination: Evidence for primary visual cortex plasticity. *Proceedings of the National Academy of Sciences: USA, 88,* 4966–4970.

Karni, A., and **Sagi, D.** (1993) The time course of learning a visual skill. *Nature, 365,* 250–252.

Katz, D. (1925) Der Aufbau der Tastwelt. *Zeitschrift fur Psychologie, 11* [see also L. E. Krueger (1970) "David Katz" Der Aufbau der Tastwelt (The world of touch): A synopsis. *Perception & Psychophysics, 7,* 337–341].

Katz, D. B., Nicolelis, M. A., and **Simon, S. A.** (2002) Gustatory processing is dynamic and distributed. *Current Opinions in Neurobiology, 12,* 448–454.

Katz, D. B., Simon, S., and **Nicolelis, M. A. L.** (2001) Dynamic and multimodal responses of gustatory cortical neurons in awake rats. *Journal of Neuroscience, 21,* 4478–4489.

Kauer, J. S. (1991) Contributions of topography and parallel processing to odor coding in the vertebrate olfactory pathway. *Trends in Neurosciences, 14,* 79–85.

Kaufman, L. (1974) *Sight and mind: An introduction to visual perception.* New York: Oxford University Press.

Kaufman, L., and **Rock, I.** (1962) The moon illusion. *Scientific American, 207,* 120–132.

Kaukoranta, E., Hari, R., and **Lounasmaa, O. V.** (1987) Responses of the human auditory cortex to vowel onset after fricative consonants. *Experimental Brain Research, 69,* 19–23.

Kayaert, G., Biederman, I., and **Vogels, R.** (2003) Shape tuning in macaque inferior temporal cortex. *Journal of Neuroscience, 23,* 3016–3027.

Keller, H. (1908a) *The world I live in.* (Reprinted in 2004 by New York Review of Books Publishers, New York.)

Keller, H. (1908b) Sense and sensibility. *Century Magazine, 75,* 566–577, 773–783.

Keller, H. (1932) Magic in your fingers, *Home Magazine,* May.

Keller, P., and **Stevens, C.** (2004) Meaning from environmental sounds: Types of signal-referent relations and their effect on recognizing auditory icons. *Journal of Experimental Psychology: Applied, 10,* 3–12.

Kellman, P. J., and **Shipley, T. F.** (1991) A theory of visual interpolation in object perception. *Cognitive Psychology, 23,* 141–221.

Kendrick, K. M., Levy, F., and **Keverne, E. B.** (1992) Changes in the sensory processing of olfactory signals induced by birth in sheep. *Science, 256,* 833–836.

Kenet, T., Bibitchkov, D., Tsodyks, M., Grinvald, A., and **Arieli, A.** (2003) Spontaneously emerging cortical representations of visual attributes. *Nature, 425,* 954–956.

Kenshalo, D. (1972) The cutaneous senses. In J. W. Kling and L. A. Riggs (eds.), *Woodworth and Schlosberg's experimental psychology,* 3rd ed., vol. 1. New York: Holt, Rinehart & Winston.

Kersten, D. (1987) Predictability and redundancy of natural images. *Journal of the Optical Society of America A,* 4, 2395–2401.

Kersten, D., Mamassian, P., and **Knill, D. C.** (1997) Moving cast shadows induce apparent motion in depth. *Perception,* 26, 171–192.

Kersten, D., Mamassian, P., and **Yuille, A.** (2004) Object perception as Bayesian inference. *Annual Review of Psychology,* 55, 271–304.

Kertsa, L. G. (1962) Voice identifications. *Nature,* 196, 1253–1257.

Keuning, J. (1968) On the nasal cycle. *International Rhinology,* 6, 99–136.

Kiang, N. Y. S. (1968) A survey of recent developments in the study of auditory physiology. *Annals of Otology, Rhinology, and Laryngology,* 77, 656–675.

Kiang, N. Y. S. (1975) Stimulus representation in the discharge pattern of auditory neurons. In E. L. Eagles (ed.), *The nervous system,* vol. 3. New York: Raven Press, 81–96.

Kim, J. S., and **Choi, S.** (2002) Altered food preference after cortical infarction: Korean style. *Cerebrovascular Diseases,* 13, 187–191.

Kim, U. K., Breslin, P. A. S., Reed, D., and **Drayna, D.** (2004) Genetics of human taste perception. *Journal of Dental Research,* 83, 448–453.

King, A. J., and **Moore, D. R.** (1991) Plasticity of auditory maps in the brain. *Trends in Neurosciences,* 14, 31–37.

Kinney, J. A., Luria, S. M., Ryan, A. P., Schlicting, C. L., and **Paulson, H. M.** (1980) The vision of submariners and national guardsmen: A longitudinal study. *American Journal of Optometry and Physiological Optics,* 57, 469–478.

Klatzky, R. L. (1998) Allocentric and egocentric spatial representations: Definitions, distinctions, and interconnections. In C. Freksa, C. Habel, & K. F. Wender (eds.), *Spatial cognition—An interdisciplinary approach to representation and processing of spatial knowledge (Lecture notes in artificial intelligence 1404).* Berlin: Springer-Verlag, 1–17.

Klatzky, R. L., Lederman, S. J., and **Metzger, V.** (1985) Identifying objects by touch: An "expert" system. *Perception & Psychophysics,* 37, 299–302.

Klinke, R., Kral, A., Heid, S., Tillein, J., and **Hartmann, R.** (1999) Recruitment of the auditory cortex in congenitally deaf cats by long-term cochlear electrostimulation. *Science,* 285, 1729–1733.

Knappmeyer, B., Thornton, I. M., and **Bülthoff, H. H.** (2003) The use of facial motion and facial form during the processing of identity. *Vision Research,* 43, 1921–1936.

Knudsen, E. I. (1998) Capacity for plasticity in the adult owl auditory system expanded by juvenile experience. *Science,* 279, 1531–1533.

Knudsen, E. I., and **Brainard, M. S.** (1995) Creating a unified representation of visual and auditory space in the brain. *Annual Review of Neuroscience,* 18, 19–43.

Knudsen, E. I., du Lac, S., and **Esterly, S. D.** (1987) Computational maps in the brain. *Annual Review of Neuroscience,* 10, 41–65.

Knudsen, E. I., and **Konishi, M.** (1978) A neural map of auditory space in the owl. *Science,* 200, 795–797.

Knudsen, E. I., and **Konishi, M.** (1980) Monaural occlusion shifts receptive-field locations of auditory midbrain units in the owl. *Journal of Neurophysiology,* 44, 687–695.

Kobatake, E., Wang, G., and **Tanaka, K.** (1998) Effects of shape-discrimination training on the selectivity of inferotemporal cells in adult monkeys. *Journal of Neurophysiology,* 80, 324–330.

Kobayakawa, T., Ogaw, A. H., Kaneda, H., Ayabe-Kanamura, S., Endo, H., and **Saito, S.** (1999) Spatio-temporal analysis of cortical activity evoked by gustatory stimulation in humans. *Chemical Senses,* 24, 201–209.

Kobayashi, H., and **Kohshima, S.** (1997) Unique morphology of the human eye. *Nature,* 387, 767–768.

Koelega, H. S., and **Koster, E. P.** (1974) Some experiments on sex differences in odor perception. *Annals of the New York Academy of Sciences,* 237, 234–246.

Koenig, W. (1950) Subjective effects in binaural hearing. *Journal of the Acoustical Society of America,* 22, 61–62.

Koffka, K. (1935) *Principles of gestalt psychology.* New York: Harcourt, Brace & World.

Köhler, W. (1920/1938) Physical gestalten. In W. D. Ellis (ed.), *A source book of gestalt psychology.* New York: Humanities Press, 17–54.

Köhler, W. (1969) *The task of gestalt psychology.* Princeton: Princeton University Press.

Kolb, B., and **Whishaw, I. Q.** (1996) *Fundamentals of human neuropsychology* (4th ed.). New York: W. H. Freeman.

Korte, M., and **Rauschecker, J. P.** (1993) Auditory spatial tuning of cortical neurons is sharpened in cats with early blindness. *Journal of Neurophysiology,* 70, 1717–1721.

Kosslyn, S. M. (1994) *Image and brain: The resolution of the imagery debate.* Cambridge: MIT Press.

Kosslyn, S. M. (2003) Understanding the mind's eye . . . and nose. *Nature Neuroscience,* 6, 1124–1125.

Kosslyn, S. M., Pascual-Leone, A., Felician, O., Camposano, S., Keenan, J. P., Thompson, W. L., Ganis, G., Sukel, K. E., and **Alpert, N. M.** (1999) The role of area 17 in visual imagery: Convergent evidence from PET and rTMS. *Science,* 284, 167–170.

Kosslyn, S. M., Sukel, K. E., and **Bly, B. M.** (1999) Squinting with the mind's eye: Effects of stimulus resolution on imaginal and perceptual comparisons. *Memory & Cognition,* 27, 276–287.

Kotz, S. A., Meyer, M., Alter, K., Besson, M., von Cramon, D. Y., and **Friederici, A. D.** (2003) On the lateralization of emotional prosody: An event-related functional MR investigation. *Brain and Language,* 86, 366–376.

Kouros-Mehr, H., Pintchovski, S., Melnyk, J., Chen, Y. J., Friedman, C., Trask, B., and **Shizuya, H.** (2001) Identification of non-functional human VNO receptor genes provides evidence for vestigiality of the human VNO. *Chemical Senses,* 26, 1167–1174.

Kovács, G., Vogels, R., and **Orban, G.** (1995) Selectivity of macaque inferior temporal neurons for partially occluded shapes. *Journal of Neuroscience,* 15, 1984–1997.

Kovács, I., and **Julesz, B.** (1993) A closed curve is much more than an incomplete one: Effect of closure in figure-ground segmentation. *Proceedings of the National Academy of Sciences: USA,* 90, 7495–7497.

Kovács, I., Kozma, P., Fehér, A., and **Benedek, G.** (1999) Late maturation of visual spatial integration in humans. *Proceedings of the National Academy of Sciences: USA,* 96, 12204–12209.

Kowler, E. (1989) Cognitive expectations, not habits, control anticipatory smooth oculomotor pursuit. *Vision Research,* 29, 1049–1058.

Kraft, J. M., and **Brainard, D. H.** (1999) Mechanisms of color constancy under nearly natural viewing. *Proceedings of the National Academy of Sciences: USA,* 96, 307–312.

Kramer, G., Walker, B., Bonebright, T., Cook, P., Flowers, J., Miner, N., Neuhoff, J., Bargar, R., Barrass, S., Berger, J., Evreinov, G., Fitch, W., Gröhn, M., Handel, S., Kaper, H., Levkowitz, H., Lodha, S., Shinn-Cunningham, B., Simoni, M., and **Tipei, S.** (1999) *The sonification report: Status of the field and research agenda.* Report prepared for the National Science Foundation by members of the International Community for Auditory Display. Santa Fe, NM: ICAD.

Kramer, M. (1989) *Making sense of wine.* New York: W. W. Morrow & Co.

Kraus, N., McGee, T. J., Carrell, T. D., Zecker, S. G., Nicol, T. G., and **Koch, D. B.** (1996) Auditory neurophysiologic responses and discrimination deficits in children with learning problems. *Science,* 273, 971–973.

Krauzlis, R. J., and **Stone, L. S.** (1999) Tracking with the mind's eye. *Trends in Neurosciences,* 22, 544–550

Kristensen, S., and **Gimsing, S.** (1988) Occupational hearing impairment in pig-breeders. *Scandinavian Audiology,* 17, 191–192.

Krueger, L. E. (1975) Familiarity effects in visual information processing. *Psychological Bulletin,* 82, 949–974.

Krumhansel, C. L. (1990) *Cognitive foundations of music pitch.* Oxford: Oxford University Press.

Kuhl, P. K. (2005) Early language acquisition: Cracking the speech code. *Nature Reviews Neuroscience,* 5, 831–843.

Kuhl, P. K., Andruski, J. E., Chistovich, I. A., Chistovich, L. A., Kozhevnikova, E. V., Ryskina, V. L., Stolyarova, E. I., Sundberg, U., and **Lacerda, F.** (1997) Cross-language analysis of phonetic units in language addressed to infants. *Science,* 277, 684–686.

Kuhl, P. K., and **Meltzoff, A. N.** (1982) The bimodal perception of speech in infancy. *Science,* 218, 1138–1141.

Kuhl, P. K., Tsao, F., and **Liu, H.** (2003) Foreign-language experience in infancy: Effects of short-term exposure and social interaction on phonetic learning. *Proceedings of the National Academy of Sciences: USA,* 100, 9096–9101.

Kühne, W. (1879/1977) Chemical processes in the retina. *Vision Research,* 17, 1273–1316.

Kujala, T., Alho, K., Huotilainen, M., Ilmoniemi, R. J., Lehtokoski, A., Leinonen, A., Rinne, T., Salonen, O., Sinkkonen, J., Standertskjold-Nordenstam, C. G., and **Naatanen, R.** (1997) Electrophysiological evidence for cross-modal plasticity in humans with early- and late-onset blindness. *Psychophysiology,* 34, 213–216.

Kulkarni, A., and **Colburn, H. S.** (1998) Role of spectral detail in sound-source localization. *Nature,* 396, 747–749.

Kuller, R., and **Mikellides, B.** (1993) Simulated studies of color, arousal and comfort. In R.W. Marans and D. Stokols (eds.), *Environmental simulation: Research and policy issues.* New York: Plenum Press, 163–190.

Kundel, H. L., and **Nodine, C. F.** (1983) A visual concept shapes image perception. *Radiology,* 146, 363–368.

Kunkler-Peck, A. J., and **Turvey, M.T.** (2000) Hearing shape. *Journal of Experimental Psychology: Human Perception & Performance,* 26, 279–294.

Künnapas, T. M. (1968) Distance perception as a function of available visual cues. *Journal of Experimental Psychology,* 77, 523–529.

Kurtenbach, W., Sternheim, C. E., and **Spillmann, L.** (1984) Change in hue of spectral colors by dilution with white light (Abney effect). *Journal of the Optical Society of America A,* 1, 365–372.

Kuthan, V. (1987) Some contributions of J. E. Purkyne to the visual physiology. *Physiologia Bohemoslovaca,* 36, 255–267.

Ladefoged, P., and **Broadbent, D. E.** (1957) Information conveyed by vowels. *Journal of the Acoustical Society of America,* 29, 98–104.

Laeng, B., Svartdal, F., and **Oelmann, H.** (2004) Does color synesthesia pose a paradox for early-selection theories of attention? *Psychological Science,* 15, 277–281.

Laing, D. G. (1983) Natural sniffing gives optimum odour perception for humans. *Perception,* 12, 99–117.

Laming, D., and **Laming, J.** (1992) F. Hegelmaier: On memory for the length of a line. *Psychological Research,* 54, 233–239.

Lamme, V. A. F. (1995) The neurophysiology of figure/ground segregation in primary visual cortex. *Journal of Neuroscience,* 15, 1605–1615.

Lancker, D. R. V., Kreiman, J., and **Cummings, J.** (1989) Voice perception deficits: Neuroanatomical correlates of phonagnosia. *Journal of Clinical and Experimental Neuropsychology,* 11, 665–674.

Land, E. H. (1959) Experiments in color vision. *Scientific American,* 200, 84–94, 96, 99.

Land, M. F., and **Furneaux, S.** (1997) The knowledge base of the oculomotor system. *Philosophical Transactions of the Royal Society of London (Series B),* 352, 1231–1239.

Landau, B. (1991) Spatial representation of objects in the young blind child. *Cognition,* 38, 145–178.

Lattner, S., Meyer, M. E., and **Friederici, A. D.** (2005) Voice perception: Sex, pitch and the right hemisphere. *Human Brain Mapping,* 24, 11–20.

Laurent, G. (1999) A systems perspective on early olfactory coding. *Science,* 286, 723–728.

Lawless, H. T., and **Engen, T.** (1977) Association to odors: Interference, memories, and verbal labeling. *Journal of Experimental Psychology,* 3, 52–59.

Lawless, H. T., Glatter, S., and **Hohn, C.** (1991) Context-dependent changes in the perception of odor quality. *Chemical Senses,* 16, 349–360.

Leclerc, C., Saint-Amour, D., Lavoie, M. E., Lassonde, M., and **Lepore, F.** (2000) Brain functional reorganization in early blind humans revealed by auditory event-related potentials. *Neuroreport,* 11, 545–550.

Lederman, S. J. (1976) The "callus-thenics" of touching. *Canadian Journal of Psychology,* 30, 82–89.

Lederman, S. J., and **Klatzky, R. L.** (1987) Hand movements: A window into haptic object recognition. *Cognitive Psychology,* 19, 342–348.

Lederman, S. J., and **Klatzky, R. L.** (1990) Haptic classification of common objects: Knowledge-driven exploration. *Cognitive Psychology,* 22, 421–459.

Lederman, S. J., and **Klatzky, R. L.** (2004) Haptic identification of common objects: Effects of constraining the manual exploration process. *Perception & Psychophysics,* 66, 618–628.

Lederman, S. J., Klatzky, R. L., and **Pawluk, D. T.** (1992) Lessons from the study of biological touch for robot haptic sensing. In H. Nicholls (ed.), *Advanced tactile sensing for robotics. (World scientific series in robotics and automated systems,* vol. 5), Singapore: World Scientific Publishing, 193–220.

Lederman, S. J., and **Taylor, M. M.** (1972) Fingertip force, surface geometry, and the perception of roughness by active touch. *Perception & Psychophysics,* 12, 401–408.

Lee, K. Y. S., van Hasselt, C. A., Chiu, S. N., and **Cheung, D. M. C.** (2002) Cantonese tone perception ability of cochlear implant children in comparison with normal-hearing children. *International Journal of Pediatric Otorhinolaryngology,* 63, 137–147.

Lee, D. N. (1976) A theory of visual control of braking based on information about time-to-collision. *Perception,* 5, 437–459.

Lee, D. N. (1980) The optic flow field: The foundation of vision. *Philosophical Transactions of the Royal Society of London (Series B),* 290, 169–179.

Lee, D. N., and **Reddish, P. E.** (1981) Plummeting gannets: A paradigm of ecological optics. *Nature,* 293, 293–294.

Lee, H. W., Hong, S. B., Seo, D. W., Tae, W. S., and **Hong S. C.** (2000) Mapping of functional organization in human visual cortex: Electrical cortical stimulation. *Neurology,* 54, 849–854.

Leehey, S. C., Moskowitz-Cook, A., Brill, S., and **Held, R.** (1975) Orientational anisotropy in infant vision. *Science,* 190, 900–902.

Leek, M. R. (2001) Adaptive procedures in psychophysical research. *Perception & Psychophysics,* 63, 1279–1292.

Lefebvre, P. P., Malgrange, B., Staecker, H., Moonen, G., and **van de Water, T. R.** (1993) Retinoic acid stimulates regeneration of mammalian auditory hair cells. *Science,* 260, 692–695.

LeGrand, Y. (1968) *Light, colour, and vision.* 2nd ed. R. W. G. Hunt and F. R. W. Hunt (trans.). London: Chapman & Hall.

Lehmkuhle, S. W., and **Fox, R.** (1977) *Global stereopsis in the cat.* Paper presented at the Association for Research in Vision and Ophthalmology, Sarasota, Fla.

Leibowitz, H. W. (1983) *A behavioral and perceptual analysis of grade crossing accidents.* Operation Lifesaver National Symposium 1982. Chicago: National Safety Council.

Leibowitz, H. W., and **Moore, D.** (1966) Role of changes in accommodation and convergence in the perception of size. *Journal of the Optical Society of America,* 56, 1120–1122.

Leibowitz, H. W., and **Owens, D. A.** (1975) Anomalous myopias and the intermediate dark focus of accommodation. *Science,* 189, 646–648.

Leibowitz, H. W., and **Owens, D. A.** (1976) Night myopia: Cause and a possible basis for amelioration. *American Journal of Optometry and Physiological Optics,* 53, 709–717.

Lennie, P. (1984) Recent developments in the physiology of color vision. *Trends in Neuroscience,* 7, 243–248.

Lennie, P. (2003) The cost of cortical computation. *Current Biology,* 13, 493–497.

Lennie, P., and **D'Zmura, M.** (1988) Mechanisms of color vision. *CRC Critical Reviews in Neurobiology,* 3, 333–400.

Lennie, P., Krauskopf, J., and **Sclar, G.** (1990) Chromatic mechanisms in striate cortex of macaque. *Journal of Neuroscience,* 10, 649–669.

Leopold, D. (2002) Distortion of olfactory perception: Diagnosis and treatment. *Chemical Senses,* 27, 611–615.

Leopold, D. A., and **Logothetis, N. K.** (1996) Activity changes in early visual cortex reflect monkeys' percepts during binocular rivalry. *Nature,* 379, 549–553.

Leopold, D. A., and **Logothetis, N. K.** (1999) Multistable phenomena: Changing views in perception. *Trends in Cognitive Sciences,* 3, 254–264.

Lerner, M. R., Gyorgyi, T. K., Reagan, J., Roby-Shemkovitz, A., Rybczynski, R., and **Vogt, R.** (1990) Peripheral events in moth olfaction. *Chemical Senses,* 15, 191–198.

Lessard, N., Paré, M., Lepore, F., and **Lassonde, M.** (1998) Early-blind human subjects localize sound sources better than sighted subjects. *Nature,* 395, 278–280.

Leventhal, A. G., Thompson, K. G., Liu, D., Zhou, Y., and **Ault, S. J.** (1995) Concomitant sensitivity to orientation, direction, and color of cells in layers 2, 3, and 4 of monkey striate cortex. *Journal of Neuroscience,* 15, 1808–1818.

Levinson, E., and **Sekuler, R.** (1976) Adaptation alters perceived direction of motion. *Vision Research,* 16, 779–781.

Levitan, I. B., and **Kaczmarek, L. K.** (1991) *The neuron: Cell and molecular biology.* New York: Oxford University Press.

Levitin, D. J., and **Rogers, S. E.** (2005) Absolute pitch: Perception, coding, and controversies. *Trends in Cognitive Sciences,* 9, 26–33.

Lewicki, M. S. (2002) Efficient coding of natural sounds. *Nature Neuroscience,* 5, 356–363.

Lewis, A., and **Del Priore, L. V.** (1988) The biophysics of visual photoreception. *Physics Today,* 41, 38–46.

Li, A., and **Zaidi, Q.** (2000) The perception of 3D shape from texture is based on patterns of oriented energy. *Vision Research,* 40, 217–242.

Li, B., Peterson, M. R., and **Freeman, R. D.** (2003) Oblique effect: A neural basis in visual cortex. *Journal of Neurophysiology,* 90, 204–217.

Li, X., Logan, R. J., and Pastore, R. E. (1991) Perception of acoustic source characteristics: Walking sounds. *Journal of the Acoustical Society of America, 90,* 3036–3049.

Liberman, A. M., Cooper, F. S., Shankweiler, D. P., and Studdert, M. (1967) Perception of the speech code. *Psychological Review,* 74, 431–461.

Liberman, M. C. (1982) The cochlear frequency map for the cat: Labelling auditory nerve fibers of known characteristics. *Journal of the Acoustical Society of America, 72,* 1441–1449.

Liégeois-Chauvel, C., Peretz, I., Babaï, M., Laguitton, V., and Chauvel, P. (1998) Contribution of different cortical areas in the temporal lobes to music processing. *Brain, 121,* 1853–1867.

Lindemann, B. (2000) A taste for umami. *Nature Neuroscience, 3,* 99–100.

Lindemann, B., Ogiwara, Y., and Ninomiya, Y. (2002) The discovery of umami. *Chemical Senses, 27,* 843–844.

Linden, D. E. J., Kallenbach, U., Heinecke, A., Singer, W., and Goebel, R. (1999) The myth of upright vision: A psychophysical and functional imaging study of adaptation to inverting spectacles. *Perception, 28,* 469–481.

Linder, M. E., and Gilman, A. G. (1992) G proteins. *Scientific American, 267,* 56–65.

Lindsey, D. T., and Brown, A. M. (2002) Color naming and the phototoxic effects of sunlight on the eye. *Psychological Science,* 13, 506–512.

Liss, J. M., Weismer, G., and Rosenbek, J. C. (1990) Selected acoustic characteristics of speech production in very old males. *Journal of Gerontology: Psychological Sciences, 45,* 35–45.

Liu, B., Metz, C. E., and Jiang, Y. (2004) An ROC comparison of four methods of combining information from multiple images of the same patient. *Medical Physics, 31,* 2552–2563.

Liu, B., and Todd, J. T. (2004) Perceptual biases in the interpretation of 3D shape from shading. *Vision Research, 44,* 2135–2145.

Liu, J., Harris, A., and Kanwisher, N. (2002) Stages of processing in face perception: An MEG study. *Nature Neuroscience, 5,* 910–916.

Livingstone, M. S. (2002) *Vision and art: The biology of seeing.* New York: H. N. Abrams.

Livingstone, M. S., and Hubel, D. H. (1981) Effects of sleep and arousal on the processing of visual information in the cat. *Nature,* 291, 554–561.

Livingstone, M. S., and Hubel, D. H. (1984) Anatomy and physiology of a color system in primate primary visual cortex. *Journal of Neuroscience, 4,* 309–356.

Livingstone, M. S., and Hubel, D. H. (1988) Segregation of form, color, movement, and depth: Anatomy, physiology, and perception. *Science, 240,* 740–749.

Locke, J. (1690/1924) *An essay concerning human understanding* (abridged and edited by A. S. Pringle-Pattison). Oxford: Clarendon Press.

Loeb, R. G., and Fitch, W. T. (2002) A laboratory evaluation of an auditory display designed to enhance intraoperative monitoring. *Anesthesia & Analgesia, 94,* 362–368.

Logothetis, N. K. (1998a) Single units and conscious vision. *Philosophical Transactions of the Royal Society of London (Series B),* 353, 1801–1818.

Logothetis, N. K. (1998b) Object vision and visual awareness. *Current Biology, 8,* 536–544.

Logothetis, N. K. (2002) The neural basis of the blood-oxygen-level-dependent functional magnetic resonance imaging signal. *Philosophical Transactions of the Royal Society of London (Series B),* 357, 1003–1037.

Logothetis, N. K., and Schall, J. D. (1989) Neuronal correlates of subjective visual perception. *Science, 245,* 761–763.

Logothetis, N. K., and Sheinberg, D. L. (1996) Visual object recognition. *Annual Review of Neuroscience, 19,* 577–621.

Loomis, J. M. (1981) Tactile pattern perception. *Perception, 10,* 5–27.

Loomis, J. M., Klatzky, R. L., and Lederman, S. J. (1991) Similarity of tactual and visual picture recognition with limited field of view. *Perception, 20,* 167–178.

Lorig, T. S., Elmes, D. G., Zald, D. H., and Pardo, J. V. (1999) A computer-controlled olfactometer for fMRI and electrophysiological studies of olfaction. *Behavior Research Methods, Instruments & Computers, 31,* 370–375.

Lotto, R. B., Williams, S. M., and Purves, D. (1999) An empirical basis for Mach bands. *Proceedings of the National Academy of Sciences: USA, 96,* 5239–5244.

Loughland, C. M., Williams, L., and Gordon, E. (2002) Visual scanpaths to positive and negative facial emotions in an outpatient schizophrenia sample. *Schizophrenia Research, 55,* 159–170.

Lu, Z. L., Williamson, S. J., and Kaufman, L. (1992) Behavioral lifetime of human auditory sensory memory predicted by physiological measures. *Science, 258,* 1668–1670.

Luck, S. J., Chelazzi, L., Hillyard, S. A., and Desimone, R. (1997) Neural mechanisms of spatial selective attention to areas V1, V2 and V4 of macaque visual cortex. *Journal of Neurophysiology, 77,* 24–42.

Luck, S. J., Vogel, E. K., and Shapiro, K. L. (1996) Word meanings can be accessed but not reported during the attentional blink. *Nature, 383,* 616–618.

Lugaz, O., Pillias, A. M., and Faurion, A. (2002) A new specific ageusia: Some humans cannot taste L-glutamate. *Chemical Senses, 27,* 105–115.

Lythgoe, J. N. (1979) *The ecology of vision.* Oxford: Clarendon Press.

Macdonald, D., and Brown, R. (1985) The smell of success. *New Scientist, 106,* 10–14.

Mach, E., (1959) *The analysis of sensations, and the relation of the physical to the psychical.* Trans. from the 1st German ed. by C. M. Williams. Rev. and supplemented from the 5th German ed. by Sydney Waterlow. With a new introduction by Thomas S. Szasz. New York. Dover Publications.

Mack, A., and Rock, I. (1998) *Inattentional blindness.* Cambridge: MIT Press.

MacMillan, N. A., and Creelman, D. C. (2004) *Detection theory: A user's guide,* 2nd ed. Mahwah: Lawrence Erlbaum Associates.

MacNichol, E. (1964) Three-pigment color vision. *Scientific American,* 211, 48–56.

Mackworth, N. H., and **Morandi, A. J.** (1967) The gaze selects informative details within pictures. *Perception & Psychophysics,* 2, 547–552.

Maeder, P. P., Meuli, R. A., Adriani, M., Bellmann, A., Fornari, E., Thiran, J.-P., Pittet, A., and **Clarke, S.** (2001) Distinct pathways involved in sound recognition and localization: A human fMRI study. *NeuroImage,* 14, 802–816.

Maffei, L., and **Fiorentini, A.** (1973) The visual cortex as a spatial frequency analyzer. *Vision Research,* 13, 1255–1267.

Mainland, J. D., Bremner, E. A., Young, N., Johnson, B. N., Khan, R. M., Bensafi, M., and **Sobel, N.** (2002) Olfactory plasticity: One nostril knows what the other learns. *Nature,* 419, 802.

Makous, W. L. (1966) Cutaneous color sensitivity: Explanation and demonstration. *Psychological Review,* 73, 280–294.

Makous, J. C., and **Middlebrooks, J. C.** (1990) Two-dimensional sound localization by human listeners. *Journal of the Acoustical Society of America,* 87, 2188–2200.

Malakoff, D. (1999) Following the scent of avian olfaction. *Science,* 286, 704–705.

Malpelli, J. G., and **Baker, F. H.** (1975) The representation of the visual field in the lateral geniculate nucleus of Macaca mulatta. *Journal of Comparative Neurology,* 161, 569–594.

Manley, G. A., Koppl, C., and **Konishi, M.** (1988) A neural map of interaural intensity differences in the brain stem of the barn owl. *Journal of Neuroscience,* 8, 2665–2676.

Manor, B. R., Gordon, E., Williams, L. M., Rennie, C. J., Bahramali, H., Latimeer, C. R., Barry, R. J., and **Meares, R. A.** (1999) Eye movements reflect impaired face processing in patients with schizophrenia. *Biological Psychiatry,* 46, 963–969.

Mansfield, R. (1974) Neural basis of orientation perception in primate vision. *Science,* 186, 1133–1135.

Marendaz, C., Stivalet, P., Barraclough, L., and **Walkowiac, P.** (1993) Effect of gravitational cues on the visual search for orientation. *Journal of Experimental Psychology: Human Perception & Performance,* 19, 1266–1277.

Marin, O. S. M. (1976) Neurobiology of language: An overview. *Annals of the New York Academy of Sciences,* 280, 900–912.

Mariotte, E. (1668/1948) The discovery of the blindspot. In W. Dennis (ed.), *Readings in the history of psychology.* New York: Appleton-Century-Crofts, 42–43.

Marks, L. E., and **Wheeler, M. E.** (1998) Attention and the detectability of weak taste stimuli. *Chemical Senses,* 23, 19–29.

Marr, D. (1976) Early processing of visual information. *Philosophical Transactions of the Royal Society of London (Series B),* 275, 483–524.

Marr, D. (1982) *Vision.* New York: W. H. Freeman.

Marron, J. A., and **Bailey, I. L.** (1982) Visual factors and orientation-mobility performance. *American Journal of Optometry and Physiological Optics,* 59, 413–426.

Marrotta, J. J., Kruyer, A., and **Goodale, M. A.** (1998) The role of head movements in the control of manual prehension. *Experimental Brain Research,* 120, 134–138.

Martin, G. (1987) The world through a starling's eye. *New Scientist,* 114, 49–51.

Martin, K. A. C. (1988) The lateral geniculate nucleus strikes back. *Trends in Neurosciences,* 11, 192–194.

Massaro, D. W., and **Cohen, M. M.** (1996) Perceiving speech from inverted faces. *Perception & Psychophysics,* 58, 1047–1065.

Massaro, D. W., and **Egan, P. B.** (1996) Perceiving affect from the voice and the face. *Psychonomic Bulletin & Review,* 3, 215–221.

Massaro, D. W., and **Stork, D. G.** (1998) Speech recognition and sensory integration. *American Scientist,* 86, 236–244.

Massof, R. W. (2003) Auditory assistive devices for the blind. *Proceedings of the 2003 International Conference on Auditory Display,* Boston, MA, USA, 6–9 July.

Masterton, R. B., and **Imig, T. J.** (1984) Neural mechanisms of sound localization. *Annual Review of Physiology,* 46, 275–280.

Masterton, R. B., Thompson, G. C., Bechtold, J. K., and **Robards, M. J.** (1975) Neuroanatomical basis of binaural phase-difference analysis for sound localization: A comparative study. *Journal of Comparative and Physiological Psychology,* 89, 379–386.

Mather, G., and **Harris, J.** (1998) Theoretical models of the motion aftereffect. In G. Mather, F. Verstraten, and S. Anstis (eds.), *The motion aftereffect: A modern perspective.* Cambridge: MIT Press, 157–185.

Mather, G., and **Moulden, B.** (1980) A simultaneous shift in apparent direction: Further evidence for a "distribution-shift" model of direction coding. *Quarterly Journal of Experimental Psychology,* 32, 325–333.

Matin, L. (1986) Visual localization and eye movements. In K. Boff, L. Kaufman, and J. Thomas (eds.), *Handbook of perception and human performance.* New York: Wiley, 20–1 to 20–45.

Maunsell, J. H. R. (1995) The brain's visual world: Representation of visual targets in cerebral cortex. *Science,* 270, 764–769.

Maunsell, J. H. R., and **Newsome, W. T.** (1987) Visual processing in monkey extrastriate cortex. *Annual Review of Neuroscience,* 10, 363–401.

Maurer, D., Lewis, T. L., Brent, H. P., and **Levin, A. V.** (1999) Rapid improvement in the acuity of infants after visual input. *Science,* 286, 108–110.

May, M. (1994) Three-dimensional mammography. *American Scientist,* 82, 421–422.

Mayr, E. (1982) *The growth of biological thought: Diversity, evolution, and inheritance.* Cambridge: Belknap Press/Harvard University Press.

McAdams, S. (1984) *Spectral fusion, spectral parsing, and the formation of auditory images.* Paris: IRCAM.

McBurney, D. H. (1978) Psychological dimensions and perceptual analyses of taste. In E. C. Carterette and M. P. Friedman (eds.), *Handbook of perception,* vol. 6A. New York: Academic Press, 125–155.

McBurney, D. H., and **Gent, J. F.** (1979) On the nature of taste qualities. *Psychological Bulletin,* 86, 151–167.

McBurney, D. H., and **Moskat, L. J.** (1975) Taste thresholds in college-age smokers and nonsmokers. *Perception & Psychophysics,* 18, 71–73.

McBurney, D. H., Smith, D. V., and **Shick, T. R.** (1972) Gustatory cross adaptation: Sourness and bitterness. *Perception & Psychophysics,* 11, 228–232.

McCabe, P. A., and **Dey, F. L.** (1965) The effect of aspirin upon auditory sensitivity. *Annals of Otology, Rhinology, and Laryngology,* 74, 312–325.

McCarley, J. S., Kramer, A. F., Wickens, C. D., Vidoni, E. D., and **Boot, W. R.** (2004) Visual skills in airport-security screening. *Psychological Science 15,* 302–306.

McConkie, G. W., and **Rayner, K.** (1975) The span of the effective stimulus during a fixation in reading. *Perception & Psychophysics,* 17, 578–586.

McDermott, H. J., and **McKay, C. M.** (1997) Musical pitch perception with electrical stimulation of the cochlea. *Journal of the Acoustical Society of America,* 101, 1622–1631.

McDermott, J., and **Adelson, E. H.** (2004) Motion perception and mid-level vision. In M. Gazzaniga (ed.), *The cognitive neurosciences,* 3rd ed. Cambridge: MIT Press.

McElheny, V. K. (1999) *Insisting on the impossible: The life of Edwin Land, and inventor of instant photography.* Reading: Perseus Books.

McFadden, D. (1982) *Tinnitus: Facts, theories and treatments.* Washington, D.C.: National Academy of Sciences Press.

McFadden, D. (1998) Sex differences in the auditory system. *Developmental Neuropsychology,* 14, 261–298.

McFadden, D., and **Callaway, N. L.** (1999) Better discrimination of small changes in commonly encountered than in less commonly encountered auditory stimuli. *Journal of Experimental Psychology: Human Perception and Performance,* 25, 543–560.

McFadden, D., and **Plattsmier, H. S.** (1983) Aspirin can potentiate the temporary hearing loss induced by intense sounds. *Hearing Research,* 9, 295–316.

McFadden, D., Plattsmier, H. S., and **Pasanen, E. G.** (1984) Aspirin-induced hearing loss as a model of sensorineural hearing loss. *Hearing Research,* 16, 251–260.

McGurk, H., and **MacDonald, J.** (1976) Hearing lips and seeing voices. *Nature,* 264, 746–748.

McIntosh, A. R., Sekuler, A. B., Penpeci, C., Rajah, M. N., Grady, C. L., Sekuler, R., and **Bennett, P. J.** (1999) Recruitment of unique neural systems supporting visual memory in normal aging. *Current Biology, 9,* 1275–1278.

McKee, S. P. (1981) A local mechanism for differential velocity detection. *Vision Research,* 21, 491–500.

McMahon, C., Neitz, J., and **Neitz, M.** (2004) Evaluating the human X-chromosome pigment gene promoter sequences as predictors of L:M cone ratio variation. *Journal of Vision, 4,* 203–208.

Mealey, L., Bridgstock, R., and **Townsend, G. C.** (1999) Symmetry and perceived facial attractiveness: A monozygotic co-twin comparison. *Journal of Personality & Social Psychology,* 76, 151–158.

Mednick, S., Nakayama, K., and **Stickgold, R.** (2003) Sleep-dependent learning: A nap is as good as a night. *Nature Neuroscience,* 6, 697–698.

Meenan, J. P., and **Miller, L. A.** (1994) Perceptual flexibility after frontal or temporal lobectomy. *Neuropsychologia,* 32, 1145–1149.

Meijer, P. B. L. (1992) An experimental system for auditory image representations. *IEEE Transactions on Biomedical Engineering,* 39, 112–121.

Meiselman, H. L., and **Dzendolet, E.** (1967) Variability in gustatory quality identification. *Perception & Psychophysics,* 2, 496–498.

Melville, H. (1851/1942) *Moby-Dick.* New York: Dodd, Mead.

Melzack, R. (1992) Phantom limbs. *Scientific American,* 266, 120–126.

Melzack, R., and **Casey, K. L.** (1968) Sensory, motivational, and central control determinants of pain. In D. R. Kenshalo (ed.), *The skin senses,* Springfield: C. C. Thomas, pp. 423–439.

Melzack, R., and **Wall, P. D.** (1965) Pain mechanisms: A new theory. *Science,* 150, 971–979.

Mendelson, J. R. (1992) Neural selectivity for interaural frequency disparity in cat primary auditory cortex. *Hearing Research,* 58, 47–56.

Mennella, J. A., and **Beauchamp, G. K.** (1999) Experience with a flavor in mother's milk modifies the infant's acceptance of flavored cereal. *Developmental Psychobiology,* 35, 197–203.

Mennella, J. A., Jagnow, C. P., and **Beauchamp, G. K.** (2001) Prenatal and postnatal flavor learning by human infants. *Pediatrics,* 107, 1–6.

Mennella, J. A., Griffin, C. E., and **Beauchamp, G. K.** (2004) Flavor programming during infancy. *Pediatrics,* 113, 840–845.

Menon, R. S., Ogawa, S., Strupp, J. P., and **Ugurbil, K.** (1997) Ocular dominance in human V1 demonstrated by functional magnetic resonance imaging. *Journal of Neurophysiology,* 77, 2780–2787.

Merbs, S. L., and **Nathans, J.** (1992) Absorption spectra of human cone pigments. *Nature,* 356, 433–435.

Merigan, W. H., and **Maunsell, J. H. R.** (1993) How parallel are the primate visual pathways? *Annual Review of Neuroscience,* 16, 369–402.

Merker, H. (1992) *Listening: Ways of hearing in a silent world.* New York: HarperCollins.

Mershon, D. H., and **Bowers, J. N.** (1979) Absolute and relative cues for the auditory perception of egocentric distance. *Perception,* 8, 311–322.

Merskey, H., and **Bogduk, N.** (1994) Classification of chronic pain, 2nd ed. In H. Merskey and N. Bogduk (eds), *IASP Task Force on Taxonomy.* Seattle: IASP Press, 209–214.

Merzenich, M. M. (1987) Dynamic neocortical processes and the origins of higher brain functions. In J. P. Changeux and M. Konishi (eds.), *Neural and molecular bases of learning.* Chichester, England: John Wiley & Sons, 337–358.

Merzenich, M. M., Jenkins, W. M., Johnston, P., Schreiner, C., Miller, S. L., and **Tallal, P.** (1996) Temporal processing deficits of language-learning impaired children ameliorated by training. *Science,* 271, 77–81.

Merzenich, M. M., Nelson, R. J., Kaas, J. H., Stryker, M. P., Jenkins, W. M., Zook, J. M., Cynader, M. S., and **Schoppmann, A.** (1987) Variability in hand surface representations in Area-3B and Area-1 in adult owl and squirrel monkeys. *Journal of Comparative Neurology,* 258, 281–296.

Metelli, F. (1974) The perception of transparency. *Scientific American,* 230, 90–98.

Middlebrooks, J. C., and **Green, D. M.** (1991) Sound localization by human listeners. *Annual Review of Psychology,* 42, 135–159.

Miller, I. J., Jr., and **Bartoshuk, L. M.** (1991) Taste perception, taste bud distribution, and spatial relationships. In T. V. Getchell, R. L. Doty, L. M. Bartoshuk, and J. B. Snow, Jr. (eds.), *Smell and taste in health and disease.* New York: Raven Press, 175–204.

Miller, I. J., Jr., and **Reedy, F. E.** (1990) Variations in human taste bud density and taste intensity perception. *Physiology & Behavior,* 47, 1213–1219.

Mills, A. W. (1960) Lateralization of high-frequency tones. *Journal of the Acoustical Society of America,* 32, 132–134.

Milner, B. (1968) Visual recognition and recall after right temporal-lobe excision in man. *Neuropsychologia,* 6, 191–209.

Mishkin, M., Ungerleider, L. G., and **Macko, K. A.** (1983) Object vision and spatial vision: Two cortical pathways. *Trends in Neurosciences,* 6, 414–417.

Mistlin, A. J., and **Perrett, D. I.** (1990) Visual and somatosensory processing in the macaque temporal cortex: The role of "expectation." *Experimental Brain Research,* 82, 437–450.

Mitchell, D. E., Freeman, R. D., Millidot, M., and **Haegerstrom, G.** (1973) Meridional amblyopia: Evidence for modification of the human visual system by early visual experience. *Vision Research,* 13, 535–558.

Mitchell, D. E., and **Ware, C.** (1974) Interocular transfer of a visual aftereffect in normal and stereoblind humans. *Journal of Physiology,* 236, 707–721.

Mitchell, R. L. C., Elliott, R., Barry, M., Cruttenden, A., and **Woodruff, P. W. R.** (2003) The neural response to emotional prosody, as revealed by functional magnetic resonance imaging. *Neuropsychologia,* 41, 1410–1421.

Mitchell, S. C. (1996) The fish-odor syndrome. *Perspectives in Biology and Medicine,* 39, 514–526.

Miyamoto, R. T., Kirk, K. I., Robbins, A. M., Todd, S., Riley, A., and **Pisoni, D. B.** (1997) Speech perception and speech intelligibility in children with multichannel cochlear implants. In W. Arnold (ed.), *Advances in Oto-Rhino-Laryngology.* Basel: S. Karger, pp. 198–203.

Miyashita, Y. (1993) Inferior temporal cortex: Where visual perception meets memory. *Annual Review of Neuroscience,* 16, 245–263.

Mody, M., Schwartz, R. G., Gravel, J. S., and **Ruben, R. J.** (1999) Speech perception and verbal memory in children with and without histories of otitis media. *Journal of Speech, Language and Hearing Research,* 42, 1069–1079.

Mojet, J., Christ-Hazelhof, E., and **Heidema, J.** (2001) Taste perception with age: Generic or specific losses in threshold sensitivity to the five basic tastes? *Chemical Senses,* 26, 845–860.

Moller, A. R. (1974) Responses of units in cochlear nucleus to sinusoidally amplitude-modulated tones. *Experimental Neurology,* 45, 104–117.

Mollon, J. D. (1987) On the origins of polymorphisms. In *Frontiers of visual science.* Washington: National Academy Press, 160–168.

Mollon, J. D. (1989) "Tho' she kneel'd in that place where they grew . . ." The uses and origins of primate colour vision. *Journal of Experimental Biology,* 146, 21–38.

Mollon, J. D. (1990) The tricks of colour. In H. Barlow, C. Blakemore and M. Weston-Smith (eds.) *Images and Understanding.* Cambridge: Cambridge University Press, 61–78.

Mollon, J. D. (1992) Worlds of difference. *Nature,* 356, 378–379.

Mombaerts, P. (2004) Genes and ligands for odorant, vomeronasal and taste receptors. *Nature Reviews Neuroscience,* 5, 263–278.

Moncrieff, R. W. (1956) Olfactory adaptation and odor likeness. *Journal of Physiology,* 133, 301–316.

Monnier, P., and **Shevell, S. K.** (2004) Chromatic induction from S-cone patterns. *Vision Research,* 44, 849–856.

Moore, B. (1986) *Frequency selectivity.* London: Academic Press.

Moore, C. M., Yantis, S., and **Vaughan, B.** (1998) Object-based visual selection: Evidence from perceptual completion. *Psychological Science,* 9, 104–110.

Moray, N. (1970) *Attention: Selective processes in vision and hearing.* New York: Academic Press.

Morgan, I. G. (2003) The biological basis of myopic refractive error. *Clinical and Experimental Optometry,* 86, 276–288.

Morgan, I. G., and **Rose, K.** (2004) How genetic is school myopia? *Progress in Retinal and Eye Research,* 24, 1–38.

Morgan, M. J., Watamaniuk, S. N. J., and **McKee, S. P.** (2000) The use of an implicit standard for measuring discrimination thresholds. *Vision Research,* 40, 2341–2349.

Morrot, G., Brochet, F., and **Dubourdieu, D.** (2001) The color of odors. *Brain and Language,* 79, 309–320.

Moscovitch. M., Winocur, G., and **Behrmann, M.** (1997) What is special about face recognition? Nineteen experiments on a person with visual object agnosia and dyslexia but normal face recognition. *Journal of Cognitive Neuroscience,* 9, 554–604.

Moses, Y., Ullman, S., and **Edelman, S.** (1996) Generalization to novel images in upright and inverted faces. *Perception,* 25, 443–461.

Moskowitz, H. R. (1978) Taste and food technology: Acceptability, aesthetics, and preference. In E. C. Carterette and M. P. Friedman (eds.), *Handbook of perception,* vol. 6A. New York: Academic Press, 157–194.

Moulton, D. G. (1974) Dynamics of cell populations in the olfactory epithelium. *Annals of the New York Academy of Sciences,* 237, 52–61.

Mountcastle, V. B. (1975) The view from within: Pathways to the study of perception. *Johns Hopkins Medical Journal,* 136, 109–131.

Mountcastle, V. B. (1984) Central nervous mechanisms in mechanoreceptive sensibility. In I. Darian-Smith (ed.), *Handbook of physiology: The nervous system III.* Bethesda, Md.: American Physiological Society, 789–878.

Mountcastle, V. B., Talbot, W. H., and **Kornhuber, H. H.** (1966) The neural transformation of mechanical stimuli delivered to the monkey's hand. In A.V.S. de Reuck and J. Knight (eds.). *Touch, Heat and Pain (A CIBA Foundation Symposium).* London: Churchill.

Movshon, J. A., Adelson, E. H., Gizzi, M. S., and Newsome, W. T. (1986) The analysis of moving visual patterns. In C. Chagas, R. Gattas, and C. G. Gross (eds.), *Pattern recognition mechanisms.* Springer-Verlag, pp. 177–151.

Movshon, J. A., and Lennie, P. (1979) Pattern-selective adaptation in visual cortical neurones. *Nature,* 278, 850–852.

Mozel, M. M., Smith, B., Smith, P., Sullivan, R., and Swender, P. (1969) Nasal chemoreception in flavor identification. *Archives of Otolaryngology,* 90, 367–373.

Mühlnickel, W., Elbert, T., Taub, E., and Flor, H. (1998) Reorganization of auditory cortex in tinnitus. *Proceedings of the National Academy of Sciences: USA,* 95, 10340–10343.

Münte, T. F., Kohlmetz, C., Nagel, W., and Altenmüller, E. (2001) Superior auditory spatial tuning in conductors. *Nature,* 409, 580.

Murphy, B. J. (1978) Pattern thresholds for moving and stationary gratings during smooth eye movement. *Vision Research,* 18, 521–530.

Murphy, C., and Cain, W. S. (1986) Odor identification: The blind are better. *Physiology & Behavior,* 37, 177–180.

Murphy, C., Cain, W. S., and Bartoshuk, L. M. (1977) Mutual action of taste and olfaction. *Sensory Processes,* 1, 204–211.

Murray, S. O., Kersten, D., Olshausen, B. A., Schrater, P., and Woods, D. L. (2002) Shape perception reduces activity in human primary visual cortex. *Proceedings of the National Academy of Sciences: USA,* 99, 15164–15169.

Nadol, J. B. (1993) Hearing loss. *New England Journal of Medicine,* 329, 1092–1102.

Nagel, T. (1974) What is it like to be a bat? *Philosophical Review,* 83, 435–450.

Naka, K. I., and Rushton, W. A. H. (1966) S-potentials from colour units in the retina of fish Cyprinidae. *Journal of Physiology,* 185, 536–555.

Nakahara, H., Zhang, L. I., and Merzenich, M. M. (2004) Specialization of primary auditory cortex processing by sound exposure in the "critical period." *Proceedings of the National Academy of Sciences: USA,* 101, 7170–7174.

Nakayama, K., and Shimojo, S. (1990) Da Vinci stereopsis: Depth and subjective occluding contours from unpaired image points. *Vision Research,* 30, 1811–1825.

Nakayama, K., Shimojo, S., and Ramachandran, V. S. (1990) Transparency: Relation to depth, subjective contours, luminance, and neon color spreading. *Perception,* 19, 497–513.

Nakayama, K., Shimojo, S., and Silverman, G. H. (1989) Stereoscopic depth: Its relation to image segmentation, grouping and the recognition of occluded objects. *Perception,* 18, 55–68.

Nathans, J. (1989) The genes for color vision. *Scientific American,* 260, 42–49.

Nathans, J. (1999) The evolution and physiology of human color vision: Insights from molecular genetic studies of visual pigments. *Neuron,* 24, 299–312.

Nawrot, M., and Blake, R. (1991) The interplay between stereopsis and structure from motion. *Perception & Psychophysics,* 49, 230–244.

Nawrot, M., and Blake, R. (1993) On the perceptual identity of dynamic stereopsis and kinetic depth. *Vision Research,* 33, 1561–1571.

Nawrot, M., Nordenstrom, B., and Olson, A. (2004) Disruption of eye movements by ethanol intoxication affects perception of depth from motion parallax. *Psychological Science,* 15, 858–865.

Neitz, J., Carroll, J., Yamauchi, Y., Neitz, M., and Williams, D. R. (2002) Color perception is mediated by a plastic neural mechanism that is adjustable in adults. *Neuron,* 35, 783–792.

Neitz, J., Neitz, M., and Jacobs, G. H. (1993) More than three different cone pigments among people with normal color vision. *Vision Research,* 33, 117–122.

Neitz, M., and Neitz, J. (1995) Numbers and ratios of visual pigment genes for normal red-green color vision. *Science,* 267, 1013–1016.

Nelken, I. (2004) Processing of complex stimuli and natural scenes in the auditory cortex. *Current Opinions in Neurobiology,* 14, 474–480.

Neuhoff, J. G. (1998) Perceptual bias for rising tones. *Nature,* 395, 123–124.

Neuhoff, J. G. (2001) An adaptive bias in the perception of looming auditory motion. *Ecological Psychology,* 13, 87–110.

Neuhoff, J. G., Kramer, G., and Wayand, J. (2002) Pitch and loudness interact in auditory displays: Can the data get lost in the map? *Journal of Experimental Psychology: Applied,* 8, 17–25.

Neumeyer, C. (1992) Tetrachromatic color vision in goldfish: Evidence from color mixture experiments. *Journal of Comparative Physiology A,* 171, 639–649.

Newsome, W. T., Britten, K. H., and Movshon, J. A. (1989) Neuronal correlates of a perceptual decision. *Nature,* 341, 52–54.

Newsome, W. T., and Paré, E. B. (1988) A selective impairment of motion perception following lesions of the middle temporal visual area (MT). *Journal of Neuroscience,* 8, 2201–2211.

Newton, I. (1704/1952) *Opticks, or a treatise of the reflections, refractions, inflections & colours of light,* 4th ed. New York: Dover.

Nicolelis, M. A. (2001) Actions from thoughts. *Nature,* 409 suppl,: 403–407.

Nicolelis, M. A., and Ribeiro, S. (2002) Multielectrode recordings: The next steps. *Current Opinions in Neurobiology,* 12, 602–606.

Niemeyer, W., and Starlinger, I. (1981) Do the blind hear better? Investigations on auditory processing in congenital or early acquired blindness: II. Central functions. *Audiology,* 20, 510–515.

Nisbett, R., and Wilson, T. D. (1977) Telling more than we can know: Verbal reports on mental processes. *Psychological Review,* 84, 231–259.

Nissen, M. J., Corkin, S., Buonanno, F. S., Growdon, J. H., Wray, S. H., and Bauer, J. A., Jr. (1985) Spatial vision in Alzheimer's disease. General findings and a case report. *Archives of Neurology,* 42, 667–671.

Nixon, J. C., and Glorig, A. (1961) Noise-induced permanent threshold shift at 2000 cps and 4000 cps. *Journal of the Acoustical Society of America,* 33, 904–908.

Nobili, R., Mammano, F., and Ashmore, J. (1998) How well do we understand the cochlea? *Trends in Neurosciences,* 21, 159–167.

Noble, W. (1983) Hearing, hearing impairment, and the audible world: A theoretical essay. *Audiology,* 22, 325–338.

Nordby, K. (1990) Vision in a complete achromat: A personal account. In R. Hess, L. Sharpe, and K. Nordby (eds.), *Night vision: Basic, clinical and applied aspects.* Cambridge: Cambridge University Press, pp. 290–315.

Norman, J. F., Dawson, T. E., and **Butler, A. K.** (2000) The effects of age upon the perception of depth and 3-D shape from differential motion and binocular disparity. *Perception,* 29, 1335–1359.

Norman, J. F., and **Lappin, J. S.** (1992) The detection of surface curvature defined by optical motion. *Perception & Psychophysics,* 51, 386–396.

Norman, J. F., Payton, S. M., Long, J. R., and **Hawkes, L. M.** (2004) Aging and the perception of biological motion. *Psychology and Aging,* 19, 219–225.

Nothdurft, H. C. (1985) Discrimination of higher-order textures. *Perception,* 14, 551–560.

NRC (1989) *Myopia: Prevalence and progression.* Washington: National Academy Press.

Nummelä, S. (1995) Scaling of the mammalian middle ear. *Hearing Research,* 85, 18–30.

Nunn, J. A., Gregory, L. J., Brammer, M., Williams, S. C. R., Parslow, D. M., Morgan, M. J., Morris, R. G., Bullmore, E. T., Baron-Cohen, S., and **Gray, J. A.** (2002) Functional magnetic resonance imaging of synesthesia: Activation of V4/V8 by spoken words. *Nature Neuroscience,* 5, 371–375.

O'Doherty, J., Rolls, E. T., Francis, S., Bowtell, R., McGlone, F., Kobal, G., Renner, B., and **Ahne G.** (2000) Sensory-specific satiety-related olfactory activation of the human orbitofrontal cortex. *Neuroreport,* 11, 399–403.

Oldfield, S. R., and **Parker, S. P. A.** (1984a) Acuity of sound localization: A topography of auditory space. I. Normal hearing conditions. *Perception,* 13, 581–600.

Oldfield, S. R., and **Parker, S. P. A.** (1984b) Acuity of sound localization: A topography of auditory space. II. Pinna cues absent. *Perception,* 13, 601–617.

Oldfield, S. R., and **Parker, S. P. A.** (1986) Acuity of sound localization: A topography of auditory space. III. Monaural hearing conditions. *Perception,* 15, 67–81.

Oliva, A., and **Schyns, P.** (1999) Diagnostic colors mediate scene recognition. *Cognitive Psychology,* 41, 176–210.

Olshausen, B. A., and **O'Connor, K. N.** (2002) A new window on sound. *Nature Neuroscience,* 5, 292–294.

Olson, H. F. (1967) *Music, physics, and engineering,* 2nd ed. New York: Dover.

O'Regan, J. K., Rensink, R. A., and **Clark, J. J.** (1999) Change-blindness as a result of "mudsplashes." *Nature,* 398, 34.

O'Shea, R. P. (1991) Thumb's rule tested: Visual angle of thumb's width is about 2 deg. *Perception,* 20, 415–418.

O'Shea, R. P., Blackburn, S. G., and **Ono, H.** (1993) Aerial perspective, contrast, and depth perception. Paper presented at the Association for Research in Vision and Opthalmology, Sarasota, Fla.

O'Shea, R. P., Blackburn, S. G., and **Ono, H.** (1994) Contrast as a depth cue. *Vision Research,* 34, 1595–1604.

O'Shea, R. P., Sekuler, R., and **Govan, D. G.** (1997) Blur and contrast as pictorial depth cues. *Perception,* 26, 599–612.

Owen, D. (1980) *Camouflage and mimicry.* Chicago: University of Chicago Press.

Owen, D. H., and **Machamer, P. K.** (1979) Bias-free improvement in wine discrimination. *Perception,* 8, 199–209.

Owens, D. A. (1984) The resting state of the eyes. *American Scientist,* 72, 378–387.

Owsley, C. J., Sekuler, R., and **Siemsen, D.** (1983) Contrast sensitivity throughout adulthood. *Vision Research,* 23, 689–699.

Packwood, J., and **Gordon, B.** (1975) Stereopsis in normal domestic cat, Siamese cat, and cat raised with alternating monocular occlusion. *Journal of Neurophysiology,* 38, 1485–1499.

Palmer, S. E. (1999) *Vision science: From photons to phenomenology.* Cambridge: MIT Press.

Palmer, S. E., Rosch, E., and **Chase, P.** (1981) Canonical perspective and the perception of objects. In J. Long and A. Baddeley (eds.), *Attention and performance,* vol. 9. Hillsdale, N.J.: Erlbaum, 135–151.

Palmeri, T. J., Blake, R., Marois, R., Flanery, M. A., and **Whetsell, Jr., W.** (2002) The perceptual reality of synesthetic colors. *Proceedings of the National Academy of Sciences: USA,* 99, 4127–4131.

Palmeri, T. J., and **Gauthier, I.** (2004) Visual object understanding. *Nature Reviews Neuroscience,* 5, 291–303.

Pangborn, R. M. (1960) Influence of color on the discrimination of sweetness. *American Journal of Psychology,* 73, 229–238.

Pantev, C., Oostenveld, R., Engelien, A., Ross, B., Roberts, L. E., and **Hoke, M.** (1998) Increased auditory representation in musicians. *Nature,* 392, 811–814.

Pantle, A. (1998) How do measues of the motion aftereffect measure up? In G. Mather, F. Verstraten and S. Anstis (eds.) *The motion aftereffect: A modern perspective.* Cambridge: MIT Press, 25–39.

Pariente, J., White, P., Frackowiak, R. S. J., and **Lewith, G.** (2005) Expectancy and belief modulate the neuronal substrates of pain treated by acupuncture. *NeuroImage,* 25, 1161–1167.

Park, D. (1999) *The fire within the eye. A historical essay on the nature and meaning of light.* Princeton, N.J.: Princeton University Press.

Parker, A. (2004) From binocular disparity to the perception of stereoscopic depth. In L. M. Chalupa and J. S. Werner (eds.), *The visual neurosciences,* vol. 1. Cambridge: MIT Press, 779–792.

Paterson, C. A. (1979) Crystalline lens. In R. E. Records (ed.), *Physiology of the human eye and visual system.* New York: Harper & Row, 232–260.

Patterson, K., and **Ralph, M.** (1999) Selective disorders of reading? *Current Opinion in Neurobiology,* 9, 235–239.

Patterson, R. D., Uppenkamp, S., Johnsrude, I. S., and **Griffiths, T. D.** (2002) The processing of temporal pitch and melody information in auditory cortex. *Neuron,* 36, 767–776.

Pavani, F., Spence, C., and **Driver, J.** (2000) Visual capture of touch: Out-of-the-body experiences with rubber gloves. *Psychological Science,* 11, 353–359.

Pavlova, M., Krägeloh-Mann, I., Sokolov, A., and **Birbaumer, N.** (2001) Recognition of point-light biological motion displays by young children. *Perception,* 30, 925–933.

Pearlman, A. L., Birch, J., and **Meadows, J. C.** (1979) Cerebral color blindness: An acquired defect in hue discrimination. *Annals of Neurology,* 5, 253–261.

Peichl, L., Behrmann, G., and **Kroger, R. H. H.** (2001) For whales and seals the ocean is not blue: A visible pigment loss in marine mammals. *European Journal of Neuroscience,* 13, 1520–1528.

Peli, E., and **Peli, T.** (1984) Image enhancement for the visually impaired. *Optical Engineering,* 23, 47–51.

Pelli, D. G. (1999) Close encounters—An artist shows that size affects shape. *Science,* 285, 844–846.

Penagos, H., Melcher, J. R., and **Oxenheam, A. J.** (2004) A neural representation of pitch salience in nonprimary human auditory cortex revealed with functional magnetic resonance imaging. *Journal of Cognitive Neuroscience,* 24, 6810–6815.

Penfield, W., and **Faulk, M. E.** (1955) The insula. Further observation on its function. *Brain,* 78, 445–470.

Penfield, W., and **Perrot, P.** (1963) The brain's record of auditory and visual experience. *Brain,* 86, 595–696.

Penhune, V. B., Zatorre, R. J., and **Evans, A. C.** (1998) Cerebellar contributions to motor timing: A PET study of auditory and visual rhythm reproduction. *Journal of Cognitive Neuroscience,* 10, 752–765.

Peretz, I. (1990) Processing of local and global musical information in unilateral brain damaged patients. *Brain,* 113, 1185–1205.

Peretz, I., Ayotte, J., Zatorre, R. J., Mehler, J., Ahad, P., Penhune, V. B., and **Jutras, B.** (2002) Congenital amusia: A disorder of fine-grained pitch discrimination. *Neuron,* 33, 185–191.

Perkins, S. (2000) Eau, brother! *Science News,* 157, 125–127.

Perky, C. W. (1910) An experimental study of imagination. *American Journal of Psychology,* 21, 422–452.

Perrett, D. I., Lee, K. J., Penton-Voak, I., Rowland, D., Yoshikawa, S., Burt, D. M., Henzi, S. P., Castles, D. L., and **Akamatsu, S.** (1998) Effects of sexual dimorphism on facial attractiveness. *Nature,* 394, 884–887.

Perrett, D. I., Oram, M. W., Harries, M. H., Bevan, R., Hietanen, J. K., Benson, P. J., and **Thomas, S.** (1991) Viewer-centered and object-centered coding of heads in the macaque temporal cortex. *Experimental Brain Research,* 86, 159–173.

Perrin, P., Perrot, C., Deviterne, D., Ragaru, B., and **Kingma, H.** (2000) Dizziness in discus throwers is related to motion sickness generated while spinning. *Acta Otolaryngology,* 120, 390–395.

Perrott, D. R., Ambarsoom, H., and **Tucker, J.** (1987) Changes in head position as a measure of auditory localization performance: Auditory psychomotor coordination under monaural and binaural listening conditions. *Journal of the Acoustical Society of America,* 82, 1637–1645.

Perry, J. S., and **Geisler, W. S.** (2002) Gaze-contingent real-time simulation of arbitrary visual fields. In B. Rogowitz and T. Pappas (eds.), *Human vision and electronic imaging,* SPIE Proceedings, San Jose.

Peterhans, E., and **von der Heydt, R.** (1991) Subjective contours—Bridging the gap between psychophysics and physiology. *Trends in Neurosciences,* 14, 112–119.

Petersen, S. E., Fox, P. T., Posner, M. I., Mintun, M., and **Raichle, M. E.** (1988) Positron emission tomographic studies of the cortical anatomy of single-word processing. *Nature,* 331, 585–589.

Pettet, M. W., McKee, S. P., and **Grzywacz, N. M.** (1998) Constraints on long range interactions mediating contour detection. *Vision Research,* 38, 865–879.

Pettigrew, J. D., and **Carter, O. L.** (2005) Perceptual rivalries as an ultradian oscillation. In D. Alais and R. Blake (eds.), *Binocular rivalry.* Cambridge: MIT Press.

Pfaffmann, C. (1955) Gustatory nerve impulses in rat, cat, and rabbit. *Journal of Neurophysiology,* 18, 429–440.

Pfaffmann, C., and **Bartoshuk, L. M.** (1989) Psychophysical mapping of a human case of left unilateral ageusia. *Chemical Senses,* 14, 738.

Pfaffmann, C., and **Bartoshuk, L. M.** (1990) Taste loss due to herpes zoster oticus: An update after 19 months. *Chemical Senses,* 15, 657–658.

Phillips, J. R., Johansson, R. S., and **Johnson, K. O.** (1992) Responses of human mechanoreceptive afferents to embossed dot arrays scanned across fingerpad skin. *Journal of Neuroscience,* 12, 827–839.

Pierce, J., and **Halpern, B. P.** (1996) Orthonasal and retronasal odorant identification based on vapor phase input from common substances. *Chemical Senses,* 21, 529–543.

Pietrini, P., Furey, M. L., Ricciardi, E., Gobbini, M. I., Wu, W. H. C., Cohen, L., Guzaaelli, M., and **Haxby, J.** (2004) Beyond sensory images: Object-based representation in the human ventral pathway. *Proceedings of the National Academy of Sciences: USA,* 101, 5658–5663.

Pinker, S. (1994) *The language instinct.* New York: William Morrow & Co.

Pinker, S. (1997) *How the mind works.* New York: Norton.

Pirenne, M. H. (1967) *Vision and the eye,* 2nd ed. London: Chapman and Hall.

Pirenne, M. H. (1970) *Optics, painting, and photography.* Cambridge: Cambridge University Press.

Platt, J. R., and **Racine, R. J.** (1985) Effect of frequency, timbre, experience, and feedback on musical tuning skills. *Perception & Psychophysics,* 38, 543–553.

Pleger, B., Foerster, A.-Y., Ragert, P., Dinse, H. R., Schwenkreis, P., Malin, J.-P., Nicolas, V., and **Tegenthoff, M.** (2003) Functional imaging of perceptual learning in human primary and secondary somatosensory cortex. *Neuron,* 40, 643–653.

Pointer, M. R., and **Atridge, G. G.** (1998) The number of discernible colours. *Color Research and Application,* 1998, 23, 52–54.

Pokorny, J., Graham, C. H., and **Lanson, R. N.** (1968) Effect of wavelength on foveal grating acuity. *Journal of the Optical Society of America,* 58, 1410–1414.

Polat, U. (1999) Functional architecture of long-range perceptual interactions. *Spatial Vision,* 12, 143–162.

Pollack, I., and **Rose, M.** (1967) Effect of head movement on the localization of sounds in the equatorial plane. *Perception & Psychophysics,* 2, 591–596.

Polyak, S. L. (1941) *The retina.* Chicago: University of Chicago Press.

Polyak, S. L. (1957) *The vertebrate visual system.* Chicago: University of Chicago Press.

Pomerantz, J. R. (1981) Perceptual organization in information processing. In M. Kubovy and J. R. Pomerantz (eds.), *Perceptual organization.* Hillsdale, N.J.: Erlbaum, 141–180.

Pons, T. P., Garraghty, P. E., Friedman, D. P., and **Mishkin, M.** (1987) Physiological evidence for serial processing in somatosensory cortex. *Science,* 237, 417–420.

Porter, R. H. (1991) Human reproduction and the mother-infant relationship. In T. V. Getchell, R. L. Doty, L. M. Bartoshuk, and J. B. Snow (eds.), *Smell and taste in health and disease.* New York: Raven Press, 429–444.

Posner, M. I. (1980) Orienting of attention. *Quarterly Journal of Experimental Psychology,* 32, 3–25.

Posner, M. I., Snyder, C. R., and **Davidson, B. J.** (1980) Attention and the detection of signals. *Journal of Experimental Psychology: General,* 109, 160–174.

Potter, M. C. (1966) On perceptual recognition. In J. S. Bruner (ed.), *Studies in cognitive growth.* New York: John Wiley & Sons, 103–134.

Prescott, J., Soo, J., Campbell, H., and **Roberts, C.** (2004) Responses of PROP taster groups to variations in sensory qualities within foods and beverages. *Physiology & Behavior,* 82, 459–469.

Press, C., Taylor-Clarke, M., Kennett, S., and **Haggard, P.** (2004) Visual enhancement of touch in spatial body representation. *Experimental Brain Research,* 154, 238–245.

Preuss, T. M., Qi, H., and **Kaas, J. H.** (1999) Distinctive compartmental organization of human primary visual cortex. *Proceedings of the National Academy of Sciences, U.S.A.,* 96, 11601–11606.

Preuss, T. M., and **Coleman, G. Q.** (2002) Human-specific organization of primary visual cortex: Alternating compartments of dense cat-301 and calbindin immunoreactivity in layer 4A. *Cerebral Cortex,* 12, 671–691.

Price, D. D. (2000) Psychological and neural mechanisms of the affective dimension of pain. *Science,* 288, 1769–1772.

Pringle, R., and **Egeth, H. E.** (1988) Mental curve tracing with elementary stimuli. *Journal of Experimental Psychology: Human Perception and Performance,* 14, 716–728.

Prinzmetal, W., Amiri, H., Allen, K., and **Edwards, T.** (1998) Phenomenology of attention: 1. Color, location, orientation, and spatial frequency. *Journal of Experimental Psychology: Human Perception & Performance,* 24, 261–282.

Pritchard, R. M., Heron, W., and **Hebb, D. O.** (1960) Visual perception approached by the method of stabilized images. *Canadian Journal of Psychology,* 14, 67–77.

Pritchard, T. C., Macaluso, D. A., and **Eslinger, P. J.** (1999) Taste perception in patients with insular cortex lesions. *Behavioral Neuroscience,* 113, 663–671.

Proust, M. (1928) *Swann's way.* New York: Random House.

Provencio, I., Rollag, M. D., and **Castrucci, A. M.** (2002) Photoreceptive net in the mammalian retina. *Nature,* 415, 493.

Provine, R., and **Fisher, K. R.** (1989) Laughing, smiling and talking: Relation to sleeping and social context in humans. *Ethology,* 83, 295–305.

Pylyshyn, Z. W., and **Storm, R. W.** (1988) Tracking multiple independent targets: Evidence for a parallel tracking mechanism. *Spatial Vision,* 3, 179–197.

Rafal, R., Smith J., Krantz J., Cohen A., and **Brennan, C.** (1990) Extrageniculate vision in hemianopic humans: Saccade inhibition by signals in the blind field. *Science,* 250, 118–121.

Raghubir, P., and **Krishna, A.** (1999) Vital dimensions in volume perception: Can the eye fool the stomach? *Journal of Marketing Research,* 36, 313–326.

Rainville, P., Duncan, G. H., Price, D. D., Carrier, B., and **Bushnell, M. C.** (1997) Pain affect encoded in human anterior cingulate but not somatosensory cortex. *Science,* 277, 968–971.

Ramachandran, V. S. (1988) Perceiving shape from shading. *Scientific American,* 259, 76–83.

Ramachandran, V. S. (1992) Blind spots. *Scientific American,* 266, 86–91.

Ramachandran, V. S., and **Anstis, S. M.** (1986) The perception of apparent motion. *Scientific American,* 254, 102–109.

Ramachandran, V. S., and **Blakeslee, S.** (1998) *Phantoms in the brain.* New York: Wm. Morrow & Co.

Ramachandran, V. S., and **Cavanagh, P.** (1987) Motion capture anisotropy. *Vision Research,* 27, 97–106.

Ramachandran, V. S., and **Hirstein, W.** (1999) The science of art: A neurological theory of aesthetic experience. *Journal of Consciousness Studies,* 6, 15–51.

Ramachandran, V. S., Rao, M. V., and **Vidyasagar, T. R.** (1973) Apparent movement with subjective contours. *Vision Research,* 13, 1399–1401.

Ramirez, I. (1990) Why do sugars taste good? *Neuroscience & Biobehavioral Reviews,* 14, 125–134.

Randolph, M., and **Semmes, J.** (1974) Behavioral consequences of selective subtotal ablations in the postcentral gyrus of the Macaca mulatta. *Brain Research,* 70, 55–70.

Rao, A. R., and **Lohse, G. L.** (1996) Toward a texture naming system: Identifying relevant dimensions of texture. *Vision Research,* 36, 1649–1670.

Ratliff, F. (1965) *Mach bands: Quantitative studies on neural networks in the retina.* San Francisco: Holden Day.

Ratliff, F. (1972) Contour and contrast. *Scientific American,* 226, 90–101.

Ratliff, F. (1984) Why Mach bands are not seen at the edges of a step. *Vision Research,* 24, 163–165.

Rauschecker, J. P. (1998) Cortical processing of complex sounds. *Current Opinion in Neurobiology,* 8, 516–521.

Rauschecker, J. P. (1999a) Auditory cortical plasticity: A comparison with other sensory systems. *Trends in Neurosciences,* 22, 74–80.

Rauschecker, J. P. (1999b) Making brain circuits listen. *Science,* 285, 1686–1687.

Rauschecker, J. P., and **Kniepert, U.** (1994) Auditory localization behavior in visually deprived cats. *European Journal of Neuroscience,* 6, 149–160.

Rauschecker, J. P., Tian, B., and **Hauser, M.** (1995) Processing of complex sounds in the macaque nonprimary auditory cortex. *Science,* 268, 111–114.

Rayner, K. (1978) Eye movements in reading and information processing. *Psychological Bulletin,* 85, 618–660.

Rayner, K. (1998) Eye movements in reading and information processing: 20 years of research. *Psychological Bulletin,* 124, 372–422.

Rayner, K., and **Bertera, J. H.** (1979) Reading without a fovea. *Science,* 206, 468–469.

Rayner, K., Inhoff, A. W., Morrison, R. E., Slowiaczek, M. L., and **Bertera, J. H.** (1981) Masking of foveal and parafoveal vision during eye fixations in reading. *Psychological Bulletin, Journal of Experimental Psychology: Human Perception and Performance,* 7, 167–179.

Rayner, K., and **Pollatsek, A.** (1987) Eye movements in reading: A tutorial review. In M. Coltheart (ed.), *Attention and performance, vol. 12: The psychology of reading.* Hove, England: Erlbaum, 327–362.

Reagan, R. (1990) *An American life.* New York: Simon & Schuster.

Recanzone, G. H., Jenkins, W. M., Hradek, G. T., and **Merzenich, M. M.** (1992a) Progressive improvement in discriminative abilities in adult owl monkeys performing a tactile frequency discrimination task. *Journal of Neurophysiology,* 67, 1015–1030.

Recanzone, G. H., Merzenich, M. M., Jenkins, W. M., Grajski, K. A., and **Dinse, H. R.** (1992b) Topographic reorganization of the hand representation in cortical area 3b of owl monkeys trained in a frequency discrimination task. *Journal of Neurophysiology,* 67, 1031–1056.

Recanzone, G. H., Schreiner, C. E., and **Merzenich, M. M.** (1993) Plasticity in the frequency representation in the primary auditory cortex following discrimination training in adult owl monkeys. *Journal of Neuroscience,* 13, 87–103.

Reeves, A. (1981) Visual imagery lowers sensitivity to hue-varying, but not luminance-varying, visual stimuli. *Perception & Psychophysics,* 29, 247–250.

Reeves, A. (1982) Letter to the editors. *Vision Research,* 22, 711.

Reeves, A. (2004) Visual adaptation. In L. M. Chalupa and J. S. Werner (eds), *The visual neurosciences.* Cambridge: MIT Press, 851–862.

Regan, B. C., Julliot, C., Simmen, B., Vienot, F., Charles-Dominique, P., and **Mollon, J. D.** (2001) Fruits, foliage and the evolution of primate colour vision. *Philosophical Transactions of the Royal Society of London (Series B),* 356, 229–283.

Regan, D. (1988) Low contrast letter charts and sinewave grating tests in ophthalmological and neurological disorders. *Clinical Vision Science,* 2, 235–250.

Regan, D. (1992) Visual judgements and misjudgements in cricket, and the art of flight. *Perception,* 21, 91–116.

Reichardt, W. (1961) Autocorrelation, a principle for the evaluation of sensory information by the central nervous system. In W. A. Rosenblith (ed.), *Sensory communication.* New York: John Wiley & Sons, 303–318.

Reichel, F. D., and **Todd, J. T.** (1990) Perceived depth inversion of smoothly curved surfaces due to image orientation. *Journal of Experimental Psychology: Human Perception and Performance,* 16, 653–664.

Reicher, G. M. (1969) Perceptual recognition as a function of meaningfulness of stimulus material. *Journal of Experimental Psychology,* 81, 275–280.

Reinagel, P. (2000) Information theory in the brain. *Current Biology,* 10, R542–R544.

Relkin, E. M., and **Doucet, J. R.** (1997) Is loudness simply proportional to the auditory nerve spike count? *Journal of the Acoustical Society of America,* 101, 2735–2740.

Rensink, R. (2002) Change detection. *Annual Review of Psychology,* 53, 245–277.

Rentschler, I., Jüttner, M., Unzicker, A., and **Landis, T.** (1999) Innate and learned components of human visual preference. *Current Biology,* 9, 665–671.

Repp, B. (1996) The art of inaccuracy: Why pianists' errors are difficult to hear. *Music Perception,* 14, 161–184.

Rezek, D. L. (1987) Olfactory deficits as a neurologic sign in dementia of the Alzheimer type. *Archives of Neurology,* 44, 1030–1032.

Ricci, C., and **Blundo, C.** (1990) Perception of ambiguous figures after focal brain lesions. *Neuropsychologia,* 28, 1163–1173.

Ricciardelli, P., Bricolo, E., Aglioti, S. M., and **Chelazzi, L.** (2002) My eyes want to look where your eyes are looking: Exploring the tendency to imitate another individual's gaze. *NeuroReport,* 13, 2259–2264.

Richards, W. (1971) The fortification illusions of migraines. *Scientific American,* 224, 88–98.

Richardson, J. T. E., and **Zucco, G. M.** (1989) Cognition and olfaction: A review. *Psychological Bulletin,* 105, 352–360.

Rieser, J. J., Ashmead, D. H., Talor, C. R., and **Youngquist, G. A.** (1990) Visual perception and the guidance of locomotion without vision of previously seen targets. *Perception,* 19, 675–689.

Riggs, L. A., and **Day, R. H.** (1980) Visual aftereffects derived from inspection of orthogonally moving patterns. *Science,* 208, 416–418.

Riggs, L. A., Ratliff, F., Cornsweet, J. C., and **Cornsweet, T. N.** (1953) The disappearance of steadily fixated visual test objects. *Journal of the Optical Society of America,* 43, 495–501.

Ringach, D. (2003) Neuroscience: States of mind. *Nature,* 425, 912–913.

Ripoll, H., and **Fleurance, P.** (1988) What does keeping one's eye on the ball mean? *Ergonomics,* 31, 1647–1654.

Rivest, J., and **Cavanagh, P.** (1996) Localizing contours defined by more than one attribute. *Vision Research,* 36, 53–66.

Rizzo, J. F., and **Wyatt, J. L.** (1997) Prospects for a visual prosthesis. *Neuroscientist,* 3, 251–262.

Rizzo, M., and **Nawrot, M.** (1998) Perception of movement and shape in Alzheimer's disease. *Brain,* 121, 2259–2270.

Rizzo, M., Reinach, S., McGehep., D., and **Dawson, J.** (1997) Simulated car crashes and crash predictors in drivers with Alzheimer's disease. *Archives of Neurology,* 54, 545–551.

Rizzolatti, G., and **Craighero, L.** (2004) The mirror-neuron system. *Annual Review of Neuroscience,* 27, 169–192.

Robertson, L. C., and **Sagiv, N.** (2005) *Synesthesia: Perspectives from cognitive neuroscience.* New York: Oxford University Press.

Robinson, D. L., Bowman, E. M., and **Kertzman, C.** (1995) Covert orienting of attention in macaques. II. Contributions of parietal cortex. *Journal of Neurophysiology,* 74, 698–712.

Rock, I., and **Mitchener, K.** (1992) Further evidence of failure of reversal of ambiguous figures by uninformed subjects. *Perception,* 21, 39–45.

Rock, I., and **Victor, J.** (1964) Vision and touch: An experimentally created conflict between the two senses. *Science,* 143, 594–596.

Röder, B., Teder-Sälajärvi, W., Sterr, A., Rösler, F., Hillyard, S. A., and **Neville, H. J.** (1999) Improved auditory spatial tuning in blind humans. *Nature,* 400, 162–166.

Rodieck, R.W. (1998) *The first steps in seeing.* Sunderland: Sinauer Associates.

Rodin, J., Bartoshuk, L., Peterson, C., and **Schank, D.** (1990) Bulimia and taste: Possible interactions. *Journal of Abnormal Psychology,* 99, 32–39.

Roelfsema, P. R., Scholte, H. S., and **Spekreijse, H.** (1999) Temporal constraints on the grouping of contour segments into spatially extended objects. *Vision Research,* 39, 1509–1529.

Rogers, B. J., and **Collett, T. S.** (1989) The appearance of surfaces specified by motion parallax and binocular disparity. *Quarterly Journal of Experimental Psychology,* 41A, 697–717.

Rogers, B. J., and **Graham, M. E.** (1979) Motion parallax as an independent cue for depth perception. *Perception,* 8, 125–134.

Rogers, B. J., and **Graham, M. E.** (1984) Aftereffects from motion parallax and stereoscopic depth: Similarities and interactions. In L. Spillmann and B. R. Wooten (eds.), *Sensory experience, adaptation, and perception.* Hillsdale, N.J.: Erlbaum, 603–619.

Roland, P. E. (1976) Focal increase of cerebral blood flow during stereognostic testing in man. *Archives of Neurology,* 33, 551–558.

Rolls, B. (1986) Sensory-specific satiety. *Nutrition Reviews,* 44, 93–101.

Rolls, B., Van Duijvenvoorde, P. M., and **Rolls, E. T.** (1984) Pleasantness changes and food intake in a varied four-course meal. *Appetite,* 5, 337–348.

Rolls, E. T. (2000) The representation of umami taste in the taste cortex. *Journal of Nutrition,* 130, 960S–965S.

Rolls, E. T., Critchley, H. D., Browning, A., and **Hernadi, I.** (1998) The neurophysiology of taste and olfaction in primates, and umami flavor. *Annals of the New York Academy of Science,* 855, 426–437.

Romanski, L. M., Tian, B., Fritz, J., Mishkin, M., Goldman-Rakic, P. S., and **Rauschecker, J. P.** (1999) Dual streams of auditory afferents target multiple domains in the primate prefrontal cortex. *Nature Neuroscience,* 2, 1131–1136.

Ronchi, V. (1970) *The nature of light: An historical survey.* Cambridge: Harvard University Press.

Roorda, A., and **Williams, D. R.** (1999) The arrangement of the three cone classes in the living human eye. *Nature,* 397, 520–522.

Roper, S. D. (1992) The microphysiology of peripheral taste organs. *Journal of Neuroscience,* 12, 1127–1134.

Rorden, C., and **Karnath, H.-O.** (2004) Using human brain lesions to infer function: A relic from a past era in the fMRI age? *Nature Review Neuroscience,* 5, 813–819.

Rose, J. E., Brugge, J. F., Anderson, D. J., and **Hind, J. E.** (1967) Phase-locked response to low-frequency tones in single auditory nerve fibers of the squirrel monkey. *Journal of Neurophysiology,* 30, 769–793.

Rossi, A. F., Rittenhouse, C. D., and **Paradiso, M. A.** (1996) The representation of brightness in primary visual cortex. *Science,* 273, 1104–1107.

Rotello, C. M., Macmillan, N. A., and **Reeder, J. A.** (2004) Sum-difference theory of remembering and knowing: A two-dimensional signal-detection model. *Psychological Review,* 111, 588–616.

Rousselet, G. A., Fabre-Thorpe, M., and **Thorpe, S. J.** (2002) Parallel processing in high-level categorization of natural images. *Nature Neuroscience,* 5, 629–630.

Royster, J. D., Royster, L. H., and **Killion, M. C.** (1991) Sound exposures and hearing thresholds of symphony orchestra musicians. *Journal of the Acoustical Society of America,* 89, 2793–2803.

Rozin, P. (1978) The use of characteristic flavorings in human culinary practice. In C. M. Apt (ed.), *Flavor: Its chemical, behavioral, and commercial aspects. Proceedings of the Arthur D. Little Symposium.* Boulder, Colo.: Westview Press, 101–128.

Rozin, P. (1979) Preference and affect in food selection. In J. H. A. Kroeze (ed.), *Preference behavior and chemoreception.* London: Information Retrieval, 289–302.

Rozin, P. (1982) "Taste-smell confusions" and the duality of the olfactory sense. *Perception & Psychophysics,* 31, 397–401.

Ruben, R. J. (1992) The ontogeny of human hearing. *Acta Otolaryngology,* 112, 192–196.

Rubin, G. S., and **Turano, K.** (1992) Reading without saccadic eye movements. *Vision Research* 32, 895–902.

Rucker, C. W. (1971) *A history of the ophthalmoscope.* Rochester, Minn.: Whiting.

Rushton, W. A. H. (1965) Visual adaptation. The Ferrier Lecture. *Proceedings of the Royal Society of London (Series B),* 162, 20–46.

Rushton, W. A. H. (1979) King Charles II and the blind spot. *Vision Research,* 19, 225.

Russel, M. J. (1976) Human olfactory communication. *Nature,* 260, 520–522.

Russell, I. J. (1987) The physiology of the organ of Corti. *British Medical Bulletin,* 43, 802–820.

Russell, J. A., Bachorowski, J. A., and **Fernández-Dols, J. M.** (2003) Facial and vocal expressions of emotion. *Annual Review of Psychology,* 54, 329–349.

Rutherford, M. D., Baron-Cohen, S., and Wheelwright, S. (2002) Reading the minds in the voice: A study with normal adults and adults with Asperger syndrome and high functioning autism. *Journal of Autism and Developmental Disorders, 32,* 189–194.

Rüttiger, L., Braun, D. I., Gegenfurtner, K. R., Petersen, D., Schönle, P., and Sharpe, L. T. (1999) Selective color constancy deficits after circumscribed unilateral brain lesions. *Journal of Neuroscience, 19,* 3094–3106.

Sacks, O. (1985) *The man who mistook his wife for a hat, and other clinical tales.* New York: Summit Books.

Sacks, O. (1995) *An anthropologist on Mars.* New York: Knopf.

Sadato, N., Pascual-Leone, A., Grafman, J., Ibanez, V., Deiber, M.-P., Dold, G., and Hallett, M. (1996) Activation of the primary visual cortex by Braille reading in blind subjects. *Nature, 380,* 526–528.

Saffran, J. R. (2003) Absolute pitch in infancy and adulthood: The role of tonal structure. *Developmental Science, 6,* 35–47.

Safire, W. (1979) Mondegreens: I led the pigeons to the flag. *New York Times Magazine,* May 27, 9–10.

Sakai, K., Hikosaka, O., Miyauchi, S., Takino, R., Tamada, T., Iwata, N. K., and Nielsen, M. (1999) Neural representation of a rhythm depends on its interval ratio. *Journal of Neuroscience, 19,* 10074–10081.

Salzman, C. D., Murasugi, C. M., Britten, K. H., and Newsome, W. T. (1992) Microstimulation in visual Area MT: Effects on direction discrimination performance. *Journal of Neuroscience, 12,* 2331–2355.

Sample, P. A., Boynton, R. M., and Weinreb, R. N. (1988) Isolating the color vision loss in primary open-angle glaucoma. *American Journal of Ophthalmology, 106,* 686–691.

Samuel, A. G. (1989) Insights from a failure of selective adaptation: Syllable-initial and syllable-final consonants are different. *Perception & Psychophysics, 45,* 485–493.

Sandhana, L. (2004) Fingertips "read" text messages. *BBC News World Edition,* Thursday, April 22.

Sary, G., Vogels, R., and Orban, G. (1993) Cue-invariant shape selectivity of macaque inferior temporal neurons. *Science, 260,* 995–997.

Sathian, K., and Zangaladze, A. (1996) Tactile spatial acuity at the human fingertip and lip: Bilateral symmetry and interdigit variability. *Neurology, 46,* 1464–1466.

Sauvan, X. M., and Peterhans, E. (1999) Orientation constancy in neurons of monkey visual cortex. *Visual Cognition, 6,* 43–54.

Savelsbergh, G. J. P., Whiting, H. T. A., and Bootsma, R. J. (1991) Grasping tau. *Journal of Experimental Psychology: Human Perception and Performance, 17,* 315–322.

Sawatari, A., and Callaway, E. M. (1996) Convergence of magno- and parvocellular pathways in layer 4B of macaque primary visual cortex. *Nature, 380,* 442–446.

Saygin, A. P., Wilson, S. M., Hagler, D. J., Jr., Bates, E., and Sereno, M. I. (2004) Point-light biological motion perception activates human premotor cortex. *Journal of Neuroscience, 24,* 6181–6188.

Schaal, B. (1988) Olfaction in infants and children: Developmental and functional perspectives. *Chemical Senses, 13,* 145–190.

Schab, F. R. (1991) Odor memory: Taking stock. *Psychological Bulletin, 109,* 242–251.

Schall, J. D. (1991) Neural basis of saccadic eye movements in primates. In A. G. Leventhal (ed.), *The neural basis of visual function.* London: Macmillan, 388–442.

Schechter, P. J., and Henkin, R. I. (1974) Abnormalities of taste and smell after head trauma. *Journal of Neurology, Neurosurgery, and Psychiatry, 37,* 802–810.

Schein, O. D., West, S., Munoz, B., Vitale, S., Maguire, M., Taylor, H. R., and Bressler, N. M. (1994) Cortical lenticular opacification: Distribution and location in a longitudinal study. *Investigative Ophthalmology & Visual Science, 35,* 363–366.

Schein, S. J., and Desimone, R. (1990) Spectral properties of V4 neurons in the macaque. *Journal of Neuroscience, 10,* 3369–3389.

Schenk, T., and Zihl, J. (1997) Visual motion perception after brain damage: II. Deficits in form-from-motion perception. *Neuropsychologia, 35,* 1299–1310.

Schiff, W. (1965) Perception of impending collision. *Psychological Monographs, 79,* 1–26.

Schiffman, H. R. (1967) Size estimation of familiar objects under informative and reduced conditions of viewing. *American Journal of Psychology, 80,* 229–235.

Schiffman, S. S. (1974) Physiochemical correlates of olfactory quality. *Science, 185,* 112–117.

Schiffman, S. S. (1997) Taste and smell losses in normal aging and disease. *Journal of the American Medical Association, 278,* 1357–1362.

Schiffman, S. S., and Erickson, R. P. (1980) The issue of primary tastes versus a taste continuum. *Neuroscience & Biobehavioral Reviews, 4,* 109–117.

Schiffman, S. S., Reynolds, M. L., and Young, F. L. (1981) *Introduction to multidimensional scaling.* New York: Academic Press.

Schiller, P. H., and Logothetis, N. K. (1990) The color-opponent and broad-band channels in the primate visual system. *Trends in Neurosciences, 13,* 392–398.

Schiller, P. H., and Colby, C. L. (1983) The responses of single cells in the lateral geniculate nucleus of the rhesus monkey to color and luminance contrast. *Vision Research, 23,* 1631–1641.

Schlagel, R. H. (1984) A reasonable reply to Hume's scepticism. *British Journal of the Philosophy of Science, 35,* 359–374.

Schmidt, E. M., Bak, M. J., Hambrecht, F. T., Kufta, C. V., O'Rourke, D. K., and Vallabhanath, P. (1996) Feasibility of a visual prosthesis for the blind based on intracortical microstimulation of the visual cortex. *Brain, 119,* 507–522.

Schneider, G. E. (1969) Two visual systems. *Science, 163,* 895–902.

Scholl, B. J. (2001) Objects and attention: The state of the art. *Cognition, 80,* 1–46. (Special issue on "Objects and attention.")

Schoups, A. A., Vogels, R., and Orban, G. A. (1995) Human perceptual learning in identifying the oblique orientation: Retinotopy, orientation specificity and monocularity. *Journal of Physiology: London, 483,* 797–810.

Schultz, G., and Melzack, R. (1991) The Charles Bonnet syndrome: "Phantom visual images." *Perception, 20,* 809–826.

Schwartz, B. S., Doty, R. L., Monroe, C., Frye, R., and Barker, S. (1989) Olfactory function in chemical workers exposed to acrylate and methacrylate vapors. *American Journal of Public Health, 79,* 613–618.

Schwartz, J.-L., Berthommier, F., and Savariaux, C. (2004) Seeing to hear better: Evidence for early audio-visual interactions in speech identification. *Cognition, 93,* B69–B78.

Schwartz, O., and Simoncelli, E. P. (2001) Natural signal statistics and sensory gain control. *Nature Neuroscience, 4,* 819–825.

Schyns, P. G., and Oliva, O. (1997) Flexible diagnosticity-driven, rather than fixed, perceptually determined scale selection and face recognition. *Perception, 26,* 1027–1038.

Scott, S. K., and Johnsrude, I. S. (2003) The neuroanatomical and functional organization of speech perception. *Trends in Neurosciences, 26,* 100–107.

Seagraves, M. A., Goldberg, M. E., Deng, S. Y., Bruce, C. J., Ungerleider, L. G., and Mishkin, M. (1987) The role of striate cortex in the guidance of eye movements in the monkey. *Journal of Neuroscience, 7,* 776–794.

Searle, J. (1987) Minds and brains without programs. In C. Blakemore and S. Greenfield (eds.) *Mindwaves.* Oxford: Blackwell, 209–233.

Segal, S. J., and Fusella, V. (1970) Influence of imaged pictures and sounds on detection of visual and auditory signals. *Journal of Experimental Psychology, 83,* 458–464.

Seifritz, E., Esposito, F., Hennel, F., Mustovic, H., Neuhoff, J. G., Bilecen, D., Tedeschi, G., Scheffler, K., and Di Salle, F. (2002) Spatiotemporal pattern of neural processing in the human auditory cortex. *Science, 297,* 1706–1708.

Seifritz, E., Neuhoff, J. G., Bilecen, D., Scheffler, K., Mustovic, H., Schachinger, H., Elefante, R., and Di Salle, F. (2002) Neural processing of auditory looming in the human brain. *Current Biology, 12,* 2147–2151.

Sekuler, A. B., and Palmer, S. E. (1992) Perception of partly occluded objects: A microgenetic analysis. *Journal of Experimental Psychology: General, 121,* 95–111.

Sekuler, A. B., and Sekuler, R. (1999) Collisions between moving visual targets: What controls alternative ways of seeing an ambiguous display? *Perception, 28,* 415–432.

Sekuler, R. (1996) Motion perception: A modern view of Wertheimer's 1912 monograph. *Perception, 25,* 1243–1258.

Sekuler, R., and Blake, R. (1999) *Star Trek on the brain: Alien minds, human minds.* New York: W. H. Freeman.

Sekuler, R., Owsley, C. J., and Berenberg, R. (1986) Contrast sensitivity during provoked visual impairment in multiple sclerosis. *Ophthalmic and Physiological Optics, 6,* 229–232.

Sekuler, R., Nash, D., and Armstrong, R. (1973) Sensitive, objective procedure for evaluating response to light touch. *Neurology, 23,* 1282–1291.

Sekuler, R., and Sekuler, A. B. (2000) Visual perception and cognition. In J. G. Evans, T. F. Williams, G. K. Wilcox, J.-P. Michel, B. L. Beattie, and G. K. Wilcock (eds.) *Oxford Textbook of Geriatric Medicine,* 2nd ed. Oxford: Oxford University Press, 874–880.

Sekuler, R., Sekuler, A. B., and Lau, R. (1997) Sound alters visual motion perception. *Nature, 385,* 308.

Sekuler, R., Watamaniuk, S. N. J., and Blake, R. (2002) Visual motion perception. In H. Pashler (Series Ed.) & S. Yantis (vol. Ed.), *Stevens' handbook of experimental psychology: vol. 1. Sensation and perception,* 3rd ed. New York: Wiley.

Sengpiel, F., Stawinski, P., and Bonhoeffer, T. (1999) Influence of experience on orientation maps in cat visual cortex. *Nature Neuroscience, 2,* 727–732.

Sergent, J. (1993) Music, the brain and Ravel. *Trends in Neurosciences, 16,* 168–171.

Sergent, J., and Poncet, M. (1990) From covert to overt recognition of faces in a prosopagnostic patient. *Brain, 113,* 989–1004.

Sergent, J., and Villemure, J.-G. (1989) Prosopagnosia in a right hemispherectomized patient. *Brain, 112,* 975–995.

Seyfarth, R. M., and Cheney, D. L. (1984) The natural vocalizations of non-human primates. *Trends in Neurosciences, 7,* 66–73.

Shams, L., Kamitani, Y., and Shimojo, S. (2000) What you see is what you hear. *Nature, 408,* 788.

Shannon, R. V., Zeng, F.-G., Kamath, V., Wygonski, J., and Ekelid, M. (1995) Speech recognition with primarily temporal cues. *Science, 270,* 303–304.

Shapley, R. (1996) Art and perception of nature: Illusory contours in the paintings of Ellsworth Kelly. *Perception, 25,* 1259–1261.

Shapley, R., and Hawken, M. (2002) Neural mechanisms for color perception in the primary visual cortex. *Current Opinion in Neurobiology, 12,* 426–432.

Sharpe, L. T., and Nordby, K. (1990) Total colour-blindness: An introduction. In R. F. Hess, L. T. Sharpe, and K. Nordby (eds.), *Night vision: Basic, clinical and applied aspects.* Cambridge: Cambridge University Press, 253–289.

Shaw, E. A. G. (1974) Transformation of sound pressure level from the free field to the eardrum in the horizontal plane. *Journal of the Acoustical Society of America, 56,* 1848–1861.

Shaw, R., and Bransford, J. (1977) Introduction: Psychological approaches to the problem of knowledge. In R. Shaw and J. Bransford (eds.), *Perceiving, acting, and knowing.* Hillsdale, N.J.: Erlbaum, 1–39.

Sheinberg, D. L., and Logothetis, N. K. (2001) Noticing familiar objects in real world scenes: The role of temporal cortical neurons in natural vision. *Journal of Neuroscience, 21,* 1340–1350.

Shepard, R. N. (1981) Psychophysical complementarity. In M. Kubovy and J. R. Pomerantz (eds.), *Perceptual organization.* Hillsdale, N.J.: Erlbaum, pp. 279–341.

Shepard, R. N., and Cooper, L. A. (1982) *Mental images and their transformations.* Cambridge: MIT Press.

Sherman, S. M., and Guillery, R. W. (2002) The role of the thalamus in the flow of information to the cortex. *Philosophical Transactions of the Royal Society of London (Series B), 357,* 1695–1708.

Sherrick, C. E. (1964) Effects of double simultaneous stimulation of the skin. *American Journal of Psychology, 77,* 42–53.

Shevell, S. K., and Wei, J. (1998) Chromatic induction: Border contrast or adaptation to surrounding light? *Vision Research, 38,* 1561–1566.

Shiffrar, M., and **Freyd, J. J.** (1990) Apparent motion of the human body. *Psychological Science, 1,* 257–264.

Shiu, L. P., and **Pashler, H.** (1992) Improvement in line orientation discrimination is retinally local but dependent on cognitive set. *Perception & Psychophysics, 52,* 582–588

Shulman, G. L., Ollinger, J. M., Akbudak, E., Conturo, T. E., Snyder, A. Z., Petersen, S. E., and **Corbetta, M.** (1999) Areas involved in encoding and applying directional expectations to moving objects. *Journal of Neuroscience, 19,* 9480–9496.

Shutty, M. S., Cunduff, G., and **DeGood, D. E.** (1992) Pain complaint and the weather: Weather sensitivity and symptom complaints in chronic pain patients. *Pain, 49,* 199–204.

Siegel, J. A., and **Siegel, W.** (1977) Absolute identification of notes and intervals by musicians. *Perception & Psychophysics, 21,* 143–152.

Siegel, R. K. (1984) Hostage hallucinations: Visual imagery induced by isolation and life-threatening stress. *Journal of Nervous and Mental Disease, 172,* 264–272.

Sigala, N., and **Logothetis, N. K.** (2002) Visual categorization shapes feature selectivity in the primate temporal cortex. *Nature, 415,* 318–320.

Simoncelli, E. P. (2003) Vision and statistics of the visual environment. *Current Opinions in Neurobiology, 13,* 144–149.

Simoncelli, E. P., and **Olshausen, B.** (2001) Natural image statistics and neural representation. *Annual Review of Neuroscience, 24,* 1193–1216.

Simons, D. J. (2000) Attentional capture and inattentional blindness. *Trends in Cognitive Sciences, 4,* 147–155.

Simons, D. J., and **Chabris, C. F.** (1999) Gorillas in our midst: Sustained inattentional blindness for dynamic events. *Perception, 28,* 1059–1074.

Simons, D. J., and **Levin, D. T.** (1998) Failure to detect changes in people in real-world interactions. *Psychonomic Bulletin & Review, 5,* 644–649.

Sinai, M. J., Ooi, T. L., and **He, Z. H.** (1998) Terrain influences the accurate judgment of distance. *Nature, 395,* 497–500.

Singer, W., Tretter, F., and **Yinon, U.** (1979) Inverted vision causes selective loss of striate cortex neurons with binocular, vertically oriented receptive fields. *Brain Research, 170,* 177–181.

Singh, M., and **Hoffman, D. D.** (1998) Part boundaries alter the perception of transparency. *Psychological Science, 9,* 370–378.

Sinnott, J., Beecher, M., Moody, D., and **Stebbins, W.** (1976) Speech and sound discrimination by monkeys and humans. *Journal of the Acoustical Society of America, 60,* 687–695.

Sivak, J. G. (1976) Optics of the eye of the "four-eyed fish" (Anableps anableps). *Vision Research, 16,* 531–534.

Sjoberg, S. A., Neitz, M., Balding, S. D., and **Neitz, J.** (1998) L-cone pigment genes expressed in normal color vision. *Vision Research, 38,* 3213–3219.

Small, D. M., Zatorre, R. J., and **Jones-Gotman, M.** (2001) Changes in taste intensity perception following anterior temporal lobe removal in humans. *Chemical Senses, 26,* 425–432.

Smith, A. T. (1994) Correspondence-based and energy-based detection of second-order motion in human vision. *Journal of the Optical Society of America A, 11,* 1940–1948.

Smith, M., Smith, L. G., and **Levinson, B.** (1982) The use of smell in differential diagnosis. *Lancet, 2,* 1452.

Smith, V. C., and **Pokorny, J.** (1975) Spectral sensitivity of the foveal cone photopigments between 400 and 500 nm. *Vision Research, 15,* 161–71.

Snowden, R. J. (1999) Visual perception: Here's mud in your eye. *Current Biology, 9,* R336–R337.

Snowden, R. J., and **Hammett, S. T.** (1996) Spatial frequency adaptation: Threshold elevation and perceived contrast. *Vision Research, 36,* 1797–1809.

Snowden, R. J., and **Verstraten, F. A. J.** (1999) Motion transparency: Making models of motion perception transparent. *Trends in Cognitive Sciences, 3,* 369–377.

Snyder, A. W., and **Barlow, H. B.** (1988) Revealing the artist's touch. *Nature, 331,* 117–118.

Snyder, S. H., Sklar, P. B., Hwang, P. M., and **Pevsner, J.** (1989) Molecular mechanisms of olfaction. *Trends in Neurosciences, 12,* 35–38.

Sobel, N., Khan, R. M., Hartley, C. A., Sullivan E. V., and **Gabrieli, J. D.** (2000) Sniffing longer rather than stronger to maintain olfactory detection threshold. *Chemical Senses, 25,* 1–8.

Sobel, N., Khan, R. M., Saltman, A., Sullivan, E. V., and **Gabrieli, J. D. E.** (1999) The world smells different to each nostril. *Nature, 402,* 35.

Sobel, N., Prabhakaran, V., Desmond, J. E., Glover, G. H., Goode, R .L., Sullivan, E. V., and **Gabrieli, J. D. E.** (1998) Sniffing and smelling: Separate subsystems in the human olfactory cortex. *Nature, 392,* 282–286.

Sobel, N., Prabhakaran, V., Zhao, Z., Desmond, J. E., Glover, G. H., Sullivan, E. V., and **Gabrieli, J. D. E.** (2000) Time course of odorant-induced activation in the human primary olfactory cortex. *Journal of Neurophysiology, 83,* 537–551.

Sobel, N., Thomason, M. E., Stappen, I., Tanner, C. M., Tetrud, J. W., Bower, J. M., Sullivan, E. V., and **Gabrieli, J. D. E.** (2001) An impairment in sniffing contributes to the olfactory impairment in Parkinson's disease. *Proceedings of the National Academy of Sciences: USA, 98,* 4154–4159.

Someya, T., Sekitani, T., Iba, S., Kato, Y., Kawaguchi, H., and **Sakurai, T.** (2004) A large-area, flexible pressure matrix with organic field-effect transistors for artificial skin applications. *Proceedings of the National Academy of Sciences: USA, 101,* 9966–9970. E-pub June 28.

Southall, J. P. C. (1937/1961) *Introduction to physiological optics.* New York: Dover.

Sowden, P. T., Davies, I. R., and **Roling, P.** (2000) Perceptual learning of the detection of features in X-ray images: A functional role for improvements in adults' visual sensitivity? *Journal of Experimental Psychology: Human Perception and Performance, 26,* 379–390.

Spalding J. A. (2004) Confessions of a colour blind physician. *Clinical and Experimental Optometry, 87,* 344–349.

Sparks, D. L. (1988) Neural cartography: Sensory and motor maps in the superior colliculus. *Brain, Behavior and Evolution, 31,* 49–56.

Spelke, E. S., Breinlinger, K., Jacobson, K., and **Phillips, A.** (1993) Gestalt relations and object perception: A developmental study. *Perception, 22,* 1483–1502.

Sperling, G., Budiansky, J., Spivak, J. G., and **Johnson, M. C.** (1971) Extremely rapid visual search: The maximum rate of scanning letters for the presence of a numeral. *Science,* 174, 307–311.

Sperling, G., and **Lu, Z. L.** (1998) A system analysis of visual motion perception. In T. Watanabe (ed.), *High-level motion processing: Computational, neurobiological, and psychophysical perspectives.* Cambridge: MIT Press, 154–183.

Sperry, R. W. (1964) Problems outstanding in the evolution of brain function. James Arthur Lecture. New York: American Museum of Natural History. Reprinted (1977) In: R. Duncan and M. Weston-Smith (Eds.), *Encyclopedia of ignorance,* pp. 423–433. Oxford: Pergamon Press.

Sperry, R. W. (1980) Mind-brain interaction: Mentalism, yes; Dualism, no. *Neurosciences,* 5, 195–206.

Spillmann, L. (1994) The Hermann grid illusion: A tool for studying human perceptive field organization. *Perception,* 23, 691–708.

Srinivasan, R. J., and **Massaro, D.W.** (2003) Perceiving prosody from the face and voice: Distinguishing statements from echoic questions in English. *Language and Speech,* 46, 1–22.

Stabell, U., Stabell, B., and **Fugelli, A.** (1992) Mechanisms of long-term dark adaptation. *Scandinavian Journal of Psychology,* 33, 12–19.

Steel, K. P. (1998) Progress in progressive hearing loss. *Science,* 279, 1870–1871.

Steel, K. P., and **Brown, S. D. M.** (1998) More deafness genes. *Science,* 280, 1403.

Stein, B. E., Wallace, M. T., and **Meredith, M. A.** (1995) Neural mechanisms mediating attention and orientation to multisensory cues. In M. S. Gazzaniga (ed.), *The cognitive neurosciences.* Cambridge: MIT Press, 683–702.

Stein, B. E., Jiang, W., and **Stanford, T. R.** (2004) Multisensory integration in single neurons of the midbrain. In G. Calvert, C. Spence and B. E. Stein (eds.), *The handbook of multisensory processes.* Cambridge: MIT Press/Bradford Books, 243–264.

Steinbach, M. J., and **Money, K. E.** (1973) Eye movements of the owl. *Vision Research,* 13, 889–891.

Steinman, R. M. (2004) Gaze control under natural conditions. In L. M. Chalupa and J. S. Werner (eds.), *The visual neurosciences,* vol. 2, MIT Press, 1339–1356.

Steinman, R. M., Kowler, E., and **Collewijn, H.** (1990) New directions for oculomotor research. *Vision Research,* 30, 1845–1864.

Steinschneider, M., Arezzo, J., and **Vaughn, H. G.** (1982) Speech-evoked activity in the auditory radiations and cortex of the awake monkey. *Brain Research,* 252, 353–365.

Sterr, A., Muller, M. M., Elbert, T., Rockstroh, B., Pantev, C., and **Taub, E.** (1998) Perceptual correlates of changes in cortical representation of fingers in blind multifinger Braille readers. *Journal of Neuroscience,* 18, 4417–4423.

Stevens, C. F. (2001) An evolutionary scaling law for the primate visual system and its basis in cortical function. *Nature,* 411, 193–195.

Stevens, J. C. (1979) Thermo-tactile interactions: Some influences of temperature on touch. In D. R. Kenshalo (ed.), *Sensory function of the skin of humans.* New York: Plenum Press.

Stevens, J. C., and **Cain, W. S.** (1986) Aging and the perception of nasal irritation. *Physiology & Behavior,* 37, 323–328.

Stevens, J. C., and **Choo, K. K.** (1998) Temperature sensitivity of the body surface over the life span. *Somatosensory and Motor Research,* 15, 13–28.

Stevens, J. C., and **Patterson, M. Q.** (1995) Dimensions of spatial acuity in the touch sense: changes over the life span. *Somatosensory and Motor Research,* 12, 29–47.

Stevens, K. A. (1981) The information content of texture gradients. *Biological Cybernetics,* 42, 95–105.

Stevens, K. A. (1983) Evidence relating subjective contours and interpretations involving interposition. *Perception,* 12, 491–500.

Stevens, K. A., and **Brookes, A.** (1988) Integrating stereopsis with monocular interpretations of planar surfaces. *Vision Research,* 28, 371–386.

Stevens, S. S. (1956) The direct estimation of sensory magnitude—Loudness. *American Journal of Psychology,* 69, 1–25.

Stevens, S. S. (1960) Psychophysics of sensory function. *American Scientist,* 48, 226–252.

Stevens, S. S. (1975) *Psychophysics: An introduction to its perceptual, neural, and social prospects.* New York: John Wiley & Sons.

Stevens, S. S., and **Newman, E. B.** (1934) The localization of pure tones. *Proceedings of the National Academy of Sciences: USA,* 20, 593–596.

Stevens, S. S., and **Warshofsky, F.** (1965) *Sound and hearing.* Morristown, N.J.: Time-Life Books.

Stewart, L., Ellison, A., Walsh, V., and **Cowey, A.** (2001) The role of transcranial magnetic stimulation (TMS) in studies of vision, attention and cognition. *Acta Psychologica,* 107, 275–291.

Stickgold, R., James, L., and **Hobson, J. A.** (2000) Visual discrimination learning requires sleep after training. *Nature Neuroscience,* 3, 1237–1238.

Stoerig, P., Ludowig, E., Meijer, P., and **Pascual-Leone, A.** (2004) Seeing through the ears? Presented at the Fourth Forum of European Neuroscience, Lisbon, Portugal. Available online at <http://www.visualprosthesis.com/voice.htm>

Stoffregen, T. A., and **Pittenger, J. B.** (1995) Human echolocation as a basic form of perception and action. *Ecological Psychology,* 7, 181–216.

Stokstad, E. (2003) Peering into ancient ears. *Science,* 302, 770–771.

Stone, H., and **Pryor, G.** (1967) Some properties of the olfactory system of man. *Perception & Psychophysics,* 2, 516–518.

Stone, J. V. (1998) Object recognition using spatiotemporal signatures. *Vision Research,* 38, 947–951.

Storr, A. (1992) *Music and the mind.* New York: Ballatine Books.

Stratton, G. M. (1897) Vision without inversion of the retinal image. *Psychological Review,* 4, 341–360.

Stypulkowski, P. H. (1990) Mechanisms of salicylate ototoxicity. *Hearing Research,* 46, 113–146.

Suga, N. (1990) Biosonar and neural computation in bats. *Scientific American,* 262, 60–68.

Sugase, Y., Yamane, S., Ueno, S., and **Kawano, K.** (1999) Global and fine information coded by single neurons in the temporal visual cortex. *Nature,* 400, 869–872.

Sugita, Y. (2004) Experience in early infancy is indispensable for color perception. *Current Biology,* 14, 1267–1271.

Summerfield, Q. (1975) How a full account of segmental perception depends on prosody and vice versa. In A. Cohen and S. G. Nooteboom (eds.), *Structure and process in speech perception.* New York: Springer-Verlag, 51–68.

Summerfield, Q. (1992) Lipreading and audio-visual speech perception. *Philosophical Transactions of the Royal Society of London (Series B),* 335, 71–78.

Súper, H., van der Togt, C., Spekreijse, H., and **Lamme, V. A. F.** (2003) Internal state of monkey primary visual cortex (V1) predicts figure-ground perception. *Journal of Neuroscience,* 23, 3407–3414.

Sur, M., Garraghty, P. E., and **Roe, A. W.** (1988) Experimentally induced visual projections into auditory thalamus and cortex. *Science,* 242, 1437–1441.

Süskind, P. (1986) *Perfume: The story of a murderer.* J. E. Woods (trans.). New York: A. A. Knopf.

Svirsky, M. A., Robbins, A. M., Kirk, K. I., Pisoni, D., and **Miyamoto, R. T.** (2000) Language development in profoundly deaf children with cochlear implants. *Psychological Science,* 11, 153–159.

Swets, J. A., Dawes, R. M., and **Monahan, J.** (2000) Psychological science can improve diagnostic decisions. *Psychological Science in the Public Interest,* 11–26.

Swets, J. A., Tanner, W. P., Jr., and **Birdsall, T. G.** (1961) Decision processes in perception. *Psychological Review,* 68, 301–340.

Swift, J. (1726/1890) *Gulliver's travels.* London: George Routledge and Sons.

Syrkin., G., and **Gur, M.** (1997) Colour and luminance interact to improve pattern recognition. *Perception,* 26, 127–140.

Tai, Y. F., Scherfler, C., Brooks, D. J., Sawamoto, N., and **Castiello, U.** (2004) The human premotor cortex is "mirror" only for biological actions. *Current Biology,* 14, 117–120.

Talamo, B. R., Rudel, R., Kosik, K. S., Lee, V. M.-Y., Adelman, L., and **Kauer, J. S.** (1989) Pathological changes in olfactory neurons in patients with Alzheimer's disease. *Nature,* 337, 736–739.

Talarico, J. M., and **Rubin, D. C.** (2003) Confidence, not consistency, characterizes flashbulb memories. *Psychological Science,* 14, 455–461.

Tallal, P., Miller, S. L., Bedi, G., Byma, G., Wang, X., Nagarajan, S. S., Schreiner, C., Jenkins, W. M., and **Merzenich, M. M.** (1996) Language comprehension in language-learning impaired children improved with acoustically modified speech. *Science,* 271, 81–84.

Tallal, P., and **Piercy, M.** (1973) Defects of non-verbal auditory perception in chilrden with developmental aphasia. *Nature,* 2412, 468–469.

Tanaka, K. (1997) Mechanisms of visual object recognition: Monkey and human studies. *Current Opinion in Neurobiology,* 7, 523–529.

Tanaka, K., Fukada, Y., and **Saito, H.** (1989) Underlying mechanisms of the response specificity of expansion/contraction and rotation cells in the dorsal part of the medial superior temporal area of the macaque monkey. *Journal of Neurophysiology,* 62, 642–656.

Tanaka, K., and **Saito, H.** (1989) Analysis of motion of the visual field by direction, expansion/contraction, and rotation cells clustered in the dorsal part of the medial superior temporal area of the macaque monkey. *Journal of Neurophysiology,* 62, 626–641.

Tanaka, T. W., and **Farah, M. J.** (1993) Parts and wholes in face recognition. *Quarterly Journal of Experimental Psychology,* 46A, 225–245.

Tanaka, Y., Kamo, T., Yoshida, M., and **Yamadori, A.** (1991) So-called cortical deafness. *Brain,* 114, 2385–2401.

Tarr, M. J. (1995) Rotating objects to recognize them: A case study on the role of viewpoint dependency in the recognition of three-dimensional objects. *Psychonomic Bulletin and Review,* 2, 55–82.

Tartter, V. C. (1991) Identifiability of vowels and speakers from whispered syllables. *Perception & Psychophysics,* 49, 365–372.

Taylor, C. A. (1965) *The physics of musical sounds.* New York: Elsevier.

Taylor, M. M., and **Williams, E.** (1966) Acoustic trauma in the sports hunter. *Laryngoscope,* 76, 969–979.

Taylor, R. (1994) Brave new nose: Sniffing out human sexual chemistry. *Journal of NIH Research,* 6, 47–51.

Taylor, W. (1988) Biological effects of the hand-arm vibration syndrome: Historical perspective and current research. *Journal of the Acoustical Society of America,* 83, 415–422.

Teghtsoonian, R., Teghtsoonian, M., Berglund, B., and **Berglund, U.** (1978) Invariance of odor strength with sniff vigor: An olfactory analogue to size constancy. *Journal of Experimental Psychology: Human Perception and Performance,* 4, 144–152.

Teller, D. Y. (1989) The domain of visual science. In L. Spillmann and J. S. Werner (eds.), *Visual perception: The neurophysiological foundations.* New York: Academic Press, 11–21.

Teller, D. Y. (1997) First glances: The vision of infants. The Friedenwald lecture. *Investigative Ophthalmology & Visual Science,* 38, 2183–203.

Teller, D. Y., and **Movshon, J. A.** (1986) Visual development. *Vision Research,* 26, 1438–1506.

Tesch-Römer, C. (1997) Psychological effects of hearing aid use in older adults. *Journal of Gerontology: Psychological Sciences,* 52B, P127–P138.

Tetewsky, S. J., and **Duffy, C. J.** (1999) Visual loss and getting lost in Alzheimer's disease. *Neurology,* 52, 958–965.

Teuber, H. L., Battersby, W. S., and **Bender, M. B.** (1960) *Visual field defects after penetrating missle wounds of the brain.* Cambridge: Harvard University Press.

Thiele, A., Henning, P., Kubischik, M., and **Hoffmann, K.-P.** (2002) Neural mechanisms of saccadic suppression. *Science,* 295, 2460–2462.

Thimbleby, H. W., and **Neesham, C.** (1993) How to play tricks with dots. *New Scientist,* 140, 26–29.

Thompson, E., Palacios, A., and **Varela, F. J.** (1992). Ways of coloring: Comparative color vision as a case study for cognitive science. *Behavioral and Brain Sciences,* 15, 1–26.

Thompson, P. (1980) Margaret Thatcher: A new illusion. *Perception,* 9, 483–484.

Thompson, P. (1998) Tuning of the motion aftereffect. In G. Mather, F. Verstraten, and S. Anstis (eds.) *The motion aftereffect: A modern perspective.* Cambridge: MIT Press, 41–55.

Thorn, F., Gwiazda, J., Cruz, A. A. V., Bauer, J. A., and **Held, R.** (1994) The development of eye alignment, convergence, and sensory binocularity in young infants. *Investigative Opthalmology & Visual Science,* 35, 544–553.

Thornbury, J. M., and **Mistretta, C. M.** (1981) Tactile sensitivity as a function of age. *Journal of Gerontology,* 36, 34–39.

Thurlow, W. R., and **Runge, P. S.** (1967) Effect of induced head movements on localization of direction of sounds. *Journal of the Acoustical Society of America,* 42, 480–488.

Timney, B., and **Muir, D. W.** (1976) Orientation anisotropy: Incidence and magnitude in Caucasian and Chinese subjects. *Science,* 193, 699–700.

Titchener, E. B. (1915) *A beginner's psychology.* New York: Macmillan.

Todd, J. T., and **Norman, J. F.** (1991) The visual perception of smoothly curved surfaces from minimal apparent motion sequences. *Perception & Psychophysics,* 50, 509–523.

Todrank, J., and **Bartoshuk, L. M.** (1991) A taste illusion: Taste sensation localized by touch. *Physiology & Behavior,* 50, 1027–1031.

Tolhurst, D. J., and **Tadmor, Y.** (1997) Contrast discrimination in complex images. *Perception,* 26, 1011–1025.

Toller, S. V. (1999) Assessing the impact of anosmia: Review of a questionnaire's findings. *Chemical Senses,* 24, 705–712.

Tong, F., and **Nakayama, K.** (1999) Robust representations for faces: Evidence from visual search. *Journal of Experimental Psychology: Human Perception & Performance,* 25, 1016–1035.

Tonndorf, J. (1987) The analogy between tinnitus and pain: A suggestion for a physiological basis of chronic tinnitus. *Hearing Research,* 28, 271–275.

Tonndorf, J. (1988) The external ear. In A. F. Jahn and J. Santos-Sacchi (eds.), *Physiology of the ear.* New York: Raven Press, 29–39.

Tootell, R. B. H., Hadjikhani, N. K., Mendola, J. D., Marrett, S., and **Dale, A. M.** (1998) From retinotopy to recognition: fMRI in human visual cortex. *Trends in Cognitive Sciences,* 2, 174–183.

Tootell, R. B. H., Mendola, J. D., Hadjikhani, N. K., Ledden, P. J., Liu, A. K., Reppas, J. B., Sereno, M. I., and **Dale, A. M.** (1997) Functional analysis of V3A and related areas in human visual cortex. *Journal of Neuroscience,* 17, 7060–7078.

Tootell, R. B. H., Reppas, J. B., Dale, A. M., Look, R. B., Sereno, M. I., Malach, R., Brady, T. J., and **Rosen, B. R.** (1995a) Visual motion aftereffect in human cortical area MT revealed by magnetic resonance imagery. *Nature,* 375, 139–141.

Tootell, R. B. H., Reppas, J. B., Kwong, K. K., Malach, R., Born, R. T., Brady, T. J., Rosen, B. R., and **Belliveau, J. W.** (1995b) Functional analysis of human MT and related visual cortical areas using magnetic resonance imaging. *Journal of Neuroscience,* 15, 3215–3230.

Torebjork, H. E., Vallbo, A. B., and **Ochoa, J. L.** (1987) Intraneural microstimulation in man: Its relation to specificity of tactile sensations. *Brain,* 110, 1509–1530.

Torrealba, F., Guillery, R. W., Eysel, U., Polley, E. H., and **Mason, C. A.** (1982) Studies of retinal representations within the cat's optic tract. *Journal of Comparative Neurology,* 211, 377–396.

Tovee, M. J. (1994) The molecular genetics and evoluton of primate colour vision. *Trends in Neuroscience,* 17, 30–37.

Tovee, M. J. (1998) Face processing: Getting by with a little help from its friends. *Current Biology,* 8, R317–R320.

Tovee, M. J., Rolls, E.T., and **Ramachandran, V. S.** (1996) Rapid visual learning in neurones of the primate temporal visual cortex. *Neuroreport,* 7, 2757–2760

Tramo, M. J. (2001) Music of the hemispheres. *Science,* 291, 54–56.

Tranel, D., and **Damasio, A. R.** (1985) Knowledge without awareness: An autonomic index of facial recognition by prosopagnosics. *Science,* 228, 1453–1454.

Tranel, D., Damasio, A. R., and **Damasio, H.** (1988) Intact recognition of facial expression, gender, and age in patients with impaired recognition of face identity. *Neurology,* 38, 690–696.

Treede, R. D., Kenshalo, D. R., Gacely, R. H., and **Jones, A. K.** (1999) The cortical representation of pain. *Pain,* 79, 105–111.

Treisman, A. (1986) Features and objects in visual processing. *Scientific American,* 255, 114–125.

Tresilian, J. R. (1999) Visually timed action: Time-out for "tau"? *Trends in Cognitive Sciences,* 3, 301–310.

Treue, S., and **Maunsell, J. H.** (1999) Effects of attention on the processing of motion in macaque middle temporal and medial superior temporal visual cortical areas. *Journal of Neuroscience,* 19, 7591–7602.

Treue, S., and **Trujillo, J. C.** (1999) Feature-based attention influences motion processing gain in macaque visual cortex. *Nature,* 399, 575–579.

Trotier, D., Eloit, C., Wassef, M., Talmain, G., Bensimon, J. L., Doving, K. B., and **Ferrand, J.** (2000) The vomeronasal cavity in adult humans. *Chemical Senses,* 25, 369–380.

Trotter, Y., Celebrini, S., Stricanne, B., Thorpe, S., and **Imbert, M.** (1992) Modulation of neural stereoscopic processing in primate area V1 by the viewing distance. *Science,* 257, 1279–1280.

Turner A. P., and **Magan, N.** (2004) Electronic noses and disease diagnostics. *Nature Reviews Microbiology,* 2, 161–166.

Turner, J., Braunstein, M. L., and **Andersen G. J.** (1995) Detection of surfaces in structure from motion. *Journal of Experimental Psychology: Human Perception & Performance,* 21, 809–821.

Uhlrich, D. J., Essock, E. A., and **Lehmkuhle, S.** (1981) Cross-species correspondence of spatial contrast sensitivity functions. *Behavioral Brain Research,* 2, 291–299.

Vaina, L. M. (1998) Complex motion perception and its deficits. *Current Opinion in Neurobiology,* 8, 494–502.

Vaina, L. M., Solomon, J., Chowdhury, S., Sinha, P., and **Belliveau, J. W.** (2001) Functional neuroanatomy of biological motion perception in humans. *Proceedings of the National Academy of Sciences: USA,* 98, 11656–11661.

Valentine, T. (1988) Upside-down faces: A review of the effect of inversion on face recognition. *British Journal of Psychology,* 79, 471–491.

Vallbo, A. B., and **Hagbarth, K. E.** (1968) Activity from skin mechanoreceptors recorded percutaneously in awake human subjects. *Experimental Neurology,* 21, 270–289.

Vallbo, A. B., and **Johansson, R. S.** (1984) Properties of cutaneous mechanoreceptors in the human hand related to touch sensation. *Human Neurobiology,* 3, 3–14.

Van Boven, R. W., Hamilton, R. H., Kauffman, T., Keenan, J. P., and **Pascual-Leone, A.** (2000) Tactile spatial resolution in blind Braille readers. *Neurology,* 54, 2230–2236.

Van Doren, C. L., Pelli, D. G., and **Verrillo, R. T.** (1987) A device for measuring tactile spatiotemporal sensitivity. *Journal of the Acoustical Society of America,* 81, 1906–1916.

Van Tonder, G. J., and **Ejima, Y.** (2000) Bottom-up clues in target finding: Why a Dalmatian may be mistaken for an elephant. *Perception,* 29, 149–157.

Varney, N. R. (1988) The prognostic significance of anosmia in patients with closed-head trauma. *Journal of Clinical and Experimental Neuropsychology,* 10, 250–254.

Vega-Bermudez, F., and **Johnson, K. O.** (2001) Differences in spatial acuity between digits. *Neurology,* 56, 1389–1391.

Verheijen, F. J. (1963) Apparent relative movement of "unsharp" and "sharp" visual patterns. *Nature,* 199, 160–161.

Verstraten, F. A., Fredericksen, R. E., and **van de Grind, W. A.** (1994) Movement aftereffect of bi-vectorial transparent motion. *Vision Research,* 34, 349–58.

Vienot, F., Brettel, H., M'Barek, A. B., and **Mollon, J. D.** (1995) What do colour-blind people see? *Nature,* 376, 127–128.

Volkmann, F. C., Riggs, L. A., and **Moore, R. K.** (1980) Eyeblinks and visual suppression. *Science,* 207, 900–902.

von der Heydt, R., Peterhans, E., and **Baumgartner, G.** (1984) Illusory contours and cortical neuron responses. *Science,* 234, 1260–1262.

von Hofson, C. (1976) The role of convergence in visual space perception. *Vision Research,* 16, 193–198.

Von Kriegstein, K., Eger, E., Kleinschmidt, A., and **Giraud, A. L.** (2003) Modulation of neural responses to speech by directing attention to voices or verbal content. *Cognitive Brain Research,* 17, 48–55.

von Melchner, L., Pallas, S. L., and **Sur, M.** (2000) Visual behaviour mediated by retinal projections directed to the auditory pathway. *Nature,* 404, 871–876.

von Noorden, G. K. (1981) New clinical aspects of stimulus deprivation amblyopia. *American Journal of Ophthalmology,* 92, 416–421.

Vos, P. G., and **Troost, J. M.** (1989) Ascending and descending melodic intervals: Statistical findings and their perceptual relevance. *Music Perception,* 6, 383–396.

Wachtler, T., Albright, T. D., and **Sejnowski, T. J.** (2001) Nonlocal interactions in color perception: Nonlinear processing of chromatic signals from remote inducers. *Vision Research,* 41, 1535–1546.

Wade, A. R., Brewer, A. A., Rieger, J. W., and **Wandell, B. A.** (2002) Functional measurements of human ventral occipital cortex: Retinotopy and colour. *Philosophical Transactions of the Royal Society of London (Series B),* 357, 963–973.

Wade, N. J. (1988) On the late invention of the stereoscope. *Perception,* 16, 785–818.

Wade, N. J. (2003) The legacy of phantom limbs. *Perception,* 32, 517–524.

Wade, N. J., and **Verstraten, F. A. J.** (1998) Introduction and historical overview. In G. Mather, F. Verstraten, and S. Anstis (eds.), *The motion aftereffect: A modern perspective.* Cambridge: MIT Press, 1–23.

Wald, G. (1950) Eye and camera. *Scientific American,* 183, 32–41.

Walker, B. N. (2002) Magnitude estimation of conceptual data dimensions for use in sonification. *Journal of Experimental Psychology: Applied,* 8, 211–221.

Walker, B. N., and **Ehrenstein, A.** (2000) Pitch and pitch change interact in auditory displays. *Journal of Experimental Psychology: Applied,* 6, 15–30.

Walker, B. N., and **Kramer, G.** (2004) Ecological psychoacoustics and auditory displays: Hearing, grouping, and meaning making. In J. G. Neuhoff (ed.), *Ecological psychoacoustics.* New York: Academic Press.

Wall, J. T. (1988) Variable organization in cortical maps of the skin as an indication of the lifelong adaptive capacities of circuits in the mammalian brain. *Trends in Neurosciences,* 12, 549–557.

Wall, P. D. (2000) *Pain: The science of suffering.* New York: Columbia University Press.

Wallace, P. (1977) Individual discrimination of humans by odor. *Physiology & Behavior,* 19, 577–579.

Wallach, H. (1935) Ueber visuell whargenommene bewegungrichtung. *Psychologische Forschung,* 20, 325–380.

Wallach, H. (1963) The perception of neutral colors. *Scientific American,* 208, 107–116.

Wallach, H., and **Floor, L.** (1971) The use of size matching to demonstrate the effectiveness of accommodation and convergence as cues for distance. *Perception & Psychophysics,* 10, 423–428.

Wallach, H., and **O'Connell, D. N.** (1953) The kinetic depth effect. *Journal of Experimental Psychology,* 45, 205–217.

Wallis, G. (1998) Temporal order in human object recognition learning. *Journal of Biological Systems,* 6, 299–313.

Walls, G. L. (1942) *The vertebrate eye and its adaptive radiation.* New York: Hafner.

Walls, G. L. (1960) Land! Land! *Psychological Bulletin,* 57, 29–48.

Walsh, V., and **Cowey, A.** (1998) Magnetic stimulation studies of visual cognition. *Trends in Cognitive Sciences,* 2, 103–110.

Walsh, V., Ellison, A., Battelli, L., and **Cowey, A.** (1998) Task-specific impairments and enhancements induced by magnetic stimulation of human visual area V5. *Proceedings of the Royal Society London (Series B),* 265, 537–543.

Wandell, B. A. (1995) *Foundations of vision.* Sunderland: Sinauer Associates.

Wandell, B. A. (1999) Computational neuroimaging of human visual cortex. *Annual Review of Neuroscience,* 22, 145–173.

Wandell, B. A. (2000) Computational neuroimaging: Color representations and processing. In M. Gazzaniga (ed.), *The new cognitive neurosciences.* Cambridge: MIT Press, 291–304.

Wang, Y., Smallwood, P. M., Cowan, M., Blesh, D., Lawler, A., and **Nathans, J.** (1999) Mutually exclusive expression of human red and green visual pigment-reporter transgenes occurs at high frequency in murine cone photoreceptors. *Proceedings of the National Academy of Sciences: USA,* 96, 5251–5256.

Ward, W. D. (1966) Temporary threshold shift in males and females. *Journal of the Acoustical Society of America,* 40, 478–485.

Ward, W. D. (1968) Susceptibility to auditory fatigue. In W. D. Neff (ed.), *Contributions to sensory physiology,* vol. 3. New York: Academic Press, 195–225.

Ward, W. D., and **Glorig, A.** (1961) A case of firecracker-induced hearing loss. *Laryngoscope,* 71, 1590–1596.

Warren, J. D., Uppenkamp, S., Patterson, R. D., and **Griffiths, T. D.** (2003) Separating pitch chroma and pitch height in the human brain. *Proceedings of the National Academy of Sciences: USA,* 100, 10038–10042.

Warren, S., Hämäläinen, H. A., and **Gardner, E. P.** (1986) Objective classification of motion- and direction-sensitive neurons in primary somatosensory cortex of awake monkeys. *Journal of Neurophysiology,* 56, 598–632.

Warren, W. H., Jr. (1984) Perceiving affordances: Visual guidance of stair climbing. *Journal of Experimental Psychology: Human Perception & Performance,* 10, 683–703.

Warren, W. H., Jr. (1998) The state of flow. In T. Watanbe (ed.), *High-level motion perception.* Cambridge: MIT Press, 316–358.

Warren, W. H., Jr., Blackwell, A. W., and **Morris, M. W.** (1989) Age differences in perceiving the direction of self-motion from optical flow. *Journal of Gerontology: Psychological Sciences,* 44, 147–153.

Warren, W. H., Jr., Morris, M. W., and **Kalish, M. L.** (1988) Perception of translational heading from optical flow. *Journal of Experimental Psychology: Human Perception and Performance,* 14, 646–660.

Warren, W. H., Jr., Young, D. S., and **Lee, D. N.** (1986) Visual control of step length during running over irregular terrain. *Journal of Experimental Psychology: Human Performance and Perception,* 12, 259–266.

Warrier, C. M., and **Zatorre, R. J.** (2002) Influence of tonal context and timbral variation on perception of pitch. *Perception & Psychophysics,* 64, 198–207.

Wasserman, G. S. (1978) *Color vision: An historical perspective.* New York: John Wiley & Sons.

Wässle, H. (1999) A patchwork of cones. *Nature,* 397, 474–475.

Wässle, H. (2004) Parallel processing in the mammalian retina. *Nature Reviews Neuroscience,* 5, 747–757.

Wässle, H., Peichl, L., and **Boycott, B. B.** (1981) Dendritic territories of cat retinal ganglion cells. *Nature,* 292, 344–345.

Watamaniuk, S. N. J., and **Heinen, S. J.** (1999) Human smooth pursuit direction discrimination. *Vision Research,* 39, 59–70.

Watson, A. B., and **Pelli, D. G.** (1983) QUEST: A Bayesian adaptive psychometric method. *Perception & Psychophysics,* 33, 113–120.

Watt, R. J., and **Andrews, D. P.** (1981) APE: Adaptive probit estimation of psychometric functions. *Current Psychological Reviews,* 1, 205–214.

Weale, R. A. (1982) *A biography of the eye.* London: Lewis.

Weale, R. A. (1986) Retinal senescence. In N. Osborne and J. Chader (eds.), *Progress in retinal research,* vol. 5. Oxford: Pergamon Press, 53–73.

Webster, M., and **Mollon, J. D.** (1995) Colour constancy influenced by contrast adaptation. *Nature,* 373, 694–698.

Weinberger, N. M. (2004) Music in the brain. *Scientific American,* 291, 88–95.

Weinstein, S. (1968) Intensive and extensive aspects of tactile sensitivity as a function of body part, sex and laterality. In D. R. Kenshalo (ed.), *The skin senses.* Springfield, Ill.: Thomas.

Weisenberger, J. M., and **Miller, J. D.** (1987) The role of tactile aids in providing information about acoustic stimuli. *Journal of the Acoustical Society of America,* 82, 906–916.

Weiskrantz, L. (1995) Blindsight—Not an island unto itself. *Current Directions in Psychological Science,* 4, 146–151.

Weisskopf, V. F. (1976) Is physics human? *Physics Today,* 29, 23–29.

Welch, R. B., and **Warren, D. H.** (1980) Immediate perceptual response to intersensory discrepancy. *Psychological Bulletin,* 88, 638–667.

Weliky, M., Bosking, W. H. and **Fitzpatrick, D.** (1996) A systematic map of direction preference in primary visual cortex. *Nature,* 379, 725–728.

Wells, D. L., and **Hepper, P. G.** (2000) The discrimination of dog odours by humans. *Perception,* 29, 111–115.

Wells, G. L., Lindsay, R. C. L., and **Ferguson, T. J.** (1979) Accuracy, confidence, and juror perceptions in eyewitness identification. *Journal of Applied Psychology,* 64, 440–448.

Wenger, M. A., Jones, F. N., and **Jones, M. H.** (1956) *Physiological psychology.* New York: Holt, Rinehart & Winston.

Werker, J. F., and **Tees, R. C.** (1992) The organization and reorganization of human speech perception. *Annual Review of Neuroscience,* 15, 377–402.

Werner, J. S., Cicerone, C. M., Kliegl, R., and **DellaRosa, D.** (1984) Spectral efficiency of blackness induction. *Journal of the Optical Society of America A,* 1, 981–986.

Wertheimer, M. (1912/1961) Experimental studies on the seeing of motion. In T. Shipley (trans. and ed.), *Classics in psychology.* New York: Philosophical Library, 1032–1088.

Wertheimer, M. (1923/1958) Principles of perceptual organization. In D. C. Beardslee and M. Wertheimer (eds.), *Readings in perception.* Princeton, N.J.: Van Nostrand, 115–135.

Wertheimer, M. (1961) Psychomotor coordination of auditory and visual space at birth. *Science,* 134, 1692–1693.

Wessinger, C. M., Van Meter, J., Tian, B., Van Lare, J., Pekar, J., and **Rauschecker, J. P.** (2001) Hierarchical organization of the human auditory cortex revealed by functional magnetic resonance imaging. *Journal of Cognitive Neuroscience,* 13, 1–7.

Westfall, R. S. (1980) *Never at rest: A biography of Isaac Newton.* Cambridge: Cambridge University Press.

Wever, E. G. (1949) *Theory of hearing.* New York: John Wiley & Sons.

Wever, E. G. (1978) *The reptile ear.* Princeton, N.J.: Princeton University Press.

Wever, E. G., and **Bray, C. W.** (1937) The perception of low tones and the resonance-volley theory. *Journal of Psychology,* 3, 101–114.

Weyl, H. (1952) *Symmetry.* Princeton, N.J.: Princeton University Press.

Wheatstone, C. (1838/1964) Some remarkable phenomena of binocular vision. In W. N. Dember (ed.), *Visual perception: The nineteenth century.* New York: John Wiley & Sons, 114–129.

Wheeler, D. D. (1970) Processes in word recognition. *Cognitive Psychology,* 1, 59–85.

White, T. H. (1939) *The sword in the stone.* New York: G. P. Putnam's Sons.

Wickens, T. D. (2001) *Elementary signal detection theory.* New York: Oxford University Press.

Wiesel, T. N., and **Hubel, D. H.** (1960) Receptive fields of ganglion cells in the cat's retina. *Journal of Physiology,* 153, 583–594.

Wiesel, T. N., and **Hubel, D. H.** (1966) Spatial and chromatic interactions in the lateral geniculate body of the rhesus monkey. *Journal of Neurophysiology,* 29, 1115–1156.

Wightman, F. L., and **Kistler, D. J.** (1980) A new "look" at auditory space perception. In G. van den Brink and F. A. Bilsen (eds.), *Psychophysical, physiological and behavioral studies in hearing.* Delft: Delft University Press, 441–448.

Wightman, F. L., and **Kistler, D. J.** (1989a) Headphones simulation of free-field listening. I. Stimulus synthesis. *Journal of the Acoustical Society of America,* 85, 858–867.

Wightman, F. L., and **Kistler, D. J.** (1989b) Headphones simulation of free-field listening: II. Psychophysical validation. *Journal of the Acoustical Society of America,* 85, 868–878.

Wightman, F. L., and **Kistler, D. J.** (1992) The dominant role of low frequency interaural time differences in sound localization. *Journal of the Acoustical Society of America,* 91, 1648–1661.

Wightman, F. L., and **Kistler, D. J.** (1998) Of Vulcan ears, human ears and "earprints." *Nature Neuroscience,* 1, 337–339.

Wilkins, P. A., and **Acton, W. I.** (1982) Noise and accidents: A review. *Annals of Occupational Hygiene,* 25, 249–260.

Williams, A. C. de C. (2002) Facial expression of pain: An evolutionary account. *Behavioral and Brain Sciences,* 25, 439–488.

Williams, D. R., MacLeod, D. I. A., and **Hayhoe, M. M.** (1981) Punctate sensitivity of the blue-sensitive mechanism. *Vision Research,* 21, 1357–1375.

Williams, D., Phillips, G., and **Sekuler, R.** (1986) Hysteresis in the perception of motion direction as evidence for neural cooperativity. *Nature,* 324, 253–255.

Williams, S. M., McCoy, A. N., and **Purves, D.** (1998) The influence of depicted illumination on brightness. *Proceedings of the National Academy of Sciences: USA,* 95, 13296–13300.

Wilmington, D., Gray, L., and **Jahrsdoerfer, R.** (1994) Binaural processing after corrected congenital unilateral conductive hearing loss. *Hearing Research,* 74, 99–114.

Wilson, B. S., Finley, C. C., Lawson, D. T., Wolford, R. D., Eddington, D. K., and **Rabinowitz, W. M.** (1991) Better speech recognition with cochlear implants. *Nature,* 352, 236–238.

Wilson, J. P., and **Sutton, G. J.** (1981) Acoustic correlates of tonal tinnitus. *CIBA Foundation Symposium,* 85, 82–107.

Wilson, H. R., Mets, M. B., Nagy, S. E., and **Kressel, A. B.** (1988) Albino spatial vision as an instance of arrested visual development. *Vision Research,* 28, 979–990.

Wilson, H. R., and **Wilkinson, F.** (2004) Spatial channels in vision and spatial pooling. In L. M Chalupa and J. S. Werner (eds.), *The visual neurosciences,* vol. 2, MIT Press, 1060–1068.

Wilson, S. M., Saygin, A. P., Sereno, M. I., and **Iacoboni, M.** (2004) Listening to speech activates motor areas involved in speech production. *Nature Neuroscience,* 7, 701–702.

Winderickx, J., Lindsey, D. T., Sanocki, E., Teller, D. Y., Motulsky, A. G., and **Deeb, S. S.** (1992) Polymorphism in red photopigment underlies variation in colour matching. *Nature,* 356, 431–433.

Winer, G. A., Cottrell, J. E., Gregg, V., Fournier, J. S., and **Bica, L. A.** (2002) Fundamentally misunderstanding visual perception: Adults' belief in visual emissions. *American Psychologist,* 57, 417–424.

Winter, R. (1976) *The smell book: Scents, sex, and society.* Philadelphia: Lippincott.

Winter, Y., Lopez, J., and **von Helversen, O.** (2003) Ultraviolet vision in a bat. *Nature,* 425, 612–614.

Wise, L. Z., and **Irvine, D. R. F.** (1985) Topographic organization of interaural intensity difference sensitivity in deep layers of cat superior colliculus: Implications for auditory spacial representation. *Journal of Neurophysiology,* 54, 185–211.

Wise, P. M., Olsson, M. J., and **Cain, W. S.** (2000) Quantification of odor quality. *Chemical Senses,* 25, 429–443.

Wist, E. R. (1976) Dark adaptation and the Hermann grid illusion. *Perception & Psychophysics,* 20, 10–12.

Witt, J. K., Proffitt, D. R., and **Epstein, W.** (2004) Perceiving distance: A role of effort and intent. *Perception,* 33, 577–590.

Wolfe, J. M. (1984) Global factors in the Hermann grid illusion. *Perception,* 13, 33–40.

Wolfson, S. S., and **Landy, M. S.** (1998) Examining edge- and region-based texture analysis mechanisms. *Vision Research,* 38, 439–446.

Wong D. L., Hockenberry-Eaton, M., Wilson, D., Winkelstein, M. L., and **Schwartz, P.** (2001) *Wong's Essentials of Pediatric Nursing,* 6th ed. St. Louis: C.V. Mosby.

Wood, J. B., and **Harkins, S. W.** (1987) Effects of age, stimulus selection, and retrieval environment on odor identification. *Journal of Gerontology,* 42, 584–588.

Woodworth, R. S. (1938) *Experimental psychology.* New York: Holt.

Woodworth, R. S., and **Schlosberg, H.** (1954) *Experimental psychology,* 2nd ed. New York: Holt.

Wright, B. A., Lombardino, L. J., King, W. M., Puranik, C. S., Leonard, C. M., and **Merzenich, M. M.** (1997) Deficits in auditory temporal and spectral resolution in language-impaired children. *Nature, 387,* 176–178.

Wright, E. (1992) The original of E. G. Boring's "Young girl mother-in-law" drawing and its relation to the pattern of a joke. *Perception, 21,* 273–275.

Wright, R. H. (1966) Why is an odour? *Nature, 209,* 551–554.

Wuerger, S., Shapley, R., and **Rubin N.** (1996) "On the visually perceived direction of motion" by Hans Wallach: 60 years later. *Perception, 25,* 1317–1367.

Wysocki, C. J., Dorries, K. M., and **Beauchamp, G. K.** (1989) Ability to perceive androstenone can be acquired by ostensibly anosmic people. *Proceedings of the National Academy of Sciences: USA, 86,* 7976–7978.

Wysocki, C. J., Pierce, J. D., and **Gilbert, A. N.** (1991) Geographic, cross-cultural, and individual variation in human olfaction. In T. V. Getchell, R. L. Doty, L. M. Bartoshuk, and J. B. Snow, Jr. (eds.), *Smell and taste in health and disease.* New York: Raven Press, 287–314.

Xiao, Y., Wang, Y., and **Felleman, D. J.** (2003) A spatially organized representation of colour in macaque cortical area V2. *Nature, 421,* 35–539.

Yang, Y., and **Blake, R.** (1991) Spatial frequency tuning of human stereopsis. *Vision Research, 31,* 1177–1189.

Yantis, S. (1992) Multielement visual tracking: Attention and perceptual organization. *Cognitive Psychology, 24,* 295–340.

Yellott, J. I., Jr. (1982) Spectral analysis of spatial sampling by photoreceptors: Topological disorder prevents aliasing. *Vision Research, 22,* 1205–1210.

Yeshurun, Y., and **Carrasco, M.** (1998) Attention improves or impairs visual performance by enhancing spatial resolution. *Nature, 396,* 72–75.

Yonas, A. (1984) Reaching as a measure of infant spatial perception. In G. Gottlieb and N. A. Krasnegor (eds.), *Measurement of audition and vision in the first year of postnatal life: A methodological review.* Norwood, N.J.: Ablex.

Yost, W. A. (1991) Auditory image perception and analysis: The basis for hearing. *Hearing Research, 56,* 8–18.

Yost, W. A. (2000) *Fundamentals of hearing: An introduction,* 4th ed. New York: Academic Press.

Yost, W. A., Patterson, R., and **Sheft, S. A.** (1996) A time domain description for the pitch strength of iterated rippled noise. *Journal of the Acoustical Society of America, 99,* 1066–1078.

Young, F. A. (1981) Primate myopia. *American Journal of Optometry and Physiological Optics, 58,* 560–566.

Young, J. P., Herath, P., Eickhoff, S., Choi, J., Grefkes, C., Zilles, K., and **Roland, P. E.** (2004) Somatotopy and attentional modulation of the human parietal and opercular regions. *Journal of Neuroscience, 24,* 5391–5399.

Young, P. T. (1928) Auditory localization with acoustical transposition of the ears. *Journal of Experimental Psychology, 11,* 399–429.

Young, T. (1801/1948) Observations on vision. In W. Dennis (ed.), *Readings in the history of psychology.* New York: Appleton-Century-Crofts, 96–101.

Yuille, A. L., and **Grzywacz, N. M.** (1988) A computational theory for the perception of coherent visual motion. *Nature, 333,* 71–74.

Yuodelis, C., and **Hendrickson, A.** (1986) A qualitative analysis of the human fovea during development. *Vision Research, 26,* 847–855.

Zacks, J. (1970) Temporal summation phenomena at threshold: Their relation to visual mechanisms. *Science, 170,* 197–199.

Zadnik, K., Satariano, W. A., Mutti, D. O., Sholtz, R. I., and **Adams, A. J.** (1994) The effect of parental history of myopia on children's eye size. *Journal of the American Medical Association, 271,* 1323–1327.

Zaidi, Q., and **Li, A.** (2002) Limitations on shape information provided by texture cues. *Vision Research, 42,* 815–835.

Zald, D. H., and **Pardo, J. V.** (1997) Emotion, olfaction, and the human amygdala: Amygdala activation during aversive olfactory stimulation. *Proceedings of the National Academy of Sciences: USA, 94,* 4119–4124.

Zald, D. H., and **Pardo, J. V.** (2002) The neural correlates of aversive auditory stimulation. *NeuroImage, 16,* 746–753.

Zatorre, R. J. (2003) Absolute pitch: A model for understanding the influence of genes and development on neural and cognitive function. *Nature Neuroscience, 6,* 692–695.

Zatorre, R. J., Belin, P., and **Penhune, V. B.** (2002) Structure and function of auditory cortex: Music and speech. *Trends in Cognitive Sciences, 6,* 37–46.

Zatorre, R. J., Bouffard, M., Ahad, P., and **Belin, P.** (2002) Where is "where" in the human auditory cortex? *Nature Neuroscience, 5,* 905–909.

Zatorre, R. J., Evans, A. C., and **Meyer, E.** (1994) Neural mechanisms underlying melodic perception and memory for pitch. *Journal of Neuroscience, 14,* 1908–1919.

Zeki, S. (1980) The representation of colours in the cerebral cortex. *Nature, 284,* 412–418.

Zeki, S. (1983) Colour coding in the cerebral cortex: The reaction of cells in monkey visual cortex to wavelengths and colours. *Neuroscience, 9,* 741–765.

Zeki, S. (1999) *Inner vision: An exploration of art and the brain.* New York: Oxford University Press

Zellner, D. A., Bartoli, A. M., and **Eckard, R.** (1991) Influence of color on odor identification and liking ratings. *American Journal of Psychology, 104,* 547–561.

Zellner, D. A., and **Durlack, P.** (2003) Effect of color on expected and experienced refreshment, intensity, and liking of beverages. *American Journal of Psychology, 116,* 633–647.

Zellner, D. A., and **Kautz, M. A.** (1990) Color affects perceived odor intensity. *Journal of Experimental Psychology: Human Perception & Performance, 16,* 391–397.

Zelman, S. (1973) Correlation of smoking history with hearing loss. *Journal of the American Medical Association, 223,* 920.

Zeng, F. G., and **Shannon, R. V.** (1994) Loudness-coding mechanisms inferred from electrical stimulation of the human auditory system. *Science,* 264, 564–566.

Zhao, G. Q., Zhang, Y., Hoon, M. A., Chandrashekar, J., Erlenbach, I., Ryba, N. J., and **Zuker, C. S.** (2003) The receptors for mammalian sweet and umami taste. *Cell,* 115, 255–266.

Zhou, Y.-D., and **Fuster, J. M.** (1996) Mnemonic neuronal activity in somatosensory cortex. *Proceedings of the National Academy of Sciences: USA,* 93, 10533–10537.

Zihl, J., von Cramon, D., and **Mai, N.** (1983) Selective disturbance of movement vision after bilateral brain damage. *Brain,* 106, 313–340.

Zihl, J., von Cramon, D., Mai, N., and **Schmid, C.** (1991) Disturbance of movement vision after bilateral posterior brain damage. Further evidence and follow up observations. *Brain,* 114, 2235–2252.

Zisman, F., and **Adams, A. J.** (1982) Spectral sensitivity of cone mechanisms in juvenile diabetes. In G. Verriest (ed.), *Colour vision deficiencies, VI. Proceedings of the Sixth Symposium of the International Research Group on Colour Vision Deficiencies.* The Hague: W. Junk, 127–131.

Zrenner, E. (1983) *Neurophysiological aspects of color vision in primates.* Berlin: Springer-Verlag.

Zverev, Y. P. (2004) Effects of caloric deprivation and satiety on sensitivity of the gustatory system. *BMC Neuroscience,* 5, 5.

Zwicker, E. (1964) Negative afterimage in hearing. *Journal of the Acoustical Society of America,* 36, 2413–2415.

Zwicker, E., and **Scharf, B.** (1965) A model of loudness summation. *Psychological Review,* 72, 3–26.

Credits

Figure 1.4 © George Gerster/Comstock, Inc.

Figure1.7 Photograph courtesy of Robert Sekuler.

Figure 1.8 Photograph courtesy of Philips Medical Systems.

Figure 1.11 © PhotoDisc/Getty Images.

Figure 2.1 (clockwise from upper left) © Gregory G. Dimijian, M.D., 1988/Photo Researchers, Inc., © Stephen Dalton/Photo Researchers, Inc., © PhotoDisc, © David M. Dennis/Animals Animals/Earth Scenes, © PhotoDisc.

Figure 2.3 Edward Wester.

Figure 2.6 (left) © PhotoDisc/Getty Images, (right) © Digital Vision/Getty Images.

Box 2.1 Courtesy of Robert Sekuler.

Figure 2.12 Glyn Cloyd.

Figure 2.14 (left) © Bettmann/CORBIS, (right) Courtesy of Welch Allyn, Inc.

Figure 2.18 © David Parker/Photo Researchers, Inc.

Figures 2.23, 2.28 Glyn Cloyd.

Figure 2.29 © Per Kjeldsen.

Figure 2.30 © Lennart Nilsson from "The Incredible Machine".

Figure 2.32 John Dowling.

Chapter 3, p. 77 From Anselm Hollo, "Age Four" in *Sojourner Microcosms: New and Selected Poems, 1959–1977* by Anselm Hollo. Copyright © 1977 Anselm Hollo. Printed here by permission of Blue Wind Press.

Figure 3.18 Lotto, Williams, and Purves. "Mach Bands as Empirically Derived Associations" in *PNAS* 96. Copyright © 1999 National Academy of Sciences, U.S.A. Used with permission.

Figure 3.19 S. M. Antis. Reprinted from "A Chart Demonstrating Variations in Acuity with Retinal Position." *Vision Research,* 1974, 14, 589–592. Used with permission from Elsevier.

Figure 3.22 Edward Adlson.

Figure 3.27 Wilson Geisler.

Figure 3.28 Stuart Anstis.

Box 3.5 Figure courtesy of Stuart Anstis.

Figure 4.5A David Calkins.

Figure 4.9 Photograph courtesy of Todd Preuss and Jon Kaas.

Figure 4.15 Jonathan Horton.

Figure 4.20 D. J. Felleman and D. C. Van Essen. "Distributed Hierarchical Procession in the Primate Cerebral Cortex" in *Cerebral Cortex,* 1991, 1, 1–17. Reprinted by permission of Oxford University Press and D. J. Felleman.

Figure 5.1 From Jim Bell in *Science* Vol. 305, Fig. 3e p. 801, 2004, NASA.

Figure 5.2 Susan Adcock.

Figure 5.3 Philippe Schyns and Aude Oliva.

Figure 5.18 Photograph courtesy of Daphne Maurer and Terry Lewis.

Figure 5.32 From Brodartz, *A Photographic Album for Artists and Designers,* 1966. © Dover Publications.

Figure 5.35 B. Julesz. From "A Brief Outline of the Texton Theory of Human Vision," *Trends in Neurosciences,* 1984, 7, 41–45. Used with permission by Elsevier.

Figure 5.36 Ellsworth Kelly *La Combe I,* 1950, Oil on canvas, 38x63 1/2 inches. Courtesy Matthew Marks Gallery, New York, NY.

Figure 5.37 Qasim Zaidi.

Figure 5.38 R. Sekuler.

Figure 5.41 Vince Ferrera.

Figure 5.44 Wilson Geisler.

Figure 6.1 NASA.

Figure 6.2 Reprinted with permission from *Anxiety Disorder,* "Social Phobics do not see eye to eye: A visuals scanpath study of emotional expression processing" Vol. 17, 2003, by Kaye Horley, et al., pages 33–44, Fig. 1B and 2B. © 2003 with permission from Elsevier.

Figure 6.3 Isabelle Bülthoff.

Figure 6.5 From Palmer, Rosch, and Chase, 1981.

Figure 6.8 Photograph courtesy of Jason Gold.

Figure 6.9 Ray Dolan.

Figure 6.10 Figure courtesy of David Sheinberg.

Figure 6.11 © Reuters/CORBIS.

Figure 6.12 Photograph courtesy of Allison B. Sekuler.

Figure 6.13 Photograph courtesy of Isabel Gauthier.

Figure 6.14 From Robert Sekuler and Randolph Blake's *Star Trek on the Brain: Alien Minds, Human Minds* (1999), New York: W.H. Freeman.

Figure 6.15 Photographs courtesy of Pierre Gosselin.

Box 6.2 Photograph courtesy of Kaye Horley.

Figure 6.19 Photographs courtesy of Ron Rensink.

Figure 6.21 Photographs and computer image processing courtesy of Lewis Harvey.

Figures 6.25, 6.26 Image courtesy of Jason McLeary.

Figure 8.1 © Bettmann/CORBIS.

Figure 8.2 © San Francisco, Assisi/ET Archive, London/SuperStock.

Figure 8.9 McGraw-Hill.

Figure 8.15 © McGraw-Hill Higher Education, John Thoeming, photographer.

Figure 8.24 © Baron Wolman/Woodfin Camp & Associates.

Figure 8.27 © Frank Sitman/Stock Boston.

Figure 8.29 Courtesy of Dennis Markley.

Figure 8.30 James Todd.

Figures 8.31, 8.32 D. Kersten, P. Mamassian, and D. Knill. "Moving Cast Shadows Induce Apparent Motion Depth." *Perception,* 1997, 26, 171–192. Used with permission.

Figure 8.33, 8.34 Roland William Fleming.

Figure 8.38 From *Perception,* 1989, Volume 18, pp. 55–68. Pion Limited, London. Used with permission from the publisher and Ken Nakayama.

Figure 8.39 Ken Nakayama.

Figure 8.42 Tom Stanford.

Box 8.2 From William Andrew Steer, *www.techmind.org/stereo/ sintro.html.* Used with permission from W. A. Steer.

Figure 10.1 © David Parker/Photo Researchers, Inc.

Figure 10.15 Photograph courtesy of David Lim.

Figure 11.3 K. P. Steel. "Progress in Progressive Hearing Loss." Reprinted with permission from *Science,* 279: 1870–1871. Copyright © 1998 AAAS.

Figure 11.20 Courtesy of Fred Wightman, University of Louisville.

Box 12.1 Figure courtesy of Jo-Anne Bachorowski.

Figure 12.7 Katharina von Kriegstein.

Figure 12.8 Mônica Zilbovicius.

Figure 12.10 The McGraw-Hill Companies, Inc./Chris Kerrigan.

Figure 12.11 Asif Ghazanfar and Nikos Logothetis.

Figures 12.12, 12.15 Courtesy of I. Peretz and K. Hyde.

Figure 12.16 Patrik N. Juslin. From "Five Facets of Musical Expression" by Patrik N. Juslin in "Emotions in Performance of a Theme by Haydn" in *Psychology of Music,* Vol. 31, #3, p. 293. Copyright © 2003 Sage Publications. Reproduced with permission from Sage Publications, Ltd.

Figure 12.17 A. J. Blood, R. J. Zatorre, P. Bermudez, and A. C. Evans. "Emotional Responses to Pleasant and Unpleasant Music Correlate with Activity in Paralimbic Brain Regions." *Neuroscience* 2, 382–387. Reprinted with permission by Nature Publishing Group © 1999 and Anne Blood.

Figure 12.18 Anne Blood.

Figure 13.3 Reproduced with permission from Pavani, Spance, and Driver, 2000.

Figure 13.4 Mark Hollins.

Figure 13.6 Courtesy of National Braille Press.

Figure 13.13 Penfield and Rasmussen, *The Cerebral Cortex of Man,* Macmillan, 1950. Copyright © 1950 Macmillan. Reprinted by permission of The Gale Group.

Figure 13.14 Ford Ebner.

Figure 13.15 © The Natural History Museum, London.

Figure 13.16 S. J. Lederman. Reprinted from "Skin and Touch." *The Encyclopedia of Human Biology.* Copyright © 1991 Academic Press. Used with permission from Elsevier.

Figure 13.17 R. Blake, K. Sobel, and T. James. "Neural Synergy between Kinetic Vision and Touch," *Psychological Science,* 15, 397–402. Used with permission from Blackwell Publishing.

Figure 13.18 Wong-Baker FACES Pain Rating Scale. Copyright © D. L. Wong and C. M. Baker. Reprinted with permission. As found in Wong, Hockenberry-Eaton, Wilson, Winkelstein and Schwartz, *Wong's Essentials of Pediatric Nursing,* 6th Edition, St. Louis, 2001, p. 1301.

Figure 14.1 Photograph courtesy of Ken Catania.

Figure 14.7 Molly Webster/© 1982. Reprinted by permission from Discover Magazine.

Figure 14.10 Noam Sobel.

Figure 14.14 W. S. Cain. "Odor Identification by Males and Females: Predictions versus Performance" in *Chemical Senses,* 7, 129–142. Reprinted by permission of Oxford University Press and the author.

Figure 15.2 (Images © Omikron/Photo Researchers, Inc.) S. M. Mader. Figure 13.5 from *Human Biology,* 8th edition. Used by permission of The McGraw-Hill Companies, Inc.

Figure 15.3 Photograph courtesy of Inglis Miller.

Figure 15.6 Photograph courtesy of Linda Bartoshuk.

Figure 15.18 Julie Mennella.

Color Plate 1 Dario Ringach.

Color Plate 2 Roger Tootell.

Color Plate 5 Philippe Schyns.

Color Plate 8 "Susan" Oil on Canvas 24x20 1987 by Chuck Close. Courtesy Pace Wildenstein Gallery, New York, NY. Photographer, Steve Lopez.

Color Plate 13 David Williams.

Color Plate 15 Beau Lotto.

Color Plate 16 Geoff Boynton.

Color Plate 17 Karl Gegenfurtner.

Color Plate 18 Donald MacLeod.

Color Plate 19 Steven Shevell.

Color Plate 20 Reproduced from Ishihara's Test for Colour Deficiency published by KANEHARA & CO., LTD., located at Tokyo in Japan. But tests for color blindness cannot be conducted with this material. For accurate testing, the original plate should be used.

Name Index

Subject Index